HARRAP'S
Spanish
AND
English
POCKET
DICTIONARY

Second Edition

Mc
Graw
Hill
Education

New York Chicago San Francisco Athens London Madrid
Mexico City Milan New Delhi Singapore Sydney Toronto

3 4 5 6 7 8 9 10   QLM/QLM 1 0 9 8 7

ISBN   978-0-07-181446-1
MHID   0-07-181446-9

Library of Congress Control Number: 2013950199

Words considered to be trademarks have been designated in this dictionary by the symbol ®. However, no judgment is implied concerning the legal status of any trademark by virtue of the presence or absence of such a symbol.

McGraw-Hill Education products are available at special quantity discounts to use as premiums and sales promotions or for use in corporate training programs. To contact a representative, please visit the Contact Us pages at www.mhprofessional.com.

Contents

Preface

The Harrap's Spanish and English Pocket Dictionary aims to provide all students of Spanish (in its different regional varieties) at beginner and intermediate level with a reliable, comprehensive and user-friendly dictionary in a compact form. The clear, systematic layout of information makes the dictionary an easy-to-use tool and its coverage of vocabulary should ensure that it becomes an invaluable resource.

The dictionary covers all essential words and phrases and packs a wealth of vocabulary into its pages. As in all Harrap dictionaries, colloquial and idiomatic language is well represented, as are words from a wide range of specialized fields, such as information technology, sports and finance.

Extra help is provided in the form of a useful supplement comprising Spanish verb conjugation tables for regular and irregular verbs, a list of English irregular verbs, as well as a Spanish conversation guide, together with guides to Spanish and English pronunciation at the beginning of the book.

Abbreviations

abbreviation	*abbr, abr*	abreviatura
adjective	*adj*	adjetivo
administration	*Admin*	administración
adverb	*adv*	adverbio
agriculture	*Agr(ic)*	agricultura
somebody, someone	*algn*	alguien
Latin American Spanish	*Am*	español de América
anatomy	*Anat*	anatomía
Andean Spanish (Bolivia, Chile, Colombia, Ecuador, Peru)	*Andes*	español andino (Bolivia, Chile, Colombia, Ecuador, Perú)
approximately	*aprox*	aproximadamente
architecture	*Archit*	arquitectura
Argentinian Spanish	*Arg*	español de Argentina
architecture	*Arquit*	arquitectura
article	*art*	artículo
astrology	*Astrol*	astrología
astronomy	*Astron*	astronomía
Australian	*Austr*	australiano
motoring	*Auto*	automóviles
auxiliary	*aux*	auxiliar
aviation	*Aviat*	aviación
biology	*Biol*	biología
Bolivian Spanish	*Bol*	español de Bolivia
botany	*Bot*	botánica
British English	*Br*	inglés británico
Central American Spanish	*CAm*	español centroamericano
Caribbean Spanish (Cuba, Puerto Rico, Dominican Republic, Venezuela)	*Carib*	español caribeño (Cuba, Puerto Rico, República Dominicana, Venezuela)
chemistry	*Chem*	químico
Chilean Spanish	*Chile*	español de Chile
cinema	*Cin(e)*	cine
Colombian Spanish	*Col*	español de Colombia
commerce	*Com(m)*	comercio
comparative	*compar*	comparativo
computers	*Comput*	informática
conjunction	*conj*	conjunción
building industry	*Constr*	construcción
sewing	*Cost*	costura
Costa Rican Spanish	*CRica*	español de Costa Rica
Spanish from the Southern Cone region (Argentina, Uruguay, Paraguay, Chile)	*CSur*	español del Cono Sur (Argentina, Uruguay, Paraguay, Chile)
Cuban Spanish	*Cuba*	español de Cuba
cookery	*Culin*	cocina
definite	*def*	definido

demonstrative	*dem*	demostrativo
sport	*Dep*	deporte
pejorative	*despec*	despectivo
definite	*det*	determinado
economics	*Econ*	economía
Ecuadorian Spanish	*Ecuad*	español de Ecuador
education	*Educ*	educación
electricity	*Elec*	electricidad
especially	*esp*	especialmente
Peninsular Spanish	*Esp*	español de España
specialist term	*Espec*	término especializado
euphemism	*Euph, Euf*	eufemismo
feminine	*f*	femenino
informal	*Fam*	familiar
pharmacy	*Farm*	farmacia
railways	*Ferroc*	ferrocarriles
figurative use	*Fig*	uso figurado
finance	*Fin*	finanzas
physics	*Fís*	física
photography	*Foto*	fotografía
feminine plural	*fpl*	plural femenino
soccer	*Ftbl, Fút*	fútbol
generally	*gen*	generalmente
geography	*Geog*	geografía
geology	*Geol*	geología
geometry	*Geom*	geometría
Guatemalan Spanish	*Guat*	español de Guatemala
history	*Hist*	historia
humorous	*Hum*	humorístico
imperative	*imperat*	imperativo
imperfect	*imperf*	imperfecto
impersonal	*impers*	impersonal
printing	*Impr*	imprenta
industry	*Ind*	industria
indefinite	*indef*	indefinido
indefinite	*indet*	indeterminado
indicative	*indic*	indicativo
infinitive	*infin*	infinitivo
computers	*Inform*	informática
insurance	*Ins*	seguros
interjection	*interj*	interjección
interrogative	*interr*	interrogativo
invariable	*inv*	invariable
ironic	*Iron, Irón*	irónico
law	*Jur*	derecho
linguistics	*Ling*	lingüística
literary	*liter*	literario
literature	*Liter*	literatura

phrase	*loc*	locución
masculine	*m*	masculino
mathematics	*Math, Mat*	matemáticas
medicine	*Med*	medicina
meteorology	*Met(eor)*	meteorología
Mexican Spanish	*Méx*	español de México
masculine and feminine	*mf/m, f*	masculino y femenino
masculine and feminine plural	*mfpl/m, fpl*	plural masculino y femenino
military	*Mil*	militar
mining	*Min*	minas
masculine plural	*mpl*	plural masculino
music	*Mus, Mús*	música
noun	*n*	nombre
nautical	*Naut, Náut*	náutica
neuter	*neut*	neutro
feminine noun	*nf*	nombre femenino
plural feminine noun	*nfpl*	nombre femenino plural
masculine noun	*nm*	nombre masculino
masculine and feminine noun	*nmf/nm, f*	nombre masculino y femenino
plural masculine noun	*nmpl*	nombre masculino plural
plural noun	*npl*	nombre plural
optics	*Opt, Ópt*	óptica
ornithology	*Ornit(h)*	ornitología
Panamanian Spanish	*Pan*	español de Panamá
Paraguayan Spanish	*Par*	español de Paraguay
pejorative	*Pej*	despectivo
personal	*pers*	personal
Peruvian Spanish	*Perú*	español de Perú
photography	*Photo*	fotografía
physics	*Phys*	física
plural	*pl*	plural
politics	*Pol*	política
possessive	*poss, poses*	posesivo
past participle	*pp*	participio pasado
prefix	*pref*	prefijo
preposition	*prep*	preposición
present	*pres*	presente
present participle	*pres p*	gerundio
Puerto Rican Spanish	*PRico*	español de Puerto Rico
pronoun	*pron*	pronombre
pasttense	*pt*	pretérito
psychology	*Psych*	psicología
chemistry	*Quím*	químico
radio	*Rad*	radio
railways	*Rail*	ferrocarriles
Dominican Spanish	*RDom*	español de la República Dominicana
relative	*rel(at)*	relativo
religion	*Rel*	religión

Spanish from the River Plate region (Argentina, Uruguay, Paraguay)	*RP*	español de los países ribereños del Río de la Plata
Salvadoran Spanish	*Salv*	español de El Salvador
somebody, someone	*sb*	alguien
Scottish	*Scot*	escocés
singular	*sing*	singular
something	*sth*	algo
subjunctive	*subj*	subjuntivo
suffix	*suff*	sufijo
superlative	*superl*	superlativo
bullfighting	*Taurom*	tauromaquia
technical	*Tech, Téc*	técnica
telephones	*Tel*	teléfonos
tennis	*Ten*	tenis
textiles	*Tex(t)*	textiles
theatre	*Th*	teatro
television	*TV*	televisión
typography	*Typ*	tipografía
university	*Univ*	universidad
Uruguayan Spanish	*Urug*	español de Uruguay
American English	*US*	inglés norteamericano
usually	*usu*	usualmente
verb	*v*	verbo
Venezuelan Spanish	*Ven*	español de Venezuela
very informal		*v fam*
intransitive verb	*vi*	verbo intransitivo
reflexive verb	*vpr*	verbo pronominal
transitive verb	*vt*	verbo transitivo
inseparable phrasal verb	*vt insep*	verbo transitivo con partícula inseparable
separable phrasal verb	*vt sep*	verbo transitivo con partícula separable
vulgar	*Vulg*	vulgar
zoology	*Zool*	zoología
culturale quivalent	≃	equivalente cultural
registered trademark	®	marca registrada

All other labels are written in full.

Spanish Pronunciation Guide

The pronunciation of most Spanish words is predictable as there is a close match between spelling and pronunciation. The table below gives an explanation of that pronunciation. In the dictionary text therefore, pronunciation is only given when the word does not follow these rules, usually because it is a word of foreign origin. In these cases, the IPA (International Phonetic Alphabet) is used (see column 2 of the table below).

Letter in Spanish	IPA Symbol	Example in Spanish	Pronunciation (example in English)
Vowels			
Note that all vowel sounds in Spanish are shorter than in English			
a	a	**a**la	Similar to the sound in "f**a**ther" but more central
e	e	**e**có	Similar to the sound in "m**e**t"
i	i	**i**ris	Like the vowel sound in "m**ea**t" but much shorter
o	o	**o**so	Like the start of "**o**we" without the 'w' sound at the end
u	u	**u**va	Like the vowel sound in "s**oo**n" but much shorter
Semiconsonants			
"i" in the diphthongs: ia, ie, io, iu	j	h**i**ato, h**i**elo, av**i**ón, v**i**uda	**y**es
"u" in the diphthongs: ua, ue, ui, uo	w	s**u**ave, f**u**ego, h**u**ida	**w**in
Consonants			
b	b	**b**om**b**a (at beginning of word or after "m")	**b**oom
	β	a**b**ajo (all other contexts)	A "**b**" pronounced without quite closing the lips completely

Letter in Spanish	IPA Symbol	Example in Spanish	Pronunciation (example in English)
c	θ (in Spain)	**c**eña (before "e") **c**inco (before "i")	**th**anks (in Spain)
	s (in Latin America and southern Spain)		**s**un (in Latin America and southern Spain)
	k	**c**asa (all other contexts)	**c**at
ch	tʃ	cau**ch**o	ar**ch**
d	d	**d**on**d**e (at beginning of word or after "n") al**d**ea (after "l")	**d**ay
	ð	a**d**orno (all other contexts)	Similar to the sound in "mo**th**er" but less strong
f	f	**f**uria	**f**ire
g	χ	**g**ema (before "e") **g**irasol (before "i")	Like an "**h**" but pronounced at the back of the throat (similar to Scottish "lo**ch**")
	g	**g**ato (at beginning of word) len**g**ua (after "n")	**g**oose
	ɣ	a**g**ua (all other contexts)	Like a "**w**" pronounced while trying to say "**g**"
j	χ	**j**abalí	Like an "**h**" but pronounced at the back of the throat (similar to Scottish "lo**ch**")
l	l	**l**ado	**l**ake
ll	j	**ll**uvia	**y**es
	ʒ		In some regions (eg the Rio de la Plata area of South America) it is pronounced like the "**s**" in "plea**s**ure"
m	m	**m**ano	**m**an
n	n	**n**ulo	**n**o
	ŋ	ma**n**co, fa**n**go (before c and g)	parki**ng**
ñ	ŋ	a**ñ**o	oni**on**

Spanish Pronunciation Guide

Letter in Spanish	IPA Symbol	Example in Spanish	Pronunciation (example in English)
p	p	**p**a**p**a	**p**ool
r	r	do**r**ado (in between vowels) habla**r** (at end of syllable or word)	A rolled "**r**" sound (similar to Scottish "**r**")
	rr	**r**osa (at beginning of word) al**r**ededor (after l) en**r**edo (after n)	A much longer rolled "**r**" sound (similar to Scottish "**r**")
rr	rr	a**rr**oyo	A much longer rolled "**r**" sound (similar to Scottish "**r**")
s	s	**s**aco	**s**ound
sh	ʃ	**sh**ow	**sh**ow
t	t	**t**ela	**t**ea
v	b	in**v**ierno (after "n")	**b**oom
	β	a**v**e (all other contexts)	A "**b**" pronounced without quite closing the lips completely
x	ks	e**x**amen	e**x**tra
y	j	a**y**er	**y**es
	ʒ		In some regions (eg the Rio de la Plata area of South America) it is pronounced like the "**s**" in "plea**s**ure"
z	θ (in Spain)	**z**apato	**th**anks (in Spain)
	s (in Latin America and southern Spain)		**s**un (in Latin America and southern Spain)

ara ilustrar la pronunciación inglesa, en este diccionario utilizamos los símbolos del AFI
Alfabeto Fonético Internacional). En el siguiente cuadro, para cada sonido del inglés hay
ejemplos de palabras en inglés y palabras en español donde aparece un sonido similar. En
es casos en los que no hay sonido similar en español, ofrecemos una explicación de cómo
ronunciar.

Carácter AFI	Ejemplo en inglés	Ejemplo en español
Consonantes		
b]	**b**abb**l**e	**b**ebé
d]	**d**ig	**d**edo
dʒ]	**g**iant, **j**ig	se pronuncia como "**ll**" en el Río de la Plata pero con una "**d**" adelante, o como "**gi**" en italiano - **Gi**ovanna
f]	**f**it, **ph**ysics	**f**aro
g]	**g**rey, bi**g**	**g**ris
h]	**h**appy	"**h**" aspirada
j]	**y**ellow	se pronuncia como "**y**" o "**ll**" en España - **y**o, **ll**uvia
k]	**c**lay, **k**ick	**c**asa
l]	**l**ip	**l**abio
	pi**ll**	pape**l**
m]	**m**u**mm**y	**m**amá
n]	**n**ip, pi**n**	**n**ada
ŋ]	si**ng**	se pronuncia como "**n**" antes de "**c**" - ba**n**co
p]	**p**i**p**	**p**a**p**á
r]	**r**ig, **wr**ite	sonido entre "**r**" y "**rr**"
s]	**s**ick, **sc**ience	**s**apo
ʃ]	**sh**ip, na**ti**on	**sh**ow
t]	**t**ip, bu**tt**	**t**ela
tʃ]	**ch**ip, ba**tch**	cau**ch**o
θ]	**th**ick	**z**apato (como se pronuncia en España)
ð]	**th**is	se pronuncia como la "**d**" de "ha**d**a" pero más fuerte

Pronunciación del inglés

Carácter AFI	Ejemplo en inglés	Ejemplo en español
[v]	**v**ague, gi**v**e	se pronuncia como "**v**" de **v**ida, con los dientes apoyados sobre el labio inferior
[w]	**w**it, **w**hy	**wh**isky
[z]	**z**ip, phy**s**ics	"**s**" con sonido zumbante
[ʒ]	plea**s**ure	se pronuncia como "**y**" o "**ll**" en el Río de la Plata - **y**o, **ll**uvia
[χ]	lo**ch**	**j**ota

Vocales

En inglés, las vocales marcadas con dos puntos son mucho más alargadas

[æ]	r**a**g	se pronuncia "**e**" con posición bucal para "**a**"
[ɑ:]	l**ar**ge	"**a**" muy alargada
[ʌ]	c**u**p	"**a**" breve y cerrada
[e]	s**e**t	se pronuncia como "**e**" de **e**l**e**fant**e** pero más corta
[ɜ:]	c**ur**tain, w**e**re	se pronuncia como una "**e**" larga con posición bucal entre "**o**" y "**e**"
[ə]	utt**er**	se pronuncia como "**e**" con posición bucal para "**o**"
[ɪ]	b**i**g, w**o**men	"**i**" breve, a medio camino entre "**e**" e "**i**"
[i:]	l**ea**k, w**ee**	"**i**" muy alargada
[ɒ]	l**o**ck	"**o**" abierta
[ɔ:]	w**a**ll, c**o**rk	"**o**" cerrada y alargada
[ʊ]	p**u**t, l**oo**k	"**u**" breve
[u:]	m**oo**n	"**u**" muy alargada

Diptongos

[aɪ]	wh**y**, h**igh**, l**ie**	**ai**re
[aʊ]	h**ow**	**au**ra
[eə]	b**ear**	"**ea**" pronunciado muy brevemente y con sonido de "**e**" más marcado que el de "**a**"
[eɪ]	d**ay**, m**a**ke, m**ai**n	r**ei**na
[əʊ]	sh**ow**, g**o**	"**ou**" como en COU
[ɪə]	h**ere**, g**ear**	h**ie**lo pronunciado con el sonido de "**i**" más marcado y alargado que el de "**e**"
[ɔɪ]	b**oy**, s**oi**l	v**oy**
[ʊə]	p**oo**r	c**ue**rno pronunciado con el sonido de "**u**" más marcado y alargado que el de "**e**"

A

A, a [eɪ] *n* **a)** [the letter] A, a *f*; *Br* AUTO
A road ≃ carretera *f* nacional **b)** MUS
A la *m*

a [eɪ] *(unstressed* [ə], *before vowel or silent h* **an)**
indef art **a)** un, una; **a man / a woman**
un hombre / una mujer; **he has a big
nose** tiene la nariz grande **b)** [omitted in Spanish] **half a litre / an hour**
medio litro / media hora; **a hundred /
thousand people** cien / mil personas;
let's have a drink vamos a beber algo;
he's a teacher es profesor; **what a pity**
qué pena **c)** [each] **60 pence a kilo** 60
peniques el kilo; **to eat grapes two
at a time** comer las uvas de dos en
dos; **three times a week** tres veces a
la semana **d)** [a certain] un / una tal; **a
Mr Rees phoned** llamó un tal Sr. Rees

A3 1. *n* [paper size] formato *m* A3
2. *adj* **A3 paper** papel *m* (de formato)
A3

A4 1. *n* [paper size] formato *m* A4
2. *adj* **A4 paper** papel *m* (de formato)
A4

aback [əˈbæk] *adv* **to be taken aback**
quedarse de una pieza (**by** por)

abandon [əˈbændən] **1.** *n* desenfreno *m*;
with reckless abandon desenfrenadamente **2.** *vt* [child] abandonar; [job]
dejar; [project] renunciar a

abbey [ˈæbɪ] *n* abadía *f*

abbreviation [əbriːvɪˈeɪʃən] *n* abreviatura *f*

abdicate [ˈæbdɪkeɪt] *vt & vi* abdicar

abdomen [ˈæbdəmən] *n* abdomen *m*

abduction [əbˈdʌkʃən] *n* rapto *m*, secuestro *m*

ability [əˈbɪlɪtɪ] *n* [capability] capacidad *f*,
aptitud *f*; [talent] talento *m*

ablaze [əˈbleɪz] *adj & adv* en llamas,
ardiendo

able [ˈeɪbəl] *adj* [capable] capaz; **will you
be able to come on Tuesday?** ¿podrás
venir el martes?

able-bodied [eɪbəlˈbɒdɪd] *adj* sano(a);
able-bodied seaman marinero *m* de
primera

abnormal [æbˈnɔːməl] *adj* anormal

aboard [əˈbɔːd] **1.** *adv* a bordo; **to go
aboard** [ship] embarcarse; [train] subir
2. *prep* a bordo de

abolish [əˈbɒlɪʃ] *vt* abolir

abolition [æbəˈlɪʃən] *n* abolición *f*

abominable [əˈbɒmɪnəbəl] *adj* abominable; [dreadful] terrible

abort [əˈbɔːt] *vt a)* MED [pregnancy] abortar **b)** *Fig* [plan, project] interrumpir,
suspender **c)** COMPUT cancelar, abortar

abortion [əˈbɔːʃən] *n* MED aborto *m*;
abortion law ley *f* del aborto; **to have
an abortion** abortar

---

about [əˈbaʊt] *adv & prep* **a)** [concerning] acerca de, sobre; **a programme
about Paris** un programa sobre París; **to be worried about sth** estar
preocupado(a) por algo; **to speak
about sth** hablar de algo; **what's it
about?** [story etc] ¿de qué trata?; *Fam*
how about a game of tennis? ¿qué te
parece un partido de tenis?

b) [around] por todas partes; **don't
leave things lying about** no dejes
las cosas por medio; **there's nobody
about** no hay nadie; **to look about** mirar alrededor; **to rush about** correr de
un lado para otro; **we went for a walk
about the town** dimos una vuelta por
el pueblo

c) [approximately] más o menos; **it's
about three o'clock** son más o menos las tres; **it's about time you got
up** ya es hora de que te levantes; **it's**

just about finished está casi terminado; **she's about forty** tiene unos
cuarenta años
d) about time too! ¡ya era hora!; **it's
about to start** está a punto de empezar; **not to be about to do sth** no estar
dispuesto(a) a hacer algo

above [ə'bʌv] adv & prep **a)** [higher
than] encima de, sobre, arriba; **100
m above sea level** 100 m sobre el nivel del mar; **it's above the door** está
encima de la puerta; **the flat above** el
piso de arriba
b) [greater than] superior(a); **amounts
above £10** cantidades superiores a las
10 libras; Fig **a policy imposed from
above** una política impuesta desde
arriba
c) above all sobre todo; **he's not above
stealing** es capaz incluso de robar
d) [in book etc] más arriba

above-board [ə'bʌv'bɔːd] adj [scheme]
legítimo(a)

above-mentioned [ə'bʌvmenʃənd]
adj susodicho(a)

abreast [ə'brest] adv **to walk three
abreast** ir de tres en fondo; Fig **to keep
abreast of things** mantenerse al día

abroad [ə'brɔːd] adv **to be abroad** estar
en el extranjero; **to go abroad** irse al
extranjero

abrupt [ə'brʌpt] adj [manner] brusco(a);
[tone] áspero(a); [change] súbito(a)

abs [æbz] npl Fam [abdominal muscles]
abdominales mpl; **I'm working on my
abs** estoy trabajando los abdominales;
to have killer abs marcar abdominales

abscess ['æbses] n absceso m; [on gum]
flemón m

absence ['æbsəns] n [of person] ausencia f; [of thing] falta f

absent ['æbsənt] adj ausente; Fig **an
absent look** una mirada distraída

absent-minded [æbsənt'maɪndɪd] adj
distraído(a)

absolute ['æbsəluːt] adj absoluto(a);
[failure] total; [truth] puro(a); **it's an
absolute disgrace** es una auténtica
vergüenza

absolutely [æbsə'luːtlɪ] **1.** adv [com-
pletely] completamente; **absolutely
wrong** totalmente equivocado(a);
absolutely not en absoluto; **you're
absolutely right** tienes toda la razón
2. interj ¡desde luego!

absorb [əb'zɔːb] vt [liquid] absorber;
[sound, blow] amortiguar; Fig **to be absorbed in sth** estar absorto(a) en algo

abstain [əb'steɪn] vi abstenerse (**from**
de)

abstract ['æbstrækt] **1.** adj abstracto(a)
2. n [of thesis etc] resumen m

absurd [əb'sɜːd] adj absurdo(a)

abundant [ə'bʌndənt] adj abundante,
rico(a) (**in** en)

abuse 1. [ə'bjuːs] n **a)** [ill-treatment]
malos tratos; [misuse] abuso m
b) [insults] injurias fpl **2.** [ə'bjuːz] vt
a) [ill-treat] maltratar; [misuse] abusar
de **b)** [insult] injuriar

abusive [əb'juːsɪv] adj [insulting] insultante

AC n **a)** (abbr of **alternating current**) corriente f alterna **b)** = **air-conditioning**

academic [ækə'demɪk] **1.** adj aca-
démico(a); [career] universitario(a);
[discussion] teórico(a); **academic year**
año m escolar **2.** n académico(a) m,f

academy [ə'kædəmɪ] n [society] academia f; SCH instituto m de enseñanza
media; **academy of music** conservatorio m

accelerate [æk'seləreɪt] **1.** vt [engine]
acelerar; [step] aligerar **2.** vi [car, en-
gine] acelerar

accelerator [æk'seləreɪtə(r)] n acelerador m

accent ['æksənt] n acento m

accept [ək'sept] vt & vi aceptar; [theory]
admitir; **do you accept that ...?** ¿estás
de acuerdo en que ...?

acceptable [ək'septəbəl] adj [satisfac-
tory] aceptable; [tolerable] admisible

access ['ækses] *n* acceso *m*; **access card** tarjeta *f* de acceso; COMPUT **access provider** proveedor *m* de acceso (a internet); **access road** carretera *f* de acceso; **to have access to sth** tener libre acceso a algo

accessible [ək'sesəbəl] *adj* [place, position] accesible; [person] asequible

accessory [ək'sesərɪ] *n* **a)** JUR cómplice *mf* **b) accessories** accesorios *mpl*; [for outfit] complementos *mpl*

accident ['æksɪdənt] *n* accidente *m*; [coincidence] casualidad *f*; **it was an accident on my part** lo hice sin querer; **car accident** accidente *m* de carretera; **by accident** por casualidad

accidental [æksɪ'dentəl] *adj* fortuito(a); [unintended] imprevisto(a)

acclaim [ə'kleɪm] **1.** *n* aclamación *f* **2.** *vt* aclamar

acclimatize [ə'klaɪmətaɪz], US **acclimate** ['æklɪmeɪt] *vt* aclimatar

accommodate [ə'kɒmədeɪt] *vt* **a)** [guests] alojar **b) to accommodate sb's wishes** complacer a algn

accommodation [əkɒmə'deɪʃən], US **accommodations** *n* [lodgings] alojamiento *m*

accompany [ə'kʌmpənɪ] *vt* acompañar

accomplice [ə'kʌmplɪs] *n* cómplice *mf*

accomplish [ə'kʌmplɪʃ] *vt* [aim] conseguir; [task, mission] llevar a cabo

accomplishment [ə'kʌmplɪʃmənt] *n* **a)** [of task] realización *f*; [of duty] cumplimiento *m* **b) accomplishments** [talents] dotes *fpl*

accord [ə'kɔːd] **1.** *n* [agreement] acuerdo *m*; **of her/his own accord** espontáneamente **2.** *vt* [honour etc] conceder

accordance [ə'kɔːdəns] *n* **in accordance with** de acuerdo con

according [ə'kɔːdɪŋ] *prep* **according to** según; **everything went according to plan** todo salió conforme a los planes

accordingly [ə'kɔːdɪŋlɪ] *adv* **a) to act accordingly** [appropriately] obrar según y conforme **b)** [therefore] así pues

accordion [ə'kɔːdɪən] *n* acordeón *m*

account [ə'kaʊnt] *n* **a)** [report] informe *m*; **by all accounts** al decir de todos **b) I was fearful on her account** sufría por ella; **it's of no account** no tiene importancia; **on account of** a causa de; **on no account** bajo ningún concepto; **to take account of, to take into account** tener en cuenta

c) COMM cuenta *f*; **to keep the accounts** llevar las cuentas; **accounts department** servicio *m* de contabilidad; **to open/close an account** abrir/cancelar una cuenta; **current account** cuenta corriente; **account number** número *m* de cuenta

■ **account for** *vt insep* [explain] explicar

accountable [ə'kaʊntəbəl] *adj* **to be accountable to sb for sth** ser responsable ante algn de algo

accountant [ə'kaʊntənt] *n Esp* contable *mf*, *Am* contador(a) *m,f*

accounting [ə'kaʊntɪŋ] *n* contabilidad *f*

accumulate [ə'kjuːmjʊleɪt] **1.** *vt* acumular; [fortune] amasar **2.** *vi* acumularse

accuracy ['ækjʊrəsɪ] *n* [of number etc] exactitud *f*; [of shot, criticism] certeza *f*

accurate ['ækjʊrət] *adj* [number] exacto(a); [shot, criticism] certero(a); [answer] correcto(a); [observation] acertado(a); [instrument] de precisión; [translation] fiel

accusation [ækjʊ'zeɪʃən] *n* acusación *f*

accuse [ə'kjuːz] *vt* acusar

accused [ə'kjuːzd] *n* **the accused** el/la acusado(a)

accustom [ə'kʌstəm] *vt* acostumbrar; **to be accustomed to doing sth** estar acostumbrado(a) a hacer algo

ace [eɪs] *n* **a)** CARDS & *Fig* as *m* **b)** [in tennis] ace *m*

ache [eɪk] **1.** *n* dolor *m*; **aches and pains** achaques *mpl* **2.** *vi* doler; **my back aches** me duele la espalda

achieve [ə'tʃiːv] *vt* [attain] conseguir, alcanzar; [accomplish] llevar a cabo, realizar

achievement [ə'tʃi:vmənt] *n* [attainment] logro *m*; [completion] realización *f*; [feat] hazaña *f*

acid ['æsɪd] **1.** *adj* ácido(a); [taste] agrio(a); [remark] mordaz; **acid rain** lluvia ácida; *Fig* **acid test** prueba decisiva **2.** *n* ácido *m*

acknowledge [ək'nɒlɪdʒ] *vt* a) [recognize] reconocer; [claim, defeat] admitir; [present] agradecer; [letter] acusar recibo de **b)** [greet] saludar

acknowledgement [ək'nɒlɪdʒmənt] *n* a) [recognition] reconocimiento *m*; [of letter] acuse *m* de recibo **b) acknowledgements** [in preface] menciones *fpl*

acne ['æknɪ] *n* acné *m*

acoustic [ə'ku:stɪk] **1.** *adj* acústico(a) **2.** *npl* **acoustics** acústica *f*

acquaint [ə'kweɪnt] *vt* **to acquaint sb with the facts** informar a algn de los detalles; **to be acquainted with the procedure** estar al corriente de como se procede; **to be acquainted with sb** conocer a algn

acquaintance [ə'kweɪntəns] *n* a) conocimiento *m*; **to make sb's acquaintance** conocer a algn **b)** [person] conocido(a) *m,f*

acquire [ə'kwaɪə(r)] *vt* adquirir

acquit [ə'kwɪt] *vt* a) *JUR* **to acquit sb of sth** absolver a algn de algo **b)** **to acquit oneself well** defenderse bien

acre ['eɪkə(r)] *n* acre *m* (= *aprox* 40,47 *áreas*)

acrobat ['ækrəbæt] *n* acróbata *mf*

acrobatic [ækrə'bætɪk] *adj* acrobático(a)

across [ə'krɒs] **1.** *adv* a través; **the river is 30 m across** el río mide 30 m de ancho; **to go across** atravesar; **to run across** atravesar corriendo **2.** *prep* a) a través de; **they live across the road** viven enfrente; **to go across the street** cruzar la calle **b)** [at the other side of] al otro lado de

acrylic [ə'krɪlɪk] *adj* acrílico(a)

act [ækt] **1.** *n* a) [action] acto *m*, acción *f*; **act of God** caso *m* de fuerza mayor

b) *JUR* **act** (*Br* of parliament *or US* of Congress) ley *f*

c) *THEAT* acto *m*; [turn in show] número *m*

2. *vt THEAT* [part] interpretar; [character] representar; *Fig* **to act the fool** hacer el tonto

3. *vi* a) *THEAT* hacer teatro; *CIN* hacer cine; *Fig* [pretend] fingir

b) [behave] comportarse

c) [take action] actuar, obrar; **to act on sb's advice** seguir el consejo de algn

d) [work] funcionar; [drug etc] actuar; **to act as a deterrent** servir de disuasivo

e) to act as director hacer de director

■ **act out** *vt sep* exteriorizar

■ **act up** *vi Fam* [machine] funcionar mal; [child] dar guerra

acting ['æktɪŋ] **1.** *adj* interino(a) **2.** *n* [profession] teatro *m*; **he's done some acting** ha hecho algo de teatro

action ['ækʃən] *n* a) [deed] acción *f*; *MIL* acción de combate; **to be out of action** [person] estar fuera de servicio; [machine] estar estropeado(a); **to take action** tomar medidas **b)** *JUR* demanda *f* **c)** *Br* TV **action replay** repetición *f*

active ['æktɪv] *adj* activo(a); [energetic] vigoroso(a); [interest] vivo(a); *LING* **active voice** voz activa

activewear ['æktɪvweə(r)] *n* ropa *f* de deporte

activity [æk'tɪvɪtɪ] *n* [of person] actividad *f*; [on street etc] bullicio *m*

actor ['æktə(r)] *n* actor *m*

actress ['æktrɪs] *n* actriz *f*

actual ['æktʃʊəl] *adj* real, verdadero(a)

actually ['æktʃʊəlɪ] *adv* [really] en efecto, realmente; [even] incluso, hasta; [in fact] de hecho

acupuncture ['ækjʊpʌŋktʃə(r)] *n* acupuntura *f*

acute [ə'kju:t] *adj* agudo(a); [pain] intenso(a); [hearing] muy fino(a); [shortage] grave; [mind] perspicaz

ad [æd] *n Fam* anuncio *m*

adapt [ə'dæpt] **1.** *vt* adaptar (**to** a); **to adapt oneself to sth** adaptarse a a algo **2.** *vi* adaptarse

adaptable [ə'dæptəbəl] *adj* [instrument] ajustable; **he's very adaptable** se amolda fácilmente a las circunstancias

adapter, adaptor [ə'dæptə(r)] *n* ELEC ladrón *m*

add [æd] **1.** *vt* [numbers] sumar; [one thing to another] añadir **2.** *vi* [count] sumar ■ **add on** *vt sep* to add sth on **(to)** añadir algo (a) ■ **add to** *vt insep* aumentar ■ **add up 1.** *vt sep* sumar **2.** *vi* [numbers] sumar; *Fig* **it doesn't add up** no tiene sentido; **it doesn't add up to much** no es gran cosa

addict ['ædɪkt] *n* adicto(a) *m,f*; *Fam* **television addict** teleadicto(a) *m,f*

addicted [ə'dɪktɪd] *adj* adicto(a); **to become addicted to sth** enviciarse con algo

addictive [ə'dɪktɪv] *adj* que crea adicción

addition [ə'dɪʃən] *n* MATH adición *f*; [increase] aumento *m*; **an addition to the family** un nuevo miembro de la familia; **in addition to** además de

additional [ə'dɪʃənəl] *adj* adicional

additive ['ædɪtɪv] *n* aditivo *m*

address [ə'dres] **1.** *n* **a)** [on letter] dirección *f*, señas *fpl* **b)** [speech] discurso *m* **2.** *vt* **a)** [letter] dirigir **b)** [speak to] dirigirse (**to** a); **to address the floor** tomar la palabra **c)** [use form of address to] tratar de

adept [ə'dept] **1.** *adj* experto(a) (**at** en) **2.** *n* experto(a) *m,f*

adequate ['ædɪkwɪt] *adj* [enough] suficiente; [satisfactory] adecuado(a)

adhere [əd'hɪə(r)] *vi* [stick] pegarse (**to** a) ■ **adhere to** *vt insep* [policy] adherirse a; [contract] cumplir con

adhesive [əd'hi:sɪv] **1.** *adj* adhesivo(a); [sticky] pegajoso(a); **adhesive tape** cinta adhesiva **2.** *n* adhesivo *m*

adjacent [ə'dʒeɪsənt] *adj* [building] contiguo(a); [land] colindante; **adjacent to** contiguo(a) a

adjective ['ædʒɪktɪv] *n* adjetivo *m*

adjoining [ə'dʒɔɪnɪŋ] *adj* contiguo(a); [land] colindante; **the adjoining room** la habitación de al lado

adjourn [ə'dʒɜ:n] **1.** *vt* [postpone] aplazar; [court] levantar **2.** *vi* aplazarse (**until** hasta)

adjust [ə'dʒʌst] **1.** *vt* [machine etc] ajustar; *Fig* [methods] variar **2.** *vi* [person] adaptarse (**to** a)

adjustable [ə'dʒʌstəbəl] *adj* ajustable

administer [əd'mɪnɪstə(r)] *vt* [country] gobernar; [justice] administrar

administration [ədmɪnɪ'streɪʃən] *n* [management, of justice] administración *f*; [governing body] dirección *f*; *US* [government] gobierno *m*, administración *f*

administrator [əd'mɪnɪstreɪtə(r)] *n* administrador(a) *m,f*

admirable [ædmərəbəl] *adj* admirable

admiral ['ædmərəl] *n* almirante *m*

admire [əd'maɪə(r)] *vt* admirar

admission [əd'mɪʃən] *n* **a)** [to school etc] ingreso *m*; [price] entrada *f* **b)** [of fact] reconocimiento *m*; [confession] confesión *f*

admit [əd'mɪt] *vt* **a)** [person] dejar entrar; **to be admitted to hospital** ser ingresado(a) en el hospital **b)** [acknowledge] reconocer; [crime, guilt] confesar

admittance [əd'mɪtəns] *n* [entry] entrada *f*

admittedly [əd'mɪtɪdlɪ] *adv* la verdad es que…

adolescent [ædə'lesənt] *n* adolescente *mf*

adopt [ə'dɒpt] *vt* adoptar; [suggestion] aceptar

adopted [ə'dɒptɪd] *adj* **adopted child** hijo(a) *m,f* adoptivo(a)

adorable [ə'dɔ:rəbəl] *adj* encantador(a)

adore [ə'dɔ:(r)] *vt* adorar

adrenalin(e) [ə'drenəlɪn] *n* adrenalina *f*

Adriatic [eɪdrɪ'ætɪk] *adj* **the Adriatic (Sea)** el (mar) Adriático

adrift [əˈdrɪft] **1.** adj ala deriva; **to feel adrift** sentirse perdido(a) **2.** adv Fig **to go adrift** ir a la deriva

ADSL n (abbr of **Asymmetric Digital Subscriber Line**) ADSL m

adult [ˈædʌlt] **1.** adj [person] adulto(a), mayor; [film, education] para adultos **2.** n adulto(a) m,f

adultery [əˈdʌltərɪ] n adulterio m

adulthood [ˈædʌlthʊd] n edad f adulta; **in adulthood** en la edad adulta

advance [ədˈvɑːns] **1.** n a) [movement] avance m; Fig [progress] progreso m; **to have sth ready in advance** tener algo preparado de antemano; **to make advances (to)** [person] insinuarse (a) **b)** [loan] anticipo m
2. adj [before time] adelantado(a); CIN & THEAT **advance bookings** reservas fpl por adelantado
3. vt **a)** [troops] avanzar; [time, date] adelantar
b) [idea] proponer; [opinion] dar
4. vi [move forward] avanzar, adelantarse; [make progress] hacer progresos; [gain promotion] ascender

advanced [ədˈvɑːnst] adj [developed] avanzado(a); [student] adelantado(a); [course] superior; Br **Advanced level** examen final o diploma en una asignatura de los estudios preuniversitarios

advantage [ədˈvɑːntɪdʒ] n ventaja f; **advantage Velasco** [in tennis] ventaja para Velasco; **to take advantage of sb/sth** abusar de algn / aprovechar algo

adventure [ədˈventʃə(r)] n aventura f; **adventure sport** deporte m de aventura

adventurous [ədˈventʃərəs] adj aventurero(a)

adverb [ˈædvɜːb] n adverbio m

adverse [ˈædvɜːs] adj [effect] desfavorable; [conditions] adverso(a); [winds] contrario(a)

advert [ˈædvɜːt] n Fam anuncio m

advertise [ˈædvətaɪz] **1.** vt anunciar **2.** vi hacer publicidad; [in newspaper] poner un anuncio; **to advertise for sth/sb** buscar algo / a algn mediante un anuncio

advertisement [ədˈvɜːtɪsmənt] n anuncio m; **advertisements** publicidad f

advertising [ˈædvətaɪzɪŋ] **1.** n publicidad f, propaganda f; [in newspaper] anuncios mpl **2.** adj publicitario(a); **advertising agency** agencia f de publicidad

advice [ədˈvaɪs] n consejos mpl; **a piece of advice** un consejo; **advice slip** [from ATM] comprobante m; **to take legal advice on a matter** consultar el caso con un abogado; **to take sb's advice** seguir los consejos de algn

advisable [ədˈvaɪzəbəl] adj aconsejable

advise [ədˈvaɪz] vt aconsejar; [on business etc] asesorar; **I advise you to do it** te aconsejo que lo hagas

adviser [ədˈvaɪzə(r)] n consejero(a) m,f; [in business etc] asesor(a) m,f

advocate 1. [ˈædvəkɪt] n Scot JUR abogado(a) m,f; [supporter] defensor(a) m,f **2.** [ˈædvəkeɪt] vt [reform] abogar por; [plan] apoyar

aerial [ˈeərɪəl] **1.** adj aéreo(a) **2.** n antena f

aerobics [eəˈrəʊbɪks] n sing aerobic m

aeroplane [ˈeərəpleɪn] n Br avión m

aerosol [ˈeərəsɒl] n aerosol m

aesthetic [iːsˈθetɪk] adj estético(a)

affair [əˈfeə(r)] n [matter] asunto m; [event] acontecimiento m; **that's my affair** eso es asunto mío; **business affairs** negocios mpl; **foreign affairs** asuntos exteriores; **love affair** aventura amorosa

affect [əˈfekt] vt [person, health] afectar; [prices, future] influir en; [touch emotionally] conmover

affected [əˈfektɪd] adj **a)** [unnatural] afectado(a) **b)** [influenced] influido(a) **c)** [touched emotionally] conmovido(a) **d)** [pretended] fingido(a)

affection [əˈfekʃən] n afecto m, cariño m

affectionate [əˈfekʃənɪt] adj cariñoso(a)

affinity [ə'fɪnɪtɪ] n afinidad f; [liking] simpatía f

affirm [ə'fɜ:m] vt afirmar, sostener

affirmative [ə'fɜ:mətɪv] **1.** adj afirmativo(a) **2.** n **he answered in the affirmative** contestó que sí

afflict [ə'flɪkt] vt afligir

affluent ['æfluənt] adj [society] opulento(a); [person] rico(a)

afford [ə'fɔ:d] vt a) [be able to buy] permitirse el lujo de; **I can't afford a new car** no puedo pagar un coche nuevo b) [be able to do] permitirse; **you can't afford to miss the opportunity** no puedes perderte la ocasión

affordable [ə'fɔ:dəbəl] adj [price, purchase] asequible

Afghanistan [æf'gænɪstɑ:n] n Afganistán

afield [ə'fi:ld] adv **far afield** muy lejos

afloat [ə'fləʊt] adv **to keep afloat** mantenerse a flote

afraid [ə'freɪd] adj a) **to be afraid** tener miedo (**of sb** a algn; **of sth** de algo); **I'm afraid of it** me da miedo b) **I'm afraid not** me temo que no; **I'm afraid so** me temo que sí; **I'm afraid you're wrong** me temo que estás equivocado(a)

afresh [ə'freʃ] adv de nuevo

Africa ['æfrɪkə] n África

African ['æfrɪkən] adj & n africano(a) (m,f); **African American** afroamericano(a) m,f

African-American adj afroamericano(a)

after ['ɑ:ftə(r)] **1.** adv después; **after all** después de todo; **soon after** poco después; **the day after** el día siguiente **2.** prep a) [later] después de; US **it's ten after five** son las cinco y diez; **soon after arriving** al poco rato de llegar; **the day after tomorrow** pasado mañana b) [behind] detrás de, tras; **after you!** ¡pase usted!; **they went in one after the other** entraron uno tras otro; **the police are after them** la policía anda tras ellos

c) [about] por; **they asked after you** preguntaron por ti; **what's he after?** ¿qué pretende? **3.** conj después (de) que; **after it happened** después de que ocurriera

after-effect ['ɑ:ftərɪfekt] n efecto secundario

afterlife ['ɑ:ftəlaɪf] n vida f después de la muerte

aftermath ['ɑ:ftəmæθ] n secuelas fpl

afternoon [ɑ:ftə'nu:n] n tarde f; **good afternoon!** ¡buenas tardes!; **in the afternoon** por la tarde

afters [ɑ:ftə(r)z] npl Br Fam postre m

after-sales service [ɑ:ftəseɪlz'sɜ:vɪs] n COMM servicio m posventa

aftershave (lotion) ['ɑ:ftəʃeɪv('ləʊʃən)] n loción f para después del afeitado or Méx rasurado

afterthought ['ɑ:ftəθɔ:t] n ocurrencia f tardía

afterward(s) ['ɑ:ftəwəd(z)] adv después, más tarde

again [ə'gen] adv a) otra vez, de nuevo; **I tried again and again** lo intenté una y otra vez; **to do sth again** volver a hacer algo; **never again!** ¡nunca más!; **now and again** de vez en cuando; **once again** otra vez b) [besides] además; **then again** por otra parte

against [ə'genst] prep a) [touching] contra b) [opposing] contra, en contra (de); **against the grain** a contrapelo; **it's against the law** es ilegal c) as against en contraste con, comparado con

age [eɪdʒ] **1.** n a) edad f; **she's eighteen years of age** tiene dieciocho años; **to be under age** ser menor de edad; **to come of age** llegar a la mayoría de edad; **age limit** límite m de edad; **old age** vejez f b) [period] época f; **the Iron Age** la Edad de Hierro c) Fam [long time] eternidad f; **it's ages since I last saw her** hace siglos que no la veo **2.** vt & vi envejecer

aged¹ [eɪdʒd] adj de or a la edad de

aged² ['eɪdʒɪd] npl **the aged** los ancianos

agency ['eɪdʒənsɪ] n a) COMM agencia f b) **by the agency of** por medio de

agenda [əˈdʒendə] n orden m del día

agent [ˈeɪdʒənt] n agente mf; [representative] representante mf

aggravate [ˈægrəveɪt] vt [worsen] agravar; [annoy] fastidiar, molestar, RP hinchar

aggressive [əˈgresɪv] adj [violent] agresivo(a), violento(a); [dynamic] dinámico(a)

aghast [əˈgɑːst] adj espantado(a)

agile [Br ˈædʒaɪl, US ˈædʒəl] adj ágil

agitate [ˈædʒɪteɪt] 1. vt [shake] agitar; Fig [worry] perturbar 2. vi POL to agitate against sth hacer campaña en contra de algo

agitated [ædʒɪteɪtɪd] adj inquieto(a), agitado(a); to be agitated estar inquieto(a) or agitado(a)

agnostic [ægˈnɒstɪk] n agnóstico(a) m,f

ago [əˈgəʊ] adv a long time ago hace mucho tiempo; as long ago as 1910 ya en 1910; a week ago hace una semana; how long ago? ¿hace cuánto tiempo?

agonizing [ˈægənaɪzɪŋ] adj [pain] atroz; [decision] desesperante

agony [ˈægənɪ] n dolor m muy fuerte; [anguish] angustia f; he was in agony with his back tenía un dolor insoportable de espalda

agree [əˈgriː] 1. vi a) [be in agreement] estar de acuerdo; [reach agreement] ponerse de acuerdo; [consent] consentir; to agree to do sth consentir en hacer algo; to agree with sb estar de acuerdo con algn b) [harmonize - things] concordar; [people] congeniar; onions don't agree with me la cebolla no me sienta bien 2. vt acordar

agreeable [əˈgriːəbəl] adj [pleasant] agradable; [person] simpático(a); [in agreement] de acuerdo

agreement [əˈgriːmənt] n [arrangement] acuerdo m; COMM contrato m; to reach an agreement llegar a un acuerdo

agricultural [ægrɪˈkʌltʃərəl] adj agrícola; [college] de agricultura

agriculture [ˈægrɪkʌltʃə(r)] n agricultura f

agritourism [ˈægrɪtʊərɪzəm] n agroturismo m

agro-industry [ˈægrəʊ-] n agroindustria f

aground [əˈgraʊnd] adv to run aground encallar, varar

ahead [əˈhed] adv [forwards] adelante; [in front] delante, Am adelante; [early] antes; go ahead! ¡adelante!; to be ahead llevar la ventaja; to go ahead ir adelante; Fig to go ahead with sth llevar algo adelante; [start] comenzar algo; to get ahead triunfar; to look ahead pensar en el futuro

aid [eɪd] 1. n ayuda f; [rescue] auxilio m; in aid of a beneficio de; to come to the aid of sb acudir en ayuda de algn; aid worker cooperante mf 2. vt ayudar; to aid and abet sb ser cómplice de algn

aide [eɪd] n ayudante mf

AIDS [eɪdz] n (abbr of Acquired Immune Deficiency Syndrome) sida m

ailing [ˈeɪlɪŋ] adj achacoso(a)

ailment [ˈeɪlmənt] n enfermedad f (leve), achaque m

aim [eɪm] 1. n [with weapon] puntería f; [target] propósito m 2. vt [gun] apuntar (at a or hacia); [attack, action] dirigir (at a or hacia) ▪ aim at vt insep [target] tirar para; to aim at doing sth tener pensado hacer algo ▪ aim to vt insep to aim to do sth tener la intención de hacer algo

aimless [ˈeɪmlɪs] adj sin objeto, sin propósito

air [eə(r)] 1. n a) aire m; Fig to be (up) in the air [plans] estar en el aire; to travel by air viajar en avión; to throw sth up in the air lanzar algo al aire; Fig it's still in the air todavía queda por resolver; AUTO air bag airbag m; air base base aérea; air bed colchón m hinchable; air conditioning aire acondicionado; Air Force Fuerzas Aéreas; air freshener ambientador m; air gun pistola f de aire comprimido; air hostess azafata f de vuelo, Am aeromoza f; air letter carta aérea; air pocket bache m; air pressure presión atmosférica; air raid ataque

aéreo; **air traffic control** control *m* de tráfico aéreo; **air traffic controller** controlador(a) *m,f* aéreo(a)
b) RADIO & TV **to be on the air** [programme] estar emitiendo, estar en antena; [person] estar transmitiendo
c) [appearance] aspecto *m*
2. *vt* **a)** [bed, clothes] airear; [room] ventilar; *Fig* [grievance] airear; [knowledge] hacer alarde de
b) [make publicly known] airear, ventilar
c) RADIO & TV emitir, transmitir
3. *vi* **a)** [clothes] secar
b) *US* RADIO & TV **the movie airs next week** la película sale la próxima semana

airbag ['eabæg] *n* AUTO Airbag® *m*

air-conditioned ['eakɒndɪʃənd] *adj* climatizado(a)

aircraft ['eakrɑ:ft] *(pl* **aircraft)** *n* avión *m*; **aircraft carrier** portaaviones *m inv*

airfield ['eafi:ld] *n* campo *m* de aviación

airline ['eəlaɪn] *n* línea aérea

airmail ['eəmeɪl] *n* correo aéreo; **by airmail** por avión

airplane ['eəpleɪn] *n US* avión *m*

airport ['eəpɔ:t] *n* aeropuerto *m*; **airport tax** tasas *fpl* de aeropuerto

airtight ['eətaɪt] *adj* hermético(a)

airy ['eərɪ] *(compar* **airier,** *superl* **airiest)** *adj* [well-ventilated] bien ventilado(a); [vague, carefree] ligero(a)

aisle [aɪl] *n* [in church] nave *f*; [in theatre] pasillo *m*

ajar [ə'dʒɑ:(r)] *adj* & *adv* entreabierto(a)

alarm [ə'lɑ:m] **1.** *n* **a)** alarma *f*; **alarm clock** despertador *m*; AUTO **car alarm** alarma *f* de coche **b)** [fear] inquietud *f*; **to cause alarm** provocar temor **2.** *vt* alarmar

alas [ə'læs] *interj* ¡ay!, ¡ay de mí!

Albania [æl'beɪnɪə] *n* Albania

Albanian [æl'beɪnɪən] **1.** *n* **a)** [person] albanés(esa) *m,f* **b)** [language] albanés *m* **2.** *adj* albanés(esa)

album ['ælbəm] *n* álbum *m*

alcohol ['ælkəhɒl] *n* alcohol *m*

alcoholic [ælkə'hɒlɪk] *adj* & *n* alcohólico(a) *(m,f)*

alcove ['ælkəʊv] *n* hueco *m*

ale [eɪl] *n* cerveza *f*; **brown / pale ale** cerveza negra / rubia

alert [ə'lɜ:t] **1.** *adj* alerta; [lively] despabilado(a) **2.** *n* alerta *m*; **to be on the alert** estar alerta **3.** *vt* **to alert sb to sth** avisar a algn de algo

A-level ['eɪlevəl] *n Br* SCH *(abbr of* **Advanced level)** *examen final o diploma en una asignatura de los estudios preuniversitarios*

algebra ['ældʒɪbrə] *n* álgebra *f*

Algeria [æl'dʒɪərɪə] *n* Argelia

Algerian [æl'dʒɪərɪən] *adj* & *n* argelino(a) *(m,f)*

alias ['eɪlɪəs] *(pl* **aliases** [-i:z]*)* **1.** *n* **a)** alias *m* **b)** COMPUT [in e-mail, on desktop] alias *m* **2.** *adv* alias

alibi ['ælɪbaɪ] *n* coartada *f*

alien ['eɪlɪən] **1.** *adj* [foreign] extranjero(a); [from space] extraterrestre; **alien to** ajeno(a) a **2.** *n* [foreigner] extranjero(a) *m,f*; [from space] extraterrestre *mf*

alienate ['eɪlɪəneɪt] *vt* **a) to alienate sb** ofender a algn; **to alienate oneself from sb** alejarse de algn **b)** JUR enajenar

alight¹ [ə'laɪt] *adj* [on fire] ardiendo(a)

alight² [ə'laɪt] *vi* [get off] apearse **(from de)**

align [ə'laɪn] *vt* alinear

alike [ə'laɪk] **1.** *adj* [similar] parecidos(as); [the same] iguales **2.** *adv* [in the same way] de la misma manera, igualmente; **dressed alike** vestidos(as) iguales

alimony ['ælɪmənɪ] *n* JUR pensión alimenticia

alive [ə'laɪv] *adj* vivo(a); *Fig* [teeming] lleno(a) **(with** de); **to be alive** estar vivo(a)

all [ɔ:l] **1.** *adj* todo(a), todos(as); **all year** (durante) todo el año; **all kinds of things** todo tipo de cosas; **at all hours**

a todas horas; **at all times** siempre; **she works all the time** siempre está trabajando; **all six of us were there** los seis estábamos allí

2. *pron* todo(a), todos(as); **after all** al fin y al cabo; **all of his work** toda su obra; **all of us** todos(as) nosotros(as); **all who saw it** todos los que lo vieron; **all you can do is wait** lo único que puedes hacer es esperar; **I don't like it at all** no me gusta en absoluto; **is that all?** ¿eso es todo?; **most of** or **above all** sobre todo; **once and for all** de una vez por todas; **thanks — not at all** gracias — de nada; **all in all** en conjunto; **that's all** ya está; **the score was one all** empataron a uno

3. *adv* **all by myself** completamente solo(a); **all at once** [suddenly] de repente; [altogether] de una vez; **all the better** tanto mejor; **not at all** [when thanked] de nada, no hay de qué; **she's not at all happy** no está nada contenta; **anything at all will do** cualquier cosa valdrá; **do you know her at all?** ¿la conoces de algo?; **he knew all along** lo sabía desde el principio; **it's all but impossible** es casi imposible; **I'm not all that tired** no estoy tan cansado(a) como eso

---

all-around [ˈɔːləraʊnd] *US adj* = **all-round**

allegation [ælɪˈɡeɪʃən] *n* alegato *m*

allege [əˈledʒ] *vt* sostener, pretender (**that** que); **it is alleged that she accepted a bribe** supuestamente aceptó un soborno

allegiance [əˈliːdʒəns] *n* lealtad *f*

allergenic [æləˈdʒenɪk] *adj* alérgeno(a)

allergic [əˈlɜːdʒɪk] *adj* alérgico(a) (**to** a)

allergy [ˈælədʒɪ] *n* alergia *f*

alleviate [əˈliːvɪeɪt] *vt* [pain] aliviar

all-expenses-paid *adj* con todos los gastos pagados

alley [ˈælɪ] *n* callejón *m*; **blind alley** callejón sin salida

alliance [əˈlaɪəns] *n* alianza *f*

allied [ˈælaɪd] *adj* aliado(a)

alligator [ˈælɪɡeɪtə(r)] *n* caimán *m*

all-night [ˈɔːlnaɪt] *adj* [café etc] abierto(a) toda la noche; [vigil] que dura toda la noche

allocate [ˈæləkeɪt] *vt* destinar (**to** para)

allot [əˈlɒt] *vt* asignar

allotment [əˈlɒtmənt] *n* a) [of time, money] asignación *f* b) Br [plot of land] huerto *m* de ocio, parcela *f* (*arrendada por el ayuntamiento para cultivo*)

all-out [ˈɔːlaʊt] **1.** *adj* [effort] supremo(a); [attack] concentrado(a) **2.** *adv* **to go all-out to do sth** emplearse a fondo para hacer algo

allow [əˈlaʊ] *vt* a) [permit] permitir; [a request] acceder a; **to allow sb to do sth** permitir que algn haga algo b) [allot -time] dejar; [money] destinar ▪ **allow for** *vt insep* tener en cuenta

allowance [əˈlaʊəns] *n* [money given] asignación *f*; *US* [pocket money] paga *f*; **to make allowances for sb/sth** disculpar a algn / tener algo en cuenta; **recommended daily allowance** [food] valor *m* diario recomendado; **tax allowance** desgravación *f* fiscal; **travel allowance** dietas *fpl* de viaje

alloy [ˈælɔɪ] *n* aleación *f*

all-purpose [ˈɔːlˈpɜːpəs] *adj* [cleaner, adhesive] multiuso

all right [ɔːlˈraɪt] **1.** *adj* [okay] bien; **thank you very much — that's all right** muchas gracias — de nada **2.** *adv* a) [well] bien b) [definitely] sin duda c) [okay] de acuerdo, vale

all-round [ˈɔːlraʊnd] *adj* [athlete etc] completo(a)

allusion [əˈluːʒən] *n* alusión *f*

ally [ˈælaɪ] **1.** *n* aliado(a) *m,f* **2.** *vt* **to ally oneself to/with sb** aliarse a/con algn

almighty [ɔːlˈmaɪtɪ] **1.** *adj* [all-powerful] todopoderoso(a) **2.** *n* **the Almighty** el Todopoderoso

almond [ˈɑːmənd] *n* almendra *f*

almost [ˈɔːlməʊst] *adv* casi

alone [əˈləʊn] **1.** *adj* solo(a); **can I speak to you alone?** ¿puedo hablar contigo a solas?; **let alone** ni mucho menos;

leave it alone! ¡no lo toques!; **leave me alone** déjame en paz; **to be alone** estar solo(a) **2.** *adv* solamente, sólo *or* solo

along [ə'lɒŋ] **1.** *adv* **come along!** ¡anda, ven!; **he'll be along in ten minutes** llegará dentro de diez minutos; **along with** junto con **2.** *prep* [the length of] a lo largo de; **to walk along the street** andar por la calle; **it's just along the street** está un poco más abajo

alongside [ə'lɒŋsaɪd] **1.** *adv* NAUT de costado **2.** *prep* al lado de

aloof [ə'luːf] **1.** *adj* [person] distante **2.** *adv* **to keep oneself aloof (from)** mantenerse a distancia (de)

aloud [ə'laʊd] *adv* en voz alta

alphabet ['ælfəbet] *n* alfabeto *m*

alphabetical [ælfə'betɪkəl] *adj* alfabético(a)

Alps [ælps] *npl* **the Alps** los Alpes

already [ɔːl'redɪ] *adv* ya

alright [ɔːl'raɪt] *adj* & *adv* = **all right**

also ['ɔːlsəʊ] *adv* también, además

altar ['ɔːltə(r)] *n* altar *m*

alter ['ɔːltə(r)] **1.** *vt* [plan] cambiar, retocar; [project] modificar; [clothing] arreglar; [timetable] revisar **2.** *vi* cambiar, cambiarse

alteration [ɔːltə'reɪʃən] *n* [to plan] cambio *m*; [to project] modificación *f*; [to clothing] arreglo *m*; [to timetable] revisión *f*; **alterations** [to building] reformas *fpl*

alternate 1. [ɔːl'tɜːnɪt] *adj* alterno(a); **on alternate days** cada dos días **2.** ['ɔːltəneɪt] *vt* alternar

alternative [ɔːl'tɜːnətɪv] **1.** *adj* alternativo(a) **2.** *n* alternativa *f*; **I have no alternative but to accept** no tengo más remedio que aceptar

alternatively [ɔːl'tɜːnətɪvlɪ] *adv* o bien; **alternatively, you could walk** o bien podrías ir andando

although [ɔːl'ðəʊ] *conj* aunque

altitude ['æltɪtjuːd] *n* altitud *f*

altogether [ɔːltə'geðə(r)] *adv* [in total] en conjunto, en total; [completely] completamente, del todo

aluminium [æljʊ'mɪnɪəm], US **aluminum** [ə'luːmɪnəm] *n* aluminio *m*

always ['ɔːlweɪz] *adv* siempre

Alwz MESSAGING *(abbr of* **always***)* smpr, 100pre

am [æm] *see* **be**

a.m. [eɪ'em] *(abbr of* **ante meridiem***)* a.m., de la mañana

amalgamate [ə'mælgəmeɪt] **1.** *vt* [metals] amalgamar **2.** *vi* [metals] amalgamarse; [companies] fusionarse

amateur ['æmətə(r)] **1.** *n* amateur *mf*, aficionado(a) *m,f* **2.** *adj* aficionado(a); *Pej* [work etc] chapucero(a)

amaze [ə'meɪz] *vt* asombrar, pasmar; **to be amazed at sth** quedarse pasmado(a) de algo

amazing [ə'meɪzɪŋ] *adj* asombroso(a), increíble

ambassador [æm'bæsədə(r)] *n* embajador(a) *m,f*

amber ['æmbə(r)] **1.** *n* ámbar *m* **2.** *adj* ambarino(a); *Br* **amber light** semáforo *m* en ámbar

ambiguous [æm'bɪgjʊəs] *adj* ambiguo(a)

ambition [æm'bɪʃən] *n* ambición *f*

ambitious [æm'bɪʃəs] *adj* ambicioso(a)

ambivalent [æm'bɪvələnt] *adj* ambivalente

ambulance ['æmbjʊləns] *n* ambulancia *f*; **ambulance man** ambulanciero *m*

ambush ['æmbʊʃ] **1.** *n* emboscada *f* **2.** *vt* tender una emboscada a; *Fig* atacar por sorpresa

AMBW MESSAGING *written abbr of* **all my best wishes**

amend [ə'mend] *vt* [law] enmendar; [error] subsanar

amends [ə'mendz] *npl* **to make amends to sb for sth** compensar a algn por algo

amenities [ə'miːnɪtɪz] *npl* comodidades *fpl*

America [ə'merɪkə] *n* [continent] América *f*; [USA] (los) Estados Unidos; **Central America** América Central,

Centroamérica f ; **North America** América del Norte, Norteamérica f; **South America** América del Sur, Sudamérica f

American [ə'merɪkən] adj & n americano(a) (m,f) ; [of USA] norteamericano(a) (m,f), estadounidense (mf) ; **North American** norteamericano(a); **South American** sudamericano(a)

amiable ['eɪmɪəbəl] adj amable, afable

amicable ['æmɪkəbəl] adj amistoso(a)

amid(st) ['æmɪd(st)] prep entre, en medio de

amiss [ə'mɪs] adj & adv mal; **there's sth amiss** algo anda mal; **to take sth amiss** tomar algo a mal

AML MESSAGING written abbr of **of all my love**

ammunition [æmjʊ'nɪʃən] n municiones fpl

among(st) [ə'mʌŋ(st)] prep entre

amoral [eɪ'mɒrəl] adj amoral

amount [ə'maʊnt] n cantidad f ; [of money] suma f ; [of bill] importe m ■ **amount to** vt insep ascender a ; Fig equivaler a

amp [æmp], **ampère** ['æmpeə(r)] n amperio m

ample ['æmpəl] adj [enough] bastante; [more than enough] abundante; [large] amplio(a)

amplifier ['æmplɪfaɪə(r)] n amplificador m

amplify ['æmplɪfaɪ] vt [essay, remarks] ampliar ; [current, volume] amplificar

amputate ['æmpjʊteɪt] vt amputar

Amtrak ['æmtræk] n compañía ferroviaria estadounidense

amuse [ə'mjuːz] vt divertir, entretener

amusement [ə'mjuːzmənt] n [enjoyment] diversión f ; [laughter] risa f ; [pastime] pasatiempo m ; **amusement arcade** salón m de juegos; **amusement park** parque m de atracciones

an [æn] (unstressed [ən]) see **a**

anaemic [ə'niːmɪk] adj anémico(a); Fig [weak] débil

anaesthetic [ænɪs'θetɪk] n anestesia f

analogy [ə'næləʤɪ] n analogía f

analyse ['ænəlaɪz] vt analizar

analysis [ə'nælɪsɪs] (pl **analyses** [ə'nælɪsiːz]) n análisis m inv

analyst ['ænəlɪst] n analista mf ; [psychoanalyst] psicoanalista mf

analyze ['ænəlaɪz] US vt = **analyse**

anarchist ['ænəkɪst] n anarquista mf

anarchy ['ænəkɪ] n anarquía f

anatomy [ə'nætəmɪ] n anatomía f

ancestor ['ænsestə(r)] n antepasado m

anchor ['æŋkə(r)] **1.** n NAUT ancla f; Fig áncora f **2.** vt NAUT anclar ; Fig [fix securely] sujetar **3.** vi anclar

anchovy [Br 'æntʃəvɪ, Am æn'tʃəʊvɪ] n anchoa f

ancient ['eɪnʃənt] adj antiguo(a)

and [ænd] (unstressed [ənd, ən]) conj y ; [before i-, hi-] e ; **a hundred and one** ciento uno; **and so on** etcétera; **Bill and Pat** Bill y Pat; **Chinese and Indian** chino e indio; **come and see us** ven a vernos; **four and a half** cuatro y medio; **she cried and cried** no paró de llorar; **try and help me** trata de ayudarme; **wait and see** espera a ver; **worse and worse** cada vez peor

Andalusia [ændə'luːzjə] n Andalucía f

anemic [ə'niːmɪk] US n = **anaemic**

anesthetic [ænɪs'θetɪk] US n = **anaesthetic**

angel ['eɪnʤəl] n ángel m

anger ['æŋgə(r)] **1.** n ira f, esp Esp enfado m, esp Am enojo m **2.** vt esp Esp enfadar, esp Am enojar

angle ['æŋgəl] n ángulo m ; Fig punto m de vista

angler ['æŋglə(r)] n pescador(a) m,f de caña

Anglican ['æŋglɪkən] adj & n anglicano(a) (m,f)

Anglo-Saxon [æŋgləʊ'sæksən] adj & n anglosajón(ona) (m,f)

angry ['æŋgrɪ] (compar **angrier**, superl **angriest**) adj [person] esp Esp enfadado(a), esp Am enojado(a) ; [voice, letter] airado(a) ; **to get angry** estar esp Esp enfadado(a) or esp Am enojado(a)

anguish ['æŋgwɪʃ] n angustia f

animal ['ænɪməl] **1.** adj animal **2.** n animal m ; Fig bestia f

animated ['ænɪmeɪtɪd] adj [lively] animado(a)

animation [ænɪ'meɪʃən] n animación f

aniseed ['ænɪsiːd] n anís m

ankle ['æŋkəl] n tobillo m ; **ankle boots** botines mpl ; **ankle socks** calcetines mpl cortos, CSur zoquetes mpl, Col medias fpl tobilleras

annex [ə'neks] vt [territory] anexionar

anniversary [ænɪ'vɜːsərɪ] n aniversario m ; **wedding anniversary** aniversario de bodas

announce [ə'naʊns] vt anunciar ; [news] comunicar ; [fact] hacer saber

announcement [ə'naʊnsmənt] n anuncio m ; [news] comunicación f ; [statement] declaración f

announcer [ə'naʊnsə(r)] n TV & RADIO locutor(a) m,f

annoy [ə'nɔɪ] vt fastidiar, molestar, esp Am enojar ; **to get annoyed** molestarse, esp Esp enfadarse, esp Am enojarse

annoying [ə'nɔɪɪŋ] adj molesto(a), fastidioso(a)

annual ['ænjʊəl] **1.** adj anual **2.** n [book] anuario m ; [plant] anual m

annually ['ænjʊəlɪ] adv anualmente

annul [ə'nʌl] vt anular

anomaly [ə'nɒməlɪ] n anomalía f

anonymous [ə'nɒnɪməs] adj anónimo(a)

anorak ['ænəræk] n anorak m

anorexia [ænə'reksɪə] n anorexia f

another [ə'nʌðə(r)] **1.** adj otro(a) ; **another one** otro(a) ; **without another word** sin más **2.** pron otro(a) ; **have another** toma otro(a) ; **to love one another** quererse el uno al otro

answer ['ɑːnsə(r)] **1.** n [to letter etc] contestación f ; [to question] respuesta f ; [to problem] solución f ; **in answer to** **your letter** contestando a su carta ; **there's no answer** [on telephone] no contestan ; [at door] no abren **2.** vt contestar a ; [problem] resolver ; [door] abrir ; [phone] contestar **3.** vi contestar, responder

■ **answer back** vi replicar ; **don't answer back!** ¡no seas respondón!

■ **answer for** vt insep responder de ; **he's got a lot to answer for** es responsable de muchas cosas

■ **answer to** vt insep [name] responder a ; [description] corresponder a

answering machine ['ɑːnsərɪŋməʃiːn] n contestador m automático

ant [ænt] n hormiga f ; **ant hill** hormiguero m

antagonize [æn'tægənaɪz] vt enemistar, malquistar

Antarctic [æn'tɑːktɪk] **1.** adj antártico(a) ; **Antarctic Ocean** océano Antártico **2.** n **the Antarctic** la Antártida

antenna [æn'tenə] n **a)** (pl antennae [æn'teniː]) [of animal, insect] antena f **b)** (pl **antennas**) TV & RADIO antena f

anthem ['ænθəm] n motete m ; **national anthem** himno m nacional

anthology [æn'θɒlədʒɪ] n antología f

antibiotic [æntɪbaɪ'ɒtɪk] n antibiótico m

anticipate [æn'tɪsɪpeɪt] vt **a)** [expect] esperar **b)** [predict] prever ; [get ahead of] anticiparse a, adelantarse a

anticipation [æntɪsɪ'peɪʃən] n [expectation] esperanza f ; [expectancy] ilusión f

anticlimax [æntɪ'klaɪmæks] n [disappointment] decepción f

anticlockwise [æntɪ'klɒkwaɪz] adv Br en sentido opuesto al de las agujas del reloj

antics ['æntɪks] npl payasadas fpl ; [naughtiness] travesuras fpl

antidote ['æntɪdəʊt] n antídoto m

antifreeze ['æntɪfriːz] n anticongelante m

antiglobalization, antiglobali-sation [ˌæntɪɡləʊbəlaɪˈzeɪʃən] **1.** n POL antiglobalización f **2.** adj POL anti-globalización (inv)

antihistamine [æntɪˈhɪstəmɪn] n an-tihistamínico m

antiperspirant [æntɪˈpɜːspɪrənt] n antitranspirante m

antiquated [ˈæntɪkweɪtɪd] adj anticuado(a)

antique [ænˈtiːk] **1.** adj antiguo(a) **2.** n antigüedad f; **antique dealer** anticuario(a) m,f; **antique shop** tien-da f de antigüedades

antisemitic [æntɪsɪˈmɪtɪk] adj [person] antisemita; [beliefs, remarks] antisemítico(a)

antiseptic [æntɪˈseptɪk] adj & n antiséptico(a) (m)

antisocial [æntɪˈsəʊʃəl] adj [delinquent] antisocial; [unsociable] insociable

antivirus [ˈæntɪvaɪrəs] adj antivirus (inv)

anxiety [æŋˈzaɪɪtɪ] n [concern] inquie-tud f; [worry] preocupación f; [fear] angustia f; [eagerness] ansia f

anxious [ˈæŋkʃəs] adj [concerned] inquieto(a); [worried] preocupado(a); [fearful] angustiado(a); [eager] ansioso(a); **to be anxious about sth** estar preocupado(a) por algo

any [ˈenɪ] **1.** adj **a)** [in questions, con-ditionals] algún(una); **are there any seats left?** ¿quedan plazas?; **have you any apples?** ¿tienes manzanas?; **have you any money?** ¿tienes (algo de) dinero? **b)** [in negative clauses] ningún(una); **I don't have any time** no tengo tiempo **c)** [no matter which] cualquier(a); **any doctor will say the same** cualquier médico te dirá lo mismo; **at any mo-ment** en cualquier momento **d)** [every] todo(a); **in any case** de todas formas **2.** pron **a)** [in questions] alguno(a); **do they have any?** ¿tienen alguno?; **I need some paper, have you any?** necesito papel, ¿tienes?

b) [in negative clauses] ninguno(a); **I don't want any** no quiero ninguno(a) **c)** [no matter which] cualquiera; **you can have any (one)** coge el / la que quieras **3.** adv **is there any more?** ¿hay más?; **I used to like it, but not any more** or **longer** antes me gustaba pero ya no; **is he any better?** ¿está mejor?

anybody [ˈenɪbɒdɪ] pron [in questions, conditionals] alguien, alguno(a); [in negative clauses] nadie, ninguno(a); [no matter who] cualquiera; **anybody but me** cualquiera menos yo; **bring anybody you like** trae a quien quieras; **do you see anybody over there?** ¿ves a alguien allí?; **I can't find anybody** no encuentro a nadie

anyhow [ˈenɪhaʊ] adv **a)** [in spite of that] en todo caso, de todas formas; [changing the subject] bueno, pues **b)** [carelessly] desordenadamente, de cualquier modo or forma

anyone [ˈenɪwʌn] pron = **anybody**

ANY1 MESSAGING written abbr of **any-one**

anyplace [ˈenɪpleɪs] US adv = **any-where**

anything [ˈenɪθɪŋ] **1.** pron [in ques-tions, conditionals] algo, alguna cosa; [in negative clauses] nada; [no matter what] cualquier cosa; **anything but that** cualquier cosa menos eso; **any-thing else?** ¿algo más?; **can I do any-thing for you?** ¿puedo ayudarte en algo?; **hardly anything** casi nada; **if anything, I'd buy the big one** de com-prar uno compraría el grande; **to run / work like anything** correr / trabajar a más no poder **2.** adv **is this anything like what you wanted?** ¿viene a ser éste lo que querías?

anytime [ˈenɪtaɪm] adv **a)** [at any time] en cualquier momento; **call me anytime** llámame en cualquier mo-mento; **they can flower anytime be-tween May and September** pueden florecer en cualquier momento entre mayo y septiembre **b)** [you're welcome] de nada, cuando quieras; **thanks for**

driving me to the airport — anytime! gracias por llevarme al aeropuerto — ¡de nada!

anyway ['enɪweɪ] *adv* = **anyhow**

anywhere ['enɪweə(r)] *adv* **a)** [in questions, conditionals - situation] en alguna parte ; [movement] a alguna parte ; **could it be anywhere else?** ¿podría estar en otro sitio? **b)** [in negative clauses - situation] en ninguna parte ; [movement] a ninguna parte ; [no matter where] dondequiera, en cualquier parte ; **go anywhere you like** ve a donde quieras ; **we aren't anywhere near finished** no hemos terminado ni mucho menos

AP ['eɪ'pi:] *n US* SCH *(abbr of* **Advanced Placement)** *examen de nivel universitario al que puede presentarse un alumno de secundaria para obtener créditos universitarios*

apart [ə'pɑːt] *adv* **a)** aparte ; **to fall apart** deshacerse ; **to take sth apart** desmontar algo **b)** [distant] alejado(a) ; [separate] separado(a) ; **to be poles apart** ser polos opuestos ; **you can't tell the twins apart** no se puede distinguir los mellizos el uno del otro **c)** **apart from** aparte de

apartment [ə'pɑːtmənt] *n US* apartamento *m*, *Esp* piso, *Arg* departamento ; **apartment block** edificio *m* or bloque *m* de apartamentos or *Esp* pisos or *Arg* departamentos

apathy ['æpəθɪ] *n* apatía *f*

ape [eɪp] **1.** *n* mono *m* **2.** *vt* imitar, copiar

aperture ['æpətʃə(r)] *n* [hole, crack] resquicio *m*, rendija *f* ; PHOTO abertura *f*

apiece [ə'piːs] *adv* cada uno(a)

apologetic [əpɒlə'dʒetɪk] *adj* [remorseful] de disculpa ; **he was very apologetic** pidió mil perdones

apologize [ə'pɒlədʒaɪz] *vi* [say sorry] disculparse ; **they apologized to us for the delay** se disculparon con nosotros por el retraso

apology [ə'pɒlədʒɪ] *n* disculpa *f*, excusa *f* ; *Fam* **what an apology for a meal!** ¡vaya birria de comida!

apostle [ə'pɒsəl] *n* apóstol *m*

apostrophe [ə'pɒstrəfɪ] *n* apóstrofo *m*

app [æp] *n* COMPUT *(abbr of* **application)** aplicación *f*, programa *m*

appal, *US* **appall** [ə'pɔːl] *vt* horrorizar

appalling [ə'pɔːlɪŋ] *adj* [horrifying] horroroso(a) ; *Fam* [very bad] pésimo(a), fatal

apparatus [æpə'reɪtəs] *n* aparato *m* ; [equipment] equipo *m*

apparel [ə'pærəl] *n US* indumentaria *f*, ropa *f*

apparent [ə'pærənt] *adj* [obvious] evidente ; [seeming] aparente ; **to become apparent** ponerse de manifiesto

apparently [ə'pærəntlɪ] *adv* [seemingly] por lo visto

appeal [ə'piːl] **1.** *n* **a)** [request] solicitud *f* ; [plea] súplica *f* **b)** [attraction] atractivo *m* ; [interest] interés *m* **c)** JUR apelación *f* **2.** *vi* **a)** [plead] rogar, suplicar (**to** a) ; **to appeal for help** solicitar ayuda **b)** [attract] atraer ; [interest] interesar ; **it doesn't appeal to me** no me dice nada **c)** JUR apelar

appealing [ə'piːlɪŋ] *adj* [moving] conmovedor(a) ; [attractive] atractivo(a) ; [tempting] atrayente

appear [ə'pɪə(r)] *vi* **a)** [become visible] aparecer ; [publicly] presentarse ; [on stage] actuar ; **to appear before a court** comparecer ante un tribunal ; **to appear on television** salir en la televisión **b)** [seem] parecer ; **he appears relaxed** parece relajado ; **so it appears** según parece

appearance [ə'pɪərəns] *n* **a)** [becoming visible] aparición *f* ; [publicly] presentación *f* ; [on stage] actuación *f* ; [before court] comparecencia *f* ; [of book etc] publicación *f* ; **to put in an appearance** hacer acto de presencia **b)** [look] apariencia *f*, aspecto *m* ; **to all appearances** al parecer

appendicitis [əpendɪ'saɪtɪs] *n* apendicitis *f*

appendix [ə'pendɪks] *(pl* **appendices)** *n* apéndice *m*

appetite ['æpɪtaɪt] *n* apetito *m* ; *Fig* deseo *m*

appetizing ['æpɪtaɪzɪŋ] *adj* apetitoso(a)

applaud [ə'plɔːd] *vt & vi* aplaudir

applause [ə'plɔːz] *n* aplausos *mpl*

apple ['æpəl] *n* manzana *f*; *US* candy **apple** manzana *f* de caramelo; **apple tree** manzano *m*

appliance [ə'plaɪəns] *n* dispositivo *m*

applicable [ə'plɪkəbəl] *adj* aplicable

applicant ['æplɪkənt] *n* [for post] candidato(a) *m,f*; [to court, for tickets] solicitante *mf*

application [æplɪ'keɪʃən] *n* a) [of cream] aplicación *f* b) [for post etc] solicitud *f*; **application form** solicitud; **job application** solicitud de empleo c) [effort] aplicación *f*; **she lacks application** no se aplica d) COMPUT aplicación *f*, programa *m*; **applications program** programa *m* de aplicaciones

applied [ə'plaɪd] *adj* aplicado(a)

apply [ə'plaɪ] 1. *vt* aplicar; [brake] echar; [law] recurrir a; [force] usar; **to apply oneself to** dedicarse a 2. *vi* a) [refer] aplicarse (**to** a) b) [for job] presentar una solicitud; [for information, to court] presentar una petición ■ **apply for** *vt insep* [post, information] solicitar; [tickets] pedir

appoint [ə'pɔɪnt] *vt* [person] nombrar; [time, place etc] fijar, señalar

appointment [ə'pɔɪntmənt] *n* a) [to post] nombramiento *m*; [post] cargo *m* b) [meeting] cita *f*; **to make an appointment with** citarse con; [at doctor's] pedir hora a

appraisal [ə'preɪzəl] *n* evaluación *f*

appreciate [ə'priːʃieɪt] 1. *vt* a) [be thankful for] agradecer b) [understand] entender c) [value] apreciar, valorar 2. *vi* [increase in value] apreciarse

appreciation [əpriːʃi'eɪʃən] *n* a) [of help, advice] agradecimiento *m*; [of difficulty] comprensión *f*; [of wine etc] aprecio *m*; [appraisal] evaluación *f* b) [increase in value] apreciación *f*

appreciative [ə'priːʃiətɪv] *adj* [thankful] agradecido(a); [responsive] apreciativo(a)

apprehend [æprɪ'hend] *vt* [arrest] detener

apprehensive [æprɪ'hensɪv] *adj* [fearful] aprensivo(a)

apprentice [ə'prentɪs] *n* aprendiz(a) *m,f*

apprenticeship [ə'prentɪsʃɪp] *n* aprendizaje *m*

approach [ə'prəʊtʃ] 1. *n* a) [coming near] acercamiento *m*; [to town] acceso *m*; **approach road** vía *f* de acceso b) [to problem] enfoque *m* 2. *vt* [come near to] acercarse a; [be similar to] aproximarse a; *Fig* [problem] abordar; [person] dirigirse a; **to approach sb about sth** dirigirse a algn a propósito de algo 3. *vi* acercarse

approachable [ə'prəʊtʃəbəl] *adj* [person] accesible

appropriate¹ [ə'prəʊprɪət] *adj* [suitable] apropiado(a), adecuado(a); [convenient] oportuno(a)

appropriate² [ə'prəʊprɪeɪt] *vt* [allocate] asignar; [steal] apropiarse de

approval [ə'pruːvəl] *n* aprobación *f*, visto bueno; COMM **to get sth on approval** adquirir algo sin compromiso de compra

approve [ə'pruːv] *vt* aprobar ■ **approve of** *vt insep* aprobar

approving [ə'pruːvɪŋ] *adj* [look etc] aprobatorio(a)

approximate 1. [ə'prɒksɪmɪt] *adj* aproximado(a) 2. [ə'prɒksɪmeɪt] *vt* aproximarse a

apricot ['eɪprɪkɒt] *n* [fruit] *Esp* albaricoque *m*, *Andes, RP* damasco *m*, *Méx* chabacano *m*; **apricot tree** *Esp* albaricoquero *m*, *Andes, RP* damasco *m*, *Méx* chabacano *m*

April ['eɪprəl] *n* abril *m*; **April Fools' Day** día *m* uno de abril, ≃ Día de los Inocentes (28 de diciembre)

apron ['eɪprən] *n* delantal *m*; [for workman] mandil *m*

apt [æpt] *adj* a) [suitable] apropiado(a); [remark] acertado(a), oportuno(a);

[name] justo(a); [description] exacto(a)
b) to be apt to do sth ser propenso(a) a hacer algo

aptitude ['æptɪtjuːd] *n* capacidad *f*; **aptitude test** prueba *f* de aptitud

aptly ['æptlɪ] *adv* acertadamente

aquarium [ə'kweərɪəm] *n* acuario *m*

Aquarius [ə'kweərɪəs] *n* Acuario *m*

aquatic [ə'kwætɪk] *adj* acuático(a)

Arab ['ærəb] *adj & n* árabe *(mf)*

Arabian [ə'reɪbɪən] *adj* árabe

Arabic ['ærəbɪk] **1.** *adj* árabe, arábigo(a); **Arabic numerals** numeración arábiga **2.** *n* [language] árabe *m*

arbitrary ['ɑːbɪtrərɪ] *adj* arbitrario(a)

arbitration [ɑːbɪ'treɪʃən] *n* arbitraje *m*

arc [ɑːk] *n* arco *m*; **arc lamp** arco voltaico

arcade [ɑː'keɪd] *n* arcada *f*; [passageway] pasaje *m*; **shopping arcade** galerías *fpl* (comerciales)

arch [ɑːtʃ] **1.** *n* **a)** ARCHIT arco *m*; [vault] bóveda *f* **b)** ANAT empeine *m* **2.** *vt* [back] arquear

archaeologist [ɑːkɪ'ɒlədʒɪst] *n* arqueólogo(a) *m,f*

archaeology [ɑːkɪ'ɒlədʒɪ] *n* arqueología *f*

archaic [ɑː'keɪɪk] *adj* arcaico(a)

archbishop [ɑːtʃ'bɪʃəp] *n* arzobispo *m*

archeologist [ɑːkɪ'ɒlədʒɪst] *US n* = **archaeologist**

archeology [ɑːkɪ'ɒlədʒɪ] *US n* = **archaeology**

archer ['ɑːtʃə(r)] *n* arquero(a) *m,f*

archetypal ['ɑːkɪtaɪpəl] *adj* arquetípico(a)

architect ['ɑːkɪtekt] *n* arquitecto(a) *m,f*

architecture ['ɑːkɪtektʃə(r)] *n* arquitectura *f*

archives ['ɑːkaɪvz] *npl* archivos *mpl*

archway ['ɑːtʃweɪ] *n* [arch] arco *m*; [vault] bóveda *f*; [in church] atrio *m*; [passage] pasaje *m*

arctic ['ɑːktɪk] **1.** *adj* ártico(a); **Arctic Circle** círculo *m* polar Ártico **2.** *n* **the Arctic** el Ártico

ardent ['ɑːdənt] *adj* [supporter etc] apasionado(a); [desire] ardiente

ardour, *US* **ardor** ['ɑːdə(r)] *n* pasión *f*, ardor *m*

are [ɑː(r)] *see* **be**

area ['eərɪə] *n* [surface] área *f*, superficie *f*; [space] extensión *f*; [region] región *f*; [of town] zona *f*; *Fig* [field] campo *m*; *US* TEL **area code** prefijo *m* local

arena [ə'riːnə] *n* [stadium] estadio *m*; [bullring] plaza *f*; [circus] pista *f*; *Fig* [stage] campo *m* de batalla

Argentina [ɑːdʒən'tiːnə] *n* Argentina

Argentine ['ɑːdʒəntaɪn], **Argentinian** [ɑːdʒən'tɪnɪən] *adj & n* argentino(a) *m,f*

arguable ['ɑːgjuəbəl] *adj* discutible

argue ['ɑːgjuː] **1.** *vt* [reason] discutir; [point of view] mantener **2.** *vi* [quarrel] discutir; [reason] argumentar, razonar; **to argue for** abogar por; **to argue against sth** ponerse en contra de algo

argument ['ɑːgjomənt] *n* [reason] argumento *m* (**for** a favor de; **against** en contra de); [quarrel] discusión *f*, disputa *f*; **for the sake of argument** por decir algo

argumentative [ɑːgjʊ'mentətɪv] *adj* **she's very argumentative** le gusta discutir por todo

Aries ['eəriːz] *n* Aries *m*

arise [ə'raɪz] (*pt* arose, *pp* arisen [ə'rɪzən]) *vi* [get up] levantarse; [happen] surgir; **should the occasion arise** si se presenta la ocasión

aristocracy [ærɪ'stɒkrəsɪ] *n* aristocracia *f*

aristocrat [*Br* 'ærɪstəkræt, *US* ə'rɪstəkræt] *n* aristócrata *mf*

arithmetic [ə'rɪθmətɪk] *n* aritmética *f*

ark [ɑːk] *n* arca *f*; **Noah's Ark** el arca de Noé

arm [ɑːm] **1.** *n* **a)** brazo *m*; [of garment] manga *f*; **to walk arm in arm** ir cogidos(as) del brazo **b)** MIL **arms** armas *fpl*; **arms race** carrera armamentística; **coat of arms** escudo *m* **2.** *vt* armar; **to arm oneself against sth** armarse contra algo

armaments ['ɑːməmənts] *npl* armamentos *mpl*

armband ['ɑːmbænd] *n* [at funeral, for swimming] brazalete *m*

armchair ['ɑːmtʃeə(r)] *n* sillón *m*

armistice ['ɑːmɪstɪs] *n* armisticio *m*

armour, *US* **armor** ['ɑːmə(r)] *n* [on vehicle] blindaje *m*; **(suit of) armour** armadura *f*

armoured car, *US* **armored car** [ɑːməd'kɑː(r)] *n* coche *m* blindado

armpit ['ɑːmpɪt] *n* axila *f*, sobaco *m*

armrest ['ɑːmrest] *n* apoyabrazos *m inv*

army ['ɑːmɪ] *n* ejército *m*

aroma [ə'rəumə] *n* aroma *m*

aromatherapy [ə,rəumə'θerəpɪ] *n* aromaterapia *f*

aromatic [ærəu'mætɪk] *adj* aromático(a)

arose [ə'rəuz] *pt of* **arise**

around [ə'raund] **1.** *adv* alrededor; **all around** por todos los lados; **are the children around?** ¿están los niños por aquí?; **he looked around** miró (a su) alrededor **2.** *prep* **a)** alrededor de; **around the corner** a la vuelta de la esquina; **around here** por aquí **b)** [approximately] aproximadamente

arouse [ə'rauz] *vt* despertar; [sexually] excitar

arrange [ə'reɪndʒ] **1.** *vt* **a)** [order] ordenar; [hair, flowers] arreglar; MUS adaptar **b)** [plan] organizar; [agree on] quedar en; **to arrange a time** fijar una hora; **arranged marriage** boda arreglada **2.** *vi* **I shall arrange for him to be there** lo arreglaré para que pueda asistir

arrangement [ə'reɪndʒmənt] *n* **a)** [display] colocación *f*; MUS adaptación *f* **b)** [agreement] acuerdo *m* **c)** **arrangements** [plans] planes *mpl*; [preparations] preparativos *mpl*

arrears [ə'rɪəz] *npl* atrasos *mpl*; **to be in arrears with the rent** estar atrasado(a)

en el pago del alquiler *or Méx* de la renta; **to be paid in arrears** cobrar con retraso

arrest [ə'rest] **1.** *n* detención *f*; **to be under arrest** estar detenido(a) **2.** *vt* [criminal] detener; *Fig* [progress] frenar

arrival [ə'raɪvəl] *n* llegada *f*; **a new arrival** un(a) recién llegado(a)

arrive [ə'raɪv] *vi* llegar (**at/in** a)

arrogance ['ærəgəns] *n* arrogancia *f*

arrogant ['ærəgənt] *adj* arrogante

arrow ['ærəu] *n* flecha *f*

arse [ɑːs] *n Br Vulg* [buttocks] culo *m*

arson ['ɑːsən] *n* incendio *m* provocado

art [ɑːt] *n* **a)** arte *m*; [drawing] dibujo *m*; **the arts** las bellas artes; **arts and crafts** artes *fpl* y oficios *mpl*; **art gallery** galería *f* de arte **b)** **arts** [branch of knowledge] letras *fpl*

artery ['ɑːtərɪ] *n* arteria *f*

arthritis [ɑː'θraɪtɪs] *n* artritis *f*

artichoke ['ɑːtɪtʃəuk] *n* alcachofa *f*, *Am* alcaucil *m*

article ['ɑːtɪkəl] *n* artículo *m*; **article of clothing** prenda *f* de vestir; JUR **articles** contrato *m* de aprendizaje

articulate¹ [ɑː'tɪkjulɪt] *adj* [speech] claro(a); [person] que se expresa bien

articulate² [ɑː'tɪkjuleɪt] *vt & vi* articular; [words] pronunciar; *Br* **articulated lorry** camión articulado

artificial [ɑːtɪ'fɪʃəl] *adj* artificial; [limb] postizo(a); **artificial intelligence** inteligencia *f* artificial

artillery [ɑː'tɪlərɪ] *n* artillería *f*

artist ['ɑːtɪst] *n* artista *mf*; [painter] pintor(a) *m,f*

artistic [ɑː'tɪstɪk] *adj* artístico(a)

arty ['ɑːtɪ] *adj Fam* [person] *que se interesa por las artes*

as [æz] (*unstressed* [əz]) **1.** *adv & conj* **a)** [comparison] **as ... as ...** tan ... como ...; **as far as** hasta; *Fig* **as far as I'm concerned** por lo que a mí respecta; **as many as** tantos(as) como; **as much as** tanto(a) como; **as tall as me** tan alto(a) como yo; **as little as £5**

tan solo 5 libras; **as soon as they arrive** en cuanto lleguen; **I'll stay as long as I can** quedaré todo el tiempo que pueda; **just as big** igual de grande; **three times as fast** tres veces más rápido; **the same as** igual que

b) [manner] como; **as a rule** por regla general; **as you know** como ya sabéis; **as you like** como quieras; **do as I say** haz lo que yo te digo; **he's working as a doctor** está trabajando de médico; **I thought as much** ya me lo suponía; **it serves as a table** sirve de mesa; **leave it as it is** déjalo tal como está; **he was dressed as a pirate** iba vestido de pirata

c) [while, when] mientras (que); **as a child** de niño(a); **as I was eating** mientras comía; **as we were leaving, we saw Pat** al salir vimos a Pat

d) [though] aunque; **be that as it may** por mucho que así sea; **young as he is** aunque es joven

e) [because] como, ya que

f) [and so] igual que; **as do I** igual que yo; **as well** también

g) [purpose] para; **so as to do sth** para hacer algo

h) **as for my brother** en cuanto a mi hermano

i) **as from, as of** a partir de

j) **to act as if** actuar como si (+ subj); **it looks as if the concert is off** parece ser que no habrá concierto

k) **it's late enough as it is** ya es muy tarde; **as it were** por así decirlo

l) **as long as** [only if] siempre que, con tal de que

m) **as regards** en cuanto a, por lo que se refiere a; **as usual** como siempre; **as yet** aún, todavía

2. rel pron **such as** tal(es) como

asap [eɪeɪeɪ'piː] adv (abbr of **as soon as possible**) cuanto antes, lo antes posible

ascend [ə'send] vi subir, ascender

ascent [ə'sent] n subida f

ascertain [æsə'teɪn] vt averiguar, enterarse de

ash¹ [æʃ] n BOT fresno m

ash² [æʃ] n ceniza f; **ash bin**, US **ash can** cubo m de la basura; REL **Ash Wednesday** miércoles m inv de ceniza

ashamed [ə'ʃeɪmd] adj avergonzado(a), Am salvo RP apenado(a); **you ought to be ashamed of yourself!** ¡debería darte vergüenza or Am salvo RP pena!

ashore [ə'ʃɔː(r)] adv [position] en tierra; **to go ashore** desembarcar; **to swim ashore** nadar hacia tierra

ashtray ['æʃtreɪ] n cenicero m

Asia ['eɪʒə] n Asia; **Asia Minor** Asia Menor

Asian ['eɪʒən] **1.** n asiático(a) m,f; Br [person from Indian subcontinent] persona de la India, Paquistán o Bangladesh **2.** adj asiático(a); Br [from Indian subcontinent] de la India, Paquistán o Bangladesh

aside [ə'saɪd] **1.** adv al lado, aparte; **to cast aside** echar a un lado; **to stand aside** apartarse **2.** prep **aside from** [apart from] aparte de; [as well as] además de **3.** n THEAT aparte m

ask [ɑːsk] **1.** vt **a)** preguntar; **to ask sb a question** hacer una pregunta a algn **b)** [request] pedir, solicitar; **she asked me to post it** me pidió que lo echara al buzón **c)** [invite] invitar **2.** vi [inquire] preguntar; [request] pedir ■ **ask after** vt insep **to ask after sb** preguntar por algn ■ **ask for** vt insep [help] pedir, solicitar; [person] preguntar por ■ **ask out** vt sep **to ask sb out** invitar a algn a salir

asleep [ə'sliːp] adj [person] dormido(a); [limb] adormecido(a); **to fall asleep** quedarse dormido(a)

asparagus [ə'spærəgəs] n inv espárragos mpl

aspect ['æspekt] n **a)** [of question] aspecto m **b)** [of building] orientación f

asphyxiate [æs'fɪksɪeɪt] **1.** vt asfixiar **2.** vi asfixiarse

aspire [ə'spaɪə(r)] vi **to aspire to** aspirar a

aspirin ['æsprɪn] n aspirina f

ass¹ [æs] n asno(a) m,f, burro(a) m,f

ass² [æs] n US Vulg culo m

assailant [ə'seɪlənt] n agresor(a) m,f, atacante mf

assassin [ə'sæsɪn] n asesino(a) m,f

assassinate [ə'sæsɪneɪt] vt asesinar

assassination [əsæsɪ'neɪʃən] n asesinato m

assault [ə'sɔːlt] **1.** n MIL ataque m (**on** a); JUR agresión f **2.** vt MIL asaltar, atacar; JUR agredir; [sexually] violar

assemble [ə'sembəl] **1.** vt [people] reunir, juntar; [furniture] montar **2.** vi [people] reunirse, juntarse

assembly [ə'semblɪ] n reunión f, asamblea f; TECH montaje m; SCH *reunión de todos los profesores y los alumnos al principio de la jornada escolar*; IND **assembly line** cadena f de montaje

assent [ə'sent] **1.** n [agreement] asentimiento m; [consent] consentimiento m; [approval] aprobación f **2.** vi asentir, consentir (**to** en)

assert [ə'sɜːt] vt afirmar; **to assert oneself** imponerse; **to assert one's rights** hacer valer sus derechos

assertion [ə'sɜːʃən] n afirmación f

assertive [ə'sɜːtɪv] adj enérgico(a)

assess [ə'ses] vt [estimate value] valorar; [damages, price] calcular; [tax] gravar; Fig [effect] evaluar

assessment [ə'sesmənt] n [of value] valoración f; [of damages etc] cálculo m; [of taxes] gravamen m; Fig juicio m

asset ['æset] n a) ventaja f; **to be an asset** [person] ser de gran valor b) FIN **assets** bienes mpl; **fixed assets** bienes raíces

assign [ə'saɪn] vt [task] asignar; [property etc] ceder; **to assign sb to a job** designar a algn para un trabajo

assignment [ə'saɪnmənt] n [allocation] asignación f; [task] tarea f; [mission] misión f; [appointment] cita f

assimilate [ə'sɪmɪleɪt] vt asimilar

assist [ə'sɪst] vt & vi ayudar

assistance [ə'sɪstəns] n ayuda f, auxilio m

assistant [ə'sɪstənt] n ayudante mf; SCH **assistant headmaster** subdirector(a) m,f; **assistant manager** subdirector(a) m,f; US SCH **assistant principal** subdirector(a) m,f; **shop assistant** dependiente(a) m,f; Br **(language) assistant** [in school] auxiliar mf de conversación; [in university] lector(a) m,f de lengua extranjera

associate¹ [ə'səʊʃɪeɪt] **1.** vt [ideas] relacionar; [companies] asociar; **to be associated with sth** estar relacionado(a) con algo **2.** vi **to associate with** tratar con

associate² [ə'səʊʃɪt] **1.** adj asociado(a) **2.** n [colleague] colega mf; [partner] socio(a) m,f; [accomplice] cómplice mf

association [əsəʊsɪ'eɪʃən] n asociación f; [company] sociedad f

assorted [ə'sɔːtɪd] adj surtido(a), variado(a)

assortment [ə'sɔːtmənt] n surtido m, variedad f

assume [ə'sjuːm] **1.** vt [power] asumir; [attitude, name] adoptar; **an assumed name** un nombre falso **2.** vi [suppose] suponer

assumption [ə'sʌmpʃən] n a) [of power] toma f; **assumption of office** toma de posesión b) [supposition] suposición f

assurance [ə'ʃʊərəns] n a) [guarantee] garantía f b) [confidence] confianza f c) Br [insurance] seguro m

assure [ə'ʃʊə(r)] vt asegurar

asterisk ['æstərɪsk] n asterisco m

asthma ['æsmə] n asma f

astonish [ə'stɒnɪʃ] vt asombrar, pasmar; **I was astonished** me quedé pasmado(a)

astonishing [ə'stɒnɪʃɪŋ] adj asombroso(a), pasmoso(a)

astonishment [ə'stɒnɪʃmənt] n asombro m; **to my astonishment** para gran sorpresa mía

astound [ə'staʊnd] vt asombrar, pasmar

astounding [ə'staʊndɪŋ] adj pasmoso(a), asombroso(a)

astray [ə'streɪ] adv **to go astray** extraviarse; Fig equivocarse; **to lead sb astray** llevar a algn por mal camino

astride [ə'straɪd] *prep* a horcajadas sobre

astrology [ə'strɒlədʒɪ] *n* astrología *f*

astronaut ['æstrənɔːt] *n* astronauta *mf*

astronomer [ə'strɒnəmə(r)] *n* astrónomo(a) *m,f*

astronomic(al) [,æstrə'nɒmɪk(l)] *adj* astronómico(a)

astronomy [ə'strɒnəmɪ] *n* astronomía *f*

astute [ə'stjuːt] *adj* astuto(a)

asylum [ə'saɪləm] *n* **a)** [protection] asilo *m*; **to seek political asylum** pedir asilo político **b) mental asylum** manicomio *m*

asylum-seeker *n* demandante *mf* de asilo

at [æt] (*unstressed* [ət]) *prep* **a)** [position] a, en; **at school/work** en el colegio / trabajo; **at the window** a la ventana; **at the top** en lo alto
b) [direction] a; **to be angry at sb** estar *esp Esp* enfadado(a) *or esp Am* enojado(a) con algn; **to laugh at sb** reírse de algn; **to look at sth/sb** mirar algo / a algn; **to shout at sb** gritarle a algn
c) [time] a; **at Easter/Christmas** en Semana Santa / Navidad; **at six o'clock** a las seis; **at night** *Esp* por la noche, *Am* en la noche; **at first** al principio; **at last** por fin; **at once** enseguida; **at that time** entonces; **at the moment** ahora
d) [manner] a, en; **at best/worst** en el mejor / peor de los casos; **at hand** a mano; **at least** por lo menos; **not at all** en absoluto; [don't mention it] de nada
e) [rate] a; **they retail at 100 euros each** se venden a 100 euros la unidad; **two at a time** de dos en dos
f) TYP & COMPUT **at sign** arroba *f*

ate [et, eɪt] *pt of* **eat**

atheist ['eɪθɪɪst] *n* ateo(a) *m,f*

Athens ['æθɪnz] *n* Atenas

athlete ['æθliːt] *n* atleta *mf*

athletic [æθ'letɪk] **1.** *adj* atlético(a); [sporty] deportista **2.** *npl* **athletics** *Br* [track and field] atletismo *m*; *US* deportes *mpl*

Atlantic [ət'læntɪk] *adj* **the Atlantic (Ocean)** el (océano) Atlántico

atlas ['ætləs] *n* atlas *m*

ATM *n* **a)** *esp US* (*abbr of* **automatic** *or* **automated teller machine**) cajero *m* automático **b)** (*abbr of* **at the moment**) de momento

atmosphere ['ætməsfɪə(r)] *n* atmósfera *f*; *Fig* [ambience] ambiente *m*

atmospheric [ætməs'ferɪk] *adj* atmosférico(a)

atom ['ætəm] *n* átomo *m*; **atom bomb** bomba atómica

atomic [ə'tɒmɪk] *adj* atómico(a)

at-risk ['æt'rɪsk] *adj* **an at-risk group** un grupo de riesgo

atrocious [ə'trəʊʃəs] *adj* atroz

atrocity [ə'trɒsɪtɪ] *n* atrocidad *f*

attach [ə'tætʃ] *vt* [stick] pegar; [fasten] sujetar; [document] adjuntar; **to attach importance to sth** dar importancia a algo; *Fig* **to be attached to** [be fond of] tener cariño a

attachment [ə'tætʃmənt] *n* **a)** TECH accesorio *m*; [action] acoplamiento *m* **b)** [fondness] apego *m* (**to** por) **c)** COMPUT [to e-mail] (archivo *m*) adjunto *or* anexo

attack [ə'tæk] **1.** *n* **a)** [assault] ataque *m*, asalto *m*; **an attack on sb's life** un atentado contra la vida de algn **b)** MED ataque *m* **2.** *vt* [assault] atacar, asaltar; *Fig* [problem] abordar; [job] emprender; *Fig* [criticize] atacar

attacker [ə'tækə(r)] *n* asaltante *mf*, agresor(a) *m,f*

attain [ə'teɪn] *vt* [aim] lograr; [rank, age] llegar a

attempt [ə'tempt] **1.** *n* intento *m*, tentativa *f*; **at the second attempt** a la segunda; **an attempt on sb's life** un atentado contra la vida de algn **2.** *vt* intentar; **to attempt to do sth** tratar de *or* intentar hacer algo; JUR **attempted murder/rape** intento *m* de asesinato / violación

attend [ə'tend] **1.** *vt* [be present at] asistir a; [care for, wait on] atender **2.** *vi* [be present] asistir; [pay attention]

prestar atención ■ **attend to** vt insep [business] ocuparse de ; [in shop]
atender a

attendance [ə'tendəns] n asistencia f

attendant [ə'tendənt] n [in cinema
etc] acomodador(a) m,f ; [in museum]
guía mf ; [in car park] vigilante(a) m,f

attention [ə'tenʃən] n **a)** atención f ;
for the attention of Miss Jones a la
atención de la Srta. Jones ; **pay attention!** ¡atiende! ; **to pay attention to sb /
sth** prestar atención a algn / algo **b)** MIL
attention! ¡firmes! ; **to stand to attention** estar firmes

attentive [ə'tentɪv] adj [listener]
atento(a) ; [helpful] solícito(a)

attic ['ætɪk] n ático m

attitude ['ætɪtju:d] n actitud f ; [position
of body] postura f ; **an attitude of mind**
un estado de ánimo

attorney [ə'tɜ:nɪ] n **a)** US [lawyer]
abogado(a) m,f ; **Attorney General**
≃ Ministro(a) m,f de Justicia ; **district attorney** fiscal mf **b)** JUR **power
of attorney** poderes mpl

attract [ə'trækt] vt atraer ; **to attract
attention** llamar la atención ; **to attract a waiter's attention** llamar a un
camarero

attraction [ə'trækʃən] n **a)** [power]
atracción f **b)** [attractive thing] atractivo m ; [charm] encanto m ; [incentive]
aliciente m ; **the main attraction** el número fuerte

attractive [ə'træktɪv] adj atractivo(a) ;
[good-looking] guapo(a) ; [idea, propos-
ition] atrayente

attribute¹ ['ætrɪbju:t] n [quality] atributo m

attribute² [ə'trɪbju:t] vt atribuir

aubergine ['əubəʒi:n] n Br berenjena f

auburn ['ɔ:bən] adj castaño rojizo (inv)

auction ['ɔ:kʃən] **1.** n subasta f **2.** vt
subastar

auctioneer [ɔ:kʃə'nɪə(r)] n subas-
tador(a) m,f

audacity [ɔ:'dæsɪtɪ] n audacia f

audible ['ɔ:dɪbəl] adj audible

audience ['ɔ:dɪəns] n **a)** [spectators] público m ; [at concert, conference] auditorio m ; [television] telespectadores mpl
b) [meeting] audiencia f

audiobook ['ɔ:dɪəubuk] n libro m de
audio

audio-visual [ɔ:dɪəu'vɪzjuəl] adj audiovisual ; **audio-visual aids** apoyo m
audiovisual

audit ['ɔ:dɪt] **1.** n revisión f de cuentas
2. vt revisar, intervenir

audition [ɔ:'dɪʃən] **1.** n prueba f **2.** vt **to
audition sb for a part** probar a algn
para un papel

auditorium [ɔ:dɪ'tɔ:rɪəm] n auditorio m

August ['ɔ:gəst] n agosto m

aunt [ɑ:nt], **auntie, aunty** ['ɑ:ntɪ] Fam
n tía f

au pair [əu'peə(r)] n **au pair (girl)** au pair f

aura ['ɔ:rə] n aura f ; REL aureola f

austere [ɒ'stɪə(r)] adj austero(a)

austerity [ɒ'sterɪtɪ] n austeridad f

Australia [ɒ'streɪlɪə] n Australia

Australian [ɒ'streɪlɪən] adj & n
australiano(a) (m,f)

Austria ['ɒstrɪə] n Austria

Austrian ['ɒstrɪən] adj & n aus-
tríaco(a) (m,f)

authentic [ɔ:'θentɪk] adj auténtico(a)

author ['ɔ:θə(r)] n autor(a) m,f

authoritarian [ɔ:θɒrɪ'teərɪən] adj
autoritario(a)

authority [ɔ:'θɒrɪtɪ] n autoridad f ; **local
authority** ayuntamiento m

authorization [ɔ:θəraɪ'zeɪʃən] n autorización f

authorize ['ɔ:θəraɪz] vt autorizar ; [pay-
ment etc] aprobar ; **to authorize sb to
do sth** autorizar a algn a hacer algo

autistic [ɔ:'tɪstɪk] adj autista

auto ['ɔ:təu] n US automóvil m, Esp coche m, Am carro m, RP auto m

autobiography [ɔ:təubaɪ'ɒgrəfɪ] n autobiografía f

autograph ['ɔ:təgrɑ:f] **1.** n autógrafo m **2.** vt [sign] firmar ; [book, photo]
dedicar

automatic [ɔ:tə'mætɪk] **1.** adj automático(a) **2.** n [car] Esp coche m or Am carro m or RP auto m (con cambio) automático; [gun] pistola automática

automobile ['ɔ:təməbi:l] n US automóvil m, Esp coche m, Am carro m, RP auto m

autonomous [ɔ:'tɒnəməs] adj autónomo(a)

autonomy [ɔ:'tɒnəmɪ] n autonomía f

autopsy ['ɔ:tɒpsɪ] n autopsía f

autumn ['ɔ:təm] n otoño m

auxiliary [ɔ:g'zɪljərɪ] adj auxiliar

availability [əveɪlə'bɪlɪtɪ] n disponibilidad f

available [ə'veɪləbəl] adj [thing] disponible; [person] libre

avalanche ['ævəlɑ:nʃ] n avalancha f

Ave (abbr of Avenue) Av., Avda.

avenge [ə'vendʒ] vt vengar

avenue ['ævɪnju:] n avenida f; Fig vía f

average ['ævərɪdʒ] **1.** n promedio m, media f; **on average** por término medio **2.** adj medio(a); [condition] regular **3.** vt sacar la media de; **he averages eight hours' work a day** trabaja una media de ocho horas al día ▪ **average out at** vt insep salir a una media de

aversion [ə'vɜ:ʃən] n [feeling] aversión f; [thing] bestia negra

avert [ə'vɜ:t] vt [eyes, thoughts] apartar (**from** de); [accident] impedir; [danger] evitar

aviation [eɪvɪ'eɪʃən] n aviación f

avid ['ævɪd] adj [reader] voraz

avocado [ævə'kɑ:dəʊ] n avocado (**pear**) aguacate m, Andes, CSur palta f

avoid [ə'vɔɪd] vt evitar; [question] eludir

avoidable [ə'vɔɪdəbəl] adj evitable

AWA MESSAGING written abbr of **a while ago**

await [ə'weɪt] vt esperar, Esp aguardar

awake [ə'weɪk] **1.** adj despierto(a); **to be awake** estar despierto(a) **2.** (pt awoke or awaked, pp awoken or awaked) vt & vi despertar

awaken [ə'weɪkən] (pt awakened, pp awoken) vt & vi = **awake**

award [ə'wɔ:d] **1.** n [prize] premio m; [medal] condecoración f; JUR indemnización f; [grant] beca f **2.** vt [prize] conceder, otorgar; [medal] dar; [damages] adjudicar

aware [ə'weə(r)] adj [informed] enterado(a); **not that I'm aware of** que yo sepa no; **to be aware of sth** ser consciente de algo; **to become aware of sth** darse cuenta de algo

awareness [ə'weənɪs] n conciencia f (**of** de)

away [ə'weɪ] adv far away lejos; **go away!** ¡lárgate!; **it's 3 miles away** está a 3 millas (de distancia); **keep away from the fire!** ¡no te acerques al fuego!; **right away** en seguida; **to be away** [absent] estar ausente; [out] estar fuera; **to die away** desvanecerse; **to give sth away** regalar algo; [secret] revelar algo; **to go away** irse; SPORT **to play away** jugar fuera; **to turn away** volver la cara; **to work away** trabajar

awe [ɔ:] n [fear] temor m; [amazement] asombro m; **he was in awe of his father** le intimidaba su padre

awesome ['ɔ:səm] adj impresionante

awful ['ɔ:fʊl] adj Fam espantoso(a); **an awful lot of people** un montón de gente, Am salvo RP harta gente

awfully ['ɔ:fʊlɪ] adv Fam terriblemente

awkward ['ɔ:kwəd] adj [clumsy] torpe; [object] incómodo(a); [moment] inoportuno(a); [situation] embarazoso(a); [problem] difícil

awning ['ɔ:nɪŋ] n [on ship] toldo m; [on shop] marquesina f

awoke [ə'wəʊk] pt of **awake**

awoken [ə'wəʊkən] pp of **awake**, **awaken**

axe, US **ax** [æks] **1.** n hacha f **2.** vt Fig [jobs] eliminar; [costs] reducir; [plan] cancelar; [person] despedir

axis ['æksɪs] (pl axes ['æksi:z]) n eje m

axle ['æksəl] n eje m; TECH árbol m

B

B, b [biː] *n* **a)** [the letter] B, b *f*; *Br* AUTO **B road** carretera secundaria **b)** MUS **B si** *m*; **B flat** si bemol

BA [biː'eɪ] *n (abbr of* **Bachelor of Arts)** [person] licenciado(a) *m,f* en Filosofía y Letras

babble ['bæbəl] *vi* (baby] balbucear; [brook] murmurar

baboon [bə'buːn] *n* zambo *m*

baby ['beɪbɪ] *n* **a)** bebé *m*, *Andes* guagua *mf*, *RP* nene(a) *m,f*; *Br* **Baby Buggy®** sillita *f* de paseo or de niño; *US* **baby buggy** or **carriage** cochecito *m* de niño; **baby face** cara *f* de niño **b)** [animal] cría *f* **c)** *Fam* [darling] querido(a) *m,f*

baby-sit ['beɪbɪsɪt] *vi* cuidar a niños, hacer de *Esp* canguro or *Am* babysitter

baby-sitter ['beɪbɪsɪtə(r)] *n* canguro *mf*, *Am* babysitter *mf*

bachelor ['bætʃələ(r)] *n* **a)** soltero *m* **b)** UNIV licenciado(a) *m,f*; **Bachelor of Arts / Science** licenciado(a) *m,f* en Filosofía y Letras / Ciencias

back [bæk] **1.** *n* **a)** [of person] espalda *f*; [of animal] lomo *m*; **back to front** al revés

b) [of book] lomo *m*; [of chair] respaldo *m*; [of coin] reverso *m*; [of hand] dorso *m*; [of house, car] parte *f* de atrás **c)** [of stage, cupboard] fondo *m*

d) FTBL defensa *mf*

e) *US* **in back (of)** [behind] en la parte de atrás (de), detrás (de); [to the rear of] al fondo (de)

2. *adj* **a)** trasero(a), de atrás; **back door** puerta *f* de atrás; **back seat** asiento *m* de detrás

b) **back rent** alquiler or *Am* renta pendiente de pago; **back pay** atrasos *mpl*
3. *adv* **a)** [to the rear] atrás; [towards the rear] hacia atrás; **back and forth** de acá para allá

b) **some years back** hace unos años
4. *vt* **a)** [support] apoyar, respaldar
b) FIN financiar
c) [bet on] apostar por
d) [car etc] dar marcha atrás a
5. *vi* **a)** [move backwards] retroceder
b) [car etc] dar marcha atrás

■ **back away** *vi* retirarse

■ **back down** *vi* echarse atrás

■ **back off** *vi* desistir

■ **back out** *vi* [withdraw] retractarse, volverse atrás

■ **back up 1.** *vt sep* **a)** [support] apoyar **b)** COMPUT [file] hacer una copia de seguridad de **2.** *vi* AUTO ir marcha atrás

backache ['bækeɪk] *n* dolor *m* de espalda

backbone ['bækbəʊn] *n* ANAT columna *f*

backer ['bækə(r)] *n* **a)** FIN promotor(a) *m,f* **b)** POL partidario(a) *m,f* **c)** [person who bets] apostante *mf*

backfire [bæk'faɪə(r)] *vi* **a)** AUTO petardear **b)** *Fig* **our plan backfired** nos salió el tiro por la culata

background ['bækgraʊnd] *n* **a)** fondo *m*; **to stay in the background** quedarse en segundo plano; **background music** música *f* de fondo **b)** [origin] origen *m*; [past] pasado *m*; [education] formación *f* **c)** [circumstances] antecedentes *mpl* **d)** [atmosphere] ambiente *m*

backlash ['bæklæʃ] *n* reacción violenta y repentina

backlog ['bæklɒg] *n* **to have a backlog of work** tener un montón de trabajo atrasado

backpack ['bækpæk] *n* mochila *f*

backside [bæk'saɪd] *n* *Fam* trasero *m*, culo *m*

backslash ['bækslæʃ] n COMPUT barra f (diagonal) inversa

backstage [bæk'steɪdʒ] adv entre bastidores

backstreet ['bækstri:t] adj [underhanded] clandestino(a)

backup ['bækʌp] **1.** adj [plan, team] de apoyo **2.** n **a)** [support] apoyo m, respaldo m **b)** COMPUT copia f seguridad **c)** US [of traffic] caravana f

backward ['bækwəd] **1.** adj **a)** [movement] hacia atrás **b)** [country] subdesarrollado(a); [child] retrasado(a) **2.** adv esp US hacia atrás

backwards ['bækwədz] adv hacia atrás; **to walk backwards** andar de espaldas

backyard [bæk'jɑːd] n patio trasero; US jardín trasero

bacon ['beɪkən] n panceta f, Méx tocino m, Esp bacon m, Esp beicon m

bacteria [bæk'tɪərɪə] npl bacterias fpl

bad [bæd] **1.** (compar **worse**, superl **worst**) adj **a)** [poor] malo(a); **to go from bad to worse** ir de mal en peor **b)** [decayed] podrido(a); **to go bad** echarse a perder **c)** that's too bad! ¡qué pena! **d)** [wicked] malo(a); **to use bad language** ser mal hablado(a) **e)** [accident] grave; [headache] fuerte **f)** [ill] enfermo(a) **g) bad debt** deuda f incobrable **2.** n lo malo

bade [beɪd] pt of **bid**

badge [bædʒ] n insignia f; [metal disc] chapa f, Br **blue badge** [for disabled drivers] tarjeta de conductor con discapacidad

badger ['bædʒə(r)] **1.** n tejón m **2.** vt acosar

badly ['bædlɪ] adv **a)** mal; **he did badly in the exam** le salió mal el examen; **to be badly off** andar mal de dinero **b)** [seriously] gravemente **c)** [very much] mucho; **to miss sb badly** echar mucho de menos a algn; **we need it badly** nos hace mucha falta

bad-mannered [bæd'mænəd] adj maleducado(a)

badminton ['bædmɪntən] n bádminton m

bad-tempered [bæd'tempəd] adj **to be bad-tempered** [temperament] tener mal genio; [temporarily] estar de mal humor

baffle ['bæfəl] **1.** vt desconcertar **2.** n TECH pantalla acústica

bag [bæg] n **a)** [large] bolsa f; [handbag] bolso m, Andes, RP cartera f, Méx bolsa; Fam **bags of** montones de; US **garbage bag** bolsa f de basura; **messenger bag** bolsa f de bandolera; **travel bag** bolsa de viaje **b)** [hunting] caza f; Fam **it's in the bag** es cosa hecha **c)** Br v Fam & Pej **old bag** [woman] bruja f **d) bags** [under eyes] ojeras fpl

bagboy ['bægbɔɪ] n US dependiente m (que ayuda a los clientes a meter las compras en las bolsas)

baggage ['bægɪdʒ] n **a)** equipaje m; **baggage control** control m de equipajes **b)** MIL bagaje m

baggy ['bægɪ] (compar **baggier**, superl **baggiest**) adj holgado(a); **baggy trousers** pantalones anchos

bagpipes ['bægpaɪps] npl gaita f

bail¹ [beɪl] n JUR fianza f; **on bail** bajo fianza; **to stand** or US **post bail for sb** salir fiador por algn ■ **bail out** vt sep Fig [person] sacar de un apuro

bail² [beɪl] vi NAUT **to bail (out)** achicar

bait [beɪt] **1.** n cebo m; **to rise to the bait** tragar el anzuelo, picar **2.** vt **a)** [for fishing] cebar **b)** [torment] hostigar

bake [beɪk] **1.** vt **a)** cocer al horno **b)** [harden] endurecer **2.** vi Fam hacer mucho calor

baked [beɪkt] adj al horno; **baked potato** patata f or Am papa f al horno

baker ['beɪkə(r)] n panadero(a) m,f

bakery ['beɪkərɪ] n panadería f

baking ['beɪkɪŋ] n cocción f; **baking dish** fuente f para horno; **baking powder** levadura f en polvo; **baking tin** molde m

balance ['bæləns] **1.** n **a)** [scales] balanza f; Fig **to hang in the balance** estar en juego

b) [equilibrium] equilibrio *m*; POL **balance of power** equilibrio de fuerzas
c) FIN saldo *m*; **balance of payments** balanza *f* de pagos; **balance sheet** balance *m*; *Br* **bank balance** saldo *m* bancario; **credit balance** saldo acreedor
d) [remainder] resto *m*
2. *vt* **a)** poner en equilibrio (**on** en)
b) [budget] equilibrar; **to balance the books** hacer el balance
c) [weigh up] sopesar
3. *vi* guardar el equilibrio
■ **balance out** *vi* [figures] corresponderse

balcony ['bælkənɪ] *n* balcón *m*; THEAT anfiteatro *m*

bald [bɔːld] *adj* **a)** [person] calvo(a)
b) [tyre] desgastado(a) **c)** [style] escueto(a)

Balearic [ˌbælɪˈærɪk] *adj* **the Balearic Islands** las (islas *fpl*) Baleares *fpl*

Balearics [ˌbælɪˈærɪks] *npl* **the Balearics** las (islas *fpl*) Baleares *fpl*

Balkans ['bɔːlkənz] *npl* **the Balkans** los Balcanes

ball[1] [bɔːl] *n* **a)** [in cricket, tennis etc] pelota *f*; FTBL balón *m*; [in billiards, golf etc] bola *f*; TECH **ball bearing** rodamiento *m* de bolas; **ball game** [in general] juego *m* de pelota; *US* [baseball match] partido *m* de béisbol *m*; **ball pit** piscina *f* de bolas; *Fig* **it's a whole new ball game** es otra historia; *Fam* **to be on the ball** ser un espabilado **b)** [of paper] bola *f*; [of wool] ovillo *m*

ball[2] [bɔːl] *n* [dance] baile *m*

ballad ['bæləd] *n* balada *f*

ballerina [bæləˈriːnə] *n* bailarina *f*

ballet ['bæleɪ] *n* ballet *m*; **ballet dancer** bailarín(ina) *m,f*

balloon [bəˈluːn] **1.** *n* **a)** globo *m* **b)** [in cartoon] bocadillo *m* **2.** *vi* hincharse; *Fig* aumentar rápidamente

ballot ['bælət] **1.** *n* votación *f*; **ballot box** urna *f*; **ballot paper** papeleta *f* (de voto), *Chile, Méx* voto *m*, *Col* tarjetón *m*, *RP* boleta *f* **2.** *vt* someter a votación

ballpark ['bɔːlpɑːk] *n* campo *m* de béisbol

ballpoint ['bɔːlpɔɪnt] *n* **ballpoint (pen)** bolígrafo *m*, *Carib, Méx* pluma *f*, *Col, Ecuad* estereográfico *m*, *CSur* lapicera *f*

ballroom ['bɔːlruːm] *n* salón *m* de baile

ballsy ['bɔːlzɪ] *adj US v Fam* con huevos

balsamic [bɔːlˈsæmɪk] *adj* **balsamic reduction** reducción *f* balsámica; **balsamic vinaigrette** vinagreta *f* de balsámico; **balsamic vinegar** vinagre *m* balsámico

Baltic ['bɔːltɪk] *adj* báltico(a); **the Baltic (Sea)** el (mar) Báltico

bamboo [bæmˈbuː] *n* bambú *m*

ban [bæn] **1.** *n* prohibición *f* **2.** *vt* **a)** [prohibit] prohibir **b)** [exclude] excluir

banal [bəˈnɑːl] *adj* banal, trivial

banana [bəˈnɑːnə] *n* plátano *m*, *CAm, Col* banano *m*, *Ven* cambur *m*, *RP* banana *f*; *Fam* **to be bananas** [mad] estar como una cabra *or Méx* destrompado *or RP* de la nuca

band [bænd] **1.** *n* **a)** [strip] tira *f*; [ribbon] cinta *f* **b)** [stripe] raya *f* **c)** [group] grupo *m*; [of youths] pandilla *f*; [of thieves] banda *f* **d)** MUS banda *f* **2.** *vi* **to band together** unirse, juntarse

bandage ['bændɪdʒ] **1.** *n* venda *f* **2.** *vt* vendar

Band-aid® ['bændeɪd] *n US Esp* tirita® *f*, *Am* curita *f*

B & B [biːənˈbiː] *n Br (abbr of bed and breakfast)* [hotel] *hostal familiar en el que el desayuno está incluido en el precio de la habitación*

bandit ['bændɪt] *n* bandido *m*

bandwagon ['bændwægən] *n Fig* **to jump on the bandwagon** subirse al tren ■ **bandy about** *vt sep* [ideas] propagar, difundir

bang [bæŋ] **1.** *n* **a)** [blow] golpe *m*
b) [noise] ruido *m*; [explosion] estallido *m*; [of gun] estampido *m*
2. *npl US* **bangs** flequillo *m*, *Am* cerquillo *m* (*corto*)
3. *vt* golpear; **to bang sth shut** cerrar algo de golpe
4. *vi* golpear; **to bang shut** cerrarse de golpe

5. *interj* [blow] ¡zas!; **bang, bang!** [of gun] ¡pum, pum!
6. *adv Fam* justo

banger ['bæŋə(r)] *n* **a)** [firework] petardo *m* **b)** *Fam* [sausage] salchicha *f* **c)** *Fam* **old banger** [car] tartana *f*

bangle ['bæŋgəl] *n* brazalete *m*

banish ['bænɪʃ] *vt* desterrar

banister ['bænɪstə(r)] *n* pasamanos *m inv*

banjo ['bændʒəʊ] *(pl* **banjos)** *n* banjo *m*

bank¹ [bæŋk] **1.** *n* **a)** COMM & FIN banco *m*; **bank account** cuenta bancaria; **bank card** tarjeta bancaria; **bank clerk** empleado(a) *m,f* de banca; **bank draft** letra bancaria; *Br* **bank holiday** fiesta *f* nacional; **bank statement** extracto *m* de cuenta **b)** [in gambling] banca *f* **c)** [store] banco *m*
2. *vt* COMM & FIN depositar, ingresar
3. *vi* COMM & FIN **to bank with** tener una cuenta en
■ **bank on** *vt insep* contar con

bank² [bæŋk] **1.** *n* **a)** [mound] loma *f*; [embankment] terraplén *m* **b)** [of river] ribera *f*; [edge] orilla *f* **2.** *vt* AVIAT ladear
3. *vi* AVIAT ladearse

banker ['bæŋkə(r)] *n* banquero(a) *m,f*

banking ['bæŋkɪŋ] *n* banca *f*

bankrupt ['bæŋkrʌpt] **1.** *adj* en quiebra; **to go bankrupt** quebrar **2.** *vt* llevar a la bancarrota

banner ['bænə(r)] *n* **a)** [flag] bandera *f* **b)** [in demonstration] pancarta *f* **c)** COMPUT banner *m*, anuncio *m*; **banner ad** banner publicitario

banquet ['bæŋkwɪt] *n* banquete *m*

banter ['bæntə(r)] **1.** *n* bromas *fpl* **2.** *vi* bromear

baptism ['bæptɪzəm] *n* bautismo *m*

Baptist ['bæptɪst] *n* bautista *mf*, bautista *mf*

baptize [bæp'taɪz, *US* 'bæptaɪz] *vt* bautizar

bar [bɑː(r)] **1.** *n* **a)** [of gold] barra *f*; [of chocolate] tableta *f*; [of soap] pastilla *f*; *US* **candy bar** [chocolate] barra *f* de chocolate; [muesli] barra *f* de cereales; COMM **bar code** código *m* de barras **b)** [of cage] barrote *m*; *Fam* **to be behind bars** estar en la cárcel **c)** JUR **the Bar** *Br* [barristers] *conjunto de los abogados que ejercen en tribunales superiores*; *US* [lawyers in general] la abogacía **d)** [pub] bar *m*; [counter] barra *f* **e)** MUS compás *m*
2. *vt* **a)** [door] atrancar; [road] cortar **b)** [exclude] excluir **(from** de) **c)** [prohibit] prohibir
3. *prep* salvo; **bar none** sin excepción

barbaric [bɑː'bærɪk] *adj* bárbaro(a)

barbecue ['bɑːbɪkjuː] **1.** *n* barbacoa *f*, *Andes, RP* asado *m* **2.** *vt* asar en la barbacoa

barbed [bɑːbd] *adj* **a)** **barbed wire** alambre *m* de púas **b)** *Fig* [remark] mordaz

barber ['bɑːbə(r)] *n* barbero(a) *m,f*; **barber's (shop)** barbería *f*

barbershop ['bɑːbəʃɒp] **1.** *n US* barbería *f* **2.** *adj* MUS [songs] *cantado por un cuarteto de voces masculinas*; **barbershop quartet** *cuarteto de voces masculinas*

bare [beə(r)] **1.** *adj* **a)** desnudo(a); [head] descubierto(a); [foot] descalzo(a); [room] sin muebles; **to lay bare** poner al descubierto; **with his bare hands** solo con las manos **b)** [basic] mero(a); **the bare minimum** lo mínimo **2.** *vt* desnudar; [uncover] descubrir

barefoot ['beəfʊt] *adj & adv* descalzo(a)

barely ['beəlɪ] *adv* apenas

bargain ['bɑːgɪn] **1.** *n* **a)** [agreement] pacto *m*; [deal] negocio *m*; **into the bargain** por añadidura, además; **to drive a hard bargain** imponer condiciones duras; **to strike a bargain** cerrar un trato **b)** [cheap purchase] ganga *f*; **bargain price** precio *m* de oferta **2.** *vi* **a)** negociar **b)** [haggle] regatear ■ **bargain for** *vt insep* esperar, contar con

barge [bɑːʤ] **1.** *n* gabarra *f* **2.** *vt Fam* **to barge into** [room] irrumpir en; [person] tropezar con ▪ **barge in** *vi Fam* **a)** [go in] entrar sin permiso **b)** [interfere] entrometerse

bark¹ [bɑːk] **1.** *n* ladrido *m* **2.** *vi* [dog] ladrar

bark² [bɑːk] *n* BOT corteza *f*

barley ['bɑːlɪ] *n* cebada *f*; **barley sugar** azúcar *m* cande

barmaid ['bɑːmeɪd] *n esp Br* camarera *f*, *Am* mesera *f*, *RP* moza *f*

barman ['bɑːmən] *n* camarero *m*, *Am* mesero *m*, *RP* mozo *m*

barn [bɑːn] *n* granero *m*; **barn dance** baile *m* popular

barnyard ['bɑːnjɑːd] *n* corral *m*

barometer [bə'rɒmɪtə(r)] *n* barómetro *m*

baron ['bærən] *n* barón *m*

baroness ['bærənɪs] *n* baronesa *f*

barracks ['bærəks] *n* MIL cuartel *m*

barrage ['bærɑːʤ] *n* **a)** [dam] presa *f* **b)** MIL barrera *f* de fuego **c)** *Fig* [of questions] lluvia *f*

barrel ['bærəl] *n* **a)** [of wine] tonel *m*; [of beer, oil] barril *m* **b)** [of firearm] cañón *m*

barren ['bærən] *adj* estéril; [land] yermo(a)

barricade [bærɪ'keɪd] **1.** *n* barricada *f* **2.** *vt* levantar barricadas; **to barricade oneself in** parapetarse

barrier ['bærɪə(r)] *n* barrera *f*

barring ['bɑːrɪŋ] *prep* salvo, excepto; **barring a miracle** a menos que ocurra un milagro

barrister ['bærɪstə(r)] *n Br* abogado(a) *m,f (que ejerce en tribunales superiores)*

barrow ['bærəʊ] *n* carretilla *f*

bartender ['bɑːtendə(r)] *n US* camarero *m*, *Am* mesero *m*, *RP* mozo *m*

barter ['bɑːtə(r)] *vt* trocar (**for** por)

base [beɪs] **1.** *n* base *f*; [foot] pie *m*; [of column] basa *f*; SPORT [of team] concentración *f*; **air /naval base** base *f* aérea /naval **2.** *vt* **a)** basar, fundar (**on** en) **b)** [troops] estacionar **3.** *adj* **a)** [despicable] bajo(a), despreciable **b)** [metals] común

baseball ['beɪsbɔːl] *n* béisbol *m*

base-jump ['beɪsʤʌmp] *vi* hacer salto base

basement ['beɪsmənt] *n* sótano *m*

bash [bæʃ] **1.** *n* [heavy blow] golpetazo *m*; [dent] bollo *m*; *Fam* [attempt] intento *m* **2.** *vt* golpear

bashful ['bæʃfʊl] *adj* tímido(a)

basic ['beɪsɪk] **1.** *adj* básico(a); **basic pay** sueldo *m* base **2.** *npl* **basics** lo fundamental

basically ['beɪsɪklɪ] *adv* fundamentalmente

basil [*Br* 'bæzəl, *US* 'beɪzəl] *n* albahaca *f*

basin ['beɪsən] *n* **a)** [for cooking] recipiente *m*, bol *m*; [for washing hands] lavabo *m*, *Am* lavamanos *m inv*; [plastic, for washing up] palangana *f*, *Esp* barreño *m* **b)** [of river] cuenca *f*

basis ['beɪsɪs] *(pl* **bases**) *n* base *f*; **on the basis of** en base a

basket ['bɑːskɪt] *n* cesta *f*; [in basketball] canasta *f*

basketball ['bɑːskɪtbɔːl] *n* baloncesto *m*

Basque [bæsk, bɑːsk] **1.** *adj* vasco(a); **Basque Country** País Vasco, Euskadi; **Basque flag** ikurriña *f*; **Basque nationalist** abertzale *mf* **2.** *n* **a)** [person] vasco(a) *m,f* **b)** [language] vasco *m*, euskera *m*

bass¹ [bæs] *n inv* [seawater] lubina *f*; [freshwater] perca *f*

bass² [beɪs] **1.** *n* **a)** [singer] bajo *m* **b)** [notes] graves *mpl*; **bass drum** bombo *m*; **bass guitar** bajo *m* **2.** *adj* bajo(a)

bassoon [bə'suːn] *n* fagot *m*

bat¹ [bæt] **1.** *n* [in cricket, baseball] bate *m*; [in table tennis] pala *f*; *Br Fam* **to**

do sth off one's own bat hacer algo por cuenta propia **2.** *vi* [in cricket, baseball] batear

bat² [bæt] *n* ZOOL murciélago *m*

bat³ [bæt] *vt Fam* **without batting an eyelid** sin pestañear

batch [bætʃ] *n* [of bread] hornada *f*; [of goods] lote *m*; COMPUT **batch processing** procesamiento *m* por lotes

bath [bɑːθ] **1.** *n* **a)** baño *m*; **to have a bath** bañarse; **bath towel** toalla *f* de baño **b)** [tub] bañera *f*, *Am* tina *f* **c)** *Br* **(swimming) baths** piscina *f*, *Méx* alberca *f*, *RP* pileta *f* **2.** *vt* bañar

bathe [beɪð] **1.** *vi* bañarse **2.** *vt* **a)** [wound] lavar **b)** **he was bathed in sweat** [covered] estaba empapado de sudor

bathing [ˈbeɪðɪŋ] *n* baño *m*; **bathing cap** gorro *m* de baño; **bathing costume** *or* **suit** traje *m* de baño, *Col* vestido *m* de baño, *RP* malla *f*; **bathing trunks** bañador *m* de hombre

bathrobe [ˈbɑːθrəʊb] *n* albornoz *m*

bathroom [ˈbɑːθruːm] *n* cuarto *m* de baño

bathtub [ˈbɑːθtʌb] *n* bañera *f*, *Am* tina *f*

baton [ˈbætən, ˈbætɒn] *n* **a)** MUS batuta *f* **b)** *Br* [of policeman] porra *f* **c)** SPORT testigo *m*

batshit [ˈbatʃɪt] *adj Fam* pirado(a)

battalion [bəˈtæljən] *n* batallón *m*

batter¹ [ˈbætə(r)] *vt* aporrear, apalear

batter² [ˈbætə(r)] *n* [in cricket, baseball] bateador(a) *m,f*

batter³ [ˈbætə(r)] **1.** *n* CULIN pasta *f* (para rebozar); **fish in batter** pescado rebozado **2.** *vt* CULIN rebozar

battered [ˈbætəd] *adj* [car] abollado(a); [person] maltratado(a)

battery [ˈbætərɪ] *n* **a)** [for torch, radio] pila *f*, AUTO batería *f* **b)** JUR **assault and battery** lesiones *fpl*

battle [ˈbætəl] **1.** *n* batalla *f*; *Fig* lucha *f*; **to do battle** librar batalla; *Fig* **battle cry** lema *m* **2.** *vi* luchar

battlefield [ˈbætəlfiːld] *n* campo *m* de batalla

battleship [ˈbætəlʃɪp] *n* acorazado *m*

baulk [bɔːk] **1.** *vt* [frustrate, defeat] frustrar, hacer fracasar **2.** *vi* **to baulk at sth** mostrarse reticente *or* echarse atrás ante algo

bawl [bɔːl] *vi* gritar, chillar

bay¹ [beɪ] *n* GEOG bahía *f*; [large] golfo *m*; **Bay of Biscay** golfo de Vizcaya; **Bay of Bengal** golfo de Bengala

bay² [beɪ] *n* **a)** [recess] hueco *m*; **bay window** ventana salediza **b)** [in factory] nave *f*; **cargo bay** bodega *f* de carga

bay³ [beɪ] *n* laurel *m*

bay⁴ [beɪ] **1.** *vi* [dog] aullar **2.** *n* ladrido *m*; *Fig* **at bay** acorralado(a); *Fig* **to keep sb at bay** mantener a algn a raya

bayonet [ˈbeɪənɪt] *n* bayoneta *f*

bazaar [bəˈzɑː(r)] *n* **a)** [market] bazar *m* **b)** **(church) bazaar** [charity sale] rastrillo benéfico

BBFN MESSAGING *written abbr of* **bye bye for now**

BBL MESSAGING *written abbr of* **be back later**

BC [biːˈsiː] *(abbr of* **before Christ)** a. de C.

Bcc *n (abbr of* **blind carbon copy)** Cci *(con copia oculta)*

BCNU MESSAGING *(abbr of* **be seeing you)** hl, ta luego

---

be [biː] *(unstressed* [bɪ]*) (pres 1st person sing* **am**; *3rd person sing* **is**; *2nd person sing & all persons pl* **are**; *pt 1st & 3rd persons sing* **was**; *2nd person sing & all persons pl* **were**; *pp* **been)**

En el inglés hablado, y en el escrito en estilo coloquial, el verbo **be** se contrae de forma que **I am** se transforma en **I'm**, **he / she / it is** se transforman en **he's / she's / it's** y **you / we / they are** se transforman en **you're / we're / they're.** Las formas negativas **is not, are not, was not** y **were not** se transforman en **isn't, aren't, wasn't** y **weren't.**

1. *vi* **a)** ser; **he is very tall** es muy alto; **Madrid is the capital** Madrid es la capital
b) [nationality, occupation] ser; **he's Italian** es italiano

c) [origin, ownership] ser; **the car is Domingo's** el coche es de Domingo
d) [price] costar; [total] ser; **a return ticket is £24** un billete de ida y vuelta cuesta £24; **how much is it?** ¿cuánto es?
e) [temporary state] estar; **how are you? — I'm very well** ¿cómo estás? — estoy muy bien; **this soup is cold** esta sopa está fría; **to be cold/afraid/hungry** [person] tener frío/miedo/hambre
f) [location] estar; **Birmingham is 200 miles from London** Birmingham está a 200 millas de Londres
g) [age] tener; **she is thirty (years old)** tiene treinta años
2. *v aux* a) [with pres participle] estar; **he is writing a letter** está escribiendo una carta; **she was singing** estaba cantando; **they are leaving next week** se van la semana que viene; **we have been waiting for a long time** hace mucho que estamos esperando
b) [passive] ser; **he was murdered** fue asesinado; **she is allowed to smoke** se le permite fumar
c) [obligation] **I am to see him this afternoon** debo verle esta tarde; **you are not to smoke here** no se puede fumar aquí
3. *v impers* a) [with 'there'] haber; **there is, there are** hay; **there was, there were** había; **there will be** habrá; **there would be** habría; **there have been a lot of complaints** ha habido muchas quejas; **there were ten of us** éramos diez
b) [with 'it'] **it's late** es tarde; **it is said that** se dice que; **who is it? — it's me** ¿quién es? — soy yo; **what is it?** ¿qué pasa?
c) [weather] **it's foggy** hay niebla; **it's cold/hot** hace frío/calor
d) [time] ser; **it's one o'clock** es la una; **it's four o'clock** son las cuatro
e) [date] **it's the 11th/Tuesday today** hoy es el 11/martes
f) [in tag questions] **it's lovely, isn't it?** es bonito, ¿no?; **you're happy, aren't you?** estás contento, ¿verdad?; **he's not very clever, is he?** no es muy listo, ¿verdad?

g) [unreal conditions] **if I was** or **were you ...** yo en tu lugar ...; **if you were a millionaire ...** si fueras millonario ...
h) [as past participle of 'go'] **I've been to Paris** he estado en París

beach [biːʃ] **1.** *n* playa *f* **2.** *vt* varar

beacon [ˈbiːkən] *n* a) AVIAT & NAUT baliza *f* b) [lighthouse] faro *m*

bead [biːd] *n* a) [of necklace etc] cuenta *f*; **glass bead** abalorio *m* b) [of liquid] gota *f*

beak [biːk] *n* a) [of bird] pico *m* b) *Fam* [nose] nariz ganchuda

beaker [ˈbiːkə(r)] *n* [tumbler] taza alta, jarra *f*

beam [biːm] **1.** *n* a) [in building] viga *f* b) [of light] rayo *m*; PHYS haz *m* **2.** *vi* a) [sun] brillar b) [smile] sonreír **3.** *vt* [broadcast] difundir, emitir

bean [biːn] *n* [vegetable] *Esp* alubia *f*, *Esp* judía *f*, *Am salvo RP* frijol *m*, *Andes, RP* poroto *m*; [of coffee] grano *m*; **to be full of beans** estar lleno(a) de vitalidad

bear[1] [beə(r)] (*pt* bore, *pp* borne) **1.** *vt* a) [carry] llevar; **to bear in mind** tener presente b) [support] sostener c) [endure] soportar, aguantar; **I can't bear him** no lo soporto d) (*pt* born, *passive only, not followed by* by) [give birth to] dar a luz; **he was born in Wakefield** nació en Wakefield **2.** *vi* [turn] girar, torcer; **to bear left** girar a la izquierda ■ **bear up** *vi* [endure] resistir

bear[2] [beə(r)] *n* [animal] oso *m*; **bear cub** osezno *m*

bearable [ˈbeərəbəl] *adj* soportable

beard [bɪəd] *n* barba *f*

bearing [ˈbeərɪŋ] *n* a) [posture] porte *m* b) [relevance] relación *f*; **to have a bearing on** estar relacionado(a) con c) TECH cojinete *m* d) NAUT **bearings** posición *f*, orientación *f*; **to get one's bearings** orientarse

beast [biːst] *n* a) [animal] bestia *f*; **beast of burden** bestia de carga b) *Fig* bestia *f*, bruto *m* c) **beasts** [cattle] reses *fpl*

beat [biːt] (*pt* beat, *pp* beaten [ˈbiːtən])
1. *vt* **a)** [hit] pegar, golpear ; [drum] tocar; *Fam* **beat it!** ¡largo!, ¡esfúmate!, *RP* ¡bórrate!
b) CULIN batir
c) [defeat] batir, vencer; **we beat them 5-2** les ganamos 5 a 2; *Fam* **it beats me** [puzzle] no lo entiendo
d) MUS [time] marcar
2. *vi* **a)** [heart] latir
b) [strike] dar golpes ; *Fam* **to beat about the bush** andarse por las ramas
3. *n* **a)** [of heart] latido *m*
b) MUS ritmo *m*, compás *m*
c) *Br* [of policeman] ronda *f*
▪ **beat down** *vi* [sun] apretar
▪ **beat off** *vt sep* rechazar
▪ **beat up** *vt sep Fam* dar una paliza a

beater [ˈbiːtə(r)] *n* **a)** [in hunting] ojeador(a) *m,f* **b)** [in cookery] batidora *f*, batidor *m*

beating [ˈbiːtɪŋ] *n* **a)** [thrashing] paliza *f* **b)** [defeat] derrota *f* **c)** [of drum] toque *m* **d)** [of heart] latido *m*

beautician [bjuːˈtɪʃən] *n* esteticista *mf*

beautiful [ˈbjuːtɪfʊl] *adj* [woman] bonita, *esp Esp* guapa; [child, animal] bonito(a), precioso(a) ; [music, dress, landscape] hermoso(a), precioso(a) ; [smell, taste] delicioso(a)

beauty [ˈbjuːtɪ] *n* belleza *f*, hermosura *f*; **beauty contest** concurso *m* de belleza; **beauty parlour** salón *m* de belleza; **beauty queen** miss *f*; **beauty salon** salón *m* de belleza; **beauty spot** [on face] lunar *m* ; [place] lugar pintoresco

beaver [ˈbiːvə(r)] **1.** *n* castor *m* **2.** *vi* **to beaver away at sth** meterse de lleno en algo

became [bɪˈkeɪm] *pt of* **become**

because [bɪˈkɒz] **1.** *conj* porque **2.** *prep* **because of** a causa de, debido a

beckon [ˈbekən] *vt & vi* llamar (con la mano); **to beckon to sb** llamar a algn con señas

become [bɪˈkʌm] (*pt* became, *pp* become) **1.** *vi* [a teacher, doctor] hacerse ; [boring, jealous, suspicious] volverse ; [old, difficult, stronger] hacerse ;

[happy, sad, thin] ponerse; **to become interested** interesarse ; **what will become of him?** ¿qué va a ser de él? **2.** *vt Formal* [of clothes, colour] sentar bien a

becoming [bɪˈkʌmɪŋ] *adj* **a)** [dress] favorecedor(a) **b)** [behaviour] conveniente, apropiado(a)

bed [bed] *n* **a)** cama *f*; **bunk bed** litera *f*; **bed linen** ropa *f* de cama; **to get out of bed** levantarse de la cama; **to go to bed** acostarse; **to make the bed** hacer la cama; *Br* **bed and breakfast** [service] cama y desayuno *m* ; [sign] pensión *f* **b)** [of river] lecho *m* ; [of sea] fondo *m* **c)** GEOL estrato *m* **d)** **(flower) bed** arriate *m*

bedclothes [ˈbedkləʊðz] *npl* ropa *f* de cama

bedding [ˈbedɪŋ] *n* ropa *f* de cama

bedraggled [bɪˈdrægəld] *adj* [wet] mojado(a) ; [dirty] ensuciado(a)

bedridden [ˈbedrɪdən] *adj* postrado(a) en cama

bedroom [ˈbedruːm] *n* [in house] dormitorio *m*, habitación *f*, cuarto *m*, *CAm, Col, Méx* recámara *f*; [in hotel] habitación *f*, *Am* cuarto *m*, *CAm, Col, Méx* recámara *f*

bedside [ˈbedsaɪd] *n* **at sb's bedside** al lado de la cama de algn; **bedside table** mesilla *f* or mesita *f* (de noche), *Andes* velador *m*, *Méx* buró *m*, *RP* mesa *f* de luz

bedsit [ˈbedsɪt] *Fam*, **bedsitter** [bedˈsɪtə(r)] *n Br* estudio *m*

bedspread [ˈbedspred] *n* colcha *f*

bedtime [ˈbedtaɪm] *n* hora *f* de acostarse

bee [biː] *n* abeja *f*

beech [biːtʃ] *n* haya *f*

beef [biːf] *n* carne *f* de vaca, *Am* carne de res; *US* **ground beef** carne *f* picada de vacuno; **roast beef** rosbif *m* ▪ **beef up** *vt sep Fam* reforzar

beefburger [ˈbiːfbɜːgə(r)] *n* hamburguesa *f*

beehive [ˈbiːhaɪv] *n* colmena *f*

been [biːn, bɪn] *pp of* **be**

beep [biːp] *Fam* **1.** *n* pitido *m* **2.** *vi* sonar

beer [bɪə(r)] n cerveza f; **a glass of beer** una caña

beet [bi:t] n US remolacha f, Méx betabel f

beetle ['bi:təl] n escarabajo m

beetroot ['bi:tru:t] n Br remolacha f, Méx betabel f

before [bɪ'fɔ:(r)] **1.** conj **a)** [earlier than] antes de que (+ subj), antes de que (+ infin); **before she goes** antes de que se vaya; **before leaving** antes de salir **b)** [rather than] antes que (+ infin) **2.** prep **a)** [place] delante de ; [in the presence of] ante **b)** [order, time] antes de; **before Christ** antes de Cristo; **before long** dentro de poco; **before 1950** antes de 1950; **I saw it before you** lo vi antes que tú **3.** adv **a)** [time] antes; **I have met him before** ya lo conozco; **not long before** poco antes; **the night before** la noche anterior **b)** [place] delante, por delante

befriend [bɪ'frend] vt trabar amistad con

beg [beg] **1.** vt **a)** [money etc] pedir **b)** [beseech] rogar, suplicar; **I beg your pardon!** ¡perdone usted!; **I beg your pardon?** ¿cómo ha dicho usted? **2.** vi **a)** [solicit] mendigar; [dog] pedir; **to beg for money** pedir limosna **b) to beg for help / mercy** [beseech] implorar ayuda / compasión

began [bɪ'gæn] pt of begin

beggar ['begə(r)] n **a)** mendigo(a) m,f **b)** Br Fam **poor beggar!** ¡pobre diablo!

begin [bɪ'gɪn] (pt began, pp begun) vt & vi empezar, comenzar; **to begin again** volver a empezar; **to begin at the beginning** empezar por el principio; **to begin doing** or **to do sth** empezar a hacer algo; **to begin with ...** [initially] para empezar ...

beginner [bɪ'gɪnə(r)] n principiante mf

beginning [bɪ'gɪnɪŋ] n **a)** principio m, comienzo m; **at the beginning of May** a principios de mayo; **from the beginning** desde el principio; **in the beginning** al principio **b)** [origin] origen m

begrudge [bɪ'grʌdʒ] vt dar de mala gana; [envy] envidiar

begun [bɪ'gʌn] pp of begin

behalf [bɪ'hɑ:f] n **on behalf of**, US **in behalf of** en nombre de, de parte de; **don't worry on my behalf** no te preocupes por mí

behave [bɪ'heɪv] vi **a)** [person] portarse, comportarse; **behave yourself!** ¡pórtate bien!; **to behave well / badly** portarse bien / mal **b)** [machine] funcionar

behaviour, US **behavior** [bɪ'heɪvjə(r)] n **a)** [of person] comportamiento m, conducta f **b)** [of machine] funcionamiento m

behind [bɪ'haɪnd] **1.** prep **a)** detrás de; **behind sb's back** a espaldas de algn; **behind the scenes** entre bastidores; **to be behind sb** apoyar a algn; **what motive was there behind the crime?** ¿cuál fue el móvil del crimen? **b) behind the times** [less advanced than] anticuado(a) **2.** adv **a)** [in the rear] detrás, atrás; **I've left my umbrella behind** se me ha olvidado el paraguas **b) to be behind with one's payments** [late] estar atrasado(a) en los pagos **3.** n Fam trasero m

beige [beɪʒ] adj & n beige m inv, Esp beis m inv

Beijing [beɪ'ʒɪŋ] n Pekín

being ['bi:ɪŋ] n **a)** ser m **b)** [existence] existencia f; **to come into being** nacer

belated [bɪ'leɪtɪd] adj tardío(a)

belch [beltʃ] **1.** vi [person] eructar **2.** vt [smoke, flames] vomitar, arrojar **3.** n eructo m

Belgian ['beldʒən] adj & n belga (mf)

Belgium ['beldʒəm] n Bélgica

belief [bɪ'li:f] n **a)** creencia f; **beyond belief** increíble **b)** [opinion] opinión f **c)** [faith] fe f **d)** [confidence] confianza f (**in** en)

believable [bɪ'li:vəbəl] adj verosímil

believe [bɪ'liːv] **1.** *vi* **a)** [have faith] creer **b) to believe in** [be in favour of] ser partidario(a) de **c)** [think] creer; **I believe so** creo que sí **2.** *vt* creer

believer [bɪ'liːvə(r)] *n* **a)** REL creyente *mf* **b)** partidario(a) *m,f* **(in** de)

belittle [bɪ'lɪtl] *vt* [person] menospreciar; [problem] minimizar

bell [bel] *n* [of church] campana *f*; [small] campanilla *f*; [of school, door, bicycle etc] timbre *m*; [on cat] cascabel *m*; [on cow] cencerro *m*; **bell jar** campana de vidrio *or Esp* cristal; **bell tower** campanario *m*; *US* SCH **bell work** trabajo *m* de timbre *(breve tarea que realizan los alumnos antes de que suene el timbre de comienzo de la clase)*; *Fig* **that rings a bell** eso me suena

bellboy ['belbɔɪ], **bellhop** ['belhɒp] *n US* botones *m inv*

bellow ['beləʊ] *vi* [bull] bramar; [person] rugir

belly ['belɪ] *n* **a)** [of person] vientre *m*, barriga *f, Chile* guata *f*; **belly flop** panzazo *m* **b)** [of animal] panza *f*

belong [bɪ'lɒŋ] *vi* **a)** pertenecer **(to** a) **b)** [be a member] ser socio(a) **(to** de); POL **to belong to a party** ser miembro de un partido **c)** [have a proper place] corresponder; **this chair belongs here** esta silla va aquí

belongings [bɪ'lɒŋɪŋz] *npl* efectos *mpl* personales

beloved [bɪ'lʌvɪd, bɪ'lʌvd] **1.** *adj* amado(a), querido(a) **2.** *n* amado(a) *m,f*

below [bɪ'ləʊ] **1.** *prep* debajo de, bajo, *Am* abajo de; **below average** por debajo de la media; **10 degrees below zero** 10 grados bajo cero **2.** *adv* abajo; **above and below** arriba y abajo; **see below** véase más abajo

below-average *adj* por debajo de la media

belt [belt] **1.** *n* **a)** cinturón *m*; **blow below the belt** golpe bajo **b)** TECH correa *f*, cinta *f* **c)** [area] zona *f* **2.** *vt Fam* pegar una paliza a ▪ **belt along** *vi*

Fam ir a todo gas ▪ **belt out** *vt sep Fam* [song] cantar a voz en grito ▪ **belt up** *vi Br Fam* callarse

beltway ['belt,weɪ] *n US* ronda *f* (de circunvalación)

bemused [bɪ'mjuːzd] *adj* perplejo(a)

bench [bentʃ] *n* **a)** [seat] banco *m* **b)** [in parliament] escaño *m* **c)** *Br* **the Bench** [judges] la magistratura **d)** SPORT banquillo *m*

benchmark ['bentʃmɑːk] *n* [for comparison] punto *m* de referencia; COMPUT **benchmark test** prueba *m* comparativa *or* de referencia

benchmarking ['bentʃmɑːkɪŋ] *n* evaluación *f* comparativa, benchmarking *m*

benchwarmer ['bentʃwɔːmə(r)] *n US Fam* SPORT calientabanquillos *mf inv*

bend [bend] *(pt & pp* **bent) 1.** *vt* doblar; [back] encorvar; [head] inclinar; *Fam* **to bend the rules** hacer una excepción **2.** *vi* **a)** doblarse; [road] torcerse **b) to bend (over)** inclinarse; *Fam* **he bends over backwards to please her** hace lo imposible por complacerla **3.** *n* [in river, road] curva *f*; [in pipe] recodo *m*; *Br Fam* **to be round the bend** estar *Esp* majara *or Am* zafado(a) ▪ **bend down** *vi* inclinarse

bender ['bendə(r)] *n Fam* [drinking binge] juerga *f*, borrachera *f*; **to go on a bender** irse de juerga

beneath [bɪ'niːθ] **1.** *prep* [below] bajo, debajo de; *Fig* **it's beneath him** es indigno de él **2.** *adv* debajo

benefactor ['benɪfæktə(r)] *n* bienhechor(a) *m,f*

beneficial [benɪ'fɪʃəl] *adj* **a)** [doing good] benéfico(a) **b)** [advantageous] beneficioso(a)

benefit ['benɪfɪt] **1.** *vt* beneficiar **2.** *vi* sacar provecho **(from** *or* **by** de) **3.** *n* **a)** [advantage] beneficio *m*, provecho *m*; **for the benefit of** en beneficio de; **I did it for your benefit** lo hice por tu bien

b) [allowance] subsidio *m*; **unemployment benefit** subsidio de desempleo
c) [event] función benéfica

benevolent [bɪ'nevələnt] *adj* benévolo(a)

benign [bɪ'naɪn] *adj* benigno(a)

bent [bent] **1.** *adj* **a)** [curved] curvado(a)
b) to be bent on doing sth [determined] estar empeñado(a) en hacer algo
c) *Br Fam* [dishonest] deshonesto(a)
2. *pt & pp of* **bend**
3. *n* [inclination] inclinación *f* (**towards** hacia)

bento ['bentəʊ] *n* bento *m*

bequeath [bɪ'kwiːð] *vt* JUR legar

bereaved [bɪ'riːvd] *npl* **the bereaved** los familiares del /de un difunto

bereavement [bɪ'riːvmənt] *n* [mourning] duelo *m*

beret ['bereɪ] *n* boina *f*

Berlin [bɜː'lɪn] *n* Berlín

berry ['berɪ] *n* baya *f*

berserk [bə'sɜːk, bə'zɜːk] *adj* **to go berserk** volverse loco(a)

berth [bɜːθ] **1.** *n* **a)** NAUT [mooring] amarradero *m*; *Fig* **to give sb a wide berth** evitar a algn **b)** [bed] litera *f* **2.** *vi* NAUT atracar

beset [bɪ'set] (*pt & pp* **beset**) *vt* acosar; **it is beset with dangers** está plagado de peligros

beside [bɪ'saɪd] *prep* **a)** [next to] al lado de, junto a **b)** [compared with] comparado con **c) he was beside himself with joy** estaba loco de alegría; **that's beside the point** eso no viene al caso; **to be beside oneself** estar fuera de sí

besides [bɪ'saɪdz] **1.** *prep* **a)** [in addition to] además de **b)** [except] excepto, menos; **no one besides me** nadie más que yo **2.** *adv* además

besiege [bɪ'siːdʒ] *vt* [city] sitiar; *Fig* asediar

best [best] **1.** (*superl of* **good**) *adj* mejor; **best man** ≃ padrino *m* de boda;
her best friend su mejor amiga; **the best thing would be to phone them** lo mejor sería llamarles; **we had to wait the best part of a year** tuvimos que esperar casi un año; **with best wishes from Mary** [in letter] con mis mejores deseos, Mary
2. (*superl of* **well**) *adv* mejor; **as best I can** lo mejor que pueda; **I like this one best** éste es el que más me gusta; **the world's best dressed man** el hombre mejor vestido del mundo
3. *n* **the best** el /la /lo mejor; **all the best!** [at the end of letter] ¡un saludo!; *RP* cariños; **at best** a lo más; **to be at one's best** estar en plena forma; **to do one's best** hacer todo lo posible; **to make the best of sth** sacar el mejor partido de algo; **to the best of my knowledge** que yo sepa

best-before *adj* **best-before date** fecha *f* de consumo preferente

best-seller [best'selə(r)] *n* best-seller *m*

bet [bet] (*pt* **bet** *or* **betted**) **1.** *n* apuesta *f* **2.** *vt* apostar **3.** *vi* apostar (**on** por); *Fam* **you bet!** ¡y tanto!

betray [bɪ'treɪ] *vt* **a)** traicionar **b)** [be unfaithful to] engañar **c)** [reveal] revelar

betrayal [bɪ'treɪəl] *n* traición *f*

better ['betə(r)] **1.** *adj* **a)** (*compar of* **good**) mejor; **the weather is better than last week** hace mejor que la semana pasada; **to be no better than …** no ser más que …; **to get better** mejorar
b) [healthier] mejor (de salud)
c) better off [better] mejor; [richer] más rico(a); **you'd be better off going home** lo mejor es que te vayas a casa
d) the better part of the day la mayor parte del día
2. (*compar of* **well**) *adv* **a)** mejor; **all the better, so much the better** tanto mejor; **better and better** cada vez mejor; **better late than never** más vale tarde que nunca
b) we had better leave más vale que nos vayamos
c) to think better of [plan] cambiar de

3. *n* mejor; **a change for the better** una mejora; **to get the better of sb** vencer a algn
4. *vt* **a)** [improve] mejorar
b) [surpass] superar

betting ['betɪŋ] *n* apuestas *fpl*; **betting shop** quiosco *m* de apuestas

between [bɪ'twiːn] **1.** *prep* entre; **between you and me** entre nosotros; **closed between one and two** cerrado de una a dos; **in between** entre **2.** *adv* **in between** [position] en medio; [time] entretanto, mientras (tanto)

beverage ['bevərɪdʒ] *n* bebida *f*

beware [bɪ'weə(r)] *vi* tener cuidado (**of** con); **beware!** ¡cuidado!; **beware of the dog** [sign] cuidado con el perro

bewildered [bɪ'wɪldəd] *adj* desconcertado(a)

beyond [bɪ'jɒnd] **1.** *prep* más allá de; **beyond belief** increíble; **beyond doubt** sin lugar a dudas; **it is beyond me why ...** no comprendo por qué ...; **it's beyond a joke** eso ya no tiene gracia; **she is beyond caring** ya no le importa; **this task is beyond me** no puedo con esta tarea **2.** *adv* más allá, más lejos

BFN, B4N MESSAGING *written abbr of* **bye for now**

B4 MESSAGING *written abbr of* **before**

BG MESSAGING *written abbr of* **big grin**

BHL8 MESSAGING *written abbr of* (**I'll) be home late**

bias ['baɪəs] *n* [tendency] tendencia *f* (**towards** hacia); [prejudice] prejuicio *m*

bias(s)ed ['baɪəst] *adj* parcial; **to be bias(s)ed against sth/sb** tener prejuicio en contra de algo/algn

bib [bɪb] *n* [for baby] babero *m*; [of apron] peto *m*

Bible ['baɪbəl] *n* Biblia *f*; *Fam & Pej* **Bible thumper** *or Br* **basher** evangelista *mf*

biblical ['bɪblɪkəl] *adj* bíblico(a)

bibliography [bɪblɪ'ɒɡrəfɪ] *n* bibliografía *f*

biceps ['baɪseps] *n* bíceps *m*

bicker ['bɪkə(r)] *vi* reñir

bicycle ['baɪsɪkəl] *n* bicicleta *f*; **bicycle pump** bomba *f* (de aire); **to go by bicycle** ir en bicicleta

bicycle-friendly *adj* = **bike-friendly**

bicycler ['baɪsɪklə(r)] *n US* ciclista *mf*

bid [bɪd] **1.** *vt* **a)** (*pt* **bid** *or* **bade**, *pp* **bid** *or* **bidden** ['bɪdən]) *Liter* [say] decir; [command] mandar, ordenar; **to bid sb farewell** despedirse de algn
b) (*pt & pp* **bid**) [at auction] pujar
2. *vi* (*pt & pp* **bid**) [at auction] pujar (**for** por)
3. *n* **a)** [offer] oferta *f*
b) [at auction] puja *f*
c) [attempt] intento *m*, tentativa *f*

bidder ['bɪdə(r)] *n* **the highest bidder** el mejor postor

bide [baɪd] (*pt* **bided** *or* **bode**, *pp* **bided**) *vt* esperar; **to bide one's time** esperar el momento oportuno

big [bɪg] **1.** *adj* grande (**gran** *before singular noun*); **a big clock** un reloj grande; **a big surprise** una gran sorpresa; **my big brother** mi hermano mayor; *Fam & Iron* **big deal!** ¿y qué?; **big business** los grandes negocios; **big dipper** montaña rusa; *US* ASTRON **Big Dipper** Osa *f* Mayor; *US* **Big Easy** apodo de Nueva Orleans; *Fam* **big gun, big shot** pez gordo; **big toe** dedo gordo del pie; *Fam* **big top** carpa *f*
2. *adv* **a)** [on a grand scale] a lo grande
b) [well] de manera excepcional

big-budget *adj* de gran presupuesto

bighead ['bɪghed] *n Fam* creído(a) *m,f*, engreído(a) *m,f*

bigot ['bɪgət] *n* intolerante *mf*

bigoted ['bɪgətɪd] *adj* intolerante

bigwig ['bɪgwɪg] *n Fam* pez gordo

bike [baɪk] *n Fam (abbr of* **bicycle** *or* **motorbike**) [bicycle] bici *f*; [motorcycle] moto *f*; *Br* **on your bike!** [go away] ¡largo!, ¡piérdete!; [don't talk nonsense] ¡no digas *Esp* chorradas *or Am* pendejadas *or RP* pavadas!

bike-friendly, bicycle-friendly
adj [area, city] en la que es fácil andar en bicicleta

bikini [bɪˈkiːnɪ] *n* bikini *m*

bilingual [baɪˈlɪŋgwəl] *adj* bilingüe

bill¹ [bɪl] **1.** *n* **a)** [for gas etc] factura *f*, recibo *m*
b) *esp Br* [in restaurant] cuenta *f*
c) POL proyecto *m* de ley; **Bill of Rights** las diez primeras enmiendas a la constitución estadounidense, relacionadas con la garantía de las libertades individuales
d) *US* [banknote] billete *m* de banco
e) [poster] cartel *m*
f) FIN **bill of exchange** letra *f* de cambio
2. *vt* **a)** [send bill to] facturar
b) THEAT programar

bill² [bɪl] *n* [of bird] pico *m*

billboard [ˈbɪlbɔːd] *n* [hoarding] cartelera *f*

billiards [ˈbɪljədz] *n sing* billar *m*

billion [ˈbɪljən] *n US* mil millones *mpl*; *Br Dated* billón *m*

billow [ˈbɪləʊ] **1.** *n* [of water] ola *f*; [of smoke] nube *f* **2.** *vi* [sea] ondear; [sail] hincharse

bin [bɪn] *n* [for storage] cajón *m*; *Br* **bread bin** panera *f*; *Br* **(rubbish) bin** cubo *m or Am* bote *m* de la basura

binary [ˈbaɪnərɪ] *adj* **binary number** número binario

bind [baɪnd] (*pt & pp* **bound**) *vt* **a)** [tie up] atar **b)** MED [bandage] vendar **c)** [book] encuadernar **d)** [require] obligar **e)** [join etc] unir ■ **bind over** *vt sep* JUR obligar legalmente

binder [ˈbaɪndə(r)] *n* [file] carpeta *f*

binding [ˈbaɪndɪŋ] *adj* [promise] comprometedor(a); [contract] vinculante

binge [bɪndʒ] *n Fam* borrachera *f*; **binge drinking** consumo excesivo de alcohol de forma esporádica; **binge eating** consumo *m* compulsivo de alimentos, atracones *mpl* compulsivos; **to go on a binge** irse de juerga

bingo [ˈbɪŋgəʊ] *n* bingo *m*

binner [ˈbɪnə(r)] *n US Fam* buscabasuras *mf inv*

binoculars [bɪˈnɒkjʊləz] *npl* prismáticos *mpl*, gemelos *mpl*

bio [ˈbaɪəʊ] *adj* bio (*inv*)

biochemistry [baɪəʊˈkemɪstrɪ] *n* bioquímica *f*

biodegradable [baɪəʊdɪˈgreɪdəbəl] *adj* biodegradable

biodiesel [ˈbaɪəʊdiːzəl] *n* biodiésel *m*

biofuel [ˈbaɪəʊfjuːl] *n* biocarburante *m*

biography [baɪˈɒgrəfɪ] *n* biografía *f*

biological [baɪəˈlɒdʒɪkəl] *adj* biológico(a); **biological warfare** guerra *f* biológica; **biological weapon** arma *f* biológica

biology [baɪˈɒlədʒɪ] *n* biología *f*

biometric [ˌbaɪəʊˈmetrɪk] *adj* biométrico(a)

bioterrorism [ˌbaɪəʊˈterərɪzm] *n* bioterrorismo *m*

bioweapon [ˈbaɪəʊwepən] *n* arma *f* biológica

bird [bɜːd] *n* **a)** pájaro *m*, ave *f*; *Fig* **to kill two birds with one stone** matar dos pájaros de un tiro; **they're birds of a feather** son tal para cual; **bird of prey** ave de rapiña; *Fam* **to be an early bird** ser madrugador(a); *Proverb* **it's the early bird that catches the worm** a quien madruga Dios le ayuda **b)** *Br Fam* [woman] nena *f*, *Arg* piba *f*

Biro® [ˈbaɪrəʊ] (*pl* **Biros**) *n Br* bolígrafo *m*, *Carib* pluma *f*, *Col, Ecuad* esferográfico *m*, *CSur* lapicera *f*, *Méx* pluma *f* (atómica)

birth [bɜːθ] *n* **a)** nacimiento *m*; [childbirth] parto *m*; **birth certificate** partida *f* de nacimiento; **birth control** [family planning] control *m* de la natalidad; [contraception] métodos anticonceptivos; **birth rate** índice *m* de natalidad; **birth sign** signo *m* del zodíaco; **what's your birth sign?** ¿de qué signo eres?; **by birth** de nacimiento; **to give birth to a child** dar a luz a un niño **b)** **of noble birth** [parentage] de noble linaje

birthday [ˈbɜːθdeɪ] *n* cumpleaños *m inv*

birthmark ['bɜːθmɑːk] n antojo m

birthparent ['bɜːθpeərənt] n [father] padre m biológico; [mother] madre f biológica

birthplace ['bɜːθpleɪs] n lugar m de nacimiento

biscuit ['bɪskɪt] n a) Br [sweet, salted] galleta f; Fam **that really takes the biscuit!** ¡eso ya es el colmo! b) US [muffin] tortita f, bollo m

bishop ['bɪʃəp] n a) REL obispo m b) [in chess] alfil m

bit¹ [bɪt] n a) [small piece] trozo m, pedazo m; **to smash sth to bits** hacer añicos algo b) [small quantity] poco m; **a bit of advice** un consejo; **bits and pieces** trastos mpl; Fig **bit by bit** poco a poco c) **a bit** [slightly] un poco; **a bit longer** un ratito más; **a bit worried** un poco preocupado d) [coin] moneda f

bit² [bɪt] n [of tool] broca f

bit³ [bɪt] n COMPUT bit m

bit⁴ [bɪt] pt of **bite**

bitch [bɪtʃ] **1.** n a) ZOOL [female] hembra f; [dog] perra f b) Fam [spiteful woman] bruja f **2.** vi Fam [complain] quejarse, Esp dar la tabarra

bite [baɪt] (pt **bit**, pp **bitten**) **1.** n a) [act] mordisco m b) [wound] mordedura f; (insect) bite picadura f c) [mouthful] bocado m d) Fam [snack] bocado m **2.** vt morder; [insect] picar; **to bite one's nails** morderse las uñas; Fam **to bite sb's head off** echarle una bronca a algn **3.** vi morder; [insect] picar

biting ['baɪtɪŋ] adj [wind] cortante; Fig [criticism] mordaz

bitten ['bɪtən] pp of **bite**

bitter ['bɪtə(r)] **1.** adj a) amargo(a) b) [weather] glacial; [wind] cortante c) [person] amargado(a) d) [struggle] enconado(a); [hatred] implacable **2.** n Br [beer] cerveza sin burbujas y de tono castaño

bitterly ['bɪtəlɪ] adv **she was bitterly disappointed** sufrió una terrible decepción

bizarre [bɪ'zɑː(r)] adj [odd] extraño(a); [eccentric] estrafalario(a)

biz(z)arro [bɪ'zɑːrəʊ] adj US Fam extraño(a)

blab [blæb] vi Fam parlotear, Esp largar, Méx platicar; [let out a secret] chivarse

black [blæk] **1.** adj a) [colour] negro(a); **a black and white television** un televisor en blanco y negro; Fig **black and blue** amoratado(a); **to put sth down in black and white** poner algo por escrito; AVIAT **black box** caja negra; **black coffee** café solo; **the Black Country** la región de los Midlands; **black eye** ojo morado; **black hole** agujero negro; **black humour** humor negro; **black magic** magia negra; **black market** mercado negro; esp Br **black pudding** morcilla f; **the Black Sea** el Mar Negro; Fig **black sheep** oveja negra b) [gloomy] negro(a); Fig **a black day** un día aciago; AUTO **black spot** punto negro
2. n a) [colour] negro m
b) [person] negro(a) m,f
3. vt a) [make black] ennegrecer
b) [polish] lustrar
c) Br [boycott] boicotear
■ **black out 1.** vt sep a) [extinguish lights in] apagar las luces de b) [censor] censurar **2.** vi [faint] desmayarse

blackberry ['blækbərɪ] n zarzamora f

blackbird ['blækbɜːd] n mirlo m

blackboard ['blækbɔːd] n pizarra f, encerado m, Am pizarrón m

blackcurrant [blæk'kʌrənt] n grosella negra f

blacken ['blækən] vt a) [make black] ennegrecer b) Fig [defame] manchar

blacklist ['blæklɪst] n lista negra

blackmail ['blækmeɪl] **1.** n chantaje m **2.** vt chantajear

blackout ['blækaʊt] n a) [of lights] apagón m b) RADIO & TV censura f c) [fainting] pérdida f de conocimiento

blacksmith ['blæksmɪθ] n herrero m

bladder ['blædə(r)] n vejiga f; **gall bladder** vesícula f biliar

blade [bleɪd] n a) [of grass] brizna f b) [of knife etc] hoja f c) [of propeller, oar] pala f

blame [bleɪm] 1. n culpa f; **to take the blame for sth** asumir la responsabilidad de algo 2. vt echar la culpa a; **he is to blame** él tiene la culpa

blameless ['bleɪmlɪs] adj [person] inocente; [conduct] intachable

blamestorm ['bleɪmstɔː(r)m] 1. n lluvia f de culpas, reunión para determinar a quién atribuir la culpa de un fracaso 2. vt **the group blamestormed to work out who was responsible for the failure of the product** el grupo se reunió para determinar a quién atribuir el fracaso del producto

blanch [blɑːntʃ] 1. vt CULIN escaldar 2. vi [go pale] palidecer, ponerse pálido(a)

bland [blænd] adj [food] soso(a)

blank [blæŋk] 1. adj a) [without writing] en blanco; FIN **blank cheque** cheque m en blanco b) [empty] vacío(a); **a blank look** una mirada inexpresiva c) **a blank refusal** [absolute] una negativa rotunda 2. n a) [space] espacio m en blanco; **to draw a blank** no tener éxito b) MIL cartucho m de fogueo c) US [form] impreso m

blanket ['blæŋkɪt] 1. n manta f, Am cobija f, Am frazada f; Fig capa f 2. adj general

blare [bleə(r)] vi resonar ▪ **blare out** vt sep pregonar

blasé [Br 'blɑːzeɪ, US blɑː'zeɪ] adj de vuelta (de todo)

blasphemous ['blæsfəməs] adj blasfemo(a)

blast [blɑːst] 1. n a) [of wind] ráfaga f b) [of horn etc] toque m; **at full blast** a toda marcha c) [explosion] explosión f d) [shock wave] onda f de choque 2. vt a) [blow up] volar; Br Fam **blast (it)!** ¡maldito sea! b) Fig [destroy] arruinar c) Fig [criticize] criticar

blasted ['blɑːstɪd] adj maldito(a)

blast-off ['blɑːstɒf] n despegue m

blatant ['bleɪtənt] adj [very obvious] evidente; [shameless] descarado(a); **a blatant lie** una mentira patente

blaze¹ [bleɪz] 1. n a) [burst of flame] llamarada f b) [fierce fire] incendio m c) [of sun] resplandor m d) Fig [of anger] arranque m 2. vi a) [fire] arder b) [sun etc] brillar

blaze² [bleɪz] vt **to blaze a trail** abrir un camino

blazer ['bleɪzə(r)] n chaqueta f sport

blazing ['bleɪzɪŋ] adj [building] en llamas; Fig **a blazing row** una discusión violenta

bleach [bliːtʃ] 1. n [household] lejía f, Arg lavandina f, CAm, Chile, Méx, Ven cloro m, Col decol m, Urug jane f 2. vt a) [whiten] blanquear; [fade] descolorir b) [hair] decolorar

bleak [bliːk] adj a) [countryside] desolado(a) b) [weather] desapacible c) [future] poco prometedor(a)

bleat [bliːt] 1. n balido m 2. vi [animal] balar

bleed [bliːd] (pt & pp bled [bled]) 1. vi sangrar 2. vt MED sangrar; Fam **to bleed sb dry** sacarle a algn hasta el último céntimo

bleep [bliːp] 1. n bip m, pitido m 2. vi pitar

bleeper ['bliːpə(r)] n Br buscapersonas m inv, Esp busca m, Méx localizador m, RP radiomensaje m

blemish ['blemɪʃ] n [flaw] defecto m; [on fruit] maca f; Fig mancha f; Fig **without blemish** sin tacha

blend [blend] 1. n mezcla f 2. vt [mix] mezclar; [colours] armonizar 3. vi [mix] mezclarse; [colours] armonizar

blender ['blendə(r)] n Esp batidora f, Am licuadora f

bless [bles] (pt & pp blessed or blest) vt a) bendecir; **bless you!** [when someone sneezes] ¡salud!, Esp ¡jesús! b) **blessed with good eyesight** dotado(a) de buena vista

blessed ['blesɪd] adj a) [holy] sagrado(a), santo(a) b) Fam [for emphasis] dichoso(a)

blessing ['blesɪŋ] n bendición f; [advantage] ventaja f; **a mixed blessing** una ventaja relativa

blew [bluː] pt of **blow**

blind [blaɪnd] **1.** adj ciego(a); **a blind man** un ciego; **a blind woman** una ciega; Fig **blind faith** fe ciega; Fig **to turn a blind eye** hacer la vista gorda; **blind alley** callejón sin salida; Br AUTO **blind corner** curva f sin visibilidad; Fam **blind date** cita a ciegas; **blind spot** ángulo muerto; **blind testing** pruebas a ciegas **2.** adv a ciegas; Fam **to get blind drunk** agarrar una curda **3.** n **a)** Br [on window] persiana f **b)** (pl) **the blind** los ciegos **4.** vt **a)** cegar, dejar ciego **b)** [dazzle] deslumbrar

blindfold ['blaɪndfəʊld] **1.** n venda f **2.** vt vendar los ojos a

blindly ['blaɪndlɪ] adv a ciegas, ciegamente

bling(-bling) ['blɪŋ'(blɪŋ)] Fam **1.** adj **a)** [jewellery] aparatoso(a) **b)** [approach, attitude] de ostentación; **the bling-bling generation** la generación obsesionada por el dinero y la apariencia **2.** n [jewellery] joyas fpl aparatosas ■ **bling out** vt US Fam [decorate] decorar en un estilo extravagante; **she's got her place all blinged out with fake leopardskin furniture** tiene el piso lleno de muebles extravagantes de piel de leopardo sintética

blink [blɪŋk] **1.** n Fam **on the blink** [machine] estropeado(a) **2.** vi **a)** [person] pestañear **b)** [light] parpadear

blissful ['blɪsfʊl] adj [happy] feliz; [marvellous] maravilloso(a)

blister ['blɪstə(r)] **1.** n [on skin] ampolla f; [on paint] burbuja f **2.** vi ampollarse

blizzard ['blɪzəd] n ventisca f

bloated ['bləʊtɪd] adj hinchado(a)

blob [blɒb] n [drop] gota f; [spot] mancha f

block [blɒk] **1.** n **a)** bloque m; [of wood] taco m; **in block capitals** en mayúsculas **b)** Br **a block of flats** un bloque de pisos **c)** [group of buildings] manzana f, Am cuadra f **d)** [obstruction] bloqueo m **2.** vt [obstruct] obstruir; **to block the way** cerrar el paso ■ **block up** vt sep bloquear, obstruir; **to get blocked up** [pipe] obstruirse

blockage ['blɒkɪdʒ] n bloqueo m, obstrucción f; [traffic jam] atasco m

blockbuster ['blɒkbʌstə(r)] n Fam exitazo m; CIN & TV gran éxito m de taquilla; [book] éxito de ventas

blog [blɒg] n (abbr of **weblog**) blog m

blogger ['blɒgə(r)] n bloguero(a) m,f

bloke [bləʊk] n Br Fam tipo m, Esp tío m

blond [blɒnd] **1.** n [man] rubio m, Méx güero m, CAm chele m, Carib catire m, Col mono m **2.** adj rubio(a), Méx güero(a), CAm chele(a), Carib catire(a), Col mono(a)

blonde [blɒnd] adj & n rubio(a) (m,f), Méx güero(a) (m,f), CAm chele(a) (m,f), Carib catire(a) (m,f), Col mono(a) (m,f)

blood [blʌd] n **a)** sangre f; **blood bank** banco m de sangre; **blood cell** glóbulo m; **blood donor** donante mf de sangre; **blood group** grupo sanguíneo; **blood pressure** tensión f arterial; US **blood sausage** morcilla f; **blood test** análisis m de sangre; **blood transfusion** transfusión f de sangre; **blood type** grupo sanguíneo; **blood vessel** vaso sanguíneo; **blue blood** sangre azul; **high / low blood pressure** hipertensión f / hipotensión f **b)** [race] sangre f, raza f

bloodshed ['blʌdʃed] n derramamiento m de sangre

bloodshot ['blʌdʃɒt] adj inyectado(a) de sangre

bloodstream ['blʌdstriːm] n corriente sanguínea

bloodthirsty ['blʌdθɜːstɪ] adj sanguinario(a)

bloody ['blʌdɪ] **1.** adj **a)** [bleeding] sanguinolento(a), sangriento(a); [bloodstained] ensangrentado(a); [battle, revolution] sangriento(a); Fig **to give sb a bloody nose** poner a algn en su sitio

b) *Br, Austr v Fam* [for emphasis] maldito(a), *Esp* puñetero(a), *Méx* pinche; **a bloody liar** un mentiroso de mierda; **bloody hell!** ¡me cago en la mar!, ¡mierda!, *Méx* ¡en la madre!
2. *adv Br, Austr v Fam* **it's bloody hot!** hace un calor del carajo *or Esp* de la leche *or RP* de mierda; **he can bloody well do it himself!** ¡que lo haga él, carajo *or Esp* joder!

bloody-minded [blʌdɪˈmaɪndɪd] *adj Br Fam* terco(a)

bloom [blu:m] **1.** *n* **a)** [flower] flor *f*; **in full bloom** en flor **b)** [on fruit] vello *m* **2.** *vi* [blossom] florecer

blooming [ˈblu:mɪŋ] *adj* **a)** [blossoming] floreciente **b)** *Br Fam* [for emphasis] condenado(a)

blossom [ˈblɒsəm] **1.** *n* [flower] flor *f* **2.** *vi* florecer; *Fig* **to blossom out** alcanzar la plenitud

blot [blɒt] **1.** *n* [of ink] borrón *m*; *Fig* mancha *f*
2. *vt* **a)** [with ink] emborronar
b) [dry] secar
3. *vi* [ink] correrse
■ **blot out** *vt sep* [memories] borrar; [view] ocultar

blotch [blɒtʃ] *n* [on skin] mancha *f*, enrojecimiento *m*

blotchy [ˈblɒtʃi] *(compar* **blotchier**, *superl* **blotchiest**) *adj* [skin etc] enrojecido(a); [paint etc] cubierto(a) de manchas

blotting-paper [ˈblɒtɪŋpeɪpə(r)] *n* papel *m* secante

blouse [blaʊz] *n* blusa *f*

blow[1] [bləʊ] *n* golpe *m*; **to come to blows** llegar a las manos; **it came as a terrible blow** fue un duro golpe

blow[2] [bləʊ] *(pt* **blew**, *pp* **blown)** **1.** *vi* **a)** [wind] soplar **b)** [fuse] fundirse **c)** [tyre] reventar **2.** *vt* **a)** [kiss] mandar **b)** [trumpet etc] tocar **c)** [one's nose] sonarse **d)** [fuse] fundir **e)** *Br Fam* [money] fundir, *RP* fumar ■ **blow away** *vt sep & vi* = **blow off** ■ **blow down** *vt sep* derribar ■ **blow off** **1.** *vt sep* [by wind] llevarse **2.** *vi* [hat] salir volando ■ **blow out 1.** *vt sep* apagar **2.** *vi* apagarse ■ **blow over** *vi* [storm] calmarse; [scandal] olvidarse ■ **blow up 1.** *vt sep* **a)** [building] volar **b)** [inflate] inflar **c)** PHOTO ampliar **2.** *vi* [explode] explotar

blown [bləʊn] *pp of* **blow**

blowout, blow out [ˈbləʊaʊt] *n* AUTO [of tyre] reventón *m*; *Fam* [meal] comilona *f*

blowtorch [ˈbləʊtɔːtʃ] *n US* soplete *m*

blue [blu:] **1.** *adj* **a)** [colour] azul; *Fig* **once in a blue moon** de uvas a peras, *RP* cada muerte de obispo; *Fam* **to scream blue murder** gritar como un loco; **blue jeans** vaqueros *mpl*, tejanos *mpl*
b) [sad] triste; **to feel blue** sentirse deprimido(a)
c) [obscene] verde; **blue joke** chiste *m* verde
2. *n* **a)** [colour] azul *m*; *Fam* **the boys in blue** los maderos
b) **out of the blue** [suddenly] de repente; [unexpectedly] como llovido del cielo

blueberry [ˈblu:bəri] *n* arándano *m*

blueprint [ˈblu:prɪnt] *n* anteproyecto *m*

Bluetooth® [ˈblu:tu:θ] *n* TEL Bluetooth® *m*

bluff [blʌf] **1.** *n* [trick] farol *m*; **to call sb's bluff** hacer que algn ponga sus cartas encima de la mesa **2.** *adj* [abrupt] brusco(a); [forthright] francote(a) **3.** *vi* tirarse un farol; **to bluff one's way through sth** hacer colar algo

blunder [ˈblʌndə(r)] **1.** *n* metedura *f or Am* metida *f* de pata; *Fam* patinazo *m* **2.** *vi* meter la pata, pegar un patinazo

blunt [blʌnt] **1.** *adj* **a)** [knife] desafilado(a); [pencil] despuntado(a); **blunt instrument** instrumento *m* contundente **b)** [frank] directo(a), francote(a); [statement] tajante **2.** *vt* [pencil] despuntar; [knife] desafilar

blur [blɜː(r)] **1.** *n* imagen *f* borrosa **2.** *vt* [shape] desdibujar; [memory] enturbiar

blurred [blɜːd] *adj* borroso(a)

blurt [blɜːt] *vt* **to blurt out** dejar escapar

blush [blʌʃ] **1.** *n* rubor *m* **2.** *vi* ruborizarse

blustery ['blʌstəri] *adj* borrascoso(a)

boar [bɔː(r)] *n* verraco *m*; **wild boar** jabalí *m*

board [bɔːd] **1.** *n* **a)** [plank] tabla *f* **b)** [work surface] mesa *f*; [blackboard] pizarra *f*, *Am* pizarrón *m*; [for games] tablero *m*; **board sports** deportes *mpl* de tabla
c) [meals] pensión *f*; **full board** pensión completa; **board and lodging** *or* *US* **room** casa *f* y comida
d) [committee] junta *f*, consejo *m*; **board of directors** consejo de administración; **board room** sala *f* del consejo
e) NAUT **on board** a bordo
f) *Fig* **above board** en regla; **across-the-board** general
2. *vt* [ship, plane etc] embarcarse en, subir a
3. *vi* **a)** [lodge] alojarse
b) [at school] estar interno(a)
■ **board up** *vt sep* tapar

boarder ['bɔːdə(r)] *n* **a)** [in boarding house] huésped *mf* **b)** [at school] interno(a) *m,f*

boarding ['bɔːdɪŋ] *n* **a)** [embarkation] embarque *m*; **boarding card**, **boarding pass** tarjeta *f* de embarque **b)** [lodging] alojamiento *m*, pensión *f*; **boarding house** pensión; **boarding school** internado *m*

boast [bəʊst] **1.** *n* jactancia *f*, alarde *m* **2.** *vi* jactarse, alardear (**about** de) **3.** *vt* presumir de, alardear de; **the town boasts an Olympic swimming pool** la ciudad disfruta de una piscina olímpica

boastful ['bəʊstfʊl] *adj* jactancioso(a), presuntuoso(a)

boat [bəʊt] *n* barco *m*; [small] barca *f*, bote *m*; [launch] lancha *f*; [large] buque *m*; *Fig* **we're all in the same boat** todos estamos en el mismo barco; **fishing boat** barco de pesca

bode¹ [bəʊd] *pt of* **bide**

bode² [bəʊd] *vt & vi* presagiar; **to bode well/ill** ser de buen/mal agüero

bodily ['bɒdɪlɪ] **1.** *adj* físico(a); **bodily harm** daños *mpl* corporales **2.** *adv* **to carry sb bodily** llevar a algn en brazos

body ['bɒdɪ] *n* **a)** cuerpo *m*; **body odour** olor *m* corporal **b)** [corpse] cadáver *m* **c)** [main part] parte *f* principal **d)** AUTO carrocería *f* **e)** [organization] organismo *m*; [profession] cuerpo *m* **f)** [group of people] conjunto *m*, grupo *m*

bodyguard ['bɒdɪgɑːd] *n* guardaespaldas *mf inv*

bodysurf ['bɒdɪsɜːf] *vi* SPORT hacer surf sin tabla

bodywork ['bɒdɪwɜːk] *n* AUTO carrocería *f*

bog [bɒg] *n* **a)** ciénaga *f* **b)** *Br Fam* [lavatory] baño *m*, *Esp* tigre *m* ■ **bog down** *vt sep* **to get bogged down** atascarse

bogus ['bəʊgəs] *adj* falso(a); **bogus company** compañía *f* fantasma

boil¹ [bɔɪl] **1.** *n* **to come to the boil** empezar a hervir
2. *vt* [water] hervir; [food] cocer; [egg] cocer, pasar por agua
3. *vi* hervir; *Fig* **to boil with rage** estar furioso(a)
■ **boil down** *vi* reducirse (**to** a)
■ **boil over** *vi* [milk] salirse

boil² [bɔɪl] *n* MED furúnculo *m*

boiled [bɔɪld] *adj* **boiled egg** huevo cocido *or* pasado por agua

boiler ['bɔɪlə(r)] *n* caldera *f*; *Br* **boiler suit** mono *m* (de trabajo), *Am* overol *m*, *CSur*, *Cuba* mameluco *m*

boiling ['bɔɪlɪŋ] *adj* **boiling water** agua hirviendo; **it's boiling hot** [food] quema; [weather] hace un calor agobiante; **boiling point** punto *m* de ebullición

boisterous ['bɔɪstərəs] *adj* **a)** [person, party] bullicioso(a) **b)** [weather] borrascoso(a)

BOL MESSAGING *(abbr of* **best of luck***)* muxa srt

bold [bəʊld] *adj* **a)** [brave] valiente **b)** [daring] audaz **c)** TYP **bold type** negrita *f*

Bolivia [bə'lɪvɪə] n Bolivia f

Bolivian [bə'lɪvɪən] adj & n boliviano(a) m,f

bolster ['bəʊlstə(r)] **1.** n [pillow] cabezal m, travesaño **2.** vt [strengthen] reforzar; [support] apoyar

bolt [bəʊlt] **1.** n **a)** [on door] cerrojo m; [small] pestillo m **b)** TECH perno m, tornillo m **c)** [of lightning] rayo m **2.** vt **a)** [lock] cerrar con cerrojo **b)** TECH sujetar con pernos **c)** Fam [food] engullir **3.** vi [person] largarse; [horse] desbocarse **4.** adv **bolt upright** derecho

bomb [bɒm] **1.** n bomba f; Br Fam **to cost a bomb** costar un ojo de la cara; **car bomb** coche-bomba m; **letter bomb** carta-bomba f; **bomb disposal squad** brigada f de artificieros; **bomb scare** amenaza f de bomba **2.** vt [city etc] bombardear; [by terrorists] volar **3.** vi Br Fam **to bomb (along)** [car] ir a toda pastilla

bombard [bɒm'bɑːd] vt bombardear

bombshell ['bɒmʃel] n **a)** MIL obús m **b)** Fig [surprise] bomba f **c)** Fam **a blonde bombshell** una rubia explosiva

bona fide [bəʊnə'faɪdɪ] adj **a)** [genuine] auténtico(a) **b)** [in good faith] bienintencionado(a)

bond [bɒnd] **1.** n **a)** [link] lazo m, vínculo m **b)** FIN bono m **c)** [binding agreement] acuerdo m **2.** vt [stick] pegar **3.** vi [form attachment] unirse (**with** a)

bone [bəʊn] **1.** n **a)** hueso m; [in fish] espina f; Fig **bone of contention** manzana f de la discordia; Fig **he made no bones about it** no trató de disimularlo; **bone china** porcelana fina **b)** **bones** [remains] restos mpl; **the bare bones** lo esencial **2.** vt [meat] deshuesar; [fish] quitar las espinas a ■ **bone up on** vt insep Fam empollar

bonfire ['bɒnfaɪə(r)] n hoguera f, fogata f; Br **Bonfire Night** fiesta del 5 de noviembre en que de noche se hacen hogueras y hay fuegos artificiales

bonkers ['bɒŋkəz] adj Br Fam **to be bonkers** estar chiflado(a) or Esp majareta

bonnet ['bɒnɪt] n **a)** [child's] gorra f **b)** Br [of car] capó m, CAm, Méx cofre m

bonus ['bəʊnəs] n **a)** [on wages] prima f **b)** FIN [on shares] dividendo m extraordinario **c)** Br INS beneficio m

boo [buː] **1.** interj ¡bu! **2.** n abucheo m **3.** vt abuchear

boob [buːb], **boo-boo** [buːbuː] n **a)** Br Fam [silly mistake] metedura for Am metida de pata **b)** v Fam **boobs** [breasts] tetas fpl **c)** US [injury] pupa f

booby-trap ['buːbɪtræp] **1.** n [explosive device] bomba f trampa or camuflada **2.** vt colocar una bomba trampa

book [bʊk] **1.** n **a)** libro m; Fig **by the book** según las reglas; **book end** sujetalibros m inv **b)** [of stamps] carpeta f; [of matches] cajetilla f **c)** COMM **books** cuentas fpl **2.** vt **a)** [reserve] reservar; [return flight] cerrar **b)** [engage] contratar **c)** [of police] poner una multa ■ **book into** vt insep [hotel] reservar una habitación en ■ **book out** vi [of hotel] marcharse ■ **book up** vt sep **booked up** [sign] completo

bookcase ['bʊkkeɪs] n librería f, estantería f

booking ['bʊkɪŋ] n esp Br [reservation] reserva f; **booking office** taquilla f, Am boletería f

bookkeeping ['bʊkkiːpɪŋ] n FIN contabilidad f

booklet ['bʊklɪt] n folleto m

bookmaker ['bʊkmeɪkə(r)] n corredor(a) m,f de apuestas

bookmark ['bʊkmɑːk] n marcador m

bookseller ['bʊkselə(r)] n librero(a) m,f

bookshelf ['bʊkʃelf] n estante m; **bookshelves** estantería f

bookshop ['bʊkʃɒp] n librería f

bookstore ['bʊkstɔː(r)] n US librería f

bookworm ['bukwɜ:m] *n Fam* ratón *m* de biblioteca

boom [bu:m] **1.** *n* **a)** [noise] estampido *m*, trueno *m* **b)** [sudden prosperity] boom *m*, auge *m* **2.** *vi* **a)** [thunder] retumbar; [cannon] tronar **b)** [prosper] estar en auge

boor ['buə(r)] *n* grosero(a) *m,f*, cafre *mf*

boost [bu:st] **1.** *n* estímulo *m*, empujón *m* **2.** *vt* **a)** [increase] aumentar **b)** to boost sb's confidence subirle la moral a algn **c)** [tourism, exports] fomentar **d)** [voltage] elevar

boot[1] [bu:t] **1.** *n* **a)** bota *f*; [short] botín *m*; *Fig* **he's too big for his boots** es muy creído; *Br Fam* **to put the boot in** pisotear; *Fam* **she got the boot** la echaron (del trabajo); **boot polish** betún *m* **b)** *Br* [of car] maletero *m*, *CAm, Méx* cajuela *f*, *CSur* baúl *m*
2. *vt Fam* **a)** FTBL [ball] chutar **b)** to boot (out) echar a patadas **c)** COMPUT arrancar
3. *vi* COMPUT **to boot (up)** arrancar

boot[2] [bu:t] *n* **to boot** además

booth [bu:ð, bu:θ] *n* **a)** [in language lab etc] cabina *f*; **telephone booth** cabina telefónica **b)** [at fair] puesto *m*

booze [bu:z] *Fam* **1.** *n* bebida *f*, *Esp* priva *f*, *RP* chupi *m* **2.** *vi* empinar el codo, *Esp* privar, *RP* chupar

border ['bɔ:də(r)] *n* **a)** borde *m*, margen *m* **b)** [frontier] frontera *f* **c)** [flowerbed] arriate *m* ■ **border on** *vt insep* **a)** GEOG lindar con **b)** *Fig* rayar en

bore[1] [bɔ:(r)] **1.** *vt* TECH taladrar, perforar **2.** *n* **a)** TECH [hole] taladro *m* **b)** [of gun] calibre *m*

bore[2] [bɔ:(r)] **1.** *vt* aburrir **2.** *n* [person] pesado(a) *m,f*, pelma *mf*; [thing] lata *f*, rollo *m*; **what a bore!** ¡qué rollo!

bore[3] [bɔ:(r)] *pt of* **bear**

boredom ['bɔ:dəm] *n* aburrimiento *m*

boring ['bɔ:rɪŋ] *adj* [uninteresting] aburrido(a); [tedious] pesado(a), latoso(a)

born [bɔ:n] **1.** *pp of* **bear**; **to be born** nacer; **I wasn't born yesterday** no nací ayer **2.** *adj* [having natural ability] nato(a); **a born poet** un poeta nato

borne [bɔ:n] *pp of* **bear**

borough ['bʌrə] *n* **a)** [town] ciudad *f*; *US* [municipality] municipio *m* **b)** *Br* [constituency] *división administrativa y electoral que comprende un municipio o un distrito urbano*

borrow ['bɒrəʊ] **1.** *vt* **a)** tomar prestado; **can I borrow your pen?** ¿me prestas *or* dejas tu bolígrafo? **b)** [ideas etc] apropiarse **2.** *vi* tomar prestado

bosom ['buzəm] *n* **a)** [breast] pecho *m*; [breasts] pechos *mpl*; **bosom friend** amigo(a) *m,f* del alma **b)** *Fig* seno *m*

boss [bɒs] **1.** *n* **a)** [head] jefe(a) *m,f*; [factory owner etc] patrón(ona) *m,f* **b)** *esp US* POL jefe *m*; *Pej* cacique *m* **2.** *vt* **to boss sb about** *or* **around** mandar sobre algn

bossy ['bɒsɪ] *(compar* **bossier**, *superl* **bossiest)** *adj Fam* mandón(ona)

bot [bɒt] *n* COMPUT bot *m*

botany ['bɒtənɪ] *n* botánica *f*

botch [bɒtʃ] **1.** *vt* chapucear; **a botched job** una chapuza **2.** *n* chapuza *f*

both [bəʊθ] **1.** *adj* ambos(as), los dos / las dos; **both men are teachers** ambos son profesores; **hold it with both hands** sujétalo con las dos manos **2.** *pron* **both (of them)** ambos(as), los dos / las dos; **both of you** vosotros dos **3.** *conj* a la vez; **both England and Spain are in Europe** tanto Inglaterra como España están en Europa

bother ['bɒðə(r)] **1.** *vt* **a)** [disturb] molestar; [be a nuisance to] dar la lata a **b)** [worry] preocupar; *Fam* **I can't be bothered** no tengo ganas
2. *vi* molestarse; **don't bother about me** no te preocupes por mí; **he didn't bother shaving** no se molestó en afeitarse
3. *n* **a)** [disturbance] molestia *f*; [nuisance] lata *f*
b) [trouble] problemas *mpl*
4. *interj Br* ¡maldito sea!

botnet ['bɒtnet] n COMPUT botnet f

bottle ['bɒtəl] **1.** n botella f ; [of perfume, ink] frasco m ; **baby's bottle** biberón m ; **bottle opener** abrebotellas m inv **2.** vt [wine] embotellar ; [fruit] enfrascar
■ **bottle out** vi Br Fam encogerse
■ **bottle up** vt sep reprimir

bottleneck ['bɒtəlnek] n AUTO embotellamiento m, atasco m

bottom ['bɒtəm] **1.** adj **a)** [lowest] más bajo(a) ; [drawer, shelf] de abajo ; AUTO **bottom gear** primera f
b) [last] último(a) ; **bottom line** FIN saldo m final ; Fig resultado m final
2. n **a)** parte f inferior ; [of sea, garden, street, box] fondo m ; [of bottle] culo m ; [of page, hill] pie m ; SCH **to be (at) the bottom of the class** ser el último /la última de la clase ; **to touch bottom** tocar fondo ; Fam **bottoms up!** ¡salud!
b) to get to the bottom of a matter llegar al meollo de una cuestión ; **who is at the bottom of all this?** ¿quién está detrás de todo esto?
c) [buttocks] trasero m
■ **bottom out** vi FIN tocar fondo

bottomless ['bɒtəmlɪs] adj [pit] sin fondo ; [mystery] insondable

bottom-of-the-range adj de gama baja

bought [bɔːt] pt & pp of **buy**

boulder ['bəʊldə(r)] n canto rodado

bounce [baʊns] **1.** vi **a)** [ball] rebotar
b) [jump] saltar
c) Fam [cheque] ser rechazado (por el banco)
2. vt [ball] botar
3. n **a)** [of ball] bote m
b) [jump] salto m
c) [energy] vitalidad f
■ **bounce back** vi [recover health] recuperarse, recobrarse

bouncer ['baʊnsə(r)] n Fam gorila m

bound¹ [baʊnd] adj **a)** [tied up] atado(a)
b) [obliged] obligado(a) **c) bound (up)** [linked] vinculado(a) (**with** a) **d) it's**

bound to happen sucederá con toda seguridad ; **it was bound to fail** estaba destinado al fracaso

bound² [baʊnd] **1.** vi saltar **2.** n salto m

bound³ [baʊnd] pt & pp of **bind**

bound⁴ [baʊnd] adj **bound for** con destino a, rumbo a ; **to be bound for** dirigirse a

boundary ['baʊndərɪ] n límite m

bounds [baʊndz] npl **beyond the bounds of reality** más allá de la realidad ; **her ambition knows no bounds** su ambición no conoce límites ; **the river is out of bounds** está prohibido bajar al río

bouquet n **a)** [of flowers] ramillete m
b) [of wine] aroma m, buqué m

bout [baʊt] n **a)** [of work] turno m ; [of illness] ataque m **b)** [in boxing] combate m

boutique [buːˈtiːk] n boutique f, tienda f

bow¹ [baʊ] **1.** vi **a)** hacer una reverencia
b) [give in] ceder **2.** n [with head, body] reverencia f ■ **bow out** vi retirarse (**of** de)

bow² [bəʊ] n **a)** SPORT & MUS arco m ; Fig **to have more than one string to one's bow** ser una persona de recursos
b) [knot] lazo m ; **bow tie** Esp pajarita f, CAm, Carib, Col corbatín m, Méx corbata f de moño

bow³ [baʊ] n NAUT proa f

bowel ['baʊəl] n **a)** intestino m **b) bowels** entrañas fpl

bowl¹ [bəʊl] n **a)** [dish] cuenco m ; [for soup] tazón m ; [for washing hands] palangana f ; [for washing clothes, dishes] barreño m ; [of toilet] taza f
b) GEOL cuenca f

bowl² [bəʊl] **1.** n bola f **2.** vt [in cricket] lanzar **3.** vi **a)** [play bowls] jugar a los bolos **b)** [in cricket] lanzar la pelota
■ **bowl over** vt sep **a)** [knock down] derribar **b)** Fig [astonish] desconcertar

bowling ['bəʊlɪŋ] n [game] bolos mpl ; **bowling alley** bolera f ; **bowling ball** bola f (de jugar a los bolos)

box¹ [bɒks] **1.** n **a)** caja f ; [large] cajón m ; [of matches] cajetilla f ; THEAT **box of-**

fice taquilla *f* **b)** THEAT palco *m* **c)** *Br Fam* [television] **the box** la tele **2.** *vt* [pack] embalar

box² [bɒks] **1.** *vi* SPORT boxear **2.** *vt* SPORT [hit] pegar; **to box sb's ears** dar un cachete a algn

boxer ['bɒksə(r)] *n* **a)** boxeador *m* **b)** [dog] bóxer *m*

boxing ['bɒksɪŋ] *n* boxeo *m*, *CAm*, *Méx* box *m*; **boxing ring** cuadrilátero *m*

boy [bɔɪ] *n* **a)** [child] niño *m*, chico *m*; [youth] joven *m*; **boy band** *grupo musical juvenil compuesto por adolescentes varones*; *Fam* **oh boy!** ¡vaya! **b)** [son] hijo *m*

boycott ['bɔɪkɒt] **1.** *n* boicot *m* **2.** *vt* boicotear

boyfriend ['bɔɪfrend] *n* novio *m*; [live-in] compañero *m*

bra [brɑː] *n* sostén *m*, *Esp* sujetador *m*, *Carib*, *Col*, *Méx* brasier *m*, *RP* corpiño *m*

brace [breɪs] **1.** *n* **a)** [clamp] abrazadera *f*, [of drill] berbiquí *m*; [for teeth] aparato *m* **b)** *Br* **braces** [for trousers] tirantes *mpl* **2.** *vt* **a)** [reinforce] reforzar **b) to brace oneself (for)** prepararse *or Chile, Méx, Ven* alistarse (para) ■ **brace up** *vi* cobrar ánimo

bracelet ['breɪslɪt] *n* pulsera *f*

bracing ['breɪsɪŋ] *adj* [wind] fresco(a); [stimulating] tonificante

bracket ['brækɪt] **1.** *n* **a)** TYP [round] paréntesis *m*; [square] corchete *m*, [curly] llave *f*; **in brackets** entre paréntesis **b)** [support] soporte *m*; [for lamp] brazo *m*; [shelf] repisa *f* **c)** [for tax] sector *m* **2.** *vt* **a)** LING [phrase etc] poner entre paréntesis **b)** [group together] agrupar, juntar

brag [bræg] *vi* jactarse (**about** de)

braid [breɪd] **1.** *vt* trenzar **2.** *n* **a)** SEWING galón *m* **b)** *esp US* [plait] trenza *f*

brain [breɪn] *n* **a)** cerebro *m*; **she's got cars on the brain** está obsesionada por los coches; MED **brain death** muerte *f* cerebral; *Fig* **brain drain** fuga *f* de cerebros; **brain wave** idea *f* genial **b)** *Fam* **brains** inteligencia *f*; **to have brains**

ser inteligente; *Br* **brains** *or US* **brain trust** grupo *m* de expertos **c)** CULIN **brains** sesos *mpl*

brainchild ['breɪntʃaɪld] *n* invento *m*, idea *f* genial

brainiac ['breɪniæk] *n US Fam* cerebrito *mf*

brainstorm ['breɪnstɔːm] *n* **a)** [outburst] arranque *m* **b)** [brainwave] genialidad *f*, lluvia *f* de ideas

brainwash ['breɪnwɒʃ] *vt* lavar el cerebro a

brainy ['breɪni] *(compar* brainier, *superl* brainiest) *adj Fam* listo(a)

brake [breɪk] **1.** *n* AUTO *(also pl)* freno *m*; **brake drum** tambor *m* del freno; **brake fluid** líquido *m* de frenos; **brake light** luz *f* de freno **2.** *vi* frenar, echar el freno

bran [bræn] *n* salvado *m*

branch [brɑːntʃ] **1.** *n* [of tree] rama *f*; [of road] bifurcación *f*; [of science etc] ramo *m*; COMM **branch (office)** sucursal *f* **2.** *vi* [road] bifurcarse ■ **branch off** *vi* desviarse ■ **branch out** *vi* diversificarse

brand [brænd] **1.** *n* **a)** COMM marca *f*; **brand name** marca de fábrica **b)** [type] clase *f* **c)** [on cattle] hierro *m* **2.** *vt* **a)** [animal] marcar con hierro candente **b)** [label] tildar

brandish ['brændɪʃ] *vt* blandir

brand-new ['brænd'njuː] *adj* flamante

brandy ['brændɪ] *n* brandy *m*, coñac *m*, *RP* cognac *m*

brash [bræʃ] *adj* **a)** [impudent] descarado(a) **b)** [reckless] temerario(a) **c)** [loud, showy] chillón(ona)

brass [brɑːs] *n* **a)** [metal] latón *m* **b)** *Br Fam* [money] *Esp* pasta *f*, *Esp*, *RP* guita *f*, *Am* plata *f*, *Méx* lana *f* **c)** MUS instrumentos *mpl* de metal; **brass band** banda *f* de metal

brat [bræt] *n Fam* mocoso(a) *m,f*

brave [breɪv] **1.** *adj* valiente, valeroso(a)
2. *n US* **(Indian) brave** guerrero *m* indio
3. *vt* **a)** [face] hacer frente a
b) [defy] desafiar

bravery ['breɪvərɪ] *n* valentía *f*, valor *m*

brawl [brɔːl] **1.** *n* reyerta *f* **2.** *vi* pelearse

Brazil [brə'zɪl] *n* (el) Brasil

Brazilian [brə'zɪlɪən] *adj* & *n* brasileño(a) *(m,f)*

BRB MESSAGING *written abbr of* **be right back**

breach [briːʧ] **1.** *n* **a)** [in wall] brecha *f* **b)** [violation] incumplimiento *m* ; **breach of confidence** abuso *m* de confianza; **breach of contract** incumplimiento de contrato; **breach of the law** violación *f* de la ley; **breach of the peace** alteración *f* del orden público **c)** [in relations] ruptura *f* **2.** *vt* violar

bread [bred] *n* **a)** pan *m* ; **bread and butter** pan con mantequilla, *Am* pan con manteca; *Fig* **our daily bread** el pan nuestro de cada día **b)** *Fam* [money] *Esp* pasta *f*, *Esp, RP* guita *f*, *Am* plata *f*, *Méx* lana *f*

breadboard ['bredbɔːd] *n* tabla *f* (para cortar el pan)

breadcrumb ['bredkrʌm] *n* miga *f* de pan; **breadcrumbs** pan rallado

breadline ['bredlaɪn] *n Fam* miseria *f*; **to be on the breadline** vivir en la miseria

breadth [bredθ] *n* **a)** [width] anchura *f*; **it is 2 m in breadth** tiene 2 m de ancho **b)** [extent] amplitud *f*

breadwinner ['bredwɪnə(r)] *n* cabeza *mf* de familia

break [breɪk] *(pt* broke, *pp* broken*)* **1.** *vt* **a)** romper; **to break a leg** romperse la pierna; **to break a record** batir un récord; *Fig* **to break sb's heart** partirle el corazón a algn

b) [fail to keep] faltar a; **to break a contract** romper un contrato; **to break the law** violar la ley

c) [destroy] destrozar; FIN arruinar

d) [interrupt] interrumpir

e) [fall] amortiguar

f) **she broke the news to him** le comunicó la noticia

2. *vi* **a)** romperse; [clouds] dispersarse; [waves] romper

b) [storm] estallar

c) [voice] cambiar

d) [health] resentirse

e) **when day breaks** al rayar el alba

f) [story] divulgarse

3. *n* **a)** [fracture] rotura *f*; [crack] grieta *f*; [opening] abertura *f*

b) [in relationship] ruptura *f*

c) [pause] pausa *f*, descanso *m* ; [at school] recreo *m*; **to take a break** descansar un rato ; [holiday] tomar unos días libres

d) *Fam* [chance] oportunidad *f*

■ **break away** *vi* **a)** [become separate] desprenderse (**from** de) **b)** [escape] escaparse

■ **break down 1.** *vt sep* **a)** [door] derribar **b)** [resistance] acabar con **c)** [costs] desglosar **2.** *vi* **a)** AUTO tener una avería **b)** [resistance] ceder **c)** [health] debilitarse **d)** [weep] ponerse a llorar

■ **break in 1.** *vt sep* acostumbrar; **to break in a pair of shoes** cogerle la forma a los zapatos **2.** *vi* [burglar] entrar por la fuerza

■ **break into** *vt insep* **a)** [burgle - house] allanar; [safe] forzar **b)** **to break into song** empezar a cantar

■ **break off 1.** *vt sep* partir **2.** *vi* **a)** [become detached] desprenderse **b)** [talks] interrumpirse **c)** [stop] pararse

■ **break out** *vi* **a)** [prisoners] escaparse **b)** [war etc] estallar; **she broke out in a rash** le salió un sarpullido

■ **break through 1.** *vt insep* **a)** [crowd] abrirse paso por; [cordon] romper **b)** [clouds] atravesar **2.** *vi* **a)** [crowd] abrirse paso **b)** [sun] salir

■ **break up 1.** *vt sep* [object] romper; [car] desguazar; [crowd] disolver **2.** *vi* **a)** [object] romperse **b)** [crowd] disolverse; [meeting] levantarse **c)** [relationship] fracasar; [couple] separarse **d)** SCH terminar

■ **break with** *vt insep* [past] romper con

breakage ['breɪkɪʤ] *n* [breaking] rotura *f*

breakdown ['breɪkdaʊn] *n* **a)** AUTO avería *f*; *Br* **breakdown truck** grúa *f*

b) (nervous) breakdown crisis nerviosa **c)** [in communications] *Esp* fallo *m*, *Am* falla *f* **d)** [analysis] análisis *m*; FIN desglose *m*

breakfast ['brekfəst] **1.** *n* desayuno *m*; **to have breakfast** desayunar **2.** *vi* desayunar

break-in ['breɪkɪn] *n* robo *m (con allanamiento de morada)*

breakthrough ['breɪkθruː] *n* paso *m* adelante, avance *m*

breast [brest] *n* [chest] pecho *m*; [of woman] pecho, seno *m*; [of chicken etc] pechuga *f*; *Fig* **to make a clean breast of it** dar la cara

breast-feed ['brestfiːd] *vt* dar el pecho a, amamantar a

breaststroke ['breststrəʊk] *n* braza *f*

breath [breθ] *n* **a)** aliento *m*; [breathing] respiración *f*; **breath freshener** spray *m* bucal; **breath test** prueba *f* de alcoholemia; **in the same breath** al mismo tiempo; **out of breath** sin aliento; **to catch one's breath** recobrar el aliento; **to draw breath** respirar; **under one's breath** en voz baja; *Fig* **to take sb's breath away** dejar pasmado a algn; AUTO **breath test** alcoholemia *f* **b) to go out for a breath of fresh air** salir a tomar el aire

Breathalyser®, *US* **Breathalyzer®** ['breθəlaɪzə(r)] *n* alcoholímetro *m*

breathe [briːð] **1.** *vt* respirar; **to breathe a sigh of relief** dar un suspiro de alivio **2.** *vi* respirar; **to breathe in** aspirar; **to breathe out** espirar; **to breathe heavily** resoplar

breathing ['briːðɪŋ] *n* respiración *f*; **breathing space** pausa *f*, respiro *m*

breathless ['breθlɪs] *adj* sin aliento, jadeante

breathtaking ['breθteɪkɪŋ] *adj* impresionante

bred [bred] **1.** *pt & pp* of **breed 2.** *adj* criado(a)

-bred *adj* (in compounds) educado(a), criado(a); **ill / well-bred** mal / bien educado(a)

breed [briːd] *(pt & pp* **bred** [bred]*)* **1.** *n* [of animal] raza *f*; *Fig* [class] clase *f* **2.** *vt* [animals] criar; *Fig* [ideas] engendrar **3.** *vi* [animals] reproducirse

breeding ['briːdɪŋ] *n* **a)** [of animals] cría *f*; *Fig* **breeding ground** caldo *m* de cultivo **b)** [of person] educación *f*

breeze [briːz] **1.** *n* brisa *f*; *Br* CONSTR **breeze block** bloque *m* de cemento **2.** *vi* **to breeze in / out** entrar / salir despreocupadamente

breezy ['briːzɪ] *(compar* **breezier**, *superl* **breeziest)** *adj* **a)** [weather] ventoso(a) **b)** [person] despreocupado(a)

brew [bruː] **1.** *vt* [beer] elaborar; [hot drink] preparar **2.** *vi* [tea] reposar; *Fig* **a storm is brewing** se prepara una tormenta; *Fam* **something's brewing** algo se está cociendo **3.** *n* **a)** [of tea] infusión *f*; *Fam* [of beer] birra *f* **b)** [magic potion] brebaje *m*

brewery ['bruːərɪ] *n* cervecería *f*

bribe [braɪb] **1.** *vt* sobornar **2.** *n* soborno *m*, *Andes*, *CSur* coima *f*, *CAm*, *Méx* mordida *f*

bribery ['braɪbərɪ] *n* soborno *m*

brick [brɪk] *n* ladrillo *m*; *Br Fam & Dated* **he's a brick** es un gran tipo

bricklayer ['brɪkleɪə(r)] *n* albañil *m*

bride [braɪd] *n* novia *f*; **the bride and groom** los novios

bridegroom ['braɪdgruːm] *n* novio *m*

bridesmaid ['braɪdzmeɪd] *n* dama *f* de honor

bridge¹ [brɪdʒ] **1.** *n* puente *m*; [of nose] caballete *m*; [of ship] puente de mando **2.** *vt* **a)** [river] tender un puente sobre **b)** [gap] llenar; *Br* FIN **bridging loan** crédito *m* a corto plazo

bridge² [brɪdʒ] *n* CARDS bridge *m*

brief [briːf] **1.** *adj* **a)** [short] breve **b)** [concise] conciso(a) **2.** *n* **a)** [report] informe *m*; **in brief** en resumen

b) JUR expediente *m*

c) MIL instrucciones *fpl*

d) briefs [for men] calzoncillos *mpl*, *Chile* fundillos *mpl*, *Méx* calzones *mpl*; [for women] *Esp* bragas *fpl*, *Chile, Col, Méx* calzones *mpl*, *RP* bombacha *f*

3. *vt* **a)** [inform] informar

b) [instruct] dar instrucciones a

briefcase ['bri:fkeɪs] *n* cartera *f*, portafolios *m inv*

briefing ['bri:fɪŋ] *n* [meeting] reunión informativa

briefly ['bri:flɪ] *adv* brevemente; **as briefly as possible** con la mayor brevedad (posible)

brigade [brɪ'geɪd] *n* brigada *f*

bright [braɪt] *adj* **a)** [light, sun, eyes] brillante; [colour] vivo(a); [day] claro(a) **b)** [cheerful] alegre **c)** [clever] listo(a), espabilado(a) **d)** [promising] prometedor(a)

brighten ['braɪtən] *vi* [prospects] mejorarse; [face] iluminarse ■ **brighten up 1.** *vt sep* [room etc] alegrar **2.** *vi* [weather] despejarse; [person] animarse

brightly ['braɪtlɪ] *adv* brillantemente

brightly-coloured *adj* de colores vivos

brilliant ['brɪljənt] **1.** *adj* brillante; *Br* [excellent] genial, *Am salvo RP* chévere, *Andes, CSur* macanudo(a), *Méx* padre, *RP* bárbaro(a) **2.** *n* brillante *m*

brim [brɪm] **1.** *n* borde *m*; [of hat] ala *f*; **full to the brim** lleno hasta el borde **2.** *vi* rebosar (**with** de) ■ **brim over** *vi* rebosar

bring [brɪŋ] (*pt & pp* brought) *vt* **a)** [carry, take] traer; [lead] llevar **b)** [cause] provocar; **he brought it upon himself** se lo buscó **c)** [persuade] convencer; **how did they bring themselves to do it?** ¿cómo llegaron a hacerlo? ■ **bring about** *vt sep* provocar ■ **bring along** *vt sep* traer ■ **bring back** *vt sep* **a)** [return] devolver **b)** [reintroduce] volver a introducir **c)** [make one remember] traerle a la memoria ■ **bring down** *vt sep* **a)** [from upstairs] bajar **b)** [government] derribar; THEAT **to bring the**

house down echar el teatro abajo con los aplausos **c)** [reduce] rebajar ■ **bring forward** *vt sep* **a)** [meeting etc] adelantar **b)** [present] presentar **c)** FIN **brought forward** suma y sigue ■ **bring in** *vt sep* **a)** [yield] dar **b)** [show in] hacer entrar **c)** [law etc] introducir; [fashion] lanzar ■ **bring off** *vt sep* lograr, conseguir ■ **bring on** *vt sep* provocar ■ **bring out** *vt sep* **a)** [publish] publicar **b)** [reveal] recalcar; **he brings out the worst in me** despierta lo peor que hay en mí ■ **bring round** *vt sep* **a)** [revive] hacer volver en sí **b)** [persuade] convencer ■ **bring to** *vt sep* reanimar ■ **bring up** *vt sep* **a)** [educate] criar, educar **b)** [subject] plantear **c)** [vomit] devolver

brink [brɪŋk] *n* [edge] borde *m*; *Fig* **on the brink of ruin** al borde de la ruina; **on the brink of tears** a punto de llorar

brisk [brɪsk] *adj* enérgico(a); [pace] rápido(a); [trade] activo(a); [weather] fresco(a)

bristle ['brɪsəl] **1.** *n* cerda *f* **2.** *vi* **a)** erizarse **b)** [show anger] enfurecer (**at** con) ■ **bristle with** *vt insep* [be full of] estar lleno(a) de

Brit [brɪt] *n (abbr of* **Briton**) *Fam* británico(a) *m,f*

Britain ['brɪtən] *n* **(Great) Britain** Gran Bretaña

British ['brɪtɪʃ] **1.** *adj* británico(a); **the British Isles** las Islas Británicas **2.** *npl* **the British** los británicos

Brittany ['brɪtənɪ] *n* Bretaña

brittle ['brɪtəl] *adj* quebradizo(a), frágil

broad [brɔːd] *adj* **a)** [wide] ancho(a); [large] extenso(a) **b) a broad hint** [clear] una indirecta clara **c)** [daylight] pleno(a) **d)** [not detailed] general **e)** [accent] marcado(a), cerrado(a)

broadband ['brɔːdbænd] **1.** *n* COMPUT banda *f* ancha; **have you got broadband?** ¿tienes (el) ADSL? **2.** *adj* COMPUT de banda ancha; **broadband Internet connection** conexión *f* internet de banda ancha

broadcast ['brɔ:dkɑ:st] **1.** n RADIO & TV emisión f **2.** (pt & pp **broadcast**) vt RADIO & TV emitir, transmitir

broaden ['brɔ:dən] vt ensanchar

broadly ['brɔ:dlı] adv en términos generales

broad-minded [brɔ:'maɪndɪd] adj liberal, tolerante

broccoli ['brɒkəlı] n brécol m

brochure ['brəʊʃə(r), 'brəʊfjʊə(r)] n folleto m

broil [brɔɪl] vt US asar a la parrilla

broke [brəʊk] **1.** adj Fam to be broke estar sin un centavo or Méx sin un peso or Esp sin blanca **2.** pt of **break**

broken ['brəʊkən] **1.** adj roto(a) **2.** pp of **break**

brokenhearted [,brəʊkn'hɑ:tɪd] adj con el corazón roto

broker ['brəʊkə(r)] n corredor m, agente mf de Bolsa

bromance ['brəʊmæns] n Fam amistad f íntima entre hombres; **there's definitely nothing gay between Jack and Mike, it's more like just bromance** no hay una relación sexual entre Jack y Mike, son solo amigos íntimos

bronchitis [brɒŋ'kaɪtɪs] n bronquitis f

bronze [brɒnz] **1.** n bronce m **2.** adj [material] de bronce; [colour] bronceado(a)

brooch [brəʊtʃ] n broche m

brood [bru:d] **1.** n [birds] cría f; Hum [children] prole m **2.** vi [hen] empollar; Fig [ponder] rumiar; Fig **to brood over a problem** darle vueltas a un problema

broody ['bru:dɪ] adj a) [pensive] pensativo(a) b) [moody] melancólico(a) c) Br Fam [woman] con ganas de tener hijos

broom [bru:m] n a) escoba f b) BOT retama f

broth [brɒθ] n caldo m

brothel ['brɒθəl] n burdel m

brother ['brʌðə(r)] n hermano m; **brothers and sisters** hermanos

brother-in-law ['brʌðərɪnlɔ:] n cuñado m

brought [brɔ:t] pt & pp of **bring**

brow [braʊ] n a) [forehead] frente f b) [eyebrow] ceja f c) [of hill] cima f

brown [braʊn] **1.** adj a) marrón, Am café; [hair, eyes] castaño(a); **brown bread** pan m integral; **brown paper** papel m de estraza; **brown sugar** azúcar moreno b) [tanned] moreno(a) **2.** n marrón m, Am color m café **3.** vt CULIN dorar; [tan] broncear

browse [braʊz] **1.** vi [in shop] mirar; [through book] hojear **2.** vt COMPUT **to browse the Web** navegar por la Web **3.** n **to have a browse (in)** dar un vistazo (a)

browser ['braʊzə(r)] n COMPUT navegador m, explorador m, browser m

BRT MESSAGING written abbr of **be right there**

bruise [bru:z] **1.** n morado m, cardenal m **2.** vt [body] contusionar; [fruit] estropear **3.** vi [body] magullarse; [fruit] estropearse

brunch [brʌntʃ] n Fam desayuno-comida m, RP brunch m

brunette [bru:'net] adj & n morena (f)

brush¹ [brʌʃ] **1.** n a) [for hair, teeth] cepillo m; ART pincel m; [for housepainting] brocha f b) [with the law] roce m **2.** vt a) cepillar; **to brush one's hair** cepillarse el pelo; **to brush one's teeth** cepillarse los dientes b) [touch lightly] rozar **3.** vi **to brush against** rozar al pasar ■ **brush aside** vt sep dejar de lado ■ **brush off** vt sep Fam no hacer caso a, Esp pasar de ■ **brush up** vt sep repasar

brush² [brʌʃ] n [undergrowth] broza f, maleza f

brush-off ['brʌʃɒf] n Fam **to give sb the brush-off** no hacer ni caso a algn

brusque [bru:sk, brʊsk] adj brusco(a); [words] áspero(a)

Brussels ['brʌsəlz] n Bruselas

brutal ['bru:təl] adj brutal, cruel

brute [bru:t] **1.** adj bruto(a); **brute force** fuerza bruta **2.** n [animal] bruto m; [person] bestia f

BSc [bi:es'si:] n (abbr of **Bachelor of Science**) [person] licenciado(a) m,f en Ciencias

BSE [bi:es'i:] n (abbr of **bovine spongiform encephalopathy**) encefalopatía f espongiforme bovina (enfermedad de las vacas locas)

BTWN MESSAGING written abbr of **between**

bubble ['bʌbəl] **1.** n burbuja f; **bubble bath** espuma f de baño; **bubble gum** chicle m; **soap bubble** pompa f de jabón **2.** vi burbujear; CULIN borbotear

bubbly ['bʌblɪ] **1.** (compar **bubblier**, superl **bubbliest**) adj efervescente **2.** n Fam champán m, cava m

buck¹ [bʌk] **1.** n ZOOL macho m; [male deer] ciervo m; [male goat] macho cabrío; Fam **to pass the buck to sb** echarle el muerto a algn **2.** vi [horse] corcovear ■ **buck up 1.** vt sep Fam **buck your ideas up!** ¡espabílate! **2.** vi [cheer up] animarse

buck² [bʌk] n US, Austr Fam dólar m

bucket ['bʌkɪt] **1.** n balde m, Esp cubo m; Br Fam **it's raining buckets** llueve a cántaros or RP a baldes **2.** vi Fam **it's bucketing (down)** llueve a cántaros or RP a baldes

buckle ['bʌkəl] **1.** n hebilla f **2.** vt abrochar con hebilla **3.** vi a) [wall, metal] combarse b) [knees] doblarse

bud [bʌd] **1.** n [shoot] brote m; [flower] capullo m **2.** vi brotar; Fig florecer

Buddhist ['bʊdɪst] n & adj budista (mf)

budding ['bʌdɪŋ] adj en ciernes

buddy ['bʌdɪ] n US Fam Esp colega mf, Am compadre, Am hermano(a), Méx cuate

budge [bʌdʒ] vi a) [move] moverse b) [yield] ceder

budgerigar ['bʌdʒərɪgɑː(r)] n periquito m

budget ['bʌdʒɪt] **1.** n presupuesto m; Br POL **the Budget** ≃ los Presupuestos Generales del Estado **2.** vi hacer un presupuesto (**for** para)

buff¹ [bʌf] **1.** adj & n [colour] color (m) de ante **2.** vt dar brillo a

buff² [bʌf] n Fam [enthusiast] aficionado(a) m,f

buffalo ['bʌfələʊ] (pl **buffaloes** or **buffalo**) n búfalo m

buffer ['bʌfə(r)] **1.** n a) [device] amortiguador m; RAIL tope m; **buffer zone** zona f de seguridad b) COMPUT memoria f intermedia, buffer m **2.** vt amortiguar

buffet¹ ['bʊfeɪ] n a) [snack bar] bar m; [at railway station] cantina f; RAIL **buffet car** coche m restaurante b) [self-service meal] bufet m libre c) [item of furniture] aparador m

buffet² ['bʌfɪt] vt golpear

bug [bʌg] **1.** n a) [insect] bicho m b) Fam [microbe] microbio m; **the flu bug** el virus de la gripe c) [hidden microphone] micrófono oculto d) COMPUT error m **2.** vt Fam a) **to bug a room** ocultar micrófonos en una habitación b) [annoy] fastidiar, molestar

bugger ['bʌgə(r)] **1.** n Br v Fam [unpleasant person] cabrón(ona) m,f; **you silly bugger** ¡qué tonto(a) eres!; **the poor bugger!** ¡pobre desgraciado!; **bugger all** nada de nada **2.** vt a) [sodomize] sodomizar b) Br v Fam **bugger (it)!** ¡carajo!, Esp ¡joder!, RP ¡la puta (digo)!

buggy ['bʌgɪ] n a) Br [baby's pushchair] sillita f de niño b) US [pram] cochecito m (de niño)

build [bɪld] **1.** (pt & pp **built**) vt construir **2.** n [physique] tipo m, físico m ■ **build up** vt sep [accumulate] acumular; **to build up a reputation** labrarse una buena reputación

builder ['bɪldə(r)] n constructor(a) m,f; [contractor] contratista mf

building ['bɪldɪŋ] n edificio m, construcción f; **building site** obra f; Br **building society** sociedad hipotecaria

build-up ['bɪldʌp] n a) [accumulation] aumento m; [of gas] acumulación f b) [publicity] propaganda f

built [bɪlt] pp of **build**

built-in ['bɪlt'ɪn] *adj* **a)** [cupboard] empotrado(a) **b)** [incorporated] incorporado(a)

built-up [bɪlt'ʌp] *adj* urbanizado(a)

bulb [bʌlb] *n* **a)** BOT bulbo *m* **b)** [light bulb] *Esp* bombilla *f*, *Andes, Méx* foco *m*, *CAm, Carib* bombillo *m*, *RP* lamparita *f*

bulge [bʌldʒ] **1.** *n* protuberancia *f*; [in pocket] bulto *m* **2.** *vi* [swell] hincharse; [be full] estar repleto(a)

bulimia [buː'lɪmɪə] *n* MED bulimia *f*

bulk [bʌlk] *n* **a)** [mass] masa *f*, volumen *m*; COMM **in bulk** a granel; **to buy sth in bulk** comprar algo al por mayor **b)** [greater part] mayor parte *f*

bulky ['bʌlkɪ] *(compar* **bulkier**, *superl* **bulkiest)** *adj* **a)** [large] voluminoso(a) **b) this crate is rather bulky** esta caja es un armatoste

bull [bʊl] *n* **a)** toro *m*; *Fig* **to take the bull by the horns** agarrar *or Esp* coger el toro por los cuernos **b)** FIN **bull market** mercado *m* al alza

bulldozer ['bʊldəʊzə(r)] *n* bulldozer *m*

bullet ['bʊlɪt] *n* bala *f*; **bullet wound** balazo *m*

bulletin ['bʊlɪtɪn] *n* boletín *m*; RADIO & TV **news bulletin** boletín de noticias; *US* **bulletin board** tablón *m* de anuncios

bullet-proof ['bʊlɪtpruːf] *adj* a prueba de balas; **bullet-proof vest** chaleco *m* antibalas

bullfight ['bʊlfaɪt] *n* corrida *f* de toros

bullion ['bʊljən] *n* [gold, silver] lingote *m*

bull's-eye ['bʊlzaɪ] *n* [of target] blanco *m*

bully ['bʊlɪ] **1.** *n* matón *m*; [at school] *Esp* abusón(ona) *m,f*, *Am* abusador(a) *m,f* **2.** *vt* [terrorize] intimidar; [bulldoze] tiranizar **3.** *interj Iron* **bully for you!** ¡bravo!

bum[1] [bʌm] *n Br Fam* [bottom] culo *m*, *Am* cola *f*

bum[2] [bʌm] *Fam* **1.** *n* **a)** *US* [tramp] vagabundo *m* **b)** [idler] holgazán(ana) *m,f* **2.** *vi* gorronear ■ **bum around** *vi Fam* vaguear

bump [bʌmp] **1.** *n* **a)** [swelling] chichón *m*; [lump] abolladura *f*; [on road] bache *m* **b)** [blow] choque *m*, golpe *m* **c)** [jolt] sacudida *f* **2.** *vt* golpear; **to bump one's head** darse un golpe en la cabeza **3.** *vi* chocar (**into** contra) ■ **bump into** *vt insep* [meet] tropezar con ■ **bump off** *vt sep Fam* liquidar

bumper ['bʌmpə(r)] **1.** *adj* abundante; *Br* **bumper issue** número *m* especial **2.** *n Br* [of car] parachoques *m inv*, *Méx* defensas *fpl*, *RP* paragolpes *mpl*; **bumper car** auto *m* de choque

bumpy ['bʌmpɪ] *(compar* **bumpier**, *superl* **bumpiest)** *adj* con muchos baches

bun [bʌn] *n* **a)** [bread] panecillo *m*; [sweet] bollo *m*; *Fig & Euph* **she's got a bun in the oven** está preñada **b)** [of hair] moño *m*

bunch [bʌntʃ] **1.** *n* [of keys] manojo *m*; [of flowers] ramo *m*; [of grapes] racimo *m*; [of people] grupo *m*; [gang] pandilla *f* **2.** *vi* **to bunch together** juntarse, agruparse

bundle ['bʌndəl] **1.** *n* [of clothes] bulto *m*, fardo *m*; [of papers] fajo *m*; [of wood] haz *m* **2.** *vt* **a)** [make a bundle of] liar, atar **b)** [push] empujar

bungalow ['bʌŋgələʊ] *n* chalé *m*, bungalow *m*

bungee ['bʌndʒiː] *n* **bungee jump(ing)** puenting *m*, puentismo *m*

bungle ['bʌŋgəl] *vt* chapucear

bunk [bʌŋk] *n* [bed] litera *f*

bunker ['bʌŋkə(r)] *n* **a)** [for coal] carbonera *f* **b)** MIL búnker *m* **c)** *Br* [on golf course] búnker *m*

bunny ['bʌnɪ] *n Fam* [baby talk] **bunny (rabbit)** conejito *m*

buoy [bɔɪ] *n* boya *f* ■ **buoy up** *vt sep* **a)** [keep afloat] mantener a flote **b)** [person, spirits] alentar, animar

buoyant ['bɔɪənt] *adj* **a)** [object] flotante **b)** FIN con tendencia alcista **c)** [optimistic] optimista

burden ['bɜːdən] **1.** *n* carga *f*; *Fig* **to be a burden to sb** ser una carga para algn **2.** *vt* cargar (**with** con)

bureau ['bjʊərəʊ] *(pl* **bureaux)** *n* **a)** [office] agencia *f*, oficina *f* **b)** *Br* [desk] escritorio *m* **c)** *US* [chest of drawers] cómoda *f*

bureaucracy [bjʊə'rɒkrəsɪ] *n* burocracia *f*

bureaucrat ['bjʊərəkræt] *n* burócrata *mf*

burger ['bɜːgə(r)] *n Fam* [hamburger] hamburguesa *f*

burglar ['bɜːglə(r)] *n* ladrón(ona) *m,f*; **burglar alarm** alarma *f* antirrobo

burgle ['bɜːgəl] *vt* robar, desvalijar

burial ['berɪəl] *n* entierro *m*

burn [bɜːn] *(pt & pp* **burnt** *or* **burned) 1.** *n* quemadura *f*
2. *vt* **a)** [heat] quemar
b) COMPUT grabar; **to burn a CD** grabar un CD
3. *vi* **a)** [fire] arder; [building, food] quemarse
b) [lamp] estar encendido(a)
c) [sore] escocer
■ **burn down 1.** *vt sep* incendiar **2.** *vi* incendiarse
■ **burn out** *vi* [person] quemarse
■ **burn up** *vt sep* [energy, calories] quemar

burner ['bɜːnə(r)] *n* quemador *m*

burning ['bɜːnɪŋ] *adj* **a)** [on fire] incendiado(a); [hot] abrasador(a) **b)** [passionate] ardiente **c) a burning question** una cuestión candente

burp [bɜːp] **1.** *n* eructo *m* **2.** *vi* eructar

burrow ['bʌrəʊ] **1.** *n* madriguera *f*; [for rabbits] conejera *f* **2.** *vi* **a)** hacer una madriguera **b)** [search] hurgar

burst [bɜːst] *(pt & pp* **burst) 1.** *n* **a)** [explosion] estallido *m*; [of tyre] reventón *m* **b)** [of applause] arranque *m*; [rage] arrebato *m*; **burst of gunfire** ráfaga *f* de tiros; **burst of laughter** carcajadas *fpl* **2.** *vt* [balloon] reventar; *Fig* **the river burst its banks** el río se salió de madre

3. *vi* **a)** reventarse; [shell] estallar
b) [enter suddenly] irrumpir (**into** en)
■ **burst into** *vt insep* **to burst into laughter / tears** echarse a reír / a llorar
■ **burst open** *vi* abrirse violentamente
■ **burst out** *vi* **to burst out laughing** echarse a reír

bury ['berɪ] *vt* **a)** enterrar; **to be buried in thought** estar absorto en pensamientos **b)** [hide] ocultar

bus [bʌs] *(pl* **buses**, *US pl* **busses)** *n* autobús *m*, *Andes* buseta *f*, *Bol, RP* colectivo *m*, *CAm, Méx* camión *m*, *CAm, Carib* guagua *f*, *Urug* ómnibus *m*, *Ven* microbusete *m*; **bendy bus** autobús *m* articulado, autobús *m* oruga; **bus conductor** cobrador(a) *m,f* de autobús; **bus driver** conductor(a) *m,f* de autobús; *Br* **bus pass** tarjeta de autobús para la tercera edad; *Br Fig* **I haven't got my bus pass yet!** ≃ ¡todavía no tengo el carnet de jubilado!; **bus stop** parada *f* de autobús

busboy ['bʌsbɔɪ] *n US* ayudante *m* de camarero

bush [bʊʃ] *n* **a)** [shrub] arbusto *m* **b)** *Austr* **the bush** el monte; *Fam* **bush telegraph** *Esp* radio *f* macuto, *Cuba, CRica, Pan* radio *f* bemba

bushy ['bʊʃɪ] *adj* espeso(a), tupido(a)

business ['bɪznɪs] *n* **a)** [commerce] negocios *mpl*; **how's business?** ¿cómo andan los negocios?; **to be away on business** estar en viaje de negocios; **business angel** padrino *m* inversor, mentor *m* empresarial; **business deal** negocio *m*; **business hours** horas *fpl* de oficina; **business incubator** incubadora *f* de empresas, vivero *m* de empresas; **business model** modelo *m* de negocio; **business park** parque *m* empresarial; **business partner** socio(a) *m,f*; **business trip** viaje *m* de negocios
b) [firm] empresa *f*
c) [matter] asunto *m*; **I mean business** estoy hablando en serio; **it's no business of mine** no es asunto mío; **to make it one's business to …** encargar-

se de …; **to get down to business** ir al grano; **to go about one's business** ocuparse de sus asuntos

businessman ['bɪznɪsmən] *n* hombre *m* de negocios

businesswoman ['bɪznɪswʊmən] *n* mujer *f* de negocios

bust[1] [bʌst] *n* **a)** [of woman] pecho *m* **b)** ART busto *m*

bust[2] [bʌst] *Fam* **1.** *vt* **a)** [break] estropear, *Esp* escacharrar **b)** [person] trincar; [place] hacer una redada en **2.** *adj* **a)** [broken] **to be bust** estar estropeado(a) *or Esp* escacharrado(a) **b) to go bust** [bankrupt] quebrar

buster ['bʌstə(r)] *n US Fam* [pal] **thanks, buster** gracias, tío

-buster *suff Fam* **crime-busters** agentes *mpl* contra la delincuencia

bustle ['bʌsəl] **1.** *n* [activity, noise] bullicio *m* **2.** *vi* **to bustle about** ir y venir

busy ['bɪzɪ] **1.** *adj* **a)** ocupado(a), atareado(a); [life] ajetreado(a); [street] concurrido(a) **b)** *esp US* TEL ocupado(a); **busy signal** señal *f* de comunicando **2.** *vt* **to busy oneself doing sth** ocuparse haciendo algo

busybody ['bɪzɪbɒdɪ] *n* entrometido(a) *m,f*

but [bʌt] **1.** *conj* **a)** pero; **but yet** a pesar de todo
b) [after negative] sino; **not two but three** no dos sino tres
2. *adv* **but for her we would have drowned** si no hubiera sido por ella, nos habríamos ahogado
3. *prep* salvo, menos; **everyone but her** todos menos ella

butcher ['bʊtʃə(r)] **1.** *n* carnicero(a) *m,f*; **butcher's (shop)** carnicería *f* **2.** *vt* [animals] matar; [people] masacrar

butler ['bʌtlə(r)] *n* mayordomo *m*

butt[1] [bʌt] *n* **a)** [of rifle] culata *f*; [of cigarette] colilla *f* **b)** *US Fam* [bottom] culo *m*

butt[2] [bʌt] **1.** *n* [with head] cabezazo *m* **2.** *vt* [hit with head] dar un cabezazo a

■ **butt in** *vi* entrar en la conversación
■ **butt out** *vi insep US Fam* **why don't you just butt out?** ¡no te metas!

butter ['bʌtə(r)] **1.** *n* mantequilla *f, RP* manteca *f*; **butter dish** mantequera *f* **2.** *vt* untar con mantequilla *or RP* manteca

butterfly ['bʌtəflaɪ] *n* mariposa *f*

buttery ['bʌtərɪ] *adj* [smell, taste] a mantequilla

buttock ['bʌtək] *n* nalga *f*; **buttocks** nalgas *fpl*

button ['bʌtən] **1.** *n* **a)** [on clothes, machine] botón *m* **b)** *US* [badge] chapa *f* **2.** *vt* **to button (up)** abrochar(se), abotonar(se)

buttonhole ['bʌtənhəʊl] *n* ojal *m*

buy [baɪ] **1.** *n* compra *f*; **a good buy** una ganga **2.** *(pt & pp bought) vt* **a)** comprar; **she bought that car from a neighbour** compró ese coche a un vecino **b)** *Fam* [believe] tragar ■ **buy off** *vt sep* sobornar ■ **buy out** *vt sep* adquirir la parte de ■ **buy up** *vt sep* comprar en grandes cantidades

buyer ['baɪə(r)] *n* comprador(a) *m,f*

buzz [bʌz] **1.** *n* **a)** [of bee] zumbido *m*; [of conversation] rumor *m* **b)** *Fam* [telephone call] telefonazo *m* **2.** *vi* zumbar

buzzer ['bʌzə(r)] *n* timbre *m*

by [baɪ] **1.** *prep* **a)** [indicating agent] por; **composed by Bach** compuesto(a) por Bach; **a film by Almodóvar** una película de Almodóvar
b) [via] por; **he left by the back door** salió por la puerta trasera
c) [manner] por; **by car / train** en coche / tren; **by credit card** con tarjeta de crédito; **by day / night** de día / noche; **by chance** por casualidad; **by oneself** solo(a); **made by hand** hecho(a) a mano
d) [amount] por; **little by little** poco a poco; **they are sold by the dozen** se venden por docenas; **to be paid by the hour** cobrar por horas; **by far** con mucho

e) [beside] al lado de, junto a; **side by side** juntos

f) to walk by a building [pass] pasar por delante de un edificio

g) [time] para; **by now** ya; **by then** para entonces; **we have to be there by nine** tenemos que estar allí para las nueve

h) MATH por

i) [according to] según; **is that O.K. by you?** ¿te viene bien?

j) [phrases] **by the way** a propósito; **bit by bit** poco a poco; **day by day** día a día; **that's by the by** eso no viene a cuento; **what do you mean by that?** ¿qué quieres decir con eso?

2. *adv* **a) to go by** [past] pasar; **she just walked by** pasó de largo

b) by and by con el tiempo; **by and large** en conjunto

by-law ['baɪlɔ:] *n* ley *f* municipal

bypass ['baɪpɑ:s] **1.** *n* **a)** [road] carretera *f* de circunvalación **b)** MED **bypass surgery** cirugía *f* de by-pass **2.** *vt* evitar

bystander ['baɪstændə(r)] *n* testigo *mf*

byte [baɪt] *n* COMPUT byte *m*, octeto *m*

C

C, c [siː] *n* **a)** [the letter] C, c **b)** MUS do *m* **c)** SCH [grade] aprobado *m*; **to get a C** [in exam, essay] sacar un aprobado

C a) *(abbr of* **celsius** *or* **centigrade)** C, centígrado **b)** *(abbr of* **century)** s., siglo; **C16** s. XVI

cab [kæb] *n* taxi *m*; **black cab** taxi negro *(típico taxi británico)*; **cab driver** taxista *mf*

cabaret ['kæbəreɪ] *n* cabaret *m*

cabbage ['kæbɪʤ] *n* col *f*, berza *f*; **red cabbage** (col) lombarda *f*

cabin ['kæbɪn] *n* **a)** [hut] choza *f*; **log cabin** cabaña *f* **b)** NAUT camarote *m* **c)** [of lorry, plane] cabina *f*

cabinet ['kæbɪnɪt] *n* **a)** [item of furniture] armario *m*; [glass-fronted] vitrina *f*; **cabinet maker** ebanista *mf* **b)** POL gabinete *m*, consejo *m* de ministros

cable ['keɪbəl] **1.** *n* cable *m*; **extension cable** alargador *m*; **cable car** teleférico *m*; **cable company** cableoperador(a) *m,f*; **cable TV** television *f* por cable **2.** *vt & vi* cablegrafiar, telegrafiar

cablecast ['keɪblkɑːst] *vt US* TV transmitir por cable

cache [kæʃ] *n* **a)** [of drugs, arms] alijo *m* **b)** COMPUT caché *f*; **cache memory** (memoria *f*) caché *f*

cactus ['kæktəs] *(pl* **cacti** ['kæktaɪ]) *n* cactus *m*

caddie ['kædɪ] *n* [in golf] cadi *m*

cadet [kə'det] *n* MIL cadete *m*

cadge [kæʤ] *vt & vi Fam* gorrear, *Esp, Méx* gorronear, *RP* garronear (**from** *or* **off** a)

café ['kæfeɪ], **cafeteria** [kæfɪ'tɪərɪə] *n* cafetería *f*

caffeine ['kæfiːn] *n* cafeína *f*

cage [keɪʤ] **1.** *n* jaula *f* **2.** *vt* enjaular

cake [keɪk] *n* pastel *m*, tarta *f*

calamity [kə'læmɪtɪ] *n* calamidad *f*

calculate ['kælkjʊleɪt] *vt* calcular

calculated ['kælkjʊleɪtɪd] *adj* intencionado(a)

calculation [kælkjʊ'leɪʃən] *n* cálculo *m*

calculator ['kælkjʊleɪtə(r)] *n* calculadora *f*

calendar ['kælɪndə(r)] *n* calendario *m*; **calendar year** año *m* natural, *Am* año *m* calendario

calf¹ [kɑːf] *(pl* **calves**) *n* [of cattle] becerro(a) *m,f*, ternero(a) *m,f*; [of other animals] cría *f*

calf² [kɑːf] *(pl* **calves**) *n* ANAT pantorilla *f*

calibre, *US* **caliber** ['kælɪbə(r)] *n* calibre *m*

call [kɔːl] **1.** *vt* **a)** [on phone] llamar, telefonear, *Am* hablar; **to call sb names** poner verde a algn; **what's he called?** ¿cómo se llama?

b) [meeting etc] convocar; **to call sth to mind** traer algo a la memoria

2. *vi* **a)** [on phone] llamar, *Am* hablar; TEL **who's calling?** ¿de parte de quién?

b) **to call at sb's (house)** pasar por casa de algn; **to call for sth /sb** pasar a recoger algo / a algn

c) [trains] parar

d) **to call for** [require] exigir; **that wasn't called for** eso no estaba justificado

3. *n* **a)** [shout - of person] llamada *f*, grito *m*, *Am* llamado *m*

b) [visit] visita *f*; **to pay a call on sb** visitar a algn

c) TEL **(phone) call** llamada *f*, *Am* llamado *m*; **call box** *Br* cabina telefónica;

US teléfono *m* de emergencia; **call center** call center *m*, centro *m* de llamadas, centro *m* de atención telefónica

■ **call away** *vt sep* **to be called away on business** tener que ausentarse por motivos de trabajo

■ **call back** *vi* [phone again] volver a llamar *or* Am hablar; [visit again] volver

■ **call in 1.** *vt sep* [doctor] llamar **2.** *vi* **a) I'll call in tomorrow** [visit] mañana me paso **b)** NAUT hacer escala (**at** en)

■ **call off** *vt sep* suspender

■ **call on** *vt insep* **a)** visitar **b) to call on sb for support** recurrir a algn en busca de apoyo

■ **call out 1.** *vt sep* **a)** [shout] gritar **b)** [doctor] hacer venir; [workers] convocar a la huelga **2.** *vi* gritar

■ **call up** *vt sep* **a)** TEL llamar, Am hablar **b)** MIL llamar a filas, reclutar

caller ['kɔːlə(r)] *n* visita *mf*; TEL persona *f* que llama; TEL **caller (ID) display** visualización *f* del nombre de la persona que llama

callous ['kæləs] *adj* insensible, duro(a)

calm [kɑːm] **1.** *adj* **a)** [weather, sea] en calma
b) [relaxed] tranquilo(a); **keep calm!** ¡tranquilo(a)!
2. *n* **a)** [of weather, sea] calma *f*
b) [tranquillity] tranquilidad *f*
3. *vt* calmar, tranquilizar
4. *vi* **to calm (down)** calmarse, tranquilizarse

calorie, calory ['kælərɪ] *n* caloría *f*

calorie-conscious *adj* **she's very calorie-conscious** tiene mucho cuidado con las calorías

calorie-controlled *adj* [diet] de control de calorías

calorie-free *adj* sin calorías

calves [kɑːvz] *pl of* **calf, calf**

camcorder ['kæmkɔːdə(r)] *n* videocámara *f* (portátil)

came [keɪm] *pt of* **come**

camel ['kæməl] *n* camello(a) *m,f*

camera ['kæmərə] *n* **a)** cámara *f or* máquina *f* fotográfica; CIN & TV cámara
b) camera phone teléfono *m* con cámara; JUR **in camera** a puerta cerrada

camouflage ['kæməflɑːʒ] **1.** *n* camuflaje *m* **2.** *vt* camuflar

camp¹ [kæmp] **1.** *n* campamento *m*; **camp bed** cama *f* plegable; **camp site** camping *m* **2.** *vi* **to go camping** ir de camping

camp² [kæmp] *adj* Fam afeminado(a); [affected] amanerado(a)

campaign [kæm'peɪn] **1.** *n* campaña *f* **2.** *vi* **to campaign for / against** hacer campaña a favor de / en contra de

campaigner [kæm'peɪnə(r)] *n* defensor(a) *m,f* (**for** de)

camper ['kæmpə(r)] *n* **a)** [person] campista *mf* **b)** US [vehicle] caravana *f*

camphone ['kæmfəʊn] *n* teléfono *m* con cámara

camping ['kæmpɪŋ] *n* **camping ground, camping site** camping *m*

campus ['kæmpəs] *n* campus *m*, ciudad universitaria

can¹ [kæn] (*unstressed* [kən]) (*pt* **could**)

El verbo **can** carece de infinitivo, de gerundio y de participio. En infinitivo o en participio, se empleará la forma correspondiente de **be able to**, por ejemplo: **he wanted to be able to speak English**; **she has always been able to swim**. En el inglés hablado, y en el escrito en estilo coloquial, la forma negativa **cannot** se transforma en **can't** y la forma negativa **could not** se transforma en **couldn't**.

v aux **a)** [be able to] poder; **he could have come** podría haber venido; **I'll phone you as soon as I can** te llamaré en cuanto pueda; **she can't do it** no puede hacerlo; **I can't understand why** no entiendo por qué
b) [know how to] saber; **can you ski?** ¿sabes esquiar?; **I can't speak English** no sé hablar inglés
c) [be permitted to] poder; **he can't go out tonight** no le dejan salir esta noche
d) [be possible] poder; **she could have forgotten** puede (ser) que lo haya ol-

vidado; **they can't be very poor** no deben ser muy pobres; **what can it be?** ¿qué será?

can² [kæn] **1.** *n* **a)** [of oil] bidón *m* **b)** [container] lata *f*, *Am* tarro *m*; **can opener** abrelatas *m inv* **2.** *vt* [fish, fruit] enlatar

Canada ['kænədə] *n* Canadá

Canadian [kə'neɪdɪən] *adj* & *n* canadiense *(mf)*

canal [kə'næl] *n* canal *m*

Canaries [kə'neərɪz] *npl* **the Canaries** las (islas *fpl*) Canarias *fpl*

canary [kə'neərɪ] *n* canario *m*

Canary *n* **the Canary Islands** las (islas *fpl*) Canarias *fpl*

cancel ['kænsəl] *vt* [train, contract] cancelar; COMM anular; [permission] retirar; [decree] revocar

cancellation [kænsɪ'leɪʃən] *n* cancelación *f*; COMM anulación *f*

cancer ['kænsə(r)] *n* **a)** MED cáncer *m*; **breast cancer** cáncer de mama; **cancer research** cancerología *f* **b)** **Cancer** [in astrology] Cáncer *m*

candid ['kændɪd] *adj* franco(a), sincero(a)

candidate ['kændɪdeɪt, 'kændɪdɪt] *n* candidato(a) *m,f*; [in exam] opositor(a) *m,f*

candle ['kændəl] *n* vela *f*; [in church] cirio *m*

candlestick ['kændəlstɪk] *n* candelero *m*, palmatoria *f*; [in church] cirial *m*

candy ['kændɪ] *n US* caramelo *m*; **candy store** confitería *f*

candyfloss ['kændɪflɒs] *n Br* algodón *m* dulce

cane [keɪn] **1.** *n* **a)** BOT caña *f*; **cane sugar** azúcar *m* de caña **b)** [wicker] mimbre *m* **c)** [walking stick] bastón *m*; [for punishment] palmeta *f* **2.** *vt* castigar con la palmeta

canine ['keɪnaɪn] *adj* ZOOL canino(a); **canine tooth** colmillo *m*

canister ['kænɪstə(r)] *n* bote *m*

cannabis ['kænəbɪs] *n* hachís *m*, cannabis *m*

canned [kænd] *adj* enlatado(a); **canned foods** conservas *fpl*

cannon ['kænən] **1.** *n* **a)** *(pl* **cannons** or **cannon)** cañón *m*; *Fig* **cannon fodder** carne *f* de cañón **b)** *Br* [in billiards, snooker] carambola *f* **2.** *vi* chocar (**into** contra)

cannot ['kænɒt, kæ'nɒt] = **can not**

canoe [kə'nuː] *n* canoa *f*; SPORT piragua *f*

canoeing [kə'nuːɪŋ] *n* piragüismo *m*; **to go canoeing** ir a hacer piragüismo

canopy ['kænəpɪ] *n* **a)** [on throne] dosel *m* **b)** [awning] toldo *m*

can't [kɑːnt] = **can not**

canteen [kæn'tiːn] *n* **a)** [restaurant] cantina *f* **b)** *Br* [set of cutlery] juego *m* de cubiertos **c)** [flask] cantimplora *f*

canvas ['kænvəs] *n* **a)** TEXT lona *f* **b)** [painting] lienzo *m*

canvass ['kænvəs] *vi* **a)** POL hacer propaganda electoral **b)** COMM hacer promoción, buscar clientes

canyon ['kænjən] *n* cañón *m*; **the Grand Canyon** el Gran Cañón

cap [kæp] **1.** *n* **a)** gorro *m*; [soldier's] gorra *f* **b)** *Br* SPORT **to win a cap for England** ser seleccionado(a) para el equipo de Inglaterra **c)** [of pen] capuchón *m*; [of bottle] tapón *m* **2.** *vt* **a)** [outdo] superar; *Fig* **to cap it all** para colmo **b)** [spending] limitar

capability [keɪpə'bɪlɪtɪ] *n* habilidad *f*

capable ['keɪpəbəl] *adj* **a)** [skilful] hábil **b)** [able] capaz (**of** de)

capacity [kə'pæsɪtɪ] *n* **a)** capacidad *f* **b)** [position] puesto *m*; **in her capacity as manageress** en calidad de gerente

cape¹ [keɪp] *n* [garment] capa *f*

cape² [keɪp] *n* GEOG cabo *m*, promontorio *m*; **Cape Horn** Cabo de Hornos; **Cape Town** Ciudad del Cabo; **Cape Verde** Cabo Verde

capeesh [kə'piːʃ] *vi US Fam* [understand] entender; **I'm not going, capeesh?** que no voy a ir, ¿entiendes?

capital ['kæpɪtəl] **1.** *n* **a)** [town] capital *f* **b)** [letter] mayúscula *f* **c)** FIN capital *m*

2. *adj* **a)** [city] capital **b) capital punishment** pena *f* capital **c) capital letter** mayúscula *f*

capitalism ['kæpɪtəlɪzəm] *n* capitalismo *m*

capitalist ['kæpɪtəlɪst] *adj & n* capitalista *(mf)*

capitalize ['kæpɪtəlaɪz] *vi* FIN capitalizar; *Fig* **to capitalize on sth** sacar provecho *or* beneficio de algo

Capricorn ['kæprɪkɔːn] *n* Capricornio *m*

capris [kə'priːz] *npl US* pantalón *m* pirata

capsize [kæp'saɪz] **1.** *vt* hacer zozobrar **2.** *vi* zozobrar

capsule ['kæpsjuːl] *n* cápsula *f*

captain ['kæptɪn] **1.** *n* capitán *m* **2.** *vt* capitanear

caption ['kæpʃən] *n* [under picture] pie *m* de foto; CIN subtítulo *m*

captivating ['kæptɪveɪtɪŋ] *adj* seductor(a)

captive ['kæptɪv] **1.** *n* cautivo(a) *m,f* **2.** *adj* cautivo(a)

captivity [kæp'tɪvɪtɪ] *n* cautiverio *m*

capture ['kæptʃə(r)] **1.** *vt* **a)** capturar, apresar; MIL [town] tomar **b)** [market] acaparar **c)** *Fig* [mood] captar **d)** COMPUT recolectar, recopilar **2.** *n* [of fugitive] captura *f*; [of town] toma *f*

car [kɑː(r)] *n* **a)** coche *m*, *Am* carro *m*, *CSur* auto *m*; *Br* **car park** parking *m*, *Esp* aparcamiento *m*; **car wash** túnel *m* de lavado **b)** *US* RAIL coche *m*

caramel ['kærəmel] *n* azúcar *m* quemado; [sweet] caramelo *m*

carat ['kærət] *n* quilate *m*

caravan ['kærəvæn] *n* **a)** *Br* [vehicle] caravana *f* **b)** [in desert] caravana *f*

carbohydrate [kɑːbəʊ'haɪdreɪt] *n* hidrato *m* de carbono, carbohidrato *m*

carbon ['kɑːbən] *n* carbono *m*; **carbon copy** copia *f* al papel carbón; *Fig* copia exacta; **carbon dioxide** dióxido *m* de carbono; **carbon footprint** huella *f* de carbono; **carbon paper** papel *m* carbón

card [kɑːd] *n* **a)** tarjeta *f*; [of cardboard] cartulina *f*; **birthday/Christmas card** tarjeta de cumpleaños/de Navidad; *US* **calling card** tarjeta *f* de visita; **cash card** tarjeta *f* de cajero automático; **landing card** carta *f* de embarque **b)** [in file] ficha *f*; [for identification] carné *m*, *CSur, Méx* credencial *m*; **card index** fichero *m* **c)** CARDS **card game** juego *m* de cartas; **pack of cards** baraja *f*, cartas *fpl*; **(playing) card** naipe *m*, carta *f*; *Fig Br* **on** *or US* **in the cards** previsto **d)** COMPUT tarjeta *f*

cardboard ['kɑːdbɔːd] *n* cartón *m*; **cardboard box** caja *f* de cartón; **cardboard cutout** recortable *m*

cardigan ['kɑːdɪgən] *n* rebeca *f*

cardinal ['kɑːdɪnəl] **1.** *n* REL cardenal *m* **2.** *adj* cardinal; **cardinal numbers** números *mpl* cardinales

care [keə(r)] **1.** *vi* [be concerned] preocuparse **(about** por); **I don't care** no me importa; *Fam* **for all I care** me trae sin cuidado; *Fam* **he couldn't care less** le importa un bledo
2. *n* **a)** [attention, protection] cuidado *m*, atención *f*; **care of ...** [on letter] al cuidado de ...; **care worker** cuidador(a) *m,f* profesional; **day care** [for elderly, disabled] servicio *m* de asistencia de día; [for children] servicio *m* de guardería; **medical care** asistencia *f* médica; **to take care of** cuidar; [business] ocuparse de
b) [carefulness] cuidado *m*; **take care** [be careful] ten cuidado; [as farewell] ¡cuídate!
c) [worry] preocupación *f*
■ **care for** *vt insep* **a)** [look after] cuidar **b)** [like] gustar, interesar; **would you care for a coffee?** ¿te apetece *or Carib, Col, Méx* provoca un café?

career [kə'rɪə(r)] **1.** *n* carrera *f* **2.** *vi* correr a toda velocidad

career-minded *adj* ambicioso(a)

carefree ['keəfriː] *adj* despreocupado(a)

careful ['keəfʊl] *adj* cuidadoso(a); [cautious] prudente; **be careful!** ¡ojo!; **to be careful** tener cuidado

carefully ['keəfʊlɪ] *adv* [painstakingly] cuidadosamente; [cautiously] con cuidado

caregiver ['keəgɪvə(r)] *n* cuidador(a) *m,f*; **primary caregiver** cuidador(a) *m,f* principal

careless ['keəlɪs] *adj* descuidado(a); [about clothes] desaliñado(a); [driving] negligente; **a careless mistake** un descuido

carer ['keərə(r)] *n* persona que cuida de un familiar enfermo o anciano, sin que necesariamente reciba compensación económica por ello; **primary carer** cuidador(a) *m,f* principal

caress [kə'res] **1.** *n* caricia *f* **2.** *vt* acariciar

caretaker ['keəteɪkə(r)] *n Br* [of building] conserje *m*, portero(a) *m,f*; [of school] conserje *m*

cargo ['kɑ:gəʊ] *(pl* **cargoes,** *US pl* **cargos)** *n* carga *f*, cargamento *m*; NAUT **cargo boat** buque *m* de carga, carguero *m*

Caribbean [kærɪ'bɪən, *US* kə'rɪbɪən] *adj* caribe, caribeño(a); **the Caribbean (Sea)** el (mar) Caribe

caricature ['kærɪkətjʊə(r)] *n* caricatura *f*

caring ['keərɪŋ] *adj* solidario(a)

carlot ['kɑ:lɒt] *n US* aparcamiento *m*

carnation [kɑ:'neɪʃən] *n* clavel *m*

carnival ['kɑ:nɪvəl] *n* carnaval *m*

carol ['kærəl] *n* villancico *m*

carp¹ [kɑ:p] *n* [fish] carpa *f*

carp² [kɑ:p] *vi* refunfuñar

carpenter ['kɑ:pɪntə(r)] *n* carpintero(a) *m,f*

carpentry ['kɑ:pɪntrɪ] *n* carpintería *f*

carpet ['kɑ:pɪt] **1.** *n* alfombra *f* **2.** *vt* [floor] *Esp* enmoquetar, *Am* alfombrar

carpool ['kɑ:pu:l] *n* uso *m* compartido del coche

carport ['kɑ:ˌpɔ:t] *n* cobertizo *m* para coches

carriage ['kærɪdʒ] *n* **a)** [horse-drawn] carruaje *m* **b)** *Br* [of train] vagón *m*, coche *m* **c)** [of gun] cureña *f* **d)** [of typewriter] carro *m* **e)** [of goods] porte *m*, transporte *m*

carrier ['kærɪə(r)] *n* **a)** [company] transportista *mf*; *Br* **carrier bag** bolsa *f* de plástico; **carrier pigeon** paloma mensajera **b)** MED portador(a) *m,f*

carrot ['kærət] *n* zanahoria *f*

carry ['kærɪ] **1.** *vt* **a)** llevar; [goods] transportar **b)** [stock] tener; [responsibility, penalty] conllevar, implicar **c)** [disease] ser portador(a) de **2.** *vi* [sound] oírse ∎ **carry away** *vt sep* llevarse; **to get carried away** entusiasmarse ∎ **carry forward** *vt sep* FIN **carried forward** suma y sigue ∎ **carry off** *vt sep* [prize] llevarse; *Fam* **to carry it off** salir airoso(a) ∎ **carry on 1.** *vt sep* continuar; [conversation] mantener **2.** *vi* **a)** continuar, seguir adelante; **carry on!** ¡adelante! **b)** *Fam* [make a fuss] hacer una escena; **don't carry on about it!** ¡no te enrolles! **c)** *Fam* **to carry on with sb** tener un lío *or Méx* una movida *or RP* un asunto con algn ∎ **carry out** *vt sep* [plan] llevar a cabo, realizar; [test] verificar

cart [kɑ:t] **1.** *n* [horse-drawn] carro *m*; [handcart] carretilla *f*; *US* [in supermarket] carrito *m* **2.** *vt* carretear

carton ['kɑ:tən] *n* [of cream etc] caja *f*

cartoon [kɑ:'tu:n] *n* [strip] tira cómica, historieta *f*; ART cartón *m*; [animated] dibujos *mpl* animados; **cartoon character** personaje *m* de dibujos animados

cartridge ['kɑ:trɪdʒ] *n* **a)** cartucho *m* **b)** [for pen] recambio *m*; **cartridge paper** papel guarro

carve [kɑ:v] *vt* **a)** [wood] tallar; [stone, metal] cincelar, esculpir **b)** [meat] trinchar

carving ['kɑ:vɪŋ] *n* **a)** ART talla *f* **b)** **carving knife** [for meat] cuchillo *m* de trinchar

cascade [kæ'skeɪd] *n* cascada *f*

case¹ [keɪs] *n* **a)** caso *m*; **a case in point** un buen ejemplo; **in any case** en cualquier caso, de todas formas; **in case of**

doubt en caso de duda; **just in case** por si acaso **b)** MED caso *m*; **case history** historial clínico **c)** JUR causa *f*

case² [keɪs] **n a)** [suitcase] maleta *f*, RP valija *f*; [small] estuche *m*; [soft] funda *f* **b) a case of wine** una caja de botellas de vino **c)** TYP **lower case** minúscula *f*; **upper case** mayúscula *f*

case-sensitive *adj* **this password is case-sensitive** esta contraseña distingue entre mayúsculas y minúsculas

cash [kæʃ] **1.** *n* dinero efectivo; **to pay cash** pagar al contado *or* en efectivo; Br **cash desk** caja *f*; **cash on delivery** entrega *f* contra reembolso; **cash dispenser**, Br **cash machine**, Br **cash point** cajero *m* (automático); **cash register** caja *f* registradora **2.** *vt* [cheque] cobrar ■ **cash in 1.** *vi* Fam & Fig **to cash in on sth** sacar provecho de algo **2.** *vt sep* hacer efectivo(a)

cashback [ˈkæʃbæk] *n* Br [in supermarket] dinero en efectivo retirado de la cuenta cuando se paga con tarjeta en un supermercado

cashew [ˈkæʃuː] *n* **cashew (nut)** anacardo *m*

cashier [kæˈʃɪə(r)] *n* cajero(a) *m,f*

cashpoint [ˈkæʃpɔɪnt] *n* Br [cash dispenser] cajero *m* (automático)

casino [kəˈsiːnəʊ] *n* casino *m*

casket [ˈkɑːskɪt] *n* [box] cofre *m*; US [coffin] ataúd *m*

casserole [ˈkæsərəʊl] *n* **a)** [container] cacerola *f* **b)** CULIN guisado *m*

cassette [kəˈset] *n* cinta *f*, casete *f*; **cassette recorder** casete *m*

cast [kɑːst] (*pt & pp* **cast**) **1.** *vt* **a)** [net, fishing line] echar, arrojar; [light] proyectar; [glance] lanzar; [vote] emitir **b)** Fig **to cast doubts on sth** poner algo en duda; **to cast suspicion on sb** levantar sospechas sobre algn **c)** [metal] moldear; **cast iron** hierro fundido **d)** THEAT [play] hacer el reparto de **2.** *n* **a)** [mould] molde *m*; [product] pieza *f*

b) MED **(plaster) cast** escayola *f*, esp Am yeso *m*
c) THEAT reparto *m*
■ **cast aside** *vt sep* Fig abandonar
■ **cast off** *vi* NAUT soltar (las) amarras

cast-iron [ˈkɑːstaɪən] *adj* de hierro fundido

castle [ˈkɑːsəl] **1.** *n* **a)** castillo *m* **b)** [in chess] torre *f* **2.** *vi* [in chess] enrocar

castrate [kæˈstreɪt] *vt* castrar

casual [ˈkæʒjʊəl] *adj* **a)** [meeting etc] fortuito(a) **b)** [worker] eventual **c)** [clothes] (de) sport **d)** [visit] de paso **e)** [person, attitude] despreocupado(a), informal

casualty [ˈkæʒjʊəltɪ] *n* **a)** MIL baja *f*; **casualties** pérdidas *fpl* **b)** [injured] herido(a) *m,f*

cat [kæt] *n* gato(a) *m,f*; Fig **to let the cat out of the bag** revelar el secreto, Esp descubrir el pastel

Catalan [ˈkætəlæn] **1.** *adj* catalán(ana) **2.** *n* **a)** [person] catalán(ana) *m,f* **b)** [language] catalán *m*

catalogue, US **catalog** [ˈkætəlɒg] **1.** *n* catálogo *m* **2.** *vt* catalogar

Catalonia [ˌkætəˈləʊnɪə] *n* Cataluña *f*

Catalonian [ˌkætəˈləʊnʃən] *adj & n* catalán(ana) *(m,f)*

catalyst [ˈkætəlɪst] *n* catalizador *m*

catapult [ˈkætəpʌlt] *n* Br tirachinas *m inv*

catastrophe [kəˈtæstrəfɪ] *n* catástrofe *f*

catch [kætʃ] (*pt & pp* **caught**) **1.** *vt* **a)** [thrown object, falling object] atrapar, Esp coger, Am agarrar; [fish] pescar; [prey, mouse, thief] atrapar, capturar; [train, bus] coger, Am agarrar; **catch (it)!** [when throwing something] ¡agárralo!, Esp ¡cógelo!; **to catch a cold** coger un resfriado; **to catch fire** [log] prenderse; [building] incendiarse; **to catch hold of** agarrar; **to catch sb's eye** captar la atención de algn; **to catch sight of** entrever
b) [surprise] pillar, sorprender
c) [hear] entender

d) to catch one's breath [hold] sostener la respiración; [recover] recuperar el aliento **2.** vi [sleeve etc] engancharse (**on** en); [fire] encenderse **3.** n a) [of ball] parada f; [of fish] presa f **b)** [on door] pestillo m **c)** [disadvantage] trampa f

■ **catch on** vi Fam **a)** [become popular] ganar popularidad **b)** [understand] caer en la cuenta

■ **catch out** vt sep Fam **to catch sb out** [discover, trick] Esp pillar or Am agarrar a algn

■ **catch up 1.** vi [close gap, get closer] **to catch up with sb** alcanzar a algn; **to catch up on sth** recuperar algo; **to catch up on sleep** recuperar el sueño perdido; **to catch up with work** ponerse al día de trabajo; [with news] ponerse al corriente (**on** de) **2.** vt sep [reach] **to catch sb up** alcanzar a algn

catching ['kætʃɪŋ] adj [disease] contagioso(a)

catchy ['kætʃɪ] (compar catchier, superl catchiest) adj Fam [tune] pegadizo(a)

categoric(al) [kætɪ'gɒrɪk(əl)] adj categórico(a)

category ['kætɪgərɪ] n categoría f

cater ['keɪtə(r)] vi **a)** to cater for [wedding etc] proveer comida para **b)** to cater for [taste] atender a

caterer ['keɪtərə(r)] n proveedor(a) m,f

catering ['keɪtərɪŋ] n abastecimiento m (de comidas por encargo)

caterpillar ['kætəpɪlə(r)] n **a)** oruga f **b) caterpillar (tractor)** tractor m de oruga

cathedral [kə'θiːdrəl] n catedral f

Catholic ['kæθəlɪk] adj & n católico(a) (m,f)

cattle ['kætəl] npl ganado m (vacuno); **cattle grid,** US **cattle guard** [sur une route] paso m canadiense (reja que impide el paso al ganado)

caught [kɔːt] pt & pp of catch

cauliflower ['kɒlɪflaʊə(r)] n coliflor f

cause [kɔːz] **1.** n **a)** [origin] causa f **b)** [reason] motivo m **c) for a good cause** por una buena causa **2.** vt causar; **to cause sb to do sth** hacer que algn haga algo

caution ['kɔːʃən] **1.** n **a)** [care] cautela f, prudencia f **b)** [warning] aviso m, advertencia f **c)** Br JUR reprensión f **2.** vt advertir, amonestar

cautious ['kɔːʃəs] adj cauteloso(a), prudente

cavalry ['kævəlrɪ] n caballería f

cave [keɪv] n cueva f ■ **cave in** vi [roof etc] derrumbarse, hundirse

cavern ['kævən] n caverna f

cavity ['kævɪtɪ] n **a)** [hole] cavidad f **b)** [in tooth] caries f inv

cc n **a)** (abbr of **cubic centimetre**) cm³ **b)** (abbr of **carbon copy**) cc

CD [siː'diː] n (abbr of **compact disc**) CD m; COMPUT **CD burner** or **writer** grabadora f de CD; **CD player** (lector m or reproductor m de) CD m

CD-ROM [siːdiː'rɒm] n COMPUT (abbr of **compact disc read-only memory**) CD-ROM m

CD-RW [siːdiːɑː'dʌblju:] n COMPUT (abbr of **compact disc rewritable**) CD-RW m

cease [siːs] **1.** vt cesar; **to cease doing** or **to do sth** dejar de hacer algo **2.** vi terminar

cease-fire [siːs'faɪə(r)] n alto m el fuego

cedar ['siːdə(r)] n cedro m

ceiling ['siːlɪŋ] n techo m

celeb [sɪ'leb] n Fam famoso(a) m,f

celebrate ['selɪbreɪt] **1.** vt [occasion] celebrar **2.** vi divertirse

celebration [selɪ'breɪʃən] n **a)** celebración f **b) celebrations** festividades fpl

celebrity [sɪ'lebrɪtɪ] n celebridad f

celery ['selərɪ] n apio m

cell [sel] n **a)** [in prison] celda f **b)** BIOL & POL célula f **c)** ELEC pila f **d)** US TEL [mobile phone] **cell (phone)** teléfono m móvil or Am celular; **cell tower** antena f de telefonía móvil; **cell site** antena f de telefonía móvil

cellar ['selə(r)] n sótano m; [for wine] bodega f

cello ['tʃeləʊ] n violoncelo m

Cellophane® ['seləfeɪn] n Br celofán m

cellphone ['selfəʊn] n teléfono m móvil or Am celular

cement [sɪ'ment] **1.** n cemento m; **cement mixer** hormigonera f **2.** vt CONSTR unir con cemento; Fig [friendship] cimentar

cemetery ['semɪtrɪ] n cementerio m

censor ['sensə(r)] **1.** n censor(a) m,f **2.** vt censurar

censorship ['sensəʃɪp] n censura f

census ['sensəs] n censo m

cent [sent] n a) centavo m, céntimo m; **euro cent** céntimo m de euro b) **per cent** por ciento

centenary [sen'tiːnərɪ] n centenario m

center ['sentər] US n & vt = **centre**

centigrade ['sentɪgreɪd] adj centígrado(a)

centimetre, US **centimeter** ['sentɪmiːtə(r)] n centímetro m

central ['sentrəl] adj central; **central heating** calefacción f central; **Central America** Centroamérica f, América f Central; **Central American** centroamericano(a) m,f; Br **central reservation** [on motorway] mediana f, Col, Méx camellón m

centralize ['sentrəlaɪz] vt centralizar

centre ['sentə(r)] **1.** n centro m; **town centre** centro de la ciudad; FTBL **centre forward** delantero centro; FTBL **centre half** medio centro; POL **centre party** partido m centrista; US **center strip** mediana f; US **activity center** centro m de actividades; **sports centre** centro deportivo **2.** vt [attention etc] centrar (**on** en)

century ['sentʃərɪ] n siglo m; **the nineteenth century** el siglo diecinueve

CEO n US (abbr of **chief executive officer**) director(a) m,f gerente, consejero(a) m,f delegado(a)

ceramic [sɪ'ræmɪk] **1.** n cerámica f **2.** adj de cerámica

cereal ['sɪərɪəl] n cereal m

ceremony ['serɪmənɪ] n ceremonia f

certain ['sɜːtən] adj a) [sure] seguro(a); **to be certain** estar seguro(a); **to make certain of sth** asegurarse de algo; **for certain** a ciencia cierta b) **to a certain extent** hasta cierto punto c) [not known] cierto(a); **a certain Miss Ward** una tal señorita Ward d) [true] cierto(a)

certainly ['sɜːtənlɪ] adv desde luego; **certainly not** de ninguna manera

certainty ['sɜːtəntɪ] n certeza f; [assurance] seguridad f

certificate [sə'tɪfɪkɪt] n certificado m; SCH diploma m; **medical certificate** certificado m médico

certify ['sɜːtɪfaɪ] vt certificar

chad [tʃæd] n US [residue from punched paper] confeti m

chain [tʃeɪn] **1.** n cadena f; Fig [of events] serie f; **chain of mountains** cordillera f; **chain reaction** reacción f en cadena; **chain saw** sierra mecánica **2.** vt **to chain (up)** encadenar

chain-smoke ['tʃeɪnsməʊk] vi fumar un pitillo tras otro

chair [tʃeə(r)] **1.** n a) silla f; [with arms] sillón m; **chair lift** telesilla m b) [position] presidencia f; UNIV cátedra f **2.** vt presidir

chairman ['tʃeəmən] n presidente m

chairperson ['tʃeəpɜːsən] n presidente(a) m,f

chalet ['ʃæleɪ] n chalet m, chalé m

chalk [tʃɔːk] n [for writing] tiza f, Méx gis m ■ **chalk up** vt sep Fam [victory etc] apuntarse

challenge ['tʃælɪndʒ] **1.** vt a) retar, desafiar; **to challenge sb to do sth** retar a algn a que haga algo b) [authority etc] poner a prueba; [statement] poner en duda c) MIL dar el alto a **2.** n a) reto m, desafío m b) MIL quién vive m

challenger ['tʃælɪndʒə(r)] n aspirante mf

chamber ['tʃeɪmbə(r)] n a) [hall] cámara f; **Chamber of Commerce** Cámara de Comercio b) MUS **chamber music** música f de cámara c) Br JUR **chambers** gabinete m

chambermaid ['tʃeɪmbəmeɪd] *n* camarera *f*

champagne [ʃæm'peɪn] *n* [French] champán *m*; [from Catalonia] cava *m*

champion ['tʃæmpɪən] *n* campeón(ona) *m,f*; *Fig* **champion of human rights** defensor(a) *m,f* de los derechos humanos

championship ['tʃæmpɪənʃɪp] *n* campeonato *m*

chance [tʃɑ:ns] **1.** *n* **a)** [fortune] casualidad *f*, azar *m*; **by chance** por casualidad; **to take a chance** arriesgarse; **chance meeting** encuentro *m* casual **b)** [likelihood] posibilidad *f*; **(the) chances are that …** lo más posible es que … **c)** [opportunity] oportunidad *f*, *Am* chance *f* **2.** *vt* arriesgar

chancellor ['tʃɑ:nsələ(r)] *n* **a)** [head of state, in embassy] canciller *m* **b)** UNIV *Br* rector(a) *m,f* honorario(a); *US* rector(a) *m,f* **c)** *Br* **Chancellor of the Exchequer** ≃ ministro(a) *m,f* de Hacienda

chandelier [ʃændɪ'lɪə(r)] *n* araña *f* (de luces)

change [tʃeɪndʒ] **1.** *vt* cambiar; **to change gear** cambiar de marcha; **to change one's mind / the subject** cambiar de opinión / de tema; **to change trains** hacer transbordo; **to get changed** cambiarse de ropa; *Fig* **to change hands** cambiar de dueño(a) **2.** *vi* cambiar, cambiarse; **to change for the better / worse** mejorar / empeorar; **to change into** convertirse en **3.** *n* **a)** cambio *m*; **for a change** para variar; **change of heart** cambio de parecer; **change of scene** cambio de aires **b)** [money] cambio *m*, *Andes, CAm, Méx* sencillo *m*, *RP* vuelto *m*; **small change** suelto *m*

■ **change over** *vi* cambiarse

changeable ['tʃeɪndʒəbəl] *adj* [weather] variable; [person] inconstante

changeover ['tʃeɪndʒəʊvə(r)] *n* conversión *f*

changing ['tʃeɪndʒɪŋ] **1.** *n* **a)** **changing room** vestuario *m* **b)** MIL relevo *m* (de la guardia) **2.** *adj* cambiante

channel ['tʃænəl] **1.** *n* **a)** GEOG canal *m*; [of river] cauce *m*; **the Channel Islands** las Islas Anglonormandas; **the English Channel** el Canal de la Mancha **b)** [administrative] vía *f* **c)** TV & RADIO canal *m*, cadena *f*; **pay channel** canal *m* de pago **2.** *vt Fig* [ideas etc] canalizar, encauzar

chant [tʃɑ:nt] **1.** *n* REL cántico *m*; [of demonstrators] slogan *m* **2.** *vt* & *vi* REL cantar; [demonstrators] corear

chaos ['keɪɒs] *n* caos *m*

chaotic [keɪ'ɒtɪk] *adj* caótico(a)

chap [tʃæp] *n Fam* [man] tipo *m*, *Esp* tío *m*; **a good chap** un buen tipo

chapel ['tʃæpəl] *n* capilla *f*

chaplain ['tʃæplɪn] *n* capellán *m*

chapter ['tʃæptə(r)] *n* **a)** capítulo *m* **b)** REL cabildo *m*

character ['kærɪktə(r)] *n* **a)** carácter *m* **b)** *Fam* [person] tipo *m* **c)** THEAT personaje *m*

characteristic [kærɪktə'rɪstɪk] **1.** *n* característica *f* **2.** *adj* característico(a)

char-broil *vt US* CULIN asar a la parrilla *(con carbón vegetal)*

charcoal ['tʃɑ:kəʊl] *n* carbón *m* vegetal; ART **charcoal drawing** carboncillo *m*; **charcoal grey** gris marengo o oscuro

charge [tʃɑ:dʒ] **1.** *vt* **a)** cobrar; **charge it to my account** cárguelo en mi cuenta **b)** **to charge sb with a crime** acusar a algn de un crimen **c)** MIL cargar contra **d)** ELEC cargar **2.** *vi* ELEC & MIL cargar; **to charge about** andar a lo loco **3.** *n* **a)** [cost] precio *m*; **free of charge** gratis **b)** **to be in charge of** estar a cargo de; **to take charge of** hacerse cargo de **c)** JUR cargo *m*, acusación *f* **d)** [explosive] carga *f* explosiva **e)** MIL carga *f* **f)** ELEC carga *f*

charger ['tʃɑːʤə(r)] n [for batteries] cargador m

charity ['tʃærɪtɪ] n caridad f; [organization] institución f benéfica

charm [tʃɑːm] **1.** n a) [quality] encanto m b) [spell] hechizo m; **lucky charm** amuleto m **2.** vt encantar

charming ['tʃɑːmɪŋ] adj encantador(a)

chart [tʃɑːt] **1.** n a) [giving information] tabla f; [graph] gráfico m b) [map] carta f de navegación c) MUS **the charts** la lista de éxitos **2.** vt AVIAT & NAUT [on map] trazar

charter ['tʃɑːtə(r)] **1.** n a) [of institution] estatutos mpl; [of rights] carta f b) **charter flight** vuelo m chárter **2.** vt [plane, boat] fletar

chartered accountant [tʃɑːtəd ə'kaʊntənt] n Br censor(a) m,f jurado(a) de cuentas, Am contador(a) m,f público(a)

chase [tʃeɪs] **1.** vt perseguir; [hunt] cazar **2.** n persecución f; [hunt] caza f

chasm ['kæzəm] n GEOG sima f; Fig abismo m

chassis ['ʃæsɪ] n chasis m inv

chaste [tʃeɪst] adj casto(a)

chat [tʃæt] **1.** n a) [informal conversation] charla f, CAm, Méx plática f; Br **chat show** coloquio m b) INTERNET charla f; **chatroom** chat m **2.** vi a) [talk informally] charlar, CAm, Méx platicar b) COMPUT charlar (**to** or **with** con) ■ **chat up** vt sep Br Fam **to chat sb up** intentar ligar con algn, RP intentar levantar a algn

chatroom n INTERNET chat m

chatter ['tʃætə(r)] **1.** vi [person] parlotear; [bird] piar; [teeth] castañetear **2.** n [of person] parloteo m; [of birds] gorjeo m; [of teeth] castañeteo m

chatty ['tʃætɪ] (compar **chattier**, superl **chattiest**) adj hablador(a)

chauffeur ['ʃəʊfə(r), ʃəʊ'fɜː(r)] n Esp chófer m, Am chofer m

chauvinist ['ʃəʊvɪnɪst] adj & n chovinista (mf); **male chauvinist** machista m

cheap [tʃiːp] **1.** adj barato(a); [fare] económico(a); [joke] de mal gusto; [contemptible] bajo(a); Fam **dirt cheap** tirado(a) **2.** n Br Fam **on the cheap** en plan barato **3.** adv barato

cheaply ['tʃiːplɪ] adv barato, en plan económico

cheat [tʃiːt] **1.** vt engañar; **to cheat sb out of sth** estafar algo a algn **2.** vi a) [at games] hacer trampa; [in exam etc] copiar(se) b) Fam [husband, wife] poner cuernos (**on** a) **3.** n [trickster] tramposo(a) m,f

check [tʃek] **1.** n a) [of documents etc] revisión f; [of facts] comprobación f b) [in chess] jaque m c) [pattern] cuadro m; **check box** casilla f d) **to keep in check** [feelings] contener; [enemy] mantener a raya e) US = **cheque 2.** vt a) repasar; [facts] comprobar, Guat, Méx checar; [tickets] controlar; [tyres, oil] revisar b) [impulse] refrenar; [growth] retardar c) [stop] detener **3.** vi comprobar, Guat, Méx checar ■ **check in 1.** vi [at airport] facturar; [at hotel] registrarse (**at** en) **2.** vt sep [luggage, coat] facturar ■ **check into** vt insep **to check into a hotel** registrarse en un hotel ■ **check out 1.** vi [of hotel] dejar el hotel **2.** vt sep [facts] verificar ■ **check up** vi **to check up on sb** hacer averiguaciones sobre algn; **to check up on sth** comprobar algo

checked [tʃekt] adj a cuadros

checkers ['tʃekərz] n sing US [game] damas fpl

check-in ['tʃekɪn] n **check-in desk** [at airport] mostrador m de facturación

checking account ['tʃekɪŋ ə'kaʊnt] n cuenta f corriente

checkout ['tʃekaʊt] n [counter] caja f

checkpoint ['tʃekpɔɪnt] n control m

checkroom ['tʃekruːm] n US [for coats, hats] guardarropa m; [for luggage] consigna f

checkup ['tʃekʌp] n MED chequeo m, examen médico

cheek [tʃi:k] n a) [of face] mejilla f b) Fam [nerve] cara f; **he's got a cheek!** ¡qué caradura!, Esp ¡vaya morro!

cheeky ['tʃi:kɪ] (compar **cheekier**, superl **cheekiest**) adj Fam fresco(a), descarado(a)

cheer [tʃɪə(r)] **1.** vi aplaudir, aclamar **2.** vt a) [applaud] vitorear, aclamar b) [make hopeful] animar **3.** n viva m; **cheers** aplausos mpl; Br Fam **cheers!** [thank you] ¡gracias!; [before drinking] ¡salud! ▪ **cheer up 1.** vi animarse **2.** vt sep **to cheer sb up** alegrar or animar a algn

cheerful ['tʃəfʊl] adj alegre

cheerleader ['tʃɪə,li:də(r)] n animadora f

cheese [tʃi:z] n queso m

cheesecake ['tʃi:zkeɪk] n tarta f de queso

cheesy ['tʃi:zɪ] (compar **cheesier**, superl **cheesiest**) adj a) [tasting of cheese] con sabor a queso b) Fam [song, TV programme] horterilla c) Fig a **cheesy grin** una sonrisa de oreja a oreja

chef [ʃef] n chef m

chemical ['kemɪkəl] **1.** n sustancia química, producto químico **2.** adj químico(a)

chemist ['kemɪst] n a) químico(a) m,f b) Br **chemist's (shop)** farmacia f; **(dispensing) chemist** farmacéutico(a) m,f

chemistry ['kemɪstrɪ] n química f

cheque [tʃek] n cheque m; **to pay by cheque** pagar con (un) cheque; **cheque book** talonario m (de cheques); Br **cheque card** tarjeta que avala los cheques

cherry ['tʃerɪ] n cereza f

chess [tʃes] n ajedrez m

chessboard ['tʃesbɔ:d] n tablero m de ajedrez

chest [tʃest] n a) ANAT pecho m b) [for linen] arca f; [for valuables] cofre m; **chest of drawers** cómoda f

chestnut ['tʃesnʌt] n [tree, colour] castaño m; [nut] castaña f

chew [tʃu:] vt masticar, mascar

chewy ['tʃu:ɪ] adj [meat, bread] correoso(a); [confectionery] gomoso(a), correoso(a)

chick [tʃɪk] n a) [young chicken] pollito m b) Fam [woman] nena f, Arg piba f, Méx chava f; **chick flick** película f para chicas; **chick lit** literatura ligera para mujeres

chicken ['tʃɪkɪn] **1.** n a) pollo m b) Fam [coward] gallina mf, Esp miedica mf **2.** vi Fam **to chicken out** acobardarse, Méx ciscarse, RP achicarse

chickenpox ['tʃɪkɪnpɒks] n varicela f

chickpea ['tʃɪkpi:] n garbanzo m

chief [tʃi:f] **1.** n jefe m **2.** adj principal

chiefly ['tʃi:flɪ] adv [above all] sobre todo; [mainly] principalmente

chilblain ['tʃɪlbleɪn] n sabañón m

child [tʃaɪld] (pl **children**) n niño(a) m,f; [son] hijo m; [daughter] hija f; **child minder** persona que cuida niños en su propia casa

childhood ['tʃaɪldhʊd] n infancia f, niñez f

childish ['tʃaɪldɪʃ] adj pueril, aniñado(a)

childlike ['tʃaɪldlaɪk] adj infantil

children ['tʃɪldrən] pl of **child**

Chilean ['tʃɪlɪən] adj & n chileno(a) (m,f)

chill [tʃɪl] **1.** adj frío(a) **2.** n a) [illness] resfriado m b) [coldness] fresco m; **there's a chill in the air** hace fresco c) [feeling of fear] escalofrío m **3.** vt a) [drink, food] poner a enfriar b) [person] causar escalofríos **4.** vi [drink, food] enfriar ▪ **chill out** vi Fam relajarse; **chill out!** ¡tranqui!

chillax [tʃɪ'læks] vi Fam & Hum **we're going to chillax at my place after the movie** nos vamos de relax a mi casa después de la peli

chilli ['tʃɪlɪ] n chilli **(pepper)** chile m, Esp guindilla f, Andes, RP ají m

chilly ['tʃɪlɪ] (compar **chillier**, superl **chilliest**) adj frío(a)

chime [tʃaɪm] **1.** n [peal] campanada f **2.** vt **to chime five o'clock** [clock] dar las cinco **3.** vi sonar ■ **chime in** vi Fam meter baza or Méx, RP la cuchara

chimney ['tʃɪmnɪ] n chimenea f; **chimney sweep** deshollinador m

chimpanzee [tʃɪmpæn'zi:] n chimpancé m

chin [tʃɪn] n barbilla f, mentón m; **double chin** papada f

china ['tʃaɪnə] n loza f, porcelana f

Chinese [tʃaɪ'ni:z] **1.** adj chino(a) **2.** n **a)** [person] chino(a) m,f **b)** [language] chino m

chink¹ [tʃɪŋk] n [opening] resquicio m; [crack] grieta f

chink² [tʃɪŋk] **1.** vi tintinear **2.** n tintineo m

chip [tʃɪp] **1.** n **a)** [of wood] astilla f; [of stone] lasca f; [in cup] mella f **b)** Br **chip shop** tienda de comida rápida que vende sobre todo pescado y patatas fritas; Br CULIN **chips** Esp patatas or Am papas fritas; **oven chips** patatas fpl fritas para horno; US **(potato) chips** [crisps] Esp patatas or Am papas fritas (de bolsa) **c)** COMPUT chip m **d)** [in gambling] ficha f **2.** vt [wood] astillar; [stone] resquebrajar; [china, glass] mellar **3.** vi [wood] astillarse; [china, glass] mellarse; [paint] desconcharse ■ **chip in** vi Fam **a)** meterse **b)** [with money] poner algo (de dinero)

chip-and-pin n Br pago con tarjeta usando el PIN

chiropodist [kɪ'rɒpədɪst] n podólogo(a) m,f, Am podiatra mf

chirp [tʃɜ:p] vi [birds] gorjear

chisel ['tʃɪzəl] n cincel m

chives [tʃaɪvz] npl cebolleta f

chlorine ['klɔ:ri:n] n cloro m

chocoholic ['tʃɒkə,hɒlɪk] n Fam adicto(a) m,f al chocolate, chocoadicto(a) m,f

chocolate ['tʃɒkəlɪt] **1.** n chocolate m; **chocolates** bombones mpl **2.** adj de chocolate

choice [tʃɔɪs] **1.** n elección f; **a wide choice** un gran surtido; **by choice** por gusto **2.** adj selecto(a)

choir ['kwaɪə(r)] n coro m, coral f

choke [tʃəuk] **1.** vt **a)** [person] ahogar **b)** [obstruct] obstruir **2.** vi ahogarse; **to choke on food** atragantarse con la comida **3.** n AUTO estárter m ■ **choke back** vt sep [emotions] tragarse

cholesterol [kə'lestərɒl] n colesterol m

choos(e)y ['tʃu:zɪ] (compar **choosier**, superl **choosiest**) adj Fam exigente

choose [tʃu:z] (pt **chose**, pp **chosen**) **1.** vt escoger, elegir; [decide on] optar por **2.** vi escoger, elegir

chop [tʃɒp] **1.** n **a)** [blow] tajo m; [with axe] hachazo m **b)** CULIN chuleta f **2.** vt **a)** [wood] cortar; [tree] talar **b)** CULIN cortar a pedacitos **c)** Fam **chops** morros mpl ■ **chop down** vt sep [tree] talar ■ **chop up** vt sep trocear

choppy ['tʃɒpɪ] (compar **choppier**, superl **choppiest**) adj [sea] picado(a)

chopsticks ['tʃɒpstɪks] npl palillos mpl

choral ['kɔ:rəl] adj coral

chord [kɔ:d] n MUS acorde m; Fig **it strikes a chord** (me) suena

chore [tʃɔ:(r)] n quehacer m, tarea f

chorus ['kɔ:rəs] n MUS & THEAT coro m; [in a song] estribillo m; **chorus girl** corista f

chose [tʃəuz] pt of **choose**

chosen ['tʃəuzən] pp of **choose**

Christ [kraɪst] n Cristo m, Jesucristo m

christen ['krɪsən] vt bautizar

christening ['krɪsənɪŋ] n bautizo m

Christian ['krɪstʃən] **1.** adj cristiano(a); **Christian name** nombre m de pila **2.** n cristiano(a) m,f

Christianity [krɪstɪ'ænɪtɪ] n cristianismo m

Christmas ['krɪsməs] n Navidad f; **merry Christmas!** ¡feliz Navidad!;

Christmas carol villancico m; **Christmas Day** día m de Navidad; **Christmas Eve** Nochebuena f

chrome [krəʊm] n cromo m

chronic ['krɒnɪk] adj crónico(a)

chronological [krɒnə'lɒdʒɪkəl] adj cronológico(a)

chubby ['tʃʌbɪ] (compar **chubbier**, superl **chubbiest**) adj rellenito(a)

chuck [tʃʌk] vt Fam tirar, Am botar; **to chuck one's job in** or up dejar el trabajo; **to chuck sb out** echar a algn; **to chuck sth away** or out tirar or Am botar algo

chuckle ['tʃʌkəl] **1.** vi reír entre dientes **2.** n sonrisita f

chum [tʃʌm] n compinche mf, compañero(a) m,f

chunk [tʃʌŋk] n Fam cacho m, pedazo m

church [tʃɜːtʃ] n iglesia f; **to go to church** ir a misa; **Church of England** Iglesia Anglicana

churchyard ['tʃɜːtʃjɑːd] n cementerio m, camposanto

churn [tʃɜːn] **1.** n [for butter] mantequera f; Br [for milk] lechera f **2.** vt [butter] hacer **3.** vi revolverse, agitarse ■ **churn out** vt sep Fam producir en serie

chute [ʃuːt] n [channel] conducto m; [slide] tobogán m

CID [siːaɪ'diː] n Br (abbr of **Criminal Investigation Department**) policía judicial británica

cider ['saɪdə(r)] n sidra f

cigar [sɪ'gɑː(r)] n puro m

cigarette [sɪgə'ret] n cigarrillo m; **cigarette case** pitillera f; **cigarette end** colilla f, Am pucho m; **cigarette holder** boquilla f; **cigarette lighter** encendedor m, Esp mechero m

cinder ['sɪndə(r)] n **cinders** cenizas fpl; **burnt to a cinder** completamente carbonizado(a)

cinema ['sɪnɪmə] n **a)** Br [building] cine m **b)** [art] cine m

cinnamon ['sɪnəmən] n canela f

circle ['sɜːkəl] **1.** n **a)** círculo m; [of people] corro m; **in business circles** en el mundo de los negocios **b)** THEAT anfiteatro m **2.** vt [surround] rodear; [move round] dar la vuelta a **3.** vi dar vueltas

circuit ['sɜːkɪt] n **a)** [journey] recorrido m **b)** ELEC circuito m **c)** Br [motor-racing track] circuito m

circular ['sɜːkjʊlə(r)] adj & n circular (f)

circulate ['sɜːkjʊleɪt] **1.** vt [news] hacer circular **2.** vi circular

circulation [sɜːkjʊ'leɪʃən] n **a)** [of blood] circulación f **b)** [of newspaper] tirada f

circumcise ['sɜːkəmsaɪz] vt circuncidar

circumference [sə'kʌmfərəns] n circunferencia f

circumstance ['sɜːkəmstəns] n [usu pl] circunstancia f; **under no circumstances** en ningún caso; **economic circumstances** situación económica

circus ['sɜːkəs] n circo m

citizen ['sɪtɪzən] n ciudadano(a) m,f

citrus ['sɪtrəs] adj **citrus fruits** agrios mpl

city ['sɪtɪ] n **a)** ciudad f; US **city council** ayuntamiento m; US **city hall** ayuntamiento m **b)** Br FIN **the City** la City (de Londres), el barrio financiero y bursátil de Londres

civics ['sɪvɪks] n [subject] educación f cívica

civil ['sɪvəl] adj **a)** civil; **civil defence** defensa f civil; **civil partner** pareja f civil; **civil rights** derechos mpl civiles; **civil servant** funcionario(a) m,f; POL **civil service** administración pública; **civil union** unión f civil **b)** [polite] cortés, educado(a)

civilian [sɪ'vɪljən] adj & n civil (mf); **civilian clothing** traje m de paisano

civilization [sɪvɪlaɪ'zeɪʃən] n civilización f

civilized ['sɪvɪlaɪzd] adj civilizado(a)

claim [kleɪm] **1.** vt **a)** [benefits, rights] reclamar; JUR [compensation] exigir **b)** [assert] afirmar **2.** n **a)** [demand] reclamación f; JUR demanda f; **to put**

in a claim reclamar una indemnización **b)** [right] derecho m **c)** [assertion] pretensión f

clam [klæm] n almeja f ■ **clam up** vi Fam callarse

clamber ['klæmbə(r)] vi trepar (**over** por)

clammy ['klæmɪ] adj [skin] húmedo(a) y frío(a); [weather] húmedo(a)

clamour, US **clamor** ['klæmə(r)] **1.** n clamor m **2.** vi clamar; **to clamour for** pedir a gritos

clamp [klæmp] **1.** n [for carpentry] tornillo m de banco; TECH abrazadera f; **wheel clamp** cepo m **2.** vt sujetar con abrazaderas ■ **clamp down on** vt insep aumentar los esfuerzos contra

clan [klæn] n clan m

clang [klæŋ] **1.** vi sonar **2.** n sonido metálico

clap [klæp] **1.** vi aplaudir **2.** n a) palmada f **b) a clap of thunder** un trueno

clapping ['klæpɪŋ] n aplausos mpl

claret ['klærət] n Br [wine] clarete m; [colour] burdeos m

clarification [klærɪfɪ'keɪʃən] n aclaración f

clarify ['klærɪfaɪ] vt aclarar

clarinet [klærɪ'net] n clarinete m

clarity ['klærɪtɪ] n claridad f

clash [klæʃ] **1.** vi a) [cymbals] sonar; [swords] chocar; Fig [disagree] estar en desacuerdo **b)** [colours] desentonar **c)** [dates] coincidir **2.** n a) [sound] sonido m **b)** [fight] choque m; Fig [conflict] conflicto m

clasp [klɑːsp] **1.** n a) [on belt] cierre m; [on necklace] broche m **b)** [grasp] apretón m; **clasp knife** navaja f **2.** vt [object] agarrar; **to clasp hands** juntar las manos

class [klɑːs] **1.** n clase f; **class struggle** lucha f de clases; US SCH **class of '84** promoción f de 1984; RAIL **first / second class ticket** billete m de primera / segunda (clase) **2.** vt clasificar

classic ['klæsɪk] **1.** adj clásico(a) **2.** n a) [author] autor clásico; [work] obra

clásica **b) the classics** [literature] las obras clásicas; **classics** [languages] clásicas fpl

classical ['klæsɪkəl] adj clásico(a)

classification [klæsɪfɪ'keɪʃən] n clasificación f

classified ['klæsɪfaɪd] adj [information] secreto(a); **classified advertisements** anuncios mpl por palabras

classify ['klæsɪfaɪ] vt clasificar

classmate ['klɑːsmeɪt] n compañero(a) m,f de clase

classroom ['klɑːsruːm] n aula f, clase f

classy ['klɑːsɪ] adj Fam con clase, elegante

clatter ['klætə(r)] **1.** vi hacer ruido; [things falling] hacer estrépito **2.** n ruido m, estrépito m

clause [klɔːz] n a) JUR cláusula f **b)** LING oración f

claustrophobic [klɔːstrə'fəʊbɪk] adj claustrofóbico(a)

claw [klɔː] **1.** n [of bird, lion] garra f; [of cat] uña f; [of crab] pinza f **2.** vt agarrar, arañar; [tear] desgarrar ■ **claw at** vt insep agarrar, arañar

clay [kleɪ] n arcilla f; **clay pigeon shooting** tiro m al plato

clean [kliːn] **1.** adj a) limpio(a) **b)** [unmarked, pure] sin defecto; **to have a clean record** no tener antecedentes (penales) **c)** [not obscene] decente **2.** adv a) **to play clean** jugar limpio; Fam **to come clean** confesarlo todo **b)** Fam por completo; **it went clean through the middle** pasó justo por el medio **3.** vt [room] limpiar; **to clean one's teeth** lavarse los dientes ■ **clean out** vt sep [room] limpiar a fondo ■ **clean up** vt sep & vi limpiar

clean-burning adj [fuel] de combustión limpia

cleaner ['kliːnə(r)] n limpiador(a) m,f

cleaning ['kliːnɪŋ] n limpieza f

clinical

cleanse [klenz] *vt* limpiar

clean-shaven [ˈkliːnˈʃeɪvən] *adj* [man, face] (bien) afeitado(a)

clear [klɪə(r)] **1.** *adj* **a)** claro(a) ; [road, day] despejado(a) ; **clear conscience** conciencia tranquila
b) [obvious] claro(a) ; **to make sth clear** aclarar algo
c) [majority] absoluto(a) ; [profit] neto(a)
d) [free] libre
2. *adv* **a)** *Fig* **loud and clear** claramente
b) **stand clear!** ¡apártese! ; **to stay clear of** evitar
3. *vt* **a)** [room] vaciar ; COMM liquidar ; **to clear one's throat** aclararse la garganta ; **to clear the table** quitar la mesa
b) [authorize] autorizar
c) [hurdle] salvar
d) **to clear sb of a charge** exculpar a algn de un delito
4. *vi* [sky] despejarse
■ **clear away** *vt sep* quitar
■ **clear off** *vi Br Fam* largarse ; **clear off!** ¡largo!
■ **clear out** *vt sep* [room] limpiar a fondo ; [cupboard] vaciar
■ **clear up 1.** *vt sep* **a)** [tidy] recoger ; [arrange] ordenar **b)** [mystery] resolver ; [misunderstanding] aclarar **2.** *vi* [weather] despejarse ; [problem] desaparecer

clearance [ˈklɪərəns] *n* **a)** [of area] despeje *m* ; COMM **clearance sale** liquidación *f* (de existencias) **b)** [space] espacio *m* libre **c)** [authorization] autorización *f*

clear-cut [klɪəˈkʌt] *adj* claro(a)

clearing [ˈklɪərɪŋ] *n* **a)** [in wood] claro *m* **b)** [of rubbish] limpieza *f* **c)** [of cheque] compensación *f*

clearly [ˈklɪəlɪ] *adv* **a)** claramente **b)** [at start of sentence] evidentemente

clef [klef] *n* clave *f* ; **bass / treble clef** clave de fa / de sol

clench [klentʃ] *vt* [teeth, fist] apretar

clergy [ˈklɜːdʒɪ] *n* clero *m*

clergyman [ˈklɜːdʒɪmən] *n* clérigo *m*

clerical [ˈklerɪkəl] *adj* **a)** REL clerical **b)** [staff, work] de oficina

clerk [klɑːk, *US* klɜːrk] *n* **a)** [office worker] oficinista *mf* ; [civil servant] funcionario(a) *m,f* **b)** *US* COMM dependiente(a) *m,f*, vendedor(a) *m,f*

clever [ˈklevə(r)] *adj* **a)** [person] inteligente, listo(a) ; **to be clever at sth** tener aptitud para algo ; *Br Fam & Pej* **clever clogs** *or* **dick** sabelotodo *mf*, *Esp* listillo(a) *m,f* **b)** [argument] ingenioso(a)

cliché [ˈkliːʃeɪ] *n* cliché *m*

click [klɪk] **1.** *n* [sound & COMPUT] clic *m* **2.** *vt* [tongue] chasquear **b)** COMPUT clicar, cliquear, hacer clic ; **to click on** clicar *or* cliquear *or* hacer clic en **3.** *vi* **it didn't click** [I didn't realize] no me di cuenta

client [ˈklaɪənt] *n* cliente *mf*

clientele [kliːɒnˈtel] *n* clientela *f*

cliff [klɪf] *n* acantilado *m*

climate [ˈklaɪmɪt] *n* clima *m* ; **climate change** cambio *m* climático

climax [ˈklaɪmæks] *n* **a)** [peak] clímax *m*, punto *m* culminante **b)** [sexual] orgasmo *m*

climb [klaɪm] **1.** *vt* [ladder] subir a ; [mountain] escalar ; [tree] trepar a
2. *vi* [plants] trepar ; AVIAT subir ; *Fig* [socially] ascender
3. *n* subida *f*, ascensión *f*
■ **climb down** *vi* bajar ; *Fig* volverse atrás

climber [ˈklaɪmə(r)] *n* alpinista *mf*, *Am* andinista *mf*

climbing [ˈklaɪmɪŋ] *n* SPORT montañismo *m*, alpinismo *m*, *Am* andinismo *m*

clinch [klɪntʃ] **1.** *vt* resolver ; [deal] cerrar **2.** *n Fam* abrazo apasionado

cling [klɪŋ] *(pt & pp* **clung)** *vi* [hang on] agarrarse ; [clothes] ajustarse ; [smell] pegarse ; **to cling together** unirse

clinic [ˈklɪnɪk] *n* [in state hospital] ambulatorio *m* ; [specialized] clínica *f*

clinical [ˈklɪnɪkəl] *adj* **a)** MED clínico(a) **b)** [detached] frío(a)

clink [klɪŋk] **1.** *vi* tintinear **2.** *n* tintineo *m*

clip¹ [klɪp] **1.** *vt* [cut] cortar; [ticket] picar **2.** *n* **a)** [of film] extracto *m* **b)** [with scissors] tijeretada *f*

clip² [klɪp] **1.** *n* [for hair] pasador *m*; [for paper] clip *m*, sujetapapeles *m inv*; [brooch] clip *f* **2.** *vt* sujetar

clippers ['klɪpəz] *npl* [for hair] maquinilla *f* para rapar; [for nails] cortaúñas *m inv*; [for hedge] tijeras *fpl* de podar

clipping ['klɪpɪŋ] *n* recorte *m*

clique [kli:k] *n Pej* camarilla *f*

cloak [kləʊk] **1.** *n* [garment] capa *f* **2.** *vt* encubrir

cloakroom ['kləʊkru:m] *n* guardarropa *m*; *Br Euph* [toilets] servicios *mpl*

clock [klɒk] **1.** *n* reloj *m* **2.** *vt* [race] cronometrar ■ **clock in, clock on** *vi* fichar (a la entrada), *Am* marcar tarjeta (a la entrada) ■ **clock off, clock out** *vi* fichar (a la salida), *Am* marcar tarjeta (a la salida) ■ **clock up** *vt sep* [mileage] hacer

clockface ['klɒkfeɪs] *n* esfera *f* del reloj

clockwise ['klɒkwaɪz] *adj & adv* en el sentido de las agujas del reloj

clockwork ['klɒkwɜ:k] *n* mecanismo *m*; **clockwork toy** juguete *m* de cuerda

clog [klɒg] **1.** *vt* obstruir; [pipe] atascar; **to get clogged up** atascarse **2.** *n* [footwear] zueco *m*

cloister ['klɔɪstə(r)] *n* claustro *m*

close¹ [kləʊs] **1.** *adj* **a)** [in space, time] cercano(a); [contact] directo(a); **close to** cerca de; **close together** juntos(as) **b)** [relationship] estrecho(a); [friend] íntimo(a) **c)** [inspection] detallado(a); [watch] atento(a) **d)** [contest] reñido(a); **a close resemblance** un gran parecido **e)** [air] cargado(a); [weather] bochornoso(a) **2.** *adv* cerca; **they live close by** or **close at hand** viven cerca; **to stand close together** estar apretados(as)

3. *prep* **close on, close to** [almost] cerca de

close² [kləʊz] **1.** *vt* **a)** cerrar; **closing time** hora *f* de cierre **b)** [end] concluir, terminar; [meeting] levantar **c)** COMPUT cerrar; **to close (a window)** cerrar (una ventana); **to close (an application)** salir (de un programa) **2.** *vi* **a)** [shut] cerrar, cerrarse **b)** [end] concluirse, terminarse **3.** *n* fin *m*, final *m* ■ **close down** *vi* [business] cerrar para siempre; *Br* RADIO & TV finalizar la emisión ■ **close in** *vi* **to close in on sb** rodear a algn

closed [kləʊzd] *adj* cerrado(a); IND **closed shop** empresa que emplea solamente a miembros de un sindicato

closet ['klɒzɪt] *n US* armario *m*

close-up ['kləʊsʌp] *n* primer plano *m*

closure ['kləʊʒə(r)] *n* cierre *m*

clot [klɒt] **1.** *n* **a)** [of blood] coágulo *m*; MED **clot on the brain** embolia *f* cerebral **b)** *Br Fam* lelo(a) *m,f*, *Esp* memo(a) *m,f* **2.** *vi* coagularse

cloth [klɒθ] *n* tela *f*, paño *m*; [rag] trapo *m*; [tablecloth] mantel *m*

clothes [kləʊðz] *npl* ropa *f*, vestidos *mpl*; **clothes brush** cepillo *m* de la ropa; **clothes hanger** percha *f*; **clothes horse** tendedero *m* plegable; **clothes line** tendedero *m*; **clothes** *Br* **peg** or *US* **pin** pinza *f*

clothing ['kləʊðɪŋ] *n* ropa *f*

cloud [klaʊd] **1.** *n* nube *f*; COMPUT **cloud computing** computación *f* en la nube **2.** *vt* nublar; *Fig* **to cloud the issue** complicar el asunto **3.** *vi* **to cloud over** nublarse

cloudy ['klaʊdɪ] *(compar* **cloudier,** *superl* **cloudiest)** *adj* **a)** [sky] nublado(a) **b)** [liquid] turbio(a)

clove¹ [kləʊv] *n* [spice] clavo *m*

clove² [kləʊv] *n* [of garlic] diente *m*

clover ['kləʊvə(r)] *n* trébol *m*

clown [klaʊn] **1.** n payaso m **2.** vi to clown (**about** or **around**) hacer el payaso

club [klʌb] **1.** n a) [society] club m; **sports club** club deportivo **b)** [nightclub] discoteca f, sala f (de fiestas) **c)** [heavy stick] garrote m, porra f; [in golf] palo m **d)** CARDS trébol m **2.** vt aporrear **3.** vi to **club together** pagar entre varios

clubbing ['klʌbɪŋ] n she loves clubbing le encanta ir a bailar (a discotecas); to go clubbing ir a bailar (a discotecas)

clue [kluː] n [sign] indicio m; [to mystery] pista f; [in crossword] clave f; Fam I haven't a clue no tengo ni idea

clump [klʌmp] n [of trees] grupo m; [of plants] mata f

clumsy ['klʌmzɪ] (compar clumsier, superl clumsiest) adj desmañado(a), torpe; [awkward] tosco(a)

clung [klʌŋ] pt & pp of cling

clunky ['klʌŋkɪ] adj a) [shoes] basto(a) **b)** [furniture] voluminoso(a)

cluster ['klʌstə(r)] **1.** n grupo m; [of grapes] racimo m **2.** vi agruparse

clusterfuck ['klʌstəfʌk] n US Vulg it was a complete clusterfuck fue una megacagada; we're in the middle of an economic clusterfuck estamos en plena jodienda económica

clutch [klʌtʃ] **1.** vt agarrar **2.** vi Fig to clutch at straws aferrarse a cualquier cosa **3.** n a) AUTO embrague m **b)** Fig to fall into sb's clutches caer en las garras de algn

clutter ['klʌtə(r)] vt to clutter (up) llenar, atestar

cm (abbr of centimetre(s)) cm

CMON MESSAGING written abbr of come on

c/o [siː'əʊ] (abbr of care of) en el domicilio de

Co a) COMM (abbr of Company) Cía. **b)** (abbr of County) condado m

coach [kəʊtʃ] **1.** n a) esp Br [bus] autobús m, Esp autocar m; [carriage] carruaje m; **coach tour** excursión f en autocar **b)** RAIL coche m, vagón m **c)** SPORT entrenador(a) m,f **2.** vt SPORT entrenar; SCH dar clases particulares a

coal [kəʊl] n carbón m, hulla f; **coal bunker** carbonera f; **coal merchant** carbonero m; **coal mine** mina f de carbón

coalition [kəʊə'lɪʃən] n coalición f

coarse [kɔːs] adj [material] basto(a); [skin] áspero(a); [language] grosero(a), ordinario(a)

coast [kəʊst] n costa f, litoral m

coat [kəʊt] **1.** n a) [overcoat] abrigo m; [jacket] chaqueta f, Méx chamarra f, RP campera f; **coat hanger** percha f **b)** [of animal] pelo m **c)** [of paint] mano f, capa f **2.** vt cubrir (**with** de); [with liquid] bañar (**with** en)

-coated [kəʊtɪd] suff plastic-coated plastificado(a); silver-coated plateado(a)

coating ['kəʊtɪŋ] n capa f, baño m

coax [kəʊks] vt engatusar

cob [kɒb] n mazorca f

cobbled ['kɒbəld] adj [path, street] adoquinado(a)

cobweb ['kɒbweb] n telaraña f

cocaine [kə'keɪn] n cocaína f

cock [kɒk] **1.** n a) ORNITH gallo m; [male bird] macho m **b)** [on gun] percutor m **c)** Vulg [penis] Esp polla f, Am verga f, Chile pico m, Méx pito m, RP pija f **2.** vt [gun] amartillar; [ears] erguir ■ **cock up** vt sep Br v Fam to cock sth up cagar or Esp joder or Méx madrear algo

cockerel ['kɒkərəl] n gallo m joven

cockney ['kɒknɪ] **1.** adj del East End londinense **2.** n persona del East End londinense

cockpit ['kɒkpɪt] n cabina f del piloto

cockroach ['kɒkrəʊtʃ] n cucaracha f

cocktail ['kɒkteɪl] n cóctel m; **cocktail lounge** bar m; **cocktail party** cóctel m; **prawn cocktail** cóctel de gambas; **Molotov cocktail** cóctel Molotov

cocky ['kɒkɪ] *(compar cockier, superl cockiest) adj Fam* gallito(a), engreído(a), *Esp* chulo(a)

cocoa ['kəʊkəʊ] n cacao m

coconut ['kəʊkənʌt] n coco m

cod [kɒd] n bacalao m; **cod liver oil** aceite m de hígado de bacalao

code [kəʊd] **1.** n código m; [symbol] clave f; TEL prefijo m **2.** vt [message] cifrar, poner en clave

coerce [kəʊ'ɜ:s] vt coaccionar

coexist [kəʊɪg'zɪst] vi coexistir

coffee ['kɒfɪ] n café m; **coffee bar/shop** cafetería f; **coffee break** descanso m; **coffee maker** cafetera f; **coffee table** mesita f de café

coffin ['kɒfɪn] n ataúd m

cog [kɒg] n diente m

cognac ['kɒnjæk] n coñac m

coherent [kəʊ'hɪərənt] adj coherente

coil [kɔɪl] **1.** vt **to coil (up)** enrollar **2.** vi enroscarse **3.** n **a)** [loop] vuelta f; [of rope] rollo m; [of hair] rizo m **b)** Br [contraceptive] espiral f **c)** ELEC carrete m, bobina f

coin [kɔɪn] **1.** n moneda f **2.** vt **a)** [money] acuñar **b)** Fig **to coin a phrase** por así decirlo

coincide [kəʊɪn'saɪd] vi coincidir (with con)

coincidence [kəʊ'ɪnsɪdəns] n coincidencia f

coke [kəʊk] n [coal] coque m

colander ['kɒləndə(r)] n colador m

cold [kəʊld] **1.** adj frío(a); **I'm cold** tengo frío; **it's cold** [weather] hace frío; [thing] está frío(a); Fig **to get cold feet (about doing sth)** entrarle miedo a algn (de hacer algo); **cold cream** crema f hidratante; Fig **it leaves me cold** ni me va ni me viene, Esp me deja

frío(a); **cold case** caso m sin resolver; **cold sore** herpes m inv labial, Esp calentura f, Méx fuego m; **cold war** guerra fría **2.** n a) frío m **b)** [illness] resfriado m, catarro m, Esp, Méx resfriado m, Andes, RP resfrío m; **to have a cold** estar acatarrado(a), tener un Esp, Méx resfriado or Andes, RP resfrío

coldness ['kəʊldnɪs] n [of weather, manner] frialdad f

coleslaw ['kəʊlslɔ:] n ensalada f de col

collaborate [kə'læbəreɪt] vi colaborar (**with** con)

collaboration [kəlæbə'reɪʃən] n also Pej colaboración f

collapse [kə'læps] **1.** vi [break down] derrumbarse; [cave in] hundirse; Fig [prices] caer en picado; MED sufrir un colapso **2.** vt [table] plegar **3.** n [breaking down] derrumbamiento m; [caving in] hundimiento m; MED colapso m

collar ['kɒlə(r)] **1.** n [of garment] cuello m; [for dog] collar m **2.** vt Fam pescar, agarrar

colleague ['kɒli:g] n colega mf

collect [kə'lekt] **1.** vt **a)** [gather] recoger **b)** [stamps etc] coleccionar **c)** [taxes] recaudar **2.** vi **a)** [people] reunirse **b)** [for charity] hacer una colecta (**for** para) **3.** adv US **to call sb collect** llamar or Am hablar a algn a cobro revertido

collection [kə'lekʃən] n **a)** [of mail] recogida f; [of money] colecta f **b)** [of stamps] colección f

collector [kə'lektə(r)] n [of stamps] coleccionista mf

college ['kɒlɪdʒ] n colegio m; Br [of university] colegio universitario; US [university] universidad f

collide [kə'laɪd] vi chocar, colisionar

collision [kə'lɪʒən] n choque m

colloquial [kə'ləʊkwɪəl] adj coloquial

Colombia [kə'lɒmbɪə] n Colombia f

Colombian [kə'lɒmbɪən] adj & n colombiano(a) (m,f)

colon[1] ['kəʊlən] n TYP dos puntos mpl

colon[2] ['kəʊlən] n ANAT colon m

colonel ['kɜːnəl] n coronel m

colonial [kə'ləʊnɪəl] adj colonial

colony ['kɒlənɪ] n colonia f

color ['kʌlər] US = **colour**

colossal [kə'lɒsəl] adj colosal

---

colour ['kʌlə(r)] **1.** n a) color m; **what colour is it?** ¿de qué color es?; **colour film/television** película f/televisión f en color; **colour scheme** combinación f de colores
b) [race] color m; **colour bar** discriminación f racial
c) **colours** Br SPORT colores mpl; MIL [flag] bandera f
2. vt colorear
3. vi **to colour (up)** ruborizarse

---

colour-blind ['kʌləblaɪnd] adj daltónico(a)

coloured ['kʌləd] adj [pencils] de colores

colourful ['kʌləfʊl] adj a) con muchos colores b) Fig lleno(a) de color; [person] pintoresco(a)

colouring ['kʌlərɪŋ] n [colour] colorido m

column ['kɒləm] n columna f

.com ['dɒtkɒm] COMPUT puntocom

coma ['kəʊmə] n coma m; **to go into a coma** entrar en coma

comb [kəʊm] **1.** n peine m **2.** vt peinar; **to comb one's hair** peinarse

combat ['kɒmbæt] **1.** n a) combate m b) **combats** pantalones mpl de camuflaje **2.** vt [enemy, disease] combatir **3.** vi combatir (**against** contra)

combination [kɒmbɪ'neɪʃən] n combinación f

combine 1. [kəm'baɪn] vt combinar **2.** [kəm'baɪn] vi combinarse; [companies] asociarse **3.** ['kɒmbaɪn] n a) COMM asociación f b) **combine harvester** cosechadora f

combustion [kəm'bʌstʃən] n combustión f

come [kʌm] (pt came, pp come) vi a) venir; [arrive] llegar; **coming!** ¡voy!; **to come and go** ir y venir; Fig **in years to come** en el futuro b) [happen] suceder; **come what may** pase lo que pase c) **I came to believe that …** llegué a creer que … ■ **come about** vi ocurrir, suceder ■ **come across 1.** vt insep [thing] encontrar por casualidad; **to come across sb** tropezar con algn **2.** vi Fig **to come across well** causar buena impresión ■ **come along** vi a) [arrive] venir; **come along!** ¡vamos!, Esp ¡venga! b) [make progress] progresar ■ **come apart** vi a) [fall to pieces] deshacerse b) [come off] caerse ■ **come at** vt insep [attack] atacar ■ **come away** vi [leave] salir; [part] desprenderse (**from** de) ■ **come back** vi [return] volver, Col, Méx regresarse ■ **come before** vt insep a) preceder b) [court] comparecer ante ■ **come by** vt insep ■ **come down** vi bajar; [rain] caer; [building] ser derribado(a); **to come down with the flu** coger la gripe ■ **come down to** vt insep reducirse a ■ **come forward** vi [advance] avanzar; [volunteer] ofrecerse ■ **come from** vt insep venir de ■ **come in** vi a) [enter] entrar; **come in!** ¡pase! b) [arrive - train] llegar; [tide] subir; Fam & Fig **where do I come in?** y yo ¿qué pinto? c) [be useful] **to come in handy** venir bien d) **to come in for** ser objeto de ■ **come into** vt insep a) [enter] entrar en b) [inherit] heredar ■ **come off 1.** vt insep [fall from] caerse de; Fam **come off it!** ¡venga ya! **2.** vi a) [fall] caerse; [stain] quitarse; [button] caerse b) Fam [take place] pasar; [succeed] salir bien; **to come off badly** salir mal ■ **come on** vi a) come on! [hurry] ¡vamos!, Esp ¡venga! b) [make progress] progresar c) [rain, illness] comenzar ■ **come out** vi a) salir (**of** de); [book] aparecer; [product] estrenarse; [facts] revelarse b) [stain] quitarse; [colour] desteñir c) **to come out against/in favour of sth** declararse en contra/a favor de algo; Br IND **to come out (on strike)** declararse en huelga

d) [turn out] salir ■ **come over 1.** *vi* venir **2.** *vt insep* **a)** [hill] aparecer en lo alto de **b)** *Fam* **what's come over you?** ¿qué te pasa? ■ **come round 1.** *vt insep* [corner] dar la vuelta a **2.** *vi* **a)** [visit] venir **b)** [regain consciousness] volver en sí **c) to come round to sb's way of thinking** dejarse convencer por algn ■ **come through 1.** *vt insep* **a)** [cross] cruzar **b)** [illness] recuperarse de ; [accident] sobrevivir **2.** *vi* [message] llegar ■ **come to 1.** *vi* [regain consciousness] volver en sí **2.** *vt insep* **a)** *Fig* **to come to one's senses** recobrar la razón **b)** [amount to] costar **c)** [arrive at] llegar a ; **to come to an end** terminar ; *Fam* **come to that** a propósito ■ **come under** *vt insep Fig* **to come under fire from sb** ser criticado(a) por algn ■ **come up 1.** *vi* **a)** [rise] subir ; [approach] acercarse (**to** a) **b)** [difficulty, question] surgir ; **to come up with a solution** encontrar una solución ; **to come up against problems** encontrarse con problemas **c)** [sun] salir **d) to come up to** igualar ; **to come up to sb's expectations** satisfacer a algn **e)** *Fam* **three chips, coming up!** ¡van tres de patatas fritas! ■ **come upon** *vt insep* = **come across**

comeback ['kʌmbæk] *n Fam* **a)** [of person] reaparición *f* ; **to make a comeback** reaparecer **b)** [answer] réplica *f*

comedian [kə'miːdɪən] *n* cómico *m*

comedy ['kɒmɪdɪ] *n* comedia *f*

comet ['kɒmɪt] *n* cometa *m*

comfort ['kʌmfət] **1.** *n* **a)** comodidad *f* ; *US* **comfort station** servicios *mpl*, *Esp* aseos *mpl*, *Am* baños *mpl* **b)** [consolation] consuelo *m* ; **to take comfort in** *or* **from sth** consolarse con algo **2.** *vt* consolar

comfortable ['kʌmfətəbəl] *adj* [chair, person, margin] cómodo(a) ; [temperature] agradable

comfortably ['kʌmfətəblɪ] *adv* [win] con facilidad ; **to be comfortably off** vivir cómodamente

comforter ['kʌmfətə(r)] *n US* [duvet] edredón *m*

comic ['kɒmɪk] **1.** *adj* cómico(a) ; **comic strip** tira cómica, historieta *f* **2.** *n* **a)** [person] cómico(a) *m,f* **b)** **comic (book)** [for children] *Esp* tebeo *m*, *Am* revista *f* de historietas ; [for adults] cómic *m*

coming ['kʌmɪŋ] **1.** *adj* [year] próximo(a) ; [generation] futuro(a) **2.** *n* venida *f*, llegada *f* ; **comings and goings** idas *fpl* y venidas ; *Fig* **coming and going** ajetreo *m*

comma ['kɒmə] *n* coma *f*

command [kə'mɑːnd] **1.** *vt* **a)** mandar **b)** [respect] infundir ; [sympathy] merecer ; [money etc] disponer de **2.** *n* **a)** [order] orden *f* ; [authority] mando *m* ; **to be at sb's command** estar a las órdenes de algn **b)** [of language] dominio *m* **c)** [disposal] disposición *f* **d)** COMPUT comando *m*, instrucción *f*

commander [kə'mɑːndə(r)] *n* comandante *m*

commandment [kə'mɑːndmənt] *n* mandamiento *m*

commemorate [kə'meməreɪt] *vt* conmemorar

commemoration [kəmemə'reɪʃən] *n* conmemoración *f* ; **in commemoration of** en conmemoración de

commence [kə'mens] *vt* & *vi Formal* comenzar

commendable [kə'mendəbəl] *adj* encomiable

comment ['kɒment] **1.** *n* comentario *m* ; **no comment** sin comentario **2.** *vi* hacer comentarios

commentary ['kɒməntərɪ] *n* comentario *m*

commentator ['kɒmənteɪtə(r)] *n* comentarista *mf*

commerce ['kɒmɜːs] *n* comercio *m*

commercial [kə'mɜːʃəl] **1.** *adj* comercial ; TV **commercial break** corte publicitario **2.** *n* TV anuncio *m*

commercialize [kə'mɜːʃəlaɪz] *vt* explotar

commiserate [kə'mɪzəreɪt] *vi* compadecerse (**with** de)

compassion

commission [kə'mɪʃən] **1.** n **a)** MIL despacho m (de oficial); **out of commission** fuera de servicio **b)** [of inquiry] comisión f; [job] encargo m **c)** [payment] comisión f **2.** vt **a)** MIL nombrar **b)** [order] encargar **c)** NAUT poner en servicio

commissioner [kə'mɪʃənə(r)] n [official] comisario m; **commissioner of police** comisario de policía

commit [kə'mɪt] vt **a)** [crime] cometer; **to commit suicide** suicidarse **b) to commit oneself (to do sth)** comprometerse (a hacer algo) **c) to commit sth to sb's care** confiar algo a algn

commitment [kə'mɪtmənt] n compromiso m

committee [kə'mɪtɪ] n comisión f, comité m

commodity [kə'mɒdɪtɪ] n producto m básico

common ['kɒmən] **1.** adj **a)** común; **that's common knowledge** eso lo sabe todo el mundo; **common law** derecho consuetudinario; **Common Market** Mercado m Común; **common room** [for students] sala f de estudiantes; [for teachers] sala f de profesores **b)** [ordinary] corriente **c)** [vulgar] ordinario(a), maleducado(a) **2.** n [land] terreno m comunal

commonly ['kɒmənlɪ] adv comúnmente

commonplace ['kɒmənpleɪs] adj corriente

Commonwealth ['kɒmənwelθ] n Br **the Commonwealth** la Commonwealth; **Commonwealth of Independent States** Comunidad f de Estados Independientes

commotion [kə'məʊʃən] n alboroto m

communal ['kɒmjʊnəl] adj comunal

commune¹ [kə'mju:n] vi [converse] conversar íntimamente; [with nature] estar en comunión (**with** con)

commune² ['kɒmju:n] n comuna f

communicate [kə'mju:nɪkeɪt] **1.** vi comunicarse (**with** con) **2.** vt comunicar

communication [kəmju:nɪ'keɪʃən] n **a)** comunicación f **b)** Br RAIL **communication cord** timbre m de alarma

communism ['kɒmjʊnɪzəm] n comunismo m

communist ['kɒmjʊnɪst] adj & n comunista (mf)

community [kə'mju:nɪtɪ] n comunidad f; [people] colectividad f; **community centre** centro m social

commute [kə'mju:t] **1.** vi viajar diariamente al lugar de trabajo **2.** vt JUR conmutar

commuter [kə'mju:tə(r)] n persona que viaja diariamente al lugar de trabajo

compact¹ 1. [kəm'pækt] adj compacto(a); [style] conciso(a) **2.** ['kɒmpækt] n [for powder] polvera f

compact² ['kɒmpækt] n POL pacto m

compact disc ['kɒmpækt'dɪsk] n disco compacto

companion [kəm'pænjən] n compañero(a) m,f

company ['kʌmpənɪ] n **a)** compañía f; **to keep sb company** hacer compañía a algn **b)** COMM empresa f, compañía f

comparable ['kɒmpərəbəl] adj comparable (**to** or **with** con)

comparative [kəm'pærətɪv] **1.** adj comparativo(a); [relative] relativo(a) **2.** n LING comparativo m

comparatively [kəm'pærətɪvlɪ] adv relativamente

compare [kəm'peə(r)] **1.** vt comparar (**to** or **with** con); **(as) compared with** en comparación con **2.** vi compararse

comparison [kəm'pærɪsən] n comparación f; **by comparison** en comparación; **there's no comparison** no se puede comparar

compartment [kəm'pɑ:tmənt] n [section] compartimiento m; RAIL departamento m

compass ['kʌmpəs] n **a)** brújula f **b) (pair of) compasses** compás m **c)** Fig [range] límites mpl

compassion [kəm'pæʃən] n compasión f

compatible [kəm'pætəbəl] *adj*
[gen & COMPUT] compatible

compatriot [kəm'pætrɪət] *n* compatriota *mf*

compel [kəm'pel] *vt* **a)** [oblige] obligar;
to compel sb to do sth obligar a algn
a hacer algo **b)** [admiration] despertar

compensate ['kɒmpənseɪt] **1.** *vt*
compensar; **to compensate sb for
sth** indemnizar a algn de algo **2.** *vi*
compensar

compensation [kɒmpən'seɪʃən] *n*
compensación *f*; [for loss] indemnización *f*

compere ['kɒmpeə(r)] *n Br* anima-
dor(a) *m,f*

compete [kəm'piːt] *vi* competir

competent ['kɒmpɪtənt] *adj* competente

competition [kɒmpɪ'tɪʃən] *n* **a)** [contest]
concurso *m* **b)** COMM competencia *f*

competitive [kəm'petɪtɪv] *adj*
competitivo(a)

competitor [kəm'petɪtə(r)] *n*
competidor(a) *m,f*

compile [kəm'paɪl] *vt* compilar, recopilar

complacent [kəm'pleɪsənt] *adj* auto-
complaciente

complain [kəm'pleɪn] *vi* quejarse (**of /
about** de)

complaint [kəm'pleɪnt] *n* **a)** queja *f*;
COMM reclamación *f* **b)** JUR demanda *f*
c) MED enfermedad *f*

complement 1. ['kɒmplɪmənt] *n*
a) complemento *m* **b)** NAUT dotación *f*
2. ['kɒmplɪment] *vt* complementar

complete [kəm'pliːt] **1.** *adj* **a)** [entire]
completo(a) **b)** [absolute] total **2.** *vt*
completar; **to complete a form** rellenar un formulario

completely [kəm'pliːtlɪ] *adv* completamente, por completo

complex ['kɒmpleks] **1.** *adj* complejo(a)
2. *n* complejo *m*; **inferiority complex**
complejo de inferioridad

complexion [kəm'plekʃən] *n* tez *f*; *Fig*
aspecto *m*

compliant [kəm'plaɪənt] *adj* **a)** [person]
dócil; [document, object] conforme
b) [compatible] compatible

complicate ['kɒmplɪkeɪt] *vt* complicar

complication [kɒmplɪ'keɪʃən] *n* complicación *f*

compliment 1. ['kɒmplɪmənt] *n* **a)** cumplido *m*; **to pay sb a compliment** hacerle un cumplido a algn **b)** **compli-
ments** saludos *mpl* **2.** ['kɒmplɪment]
vt felicitar; **to compliment sb on sth**
felicitar a algn por algo

complimentary [kɒmplɪ'mentərɪ] *adj*
a) [praising] elogioso(a) **b)** [free] gratis

comply [kəm'plaɪ] *vi* obedecer; **to
comply with** [order] cumplir con; [re-
quest] acceder a

component [kəm'pəʊnənt] **1.** *n* componente *m* **2.** *adj* componente; **component part** parte *f*

compose [kəm'pəʊz] *vt & vi* **a)** componer; **to be composed of** componerse
de **b)** **to compose oneself** calmarse

composed [kəm'pəʊzd] *adj* [calm]
sereno(a)

composer [kəm'pəʊzə(r)] *n* composi-
tor(a) *m,f*

composition [kɒmpə'zɪʃən] *n* composición *f*; [essay] redacción *f*

compost ['kɒmpɒst] *n* abono *m*

composure [kəm'pəʊʒə(r)] *n* calma *f*,
serenidad *f*

compound[1] **1.** ['kɒmpaʊnd] *n* compuesto *m*
2. ['kɒmpaʊnd] *adj* compuesto(a); [frac-
ture] complicado(a)
3. [kəm'paʊnd] *vt* [problem] agravar

compound[2] ['kɒmpaʊnd] *n* [enclosure]
recinto *m*

comprehend [kɒmprɪ'hend] *vt* comprender

comprehensive [kɒmprɪ'hensɪv]
adj **a)** [knowledge] amplio(a); [study]
detallado(a) **b)** INS a todo riesgo **c)** *Br*
comprehensive school ≃ instituto *m*
de segunda enseñanza

compress 1. [kəm'pres] *vt* comprimir
2. ['kɒmpres] *n* compresa *f*

comprise [kəm'praɪz] *vt* comprender; [consist of] constar de

compromise ['kɒmprəmaɪz] **1.** *n* solución *f* negociada; **to reach a compromise** llegar a un acuerdo **2.** *vi* [two people] llegar a un acuerdo; [individual] transigir **3.** *vt* [person] comprometer

compulsion [kəm'pʌlʃən] *n* obligación *f*

compulsive [kəm'pʌlsɪv] *adj* compulsivo(a)

compulsory [kəm'pʌlsərɪ] *adj* obligatorio(a)

computer [kəm'pjuːtə(r)] *n Esp* ordenador *m*, *Am* computadora *f*; **personal computer** ordenador personal, *Am* computadora personal; **computer programmer** programador(a) *m,f*; **computer science** informática *f*

computerize [kəm'pjuːtəraɪz] *vt* informatizar, *Am* computarizar, *Am* computadorizar

computing [kəm'pjuːtɪŋ] *n* informática *f*, *Am* computación *f*

con [kɒn] *Fam* **1.** *vt* timar, *RP* cagar **2.** *n* timo *m*, *Andes*, *RP* truchada *f*; **con man** timador *m*, *Andes*, *RP* cagador *m*

conceal [kən'siːl] *vt* ocultar; [emotions] disimular

concede [kən'siːd] *vt* conceder

conceited [kən'siːtɪd] *adj* presuntuoso(a)

conceivable [kən'siːvəbəl] *adj* concebible

conceive [kən'siːv] *vt & vi* concebir

concentrate ['kɒnsəntreɪt] **1.** *vt* concentrar **2.** *vi* **to concentrate on sth** concentrarse en algo

concentration [kɒnsən'treɪʃən] *n* concentración *f*; **concentration camp** campo *m* de concentración

concept ['kɒnsept] *n* concepto *m*

concern [kən'sɜːn] **1.** *vt* **a)** concernir, afectar; **as far as I'm concerned** por lo que a mí se refiere **b)** [worry] preocupar **2.** *n* **a)** **it's no concern of mine** no es asunto mío **b)** [worry] preocupación *f* **c)** COMM negocio *m*

concerned [kən'sɜːnd] *adj* **a)** [affected] afectado(a) **b)** [worried] preocupado(a) (**about** por)

concerning [kən'sɜːnɪŋ] *prep* con respecto a, en cuanto a

concert ['kɒnsət, 'kɒnsɜːt] *n* MUS concierto *m*; **concert hall** sala *f* de conciertos

concerto [kən'tʃɜːtəʊ] *n* concierto *m*

concession [kən'seʃən] *n* **a)** concesión *f*; **tax concession** privilegio *m* fiscal **b)** COMM reducción *f*

conciliatory [kən'sɪlɪətərɪ] *adj* conciliador(a)

concise [kən'saɪs] *adj* conciso(a)

conclude [kən'kluːd] *vt & vi* concluir

conclusion [kən'kluːʒən] *n* conclusión *f*; **to reach a conclusion** llegar a una conclusión

conclusive [kən'kluːsɪv] *adj* concluyente

concoction [kən'kɒkʃən] *n* [mixture] mezcolanza *f*; *Pej* [brew] brebaje *m*

concourse ['kɒŋkɔːs] *n* explanada *f*

concrete ['kɒnkriːt] **1.** *n* hormigón *m*, *Am* concreto *m*; **concrete mixer** hormigonera *f* **2.** *adj* **a)** [definite] concreto(a) **b)** [made of concrete] de hormigón

concur [kən'kɜː(r)] *vi* **a)** **to concur with** [agree] estar de acuerdo con **b)** [coincide] coincidir

concussion [kən'kʌʃən] *n* conmoción *f* cerebral

condemn [kən'dem] *vt* condenar

condensation [kɒnden'seɪʃən] *n* condensación *f*

condense [kən'dens] **1.** *vt* condensar **2.** *vi* condensarse

condescending [kɒndɪ'sendɪŋ] *adj* condescendiente

condition [kən'dɪʃən] **1.** *n* condición *f*; **to be in good condition** estar en buen estado; **on condition that ...** a condición de que ...; **on one condition** con una condición; **heart condition** enfermedad cardíaca; **conditions** [circumstances] circunstancias *fpl* **2.** *vt* condicionar

conditional [kən'dıʃənəl] *adj* condicional

conditioner [kən'dıʃənə(r)] *n* acondicionador *m*

condolences [kən'dəʊlənsız] *npl* pésame *m*; **please accept my condolences** le acompaño en el sentimiento

condom ['kɒndəm] *n* preservativo *m*

condominium [kɒndə'mınıəm] *n US* [building] *bloque de apartamentos poseídos por diferentes propietarios*; [apartment] apartamento *m*, *Esp* piso *m*, *Arg* departamento *m (en propiedad)*

condone [kən'dəʊn] *vt* perdonar, consentir

conducive [kən'dju:sıv] *adj* conducente

conduct 1. ['kɒndʌkt] *n* [behaviour] conducta *f*, comportamiento *m* **2.** [kən'dʌkt] *vt* [lead] guiar; [business, orchestra] dirigir; **conducted tour** visita acompañada; **to conduct oneself** comportarse

conductor [kən'dʌktə(r)] *n* **a)** *Br* [on bus] cobrador(a) *m,f*, *RP* guarda *mf* **b)** *US* RAIL revisor(a) *m,f* **c)** MUS director(a) *m,f* **d)** PHYS conductor *m*

cone [kəʊn] *n* **a)** cono *m*; **ice-cream cone** cucurucho *m* **b)** BOT piña *f*

confectionery [kən'fekʃənərı] *n* dulces *mpl*

confederation [kənfedə'reıʃən] *n* confederación *f*

confer [kən'fɜ:(r)] **1.** *vt* **to confer a title on sb** conferir un título a algn **2.** *vi* consultar

conference ['kɒnfərəns] *n* conferencia *f*

confess [kən'fes] **1.** *vi* confesar; REL confesarse **2.** *vt* confesar

confession [kən'feʃən] *n* confesión *f*

confetti [kən'fetı] *n* confeti *m*

confide [kən'faıd] *vi* **to confide in sb** confiar en algn

confidence ['kɒnfıdəns] *n* **a)** confianza *f*; **vote of confidence /no confidence** voto *m* de confianza /de censura; **confidence trick** camelo *m* **b)** [secret] confidencia *f*; **in confidence** en confianza

confident ['kɒnfıdənt] *adj* seguro(a)

confidential [kɒnfı'denʃəl] *adj* [secret] confidencial; [entrusted] de confianza

confidently ['kɒnfıdəntlı] *adv* con seguridad

configure [kən'fıgə] *vt* [gen & COMPUT] configurar

confine [kən'faın] *vt* encerrar; *Fig* limitar

confirm [kən'fɜ:m] *vt* confirmar

confirmation [kɒnfə'meıʃən] *n* confirmación *f*

confirmed [kən'fɜ:md] *adj* empedernido(a)

confiscate ['kɒnfıskeıt] *vt* confiscar

conflict 1. ['kɒnflıkt] *n* conflicto *m* **2.** [kən'flıkt] *vi* chocar (**with** con)

conflicting [kən'flıktıŋ] *adj* contradictorio(a)

conform [kən'fɔ:m] *vi* conformarse; **to conform to** *or* **with** [customs] amoldarse a; [rules] someterse a

confront [kən'frʌnt] *vt* hacer frente a

confrontation [kɒnfrʌn'teıʃən] *n* confrontación *f*

confuse [kən'fju:z] *vt* [person] despistar; [thing] confundir (**with** con); **to get confused** confundirse

confused [kən'fju:zd] *adj* [person] confundido(a); [mind, ideas] confuso(a)

confusing [kən'fju:zıŋ] *adj* confuso(a)

confusion [kən'fju:ʒən] *n* confusión *f*

congested [kən'dʒestıd] *adj* **a)** [street] repleto(a) de gente; [city] superpoblado(a) **b)** MED congestionado(a)

congestion [kən'dʒestʃən] *n* congestión *f*; *Br* **congestion zone** *zona del centro de Londres en la que se aplica la tasa de congestión al tráfico*

congratulate [kən'grætjʊleıt] *vt* felicitar

congratulations [kəngrætjʊ'leɪʃənz] *npl* felicitaciones *fpl*; **congratulations!** ¡enhorabuena!

congregate ['kɒŋgrɪgeɪt] *vi* congregarse

congregation [kɒŋgrɪ'geɪʃən] *n* [group] congregación *f*; REL fieles *mpl*

congress ['kɒŋgres] *n* **a)** [conference] congreso *m* **b)** US POL **Congress** el Congreso *(de los Estados Unidos)*

congressman ['kɒŋgresmən] *(pl* **congressmen** [-mən]) *n* US POL congresista *m*

congresswoman ['kɒŋgres,wʊmən] *(pl* **congresswomen** [-,wɪmɪn]) *n* US POL congresista *f*

conifer ['kɒnɪfə(r)] *n* conífera *f*

conjunction [kən'dʒʌŋkʃən] *n* conjunción *f*; *Fig* **in conjunction with** conjuntamente con

connect [kə'nekt] **1.** *vt* **a)** [join] juntar, unir; [wires] empalmar; *Fig* **to be connected by marriage** estar emparentado(a) por matrimonio **b)** [install] instalar; ELEC conectar **c)** TEL [person] pasar, *Esp* poner **d)** *Fig* [associate] asociar **2.** *vi* unirse; [rooms] comunicarse; [train, flight] enlazar *or* empalmar (**with** con)

connected [kə'nektɪd] *adj* unido(a); [events] relacionado(a); *Fig* **to be well connected** [person - socially] estar bien relacionado(a)

connection [kə'nekʃən] *n* **a)** [joint] juntura *f*, unión *f*; ELEC conexión *f*; TEL instalación *f* **b)** RAIL correspondencia *f* **c)** *Fig* [of ideas] relación *f*; **in connection with** [regarding] con respecto a **d)** [person] contacto *m*

connoisseur [kɒnɪ's3:(r)] *n* conocedor(a) *m,f*

connotation [kɒnə'teɪʃən] *n* connotación *f*

conquer ['kɒŋkə(r)] *vt* [enemy, bad habit] vencer; [country] conquistar

conquest ['kɒŋkwest] *n* conquista *f*

conscience ['kɒnʃəns] *n* conciencia *f*; **to have a clear conscience** tener la conciencia tranquila; **to have a guilty conscience** sentirse culpable

conscientious [kɒnʃɪ'enʃəs] *adj* concienzudo(a); **conscientious objector** objetor(a) *m,f* de conciencia

conscious ['kɒnʃəs] *adj* [aware] consciente; [choice etc] deliberado(a)

consciousness ['kɒnʃəsnɪs] *n* MED conocimiento *m*; [awareness] conciencia *f*

conscript ['kɒnskrɪpt] *n* recluta *m*

conscription [kən'skrɪpʃən] *n* servicio *m* militar obligatorio

consecutive [kən'sekjʊtɪv] *adj* consecutivo(a)

consensus [kən'sensəs] *n* consenso *m*

consent [kən'sent] **1.** *n* consentimiento *m*; **by common consent** de común acuerdo **2.** *vi* consentir (**to** en)

consequence ['kɒnsɪkwəns] *n* consecuencia *f*

consequently ['kɒnsɪkwəntlɪ] *adv* por consiguiente

conservation [kɒnsə'veɪʃən] *n* conservación *f*

conservative [kən's3:vətɪv] **1.** *adj* cauteloso(a) **2.** *adj & n Br* POL **Conservative** conservador(a) *(m,f)*

conservatory [kən's3:vətrɪ] *n* **a)** [greenhouse] invernadero *m* **b)** MUS conservatorio *m*

conserve **1.** [kən's3:v] *vt* conservar **2.** ['kɒns3:v] *n* conserva *f*

consider [kən'sɪdə(r)] *vt* **a)** [ponder on, regard] considerar; **to consider doing sth** pensar hacer algo **b)** [keep in mind] tener en cuenta

considerable [kən'sɪdərəbəl] *adj* considerable

considerably [kən'sɪdərəblɪ] *adv* bastante

considerate [kən'sɪdərɪt] *adj* considerado(a)

consideration [kənsɪdə'reɪʃən] *n* consideración *f*; **without due consideration** sin reflexión

considering [kən'sɪdərɪŋ] *prep* teniendo en cuenta

consignment [kən'saɪnmənt] *n* envío *m*

consist [kən'sɪst] *vi* **to consist of** consistir en

consistency [kən'sɪstənsɪ] *n* **a)** [of actions] consecuencia *f* **b)** [of mixture] consistencia *f*

consistent [kən'sɪstənt] *adj* consecuente; **consistent with** de acuerdo con

consolation [kɒnsə'leɪʃən] *n* consuelo *m*; **consolation prize** premio *m* de consolación

console¹ [kən'səʊl] *vt* consolar

console² ['kɒnsəʊl] *n* [control panel, COMPUT & MUS] consola *f*; **games console** consola de juegos

consolidate [kən'sɒlɪdeɪt] **1.** *vt* consolidar **2.** *vi* consolidarse

consonant ['kɒnsənənt] *n* consonante *f*

conspicuous [kən'spɪkjʊəs] *adj* [striking] llamativo(a); [easily seen] visible; [mistake] evidente

conspiracy [kən'spɪrəsɪ] *n* conjura *f*

conspire [kən'spaɪə(r)] *vi* conspirar

constable ['kʌnstəbəl] *n Br* policía *mf*; **chief constable** jefe *m* de policía

constant ['kɒnstənt] **1.** *adj* constante; [continuous] incesante; [loyal] fiel, leal **2.** *n* constante *f*

constellation [kɒnstɪ'leɪʃən] *n* constelación *f*

constipated ['kɒnstɪpeɪtɪd] *adj* **to be constipated** estar estreñido(a)

constituency [kən'stɪtjʊənsɪ] *n* circunscripción *f* electoral

constituent [kən'stɪtjʊənt] **1.** *adj* [component] constituyente **2.** *n* **a)** [part] componente *m* **b)** POL votante *mf*

constitute ['kɒnstɪtjuːt] *vt* constituir

constitution [kɒnstɪ'tjuːʃən] *n* constitución *f*

constraint [kən'streɪnt] *n* coacción *f*; **to feel constraint in sb's presence** sentirse cohibido(a) ante algn

construct [kən'strʌkt] *vt* construir

construction [kən'strʌkʃən] *n* construcción *f*

constructive [kən'strʌktɪv] *adj* constructivo(a)

consul ['kɒnsəl] *n* cónsul *mf*

consulate ['kɒnsjʊlɪt] *n* consulado *m*

consult [kən'sʌlt] *vt* & *vi* consultar (**about** sobre)

consultant [kən'sʌltənt] *n* MED especialista *mf*; COMM & IND asesor(a) *m,f*

consultation [kɒnsəl'teɪʃən] *n* consulta *f*

consulting *adj* **consulting fee** honorarios *mpl* de asesoría

consume [kən'sjuːm] *vt* consumir

consumer [kən'sjuːmə(r)] *n* consumidor(a) *m,f*; **consumer goods** bienes *mpl* de consumo

consumption [kən'sʌmpʃən] *n* **a)** [of food] consumo *m*; **fit for consumption** apto(a) para el consumo **b)** MED tisis *f*

contact ['kɒntækt] **1.** *n* contacto *m*; **contact lens** lente *f* de contacto, *Esp* lentilla *f*, *Méx* pupilente *f* **2.** *vt* ponerse en contacto con

contagious [kən'teɪdʒəs] *adj* contagioso(a)

contain [kən'teɪn] *vt* contener; **to contain oneself** contenerse

container [kən'teɪnə(r)] *n* **a)** [box, package] recipiente *m*; [bottle] envase *m* **b)** NAUT contenedor *m*

contaminate [kən'tæmɪneɪt] *vt* contaminar

contemplate ['kɒntempleɪt] *vt* **a)** [consider] considerar, pensar en **b)** [look at] contemplar

contemporary [kən'tempərərɪ] *adj* & *n* contemporáneo(a) *(m,f)*

contempt [kən'tempt] *n* desprecio *m*; **to hold in contempt** despreciar; **contempt of court** desacato *m* a los tribunales

contend [kən'tend] **1.** *vi* competir; *Fig* **there are many problems to contend with** se han planteado muchos problemas **2.** *vt* afirmar

content¹ ['kɒntent] *n* contenido *m*; **table of contents** índice *m* de materias

content² [kən'tent] **1.** *adj* contento(a) **2.** *vt* contentar **3.** *n* contento *m*; **to one's heart's content** todo lo que uno quiera

contented [kən'tentɪd] *adj* contento(a), satisfecho(a)

contest 1. ['kɒntest] *n* concurso *m*; SPORT prueba *f* **2.** [kən'test] *vt* **a)** [matter] rebatir; [verdict] impugnar; *Fig* [will] disputar **b)** POL [seat] luchar por

contestant [kən'testənt] *n* concursante *mf*

context ['kɒntekst] *n* contexto *m*

context-sensitive *adj* COMPUT dependiente del contexto

continent ['kɒntɪnənt] *n* continente *m*; *Br* **(on) the Continent** (en) Europa

continental [kɒntɪ'nentəl] *adj* **a)** continental; **continental shelf** plataforma *f* continental **b)** *Br* de la Europa continental; **continental quilt** edredón *m* de pluma

contingency [kən'tɪndʒənsɪ] *n* contingencia *f*; **contingency plans** planes *mpl* para casos de emergencia

contingent [kən'tɪndʒənt] *adj* & *n* contingente (*m*)

continual [kən'tɪnjʊəl] *adj* continuo(a), constante

continue [kən'tɪnjuː] *vt* & *vi* continuar, seguir; **to continue to do sth** seguir *or* continuar haciendo algo

continuous [kən'tɪnjʊəs] *adj* continuo(a)

contour ['kɒntʊə(r)] *n* contorno *m*; **contour line** línea *f* de nivel

contraception [kɒntrə'sepʃən] *n* anticoncepción *f*

contraceptive [kɒntrə'septɪv] *adj* & *n* anticonceptivo (*m*)

contract 1. [kən'trækt] *vi* PHYS contraerse

2. [kən'trækt] *vt* **a)** contraer **b) to contract to do sth** [make agreement] comprometerse por contrato a hacer algo

3. ['kɒntrækt] *n* contrato *m*; **to enter into a contract** hacer un contrato

contractor [kən'træktə(r)] *n* contratista *mf*

contradict [kɒntrə'dɪkt] *vt* contradecir

contradictory [kɒntrə'dɪktərɪ] *adj* contradictorio(a)

contraption [kən'træpʃən] *n* *Fam* cacharro *m*

contrary ['kɒntrərɪ] **1.** *adj* **a)** [opposite] contrario(a) **b)** [kən'treərɪ] [awkward] terco(a) **2.** *n* **on the contrary** todo lo contrario; **unless I tell you to the contrary** a menos que te diga lo contrario **3.** *adv* **contrary to** en contra de

contrast 1. [kən'trɑːst] *vi* contrastar **2.** ['kɒntrɑːst] *n* contraste *m*

contribute [kən'trɪbjuːt] **1.** *vt* [money] contribuir con; [ideas, information] aportar **2.** *vi* **a)** contribuir; [in discussion] participar **b)** PRESS colaborar (**to** en)

contribution [kɒntrɪ'bjuːʃən] *n* **a)** [of money] contribución *f*; [of ideas etc] aportación *f* **b)** PRESS colaboración *f*

contributor [kən'trɪbjʊtə(r)] *n* [to newspaper] colaborador(a) *m,f*

contrive [kən'traɪv] *vt* inventar, idear; **to contrive to do sth** buscar la forma de hacer algo

contrived [kən'traɪvd] *adj* artificial, forzado(a)

control [kən'trəʊl] **1.** *vt* controlar; [person, animal] dominar; [vehicle] manejar; **to control one's temper** controlarse **2.** *n* **a)** [power] control *m*, dominio *m*; **out of control** fuera de control; **to be in control** estar al mando; **to be under control** [situation] estar bajo control; **to go out of control** descontrolarse; **to lose control** perder los estribos **b)** AUTO & AVIAT [device] mando *m*; RADIO & TV botón *m* de control; **control panel** tablero *m* de instrumentos; **control room** sala *f* de control; AVIAT **control tower** torre *f* de control

controversial [kɒntrə'vɜːʃəl] *adj* controvertido(a), polémico(a)

controversy ['kɒntrəvɜːsɪ, kən'trɒvəsɪ] *n* polémica *f*

convalescence [kɒnvə'lesəns] *n* convalecencia *f*

convenience [kən'viːnɪəns] *n* conveniencia *f*, comodidad *f*; **all modern conveniences** todas las comodidades; **at your convenience** cuando le convenga; **convenience food** comida precocinada; *US* **convenience store** *pequeño supermercado de barrio*; *Br* **public conveniences** [toilets] servicio *m* público, *Esp* aseos *mpl*, *Am* baños *mpl* públicos

convenient [kən'viːnɪənt] *adj* [time, arrangement] conveniente, oportuno(a); [place] bien situado(a)

convention [kən'venʃən] *n* convención *f*

conventional [kən'venʃənəl] *adj* clásico(a); [behaviour] convencional

converge [kən'vɜːdʒ] *vi* convergir

conversation [kɒnvə'seɪʃən] *n* conversación *f*, *CAm*, *Méx* plática *f*

conversion [kən'vɜːʃən] *n* MATH & REL conversión *f* (**to a**; **into** en)

convert 1. [kən'vɜːt] *vt* **a)** [change] **to convert sth to** *or* **into** convertir algo en; REL **to convert sb (to)** convertir a algn **b)** [building, ship] **to convert sth to** *or* **into** convertir algo en **2.** [kən'vɜːt] *vi* **to convert from sth to sth** convertirse de algo a algo **3.** ['kɒnvɜːt] *n* converso(a) *m,f*

convertible [kən'vɜːtəbəl] **1.** *adj* convertible **2.** *n* [car] descapotable *m*, *Am* convertible *m*

convey [kən'veɪ] *vt* **a)** [carry] transportar **b)** [sound] transmitir; [idea] comunicar

conveyor [kən'veɪə(r)] *n* **conveyor belt** cinta transportadora

convict 1. [kən'vɪkt] *vt* declarar culpable a, condenar **2.** ['kɒnvɪkt] *n* presidiario(a) *m,f*

conviction [kən'vɪkʃən] *n* **a)** [belief] creencia *f*, convicción *f* **b)** JUR condena *f*

convince [kən'vɪns] *vt* convencer

convincing [kən'vɪnsɪŋ] *adj* convincente

convoy ['kɒnvɔɪ] *n* convoy *m*

cook [kʊk] **1.** *vt* cocinar, guisar; [dinner] preparar; *Fam* **to cook the books** falsificar las cuentas **2.** *vi* [person] cocinar, guisar; [food] cocerse **3.** *n* cocinero(a) *m,f*

cookbook ['kʊkbʊk] *n* *US* libro *m* de cocina

cooker ['kʊkə(r)] *n* cocina *f*, *Col*, *Méx*, *Ven* estufa *f*

cookery ['kʊkərɪ] *n* cocina *f*; **cookery book** libro *m* de cocina

cookie ['kʊkɪ] *n* **a)** *US* [biscuit] galleta *f* **b)** COMPUT cookie *f*

cooking ['kʊkɪŋ] *n* cocina *f*

cool [kuːl] **1.** *adj* **a)** fresco(a); **it's cool** [weather] hace fresquito **b)** *Fig* [calm] tranquilo(a); [reserved] frío(a) **2.** *n* **a)** [coolness] fresco *m* **b)** *Fam* **to lose one's cool** perder la calma **3.** *vt* [air] refrescar; [drink] enfriar **4.** *adv* *Fam* **to play it cool** aparentar calma

■ **cool down**, **cool off** *vi Fig* calmarse; [feelings] enfriarse

cooler ['kuːlə(r)] *n* *US* nevera *f* portátil

coop [kuːp] **1.** *n* gallinero *m* **2.** *vt* **to coop (up)** encerrar

co-op ['kəʊɒp] *n* cooperativa *f*

co-operate [kəʊ'ɒpəreɪt] *vi* cooperar

co-operation [kəʊɒpə'reɪʃən] *n* cooperación *f*

co-ordinate 1. [kəʊ'ɔːdɪneɪt] *vt* coordinar **2.** [kəʊ'ɔːdɪnɪt] *n* **a)** MATH coordenada *f* **b)** **co-ordinates** [clothes] conjunto *m*

co-ordination [kəʊɔːdɪ'neɪʃən] *n* coordinación *f*

cop [kɒp] *Fam* **1.** *n* [policeman] poli *m* **2.** *vt Br* **you'll cop it** te vas a ganar una buena ▪ **cop out** *vi Fam* zafarse, *Esp* escaquearse, *RP* zafar

co-parenting *n* coparentalidad *f*

cope [kəʊp] *vi* arreglárselas; **to cope with** [person, work] poder con ; [problem] hacer frente a

copier ['kɒpɪə(r)] *n* [photocopying machine] fotocopiadora *f*

copper¹ ['kɒpə(r)] **1.** *n* [metal] cobre *m* **2.** *adj* [colour] cobrizo(a)

copper² ['kɒpə(r)] *n Fam* poli *mf*

copy ['kɒpɪ] **1.** *n* **a)** copia *f* **b)** [of book] ejemplar *m* **2.** *vt & vi* copiar

copyright ['kɒpɪraɪt] *n* copyright *m*, derechos *mpl* de autor

coral ['kɒrəl] *n* coral *m*; **coral reef** arrecife *m* de coral

cord [kɔːd] *n* **a)** [string] cuerda *f*; ELEC cordón *m* **b)** TEXT [corduroy] pana *f*; **cords** pantalones *mpl* de pana

cordial ['kɔːdɪəl] **1.** *adj* cordial **2.** *n* licor *m*

cordon ['kɔːdən] **1.** *n* cordón *m* **2.** *vt* **to cordon off a street** acordonar una calle

corduroy ['kɔːdərɔɪ] *n* pana *f*

core [kɔː(r)] **1.** *n* [of fruit] corazón *m*; ELEC núcleo *m*; *Fig* **the hard core** los incondicionales **2.** *vt* quitarle el corazón a

cork [kɔːk] *n* corcho *m*; **cork oak** alcornoque *m*

corkscrew ['kɔːkskruː] *n* sacacorchos *m inv*

corn¹ [kɔːn] *n* **a)** *Br* [wheat] trigo *m* **b)** [maize] maíz *m*, *Andes, RP* choclo *m*; **corn bread** pan *m* de maíz *or Andes, RP* choclo; **corn on the cob** mazorca *f* de maíz *or Andes, RP* choclo, *Méx* elote *m*

corn² [kɔːn] *n* MED callo *m*

corner ['kɔːnə(r)] **1.** *n* **a)** [of street] esquina *f*; [bend in road] curva *f*; **round the corner** a la vuelta de la esquina; FTBL **corner kick** córner *m*; **corner** *Br* **shop** *or US* **store** tienda pequeña de barrio

b) [of room] rincón *m* **2.** *vt* **a)** [enemy] arrinconar **b)** COMM acaparar **3.** *vi* AUTO tomar una curva

cornet [*Br* 'kɔːnɪt, *US* kɔː'net] *n* **a)** MUS corneta *f* **b)** *Br* [for ice cream] cucurucho *m*

cornfed ['kɔːnfed] *adj US Fam* paleto(a), de pueblo; **it's about a cornfed girl who makes it big in Manhattan** trata de una chica de pueblo que triunfa en Manhattan

cornflakes ['kɔːnfleɪks] *npl* copos *mpl* de maíz, cornflakes *mpl*

cornstarch ['kɔːnstɑːtʃ] *n US* harina *f* de maíz *or Andes, RP* choclo, maicena® *f*

corny ['kɔːnɪ] *(compar* **cornier**, *superl* **corniest)** *adj Fam* gastado(a)

coronary ['kɒrənərɪ] *adj* coronario(a); **coronary thrombosis** trombosis coronaria

coronation [kɒrə'neɪʃən] *n* coronación *f*

corporal¹ ['kɔːpərəl] *adj* corporal; **corporal punishment** castigo *m* corporal

corporal² ['kɔːpərəl] *n* MIL cabo *m*

corporate ['kɔːpərɪt] *adj* corporativo(a)

corporation [kɔːpə'reɪʃən] *n* **a)** [business] sociedad anónima **b)** [of city] ayuntamiento *m*

corps [kɔː(r)] *(pl* **corps** [kɔːz]*) n* cuerpo *m*

corpse [kɔːps] *n* cadáver *m*

correct [kə'rekt] **1.** *vt* **a)** [mistake] corregir **b)** [child] reprender **2.** *adj* correcto(a), exacto(a); [behaviour] formal

correction [kə'rekʃən] *n* corrección *f*

correspond [kɒrɪ'spɒnd] *vi* **a)** corresponder; **to correspond to** equivaler a **b)** [by letter] escribirse

correspondence [kɒrɪ'spɒndəns] *n* correspondencia *f*; **correspondence course** curso *m* por correspondencia

corresponding [kɒrɪ'spɒndɪŋ] *adj* correspondiente

corridor ['kɒrɪdɔː(r)] *n* pasillo *m*

corrosion [kə'rəʊʒən] *n* corrosión *f*

corrugated ['kɒrʊɡeɪtɪd] *adj* **corrugated iron** hierro ondulado

corrupt [kə'rʌpt] **1.** *adj* **a)** [person] corrompido(a), corrupto(a); [actions] deshonesto(a) **b)** COMPUT corrupto(a) **2.** *vt & vi* corromper

corruption [kə'rʌpʃən] *n* corrupción *f*

Corsica ['kɔːsɪkə] *n* Córcega

cos [kɒs] *n Br* **cos (lettuce)** lechuga *f* romana

cosmetic [kɒz'metɪk] **1.** *n* cosmético *m* **2.** *adj* cosmético(a); **cosmetic surgery** cirugía plástica

cosmopolitan [kɒzmə'pɒlɪtən] *adj* cosmopolita

cost [kɒst] **1.** *n* [price] costo *m*, *Esp* coste *m*; **cost of living** costo *or Esp* coste de la vida; **administrative costs** gastos *mpl* de administración *or* de gestión; **to count the cost** considerar las desventajas; **at all costs** a toda costa **2.** (*pt & pp* **cost**) *vt & vi* costar, valer; **how much does it cost?** ¿cuánto cuesta?; **whatever it costs** cueste lo que cueste **3.** (*pt & pp* **costed**) *vt* COMM & IND calcular el costo *or Esp* coste de

Costa Rica [ˌkɒstə'riːkə] *n* Costa Rica *f*

Costa Rican [ˌkɒstə'riːkən] *adj & n* costarricense (*mf*)

costly ['kɒstlɪ] (*compar* **costlier**, *superl* **costliest**) *adj* costoso(a)

costume ['kɒstjuːm] *n* traje *m*; **(swimming) costume** traje *m* de baño, *Esp* bañador *m*, *RP* malla *f*; **costume jewellery** bisutería *f*

cosy ['kəʊzɪ] (*compar* **cosier**, *superl* **cosiest**) *adj* [atmosphere] acogedor(a); [bed] calentito(a); **it's cosy in here** aquí se está bien

cot [kɒt] *n* **a)** *Br* [for child] cuna *f* **b)** *US* [folding bed] catre *m*, cama *f* plegable

cottage ['kɒtɪdʒ] *n* casa *f* de campo; **cottage cheese** queso fresco; **cottage industry** industria casera; *Br* **cottage pie** *pastel de carne picada y puré de (Esp) patata o (Am) papa*

cotton ['kɒtən] *n* algodón *m*, *Am* cotón *m*; **a cotton shirt** una camisa de algodón; **cotton bud** bastoncillo *m* (de algodón); *US* **cotton candy** algodón dulce; *Br* **cotton wool** algodón (hidrófilo) ■ **cotton on** *vi Fam* enterarse, *Esp* coscarse, *RP* captar

couch [kaʊtʃ] *n* sofá *m*; [in surgery] camilla *f*

couchette [kuː'ʃet] *n* RAIL litera *f*

cough [kɒf] **1.** *vi* toser **2.** *n* tos *f*; **cough drop** pastilla *f* para la tos; **cough mixture** *or* **syrup** jarabe *m* para la tos ■ **cough up** *vt sep Fam* [money] poner, *Esp* apoquinar, *RP* garpar

could [kʊd] *v aux see* **can**

council ['kaʊnsəl] *n* [body] consejo *m*; *Br* **council estate** barrio *m* de viviendas sociales; *Br* **council house** vivienda *f* de protección oficial; **town council** consejo municipal, ayuntamiento *m*

councillor, *US* **councilor** ['kaʊnsələ(r)] *n* concejal *mf*

counselling ['kaʊnsəlɪŋ] *n* apoyo *m* psicológico, orientación *f* psicológica

count¹ [kaʊnt] **1.** *vt* **a)** contar **b)** *Fig* **to count oneself lucky** considerarse afortunado(a) **2.** *vi* contar; **that doesn't count** eso no vale; **to count to ten** contar hasta diez **3.** *n* **a)** cuenta *f*; [total] recuento *m* **b)** JUR cargo *m* ■ **count on** *vt insep* contar con

count² [kaʊnt] *n* [nobleman] conde *m*

countdown ['kaʊntdaʊn] *n* cuenta *f* atrás

counter¹ ['kaʊntə(r)] *n* **a)** [in shop] mostrador *m*; [in bank] ventanilla *f* **b)** [in board games] ficha *f*

counter² ['kaʊntə(r)] *n* contador *m*

counter³ ['kaʊntə(r)] **1.** *adv* **counter to** en contra de **2.** *vt* [attack] contestar a; [trend] contrarrestar **3.** *vi* contestar

counterattack ['kaʊntərətæk] *n* contraataque *m*

counter-clockwise ['kaʊntə'klɒkwaɪz] *adv US* en sentido opuesto al de las agujas del reloj

counterfeit ['kaʊntəfɪt] **1.** *adj* falsificado(a); **counterfeit coin** moneda falsa **2.** *n* falsificación *f* **3.** *vt* falsificar

counterpart ['kaʊntəpɑːt] *n* homólogo(a) *m,f*

counterproposal ['kaʊntəprəˌpəʊzl] *n* contrapropuesta *f*

countless ['kaʊntlɪs] *adj* innumerable, incontable

country ['kʌntrɪ] *n* a) [state] país *m*; **native country** patria *f* b) [rural area] campo *m*; **country dancing** baile *m* popular

countryman ['kʌntrɪmən] *n* a) [rural] hombre *m* del campo b) [compatriot] compatriota *m*

countryside ['kʌntrɪsaɪd] *n* [area] campo *m*; [scenery] paisaje *m*

county ['kaʊntɪ] *n* condado *m*

coup [kuː] (*pl* coups [kuːz]) *n* golpe *m*; **coup d'état** golpe de estado

couple ['kʌpl] **1.** *n* a) [of people] pareja *f*; **a married couple** un matrimonio b) [of things] par *m*; *Fam* **a couple of times** un par de veces **2.** *vt* [wagons] enganchar

coupon ['kuːpɒn] *n* a) cupón *m* b) *Br* FTBL quiniela *f*

courage ['kʌrɪdʒ] *n* coraje *m*, valentía *f*

courageous [kə'reɪdʒəs] *adj* valeroso(a), valiente

courgette [kʊə'ʒet] *n Br* calabacín *m*, *CSur* zapallito *m*, *Méx* calabacita *f*

courier ['kʊrɪə(r)] *n* a) [messenger] mensajero(a) *m,f* b) [guide] guía *mf* turístico(a)

course [kɔːs] *n* a) [of river] curso *m*; NAUT & AVIAT rumbo *m* b) *Fig* desarrollo *m*; **in the course of construction** en vías de construcción; **in the course of time** con el tiempo c) [series] ciclo *m*; **a course of treatment** un tratamiento d) SCH curso *m*; UNIV asignatura *f* e) [for golf] *Esp* campo *m*, *Am* cancha *f*; [for horse-racing] hipódromo *m* f) CULIN plato *m*

g) **of course** claro, por supuesto; **of course not!** ¡claro que no!

court [kɔːt] **1.** *n* a) JUR tribunal *m*; **court martial** consejo *m* de guerra; **court order** orden *f* judicial b) [royal] corte *f* c) SPORT pista *f*, cancha *f* **2.** *vt* [woman] hacer la corte a; *Fig* **to court danger** buscar el peligro; *Fig* **to court disaster** exponerse al desastre **3.** *vi* [couple] tener relaciones

courteous ['kɜːtɪəs] *adj* cortés

courtesy ['kɜːtɪsɪ] *n* a) cortesía *f*, educación *f*; **courtesy car** coche *m* de cortesía *or* de sustitución; **courtesy coach** autocar *m* de cortesía *or* de sustitución b) **by courtesy of** por cortesía de

courthouse ['kɔːthaʊs] *n US* palacio *m* de justicia

courtroom ['kɔːtruːm] *n* sala *f* de justicia

courtyard ['kɔːtjɑːd] *n* patio *m*

cousin ['kʌzən] *n* primo(a) *m,f*; **first cousin** primo(a) hermano(a)

cover ['kʌvə(r)] **1.** *vt* a) cubrir (**with** de); [furniture] revestir (**with** de); [with lid] tapar b) [hide] disimular c) [protect] abrigar d) [distance] recorrer e) PRESS investigar f) [deal with] abarcar g) [include] incluir **2.** *vi* **to cover for sb** sustituir a algn **3.** *n* a) cubierta *f*; [lid] tapa *f*; [on bed] manta *f*, *Am* frazada *f*, cobija *f*; [of chair etc] funda *f* b) [of book] tapa *f*; [of magazine] portada *f* c) [in restaurant] cubierto *m* d) [protection] abrigo *m*; **to take cover** abrigarse; **under cover** al abrigo; [indoors] bajo techo

■ **cover up 1.** *vt sep* a) cubrir b) [crime] encubrir **2.** *vi* a) [person] abrigarse b) **to cover up for sb** encubrir a algn

coverage ['kʌvərɪdʒ] *n* cobertura *f*

coveralls [ˈkʌvərɔːlz] npl US mono m (de trabajo), Am overol m

covering [ˈkʌvərɪŋ] **1.** n cubierta f, envoltura f **2.** adj [letter] explicatorio(a)

cover-up [ˈkʌvərʌp] n encubrimiento m

cow¹ [kaʊ] n vaca f; Pej [woman] arpía f, bruja f

cow² [kaʊ] vt intimidar

coward [ˈkaʊəd] n cobarde mf

cowboy [ˈkaʊbɔɪ] n vaquero m

cower [ˈkaʊə(r)] vi [with fear] encogerse

COZ MESSAGING (abbr of **because**) pq, xq

cozy [ˈkəʊzɪ] US adj = **cosy**

CPA [siːpiːˈeɪ] n US (abbr of **certified public accountant**) Esp censor(a) m, f jurado(a) de cuentas, Am contador(a) m, f público(a)

crab [kræb] n a) cangrejo m, Am jaiba f b) **crab apple** manzana f silvestre

crack [kræk] **1.** vt a) [cup] partir; [bone] fracturar; [nut] cascar; [safe] forzar b) [whip] hacer restallar c) Fig [problem] dar con la solución de; [joke] contar **2.** vi a) [glass] partirse; [wall] agrietarse b) [whip] restallar c) Fam **to get cracking on sth** ponerse a hacer algo **3.** n a) [in cup] raja f; [in wall, ground] grieta f b) [of whip] restallido m; [of gun] detonación f c) Fam [drug] crack m **4.** adj Fam de primera ■ **crack down on** vt insep atajar con mano dura ■ **crack up** vi Fam & Fig [go mad] desquiciarse; [with laughter] partirse de risa, Méx atacarse de risa

cracker [ˈkrækə(r)] n a) [biscuit] galleta salada b) [firework] petardo m

crackle [ˈkrækəl] vi crujir; [fire] crepitar

cradle [ˈkreɪdəl] n [baby's] cuna f

craft [krɑːft] n a) [occupation] oficio m; [art] arte m; [skill] destreza f b) [cunning] maña f c) NAUT embarcación f

craftsman [ˈkrɑːftsmən] n artesano m

craftsmanship [ˈkrɑːftsmənʃɪp] n arte f

crafty [ˈkrɑːftɪ] (compar **craftier**, superl **craftiest**) adj astuto(a)

cram [kræm] **1.** vt atiborrar; **crammed with** atestado(a) de **2.** vi Fam SCH matarse estudiando, Esp empollar, RP tragar; US SCH **cram school** colegio privado especializado en preparar a los alumnos para los exámenes

cramp¹ [kræmp] n MED calambre m; **cramps** retortijones mpl

cramp² [kræmp] vt [development etc] poner trabas a

cramped [kræmpt] adj atestado(a); [writing] apretado(a)

crane [kreɪn] **1.** n a) ZOOL grulla f común b) [device] grúa f **2.** vt estirar

crank [kræŋk] n a) TECH manivela f b) Fam [eccentric] tío raro

crapfest [ˈkræpfest] n v Fam porquería f de fiesta; **it was a crapfest** fue una porquería de fiesta

crapware [ˈkræpweə(r)] n v Fam COMPUT programas mpl basura

crash [kræʃ] **1.** vt a) **to crash one's car** tener un accidente con el coche or Am carro or CSur auto b) COMPUT colgar **2.** vi a) [car, plane] estrellarse; [collide] chocar; **to crash into** estrellarse contra b) COMM quebrar c) COMPUT fallar, colgarse **3.** n a) [noise] estrépito m b) [collision] choque m; **car/plane crash** accidente m de coche /avión; Fig **crash course** curso intensivo; **crash helmet** casco m protector c) COMM quiebra f d) COMPUT fallo m

crate [kreɪt] n caja f, cajón m (para embalaje)

crater [ˈkreɪtə(r)] n cráter m

craving [ˈkreɪvɪŋ] n ansia f; [in pregnancy] antojo m

crawl [krɔːl] **1.** *vi* [baby] gatear; [vehicle] avanzar lentamente; *Fig* **to crawl to sb** arrastrarse a los pies de algn **2.** *n* [swimming] crol *m*

crayon ['kreɪɒn] *n* cera *f*

craze [kreɪz] *n* manía *f*; [fashion] moda *f*; **it's the latest craze** es el último grito

crazy ['kreɪzi] *(compar* **crazier,** *superl* **craziest)** *adj Fam* loco(a), chalado(a)

creak [kriːk] *vi* [floor] crujir; [hinge] chirriar

cream [kriːm] **1.** *n* **a)** [of milk] *Esp* nata *f*, *Am* crema *f* (de leche); **cream-coloured** color crema; *Fig* **the cream** la flor y nata; **cream cheese** queso *m* blanco para untar **b)** [cosmetic] crema *f* **2.** *vt* **a)** [milk] desnatar **b)** CULIN batir; **creamed potatoes** puré *m* de patatas *or Am* papas

creamy ['kriːmɪ] *(compar* **creamier,** *superl* **creamiest)** *adj* cremoso(a)

crease [kriːs] **1.** *n* [wrinkle] arruga *f*; [fold] pliegue *m*; [on trousers] raya *f* **2.** *vt* [clothes] arrugar **3.** *vi* arrugarse

create [kriːˈeɪt] *vt* crear

creation [kriːˈeɪʃən] *n* creación *f*

creative [kriːˈeɪtɪv] *adj* [person] creativo(a)

creator [kriːˈeɪtə(r)] *n* creador(a) *m,f*

creature ['kriːtʃə(r)] *n* [animal] criatura *f*

crèche [kreɪʃ, kreʃ] *n Br* guardería *f* (infantil)

credentials [krɪˈdenʃəlz] *npl* credenciales *fpl*

credibility [kredɪˈbɪlɪtɪ] *n* credibilidad *f*

credible ['kredɪbəl] *adj* creíble

credit ['kredɪt] **1.** *n* **a)** COMM crédito *m*; **on credit** a crédito; **credit card** tarjeta *f* de crédito; **credit crunch** crisis *f* del crédito **b) to give credit to sb for sth** reconocer algo a algn **c)** [benefit] honor *m*; **to be a credit to** hacer honor a **d)** CIN & TV **credits** créditos *mpl* **2.** *vt* **a)** COMM abonar **b)** [believe] creer **c)** *Fig* atribuir; **he is credited with having** se le atribuye haber

creek [kriːk] *n* **a)** *Br* cala *f* **b)** *US, Austr* riachuelo *m*

creep [kriːp] **1.** *(pt & pp* **crept)** *vi* andar silenciosamente; [insect] arrastrarse; [plant] trepar; **to creep up on sb** sorprender a algn **2.** *n Fam* [unpleasant person] asqueroso(a) *m,f*; *Br* [obsequious person] pelota *mf*, *Am* arrastrado(a) *m,f*, *Méx* lambiscón(ona) *m,f*, *RP* chupamedias *mf inv*

creepy ['kriːpɪ] *(compar* **creepier,** *superl* **creepiest)** *adj Fam* espeluznante

creepy-crawly [-ˈkrɔːlɪ] *n Fam* bicho *m* *(que repta)*

cremation [krɪˈmeɪʃən] *n* incineración *f*, cremación *f*

crematorium [kreməˈtɔːrɪəm] *n* crematorio *m*

crept [krept] *pt & pp of* **creep**

crescent ['kresənt] **1.** *n* [shape] medialuna *f*; *Br* [street] calle *f* en medialuna **2.** *adj* creciente

crest [krest] *n* **a)** [of cock, wave] cresta *f*; [on helmet] penacho *m*; [of hill] cima *f* **b)** [heraldic] blasón *m*

Crete [kriːt] *n* Creta

crevice ['krevɪs] *n* grieta *f*, hendedura *f*

crew [kruː] *n* AVIAT & NAUT tripulación *f*; **crew cut** corte *m* al rape; **crew-neck sweater** jersey *m* con cuello redondo

crib [krɪb] **1.** *n* **a)** [manger] pesebre *m* **b)** [for baby] cuna *f* **c)** *Fam* [in exam] *Esp Ven* chuleta *f*, *Arg* machete *m*, *Col, Méx* acordeón *m* **2.** *vt Fam* **a)** [copy] copiar **b)** [steal] quitar

cricket¹ ['krɪkɪt] *n* [insect] grillo *m*

cricket² ['krɪkɪt] *n* SPORT cricket *m*

crime [kraɪm] *n* delincuencia *f*; [offence] delito *m*

criminal ['krɪmɪnəl] *adj & n* criminal *(mf)*; **criminal law** derecho *m* penal; **criminal record** antecedentes *mpl* penales

crimson ['krɪmzən] *adj & n* carmesí *(m)*

cringe [krɪndʒ] *vi* abatirse, encogerse

crinkle ['krɪŋkəl] *vt* fruncir, arrugar

cripple ['krɪpəl] **1.** n lisiado(a) m,f, mutilado(a) m,f **2.** vt mutilar, dejar cojo(a); Fig paralizar

crisis ['kraɪsɪs] (pl **crises** ['kraɪsi:z]) n crisis f inv

crisp [krɪsp] **1.** adj crujiente; [lettuce] fresco(a); [banknote] nuevo(a); [weather] frío(a) y seco(a); Fig [style] directo(a) **2.** n Br **crisps** patatas or Am papas fritas (de bolsa)

criterion [kraɪ'tɪərɪən] (pl **criteria** [kraɪ'tɪərɪə]) n criterio m

critic ['krɪtɪk] n ART & THEAT crítico(a) m,f

critical ['krɪtɪkəl] adj crítico(a)

critically ['krɪtɪkəlɪ] adv críticamente; **critically ill** gravemente enfermo(a)

criticism ['krɪtɪsɪzəm] n crítica f

criticize ['krɪtɪsaɪz] vt criticar

croak [krəʊk] vi [frog] croar; [raven] graznar; [person] hablar con voz ronca

Croatia [krəʊ'eɪʃə] n Croacia f

crockery ['krɒkərɪ] n loza f

crocodile ['krɒkədaɪl] n cocodrilo m

crocus ['krəʊkəs] n azafrán m

cromulent ['krɒmjʊlənt] adj Hum **it's a perfectly cromulent word** es una palabra perfectamente válida

crook [krʊk] **1.** n a) [of shepherd] cayado m b) Fam caco m **2.** vt [arm] doblar

crooked ['krʊkɪd] adj a) [stick, picture] torcido(a); [path] tortuoso(a) b) Fam [dishonest] deshonesto(a)

crop [krɒp] **1.** n a) cultivo m; [harvest] cosecha f; [of hair] mata f b) [whip] fusta f **2.** vt [hair] rapar; [grass] cortar
 ■ **crop up** vi Fam surgir, presentarse

cropped ['krɒpt] adj **cropped hair** pelo m corto; **cropped trousers** pantalones mpl pesqueros or piratas

cross [krɒs] **1.** n a) cruz f
b) [breeds] cruce m, Am cruza f
2. vt a) cruzar
b) REL **to cross oneself** hacer la señal de la cruz; Fam **cross my heart!** ¡te lo juro!
3. vi cruzar; [roads] cruzarse; **to cross over** cruzar

4. adj [annoyed] esp Esp enfadado(a), esp Am enojado(a)
 ■ **cross off**, **cross out** vt sep tachar, rayar

cross-country 1. ['krɒskʌntrɪ] adj **cross-country race** cros m **2.** [krɒs'kʌntrɪ] adv campo través

crossing ['krɒsɪŋ] n cruce m; US **crossing guard** persona encargada de ayudar a cruzar la calle a los colegiales; **pedestrian crossing** paso m de peatones; **sea crossing** travesía f

cross-platform adj multiplataforma (inv)

crossroads ['krɒsrəʊdz] n cruce m; Fig encrucijada f

cross-section ['krɒs'sekʃən] n sección f transversal

crosstown adj **crosstown street** calle f transversal

crossword ['krɒswɜːd] n **crossword (puzzle)** crucigrama m

crotch [krɒtʃ] n entrepierna f

crouch [kraʊtʃ] vi **to crouch (down)** agacharse

crow¹ [krəʊ] n cuervo m; Fig **as the crow flies** en línea recta; **crow's-feet** patas fpl de gallo

crow² [krəʊ] **1.** vi a) [cock] cantar; Fig **to crow over sth** jactarse de algo b) [baby] balbucir **2.** n [of cock] canto m

crowbar ['krəʊbɑː(r)] n palanca f

crowd [kraʊd] **1.** n muchedumbre f; Fam [gang] pandilla f, Méx bola f, RP barra f; **the crowd** el populacho **2.** vt [streets] llenar
3. vi apiñarse; **to crowd in/out** entrar / salir en tropel

crowded ['kraʊdɪd] adj atestado(a), lleno(a)

crown [kraʊn] **1.** n a) [of king] corona f; **the crown jewels** las joyas de la corona b) [of head] coronilla f **2.** vt coronar

crucial ['kruːʃəl] adj decisivo(a)

crucifix ['kruːsɪfɪks] n crucifijo m

crucify ['kruːsɪfaɪ] vt crucificar

crude [kru:d] *adj* **a)** [manners, style] tosco(a), grosero(a); [tool] primitivo(a) **b) crude oil** crudo *m*

cruel [kru:əl] *adj* cruel (**to** con)

cruelty ['kru:əltɪ] *n* crueldad *f* (**to** hacia)

cruise [kru:z] **1.** *vi* **a)** NAUT hacer un crucero **b)** AUTO viajar a velocidad constante; AVIAT viajar a velocidad de crucero **2.** *n* **a)** NAUT crucero *m* **b) cruise missile** misil teledirigido

crumb [krʌm] *n* miga *f*, migaja *f*

crumble ['krʌmbəl] **1.** *vt* desmigar **2.** *vi* [wall] desmoronarse; *Fig* [hopes] desvanecerse

crummy ['krʌmɪ] *(compar* **crummier**, *superl* **crummiest**) *adj Fam* cutre

crumpet ['krʌmpɪt] *n* torta pequeña que se come con mantequilla

crumple ['krʌmpəl] *vt* arrugar

crunch [krʌntʃ] **1.** *vt* [food] ronchar; [with feet] hacer crujir **2.** *n Fam* **when it comes to the crunch** a la hora de la verdad

crusade [kru:'seɪd] *n* cruzada *f*

crush [krʌʃ] **1.** *vt* aplastar; [wrinkle] arrugar; [grind] moler; [squeeze] exprimir **2.** *n* **a)** [of people] gentío *m* **b) orange crush** naranjada *f*

crust [krʌst] *n* corteza *f*

crutch [krʌtʃ] *n* MED muleta *f*; *Fig* apoyo *m*

cry [kraɪ] [*pt & pp* **cried**] **1.** *vi* **a)** gritar **b)** [weep] llorar **2.** *vt* gritar; *Fig* **to cry wolf** dar una falsa alarma **3.** *n* **a)** grito *m* **b)** [weep] llanto *m*
■ **cry off** *vi Fam* rajarse
■ **cry out** *vi* gritar; **to cry out for sth** pedir algo a gritos

crypt [krɪpt] *n* cripta *f*

crystal ['krɪstəl] *n* cristal *m*

CSR *n* (*abbr of* **Corporate Social Responsibility**) RSC *f* (*Responsabilidad Social Corporativa*)

CTR *n abbr of* **click-through rate**

CU@ MESSAGING *written abbr of* **see you at**

cub [kʌb] *n* **a)** [animal] cachorro *m* **b)** [junior scout] niño *m* explorador

Cuba ['kju:bə] *n* Cuba

Cuban ['kju:bən] *adj & n* cubano(a) *(m,f)*

cube [kju:b] **1.** *n* cubo *m*; [of sugar] terrón *m*; **cube root** raíz cúbica **2.** *vt* MATH elevar al cubo

cubic ['kju:bɪk] *adj* cúbico(a)

cubicle ['kju:bɪkəl] *n* cubículo *m*; [at swimming pool] caseta *f*

cuckoo ['kʊku:] **1.** *n* cuco *m*; **cuckoo clock** reloj *m* de cuco; *RP* reloj *m* cucú **2.** *adj Fam* [mad] **to be cuckoo** estar pirado(a), *Méx* estar zafado(a)

cucumber ['kju:kʌmbə(r)] *n* pepino *m*

cuddle ['kʌdəl] **1.** *vt* abrazar **2.** *vi* abrazarse

cue¹ [kju:] *n* THEAT pie *m*

cue² [kju:] *n* [in billiards] taco *m*; **cue ball** bola blanca

cuff¹ [kʌf] *n* [of sleeve] puño *m*; *US* [of trousers] dobladillo *m*; **cuff link** gemelo *m*; *Fig* **to do sth off the cuff** improvisar algo

cuff² [kʌf] **1.** *vt* [hit] dar un sopapo *or Am* una cachetada a **2.** *n* [blow] cachete *m*, cate *m*

CUL MESSAGING (*abbr of* **see you later**) hl, ta luego

cul-de-sac ['kʌldəsæk] *n* callejón *m* sin salida

CUL8R (*abbr of* **see you later**) MESSAGING hl, ta luego

culinary ['kʌlɪnərɪ] *adj* culinario(a)

culminate ['kʌlmɪneɪt] *vi* **to culminate in** terminar en

culprit ['kʌlprɪt] *n* culpable *mf*

cult [kʌlt] *n* culto *m*; **cult figure** ídolo *m*

cultivate ['kʌltɪveɪt] *vt* cultivar

cultivated ['kʌltɪveɪtɪd] *adj* [person] culto(a)

cultural ['kʌltʃərəl] *adj* cultural

culture ['kʌltʃə(r)] *n* cultura *f*

cultured ['kʌltʃəd] *adj* = **cultivated**

cumbersome ['kʌmbəsəm] *adj* [awkward] incómodo(a); [bulky] voluminoso(a)

cunning ['kʌnɪŋ] **1.** *adj* astuto(a) **2.** *n* astucia *f*

cup [kʌp] **1.** *n* taza *f*; SPORT copa *f*; **Cup Final** final *f* de copa; **cup tie** partido *m* de copa **2.** *vt* [hands] ahuecar

cupboard ['kʌbəd] *n* armario *m*; [on wall] alacena *f*

cupcake ['kʌpkeɪk] *n* [cake] ≈ magdalena *f*

curable ['kjʊərəbəl] *adj* curable

curate ['kjʊərɪt] *n* coadjutor *m*

curb [kɜːb] **1.** *n* **a)** [limit] freno *m* **b)** US [kerb] bordillo *m* (de la acera), *Chile* solera *f*, *Col*, *Perú* sardinel *m*, *CSur* cordón *m* (de la vereda), *Méx* borde *m* (de la banqueta) **2.** *vt* [horse] refrenar; *Fig* [public spending] contener

cure [kjʊə(r)] **1.** *vt* curar **2.** *n* [remedy] cura *f*, remedio *m*

curiosity [kjʊərɪˈɒsɪtɪ] *n* curiosidad *f*

curious ['kjʊərɪəs] *adj* **a)** [inquisitive] curioso(a) **b)** [odd] extraño(a)

curl [kɜːl] **1.** *vt* [hair] rizar; [lip] fruncir **2.** *vi* rizarse **3.** *n* [of hair] rizo *m*, *Andes*, *RP* rulo *m*; [of smoke] espiral *f*

■ **curl up** *vi* enroscarse

curler ['kɜːlə(r)] *n* [for hair] rulo *m*, *Chile* tubo *m*, *RP* rulero *m*, *Ven* rollo *m*

curly ['kɜːlɪ] *(compar* **curlier**, *superl* **curliest)** *adj* rizado(a), *Chile*, *Col* crespo(a), *Méx* quebrado(a), *RP* enrulado(a)

currant ['kʌrənt] *n* pasa *f* (de Corinto)

currency ['kʌrənsɪ] *n* **a)** moneda *f*; **foreign currency** divisa *f* **b)** **to gain currency** cobrar fuerza

current ['kʌrənt] **1.** *adj* **a)** [opinion] general; [word] en uso; [year] en curso; *Br* **current account** cuenta *f* corriente; **current affairs** actualidad *f* (política); FIN **current assets** activo *m* disponible **b)** **the current issue** [of magazine, newspaper] el último número **2.** *n* corriente *f*

currently ['kʌrəntlɪ] *adv* actualmente

curriculum [kəˈrɪkjʊləm] *(pl* **curricula** [kəˈrɪkjʊlə]*) n* plan *m* de estudios; *esp Br* **curriculum vitae** currículum *m* (vitae)

curry¹ ['kʌrɪ] *n* curry *m*; **curry powder** curry *m*; **chicken curry** pollo *m* al curry

curry² ['kʌrɪ] *vt* **to curry favour with** congraciarse con

curse [kɜːs] **1.** *n* maldición *f*; [oath] palabrota *f*; *Figazote m*; *US* **curse word** juramento *m* **2.** *vt* maldecir **3.** *vi* blasfemar

cursor ['kɜːsə(r)] *n* cursor *m*

cursory ['kɜːsərɪ] *adj* rápido(a)

curt [kɜːt] *adj* brusco(a), seco(a)

curtail [kɜːˈteɪl] *vt* [expenses] reducir; [text] acortar

curtain ['kɜːtən] *n* cortina *f*; THEAT telón *m*; *Fig* velo *m*; **shower curtain** cortina *f* de ducha

curts(e)y ['kɜːtsɪ] *(pl* **curtseys** *or* **curtsies**, *pt & pp* **curtseyed** *or* **curtsied)** **1.** *n* reverencia *f* **2.** *vi* hacer una reverencia (**to** a)

curve [kɜːv] **1.** *n* curva *f*; *US* SCH **curve grading** *evaluación por campana de Gauss* **2.** *vt* encorvar **3.** *vi* torcerse, describir una curva

cushion ['kʊʃən] **1.** *n* cojín *m*; [large] almohadón *m*; [of billiard table] banda *f* **2.** *vt* *Fig* amortiguar; [person] proteger

custard ['kʌstəd] *n* natillas *fpl*; **custard powder** polvos *mpl* para hacer natillas

custody ['kʌstədɪ] *n* custodia *f*; **to take into custody** detener

custom ['kʌstəm] *n* **a)** [habit] costumbre *f* **b)** COMM clientela *f*

customary ['kʌstəmərɪ] *adj* habitual

custom-designed *adj* **custom-designed vacations** vacaciones *fpl* a medida

customer ['kʌstəmə(r)] *n* cliente *mf*

customs ['kʌstəmz] *n sing or pl* aduana *f*; **customs duty** derechos *mpl* de aduana; **customs officer** agente *mf* de aduana

cut [kʌt] *(pt & pp* **cut)** **1.** *n* **a)** corte *m*; [in skin] cortadura *f*; [wound] herida *f*; [with knife] cuchillada *f* **b)** [of meat] clase *f* de carne

c) [reduction] reducción f
2. vt **a)** cortar; [stone] tallar; [record] grabar; **to cut one's finger** cortarse el dedo; Fig **to cut a long story short** en resumidas cuentas; Fig **to cut corners** recortar presupuestos
b) [reduce] reducir
c) [divide up] dividir (**into** en)
3. vi [of knife, scissors] cortar

■ **cut back 1.** vt sep **a)** [prune] podar **b)** [reduce] reducir, disminuir, recortar **2.** vi **to cut back on** reducir, disminuir, recortar

■ **cut down 1.** vt sep **a)** [chop down] cortar; [tree] talar **b)** [reduce] reducir, disminuir, recortar **2.** vt insep **to cut down on** reducir; **to cut down on smoking/eating/spending** fumar / comer /gastar menos

■ **cut in** vi [driver] adelantar bruscamente

■ **cut off** vt sep [water etc] cortar; [place] aislar; [heir] excluir; TEL **I've been cut off** me han cortado (la comunicación)

■ **cut out 1.** vt sep **a)** [from newspaper] recortar; **to be cut out for sth** [person] estar hecho(a) para algo **b)** [delete] suprimir **2.** vi [engine] calarse

■ **cut up** vt sep cortar en pedazos

cutback [ˈkʌtbæk] n reducción f (**in** de)
cute [kjuːt] adj mono(a), lindo(a); US Fam & Pej listillo(a)
cutlery [ˈkʌtlərɪ] n cubiertos mpl
cutting [ˈkʌtɪŋ] **1.** n corte m, cortadura f; [from newspaper] recorte m; RAIL tajo m; US **cutting board** tabla f de cortar **2.** adj cortante; [remark] mordaz

cutting-edge adj [technology] punta (inv)
CV, cv [siːˈviː] n (abbr of **curriculum vitae**) CV m
CYA MESSAGING (abbr of **see you around** or **see ya**) hl, ta luego
cyberbully [ˈsaɪb(r)ˌbʊlɪ] n INTERNET ciberacosador(a) m,f
cyberbullying [ˈsaɪbəbʊlɪɪŋ] n INTERNET ciberacoso m
cybercafe [ˈsaɪbəkæfeɪ] n COMPUT cibercafé m
cybershopping [ˈsaɪbəʃɒpɪŋ] n INTERNET compras fpl por internet
cyberspace [ˈsaɪbəspeɪs] n COMPUT ciberespacio m
cyberstalk [ˈsaɪbə(r)ˌstɔːk] vt INTERNET ciberacosar
cycle [ˈsaɪkəl] **1.** n **a)** ciclo m **b)** [bicycle] bicicleta f; [motorcycle] moto f **2.** vi ir en bicicleta
cycling [ˈsaɪklɪŋ] n ciclismo m
cyclist [ˈsaɪklɪst] n ciclista mf
cylinder [ˈsɪlɪndə(r)] n **a)** cilindro m **b)** [for gas] bombona f
cymbal [ˈsɪmbəl] n címbalo m, platillo m
cynical [ˈsɪnɪkəl] adj **a)** [sceptical] descreído(a), suspicaz **b)** [unscrupulous] desaprensivo(a), sin escrúpulos
Cyprus [ˈsaɪprəs] n Chipre
cyst [sɪst] n quiste m
Czech [tʃek] **1.** adj checo(a); **the Czech Republic** la República Checa **2.** n **a)** [person] checo(a) m,f **b)** [language] checo m

D

D, d [di:] *n* a) [the letter] D, d *f* b) MUS D re *m*

dab [dæb] **1.** *n* [small quantity] toque *m* **2.** *vt* a) [apply] aplicar b) [touch lightly] tocar ligeramente

dabble ['dæbəl] *vi* to dabble in politics meterse en política

dad [dæd], **daddy** ['dædɪ] *n Fam* papá *m*

dadager ['dædədʒə(r)] *n US Fam* padre *m* y mánager

daffodil ['dæfədɪl] *n* narciso *m*

daft [dɑːft] *adj Br Fam* [persona, idea] tonto(a), *Am* sonso(a), *Am* zonzo(a)

dagger ['dægə(r)] *n* puñal *m*, daga *f*

daily ['deɪlɪ] **1.** *adj* diario(a), cotidiano(a)
2. *adv* diariamente; **three times daily** tres veces al día
3. *n* a) [newspaper] diario *m*
b) *Br Fam* [cleaning lady] asistenta *f*

dairy ['deərɪ] *n* [on farm] vaquería *f*; [shop] lechería *f*; **dairy farming** industria lechera; **dairy produce** productos lácteos

daisy ['deɪzɪ] *n* margarita *f*

dam [dæm] **1.** *n* [barrier] dique *m*; [lake] presa *f* **2.** *vt* [water] represar ▪ **dam up** *vt sep Fig* [emotion] contener

damage ['dæmɪdʒ] **1.** *n* a) [to health, reputation] perjuicio *m*; [to relationship] deterioro *m* b) JUR **damages** daños *mpl* y perjuicios *mpl* **2.** *vt* [harm] dañar, hacer daño a; [spoil] estropear; [undermine] perjudicar

damaging ['dæmɪdʒɪŋ] *adj* perjudicial

damn [dæm] **1.** *vt* condenar; **well, I'll be damned!** ¡vaya por Dios!
2. *interj Fam* **damn (it)!** ¡maldito(a) sea!
3. *n Fam* **I don't give a damn** me importa un bledo
4. *adj Fam* maldito(a)
5. *adv Fam* muy, sumamente

damned [dæmd] *adj & adv* = **damn**

damp [dæmp] **1.** *adj* húmedo(a); [wet] mojado(a) **2.** *n* humedad *f* **3.** *vt* a) [for ironing] humedecer b) to damp (down) [fire] sofocar; *Fig* [violence] frenar

dampen ['dæmpən] *vt* humedecer; *Fig* frenar

dance [dɑːns] **1.** *n* baile *m*; [classical, tribal] danza *f*; **dance band** orquesta *f* de baile; **dance floor** pista *f* de baile; **dance hall** salón *m* de baile **2.** *vi & vt* bailar

dancesport ['dɑːnspɔːt] *n* baile *m* deportivo, baile *m* de competición

dancing ['dɑːnsɪŋ] *n* baile *m*; **pole dancing** baile *m* en barra

dandelion ['dændɪlaɪən] *n* diente *m* de león

dandruff ['dændrəf] *n* caspa *f*

Dane [deɪn] *n* danés(esa) *m,f*

danger ['deɪndʒə(r)] *n* a) [risk] riesgo *m*; [of war etc] amenaza *f* b) [peril] peligro *m*; **danger** [sign] peligro; **out of danger** fuera de peligro

dangerous ['deɪndʒərəs] *adj* peligroso(a); [risky] arriesgado(a); [harmful] nocivo(a); [illness] grave

dangle ['dæŋgəl] **1.** *vi* [hang] colgar; [swing] balancearse **2.** *vt* [legs] colgar; [bait] dejar colgado(a); [swing] balancear en el aire

Danish ['deɪnɪʃ] **1.** *adj* danés(esa); **Danish pastry** pastel *m* de hojaldre **2.** *n* [language] danés *m*

dare [deə(r)] **1.** *vi* atreverse, osar; **he doesn't dare be late** no se atreve a llegar tarde ; **how dare you!** ¿cómo te atreves? ; *esp Br* **I dare say** quizás ; *Iron* ya (lo creo) **2.** *vt* [challenge] desafiar **3.** *n* desafío *m*

daring ['deərɪŋ] **1.** *adj* a) [bold] audaz, osado(a) b) [clothes] atrevido(a) **2.** *n* atrevimiento *m*, osadía *f*

dark [dɑːk] **1.** *adj* a) [room, colour] oscuro(a) ; [hair, complexion] moreno(a) ; [eyes, future] negro(a) b) *Fig* [gloomy] triste c) *Fig* [sinister] siniestro(a) **2.** *n* a) [darkness] oscuridad *f*, tinieblas *fpl* ; **after dark** después del anochecer b) *Fig* **to be in the dark (about sth)** *Esp* estar in albis (sobre algo), *Am* no tener ni idea (sobre algo)

darken ['dɑːkən] **1.** *vt* [sky] oscurecer ; [colour] hacer más oscuro(a) **2.** *vi* oscurecerse ; [sky] nublarse ; *Fig* [face] ensombrecerse

darkness ['dɑːknɪs] *n* oscuridad *f*, tinieblas *fpl*

darling ['dɑːlɪŋ] *adj* & *n* querido(a) (*m,f*)

darn [dɑːn] **1.** *vt* zurcir **2.** *n* zurcido *m*

dart [dɑːt] **1.** *n* a) [missile] dardo *m* b) **darts** (*sing*) dardos *mpl* **2.** *vi* [fly about] revolotear ; **to dart in / out** entrar / salir corriendo

dash [dæʃ] **1.** *n* a) [rush] carrera *f* b) *esp US* [race] sprint *m* c) [small amount] poquito *m* ; [of salt] pizca *f* ; [of liquid] gota *f* d) TYP guión largo ; [hyphen] guión **2.** *vt* [throw] arrojar **3.** *vi* [rush] correr ; **to dash around** correr de un lado a otro ; **to dash out** salir corriendo
■ **dash off** *vi* salir corriendo

dashboard ['dæʃbɔːd] *n* tablero *m* de mandos, *Esp* salpicadero *m*

data ['deɪtə, 'dɑːtə] *npl* datos *mpl* ; **data bank** *or* **base** banco *m* de datos ; TEL **data cap** límite *m* de consumo de datos (*en móvil*) ; **data processing** [act]

proceso *m* de datos ; [science] informática *f* ; **data protection act** ley *f* de informática

date[1] [deɪt] **1.** *n* a) fecha *f* ; **what's the date today?** ¿a qué (fecha) estamos hoy?, ¿qué fecha es hoy?, *Am* ¿a cómo estamos? ; **out of date** [ideas] anticuado(a) ; [expression] desusado(a) ; [invalid] caducado(a) ; **to date** hasta la fecha ; *Fig* **to be up to date** estar al día ; **date of birth** fecha de nacimiento b) [social event] compromiso *m* ; *Fam* [with girl, boy] cita *f* c) *US Fam* [person dated] ligue *m* **2.** *vt* [ruins] datar **3.** *vi* [ideas] quedar anticuado(a)
■ **date back to**, **date from** *vt insep* remontar a, datar de

date[2] [deɪt] *n* [fruit] dátil *m* ; **date palm** datilera *f*

datebook ['deɪtbʊk] *n US* agenda *f*

dated ['deɪtɪd] *adj* [idea] anticuado(a) ; [fashion] pasado(a) de moda ; [expression] desusado(a)

daughter ['dɔːtə(r)] *n* hija *f*

daughter-in-law ['dɔːtərɪnlɔː] *n* nuera *f*, hija política

dawdle ['dɔːdəl] *vi Fam* [walk slowly] andar despacio ; [waste time] perder el tiempo

dawn [dɔːn] **1.** *n* alba *f*, amanecer *m* **2.** *vi* a) [day] amanecer b) *Fig* [age, hope] comenzar c) *Fig* **suddenly it dawned on him that ...** de repente cayó en la cuenta de que ...

day [deɪ] *n* a) día *m* ; **one of these days** un día de éstos ; **(on) the next** *or* **following day** el or al día siguiente ; **the day after tomorrow** pasado mañana ; **the day before yesterday** anteayer ; **the other day** el otro día b) [daylight] día *m* ; **by day** de día c) [era] **in those days** en aquellos tiempos ; **these days** hoy (en) día

daybreak ['deɪbreɪk] *n* amanecer *m*

day-care *adj* a) [for elderly, disabled] de asistencia de día b) [for children] de guardería

daydream ['deɪdri:m] **1.** n ensueño m; [vain hope] fantasía f **2.** vi soñar despierto(a); [hope vainly] hacerse ilusiones

daylight ['deɪlaɪt] n luz f del día; **in broad daylight** en pleno día; **to scare the (living) daylights out of sb** pegarle a algn un susto de muerte

daypack ['deɪpæk] n mochila m pequeña

days adv de día

daytime ['deɪtaɪm] n día m; **in the daytime** de día

daze [deɪz] n aturdimiento m; **in a daze** aturdido(a)

dazzle ['dæzəl] vt deslumbrar

dead [ded] **1.** adj a) muerto(a); **to be dead** estar muerto(a); **dead man** muerto m
b) [machine] averiado(a); [phone] cortado(a)
c) [numb] entumecido(a); [limb] adormecido(a); **my leg's gone dead** se me ha dormido la pierna
d) [silence, secrecy] total; **dead end** callejón m sin salida
2. adv [very] muy; Fam **you're dead right** tienes toda la razón; **to stop dead** pararse en seco
3. n **the dead** pl los muertos

deadline ['dedlaɪn] n [date] fecha f tope; [time] hora f tope; **we have to meet the deadline** tenemos que hacerlo dentro del plazo

deadlock ['dedlɒk] n punto muerto

deadly ['dedlɪ] (compar **deadlier**, superl **deadliest**) **1.** adj mortal; [weapon] mortífero(a); [aim] certero(a) **2.** adv [extremely] terriblemente, sumamente

deaf [def] **1.** adj sordo(a); Fig **to turn a deaf ear** hacerse el sordo; **deaf mute** sordomudo(a) m,f **2.** npl **the deaf** los sordos; **the deaf and dumb** los sordomudos

deafen ['defən] vt ensordecer

deal [di:l] **1.** n a) COMM & POL trato m, pacto m; **business deal** negocio m, transacción f; **to do a deal with sb**

[transaction] cerrar un trato con algn; [agreement] pactar algo con algn; Fam **it's a deal!** ¡trato hecho! **b)** [amount] cantidad f; **a good deal of criticism** muchas críticas; **a good deal slower** mucho más despacio **c)** CARDS reparto m. (pt & pp **dealt**) vt a) CARDS dar (**to** a) **b) to deal sb a blow** asestarle un golpe a algn ■ **deal in** vt insep [goods] comerciar en, tratar en; [drugs] traficar con ■ **deal out** vt sep repartir ■ **deal with** vt insep [firm, person] tratar con; [subject, problem] abordar, ocuparse de; [in book etc] tratar de

dealer ['di:lə(r)] n a) COMM [in goods] comerciante mf; [in drugs] traficante mf **b)** CARDS repartidor(a) m,f

dealings ['di:lɪŋz] npl a) [relations] trato m **b)** COMM negocios mpl

dealt [delt] pt & pp of **deal**

dean ['di:n] n a) decano(a) m,f **b)** US administrador encargado de aconsejar y disciplinar a los alumnos

dear [dɪə(r)] **1.** adj a) [loved] querido(a); **Dear Andrew** [in letter] Querido Andrew; Formal **Dear Madam** Estimada señora; Formal **Dear Sir(s)** Muy señor(es) mío(s) **b)** [expensive] caro(a) **2.** n querido(a) m,f; **my dear** mi vida **3.** interj **oh dear!, dear me!** [surprise] ¡caramba!; [disappointment] ¡qué pena!

dearly ['dɪəlɪ] adv muchísimo; Fig **he paid dearly for his mistake** su error le costó caro

death [deθ] n muerte f; Formal fallecimiento m; Fam **to be bored to death** aburrirse como una ostra; Fam **to be scared to death** estar muerto(a) de miedo; Fam & Fig **to be sick to death of** estar hasta la coronilla de; **death certificate** certificado m de defunción; **death penalty, death sentence** pena f de muerte

debatable [dɪ'beɪtəbəl] adj discutible

debate [dɪ'beɪt] **1.** n debate m; **a heated debate** una discusión acalorada **2.** vt a) [discuss] discutir **b)** [wonder about] dar vueltas a **3.** vi discutir

debit ['debɪt] **1.** n débito m; **debit balance** saldo negativo **2.** vt **debit Mr Jones with £20** cargar la suma de 20 libras en la cuenta del Sr. Jones

debris ['debri:, 'deɪbri:] n sing escombros mpl

debt [det] n deuda f; **to be deeply in debt** estar cargado(a) de deudas; Fig **to be in sb's debt** estar en deuda con algn

debtor ['detə(r)] n deudor(a) m,f

debug [,di:'bʌg] vt COMPUT [program] eliminar fallos, depurar

debut ['debju:, 'deɪbju:] n debut m; **to make one's debut** debutar

decade [de'keɪd, 'dekeɪd] n decenio m, década f

decadent ['dekədənt] adj decadente

decaffeinated [dɪ'kæfɪneɪtɪd] adj descafeinado(a)

decay [dɪ'keɪ] **1.** n [of food, body] descomposición f; [of teeth] caries f inv; [of buildings] desmoronamiento m; Fig decadencia f **2.** vi descomponerse; [teeth] cariarse; [building] deteriorarse; Fig corromperse

deceased [dɪ'si:st] adj Formal difunto(a), fallecido(a)

deceit [dɪ'si:t] n a) [dishonesty] falta f de honradez, falsedad f b) [trick] engaño m, mentira f

deceitful [dɪ'si:tfʊl] adj falso(a)

deceive [dɪ'si:v] vt [mislead] engañar; [lie to] mentir

December [dɪ'sembə(r)] n diciembre m

decency ['di:sənsɪ] n decencia f; [modesty] pudor m; [morality] moralidad f

decent ['di:sənt] adj decente; [person] honrado(a); Fam [kind] simpático(a)

deception [dɪ'sepʃən] n engaño m

deceptive [dɪ'septɪv] adj engañoso(a)

decide [dɪ'saɪd] **1.** vt a) decidir; **to decide to do sth** decidir hacer algo b) [matter, question] resolver, determinar **2.** vi [reach decision] decidirse; **to decide against sth** decidirse en contra de algo ■ **decide on** vt insep [choose] optar por

decimal ['desɪməl] **1.** adj decimal; **decimal point** coma f (de fracción decimal) **2.** n decimal m

decipher [dɪ'saɪfə(r)] vt descifrar

decision [dɪ'sɪʒən] n a) decisión f; JUR fallo m; **to come to a decision** llegar a una decisión; **to make a decision** tomar una decisión b) [resolution] resolución f

decisive [dɪ'saɪsɪv] adj a) [resolute] decidido(a), resuelto(a) b) [conclusive] decisivo(a)

deck [dek] **1.** n a) [of ship] cubierta f; **deck chair** tumbona f b) [of bus] piso m; **top deck** piso de arriba c) esp US [of cards] baraja f d) [of record player] plato m **2.** vt **to deck out** adornar

decking ['dekɪŋ] n terraza f entarimada or de madera

declaration [deklə'reɪʃən] n declaración f

declare [dɪ'kleə(r)] vt declarar; [winner, innocence] proclamar; [decision] manifestar

decline [dɪ'klaɪn] **1.** n a) [decrease] disminución f
b) [deterioration] deterioro m; [of health] empeoramiento m; **to fall into decline** empezar a decaer
2. vi a) [decrease] disminuir; [amount] bajar; [business] decaer
b) [deteriorate] deteriorarse; [health] empeorar
c) [refuse] negarse
3. vt a) [refuse] rechazar
b) LING declinar

décor ['deɪkɔ:(r)] n decoración f; THEAT decorado m

decorate ['dekəreɪt] vt a) [adorn] decorar, adornar (**with** con) b) [paint] pintar; [wallpaper] empapelar c) [honour] condecorar

decoration [dekə'reɪʃən] n a) [decor] decoración f; **Christmas decorations** adornos navideños b) [medal] condecoración f

decorative ['dekərətɪv] adj decorativo(a)

decrease 1. ['diːkriːs] *n* disminución *f*; [in speed, size, price] reducción *f* **2.** [dɪ'kriːs] *vi* disminuir; [strength] menguar; [price, temperature] bajar; [speed, size] reducir **3.** [dɪ'kriːs] *vt* disminuir, reducir; [price, temperature] bajar

decree [dɪ'kriː] **1.** *n* **a)** POL & REL decreto *m* **b)** *esp US* JUR sentencia *f*; **decree absolute** sentencia definitiva de divorcio; **decree nisi** sentencia provisional de divorcio **2.** *vt* POL & REL decretar, pronunciar

decrepit [dɪ'krepɪt] *adj* decrépito(a)

dedicate ['dedɪkeɪt] *vt* consagrar, dedicar

dedicated ['dedɪkeɪtɪd] *adj* **a)** ardiente; **dedicated to** entregado(a) a **b)** COMPUT dedicado(a), especializado(a)

dedication [dedɪ'keɪʃən] *n* [act] dedicación *f*; [commitment] entrega *f*; [in book] dedicatoria *f*

deduce [dɪ'djuːs] *vt* deducir (**from** de)

deduct [dɪ'dʌkt] *vt* descontar (**from** de)

deduction [dɪ'dʌkʃən] *n* **a)** [conclusion] conclusión *f* **b)** [subtraction] descuento *m*

deed [diːd] *n* **a)** [act] acto *m*; [feat] hazaña *f* **b)** JUR escritura *f*; **title deeds** título *m* de propiedad

deep [diːp] **1.** *adj* **a)** profundo(a); [breath, sigh] hondo(a); **it's 10 m deep** tiene 10 m de profundidad **b)** [voice] grave **c)** [colour] oscuro(a) **d)** [serious] grave **2.** *adv* **to be deep in thought** estar absorto(a); **to look deep into sb's eyes** penetrar a algn con la mirada

deepen ['diːpən] **1.** *vt* [well] profundizar, ahondar; *Fig* [knowledge] aumentar **2.** *vi* [river etc] hacerse más hondo *or* profundo; *Fig* [knowledge] aumentar; [colour, emotion] intensificarse; [sound, voice] hacerse más grave

deep-freeze [diːp'friːz] **1.** *n* congelador *m* **2.** *vt* congelar

deep-fry *vt* freír *(con aceite abundante)*

deeply ['diːplɪ] *adv* profundamente; [breathe] hondo; **to be deeply in debt** estar cargado(a) de deudas

deer [dɪə(r)] *n inv* ciervo *m*

deface [dɪ'feɪs] *vt* [book, poster] garabatear

default [dɪ'fɔːlt] **1.** *vi* **a)** [not act] faltar a sus compromisos **b)** JUR estar en rebeldía **c)** [not pay] suspender pagos **2.** *n* **a)** [failure to act] omisión *f* **b)** [failure to pay] incumplimiento *m* de pago **c)** JUR rebeldía *f*; **in default of** a falta de; **to win by default** ganar por incomparecencia del adversario **d)** COMPUT valor *m* predeterminado

defeat [dɪ'fiːt] **1.** *vt* **a)** derrotar, vencer; [motion] rechazar **b)** *Fig* frustrar **2.** *n* **a)** [of army, team] derrota *f*; [of motion] rechazo *m* **b)** *Fig* fracaso *m*

defect 1. ['diːfekt] *n* defecto *m*; [flaw] desperfecto *m* **2.** [dɪ'fekt] *vi* desertar (**from** de); [from country] huir

defective [dɪ'fektɪv] *adj* [faulty] defectuoso(a); [flawed] con desperfectos; [lacking] incompleto(a)

defence [dɪ'fens] *n* **a)** [gen & POL] defensa *f*; **to come to sb's defence** salir en defensa de algn **b)** (*usu sing*) JUR defensa *f* **c)** [US 'diːfens] SPORT **the defence** la defensa

defend [dɪ'fend] *vt* defender

defendant [dɪ'fendənt] *n* JUR acusado(a) *m,f*

defender [dɪ'fendə(r)] *n* defensor(a) *m,f*; SPORT defensa *mf*

defense [dɪ'fens, 'diːfens] *US n* = **defence**

defensive [dɪ'fensɪv] **1.** *adj* defensivo(a) **2.** *n* **to be on the defensive** estar a la defensiva

defer¹ [dɪ'fɜː(r)] *vt* aplazar, retrasar

defer² [dɪ'fɜː(r)] *vi* **to defer to** deferir a

defiance [dɪ'faɪəns] *n* **a)** [challenge] desafío *m*; **in defiance of** a despecho de **b)** [resistance] resistencia *f*

defiant [dɪ'faɪənt] *adj* [challenging] desafiante; [bold] insolente

deliver

deficiency [dɪ'fɪʃənsɪ] n a) [lack] falta f, carencia f b) [shortcoming] defecto m

deficient [dɪ'fɪʃənt] adj deficiente; **to be deficient in sth** carecer de algo

deficit ['defɪsɪt] n déficit m

define [dɪ'faɪn] vt definir; [duties, powers] delimitar

definite ['defɪnɪt] adj a) [clear] claro(a); [progress] notable b) [date, place] determinado(a); **is it definite?** ¿es seguro?

definitely ['defɪnɪtlɪ] **1.** adv sin duda; **he was definitely drunk** no cabe duda de que estaba borracho **2.** interj ¡desde luego!

definition [defɪ'nɪʃən] n definición f; **by definition** por definición

deflect [dɪ'flekt] vt desviar

deformed [dɪ'fɔːmd] adj deforme

defragment [ˌdiːfræg'ment] vt COMPUT desfragmentar

defraud [dɪ'frɔːd] vt estafar

defriend [diː'frend] vt Fam INTERNET [in social network] borrar (de los amigos)

defrost [diː'frɒst] vt a) [freezer, food] descongelar b) US [windscreen] desempañar

defy [dɪ'faɪ] vt a) [person] desafiar; [law, order] contravenir b) [challenge] retar, desafiar

degenerate 1. [dɪ'dʒenəreɪt] vi degenerar (**into** en) **2.** [dɪ'dʒenərɪt] adj & n degenerado(a) (m,f)

degrading [dɪ'greɪdɪŋ] adj degradante

degree [dɪ'griː] n a) grado m; **to some degree** hasta cierto punto b) [stage] etapa f; **by degrees** poco a poco c) [qualification] título m; [doctorate] doctorado m; Br **bachelor's degree** ≈ grado m; **to have a degree in science** ser licenciado(a) en ciencias

dehydrated [diːhaɪ'dreɪtɪd] adj [person] deshidratado(a); [vegetables] seco(a)

dejected [dɪ'dʒektɪd] adj desalentado(a), abatido(a)

delay [dɪ'leɪ] **1.** vt a) [flight, train] retrasar; [person] entretener; **delayed action** acción retardada
b) [postpone] aplazar
2. vi **don't delay** no lo deje para más tarde
3. n retraso m, Am demora f

delegate 1. ['delɪgɪt] n delegado(a) m,f **2.** ['delɪgeɪt] vt delegar (**to** en); **to delegate sb to do sth** encargar a algn que haga algo

delegation [delɪ'geɪʃən] n delegación f

delete [dɪ'liːt] vt tachar, suprimir

deliberate 1. [dɪ'lɪbərɪt] adj [intentional] deliberado(a), intencionado(a); [studied] premeditado(a); [careful] prudente; [unhurried] pausado(a) **2.** [dɪ'lɪbəreɪt] vt deliberar **3.** vi deliberar (**on** or **about** sobre)

deliberately [dɪ'lɪbərɪtlɪ] adv [intentionally] a propósito; [unhurriedly] pausadamente

delicacy ['delɪkəsɪ] n a) delicadeza f b) [food] manjar m (exquisito)

delicate ['delɪkɪt] adj delicado(a); [handiwork] fino(a); [instrument] sensible; [flavour] sutil

delicatessen [delɪkə'tesən] n [shop] tienda de ultramarinos or (Am) enlatados de calidad

delicious [dɪ'lɪʃəs] adj delicioso(a)

delight [dɪ'laɪt] **1.** n a) [pleasure] placer m; **he took delight in it** le encantó b) [source of pleasure] encanto m, delicia f **2.** vt encantar

delighted [dɪ'laɪtɪd] adj encantado(a); [smile] de alegría; **I'm delighted to see you** me alegro mucho de verte

delightful [dɪ'laɪtfʊl] adj encantador(a); [view, person] muy agradable; [meal, weather] delicioso(a)

delinquent [dɪ'lɪŋkwənt] adj & n delincuente (mf)

delirious [dɪ'lɪrɪəs] adj delirante

deliver [dɪ'lɪvə(r)] vt a) [goods] repartir, entregar; [message] dar; [order]

despachar **b)** [blow] asestar ; [speech, verdict] pronunciar **c)** MED ayudar en el nacimiento de **d)** Formal [rescue] liberar

delivery [dɪˈlɪvərɪ] n **a)** [of goods] reparto m, entrega f; **delivery vehicle** vehículo m de reparto **b)** [of speech] declamación f **c)** [of baby] parto m

delude [dɪˈluːd] vt engañar ; **don't delude yourself** no te hagas ilusiones

delusion [dɪˈluːʒən] n **a)** [state, act] engaño m **b)** [false belief] ilusión f (vana) ; **delusions of grandeur** delirios mpl de grandeza

de luxe [dəˈlʌks, dəˈluks] adj de lujo (inv)

demand [dɪˈmɑːnd] **1.** n **a)** solicitud f; [for pay rise, rights] reclamación f; [need] necesidad f; **on demand** a petición **b)** [claim] exigencia f; **to be in demand** ser solicitado(a) **c)** ECON demanda f **2.** vt **a)** exigir ; [rights] reclamar ; **to demand that ...** insistir en que ... (+ subj) **b)** [need] requerir

demanding [dɪˈmɑːndɪŋ] adj **a)** [person] exigente **b)** [job] agotador(a)

demeaning [dɪˈmiːnɪŋ] adj Formal humillante

demo [ˈdeməʊ] n Fam manifestación f; **demo tape** maqueta f

democracy [dɪˈmɒkrəsɪ] n democracia f

democratic [deməˈkrætɪk] adj democrático(a) ; US POL **Democratic party** partido m demócrata

demolish [dɪˈmɒlɪʃ] vt [building] derribar, demoler ; Fig [theory, proposal] echar por tierra

demon [ˈdiːmən] n demonio m

demonstrate [ˈdemənstreɪt] **1.** vt demostrar **2.** vi POL manifestarse

demonstration [demənˈstreɪʃən] n **a)** [proof] demostración f, prueba f **b)** [explanation] explicación f **c)** POL manifestación f

demonstrator [ˈdemənstreɪtə(r)] n manifestante mf

demoralize [dɪˈmɒrəlaɪz] vt desmoralizar

den [den] n **a)** [of animal] guarida f **b)** Fam [study] estudio m

denial [dɪˈnaɪəl] n **a)** [of charge] desmentido m **b)** [of rights] denegación f; [of request] negativa f

denim [ˈdenɪm] n tela f vaquera ; **denims** [jeans] vaqueros mpl, Andes, Ven bluyíns mpl, Méx pantalones mpl de mezclilla ; **denim skirt / shirt** falda f / camisa f vaquera

Denmark [ˈdenmɑːk] n Dinamarca f

denomination [dɪnɒmɪˈneɪʃən] n **a)** REL confesión f **b)** FIN [of coins] valor m

denounce [dɪˈnaʊns] vt denunciar ; [criticize] censurar

dense [dens] adj **a)** denso(a) ; [crowd] numeroso(a) **b)** Fam [stupid] torpe

dent [dent] **1.** n abolladura f **2.** vt [car] abollar

dental [ˈdentəl] adj dental ; **dental floss** hilo m dental ; **dental surgeon** odontólogo(a) m,f; **dental surgery** [place] clínica f dental ; [treatment] cirugía f dental

dentist [ˈdentɪst] n dentista mf

denture [ˈdentʃə(r)] n [usu pl] dentadura f postiza

deny [dɪˈnaɪ] vt **a)** [repudiate] negar ; [rumour, report] desmentir ; [charge] rechazar **b)** [refuse] negar

deodorant [diːˈəʊdərənt] n desodorante m

deodorizer [diːˈəʊdəraɪzə(r)] n [for home] desodorizante m

depart [dɪˈpɑːt] vi marcharse, irse ; Fig [from subject] desviarse (**from** de)

department [dɪˈpɑːtmənt] n sección f; [in university] departamento m ; [in government] ministerio m ; **department store** grandes almacenes mpl; US **Department of the Interior** Ministerio m del Interior

departure [dɪˈpɑːtʃə(r)] n partida f; AVIAT & RAIL salida f; AVIAT **departure lounge** sala f de embarque

depend [dɪˈpend] **1.** vi [rely] fiarse (**on** or **upon** de) **2.** v impers [be determined by]

depender (**on** or **upon** de); **it depends on the weather** según el tiempo que haga; **that depends** según

dependant [dɪ'pendənt] n dependiente mf

dependent [dɪ'pendənt] **1.** adj dependiente; **to be dependent on sth** depender de algo **2.** n US = **dependant**

depict [dɪ'pɪkt] vt ART representar; Fig describir

deplorable [dɪ'plɔːrəbəl] adj lamentable

deploy [dɪ'plɔɪ] vt MIL desplegar; Fig utilizar

deport [dɪ'pɔːt] vt expulsar (**from** de; **to** a)

deposit [dɪ'pɒzɪt] **1.** n a) sedimento m; MINING yacimiento m; [in wine] poso m b) [in bank] depósito m; Br **deposit account** cuenta f de ahorros c) [returnable] señal f, fianza f; [first payment] entrega f inicial, Esp entrada f **2.** vt depositar; [in bank account] Esp ingresar, Am depositar

depot [Br 'depəʊ, US 'diːpəʊ] n almacén m; MIL depósito m; Br [for keeping and repairing buses] cochera f; US [bus station] estación f de autobuses, CAm, Méx central f camionera

depress [dɪ'pres] vt a) [person] deprimir b) ECON [profits] reducir; [trade] dificultar c) Formal [switch, lever etc] presionar; [clutch, piano pedal] pisar

depressed [dɪ'prest] adj a) [person] deprimido(a); **to get depressed** deprimirse b) [market] en crisis c) [surface] hundido(a)

depression [dɪ'preʃən] n depresión f

deprive [dɪ'praɪv] vt privar (**of** de)

deprived [dɪ'praɪvd] adj necesitado(a)

depth [depθ] n a) profundidad f b) Fig [of emotion] intensidad f; [of thought] complejidad f; **to be in the depths of despair** estar completamente desesperado(a); **in depth** a fondo

deputy ['depjʊtɪ] n a) [substitute] suplente mf; **deputy chairman** vicepresidente m; **deputy head** subdirector(a) m,f b) POL diputado(a) m,f

derail [dɪ'reɪl] vt hacer descarrilar

derelict ['derɪlɪkt] adj abandonado(a), en ruinas

derive [dɪ'raɪv] **1.** vt sacar **2.** vi [word] derivarse (**from** de); [skill] provenir (**from** de)

descend [dɪ'send] **1.** vi descender; **to descend from** [be related to] descender de **2.** vt [stairs] bajar

descendant [dɪ'sendənt] n descendiente mf

descent [dɪ'sent] n a) descenso m b) [slope] declive m c) [ancestry] ascendencia f

describe [dɪ'skraɪb] vt a) describir b) [circle] trazar

description [dɪ'skrɪpʃən] n a) descripción f; **to defy description** superar la descripción b) [type] clase f

desert[1] ['dezət] n desierto m

desert[2] [dɪ'zɜːt] **1.** vt [place, family] abandonar **2.** vi MIL desertar (**from** de)

deserted [dɪ'zɜːtɪd] adj desierto(a)

deserve [dɪ'zɜːv] vt merecer, merecerse, Am ameritar

deserving [dɪ'zɜːvɪŋ] adj [person] de valía; [cause] meritorio(a)

design [dɪ'zaɪn] **1.** n a) [of car, furniture, clothes] diseño m b) [drawing, blueprint] plano m c) [layout] disposición f d) [pattern] dibujo m e) Fig [scheme] intención f; **by design** a propósito; Fam **to have designs on** tener puestas las miras en **2.** vt diseñar

designate 1. ['dezɪgneɪt] vt a) [appoint] designar, nombrar b) Formal [boundary] señalar **2.** ['dezɪgnɪt] adj designado(a)

designer [dɪ'zaɪnə(r)] n ART diseñador(a) m,f; **designer jeans** pantalones mpl de marca

desirable [dɪ'zaɪərəbəl] adj deseable; [asset, offer] atractivo(a)

desire [dɪ'zaɪə(r)] **1.** n deseo m; **I feel no desire to go** no me *Esp* apetece or *Carib, Col, Méx* provoca nada ir, no tengo nada de ganas de ir **2.** vt desear

desk [desk] n [in school] pupitre m; [in office] escritorio m; *US* **desk clerk** recepcionista mf; **desk job** trabajo m de oficina; **news desk** redacción f; **reception desk** recepción f

desktop ['desktɒp] n COMPUT escritorio m; **desktop computer** *Esp* ordenador m or *Am* computadora f de sobremesa; **desktop publishing** autoedición f

desolate ['desəlɪt] adj **a)** [uninhabited] desierto(a); [barren] yermo(a) **b)** [person] desconsolado(a)

despair [dɪ'speə(r)] **1.** n desesperación f; **to drive sb to despair** desesperar a algn **2.** vi desesperar(se) **(of** de)

despatch [dɪ'spætʃ] n & vt = **dispatch**

desperate ['despərɪt] adj **a)** desesperado(a); [struggle] encarnizado(a) **b)** [need] apremiante

desperately ['despərɪtlɪ] adv [recklessly] desesperadamente; [struggle] encarnizadamente; [ill] gravemente; [in love] locamente; [difficult] sumamente

despicable [dɪ'spɪkəbəl] adj despreciable; [behaviour] indigno(a)

despise [dɪ'spaɪz] vt despreciar, menospreciar

despite [dɪ'spaɪt] prep *Formal* a pesar de

dessert [dɪ'zɜːt] n postre m; **dessert wine** vino m dulce

dessertspoon [dɪ'zɜːtspuːn] n **a)** cuchara f de postre **b)** **dessertspoon(ful)** [measure] cucharada f de postre

destination [destɪ'neɪʃən] n destino m

destined ['destɪnd] adj **a)** **destined to fail** condenado(a) al fracaso **b)** [bound] con destino **(for** a)

destiny ['destɪnɪ] n destino m

destitute ['destɪtjuːt] adj indigente

destroy [dɪ'strɔɪ] vt destruir; [vehicle, old furniture] destrozar

destruction [dɪ'strʌkʃən] n destrucción f; *Fig* ruina f

destructive [dɪ'strʌktɪv] adj [gale etc] destructor(a); [tendency, criticism] destructivo(a)

detach [dɪ'tætʃ] vt [remove] separar

detachable [dɪ'tætʃəbəl] adj separable **(from** de)

detached [dɪ'tætʃt] adj **a)** [separated] separado(a); *esp Br* **detached house** casa f independiente **b)** [impartial] objetivo(a)

detail [*Br* 'diːteɪl, *US* dɪ'teɪl] **1.** n **a)** detalle m, pormenor m; **without going into detail(s)** sin entrar en detalles; **details** [information] información f; **bank details** datos bancarios **b)** MIL destacamento m **2.** vt **a)** [list] detallar, enumerar **b)** MIL [appoint] destacar

detailed ['diːteɪld] adj detallado(a), minucioso(a)

detailing ['diːteɪlɪŋ] n *US* [thorough cleaning] limpieza f completa

detain [dɪ'teɪn] vt **a)** JUR detener **b)** [delay] retener

detect [dɪ'tekt] vt **a)** [error, movement] advertir; [difference] notar; [smell, sound] percibir **b)** [discover] descubrir; [enemy ship] detectar; [position] localizar

detective [dɪ'tektɪv] n detective mf; **detective story** novela policíaca

detector [dɪ'tektə(r)] n aparato m detector

detention [dɪ'tenʃən] n [of suspect etc] detención f, arresto m; SCH **to get detention** quedarse castigado(a)

deter [dɪ'tɜː(r)] vt [dissuade] disuadir **(from** de); [stop] impedir

detergent [dɪ'tɜːdʒənt] n detergente m

deteriorate [dɪ'tɪərɪəreɪt] vi deteriorarse

determine [dɪ'tɜːmɪn] vt determinar

determined [dɪ'tɜːmɪnd] adj [person] decidido(a); [effort] enérgico(a)

deterrent [dɪ'terənt] **1.** adj disuasivo(a) **2.** n fuerza disuasoria

detest [dɪ'test] vt detestar, odiar

detonate ['detəneɪt] vt & vi detonar

detour ['di:tʊə(r)] n desvío m

detract [dɪ'trækt] vi quitar mérito (**from** a)

devaluation [di:vælju:'eɪʃən] n devaluación f

devastate ['devəsteɪt] vt [city, area] asolar; Fig [person] desolar

devastating ['devəsteɪtɪŋ] adj [fire] devastador(a); [wind, flood] arrollador(a)

develop [dɪ'veləp] **1.** vt a) desarrollar; [trade] fomentar; [skill] perfeccionar; [plan] elaborar; [habit] contraer; [interest] mostrar b) [natural resources] aprovechar; CONSTR [site] urbanizar c) PHOTO revelar **2.** vi a) [body, industry] desarrollarse; [system] perfeccionarse; [interest] crecer b) [appear] crearse; [evolve] evolucionar

developer [dɪ'veləpə(r)] n (**property**) **developer** inmobiliaria f

development [dɪ'veləpmənt] n a) desarrollo m; [of trade] fomento m; [of skill] perfección f; [of character] formación f b) [advance] avance m c) **there are no new developments** no hay ninguna novedad d) [exploitation] explotación f e) CONSTR urbanización f

deviate ['di:vɪeɪt] vi desviarse (**from** de)

device [dɪ'vaɪs] n a) aparato m; [mechanism] mecanismo m b) [trick, scheme] ardid m

devil ['devəl] n diablo m, demonio m; **devil's advocate** abogado(a) m,f del diablo; Fam **where the devil did you put it?** ¿dónde demonios lo pusiste?; **you lucky devil!** ¡vaya suerte que tienes!

devious ['di:vɪəs] adj a) [winding] tortuoso(a) b) esp Pej [person] taimado(a)

devise [dɪ'vaɪz] vt idear, concebir

devoid [dɪ'vɔɪd] adj desprovisto(a) (**of** de)

devote [dɪ'vəʊt] vt dedicar; **she devoted her life to helping the poor** consagró su vida a la ayuda de los pobres

devoted [dɪ'vəʊtɪd] adj fiel, leal (**to** a)

devotion [dɪ'vəʊʃən] n devoción f; [to cause] dedicación f

devour [dɪ'vaʊə(r)] vt devorar

devout [dɪ'vaʊt] adj devoto(a)

dew [dju:] n rocío m

diabetes [daɪə'bi:ti:z, daɪə'bi:tɪs] n diabetes f

diabetic [daɪə'betɪk] adj & n diabético(a) (m,f)

diagnose ['daɪəgnəʊz] vt diagnosticar

diagnosis [daɪəg'nəʊsɪs] (pl **diagnoses** [daɪəg'nəʊsi:z]) n diagnóstico m

diagonal [daɪ'ægənəl] adj & n diagonal (f)

diagonally [daɪ'ægənəlɪ] adv en diagonal, diagonalmente

diagram ['daɪəgræm] n diagrama m; [of process, system] esquema m; [of workings] gráfico m

dial ['daɪəl, daɪl] **1.** n [of clock] esfera f; [of radio] cuadrante m; [of telephone] disco m; [of machine] botón m selector **2.** vt & vi TEL marcar, Andes, CSur discar; Br **dialling** or US **dial code** prefijo m; Br **dialling** or US **dial tone** señal f de marcar or Andes, CSur discar

dialect ['daɪəlekt] n dialecto m

dialogue, US **dialog** ['daɪəlɒg] n diálogo m

diameter [daɪ'æmɪtə(r)] n diámetro m

diamond ['daɪəmənd] n a) [shape] rombo m

diaper ['daɪəpə(r)] n US pañal m

diarrhoea, US **diarrhea** [daɪə'rɪə] n diarrea f

diary ['daɪərɪ] n a) diario m; **to keep a diary** llevar un diario b) Br [for appointments] agenda f

dice [daɪs] **1.** (pl **dice**) n dado m **2.** vt CULIN cortar en cuadritos

dictate 1. [dɪk'teɪt] vt [letter, order] dictar
2. [dɪk'teɪt] vi **to dictate to sb** dar órdenes a algn
3. ['dɪkteɪt] n Fig **the dictates of conscience** los dictados de la conciencia

dictation [dɪk'teɪʃən] n dictado m

dictator [dɪk'teɪtə(r)] n dictador(a) m,f

dictionary ['dɪkʃənərɪ] n diccionario m

did [dɪd] pt of **do**

die [daɪ] vi morir, morirse; Fam & Fig **to be dying for sth/to do sth** morirse por algo/de ganas de hacer algo ▪ **die away** vi desvanecerse ▪ **die down** vi [fire] extinguirse; [wind] amainar; [noise, excitement] disminuir ▪ **die off** vi morir uno por uno ▪ **die out** vi extinguirse

diesel ['diːzəl] n a) [oil] gasoil m; **diesel engine** motor m diesel b) Fam [vehicle] vehículo m diesel

diet ['daɪət] **1.** n [normal food] dieta f; [selected food] régimen m; **to be on a diet** estar a régimen **2.** vi estar a régimen

differ ['dɪfə(r)] vi [be unlike] ser distinto(a); [disagree] discrepar

difference ['dɪfərəns] n a) [dissimilarity] diferencia f; **it makes no difference (to me)** (me) da igual; **what difference does it make?** ¿qué más da? b) [disagreement] desacuerdo m

different ['dɪfərənt] adj diferente, distinto(a); **you look different** pareces otro(a)

differentiate [dɪfə'renʃɪeɪt] **1.** vt distinguir, diferenciar (**from** de) **2.** vi distinguir (**between** entre)

differently ['dɪfərəntlɪ] adv de otra manera

difficult ['dɪfɪkəlt] adj difícil

difficulty ['dɪfɪkəltɪ] n dificultad f; [problem] problema m; **to be in difficulties** estar en un apuro

dig [dɪg] (pt & pp **dug**) **1.** n a) [poke] codazo m
b) Fam [gibe] pulla f
2. vt a) [earth] cavar; [tunnel] excavar
b) Fam & Fig **to dig one's heels in** mantenerse en sus trece
3. vi [person] cavar; [animal] escarbar
▪ **dig in** vi MIL atrincherarse
▪ **dig out** vt sep Fig [old suit] sacar; [information] descubrir

▪ **dig up** vt sep [weeds] arrancar; [buried object] desenterrar; [road] levantar; Fig sacar a relucir

digest 1. ['daɪdʒest] n [summary] resumen m **2.** [dɪ'dʒest] vt [food] digerir; Fig [facts] asimilar

digestion [dɪ'dʒestʃən] n digestión f

digibox ['dɪdʒɪbɒks] n Br TV decodificador m

digit ['dɪdʒɪt] n a) MATH dígito m b) Formal ANAT dedo m

digital ['dɪdʒɪtəl] adj digital; **digital camcorder** videocámara f digital; **digital camera** cámara f digital; **digital divide, digital gap** brecha f digital; **digital radio** radio f digital; **digital television** televisión f digital

dignified ['dɪgnɪfaɪd] adj [manner] solemne, serio(a); [appearance] majestuoso(a)

dignity ['dɪgnɪtɪ] n dignidad f

digs [dɪgz] npl Br Fam habitación f (de alquiler)

dilapidated [dɪ'læpɪdeɪtɪd] adj en mal estado

dilemma [dɪ'lemə, daɪ'lemə] n dilema m

diligent ['dɪlɪdʒənt] adj [worker] diligente; [inquiries, search] esmerado(a)

dilute [daɪ'luːt] **1.** vt diluir; [wine, milk] aguar; Fig [effect, influence] atenuar **2.** vi diluirse

dim [dɪm] **1.** (compar **dimmer**, superl **dimmest**) adj a) [light] débil, tenue; [room] oscuro(a); [outline] borroso(a); [eyesight] defectuoso(a); Fig [memory] vago(a); Fig [future] sombrío(a) b) Fam [stupid] tonto, corto de alcances, Am sonso(a)
2. vt [light] bajar
3. vi [light] bajarse; [sight] nublarse; Fig [joy] extinguirse

dime [daɪm] n US moneda f de diez centavos

dimension [daɪ'menʃən] n dimensión f

diminish [dɪ'mɪnɪʃ] vt & vi disminuir

dimple ['dɪmpəl] n hoyuelo m

disappear

din [dɪn] n [of crowd] alboroto m ; [of machinery] estruendo m

dine [daɪn] vi Formal cenar ; **to dine out** cenar fuera

diner ['daɪnə(r)] n a) [person] comensal mf b) US [restaurant] restaurante barato

dinghy ['dɪŋɪ] n bote m ; **(rubber) dinghy** bote neumático

dingy ['dɪndʒɪ] (compar dingier, superl dingiest) adj a) [dark] oscuro(a) b) [dirty] sucio(a) c) [colour] desteñido(a)

dining car ['daɪnɪŋkɑ:(r)] n vagón m restaurante

dining room ['daɪnɪŋru:m] n comedor m

dinner ['dɪnə(r)] n [at midday] comida f ; [in evening] cena f ; **dinner jacket** smoking m ; **dinner service** vajilla f ; **dinner table** mesa f de comedor

dinosaur ['daɪnəsɔ:(r)] n dinosaurio m

dip [dɪp] **1.** n a) Fam [bathe] chapuzón m **b)** [of road] pendiente f ; [in ground] depresión f
c) CULIN salsa f
2. vt a) bañar ; [spoon, hand] meter
b) Br AUTO **to dip one's headlights** poner las luces de cruce
3. vi [road] bajar
■ **dip into** vt insep **a)** [savings] echar mano de **b)** [book] hojear

diploma [dɪ'pləʊmə] n diploma m

diplomat ['dɪpləmæt] n diplomático(a) m,f

diplomatic [dɪplə'mætɪk] adj diplomático(a)

dire ['daɪə(r)] adj [urgent] extremo(a) ; [serious] grave

direct [dɪ'rekt, daɪ'rekt] **1.** adj
a) directo(a) ; **direct current** corriente continua
b) the direct opposite todo lo contrario
2. adv directamente
3. vt a) dirigir ; **can you direct me to a bank?** ¿me puede indicar dónde hay un banco?

b) Formal [order] mandar

direction [dɪ'rekʃən, daɪ'rekʃən] n a) dirección f ; **sense of direction** sentido m de la orientación **b) directions** [to place] señas fpl ; **directions for use** modo m de empleo **c)** THEAT puesta f en escena

directly [dɪ'rektlɪ, daɪ'rektlɪ] **1.** adv **a)** [above etc] exactamente, justo **b)** [speak] francamente **c)** [descend] directamente **d)** [come] en seguida **2.** conj Fam en cuanto

director [dɪ'rektə(r), daɪ'rektə(r)] n director(a) m,f

directory [dɪ'rektərɪ, daɪ'rektərɪ] n a) TEL guía telefónica, Am directorio m de teléfonos ; **directory enquiries** (servicio m de) información f **b)** COMPUT directorio m

dirt [dɜ:t] n suciedad f ; Br **dog dirt** caca f de perro

dirty ['dɜ:tɪ] **1.** (compar dirtier, superl dirtiest) adj **a)** sucio(a) **b) to give sb a dirty look** fulminar a algn con la mirada **c)** [joke] verde ; [mind] pervertido(a) ; **dirty word** palabrota f ; **dirty old man** viejo m verde **2.** vt ensuciar

dis [dɪs] US Fam vt = diss

disability [dɪsə'bɪlɪtɪ] n incapacidad f, discapacidad f ; **disability pension** pensión f por invalidez

disabled [dɪ'seɪbəld] **1.** adj minusválido(a) **2.** npl **the disabled** los minusválidos

disadvantage [dɪsəd'vɑ:ntɪdʒ] n desventaja f ; [obstacle] inconveniente m

disagree [dɪsə'gri:] vi a) [differ] no estar de acuerdo (**with** con) ; **to disagree on** or **over sth** reñir por algo **b)** [not match] discrepar (**with** de or con) **c) garlic disagrees with me** el ajo no me sienta bien

disagreeable [dɪsə'gri:əbəl] adj desagradable

disagreement [dɪsə'gri:mənt] n a) desacuerdo m ; [argument] riña f **b)** [non-correspondence] discrepancia f

disappear [dɪsə'pɪə(r)] vi desaparecer

disappearance [dɪsə'pɪərəns] *n* desaparición *f*

disappoint [dɪsə'pɔɪnt] *vt* [person] decepcionar, defraudar; [hope, ambition] frustrar

disappointing [dɪsə'pɔɪntɪŋ] *adj* decepcionante

disappointment [dɪsə'pɔɪntmənt] *n* decepción *f*

disapproval [dɪsə'pruːvəl] *n* desaprobación *f*

disapprove [dɪsə'pruːv] *vi* **to disapprove of** desaprobar

disaster [dɪ'zɑːstə(r)] *n* desastre *m*

disastrous [dɪ'zɑːstrəs] *adj* desastroso(a)

disbelief [dɪsbɪ'liːf] *n* incredulidad *f*

disc [dɪsk] *n* disco *m*; COMPUT disquete *m*; **disc jockey** disc-jockey *mf*, pinchadiscos *mfinv*

discard [dɪs'kɑːd] *vt* [old things] deshacerse de; [plan] descartar

discern [dɪ'sɜːn] *vt* [shape, difference] percibir; [truth] darse cuenta de

discerning [dɪ'sɜːnɪŋ] *adj* [person] perspicaz; [taste] refinado(a)

discharge *Formal* **1.** [dɪs'tʃɑːdʒ] *vt* [prisoner] soltar; [patient] dar de alta a; [soldier] licenciar; [employee] despedir; [gun] descargar **2.** ['dɪstʃɑːdʒ] *n* **a)** [of current, load, gun] descarga *f*; [of gases] escape *m* **b)** [of prisoner] liberación *f*; [of patient] alta *f*; [of soldier] licencia *f*

disciple [dɪ'saɪpəl] *n* discípulo(a) *m,f*

discipline ['dɪsɪplɪn] **1.** *n* disciplina *f* **2.** *vt* [child] castigar; [worker] sancionar; [official] expedientar

disclose [dɪs'kləʊz] *vt* revelar

disco ['dɪskəʊ] *n* Fam (abbr of **discotheque**) disco *f*

discomfort [dɪs'kʌmfət] *n* **a)** [lack of comfort] incomodidad *f* **b)** [pain] malestar *m* **c)** [unease] inquietud *f*

disconcerting [dɪskən'sɜːtɪŋ] *adj* desconcertante

disconnect [dɪskə'nekt] *vt* desconectar (**from** de); [gas, electricity] cortar

discontented [dɪskən'tentɪd] *adj* descontento(a)

discontinue [ˌdɪskən'tɪnjuː] *vt* suspender, interrumpir; [product] dejar de fabricar

discotheque ['dɪskətek] *n* discoteca *f*

discount 1. ['dɪskaʊnt] *n* descuento *m* **2.** [dɪs'kaʊnt] *vt* **a)** [price] rebajar **b)** [view, suggestion] descartar

discourage [dɪs'kʌrɪdʒ] *vt* [dishearten] desanimar; [advances] rechazar

discover [dɪ'skʌvə(r)] *vt* descubrir; [missing person, object] encontrar

discovery [dɪ'skʌvərɪ] *n* descubrimiento *m*

discredit [dɪs'kredɪt] **1.** *n* descrédito *m* **2.** *vt* [person, régime] desacreditar; [theory] poner en duda

discreet [dɪ'skriːt] *adj* discreto(a); [distance, silence] prudente; [hat, house] modesto(a)

discretion [dɪ'skreʃən] *n* discreción *f*; [prudence] prudencia *f*; **at the discretion of ...** a juicio de ...

discriminate [dɪ'skrɪmɪneɪt] *vi* discriminar (**between** entre); **to discriminate against sth/sb** discriminar algo/a algn

discrimination [dɪskrɪmɪ'neɪʃən] *n* **a)** [bias] discriminación *f* **b)** [distinction] diferenciación *f*

discus ['dɪskəs] *n* disco *m* (*para lanzamientos*)

discuss [dɪ'skʌs] *vt* discutir; [in writing] tratar de

discussion [dɪ'skʌʃən] *n* discusión *f*; INTERNET **discussion forum** foro *m* de discusión; INTERNET **discussion group** grupo *m* de discusión; INTERNET **discussion thread** hilo *m* de discusión

disdain [dɪs'deɪn] *Formal* **1.** *n* desdén *m* **2.** *vt* desdeñar

disease [dɪ'ziːz] *n* enfermedad *f*; Fig mal *m*

disembark [dɪsɪm'bɑːk] *vt* & *vi* desembarcar

disfigure [dɪs'fɪgə(r)] *vt* desfigurar

disgrace [dɪs'greɪs] **1.** n a) [disfavour] desgracia f; **to be in disgrace** estar desacreditado(a); **to fall into disgrace** caer en desgracia b) [shame] vergüenza f, escándalo m **2.** vt deshonrar, desacreditar

disgraceful [dɪs'greɪsfʊl] adj vergonzoso(a)

disgruntled [dɪs'grʌntəld] adj contrariado(a), disgustado(a)

disguise [dɪs'gaɪz] **1.** n disfraz m; **in disguise** disfrazado(a) **2.** vt a) [person] disfrazar (**as** de) b) [feelings] disimular

disgust [dɪs'gʌst] **1.** n a) [loathing] repugnancia f, asco m b) [strong disapproval] indignación f **2.** vt a) [revolt] repugnar, dar asco a b) [offend] indignar

disgusting [dɪs'gʌstɪŋ] adj asqueroso(a), repugnante; [behaviour, state of affairs] intolerable

dish [dɪʃ] n [for serving] fuente f; [course] plato m; **to wash** or **do the dishes** fregar los platos ■ **dish out** vt sep Fam [food] servir; [books, advice] repartir; **to dish it out (to sb)** [criticize] criticar (a algn) ■ **dish up** vt sep [meal] servir

dishcloth ['dɪʃklɒθ] n [for washing] bayeta f; [for drying] paño m (de cocina), CAm secador m, Méx trapón m, RP repasador m

dishevelled, US **disheveled** [dɪ'ʃevəld] adj [hair] despeinado(a); [appearance] desaliñado(a)

dishonest [dɪs'ɒnɪst] adj [person] poco honrado(a); [means] fraudulento(a)

dishonesty [dɪs'ɒnɪstɪ] n [of person] falta f de honradez

dishonourable, US **dishonorable** [dɪs'ɒnərəbəl] adj deshonroso(a)

dishtowel ['dɪʃtaʊəl] n paño m (de cocina), CAm secador m, Méx trapón m, RP repasador m

dishwasher ['dɪʃwɒʃə(r)] n lavaplatos m inv; [person] lavaplatos mf inv

dishwater ['dɪʃˌwɔːtə(r)] n agua f de fregar (los platos)

disillusion [dɪsɪ'luːʒən] vt desilusionar

disinfect [dɪsɪn'fekt] vt desinfectar

disinfectant [dɪsɪn'fektənt] n desinfectante m

disintegrate [dɪs'ɪntɪgreɪt] vi desintegrarse

disinterested [dɪs'ɪntrɪstɪd] adj desinteresado(a)

disjointed [dɪs'dʒɔɪntɪd] adj inconexo(a)

disk [dɪsk] n a) COMPUT disco m; **on disk** en disco; **disk drive** disquetera f, disketera f b) US = **disc**

diskette [dɪs'ket] n COMPUT disquete m

dislike [dɪs'laɪk] **1.** n antipatía f, aversión f (**of** a or hacia) **2.** vt tener antipatía or aversión a or hacia

dislocate ['dɪsləkeɪt] vt [joint] dislocar

dislodge [dɪs'lɒdʒ] vt sacar

disloyal [dɪs'lɔɪəl] adj desleal

dismal ['dɪzməl] adj a) [prospect] sombrío(a); [place, weather] deprimente; [person] triste b) [failure] horroroso(a)

dismantle [dɪs'mæntəl] vt desmontar

dismay [dɪs'meɪ] **1.** n consternación f **2.** vt consternar

dismiss [dɪs'mɪs] vt a) [idea] descartar b) [employee] despedir; [official] destituir c) **to dismiss sb** [from room, presence] dar permiso a algn para retirarse d) JUR [case] sobreseer

dismissal [dɪs'mɪsəl] n a) [of employee] despido m; [of official] destitución f b) JUR [of case] sobreseimiento m

dismount [dɪs'maʊnt] vi Formal apearse (**from** de)

disobedient [dɪsə'biːdɪənt] adj desobediente

disobey [dɪsə'beɪ] vt & vi desobedecer; [law] violar

disorder [dɪs'ɔːdə(r)] n a) [untidiness] desorden m b) [riot] disturbio m c) [of organ, mind] trastorno m; [of speech] defecto m

disorderly [dɪs'ɔːdəlɪ] adj a) [untidy] desordenado(a) b) [meeting] alborotado(a); [conduct] escandaloso(a)

disorganized [dɪsˈɔːɡənaɪzd] *adj* desorganizado(a)

disorient [dɪsˈɔːrɪənt], **disorientate** [dɪsˈɔːrɪənteɪt] *vt* desorientar

disown [dɪsˈəʊn] *vt* desconocer

dispatch [dɪˈspætʃ] **1.** *n* **a)** [official message] despacho *m*; [journalist's report] reportaje *m*; [military message] parte *m* **b)** [of mail] envío *m*; [of goods] consignación *f* **2.** *vt* **a)** [mail] enviar; [goods] expedir **b)** *Fam* [food] zamparse; [job] despachar

dispel [dɪˈspel] *vt* disipar

dispensary [dɪˈspensərɪ] *n* dispensario *m*

dispense [dɪˈspens] *vt* [supplies] repartir; [justice] administrar ∎ **dispense with** *vt insep* [do without] prescindir de

dispenser [dɪˈspensə(r)] *n* máquina expendedora; **cash dispenser** cajero automático; **soap dispenser** dosificador *m* de jabón

disperse [dɪˈspɜːs] **1.** *vt* dispersar **2.** *vi* dispersarse; [fog] disiparse

display [dɪˈspleɪ] **1.** *n* **a)** [exhibition] exposición *f*; [of feelings, skills] demostración *f*; [of force] despliegue *m*; **display window** escaparate *m*, *Am* vidriera *f*, *Chile, Col, Méx* vitrina *f*; **military display** desfile *m* militar **b)** COMPUT [device] pantalla *f* (de visualización); [information displayed] visualización *f* **2.** *vt* **a)** mostrar; [goods] exponer; COMPUT visualizar **b)** [feelings] manifestar

disposable [dɪˈspəʊzəbəl] *adj* **a)** [throwaway] desechable, de usar y tirar; **disposable camera** cámara *f* deshechable *or* de usar y tirar **b)** [available] disponible

disposal [dɪˈspəʊzəl] *n* [of rubbish] eliminación *f*; **at my disposal** [available] a mi disposición

dispose [dɪˈspəʊz] **1.** *vi* **to dispose of** [remove] eliminar; [rubbish] tirar; [unwanted object] deshacerse de; [matter] resolver; [sell] vender; [property] traspasar **2.** *vt* *Formal* [arrange] disponer

disposition [dɪspəˈzɪʃən] *n* **a)** [temperament] genio *m* **b)** *Formal* [arrangement] disposición *f*

dispossess [dɪspəˈzes] *vt* desposeer (**of** de)

disproportionate [dɪsprəˈpɔːʃənɪt] *adj* desproporcionado(a) (**to** a)

disprove [dɪsˈpruːv] *vt* refutar

dispute **1.** [ˈdɪspjuːt] *n* [disagreement] discusión *f*; [quarrel] disputa *f*; **industrial dispute** conflicto *m* laboral **2.** [dɪˈspjuːt] *vt* [claim] refutar; [territory] disputar; [matter] discutir **3.** *vi* discutir (**about** *or* **over** de *or* sobre)

disqualify [dɪsˈkwɒlɪfaɪ] *vt* **a)** SPORT descalificar **b)** [make ineligible] incapacitar

disregard [dɪsrɪˈɡɑːd] **1.** *n* indiferencia *f*; [for safety] despreocupación *f* **2.** *vt* descuidar; [ignore] ignorar

disrespectful [dɪsrɪˈspektfʊl] *adj* irrespetuoso(a)

disrupt [dɪsˈrʌpt] *vt* [meeting, traffic] interrumpir; [schedule etc] desbaratar

disruption [dɪsˈrʌpʃən] *n* [of meeting, traffic] interrupción *f*; [of schedule etc] desbaratamiento *m*

disruptive [dɪsˈrʌptɪv] *adj* **to be disruptive** ocasionar trastornos

diss [dɪs] *vt* **a)** *US Fam* pasar de; **she dissed me** pasó de mí **b)** (*abbr of* **disrespect**) insultar, ofender; **she dissed me** me trató con desdén

dissatisfaction [dɪssætɪsˈfækʃən] *n* descontento *m*, insatisfacción *f*

dissatisfied [dɪsˈsætɪsfaɪd] *adj* descontento(a)

dissent [dɪˈsent] **1.** *n* disentimiento *m* **2.** *vi* disentir

dissertation [dɪsəˈteɪʃən] *n* UNIV *Br* [for higher degree] tesina *f*; *US* [doctoral] tesis *f*

dissident [ˈdɪsɪdənt] *adj* & *n* disidente (*mf*)

dissimilar [dɪˈsɪmɪlə(r)] *adj* distinto(a)

diverse

dissociate [dɪˈsəʊʃɪeɪt] *vt* to dissociate oneself distanciarse

dissolute [ˈdɪsəluːt] *adj* disoluto(a)

dissolve [dɪˈzɒlv] **1.** *vt* disolver **2.** *vi* disolverse

dissuade [dɪˈsweɪd] *vt* disuadir (**from** de)

distance [ˈdɪstəns] **1.** *n* distancia *f*; **in the distance** a lo lejos; *Fam* **to stay the distance** completar la prueba **2.** *vt* to **distance oneself (from)** distanciarse (de)

distant [ˈdɪstənt] *adj* **a)** [place, time] lejano(a); [look] distraído(a) **b)** [aloof] distante, frío(a)

distasteful [dɪsˈteɪstfʊl] *adj* desagradable

distil, *US* **distill** [dɪsˈtɪl] *vt* destilar

distinct [dɪˈstɪŋkt] *adj* **a)** [different] diferente; **as distinct from** a diferencia de **b)** [smell, change] marcado(a); [idea, intention] claro(a)

distinction [dɪˈstɪŋkʃən] *n* **a)** [difference] diferencia *f* **b)** [excellence] distinción *f* **c)** *SCH* sobresaliente *m*

distinctive [dɪˈstɪŋktɪv] *adj* distintivo(a)

distinctly [dɪsˈtɪŋktlɪ] *adv* **a)** [clearly - speak, hear] claramente, con claridad **b)** [decidedly - better, easier] claramente; [stupid, ill-mannered] verdaderamente

distinguish [dɪˈstɪŋgwɪʃ] *vt* distinguir

distinguished [dɪˈstɪŋgwɪʃt] *adj* distinguido(a)

distort [dɪsˈtɔːt] *vt* [misrepresent] deformar; [words] tergiversar

distract [dɪˈstrækt] *vt* distraer

distracted [dɪˈstræktɪd] *adj* distraído(a)

distraction [dɪˈstrækʃən] *n* [interruption] distracción *f*; [confusion] confusión *f*; **to drive sb to distraction** sacar a algn de quicio

distraught [dɪsˈtrɔːt] *adj* [anguished] afligido(a)

distress [dɪˈstres] **1.** *n* [mental] angustia *f*; [physical] dolor *m*; **distress signal** señal *f* de socorro **2.** *vt* [upset] apenar

distressing [dɪˈstresɪŋ] *adj* penoso(a)

distribute [dɪˈstrɪbjuːt] *vt* distribuir, repartir

distribution [dɪstrɪˈbjuːʃən] *n* distribución *f*

distributor [dɪˈstrɪbjʊtə(r)] *n* **a)** COMM distribuidor(a) *m,f*, **b)** AUTO distribuidor *m*, *Esp* delco® *m*

district [ˈdɪstrɪkt] *n* [of country] región *f*; [of town] barrio *m*; *US* **district attorney** fiscal *m*; **district council** corporación *f* local; *Br* **district nurse** practicante *mf*

distrust [dɪsˈtrʌst] **1.** *n* recelo *m* **2.** *vt* desconfiar de

disturb [dɪˈstɜːb] *vt* **a)** [inconvenience] molestar **b)** [silence] romper; [sleep] interrumpir **c)** [worry] perturbar **d)** [papers] desordenar

disturbance [dɪˈstɜːbəns] *n* **a)** [of routine] alteración *f* **b)** [commotion] disturbio *m*, alboroto *m*

disturbing [dɪˈstɜːbɪŋ] *adj* inquietante

disuse [dɪsˈjuːs] *n* desuso *m*

ditch [dɪtʃ] **1.** *n* zanja *f*; [at roadside] cuneta *f*; [for irrigation] acequia *f* **2.** *vt* *Fam* [plan, friend] abandonar

ditto [ˈdɪtəʊ] *adv* ídem, lo mismo

dive [daɪv] **1.** *n* **a)** [into water] salto *m* de cabeza; [of submarine] inmersión *f*; [of plane] *Esp* picado *m*, *Am* picada *f*; *SPORT* salto **b)** *Fam* [bar] antro *m* **2.** *vi* **a)** [from poolside, diving board] tirarse de cabeza; [submarine] sumergirse; [plane] lanzarse en *Esp* picado *or Am* picada; *SPORT* saltar **b)** [move quickly] **he dived for the phone** se precipitó hacia el teléfono

diver [ˈdaɪvə(r)] *n* [person] buceador(a) *m,f*; [professional] buzo *m*; *SPORT* saltador(a) *m,f*

diverge [daɪˈvɜːdʒ] *vi* divergir

diverse [daɪˈvɜːs] *adj* [varied] diverso(a), variado(a); [different] distinto(a), diferente

diversify [daɪˈvɜːsɪfaɪ] **1.** *vt* diversificar **2.** *vi* [company] diversificarse

diversion [daɪˈvɜːʃən] *n* **a)** [distraction] distracción *f* **b)** *Br* [detour] desvío *m*

diversity [daɪˈvɜːsɪtɪ] *n* diversidad *f*

divert [daɪˈvɜːt] *vt* desviar

divide [dɪˈvaɪd] **1.** *vt* dividir **2.** *vi* [road, stream] bifurcarse **3.** *n* división *f*, diferencia *f*

divine [dɪˈvaɪn] *adj* divino(a)

diving board [ˈdaɪvɪŋbɔːd] *n* trampolín *m*

division [dɪˈvɪʒən] *n* **a)** división *f* **b)** [sharing] reparto *m* **c)** [of organization] sección *f*

divorce [dɪˈvɔːs] **1.** *n* divorcio *m* **2.** *vt* **she divorced him, she got divorced from him** se divorció de él **3.** *vi* divorciarse

divorcé [dɪˈvɔːseɪ] *n* divorciado *m*

divorcée [dɪvɔːˈsiː] *n* divorciada *f*

divulge [daɪˈvʌldʒ] *vt Formal* divulgar, revelar

DIY [diːaɪˈwaɪ] *n Br (abbr of* **do-it-yourself***)* bricolaje *m*

dizzy [ˈdɪzɪ] *(compar* dizzier, *superl* dizziest*)adj* **a)** [person - unwell] mareado(a) **b)** [height, pace] vertiginoso(a)

DJ [ˈdiːdʒeɪ] *n Fam (abbr of* **disc jockey***)* pinchadiscos *mf inv,* disc-jockey *mf*

Dk, DK MESSAGING *(abbr of* **don't know***)* no c

DNA *n (abbr of* **deoxyribonucleic acid***)* ADN *m (ácido desoxirribonucleico)*

DNS [ˌdiːenˈes] *n* COMPUT *(abbr of* **Domain Name System***)* DNS *m (Sistema de Nombres de Dominio)*

do [duː] *(unstressed* [dʊ, də]*) (3rd person sing pres* **does**, *pt* **did**, *pp* **done***)*

En el inglés hablado, y en el escrito en estilo coloquial, las formas negativas **do not**, **does not** y **did not** se transforman en **don't**, **doesn't** y **didn't**.

1. *v aux* **a)** [in negatives and questions - not translated in Spanish] **do you want some coffee?** ¿quieres café?; **do you drive?** ¿tienes carnet de conducir?; **don't you want to come?** ¿no quieres venir?; **he doesn't smoke** no fuma **b)** [emphatic - not translated in Spanish] **do come with us!** ¡ánimo, vente con nosotros!; **I do like your bag** me encanta tu bolso **c)** [substituting main verb in sentence - not translated in Spanish] **neither / so do I** yo tampoco / también; **I'll go if you do** si vas tú, voy yo; **I think it's dear, but he doesn't** a mí me parece caro pero a él no; **who went? — I did** ¿quién asistió? — yo **d)** [in question tags] **he refused, didn't he?** dijo que no, ¿verdad?; **I don't like it, do you?** a mí no me gusta, ¿y a ti? **2.** *vt* hacer; [task] realizar; [duty] cumplir con; **to do one's best** hacer todo lo posible; **to do sth again** volver a hacer algo; **to do sth for sb** hacer algo por algn; **to do the cooking / cleaning** cocinar / limpiar; **what can I do for you?** ¿en qué puedo servirle?; **what do you do (for a living)?** ¿a qué te dedicas?; *Fam* **he's done it!** ¡lo ha conseguido!

do, unido a muchos nombres, expresa actividades, como **to do the gardening, to do the ironing**, etc. En este diccionario, estas estructuras se encuentran bajo los nombres respectivos.

3. *vi* **a)** [act] hacer; **do as I tell you** haz lo que te digo; **you did right** hiciste bien **b)** [with adverb] **he did badly in the exams** los exámenes le salieron mal; **how are you doing?** ¿qué tal?; **how do you do?** [greeting] ¿cómo está usted?; [answer] mucho gusto; **to do well** [person] tener éxito; [business] ir bien **c)** **£5 will do** [suffice] con 5 libras será suficiente; *Fam* **that will do!** ¡basta ya! **d)** **this cushion will do as a pillow** [be suitable] este cojín servirá de almohada; **this won't do** esto no puede ser **4.** *n Br Fam* [party] fiesta *f*; [event] ceremonia *f*

■ **do away with** *vt insep* **a)** [abolish] abolir; [discard] deshacerse de **b)** [kill] asesinar

■ **do down** *vt sep Br* [criticize] desacreditar, menospreciar

■ **do for** *vt insep Fam* [destroy, ruin] arruinar; *Fig***I'm done for if I don't finish this** estoy perdido(a) si no acabo esto

■ **do in** *vt sep Fam* **a)** [kill] cargarse **b)** *esp Br***I'm done in** [exhausted] estoy hecho(a) polvo

■ **do out of** *vt sep Fam* **to do sb out of sth** estafar algo a algn

■ **do over** *vt sep Fam* **a)** *US* [repeat] repetir **b)** *Br* [thrash] dar una paliza a

■ **do up** *vt sep* **a)** [wrap] envolver **b)** [belt etc] abrochar; [laces] atar **c)** [dress up] arreglar **d)** *Fam* [redecorate] renovar

■ **do with** *vt insep* **a) I could do with a rest** [need] un descanso no me vendría nada mal **b) to have** *or* **be to do with** [concern] tener que ver con

■ **do without 1.** *vt insep* pasarse sin, prescindir de **2.** *vi* arreglárselas

docile [ˈdəʊsaɪl] *adj* dócil; [animal] manso(a)

dock¹ [dɒk] **1.** *n* NAUT **the docks** el muelle **2.** *vi* **a)** [ship] atracar **b)** [spacecraft] acoplarse

dock² [dɒk] *vt* [reduce] descontar

dock³ [dɒk] *n* JUR banquillo *m* (de los acusados)

docking [ˈdɒkɪŋ] *n* **a)** [in space] acoplamiento *m* **b)** COMPUT **docking station** estación *m* base

doctor [ˈdɒktə(r)] **1.** *n* **a)** MED médico(a) *m,f* **b)** UNIV doctor(a) *m,f*; **Doctor of Law** doctor en derecho **2.** *vt Pej* [figures] falsificar; [text] arreglar; [drink etc] adulterar

doctorate [ˈdɒktərɪt] *n* doctorado *m*

document [ˈdɒkjʊmənt] **1.** *n* documento *m*; **documents** documentación *f* **2.** *vt* documentar

documentary [dɒkjʊˈmentərɪ] *adj & n* documental (*m*)

dodge [dɒdʒ] **1.** *vt* **a)** [blow] esquivar; [pursuer] despistar; *Fig* eludir **b)** *Fam* **to dodge one's taxes** engañar a Hacienda **2.** *vi* [move aside] echarse a un lado **3.** *n* **a)** [movement] regate *m* **b)** *Fam* [trick] truco *m*

dodgy [ˈdɒdʒɪ] *(compar* **dodgier***, superl* **dodgiest***) adj Br Fam* [risky] peligroso(a), *Esp* chungo; [untrustworthy] dudoso; **a dodgy business deal** un chanchullo; **the engine sounds a bit dodgy** el motor no suena nada bien

does [dʌz] *see* **do**

doesn't [ˈdʌzənt] = **does not**

dog [dɒg] **1.** *n* **a)** [animal] perro(a) *m,f*; **assistance dog** perro *m* guía; **attack dog** perro *m* de ataque **b)** [food] *US* **corn dog** *perrito caliente envuelto en harina de maíz y frito*; **hot dog** perrito *m* caliente, *Col, Méx* perro *m* caliente, *RP* pancho *m* **2.** *vt* acosar; **to dog sb's footsteps** seguir los pasos de algn

dogged [ˈdɒgɪd] *adj* obstinado(a), tenaz

doggone [ˈdɑːgɑːn] *interj US Fam* **doggone (it)!** ¡maldita sea!

doing [ˈduːɪŋ] *n* **a)** [action] obra *f*; **it was none of my doing** yo no tuve nada que ver; *Fig* **it took some doing** costó trabajo hacerlo **b) doings** [activities] actividades *fpl*

do-it-yourself [duːɪtjəˈself] *n* bricolaje *m*

dole [dəʊl] *Fam* **1.** *n Br* subsidio *m* de desempleo, *Esp* paro *m*; **to be on the dole** cobrar el subsidio de desempleo *or Esp* el paro; **to go on the dole** apuntarse para cobrar el desempleo, *Esp* apuntarse al paro **2.** *vt* **to dole (out)** repartir

doll [dɒl] **1.** *n* **a)** [toy] muñeca *f* **b)** *US Fam* [girl] muñeca *f* **2.** *vt Fam* **to doll oneself up** ponerse guapa

dollar [ˈdɒlə(r)] *n* dólar *m*; **to pay top dollar for sth** pagar una pasta por algo

dolphin [ˈdɒlfɪn] *n* delfín *m*

domain [dəˈmeɪn] *n* **a)** [sphere] campo *m*, esfera *f*; **that's not my domain** no es de mi competencia **b)** [territory] dominio *m* **c)** COMPUT dominio *m*; **domain name** nombre *m* de dominio

dome [dəʊm] *n* [roof] cúpula *f*; [ceiling] bóveda *f*

domestic [də'mestɪk] *adj* **a)** [appliance, pet] doméstico(a); **domestic science** economía doméstica **b)** [home-loving] casero(a) **c)** [flight, news] nacional; [trade, policy] interior

dominant ['dɒmɪnənt] *adj* dominante

dominate ['dɒmɪneɪt] *vt & vi* dominar

domineering [dɒmɪ'nɪərɪŋ] *adj* dominante

domino ['dɒmɪnəʊ] (*pl* **dominoes**) *n* [piece] ficha *f* de dominó; **dominoes** [game] dominó *m*

donate [dəʊ'neɪt] *vt* donar

donation [dəʊ'neɪʃən] *n* donativo *m*

done [dʌn] **1.** *adj* **a)** [finished] terminado(a); **it's over and done with** se acabó **b)** *Fam* [tired] rendido(a) **c)** [meat] hecho(a); [vegetables] cocido(a) **2.** *pp of* **do**

donkey ['dɒŋkɪ] *n* burro(a) *m,f*

donor ['dəʊnə(r)] *n* donante *mf*

don't [dəʊnt] = **do not**

doom [du:m] **1.** *n* [fate] destino *m* (funesto); [ruin] perdición *f*; [death] muerte *f* **2.** *vt* [destine] destinar; **doomed to failure** condenado(a) al fracaso

door [dɔ:(r)] *n* puerta *f*; **front/back door** puerta principal / trasera; *Fig* **behind closed doors** a puerta cerrada; **door handle** manilla *f* (de la puerta); **door knocker** picaporte *m*; **next door (to)** (en) la casa de al lado (de)

doorbell ['dɔ:bel] *n* timbre *m* (de la puerta)

doorknob ['dɔ:nɒb] *n* pomo *m*

doorman ['dɔ:mən] *n* portero *m*

doormat ['dɔ:mæt] *n* felpudo *m*, esterilla *f*

doorstep ['dɔ:step] *n* peldaño *m*; *Fig* **on one's doorstep** a la vuelta de la esquina

door-to-door ['dɔ:tə'dɔ:(r)] *adj* a domicilio

doorway ['dɔ:weɪ] *n* portal *m*, entrada *f*

doozy ['du:zɪ] *n US Fam* **wow, that bruise is a real doozy!** ¡hala! ¡vaya pasada de moratón!; **I'm having a doozy of a problem with this camera** tengo un problemazo con esta cámara; **it's a doozy of a challenge** es una pasada de reto

dope [dəʊp] **1.** *n* **a)** *Fam* [drug] chocolate *m* **b)** *Fam* [person] tonto(a) *mf*, *Am* zonzo(a) *m,f* **2.** *vt* [food, drink] adulterar con drogas; SPORT dopar

dork [dɔ:k] *n US Fam* [idiot] pazguato(a) *m,f*; [studious person] gafapasta *mf*, nerd *mf*

dormitory ['dɔ:mɪtərɪ] *n* **a)** [in school] dormitorio *m* **b)** *US* [in university] colegio *m* mayor

dosage ['dəʊsɪdʒ] *n Formal* [amount] dosis *finv*

dose [dəʊs] **1.** *n* dosis *finv* **2.** *vt* [patient] medicar

dossier ['dɒsɪeɪ] *n* expediente *m*

dot [dɒt] **1.** *n* punto *m*; **on the dot** en punto; COMPUT **dot matrix printer** impresora *f* matricial *or* de agujas **2.** *vt* **a)** *Fam* **to dot one's i's and cross one's t's** poner los puntos sobre las íes **b)** [scatter] esparcir, salpicar

dotcom ['dɒtkɒm] *n* puntocom *f*

dote [dəʊt] *vi* **to dote on sb** chochear con algn

double ['dʌbəl] **1.** *adj* doble; **it's double the price** cuesta dos veces más; **double bass** contrabajo *m*; **double bed** cama *f* de matrimonio; *Br* **double cream** *Esp* nata *f* para montar, *Am* crema líquida enriquecida, *RP* crema *f* doble

2. *adv* doble; **folded double** doblado(a) por la mitad; **to earn double** ganar el doble

3. *n* vivo retrato *m*; CIN & THEAT doble *m*

4. *vt* doblar; *Fig* [efforts] redoblar

5. *vi* **a)** [increase] doblarse

b) **to double as** [serve] hacer las veces de

■ **double back** *vi* **to double back on one's tracks** volver sobre sus pasos

■ **double up 1.** *vt sep* [bend] doblar **2.** *vi* **a)** [bend] doblarse **b)** [share room] compartir la habitación (**with** con)

double-cross [dʌbəl'krɒs] *Fam* **1.** *vt* engañar, traicionar **2.** *n* engaño *m*, traición *f*

double-glazing ['dʌbəl'gleɪzɪŋ] *n* doble acristalamiento *m*

doubt [daʊt] **1.** *n* duda *f*; **beyond (all) doubt** sin duda alguna; **no doubt** sin duda; **there's no doubt about it** no cabe la menor duda; **to be in doubt about sth** dudar algo; **to be open to doubt** [fact] ser dudoso(a); [outcome] ser incierto(a) **2.** *vt* **a)** [distrust] desconfiar de **b)** [not be sure of] dudar; **I doubt if** *or* **whether he'll come** dudo que venga

doubtful ['daʊtfʊl] *adj* **a)** [future] dudoso(a); [look] dubitativo(a); **I'm a bit doubtful about it** no me convence del todo; **it's doubtful whether …** no se sabe seguro si … **b)** [questionable] sospechoso(a)

doubtless ['daʊtlɪs] *adv* sin duda, seguramente

dough [dəʊ] *n* **a)** [for bread] masa *f* **b)** *Fam* [money] *Esp* pasta *f*, *Esp, RP* guita *f*, *Am* plata *f*, *Méx* lana *f*

doughnut ['dəʊnʌt] *n* rosquilla *f*, dónut® *m*

dove [dʌv] *n* paloma *f*

dowdy ['daʊdɪ] *(compar* **dowdier***, superl* **dowdiest***) adj* poco elegante

down [daʊn] **1.** *prep* **a)** [to or at a lower level] **down the river** río abajo; **to go down the road** bajar la calle **b)** [along] por
2. *adv* **a)** [to lower level] (hacia) abajo; [to floor] al suelo; [to ground] a tierra; **sales are down by 5 per cent** las ventas han bajado un 5 por ciento; **to fall down** caerse
b) [at lower level] abajo; **down there** allí abajo; *Fam & Fig* **to feel down** estar deprimido(a); *Br Fam* **down under** en Australia y Nueva Zelanda
3. *adj* [payment] al contado; [on property] de entrada
4. *vt Fam* [drink] tomarse de un trago; [food] zamparse

down-and-out ['daʊnən'aʊt] **1.** *adj* en las últimas **2.** *n* vagabundo(a) *m,f*

downcast ['daʊnkɑːst] *adj* abatido(a)

downfall ['daʊnfɔːl] *n* [of regime] caída *f*; [of person] perdición *f*

downhearted [daʊn'hɑːtɪd] *adj* desalentado(a)

downhill [daʊn'hɪl] **1.** *adj* [skiing] de descenso; *Fam* **after his first exam, the rest were all downhill** después del primer examen, los demás le fueron sobre ruedas **2.** *adv* **to go downhill** ir cuesta abajo; *Fig* [standards] deteriorarse

download ['daʊn'ləʊd] **1.** *n* COMPUT descarga *f*, *Fam* bajada *f* **2.** *vt* COMPUT descargar, *Fam* bajar

downloadable [,daʊn'ləʊdəbl] *adj* COMPUT descargable

downpour ['daʊnpɔː(r)] *n* chaparrón *m*

downright ['daʊnraɪt] *Fam* **1.** *adj* [blunt] tajante; [categorical] categórico(a); **it's a downright lie** es una mentira y gorda **2.** *adv* [totally] completamente

downstairs **1.** [daʊn'steəz] *adv* abajo; [to ground floor] a la planta baja; **to go downstairs** bajar la escalera **2.** ['daʊnsteəz] *adj* [on ground floor] de la planta baja

downtime ['daʊntaɪm] *n* **a)** tiempo *m* de inactividad **b)** *US Fig* [time for relaxing] **on the weekends I need some downtime** los fines de semana necesito parar y descansar

down-to-earth [daʊntʊ'ɜːθ] *adj* realista

downtown [daʊn'taʊn] *adv US* en el centro (de la ciudad)

downward ['daʊnwəd] **1.** *adj* [slope] descendente; [look] hacia abajo; FIN [tendency] a la baja **2.** *adv* = **downwards**

downwards ['daʊnwədz] *adv* hacia abajo

doze [dəʊz] **1.** *vi* dormitar **2.** *n* cabezada *f*; **to have a doze** echar una cabezada ■ **doze off** *vi* quedarse dormido(a)

dozen ['dʌzən] n docena f; **half a dozen/a dozen eggs** media docena / una docena de huevos; Fam **dozens of** un montón de

Dr (abbr of **Doctor**) Dr., Dra.

drab [dræb] (compar **drabber**, superl **drabbest**) adj a) [ugly] feo(a); [dreary] monótono(a), gris b) [colour] pardo(a)

draft [drɑːft] 1. n a) borrador m b) US servicio militar obligatorio c) US = **draught** 2. vt a) hacer un borrador de b) US MIL reclutar

drag [dræg] 1. vt a) [pull] arrastrar b) COMPUT arrastrar; **to drag and drop** arrastrar y soltar 2. vi [trail] arrastrarse 3. n Fam [nuisance] lata f ■ **drag off** vt sep llevarse arrastrando ■ **drag on** vi [war, strike] hacerse interminable ■ **drag out** vt sep [speech etc] alargar

dragon ['drægən] n dragón m

drain [dreɪn] 1. n a) [for water] desagüe m; [for sewage] alcantarilla f b) [grating] sumidero m c) Fig **the boys are a drain on her strength** los niños la dejan agotada 2. vt a) [marsh etc] avenar; [reservoir] desecar b) [crockery] escurrir c) [empty - glass] apurar; Fig [capital etc] agotar 3. vi a) [crockery] escurrirse b) **to drain (away)** [liquid] irse

drainpipe ['dreɪnpaɪp] n tubo m de desagüe

drama ['drɑːmə] n a) [play] obra f de teatro; Fig drama m b) [subject] teatro m

dramatic [drə'mætɪk] adj a) [change] impresionante; [moment] emocionante b) THEAT dramático(a), teatral

drank [dræŋk] pt of **drink**

drape [dreɪp] 1. vt **to drape sth over sth** colgar algo sobre algo; **draped with** cubierto(a) de 2. n a) [of fabric] caída f b) US cortina f

drastic ['dræstɪk] adj a) [measures] drástico(a), severo(a) b) [change] radical

draught [drɑːft] n a) [of cold air] corriente f (de aire) b) [of liquid] trago m; **draught (beer)** cerveza f de barril c) Br **draughts** [game] damas fpl

draw [drɔː] (pt **drew**, pp **drawn**) 1. vt a) [picture] dibujar; [line] trazar b) [pull] tirar de; [train, carriage] arrastrar; [curtains - open] descorrer; [close] correr; [blinds] bajar c) [extract] sacar; [salary] cobrar; [cheque] librar d) [attract] atraer; [attention] llamar e) Fig [strength] sacar f) [comparison] hacer; [conclusion] sacar 2. vi a) [sketch] dibujar b) [move] **the train drew into/out of the station** el tren entró en/salió de la estación; **to draw apart (from)** separarse (de) c) SPORT **they drew two all** empataron a dos 3. n a) [raffle] sorteo m b) SPORT empate m c) [attraction] atracción f ■ **draw in** vi [days] acortarse ■ **draw on** vt insep [savings] recurrir a; [experience] aprovecharse de ■ **draw out** vt sep a) [make long] alargar b) [encourage to speak] desatar la lengua a c) [from pocket, drawer etc] sacar ■ **draw up** vt sep [contract] preparar; [plan] esbozar

drawback ['drɔːbæk] n desventaja f, inconveniente m

drawer ['drɔːə(r)] n cajón m

drawing ['drɔːɪŋ] n dibujo m; **drawing board** mesa f de dibujo; Br **drawing pin** Esp chincheta f, Am chinche m; Formal **drawing room** sala f de estar

drawl [drɔːl] 1. vi hablar arrastrando las palabras 2. n voz cansina; US a **Southern drawl** un acento sureño

drawn [drɔːn] 1. adj [tired] ojeroso(a) 2. pp of **draw**

dread [dred] 1. vt temer a, tener pavor a 2. n temor m

dreadful ['dredful] *adj* a) [shocking] espantoso(a) b) *Fam* [awful] fatal; **how dreadful!** ¡qué horror!

dreadfully ['dredfulɪ] *adv Fam* terriblemente

dream [driːm] *(pt & pp* **dreamed** *or* **dreamt) 1.** *n* a) [sleep] sueño *m*
b) [daydream] ensueño *m*
c) *Fam* [marvel] maravilla *f* **2.** *vt* soñar
3. *vi* soñar **(of** *or* **about** con)

dreary ['drɪərɪ] *(compar* **drearier,** *superl* **dreariest)** *adj* a) [gloomy] triste
b) *Fam* [boring] aburrido(a), pesado(a)

drench [drentʃ] *vt* empapar

dress [dres] **1.** *n* a) [frock] vestido *m*
b) [clothing] ropa *f*; **dress rehearsal** ensayo *m* general; **dress shirt** camisa *f* de etiqueta **2.** *vt* a) [person] vestir; **he was dressed in a grey suit** llevaba (puesto) un traje gris b) [salad] aderezar, *Esp* aliñar c) [wound] vendar
3. *vi* vestirse ■ **dress up 1.** *vi* a) [in disguise] disfrazarse **(as** de) b) [in best clothes] vestirse elegante **2.** *vt sep Fig* disfrazar

dressing ['dresɪŋ] *n* a) [bandage] vendaje *m* b) **(salad) dressing** aliño *m*
c) **dressing gown** bata *f*; **dressing room** THEAT camerino *m*; SPORT vestuario *m*; **dressing table** tocador *m*

drew [druː] *pt of* **draw**

dribble ['drɪbəl] **1.** *vi* a) [baby] babear
b) [liquid] gotear **2.** *vt* SPORT [ball] driblar **3.** *n* [saliva] saliva *f*; [of water, blood] gotas *fpl*

dried [draɪd] *adj* [fruit] seco(a); [milk] en polvo

drier ['draɪə(r)] *n* = **dryer**

drift [drɪft] **1.** *vi* a) [boat] ir a la deriva; *Fig* [person] ir sin rumbo, vagar; **they drifted away** se marcharon poco a poco
b) [snow] amontonarse **2.** *n* a) [flow] flujo *m* b) [of snow] ventisquero *m*; [of sand] montón *m* c) *Fig* [meaning] idea *f*

drill [drɪl] **1.** *n* a) [hand tool] taladro *m*; MINING barrena *f*; **dentist's drill** fresa *f*; **pneumatic drill** martillo neumático
b) MIL instrucción *f* **2.** *vt* a) [wood etc] taladrar
b) [soldiers, children] instruir **3.** *vi* [by hand] taladrar; [for oil, coal] perforar, sondar

drilling ['drɪlɪŋ] *n* **drilling platform** plataforma *f* de perforación (petrolífera); **drilling rig** torre *f* de perforación (petrolífera)

drink [drɪŋk] *(pt* **drank,** *pp* **drunk) 1.** *vt* beber **2.** *vi* beber; **to have sth to drink** tomarse algo; **to drink to sth/sb** brindar por algo /algn **3.** *n* bebida *f*; [alcoholic] copa *f*

drink-driver *n Br* conductor(a) *m,f* borracho(a)

drinking ['drɪŋkɪŋ] *n* **drinking water** agua *f* potable

drip [drɪp] **1.** *n* a) [drop] goteo *m* b) MED gota a gota *m inv* c) *Fam* [person] necio(a) *m,f* **2.** *vi* gotear; **he was dripping with sweat** el sudor le caía a gotas

drive [draɪv] *(pt* **drove,** *pp* **driven) 1.** *vt*
a) [vehicle] conducir, *Am* manejar; [person] llevar
b) [power] impulsar
c) [compel] forzar, obligar; **to drive sb mad** volver loco(a) a algn; **to drive off** rechazar
2. *vi* AUTO conducir, *Am* manejar
3. *n* a) [trip] paseo *m* en coche *or Am* carro *or CSur* auto; **to go for a drive** dar una vuelta en coche *or Am* carro *or CSur* auto
b) [to house] camino *m* de entrada
c) [campaign] campaña *f*
d) [energy] energía *f*, vigor *m*
e) COMPUT unidad *f* de disco; **flash drive** memoria *f* USB

drivel ['drɪvəl] *n Fam Esp* chorradas *fpl*, *CAm, Méx* babosadas *fpl*, *Chile* leseras *fpl*, *CSur, Perú, Ven* macanas *fpl*

driven ['drɪvən] *pp of* **drive**

driver ['draɪvə(r)] *n* [of car, bus] conductor(a) *m,f*; [of train] maquinista *mf*, *Am* chofer *mf*; [of lorry] camionero(a) *m,f*; [of racing car] piloto *mf*; *US* **driver's license** *Esp* carné *m* or permiso *m* de conducir, *Bol, Ecuad, Perú* brevet *m*, *Carib* licencia *f* de conducir, *Méx* licencia *f* de manejar or para conducir, *RP* permiso *m* de conductor

driveway ['draɪweɪ] *n* [to house] camino *m* de entrada

driving ['draɪvɪŋ] **1.** *n* conducción *f*, *Am* manejo *m*; **driving instructor** profesor(a) *m,f* de autoescuela; *Br* **driving licence** *Esp* carné *m* or permiso *m* de conducir, *Bol, Ecuad, Perú* brevet *m*, *Carib* licencia *f* de conducir, *Méx* licencia *f* de manejar or para conducir, *RP* permiso *m* de conductor; **driving school** autoescuela *f*; **driving test** examen *m* de conducir **2.** *adj* **driving force** fuerza *f* motriz

drizzle ['drɪzəl] **1.** *n* llovizna *f*, *Andes, RP* garúa *f* **2.** *vi* lloviznar, chispear, *Andes, RP* garuar

droop [druːp] *vi* [flower] marchitarse; [eyelids] caerse

drop [drɒp] **1.** *n* **a)** [of liquid] gota *f*; **eye drops** colirio *m*
b) [descent] desnivel *m*
c) [in price] bajada *f*; [in temperature] descenso *m*
2. *vt* **a)** [let fall] dejar caer; [lower] bajar; [reduce] disminuir; **to drop a hint** soltar una indirecta
b) [abandon - subject, charge etc] abandonar, dejar; *SPORT* **he was dropped from the team** le echaron del equipo **3.** *vi* [object] caerse; [person] tirarse; [voice, price, temperature] bajar; [wind] amainar; [speed] disminuir
■ **drop by**, **drop in** *vi Fam* [visit] pasarse (**at** por)
■ **drop off 1.** *vi Fam* [fall asleep] quedarse dormido(a) **2.** *vt sep* [deliver] dejar
■ **drop out** *vi* [from college] dejar los estudios; [from society] marginarse; [from competition] retirarse
■ **drop round** *vi Fam* = **drop by**

drop-off *n* **a)** [decrease] descenso *m*; **a drop-off in sales** un descenso de las ventas **b)** *US* [descent] descenso *m*,

pendiente *f*; **there's a sharp drop-off in the road** la carretera desciende abruptamente, hay una pendiente abrupta en la carretera

drought [draʊt] *n* sequía *f*

drove [drəʊv] **1.** *n* [of cattle] manada *f* **2.** *pt of* **drive**

drown [draʊn] **1.** *vt* **a)** ahogar **b)** [place] inundar **2.** *vi* ahogarse; **he (was) drowned** murió ahogado

drowsy ['draʊzɪ] *(compar* **drowsier**, *superl* **drowsiest)** *adj* soñoliento(a); **to feel drowsy** tener sueño

drug [drʌg] **1.** *n* **a)** [medicine] medicamento *m* **b)** [narcotic] droga *f*, estupefaciente *m*; **to be on drugs** drogarse; **drug addict** drogadicto(a) *m,f*; **drug addiction** drogadicción *f*; **drug squad** brigada *f* antidroga **2.** *vt* [person] drogar; [food, drink] adulterar con drogas

druggist ['drʌgɪst] *n US* farmacéutico(a) *m,f*

drugstore ['drʌgstɔːr] *n US* establecimiento donde se compran medicamentos, periódicos, etc

drum [drʌm] **1.** *n* **a)** tambor *m*; **to play the drums** tocar la batería
b) [container] bidón *m*
2. *vi Fig* [with fingers] tabalear
3. *vt Fig* **to drum sth into sb** enseñar algo a algn a machamartillo
■ **drum up** *vt sep Fam* solicitar

drummer ['drʌmə(r)] *n* [in band] tambor *mf*; [in pop group] batería *mf*, *Am* baterista *mf*

drumstick ['drʌmstɪk] *n* **a)** *MUS* baqueta *f* **b)** [chicken leg] muslo *m*

drunk [drʌŋk] **1.** *adj* borracho(a); **to get drunk** emborracharse **2.** *n* borracho(a) *m,f* **3.** *pp of* **drink**

drunkard ['drʌŋkəd] *n* borracho(a) *m,f*

drunken ['drʌŋkən] *adj* [person] borracho(a); **drunken brawl** trifulca *f* de borrachos

dry [draɪ] *(pt & pp* dried*)* **1.** *(compar* drier or dryer, *superl* driest or dryest*) adj*
a) seco(a); *US* dry goods store mercería *f*, tienda *f* de confección
b) [wry] socarrón(ona)
2. *vt* secar
3. *vi* to dry (off) secarse

dry-clean [draɪˈkliːn] *vt* limpiar or lavar en seco

dryer [ˈdraɪə(r)] *n* secadora *f*

dual [ˈdjʊəl] *adj* doble; *Br* dual carriageway [road] (tramo *m* de) autovía *f*

dual-core *adj* dual-core processor procesador *m* de doble núcleo

dub¹ [dʌb] *vt* [subtitle] doblar (into a)

dub² [dʌb] *vt* a) [give nickname to] apodar b) [knight] armar

dubious [ˈdjuːbɪəs] *adj* a) [morals etc] dudoso(a); [compliment] equívoco(a) b) [doubting] indeciso(a)

duchess [ˈdʌtʃɪs] *n* duquesa *f*

duck¹ [dʌk] *n* pato(a) *m,f*; CULIN pato *m*

duck² [dʌk] **1.** *vt* a) [submerge] dar una ahogadilla a b) [evade] esquivar **2.** *vi* a) [evade blow] esquivar b) *Fam* to duck (out) rajarse

duckling [ˈdʌklɪŋ] *n* patito *m*

due [djuː] *adj* a) [expected] esperado(a); the train is due (to arrive) at ten el tren debe llegar a las diez b) *Formal* [proper] debido(a); in due course a su debido tiempo c) [owing] pagadero(a); how much are you due? [owed] ¿cuánto te deben? d) to be due to [caused by] deberse a; due to [because of] debido de

duel [ˈdjuːəl] *n* duelo *m*

duet [djuːˈet] *n* dúo *m*

duffel [ˈdʌfəl] *n* duffel bag petate *m*; duffel coat trenca *f*

dug [dʌg] *pt & pp of* dig

duke [djuːk] *n* duque *m*

dull [dʌl] **1.** *adj* a) [boring] pesado(a); [place] sin interés b) [light] apagado(a); [weather] gris c) [sound, ache] sordo(a) d) [not intelligent] tonto(a), torpe, *Am* sonso(a) **2.** *vt* [pain] aliviar

duly [ˈdjuːlɪ] *adv Formal* [properly] debidamente; [as expected] como era de esperar; [in due course] a su debido tiempo

dumb [dʌm] **1.** *adj* a) MED mudo(a) b) *Fam* [stupid] tonto(a) **2.** *npl* the dumb los mudos

dumbfounded [dʌmˈfaʊndɪd], **dumbstruck** [ˈdʌmstrʌk] *adj* pasmado(a)

dummy [ˈdʌmɪ] *n* a) [sham] imitación *f* b) [in shop window] maniquí *m*; [of ventriloquist] muñeco *m* c) *Br* [for baby] chupete *m*

dump [dʌmp] **1.** *n* a) [tip] vertedero *m*; [for old cars] cementerio *m* (de coches) b) *Fam & Pej* [place] estercolero *m*; [town] poblacho *m*; [dwelling] tugurio *m* c) MIL depósito *m* **2.** *vt* a) [rubbish] verter; [truck contents] descargar b) [person] dejar; COMM inundar el mercado con c) COMPUT [transfer] copiar de memoria interna

dumpling [ˈdʌmplɪŋ] *n* CULIN *bola de masa hervida*

dune [djuːn] *n* (sand) dune duna *f*

dung [dʌŋ] *n* estiércol *m*

dungarees [dʌŋɡəˈriːz] *npl* mono *m*

dupe [djuːp] **1.** *vt* engañar **2.** *n* ingenuo(a) *m,f*

duplex [ˈdjuːpleks] *n US* [house] casa adosada; duplex apartment dúplex *m inv*

duplicate 1. [ˈdjuːplɪkeɪt] *vt* a) [copy] duplicar; [film, tape] reproducir b) [repeat] repetir **2.** [ˈdjuːplɪkɪt] *n* duplicado *m*; in duplicate por duplicado

durable [ˈdjʊərəbəl] *adj* duradero(a)

duration [djʊˈreɪʃən] *n Formal* duración *f*

during [ˈdjʊərɪŋ] *prep* durante

dusk [dʌsk] *n Formal* crepúsculo *m*; at dusk al anochecer

dust [dʌst] **1.** *n* polvo *m*; dust cloud polvareda *f*; dust jacket sobrecubierta *f* **2.** *vt* a) [furniture] quitar el polvo a b) [cake] espolvorear

dustbin [ˈdʌstbɪn] *n Br* cubo *m* or *Am* bote *m* de la basura

duster ['dʌstə(r)] *n Br* [cloth] trapo *m or* bayeta *f* (del polvo); **feather duster** plumero *m*

dustman ['dʌstmən] *n Br* basurero *m*

dustpan ['dʌstpæn] *n* recogedor *m*

dusty ['dʌstɪ] *(compar* **dustier**, *superl* **dustiest)** *adj* polvoriento(a)

Dutch [dʌtʃ] **1.** *adj* holandés(esa); *Fig* **Dutch cap** diafragma *m*
2. *n* **a)** *(pl)* **the Dutch** los holandeses
b) [language] holandés *m*; **it's double Dutch to me** me suena a chino
3. *adv Fam* **to go Dutch** pagar cada uno lo suyo, *Esp* pagar a escote

duty ['dju:tɪ] *n* **a)** deber *m*; **to do one's duty** cumplir con su deber **b)** [task] función *f* **c)** **to be on duty** estar de servicio; MED & MIL estar de guardia **d)** [tax] impuesto *m*

duty-free [dju:tɪ'fri:] *adj* libre de impuestos

duvet ['du:veɪ] *n Br* edredón *m*

DVD [di:vi:'di:] *n* COMPUT *(abbr of* **Digital Versatile Disk, Digital Video Disk)** DVD *m*; **DVD burner** grabadora *f* de DVD; **DVD player** lector *m* de DVD

DVR *n (abbr of* **digital video recorder)** DVR *m*

dwarf [dwɔ:f] **1.** *(pl* **dwarves** [dwɔ:vz]) *n* [person] enano(a) *m,f* **2.** *vt* hacer parecer pequeño(a) a

dwell [dwel] *(pt & pp* **dwelt** [dwelt]) *vi Formal* morar ■ **dwell on** *vt insep* hablar extensamente de; **let's not dwell on it** olvidémoslo

dwindle ['dwɪndəl] *vi* menguar, disminuir

dye [daɪ] *(pt & pp* **dyed**, *pres p* **dyeing) 1.** *n* tinte *m* **2.** *vt* teñir; **to dye one's hair black** teñirse el pelo de negro

dying ['daɪɪŋ] *adj* [person] moribundo(a), agonizante; *Fig* [custom] en vías de desaparición

dynamic [daɪ'næmɪk] *adj* dinámico(a)

dynamite ['daɪnəmaɪt] *n* dinamita *f*

dynamo ['daɪnəməʊ] *n* dínamo *f*

dyslexia [dɪs'leksɪə] *n* dislexia *f*

E

E, e [i:] *n* a) [the letter] E, e *f* **b)** MUS E mi *m*

E [i:] *n* a) *(abbr of* **east)** E **b)** *Fam (abbr of* **ec-stasy)** [drug] éxtasis *m inv*

each [i:tʃ] **1.** *adj* cada; **each day /month** todos los días /meses; **each person** cada cual; **each time I see him** cada vez que lo veo **2.** *pron* a) cada uno(a); **£2 each** 2 libras cada uno; **we bought one each** nos compramos uno cada uno **b) each other** el uno al otro; **they hate each other** se odian

eager ['i:gə(r)] *adj* [anxious] impaciente; [desirous] deseoso(a); **eager to begin** impaciente por empezar; **to be eager for success** codiciar el éxito

eagerly ['i:gəlɪ] *adv* [anxiously] con impaciencia; [keenly] con ilusión

eagle ['i:gəl] *n* águila *f*

ear [ɪə(r)] *n* a) oreja *f*; [sense of hearing] oído *m* b) [of corn etc] espiga *f*

earache ['ɪəreɪk] *n* dolor *m* de oídos

eardrum ['ɪədrʌm] *n* tímpano *m*

early ['ɜ:lɪ] *(compar* **earlier,** *superl* **earliest)* **1.** *adj* a) [before the usual time] temprano(a); **to have an early night** acostarse pronto; **you're early!** ¡qué pronto has venido!
b) [at first stage, period] **at an early age** siendo joven; **in early July** a principios de julio; **early work** obra de juventud; **in her early forties** a los cuarenta y pocos
2. *adv* a) [before the expected time] temprano, *Esp* pronto; **earlier on** antes; **five minutes early** con cinco minutos de adelanto
b) [near the beginning] **as early as 1914** ya en 1914; **as early as possible** tan pronto como sea posible; **to book early** reservar con tiempo; **early on** temprano

earmark ['ɪəmɑ:k] *vt* destinar (**for** para *or* a)

earn [ɜ:n] *vt* a) [money] ganar; **to earn one's living** ganarse la vida **b)** [reputation] ganarse **c) to earn interest** cobrar interés *or* intereses

earnest ['ɜ:nɪst] **1.** *adj* serio(a), formal **2.** *n* **in earnest** de veras, en serio

earnings ['ɜ:nɪŋz] *npl* ingresos *mpl*

earphones ['ɪəfəʊnz] *npl* auriculares *mpl*

earring ['ɪərɪŋ] *n* pendiente *m*, *Am* arete *m*

earshot ['ɪəʃɒt] *n* **out of earshot** fuera del alcance del oído; **within earshot** al alcance del oído

earth [ɜ:θ] **1.** *n* a) tierra *f*; *Fig* **to be down to earth** ser práctico; *Fam* **where /why on earth ...?** ¿pero dónde /por qué demonios ...? **b)** *Br* ELEC toma *f* de tierra **2.** *vt* *Br* ELEC conectar a tierra

earthquake ['ɜ:θkweɪk] *n* terremoto *m*

ease [i:z] **1.** *n* a) [freedom from discomfort] tranquilidad *f*; **at ease** relajado(a) **b)** [lack of difficulty] facilidad *f* **2.** *vt* [pain] aliviar ■ **ease off, ease up** *vi* a) [decrease] disminuir **b)** [slow down] ir más despacio

easily ['i:zɪlɪ] *adv* fácilmente; **easily the best** con mucho el mejor

east [i:st] **1.** *n* este *m*; **the Middle East** el Oriente Medio **2.** *adj* del este, oriental; **East Germany** Alemania Oriental **3.** *adv* al *or* hacia el este

Easter ['i:stə(r)] *n* Semana Santa, Pascua *f*; **Easter egg** huevo *m* de Pascua; **Easter Sunday** Domingo *m* de Resurrección

easterly ['i:stəlɪ] *adj* [from the east] del este ; [to the east] hacia al este

eastern ['i:stən] *adj* oriental, del este

eastward(s) ['i:stwəd(z)] *adv* hacia el este

easy ['i:zɪ] (*compar* **easier**, *superl* **easiest**) **1.** *adj* a) [simple] fácil, sencillo(a) b) [unworried, comfortable] cómodo(a), tranquilo(a); *US* **Big Easy** apodo de Nueva Orleans; *Fam* **I'm easy!** ¡me da lo mismo!; **easy chair** butacón *m* **2.** *adv* **go easy on the wine** no te pases con el vino; *Fam* **to take things easy** tomarse las cosas con calma; *Fam* **take it easy!** ¡tranquilo!

easy-going [i:zɪ'ɡəʊɪŋ] *adj* [calm] tranquilo(a) ; [lax] despreocupado(a) ; [undemanding] poco exigente

eat [i:t] (*pt* **ate**, *pp* **eaten** ['i:tən]) *vt* comer ■ **eat away** *vt sep* desgastar ; [metal] corroer ■ **eat into** *vt insep* a) [wood] roer b) *Fig* [savings] consumir ■ **eat out** *vi* comer fuera ■ **eat up** *vt sep* a) [meal] terminar b) *Fig* [petrol] consumir ; [miles] recorrer rápidamente

eating ['i:tɪŋ] *adj* a) [for eating] **eating apple / pear** manzana *f* / pera *f* de mesa; **eating place** *or* **house** restaurante *m*, casa *f* de comidas b) [of eating] **eating disorder** trastorno *m* alimenticio; **eating habits** hábitos *mpl* alimenticios

eavesdrop ['i:vzdrɒp] *vi* escuchar disimuladamente

ebb [eb] **1.** *n* reflujo *m*; **ebb and flow** flujo y reflujo ; *Fig* **to be at a low ebb** estar decaído **2.** *vi* a) [tide] bajar ; **to ebb and flow** subir y bajar b) *Fig* **to ebb away** decaer

e-book *n* libro *m* electrónico, e-book *m*; **e-book reader** lector(a) *m,f* de libros electrónicos *or* de e-books

e-business *n* a) [company] ciberempresa *f*, negocio *m* electrónico b) [trade] cibercomercio *m*, comercio *m* electrónico

EC *n* (*abbr of* **European Community**) CE *f* (*Comunidad Europea*)

e-card *n* COMPUT tarjeta *f* electrónica

eccentric [ɪk'sentrɪk] *adj* & *n* excéntrico(a) *(m,f)*

echo ['ekəʊ] **1.** (*pl* **echoes**) *n* eco *m* **2.** *vt* [repeat] repetir **3.** *vi* resonar, hacer eco

eclipse [ɪ'klɪps] **1.** *n* eclipse *m* **2.** *vt* eclipsar

eco-house *n* casa *f* ecológica

ecological [i:kə'lɒdʒɪkəl] *adj* ecológico(a)

e-commerce *n* cibercomercio *m*, comercio *m* electrónico

economic [i:kə'nɒmɪk] *adj* económico(a) ; [profitable] rentable

economical [i:kə'nɒmɪkəl] *adj* económico(a)

economics [i:kə'nɒmɪks] *n sing* [science] economía *f*; SCH (ciencias *fpl*) económicas *fpl*

economize [ɪ'kɒnəmaɪz] *vi* economizar

economy [ɪ'kɒnəmɪ] *n* a) **the economy** la economía b) [saving] ahorro *m*; **economy class** clase *f* turista

ecorefill [i:kəʊ'ri:fɪl] *n* ecorrecarga *f*

ecotourism ['i:kəʊ,tʊərɪzm] *n* ecoturismo *m*, turismo *m* verde *or* ecológico

eco-town *n* ciudad *f* ecológica, eco-ciudad *f*

ecstasy ['ekstəsɪ] *n* éxtasis *m*

Ecuador ['ekwədɔ:(r)] *n* Ecuador *m*

Ecuadoran [,ekwə'dɔ:rən], **Ecuadorian** [,ekwə'dɔ:rɪən] *adj* & *n* ecuatoriano(a) *(m,f)*

edge [edʒ] **1.** *n* borde *m*; [of knife] filo *m*; [of coin] canto *m*; [of water] orilla *f*; **on the edge of town** en las afueras de la ciudad **2.** *vt* SEWING ribetear **3.** *vi* **to edge forward** avanzar poco a poco

edgy ['edʒɪ] (*compar* **edgier**, *superl* **edgiest**) *adj* nervioso(a)

edible ['edɪbəl] *adj* comestible

Edinburgh ['edɪnbrə] *n* Edimburgo

edit ['edɪt] *vt* a) [prepare for printing] preparar para la imprenta b) [rewrite] corregir c) PRESS ser redactor(a) de d) CIN, RADIO & TV montar ; [cut] cortar

elaborate

edition [ɪ'dɪʃən] n edición f; Fam **dead tree edition** edición f en papel, edición f impresa

editor ['edɪtə(r)] n [of book] editor(a) m,f; PRESS redactor(a) m,f; CIN, RADIO & TV montador(a) m,f

educate ['edjukeɪt] vt educar

educated ['edjukeɪtɪd] adj culto(a)

education [edju'keɪʃən] n a) [schooling] enseñanza f; **Ministry of Education** Ministerio m de Educación b) [training] formación f c) [studies] estudios mpl d) [culture] cultura f

educational [edju'keɪʃənəl] adj educativo(a), educacional

EEA n (abbr of **European Economic Area**) EEE m (Espacio Económico Europeo)

EEC n (abbr of **European Economic Community**) CEE f (Comunidad Económica Europea)

eel [iːl] n anguila f

eerie ['ɪərɪ] (compar eerier, superl eeriest) adj siniestro(a)

effect [ɪ'fekt] 1. n a) efecto m; **in effect** efectivamente; **to come into effect** entrar en vigor; **to have an effect on** afectar a; **to take effect** [drug] surtir efecto; [law] entrar en vigor b) [impression] impresión f 2. vt Formal provocar

effective [ɪ'fektɪv] adj a) [successful] eficaz b) [real] efectivo(a) c) [impressive] impresionante

effectively [ɪ'fektɪvlɪ] adv a) [successfully] eficazmente b) [in fact] en efecto

efficient [ɪ'fɪʃənt] adj eficaz, eficiente; [machine] de buen rendimiento

effort ['efət] n a) esfuerzo m; **to make an effort** hacer un esfuerzo, esforzarse b) [attempt] intento m

e.g. [iː'dʒiː] (abbr of **exempli gratia**) p. ej.

egg [eg] 1. n huevo m, CAm, Méx blanquillo m; **egg cup** huevera f; **egg timer** reloj m de arena; **egg white** clara f de huevo 2. vt **to egg sb on (to do sth)** empujar a algn (a hacer algo)

eggplant ['egplɑːnt] n US berenjena f

eggy ['egɪ] adj **an eggy taste/smell** un sabor/olor a huevo; **eggy bread** ≃ torrijas (sin azúcar)

ego ['iːgəu,'egəu] n a) ego m; Fam **ego trip** autobombo m b) Fam amor propio

egoist ['iːgəuɪst] n egoista mf

Egypt ['iːdʒɪpt] n Egipto

Egyptian [ɪ'dʒɪpʃən] adj & n egipcio(a) (m,f)

eight [eɪt] adj & n ocho (m inv)

eighteen [eɪ'tiːn] adj & n dieciocho (m inv)

eighteenth [eɪ'tiːnθ] 1. adj & n decimoctavo (m,f) 2. n [fraction] decimoctavo m

eighth [eɪtθ] 1. adj & n octavo(a) (m,f) 2. n [fraction] octavo m

eighty ['eɪtɪ] adj & n ochenta (m inv)

either ['aɪðə(r), 'iːðə(r)] 1. pron a) [affirmative] cualquiera; **either of them** cualquiera de los dos; **either of us** cualquiera de nosotros dos
b) [negative] ninguno/ninguna, ni el uno ni el otro/ni la una ni la otra; **I don't want either of them** no quiero ninguno de los dos
2. adj [both] cada, los dos/las dos; **on either side** en ambos lados; **in either case** en cualquier de los dos casos
3. conj o; **either ... or ...** o ... o ...; **either Friday or Saturday** o (bien) el viernes o el sábado
4. adv [after negative] tampoco; **I don't want to do it either** yo tampoco quiero hacerlo

eject [ɪ'dʒekt] 1. vt expulsar 2. vi AVIAT eyectarse

elaborate 1. [ɪ'læbəreɪt] vt a) [devise] elaborar
b) [explain] explicar detalladamente
2. [ɪ'læbəreɪt] vi explicarse; **to elaborate on sth** explicar algo con más detalles
3. [ɪ'læbərɪt] adj a) [complicated] complicado(a)
b) [detailed] detallado(a); [style] esmerado(a)

elastic [ɪ'læstɪk] **1.** *adj* elástico(a) ; *Fig* flexible ; **elastic band** goma elástica **2.** *n* elástico *m*

elbow ['elbəʊ] **1. n a)** codo *m* ; *Fig* **elbow room** espacio *m* **b)** [bend] recodo *m* **2.** *vt* **to elbow sb** dar un codazo a algn

elder[1] ['eldə(r)] **1.** *adj* mayor **2.** *n* **the elders** los ancianos

elder[2] ['eldə(r)] *n* BOT saúco *m*

elderly ['eldəlɪ] **1.** *adj* anciano(a) **2.** *npl* **the elderly** los ancianos

eldest ['eldɪst] **1.** *adj* mayor **2.** *n* **the eldest** el /la mayor

elect [ɪ'lekt] **1.** *vt* **a)** POL elegir **b)** [choose] **to elect to do sth** decidir hacer algo **2.** *adj* **the president elect** el presidente electo

election [ɪ'lekʃən] **1.** *n* elección *f* ; **general election** elecciones *fpl* generales **2.** *adj* electoral

electorate [ɪ'lektərɪt] *n* electorado *m*

electric [ɪ'lektrɪk] *adj* **a)** eléctrico(a) ; **electric blanket** manta eléctrica, *Am* frazada eléctrica ; **electric chair** silla eléctrica ; **electric shock** electrochoque *m* **b)** *Fig* electrizante

electrical [ɪ'lektrɪkəl] *adj* eléctrico(a)

electrician [ɪlek'trɪʃən] *n* electricista *mf*

electricity [ɪlek'trɪsɪtɪ] *n* electricidad *f* ; **electricity bill** recibo *m* de la luz

electronic [ɪlek'trɒnɪk] *adj* electrónico(a) ; **electronic banking** banca electrónica, telebanca *f* ; **electronic mail** correo *m* electrónico

electronics [ɪlek'trɒnɪks] **1.** *n sing* [science] electrónica *f* **2.** *npl* [of machine] componentes *mpl* electrónicos

elegant ['elɪgənt] *adj* elegante

element ['elɪmənt] *n* **a)** elemento *m* **b)** [part] parte *f* **c)** [electrical] resistencia *f* **d)** *Fam & Fig* **to be in one's element** estar en su salsa

elementary [elɪ'mentərɪ] *adj* [basic] elemental ; [not developed] rudimentario(a) ; [easy] fácil ; *US* **elementary school** escuela *f* primaria

elephant ['elɪfənt] *n* elefante *m*

elevate ['elɪveɪt] *vt* elevar ; [in rank] ascender

elevator ['elɪveɪtər] *n US* ascensor *m*

eleven [ɪ'levən] *adj & n* once (*m inv*)

eleventh [ɪ'levənθ] **1.** *adj & n* undécimo(a) (*m,f*) **2.** *n* [fraction] undécimo *m*

elicit [ɪ'lɪsɪt] *vt* obtener

eligible ['elɪdʒəbəl] *adj* apto(a) ; **he isn't eligible to vote** no tiene derecho al voto

eliminate [ɪ'lɪmɪneɪt] *vt* eliminar

elite [ɪ'liːt] *n* elite *f*

eloquent ['eləkwənt] *adj* elocuente

El Salvador [el'sælvədɔ:(r)] *n* El Salvador *m*

else [els] *adv* **a)** **anyone else** alguien más ; **anything else?** ¿algo más? ; **everything else** todo lo demás ; **no one else** nadie más ; **someone else** otro(a) ; **something else** otra cosa, algo más ; **somewhere else** en otra parte ; **what else?** ¿qué más? ; **where else?** ¿en qué otro sitio? **b)** **or else** [otherwise] si no

elsewhere [els'weə(r)] *adv* en otra parte

elude [ɪ'luːd] *vt* **a)** [escape] eludir ; **his name eludes me** no consigo acordarme de su nombre **b)** [avoid] esquivar

e-mail ['iːmeɪl] **1.** *n* COMPUT [system] correo *m* (electrónico) ; [message] (mensaje *m* por) correo (electrónico) ; **e-mail address** dirección *f* de correo (electrónico) **2.** *vt* COMPUT [person] enviar un correo (electrónico) a ; [file] enviar por correo (electrónico)

embankment [ɪm'bæŋkmənt] *n* **a)** [made of earth] terraplén *m* **b)** [of river] dique *m*

embargo [em'bɑːgəʊ] *(pl* **embargoes)** *n* embargo *m*

embark [em'bɑːk] **1.** *vt* [merchandise] embarcar **2.** *vi* embarcar, embarcarse ; *Fig* **to embark upon** emprender ; [sth difficult] embarcarse en

embarrass [ɪm'bærəs] *vt* avergonzar, *Am salvo RP* apenar

embarrassing [ɪmˈbærəsɪŋ] *adj* embarazoso(a), *Am salvo RP* penoso(a)

embassy [ˈembəsɪ] *n* embajada *f*

ember [ˈembə(r)] *n* ascua *f*, rescoldo *m*

emblem [ˈembləm] *n* emblema *m*

embrace [ɪmˈbreɪs] **1.** *vt* **a)** abrazar **b)** [accept] adoptar **c)** [include] abarcar **2.** *vi* abrazarse **3.** *n* abrazo *m*

embroider [ɪmˈbrɔɪdə(r)] *vt* **a)** SEWING bordar **b)** *Fig* [story, truth] adornar, embellecer

embroidery [ɪmˈbrɔɪdərɪ] *n* bordado *m*

embryo [ˈembrɪəʊ] *n* embrión *m*

emerald [ˈemərəld] *n* esmeralda *f*

emerge [ɪˈmɜːdʒ] *vi* salir; [problem] surgir; **it emerged that ...** resultó que ...

emergency [ɪˈmɜːdʒənsɪ] *n* emergencia *f*; MED urgencia *f*; **in an emergency** en caso de emergencia; **emergency brake** freno *m* de emergencia; *US* [handbrake] freno *m* de mano; **emergency exit** salida *f* de emergencia; **emergency landing** aterrizaje forzoso; **emergency measures** medidas *fpl* de urgencia; *US* **emergency room** sala *f* de urgencias; AUTO **emergency stop** frenazo *m* en seco; **emergency telephone** teléfono *m* de urgencias; POL **state of emergency** estado *m* de excepción

emigrant [ˈemɪgrənt] *n* emigrante *mf*

emigrate [ˈemɪgreɪt] *vi* emigrar

eminent [ˈemɪnənt] *adj* eminente

emit [ɪˈmɪt] *vt* [signals] emitir; [smells] despedir; [sound] producir

e-money *n* dinero *m* electrónico

emotion [ɪˈməʊʃən] *n* emoción *f*

emotional [ɪˈməʊʃənəl] *adj* **a)** emocional **b)** [moving] conmovedor(a)

emotive [ɪˈməʊtɪv] *adj* emotivo(a)

empathy [ˈempəθɪ] *n* identificación *f*

emperor [ˈempərə(r)] *n* emperador *m*

emphasis [ˈemfəsɪs] *(pl* **emphases** [ˈemfəsiːz]*) n* énfasis *m*; **to place emphasis on sth** hacer hincapié en algo

emphasize [ˈemfəsaɪz] *vt* subrayar, hacer hincapié en; [insist] insistir; [highlight] hacer resaltar

emphatic [emˈfætɪk] *adj* [forceful] enfático(a); [convinced] categórico(a)

empire [ˈempaɪə(r)] *n* imperio *m*

employ [ɪmˈplɔɪ] *vt* emplear; [time] ocupar

employee [emˈplɔiː, emplɔɪˈiː] *n* empleado(a) *m,f*

employer [ɪmˈplɔɪə(r)] *n* patrón(ona) *m,f*

employment [ɪmˈplɔɪmənt] *n* empleo *m*; **employment agency** agencia *f* de colocaciones; **full employment** pleno empleo

emptiness [ˈemptɪnɪs] *n* vacío *m*

empty [ˈemptɪ] **1.** *(compar* **emptier**, *superl* **emptiest***) adj* vacío(a); **an empty house** una casa deshabitada; **empty promises** promesas *fpl* vanas **2.** *vt* vaciar **3.** *vi* **a)** vaciarse **b)** [river] desembocar **(into en) 4.** *npl* **empties** envases vacíos

empty-handed [emptɪˈhændɪd] *adj* con las manos vacías

emulate [ˈemjʊleɪt] *vt* emular

enable [ɪnˈeɪbəl] *vt* permitir

enabled [ɪˈneɪbəld] *adj* COMPUT [option] activado(a)

enamel [ɪˈnæməl] *n* esmalte *m*

enchanting [ɪnˈtʃɑːntɪŋ] *adj* encantador(a)

encircle [ɪnˈsɜːkəl] *vt* rodear

enclose [ɪnˈkləʊz] *vt* **a)** [surround] rodear **b)** [fence in] cercar **c)** [in envelope] adjuntar; **please find enclosed** le enviamos adjunto

enclosure [ɪnˈkləʊʒə(r)] *n* **a)** [fenced area] cercado *m* **b)** [in envelope] documento adjunto **c)** [of racecourse] recinto *m*

encore [ˈɒŋkɔː(r)] **1.** *interj* ¡otra!, ¡bis! **2.** *n* repetición *f*, bis *m*

encounter [ɪnˈkaʊntə(r)] **1.** *n* [meeting] encuentro *m* **2.** *vt* encontrar, encontrarse con; [problems] tropezar con

encourage [ɪnˈkʌrɪdʒ] *vt* **a)** [person] animar **b)** [tourism, trade] fomentar

encouragement [ɪnˈkʌrɪdʒmənt] n estímulo m

encrypt [enˈkrɪpt] vt COMPUT encriptar, codificar

encryption [enˈkrɪpʃn] n COMPUT encriptación f, codificación f

encyclop(a)edia [ensaɪkləʊˈpiːdɪə] n enciclopedia f

end [end] **1.** n a) [of stick] punta f; [of street] final m; [of table] extremo m; *Fig* **to make ends meet** llegar a final de mes
b) [conclusion] fin m, final m; **from end to end** de un extremo al otro; **in the end** al final; **for hours on end** hora tras hora; **to bring an end to sth** poner fin a algo; **to put an end to** acabar con c) [aim] objetivo m, fin m
2. vt acabar, terminar
3. vi acabarse, terminarse

■ **end up** vi terminar; **it ended up in the dustbin** fue a parar al cubo de la basura; **to end up doing sth** terminar por hacer algo

endanger [ɪnˈdeɪndʒə(r)] vt poner en peligro

endearing [ɪnˈdɪərɪŋ] adj simpático(a)

endeavour, US **endeavor** [ɪnˈdevə(r)] **1.** n esfuerzo m **2.** vt intentar, procurar

ending [ˈendɪŋ] n final m

endless [ˈendlɪs] adj interminable

end-of-year adj de fin de año

endorse [ɪnˈdɔːs] vt a) [document, cheque] endosar b) [approve - opinion, action] apoyar, respaldar

endorsement [ɪnˈdɔːsmənt] n a) [on document, cheque] endoso m b) Br [on driving licence] infracción f anotada c) [approval] aprobación f

endow [ɪnˈdaʊ] vt dotar; **to be endowed with** estar dotado(a) de

endurance [ɪnˈdjʊərəns] n resistencia f

endure [ɪnˈdjʊə(r)] **1.** vt [bear] aguantar, soportar **2.** vi perdurar

enemy [ˈenəmɪ] adj & n enemigo(a) (m,f)

energetic [enədˈʒetɪk] adj enérgico(a)

energy [ˈenədʒɪ] n energía f

energy-saving adj [device] para ahorrar energía; **energy-saving bulb** bombilla f de bajo consumo

enforce [ɪnˈfɔːs] vt [law] hacer cumplir

engage [ɪnˈgeɪdʒ] vt a) [hire] contratar b) [attention] llamar c) [in conversation] entablar

engaged [ɪnˈgeɪdʒd] adj a) [betrothed] prometido(a); **to get engaged** prometerse b) [busy] ocupado(a); Br TEL **it's engaged** está comunicando

engagement [ɪnˈgeɪdʒmənt] n a) [betrothal] petición f de mano; [period] noviazgo m; **engagement ring** anillo m de compromiso b) [appointment] cita f c) MIL combate m

engine [ˈendʒɪn] n motor m; RAIL locomotora f; **engine room** sala f de máquinas; **engine driver** maquinista mf

engineer [endʒɪˈnɪə(r)] **1.** n a) ingeniero(a) m,f; **civil engineer** ingeniero de caminos b) US RAIL maquinista mf **2.** vt Fig [contrive] maquinar

engineering [endʒɪˈnɪərɪŋ] n ingeniería f; **electrical engineering** electrotecnia f; **civil engineering** ingeniería civil

England [ˈɪŋglənd] n Inglaterra

English [ˈɪŋglɪʃ] **1.** adj inglés(esa) **2.** n a) [language] inglés m b) (pl) **the English** los ingleses

Englishman [ˈɪŋglɪʃmən] n inglés m

English-speaking [ˈɪŋglɪʃspiːkɪŋ] adj de habla inglesa

Englishwoman [ˈɪŋglɪʃwʊmən] n inglesa f

engraving [ɪnˈgreɪvɪŋ] n grabado m

engrossed [ɪnˈgrəʊst] adj absorto(a) (**in** en)

engulf [ɪnˈgʌlf] vt tragarse

enhance [ɪnˈhɑːns] vt [beauty] realzar; [power, chances] aumentar

enigma [ɪˈnɪgmə] n enigma m

enjoy [ɪnˈdʒɔɪ] vt a) disfrutar de; **to enjoy oneself** pasarlo bien b) [benefit from] gozar de

enjoyable [ɪnˈdʒɔɪəbəl] adj agradable; [amusing] divertido(a)

enjoyment [ɪnˈdʒɔɪmənt] *n* placer *m*, gusto *m*

enlarge [ɪnˈlɑːdʒ] **1.** *vt* extender, ampliar ; PHOTO ampliar **2.** *vi* **to enlarge upon a subject** extenderse sobre un tema

enlargement [ɪnˈlɑːdʒmənt] *n* PHOTO ampliación *f*

enlighten [ɪnˈlaɪtən] *vt* iluminar

enlist [ɪnˈlɪst] **1.** *vt* MIL reclutar ; **to enlist sb's help** conseguir ayuda de algn **2.** *vi* MIL alistarse

enormous [ɪˈnɔːməs] *adj* enorme

enormously [ɪˈnɔːməslɪ] *adv* enormemente ; **I enjoyed myself enormously** lo pasé genial

enough [ɪˈnʌf] **1.** *adj* bastante, suficiente ; **enough books** bastantes libros ; **enough money** bastante dinero ; **have we got enough petrol?** ¿tenemos suficiente gasolina?
2. *adv* bastante ; **oddly enough ...** lo curioso es que ... ; **sure enough** en efecto
3. *pron* lo bastante, lo suficiente ; **enough to live on** lo suficiente para vivir ; **it isn't enough** no basta ; **more than enough** más que suficiente ; *Fam* **I've had enough!** ¡estoy harto!

enquire [ɪnˈkwaɪə(r)] *vi* preguntar

enquiry [ɪnˈkwaɪərɪ] *n* **a)** [question] pregunta *f* ; **to make an enquiry** preguntar ; **enquiries** información *f* **b)** [investigation] investigación *f*

enrage [ɪnˈreɪdʒ] *vt* enfurecer

enrich [ɪnˈrɪtʃ] *vt* enriquecer

enrol, *US* **enroll** [ɪnˈrəʊl] **1.** *vt* matricular, inscribir **2.** *vi* matricularse, inscribirse

enrolment, *US* **enrollment** [ɪnˈrəʊlmənt] *n* matrícula *f*

ensue [ɪnˈsjuː] *vi* **a)** [follow] seguir **b)** [result] resultar (**from** de)

ensure [ɪnˈʃʊə(r)] *vt* asegurar

entail [ɪnˈteɪl] *vt* [involve] suponer

entangle [ɪnˈtæŋgəl] *vt* enredar

enter [ˈentə(r)] **1.** *vt* **a)** [go into] entrar en ; *Fig* [join] ingresar en **b)** [write down]
apuntar, anotar **c)** COMPUT dar entrada a **2.** *vi* entrar ■ **enter into** *vt insep* **a)** [agreement] firmar ; [negotiations] iniciar ; [bargain] cerrar **b)** [relations] establecer ; [conversation] entablar

enterprise [ˈentəpraɪz] *n* empresa *f* ; **free enterprise** libre empresa ; **private enterprise** iniciativa privada ; [as a whole] sector privado ; **public enterprise** el sector público

enterprising [ˈentəpraɪzɪŋ] *adj* emprendedor(a)

entertain [entəˈteɪn] **1.** *vt* **a)** [amuse] divertir **b)** [consider] considerar ; **to entertain an idea** abrigar una idea **2.** *vi* tener invitados

entertainer [entəˈteɪnə(r)] *n* artista *mf*

entertainment [entəˈteɪnmənt] *n* **a)** diversión *f* **b)** THEAT espectáculo *m*

enthusiasm [ɪnˈθjuːzɪæzəm] *n* entusiasmo *m*

enthusiast [ɪnˈθjuːzɪæst] *n* entusiasta *mf*

enthusiastic [ɪnθjuːzɪˈæstɪk] *adj* entusiasta ; [praise] caluroso(a) ; **to be enthusiastic about sth** entusiasmarse por algo

entice [ɪnˈtaɪs] *vt* seducir, atraer

entire [ɪnˈtaɪə(r)] *adj* entero(a), todo(a)

entirely [ɪnˈtaɪəlɪ] *adv* **a)** [completely] totalmente **b)** [solely] exclusivamente

entitle [ɪnˈtaɪtəl] *vt* **a)** dar derecho a ; **to be entitled to** tener derecho a **b)** [book etc] titular

entrance¹ [ˈentrəns] *n* **a)** entrada *f* ; **entrance fee** [to museum etc] entrada ; [to organization] cuota *f* **b)** [admission] ingreso *m* ; **entrance examination** examen *m* de ingreso

entrance² [ɪnˈtrɑːns] *vt* encantar

entrant [ˈentrənt] *n* [in competition] participante *mf* ; [applicant] aspirante *mf*

entrée [ˈɒntreɪ] *n Br* [first course] entrada *f*, primer plato *m* ; *US* [main course] plato principal

entrepreneur [ɒntrəprəˈnɜː(r)] *n* empresario(a) *m,f*

entrust [ɪn'trʌst] *vt* encargar (**with** de); **to entrust sth to sb** dejar algo al cuidado de algn

entry ['entrɪ] *n* **a)** [entrance] entrada *f*; **no entry** [sign] dirección prohibida **b)** [in competition] participante *mf*

enuf MESSAGING *written abbr of* **enough**

envelope ['envələʊp] *n* sobre *m*

envious ['envɪəs] *adj* envidioso(a); **to feel envious** tener envidia

environment [ɪn'vaɪərənmənt] *n* medio *m* ambiente

environmental [ɪnvaɪərən'mentəl] *adj* medioambiental

envisage [ɪn'vɪzɪʤ] *vt* [imagine] imaginarse; [foresee] prever

envoy ['envɔɪ] *n* enviado(a) *m,f*

envy ['envɪ] **1.** *n* envidia *f* **2.** *vt* envidiar, tener envidia de

ephemeral [ɪ'femərəl] *adj* efímero(a)

epic ['epɪk] **1.** *n* epopeya *f* **2.** *adj* épico(a)

epidemic [epɪ'demɪk] *n* epidemia *f*; *Fig* [of crime etc] ola *f*

epilepsy ['epɪlepsɪ] *n* epilepsia *f*

episode ['epɪsəʊd] *n* episodio *m*

epitaph ['epɪtɑːf] *n* epitafio *m*

epoch ['iːpɒk] *n* época *f*

equal ['iːkwəl] **1.** *adj* igual; **to be equal to the occasion** estar a la altura de las circunstancias; **equal pay** igualdad *f* de salarios
2. *n* igual *mf*; **to treat sb as an equal** tratar a algn de igual a igual
3. (*pt & pp* **equalled**, *US pt & pp* **equaled**) *vt* **a)** MATH equivaler
b) [match] igualar

equality [iː'kwɒlɪtɪ] *n* igualdad *f*

equalize ['iːkwəlaɪz] **1.** *vi* FTBL empatar **2.** *vt* igualar

equally ['iːkwəlɪ] *adv* igualmente; **equally pretty** igual de bonito; **to share sth equally** dividir algo en partes iguales

equation [ɪ'kweɪʒən, ɪ'kweɪʃən] *n* MATH ecuación *f*

equator [ɪ'kweɪtə(r)] *n* ecuador *m*

equilibrium [iːkwɪ'lɪbrɪəm] *n* equilibrio *m*

equip [ɪ'kwɪp] *vt* [with tools, machines] equipar; [with food] proveer

equipment [ɪ'kwɪpmənt] *n* [materials] equipo *m*; **office equipment** material *m* de oficina

equivalent [ɪ'kwɪvələnt] *adj & n* equivalente (*m*); **to be equivalent to** equivaler a, ser equivalente a

ER a) (*abbr of* **Elizabeth Regina**) *emblema de la reina Isabel II* **b)** *US* (*abbr of* **Emergency Room**) urgencias *fpl*

era ['ɪərə] *n* era *f*

eradicate [ɪ'rædɪkeɪt] *vt* erradicar

erase [ɪ'reɪz] *vt* borrar

eraser [*Br* ɪ'reɪzə(r), *US* ɪ'reɪsər] *n* goma *f* de borrar

ereader ['iːriːdə(r)] *n* lector *m* electrónico

erect [ɪ'rekt] **1.** *adj* **a)** [upright] erguido(a) **b)** [penis] erecto(a) **2.** *vt* [monument] levantar, erigir

erode [ɪ'rəʊd] *vt* **a)** [rock, soil] erosionar **b)** [metal] corroer, desgastar; *Fig* [power, confidence] hacer perder

erosion [ɪ'rəʊʒən] *n* GEOL erosión *f*

erotic [ɪ'rɒtɪk] *adj* erótico(a)

errand ['erənd] *n* recado *m*; **errand boy** recadero *m*

erratic [ɪ'rætɪk] *adj* [performance, behaviour] irregular; [weather] muy variable; [person] caprichoso(a)

error ['erə(r)] *n* error *m*, equivocación *f*

erupt [ɪ'rʌpt] *vi* **a)** [volcano] entrar en erupción; [violence] estallar **b)** **his skin erupted in a rash** le salió una erupción

eruption [ɪ'rʌpʃən] *n* erupción *f*

escalate ['eskəleɪt] *vi* [war] intensificarse; [prices] aumentar; [change] convertirse (**into** en)

escalator ['eskəleɪtə(r)] *n* escalera mecánica

escapade ['eskəpeɪd] *n* aventura *f*

escape [ɪ'skeɪp] **1.** *n* huída *f*, fuga *f*; [of gas] escape *m*; **escape lane** vía *f* de frenado; **escape route** vía *f* de escape

2. *vi* escaparse

3. *vt* **a)** [avoid] evitar, huir de; **to escape punishment** librarse del castigo **b)** *Fig* **his name escapes me** no recuerdo su nombre

escort 1. ['eskɔːt] *n* **a)** [companion] acompañante *mf* **b)** MIL escolta *f* **c)** [prostitute] prostituto(a) *m,f* **2.** [ɪˈskɔːt] *vt* **a)** [accompany] acompañar **b)** [protect] escoltar

e-signature *n* firma *f* electrónica

Eskimo ['eskɪməʊ] *adj* & *n* esquimal (*mf*)

ESOL ['iːsɒl] *n US* SCH (*abbr of* **English for Speakers of Other Languages**) inglés *m* como segunda lengua

especially [ɪˈspeʃəlɪ] *adv* especialmente, sobre todo

espresso [eˈspresəʊ] *n* café *m* exprés

essay ['eseɪ] *n* SCH redacción *f*

essence ['esəns] *n* esencia *f*; **in essence** esencialmente

essential [ɪˈsenʃəl] **1.** *adj* esencial, imprescindible **2.** *n* necesidad básica; **the essentials** lo fundamental

establish [ɪˈstæblɪʃ] *vt* **a)** [found] establecer; [business] montar **b)** JUR **to establish a fact** probar un hecho; **to establish the truth** demostrar la verdad

established [ɪˈstæblɪʃt] *adj* [person] establecido(a); [fact] conocido(a)

establishment [ɪˈstæblɪʃmənt] *n* establecimiento *m*; **the Establishment** el sistema

estate [ɪˈsteɪt] *n* **a)** [land] finca *f*; *Br* **estate agent** agente *mf* inmobiliario(a); *Br* **estate (car)** ranchera *f*, *Esp* coche *m* modelo familiar **b)** *Br* [housing] **estate** urbanización *f* **c)** JUR [of deceased person] herencia *f*

esteem [ɪˈstiːm] **1.** *n* **to hold sb in great esteem** apreciar mucho a algn **2.** *vt* estimar

esthetic [esˈθetɪk] *US adj* = **aesthetic**

estimate 1. ['estɪmɪt] *n* [calculation] cálculo *m*; [likely cost of work] presupuesto *m*; **rough estimate** cálculo aproximado **2.** ['estɪmeɪt] *vt* calcular; *Fig* pensar, creer

estuary ['estjʊərɪ] *n* estuario *m*

etc [etˈsetrə] *adv* (*abbr of* **et cetera**) etc., etcétera

etching ['etʃɪŋ] *n* aguafuerte *m*

eternal [ɪˈtɜːnəl] *adj* eterno(a), incesante; **eternal triangle** triángulo amoroso

eternity [ɪˈtɜːnɪtɪ] *n* eternidad *f*

ethical ['eθɪkəl] *adj* ético(a)

ethics ['eθɪks] *n* ética *f*

ethnic ['eθnɪk] *adj* étnico(a)

e-ticket *n* billete *m* electrónico

etiquette ['etɪket] *n* protocolo *m*, etiqueta *f*

e-trade *n* cibercomercio *m*, comercio *m* electrónico

E2EG MESSAGING *written abbr of* **ear to ear grin**

EU [iːˈjuː] *n* (*abbr of* **European Union**) UE *f*

euphemism ['juːfɪmɪzəm] *n* eufemismo *m*

euro ['jʊərəʊ] *n* (*pl* **euros**) *n* [European currency] euro *m*

Europe ['jʊərəp] *n* Europa

European [jʊərəˈpiːən] *adj* & *n* europeo(a) (*m,f*); **European Community** Comunidad *f* Europea; **European Union** Unión *f* Europea

evacuate [ɪˈvækjʊeɪt] *vt* evacuar

evade [ɪˈveɪd] *vt* evadir

evaluate [ɪˈvæljʊeɪt] *vt* evaluar

evangelical [iːvænˈdʒelɪkəl] *adj* evangélico(a)

evaporate [ɪˈvæpəreɪt] **1.** *vt* evaporar; **evaporated milk** leche condensada sin endulzar **2.** *vi* evaporarse; *Fig* desvanecerse

evasive [ɪˈveɪsɪv] *adj* evasivo(a)

eve [iːv] *n* víspera *f*; **on the eve of** en vísperas de

even ['iːvən] **1.** *adj* **a)** [smooth] liso(a); [level] llano(a) **b)** [regular] uniforme

c) [equally balanced] igual; **to get even with sb** desquitarse con algn
d) [number] par
e) [at the same level] a nivel
f) [quantity] exacto(a)
2. *adv* **a)** incluso, hasta, aun; **even now** incluso ahora; **even so** aun así; **even the children knew** hasta los niños lo sabían
b) [negative] ni siquiera; **she can't even write her name** ni siquiera sabe escribir su nombre
c) [before comparative] aun, todavía; **even worse** aun peor
d) even if incluso si; **even though** aunque
3. *vt* igualar

evening ['i:vnɪŋ] *n* **a)** [early] tarde *f*; [late] noche *f*; **in the evening** por la tarde; **tomorrow evening** mañana por la tarde; **evening class** clase nocturna; **evening dress** [for man] traje *m* de etiqueta; [for woman] traje de noche; **evening paper** periódico vespertino
b) [greeting] **good evening!** [early] ¡buenas tardes!; [late] ¡buenas noches!

evenly ['i:vənlı] *adv* [uniformly] uniformemente; [fairly] equitativamente

event [ɪ'vent] *n* **a)** [happening] suceso *m*, acontecimiento *m* **b)** [case] caso *m*; **in the event of fire** en caso de incendio **c)** SPORT prueba *f*

eventful [ɪ'ventfʊl] *adj* **an eventful day** [busy] un día agitado; [memorable] un día memorable

eventual [ɪ'ventʃʊəl] *adj* [ultimate] final; [resulting] consiguiente

eventuality [ɪventʃʊ'ælɪtɪ] *n* eventualidad *f*

eventually [ɪ'ventʃʊəlɪ] *adv* finalmente

ever ['evə(r)] *adv* **a)** nunca, jamás; **stronger than ever** más fuerte que nunca **b)** [interrogative] alguna vez; **have you ever been there?** ¿has estado allí alguna vez? **c)** [always] siempre; **for ever** para siempre **d)** [emphasis] **how ever did you manage it?** ¿cómo diablos lo conseguiste?; **thank you ever so much** muchísimas gracias

evergreen ['evəgri:n] **1.** *adj* de hoja perenne **2.** *n* árbol *m* / planta *f* de hoja perenne

everlasting [evə'lɑ:stɪŋ] *adj* eterno(a)

every ['evrɪ] *adj* **a)** [each] cada; **every now and then** de vez en cuando; **every day** todos los días; **every other day** cada dos días; **every one of you** todos(as) vosotros(as); **every citizen** todo ciudadano **b) you had every right to be angry** tenías toda la razón para estar *esp Esp* enfadado *or esp Am* enojado

everybody ['evrɪbɒdɪ] *pron* todo el mundo, todos(as)

everyday ['evrɪdeɪ] *adj* diario(a), de todos los días; **an everyday occurrence** un suceso cotidiano

everyone ['evrɪwʌn] *pron* todo el mundo, todos(as)

everyplace ['evrɪpleɪs] *US adv* = **everywhere**

everything ['evrɪθɪŋ] *pron* todo; **he eats everything** come de todo; **she means everything to me** ella lo es todo para mí

everywhere ['evrɪweə(r)] *adv* en todas partes, por todas partes

evict [ɪ'vɪkt] *vt* desahuciar

evidence ['evɪdəns] *n* **a)** [proof] evidencia *f* **b)** JUR testimonio *m*; **to give evidence** prestar declaración **c)** [sign] indicio *m*, señal *f*; **to be in evidence** dejarse notar

evident ['evɪdənt] *adj* evidente, manifiesto(a)

evidently ['evɪdəntlɪ] *adv* evidentemente, al parecer

evil ['i:vəl] **1.** *adj* [wicked] malo(a), malvado(a); [harmful] nocivo(a); [unfortunate] aciago(a) **2.** *n* mal *m*

evocative [ɪ'vɒkətɪv] *adj* evocador(a)

evoke [ɪ'vəʊk] *vt* evocar

evolution [i:və'lu:ʃən] *n* evolución *f*; BIOL desarrollo *m*

evolve [ɪ'vɒlv] **1.** *vi* [species] evolucionar; [ideas] desarrollarse **2.** *vt* desarrollar

EVRY1 MESSAGING *written abbr of* **everyone**

e-wallet *n* monedero *m* electrónico

ewe [juː] *n* oveja *f*

ex [eks] *n* **her ex** su exmarido; **his ex** su exmujer

ex- [eks] *pref* ex, antiguo(a); **ex-minister** exministro *m*

exact [ɪgˈzækt] **1.** *adj* [accurate] exacto(a); [definition] preciso(a); **this exact spot** este mismo lugar **2.** *vt* exigir

exactly [ɪgˈzæktlɪ] *adv* exactamente, precisamente; **exactly!** ¡exacto!

exaggerate [ɪgˈzædʒəreɪt] *vi & vt* exagerar

exam [ɪgˈzæm] *n Fam* examen *m*

examination [ɪgzæmɪˈneɪʃən] *n* a) SCH examen *m*; **to sit an examination** hacer un examen **b)** MED reconocimiento *m* **c)** JUR interrogatorio *m*

examine [ɪgˈzæmɪn] *vt* SCH examinar; [customs] registrar; MED hacer un reconocimiento médico a; JUR interrogar

example [ɪgˈzɑːmpəl] *n* ejemplo *m*; [specimen] ejemplar *m*; **for example** por ejemplo

exasperate [ɪgˈzɑːspəreɪt] *vt* exasperar

excavate [ˈekskəveɪt] *vt* excavar

exceed [ekˈsiːd] *vt* exceder, sobrepasar

exceedingly [ekˈsiːdɪŋlɪ] *adv* extremadamente, sumamente

excel [ɪkˈsel] **1.** *vi* sobresalir **2.** *vt* superar

excellent [ˈeksələnt] *adj* excelente

except [ɪkˈsept] **1.** *prep* excepto, salvo; **except for the little ones** excepto los pequeños; **except that ...** salvo que ... **2.** *vt* exceptuar

exception [ɪkˈsepʃən] *n* a) excepción *f*; **with the exception of** a excepción de; **without exception** sin excepción **b)** [objection] objeción *f*; **to take exception to sth** ofenderse por algo

exceptional [ɪkˈsepʃənəl] *adj* excepcional

excerpt [ˈeksɜːpt] *n* extracto *m*

excess 1. [ɪkˈses] *n* exceso *m* **2.** [ˈekses] *adj* excedente; **excess baggage** exceso *m* de equipaje; **excess fare** suplemento *m*

excessive [ɪkˈsesɪv] *adj* excesivo(a)

exchange [ɪksˈtʃeɪndʒ] **1.** *n* a) cambio *m*; **exchange of ideas** intercambio *m* de ideas; **in exchange for** a cambio de **b)** FIN **exchange rate** tipo *m* de cambio **c) (telephone) exchange** central telefónica **2.** *vt* a) intercambiar; **to exchange blows** golpearse **b)** [prisoners] canjear

exchequer [ɪksˈtʃekə(r)] *n Br* **the Exchequer** Hacienda *f*; **Chancellor of the Exchequer** Ministro *m* de Hacienda

excitable [ɪkˈsaɪtəbəl] *adj* excitable

excite [ɪkˈsaɪt] *vt* [person] entusiasmar, emocionar; [stimulate] excitar

excited [ɪkˈsaɪtɪd] *adj* entusiasmado(a), emocionado(a)

excitement [ɪkˈsaɪtmənt] *n* [stimulation] excitación *f*; [emotion] emoción *f*; [commotion] agitación *f*

exciting [ɪkˈsaɪtɪŋ] *adj* apasionante, emocionante

exclaim [ɪkˈskleɪm] **1.** *vi* exclamar **2.** *vt* gritar

exclamation [eksκləˈmeɪʃən] *n* exclamación *f*; **exclamation** *Br* **mark** *or US* **point** signo *m* de admiración

exclude [ɪkˈskluːd] *vt* excluir; [from club] no admitir

exclusive [ɪkˈskluːsɪv] **1.** *adj* exclusivo(a); [neighbourhood] selecto(a); [club] cerrado(a) **2.** *n* PRESS exclusiva *f*

excruciating [ɪkˈskruːʃɪeɪtɪŋ] *adj* insoportable

excursion [ɪkˈskɜːʃən] *n* excursión *f*

excuse 1. [ɪkˈskjuːz] *vt* a) perdonar, disculpar; **excuse me!** [to attract attention] ¡perdón!, ¡oiga (por favor)!; [when trying to get past] con permiso; **may I be excused for a moment?** ¿puedo salir un momento? **b)** [exempt] dispensar **c)** [justify] justificar **2.** [ɪkˈskjuːs] *n* excusa *f*; **to make an excuse** dar excusas

execute ['eksɪkju:t] *vt* **a)** [order] cumplir ; [task] realizar **b)** JUR cumplir **c)** [person] ejecutar

execution [eksɪ'kju:ʃən] *n* **a)** [of order] cumplimiento *m* ; [of task] realización *f* **b)** JUR cumplimiento *m* **c)** [of person] ejecución *f*

executive [ɪg'zekjʊtɪv] **1.** *adj* ejecutivo(a) **2.** *n* ejecutivo(a) *m,f* ; **account executive** responsable *mf* de grandes cuentas

exemplify [ɪg'zemplɪfaɪ] *vt* ejemplificar

exempt [ɪg'zempt] **1.** *vt* eximir (**from** de) **2.** *adj* exento(a) ; **exempt from tax** libre de impuesto

exemption [ɪg'zempʃən] *n* exención *f*

exercise ['eksəsaɪz] **1.** *n* ejercicio *m* ; **exercise book** cuaderno *m* **2.** *vt* **a)** [rights, duties] ejercer **b)** [dog] sacar de paseo **3.** *vi* hacer ejercicio

exert [ɪg'zɜ:t] *vt* [influence] ejercer ; **to exert oneself** esforzarse

exertion [ɪg'zɜ:ʃən] *n* esfuerzo *m*

exhale [eks'heɪl] **1.** *vt* [breathe] exhalar **2.** *vi* espirar

exhaust [ɪg'zɔ:st] **1.** *vt* agotar **2.** *n* [gas] gases *mpl* de combustión ; **exhaust pipe** tubo *m* de escape

exhausted [ɪg'zɔ:stɪd] *adj* agotado(a)

exhausting [ɪg'zɔ:stɪŋ] *adj* agotador(a)

exhaustive [ɪg'zɔ:stɪv] *adj* exhaustivo(a)

exhibit [ɪg'zɪbɪt] **1.** *n* ART objeto expuesto ; JUR prueba *f* instrumental **2.** *vt* ART exponer ; [surprise etc] mostrar

exhibition [eksɪ'bɪʃən] *n* exposición *f*

exhilarating [ɪg'zɪləreɪtɪŋ] *adj* estimulante

exile ['eksaɪl] **1.** *n* **a)** [banishment] exilio *m* **b)** [person] exiliado(a) *m,f* **2.** *vt* exiliar

exist [ɪg'zɪst] *vi* existir ; [have little money] malvivir

existence [ɪg'zɪstəns] *n* existencia *f*

existing [ɪg'zɪstɪŋ] *adj* existente, actual

exit ['eksɪt] **1.** *n* **a)** salida *f* **b)** THEAT mutis *m* **2.** *vi* THEAT hacer mutis

exorbitant [ɪg'zɔ:bɪtənt] *adj* exorbitante, desorbitado(a)

exotic [ɪg'zɒtɪk] *adj* exótico(a)

expand [ɪk'spænd] **1.** *vt* [enlarge] ampliar ; [gas, metal] dilatar **2.** *vi* [grow] ampliarse ; [metal] dilatarse ; [become more friendly] abrirse ■ **expand on** *vt insep* ampliar

expanse [ɪk'spæns] *n* extensión *f*

expatriate 1. [eks'pætrɪɪt] *adj & n* expatriado(a) *(m,f)* **2.** [eks'pætrɪeɪt] *vt* expatriar

expect [ɪk'spekt] **1.** *vt* **a)** [anticipate] esperar ; **I half-expected that to happen** suponía que iba a ocurrir **b)** [demand] contar con **c)** [suppose] suponer **2.** *vi Fam* **to be expecting** estar embarazada

expectation [ekspek'teɪʃən] *n* esperanza *f* ; **contrary to expectation** contrariamente a lo que se esperaba

expedient [ɪk'spi:dɪənt] **1.** *adj* conveniente, oportuno(a) **2.** *n* expediente *m*, recurso *m*

expedition [ekspɪ'dɪʃən] *n* expedición *f*

expel [ɪk'spel] *vt* expulsar

expend [ɪk'spend] *vt* gastar

expendable [ɪk'spendəbəl] *adj* prescindible

expenditure [ɪk'spendɪtʃə(r)] *n* desembolso *m*

expense [ɪk'spens] *n* gasto *m* ; **all expenses paid** con todos los gastos pagados ; **to spare no expense** no escatimar gastos ; *Fig* **at the expense of** a costa de ; **expense account** cuenta *f* de gastos de representación

expensive [ɪk'spensɪv] *adj* caro(a), costoso(a)

experience [ɪk'spɪərɪəns] **1.** *n* experiencia *f* **2.** *vt* [sensation] experimentar ; [difficulty, loss] sufrir

experienced [ɪk'spɪərɪənst] *adj* experimentado(a)

experiment [ɪk'sperɪmənt] **1.** n experimento m **2.** vi experimentar, hacer experimentos (**on** or **with** con)

expert ['ekspɜːt] **1.** adj experto(a) **2.** n experto(a) m,f, especialista mf

expertise [ekspɜː'tiːz] n pericia f

expire [ɪk'spaɪə(r)] vi **a)** [die] expirar; [mandate] terminar **b)** COMM & INS vencer; [ticket] caducar

expiry [ɪk'spaɪərɪ] n vencimiento m; **expiry date** fecha f de caducidad

explain [ɪk'spleɪn] **1.** vt explicar; [clarify] aclarar; **to explain oneself** justificarse **2.** vi explicarse

explanation [eksplə'neɪʃən] n explicación f; [clarification] aclaración f

explanatory [ɪk'splænətərɪ] adj explicativo(a), aclaratorio(a)

explicit [ɪk'splɪsɪt] adj explícito(a)

explode [ɪk'spləʊd] **1.** vt a) [bomb] hacer explotar **b)** Fig [theory] echar por tierra **2.** vi [bomb] estallar, explotar; Fig **to explode with** or **in anger** montar en cólera

exploit 1. ['eksplɔɪt] n proeza f, hazaña f **2.** [ek'splɔɪt] vt explotar

exploitation [eksplɔɪ'teɪʃən] n explotación f

explore [ɪk'splɔː(r)] vt explorar

explosion [ɪk'spləʊʒən] n explosión f

explosive [ɪk'spləʊsɪv] **1.** adj explosivo(a); **explosive issue** asunto delicado **2.** n explosivo m

exporter [ek'spɔːtə(r)] n exportador(a) m,f

expose [ɪk'spəʊz] vt [uncover] exponer; [secret] revelar; [plot] descubrir; **to expose oneself** exhibirse desnudo

exposure [ɪk'spəʊʒə(r)] n **a)** [to light, cold, heat] exposición f; **to die of exposure** morir de frío **b)** PHOTO fotografía f; **exposure meter** fotómetro m **c)** [of criminal] descubrimiento m

express [ɪk'spres] **1.** adj **a)** [explicit] expreso(a)
b) Br [letter] urgente; **express train** expreso m
2. n RAIL expreso m
3. vt expresar
4. adv **send it express** mándalo urgente

expression [ɪk'spreʃən] n expresión f

expressive [ɪks'presɪv] adj expresivo(a)

expressway [ɪk'spresweɪ] n US autopista f

expulsion [ɪk'spʌlʃən] n expulsión f

exquisite [ɪk'skwɪzɪt] adj exquisito(a)

extend [ɪk'stend] **1.** vt a) [enlarge] ampliar; [lengthen] alargar; [increase] aumentar; Fig **the prohibition was extended to cover cigarettes** extendieron la prohibición a los cigarrillos **b)** [give] rendir, dar; **to extend a welcome to sb** recibir a algn **c)** [prolong] prolongar **2.** vi a) [stretch] extenderse **b)** [last] prolongarse

extension [ɪk'stenʃən] n a) extensión f; [of time] prórroga f **b)** CONSTR anexo m

extensive [ɪk'stensɪv] adj extenso(a)

extent [ɪk'stent] n **a)** [area] extensión f **b) to some extent** hasta cierto punto; **to a large extent** en gran parte; **to a lesser extent** en menor grado; **to such an extent** hasta tal punto

exterior [ɪk'stɪərɪə(r)] **1.** adj exterior, externo(a) **2.** n exterior m

exterminate [ɪk'stɜːmɪneɪt] vt exterminar

external [ɪk'stɜːnəl] adj externo(a), exterior

extinct [ɪk'stɪŋkt] adj extinguido(a)

extinguish [ɪk'stɪŋgwɪʃ] vt extinguir, apagar

extinguisher [ɪk'stɪŋgwɪʃə(r)] n extintor m

extortionate [ɪk'stɔːʃənɪt] adj desorbitado(a)

extra ['ekstrə] **1.** adj extra; [spare] de sobra; **extra time** [in soccer match] prórroga f
2. adv extra; **extra fine** extra fino
3. n [additional charge] suplemento m; CIN extra mf; [newspaper] edición f especial

extract 1. ['ekstrækt] *n* extracto *m*
2. [ɪk'strækt] *vt* [tooth, information] extraer; [confession] arrancar

extracurricular [ekstrəkə'rɪkjʊlə(r)] *adj* extracurricular

extraordinary [ɪk'strɔːdənərɪ] *adj* [meeting] extraordinario(a); [behaviour etc] extraño(a)

extravagance [ɪk'strævəgəns] *n* [with money] derroche *m*; [of behaviour] extravagancia *f*

extravagant [ɪk'strævəgənt] *adj* [wasteful] derrochador(a); [excessive] exagerado(a); [luxurious] lujoso(a)

extreme [ɪk'striːm] **1.** *adj* extremo(a); **an extreme case** un caso excepcional; **to hold extreme views** tener opiniones radicales **2.** *n* extremo *m*; **in the extreme** en sumo grado

extremist [ɪk'striːmɪst] *n* extremista *mf*

extrovert ['ekstrəvɜːt] *adj & n* extrovertido(a) *(m,f)*

exuberant [ɪg'zjuːbərənt] *adj* exuberante

eye [aɪ] **1.** *n* ojo *m*; *Fig* **not to take one's eyes off sb/sth** no quitar la vista de encima a algn/algo; *Fig* **to catch sb's eye** llamar la atención a algn; *Fig* **to have an eye for** tener buen ojo para; *Fig* **to turn a blind eye (to)** hacer la vista gorda (a); *Fig* **with an eye to** con miras a; **to keep an eye on sb/sth** vigilar a algn/algo; **black eye** ojo morado; *US* **eye doctor** óptico(a) *m,f* **2.** *vt* observar

eyebrow ['aɪbraʊ] *n* ceja *f*

eyelash ['aɪlæʃ] *n* pestaña *f*

eyelid ['aɪlɪd] *n* párpado *m*

eyeliner ['aɪlaɪnə(r)] *n* lápiz *m* de ojos

eye-opening *adj Fam* revelador(a)

eyeshadow ['aɪʃædəʊ] *n* sombra *f* de ojos

eyesight ['aɪsaɪt] *n* vista *f*

eyesore ['aɪsɔː(r)] *n* monstruosidad *f*

eyewitness ['aɪwɪtnɪs] *n* testigo *mf* ocular

EZ, EZY MESSAGING *(abr of* **easy***)* fcl

F

F, f [ef] *n* **a)** [the letter] F, f *f* **b)** MUS **F** fa *m*

F [ef] *(abbr of* **Fahrenheit***)* F

fab [fæb] *adj Fam* genial

fable ['feɪbəl] *n* fábula *f*

fabric ['fæbrɪk] *n* **a)** TEXT tejido *m* **b)** CONSTR estructura *f*

fabulous ['fæbjʊləs] *adj* fabuloso(a)

face [feɪs] **1.** *n* **a)** cara *f*, rostro *m*; **face to face** cara a cara; **face cloth** paño *m*
b) [expression] cara *f*, expresión *f*; **to pull faces** hacer muecas
c) [surface] superficie *f*; [of card, coin] cara *f*; [of watch] esfera *f*; **face down / up** boca abajo / arriba
d) [appearance] aspecto *m*; **to lose face** desprestigiarse; **to save face** salvar las apariencias
2. *vt* **a)** [look on to] dar a; [be opposite] estar enfrente de
b) to face the wall / window [person] estar de cara a la pared / ventana
c) [problem] hacer frente a; **to face up to** hacer cara a
3. *vi* **to face on to** dar a; **to face towards** mirar hacia; **face this way** vuélvase de este lado

faceless ['feɪslɪs] *adj* anónimo(a)

facelift ['feɪslɪft] *n* MED lifting *m*; *Fig* renovación *f*

facepalm ['feɪspɑːm] *Fam* **1.** *n* **it was a bit of a facepalm moment** en ese momento habrá querido que me tragara la tierra **2.** *interj* ¡tierra, trágame!

facetious [fə'siːʃəs] *adj* bromista

facial ['feɪʃəl] *adj* facial

facilitate [fə'sɪlɪteɪt] *vt* facilitar

facility [fə'sɪlɪtɪ] *n* **a)** [ease] facilidad *f* **b) facilities** [means] facilidades *fpl*; **credit facilities** facilidades de crédito **c) facilities** [rooms, equipment] instalaciones *fpl*; **cooking facilities** derecho *m* a cocina

fact [fækt] *n* hecho *m*; **as a matter of fact** de hecho; **the fact that he confessed** el hecho de que confesara; **in fact** en realidad

faction ['fækʃən] *n* [group] facción *f*

factor ['fæktə(r)] *n* factor *m*

factory ['fæktərɪ] *n* fábrica *f*

factual ['fæktʃʊəl] *adj* **a factual error** un error de hecho

faculty ['fækəltɪ] *n* **a)** facultad *f* **b)** US UNIV profesorado *m*, cuerpo *m* docente

fad [fæd] *n Fam* [craze] moda pasajera; [whim] capricho *m*

fade [feɪd] *vi* [colour] desteñirse; [flower] marchitarse; [light] apagarse ■ **fade away** *vi* desvanecerse ■ **fade in, fade out** *vt sep* CIN & TV fundir

fag [fæg] *n* **a)** *Br Fam* [cigarette] pitillo *m* **b)** *US v Fam* [homosexual] marica *m*

fail [feɪl] **1.** *n* **a)** [in exam] *Esp* suspenso *m*, *Am* reprobado *m*
b) without fail sin falta
2. *vt* **a) don't fail me** no me falles
b) [exam] suspender
c) [be unable] no lograr
d) [neglect] dejar de
3. *vi* **a)** [show, film] fracasar; [in exam] *Esp* suspender, *Am* reprobar; [brakes] fallar
b) [business] quebrar
c) [health] deteriorarse

failing ['feɪlɪŋ] **1.** *n* **a)** [shortcoming] defecto *m* **b)** [weakness] punto *m* débil **2.** *prep* a falta de

failure ['feɪljə(r)] *n* **a)** fracaso *m* **b)** COMM quiebra *f* **c)** SCH suspenso *m* **d)** [person] fracasado(a) *m,f*

faint [feɪnt] **1.** *adj* **a)** [sound] débil ; [colour] pálido(a) ; [outline] borroso(a) ; [recollection] vago(a) **b)** [giddy] mareado(a) **2.** *n* desmayo *m* **3.** *vi* desmayarse

fair¹ [feə(r)] **1.** *adj* **a)** [impartial] imparcial ; [just] justo(a) ; **it's not fair** no hay derecho ; *Fam* **fair enough!** de acuerdo, *Esp* vale **b)** [hair] rubio(a), *Méx* güero(a) ; [skin] claro(a) **c)** [weather] bueno(a) **d)** [beautiful] bello(a) **e) a fair number** un buen número ; **he has a fair chance** tiene bastantes probabilidades **2.** *adv* **to play fair** jugar limpio

fair² [feə(r)] *n* **a)** *Br* [funfair] feria *f* **b) trade fair** feria de muestras

fairground ['feəgraʊnd] *n* real *m* de la feria

fairly ['feəlɪ] *adv* **a)** [justly] justamente **b)** [moderately] bastante

fairy ['feərɪ] *n* **a)** hada *f*; **fairy godmother** hada madrina ; **fairy tale** cuento *m* de hadas **b)** *Fam & Pej* marica *m*

faith [feɪθ] *n* **a)** *REL* fe *f* **b)** [trust] confianza *f*; **in good faith** de buena fe

faithful ['feɪθfʊl] **1.** *adj* fiel **2.** *npl* **the faithful** los fieles

faithfully ['feɪθfʊlɪ] *adv* fielmente ; **yours faithfully** [in letter] le saluda atentamente

fake [feɪk] **1.** *adj* falso(a) **2.** *n* **a)** [object] falsificación *f* **b)** [person] impostor(a) *m,f* **3.** *vt* **a)** [forge] falsificar **b)** [feign] fingir **4.** *vi* [pretend] fingir

fall [fɔːl] **1.** *n* **a)** caída *f*; **fall of snow** nevada *f* **b)** [decrease] baja *f* **c)** *US* [autumn] otoño *m* **d)** [usu pl] cascada *f*; **Niagara Falls** las cataratas del Niágara **2.** *vi* (*pt* **fell**, *pp* **fallen**) *vi* **a)** caer, caerse ; **they fall into two categories** se dividen en dos categorías ; *Fig* **night was falling** anochecía ; *Fig* **to fall short (of)** no alcanzar

b) [in battle] caer **c)** [temperature, prices] bajar **d) to fall asleep** dormirse ; **to fall ill** caer enfermo(a), enfermar, *RP, Ven* enfermarse ; **to fall in love** enamorarse

■ **fall back** *vi* replegarse

■ **fall back on** *vt insep* echar mano a, recurrir a

■ **fall behind** *vi* [in race] quedarse atrás ; **to fall behind with one's work** retrasarse en el trabajo

■ **fall down** *vi* **a)** [picture etc] caerse **b)** [building] derrumbarse

■ **fall for** *vt insep* **a)** [person] enamorarse de **b)** [trick] dejarse engañar por

■ **fall in** *vi* **a)** [roof] desplomarse **b)** *MIL* formar filas

■ **fall off 1.** *vi* **a)** [drop off] caerse **b)** [part] desprenderse **c)** [diminish] disminuir **2.** *vt insep* **to fall off sth** caerse de algo

■ **fall out** *vi* **a)** [hair] caerse **b)** *MIL* romper filas **c)** [quarrel] pelearse

■ **fall over** *vi* caerse

■ **fall through** *vi* [plan] fracasar

fallacy ['fæləsɪ] *n* falacia *f*

fallen ['fɔːlən] *pp of* **fall**

fallible ['fælɪbəl] *adj* falible

false [fɔːls] *adj* falso(a) ; **false teeth** dentadura postiza ; **false alarm** falsa alarma

falsify ['fɔːlsɪfaɪ] *vt* [records, accounts] falsificar ; [story] falsear

falter ['fɔːltə(r)] *vi* vacilar ; [voice] fallar

fame [feɪm] *n* fama *f*

familiar [fə'mɪlɪə(r)] *adj* **a)** [common] familiar, conocido(a) ; **his face is familiar** su cara me suena **b)** [aware, knowledgeable] enterado(a), al corriente (**with** de) **c) to be on familiar terms with sb** [know well] tener confianza con algn

familiarize [fə'mɪljəraɪz] *vt* **a)** [become acquainted] familiarizar (**with** con) ; **to familiarize oneself with sth** familiarizarse con algo **b)** [make widely known] popularizar

family ['fæmɪlɪ] *n* familia *f*; **family allowance** subsidio *m* familiar; **family doctor** médico *m* de cabecera; **family man** hombre hogareño; **family planning** planificación *f* familiar; **family tree** árbol genealógico

family-friendly *adj* [pub, hotel, campsite] familiar; [policy, proposal] de apoyo a las familias; [show, entertainment] para toda la familia

family-size(d) *adj* [jar, packet] (de tamaño) familiar

famine ['fæmɪn] *n* hambre *f*, escasez *f* de alimentos

famished ['fæmɪʃt] *adj Fam* muerto(a) de hambre

famous ['feɪməs] *adj* célebre, famoso(a) (**for** por)

fan [fæn] **1.** *n* **a)** abanico *m*; ELEC ventilador *m* **b)** [person] aficionado(a) *m,f*; [of pop star etc] fan *mf*; **fan club** club *m* de fans; **football fan** hincha *mf* **2.** *vt* **a)** abanicar **b)** [fire, passions] avivar ■ **fan out** *vi* [troops] desplegarse en abanico

fanatic [fə'nætɪk] *adj & n* fanático(a) (*m,f*)

fanciful ['fænsɪfʊl] *adj* **a)** [person] caprichoso(a) **b)** [idea] fantástico(a)

fancy ['fænsɪ] **1.** *(compar* fancier, *superl* fanciest) *adj* de fantasía; **fancy dress** disfraz *m* **2.** *n* **a)** [imagination] fantasía *f* **b)** [whim] capricho *m*, antojo *m*; **to take a fancy to sb** cogerle cariño a algn; **to take a fancy to sth** encapricharse con algo **3.** *vt* **a)** [imagine] imaginarse; *Fam* **fancy seeing you here!** ¡qué casualidad verte por aquí! **b)** [like, want] apetecer; **do you fancy a drink?** ¿te apetece una copa?; *Br Fam* **I fancy her** ella me gusta

fanfare ['fænfeə(r)] *n* fanfarria *f*

fan-shaped *adj* en abanico

fantastic [fæn'tæstɪk] *adj* fantástico(a)

fantasy ['fæntəsɪ] *n* fantasía *f*

FAQ [fak, efer'kjuː] *n* COMPUT *(abbr of* frequently asked questions*)* PMF *fpl (preguntas más frecuentes)*

far [fɑː(r)] *(compar* farther *or* further, *superl* farthest *or* furthest) **1.** *adj* **a)** [distant] lejano(a); **the Far East** el Lejano Oriente
b) at the far end en el otro extremo
c) the far left la extrema izquierda
2. *adv* **a)** [distant] lejos; **far off** a lo lejos; **farther back / north** más atrás / al norte; **how far is it to Cardiff?** ¿cuánto hay de aquí a Cardiff?; **as far as I know** que yo sepa; **as far as possible** en lo posible; *Fig* **far from complaining, he seemed pleased** lejos de quejarse, parecía contento; *Fam* **to go too far** pasarse de la raya
b) [in time] **as far back as the fifties** ya en los años cincuenta; **so far** hasta ahora
c) [much] mucho; **by far** con diferencia *or* mucho, *RP* por lejos; **far cleverer** mucho más listo(a); **far too much** demasiado

faraway ['fɑːrəweɪ] *adj* lejano(a), remoto(a)

farce [fɑːs] *n* farsa *f*

farcical ['fɑːsɪkəl] *adj* absurdo(a)

fare [feə(r)] **1.** *n* **a)** [ticket price] tarifa *f*, precio *m* del billete; [for boat] pasaje *m*; **half fare** media tarifa **b)** [passenger] pasajero(a) *m,f* **c)** [food] comida *f* **2.** *vi* **how did you fare?** ¿qué tal te fue?

farewell [feə'wel] **1.** *interj Liter* ¡adiós! **2.** *n* despedida *f*

far-fetched [fɑː'fetʃt] *adj* rebuscado(a)

farm [fɑːm] **1.** *n* [small] granja *f*; [large] hacienda *f*, *CSur* estancia *f* **2.** *vt* cultivar, labrar ■ **farm out** *vt sep* encargar fuera

farmer ['fɑːmə(r)] *n* granjero(a) *m,f*, *Am* hacendado(a) *m,f*

farmhouse ['fɑːmhaʊs] *n* granja *f*, *Am* hacienda *f*

farming ['fɑːmɪŋ] **1.** *n* **a)** [agriculture] agricultura *f* **b)** [of land] cultivo *m*, labranza *f* **2.** *adj* agrícola

farmyard ['fɑːmjɑːd] *n* corral *m*

far-reaching [fɑː'riːtʃɪŋ] *adj* de gran alcance

far(-)sighted [fɑːˈsaɪtɪd] *adj* **a)** [person] previsor(ora), con visión de futuro; [plan] con miras al futuro **b)** *US* [long-sighted] hipermétrope

fart [fɑːt] *Fam* **1.** *n* pedo *m* **2.** *vi* tirarse un pedo

farther [ˈfɑːðə(r)] *adj* & *adv compar of* **far**

farthest [ˈfɑːðɪst] *adj* & *adv superl of* **far**

fascinate [ˈfæsɪneɪt] *vt* fascinar

fascinating [ˈfæsɪneɪtɪŋ] *adj* fascinante

fascist [ˈfæʃɪst] *adj* & *n* fascista *(mf)*

fashion [ˈfæʃən] **1.** *n* **a)** [manner] manera *f*, modo *m*; **after a fashion** más o menos **b)** [latest style] moda *f*; **to go/be out of fashion** pasar/no estar de moda; **fashion designer** diseñador(a) *m,f* de modas; **fashion parade** desfile *m* de modelos **2.** *vt* [metal] labrar; [clay] formar

fashionable [ˈfæʃənəbəl] *adj* **a)** de moda **b)** [area, hotel] elegante

fast¹ [fɑːst] **1.** *adj* **a)** [quick] rápido(a) **b) hard and fast rules** reglas estrictas **c)** [clock] adelantado(a) **2.** *adv* **a)** rápidamente, deprisa; **how fast?** ¿a qué velocidad? **b)** [securely] firmemente; **fast asleep** profundamente dormido(a)

fast² [fɑːst] **1.** *n* ayuno *m* **2.** *vi* ayunar

fasten [ˈfɑːsən] **1.** *vt* **a)** [attach] sujetar; [fix] fijar **b)** [belt] abrochar; [bag] asegurar; [shoelaces] atar **2.** *vi* [dress] abrocharse

fastener [ˈfɑːsənə(r)] *n* cierre *m*

fast-paced [fɑːstˈpeɪst] *adj* [novel, film, TV show] de ritmo trepidante

fat [fæt] **1.** *(compar* **fatter**, *superl* **fattest)** *adj* **a)** gordo(a) **b)** [book, file] grueso(a) **c)** [meat] que tiene mucha grasa **2.** *n* grasa *f*; **cooking fat** manteca *f* de cerdo

fatal [ˈfeɪtəl] *adj* **a)** [accident, illness] mortal **b)** [ill-fated] fatal, funesto(a) **c)** [fateful] fatídico(a)

fatality [fəˈtælɪtɪ] *n* víctima *f* mortal

fatally [ˈfeɪtəlɪ] *adv* **fatally wounded** mortalmente herido(a)

fate [feɪt] *n* destino *m*, suerte *f*

fateful [ˈfeɪtfʊl] *adj* fatídico(a), aciago(a)

father [ˈfɑːðə(r)] *n* **a)** padre *m*; **my father and mother** mis padres; **Father Christmas** Papá *m* Noel **b)** REL padre *m*

fatherhood [ˈfɑːðəhʊd] *n* paternidad *f*

father-in-law [ˈfɑːðərɪnlɔː] *n* suegro *m*

fatigue [fəˈtiːg] *n* **a)** [tiredness] fatiga *f* **b)** MIL faena *f*; **fatigue dress** traje *m* de faena

fatten [ˈfætən] *vt* engordar

fattening [ˈfætənɪŋ] *adj* que engorda

fatty [ˈfætɪ] **1.** *adj* [food] graso(a); ANAT [tissue] adiposo(a) **2.** *n Fam* [person] gordinflón(ona) *m,f*

faucet [ˈfɔːsɪt] *n US Esp* grifo *m*, *Chile, Col, Méx* llave *f*, *RP* canilla *f*

fault [fɔːlt] **1.** *n* **a)** [defect] defecto *m*; [in merchandise] desperfecto *m* **b)** [blame] culpa *f*; **to be at fault** tener la culpa **c)** [mistake] error *m* **d)** GEOL falla *f* **2.** *vt* criticar

faultless [ˈfɔːltlɪs] *adj* intachable

faulty [ˈfɔːltɪ] *adj* defectuoso(a)

favour, *US* **favor** [ˈfeɪvə(r)] **1.** *n* **a)** favor *m*; **in favour of** a favor de; **to be in favour with sb** gozar del favor de algn; **to ask sb a favour** pedirle un favor a algn **b) 1-0 in our favour** [advantage] 1-0 a favor nuestro **2.** *vt* **a)** [person] favorecer **b)** [approve] estar a favor de

favourable, *US* **favorable** [ˈfeɪvərəbəl] *adj* favorable

favourite, *US* **favorite** [ˈfeɪvərɪt] **1.** *adj* favorito(a) **2.** *n* **a)** favorito(a) *(m,f)* **b)** COMPUT **favourites**, **favorites** favoritos *mpl*

favouritism, *US* **favoritism** [ˈfeɪvərɪtɪzəm] *n* favoritismo *m*

fawn¹ [fɔːn] **1.** *adj* (de) color café claro **2.** *n* **a)** ZOOL cervato *m* **b)** color *m* café claro

fawn² [fɔːn] *vi* adular (**on** a)

fax [fæks] **1.** *n* [machine, message] fax *m*; **fax modem** modem *m* fax **2.** *vt* mandar por fax

fear [fɪə(r)] **1.** *n* miedo *m*, temor *m*; **for fear of** por temor a; *Fam* **no fear!** ¡ni pensarlo!

2. *vt* temer; **I fear it's too late** me temo que ya es tarde
3. *vi* temer (**for** por)

fearful ['fɪəfʊl] *adj* **a)** [person] temeroso(a) **b)** [frightening] espantoso(a)

fearless ['fɪəlɪs] *adj* intrépido(a)

feasible ['fiːzəbəl] *adj* [practicable] factible; [possible] viable

feast [fiːst] *n* **a)** banquete *m*; *Fam* comilona *f* **b)** REL **feast day** fiesta *f* de guardar

feat [fiːt] *n* hazaña *f*

feather ['feðə(r)] **1.** *n* pluma *f*; **feather duster** plumero *m* **2.** *vt Fam* **to feather one's nest** hacer su agosto

feature ['fiːtʃə(r)] **1.** *n* **a)** [of face] rasgo *m*, facción *f*
b) [characteristic] característica *f*
c) feature film largometraje *m*
d) PRESS crónica *f* especial
2. *vt* **a)** poner de relieve
b) CIN tener como protagonista a
3. *vi* figurar

February ['februərɪ] *n* febrero *m*

fed [fed] **1.** *adj Fam* **fed up (with)** harto(a) (de) **2.** *pt & pp of* **feed**

federal ['fedərəl] *adj* federal; *US* **Federal Agent** agente *mf* federal

federation [fedə'reɪʃən] *n* federación *f*

fee [fiː] *n* [of lawyer, doctor] honorarios *mpl*; FTBL **transfer fee** prima *f* de traslado; UNIV **tuition fees** derechos *mpl* de matrícula

feeble ['fiːbəl] *adj* débil

feed [fiːd] (*pt & pp* **fed**) **1.** *vt* **a)** [give food to] dar de comer a; *Fig* [fire] alimentar; **to feed a baby** [breast-feed] amamantar a un bebé; [with bottle] dar el biberón a un bebé
b) ELEC alimentar
c) [insert] introducir
2. *vi* [cows, sheep] pacer; **to feed on sth** [person] comer algo
3. *n* **a)** [food] comida *f*; **cattle feed** pienso *m*
b) TECH alimentación *f*
■ **feed up** *vt sep* cebar

feedback ['fiːdbæk] *n* **a)** TECH feedback *m* **b)** *Fig* reacción *f*

feel [fiːl] (*pt & pp* **felt**) **1.** *vi* **a)** [emotion, sensation] sentir; **how do you feel?** ¿qué tal te encuentras?; **I feel bad about it** me da pena; **to feel happy / uncomfortable** sentirse feliz / incómodo; **to feel cold / sleepy** tener frío / sueño
b) [seem] **your hand feels cold** tienes la mano fría; **it feels like summer** parece verano
c) [opinion] opinar; **I feel sure that ...** estoy seguro(a) de que ...
d) I feel like an ice cream me tomaría *or Esp* me apetece un helado, *Carib, Col, Méx* me provoca un sorbete; **to feel like doing sth** tener ganas de hacer algo
2. *vt* **a)** [touch] tocar
b) she feels a failure se siente inútil
c) [notice, be aware of] notar
3. *n* **a)** [touch, sensation] tacto *m*; *Fig* **to get the feel for sth** *Esp* cogerle el truco a algo, *Am* agarrar la onda a algo
b) [atmosphere] ambiente *m*
■ **feel for** *vt insep* **a)** [search for] buscar **b)** [have sympathy for] compadecer

feeling ['fiːlɪŋ] **1.** *n* **a)** [emotion] sentimiento *m*; **ill feeling** rencor *m*
b) [compassion] compasión *f* **c) I had the feeling that ...** [impression] tuve la impresión de que ... **d)** [sensitivity] sensibilidad *f* **e)** [opinion] opinión *f*; **to express one's feelings** expresar sus opiniones **2.** *adj* sensible, compasivo(a)

feet [fiːt] *pl of* **foot**

feign [feɪn] *vt* fingir

feline ['fiːlaɪn] **1.** *n* felino *m*, félido *m* **2.** *adj* felino(a)

fell¹ [fel] *pt of* **fall**

fell² [fel] *vt* [trees] talar; *Fig* [enemy] derribar

fellow ['feləʊ] *n* **a)** [companion] compañero(a) *m,f*; **fellow citizen** conciudadano(a) *m,f*; **fellow countryman / countrywoman** compatriota *mf*; **fellow men** prójimos *mpl*; **fellow passenger / student** compañero(a) *m,f* de viaje / estudios **b)** *Fam* [chap] tipo *m*, tío *m* **c)** [of society] socio(a) *m,f*

fellowship ['feləʊʃɪp] n a) [comradeship] camaradería f b) UNIV beca f de investigación

felony ['felənɪ] n US JUR crimen m, delito m grave

felt[1] [felt] pt & pp of **feel**

felt[2] [felt] n TEXT fieltro m

felt-tip(ped) ['felttɪp(t)] adj **felt-tip(ped) pen** rotulador m

female ['fi:meɪl] **1.** adj a) ZOOL hembra b) femenino(a) **2.** n a) ZOOL hembra f b) [woman] mujer f; [girl] chica f

femidom n preservativo m femenino

feminine ['femɪnɪn] adj femenino(a)

feminist ['femɪnɪst] adj & n feminista (mf)

fence [fens] **1.** n cerca f, valla f; Fig **to sit on the fence** ver los toros desde la barrera **2.** vi SPORT practicar la esgrima ■ **fence in** vt sep meter en un cercado

fencing ['fensɪŋ] n SPORT esgrima f

fend [fend] vi **to fend for oneself** valerse por sí mismo ■ **fend off** vt sep [blow] parar; [question] rehuir; [attack] rechazar

fender ['fendə(r)] n a) [fireplace] pantalla f b) US AUTO Esp, Bol, RP guardabarros mpl, Andes, CAm, Carib guardafango m, Méx salpicadera f c) NAUT defensa f

ferment [fə'ment] vt & vi fermentar

ferocious [fə'rəʊʃəs] adj feroz

ferret ['ferɪt] **1.** n hurón m **2.** vi huronear, husmear ■ **ferret out** vt sep descubrir

Ferris wheel ['ferɪs-] n US noria f

ferry ['ferɪ] **1.** n a) [small] barca f de pasaje b) [large, for cars] transbordador m, ferry m **2.** vt transportar

fertile ['fɜ:taɪl] adj fértil

fertilizer ['fɜ:tɪlaɪzə(r)] n abono m

fervent ['fɜ:vənt] adj ferviente

fest [fest] n Fam **crazy shopping fest** locura f de compras

festival ['festɪvəl] n [event] festival m; [celebration] fiesta f

festive ['festɪv] adj festivo(a); **the festive season** las fiestas de Navidad

festivity [fe'stɪvɪtɪ] n **the festivities** las fiestas

fetch [fetʃ] vt a) [go for] ir a buscar b) [bring] traer c) **how much did it fetch?** [sell for] ¿por cuánto se vendió?

fete [feɪt] **1.** n fiesta f **2.** vt festejar

fetus ['fi:təs] US n = **foetus**

feud [fju:d] **1.** n enemistad duradera **2.** vi pelear

fever ['fi:və(r)] n fiebre f

feverish ['fi:vərɪʃ] adj febril

few [fju:] **1.** adj a) [not many] pocos(as); **as few as** solamente
b) [some] algunos(as), unos(as) cuantos(as); **a few books** unos or algunos libros; **she has fewer books than I thought** tiene menos libros de lo que pensaba; **for the past few years** durante estos últimos años; **in the next few days** dentro de unos días; **quite a few** bastantes
2. pron a) [not many] pocos(as); **there are too few** no hay suficientes
b) **a few** [some] algunos(as), unos(as) cuantos(as); **who has the fewest?** ¿quién tiene menos?

fiancé [fɪ'ɒnseɪ] n prometido m

fiancée [fɪ'ɒnseɪ] n prometida f

fiasco [fɪ'æskəʊ] (Br pl **fiascos**, US pl **fiascoes**) n fiasco m

fib [fɪb] Fam **1.** n trola f **2.** vi contar trolas

fibre, US **fiber** ['faɪbə(r)] n fibra f

fickle ['fɪkəl] adj inconstante, voluble

fiction ['fɪkʃən] n ficción f

fictional ['fɪkʃənəl] adj a) LITER novelesco(a) b) [imaginative] ficticio(a)

fictitious [fɪk'tɪʃəs] adj ficticio(a)

fiddle ['fɪdəl] **1.** n a) [violin] violín m (en música folk) b) esp Br Fam [swindle] timo m **2.** vt Br Fam amañar **3.** vi juguetear (**with** con) ■ **fiddle about** vi perder tiempo

fiddly ['fɪdlɪ] adj Fam laborioso(a)

fidget ['fɪdʒɪt] vi a) moverse; **stop fidgeting!** ¡estáte quieto! b) jugar (**with** con)

field [fi:ld] **1.** n a) campo m; **field glasses** gemelos mpl; **field marshal**

mariscal *m* de campo; *US* SPORT **to play left field** jugar de exterior izquierdo; *Fam & Fig* **to be out in left field** ser un(a) excéntrico(a) **b)** GEOL & MINING yacimiento *m* **c)** COMPUT campo *m* **d)** **field trip** viaje *m* de estudios; **field work** trabajo *m* de campo **2.** *vt* **a)** SPORT [ball] parar y devolver **b)** [team] presentar

fierce [fɪəs] *adj* [animal] feroz; [argument] acalorado(a); [heat, competition] intenso(a); [wind] violento(a)

fiery ['faɪərɪ] *adj* [temper] fogoso(a); [speech] acalorado(a); [colour] encendido(a)

fifteen [fɪf'tiːn] *adj & n* quince (*m inv*)

fifteenth [fɪf'tiːnθ] **1.** *adj & n* decimoquinto(a) (*m,f*) **2.** *n* [fraction] quinzavo *m*

fifth [fɪfθ] **1.** *adj & n* quinto(a) (*m,f*) **2.** *n* [fraction] quinto *m*

fifty ['fɪftɪ] *adj & n* cincuenta (*m inv*)

fifty-fifty *adj* al cincuenta por ciento; **a fifty-fifty chance** una cincuenta por ciento de probabilidades

fig¹ [fɪg] *n* [fruit] higo *m*

fig² [fɪg] (*abbr of* **figure**) fig

fight [faɪt] (*pt & pp* **fought**) **1.** *vt* **a)** pelear(se) con, luchar con; [of boxer] enfrentarse a, luchar con; [of bullfighter] lidiar; *Fig* [corruption] combatir **b)** [battle] librar; [war] hacer **c)** [decision] recurrir contra **2.** *vi* **a)** pelear(se), luchar **b)** [quarrel] reñir; **to fight over sth** disputarse la posesión de algo **c)** *Fig* [struggle] luchar (**for /against** por /contra) **3.** *n* **a)** pelea *f*, lucha *f*; [in boxing] combate *m* **b)** [quarrel] riña *f* **c)** *Fig* [struggle] lucha *f*
■ **fight back 1.** *vt sep* [tears] contener **2.** *vt insep* reprimir **3.** *vi* contraatacar, devolver el golpe
■ **fight off** *vt sep* **a)** [attack] rechazar **b)** [illness] cortar
■ **fight out** *vt sep* discutir

fighter ['faɪtə(r)] *n* **a)** [person] combatiente *mf*; [in boxing] púgil *m* **b)** *Fig*

luchador(a) *m,f*; **fighter (plane)** (avión *m* de) caza *m*; **fighter bomber** cazabombardero *m*

figment ['fɪgmənt] *n* **it's a figment of your imagination** es un producto de tu imaginación

figurative ['fɪgərətɪv] *adj* figurado(a)

figure ['fɪgə(r), *US* 'fɪgjər] **1.** *n* **a)** [form, outline] forma *f*, silueta *f* **b)** [shape, statue, character] figura *f*; **she has a good figure** tiene buen tipo **c)** [in book] dibujo *m* **d)** **figure of speech** figura retórica **e)** MATH cifra *f*; *Br* **to be in(to) double figures** ser igual o superior a diez, alcanzar o superar la decena **2.** *vt US Fam* pensar, figurarse **3.** *vi* **a)** [appear - in list, book] figurar **b)** *Fam* [make sense] **that figures!** (es) normal or lógico
■ **figure out** *vt sep Fam* comprender; **I can't figure it out** no me lo explico

file [faɪl] **1.** *n* **a)** [tool] lima *f* **b)** [folder] carpeta *f* **c)** [archive, of computer] archivo *m*; **box file** archivador *m*; **native file** archivo *m* nativo; **on file** archivado(a) **d)** [line] fila *f*; **in single file** en fila india **2.** *vt* **a)** [smooth] limar **b)** [put away] archivar **3.** *vi* **to file past** desfilar

filename *n* nombre *m* de archivo

filing ['faɪlɪŋ] *n* clasificación *f*; **filing cabinet** archivador *m*; [for cards] fichero *m*

fill [fɪl] **1.** *vt* **a)** [space, time] llenar (**with** de) **b)** [post, requirements] cubrir **c)** CULIN rellenar **2.** *vi* llenarse (**with** de) **3.** *n* **to eat one's fill** comer hasta hartarse
■ **fill in 1.** *vt sep* **a)** [space, form] rellenar **b)** *Fam* [inform] poner al corriente (**on** de) **c)** [time] pasar **2.** *vi* **to fill in for sb** sustituir a algn
■ **fill out 1.** *vt sep US* [form] llenar **2.** *vi Fam* engordar

■ **fill up 1.** *vt sep* llenar hasta arriba; *Fam* AUTO **fill her up!** ¡llénelo! **2.** *vi* llenarse

fillet ['fɪlɪt] *n* filete *m*; **fillet steak** filete

filling ['fɪlɪŋ] **1.** *adj* que llena mucho **2.** *n* **a)** [stuffing] relleno *m* **b)** [in tooth] empaste *m* **c)** *Br* **filling station** gasolinera *f*, estación *f* de servicio, *Andes, Ven* bomba *f*, *Méx* gasolinería *f*, *Perú* grifo *m*

film [fɪlm] **1.** *n* **a)** *esp Br* [at cinema] película *f*; **film star** estrella *f* de cine **b)** [layer] capa *f* **c)** [photographic] **a (roll of) film** [for camera] un rollo, un carrete **2.** *vt* CIN filmar **3.** *vi* CIN rodar

filter ['fɪltə(r)] **1.** *n* filtro *m*; AUTO **filter lane** carril *m* de acceso **2.** *vt* filtrar ■ **filter through** *vi Fig* filtrarse (**to** a)

filth [fɪlθ] *n* [dirt] porquería *f*; *Fig* porquerías *fpl*

filthy ['fɪlθɪ] *(compar* **filthier**, *superl* **filthiest)** *adj* **a)** [dirty] asqueroso(a) **b)** [obscene] obsceno(a)

fin [fɪn] *n* ZOOL & AVIAT aleta *f*

final ['faɪnəl] **1.** *adj* **a)** [last] último(a), final **b)** [definitive] definitivo(a) **2.** *n* **a)** SPORT final *f* **b)** UNIV **finals** *Br* exámenes *mpl* de fin de carrera; *US* exámenes *mpl* finales

finalist ['faɪnəlɪst] *n* finalista *mf*

finalize ['faɪnəlaɪz] *vt* ultimar; [date] fijar

finally ['faɪnəlɪ] *adv* [lastly] por último; [at last] por fin

finance ['faɪnæns, fɪ'næns] **1.** *n* **a)** finanzas *fpl* **b)** **finances** fondos *mpl* **2.** *vt* financiar

financial [faɪ'nænʃəl, fɪ'nænʃəl] *adj* financiero(a); **financial crisis** crisis económica; *Br* **financial year** [for budget] ejercicio *m* (económico); [for tax] año *m* fiscal

financier [faɪ'nænsɪə(r), fɪ'nænsɪə(r)] *n* financiero(a) *m,f*

find [faɪnd] **1.** *(pt & pp* **found)** *vt* **a)** [locate] encontrar **b)** [think] encontrar **c)** [discover] descubrir **d)** JUR **to find sb guilty / not guilty** declarar culpable / inocente a algn **e)** **I can't find the courage to tell him** no tengo valor

para decírselo; **I found it impossible to get away** me resultó imposible irme **2.** *n* hallazgo *m* ■ **find out 1.** *vt sep* **a)** [inquire] averiguar **b)** [discover] descubrir **2.** *vi* **a) to find out about sth** informarse sobre algo **b)** [discover] enterarse

findings ['faɪndɪŋz] *npl* conclusiones *fpl*

fine¹ [faɪn] **1.** *n* multa *f* **2.** *vt* multar

fine² [faɪn] **1.** *adj* **a)** [delicate etc] fino(a) **b)** [subtle] sutil **c)** [excellent] excelente **d)** [weather] bueno(a) **e)** [all right] bien **2.** *adv Fam* muy bien **3.** *interj* ¡vale!

finger ['fɪŋɡə(r)] **1.** *n* dedo *m* (de la mano) **2.** *vt* tocar; *Pej* manosear

fingerless ['fɪŋɡələs] *adj* **fingerless glove** mitón *m*

fingernail ['fɪŋɡəneɪl] *n* uña *f*

fingertip ['fɪŋɡətɪp] *n* punta *f* or yema *f* del dedo

finish ['fɪnɪʃ] **1.** *n* **a)** fin *m*; [of race] llegada *f* **b)** [surface] acabado *m* **2.** *vt* **a)** [complete] acabar, terminar; **to finish doing sth** terminar de hacer algo **b)** [use up] agotar **3.** *vi* acabar, terminar; **to finish second** quedar el segundo ■ **finish off** *vt sep* **a)** [complete] terminar completamente **b)** *Fam* [kill] rematar ■ **finish up 1.** *vt sep* acabar, agotar **2.** *vi* **to finish up in jail** ir a parar a la cárcel

finished ['fɪnɪʃt] *adj* **a)** [product] acabado(a) **b)** *Fam* [exhausted] rendido(a)

finishing ['fɪnɪʃɪŋ] *adj* **to put the finishing touch(es) to sth** darle los últimos toques a algo; **finishing line** (línea *f* de) meta *f*; **finishing school** *escuela privada de modales para señoritas*

finite ['faɪnaɪt] *adj* finito(a); [verb] conjugable

Finland [ˈfɪnlənd] n Finlandia

Finn [fɪn] n finlandés(esa) m,f

Finnish [ˈfɪnɪʃ] **1.** adj finlandés(esa) **2.** n [language] finlandés m

fir [fɜː(r)] n abeto m

fire [ˈfaɪə(r)] **1.** n **a)** fuego m **b)** [accident etc] incendio m; **to be on fire** estar en llamas; **to catch fire** incendiarse; **fire alarm** alarma f de incendios; Br **fire brigade,** US **fire department** (cuerpo m de) bomberos mpl; **fire engine** coche m de bomberos; **fire escape** escalera f de incendios; **fire station** parque m de bomberos **c)** [heater] estufa f **d)** MIL fuego m; **to open fire** abrir fuego **2.** vt **a)** [gun] disparar (**at** a); [rocket] lanzar; Fig **to fire questions at sb** bombardear a algn a preguntas **b)** Fam [dismiss] despedir **3.** vi [shoot] disparar (**at** sobre)

firearm [ˈfaɪərɑːm] n arma f de fuego

fireman [ˈfaɪəmən] n bombero m

fireplace [ˈfaɪəpleɪs] n chimenea f; [hearth] hogar m

fire-retardant adj ignífugo(a)

firewall [ˈfaɪəwɔːl] n COMPUT cortafuego(s) m

firewood [ˈfaɪəwʊd] n leña f

fireworks [ˈfaɪəwɜːks] npl fuegos mpl artificiales

firm [fɜːm] **1.** adj firme; **to be firm with sb** [strict] tratar a algn con firmeza **2.** n COMM empresa f, firma f

firmly [ˈfɜːmlɪ] adv firmemente

first [fɜːst] **1.** adj primero(a); [before masculine singular noun] primer; **Charles the First** Carlos Primero; **for the first time** por primera vez; **in the first place** en primer lugar; **first aid** primeros auxilios; **first floor** Br primer piso; US planta baja **2.** adv [before anything else] primero; **first of all** en primer lugar **3.** n **a) the first** el primero / la primera; **the first of April** el primero or Esp el uno de abril **b) at first** al principio; **from the (very) first** desde el principio **c)** AUTO primera f

first-class [ˈfɜːstˈklɑːs] **1.** adj de primera clase **2.** adv **to travel first-class** viajar en primera

firstly [ˈfɜːstlɪ] adv en primer lugar

first-rate [ˈfɜːstreɪt] adj de primera

fish [fɪʃ] **1.** (pl **fish**) n **a)** pez m; Fam **big fish** pez m gordo; **fish factory** piscifactoría f; **fish shop** pescadería f **b)** CULIN pescado m; Br **fish and chips** pescado frito con patatas o (Am) papas fritas; **fish** Br **finger** or US **stick** palito m de pescado **2.** vi pescar; Fig **to fish in one's pocket for sth** buscar algo en el bolsillo

fisherman [ˈfɪʃəmən] n pescador m

fishing [ˈfɪʃɪŋ] n pesca f; **to go fishing** ir de pesca; **fishing net** red f de pesca; **fishing rod** caña f de pescar; **fishing tackle** aparejo m de pescar

fishmonger [ˈfɪʃmʌŋgə(r)] n Br pescadero(a) m,f; **fishmonger's (shop)** pescadería f

fishy [ˈfɪʃɪ] (compar **fishier,** superl **fishiest**) adj de pescado; Fam [suspicious] sospechoso(a)

fist [fɪst] n puño m

fit¹ [fɪt] **1.** vt **a)** ir bien a; **that suit doesn't fit you** ese traje no te entalla; **the key doesn't fit the lock** la llave no es de esta cerradura; Fig **she doesn't fit the description** no responde a la descripción **b)** [install] colocar; **a car fitted with a radio** un coche provisto de radio **2.** vi **a)** [be of right size] caber **b)** [facts etc] cuadrar **3.** adj **a)** [suitable] apto(a), adecuado(a) (**for** para); **are you fit to drive?** ¿estás en condiciones de conducir? **b)** [healthy] en (plena) forma; **to keep fit** mantenerse en forma **4.** n ajuste m; **to be a good fit** encajar bien

▪ **fit in 1.** vi **a) he didn't fit in with his colleagues** no encajó con sus compañeros de trabajo **b)** [tally] cuadrar (**with** con) **2.** *vt sep* [find time for] encontrar un hueco para

fit² [fɪt] *n* **a)** MED ataque *m* **b)** *Fig* arrebato *m*; **fit of anger** arranque *m* de cólera; *Fig* **by fits and starts** a trompicones

FITB MESSAGING *written abbr of* **fill in the blank**

fitness ['fɪtnɪs] *n* **a)** [aptitude] aptitud *f*, capacidad *f* **b)** [health] (buen) estado físico

fitted ['fɪtɪd] *adj* empotrado(a); **fitted carpet** moqueta *f*; **fitted cupboard** armario empotrado

fitting ['fɪtɪŋ] **1.** *adj* apropiado(a) **2.** *n* **a)** [of dress] prueba *f*; **fitting room** probador *m* **b)** [usu pl] accesorio *m*; **light fittings** apliques eléctricos

five [faɪv] *adj & n* cinco (*m inv*)

fix [fɪks] **1.** *n* **a)** *Fam* **to be in a fix** estar en un apuro **b)** *Fam* [drugs] chute *m* **2.** *vt* **a)** [fasten] fijar, asegurar **b)** [date, price] fijar; [limit] señalar **c)** [repair] arreglar **d)** *US* [food, drink] preparar ■ **fix up** *vt sep* [arrange] arreglar; **to fix sb up with sth** proveer a algn de algo

fixed [fɪkst] *adj* **a)** fijo(a); **fixed price** precio *m* fijo **b)** *Fam* [match etc] amañado(a)

fixture ['fɪkstʃə(r)] *n* **a)** *Br* [in football] encuentro *m* **b)** **fixtures** [in building] accesorios *mpl*

fizz [fɪz] **1.** *n* burbujeo *m* **2.** *vi* burbujear ■ **fizzle out** ['fɪzəl] *vi Fam* [plan] quedarse en nada *or Esp* en agua de borrajas

fizzy ['fɪzɪ] (*compar* **fizzier**, *superl* **fizziest**) *adj* [water] con gas

flabbergasted ['flæbəgɑːstɪd] *adj* pasmado(a)

flabby ['flæbɪ] (*compar* **flabbier**, *superl* **flabbiest**) *adj* fofo(a)

flag [flæg] **1.** *n* bandera *f*; NAUT pabellón *m*
2. *vt Fig* **to flag down a car** hacer señales a un coche para que pare
3. *vi* [interest] decaer; [conversation] languidecer

flagstone ['flægstəʊn] *n* losa *f*

flair [fleə(r)] *n* facilidad *f*

flake [fleɪk] **1.** *n* [of snow] copo *m*; [of skin, soap] escama *f*; [of paint] desconchón *m* **2.** *vi* [skin] descamarse; [paint] desconcharse

flamboyant [flæm'bɔɪənt] *adj* extravagante

flame [fleɪm] *n* **a)** [of fire] llama *f*; **to go up in flames** incendiarse **b)** COMPUT llamarada *f (mensaje ofensivo)*

flamingo [flə'mɪŋgəʊ] *n* flamenco *m*

flammable ['flæməbəl] *adj* inflamable

flan [flæn] *n* tarta *f*; **fruit flan** tarta de fruta

flank [flæŋk] **1.** *n* **a)** [of animal] ijada *f* **b)** MIL flanco *m* **2.** *vt* flanquear

flannel ['flænəl] *n* **a)** TEXT franela *f* **b)** *Br* [face cloth] toallita *f*

flap [flæp] **1.** *vt* [wings, arms] batir
2. *vi* [wings] aletear; [flag] ondear
3. *n* **a)** [of envelope, pocket] solapa *f*; [of tent] faldón *m*
b) [of wing] aletazo *m*
c) *Fam* **to get into a flap** ponerse nervioso(a)

flare [fleə(r)] **1.** *n* **a)** [flame] llamarada *f* **b)** MIL & NAUT bengala *f* **2.** *vi* **to flare (up)** [fire] llamear; *Fig* [person] encolerizarse; [trouble] estallar

flared [fleəd] *adj* [trousers etc] acampanado(a)

flash [flæʃ] **1.** *n* **a)** [of light] destello *m*; [of lightning] relámpago *m*; *Fig* **in a flash** en un santiamén
b) **news flash** noticia *f* de última hora
c) PHOTO flash *m*
2. *adj Br Fam* [showy] llamativo(a), ostentoso(a)
3. *vt* **a)** [torch] dirigir
b) RADIO & TV transmitir
4. *vi* **a)** [light] destellar
b) **a car flashed past** un coche pasó como un rayo

flashback ['flæʃbæk] *n* flashback *m*

flashlight ['flæʃlaɪt] *n US* linterna *f*

flashy ['flæʃɪ] *(compar* **flashier**, *superl* **flashiest)** *adj Fam* chillón(ona)

flask [flɑːsk, flæsk] *n* frasco *m*; **(Thermos®) flask** termo *m*

flat [flæt] **1.** *(compar* **flatter**, *superl* **flattest)** *adj* **a)** [surface] llano(a)
b) [beer] sin gas
c) [battery] descargado(a); [tyre] desinflado(a)
d) [rate] fijo(a)
e) [dull] soso(a)
f) MUS **B flat** si *m* bemol
2. *adv* **a) to fall flat on one's face** caerse de bruces
b) in ten seconds flat en diez segundos justos
c) *Fam* **to go flat out** ir a todo gas
3. *n* **a)** *Br* [apartment] apartamento *m*, *Esp* piso *m*, *Arg* departamento *m*
b) *US* AUTO pinchazo *m*

flatline ['flætlaɪn] *vi US Fam* [die] morir

flatly ['flætlɪ] *adv* rotundamente

flat-pack 1. *n* mueble *m* en kit, mueble *m* en paquete plano; **it comes as a flat-pack** lo mandan en kit *or* en paquete plano **2.** *adj* **flat-pack furniture** muebles *mpl* en kit, muebles *m* en paquete plano

flatten ['flætən] *vt* **a)** [make level] allanar **b)** [crush] aplastar

flatter ['flætə(r)] *vt* **a)** adular, halagar **b)** [clothes, portrait] favorecer **c) to flatter oneself** hacerse ilusiones

flattering ['flætərɪŋ] *adj* **a)** [words] halagador(a) **b)** [dress, portrait] favorecedor(a)

flattery ['flætərɪ] *n* adulación *f*, halago *m*

flaunt [flɔːnt] *vt* hacer alarde de

flavour, *US* **flavor** ['fleɪvə(r)] **1.** *n* sabor *m* **2.** *vt* CULIN sazonar (**with** con)

flavouring, *US* **flavoring** ['fleɪvərɪŋ] *n* condimento *m*; **artificial flavouring** aroma *m* artificial

flaw [flɔː] *n* [failing] defecto *m*; [fault] desperfecto *m*

flawed [flɔːd] *adj* defectuoso(a)

flawless ['flɔːlɪs] *adj* perfecto(a)

flea [fliː] *n* pulga *f*; **flea market** rastro *m*

fled [fled] *pt & pp of* **flee**

flee [fliː] *(pt & pp* **fled)** **1.** *vt* huir de **2.** *vi* huir (**from** de)

fleece [fliːs] **1.** *n* **a)** [sheep's coat] lana *f* **b)** [sheared] vellón *m* **2.** *vt Fam* [cheat] sangrar

fleet [fliːt] *n* **a)** flota *f* **b) Fleet Street** *calle de la City de Londres que a menudo se emplea para designar a la prensa británica*

fleeting ['fliːtɪŋ] *adj* fugaz

Flemish ['flemɪʃ] **1.** *adj* flamenco(a) **2.** *n* [language] flamenco *m*

flesh [fleʃ] *n* **a)** carne *f*; *Fig* **in the flesh** en persona; *Fig* **to be of flesh and blood** ser de carne y hueso; **flesh wound** herida *f* superficial **b)** [of fruit] pulpa *f*

flew [fluː] *pt of* **fly**

flex [fleks] **1.** *n Br* ELEC cable *m* **2.** *vt* [muscles] flexionar

flexible ['fleksɪbəl] *adj* flexible

flexitime ['fleksɪtaɪm], *US* **flextime** ['flekstaɪm] *n* horario *m* flexible

flick [flɪk] **1.** *n* movimiento rápido; [of finger] capirotazo *m* **2.** *vt* [with finger] dar un capirotazo a ■ **flick through** *vt insep* [book] hojear

flicker ['flɪkə(r)] **1.** *n* **a)** parpadeo *m*; [of light] titileo *m* **b)** *Fig* **a flicker of hope** un destello de esperanza **2.** *vi* [eyes] parpadear; [flame] vacilar

flier ['flaɪə(r)] *n* aviador(a) *m,f*

flight [flaɪt] *n* **a)** vuelo *m*; **flight path** trayectoria *f* de vuelo **b)** [of ball] trayectoria *f* **c)** [escape] huida *f*, fuga *f*; **to take flight** darse a la fuga **d)** [of stairs] tramo *m*

flimsy ['flɪmzɪ] *(compar* **flimsier**, *superl* **flimsiest)** *adj* [cloth] ligero(a); [paper] fino(a); [structure] poco sólido(a); [excuse] poco convincente

flinch [flɪntʃ] *vi* [wince] estremecerse

fling [flɪŋ] **1.** *(pt & pp* **flung)** *vt* arrojar **2.** *n Fam* **to have a fling** echar una cana al aire

flint [flɪnt] *n* **a)** [stone] pedernal *m* **b)** [in lighter] piedra *f* de mechero

flip [flɪp] **1.** n (flick) capirotazo m; **flip chart** flip chart m, pizarra f de conferencia (con bloc); **flip side** [of record] cara f B; [of situation] inconveniente m **2.** vt [toss] tirar (al aire); **to flip a coin** echar a cara o cruz

flip-flop ['flɪpflɒp] n **a)** COMPUT báscula f biestable **b)** Br [footwear] chancla f

flippant ['flɪpənt] adj frívolo(a)

flipper ['flɪpə(r)] n aleta f

flirt [flɜːt] **1.** n coqueto(a) m,f **2.** vi flirtear, coquetear; **to flirt with death** jugar con la muerte

float [fləʊt] **1.** n **a)** [on fishing line, as swimming aid] flotador m **b)** [in procession] carroza f **2.** vt **a)** poner a flote **b)** [shares] emitir; [currency, business] hacer flotar **3.** vi flotar

floaty ['fləʊtɪ] adj **floaty dress / skirt** vestido m vaporoso / falda f vaporosa

flock [flɒk] **1.** n ZOOL rebaño m; ORNITH bandada f; REL grey f; [crowd] multitud f **2.** vi acudir en masa

flood [flʌd] **1.** n inundación f; [of river] riada f; Fig torrente m **2.** vt inundar **3.** vi [river] desbordarse; Fig **to flood in** entrar a raudales

floodlight ['flʌdlaɪt] n foco m

floor [flɔː(r)] **1.** n **a)** [of room] suelo m; **dance floor** pista f de baile **b)** [of ocean, forest] fondo m **c)** [storey] piso m; **first floor** Br primer piso; US planta baja; Br **ground floor** planta baja **2.** vt Fig dejar perplejo(a)

floorboard ['flɔːbɔːd] n tabla f (del suelo)

flop [flɒp] **1.** n Fam fracaso m **2.** vi **a)** **to flop down on the bed** tumbarse en la cama **b)** Fam fracasar

floppy ['flɒpɪ] (compar **floppier**, superl **floppiest**) adj flojo(a); COMPUT **floppy disk** disco m flexible

florist ['flɒrɪst] n florista mf; **florist's shop** floristería f

flouncy ['flaʊnsɪ] adj [dress, skirt] con mucho vuelo

flour ['flaʊə(r)] n harina f

flourish ['flʌrɪʃ] **1.** n **a)** [gesture] ademán m (teatral) **b)** [under signature] rúbrica f **2.** vt [brandish] agitar **3.** vi [thrive] florecer; [plant] crecer

flow [fləʊ] **1.** n flujo m; [of river] corriente f; [of traffic] circulación f; [of capital] movimiento m; [of people, goods] afluencia f; **flow chart** diagrama m de flujo; COMPUT organigrama m **2.** vi [blood, river] fluir; [sea] subir; [traffic] circular

flower ['flaʊə(r)] **1.** n flor f; **flower bed** arriate m **2.** vi florecer

flowery ['flaʊərɪ] adj Fig florido(a)

flowing ['fləʊɪŋ] adj [hair] suelto(a); [dress] de mucho vuelo; [style] fluido(a); [shape, movement] natural

flown [fləʊn] pp of **fly**

flu [fluː] n (abbr of **influenza**) gripe f; **bird flu** gripe aviar

fluctuate ['flʌktjʊeɪt] vi fluctuar

fluent ['fluːənt] adj **a)** **he speaks fluent German** habla el alemán con soltura **b)** [eloquent] fluido(a)

fluff [flʌf] **1.** n [down] pelusa f **2.** vt Fam **to fluff sth** hacer algo mal

fluffy ['flʌfɪ] (compar **fluffier**, superl **fluffiest**) adj [pillow] mullido(a); [toy] de peluche; [cake] esponjoso(a)

fluid ['fluːɪd] **1.** adj [movement] natural; [style, prose] fluido(a); [situation] incierto(a) **2.** n fluido m, líquido m

fluke [fluːk] n Fam chiripa f; **by a fluke** por chiripa

flung [flʌŋ] pt & pp of **fling**

flunk [flʌŋk] vt & vi US Fam Esp catear, Am reprobar, Méx tronar

fluorescent [flʊəˈresənt] adj fluorescente

fluoride ['flʊəraɪd] n fluoruro m

flurry ['flʌrɪ] n **a)** [of wind] ráfaga f; [of snow] nevasca f **b)** Fig [bustle] agitación f

flush [flʌʃ] **1.** adj **flush with** [level] a ras de **2.** n [blush] rubor m

3. *vt* **to flush the lavatory** tirar de la cadena
4. *vi* [blush] ruborizarse

fluster ['flʌstə(r)] *vt* **to get flustered** ponerse nervioso(a)

flute [flu:t] *n* flauta *f*

flutter ['flʌtə(r)] **1.** *vi* [leaves, birds] revolotear ; [flag] ondear **2.** *n Br Fam* [bet] apuesta *f*

fly¹ [flaɪ] *(pt* **flew***, pp* **flown***)* **1.** *vt* **a)** AVIAT pilotar
b) [merchandise, troops] transportar
c) [distance] recorrer
d) [kite] hacer volar
2. *vi* **a)** [bird, plane] volar
b) [go by plane] ir en avión
c) [flag] ondear
d) **to fly into a rage** montar en cólera
e) *Fam* **to go flying** [fall] caerse
3. *npl* **flies** bragueta *f*

fly² [flaɪ] *n* [insect] mosca *f* ; **fly spray** spray *m* matamoscas

flying ['flaɪɪŋ] **1.** *adj* volador(a) ; [rapid] rápido(a) ; **a flying visit** una visita relámpago ; *Fig* **to come out of an affair with flying colours** salir airoso(a) de un asunto ; *Fig* **to get off to a flying start** empezar con buen pie ; **flying saucer** platillo *m* volante **2.** *n* **a)** [action] vuelo *m* **b)** [aviation] aviación *f*

flyover ['flaɪəʊvə(r)] *n Br* paso elevado

foal [fəʊl] *n* potro(a) *m,f*

foam [fəʊm] **1.** *n* espuma *f* ; **foam bath** espuma de baño ; **foam rubber** goma espuma **2.** *vi* hacer espuma

focus ['fəʊkəs] **1.** *vt* centrarse **(on** en**)** **2.** *vi* enfocar ; **to focus on sth** PHOTO enfocar algo ; *Fig* centrarse en algo **3.** *(pl* **focuses***) n* foco *m* ; **to be in focus / out of focus** estar enfocado(a) / desenfocado(a)

foetus ['fi:təs] *n* feto *m*

fog [fɒg] *n* niebla *f* ; [at sea] bruma *f*

foggy ['fɒgɪ] *(compar* **foggier***, superl* **foggiest***) adj* **it is foggy** hay niebla ; *Fam* **I haven't the foggiest (idea)** no tengo la más mínima idea

foglamp ['fɒglæmp]*, US* **foglight** ['fɒglaɪt] *n* faro *m* antiniebla

foil [fɔɪl] **1.** *n* **a)** **aluminium foil** papel *m* de aluminio **b)** [in fencing] florete *m* **2.** *vt* [plot] desbaratar

fold [fəʊld] **1.** *n* [crease] pliegue *m* **2.** *vt* plegar, doblar ; **to fold one's arms** cruzar los brazos **3.** *vi* **to fold (up)** [chair etc] plegarse ; COMM quebrar

folder ['fəʊldə(r)] *n* carpeta *f*

folding ['fəʊldɪŋ] *adj* [chair etc] plegable

foliage ['fəʊlɪɪdʒ] *n* follaje *m*

folk [fəʊk] **1.** *npl Fam* **a)** [people] gente *f* **b)** **my/your folks** mi /tu familia ; *US* [parents] mis /tus padres **2.** *adj* popular ; **folk music** música *f* folk ; **folk song** canción *f* popular

follow ['fɒləʊ] **1.** *vt* seguir ; [pursue] perseguir ; [understand] comprender ; [way of life] llevar **2.** *vi* **a)** [come after] seguir ; **as follows** como sigue **b)** [result] resultar ; **that doesn't follow** eso no es lógico **c)** [understand] entender ▪ **follow through, follow up** *vt sep* [idea] llevar a cabo ; [clue] investigar

follower ['fɒləʊə(r)] *n* seguidor(a) *m,f*

following ['fɒləʊɪŋ] **1.** *adj* siguiente **2.** *n* seguidores *mpl*

follow-up *n* continuación *f*

folly ['fɒlɪ] *n* locura *f*, desatino *m*

FOMCL MESSAGING *written abbr of* **fell off my chair laughing**

fond [fɒnd] *adj* [loving] cariñoso(a) ; **to be fond of sb** tenerle mucho cariño a algn ; **to be fond of doing sth** ser aficionado(a) a hacer algo

fondle ['fɒndəl] *vt* acariciar

fondly ['fɒndlɪ] *adv* **a)** [lovingly] cariñosamente **b)** [naively] **to fondly imagine that...** creer ingenuamente que...

font [fɒnt] *n* **a)** REL [in church] pila *f* **b)** COMPUT & TYP fuente *f*

food [fu:d] *n* comida *f* ; **food chain** cadena trófica ; **food hall** departamento *m* de alimentación ; **food poisoning** intoxicación alimenticia ; **food safety** seguridad *f* alimentaria

foodstuffs ['fu:dstʌfs] *npl* productos alimenticios

fool [fu:l] **1.** *n* **a)** tonto(a) *m,f*, imbécil *mf*; **to make a fool of sb** poner a algn en ridículo
b) CULIN ≃ mousse *f* de fruta
2. *vt* [deceive] engañar
3. *vi* [joke] bromear; **to fool about** or **around** hacer el tonto

foolish ['fu:lɪʃ] *adj* estúpido(a)

foolproof ['fu:lpru:f] *adj* infalible

foot [fʊt] **1.** *(pl* **feet**) *n* pie *m*; ZOOL pata *f*; **on foot** a pie, *Esp* andando **2.** *vt* [bill] pagar

football ['fʊtbɔ:l] *n* **a)** [soccer] fútbol *m*; **bar football** futbolín *m*; *US* **football field** campo *m* de fútbol (americano); **football ground** campo *m* de fútbol; **football match** partido *m* de fútbol; *Br* **football pools** quinielas *fpl* **b)** [ball] balón *m*

footballer ['fʊtbɔ:lə(r)] *n* futbolista *mf*

footbridge ['fʊtbrɪdʒ] *n* puente *m* para peatones

foothold ['fʊthəʊld] *n Fig* **to gain a foothold** afianzarse en una posición

footnote ['fʊtnəʊt] *n* nota *f* a pie de página

footpath ['fʊtpɑ:θ] *n* [track] sendero *m*

footstep ['fʊtstep] *n* paso *m*

footwear ['fʊtweə(r)] *n* calzado *m*

for [fɔ:(r)] *(unstressed* [fə(r)]) **1.** *prep*
a) [intended] para; **curtains for the bedroom** cortinas para el dormitorio
b) [representing] por; **a cheque for £10** un cheque de 10 libras; **what's the Spanish for "rivet"?** ¿cómo se dice "rivet" en español?
c) [purpose] para; **what's this for?** ¿para qué sirve esto?
d) [because of] por; **famous for its cuisine** famoso(a) por su cocina
e) [on behalf of] por; **will you do it for me?** ¿lo harás por mí?
f) [during] por, durante; **I shall stay for two weeks** me quedaré dos semanas; **I've been here for three months** hace tres meses que estoy aquí
g) [distance] **I walked for 10 km** caminé 10 km
h) [at a point in time] para; **I can do it for next Monday** puedo hacerlo para el lunes que viene; **for the last time** por última vez
i) [destination] para
j) [in exchange] por; **I got the car for £500** conseguí el coche por 500 libras; **how much did you sell it for?** ¿por cuánto lo vendiste?
k) [in favour of] a favor de; **are you for or against?** ¿estás a favor o en contra?; **to vote for sb** votar a algn
l) [to obtain] para; **to run for the bus** correr para coger el autobús; **to send sb for water** mandar a algn a por agua
m) [with respect to] en cuanto a; **as for him** en cuanto a él; **for all I know** que yo sepa
n) [despite] a pesar de; **he's tall for his age** está muy alto para su edad
o) [towards] hacia, por; **his love for you** su amor por ti
p) [as] por; **what do you use for fuel?** ¿qué utilizan como combustible?
q) [+ object + infin] **it's time for you to go** es hora de que os marchéis; **it's easy for him to say that** le es fácil decir eso
2. *conj* [since, as] ya que, puesto que

forbid [fə'bɪd] *(pt* **forbade** [fə'bæd], *pp* **forbidden** [fə'bɪdən]) *vt* prohibir; **to forbid sb to do sth** prohibirle a algn hacer algo

force [fɔ:s] **1.** *n* **a)** fuerza *f*; **by force** por la fuerza; **to come into force** entrar en vigor **b)** MIL cuerpo *m*; **the (armed) forces** las fuerzas armadas; **the police force** la policía **2.** *vt* forzar; **to force sb to do sth** forzar a algn a hacer algo

forceful ['fɔ:sfʊl] *adj* **a)** [person] enérgico(a) **b)** [argument] convincente

ford [fɔ:d] **1.** *n* vado *m* **2.** *vt* vadear

forearm ['fɔ:rɑ:m] *n* antebrazo *m*

forecast ['fɔ:kɑ:st] **1.** *n* pronóstico *m* **2.** *(pt & pp* **forecast** or **forecasted**) *vt* pronosticar

forefinger ['fɔ:fɪŋgə(r)] *n* (dedo *m*) índice *m*

forefront ['fɔ:frʌnt] *n* **in the forefront** a la vanguardia

forego [fɔ:'gəʊ] *(pt* **forewent**, *pp* **foregone** [fɔ:'gɒn]) *vt Formal* renunciar a

foreground ['fɔ:graʊnd] *n* primer plano

forehead ['fɒrɪd, 'fɔ:hed] *n* frente *f*

foreign ['fɒrɪn] *adj* extranjero(a); [trade, policy] exterior; **foreign exchange** divisas *fpl*; *Br* **the Foreign Office** el Ministerio de Asuntos Exteriores; **foreign body** cuerpo extraño

foreigner ['fɒrɪnə(r)] *n* extranjero(a) *m,f*

foreman ['fɔ:mən] *n* **a)** IND capataz *m* **b)** JUR presidente *m* del jurado

foremost ['fɔ:məʊst] *adj* principal; **first and foremost** ante todo

forerunner ['fɔ:rʌnə(r)] *n* precursor(a) *m,f*

foresee [fɔ:'si:] *(pt* **foresaw** [fɔ:'sɔ:], *pp* **foreseen** [fɔ:'si:n]) *vt* prever

foresight ['fɔ:saɪt] *n* previsión *f*

forest ['fɒrɪst] *n* bosque *m*

forestall [fɔ:'stɔ:l] *vt* [plan] anticiparse a; [danger] prevenir

foretell [fɔ:'tel] *(pt & pp* **foretold** [fɔ:'təʊld]) *vt* presagiar

forever [fə'revə(r)] *adv* **a)** [eternally] siempre **b)** [for good] para siempre **c)** *Fam* [ages] siglos *mpl*

forewarning [,fɔ:'wɔ:nɪŋ] *n* advertencia *f* anticipada

forewent [fɔ:'went] *pp of* **forego**

foreword ['fɔ:wɜ:d] *n* prefacio *m*

forfeit ['fɔ:fɪt] **1.** *n* [penalty] pena *f*; [in games] prenda *f* **2.** *vt* perder

forgave [fə'geɪv] *pt of* **forgive**

forge [fɔ:dʒ] **1.** *n* **a)** [furnace] fragua *f* **b)** [blacksmith's] herrería *f* **2.** *vt* **a)** [counterfeit] falsificar **b)** [metal] forjar **3.** *vi* **to forge ahead** hacer grandes progresos

forged [fɔ:dʒd] *adj* [banknote, letter] falso(a), falsificado(a)

forgery ['fɔ:dʒərɪ] *n* falsificación *f*

forget [fə'get] *(pt* **forgot**, *pp* **forgotten**) **1.** *vt* olvidar, olvidarse de; **I've forgotten my key** he olvidado la llave **2.** *vi* olvidarse

forgetful [fə'getfʊl] *adj* olvidadizo(a)

forgive [fə'gɪv] *(pt* **forgave**, *pp* **forgiven** [fə'gɪvən]) *vt* perdonar; **to forgive sb for sth** perdonarle algo a algn

forgiveness [fə'gɪvnɪs] *n* perdón *m*

forgo [fɔ:'gəʊ] *Formal vt* = **forego**

forgot [fə'gɒt] *pt of* **forget**

forgotten [fə'gɒtən] *pp of* **forget**

fork [fɔ:k] **1.** *n* **a)** [cutlery] tenedor *m* **b)** [in road] bifurcación *f* **2.** *vi* [roads] bifurcarse ■ **fork out** *vt sep Fam* [money] aflojar, *Esp* apoquinar, *RP* garpar

forlorn [fə'lɔ:n] *adj* [forsaken] abandonado(a); [desolate] triste; [without hope] desesperado(a)

form [fɔ:m] **1.** *n* **a)** [shape] forma *f* **b)** [type] clase *f* **c)** [document] formulario *m* **d)** **on (top) form** en (plena) forma; **off form** en baja forma **e)** *Br* SCH clase *f*; **the first form** el primer curso **2.** *vt* formar; **to form an impression** formarse una impresión **3.** *vi* formarse

formal ['fɔ:məl] *adj* **a)** [official] oficial; **a formal application** una solicitud en forma **b)** [party, dress] de etiqueta **c)** [ordered] formal **d)** [person] formalista

formality [fɔ:'mælɪtɪ] *n* formalidad *f*

formally ['fɔ:məlɪ] *adv* oficialmente

format ['fɔ:mæt] **1.** *n* formato *m* **2.** *vt* COMPUT formatear

formation [fɔ:'meɪʃən] *n* formación *f*

former ['fɔ:mə(r)] *adj* **a)** [time] anterior **b)** [one-time] antiguo(a); [person] ex; **the former champion** el ex-campeón **c)** [first] aquél /aquélla; **Peter and Lisa came, the former wearing a hat** vinieron Peter y Lisa, aquél llevaba sombrero

formerly ['fɔ:məlɪ] *adv* antiguamente

formidable [ˈfɔːmɪdəbəl] *adj* [prodigious] formidable ; [daunting] terrible

formula [ˈfɔːmjʊlə] *n* fórmula *f*

formulate [ˈfɔːmjʊleɪt] *vt* formular

fort [fɔːt] *n* fortaleza *f*

forth [fɔːθ] *adv Formal* **and so forth** y así sucesivamente; **to go back and forth** ir de acá para allá

forthcoming [fɔːθˈkʌmɪŋ] *adj* **a)** [event] próximo(a) **b) no money was forthcoming** no hubo oferta de dinero **c)** [communicative] comunicativo(a)

fortieth [ˈfɔːtɪəθ] *n* & *adj* cuadragésimo(a) *(m,f)*

fortification [fɔːtɪfɪˈkeɪʃən] *n* fortificación *f*

fortify [ˈfɔːtɪfaɪ] *vt* fortificar

fortnight [ˈfɔːtnaɪt] *n Br* quincena *f*

fortress [ˈfɔːtrɪs] *n* fortaleza *f*

fortunate [ˈfɔːtʃənɪt] *adj* afortunado(a); **it was fortunate that he came** fue una suerte que viniera

fortunately [ˈfɔːtʃənɪtlɪ] *adv* afortunadamente

fortune [ˈfɔːtʃən] *n* **a)** [luck, fate] suerte *f*; **to tell sb's fortune** echar la buenaventura a algn **b)** [money] fortuna *f*

fortune-teller [ˈfɔːtʃəntelə(r)] *n* adivino(a) *m,f*

forty [ˈfɔːtɪ] *adj* & *n* cuarenta *(m inv)*

forum [ˈfɔːrəm] *n* foro *m*

forward [ˈfɔːwəd] **1.** *adv* **a)** (*also* **forwards**) [direction and movement] hacia adelante
b) *Fig* **to come forward** ofrecerse
c) from this day forward de ahora en adelante
2. *adj* **a)** [movement] hacia adelante ; [position] delantero(a)
b) [person] fresco(a)
3. *n* SPORT delantero(a) *m,f*
4. *vt* **a)** [send on] remitir
b) *Formal* [send goods] expedir
c) *Formal* [further] fomentar

fossil [ˈfɒsəl] *n* fósil *m*; **fossil fuel** combustible *m* fósil

foster [ˈfɒstə(r)] **1.** *vt* **a)** [child] criar **b)** *Formal* [hopes] abrigar ; [relations] fomentar **2.** *adj* **foster child** hijo(a) adoptivo(a); **foster father** padre adoptivo; **foster mother** madre adoptiva; **foster parents** padres adoptivos

fought [fɔːt] *pt & pp of* **fight**

foul [faʊl] **1.** *adj* **a)** [smell] fétido(a) ; [taste] asqueroso(a) **b)** [deed] atroz; [weather] de perros **c)** [language] grosero(a) **d)** SPORT **foul play** juego sucio **2.** *n* SPORT falta *f* **3.** *vt* **a)** [dirty] ensuciar ; [air] contaminar **b)** SPORT cometer una falta contra

found[1] [faʊnd] *pt & pp of* **find**

found[2] [faʊnd] *vt* [establish] fundar

foundation [faʊnˈdeɪʃən] *n* **a)** [establishment] fundación *f* **b)** [basis] fundamento *m* **c)** CONSTR **foundations** cimientos *mpl*

founder[1] [ˈfaʊndə(r)] *n* fundador(a) *m,f*

founder[2] [ˈfaʊndə(r)] *vi* **a)** *Formal* [sink] hundirse **b)** *Fig* [plan, hopes] fracasar

fountain [ˈfaʊntɪn] *n* [structure] fuente *f*; [jet] surtidor *m*; **fountain pen** pluma estilográfica, *CSur* lapicera *f* fuente, *Perú* lapicero *m*

four [fɔː(r)] *adj* & *n* cuatro *(m inv)*; **on all fours** a gatas

4 MESSAGING *(abbr of* **for***)* x *(por)*, xra *(para)*

4eva, **4E** *(abbr of* **for ever***)* MESSAGING xra smpr *or* 100pre

4gv MESSAGING *written abbr of* **forgive**

4gvn *(abbr of* **forgiven***)* MESSAGING xdon

fourteen [fɔːˈtiːn] *adj* & *n* catorce *(m inv)*

fourteenth [fɔːˈtiːnθ] **1.** *adj* & *n* decimocuarto(a) *(m,f)* **2.** *n* [fraction] catorceavo *m*

fourth [fɔːθ] **1.** *adj* & *n* cuarto(a) *(m,f)* **2.** *n* **a)** [fraction] cuarto *m* **b)** AUTO cuarta *f* (velocidad) **c) the Fourth of July** Día de la Independencia estadounidense que se celebra el 4 de julio

four-wheel *adj* **with four-wheel drive** con tracción en las cuatro ruedas

fowl [faʊl] *(pl* **fowl***) n* ave *f* de corral

fox [fɒks] **1.** n zorro(a) m,f **2.** vt a) [perplex] dejar perplejo(a) **b)** [deceive] engañar

foyer [ˈfɔɪeɪ,ˈfɔɪə(r)] n vestíbulo m

fraction [ˈfrækʃən] n fracción f

fracture [ˈfræktʃə(r)] **1.** n fractura f **2.** vt fracturar

fragile [ˈfrædʒaɪl] adj frágil

fragment [ˈfrægmənt] n fragmento m

fragrance [ˈfreɪgrəns] n fragancia f, perfume m

fragrance-free adj sin perfume

fragrant adj **fragrant rice** arroz m aromático

frail [freɪl] adj frágil, delicado(a)

frame [freɪm] **1.** n a) [of window, door, picture] marco m ; [of machine] armazón m ; [of bicycle] cuadro m ; [of spectacles] montura f; **photo frame** marco m para foto; Fig **frame of mind** estado m de ánimo **b)** CIN & TV fotograma m **2.** vt a) [picture] enmarcar **b)** [question] formular **c)** Fam [innocent person] incriminar

framework [ˈfreɪmwɜːk] n Fig **within the framework of ...** dentro del marco de ...

franc [fræŋk] n franco m

France [frɑːns] n Francia f

franchise [ˈfræntʃaɪz] n a) POL derecho m al voto **b)** COMM concesión f, licencia f

frank [fræŋk] **1.** adj franco(a) **2.** vt [mail] franquear

frankly [ˈfræŋklɪ] adv francamente

frantic [ˈfræntɪk] adj [anxious] desesperado(a) ; [hectic] frenético(a)

frape [freɪp] vt Fam usar la cuenta de Facebook de otra persona colgando algo en su perfil o cambiando su información

fraternize [ˈfrætənaɪz] vi confraternizar (**with** con)

fraud [frɔːd] n a) fraude m **b)** [person] impostor(a) m,f

fraught [frɔːt] adj a) [full] cargado(a) (**with** de) **b)** [tense] nervioso(a)

fray[1] [freɪ] vi a) [cloth] deshilacharse **b)** [nerves] crisparse; **his temper frequently frayed** se irritaba a menudo

fray[2] [freɪ] n combate m

freak [friːk] **1.** n a) [monster] monstruo m
b) Fam [eccentric] estrafalario(a) m,f
c) Fam [fan] fanático(a) m,f
2. adj a) [unexpected] inesperado(a)
b) [unusual] insólito(a)
■ **freak out** vi Fam a) [get angry] ponerse hecho(a) una furia **b)** [panic] entrarle el pánico

freckle [ˈfrekəl] n peca f

free [friː] **1.** adj a) libre ; **to set sb free** poner en libertad a algn; **free kick** tiro m libre; **free speech** libertad f de expresión; **free will** libre albedrío m **b)** **free (of charge)** [gratis] gratuito(a); **free gift** obsequio m **2.** adv a) **(for) free** gratis **b)** [loose] suelto(a) **3.** vt a) [liberate] poner en libertad **b)** [let loose, work loose] soltar **c)** [untie] desatar **d)** [exempt] eximir (**from** de)

freedom [ˈfriːdəm] n a) [liberty] libertad f; **freedom of the press** libertad de prensa **b)** [exemption] exención f

freelance [ˈfriːlɑːns] adj independiente

freely [ˈfriːlɪ] adv a) libremente **b)** [openly] abiertamente

freemium [ˈfriːmɪəm] adj **a freemium business model** un (modelo de negocio) freemium

free-range [ˈfriːreɪndʒ] adj Br de granja

freeway [ˈfriːweɪ] n US autopista f

freeze [friːz] (pt **froze**, pp **frozen**) **1.** vt congelar
2. n MET helada f; **price freeze** congelación f de precios; TV & CIN **freeze frame** imagen congelada
3. vi [liquid] helarse ; [food] congelarse

freezer [ˈfriːzə(r)] n congelador m

freezing [ˈfriːzɪŋ] adj a) glacial **b)** **freezing point** punto m de congelación ; **above/below freezing point** sobre / bajo cero

freight [freɪt] n a) [transport] transporte m b) [goods, price] flete m; US **freight car** vagón m; US **freight elevator** montacargas m inv; **freight train** tren m de mercancías

French [frentʃ] **1.** adj francés(esa); **French bean** judía f verde, Bol, RP chaucha f, CAm ejote m, Col, Cuba habichuela f, Chile poroto m verde, Ven vainita f; **French dressing** vinagreta f; US **French fries** patatas fpl or Am papas fpl fritas; Br **French stick** barra f de pan; **French window** puerta f vidriera **2.** n a) [language] francés m b) (pl) **the French** los franceses

Frenchman ['frentʃmən] n francés m

Frenchwoman ['frentʃwʊmən] n francesa f

frenemy ['frenəmɪ] n Fam Emily and Susan are frenemies; they like each other but they're working on competing products Emily y Susan son amigas y rivales; se tienen cariño pero trabajan en productos que compiten entre sí

frenzy ['frenzɪ] n frenesí m

frequency ['fri:kwənsɪ] n frecuencia f

frequent 1. ['fri:kwənt] adj frecuente **2.** [frɪ'kwent] vt frecuentar

frequently ['fri:kwəntlɪ] adv frecuentemente, a menudo

fresh [freʃ] adj a) fresco(a); **fresh water** agua f dulce; **fresh bread** pan m del día b) [new] nuevo(a) c) [air] puro(a); **in the fresh air** al aire libre d) US Fam [cheeky] fresco(a)

freshly ['freʃlɪ] adv recién, recientemente

freshman ['freʃmæn] (pl **freshmen** [-mən]) n US SCH & UNIV novato(a) m,f, estudiante mf de primer año

freshwater ['freʃˌwɔːtə(r)] adj de agua dulce

fret [fret] vi preocuparse (**about** por)

friction ['frɪkʃən] n fricción f

Friday ['fraɪdɪ] n viernes m

fridge [frɪdʒ] n esp Br nevera f, frigorífico m, Andes frigider m, RP heladera f

fried [fraɪd] adj frito(a)

friend [frend] n amigo(a) m,f; **a friend of mine** un(a) amigo(a) mío(a); **to make friends with sb** hacerse amigo(a) de algn; **to make friends again** hacer las paces

friendly ['frendlɪ] (compar **friendlier**, superl **friendliest**) adj [person] simpático(a); [atmosphere] acogedor(a); **friendly advice** consejo m de amigo; **friendly nation** nación amiga

friendship ['frendʃɪp] n amistad f

friendzone ['frendzəʊn] Fam **1.** n zona f de amistad; **Alan really likes Emily but he's been stuck in the friendzone for way too long** a Alan le gusta mucho Emily pero llevan demasiado tiempo siendo solo amigos **2.** vt **to friendzone sb** poner a algn en la zona de amistad, hacer comprender a algn que solo se desea ser su amigo

fright [fraɪt] n a) [fear] miedo m; **to take fright** asustarse b) [shock] susto m; **to get a fright** pegarse un susto

frighten ['fraɪtən] vt asustar ■ **frighten away**, **frighten off** vt sep ahuyentar

frightened ['fraɪtənd] adj asustado(a); **to be frightened of sb** tenerle miedo a algn

frightening ['fraɪtənɪŋ] adj espantoso(a)

frightful ['fraɪtfʊl] adj espantoso(a), horroroso(a)

frill [frɪl] n [on dress] volante m; Fig **frills** [decorations] adornos mpl

fringe [frɪndʒ] n a) Br [of hair] flequillo m, Am cerquillo m b) [edge] borde m; Fig **on the fringe of society** al margen de la sociedad; **fringe theatre** teatro m experimental; **fringe benefits** extras mpl

frisk [frɪsk] vt Fam [search] registrar

frisky ['frɪskɪ] (compar **friskier**, superl **friskiest**) adj a) [children, animals] juguetón(ona) b) [adult] vivo(a)

fritter ['frɪtə(r)] n buñuelo m ■ **fritter away** vt sep malgastar

frivolous ['frɪvələs] adj frívolo(a)

frizzy ['frɪzɪ] *(compar* **frizzier**, *superl* **frizziest**) *adj* crespo(a)

frog [frɒg] *n* rana *f*

frolic ['frɒlɪk] *vi* retozar, juguetear

from [frɒm] (*unstressed* [frəm]) *prep*
a) [time] desde, a partir de; **from now on** a partir de ahora; **from Monday to Friday** de lunes a viernes; **from the 8th to the 17th** desde el 8 hasta el 17
b) [price, number] desde, de; **a number from one to ten** un número del uno a diez
c) [origin] de; **a letter from her father** una carta de su padre; **from English into Spanish** del inglés al español; **he's from Malaga** es de Málaga; **the train from Bilbao** el tren procedente de Bilbao; **from now on** desde ahora, a partir de ahora; **from then on** desde entonces, a partir de entonces
d) [distance] de; **the town is 4 miles from the coast** el pueblo está a 4 millas de la costa
e) [out of] de; **bread is made from flour** el pan se hace con harina
f) [remove, subtract] a; **he took the book from the child** le quitó el libro al niño; **take three from five** restar tres a cinco
g) [according to] según, por; **from what the author said** según lo que dijo el autor
h) [position] desde, de; **from here** desde aquí
i) **can you tell margarine from butter?** ¿puedes distinguir entre la margarina y la mantequilla?

front [frʌnt] **1.** *n* a) parte delantera; **in front (of)** delante (de) b) [of building] fachada *f* c) MIL, POL & MET frente *m* d) [seaside] paseo marítimo e) *Fig* **she put on a brave front** hizo de tripas corazón **2.** *adj* delantero(a), de delante; **front door** puerta *f* principal; **front seat** asiento *m* de delante; *US* **front yard** jardín *m* delantero

frontier ['frʌntɪə(r)] *n* frontera *f*

frost [frɒst] **1.** *n* a) [covering] escarcha *f* b) [freezing] helada *f* **2.** *vt US* CULIN recubrir con azúcar glas ■ **frost over** *vi* escarchar

frostbite ['frɒstbaɪt] *n* congelación *f*

frosting ['frɒstɪŋ] *n US* glaseado *m*

frosty ['frɒstɪ] *(compar* **frostier**, *superl* **frostiest**) *adj* a) **it will be a frosty night tonight** esta noche habrá helada b) *Fig* glacial

froth [frɒθ] **1.** *n* espuma *f*; [from mouth] espumarajos *mpl* **2.** *vi* espumar

frothy ['frɒθɪ] *(compar* **frothier**, *superl* **frothiest**) *adj* espumoso(a)

frown [fraʊn] *vi* fruncir el ceño ■ **frown upon** *vt insep* desaprobar

froyo ['frəʊˌjəʊ] *n Fam* yogur *m* helado

froze [frəʊz] *pt of* **freeze**

frozen ['frəʊzən] **1.** *adj* [liquid, feet etc] helado(a); [food] congelado(a) **2.** *pp of* **freeze**

fructose ['frʌktəʊs] *n* fructosa *f*

fruit [fruːt] *n* a) BOT fruto *m* b) [apple, orange etc] fruta *f*; **fruit bowl** frutero *m*; **fruit cake** pastel *m* con fruto seco; **fruit machine** (máquina *f*) tragaperras *f inv*; **fruit salad** macedonia *f* de frutas c) **fruits** [rewards] frutos *mpl*

fruitful ['fruːtfʊl] *adj Fig* provechoso(a)

fruitless ['fruːtlɪs] *adj* infructuoso(a)

frustrate [frʌˈstreɪt] *vt* frustrar

frustrating [frʌsˈtreɪtɪŋ] *adj* frustrante

frustration [frʌsˈtreɪʃən] *n* frustración *f*

fry[1] [fraɪ] *(pt & pp* **fried**) **1.** *vt* freír **2.** *vi Fig* asarse

fry[2] [fraɪ] *npl* **small fry** gente *f* de poca monta

frying pan ['fraɪŋpæn], *US* **fry-pan** ['fraɪpæn] *n* sartén *f*

ft *(abbr of* **foot)** pie *m*; *(abbr of* **feet)** pies *mpl*

F2F, FTF MESSAGING *written abbr of* face to face

fudge [fʌdʒ] **1.** *n* CULIN *dulce hecho con azúcar, leche y mantequilla* **2.** *vt* [figures] amañar

fuel ['fjʊəl] **1.** n combustible m ; [for engines] carburante m ; **fuel tank** depósito m de combustible **2.** vt Fig [ambition] estimular ; [difficult situation] empeorar

fugitive ['fju:dʒɪtɪv] n Formal fugitivo(a) m,f

fugly ['fʌɡlɪ] adj v Fam (abbr of **fucking ugly**) feo(a) de la hostia ; **she's really fugly** es más fea que pegar a un padre

fulfil, US **fulfill** [fʊl'fɪl] vt a) [task, ambition] realizar ; [promise] cumplir ; [role] desempeñar b) [wishes] satisfacer

fulfilment, US **fulfillment** [fʊl'fɪlmənt] n a) [of ambition] realización f b) [of duty, promise] cumplimiento m

full [fʊl] **1.** adj a) lleno(a) ; **full of** lleno(a) de ; **I'm full (up)** no puedo más b) [complete] completo(a) ; **at full speed** a toda velocidad ; **full employment** pleno empleo ; **full moon** luna llena ; **full stop** punto m **2.** n **in full** en su totalidad ; **name in full** nombre y apellidos completos **3.** adv **full well** perfectamente

full-fat adj entero(a)

full-scale ['fʊlskeɪl] adj a) [model] de tamaño natural b) **full-scale search** registro m a fondo ; **full-scale war** guerra generalizada or total

full-time ['fʊl'taɪm] **1.** adj de jornada completa **2.** adv **to work full-time** trabajar a tiempo completo

fully ['fʊlɪ] adv completamente

fully-equiped adj totalmente equipado(a)

fully-fitted adj [kitchen] integral

fumble ['fʌmbəl] vi hurgar ; **to fumble for sth** buscar algo a tientas ; **to fumble with sth** manejar algo con torpeza

fume [fju:m] **1.** n (usu pl) humo m **2.** vi despedir humo

fun [fʌn] **1.** n [amusement] diversión f ; **in** or **for fun** en broma ; **to have fun** divertirse, pasarlo bien ; **to make fun of sb** reírse de algn **2.** adj divertido(a)

function ['fʌŋkʃən] **1.** n a) función f b) [ceremony] acto m ; [party] recepción f **2.** vi funcionar

functional ['fʌŋkʃənəl] adj funcional

fund [fʌnd] **1.** n a) COMM fondo m b) **funds** fondos mpl **2.** vt [finance] financiar

fundamental [fʌndə'mentəl] **1.** adj fundamental **2.** npl **fundamentals** los fundamentos

funeral ['fju:nərəl] n funeral m ; US **funeral home** funeraria f ; **funeral march** marcha f fúnebre ; Br **funeral parlour** funeraria f ; **funeral service** misa f de cuerpo presente

funfair ['fʌnfeə(r)] n Br parque m de atracciones

fun-filled adj divertido(a)

fungus ['fʌŋɡəs] (pl **fungi** ['fʌŋɡaɪ]) n a) BOT hongo m b) MED fungo m

funnel ['fʌnəl] **1.** n a) [for liquids] embudo m b) NAUT chimenea f **2.** (pt & pp **funnelled**, US pt & pp **funneled**) vt Fig [funds, energy] encauzar

funny ['fʌnɪ] (compar **funnier**, superl **funniest**) adj a) [peculiar] raro(a), extraño(a) ; **that's funny!** ¡qué raro! b) [amusing] divertido(a), gracioso(a) ; **I found it very funny** me hizo mucha gracia c) Fam [ill] mal

fun-packed adj divertido(a)

fur [fɜ:(r)] **1.** n a) [of living animal] pelo m b) [of dead animal] piel f c) [in kettle, on tongue] sarro m **2.** adj de piel ; **fur coat** abrigo m de pieles

furious ['fjʊərɪəs] adj a) [angry] furioso(a) b) [vigorous] violento(a)

furnace ['fɜ:nɪs] n horno m

furnish ['fɜ:nɪʃ] vt a) [house] amueblar b) Formal [food] suministrar ; [details] facilitar

furnishings ['fɜ:nɪʃɪŋz] npl a) muebles mpl b) [fittings] accesorios mpl

furniture ['fɜ:nɪtʃə(r)] n muebles mpl ; **a piece of furniture** un mueble

furrow ['fʌrəʊ] n AGR surco m ; [on forehead] arruga f

furry ['fɜːrɪ] *(compar* furrier, *superl* furriest) *adj* a) [hairy] peludo(a) b) [tongue, kettle] sarroso(a)

further ['fɜːðə(r)] *(compar of* far) **1.** *adj* a) [new] nuevo(a); **until further notice** hasta nuevo aviso
b) [additional] otro(a), adicional
c) [later] posterior; *Br* **further education** estudios *mpl* superiores
2. *adv* a) [more] más; **further back** más atrás; **further along** más adelante
b) *Formal* [besides] además
3. *vt* fomentar

furthermore [fɜːðə'mɔː(r)] *adv Formal* además

furthest ['fɜːðɪst] **1.** *adj* (*superl of* far) más lejano(a) **2.** *adv* más lejos

furtive ['fɜːtɪv] *adj* furtivo(a)

fury ['fjʊərɪ] *n* furia *f*, furor *m*

fuse [fjuːz] **1.** *n* a) ELEC fusible *m*; **fuse box** caja *f* de fusibles
b) [of bomb] mecha *f*
2. *vi* a) *Br* ELEC **the lights fused** se fundieron los plomos
b) *Fig* [merge] fusionarse
c) [melt] fundirse

3. *vt* a) *Br* ELEC **a surge of power fused the lights** se fundieron los plomos y se fue la luz por una subida de corriente
b) *Fig* [merge] fusionar
c) [melt] fundir

fusion ['fjuːʒən] *n* fusión *f*

fuss [fʌs] **1.** *n* [commotion] jaleo *m*; **to kick up a fuss** armar un escándalo; **stop making a fuss** [complaining] deja ya de quejarte; **to make a fuss of** [pay attention to] mimar a **2.** *vi* preocuparse (**about** por)

fussy ['fʌsɪ] *(compar* fussier, *superl* fussiest) *adj* exigente; [nitpicking] quisquilloso(a)

futile ['fjuːtaɪl] *adj* inútil, vano(a)

futon ['fuːtɒn] *n* futón *m*

future ['fjuːtʃə(r)] **1.** *n* futuro *m*, porvenir *m*; **in the near future** en un futuro próximo; **in future** de aquí en adelante **2.** *adj* futuro(a)

fuze [fjuːz] *US n*, *vi* & *vt* = **fuse**

fuzzy ['fʌzɪ] *(compar* fuzzier, *superl* fuzziest) *adj* a) [hair] muy rizado(a)
b) [blurred] borroso(a)

FWIW *n* MESSAGING *written abbr of* **for what it's worth**

G

G, g [dʒiː] *n* **a)** [the letter] G, g *f* **b)** MUS G sol *m*

G [dʒiː] *adj* US CIN ≃ (apta) para todos los públicos

gabble ['gæbəl] **1.** *n* chapurreo *m* **2.** *vi* hablar atropelladamente

gadget ['gædʒɪt] *n* artilugio *m*, aparato *m*

gaffe [gæf] *n* metedura *f* de pata, desliz *m*; **to make a gaffe** meter la pata, patinar

gag [gæg] **1.** *n* **a)** mordaza *f* **b)** *Fam* [joke] chiste *m* **2.** *vt* amordazar

gage [geɪdʒ] US *n* & *vt* = **gauge**

gaily ['geɪlɪ] *adv* alegremente

gain [geɪn] **1.** *n* ganancia *f*, beneficio *m*; [increase] aumento *m* **2.** *vt* ganar; *Fig* **to gain ground** ganar terreno; **to gain speed** ganar velocidad, acelerar; **to gain weight** aumentar de peso

gala ['gɑːlə, 'geɪlə] *n* gala *f*, fiesta *f*

galaxy ['gæləksɪ] *n* galaxia *f*

gale [geɪl] *n* vendaval *m*

gallant ['gælənt] *adj* [brave] valiente; (*also* [gə'lænt]) [chivalrous] galante

gallery ['gælərɪ] *n* **a)** galería *f* **b)** THEAT gallinero *m* **c)** [court] tribuna *f*

gallon ['gælən] *n* galón *m* (*Br* = 4,55 *l*; US = 3,79 *l*)

gallop ['gæləp] **1.** *n* galope *m* **2.** *vi* galopar

gamble ['gæmbəl] **1.** *n* [risk] riesgo *m*; [risky undertaking] empresa arriesgada; [bet] apuesta *f* **2.** *vi* [bet] jugar; [take a risk] arriesgarse

gambler ['gæmblə(r)] *n* jugador(a) *m,f*

gambling ['gæmblɪŋ] *n* juego *m*

game [geɪm] **1.** *n* **a)** juego *m*; **game of chance** juego de azar **b)** [match] partido *m*; [of bridge] partida *f* **c)** games

[sporting event] juegos *mpl*; *Br* [school subject] deportes *mpl* **d)** [hunting] caza *f*; *Fig* presa *f* **2.** *adj* **game for anything** dispuesto(a) a todo

gamer ['geɪmə(r)] *n* **a)** [who plays computer games] *aficionado a los juegos de ordenador* **b)** US [athlete, sportsperson] jugador(a) *m,f* competitivo(a)

gaming ['geɪmɪŋ] *n* [video games] juegos *mpl* de ordenador

gang [gæŋ] *n* [of criminals] banda *f*; [of youths] pandilla *f*; [of workers] cuadrilla *f* ▪ **gang up** *vi Fam* confabularse (**on** contra)

gangplank ['gæŋplæŋk] *n* pasarela *f*

gangsta ['gæŋstə] *n* **a)** [music] **gangsta (rap)** gangsta rap *m* **b)** [rapper] rapero(a) *m,f* gangsta **c)** US [gang member] miembro *m* de un gang

gangster ['gæŋstə(r)] *n* gángster *m*

gangway ['gæŋweɪ] *n* NAUT pasarela *f*; THEAT pasillo *m*

gaol [dʒeɪl] *Br n* & *vt* = **jail**

gap [gæp] *n* **a)** abertura *f*, hueco *m*; [blank space] blanco *m* **b)** [in time] intervalo *m*; [emptiness] vacío *m* **c)** [gulf] diferencia *f* **d)** [deficiency] laguna *f*

gape [geɪp] *vi* [person] quedarse boquiabierto(a), mirar boquiabierto(a); [thing] estar abierto(a)

garage ['gærɑːʒ, 'gærɪdʒ, US gə'rɑːʒ] *n* garaje *m*; [for repairs] taller mecánico; [filling station] gasolinera *f*, estación *f* de servicio, *Andes, Ven* bomba *f*, *Méx* gasolinería *f*, *Perú* grifo *m*

garbage ['gɑːbɪdʒ] *n* US basura *f*, *Méx* cochera *f*; *Fig* tonterías *fpl*

garbanzo [gɑː'bɑːnzəʊ] (*pl* **garbanzos**) *n* US **garbanzo (bean)** garbanzo *m*

garbled ['gɑ:bəld] *adj* embrollado(a); **garbled account** relato confuso

garden ['gɑ:dən] *n* jardín *m*; **garden centre** centro *m* de jardinería; **garden party** recepción *f* al aire libre

gardener ['gɑ:dənə(r)] *n* jardinero(a) *m,f*

gardening ['gɑ:dənɪŋ] *n* jardinería *f*; **his mother does the gardening** su madre es la que cuida el jardín

gargle ['gɑ:gəl] *vi* hacer gárgaras

garish ['geərɪʃ] *adj* chillón(ona)

garland ['gɑ:lənd] *n* guirnalda *f*

garlic ['gɑ:lɪk] *n* ajo *m*

garment ['gɑ:mənt] *n* prenda *f*

garnish ['gɑ:nɪʃ] *vt* guarnecer

garter ['gɑ:tə(r)] *n* liga *f*

gas [gæs] **1.** *n* **a)** gas *m*; **gas cooker** cocina *f* de gas; **gas fire** estufa *f* de gas; **gas mask** careta *f* antigás; **gas ring** hornillo *m* de gas
b) *US* gasolina *f*, *RP* nafta *f*; **gas pump** surtidor *m* de gasolina; **gas refill** cartucho *m* de gas; **gas station** gasolinera *f*, estación *f* de servicio, *Andes, Ven* bomba *f*, *Méx* gasolinería *f*, *Perú* grifo *m*; **gas tank** depósito *m* de la gasolina
2. *vt* [asphyxiate] asfixiar con gas
3. *vi Fam* [talk] charlotear

gash [gæʃ] **1.** *n* herida profunda **2.** *vt* hacer un corte en; **he gashed his forehead** se hizo una herida en la frente

gasoline ['gæsəli:n] *n US* gasolina *f*, *RP* nafta *f*

gasp [gɑ:sp] **1.** *n* [cry] grito sordo; [breath] bocanada *f*; *Fig* **to be at one's last gasp** estar en las últimas **2.** *vi* [in surprise] quedar boquiabierto(a); [breathe] jadear

gassy ['gæsɪ] *(compar* gassier, *superl* gassiest) *adj* gaseoso(a)

gastric ['gæstrɪk] *adj* gástrico(a)

gate [geɪt] *n* **a)** puerta *f* **b)** [at football ground] entrada *f*; **gate (money)** taquilla *f* **c)** [attendance] entrada *f*

gateau ['gætəʊ] *(pl* gateaux ['gætəʊz]) *n* pastel *m* con nata

gatecrash ['geɪtkræʃ] **1.** *vt* colarse en **2.** *vi* colarse

gateway ['geɪtweɪ] *n* puerta *f*; *Fig* pasaporte *m*

gather ['gæðə(r)] **1.** *vt* **a)** [collect] juntar; [pick] coger; [pick up] recoger **b)** [bring together] reunir **c)** [harvest] cosechar **d) to gather speed** ir ganando velocidad; **to gather strength** cobrar fuerzas **e)** [understand] suponer; **I gather that ...** tengo entendido que ... **2.** *vi* **a)** [come together] reunirse **b)** [form] formarse
■ **gather round** *vi* agruparse

gathering ['gæðərɪŋ] **1.** *adj* creciente **2.** *n* reunión *f*

gauge [geɪdʒ] **1.** *n* **a)** [measure] medida *f* estándar; [of gun, wire] calibre *m* **b)** [calibrator] indicador *m* **c)** *Fig* [indication] indicación *f* **2.** *vt* **a)** [measure] medir, calibrar **b)** *Fig* [judge] juzgar

gaunt [gɔ:nt] *adj* [lean] demacrado(a); [desolate] lúgubre

gauze [gɔ:z] *n* gasa *f*

gave [geɪv] *pt of* give

gay [geɪ] *adj* **a)** [homosexual] gay **b)** [happy] alegre

gaze [geɪz] **1.** *n* mirada fija **2.** *vi* mirar fijamente

GB [dʒi:'bi:] *(abbr of* Great Britain*)* GB

GCSE [dʒi:si:es'i:] *n Br (abbr of* General Certificate of Secondary Education*)* certificado de enseñanza secundaria

gear [gɪə(r)] **1.** *n* **a)** [equipment] equipo *m* **b)** *Fam* [belongings] bártulos *mpl* **c)** *Fam* [clothing] ropa *f* **d)** TECH engranaje *m* **e)** AUTO velocidad *f*, marcha *f*; **first gear** primera *f* (velocidad *f*); **gear lever** *or US* **shift** palanca *f* de cambio **2.** *vt* ajustar, adaptar

gearbox ['gɪəbɒks] *n* caja *f* de cambios

geek [gi:k], **geekazoid** [*US* 'gi:kəzɔɪd] *n Fam* geek *mf*, friki *mf* informático(a)

geeky [gi:ki], **geekazoid** [*US* 'gi:kəzɔɪd] *adj Fam* fanático(a) de los ordenadores *or US* de las computadoras

geese [gi:s] *pl of* goose

gel [dʒel] **1.** *n* gel *m*; [for hair] gomina *f* **2.** *vi Fig* [ideas etc] cuajar **3.** *vt* [hair] engominar

gelatin [ˈdʒelətɪn] n gelatina f

gem [dʒem] n piedra preciosa ; Fig [person] joya f

Gemini [ˈdʒemɪnaɪ] n Géminis m inv

gender [ˈdʒendə(r)] n género m

gene [dʒiːn] n gene m, gen m

general [ˈdʒenərəl] **1.** adj general; **general knowledge** conocimientos mpl generales; **in general** en general; **the general public** el público; **general practitioner** médico m de cabecera **2.** n MIL general m; US **general of the army** mariscal m de campo

generalization [dʒenərəlaɪˈzeɪʃən] n generalización f

generalize [ˈdʒenərəlaɪz] vt & vi generalizar

generally [ˈdʒenərəlɪ] adv generalmente, en general

generate [ˈdʒenəreɪt] vt generar

generation [dʒenəˈreɪʃən] n generación f; **generation gap** abismo m or conflicto m generacional

generator [ˈdʒenəreɪtə(r)] n generador m

generic [dʒɪˈnerɪk] adj genérico(a); **generic brand / product** marca f genérica / producto m genérico

generosity [dʒenəˈrɒsɪtɪ] n generosidad f

genetic [dʒɪˈnetɪk] adj genético(a); **genetic engineering** ingeniería genética

genetics [dʒɪˈnetɪks] n sing genética f

gengineering [ˌdʒendʒɪˈnɪərɪŋ] n ingeniería f genética

genitals [ˈdʒenɪtəlz] npl órganos mpl genitales

genius [ˈdʒiːnjəs, ˈdʒiːnɪəs] n a) [person] genio m b) [gift] don m

gent [dʒent] n Br Fam (abbr of gentleman) señor m, caballero m; **the gents** los servicios (de caballeros)

gentle [ˈdʒentəl] adj dulce, tierno(a); [breeze] suave

gentleman [ˈdʒentəlmən] n caballero m; **gentleman's agreement** pacto m de caballeros

gently [ˈdʒentlɪ] adv con cuidado

genuine [ˈdʒenjuɪn] adj auténtico(a), genuino(a); [sincere] sincero(a)

genuinely [ˈdʒenjuɪnlɪ] adv auténticamente

geographic(al) [dʒɪəˈgræfɪk(əl)] adj geográfico(a)

geography [dʒɪˈɒgrəfɪ, ˈdʒɒɡrəfɪ] n geografía f

geologic(al) [dʒɪəˈlɒdʒɪk(əl)] adj geológico(a)

geology [dʒɪˈɒlədʒɪ] n geología f

geometric(al) [dʒɪəˈmetrɪk(əl)] adj geométrico(a)

geometry [dʒɪˈɒmɪtrɪ] n geometría f

geotag [ˈdʒiːəʊˌtæg] n [photo, video] geolocalizar

geriatric [dʒerɪˈætrɪk] adj geriátrico(a)

germ [dʒɜːm] n a) BIOL & Fig germen m b) MED microbio m

German [ˈdʒɜːmən] **1.** adj alemán(ana); **German measles** rubeola f **2.** n a) alemán(ana) m,f b) [language] alemán m

Germany [ˈdʒɜːmənɪ] n Alemania

germinate [ˈdʒɜːmɪneɪt] vi germinar

gesticulate [dʒeˈstɪkjʊleɪt] vi gesticular

gesture [ˈdʒestʃə(r)] **1.** n gesto m, ademán m; **it's an empty gesture** es pura formalidad **2.** vi gesticular, hacer gestos

get [get] (pt & pp **got**, US pp **gotten**) **1.** vt a) [obtain] obtener, conseguir ; [receive] recibir ; [earn] ganar
b) [fetch - something] traer ; [somebody] ir a por ; **can I get you something to eat?** ¿quieres comer algo? ; **get the police!** ¡llama a la policía!
c) [bus, train] coger, Am agarrar
d) [have done] **get him to call me** dile que me llame; **to get sb to agree to sth** conseguir que algn acepte algo; **to get one's hair cut** cortarse el pelo
e) have got, have got to see **have**
f) Fam [understand] entender

2. *vi* **a)** [become] ponerse ; **to get dressed** vestirse ; **to get drunk** emborracharse ; **to get married** casarse ; **to get paid** cobrar

b) to get to [arrive, come to] llegar a ; **to get to know sb** llegar a conocer a algn

■ **get about** *vi* [person] salir ; [news] difundirse

■ **get across** *vt sep* [idea etc] hacer comprender

■ **get ahead** *vi* progresar

■ **get along** *vi* **a)** [leave] marcharse **b)** [manage] arreglárselas **c)** [two people] llevarse bien

■ **get around** *vi* **a)** [person] salir ; [travel] viajar ; [news] difundirse **b)** [eventually do] **to get around to (doing) sth** encontrar el momento de hacer algo ; *see* **get about**, **get round**

■ **get at** *vt insep* **a)** [reach] alcanzar **b)** [insinuate] insinuar ; **what are you getting at?** ¿a dónde quieres llegar?

■ **get away** *vi* escaparse

■ **get away with** *vt insep* salir impune de

■ **get back 1.** *vi* **a)** [return] regresar, volver **b) get back!** [move backwards] ¡atrás! **2.** *vt sep* [recover] recuperar ; *Fam* **to get one's own back on sb** vengarse de algn

■ **get back to** *vt insep* volver a

■ **get by** *vi* [manage] arreglárselas ; **she can get by in French** sabe defenderse en francés

■ **get down 1.** *vt sep* [depress] deprimir **2.** *vi* [descend] bajar

■ **get down to** *vt insep* ponerse a ; **to get down to the facts** ir al grano

■ **get in 1.** *vi* **a)** [arrive] llegar **b)** POL ser elegido(a) **2.** *vt sep* **a)** [buy] comprar **b)** [collect] recoger

■ **get into** *vt insep Fig* **to get into bad habits** adquirir malas costumbres ; **to get into trouble** meterse en un lío

■ **get off 1.** *vt insep* [bus etc] bajarse de **2.** *vt sep* [remove] quitarse **3.** *vi* **a)** [leave] bajarse ; *Fam* **get off!** ¡fuera! **b)** [escape] **to get off to a good start** [begin] empezar bien **c)** [escape]

■ **get on 1.** *vt insep* [board] subir a **2.** *vi* **a)** [board] subirse **b)** [make progress] hacer progresos ; **how are you getting on?** ¿cómo te van las cosas? **c) to get on (well) (with sb)** llevarse bien (con algn) **d)** [continue] seguir ; **to get on with one's work** seguir trabajando

■ **get on to** *vt insep* **a)** [find a person] localizar ; [find out] descubrir **b)** [continue] pasar a

■ **get out 1.** *vt sep* [object] sacar **2.** *vi* **a)** [room etc] salir (**of** de) ; [train] bajar (**of** de) **b)** [escape] escaparse (**of** de) ; **to get out of an obligation** librarse de un compromiso **c)** [news] difundirse ; [secret] hacerse público

■ **get over 1.** *vt insep* **a)** [illness] recuperarse de **b)** [difficulty] vencer **2.** *vt sep* [convey] hacer comprender

■ **get round 1.** *vt insep* **a)** [overcome] sortear, eludir ; [problem] salvar ; [difficulty] vencer **b)** [rule] soslayar **2.** *vi* [person] salir ; [travel] viajar ; [news] difundirse

■ **get round to** *vt insep* **if I get round to it** si tengo tiempo

■ **get through 1.** *vi* **a)** [message] llegar **b)** SCH aprobar **c)** TEL **to get through to sb** conseguir comunicar con algn **2.** *vt insep* **a) to get through a lot of work** trabajar mucho **b)** [consume] consumir

■ **get to** *vt insep Fam* [annoy] fastidiar

■ **get together 1.** *vi* [people] juntarse, reunirse **2.** *vt sep* [people] juntar, reunir

■ **get up 1.** *vi* [rise] levantarse, *Am* pararse **2.** *vt sep* [wake] despertar **3.** *vt insep* [petition, demonstration] organizar

■ **get up to** *vt insep* hacer ; **to get up to mischief** hacer de las suyas

getaway ['getəweɪ] *n* fuga *f* ; **to make one's getaway** fugarse

get-together ['gettəgeðə(r)] *n* reunión *f*

GF MESSAGING *written abbr of* **girlfriend**

ghastly ['gɑːstlɪ] *(compar* **ghastlier**, *superl* **ghastliest***) adj* horrible, espantoso(a)

gherkin ['gɜːkɪn] *n* pepinillo *m*

ghetto ['getəʊ] *n* gueto *m*

ghost [gəʊst] *n* fantasma *m*; **ghost story** cuento *m* de fantasmas; **ghost town** pueblo *m* fantasma

giant ['dʒaɪənt] *adj & n* gigante *(m)*

gibe [dʒaɪb] **1.** *n* mofa *f* **2.** *vi* mofarse (at de)

giddy ['gɪdɪ] *(compar* **giddier**, *superl* **giddiest***) adj* mareado(a); **it makes me giddy** me da vértigo; **to feel giddy** sentirse mareado(a)

gift [gɪft] *n* **a)** regalo *m*; COMM obsequio *m*; **gift token** vale *m* **b)** [talent] don *m*; **to have a gift for music** estar muy dotado(a) para la música

gifted ['gɪftɪd] *adj* dotado(a)

gig [gɪg] *n Fam* MUS actuación *f*

gigabyte ['gaɪgəbaɪt] *n* COMPUT gigabyte *m*

gigantic [dʒaɪˈgæntɪk] *adj* gigantesco(a)

giggle ['gɪgəl] **1.** *n* **a)** risita *f* **b)** [lark] broma *f*, diversión *f* **2.** *vi* reírse tontamente

gilt [gɪlt] **1.** *adj* dorado(a) **2.** *n* [colour] dorado *m*

gimmick ['gɪmɪk] *n* truco *m*; [in advertising] reclamo *m*

gimp [gɪmp] *n US Fam* **a)** *Pej* [person] cojo(a) *m,f* **b)** [object] trencilla *f*

gin [dʒɪn] *n* ginebra *f*; **gin and tonic** gin tonic *m*

ginger ['dʒɪndʒə(r)] **1.** *n* jengibre *m*; **ginger ale** ginger ale *m* **2.** *adj* **a)** de jengibre **b)** [hair] pelirrojo(a)

gipsy ['dʒɪpsɪ] *adj & n* gitano(a) *(m,f)*

giraffe [dʒɪˈrɑːf] *n* jirafa *f*

girl [gɜːl] *n* **a)** chica *f*, joven *f*; [child] niña *f*; *Br* **girl guide**, *US* **girl scout** exploradora *f* **b)** [daughter] hija *f* **c)** [sweetheart] novia *f*

girlfriend ['gɜːlfrend] *n* **a)** [lover] novia *f* **b)** [female friend] amiga *f*

girlish ['gɜːlɪʃ] *adj* **a)** de niña **b)** [effeminate] afeminado(a)

giro ['dʒaɪrəʊ] *n Br Fam* [unemployment cheque] cheque *m* del desempleo *or Esp* paro

gist [dʒɪst] *n* esencia *f*; **did you get the gist of what he was saying?** ¿cogiste la idea de lo que decía?

give [gɪv] *(pt* **gave**, *pp* **given***)* **1.** *n* [elasticity] elasticidad *f* **2.** *vt* **a)** dar; **to give sth to sb** dar algo a algn; **to give a start** pegar un salto; **to give sb a present** regalar algo a algn; **to give sb sth to eat** dar de comer a algn **b)** [pay] pagar **c)** [speech] pronunciar **d)** [grant] otorgar; **to give sb one's attention** prestar atención a algn **e)** [yield] ceder; **to give way** AUTO ceder el paso; *Fig* ceder; [legs] flaquear **3.** *vi* [yield] ceder; [fabric] dar de sí

■ **give away** *vt sep* **a)** repartir; [present] regalar **b)** [disclose] revelar; **to give the game away** descubrir el pastel **c)** [betray] traicionar

■ **give back** *vt sep* devolver

■ **give in 1.** *vi* **a)** [admit defeat] darse por vencido(a); [surrender] rendirse **b)** **to give in to** ceder ante **2.** *vt sep* [hand in] entregar

■ **give off** *vt sep* [smell etc] despedir

■ **give out** *vt sep* distribuir, repartir

■ **give over** *vt sep* [hand over] entregar; [devote] dedicar

■ **give up 1.** *vt sep* **a)** [idea] abandonar; **to give up smoking** dejar de fumar **b)** [hand over] entregar; **to give oneself up** entregarse **2.** *vi* [admit defeat] darse por vencido(a), rendirse

■ **give up on** *vt insep* darse por vencido con

given ['gɪvən] **1.** *adj* **a)** [particular] dado(a); *US* **given name** nombre *m* de pila; **at a given time** en un momento dado **b)** **given to** dado(a) a **2.** *conj* **a)** [considering] dado(a) **b)** [if] si **3.** *pp of* **give**

glad [glæd] *(compar* **gladder**, *superl* **gladdest***) adj* contento(a); [happy] alegre; **he'll be only too glad to help you** tendrá mucho gusto en ayudarle; **to be glad** alegrarse

glamorous ['glæmərəs] *adj* atractivo(a), encantador(a)

glance [glɑ:ns] **1.** *n* mirada *f*, vistazo *m*; **at a glance** de un vistazo; **at first glance** a primera vista **2.** *vi* echar un vistazo (**at** a) ▪ **glance off** *vt insep* [of ball etc] rebotar de

gland [glænd] *n* glándula *f*

glare [gleə(r)] **1.** *n* [light] luz *f* deslumbrante; [dazzle] deslumbramiento *m*; [look] mirada *f* feroz **2.** *vi* [dazzle] deslumbrar; [look] lanzar una mirada furiosa (**at** a)

glaring ['gleərɪŋ] *adj* [light] deslumbrante; [colour] chillón(ona); [obvious] evidente

glass [glɑ:s] *n* **a)** [material] vidrio *m*; **pane of glass** cristal *m* **b)** [drinking vessel] vaso *m*; **wine glass** copa *f* (para vino) **c)** **glasses** gafas *fpl*, *Am* lentes *mpl*, anteojos *mpl*; **to wear glasses** llevar gafas *or Am* lentes *or* anteojos

glaze [gleɪz] **1.** *n* [varnish] barniz *m*; [for pottery] vidriado *m* **2.** *vt* **a)** [windows] acristalar **b)** [varnish] barnizar; [ceramics] vidriar **c)** CULIN glasear

gleam [gli:m] **1.** *n* **a)** destello *m* **b)** *Fig* [glimmer] rayo *m* **2.** *vi* brillar, relucir

glean [gli:n] *vt Fig* recoger, cosechar

glee [gli:] *n* gozo *m*

glen [glen] *n* cañada *f*

glide [glaɪd] *vi* **a)** [slip, slide] deslizarse **b)** AVIAT planear

glider ['glaɪdə(r)] *n* planeador *m*

gliding ['glaɪdɪŋ] *n* vuelo *m* sin motor

glimmer ['glɪmə(r)] *n* **a)** [light] luz *f* tenue **b)** *Fig* [trace] destello *m*

glimpse [glɪmps] **1.** *n* atisbo *m* **2.** *vt* atisbar

glint [glɪnt] **1.** *n* destello *m*, centelleo *m*; **he had a glint in his eye** le brillaban los ojos **2.** *vi* destellar, centellear

glisten ['glɪsən] *vi* relucir, brillar

glitter ['glɪtə(r)] **1.** *n* brillo *m* **2.** *vi* relucir

gloat [gləʊt] *vi* jactarse; **to gloat over another's misfortune** recrearse con la desgracia de otro

global ['gləʊbəl] *adj* **a)** [of the world] mundial; **global market** mercado *m* mundial *or* global **b)** [overall] global

globalization [gləʊbəlaɪ'zeɪʃən] *n* mundialización *f*, globalización *f*

globe [gləʊb] *n* globo *m*, esfera *f*

gloom [glu:m] *n* [obscurity] penumbra *f*; [melancholy] melancolía *f*; [despair] desolación *f*

gloomy ['glu:mɪ] *(compar* gloomier, *superl* gloomiest*) adj* [dark] oscuro(a); [weather] gris; [dismal] deprimente; [despairing] pesimista; [sad] triste

glorious ['glɔ:rɪəs] *adj* [momentous] glorioso(a); [splendid] magnífico(a), espléndido(a)

glory ['glɔ:rɪ] *n* gloria *f*; *Fig* [splendour] esplendor *m*; *Fig* [triumph] triunfo *m*

gloss [glɒs] **1.** *n* **a)** [explanation] glosa *f* **b)** [sheen] brillo *m*; **gloss (paint)** pintura *f* brillante **2.** *vi* glosar ▪ **gloss over** *vt insep Fig* encubrir

glossary ['glɒsərɪ] *n* glosario *m*

glossy ['glɒsɪ] *(compar* glossier, *superl* glossiest*) adj* lustroso(a); **glossy magazine** revista *f* de lujo

glove [glʌv] *n* guante *m*; AUTO **glove compartment** guantera *f*

glow [gləʊ] **1.** *n* brillo *m*; [of fire] incandescencia *f*; [of sun] arrebol *m*; [heat] calor *m*; [light] luz *f*; [in cheeks] rubor *m* **2.** *vi* brillar; [fire] arder

glowing ['gləʊɪŋ] *adj* **a)** [fire] incandescente; [colour] vivo(a); [light] brillante **b)** [cheeks] encendido(a) **c)** *Fig* [report] entusiasta

glue [glu:] **1.** *n* pegamento *m*, cola *f* **2.** *vt* pegar (**to** a)

glug [glʌg] *Fam* **1.** *n* glug (glug) gluglú *m*; **he took a long glug of lemonade** dio un largo trago de limonada **2.** *(pt & pp* glugged, *pres p* glugging*) vi* tragar

glum [glʌm] *(compar* glummer, *superl* glummest*) adj* alicaído(a)

glutton ['glʌtən] *n* glotón(ona) *m,f*

GM [dʒi:'em] *adj (abbr of* **genetically modified***)* transgénico(a), modificado(a) genéticamente; **GM food** (alimentos) transgénicos

GMT [ˌdʒiːemˈtiː] n (abbr of **Greenwich Mean Time**) hora f del meridiano de Greenwich

gnat [næt] n mosquito m

gnaw [nɔː] vt & vi [chew] roer

go [gəʊ] (3rd person sing pres **goes**) (pt **went**, pp **gone**) **1.** vi **a)** ir; **to go for a walk** (ir a) dar un paseo
b) [depart] irse, marcharse
c) [function] funcionar
d) [be sold] venderse
e) [become] quedarse, volverse; **to go blind** quedarse ciego(a); **to go mad** volverse loco(a)
f) [progress] ir, marchar; **everything went well** todo salió bien; **how's it going?** ¿qué tal (te van las cosas)?
g) to be going to [in the future] ir a; [on the point of] estar a punto de
h) [fit] caber
i) [be available] quedar; **I'll take whatever's going** me conformo con lo que hay
j) [be acceptable] valer; **anything goes** todo vale
k) [time] pasar; **there are only two weeks to go** solo quedan dos semanas, no quedan más que dos semanas
l) [say] decir; **as the saying goes** según el dicho
m) to let sth go soltar algo
2. vt **a)** [travel] hacer, recorrer
b) to go it alone apañárselas solo
3. n **a)** [energy] energía f, dinamismo m
b) [try] intento m; **to have a go at sth** probar suerte con algo; **to have a go at sb** criticar a algn
c) [turn] turno m; **it's your go** te toca a ti
d) to make a go of sth tener éxito en algo

■ **go about 1.** vt insep **a)** [task] emprender; **how do you go about it?** ¿cómo hay que hacerlo? **b) to go about one's business** ocuparse de sus asuntos **2.** vi [rumour] correr

■ **go after** vt insep [pursue] ir tras

■ **go against** vt insep [oppose] ir en contra de; [verdict] ser desfavorable a

■ **go ahead** vi **a)** [proceed] proceder **b) we'll go on ahead** iremos delante

■ **go along 1.** vt insep [street] pasar por **2.** vi [progress] progresar

■ **go along with** vt insep **a)** [agree with] estar de acuerdo con **b)** [accompany] acompañar

■ **go around** vi **a)** [rumour] correr **b) there's enough to go around** hay para todos

■ **go away** vi marcharse

■ **go back** vi **a)** [return] volver, regresar **b)** Fig **to go back to** [date from] datar de

■ **go back on** vt insep **to go back on one's word** faltar a su palabra

■ **go back to** vt insep volver a

■ **go by 1.** vi [time] pasar; **as time goes by** con el tiempo **2.** vt insep **a)** [be guided by] guiarse por **b)** [judge from] juzgar por; **going by...** a juzgar por..

■ **go down** vi **a)** [get lower, descend] bajar; [sun] ponerse; [ship] hundirse; [tyre, balloon] desinflarse **b)** [diminish] disminuir; [temperature] bajar **c)** [be accepted] **to go down well / badly** ser bien / mal acogido(a)

■ **go for** vt insep **a)** [attack] lanzarse sobre **b)** [fetch] ir por

■ **go in** vi entrar

■ **go in for** vt insep [exam] presentarse a; [hobby] dedicarse a

■ **go into** vt insep **a)** [enter] entrar en; **to go into journalism** dedicarse al periodismo **b)** [study] examinar; [matter] investigar

■ **go off 1.** vi **a)** [leave] irse, marcharse **b)** [bomb] explotar; [gun] dispararse; [alarm] sonar **c)** [food] pasarse **2.** vt insep Fam **to go off sth** perder el gusto or el interés por algo

■ **go on 1.** vi **a)** [continue] seguir, continuar; **to go on talking** seguir hablando; Fam **to go on and on about sth** no parar de hablar sobre algo; [complain] quejarse constantemente de algo **b)** [proceed to further activity] **to go on to sth** pasar a algo; **to go on to do sth** hacer algo después **c)** [take place, happen] transcurrir, pasar **d)** [light] encenderse, *Am* prenderse; [heating] ponerse en marcha **2.** *vt insep* [be guided by] basarse en

■ **go on at** *vt insep Br Fam* [nag] dar la lata a

■ **go out** *vi* **a)** [leave] salir; **to go out for a meal** comer *or* cenar fuera **b)** [boy and girl] salir juntos **c)** [fire, light] apagarse **d)** [tide] bajar

■ **go over** *vt insep* [revise] repasar

■ **go over to** *vt insep* **a)** acercarse a; **to go over to the enemy** pasarse al enemigo **b)** [switch to] pasar a

■ **go round** *vi* **a)** [revolve] dar vueltas **b) to go round to sb's house** pasar por casa de algn

■ **go through 1.** *vi* [bill] ser aprobado(a) **2.** *vt insep* **a)** [examine] examinar; [search] registrar **b)** [rehearse] ensayar **c)** [spend] gastar **d)** [list etc] explicar **e)** [endure] sufrir

■ **go through with** *vt insep* llevar a cabo

■ **go toward(s)** *vt insep* contribuir a

■ **go under** *vi* **a)** [ship] hundirse **b)** [business] fracasar

■ **go up 1.** *vi* **a)** [price etc] subir **b) to go up to sb** acercarse a algn **c)** [in a lift] subir **2.** *vt insep* subir

■ **go with** *vt insep* **a)** [accompany] ir con **b)** [colours] hacer juego con

■ **go without 1.** *vt insep* pasarse sin, prescindir de **2.** *vi* arreglarse

go-ahead ['gəʊəhed] *n Fam* **to give sb the go-ahead** dar luz verde a algn

goal [gəʊl] *n* **a)** SPORT gol *m*; **goal post** poste *m* **b)** [aim, objective] meta *f*, objetivo *m*

goalkeeper ['gəʊlki:pə(r)] *n* portero(a) *m,f*

goat [gəʊt] *n* [female] cabra *f*; [male] macho cabrío

gobble ['gɒbəl] *vt* engullir

goblet ['gɒblɪt] *n* copa *f*

god [gɒd] *n* dios *m*; **God** Dios; **(my) God!** ¡Dios mío!

goddammit [ˌgɒd'dæmɪt] *interj v Fam* ¡maldita sea!

goddam(n) ['gɒdæm] *US Fam* **1.** *adj* maldito(a), dichoso(a), *Méx* pinche **2.** *adv* **that was goddam(n) stupid!** ¡eso fue una auténtica estupidez!

goddaughter ['gɒddɔːtə(r)] *n* ahijada *f*

goddess ['gɒdɪs] *n* diosa *f*

godfather ['gɒdfɑːðə(r)] *n* padrino *m*

godmother ['gɒdmʌðə(r)] *n* madrina *f*

godsend ['gɒdsend] *n* regalo inesperado

godson ['gɒdsʌn] *n* ahijado *m*

goes [gəʊz] *see* **go**

go-getting [-'getɪŋ] *adj Fam* [person] dispuesto(a), resuelto(a)

goggles ['gɒgəlz] *npl* gafas *fpl* protectoras, *CSur* antiparras *fpl*

going ['gəʊɪŋ] **1.** *adj* **a)** [price] corriente; **the going rate** el precio medio **b) a going concern** un negocio que marcha bien **c) to get** *or* **be going** marcharse **d) to keep going** resistir **2.** *n* **to get out while the going is good** retirarse antes que sea demasiado tarde

going-away *adj* [party, present] de despedida

going-over (*pl* **goings-over**) *n Fam* **a)** [checkup] revisión *f*, comprobación *f*; [cleanup] limpieza *f*; **the house needs a good going-over** la casa necesita una buena limpieza **b) to give sb a (good) going-over** [scolding] echar a algn una (buena) bronca; [beating] dar a algn una (buena) paliza

goings-on [ˌgəʊɪŋz'ɒn] *npl Fam* tejemanejes *mpl*

gold [gəʊld] **1.** *n* oro *m*; **gold leaf** pan *m* de oro; **gold medal** medalla *f* de oro; **gold mine** mina *f* de oro. **2.** *adj* de oro; [colour] oro, dorado(a)

golden ['gəʊldən] *adj* de oro; [colour] dorado(a); *Fig* **a golden opportunity** una excelente oportunidad; ORNITH **golden eagle** águila *f* real; *Fig* **golden handshake** indemnización *f* por despido; **golden wedding** bodas *fpl* de oro

goldfish ['gəʊldfɪʃ] *n* pez *m* de colores

gold-plated [ˌgəʊld'pleɪtɪd] *adj* chapado(a) en oro

goldsmith ['gəʊldsmɪθ] n orfebre m

golf [gɒlf] n golf m; **golf ball** pelota f de golf; **golf club** [stick] palo m de golf; [place] club m de golf; **golf course** campo m de golf

golfer ['gɒlfə(r)] n golfista mf

gone [gɒn] **1.** adj desaparecido(a) **2.** pp of **go**

gong [gɒŋ] n gong m

good [gʊd] **1.** (compar **better**, superl **best**) adj **a)** [before noun] buen(a); [after noun] bueno(a); **a good book** un buen libro; **good afternoon / evening** buenas tardes; **good morning** buenos días; **good night** buenas noches; **it looks good** tiene buena pinta; **to feel good** sentirse bien; **to smell good** oler bien; **to have a good time** pasarlo bien **b)** [kind] amable
c) [morally correct] correcto(a); **be good!** ¡pórtate bien!
d) **he's good at languages** tiene facilidad para los idiomas
e) [attractive] bonito(a); **good looks** atractivo m, belleza f
f) [propitious] propicio(a)
g) [character] agradable; **he's in a good mood** está de buen humor
2. n **a)** bien m; **good and evil** el bien y el mal; **to do good** hacer el bien
b) [advantage] bien m, provecho m; **for your own good** para tu propio bien; **it's no good waiting** no sirve de nada esperar; **it will do you good** te hará bien
c) COMM **goods** artículos mpl, géneros mpl; **goods train** tren m de mercancías; **goods vehicle** vehículo m de mercancías
3. adv **she's gone for good** se ha ido para siempre
4. interj ¡muy bien!

goodbye [gʊd'baɪ] **1.** interj ¡adiós! **2.** n adiós m, despedida f; **to say goodbye to sb** despedirse de algn

good-for-nothing ['gʊdfənʌθɪŋ] adj & n inútil (mf)

good-looking [gʊd'lʊkɪŋ] adj guapo(a)

goodness ['gʊdnɪs] n bondad f; **my goodness!** ¡Dios mío!; **thank goodness!** ¡gracias a Dios!; **for goodness sake!** ¡por Dios!

goodwill [gʊd'wɪl] n **a)** buena voluntad f **b)** COMM [reputation] buen nombre m

goof [guːf] US Fam **1.** n [mistake] metedura f de pata **2.** vi meter la pata ■ **goof around** vi US Fam hacer el ganso

Google® ['guːgl] vt [look up using Google] buscar en Google®; **I'll Google that** ya lo busco en Google

goose [guːs] (pl **geese**) n ganso m, oca f

gooseberry ['gʊzbərɪ, 'guːsbərɪ] n uva espina, grosella espinosa; Br Fam **to play gooseberry** Esp hacer de carabina or de sujetavelas, Méx hacer mal tercio, RP estar de paleta

gooseflesh ['guːsfleʃ] n carne f de gallina

goosepimples ['guːspɪmpəlz] npl carne f de gallina

gorge [gɔːdʒ] **1.** n desfiladero m **2.** vt & vi **to gorge (oneself) (on)** atiborrarse (de)

gorgeous ['gɔːdʒəs] adj magnífico(a), estupendo(a); [person] atractivo(a), guapo(a)

gorilla [gə'rɪlə] n gorila m

gory ['gɔːrɪ] (compar **gorier**, superl **goriest**) adj sangriento(a)

gosh [gɒʃ] interj Fam ¡cielos!, ¡caray!

go-slow [gəʊ'sləʊ] n Br huelga f de celo

gospel ['gɒspəl] n **the Gospel** el Evangelio; Fam **it's the gospel truth** es la pura verdad

gossip ['gɒsɪp] **1.** n **a)** [rumour] cotilleo m; **gossip column** ecos mpl de sociedad **b)** [person] chismoso(a) m,f, cotilla mf **2.** vi [natter] cotillear, chismorrear

got [gɒt] pt & pp of **get**

go-to adj US Fam **he's your go-to guy** él es la persona a quien acudir

gotten ['gɒtən] US pp of **get**

gourmet ['gʊəmeɪ] n gourmet mf

govern ['gʌvən] vt **a)** gobernar **b)** [determine] determinar

government ['gʌvənmənt] *n* gobierno *m*

governor ['gʌvənə(r)] *n* [ruler] gobernador(a) *m,f*; [of prison] director(a) *m,f*; [of school] administrador(a) *m,f*

gown [gaʊn] *n* [dress] vestido largo; JUR & UNIV toga *f*

GP [dʒi:'pi:] *n Br (abbr of general practitioner)* médico(a) *m,f* de familia *or* de cabecera

GPS [,dʒi:pi:'es] *n (abbr of Global Positioning System)* GPS *m*

grab [græb] **1.** *n* agarrón *m*; *Fam* **to be up for grabs** estar disponible **2.** *vt* **a)** agarrar; **to grab hold of sb** agarrarse a algn **b)** *Fig* **grab a bottle of wine** píllate una botella de vino **c)** *Fig* **how does that grab you?** ¿qué te parece?

grace [greɪs] **1.** *n* **a)** gracia *f* **b) to say grace** bendecir la mesa **c) five days' grace** [reprieve] un plazo de cinco días **d)** [elegance] elegancia *f* **2.** *vt* **a)** [adorn] adornar **b)** [honour] honrar

graceful ['greɪsfʊl] *adj* elegante; [movement] garboso(a)

gracious ['greɪʃəs] **1.** *adj* **a)** [elegant] elegante **b)** [courteous] cortés **c)** [kind] amable **2.** *interj* **good gracious (me)!, goodness gracious!** ¡santo cielo!

grade [greɪd] **1.** *n* **a)** [quality] grado *m*; [rank] categoría *f*; MIL rango *m* **b)** *US* SCH [mark] nota *f* **c)** *US* SCH [class] clase *f*; **grade school** escuela *f* primaria; **first grade** *primer curso de enseñanza primaria en Estados Unidos*; **second grade** *segundo curso de enseñanza primaria en Estados Unidos*; **third grade** *tercer curso de enseñanza primaria en Estados Unidos*; **fourth grade** *cuarto curso de enseñanza primaria en Estados Unidos*; **fifth grade** *quinto curso de enseñanza primaria en Estados Unidos*; **sixth grade** *sexto curso de enseñanza primaria en Estados Unidos*; **seventh grade** *séptimo curso de enseñanza primaria en Estados Unidos*; **eighth grade** *octavo curso de enseñanza primaria en Estados Unidos*; **ninth grade** *primer curso de enseñanza secundaria en Estados Unidos*; **tenth grade** *segundo curso de enseñanza secundaria en Estados Unidos*; **eleventh grade** *tercer curso de enseñanza secundaria en Estados Unidos*; **twelfth grade** *cuarto curso de enseñanza secundaria en Estados Unidos* **d)** [level] nivel *m* **e)** *US* **grade crossing** paso *m* a nivel **2.** *vt* clasificar

gradient ['greɪdɪənt] *n* [graph] declive *m*; [hill] cuesta *f*, pendiente *f*

gradual ['grædjʊəl] *adj* gradual, progresivo(a)

gradually ['grædjʊəlɪ] *adv* poco a poco

graduate 1. ['grædjʊɪt] *n* UNIV licenciado(a) *m,f*; *US* [from high school] ≃ bachiller *mf* **2.** ['grædjʊeɪt] *vi* **a)** UNIV licenciarse (**in** en) **b)** *US* [from high school] ≃ sacar el bachillerato

graduation [grædjʊ'eɪʃən] *n* graduación *f*; UNIV **graduation ceremony** ceremonia *f* de entrega de los títulos

graffiti [grə'fi:ti:] *npl* grafiti *mpl*

graham ['greɪəm] *adj US* **graham cracker** galleta integral

grain [greɪn] *n* **a)** [cereals] cereales *mpl* **b)** [particle] grano *m*; *Fig* **there's not a grain of truth in it** no tiene ni pizca de verdad **c)** [in wood] fibra *f*; [in stone] veta *f*; [in leather] flor *f*; *Fig* **to go against the grain** ir a contrapelo

gram [græm] *n* gramo *m*

grammar ['græmə(r)] *n* gramática *f*; **grammar (book)** libro *m* de gramática; *Br* **grammar school** instituto *m* de enseñanza secundaria (*al que solo se accede después de superar un examen de ingreso*)

grammatical [grə'mætɪkəl] *adj* gramatical

gramme [græm] *n* gramo *m*

grand [grænd] **1.** *adj* **a)** grande; [before singular noun] gran; **grand piano** piano *m* de cola **b)** [splendid] grandioso(a), magnífico(a); [impressive] impresionante **c) grand total** total *m* **d)** *Fam* [wonderful] genial, *Am salvo RP* chévere, *Méx* padre, *RP* bárbaro(a) **2.** *n Fam* mil libras *fpl*; *US* mil dólares *mpl*

grandad ['grændæd] *n Fam* abuelo *m*

grandchild ['græntʃaɪld] *n* nieto(a) *m,f*

granddad ['grændæd] *n Fam* abuelo *m*

granddaughter ['grændɔ:tə(r)] n nieta f

grandfather ['grænfɑ:ðə(r)] n abuelo m; **grandfather clock** reloj m de caja

grandma ['grænmɑ:] n Fam abuelita f

grandmother ['grænmʌðə(r)] n abuela f

grandpa ['grænpɑ:] n Fam abuelito m

grandparents ['grænpeərənts] npl abuelos mpl

grandson ['grænsʌn] n nieto m

grandstand ['grænstænd] n tribuna f

granite ['grænɪt] n granito m

granny ['grænɪ] n Fam abuelita f

grant [grɑ:nt] **1.** vt a) [allow] conceder, otorgar b) [admit] admitir; **to take sb for granted** no apreciar a algn en lo que vale; **to take sth for granted** dar algo por sentado **2.** n SCH beca f; [subsidy] subvención f

grape [greɪp] n uva f; **grape juice** mosto m

grapefruit ['greɪpfru:t] n pomelo m, Am toronja f

graph [grɑ:f, græf] n gráfica f

graphic ['græfɪk] adj gráfico(a); **graphic arts** artes gráficas; **graphic designer** grafista mf

graphics ['græfɪks] n a) [study] grafismo m b) (pl) COMPUT gráficas fpl

grapple ['græpəl] **1.** vi [struggle] luchar cuerpo a cuerpo (**with** con); Fig **to grapple with a problem** intentar resolver un problema **2.** n [hook] garfio m

grasp [grɑ:sp] **1.** vt a) agarrar b) [understand] comprender **2.** n a) [grip] agarrón m b) [understanding] comprensión f; **within sb's grasp** al alcance de algn

grass [grɑ:s] n hierba f; [lawn] césped m; Fig **grass roots** base f

grasshopper ['grɑ:shɒpə(r)] n saltamontes m inv

grassy ['grɑ:sɪ] (compar grassier, superl grassiest) adj cubierto(a) de hierba

grate[1] [greɪt] **1.** vt CULIN rallar **2.** vi chirriar

grate[2] [greɪt] n a) [in fireplace] rejilla f b) [fireplace] chimenea f c) CONSTR rejilla f, reja f

grateful ['greɪtfʊl] adj agradecido(a); **to be grateful for** agradecer

grater ['greɪtə(r)] n CULIN rallador m

gratify ['grætɪfaɪ] vt a) [please] complacer b) [yield to] sucumbir a

gratifying ['grætɪfaɪɪŋ] adj grato(a)

grating[1] ['greɪtɪŋ] n rejilla f, reja f

grating[2] ['greɪtɪŋ] adj chirriante; [tone] áspero(a)

gratitude ['grætɪtju:d] n agradecimiento m

gratuitous [grə'tju:ɪtəs] adj gratuito(a)

grave[1] [greɪv] n sepultura f, tumba f

grave[2] [greɪv] adj [look etc] serio(a); [situation] grave

gravel ['grævəl] n grava f, gravilla f

gravestone ['greɪvstəʊn] n lápida f sepulcral

graveyard ['greɪvjɑ:d] n cementerio m

gravity ['grævɪtɪ] n gravedad f

gravy ['greɪvɪ] n salsa f, jugo m (de la carne)

gray [greɪ] US adj & n = **grey**

graze[1] [greɪz] vi pacer, pastar

graze[2] [greɪz] **1.** vt [scratch] rasguñar; [brush against] rozar **2.** n rasguño m

grease [gri:s, gri:z] **1.** n grasa f **2.** vt engrasar

greasy ['gri:sɪ, 'gri:zɪ] (compar greasier, superl greasiest) adj a) [oily] grasiento(a); [hair, food] graso(a) b) [slippery] resbaladizo(a) c) Fam [ingratiating] pelotillero(a)

great [greɪt] **1.** adj a) grande; [before singular noun] gran; [pain, heat] fuerte; **a great many** muchos(as); **Great Britain** Gran Bretaña; Br **Great Bear** Osa f Mayor
b) Fam [excellent] genial, Am salvo RP chévere, Méx padre, RP bárbaro(a); **to have a great time** pasarlo muy bien **2.** adv Fam muy bien, estupendamente

great-grandfather [greɪt'græn-
fɑːðə(r)] n bisabuelo m

great-grandmother [greɪt'græn-
mʌðə(r)] n bisabuela f

greatly ['greɪtlɪ] adv muy, mucho

Greece [griːs] n Grecia

greed [griːd], **greediness** ['griːdɪnɪs]
n [for food] gula f; [for money] codicia f,
avaricia f

greedy ['griːdɪ] (compar greedier, superl
greediest) adj [for food] glotón(ona);
[for money] codicioso(a) (for de)

Greek [griːk] 1. adj griego(a) 2. n
a) [person] griego(a) m,f b) [language]
griego m

green [griːn] 1. n a) [colour] verde m
b) [in golf] campo m; **village green**
plaza f (del pueblo)
c) **greens** verdura f, verduras fpl
2. adj a) verde; **green bean** judía f verde, Bol, RP chaucha f, CAm ejote m, Col,
Cuba habichuela f, Chile poroto m verde,
Ven vainita f; **green belt** zona f verde;
US **green card** [work permit] permiso m
de trabajo; **green pepper** pimiento m
verde; **she was green with envy** se la
comía la envidia
b) [inexperienced] verde, novato(a);
[gullible] crédulo(a)
c) POL **Green Party** Partido m Verde

greenery ['griːnərɪ] n follaje m

greengrocer ['griːnɡrəʊsə(r)] n Br
verdulero(a) m,f

greenhouse ['griːnhaʊs] n invernadero m; **greenhouse effect** efecto
invernadero

greenlight ['griːnlaɪt] vt dar luz verde a

greet [griːt] vt [wave at] saludar; [re-
ceive] recibir; [welcome] dar la bienvenida a

greeting ['griːtɪŋ] n a) saludo m; **greetings card**, US **greeting card** tarjeta f
de felicitación b) [reception] recibimiento m; [welcome] bienvenida f

GR8 MESSAGING written abbr of **great**

grenade [ɡrɪ'neɪd] n granada f

grew [ɡruː] pt of **grow**

grey [greɪ] 1. adj [colour] gris; [hair]
cano(a); [sky] nublado(a); **grey matter** materia f gris 2. n a) [colour] gris m
b) [horse] caballo tordo

grey-haired ['greɪheəd] adj canoso(a)

greyhound ['greɪhaʊnd] n galgo m

grid [ɡrɪd] n a) [on map] cuadrícula f
b) [of electricity etc] red f nacional c) [for
cooking] parrilla f

griddle ['ɡrɪdəl] n [for cooking] plancha f

grief [griːf] n dolor m, pena f; Fam **to
come to grief** [car, driver] sufrir un
accidente; [plans] irse al traste

grievance ['griːvəns] n [wrong] agravio m; [resentment] queja f

grieve [griːv] 1. vt apenar, dar pena a
2. vi apenarse, afligirse; **to grieve for
sb** llorar la muerte de algn

grill [ɡrɪl] 1. vt a) CULIN asar (a la parrilla)
b) Fam [interrogate] interrogar dura-
mente 2. n Br [on cooker] grill m; [for
open fire] parrilla f; [dish] parrillada f

grill(e) [ɡrɪl] n [grating] reja f

grilling ['ɡrɪlɪŋ] n Br [of food] cocina f
a la parrilla

grim [ɡrɪm] (compar grimmer, superl
grimmest) adj a) [sinister] macabro(a);
[landscape] lúgubre b) [person]
ceñudo(a) c) Fam [unpleasant] desagradable

grimace [ɡrɪ'meɪs] 1. n mueca f 2. vi
hacer una mueca

grime [ɡraɪm] n mugre f, porquería f

grimy ['ɡraɪmɪ] (compar grimier, superl
grimiest) adj mugriento(a)

grin [ɡrɪn] 1. vi sonreír abiertamente
2. n sonrisa abierta

grind [ɡraɪnd] (pt & pp ground) 1. vt [mill]
moler; [crush] triturar; [sharpen] afilar; US [meat] picar
2. vi a) rechinar; Fig **to grind to a halt**
[vehicle] pararse lentamente; [produc-
tion etc] pararse poco a poco
b) US Fam empollar
3. n a) Fam **the daily grind** la rutina
cotidiana
b) US Fam [studious pupil] em-
pollón(ona) m,f

grinder ['graɪndə(r)] n [for coffee, pepper] molinillo m; [crusher] trituradora f; [for sharpening] afilador m

grip [grɪp] **1.** n a) [hold] agarrón m; [handshake] apretón m; **to get to grips with a problem** superar un problema b) [handle - of oar, handlebars, racket] empuñadura f c) US [bag] bolsa f de viaje **2.** vt a) agarrar, asir; [hand] apretar b) Fig [of film, story] captar la atención de; **to be gripped by fear** ser presa del miedo

gripping ['grɪpɪŋ] adj [film, story] apasionante

grisly ['grɪzlɪ] (compar **grislier**, superl **grisliest**) adj espeluznante

gristle ['grɪsəl] n cartílago m, ternilla f

grit [grɪt] **1.** n a) [gravel] grava f b) Fam [courage] valor m **2.** vt Fig **to grit one's teeth** apretar los dientes

groan [grəʊn] **1.** n a) [of pain] gemido m b) Fam [of disapproval] gruñido m **2.** vi a) [in pain] gemir b) Fam [complain] quejarse (**about** de)

grocer ['grəʊsə(r)] n tendero(a) m,f; Br **grocer's (shop)** tienda f de comestibles or de ultramarinos, Andes, CSur bodega f, CAm, Méx (tienda f de) abarrotes mpl

groceries ['grəʊsərɪz] npl comestibles mpl

grocery ['grəʊsərɪ] n esp US **grocery (shop** or **store)** tienda f de alimentación, Andes, CSur bodega f, CAm, Méx (tienda f de) abarrotes mpl

groin [grɔɪn] n ingle f

groom [gru:m] **1.** n a) mozo m de cuadra b) [bridegroom] novio m **2.** vt [horse] almohazar; [clothes, appearance] cuidar

groove [gru:v] n [furrow etc] ranura f; [of record] surco m

grope [grəʊp] vi a) [search about] andar a tientas; **to grope for sth** buscar algo a tientas b) Fam [fondle] meter mano

gross [grəʊs] **1.** adj a) grosero(a); [joke] verde b) [fat] obeso(a) c) [flagrant] flagrante; [ignorance] craso(a)

d) COMM & ECON bruto(a); **gross national product** producto nacional bruto **2.** vt COMM recaudar (en bruto)

grossly ['grəʊslɪ] adv enormemente

grotesque [grəʊ'tesk] adj grotesco(a)

ground¹ [graʊnd] **1.** n a) suelo m, tierra f; **at ground level** al nivel del suelo; Br **ground floor** planta baja b) [terrain] terreno m c) US ELEC toma f de tierra d) **grounds** [gardens] jardines mpl e) **grounds** [reason] motivo m f) **grounds** [sediment] poso m **2.** vt a) AVIAT obligar a quedarse en tierra; NAUT varar b) US ELEC conectar con tierra

ground² [graʊnd] **1.** adj [coffee] molido(a); US [meat] Esp, RP picado(a), Am molido(a) **2.** pt & pp of **grind**

grounded ['graʊndɪd] adj a) **to be grounded** [emotionally stable] tener los pies en la tierra b) castigado(a) sin salir

grounding ['graʊndɪŋ] n base f; **to have a good grounding in** tener buenos conocimientos de

groundwork ['graʊndwɜ:k] n trabajo preparatorio

group [gru:p] **1.** n grupo m, conjunto m **2.** vt agrupar, juntar (**into** en) **3.** vi **to group (together)** agruparse, juntarse

grovel ['grɒvəl] (pt & pp **grovelled**, US pt & pp **groveled**) vi humillarse (**to** ante); [crawl] arrastrarse (**to** ante)

grow [grəʊ] (pt **grew**, pp **grown**) **1.** vt [cultivate] cultivar; **to grow a beard** dejarse (crecer) la barba **2.** vi a) crecer; [increase] aumentar b) [become] hacerse, volverse; **to grow accustomed to** acostumbrarse a; **to grow dark** oscurecer; **to grow old** envejecer

grower ['grəʊə(r)] n cultivador(a) m,f

growl [graʊl] **1.** vi gruñir **2.** n gruñido m

grown [grəʊn] **1.** adj crecido(a), adulto(a) **2.** pp of **grow**

grown-up ['grəʊnʌp] adj & n adulto(a) (m,f); **the grown-ups** los mayores

growth [grəʊθ] n a) crecimiento m; [increase] aumento m; [development] desarrollo m b) MED bulto m

grub [grʌb] n a) [larva] gusano m b) Fam [food] papeo m

grubby ['grʌbɪ] (compar **grubbier**, superl **grubbiest**) adj sucio(a)

grudge [grʌdʒ] 1. n rencor m; **to bear sb a grudge** guardar rencor a algn 2. vt [give unwillingly] dar a regañadientes; **he grudges me my success** me envidia el éxito

grudgingly ['grʌdʒɪŋlɪ] adv a regañadientes

gruelling, US **grueling** ['gru:əlɪŋ] adj penoso(a)

gruesome ['gru:səm] adj espantoso(a), horrible

gruff [grʌf] adj [manner] brusco(a); [voice] áspero(a)

grumble ['grʌmbəl] 1. vi refunfuñar 2. n queja f

grumpy ['grʌmpɪ] (compar **grumpier**, superl **grumpiest**) adj gruñón(ona)

grunt [grʌnt] 1. vi gruñir 2. n gruñido m

GTG, G2G MESSAGING written abbr of **got to go**

GTSY MESSAGING written abbr of **glad to see you**

guarantee [gærən'ti:] 1. n garantía f; [certificate] certificado m de garantía 2. vt garantizar; [assure] asegurar

guard [gɑ:d] 1. vt a) [protect] defender, proteger; [keep watch over] vigilar b) [control] guardar
2. vi protegerse (**against** de or contra)
3. n a) **to be on one's guard** estar en guardia; **to catch sb off his guard** coger desprevenido a algn b) [sentry] guardia mf; **guard dog** perro m guardián c) Br RAIL jefe m de tren; **guard's van** furgón m de cola d) [on machine] dispositivo m de seguridad; **fire guard** pantalla f

guardian ['gɑ:dɪən] n a) guardián(ana) m,f; **guardian angel** ángel m de la guarda b) JUR [of minor] tutor(a) m,f

Guatemala [ˌgwɑ:tə'mɑ:lə] n Guatemala f

Guatemalan [ˌgwɑ:tə'mɑ:lən] adj & n guatemalteco(a) (m,f)

GUDLUK (abbr of **good luck**) MESSAGING bna srte

guer(r)illa [gə'rɪlə] n guerrillero(a) m,f; **guer(r)illa warfare** guerra f de guerrillas

guess [ges] 1. vt & vi a) adivinar; **I guessed as much** me lo imaginaba; **to guess right/wrong** acertar / no acertar b) US Fam pensar, suponer; **I guess so** supongo que sí 2. n conjetura f; [estimate] cálculo m; **at a rough guess** a ojo de buen cubero; **to have** or **make a guess** intentar adivinar

guesswork ['gesws:k] n conjetura f

guest [gest] n [at home] invitado(a) m,f; [in hotel] cliente mf, huésped(a) mf; **guest artist** artista mf invitado(a); **guest room** cuarto m de los invitados

guesthouse ['gesthaʊs] n casa f de huéspedes

guidance ['gaɪdəns] n orientación f, consejos mpl; **for your guidance** a título de información

guide [gaɪd] 1. vt guiar, dirigir 2. n a) [person] guía mf; Br **girl guide** exploradora f; **guide dog** perro lazarillo b) [guidebook] guía f

guided ['gaɪdɪd] adj dirigido(a); **guided tour** visita con guía; **guided missile** misil teledirigido

guideline ['gaɪdlaɪn] n pauta f

guild [gɪld] n gremio m

guilt [gɪlt] n a) culpa f b) JUR culpabilidad f

guilty ['gɪltɪ] (compar **guiltier**, superl **guiltiest**) adj culpable (**of** de); **to have a guilty conscience** remorderle a uno la conciencia

guinea¹ ['gɪnɪ] n **guinea pig** conejillo m de Indias, cobayo m; Fig **to act as a guinea pig** servir de conejillo de Indias

guinea² ['gɪnɪ] *n Br* [coin] guinea *f* (*= 21 chelines*)

guise [gaɪz] *n* **under the guise of** so pretexto de

guitar [gɪ'tɑː(r)] *n* guitarra *f*

guitarist [gɪ'tɑːrɪst] *n* guitarrista *mf*

gulf [gʌlf] *n* **a)** golfo *m*; **Gulf of Mexico** Golfo de Méjico; **Gulf Stream** corriente *f* del Golfo de Méjico; **the Gulf War** la guerra del Golfo **b)** *Fig* abismo *m*

gull [gʌl] *n* gaviota *f*

gullible ['gʌləbəl] *adj* crédulo(a)

gulp [gʌlp] **1.** *n* trago *m*
2. *vt* tragar; **to gulp sth down** [drink] tomarse algo de un trago; [food] engullir algo
3. *vi* **a)** [swallow air] tragar aire **b)** *Fig* [with fear] tragar saliva

gum¹ [gʌm] **1.** *n* goma *f* **2.** *vt* pegar con goma

gum² [gʌm] *n* ANAT encía *f*

gun [gʌn] *n* arma *f* de fuego; [handgun] pistola *f*, revólver *m*; [rifle] fusil *m*, escopeta *f*; [cannon] cañón *m*; *Fam* **the big guns** los peces gordos ■ **gun down** *vt sep* matar a tiros

gunfire ['gʌnfaɪə(r)] *n* tiros *mpl*

gunpowder ['gʌnpaʊdə(r)] *n* pólvora *f*

gunshot ['gʌnʃɒt] *n* disparo *m*, tiro *m*

gurgle ['gɜːgəl] *vi* [baby] gorjear; [liquid] gorgotear; [stream] murmurar

gush [gʌʃ] **1.** *vi* **a)** brotar **b)** *Fig* **to gush over sb** enjabonar a algn **2.** *n* [of water] chorro *m*; [of words] torrente *m*

gust [gʌst] *n* [of wind] ráfaga *f*, racha *f*

gusto ['gʌstəʊ] *n* entusiasmo *m*

gut [gʌt] **1.** *n* **a)** ANAT intestino *m* **b)** guts [entrails] tripas *fpl*; *Fam* **to have guts** tener agallas **2.** *vt* **a)** [fish] destripar **b)** [destroy] destruir por dentro **3.** *adj Fam* **gut reaction** reacción *f* visceral

gutter ['gʌtə(r)] *n* [in street] arroyo *m*; [on roof] canalón *m*; *Fig* **gutter press** prensa amarilla

guy¹ [gaɪ] *n Fam* tipo *m*, tío *m*

guy² [gaɪ] *n* [rope] viento *m*, cuerda *f*

Guyana [gaɪ'ænə] *n* Guyana *f*

guzzle ['gʌzəl] *vt* & *vi Fam* [food etc] zamparse; [car] tragar mucho

gym [dʒɪm] *n Fam* **a)** [gymnasium] gimnasio *m* **b)** [gymnastics] gimnasia *f*; **gym shoes** zapatillas *fpl* de deporte

gymnasium [dʒɪm'neɪzɪəm] *n* gimnasio *m*

gymnastics [dʒɪm'næstɪks] *n sing* gimnasia *f*

gynaecologist, *US* **gynecologist** [gaɪnɪ'kɒlədʒɪst] *n* ginecólogo(a) *m,f*

gypsy ['dʒɪpsɪ] *adj* & *n* gitano(a) *(m,f)*

gyrate [dʒaɪ'reɪt] *vi* girar

H

H, h [eɪtʃ] *n* [the letter] H, h *f*

habit ['hæbɪt] *n* **a)** costumbre *f* **b)** [garment] hábito *m*

habitat ['hæbɪtæt] *n* hábitat *m*

habitual [hə'bɪtjuəl] *adj* habitual ; [drinker, liar] empedernido(a)

hack¹ [hæk] **1.** *n* [cut] corte *m* ; [with axe] hachazo *m* **2.** *vt* [with knife, axe] cortar; [kick] dar un puntapié a ▪ **hack into** *vt insep* COMPUT piratear, hackear

hack² [hæk] *n Fam* [writer] escritorzuelo(a) *m,f* ; [journalist] gacetillero(a) *m,f*

hacker ['hækə(r)] *n* COMPUT pirata *mf* informático(a), hacker *mf* ; **ethical hacker** hacker *mf* ético(a)

hacktivism ['hæktɪ,vɪzəm] *n* hacktivismo *m*

hacktivist ['hæktɪ,vɪst] *n* hacktivista *mf*

had [hæd] *pt & pp of* **have**

haemorrhage ['hemərɪdʒ] *n* hemorragia *f*

haemorrhoids ['hemərɔɪdz] *npl* hemorroides *fpl*

hag [hæg] *n Pej* bruja *f*, arpía *f*

haggard ['hægəd] *adj* ojeroso(a)

haggle ['hægəl] *vi* regatear

hail¹ [heɪl] **1.** *n* granizo *m* ; *Fig* **a hail of bullets / insults** una lluvia de balas / insultos **2.** *vi* granizar

hail² [heɪl] **1.** *vt* **a)** [taxi etc] parar **b)** [acclaim] aclamar **2.** *vi* **to hail from** [originate] ser nativo(a) de

hair [heə(r)] *n* [strand] pelo *m*, cabello *m* ; [mass] pelo, cabellos *mpl* ; [on arm, leg] vello *m* ; **hair conditioner** acondicionador *m* ; **hair wax** cera *f* para el pelo; **to have long hair** tener el pelo largo

hairbrush ['heəbrʌʃ] *n* cepillo *m* (para el pelo)

haircut ['heəkʌt] *n* corte *m* de pelo; **to have a haircut** cortarse el pelo

hairdo ['heədu:] *n Fam* peinado *m*

hairdresser ['heədresə(r)] *n* peluquero(a) *m,f* ; **hairdresser's (shop)** peluquería *f*

hairdryer, hairdrier ['heədraɪə(r)] *n* secador *m* (de pelo)

hairgrip ['heəgrɪp] *n Br* horquilla *f*

hairpin ['heəpɪn] *n* horquilla *f* ; **hairpin bend** curva muy cerrada

hairspray ['heəspreɪ] *n* laca *f* (para el pelo)

hairstyle ['heəstaɪl] *n* peinado *m*, corte *m* de pelo

hairy ['heəri] *(compar* hairier, *superl* hairiest) *adj* **a)** [with hair] peludo(a) **b)** *Fig* [frightening] enervante, espantoso(a)

HAK *(abbr of* hugs and kisses) MESSAGING bss

half [hɑːf] **1.** *(pl* halves) *n* mitad *f* ; SPORT [period] tiempo *m* ; **he's four and a half** tiene cuatro años y medio; **to cut in half** cortar por la mitad **2.** *adj* medio(a); **half a dozen / an hour** media docena / hora; **half board** media pensión; **half fare** media tarifa; **half term** medio trimestre **3.** *adv* medio, a medias ; **half asleep** medio dormido(a)

half-baked [-'beɪkt] *adj Fam & Fig* [idea, project] chapucero(a) ; **they made a half-baked attempt to improve security** hicieron un medio intento de mejorar la seguridad

half-bottle *n* media botella *f*

half-brother *n* medio hermano *m*

half-caste ['hɑːfkɑːst] *adj & n* mestizo(a) *(m,f)*

half-hearted [hɑːfˈhɑːtɪd] *adj* poco
entusiasta

half-hour [hɑːfˈaʊə(r)] *n* media hora

half-sister *n* medio hermana *f*

half-time [hɑːfˈtaɪm] *n* descanso *m*

half-way [ˈhɑːfweɪ] *adj* intermedio(a)
■ **halfway** [hɑːfˈweɪ] *adv* a medio camino, a mitad de camino

hall [hɔːl] *n* a) [lobby] vestíbulo *m*
b) [building] sala *f*; *Br* UNIV **hall of residence** residencia *f* de estudiantes, *Esp*
colegio *m* mayor

hallo [həˈləʊ] *interj* ¡hola!

Hallowe(')en [hæləʊˈiːn] *n* víspera *f* de
Todos los Santos

hallucination [həluːsɪˈneɪʃən] *n* alucinación *f*

hallway [ˈhɔːlweɪ] *n* vestíbulo *m*

halo [ˈheɪləʊ] *n* a) REL aureola *f* b) ASTRON
halo *m*

halt [hɔːlt] **1.** *n* [stop] alto *m*, parada *f*; **to
call a halt to sth** poner fin a algo
2. *vt* parar
3. *vi* pararse

halve [hɑːv] *vt* a) partir por la mitad;
[reduce by half] reducir a la mitad
b) [share] compartir

ham [hæm] *n* jamón *m*; **boiled ham**
jamón de York; **Parma** *or* **cured ham**
jamón serrano

hamburger [ˈhæmbɜːgə(r)] *n* hamburguesa *f*

hammer [ˈhæmə(r)] **1.** *n* a) martillo *m*
b) [of gun] percusor *m*
2. *vt* a) martillar; [nail] clavar; *Fig* **to
hammer home** insistir sobre
b) *Fam* [defeat] dar una paliza a
3. *vi* martillar, dar golpes

hammock [ˈhæmək] *n* hamaca *f*; NAUT
coy *m*

hamper¹ [ˈhæmpə(r)] *n* cesta *f*

hamper² [ˈhæmpə(r)] *vt* estorbar, dificultar

hamster [ˈhæmstə(r)] *n* hámster *m*

hand [hænd] **1.** *n* a) mano *f*; **by hand** a
mano; **(close) at hand** a mano; **hands
up!** ¡manos arriba!; **on the one /other
hand** por una /otra parte; *Fig* **to get out
of hand** descontrolarse; *Fig* **to wash
one's hands of sth** lavarse las manos
de algo; *Fig* **to give sb a hand** echarle
una mano a algn; **hand grenade** granada *f* de mano
b) [worker] trabajador(a) *m,f*; NAUT
tripulante *m*
c) [of clock] aguja *f*
d) [handwriting] letra *f*
2. *vt* [give] dar, entregar
■ **hand back** *vt sep* devolver
■ **hand down** *vt sep* dejar en herencia
■ **hand in** *vt sep* [homework] entregar; [resignation] presentar
■ **hand out** *vt sep* repartir
■ **hand over** *vt sep* entregar
■ **hand round** *vt sep* repartir

handbag [ˈhændbæg] *n Br* [woman's] *Esp*
bolso *m*, *Col, CSur* cartera *f*, *Méx* bolsa *f*

handbook [ˈhændbʊk] *n* manual *m*

handbrake [ˈhændbreɪk] *n* freno *m* de
mano

handful [ˈhændfʊl] *n* puñado *m*

hand-held [hændˈheld] *adj* de mano,
portátil; **hand-held computer** *Esp*
ordenador *m or Am* computadora *f* de
bolsillo

handicap [ˈhændɪkæp] **1.** *n* a) MED
minusvalía *f* b) SPORT hándicap *m*,
desventaja *f* **2.** *vt* impedir

handicapped [ˈhændɪkæpt] *adj*
a) [physically] minusválido(a); [men-
tally] retrasado(a) b) SPORT en desventaja c) *Fig* desfavorecido(a)

handicraft [ˈhændɪkrɑːft] *n* artesanía *f*

H&K (*abbr of* **hugs and kisses**)
MESSAGING bss

handkerchief [ˈhæŋkətʃiːf] *n* pañuelo *m*

handle [ˈhændəl] **1.** *n* [of knife] mango *m*; [of cup] asa *f*; [of door] pomo *m*;
[of drawer] tirador *m* **2.** *vt* a) manejar;
handle with care [sign] frágil b) [prob-
lem] encargarse de; [people] tratar; *Fam*
[put up with] soportar

handmade [hænd'meɪd] *adj* hecho(a) a mano

hand-out ['hændaʊt] *n* a) [leaflet] folleto *m*; PRESS nota *f* de prensa b) [charity] limosna *f*

hands-free [hænds-] *adj* [phone] manos libres (*inv*)

handshake ['hændʃeɪk] *n* apretón *m* de manos

handsome ['hænsəm] *adj* a) [person] guapo(a) b) [substantial] considerable

handwriting ['hændraɪtɪŋ] *n* letra *f*

handwritten ['hændrɪtən] *adj* manuscrito(a), escrito(a) a mano

handy ['hændɪ] (*compar* **handier**, *superl* **handiest**) *adj* a) [useful] útil, práctico(a); [nearby] a mano b) [dextrous] diestro(a)

handyman ['hændɪmæn] *n* [person good at odd jobs] persona *f* habilidosa, *Esp* manitas *mf inv*

hang [hæŋ] (*pt & pp* **hung**) **1.** *vt* a) colgar b) [head] bajar c) (*pt & pp* **hanged**) ahorcar; **to hang oneself** ahorcarse **2.** *vi* a) colgar (**from** de); [in air] flotar b) (*pt & pp* **hanged**) [criminal] ser ahorcado(a) ■ **hang about** *vi Fam* a) perder el tiempo b) [wait] esperar ■ **hang around** *vi Fam* a) esperar b) frecuentar; **where does he hang around?** ¿a qué lugares suele ir? ■ **hang on** *vi* a) agarrarse b) [wait] esperar ■ **hang out 1.** *vt sep* [washing] tender **2.** *vi Fam* [frequent] frecuentar ■ **hang together** *vi* [ideas] ser coherente ■ **hang up** *vt sep* [picture, telephone] colgar

hanger ['hæŋə(r)] *n* percha *f*

hang-glider ['hæŋglaɪdə(r)] *n* ala delta

hang-gliding ['hæŋglaɪdɪŋ] *n* vuelo *m* libre

hangover ['hæŋəʊvə(r)] *n* resaca *f*

hang-up ['hæŋʌp] *n Fam* [complex] complejo *m*

hankie, hanky ['hæŋkɪ] *n Fam* pañuelo *m*

haphazard [hæp'hæzəd] *adj* caótico(a), desordenado(a)

happen ['hæpən] *vi* suceder, ocurrir; **it so happens that** lo que pasa es que; **if you happen to see my friend** si por casualidad ves a mi amigo

happily ['hæpɪlɪ] *adv* [with pleasure] felizmente; [fortunately] afortunadamente

happiness ['hæpɪnɪs] *n* felicidad *f*

happy ['hæpɪ] (*compar* **happier**, *superl* **happiest**) *adj* [cheerful] feliz, contento(a); [fortunate] afortunado(a); **happy birthday!** ¡feliz cumpleaños!

harass ['hærəs] *vt* acosar

harassment ['hærəsmənt, hə'ræsmənt] *n* hostigamiento *m*, acoso *m*; **sexual harassment** acoso *m* sexual

harbour, *US* **harbor** ['hɑːbə(r)] **1.** *n* puerto *m* **2.** *vt* a) [criminal] encubrir b) [doubts] abrigar

hard [hɑːd] **1.** *adj* a) duro(a); [solid] sólido(a); COMPUT **hard copy** copia *f* en papel; COMPUT **hard disk** disco *m* duro; *Br* AUTO **hard shoulder** *Esp* arcén *m*, *Andes* berma *f*, *Méx* acotamiento *m*, *RP* banquina *f* b) [difficult] difícil; **hard of hearing** duro(a) de oído; *Fam & Fig* **to be hard up** estar sin blanca c) [harsh] severo(a); [strict] estricto(a); **hard drugs** droga dura; POL **hard left** extrema izquierda; **hard sell** promoción *f* de venta agresiva d) **a hard worker** un trabajador concienzudo e) **hard luck!** ¡mala suerte! f) **hard evidence** pruebas definitivas; **hard currency** divisa *f* fuerte **2.** *adv* a) [hit] fuerte b) [work] mucho

hardback ['hɑːdbæk], **hardcover** ['hɑːdkʌvə(r)] *n* edición *f* de tapas duras

hardball ['hɑːdbɔːl] *n US* [baseball] béisbol *m*

hard-boiled ['hɑːdbɔɪld] *adj* duro(a)

hardcover *n* = **hardback**

harden ['hɑːdən] **1.** *vt* endurecer **2.** *vi* endurecerse

hard-hit *adj* muy afectado(a), muy perjudicado(a)

hardly ['hɑːdlɪ] adv apenas ; **hardly anyone /ever** casi nadie /nunca ; **he had hardly begun when ...** apenas había comenzado cuando ...; **I can hardly believe it** apenas lo puedo creer

hardware ['hɑːdweə(r)] n a) [goods] ferretería f; US **hardware store** [ironmonger's] ferretería b) COMPUT hardware m

hardwearing [hɑːd'weərɪŋ] adj duradero(a)

hardworking ['hɑːdwɜːkɪŋ] adj muy trabajador(a)

hardy ['hɑːdɪ] (compar **hardier**, superl **hardiest**) adj [person] robusto(a), fuerte ; [plant] resistente

hare [heə(r)] 1. n liebre f 2. vi correr muy de prisa

harm [hɑːm] 1. n daño m, perjuicio m ; **to be out of harm's way** estar a salvo 2. vt hacer daño a, perjudicar

harmful ['hɑːmfʊl] adj perjudicial (**to** para)

harmless ['hɑːmlɪs] adj inofensivo(a)

harmonica [hɑː'mɒnɪkə] n armónica f

harmonious [hɑː'məʊnɪəs] adj armonioso(a)

harmonize ['hɑːmənaɪz] vt & vi armonizar

harmony ['hɑːmənɪ] n armonía f

harness ['hɑːnɪs] 1. n [for horse] arreos mpl 2. vt a) [horse] enjaezar b) Fig [resources etc] aprovechar

harp [hɑːp] n arpa f ■ **harp on** vi Fam hablar sin parar

harrowing ['hærəʊɪŋ] adj angustioso(a)

harsh [hɑːʃ] adj severo(a) ; [voice] áspero(a) ; [sound] discordante

harvest ['hɑːvɪst] 1. n cosecha f ; [of grapes] vendimia f 2. vt cosechar, recoger

has [hæz] 3rd person sing pres see **have**

has-been ['hæzbiːn] n Fam & Pej vieja gloria f

hash n COMPUT función f hash ; **hash key** (tecla f) almohadilla f

hashtag ['hæʃtæg] n COMPUT hashtag m

hassle ['hæsəl] Fam 1. n a) [nuisance] rollo m b) [problem] lío m c) [wrangle] bronca f 2. vt fastidiar

haste [heɪst] n Formal prisa f ; **to make haste** darse prisa

hasten ['heɪsən] vi apresurarse

hastily ['heɪstɪlɪ] adv [quickly] de prisa

hasty ['heɪstɪ] (compar **hastier**, superl **hastiest**) adj apresurado(a) ; [rash] precipitado(a)

hat [hæt] n sombrero m

hatch¹ [hætʃ] n escotilla f ; **serving hatch** ventanilla f

hatch² [hætʃ] 1. vt a) [eggs] empollar b) Fig [plan] tramar 2. vi **to hatch (out)** salirse del huevo

hatchback ['hætʃbæk] n coche m de 3 /5 puertas

hate [heɪt] 1. n odio m 2. vt odiar

hateful ['heɪtfʊl] adj odioso(a)

hatred ['heɪtrɪd] n odio m

haughty ['hɔːtɪ] (compar **haughtier**, superl **haughtiest**) adj altanero(a), arrogante

haul [hɔːl] 1. n a) [journey] trayecto m b) [of fish] redada f c) [loot] botín m 2. vt a) tirar ; [drag] arrastrar b) [transport] acarrear ■ **haul up** vt sep Fam [to court] llevar

haunt [hɔːnt] 1. n guarida f 2. vt a) [of ghost] aparecerse en b) Fig atormentar c) [frequent] frecuentar

haunted ['hɔːntɪd] adj encantado(a), embrujado(a)

have [hæv] (3rd person sing pres **has**) (pt & pp **had**)

En el inglés hablado, y en el escrito en estilo coloquial, el verbo auxiliar **have** se contrae de forma que **I have** se transforma en **I've**, **he /she /it has** se transforman en **he's /she's /it's** y **you /we /they have** se transforman en **you've /we've / they've**. Las formas de pasado **I /you / he** etc **had** se transforman en **I'd, you'd, he'd** etc. Las formas negativas **has not, have not** y **had not** se transforman en **hasn't, haven't** y **hadn't**.

1. vt a) [possess] tener ; **have you got a car?** ¿tienes coche?

headband

b) [get, experience, suffer] tener; **to have a holiday** tomarse unas vacaciones

c) [partake of - drink] tomar; **to have breakfast/lunch/dinner** desayunar / comer /cenar; **to have a bath/shave** bañarse /afeitarse

d) to have (got) to [obligation] tener que, deber

e) [make happen] hacer que; **I'll have someone come round** haré que venga alguien

f) [receive] recibir; **to have people round** invitar a gente

g) [party, meeting] hacer, celebrar

h) to have a baby tener un niño

i) we won't have it [allow] no lo consentiremos

j) [hold] tener; *Fig* **to have sth against sb** tener algo en contra de algn

k) *Fam* [deceive] engañar

l) you'd better stay más vale que te quedes

2. *v aux* **a)** [compound] haber; **I had been waiting for half an hour** hacía media hora que esperaba; **he hasn't eaten yet** no ha comido aún; **she had broken the window** había roto el cristal; **we have lived here for ten years** hace diez años que vivimos aquí; **so I have!** [emphatic] ¡ay, sí!, es verdad; **yes I have!** ¡que sí!

b) [tag questions] **you haven't seen my book, have you?** no has visto mi libro, ¿verdad?; **he's been to France, hasn't he?** ha estado en Francia, ¿verdad? *or* ¿no?

c) to have just done acabar de hacer

■ **have on** *vt sep* **a)** [wear] vestir **b)** *Fam* **to have sb on** tomarle el pelo *or Esp, Carib, Méx* vacilar a algn

■ **have out** *vt sep Fam* **to have it out with sb** ajustar cuentas con algn

■ **have over** *vt sep* [invite] recibir

haven ['heɪvən] *n* puerto *m*; *Fig* refugio *m*

havoc ['hævək] *n* **to play havoc with** hacer estragos en

hawk [hɔːk] *n* ORNITH & POL halcón *m*

hay [heɪ] *n* heno *m*; **hay fever** fiebre *f* del heno

haystack ['heɪstæk] *n* almiar *m*

haywire ['heɪwaɪə(r)] *adj Fam* en desorden; **to go haywire** [machine etc] estropearse; [person] volverse loco(a)

hazard ['hæzəd] **1.** *n* peligro *m*, riesgo *m*; [in golf] obstáculo *m* **2.** *vt Formal* arriesgar; **to hazard a guess** intentar adivinar

hazardous ['hæzədəs] *adj* arriesgado(a), peligroso(a)

haze [heɪz] *n* [mist] neblina *f*; *Fig* [blur] confusión *f*

hazelnut ['heɪzəlnʌt] *n* avellana *f*

Hazmat ['hæzmæt] *n US abbr of* **hazardous material**; *US* **Hazmat suit** traje *m* de protección química

hazy ['heɪzɪ] *(compar* **hazier**, *superl* **haziest)** *adj* nebuloso(a)

HD *adj* **a)** COMPUT *(abbr of* **high density)** HD **b)** *(abbr of* **high definition)** HD

HDTV *n (abbr of* **high-definition television)** televisión *f* de alta definición

HDV *n (abbr of* **high definition video)** HDV *m*

he [hiː] *pers pron* él *(usually omitted in Spanish, except for contrast)*; **he did it** ha sido él; **he who** el que

head [hed] **1.** *n* **a)** cabeza *f*; [mind] mente *f*; **£3 a head** [each] 3 libras por cabeza; *Fig* **to lose one's head** perder la cabeza; **success went to his head** se le subió el éxito a la cabeza

b) [of nail] cabeza *f*; [of beer] espuma *f*

c) [boss] cabeza *m*; [of company] director(a) *m,f*; *Br* **head (teacher)** director(a) *m,f*

d) [of coin] cara *f*; **heads or tails** cara o cruz

2. *adj* principal; **head office** oficina *f* central

3. *vt* **a)** [list etc] encabezar

b) FTBL cabecear

■ **head for** *vt insep* dirigirse hacia

■ **head off 1.** *vi* irse **2.** *vt sep* [avert] evitar

headache ['hedeɪk] *n* dolor *m* de cabeza; *Fig* quebradero *m* de cabeza

headband ['hedbænd] *n* cinta *f* para la cabeza

headed ['hedɪd] *adj Br* **headed notepaper** papel *m* con membrete

header ['hedə(r)] *n* FTBL cabezazo *m*

heading ['hedɪŋ] *n* título *m*; [of letter] membrete *m*

headlamp ['hedlæmp] *n* faro *m*

headlight ['hedlaɪt] *n* faro *m*; **dipped headlights** luces *fpl* de cruce

headline ['hedlaɪn] *n* titular *m*; **the headlines** [on radio, TV] los titulares

headlong ['hedlɒŋ] *adj & adv* de cabeza; **to rush headlong into sth** lanzarse a hacer algo sin pensar

headmaster [hed'mɑ:stə(r)] *n* director *m*

headmistress [hed'mɪstrɪs] *n* directora *f*

headphone ['hedfəʊn] *n* auricular *m*; **headphone jack** conector *m* de auriculares, jack *m* de auriculares

headquarters ['hedkwɔ:təz] *npl* **a)** oficina *f* central, sede *f* **b)** MIL cuartel *m* general

headstrong ['hedstrɒŋ] *adj* testarudo(a)

heady ['hedɪ] *(compar* **headier**, *superl* **headiest)** *adj* embriagador(a)

heal [hi:l] **1.** *vi* cicatrizar **2.** *vt* [wound] curar

health [helθ] *n* salud *f*; *Fig* prosperidad *f*; **to be in good / bad health** estar bien / mal de salud; **your good health!** ¡salud!; **health care** servicios *mpl* médicos; **health club** gimnasio *m*; **health foods** alimentos *mpl* naturales; **health food shop** tienda *f* de alimentos naturales; *Br* **the Health Service** el sistema de sanidad pública británico

healthy ['helθɪ] *(compar* **healthier**, *superl* **healthiest)** *adj* sano(a); [good for health] saludable; [thriving] próspero(a)

heap [hi:p] **1.** *n* montón *m* **2.** *vt* amontonar; *Fig* **to heap praise on sb** colmar a algn de alabanzas; **a heaped spoonful** una cucharada colmada

hear [hɪə(r)] *(pt & pp* **heard** [hɜ:d]) **1.** *vt* **a)** oír **b)** [listen to] escuchar **c)** [find out] enterarse **d)** JUR ver; [evidence] oír **2.** *vi* **to hear from sb** tener noticias de algn

hearing ['hɪərɪŋ] *n* **a)** oído *m*; **hearing aid** audífono *m* **b)** JUR audiencia *f*

hearse [hɜ:s] *n* coche *m* fúnebre

heart [hɑ:t] *n* **a)** corazón *m*; MED **heart attack** infarto *m* de miocardio; MED **heart disease** cardiopatía *f*; MED **heart failure** paro *m* cardíaco; **heart transplant** trasplante *m* de corazón; **a broken heart** un corazón roto; **at heart** en el fondo; **to take sth to heart** tomarse algo a pecho; **to have a good heart** [be kind] tener buen corazón **b)** [courage] valor *m*; **to lose heart** desanimarse **c)** [core] meollo *m*; [of lettuce] cogollo *m*

heartache ['hɑ:teɪk] *n* dolor *m*, tristeza *f*

heartbeat ['hɑ:tbi:t] *n* latido *m* del corazón

heart-breaking ['hɑ:tbreɪkɪŋ] *adj* desgarrador(a)

heart-broken ['hɑ:tbrəʊkən] *adj* hundido(a); **he's heart-broken** tiene el corazón destrozado

heartening ['hɑ:tənɪŋ] *adj* alentador(a)

hearth [hɑ:θ] *n* **a)** [fireplace] chimenea *f* **b)** *Formal* [home] hogar *m*

hearty ['hɑ:tɪ] *(compar* **heartier**, *superl* **heartiest)** *adj* [person] francote; [meal] abundante; [welcome] cordial; **to have a hearty appetite** ser de buen comer

heat [hi:t] **1.** *n* **a)** calor *m* **b)** SPORT eliminatoria *f* **c)** ZOOL **on heat** en celo **2.** *vt* calentar ■ **heat up** *vi* **a)** [warm up] calentarse **b)** [increase excitement] acalorarse

heated ['hi:tɪd] *adj Fig* [argument] acalorado(a)

heater ['hi:tə(r)] *n* calentador *m*

heath [hi:θ] *n* [land] brezal *m*

heather ['heðə(r)] *n* brezo *m*

heating ['hi:tɪŋ] *n* calefacción *f*

heave [hi:v] **1.** *n* [pull] tirón *m*; [push] empujón *m*

2. *vt* **a)** [lift] levantar ; [haul] tirar ; [push] empujar
b) [throw] arrojar
3. *vi* subir y bajar

heaven ['hevən] **1.** *n* **a)** cielo *m* ; **for heaven's sake!** ¡por Dios! ; **heaven on earth** un paraíso en la tierra **b)** **heavens** cielo *m* **2.** *interj* **good heavens!** ¡por Dios!

heavily ['hevɪlɪ] *adv* **it rained heavily** llovió mucho ; **to sleep heavily** dormir profundamente

heavy ['hevɪ] **1.** *(compar* **heavier**, *superl* **heaviest)** *adj* pesado(a) ; [rain, meal] fuerte ; [traffic] denso(a) ; [loss] grande ; **heavy going** duro(a) ; **is it heavy?** ¿pesa mucho? ; **a heavy drinker / smoker** un(a) bebedor(a) / fumador(a) empedernido(a) ; MUS **heavy metal** heavy metal *m* **2.** *n* *Fam* gorila *m*

heavyweight ['hevɪweɪt] *n* peso pesado

Hebrew ['hi:bru:] **1.** *adj* hebreo(a) **2.** *n* [language] hebreo *m*

Hebrides ['hebrɪdi:z] *npl* **the Hebrides** las (islas *fpl*) Hébridas *fpl*

heckle ['hekəl] *vt* interrumpir

hectic ['hektɪk] *adj* agitado(a)

hedge [hedʒ] **1.** *n* seto *m* **2.** *vt* cercar con un seto ; *Fig* **to hedge one's bets** cubrirse

hedgehog ['hedʒhɒg] *n* erizo *m*

hedgerow ['hedʒrəʊ] *n* seto vivo

heed [hi:d] *n* **to take heed of** hacer caso de

heel [hi:l] *n* [of foot] talón *m* ; [of shoe] tacón *m* ; [of palm] pulpejo *m* ; *Fig* **to be on sb's heels** pisarle los talones a algn ; **high heels** zapatos *mpl* de tacón alto

hefty ['heftɪ] *(compar* **heftier**, *superl* **heftiest)** *adj* **a)** [person] fornido(a) ; [package] pesado(a) **b)** [large] grande

height [haɪt] *n* **a)** altura *f* ; [of person] estatura *f* ; AVIAT **to gain / lose height** subir / bajar ; **what height are you?** ¿cuánto mides? ; *Fig* **the height of ignorance** el colmo de la ignorancia **b)** GEOG cumbre *f*

H8 MESSAGING *written abbr of* **hate**

heighten ['haɪtən] *vt* [intensify] realzar ; [increase] aumentar

heir [eə(r)] *n* heredero *m*

heiress ['eərɪs] *n* heredera *f*

heirloom ['eəlu:m] *n* reliquia *f* de familia

held [held] *pt & pp of* **hold**

helicopter ['helɪkɒptə(r)] *n* helicóptero *m*

hell [hel] **1.** *n* **a)** infierno *m* **b)** *Fam* [for emphasis] **he's a hell of a nice guy** es un tipo de primera, es una pasada de tío ; *Fam* **a hell of a party** una fiesta estupenda ; **what / where / why the hell…?** ¿qué / dónde / por qué demonios…? ; *Fam* **what the hell are you doing?** ¿qué diablos estás haciendo? ; *Fam* **she's had a hell of a day** ha tenido un día fatal ; *Fam* **it was a journey from hell!** ¡el viaje fue una pesadilla! **c)** *Fam* **to do sth for the hell of it** hacer algo porque sí ; *Fam* **to give sb hell** [verbally] poner a algn como un trapo ; *v Fam* **go to hell!** ¡vete a la mierda! **2.** *interj* *Fam* ¡mierda!

hello [hə'ləʊ, he'ləʊ] *interj* ¡hola! ; [when answering phone] ¿sí?, ¡diga?, *Am* ¿aló?, *Méx* ¿bueno? ; [showing surprise] ¡hala!

helm [helm] *n* timón *m* ; **to be at the helm** llevar el timón

helmet ['helmɪt] *n* casco *m*

help [help] **1.** *n* **a)** [assistance] ayuda *f* ; **(daily) help** asistenta *f* ; COMPUT **help button** tecla *f* de ayuda ; **he gave me a lot of help** me ayudó mucho ; **with the help of sth** con la ayuda de algo ; **with sb's help** con la ayuda de algn ; **to be of help** ser de ayuda, ayudar **b)** [emergency aid] socorro *m* **c)** [useful person or object] **to be a help** ayudar **2.** *interj* ¡socorro!, ¡ayuda! **3.** *vt* **a)** [assist] ayudar ; **to help sb (to) do sth** ayudar a algn a hacer algo ; **to help sb with sth** ayudar a algn con algo ; **can I help you?** [in shop] ¿qué desea?, ¿en qué puedo servirle? **b)** [alleviate] aliviar **c)** **help yourself!** [to food etc] ¡sírvete! **d)** [avoid] evitar ; **I can't help it** no lo puedo remediar ; **I couldn't help laughing** no pude evitar reírme **e)** **to help oneself (to sth)**

servirse (algo) **4.** *vi* ayudar ■ **help out** *vt sep* & *vi* ayudar; **to help sb out** ayudar a algn

helper ['helpə(r)] *n* ayudante(a) *m,f*

helpful ['helpfʊl] *adj* [person] amable; [thing] útil

helping ['helpɪŋ] *n* ración *f*; **who wants a second helping?** ¿quién quiere repetir?

helpless ['helplɪs] *adj* [defenceless] desamparado(a); [powerless] incapaz

helpline ['helplaɪn] *n* teléfono *m* de asistencia or ayuda

hem [hem] **1.** *n* SEWING dobladillo *m* **2.** *vt* SEWING hacer un dobladillo a ■ **hem in** *vt sep* cercar, rodear

hemisphere ['hemɪsfɪə(r)] *n* hemisferio *m*

hemorrhage ['hemərɪʤ] *US n* = **haemorrhage**

hemorrhoids ['hemərɔɪdz] *US npl* = **haemorrhoids**

hen [hen] *n* gallina *f*; *Fam* **hen party** or **night** despedida *f* de soltera

hence [hens] *adv Formal* **a)** **six months hence** [from now] de aquí a seis meses **b)** [consequently] por lo tanto

her [hɜː(r)] *(unstressed* [hə(r)]*)* **1.** *poss adj* [one thing] su; [more than one] sus; [to distinguish] de ella; **are they her books or his?** ¿los libros son de ella o de él?; **she has cut her finger** se ha cortado el dedo

2. *pers pron* **a)** [direct object] la; **I saw her recently** la vi hace poco **b)** [indirect object] le; [with other third person pronouns] se; **he gave her money** le dio dinero; **they handed it to her** se lo entregaron **c)** [after prep] ella; **for her** para ella **d)** *Fam* [as subject] ella; **look, it's her!** ¡mira, es ella!

herb [hɜːb, *US* ɜːrb] *n* hierba *f*; **herb tea** infusión *f*

herbal ['hɜːbəl] *adj* herbario(a); **herbal remedies** curas *fpl* de hierbas

herd [hɜːd] *n* [of cattle] manada *f*; [of goats] rebaño *m*; *Fig* [large group] multitud *f*

here [hɪə(r)] **1.** *adv* aquí; **come here** ven aquí; **here!** ¡presente!; **here goes!** ¡vamos a ver!; **here's to success!** ¡brindemos por el éxito!; **here you are!** ¡toma! **2.** *interj* **look here, you can't do that!** ¡oiga, que no se permite hacer eso!

hereafter [hɪər'ɑːftə(r)] *Formal* **1.** *adv* de ahora en adelante **2.** *n* **the hereafter** la otra vida, el más allá

hereditary [hɪ'redɪtərɪ] *adj* hereditario(a)

heritage ['herɪtɪʤ] *n* patrimonio *m*; JUR herencia *f*

hero ['hɪərəʊ] *(pl* **heroes***)* *n* héroe *m*; [in novel] protagonista *m*; **hero worship** idolatría *f*

heroic [hɪ'rəʊɪk] *adj* heroico(a)

heroin ['herəʊɪn] *n* heroína *f*

heroine ['herəʊɪn] *n* heroína *f*; [in novel] protagonista *f*

herring ['herɪŋ] *n* arenque *m*

hers [hɜːz] *poss pron* **a)** [attribute - one thing] suyo(a); [more than one] suyos(as); [to distinguish] de ella; **they are hers, not his** son de ella, no de él **b)** [noun reference - one thing] el suyo / la suya; [more than one] los suyos / las suyas; **my car is blue and hers is red** mi coche es azul y el suyo es rojo

herself [hɜː'self] *pers pron* **a)** [reflexive] se; **she dressed herself** se vistió **b)** [alone] ella sola; **she was by herself** estaba sola **c)** [emphatic] ella misma

hesitant ['hezɪtənt] *adj* vacilante

hesitate ['hezɪteɪt] *vi* vacilar

hesitation [hezɪ'teɪʃən] *n* indecisión *f*

heterosexual [hetərəʊ'seksjʊəl] *adj* & *n* heterosexual *(mf)*

hexagon ['heksəgən] *n* hexágono *m*

hey [heɪ] *interj* ¡oye!, ¡oiga!

hi [haɪ] *interj Fam* ¡hola!

hibernate ['haɪbəneɪt] *vi* hibernar

him

hiccup, hiccough ['hɪkʌp] **1.** n hipo m; Fam [minor problem] problemilla m; **to have (the) hiccups** tener hipo **2.** vi tener hipo

hide¹ [haɪd] (pt hid [hɪd], pp hidden ['hɪdən]) **1.** vt [conceal] esconder; [obscure] ocultar
2. vi esconderse, ocultarse
3. n puesto m

hide² [haɪd] n [of animal] piel f

hide-and-seek [haɪdən'siːk] n escondite m

hideous ['hɪdɪəs] adj [horrific] horroroso(a); [extremely ugly] espantoso(a)

hide-out ['haɪdaʊt] n escondrijo m, guarida f

hiding¹ ['haɪdɪŋ] n **to go into hiding** esconderse

hiding² ['haɪdɪŋ] n Fam paliza f

hierarchy ['haɪərɑːkɪ] n jerarquía f

hi-fi ['haɪfaɪ] n hifi m; **hi-fi equipment** equipo m de alta fidelidad

high [haɪ] **1.** adj **a)** alto(a); **how high is that wall?** ¿qué altura tiene esa pared?; **it's 3 feet high** tiene 3 pies de alto; **high chair** trona f; **high jump** salto m de altura; **high wind** viento m fuerte
b) [elevated] elevado(a); **high prices** precios elevados
c) [important] importante; **to have a high opinion of sb** tener muy buena opinión de algn; **high school** instituto m de enseñanza media; Br **the High Street** la Calle Mayor
d) Fam [drugged] colocado(a)
2. adv alto; **to fly high** volar a gran altura
3. n [high point] punto máximo

highbrow ['haɪbraʊ] adj & n intelectual (mf)

high-class ['haɪklɑːs] adj de alta categoría

high-definition adj de alta definición

higher ['haɪə(r)] adj superior; **higher education** enseñanza f superior

high-fibre adj [food, diet] rico(a) en fibra

highlands ['haɪləndz] npl tierras altas

highlight ['haɪlaɪt] **1.** n **a)** [in hair] reflejo m **b)** [of event] atracción f principal
2. vt **a)** hacer resaltar **b)** [text] marcar con un rotulador fosforescente **c)** COMPUT seleccionar, resaltar

highly ['haɪlɪ] adv [very] sumamente; **to speak highly of sb** hablar muy bien de algn

Highness ['haɪnɪs] n alteza mf; **Your Highness** Su Alteza

high-powered ['haɪpaʊəd] adj [person] dinámico(a)

high-res [haɪrez] adj Fam abbr of **high-resolution**

high-rise ['haɪraɪz] adj **high-rise building** rascacielos m inv

high-speed ['haɪspiːd] adj **high-speed lens** objetivo ultrarrápido; **high-speed train** tren m de alta velocidad

high-tech ['haɪtek] adj de alta tecnología

highway ['haɪweɪ] n US carretera f, autopista f; Br **Highway Code** código m de la circulación

hijack ['haɪdʒæk] **1.** vt secuestrar **2.** n secuestro m

hijacker ['haɪdʒækə(r)] n secuestrador(a) m,f; [of planes] pirata mf del aire

hike [haɪk] **1.** n **a)** [walk] excursión f **b)** **price hike** aumento m de precio **2.** vi ir de excursión

hiker ['haɪkə(r)] n excursionista mf

hiking ['haɪkɪŋ] n senderismo m, excursionismo m; **hiking boots** botas fpl de montaña

hilarious [hɪ'leərɪəs] adj graciosísimo(a)

hill [hɪl] n colina f; [slope] cuesta f

hillside ['hɪlsaɪd] n ladera f

hilly ['hɪlɪ] (compar hillier, superl hilliest) adj accidentado(a)

him [hɪm] pers pron **a)** [direct object] lo, le; **hit him!** ¡pégale!; **she loves him** lo quiere **b)** [indirect object] le; [with other third person pronouns] se; **give him the**

money dale el dinero; **give it to him** dáselo **c)** [after prep] él; **it's not like him to say that** no es propio de él decir eso **d)** *Fam* [as subject] él; **it's him** es él

himself [hɪm'self] *pers pron* **a)** [reflexive] se; **he hurt himself** se hizo daño **b)** [alone] él solo; **by himself** solo **c)** [emphatic] él mismo

hind¹ [haɪnd] *adj* trasero(a); **hind legs** patas traseras

hind² [haɪnd] *n* ZOOL cierva *f*

hinder ['hɪndə(r)] *vt* dificultar, estorbar; **to hinder sb from doing sth** impedir a algn hacer algo

hindrance ['hɪndrəns] *n* estorbo *m*

hindsight ['haɪndsaɪt] *n* **with hindsight** en retrospectiva

Hindu [hɪn'duː, 'hɪnduː] *adj & n* hindú *(mf)*

hinge [hɪndʒ] **1.** *n* bisagra *f*; *Fig* eje *m* **2.** *vt* engoznar ■ **hinge on** *vt insep* depender de

hint [hɪnt] **1.** *n* **a)** indirecta *f*; **to take the hint** coger la indirecta **b)** [clue] pista *f* **c)** [trace] pizca *f* **d)** [advice] consejo *m* **2.** *vi* **a)** lanzar indirectas **b)** [imply] insinuar algo

hip¹ [hɪp] *n* cadera *f*; **hip flask** petaca *f*

hip² [hɪp] *adj Fam* en la onda

hippie ['hɪpɪ] *adj & n Fam* hippy *(mf)*

hippopotamus [hɪpə'pɒtəməs] *n* hipopótamo *m*

hire ['haɪə(r)] **1.** *n Br* alquiler *m*; **bicycles for hire** se alquilan bicicletas; **taxi for hire** taxi *m* libre; **hire purchase** compra *f* a plazos **2.** *vt* **a)** *Br* [rent] alquilar, *Méx* rentar **b)** [employ] contratar ■ **hire out** *vt sep* [car] alquilar, *Méx* rentar; [people] contratar

hired ['haɪəd] *adj* alquilado(a); **hired help** [for housework] asistente(a) *m,f*

his [hɪz] **1.** *poss adj* [one thing] su; [more than one] sus; [to distinguish] de él; **he washed his face** se lavó la cara; **is it his dog or hers?** ¿el perro es de él o de ella? **2.** *poss pron* **a)** [attribute - one thing] suyo(a); [more than one] suyos(as); [to distinguish] de él; **they are his, not hers** son de él, no de ella

b) [noun reference - one thing] el suyo/la suya; [more than one] los suyos/las suyas; **my car is blue and his is red** mi coche es azul y el suyo es rojo

Hispanic [hɪ'spænɪk] **1.** *adj* hispánico(a) **2.** *n US* hispano(a) *m,f*, latino(a) *m,f*

hiss [hɪs] **1.** *n* siseo *m*; THEAT silbido *m* **2.** *vt & vi* silbar

hissy ['hɪsɪ] *Fam* **1.** *n* rabieta *f* **2.** *adj* **to have a hissy fit** coger *or Am* agarrar una rabieta

historian [hɪ'stɔːrɪən] *n* historiador(a) *m,f*

historic [hɪ'stɒrɪk] *adj* histórico(a)

historical [hɪ'stɒrɪkəl] *adj* histórico(a); **historical novel** novela histórica

history ['hɪstərɪ] *n* **a)** historia *f* **b)** COMPUT historial *m*

hit [hɪt] **1.** *n* **a)** [blow] golpe *m*; **direct hit** impacto directo; *Fam* **hit list** lista negra; *Fam* **hit man** asesino *m* a sueldo **b)** [success] éxito *m*; **hit parade** lista *f* de éxitos **c)** COMPUT [visit to web site] acceso *m*, visita *f* **2.** *(pt & pp hit) vt* **a)** [strike] golpear, pegar; **he was hit in the leg** le dieron en la pierna; **the car hit the kerb** el coche chocó contra el bordillo **b)** [affect] afectar **c) to hit the headlines** ser noticia ■ **hit back** *vi* [reply to criticism] replicar ■ **hit on** *vt insep* dar con; **we hit on the idea of ...** se nos ocurrió la idea de ... ■ **hit out** *vi* **to hit out at sb** atacar a algn ■ **hit upon** *vt insep* = **hit on**

hitch [hɪtʃ] **1.** *n* dificultad *f* **2.** *vt* [fasten] atar **3.** *vi Fam* [hitch-hike] hacer autostop ■ **hitch up** *vt sep* remangarse

hitch-hike ['hɪtʃhaɪk] *vi* hacer autostop *or* dedo

hitch-hiker ['hɪtʃhaɪkə(r)] *n* autostopista *mf*

HIV [eɪtʃaɪ'viː] n (abbr of **human immunodeficiency virus**) VIH m; **HIV positive/negative** seropositivo(a) / seronegativo(a)

hive [haɪv] n colmena f; Fig lugar muy activo

hoard [hɔːd] **1.** n [provisions] reservas fpl; [money etc] tesoro m **2.** vt [objects] acumular; [money] atesorar

hoarding ['hɔːdɪŋ] n [temporary fence] valla f; Br [billboard] valla publicitaria

hoarse [hɔːs] adj ronco(a); **to be hoarse** tener la voz ronca

hoax [həʊks] n [joke] broma pesada; [trick] engaño m

hobby ['hɒbɪ] n pasatiempo m, afición f

hockey ['hɒkɪ] n Br [on grass] hockey m (sobre hierba or Am césped); US [on ice] hockey (sobre hielo); US **field hockey** hockey m sobre hierba; US **hockey mom** madre f dedicada a sus hijos (que dedica gran parte de su tiempo a llevar a sus hijos a jugar al hockey sobre hielo)

hog [hɒg] **1.** n cerdo m, puerco m; Fam **to go the whole hog** liarse la manta a la cabeza **2.** vt Fam acaparar

ho-hum [həʊ'hʌm] adj US Fam **a)** [mediocre] mediocre; **it's a pretty ho-hum affair** un asunto bastante mediocre **b)** [unenthusiastic] poco entusiasta; **I was pretty ho-hum about it** no me emocionaba el tema

hoist [hɔɪst] **1.** n [crane] grúa f; [lift] montacargas m inv **2.** vt levantar, subir

hold [həʊld] (pt & pp held) **1.** vt **a)** [keep in hand] aguantar, tener (en la mano); [grip] agarrar; [support - weight] soportar; [opinion] sostener; **to hold sb** abrazar a algn; **to hold sb's hand** cogerle la mano a algn

b) [contain] dar cabida a; **the jug holds a litre** en la jarra cabe un litro

c) [meeting] celebrar; [conversation] mantener

d) to hold office ocupar un puesto

e) he was held for two hours at the police station estuvo detenido durante dos horas en la comisaría; **to hold one's breath** contener la respiración; **to hold sb hostage** retener a algn como rehén

f) TEL **to hold the line** no colgar

2. vi [rope] aguantar

3. n **a) to get hold of** [grip] coger, agarrar; Fig localizar

b) NAUT bodega f

c) [in wrestling] llave f

■ **hold back 1.** vt sep [crowd] contener; [feelings] reprimir; [truth] ocultar; **I don't want to hold you back** [delay] no quiero entretenerte **2.** vi [hesitate] vacilar

■ **hold down** vt sep **a)** [control] dominar **b)** Fam [job] desempeñar

■ **hold off** vt sep mantener a distancia

■ **hold on** vi **a)** [keep a firm grasp] agarrarse bien **b)** [wait] esperar; TEL **hold on!** ¡no cuelgue!

■ **hold out 1.** vt sep [hand] tender **2.** vi [last - things] durar; [person] resistir

■ **hold up** vt sep **a)** [rob - train] asaltar; [bank] atracar **b)** [delay] retrasar **c)** [raise] levantar **d)** [support] apuntalar

holdall ['həʊldɔːl] n esp Br bolsa f (de viaje o de deporte)

holder ['həʊldə(r)] n **a)** [receptacle] recipiente m **b)** [owner] poseedor(a) m,f; [of passport] titular mf; **account holder** titular mf; **record holder** plusmarquista mf

hold-up ['həʊldʌp] n **a)** [robbery] atraco m **b)** [delay] retraso m; [in traffic] atasco m

hole [həʊl] n **a)** agujero m; [large] hoyo m; [in the road] bache m **b)** [in golf] hoyo m **c)** Fam [of place] antro m

holiday ['hɒlɪdeɪ] **1.** n [one day] Esp [día m de] fiesta, Am feriado m; Br [several days] vacaciones fpl; **to be/go on holiday** estar/irse de vacaciones; **holiday let** alquiler m de vacaciones; **holiday resort** lugar turístico **2.** vi Br pasar las vacaciones; [in summer] veranear

holidaymaker ['hɒlɪdeɪmeɪkə(r)] n esp Br turista mf; [in summer] veraneante mf

Holland ['hɒlənd] n Holanda

hollow ['hɒləʊ] **1.** *adj* **a)** hueco(a) **b)** [cheeks, eyes] hundido(a) **c)** *Fig* [insincere] falso(a) ; [empty] vacío(a) **2.** *n* hueco *m* ; GEOG hondonada *f* **3.** *vt* **to hollow (out)** hacer un hueco en

holly ['hɒlɪ] *n* acebo *m*

holy ['həʊlɪ] *adj* sagrado(a), santo(a) ; [blessed] bendito(a) ; **Holy Ghost** Espíritu Santo; **Holy Land** Tierra Santa; **Holy See** Santa Sede

homage ['hɒmɪdʒ] *n* homenaje *m*; **to pay homage to sb** rendir homenaje a algn

home [həʊm] **1.** *n* **a)** casa *f*, hogar *m*; **at home** en casa ; *Fig* **make yourself at home!** ¡estás en tu casa!; *Fig* **to feel at home** estar a gusto; **home banking** telebanco *m*; COMPUT **home page** [initial page] portada *f*, página *f* inicial o de inicio; [personal page] página personal; **home shopping** telecompra *f*; **old people's home** hogar *m* de ancianos **b)** [institution] residencia *f*; **old people's home** residencia de ancianos **c)** SPORT **to play at home** jugar en casa **2.** *adj* **a)** [domestic] del hogar; *Br* **home help** asistenta *f* **b)** POL interior; *Br* **Home Office** Ministerio *m* del Interior; *Br* **Home Secretary** Ministro(a) *m,f* del Interior **c)** [native] natal **3.** *adv* en casa; **to go home** irse a casa; **to leave home** irse de casa
  ■ **home in on** *vt insep* dirigirse a ; *Fig* [problem, question, solution] centrarse en

homeland ['həʊmlænd] *n* patria *f* ; [birthplace] tierra *f* natal

homeless ['həʊmlɪs] **1.** *adj* sin techo **2.** *npl* **the homeless** los sin techo

homely ['həʊmlɪ] *(compar* **homelier**, *superl* **homeliest)** *adj* **a)** *Br* [person] casero(a) ; [atmosphere] familiar **b)** *US* [ugly] feúcho(a)

home-made ['həʊmmeɪd] *adj* casero(a)

homeschooling ['həʊm,skuːlɪŋ] *n US* SCH educación *f* en casa

homesick ['həʊmsɪk] *adj* **to be homesick** tener morriña

homeward(s) ['həʊmwəd(z)] *adv* hacia casa

homeware ['həʊmweə(r)] *n* artículos *mpl* para el hogar

homework ['həʊmwɜːk] *n* deberes *mpl*

homeworking ['həʊm,wɜːkɪŋ] *n* trabajo *m* en casa

homicide ['hɒmɪsaɪd] *n* homicidio *m*

homosexual [həʊməʊ'seksjʊəl] *adj* & *n* homosexual *(mf)*

honcho ['hɒntʃəʊ] *n US Fam* [boss] jefe *m*

Honduran [hɒn'djʊərən] *adj* & *n* hondureño(a) *(m,f)*

Honduras [hɒn'djʊərəs] *n* Honduras *f*

honest ['ɒnɪst] **1.** *adj* [trustworthy] honrado(a) ; [sincere] sincero(a), franco(a) ; [fair] justo(a) ; **the honest truth** la pura verdad; **to be honest…** la verdad es que… **2.** *adv Fam* = **honestly**

honestly ['ɒnɪstlɪ] *adv* honradamente; [question] ¿de verdad? ; [exclamation] ¡hay que ver!; **honestly, it doesn't matter** de verdad, no tiene importancia

honesty ['ɒnɪstɪ] *n* honradez *f*

honey ['hʌnɪ] *n* miel *f* ; *esp US Fam* [endearment] cariño *m*

honeymoon ['hʌnɪmuːn] *n* luna *f* de miel

honk [hɒŋk] *vi* AUTO tocar la bocina

honking ['hɒŋkɪŋ] *adj Fam* **a)** [huge] enorme; **he's bought a honking great plasma screen** ha comprado una pantalla de plasma enorme **b)** [brilliant] enorme; **that's a honking great idea** es una idea enorme

honor ['ɒnə(r)] *US n* = **honour**

honorable ['ɒnərəbəl] *US adj* = **honourable**

honorary ['ɒnərərɪ] *adj* [member] honorario(a) ; [duties] honorífico(a)

honour ['ɒnə(r)] **1.** *n* **a)** honor *m* **b)** *US* JUR **Her Honour / His Honour / Your Honour** Su Señoría *f* **c)** MIL **honours** honores *mpl* **d) Honours degree** licenciatura *f* superior **2.** *vt* **a)** [respect] honrar **b)** [obligation] cumplir con

honourable ['ɒnərəbəl] *adj* [person] honrado(a) ; [action] honroso(a)

hood [hʊd] n a) [of garment] capucha f b) Br [of car, pram] capota f; US [car bonnet] capó m c) US Fam [gangster] matón(ona) m,f

hoof [hu:f] (pl hoofs or hooves) n [of horse] casco m; [of cow, sheep] pezuña f

hook [hʊk] 1. n a) gancho m; [in fishing] anzuelo m; SEWING hooks and eyes corchetes mpl; to take the phone off the hook descolgar el teléfono b) [in boxing] gancho m 2. vt enganchar ▪ hook up vt sep & vi RADIO, TV & COMPUT conectar (with con)

hooked [hʊkt] adj a) [nose] aguileño(a) b) Fam [addicted] enganchado(a) (on a); to get hooked engancharse

hooligan ['hu:lɪgən] n Fam gamberro(a) m,f

hoot [hu:t] 1. n a) ululato m; Fam hoots of laughter carcajadas fpl; Fam I don't care a hoot me importa un pepino b) [of car horn] bocinazo m 2. vi a) [owl] ulular b) [car] dar un bocinazo; [train] silbar; [siren] pitar

hooter ['hu:tə(r)] n Br [of car] bocina f; [of ship, factory] sirena f

Hoover® ['hu:və(r)] Br 1. n aspiradora f 2. vt to Hoover® pasar la aspiradora por

hooves [hu:vz] pl of hoof

hop¹ [hɒp] 1. vi saltar; to hop on one leg andar a la pata coja 2. n [small jump] brinco m

hop² [hɒp] n BOT lúpulo m

hope [həʊp] 1. n esperanza f; [false] ilusión f; to have little hope of doing sth tener pocas posibilidades de hacer algo 2. vt & vi esperar; I hope so/not espero que sí/no; we hope you're well esperamos que estés bien

hopeful ['həʊpfʊl] adj [confident] optimista; [promising] prometedor(a)

hopefully ['həʊpfʊlɪ] adv a) [confidently] con optimismo b) hopefully the weather will be fine [it is hoped] esperemos que haga buen tiempo

hopeless ['həʊplɪs] adj desesperado(a); Fam to be hopeless at sports ser negado(a) para los deportes

horde [hɔ:d] n multitud f

horizon [hə'raɪzən] n horizonte m

horizontal [hɒrɪ'zɒntəl] adj horizontal

hormone ['hɔ:məʊn] n hormona f

horn [hɔ:n] n a) cuerno m b) Fam MUS trompeta f; French horn trompa f; hunting horn cuerno m de caza c) AUTO bocina f

horoscope ['hɒrəskəʊp] n horóscopo m

horrendous [hɒ'rendəs] adj horrendo(a)

horrible ['hɒrəbəl] adj horrible

horrid ['hɒrɪd] adj horrible

horrific [hə'rɪfɪk] adj horrendo(a)

horrify ['hɒrɪfaɪ] vt horrorizar

horror ['hɒrə(r)] n horror m; Fam a little horror un diablillo; horror film película f de miedo or de terror

horse [hɔ:s] n a) [animal] caballo m; horse race carrera f de caballos b) [tree] horse chestnut castaño m de Indias c) Fam & Fig to get on one's high horse echar un sermón

horseback ['hɔ:sbæk] n on horseback a caballo; US horseback riding equitación f

horsepower ['hɔ:spaʊə(r)] n caballo m (de vapor)

horseradish ['hɔ:s,rædɪʃ] n [plant] rábano m picante

horticulture ['hɔ:tɪkʌltʃə(r)] n horticultura f

hose [həʊz] n [pipe] manguera f

hosepipe ['həʊzpaɪp] n manguera f

hospitable ['hɒspɪtəbəl, hɒ'spɪtəbəl] adj hospitalario(a); hospitable atmosphere ambiente acogedor

hospital ['hɒspɪtəl] n hospital m

hospitality [hɒspɪ'tælɪtɪ] n hospitalidad f

host¹ [həʊst] 1. n a) [at home] anfitrión m b) THEAT & TV presentador m c) BIOL huésped m 2. vt THEAT & TV presentar

host² [həʊst] n [large number] montón m

hostage ['hɒstɪdʒ] n rehén m

hostel ['hɒstəl] n hostal m

hostess ['həʊstɪs] *n* **a)** [at home etc] anfitriona *f* **b)** THEAT & TV presentadora *f* **c) (air) hostess** azafata *f*

hostile ['hɒstaɪl, *US* 'hɒstəl] *adj* hostil

hostility [hɒ'stɪlɪtɪ] *n* hostilidad *f*

hosting ['hɒstɪŋ] *n* COMPUT [of web site] alojamiento *m*, hosting *m*; **hosting charge** costes *mpl* de alojamiento

hot [hɒt] *(compar* **hotter**, *superl* **hottest)** *adj* **a)** caliente; *Fig* **hot line** teléfono rojo **b)** [weather] caluroso(a); **it's very hot** hace mucho calor; **to feel hot** tener calor **c)** [spicy] picante; **hot dog** perrito *m* caliente, *Col, Méx* perro *m* caliente, *RP* pancho *m* **d)** [temper] fuerte **e)** *Fam* [good] bueno(a); **it's not so hot** no es nada del otro mundo **f)** [popular] popular ∎ **hot up** *vi Fam* [situation, contest] *Esp* calentarse, *Am* ponerse bravo(a)

hotcake ['hɒtkeɪk] *n US* crepe *f*, panqueque *m*, *Esp* tortita *f*

hotel [həʊ'tel] *n* hotel *m*

hot-headed [hɒt'hedɪd] *adj* impetuoso(a)

hotplate ['hɒtpleɪt] *n* [cooker] placa *f* de cocina; [to keep food warm] calientaplatos *m inv*

hotspot [hɒtspɒt] *n* [dangerous area] zona *f* conflictiva

hound [haʊnd] **1.** *n* perro *m* de caza **2.** *vt* acosar

hour ['aʊə(r)] *n* **a)** [period of time] hora *f*; **60 miles an hour** 60 millas por hora; **by the hour** por horas; **hour hand** manecilla *f* **b) hours** [of business] horario *m*

hourly ['aʊəlɪ] **1.** *adj* cada hora **2.** *adv* por horas

house 1. [haʊs] *n* **a)** casa *f*; **at my house** en mi casa; *Fig* **on the house** cortesía de la casa; **house plant** planta *f* de interior **b)** POL **House of Commons** Cámara *f* de los Comunes; **House of Lords** Cámara de los Lores; *US* **House of Representatives** Cámara de Representantes; **Houses of Parliament** Parlamento *m* **c)** [company] empresa *f*; **publishing house** editorial *f* **d)** THEAT sala *f* **2.** [haʊz] *vt* alojar; [store] guardar

housebound ['haʊsbaʊnd] *adj* to be **housebound** estar confinado(a) en casa

household ['haʊshəʊld] *n* hogar *m*; **household products** productos domésticos

housekeeper ['haʊskiːpə(r)] *n* ama *f* de llaves

housekeeping ['haʊskiːpɪŋ] *n* administración doméstica; **housekeeping money** dinero *m* para los gastos domésticos

house-sitter *n persona que cuida una casa en ausencia de sus ocupantes*

house-train ['haʊstreɪn] *vt* [pet] educar

house-warming ['haʊswɔːmɪŋ] *n* **house-warming (party)** fiesta *f* de inauguración

housewife ['haʊswaɪf] *n* ama *f* de casa

housework ['haʊswɜːk] *n* trabajo doméstico

housing ['haʊzɪŋ] *n* vivienda *f*; *US* **housing development** urbanización *f*; *Br* **housing estate** [public housing] ≈ viviendas *fpl* de protección oficial; [private housing] urbanización *f*, *Am* condominio *m*

hovel ['hʌvəl, 'hɒvəl] *n* casucha *f*

hover ['hɒvə(r)] *vi* [bird] cernerse; [aircraft] permanecer inmóvil (en el aire)

hovercraft ['hɒvəkrɑːft] *n* aerodeslizador *m*

how [haʊ] *adv* **a)** [direct question] ¿cómo?; **how are you?** ¿cómo estás?; *Fam* **how come?** ¿por qué?
b) [indirect question] cómo
c) [very] qué; **how funny!** ¡qué divertido!
d) [suggestion] **how about a drink?** ¿y si tomamos algo?; **how about going to the cinema?** ¿te apetece ir al cine?; **how about you?** ¿y tú?
e) [quantity] cuánto; **how old is she?** ¿cuántos años tiene?; **how tall are you?** ¿cuánto mides?; **how many days?** ¿cuántos días?; **how many**

nights? ¿cuántas noches?; **how much does it cost?** ¿cuánto cuesta?; **how much water?** ¿cuánta agua?

however [haʊ'evə(r)] *adv* **a)** [nevertheless] no obstante, sin embargo **b)** [with adjective] **however difficult it may be** por difícil que sea; **however much** por mucho que (+ *subj*)

howl [haʊl] **1.** *n* aullido *m* **2.** *vi* aullar

HP, hp [eɪtʃ'pi:] *n* **a)** *Br* (abbr of **hire purchase**) compra *f* a plazos **b)** (abbr of **horsepower**) cv *mpl*

HQ [eɪtʃ'kju:] *n* (abbr of **headquarters**) sede *f*, central *f*

HR *n* (abbr of **human resources**) RRHH (recursos humanos)

HRU MESSAGING (abbr of **how are you?**) q tal?, qtl?

h2cus MESSAGING written abbr of **hope to see you soon**

hub [hʌb] *n* AUTO cubo *m*; Fig eje *m*

hubcap ['hʌbkæp] *n* AUTO tapacubos *m* inv

huddle ['hʌdəl] **1.** *n* grupo *m* **2.** *vi* to **huddle (up** or **together)** acurrucarse

huff [hʌf] *n* **to be in a huff** estar de mala uva

hug [hʌg] **1.** *vt* abrazar **2.** *n* abrazo *m*; **free hugs** abrazos *mpl* gratis

huge [hju:dʒ] *adj* enorme

hull [hʌl] *n* NAUT casco *m*

hullo [hʌ'ləʊ] *interj* Br ¡hola!

hum [hʌm] **1.** *vt* [tune] tararear **2.** *vi* [bees, engine] zumbar; [sing] tararear **3.** *n* [of bees] zumbido *m*

human ['hju:mən] **1.** *adj* humano(a); **human race** raza humana; **human being** ser humano **2.** *n* ser humano

humane [hju:'meɪn] *adj* humano(a)

humanity [hju:'mænɪtɪ] *n* **a)** humanidad *f* **b)** UNIV **the humanities** las humanidades

humble ['hʌmbəl] **1.** *adj* humilde **2.** *vt* humillar

humid ['hju:mɪd] *adj* húmedo(a)

humidity [hju:'mɪdɪtɪ] *n* humedad *f*

humiliate [hju:'mɪlɪeɪt] *vt* humillar

humiliation [hju:mɪlɪ'eɪʃən] *n* humillación *f*

humility [hju:'mɪlɪtɪ] *n* humildad *f*

humongous [hju:'mʌŋgəs] *adj* US Fam enorme

humor ['hju:mə(r)] *US n* = **humour**

humorous ['hju:mərəs] *adj* [writer] humorístico(a); [person, story] gracioso(a), divertido(a)

humour ['hju:mə(r)] **1.** *n* humor *m* **2.** *vt* seguir la corriente a

hump [hʌmp] **1.** *n* **a)** [on back] joroba *f* **b)** [small hill] montículo *m* **2.** *vt* esp Br Fam [carry] acarrear

hunch [hʌntʃ] *n* Fam corazonada *f*

hundred ['hʌndrəd] **1.** *n* cien *m*, ciento *m*; [rough number] centenar *m*; **a hundred and twenty-five** ciento veinticinco; **five hundred** quinientos **2.** *adj* cien; **a hundred people** cien personas; **a hundred percent** cien por cien; **two hundred chairs** doscientas sillas

hundredth ['hʌndrədθ] *adj & n* centésimo(a) (*m,f*)

hundredweight ['hʌndrədweɪt] *n* Br = 50,8 kg; US = 45,36 kg

hung [hʌŋ] **1.** *adj* Fam **a) hung over** con resaca **b) hung up** acomplejado(a) **2.** *pt & pp of* **hang**

Hungarian [hʌŋ'geərɪən] *adj & n* húngaro(a) (*m,f*)

Hungary ['hʌŋgərɪ] *n* Hungría

hunger ['hʌŋgə(r)] **1.** *n* hambre *f*; **hunger strike** huelga *f* de hambre **2.** *vi* Fig tener hambre (**for** de)

hungry ['hʌŋgrɪ] (compar **hungrier**, superl **hungriest**) *adj* hambriento(a); **to be hungry** tener hambre; **to go hungry** pasar hambre

hunk [hʌŋk] *n* **a)** [piece] buen pedazo *m* **b)** Fam [man] machote *m*

hunt [hʌnt] **1.** *vt* cazar **2.** *vi* [for game] cazar; [search] buscar **3.** *n* caza *f*; [search] búsqueda *f* ■ **hunt down** *vt sep* perseguir

hunter ['hʌntə(r)] *n* cazador(a) *m,f*

hunting ['hʌntɪŋ] n caza f; [expedition] cacería f

hurdle ['hɜːdəl] n SPORT valla f; Fig obstáculo m

hurl [hɜːl] vt arrojar, lanzar

hurrah [huˈrɑː], **hurray** [huˈreɪ] interj ¡hurra!; **hurrah for John!** ¡viva John!

hurricane ['hʌrɪkən, US 'hʌrɪkeɪn] n huracán m

hurried ['hʌrɪd] adj apresurado(a); [action etc] hecho(a) deprisa

hurry ['hʌrɪ] **1.** vi darse prisa, apresurarse, Am apurarse
2. vt meter prisa a
3. n **to be in a hurry** tener prisa or Am apuro

hurt [hɜːt] (pt & pp hurt) **1.** vt hacer daño a; [wound] herir; [feelings] ofender
2. vi doler; **my arm hurts** me duele el brazo
3. adj [physically] herido(a); [mentally] dolido(a)

hurtful ['hɜːtfʊl] adj hiriente

hurtle ['hɜːtəl] vi lanzarse; **to hurtle down** desplomarse

husband ['hʌzbənd] n marido m, esposo m

hush [hʌʃ] **1.** vt callar; **to hush sth up** echar tierra a un asunto **2.** n silencio m **3.** interj ¡silencio!

husky[1] ['hʌskɪ] (compar huskier, superl huskiest) adj ronco(a)

husky[2] ['hʌskɪ] n [dog] perro m esquimal

hustle ['hʌsəl] **1.** vt a) [jostle] empujar b) Fam meter prisa a **2.** n bullicio m; **hustle and bustle** ajetreo m

hustler ['hʌslə(r)] n Fam [swindler] estafador(a) m,f

hut [hʌt] n cabaña f; [shed] cobertizo m; MIL barraca f

huzzah [həˈzɑː] interj ¡hurra!

hybrid ['haɪbrɪd] adj & n híbrido(a) (m,f)

hydrogen ['haɪdrədʒən] n hidrógeno m

hygiene ['haɪdʒiːn] n higiene f

hygienic [haɪˈdʒiːnɪk] adj higiénico(a)

hymn [hɪm] n himno m; **hymn book** cantoral m

hype [haɪp] n Fam campaña publicitaria, movida f

hyper- ['haɪpə(r)] pref hiper-; **hyperactive** hiperactivo(a)

hypermarket ['haɪpəmɑːkɪt] n Br hipermercado m

hyphen ['haɪfən] n guión m

hypnotize ['hɪpnətaɪz] vt hipnotizar

hypochondriac [haɪpəˈkɒndriæk] adj & n hipocondríaco(a) (m,f)

hypocrisy [hɪˈpɒkrəsɪ] n hipocresía f

hypocrite ['hɪpəkrɪt] n hipócrita mf

hypocritical [hɪpəˈkrɪtɪkəl] adj hipócrita

hypothesis [haɪˈpɒθɪsɪs] (pl **hypotheses** [haɪˈpɒθɪsiːz]) n hipótesis f

hypothetic(al) [haɪpəˈθetɪk(əl)] adj hipotético(a)

hysterical [hɪˈsterɪkəl] adj histérico(a)

hysterics [hɪˈsterɪks] npl **a)** ataque m de histeria **b)** Fam [of laughter] ataque m de risa

I, i [aɪ] *n* [the letter] I, i *f*

I [aɪ] *pers pron* yo *(usually omitted in Spanish, except for contrast)*; **I know her** (yo) la conozco

ice [aɪs] **1.** *n* hielo *m*; **ice axe** pico *m* (de alpinista); **ice cream** helado *m*, *Am* sorbete; **ice cube** cubito *m* de hielo; **ice hockey** hockey *m* sobre hielo; *Br* **ice lolly** polo *m*; **ice rink** pista *f* de patinaje; **ice skate** patín *m* de cuchilla **2.** *vt* [cake] alcorzar ▪ **ice over, ice up** *vi* [pond etc] helarse; [windscreen, plane wings] cubrirse de hielo

iceberg ['aɪsbɜːg] *n* iceberg *m*

icebox ['aɪsbɒks] *n* **a)** *Br* [compartment of fridge] congelador *m* **b)** *US* [fridge] nevera *f*, *Méx* refrigerador *m*, *RP* heladera *f*

Iceland ['aɪslənd] *n* Islandia

ice-skating ['aɪsskeɪtɪŋ] *n* patinaje *m* sobre hielo

icicle ['aɪsɪkəl] *n* carámbano *m*

icing ['aɪsɪŋ] *n* alcorza *f*; *Br* **icing sugar** azúcar *m Esp*, *Méx* glas *or Chile* flor *or RP* impalpable

icon ['aɪkɒn] *n* [gen & COMPUT] icono *m*

icy ['aɪsɪ] *(compar* **icier***, superl* **iciest***) adj* [road etc] helado(a); *Fig* [smile] glacial

ID [aɪ'diː] *n US* documentación *f*; **ID card** DNI *m*

I'd [aɪd] **a)** = **I would b)** = **I had**

idea [aɪ'dɪə] *n* **a)** idea *f* **b)** [aim] intención *f* **c)** [impression] impresión *f*

ideal [aɪ'dɪəl] *adj* & *n* ideal *(m)*

idealistic [aɪdɪə'lɪstɪk] *adj* idealista

ideally [aɪ'dɪəlɪ] *adv* **a)** [perfectly] perfectamente **b)** [in the best conditions] de ser posible

identical [aɪ'dentɪkəl] *adj* idéntico(a)

identification [aɪdentɪfɪ'keɪʃən] *n* **a)** identificación *f* **b)** [papers] documentación *f*

identify [aɪ'dentɪfaɪ] **1.** *vt* [body] identificar; [cause] descubrir **2.** *vi* identificarse **(with** con)

identity [aɪ'dentɪtɪ] *n* identidad *f*; **identity card** carné *m* de identidad; **identity theft** robo *m* de identidad; **proof of identity** prueba *f* de identidad

ideology [aɪdɪ'ɒlədʒɪ] *n* ideología *f*

idiom ['ɪdɪəm] *n* modismo *m*; *Fig* [style] lenguaje *m*

idiot ['ɪdɪət] *n* idiota *mf*, tonto(a) *m,f*

idiotic [ɪdɪ'ɒtɪk] *adj* [behaviour] idiota, tonto(a); [joke, plan] estúpido(a)

IDK MESSAGING *written abbr of* **I don't know**

idle ['aɪdəl] **1.** *adj* holgazán(ana); [not working-person] desempleado(a); [machinery] parado(a); [gossip] frívolo(a); [threat] vano(a) **2.** *vi* [engine] funcionar en vacío ▪ **idle away** *vt sep* [time] desperdiciar

idol ['aɪdəl] *n* ídolo *m*

idolize ['aɪdəlaɪz] *vt* idolatrar

i.e. *(abbr of* **id est***)* i.e.

if [ɪf] **1.** *conj* **a)** si; **if not** si no; **if so** de ser así; **if I were you** yo en tu lugar; **if only she were here!** ¡ojalá estuviera aquí! **b)** [whenever] si; **if you need help, ask** siempre que necesites ayuda, pídela **2.** *n* **ifs and buts** pegas *fpl*

ignition [ɪg'nɪʃən] *n* ignición *f*; AUTO encendido *m*; **ignition key** llave *f* de contacto

ignorance ['ɪgnərəns] *n* ignorancia *f*

ignorant ['ɪgnərənt] *adj* ignorante **(of** de); **to be ignorant of the facts** ignorar *or* desconocer los hechos

ignore

ignore [ɪgˈnɔː(r)] *vt* [warning, remark] no hacer caso de ; [behaviour, fact] pasar por alto

ill [ɪl] **1.** *adj* **a)** enfermo(a) ; **to feel ill** encontrarse mal
b) [bad] malo(a) ; **ill feeling** resentimiento *m* ; **ill will** mala voluntad
2. *n* mal *m*
3. *adv* difícilmente

I'll [aɪl] **a)** = **I shall b)** = **I will**

illegal [ɪˈliːgəl] *adj* ilegal

illegible [ɪˈledʒɪbəl] *adj* ilegible

illegitimate [ɪlɪˈdʒɪtɪmɪt] *adj* ilegítimo(a)

ill-fitting *adj* [garment, lid, window] que no ajusta bien

ill-humoured, *US* **ill-humored** *adj* malhumorado(a)

illicit [ɪˈlɪsɪt] *adj* ilícito(a)

ill-intentioned [-ɪnˈtenʃənd] *adj* malintencionado(a)

illiterate [ɪˈlɪtərɪt] *adj* [person] analfabeto(a) ; *Fam* [uneducated] inculto(a)

ill-matched *adj* que no pega

illness [ˈɪlnɪs] *n* enfermedad *f*

illogical [ɪˈlɒdʒɪkəl] *adj* ilógico(a)

illuminate [ɪˈluːmɪneɪt] *vt* **a)** [light up] iluminar, alumbrar ; *Fig* [clarify] aclarar
b) [manuscript] iluminar

illusion [ɪˈluːʒən] *n* ilusión *f* ; **to be under the illusion that ...** engañarse pensando que ...

illustrate [ˈɪləstreɪt] *vt* ilustrar

illustration [ɪləˈstreɪʃən] *n* ilustración *f* ; [example] ejemplo *m*

image [ˈɪmɪdʒ] *n* imagen *f*

imaginary [ɪˈmædʒɪnərɪ] *adj* imaginario(a)

imagination [ɪmædʒɪˈneɪʃən] *n* imaginación *f* ; [inventiveness] inventiva *f*

imaginative [ɪˈmædʒɪnətɪv] *adj* imaginativo(a)

imagine [ɪˈmædʒɪn] *vt* [visualize] imaginar ; [think] suponer, imaginarse ; **just imagine!** ¡imagínate!

imitate [ˈɪmɪteɪt] *vt* imitar

imitation [ɪmɪˈteɪʃən] **1.** *n* imitación *f*, copia *f* ; *Pej* remedo *m* **2.** *adj* de imitación

immaculate [ɪˈmækjʊlɪt] *adj* [clean] inmaculado(a) ; [tidy] perfectamente ordenado(a) ; [clothes] impecable ; [work] perfecto(a) ; **the Immaculate Conception** la Inmaculada Concepción

immature [ɪməˈtjʊə(r)] *adj* inmaduro(a)

immediate [ɪˈmiːdɪət] *adj* **a)** inmediato(a) ; [urgent] urgente **b)** [close] cercano(a) ; [danger] inminente **c)** [cause] primero(a)

immediately [ɪˈmiːdɪətlɪ] **1.** *adv* **a)** inmediatamente **b)** [directly] directamente **2.** *conj* en cuanto

immense [ɪˈmens] *adj* inmenso(a), enorme

immensely [ɪˈmenslɪ] *adv* [rich] enormemente ; [interesting, difficult] sumamente

immerse [ɪˈmɜːs] *vt* sumergir (**in** en) ; *Fig* **to be immersed in sth** estar absorto(a) en algo

immigrant [ˈɪmɪgrənt] *adj & n* inmigrante *(mf)*

immigrate [ˈɪmɪgreɪt] *vi* inmigrar

immigration [ɪmɪˈgreɪʃən] *n* inmigración *f*

imminent [ˈɪmɪnənt] *adj* inminente

immobile [ɪˈməʊbaɪl] *adj* inmóvil

immoral [ɪˈmɒrəl] *adj* inmoral

immortal [ɪˈmɔːtəl] *adj* inmortal

immune [ɪˈmjuːn] *adj* inmune ; [exempt] exento(a) ; **immune system** sistema *m* inmunológico

immunize [ˈɪmjʊnaɪz] *vt* inmunizar (**against** contra)

IMO MESSAGING *written abbr of* **in my opinion**

impact [ˈɪmpækt] *n* impacto *m* ; [crash] choque *m*

impair [ɪmˈpeə(r)] *vt* perjudicar ; [sight etc] dañar

impartial [ɪmˈpɑːʃəl] *adj* imparcial

impassive [ɪmˈpæsɪv] *adj* impasible

impatient [ɪmˈpeɪʃənt] *adj* impaciente; [fretful] irritable; **to get impatient** perder la paciencia

impending [ɪmˈpendɪŋ] *adj Formal* inminente

imperative [ɪmˈperətɪv] **1.** *adj Formal* imperativo(a); [tone] imperioso(a); [urgent] urgente **2.** *n* LING imperativo *m*

imperfect [ɪmˈpɜːfɪkt] **1.** *adj* imperfecto(a); [goods] defectuoso(a) **2.** *n* LING imperfecto *m*

imperial [ɪmˈpɪərɪəl] *adj* **a)** imperial **b)** [measure] **imperial gallon** galón británico *(aprox 4,546 l)*

impersonal [ɪmˈpɜːsənəl] *adj* impersonal

impersonate [ɪmˈpɜːsəneɪt] *vt* hacerse pasar por; [famous people] imitar

impertinent [ɪmˈpɜːtɪnənt] *adj* impertinente

impetus [ˈɪmpɪtəs] *n* ímpetu *m*; *Fig* impulso *m*

implant 1. [ɪmˈplɑːnt] *vt* MED implantar **2.** [ˈɪmplɑːnt] *n* MED implantación *f*

implement 1. [ˈɪmplɪmənt] *n* [tool] herramienta *f*; [instrument] instrumento *m*; **farm implements** aperos *mpl* de labranza **2.** [ˈɪmplɪment] *vt* [decision, plan] llevar a cabo; [law, policy] aplicar

implicate [ˈɪmplɪkeɪt] *vt* implicar (**in** en)

implication [ɪmplɪˈkeɪʃən] *n* implicación *f*; [consequence] consecuencia *f*

implicit [ɪmˈplɪsɪt] *adj* [implied] implícito(a); [trust] absoluto(a); [faith] incondicional

implore [ɪmˈplɔː(r)] *vt* implorar, suplicar

imply [ɪmˈplaɪ] *vt* **a)** [involve] implicar **b)** [hint] dar a entender; [mean] significar

impolite [ɪmpəˈlaɪt] *adj* maleducado(a)

import 1. [ˈɪmpɔːt] *n* **a)** COMM [usu pl] importación *f*; **import duty** derechos *mpl* de importación **b)** *Formal* [meaning] sentido *m* **2.** [ɪmˈpɔːt] *vt* COMM & COMPUT importar

importance [ɪmˈpɔːtəns] *n* importancia *f*; [standing] envergadura *f*; **of little importance** de poca monta

important [ɪmˈpɔːtənt] *adj* importante; **it's not important** no importa

importer [ɪmˈpɔːtə(r)] *n* COMM importador(a) *m,f*

impose [ɪmˈpəʊz] **1.** *vt* imponer (**on** *or* **upon** a) **2.** *vi* **to impose on** *or* **upon** [take advantage of] abusar de

imposing [ɪmˈpəʊzɪŋ] *adj* imponente, impresionante

imposition [ɪmpəˈzɪʃən] *n* [of tax etc] imposición *f*; [unfair demand] abuso *m*; **would it be an imposition if ...?** ¿le molestaría si ...?

impossibility [ɪmpɒsəˈbɪlɪtɪ] *n* imposibilidad *f*

impossible [ɪmˈpɒsəbəl] **1.** *adj* imposible; [person] insoportable **2.** *n* **to do the impossible** hacer lo imposible

impostor [ɪmˈpɒstə(r)] *n* impostor(a) *m,f*

impotent [ˈɪmpətənt] *adj* impotente

impractical [ɪmˈpræktɪkəl] *adj* [person] poco práctico(a); [project, solution etc] poco viable

imprecise [ɪmprɪˈsaɪs] *adj* impreciso(a)

impress [ɪmˈpres] *vt* **a)** impresionar; **to impress sb favourably / unfavourably** dar a algn buena / mala impresión **b)** [mark] imprimir (**on** en); [pattern] estampar (**on** en); *Fig* **to impress sth on sb** convencer a algn de la importancia de algo

impression [ɪmˈpreʃən] *n* **a)** impresión *f*; **to be under the impression that ...** tener la impresión de que ...; **to give the impression of ...** dar la impresión de ... **b)** [imprint] marca *f*; [in snow] huella *f* **c)** [imitation] imitación *f*

impressive [ɪmˈpresɪv] *adj* impresionante

imprint 1. [ɪmˈprɪnt] *vt* [mark] dejar huella (**on** en) **2.** [ˈɪmprɪnt] *n* **a)** [mark] marca *f*; [left by foot etc] huella *f* **b)** [publisher's name] pie *m* de imprenta

imprison [ɪmˈprɪzən] *vt* encarcelar

imprisonment [ɪm'prɪzənmənt] *n* encarcelamiento *m*

improbable [ɪm'prɒbəbəl] *adj* [event] improbable; [story] inverosímil

improper [ɪm'prɒpə(r)] *adj* **a)** impropio(a); [method] inadecuado(a) **b)** [indecent] indecente; [behaviour] deshonesto(a) **c)** [wrong] incorrecto(a)

improve [ɪm'pruːv] **1.** *vt* mejorar; [knowledge] perfeccionar; [mind] cultivar; [increase] aumentar **2.** *vi* mejorarse; [increase] aumentar ■ **improve on** *vt insep* superar; [offer, bid] sobrepujar

improvement [ɪm'pruːvmənt] *n* mejora *f*; [in skill] perfeccionamiento *m*; [increase] aumento *m*

improvise ['ɪmprəvaɪz] *vt* & *vi* improvisar

impudent ['ɪmpjʊdənt] *adj* insolente

impulse ['ɪmpʌls] *n* impulso *m*; **to act on (an) impulse** dejarse llevar por un impulso

impulsive [ɪm'pʌlsɪv] *adj* irreflexivo(a)

impurity [ɪm'pjʊərɪtɪ] *n* **a)** [of act] deshonestidad *f* **b)** (*usu pl*) [in air, substance] impureza *f*

in [ɪn] **1.** *prep* **a)** [place] en; [within] dentro de; **in bed** en la cama; **in Brazil** en Brasil; **in prison** en la cárcel
b) [motion] en; **she arrived in Paris** llegó a París
c) [time-during] en, durante; **I haven't seen her in years** hace años que no la veo; **in May/1945** en mayo/1945; **in spring** en primavera; **in the daytime** durante el día; **in the morning** por la mañana; **at ten in the morning** a las diez de la mañana
d) [time-within] dentro de; **I arrived in time** llegué a tiempo
e) [time-after] al cabo de
f) [manner] en; **in a loud/quiet voice** en voz alta/baja; **in fashion** de moda; **in French** en francés; **in writing** por escrito; **write in pencil** escribe con lápiz
g) [wearing] en; **dressed in blue** vestido(a) de azul; **in uniform** de uniforme

h) [weather etc] a, en; **in the rain** bajo la lluvia; **in the sun** al sol; **in darkness** en la oscuridad; **in daylight** a la luz del día
i) [state, emotion] en; **in danger/public/silence** en peligro/público/silencio; **in love** enamorado(a); **in tears** llorando
j) [ratio, numbers] de; **in threes** de tres en tres; **one in six** uno de cada seis; **2 m in length** 2 m de largo
k) [after superlative] de; **the smallest car in the world** el coche más pequeño del mundo
l) [phrases] **in all** en total; **in itself/himself/herself** en sí; **in that...** dado que...
2. *adv* **in here/there** aquí/allí dentro; **let's go in** vamos adentro; **to be in** [at home] estar (en casa); [at work] estar; [tide] estar alta; *Fam* [in fashion] estar de moda; **the bus is in** el autobús ha llegado; *Fam* **to be in on sth** estar enterado(a) de algo
3. *adj Fam* **a)** [fashionable - place] de moda; [clothes] del último grito
b) **an in joke** una broma privada
4. *n Fam* **ins and outs** detalles *mpl*

inability [ɪnə'bɪlɪtɪ] *n* incapacidad *f*

inaccessible [ɪnæk'sesəbəl] *adj* inaccesible

inaccurate [ɪn'ækjʊrɪt] *adj* inexacto(a); [statement] erróneo(a); [figures, total] incorrecto(a)

inadequate [ɪn'ædɪkwɪt] *adj* **a)** [lacking] insuficiente **b)** [not capable] incapaz; [unsuitable] inadecuado(a) **c)** [defective] defectuoso(a)

inanimate [ɪn'ænɪmɪt] *adj* inanimado(a)

inappropriate [ɪnə'prəʊprɪɪt] *adj* inoportuno(a); [behaviour] poco apropiado(a)

inauguration [ɪnɔːgjʊ'reɪʃən] *n* [of building] inauguración *f*; [of president] investidura *f*

inbox ['ɪnbɒks] *n* COMPUT buzón *m* de entrada

Inc, inc *US* COMM (*abbr of* **Incorporated**) ≃ S.A.

incalculable [ɪnˈkælkjʊləbəl] *adj* incalculable

incapable [ɪnˈkeɪpəbəl] *adj* incapaz

incense¹ [ˈɪnsens] *n* incienso *m*

incense² [ɪnˈsens] *vt* enfurecer, sacar de quicio

incentive [ɪnˈsentɪv] *n* incentivo *m*

incentive-based *adj* basado(a) en incentivos

incest [ˈɪnsest] *n* incesto *m*

inch [ɪntʃ] *n* pulgada *f*; *Fig* **inch by inch** poco a poco; *Fig* **she wouldn't give an inch** no quería ceder ni un ápice ▪ **inch forward** *vt sep* & *vi* avanzar poco a poco

incident [ˈɪnsɪdənt] *n* incidente *m*

incidental [ɪnsɪˈdentəl] *adj* [accessory] incidental, accesorio(a); [risk] inherente (**to** a); **incidental music** música *f* de fondo

incidentally [ɪnsɪˈdentəlɪ] *adv* a propósito

incinerator [ɪnˈsɪnəreɪtə(r)] *n* incinerador *m*

incision [ɪnˈsɪʒən] *n* incisión *f*

incisive [ɪnˈsaɪsɪv] *adj* [comment] incisivo(a); [reply] tajante; [mind] penetrante

incite [ɪnˈsaɪt] *vt* incitar; **to incite sb to do sth** incitar a algn a hacer algo

inclination [ɪnklɪˈneɪʃən] *n* inclinación *f*; **my inclination is to stay** yo prefiero quedarme

incline [ɪnˈklaɪn] **1.** *vt* **a)** **I'm inclined to believe him** me inclino a creerlo; **she's inclined to be aggressive** tiende a ser agresiva
b) [head etc] inclinar
2. *vi* [slope] inclinarse
3. [ˈɪnklaɪn] *n* [slope] pendiente *f*

include [ɪnˈkluːd] *vt* incluir (**in** en); [in price] comprender (**in** en); [in list] figurar (**in** en)

including [ɪnˈkluːdɪŋ] *prep* incluso, inclusive

inclusive [ɪnˈkluːsɪv] *adj* inclusivo(a); **pages 6 to 10 inclusive** de la página 6 a la 10, ambas inclusive; **the rent is inclusive of bills** el alquiler incluye las facturas

incoherent [ɪnkəʊˈhɪərənt] *adj* incoherente

income [ˈɪnkʌm] *n* ingresos *mpl*; [from investment] réditos *mpl*; **annual income** ingresos *mpl* anuales; **income tax** impuesto *m* sobre la renta; **income tax return** declaración *f* de la renta

incomparable [ɪnˈkɒmpərəbəl] *adj* incomparable, sin par

incompatible [ɪnkəmˈpætəbəl] *adj* incompatible (**with** con)

incompetent [ɪnˈkɒmpɪtənt] *adj* incompetente

incomplete [ɪnkəmˈpliːt] *adj* incompleto(a)

incomprehensible [ɪnkɒmprɪˈhensəbəl] *adj* incomprensible

inconceivable [ɪnkənˈsiːvəbəl] *adj* inconcebible

inconclusive [ɪnkənˈkluːsɪv] *adj* [vote] no decisivo(a); [proof] no concluyente

inconsiderate [ɪnkənˈsɪdərɪt] *adj* desconsiderado(a); **how inconsiderate of you!** ¡qué falta de consideración por tu parte!

inconsistent [ɪnkənˈsɪstənt] *adj* inconsecuente; [contradictory] contradictorio(a); **your evidence is inconsistent with the facts** su testimonio no concuerda con los hechos

inconspicuous [ɪnkənˈspɪkjʊəs] *adj* que pasa desapercibido(a); [discreet] discreto(a)

inconvenience [ɪnkənˈviːnɪəns] **1.** *n* inconveniente *f*; [annoyance] molestia *f*
2. *vt* [annoy] molestar; [cause difficulty to] incomodar

inconvenient [ɪnkənˈviːnɪənt] *adj* molesto(a); [time] inoportuno(a); [design] poco práctico(a)

incorporate [ɪnˈkɔːpəreɪt] *vt* incorporar (**in** *or* **into** a); [include] incluir; [contain] contener

incorrect

incorrect [ɪnkəˈrekt] *adj* incorrecto(a)

increase 1. [ˈɪnkriːs] *n* aumento *m*; [in number] incremento *m*; [in price etc] subida *f* **2.** [ɪnˈkriːs] *vt* aumentar; [price etc] subir **3.** [ɪnˈkriːs] *vi* aumentar

increasing [ɪnˈkriːsɪŋ] *adj* creciente

increasingly [ɪnˈkriːsɪŋlɪ] *adv* cada vez más

incredible [ɪnˈkredəbəl] *adj* increíble

incredulous [ɪnˈkredjʊləs] *adj* incrédulo(a)

increment [ˈɪnkrɪmənt] *n* incremento *m*

incriminate [ɪnˈkrɪmɪneɪt] *vt* incriminar

incriminating [ɪnˈkrɪmɪneɪtɪŋ] *adj* incriminatorio(a)

incubator [ˈɪnkjʊbeɪtə(r)] *n* incubadora *f*

incur [ɪnˈkɜː(r)] *vt* [blame] incurrir en; [risk] correr; [debt] contraer; [loss] sufrir

incurable [ɪnˈkjʊərəbəl] *adj* incurable

indebted [ɪnˈdetɪd] *adj* endeudado(a); *Fig* [grateful] agradecido(a); *Fig* **to be indebted to sb** estar en deuda con algn

indecent [ɪnˈdiːsənt] *adj* indecente; **indecent assault** atentado *m* contra el pudor; **indecent exposure** exhibicionismo *m*

indecisive [ɪndɪˈsaɪsɪv] *adj* [person] indeciso(a); [evidence] poco concluyente; [victory] no decisivo(a)

indeed [ɪnˈdiːd] *adv* **a)** *Formal* [in fact] efectivamente, en realidad **b) I'm very sorry indeed** lo siento de veras; **it's very hard indeed** es verdaderamente difícil; **thank you very much indeed** muchísimas gracias

indefinite [ɪnˈdefɪnɪt] *adj* indefinido(a)

indefinitely [ɪnˈdefɪnɪtlɪ] *adv* indefinidamente

independence [ɪndɪˈpendəns] *n* independencia *f*; *US* **Independence Day** *fiesta de la independencia en Estados Unidos, el cuatro de julio*

independent [ɪndɪˈpendənt] *adj* independiente; *Br* **independent school** colegio *m* privado; **to become independent** independizarse

indescribable [ɪndɪsˈkraɪbəbəl] *adj* [pain, beauty] indescriptible

indestructible [ɪndɪˈstrʌktəbəl] *adj* indestructible

index [ˈɪndeks] **1.** *(pl* **indexes** *or* **indices)** *n* **a)** [in book] índice *m*; [in library] catálogo *m*; **index card** ficha *f* **b)** MATH exponente *m*; ECON índice *m* **c) index finger** dedo *m* índice **2.** *vt* catalogar

India [ˈɪndɪə] *n* (la) India

Indian [ˈɪndɪən] *adj* & *n* [of America] indio(a) *(m,f)*, *Am* indígena *(mf)*; [of India] hindú *(mf)*; **Indian Ocean** Océano Índico; **Indian Summer** veranillo *m* de San Martín

indicate [ˈɪndɪkeɪt] **1.** *vt* indicar **2.** *vi* AUTO poner el intermitente

indication [ɪndɪˈkeɪʃən] *n* indicio *m*

indicator [ˈɪndɪkeɪtə(r)] *n* indicador *m*; *Br* AUTO intermitente *m*

indifferent [ɪnˈdɪfərənt] *adj* **a)** [uninterested] indiferente **b)** [mediocre] regular

indigestion [ɪndɪˈdʒestʃən] *n* indigestión *f*; **to suffer from indigestion** tener un empacho

indignant [ɪnˈdɪgnənt] *adj* indignado(a); [look] de indignación; **to get indignant about sth** indignarse por algo

indirect [ɪndɪˈrekt, ɪndaɪˈrekt] *adj* indirecto(a)

indiscreet [ɪndɪsˈkriːt] *adj* indiscreto(a)

indiscriminate [ɪndɪsˈkrɪmɪnɪt] *adj* indiscriminado(a)

indispensable [ɪndɪsˈpensəbəl] *adj* indispensable, imprescindible

indisputable [ɪndɪsˈpjuːtəbəl] *adj* indiscutible, incontestable

indistinct [ɪndɪsˈtɪŋkt] *adj* indistinto(a); [memory] confuso(a), vago(a); [shape etc] borroso(a)

indistinguishable [ɪndɪsˈtɪŋgwɪʃəbəl] *adj* indistinguible

individual [ɪndɪ'vɪdjʊəl] **1.** *adj* **a)** [separate] individual; [for one] particular; [personal] personal **b)** [characteristic] particular; [original] original **2.** *n* [person] individuo *m*; **private individual** particular *m*

indoctrinate [ɪn'dɒktrɪneɪt] *vt* adoctrinar

Indonesia [ɪndəʊ'niːzɪə] *n* Indonesia

indoor ['ɪndɔː(r)] *adj* [plant] de interior; **indoor football** fútbol *m* sala; **indoor pool** piscina cubierta

indoors [ɪn'dɔːz] *adv* [inside] dentro (de casa); [at home] en casa; **let's go indoors** vamos adentro

induce [ɪn'djuːs] *vt* **a)** [persuade] inducir, persuadir **b)** [cause] producir; MED [labour] provocar

induction [ɪn'dʌkʃn] *n* inducción *f*; **induction hob** placa *f* de inducción

indulge [ɪn'dʌldʒ] **1.** *vt* **a)** [child] consentir; [person] complacer; **to indulge oneself** darse gusto **b)** [whim] ceder a, satisfacer **2.** *vi* darse el gusto (**in** de)

indulgent [ɪn'dʌldʒənt] *adj* indulgente

industrial [ɪn'dʌstrɪəl] *adj* industrial; **to take industrial action** declararse en huelga; *Br* **industrial estate**, *US* **industrial park** polígono *m* industrial

industrialist [ɪn'dʌstrɪəlɪst] *n* industrial *mf*

industrialize [ɪn'dʌstrɪəlaɪz] *vt* industrializar; **to become industrialized** industrializarse

industrious [ɪn'dʌstrɪəs] *adj* trabajador(a)

industry ['ɪndəstrɪ] *n* **a)** industria *f* **b)** [diligence] aplicación *f*

inedible [ɪn'edəbəl] *adj* incomible

ineffective [ɪnɪ'fektɪv] *adj* ineficaz

ineffectual [ɪnɪ'fektʃʊəl] *adj* [aim, protest] ineficaz; [person] incompetente

inefficient [ɪnɪ'fɪʃənt] *adj* ineficaz; [person] inepto(a)

inept [ɪn'ept] *adj* [person] inepto(a); [remark] estúpido(a)

inequality [ɪnɪ'kwɒlɪtɪ] *n* desigualdad *f*

inert [ɪn'ɜːt] *adj* inerte

inescapable [ɪnɪ'skeɪpəbəl] *adj* ineludible

inevitable [ɪn'evɪtəbəl] *adj* inevitable

inexcusable [ɪnɪk'skjuːzəbəl] *adj* inexcusable, imperdonable

inexpensive [ɪnɪk'spensɪv] *adj* económico(a)

inexperienced [ɪnɪk'spɪərɪənst] *adj* inexperto(a)

inexplicable [ɪnɪk'splɪkəbəl] *adj* inexplicable

infallible [ɪn'fæləbəl] *adj* infalible

infamous ['ɪnfəməs] *adj* infame

infant ['ɪnfənt] *n* niño(a) *m,f*; *Br* **infant school** parvulario *m*

infantry ['ɪnfəntrɪ] *n* infantería *f*

infatuated [ɪn'fætjʊeɪtɪd] *adj* encaprichado(a)

infect [ɪn'fekt] *vt* [cut] infectar; [water] contaminar; [person] contagiar

infection [ɪn'fekʃən] *n* [of cut] infección *f*; [of water] contaminación *f*; [with illness] contagio *m*

infectious [ɪn'fekʃəs] *adj* [disease] infeccioso(a); *Fig* contagioso(a)

infer [ɪn'fɜː(r)] *vt* inferir (**from** de)

inferior [ɪn'fɪərɪə(r)] **1.** *adj* inferior (**to** a) **2.** *n Pej* inferior *mf*

inferiority [ɪnfɪərɪ'ɒrɪtɪ] *n* inferioridad *f*

infest [ɪn'fest] *vt* infestar, plagar (**with** de)

infidelity [ɪnfɪ'delɪtɪ] *n* infidelidad *f*

infiltrate ['ɪnfɪltreɪt] *vt* infiltrarse (**into** en)

infinite ['ɪnfɪnɪt] *adj* infinito(a)

infinitive [ɪn'fɪnɪtɪv] *n* infinitivo *m*

infinity [ɪn'fɪnɪtɪ] *n* infinidad *f*; MATH infinito *m*

infirmary [ɪn'fɜːmərɪ] *n* hospital *m*

inflamed [ɪn'fleɪmd] *adj* inflamado(a); **to become inflamed** inflamarse

inflammable [ɪn'flæməbəl] *adj* [material] inflamable; *Fig* [situation] explosivo(a)

inflammation [ɪnfləˈmeɪʃən] n inflamación f

inflatable [ɪnˈfleɪtəbəl] adj inflable

inflate [ɪnˈfleɪt] **1.** vt inflar **2.** vi inflarse

inflation [ɪnˈfleɪʃən] n inflación f

inflexible [ɪnˈfleksəbəl] adj inflexible

inflict [ɪnˈflɪkt] vt [blow] asestar (**on** a); [damage] causar (**on** a); [defeat] infligir (**on** a)

influence [ˈɪnfluəns] **1.** n influencia f; Fam **to be under the influence** llevar una copa de más **2.** vt influir en

influential [ɪnfluˈenʃəl] adj influyente

influenza [ɪnfluˈenzə] n gripe f

influx [ˈɪnflʌks] n afluencia f

info [ˈɪnfəʊ] n Fam información f

inform [ɪnˈfɔːm] **1.** vt informar (**of** or **about** de or sobre); [police] avisar (**of** or **about** de) **2.** vi **to inform against** or **on** denunciar

informal [ɪnˈfɔːməl] adj **a)** [occasion, behaviour] informal; [language, treatment] familiar **b)** [unofficial] no oficial

informality [ɪnfɔːˈmælɪtɪ] n [of occasion, behaviour] sencillez f; [of treatment] familiaridad f

information [ɪnfəˈmeɪʃən] n información f; [details] detalles mpl; [facts] datos mpl; [knowledge] conocimientos mpl; [news] noticias fpl; **a piece of information** un dato; **information bureau** centro m de información; **information desk** mostrador m de información; **information (super)highway** autopista f de la información; **information technology** informática f, tecnologías fpl de la información

informative [ɪnˈfɔːmətɪv] adj informativo(a)

infrequent [ɪnˈfriːkwənt] adj infrecuente

infringe [ɪnˈfrɪndʒ] **1.** vt [law, rule] infringir; [copyright] no respetar **2.** vi **to infringe on** or **upon** [rights] violar; [privacy] invadir

infuriating [ɪnˈfjʊərɪeɪtɪŋ] adj exasperante

ingenious [ɪnˈdʒiːnɪəs] adj ingenioso(a)

ingrained [ɪnˈɡreɪnd] adj Fig arraigado(a)

ingredient [ɪnˈɡriːdɪənt] n ingrediente m

inhabit [ɪnˈhæbɪt] vt vivir en, ocupar

inhabitant [ɪnˈhæbɪtənt] n habitante mf

inhale [ɪnˈheɪl] **1.** vt [gas] inhalar; [air] aspirar **2.** vi aspirar; [smoker] tragar el humo

inherent [ɪnˈhɪərənt] adj inherente

inherit [ɪnˈherɪt] vt heredar (**from** de)

inheritance [ɪnˈherɪtəns] n herencia f

inhibit [ɪnˈhɪbɪt] vt [freedom] limitar; [person] cohibir; **to inhibit sb from doing sth** impedir a algn hacer algo

inhibition [ɪnhɪˈbɪʃən] n cohibición f

inhospitable [ɪnhɒˈspɪtəbəl] adj inhospitalario(a); [climate, place] inhóspito(a)

inhuman [ɪnˈhjuːmən] adj inhumano(a)

inhumane [ɪnhjuːˈmeɪn] adj inhumano(a)

initial [ɪˈnɪʃəl] **1.** adj inicial, primero(a) **2.** n **a)** inicial f **b) initials** [of name] iniciales fpl; [of abbreviation] siglas fpl **3.** (pt & pp **initialled**, US pt & pp **initialed**) vt firmar con las iniciales

initially [ɪˈnɪʃəlɪ] adv al principio

initiate [ɪˈnɪʃɪeɪt] vt **a)** iniciar; [reform] promover; [lawsuit] entablar **b)** [into society] admitir (**into** en); [into knowledge] iniciar (**into** en)

initiative [ɪˈnɪʃətɪv] n iniciativa f

inject [ɪnˈdʒekt] vt **a)** [drug etc] inyectar **b)** Fig [capital] invertir; [life, hope] infundir

injection [ɪnˈdʒekʃən] n **a)** inyección f **b)** Fig [of capital] inversión f

injure [ˈɪndʒə(r)] vt herir; **to injure oneself** hacerse daño; Fig [health, reputation] perjudicar

injured [ˈɪndʒəd] **1.** adj herido(a); Fig [look, tone] ofendido(a) **2.** npl **the injured** los heridos

injury ['ɪndʒərɪ] n [hurt] herida f; Fig [harm] daño m; SPORT **injury time** (tiempo m de) descuento m

injustice [ɪn'dʒʌstɪs] n injusticia f

ink [ɪŋk] n tinta f; **invisible ink** tinta simpática

inkjet ['ɪŋkdʒet] n COMPUT **inkjet printer** impresora f de chorro de tinta

inland 1. ['ɪnlənd] adj (del) interior; Br **Inland Revenue** ≃ Hacienda f **2.** [ɪn'lænd] adv [travel] tierra adentro

in-laws ['ɪnlɔːz] npl Fam familia f política

inlet ['ɪnlet] n a) [in coastline] ensenada f, cala f b) [in pipe, machine] entrada f, admisión f

inmate ['ɪnmeɪt] n [of prison] preso(a) m,f; [of hospital] enfermo(a) m,f; [of asylum, camp] internado(a) m,f

inn [ɪn] n [with lodging] posada f, mesón m

innate [ɪ'neɪt] adj innato(a)

inner ['ɪnə(r)] adj a) [region] interior; [structure] interno(a); **inner city** zona urbana desfavorecida; **inner tube** cámara f de aire b) Fig [thoughts] íntimo(a); [peace etc] interior

innermost ['ɪnəməʊst] adj [room] más interior; Fig [thoughts] más íntimo(a)

innocent ['ɪnəsənt] adj & n inocente (mf)

innovate ['ɪnəveɪt] vi & vt innovar

innovation [ɪnə'veɪʃən] n novedad f

innumerable [ɪ'njuːmərəbəl] adj innumerable

inoculate [ɪ'nɒkjʊleɪt] vt inocular

inoculation [ɪnɒkjʊ'leɪʃən] n inoculación f

inpatient ['ɪnpeɪʃənt] n interno(a) m,f

input ['ɪnpʊt] n [of resources] inversión f; [of power] entrada f; COMPUT [of data] input m, entrada

inquest ['ɪnkwest] n investigación f judicial

inquire [ɪn'kwaɪə(r)] **1.** vt preguntar; [find out] averiguar **2.** vi preguntar (about por); [find out] informarse (about de) ▪ **inquire after** vt insep preguntar por ▪ **inquire into** vt insep investigar, indagar

inquiry [ɪn'kwaɪərɪ] n a) pregunta f; Br **inquiry desk** mostrador m de información b) [investigation] investigación f c) **inquiries** [sign] información

inquisitive [ɪn'kwɪzɪtɪv] adj [curious] curioso(a); [questioning] preguntón(ona)

insane [ɪn'seɪn] adj loco(a); [act] insensato(a); Fig **to drive sb insane** volver loco(a) a algn

inscription [ɪn'skrɪpʃən] n [on stone, coin] inscripción f; [in book, on photo] dedicatoria f

insect ['ɪnsekt] n insecto m; **insect bite** picadura f

insecure [ɪnsɪ'kjʊə(r)] adj inseguro(a)

insensitive [ɪn'sensɪtɪv] adj insensible

inseparable [ɪn'sepərəbəl] adj inseparable

insert 1. ['ɪnsɜːt] n encarte m **2.** [ɪn'sɜːt] vt introducir

inside [ɪn'saɪd] **1.** n a) interior m; **on the inside** por dentro; **to turn sth inside out** volver algo al revés b) Fam **insides** tripas fpl **2.** ['ɪnsaɪd] adj interior; AUTO **inside lane** carril m interior **3.** adv [be] dentro, adentro; [run etc] (hacia) adentro; **to come inside** entrar **4.** prep a) [place] dentro de b) Fam **inside (of)** [time] en menos de

insider [ɪn'saɪdə(r)] n **insider dealing** uso indebido de información privilegiada y confidencial para operaciones comerciales

insight ['ɪnsaɪt] n perspicacia f

insignificant [ɪnsɪg'nɪfɪkənt] adj insignificante

insincere [ɪnsɪn'sɪə(r)] adj poco sincero(a)

insinuate [ɪn'sɪnjʊeɪt] vt insinuar

insipid [ɪn'sɪpɪd] adj soso(a), insulso(a)

insist [ɪn'sɪst] **1.** *vi* insistir (**on** en); [argue] obstinarse (**on** en) **2.** *vt* to insist that … insistir en que …

insistence [ɪn'sɪstəns] *n* insistencia *f*

insistent [ɪn'sɪstənt] *adj* insistente

in so far as [ɪnsəʊ'fɑːrəz] *adv* en tanto que

insolent ['ɪnsələnt] *adj* insolente

insoluble [ɪn'sɒljʊbəl] *adj* insoluble

insolvent [ɪn'sɒlvənt] *adj* FIN insolvente

insomnia [ɪn'sɒmnɪə] *n* insomnio *m*

inspect [ɪn'spekt] *vt* inspeccionar, examinar; [troops] pasar revista a

inspector [ɪn'spektə(r)] *n* inspector(a) *m,f*; *Br* [on bus, train] revisor(a) *m,f*

inspiration [ɪnspɪ'reɪʃən] *n* inspiración *f*; **to get inspiration from sb / sth** inspirarse en algn / algo

inspire [ɪn'spaɪə(r)] *vt* **a)** inspirar; **to inspire respect in sb** infundir respeto a algn **b) to inspire sb to do sth** animar a algn a hacer algo

instability [ɪnstə'bɪlɪtɪ] *n* inestabilidad *f*

install, *US* **instal** [ɪn'stɔːl] *vt* [machinery, person & COMPUT] instalar

instalment, *US* **installment** [ɪn'stɔːlmənt] *n* **a)** [of payment] plazo *m*; **to pay by instalments** pagar a plazos; *US* **instalment plan** venta *f* / compra *f* a plazos **b)** [of novel, programme] entrega *f*; [of journal] fascículo *m*

instance ['ɪnstəns] *n* caso *m*, ejemplo *m*; **for instance** por ejemplo; **in the first instance** en primer lugar

instant ['ɪnstənt] **1.** *n* [moment] instante *m*, momento *m*; **in an instant** en un instante **2.** *adj* inmediato(a); [coffee, meal] instantáneo(a); **instant access** de acceso inmediato; **instant messaging** mensajería *f* instantánea

instantaneous [ɪnstən'teɪnɪəs] *adj* instantáneo(a)

instantly ['ɪnstəntlɪ] *adv* inmediatamente

instead [ɪn'sted] **1.** *adv* en cambio **2.** *prep* **instead of** en vez de, en lugar de

instigate ['ɪnstɪgeɪt] *vt* [strike, violence] instigar; [inquiry, changes] iniciar

instinct ['ɪnstɪŋkt] *n* instinto *m*

instinctive [ɪn'stɪŋktɪv] *adj* instintivo(a)

institute ['ɪnstɪtjuːt] **1.** *n* instituto *m*; [centre] centro *m*; [professional body] colegio *m* **2.** *vt Formal* **a)** [system] establecer **b)** [start] iniciar; [proceedings] entablar

institution [ɪnstɪ'tjuːʃən] *n* **a)** institución *f* **b)** [home] asilo *m*; [asylum] manicomio *m*

instruct [ɪn'strʌkt] *vt* instruir; [order] mandar; **I am instructed to say that** … me han encargado decir que …

instruction [ɪn'strʌkʃən] *n* **a)** instrucción *f* **b) instructions** instrucciones *fpl*; **instructions for use** modo de empleo

instructor [ɪn'strʌktə(r)] *n* instructor(a) *m,f*; [of driving] profesor(a) *m,f*

instrument ['ɪnstrəmənt] *n* instrumento *m*; **instrument panel** tablero *m* de mandos

instrumental [ɪnstrə'mentəl] *adj* **a)** MUS instrumental **b) to be instrumental in sth** contribuir decisivamente a algo

insufficient [ɪnsə'fɪʃənt] *adj* insuficiente

insulate ['ɪnsjʊleɪt] *vt* aislar (**against** or **from** de)

insulation [ɪnsjʊ'leɪʃən] *n* aislamiento *m*

insulin ['ɪnsjʊlɪn] *n* insulina *f*

insult **1.** ['ɪnsʌlt] *n* [words] insulto *m*; [action] afrenta *f*, ofensa *f* **2.** [ɪn'sʌlt] *vt* insultar, ofender

insurance [ɪn'ʃʊərəns] *n* seguro *m*; **fire insurance** seguro contra incendios; **insurance broker** agente *mf* de seguros; **insurance company** compañía *f* de seguros; **insurance policy** póliza *f* (de seguros); **private health insurance** seguro médico privado

insure [ɪn'ʃʊə(r)] *vt* asegurar (**against** contra)

intact [ɪn'tækt] *adj* intacto(a)

intake ['ɪnteɪk] *n* **a)** [of air, water] entrada *f*; [of electricity etc] toma *f* **b)** [of food, calories] consumo *m* **c)** [of students, recruits] número *m* de admitidos

integral ['ɪntɪɡrəl] **1.** *adj* **a)** [intrinsic] integrante **b)** [whole] íntegro(a) **c)** MATH integral **2.** *n* MATH integral *f*

integrate ['ɪntɪɡreɪt] **1.** *vt* integrar **2.** *vi* integrarse

integrity [ɪn'teɡrɪtɪ] *n* integridad *f*, honradez *f*

intellect ['ɪntɪlekt] *n* intelecto *m*

intellectual [ɪntɪ'lektʃʊəl] *adj & n* intelectual *(mf)*

intelligence [ɪn'telɪdʒəns] *n* **a)** inteligencia *f* **b)** [information] información *f*

intelligent [ɪn'telɪdʒənt] *adj* inteligente

intelligible [ɪn'telɪdʒəbəl] *adj* inteligible

intend [ɪn'tend] *vt* **a)** [mean] tener la intención de **b)** to intend sth for sb destinar algo a algn

intended [ɪn'tendɪd] *adj* [planned] previsto(a)

intense [ɪn'tens] *adj* intenso(a); [person] muy serio(a)

intensify [ɪn'tensɪfaɪ] *vt* [search] intensificar; [effort] redoblar; [production, pollution] aumentar

intensity [ɪn'tensɪtɪ] *n* intensidad *f*

intensive [ɪn'tensɪv] *adj* intensivo(a); MED **intensive care unit** unidad *f* de vigilancia intensiva

intent [ɪn'tent] **1.** *adj* [absorbed] absorto(a); [gaze etc] atento(a); **to be intent on doing sth** estar resuelto(a) a hacer algo **2.** *n Formal* intención *f*, propósito *m*; **to all intents and purposes** a todos los efectos

intention [ɪn'tenʃən] *n* intención *f*

intentional [ɪn'tenʃənəl] *adj* deliberado(a)

interact [ɪntər'ækt] *vi* [people] interrelacionarse

interactive [ɪntər'æktɪv] *adj* interactivo(a); **interactive whiteboard** pizarra *f* interactiva

intercept [ɪntə'sept] *vt* interceptar

interchange 1. ['ɪntətʃeɪndʒ] *n* **a)** [exchange] intercambio *m* **b)** [on motorway] cruce *m* **2.** [ɪntə'tʃeɪndʒ] *vt* intercambiar (**with** con)

interchangeable [ɪntə'tʃeɪndʒəbəl] *adj* intercambiable

intercom ['ɪntəkɒm] *n* portero automático

intercourse ['ɪntəkɔːs] *n* **a)** [dealings] trato *m* **b)** [sexual] relaciones *fpl* sexuales

interest ['ɪntrɪst] **1.** *n* **a)** interés *m* **b)** [advantage] provecho *m*; **in the interest of** en pro de **c)** COMM [share] participación *f* **d)** FIN interés *m*; **interest rate** tipo *m* de interés **2.** *vt* interesar; **he's interested in politics** le interesa la política

interesting ['ɪntrɪstɪŋ] *adj* interesante

interface ['ɪntəfeɪs] *n* **a)** [interaction] interacción *f* **b)** COMPUT interfaz *f*

interfere [ɪntə'fɪə(r)] *vi* **a)** [meddle] entrometerse (**in** en); **to interfere with** [hinder] dificultar; [spoil] estropear; [prevent] impedir **b)** RADIO & TV interferir (**with** con)

interference [ɪntə'fɪərəns] *n* [meddling] intromisión *f*; [hindrance] estorbo *m*; RADIO & TV interferencia *f*

interim ['ɪntərɪm] **1.** *n Formal* **in the interim** en el ínterin **2.** *adj* interino(a), provisional

interior [ɪn'tɪərɪə(r)] **1.** *adj* interior **2.** *n* interior *m*; **interior design** diseño *m* de interiores

interlude ['ɪntəluːd] *n* [break] intervalo *m*; CIN & THEAT intermedio *m*; MUS interludio *m*

intermediary [ɪntə'miːdɪərɪ] *n* intermediario(a) *m,f*

intermediate [ɪntə'miːdɪt] *adj* intermedio(a)

intermission [ɪntə'mɪʃən] *n* CIN & THEAT intermedio *m*

intern 1. [ɪn'tɜːn] *vt* recluir **2.** ['ɪntɜːn] *n US* MED médico(a) *m,f* interno(a) residente

internal [ɪn'tɜ:nəl] *adj* interior; [dispute, injury] interno(a); *US* **Internal Revenue Service** ≃ Hacienda *f*

international [ɪntə'næʃənəl] **1.** *adj* internacional **2.** *n* SPORT [player] internacional *mf*; [match] partido *m* internacional

Internet ['ɪntənet] *n* COMPUT **the Internet** internet; **it's on the Internet** está en internet; **Internet access provider** proveedor *m* de acceso a internet; **Internet address** dirección *f* de internet; **Internet café** cibercafé *m*; **Internet service provider** proveedor *m* de (acceso a) internet

interpret [ɪn'tɜ:prɪt] **1.** *vt* interpretar **2.** *vi* actuar de intérprete

interpretation [ɪntɜ:prɪ'teɪʃən] *n* interpretación *f*

interpreter [ɪn'tɜ:prɪtə(r)] *n* intérprete *mf*

interrogate [ɪn'terəgeɪt] *vt* interrogar

interrogation [ɪnterə'geɪʃən] *n* interrogatorio *m*

interrupt [ɪntə'rʌpt] *vt & vi* interrumpir

interruption [ɪntə'rʌpʃən] *n* interrupción *f*

intersect [ɪntə'sekt] **1.** *vt* cruzar **2.** *vi* cruzarse

intersection [ɪntə'sekʃən] *n* **a)** [crossroads] cruce *m* **b)** [of two lines] intersección *f*

interstate ['ɪntəsteɪt] *n US* autopista *f* interestatal

interval ['ɪntəvəl] *n* **a)** [of time, space] intervalo *m*; **at intervals** [time, space] a intervalos; [time] de vez en cuando **b)** *Br* CIN & THEAT intermedio *m*

intervene [ɪntə'vi:n] *vi* **a)** [person] intervenir (**in** en) **b)** [event] sobrevenir **c)** [time] transcurrir

intervention [ɪntə'venʃən] *n* intervención *f*

interview ['ɪntəvju:] **1.** *n* entrevista *f*; **to give an interview** conceder una entrevista **2.** *vt* entrevistar

interviewer ['ɪntəvju:ə(r)] *n* entrevistador(a) *m,f*

intestine [ɪn'testɪn] *n* [usu pl] intestino *m*; **large/small intestine** intestino grueso/delgado

intimate¹ ['ɪntɪmɪt] *adj* íntimo(a); [knowledge] profundo(a)

intimate² ['ɪntɪmeɪt] *vt Formal* dar a entender

intimidate [ɪn'tɪmɪdeɪt] *vt* intimidar

into ['ɪntu:] (*unstressed* ['ɪntə]) *prep* **a)** [motion] en, a, con; **he fell into the water** se cayó al agua; **to go into a house** entrar en una casa **b)** [state] en, a; **to change pounds into euros** cambiar libras en *or* por euros; **to translate sth into French** traducir algo al francés **c)** [to divide sth into three** dividir algo en tres **d)** *Fam* **to be into sth** ser aficionado(a) a algo

intolerable [ɪn'tɒlərəbəl] *adj* intolerable

intolerance [ɪn'tɒlərəns] *n* intolerancia *f*

intolerant [ɪn'tɒlərənt] *adj* intolerante

intonation [ɪntə'neɪʃən] *n* entonación *f*

intoxicated [ɪn'tɒksɪkeɪtɪd] *adj* borracho(a)

intransitive [ɪn'trænsɪtɪv] *adj* intransitivo(a)

intrigue 1. [ɪn'tri:g, 'ɪntri:g] *n* intriga *f* **2.** [ɪn'tri:g] *vt* intrigar **3.** [ɪn'tri:g] *vi* intrigar, conspirar

introduce [ɪntrə'dju:s] *vt* **a)** [person, programme] presentar (**to** a) **b)** [bring in] introducir (**into** *or* **to** en); COMM lanzar (**into** *or* **to** a); [topic] proponer

introduction [ɪntrə'dʌkʃən] *n* **a)** [of person, programme] presentación *f*; [in book] introducción *f* **b)** [bringing in] introducción *f*; COMM [of product] lanzamiento *m*

introductory [ɪntrə'dʌktərɪ] *adj* introductorio(a); [remarks] preliminar; COMM de lanzamiento

introvert ['ɪntrəvɜ:t] *n* introvertido(a) *m,f*

intrude [ɪn'tru:d] *vi* entrometerse (**into** *or* **on** en); [disturb] molestar

intruder [ɪn'tru:də(r)] *n* intruso(a) *m,f*

intrusion [ɪn'tru:ʒən] *n* incursión *f*

intuition [ɪntjʊ'ɪʃən] n intuición f

inundate ['ɪnʌndeɪt] vt inundar (**with** de)

invade [ɪn'veɪd] vt invadir

invader [ɪn'veɪdə(r)] n invasor(a) m,f

invalid¹ ['ɪnvəlɪd] n [disabled person] minusválido(a) m,f; [sick person] enfermo(a) m,f

invalid² [ɪn'vælɪd] adj inválido(a), nulo(a)

invalidate [ɪn'vælɪdeɪt] vt invalidar

invaluable [ɪn'væljʊəbəl] adj inestimable

invariably [ɪn'veərɪəblɪ] adv invariablemente

invasion [ɪn'veɪʒən] n invasión f

invent [ɪn'vent] vt inventar

invention [ɪn'venʃən] n invento m; [creativity] inventiva f; [lie] mentira f

inventor [ɪn'ventə(r)] n inventor(a) m,f

inventory ['ɪnvəntərɪ] n inventario m

invest [ɪn'vest] **1.** vt invertir (**in** en); **to invest sb with sth** conferir algo a algn **2.** vi invertir (**in** en)

investigate [ɪn'vestɪgeɪt] vt [crime, subject] investigar; [cause, possibility] estudiar

investigation [ɪnvestɪ'geɪʃən] n [of crime] investigación f; [of cause] examen m

investigator [ɪn'vestɪgeɪtə(r)] n investigador(a) m,f; **private investigator** detective privado

investment [ɪn'vestmənt] n inversión f

investor [ɪn'vestə(r)] n inversor(a) m,f

invigorating [ɪn'vɪgəreɪtɪŋ] adj vigorizante

invincible [ɪn'vɪnsəbəl] adj invencible

invisible [ɪn'vɪzəbəl] adj invisible

invitation [ɪnvɪ'teɪʃən] n invitación f

invite [ɪn'vaɪt] vt **a)** invitar (**to** a) **b)** [comments etc] solicitar; [criticism] provocar; **to invite trouble** buscarse problemas

invoice ['ɪnvɔɪs] **1.** n factura f **2.** vt facturar

invoke [ɪn'vəʊk] vt Formal invocar

involuntary [ɪn'vɒləntərɪ] adj involuntario(a)

involve [ɪn'vɒlv] vt **a)** [concern] implicar (**in** en); **the issues involved** las cuestiones en juego; **to be involved in an accident** sufrir un accidente **b)** [entail] suponer, implicar; [trouble, risk] acarrear

involved [ɪn'vɒlvd] adj [complicated] complicado(a); Fam [romantically attached] enredado(a), liado(a)

involvement [ɪn'vɒlvmənt] n [participation] participación f; [in crime] implicación f

invulnerable [ɪn'vʌlnərəbəl] adj invulnerable

inward ['ɪnwəd] **1.** adj interior **2.** adv = **inwards**

inwards ['ɪnwədz] adv hacia dentro

iodine ['aɪədiːn] n yodo m

IOU [aɪəʊ'juː] n (abbr of **I owe you**) pagaré m

IP n (abbr of **Internet Protocol**) IP **address** dirección f IP

iPod® ['aɪpɒd] n iPod® m

iPodder ['aɪpɒdə(r)] n usuario(a) m,f de iPod

IQ [aɪ'kjuː] n (abbr of **intelligence quotient**) CI m

IRA [aɪɑː'reɪ] n **a)** (abbr of **Irish Republican Army**) IRA m **b)** US (abbr of **individual retirement account**) cuenta f de retiro or jubilación individual

Iran [ɪ'rɑːn] n Irán

Iraq [ɪ'rɑːk] n Irak

irate [aɪ'reɪt] adj airado(a), furioso(a)

IRC n (abbr of **Internet Relay Chat**) IRC m (charla en tiempo real)

Ireland ['aɪələnd] n Irlanda; **Republic of Ireland** República de Irlanda

iris ['aɪərɪs] n **a)** ANAT iris m inv **b)** BOT lirio m

Irish ['aɪrɪʃ] **1.** adj irlandés(esa); **Irish coffee** café m irlandés; **Irish Sea** Mar m de Irlanda **2.** n **a)** [language] irlandés m **b)** (pl) **the Irish** los irlandeses

Irishman ['aɪrɪʃmən] *n* irlandés *m*

Irishwoman ['aɪrɪʃwʊmən] *n* irlandesa *f*

iron ['aɪən] **1.** *n* **a)** hierro *m*; **the iron and steel industry** la industria siderúrgica **b)** [for clothes] plancha *f* **2.** *vt* [clothes] planchar ▪ **iron out** *vt sep* **a)** [crease] planchar **b)** *Fam & Fig* [problem] resolver

ironic(al) [aɪ'rɒnɪk(əl)] *adj* irónico(a)

ironing ['aɪənɪŋ] *n* **a) to do the ironing** planchar; **ironing board** mesa *f* de la plancha **b)** [clothes to be ironed] ropa *f* para planchar; [clothes ironed] ropa planchada

ironmonger ['aɪənmʌŋgə(r)] *n Br* ferretero(a) *m,f*; **ironmonger's (shop)** ferretería *f*

irony ['aɪrənɪ] *n* ironía *f*

irrational [ɪ'ræʃənəl] *adj* irracional

irregular [ɪ'regjʊlə(r)] *adj* **a)** irregular; [abnormal] anormal **b)** [uneven] desigual

irrelevant [ɪ'reləvənt] *adj* no pertinente

irresistible [ɪrɪ'zɪstəbəl] *adj* irresistible

irrespective [ɪrɪ'spektɪv] *adj* **irrespective of** sin tener en cuenta

irresponsible [ɪrɪ'spɒnsəbəl] *adj* irresponsable

irreverent [ɪ'revərənt] *adj* irreverente

irrigate ['ɪrɪgeɪt] *vt* regar

irritable ['ɪrɪtəbəl] *adj* irritable

irritate ['ɪrɪteɪt] *vt* [annoy] fastidiar; MED irritar

irritating ['ɪrɪteɪtɪŋ] *adj* irritante

is [ɪz] *see* **be**

Islam ['ɪzlɑːm] *n* Islam *m*

Islamic [ɪz'læmɪk] *adj* islámico(a)

island ['aɪlənd] *n* isla *f*; **(traffic) island** isleta *f*

isle [aɪl] *n* isla *f*

isn't ['ɪzənt] = **is not**

isolate ['aɪsəleɪt] *vt* aislar **(from** de)

isolated ['aɪsəleɪtɪd] *adj* aislado(a)

isolation [aɪsə'leɪʃən] *n* aislamiento *m*

ISP [aɪes'piː] *n* COMPUT *(abbr of* **Internet Service Provider)** PSI *m*

Israel ['ɪzreɪəl] *n* Israel

Israeli [ɪz'reɪlɪ] *adj & n* israelí *(mf)*

ISS ['aɪes'es] *n US* SCH *(abbr of* **In School Suspension)** expulsión *f* temporal de clase *(pero permaneciendo en el centro)*

issue ['ɪʃuː] **1.** *n* **a)** [matter] cuestión *f*; **to take issue with sb (over sth)** manifestar su desacuerdo con algn (en algo) **b)** [of magazine] ejemplar *m* **c)** *Formal* [outcome] resultado *m* **d)** JUR [offspring] descendencia *f* **2.** *vt* **a)** [book] publicar; [banknotes etc] emitir; [passport] expedir **b)** [supplies] repartir **c)** [order, instructions] dar; [warrant] dictar

it [ɪt] *pers pron* **a)** [subject] él /ella /ello *(usually omitted in Spanish, except for contrast)*; **it's here** está aquí
b) [direct object] lo /la; **I don't believe it** no me lo creo; **I liked the house and bought it** me gustó la casa y la compré
c) [indirect object] le; **give it a kick** dale una patada
d) [after prep] él /ella /ello; **I saw the beach and ran towards it** vi la playa y fui corriendo hacia ella; **we'll talk about it later** ya hablaremos de ello
e) [abstract] ello; **let's get down to it!** ¡vamos a ello!
f) [impersonal] **it's late** es tarde; **it's me** soy yo; **it's raining** está lloviendo; **it's 2 miles to town** hay 2 millas de aquí al pueblo; **who is it?** ¿quién es?

IT *n (abbr of* **information technology)** informática *f*

Italian [ɪ'tæljən] **1.** *adj* italiano(a) **2.** *n* **a)** [person] italiano(a) *m,f* **b)** [language] italiano *m*

italic [ɪ'tælɪk] *n* cursiva *f*

Italy ['ɪtəlɪ] *n* Italia

itch [ɪtʃ] **1.** *n* picor *m*; *Fig* **an itch to travel** unas ganas locas de viajar **2.** *vi* **a)** [skin] picar **b)** *Fig* anhelar; *Fam* **to be itching to do sth** tener muchas ganas de hacer algo

itchy ['ɪtʃɪ] *adj* que pica; **to be itchy** picar

item ['aɪtəm] *n* **a)** [in list] artículo *m*; [in collection] pieza *f*; **item of clothing** prenda *f* de vestir **b)** [on agenda] asunto *m*; [in show] número *m*; **news item** noticia *f*

itemize ['aɪtəmaɪz] *vt* detallar

it-girl *n Fam* joven cuya ocupación es ser famosa; **she's the it-girl** es la chica de la que habla todo el mundo

itinerary [aɪ'tɪnərərɪ] *n* itinerario *m*

its [ɪts] *poss adj* [one thing] su; [more than one] sus

itself [ɪt'self] *pers pron* **a)** [reflexive] se; **the cat scratched itself** el gato se arañó **b)** [emphatic] él mismo / ella misma / ello mismo; [after prep] sí (mismo(a)); **in itself** en sí

ivory ['aɪvərɪ] *n* marfil *m*

ivy ['aɪvɪ] *n* hiedra *f*

IWB *n* = interactive whiteboard

IYD MESSAGING *written abbr of* **in your dreams**

J

J, j [dʒeɪ] *n* [the letter] J, j *f*

jab [dʒæb] **1.** *n* pinchazo *m* ; [poke] golpe seco **2.** *vt* pinchar ; [with fist] dar un puñetazo a

jack [dʒæk] *n* **a)** AUTO gato *m* **b)** CARDS sota *f* **c)** [bowls] boliche *m* ■ **jack in** *vt sep Br Fam* [job] dejar ■ **jack up** *vt sep Fam* [price, salaries] subir

jacket [ˈdʒækɪt] *n* **a)** [coat - formal] chaqueta *f*, americana *f*, *Am* saco *m* ; [casual] cazadora *f* ; [bomber jacket] cazadora *f* **b)** [of book] sobrecubierta *f* ; *US* [of record] funda *f* **c) jacket potatoes** patatas *fpl* or *Am* papas *fpl* al horno

jackpot [ˈdʒækpɒt] *n* (premio *m*) gordo *m*

jagged [ˈdʒægɪd] *adj* dentado(a)

jail [dʒeɪl] **1.** *n* cárcel *f*, prisión *f* **2.** *vt* encarcelar

jam¹ [dʒæm] *n* CULIN mermelada *f*

jam² [dʒæm] **1.** *n* [blockage] atasco *m* ; *Fam* [fix] apuro *m* **2.** *vt* **a)** [cram] meter a la fuerza **b)** [block] atascar ; RADIO interferir **3.** *vi* [door] atrancarse ; [brakes] agarrotarse

jammin' [ˈdʒæmɪn] *adj US Fam* [doing well] **we're jammin'** vamos super bien

jam-packed [dʒæmˈpækt] *adj Fam* [with people] atestado(a) ; [with things] atiborrado(a)

jangle [ˈdʒæŋgəl] *vi* tintinear

janitor [ˈdʒænɪtə(r)] *n US, Scot* [caretaker] conserje *m*, bedel *m*

January [ˈdʒænjuərɪ] *n* enero *m*

Japan [dʒəˈpæn] *n* (el) Japón

Japanese [dʒæpəˈniːz] **1.** *adj* japonés(esa) **2.** *n* [person] japonés(esa) *m,f* ; [language] japonés *m*

jar¹ [dʒɑː(r)] *n* [container] tarro *m* ; *Br Fam* **to have a jar** tomar una copa

jar² [dʒɑː(r)] *vi* [sounds] chirriar ; [appearance] chocar ; [colours] desentonar ; *Fig* **to jar on one's nerves** ponerle a uno los nervios de punta

jargon [ˈdʒɑːgən] *n* jerga *f*, argot *m*

jaunt [dʒɔːnt] *n* [walk] paseo *m* ; [trip] excursión *f*

javelin [ˈdʒævəlɪn] *n* jabalina *f*

jaw [dʒɔː] **1.** *n* mandíbula *f* **2.** *vi Fam* estar de palique

jaywalking [ˈdʒeɪwɔːkɪŋ] *n* imprudencia *f* peatonal

jazz [dʒæz] *n* jazz *m* ■ **jazz up** *vt sep* alegrar ; [premises] arreglar

jealous [ˈdʒeləs] *adj* celoso(a) ; [envious] envidioso(a) ; **to be jealous of ...** tener celos de ...

jealousy [ˈdʒeləsɪ] *n* celos *mpl* ; [envy] envidia *f*

jeans [dʒiːnz] *npl* vaqueros *mpl*, tejanos *mpl*

Jeep® [dʒiːp] *n* jeep *m*, todo terreno *m* inv

jeer [dʒɪə(r)] **1.** *n* [boo] abucheo *m* ; [mocking] mofa *f* **2.** *vi* [boo] abuchear ; [mock] burlarse

jeering [ˈdʒɪərɪŋ] *adj* burlón(ona)

jeez [dʒiːz] *interj US Fam* ¡caray!

Jell-O®, jello [ˈdʒeləʊ] *n US* gelatina *f*

jelly [ˈdʒelɪ] *n Br* [dessert] gelatina *f* ; *esp US* [jam] mermelada *f*, confitura *f*

jellyfish [ˈdʒelɪfɪʃ] *n* medusa *f*

jeopardize [ˈdʒepədaɪz] *vt* poner en peligro ; [agreement etc] comprometer

jeopardy [ˈdʒepədɪ] *n* riesgo *m*, peligro *m*

jerk [dʒɜːk] **1.** *n* **a)** [jolt] sacudida *f*; [pull] tirón *m*
b) *Pej* [idiot] imbécil *mf*
2. *vt* [shake] sacudir; [pull] dar un tirón a
3. *vi* [move suddenly] dar una sacudida

jersey ['dʒɜːzɪ] *n* jersey *m*, suéter *m*, pulóver *m*, *Andes* chompa *f*, *Urug* buzo *m*

jest [dʒest] **1.** *n* broma *f* **2.** *vi* bromear

Jesus ['dʒiːzəs] *n* Jesús *m*; **Jesus Christ** Jesucristo *m*

jet¹ [dʒet] **1.** *n* **a)** [stream of water] chorro *m* **b)** [spout] surtidor *m* **c)** AVIAT reactor *m*; **jet engine** reactor *m*; **jet lag** *cansancio debido al desfase horario*; **jet ski** moto náutica *or* acuática **2.** *vi* *Fam* volar

jet² [dʒet] *n* **jet black** negro(a) como el azabache

jetty ['dʒetɪ] *n* muelle *m*, malecón *m*

Jew [dʒuː] *n* judío(a) *m,f*

jeweller, *US* **jeweler** ['dʒuːələ(r)] *n* joyero(a) *m,f*; **jeweller's (shop)** joyería *f*

jewellery, *US* **jewelry** ['dʒuːəlrɪ] *n* joyas *fpl*, alhajas *fpl*

Jewish ['dʒuːɪʃ] *adj* judío(a)

jibe [dʒaɪb] *n* & *vi* = **gibe**

jiffy ['dʒɪfɪ] *n* *Fam* momento *m*; **in a jiffy** en un santiamén; **just a jiffy!** ¡un momento!

jigsaw ['dʒɪgsɔː] *n* [puzzle] rompecabezas *m inv*

jingle ['dʒɪŋgəl] **1.** *n* RADIO & TV *canción que acompaña a un anuncio* **2.** *vi* tintinear

jinx [dʒɪŋks] **1.** *n* [person] gafe *mf* **2.** *vt* gafar

JIT *adj (abbr of just in time)* justo a tiempo, JAT

jitters ['dʒɪtəz] *npl* *Fam* **to get the jitters** tener canguelo

JK MESSAGING *written abbr of* **just kidding**

job [dʒɒb] *n* **a)** trabajo *m*; [task] tarea *f* **b)** [occupation] (puesto *m* de) trabajo *m*, empleo *m*; [trade] oficio *m*; *US* **job office** oficina *f* de empleo; **job sharing** trabajo compartido a tiempo parcial
c) *Fam* **we had a job to ...** nos costó (trabajo) ... **d)** *Br Fam* **it's a good job that ...** menos mal que ...

jobless ['dʒɒblɪs] *adj* parado(a)

job-share 1. *n* trabajo *m* compartido **2.** *vi* compartir el trabajo

jockey ['dʒɒkɪ] **1.** *n* jinete *m*, jockey *m* **2.** *vi* **to jockey for position** luchar para conseguir una posición aventajada

jog [dʒɒg] **1.** *n* trote *m* **2.** *vt* empujar; *Fig* [memory] refrescar **3.** *vi* SPORT hacer footing

jogging ['dʒɒgɪŋ] *n* footing *m*

john [dʒɒn] *n* *US Fam* **the john** [lavatory] el váter

join [dʒɔɪn] **1.** *vt* **a)** juntar; **to join forces with sb** unir fuerzas con algn
b) [road] empalmar con; [river] desembocar en
c) [meet] reunirse con
d) [group] unirse a; [institution] entrar; [army] alistarse a
e) [party] afiliarse a; [club] hacerse socio(a) de
2. *vi* **a)** unirse
b) [roads] empalmar; [rivers] confluir
c) [become member of political party] afiliarse; [become member of club] hacerse socio(a)
3. *n* juntura *f*
■ **join in 1.** *vi* participar, tomar parte; [debate] intervenir **2.** *vt insep* participar en, tomar parte en
■ **join up 1.** *vt sep* juntar **2.** *vi* [of roads] unirse; MIL alistarse

joiner ['dʒɔɪnə(r)] *n* *Br* carpintero(a) *m,f*

joint [dʒɔɪnt] **1.** *n* **a)** juntura *f*, unión *f*; TECH & ANAT articulación *f* **b)** CULIN *corte de carne para asar*; [once roasted] asado *m* **c)** *Fam* [nightclub etc] garito *m* **d)** *Fam* [drug] porro *m* **2.** *adj* colectivo(a); **joint (bank) account** cuenta conjunta; **joint venture** empresa conjunta

jointly ['dʒɔɪntlɪ] *adv* conjuntamente, en común

joke [dʒəʊk] **1.** *n* **a)** chiste *m*; [prank] broma *f*; **to play a joke on sb** gastarle una broma a algn; **to tell a joke** contar un chiste **b)** *Fam* [person] hazmerreír *m*, payaso(a) *m,f*; **to be a joke** [thing] ser de chiste **2.** *vi* estar de broma; **you must be joking!** ¡no hablarás en serio!

joker ['dʒəʊkə(r)] *n* **a)** bromista *mf* **b)** CARDS comodín *m*

jolly ['dʒɒlɪ] *(compar* **jollier**, *superl* **jolliest)** **1.** *adj* alegre **2.** *adv Br Fam* [very] bien; **she played jolly well** jugó muy bien

jolt [dʒəʊlt] **1.** *n* **a)** sacudida *f*; [pull] tirón *m* **b)** *Fig* [fright] susto *m* **2.** *vi* moverse a sacudidas **3.** *vt* sacudir

jostle ['dʒɒsəl] **1.** *vi* dar empujones **2.** *vt* dar empujones a ■ **jot down** [dʒɒt] *vt sep* apuntar

jotter ['dʒɒtə(r)] *n Br* bloc *m*

journal ['dʒɜ:nəl] *n* **a)** revista *f* **b)** [diary] diario *m* **c)** [newspaper] periódico *m*

journalism ['dʒɜ:nəlɪzəm] *n* periodismo *m*

journalist ['dʒɜ:nəlɪst] *n* periodista *mf*

journey ['dʒɜ:nɪ] **1.** *n* viaje *m*; [distance] trayecto *m* **2.** *vi Formal* viajar

joy [dʒɔɪ] *n* alegría *f*; [pleasure] placer *m*

joyful ['dʒɔɪfʊl] *adj* alegre, contento(a)

joyride ['dʒɔɪraɪd] *n Fam* paseo *m* en un coche robado

joystick ['dʒɔɪstɪk] *n* AVIAT palanca *f* de mando; [of video game] joystick *m*

JPEG *n (abbr of* **joint picture expert group)** COMPUT (formato *m*) JPEG *m*

jubilant ['dʒu:bɪlənt] *adj* jubiloso(a)

jubilee ['dʒu:bɪli:] *n* festejos *mpl*; **golden jubilee** quincuagésimo aniversario

judge [dʒʌdʒ] **1.** *n* juez *mf*, jueza *f*; [in competition] jurado *m* **2.** *vt* **a)** JUR juzgar **b)** [estimate] considerar **c)** [competition] actuar de juez de **d)** [assess] juzgar **3.** *vi* juzgar; **judging from what you say** a juzgar por lo que dices

judg(e)ment ['dʒʌdʒmənt] *n* **a)** JUR sentencia *f*, fallo *m* **b)** [opinion] juicio *m* **c)** [ability] buen juicio *m*

judicial [dʒu:'dɪʃəl] *adj* judicial

judo ['dʒu:dəʊ] *n* judo *m*

jug [dʒʌg] *n Br* jarra *f*; **milk jug** jarra de leche

juggle ['dʒʌgəl] *vi* [perform] hacer juegos malabares **(with** con); *Fig* [responsibilities] ajustar

juggler ['dʒʌglə(r)] *n* malabarista *mf*

juice [dʒu:s] *n* [of fruit] zumo *m*, *Am* jugo *m*; [of meat] jugo

juicy ['dʒu:sɪ] *(compar* **juicier**, *superl* **juiciest)** *adj* **a)** jugoso(a) **b)** *Fam & Fig* picante

jukebox ['dʒu:kbɒks] *n* rocola *f*

July [dʒu:'laɪ, dʒə'laɪ] *n* julio *m*

jumble ['dʒʌmbəl] **1.** *n* revoltijo *m*; *Br* **jumble sale** rastrillo *m* benéfico **2.** *vt* revolver

jumbo ['dʒʌmbəʊ] *n* **jumbo (jet)** jumbo *m*

jump [dʒʌmp] **1.** *n* salto *m*; [sudden increase] subida repentina; *Br* AUTO **jump leads** cables *mpl* de emergencia; **jump suit** mono *m* **2.** *vi* **a)** saltar, dar un salto; *Fig* **to jump to conclusions** sacar conclusiones precipitadas **b)** *Fig* [start] sobresaltarse **c)** [increase] aumentar de golpe **3.** *vt* saltar; *Br* **to jump the queue** colarse; *US* **to jump rope** saltar a la comba ■ **jump at** *vt insep* aceptar sin pensarlo

jumper ['dʒʌmpə(r)] *n* **a)** *Br* [sweater] suéter *m*, *Esp* jersey *m*, *RP* pulóver *m* **b)** *US* [dress] *Esp* pichi *m*, *CSur*, *Méx* jumper *m* **c)** *US* AUTO **jumper cables** cables *mpl* de emergencia

jumpy ['dʒʌmpɪ] *(compar* **jumpier**, *superl* **jumpiest)** *adj Fam* nervioso(a)

junction ['dʒʌŋkʃən] *n* [of roads] cruce *m*; RAIL & ELEC empalme *m*

June [dʒu:n] *n* junio *m*

jungle ['dʒʌŋgəl] *n* jungla *f*, selva *f*; *Fig* laberinto *m*; **the concrete jungle** la jungla de asfalto

junior ['dʒu:nɪə(r)] **1.** *adj* **a)** [son of] hijo; **David Hughes Junior** David Hughes hijo **b)** *US* **junior high (school)** [between 11 and 15] escuela secundaria; *Br* **junior school** [between 7 and 11] escuela primaria; **junior team** equipo *m* juvenil **c)** [lower in rank] subalterno(a) **2.** *n* **a)** [person of lower rank] subalterno(a) *m, f* **b)** [younger person] menor *mf*

junk [dʒʌŋk] *n* **a)** *Fam* trastos *mpl*; **junk food** comida basura; **junk mail** [e-mail] correo *m* basura; [postal] propaganda *f* (por correo); **junk shop** tienda *f* de segunda mano **b)** [boat] junco *m*

junkie [ˈdʒʌŋkɪ] *n Fam* yonqui *mf*

jury [ˈdʒʊərɪ] *n* jurado *m*

just [dʒʌst] **1.** *adj* [fair] justo(a); *Formal* [well-founded] justificado(a)
2. *adv* **a)** he had **just arrived** acababa de llegar
b) [at this very moment] ahora mismo, en este momento; **he was just leaving when ...** estaba a punto de salir cuando ... ; **I'm just coming!** ¡ya voy!
c) [only] solamente; **just in case** por si acaso; **just a minute!** ¡un momento!

d) [barely] por poco; **just about** casi; **just enough** justo lo suficiente
e) [emphatic] **it's just fantastic!** ¡es sencillamente fantástico!
f) [exactly] exactamente, justo; **just as I thought** me lo figuraba; **just as fast as** tan rápido como

justice [ˈdʒʌstɪs] *n* **a)** justicia *f*; **you didn't do yourself justice** no diste lo mejor de ti **b)** *US* [judge] juez *mf*; *Br* **Justice of the Peace** juez de paz

justifiable [ˈdʒʌstɪfaɪəbəl] *adj* justificable

justification [dʒʌstɪfɪˈkeɪʃən] *n* justificación *f*

justify [ˈdʒʌstɪfaɪ] *vt* justificar

jut [dʒʌt] *vi* sobresalir; **to jut out over** proyectarse sobre

juvenile [ˈdʒuːvənaɪl] **1.** *adj* **a)** juvenil; **juvenile court** tribunal *m* de menores; **juvenile delinquent** delincuente *mf* juvenil **b)** [immature] infantil **2.** *n* menor *mf*, joven *mf*

juxtapose [dʒʌkstəˈpəʊz] *vt* yuxtaponer

K

K, k [keɪ] *n* [the letter] K, k *f*

K *(abbr of* **Kilo(s)***)* K

kahuna [kə'hu:nə] *n US Fam* **the big kahuna** el capo

kangaroo [kæŋgə'ru:] *n* canguro *m*

karate [kə'rɑ:tɪ] *n* kárate *m*

kB, KB *n* COMPUT *(abbr of* **kilobyte(s)***)* KB *m*

kebab [kə'bæb] *n* CULIN pincho moruno, brocheta *f*

keel [ki:l] *n* quilla *f*; *Fig* **to be on an even keel** estar en calma ■ **keel over** *vi Fam* desmayarse

keen [ki:n] *adj* **a)** [eager] entusiasta **b)** [intense] profundo(a) **c)** [mind, senses] agudo(a); [look] penetrante; [blade] afilado(a); [competition] fuerte

keep [ki:p] *(pt & pp* kept*)* **1.** *n* **a) to earn one's keep** ganarse el pan **b)** *Fam* **for keeps** para siempre **2.** *vt* **a)** guardar; **to keep one's room tidy** mantener su cuarto limpio **b)** [not give back] quedarse con **c)** [detain] detener; **to keep sb waiting** hacer esperar a algn **d)** [animals] criar **e)** [the law] observar; [promise] cumplir **f)** [secret] guardar **g)** [diary, accounts] llevar **h)** [prevent] **to keep sb from doing sth** impedir a algn hacer algo **i)** [own, manage] tener; [shop, hotel] llevar **3.** *vi* **a)** [remain] seguir; **keep still!** ¡estáte quieto(a)!; **to keep fit** mantenerse en forma; **to keep going** seguir adelante **b)** [do frequently] no dejar de; **she keeps forgetting her keys** siempre se olvida las llaves **c)** [food] conservarse ■ **keep at** *vt insep* perseverar en

■ **keep away 1.** *vt sep* mantener a distancia **2.** *vi* mantenerse a distancia

■ **keep back** *vt sep* [information] ocultar, callar; [money etc] retener

■ **keep down** *vt sep* **to keep prices down** mantener los precios bajos

■ **keep from** *vt insep* evitar; **I couldn't keep from laughing** no podía contener la risa

■ **keep in with** *vt insep* **to keep in with sb** mantener buenas relaciones con algn

■ **keep off 1.** *vt insep* **keep off the grass** [sign] prohibido pisar la hierba **2.** *vt sep* [dogs, birds, trespassers] alejar; [rain, sun] proteger de; **this cream will keep the mosquitoes off** esta crema te protegerá contra los mosquitos; **keep your hands off!** ¡no lo toques!

■ **keep on 1.** *vt sep* **a)** [clothes etc] no quitarse; **to keep an eye on sth / sb** vigilar algo /a algn **b)** [continue to employ] no despedir a **2.** *vi* [continue to do] seguir

■ **keep out 1.** *vt sep* no dejar pasar **2.** *vi* no entrar; **keep out!** [sign] ¡prohibida la entrada!

■ **keep to** *vt insep* [subject] limitarse a; **to keep to one's room** quedarse en el cuarto; **keep to the point!** ¡cíñete a la cuestión!; **to keep to the left** circular por la izquierda

■ **keep up 1.** *vt sep* **a)** [continue to do] continuar; **keep it up!** ¡sigue así! **b)** [maintain] mantener; **to keep up appearances** guardar las apariencias **c)** [prevent from sleeping] mantener despierto(a) **2.** *vt sep* [continue to do] continuar; [maintain] mantener **3.** *vi* [maintain pace, level] **to keep up (with sb)** mantener el ritmo (de algn)

kind

■ **keep up with** *vt insep* to keep up with the times estar al día

keeper ['kiːpə(r)] *n* [in zoo] guarda *mf*; [in record office] archivero(a) *m,f*; [in museum] conservador(a) *m,f*

keeping ['kiːpɪŋ] *n* **a)** [care] cuidado *m* **b) in keeping with** en armonía con; **out of keeping with** en desacuerdo con

kennel ['kenəl] *n* caseta *f* para perros; **kennels** hotel *m* de perros

kept [kept] *pt & pp of* **keep**

kerb [kɜːb] *n Br* bordillo *m* (de la acera), *Chile* solera *f*, *Col, Perú* sardinel *m*, *CSur* cordón *m* (de la vereda), *Méx* borde *m* (de la banqueta)

kernel ['kɜːnəl] *n* [of fruit, nut] pepita *f*; [of wheat] grano *m*; *Fig* meollo *m*

kerosene, kerosine ['kerəsiːn] *n US* queroseno *m*

ketchup ['ketʃəp] *n* ketchup *m*, salsa *f* de tomate

kettle ['ketəl] *n* hervidor *m*; **that's a different kettle of fish** eso es harina de otro costal

kewl *adj US Fam* cool

key [kiː] **1.** *n* **a)** [for lock] llave *f*; **key ring** llavero *m* **b)** [of piano, typewriter] tecla *f*; COMPUT **delete key** tecla *f* de borrado or supresión; COMPUT **enter key** (tecla *f*) de introducción de datos, (tecla *f*) enter *m*; **hash key** tecla *f* (de) almohadilla **c)** MUS tono *m* **2.** *adj* clave **3.** *vt* COMPUT teclear

■ **key in** *vt sep* COMPUT introducir

keyboard ['kiːbɔːd] *n* teclado *m*

keyguard ['kiːgaːd] *n* [on mobile phone] bloqueo *m* del teclado

keyhole ['kiːhəʊl] *n* ojo *m* de la cerradura

keypad ['kiːpæd] *n* COMPUT teclado *m* numérico

keypal ['kiːpæl] *n* INTERNET amigo(a) *m,f* por internet

khaki ['kaːkiː] *adj & n* caqui (*m*)

kick [kɪk] **1.** *n* [from person] patada *f*, puntapié *m*; [from horse etc] coz *f* **2.** *vi* [animal] cocear; [person] dar patadas **3.** *vt* dar un puntapié a

■ **kick off** *vi Fam* empezar; FTBL sacar

■ **kick out** *vt sep* echar a patadas

■ **kick up** *vt insep Fam* **to kick up a fuss** armar or *Esp* montar un alboroto

kickboxing ['kɪkbɒksɪŋ] *n* kick boxing *m*

kick-off ['kɪkɒf] *n* FTBL saque *m* inicial

kid¹ [kɪd] *n* **a)** ZOOL cabrito *m*; *Fig* **to handle sb with kid gloves** tratar a algn con guante blanco **b)** *Fam* niño(a) *m,f*, *CAm* chavalo(a) *m,f*, *Méx* chavo(a) *mf*; **the kids** los críos

kid² [kɪd] **1.** *vi Fam* tomar el pelo; **no kidding!** ¡va en serio! **2.** *vt* tomar el pelo a; **to kid oneself** [fool] hacerse ilusiones

kidnap ['kɪdnæp] *vt* secuestrar

kidnapper ['kɪdnæpə(r)] *n* secuestrador(a) *m,f*

kidnapping ['kɪdnæpɪŋ] *n* secuestro *m*

kidney ['kɪdnɪ] *n* riñón *m*

kidult ['kɪdʌlt] *n Fam* niño(a) *m,f* grande

kill [kɪl] *vt* matar; *Fig* **to kill time** pasar el rato; *Fam* **my feet are killing me!** ¡cómo me duelen los pies! ■ **kill off** *vt sep* exterminar

killer ['kɪlə(r)] *n* asesino(a) *m,f*; **killer whale** orca *f*

killing ['kɪlɪŋ] *n* asesinato *m*; *Fig* **to make a killing** forrarse de dinero

killjoy ['kɪldʒɔɪ] *n* aguafiestas *mf inv*

kilo ['kiːləʊ] *n* kilo *m*

kilobyte ['kɪləbaɪt] *n* COMPUT kilobyte *m*

kilogram(me) ['kɪləʊgræm] *n* kilogramo *m*

kilometre, *US* **kilometer** [kɪ'lɒmɪtə(r)] *n* kilómetro *m*

kilt [kɪlt] *n* falda escocesa, kilt *m*

kin [kɪn] *n* familiares *mpl*, parientes *mpl*

kind¹ [kaɪnd] **1.** *n* tipo *m*, clase *f*; **they are two of a kind** son tal para cual; **in**

kind [payment] en especie; [treatment] con la misma moneda **2.** adv Fam **kind of** en cierta manera

kind² [kaɪnd] adj amable, simpático(a); Formal **would you be so kind as to …?** ¿me haría usted el favor de …?

kindergarten [ˈkɪndəgɑːtən] n jardín m de infancia

kindly [ˈkaɪndlɪ] **1.** (compar **kindlier**, superl **kindliest**) adj amable, bondadoso(a) **2.** adv Formal [please] por favor; **kindly remit a cheque** sírvase enviar cheque; **to look kindly on** aprobar

kindness [ˈkaɪndnɪs] n bondad f, amabilidad f

king [kɪŋ] n rey m; [draughts] dama f

kingdom [ˈkɪŋdəm] n reino m

kiosk [ˈkiːɒsk] n quiosco m

kip [kɪp] Br Fam **1.** n **to have a kip** echar un sueño **2.** (pt & pp **kipped**) vi dormir

kipper [ˈkɪpə(r)] n arenque m ahumado

kiss [kɪs] **1.** n beso m
2. vt besar
3. vi besarse

kit [kɪt] n **a)** [gear] equipo m; MIL avíos mpl **b)** [clothing] ropa f **c)** [toy model] maqueta f ■ **kit out** vt sep equipar

kitchen [ˈkɪtʃɪn] n cocina f; **kitchen sink** fregadero m

kite [kaɪt] n **a)** [toy] cometa f **b)** ORNITH milano m

kitesurfing [ˈkaɪtsɜːfɪŋ] n kitesurf m

kitten [ˈkɪtən] n gatito(a) m,f

kitty [ˈkɪtɪ] n [money] fondo m común; CARDS bote m

kiwi [ˈkiːwiː] n BOT & ORNITH kiwi m

KK MESSAGING OK

klutz [klʌts] n US Fam [stupid person] bobo(a) m,f, Esp chorra mf; [clumsy person] torpe, Esp patoso(a) m,f

km (pl **km** or **kms**) (abbr of **kilometre(s)**) km

knack [næk] n **to get the knack of doing sth** cogerle el truquillo a algo

knackered [ˈnækəd] adj Br Fam **to be knackered** [tired] estar reventado(a) or hecho(a) polvo; [broken, damaged] estar hecho(a) polvo

knapsack [ˈnæpsæk] n mochila f

knead [niːd] vt dar masaje a; [bread etc] amasar

knee [niː] **1.** n rodilla f **2.** vt dar un rodillazo a

kneecap [ˈniːkæp] **1.** n rótula f **2.** vt romper la rótula a

kneel [niːl] (pt & pp **knelt**) vi **to kneel (down)** arrodillarse

knelt [nelt] pt & pp of **kneel**

knew [njuː] pt of **know**

knickers [ˈnɪkəz] npl Br bragas fpl, Chile, Col, Méx calzones mpl, RP bombacha f

knick-knack [ˈnɪknæk] n Fam chuchería f, baratija f

knife [naɪf] **1.** (pl **knives**) n cuchillo m **2.** vt apuñalar, dar una puñalada a

knight [naɪt] **1.** n HIST caballero m; [in chess] caballo m **2.** vt armar caballero

knit [nɪt] (pt & pp **knitted** or **knit**) **1.** vt **a)** tejer **b)** **to knit (together)** [join] juntar; Fig **to knit one's brow** fruncir el ceño **2.** vi **a)** tejer, hacer punto **b)** [bone] soldarse

knitting [ˈnɪtɪŋ] n punto m; **knitting machine** máquina f de tejer; **knitting needle** aguja f de tejer

knives [naɪvz] pl of **knife**

knob [nɒb] n **a)** [of stick] puño m; [of drawer] tirador m; [button] botón m **b)** [small portion] trozo m

knock [nɒk] **1.** n golpe m; Fig revés m
2. vt **a)** golpear
b) Fam [criticize] criticar
3. vi chocar (**against** or **into** contra); [at door] llamar (**at** a)
■ **knock down** vt sep **a)** [demolish] derribar **b)** AUTO atropellar **c)** [price] rebajar
■ **knock off 1.** vt sep **a)** tirar **b)** Fam [steal] Esp mangar, Am volar **c)** Fam [kill] asesinar a, Esp cepillarse a **2.** vi Fam **they knock off at five** se piran a las cinco

■ **knock out** *vt sep* **a)** [make unconscious] dejar sin conocimiento; [in boxing] poner fuera de combate, derrotar por K.O. **b)** [surprise] dejar pasmado(a)
■ **knock over** *vt sep* [cup] volcar; [with car] atropellar

knocker ['nɒkə(r)] *n* [on door] aldaba *f*
knockout ['nɒkaʊt] *n* **a)** [in boxing] K.O. *m*, knock-out *m* **b)** *Fam* maravilla *f*
knot [nɒt] **1.** *n* nudo *m*; [group of people] curro *m* **2.** *vt* anudar
know [nəʊ] *(pt* knew, *pp* known) *vt & vi* **a)** saber; **as far as I know** que yo sepa; **she knows how to ski** sabe esquiar; **to get to know sth** enterarse de algo; **to let sb know** avisar al algn **b)** [be acquainted with] conocer; **we got to know each other at the party** nos conocimos en la fiesta
know-how ['nəʊhaʊ] *n Fam* conocimiento práctico
knowingly ['nəʊɪŋlɪ] *adv* [shrewdly] a sabiendas; [deliberately] deliberadamente

know-it-all ['nəʊɪtɔ:l] *n Fam* sabihondo(a) *m,f*, sabelotodo *mf*
knowledge ['nɒlɪdʒ] *n* **a)** conocimiento *m*; **without my knowledge** sin saberlo yo **b)** [learning] conocimientos *mpl*
knowledgeable ['nɒlɪdʒəbəl] *adj* erudito(a); **knowledgeable about** muy entendido(a) en
known [nəʊn] **1.** *adj* conocido(a) **2.** *pp of* **know**
knuckle ['nʌkəl] *n* ANAT nudillo *m*; CULIN hueso *m* ■ **knuckle down** *vi Fam* ponerse a trabajar en serio
Koran [kɔːˈrɑːn] *n* Corán *m*
Korea [kəˈriːə] *n* Corea
kosher ['kəʊʃə(r)] *adj* **a)** [meat] kosher (*inv*), conforme a la ley judaica **b)** *Fam* [reputable] legal
KOTC MESSAGING (*abbr of* **kiss on the cheek**) bss
KOTL MESSAGING *written abbr of* **kiss on the lips**

L, l [el] *n* [the letter] L, l *f*

lab [læb] *n Fam (abbr of laboratory)* laboratorio *m*

label ['leɪbəl] **1.** *n* etiqueta *f*; **record label** ≃ casa discográfica **2.** *(pt & pp* **labelled**, *US pt & pp* **labeled)** *vt* poner etiqueta a

labor ['leɪbə(r)] *US n* = **labour**

laboratory [lə'bɒrətərɪ, *US* 'læbrətɔːrɪ] *n* laboratorio *m*

laborer ['leɪbərə(r)] *US n* = **labourer**

laborious [lə'bɔːrɪəs] *adj* penoso(a)

labour *US* **labor** ['leɪbə(r)] **1.** *n* **a)** [work] trabajo *m*
b) [workforce] mano *f* de obra
c) the Labour Party el Partido Laborista
d) Labor Day *fiesta del trabajo en Estados Unidos (primer lunes de septiembre) que marca simbólicamente el fin del verano y durante la que se llevan a cabo diversas actividades de ocio: picnics y barbacoas en familia, fuegos artificiales, etc. En algunas ciudades se celebra también un desfile, denominado* **Labor Day Parade.**
e) [childbirth] **to be in labour** estar de parto
f) labours esfuerzos *mpl*
2. *adj* laboral
3. *vt* [stress, linger on] machacar; [a point] insistir en
4. *vi* [work] trabajar (duro)

labourer ['leɪbərə(r)] *n* peón *m*; **farm labourer** peón *m* agrícola

labyrinth ['læbərɪnθ] *n* laberinto *m*

lace [leɪs] **1.** *n* **a)** [fabric] encaje *m*
b) laces cordones *mpl* **2.** *vt* **a)** [shoes] atar (los cordones de) **b)** [add spirits to] echar licor a ▪ **lace up** *vt sep* atar con cordones

lack [læk] **1.** *n* falta *f*, escasez *f*; **for lack of** por falta de
2. *vt* carecer de
3. *vi* carecer (**in** de)

lad [læd] *n Fam* chaval *m*, muchacho *m*; **(stable) lad** mozo *m* de cuadra

ladder ['lædə(r)] **1.** *n* **a)** escalera *f* (de mano); *Fig* escala *f* **b)** [in stocking] carrera *f* **2.** *vt* **I've laddered my stocking** me he hecho una carrera en las medias

laddish ['lædɪʃ] *adj Br* referente a un estilo de vida en el que abundan las salidas con los amigos, el alcohol y las actitudes machistas

laden ['leɪdən] *adj* cargado(a) (**with** de)

lady ['leɪdɪ] *n* señora *f*; *POL* **First Lady** primera dama; **Ladies** [sign on WC] Señoras; **ladies and gentlemen!** ¡señoras y señores!; **Lady Brown** Lady Brown

ladybird ['leɪdɪbɜːd], *US* **ladybug** ['leɪdɪbʌg] *n* mariquita *f*

ladyfinger ['leɪdɪfɪŋgə(r)] *n US* [biscuit] bizcocho *m* de soletilla

lag [læg] **1.** *n* **time lag** demora *f*
2. *vi* **to lag (behind)** quedarse atrás, retrasarse
3. *vt* TECH revestir

lager ['lɑːgə(r)] *n* cerveza rubia

lagoon [lə'guːn] *n* laguna *f*

laid [leɪd] *pt & pp of* **lay**

lain [leɪn] *pp of* **lie**

lair [leə(r)] *n* guarida *f*

lake [leɪk] *n* lago *m*

lamb [læm] *n* cordero *m*; [meat] carne *f* de cordero; **lamb chop** chuleta *f* de cordero; **lamb's wool** lana *f* de cordero

lame [leɪm] *adj* **a)** cojo(a) **b)** *Fig* [excuse] poco convincente; [argument] flojo(a)

lament [lə'ment] **1.** *n* MUS elegia *f* **2.** *vt* [death] llorar, lamentar **3.** *vi* llorar (**for** a), lamentarse (**over** de)

laminated ['læmɪneɪtɪd] *adj* [metal] laminado(a) ; [glass] inastillable ; [paper] plastificado(a)

lamp-post ['læmppəʊst] *n* farola *f*

lampshade ['læmpʃeɪd] *n* pantalla *f*

lance [lɑːns] **1.** *n* lanza *f*; Br MIL **lance corporal** cabo interino ; MED lanceta *f* **2.** *vt* MED abrir con lanceta

land [lænd] **1.** *n* **a)** tierra *f*; [soil] suelo *m*; **by land** por tierra
b) [country] país *m*
c) [property] tierras *fpl*; [estate] finca *f*; **piece of land** terreno *m*
2. *vt* **a)** [plane] hacer aterrizar
b) [disembark] desembarcar
c) *Fam* [obtain] conseguir ; [contract] ganar
d) *Fam* **she got landed with the responsibility** tuvo que cargar con la responsabilidad
e) *Fam* [blow] asestar
3. *vi* **a)** [plane] aterrizar
b) [disembark] desembarcar
■ **land up** *vi Fam* ir a parar

landing ['lændɪŋ] *n* **a)** [of staircase] rellano **b)** [of plane] aterrizaje *m*; **landing strip** pista *f* de aterrizaje **c)** [of passengers] desembarco *m*; **landing stage** desembarcadero *m*

landlady ['lændleɪdɪ] *n* [of flat] dueña *f*, propietaria *f*; [of boarding house] patrona *f*; [of pub] dueña

landlord ['lændlɔːd] *n* [of flat] dueño *m*, propietario *m*; [of pub] patrón *m*, dueño

landmark ['lændmɑːk] *n* **a)** señal *f*, marca *f*; [well-known place] lugar muy conocido **b)** *Fig* hito *m*

landowner ['lændəʊnə(r)] *n* terrateniente *mf*

landscape ['lændskeɪp] **1.** *n* paisaje *m* **2.** *vt* ajardinar

landslide ['lændslaɪd] *n* desprendimiento *m* de tierras; **landslide victory** victoria arrolladora

lane [leɪn] *n* [in country] camino *m*; [in town] callejón *m*; [of motorway] carril *m*; SPORT calle *f*; NAUT ruta *f*; **bike** or **cycle lane** carril *m* bici

language ['læŋgwɪdʒ] *n* **a)** lenguaje *m*; **bad language** palabrotas *fpl* **b)** [of a country] idioma *m*, lengua *f*; **language laboratory** laboratorio *m* de idiomas; **language school** academia *f* de idiomas

languish ['læŋgwɪʃ] *vi* languidecer ; [project, plan etc] quedar abandonado(a) ; [in prison] pudrirse

lanky ['læŋkɪ] *(compar* **lankier***, super* **lankiest)** *adj* larguirucho(a)

lantern ['læntən] *n* farol *m*; **paper lantern** farolillo *m* de papel

lap¹ [læp] *n* ANAT regazo *m*

lap² [læp] **1.** *n* [circuit] vuelta *f*; *Fig* etapa *f* **2.** *vt* [overtake] doblar

lap³ [læp] *(pt & pp* **lapped) 1.** *vt* [of cat] **to lap (up)** beber a lengüetadas **2.** *vi* [waves] lamer, besar

lapel [lə'pel] *n* solapa *f*

lapse [læps] **1.** *n* **a)** [of time] lapso *m* **b)** [error] error *m*, desliz *m*; [of memory] fallo *m* **2.** *vi* **a)** [time] pasar, transcurrir **b)** [expire] caducar **c)** [err] cometer un error ; [fall back] caer (**into** en)

laptop ['læptɒp] *n* COMPUT **laptop (computer)** *Esp* ordenador *m* or *Am* computadora *f* portátil

larceny ['lɑːsənɪ] *n* JUR (delito *m* de) robo *m* or latrocinio *m*

lard [lɑːd] *n* manteca *f* de cerdo

larder ['lɑːdə(r)] *n* despensa *f*

large [lɑːdʒ] **1.** *adj* grande ; [amount] importante ; [extensive] amplio(a); **by and large** por lo general **2.** *n* **to be at large** andar suelto(a); **the public at large** el público en general

largely ['lɑːdʒlɪ] *adv* [mainly] en gran parte ; [chiefly] principalmente

large-scale ['lɑːdʒskeɪl] *adj* [project, problem etc] de gran envergadura ; [map] a gran escala

lark¹ [lɑːk] *n* ORNITH alondra *f*

lark² [lɑːk] n Fam [joke] broma f; **what a lark!** ¡qué risa! ▪ **lark about**, **lark around** vi Fam hacer el tonto

laryngitis [lærɪnˈdʒaɪtɪs] n laringitis f

laser [ˈleɪzə(r)] n láser m; **laser printer** impresora f láser; **laser weapon** arma f láser

lash [læʃ] **1.** n a) [eyelash] pestaña f b) [blow with whip] latigazo m **2.** vt a) [beat] azotar b) [rain] azotar c) [tie] atar ▪ **lash out** vi a) [with fists] repartir golpes a diestro y siniestro; [verbally] criticar (**at** a) b) Fam [spend money] tirar or Am salvo RP botar la casa por la ventana

lass [læs] n Fam chavala f, muchacha f

last [lɑːst] **1.** adj a) [final] último(a), final; **down to the last detail / penny** hasta el último detalle / penique; Fam **the last straw** el colmo
b) [most recent] último(a)
c) [past] pasado(a); [previous] anterior; **last but one** penúltimo(a); **last month** el mes pasado; **last night** anoche
2. adv a) [most recently] la última vez; **when I last saw her** la última vez que la vi
b) [at the end] en último lugar; [in race etc] último; **at (long) last** por fin; **last but not least** el último en orden pero no en importancia
3. n **the last** el último / la última; **the last I saw of him** la última vez que le vi
4. pron **the Sunday before last** hace dos domingos; **the year before last** hace dos años; **the last but one** el / la penúltimo(a) m,f; **to leave sth till last** dejar algo para el final
5. vi a) [time] durar
b) [hold out] aguantar
c) [be enough for] llegar, alcanzar

lasting [ˈlɑːstɪŋ] adj duradero(a)

lastly [ˈlɑːstlɪ] adv por último, finalmente

latch [lætʃ] n picaporte m, pestillo m

late [leɪt] **1.** adj a) [not on time] tardío(a); [hour] avanzado(a); **to be five minutes late** llegar con cinco minutos de retraso
b) [far on in time] tarde; **in late autumn** a finales del otoño; **in the late afternoon** a última hora de la tarde; **she's in her late twenties** ronda los treinta
c) [dead] difunto(a)
2. adv a) [not on time] tarde; **to arrive late** llegar tarde
b) [far on in time] tarde; **late at night** a altas horas de la noche; **late in life** a una edad avanzada
c) **as late as 1950** todavía en 1950; **of late** últimamente

latecomer [ˈleɪtkʌmə(r)] n tardón(ona) m,f

lately [ˈleɪtlɪ] adv últimamente, recientemente

lather [ˈlɑːðə(r)] **1.** n [of soap] espuma f; [horse's sweat] sudor m **2.** vt [with soap] enjabonar

Latin [ˈlætɪn] **1.** adj & n latino(a) (m,f); **Latin America** América Latina, Latinoamérica; **Latin American** latinoamericano(a) (m,f) **2.** n [language] latín m

latitude [ˈlætɪtjuːd] n latitud f

latter [ˈlætə(r)] **1.** adj a) [last] último(a) b) [second of two] segundo(a) **2.** pron éste(a); **the former ... the latter** aquél ... éste / aquélla ... ésta

lattice [ˈlætɪs] n enrejado m, rejilla f

laudable [ˈlɔːdəbəl] adj loable

laugh [lɑːf] **1.** n risa f; [guffaw] carcajada f; **laugh lines** líneas fpl de la sonrisa; **for a laugh** para divertirse **2.** vi reír, reírse ▪ **laugh at** vt insep to laugh at sb / sth reírse de algn / algo ▪ **laugh about** vt insep to laugh about sb / sth reírse de algn / algo ▪ **laugh off** vt sep tomar a risa

laughable [ˈlɑːfəbəl] adj [situation, suggestion] ridículo(a); [amount, offer] irrisorio(a)

laughter [ˈlɑːftə(r)] n risa f

launch [lɔːntʃ] **1.** n a) [vessel] lancha f b) [of product] lanzamiento f **2.** vt a) [attack, rocket, new product] lanzar; [ship] botar b) [company] fundar; [scheme] iniciar

laund(e)rette [lɔːndəˈret], *US* **Laundromat®** [ˈlɔːndrəmæt] *n* lavandería *f*

laundry [ˈlɔːndrɪ] *n* a) [place] lavandería *f* b) [dirty clothes] ropa sucia; **to do the laundry** lavar la ropa

lava [ˈlɑːvə] *n* lava *f*

lavatory [ˈlævətərɪ] *n* a) excusado *m*, retrete *m*; *Br* **lavatory seat** tapa *f* del inodoro b) [room] baño *m*; **public lavatory** servicios *mpl*, aseos *mpl*

lavender [ˈlævəndə(r)] *n* lavanda *f*

lavish [ˈlævɪʃ] **1.** *adj* a) [generous] pródigo(a) b) [abundant] abundante c) [luxurious] lujoso(a) **2.** *vt* **to lavish praise on sb** colmar de alabanzas a algn; **to lavish attention on sb** prodigarse en atenciones con algn

law [lɔː] *n* a) ley *f*; **by law** según la ley; **law and order** el orden público; **to lay down the law** dictar la ley b) [as subject] derecho *m*; **law court** tribunal *m* de justicia c) *Fam* **the law** los maderos

lawful [ˈlɔːfʊl] *adj* legal; [permitted by law] lícito(a); [legitimate] legítimo(a)

lawn [lɔːn] *n* césped *m*; **lawn tennis** tenis *m* sobre hierba

lawsuit [ˈlɔːsjuːt] *n* pleito *m*

lawyer [ˈlɔːjə(r)] *n* abogado(a) *m,f*; **lawyer's office** bufete *m* de abogados

lax [læks] *adj* [not strict] relajado(a); [not demanding] poco exigente; [careless] descuidado(a)

laxative [ˈlæksətɪv] *adj & n* laxante *(m)*

lay¹ [leɪ] *adj* a) REL laico(a) b) [nonspecialist] lego(a)

lay² [leɪ] *(pt & pp* **laid)** **1.** *vt* a) [place] poner, colocar; [cable, trap] tender; [foundations] echar b) [fire] preparar; [table] poner c) [eggs] poner **2.** *pt of* **lie** ▪ **lay down** *vt sep* a) [put down] poner; [let go] dejar; **to lay down one's arms** rendir las armas b) [establish] fijar, imponer; [principles] sentar ▪ **lay into** *vt insep Fam* [physically] dar una paliza a; [verbally] arremeter contra ▪ **lay off 1.** *vt sep* [dismiss] despedir **2.** *vt insep Fam* dejar en paz ▪ **lay on** *vt sep* [provide] proveer de; [food] preparar

▪ **lay out** *vt sep* a) [open out] extender b) [arrange] disponer c) [ideas] exponer d) [plan] trazar e) *Fam* [spend] gastar

layabout [ˈleɪəbaʊt] *n Fam* vago(a) *m,f*

lay-by [ˈleɪbaɪ] *n Br* área *f* de descanso

layer [ˈleɪə(r)] *n* capa *f*

layman [ˈleɪmən] *n* lego(a) *m,f*

layout [ˈleɪaʊt] *n* [arrangement] disposición *f*; [presentation] presentación *f*; TYP composición *f*; [plan] diseño *m*, trazado *m*

lazy [ˈleɪzɪ] *(compar* **lazier**, *superl* **laziest)** *adj* perezoso(a), holgazán(ana); **at a lazy pace** a paso lento

lb *(abbr of* **pound)** libra *f*

L-driver *Br n* = **learner-driver**

lead¹ [led] *n* a) [metal] plomo *m* b) [in pencil] mina *f*

lead² [liːd] *(pt & pp* **led)** **1.** *n* a) [front position] delantera *f*; [advantage] ventaja *f*; **to take the lead** [in race] tomar la delantera b) [clue] pista *f* c) THEAT primer papel *m* d) [leash] correa *f* e) ELEC cable *m* **2.** *vt* a) [conduct] llevar, conducir b) [be the leader of] dirigir, encabezar c) [influence] llevar a; **this leads me to believe that** esto me lleva a creer que d) [life] llevar **3.** *vi* a) [road] llevar, conducir (**to** a) b) [go first] ir delante; [in race] llevar la delantera c) **to lead to** llevar a ▪ **lead away** *vt* llevar ▪ **lead on 1.** *vi* [go ahead] ir adelante **2.** *vt sep* [deceive] engañar, timar ▪ **lead up to** *vt insep* llevar a

leader [ˈliːdə(r)] *n* a) jefe(a) *m,f*, líder *mf*; [in race] líder b) PRESS editorial *m*, artículo *m* de fondo

leadership [ˈliːdəʃɪp] *n* a) [command] dirección *f*, mando *m*; POL liderazgo *m* b) [leaders] dirigentes *mpl*, cúpula *f*

leading [ˈliːdɪŋ] *adj* a) [main] principal b) [outstanding] destacado(a)

leaf [liːf] *(pl* **leaves***) n* hoja *f*; **to turn over a new leaf** hacer borrón y cuenta nueva
■ **leaf through** *vt insep* hojear

leaflet [ˈliːflɪt] *n* folleto *m*

league [liːg] *n* **a)** [alliance] alianza *f*; [association] sociedad *f*; *Fam* **to be in league with sb** estar conchabado(a) con algn **b)** SPORT liga *f*

leak [liːk] **1.** *n* **a)** [hole] agujero *m*; [in roof] gotera *f*
b) [of gas, liquid] fuga *f*, escape *m*; [of information] filtración *f*
2. *vi* **a)** [container] tener un agujero; [pipe] tener un escape; [roof] gotear; [boat] hacer agua
b) [gas, liquid] escaparse; [information] filtrarse; [news] trascender
3. *vt* [information] filtrar (**to** a)

leaky [ˈliːkɪ] *(compar* **leakier**, *superl* **leakiest**) *adj* [container] agujereado(a); [roof] que tiene goteras; [ship] que hace agua

lean¹ [liːn] *adj* [meat] magro(a); [person] flaco(a); [harvest] escaso(a)

lean² [liːn] *(pt & pp* **leaned** *or* **leant** [lent]) **1.** *vi* **a)** inclinarse **b) to lean on/against** apoyarse en/contra; *Fig* **to lean on sb** [pressurize] presionar a algn; [depend] depender de algn **2.** *vt* apoyar (**on** en)
■ **lean back** *vi* reclinarse ■ **lean forward** *vi* inclinarse hacia delante
■ **lean over** *vi* inclinarse

leaning [ˈliːnɪŋ] **1.** *adj* inclinado(a) **2.** *n* *Fig* [tendency] inclinación *f*, tendencia *f*

leap [liːp] **1.** *n* [jump] salto *m*; *Fig* paso *m*; **leap year** año bisiesto **2.** *(pt & pp* **leaped** *or* **leapt** [lept]*)* *vi* saltar; *Fig* **her heart leapt** su corazón dio un vuelco ■ **leap at** *vt insep Fig* [chance] no dejar escapar

learn [lɜːn] *(pt & pp* **learned** *or* **learnt** [lɜːnt]*)*
1. *vt* **a)** aprender; **to learn (how) to ski** aprender a esquiar **b) to learn that** enterarse de que **2.** *vi* **a)** aprender **b) to learn about** *or* **of** [find out] enterarse de

learned [ˈlɜːnɪd] *adj* erudito(a)

learner [ˈlɜːnə(r)] *n* [beginner] principiante *mf*; **learner driver** conductor(ora) *m,f* en prácticas

learner-driver *n* *Br* conductor(ora) *m,f* en prácticas

learning [ˈlɜːnɪŋ] *n* [knowledge] conocimientos *mpl*; [erudition] saber *m*

lease [liːs] **1.** *n* contrato *m* de arrendamiento; *Fig* **to give sb a new lease** *Br* **of** *or US* **on life** dar nueva vida a algn
2. *vt* arrendar

leash [liːʃ] *n* correa *f*

least [liːst] *(superl* of **little**) **1.** *adj* menor, mínimo(a); **he has the least time** él es quien menos tiempo tiene
2. *adv* menos; **least of all him** él menos que nadie
3. *n* **the least** lo menos; **at least** por lo menos, al menos; **to say the least** por no decir más

leather [ˈleðə(r)] **1.** *n* piel *f*, cuero *m*
2. *adj* de piel

leave¹ [liːv] *(pt & pp* **left***)* **1.** *vt* **a)** dejar; [go away from] abandonar; [go out of] salir de
b) leave him alone! ¡déjale en paz!; *Fam* **leave it to me** yo me encargo
c) [bequeath] legar
d) [forget] dejarse, olvidarse
e) I have two biscuits left me quedan dos galletas
f) to be left over sobrar
2. *vi* [go away] irse, marcharse; [go out] salir; **the train leaves in five minutes** el tren sale dentro de cinco minutos
■ **leave aside** *vt sep* dejar a un lado; **leaving aside the question of cost** dejando a un lado la cuestión del coste
■ **leave behind** *vt sep* **a)** dejar atrás **b)** [forget] olvidarse
■ **leave on** *vt sep* **a)** [clothes] dejar puesto(a) **b)** [lights, radio] dejar encendido(a) *or Am* prendido(a)
■ **leave out** *vt sep* [omit] omitir; *Fig* **to feel left out** sentirse excluido(a)

leave² [liːv] *n* **a)** [permission] permiso *m*; **family leave** permiso *m* parental **b)** [time off] vacaciones *fpl*; MIL **on leave** de permiso; **leave of absence** excedencia *f* **c) to take one's leave of sb** despedirse de algn

leaves [li:vz] *pl of* **leaf**

Lebanon ['lebənən] *n* **(the) Lebanon** (el) Líbano

lecherous ['letʃərəs] *adj* lascivo(a)

lecture ['lektʃə(r)] **1.** *n* **a)** conferencia *f*; UNIV clase *f*; **to give a lecture (on)** dar una conferencia (sobre); **lecture hall, lecture room, lecture theatre** sala *f* de conferencias; UNIV aula *f*
b) [rebuke] sermón *m*
2. *vi* dar una conferencia; UNIV dar clases
3. *vt* [reproach] sermonear

lecturer ['lektʃərə(r)] *n* conferenciante *mf*; *Br* UNIV profesor(a) *m,f* de universidad

led [led] *pt & pp of* **lead**

ledge [ledʒ] *n* **a)** [shelf] repisa *f*; [of window] alféizar *m* **b)** [on mountain] saliente *m*

ledger ['ledʒə(r)] *n* libro *m* mayor

leek [li:k] *n* puerro *m*

leer [lɪə(r)] *vi* mirar con lascivia

leeway ['li:weɪ] *n* libertad *f*; **this gives me a certain amount of leeway** esto me da cierto margen de libertad

left[1] [left] **1.** *adj* izquierdo(a); POL **left wing** izquierda *f*
2. *adv* a la izquierda
3. *n* **a)** izquierda *f*; **on the left** a mano izquierda
b) POL **to be on the left** ser de izquierdas

left[2] [left] *pt & pp of* **leave**

left-hand ['lefthænd] *adj* **left-hand drive** con el volante a la izquierda; **on the left-hand side** a mano izquierda

left-handed [left'hændɪd] *adj* zurdo(a)

left-luggage [left'lʌgɪdʒ] *n Br* **left-luggage office** consigna *f*

leftovers ['leftəʊvəz] *npl* sobras *fpl*

left-wing ['leftwɪŋ] *adj* de izquierdas, izquierdista

leg [leg] *n* **a)** [of person] pierna *f*; [of animal, table] pata *f*; CULIN [of lamb] pierna *f*; [of trousers] pernera *f* **b)** [stage] etapa *f*

legacy ['legəsɪ] *n* herencia *f*, legado *m*

legal ['li:gəl] *adj* **a)** legal; [permitted by law] lícito(a); **legal tender** moneda *f* de curso legal **b)** [relating to the law] jurídico(a); **legal aid** asesoramiento jurídico gratuito; **legal dispute** contencioso *m*; *US* **legal holiday** fiesta *f* nacional

legalize ['li:gəlaɪz] *vt* legalizar

legally ['li:gəlɪ] *adv* legalmente

legend ['ledʒənd] *n* leyenda *f*

legendary ['ledʒəndərɪ] *adj* legendario(a)

leggings ['legɪŋz] *npl* polainas *fpl*

legible ['ledʒəbəl] *adj* legible

legionella [,li:dʒə'nelə] *n* legionelosis *f*

legislation [ledʒɪs'leɪʃən] *n* legislación *f*

legislative ['ledʒɪslətɪv] *adj* legislativo(a)

legitimate [lɪ'dʒɪtɪmɪt] *adj* legítimo(a)

L8r, L8R *(abbr of* **later**) MESSAGING + tdr

leisure ['leʒə(r), *US* 'li:ʒər] *n* ocio *m*, tiempo *m* libre; **at leisure** con calma; **do it at your leisure** hazlo cuando tengas tiempo; **leisure activities** pasatiempos *mpl*; **leisure centre** centro recreativo

leisurely ['leʒəlɪ, *US* 'li:ʒərlɪ] *adj* [unhurried] tranquilo(a); [slow] lento(a)

lemon ['lemən] *n* limón *m*; **lemon curd** crema *f* de limón; **lemon juice** zumo *m* de limón; **lemon tea** té *m* con limón

lemonade [lemə'neɪd] *n* [still] limonada *f*; *Br* [fizzy] *Esp, Arg* gaseosa *f*, *Am* gaseosa *f* de lima or limón

lend [lend] *(pt & pp* **lent**) *vt* prestar; **to lend oneself / itself to sth** prestarse a or para algo

lender ['lendə(r)] *n* FIN prestamista *mf*

length [leŋkθ, leŋθ] *n* **a)** longitud *f*, largo *m*; **it is 5 m in length** tiene 5 m de largo; *Fig* **to go to any lengths to achieve sth** hacer lo que sea para conseguir algo

b) [duration] duración f **c)** [of string] trozo m ; [of cloth] retal m **d) at length** [finally] finalmente ; [in depth] a fondo

lengthen ['leŋkθən, 'leŋθən] **1.** vt alargar ; [lifetime] prolongar **2.** vi alargarse ; [lifetime] prolongarse

lengthy ['leŋkθɪ, 'leŋθɪ] (compar **lengthier,** superl **lengthiest**) adj largo(a) ; [film, illness] de larga duración ; [meeting, discussion] prolongado(a)

lenient ['li:nɪənt] adj indulgente

lens [lenz] n [of eye] cristalino m ; [of spectacles] lente f ; PHOTO objetivo m

lent [lent] pt & pp of **lend**

lentil ['lentɪl] n lenteja f

Leo ['li:əʊ] n Leo m

leopard ['lepəd] n leopardo m

leotard ['li:ətɑ:d] n leotardo m

lesbian ['lezbɪən] adj & n lesbiana (f)

less [les] **1.** (compar of **little**) adj menos **2.** pron menos ; **the less said about it, the better** cuanto menos se hable de eso mejor
3. adv menos ; **less and less** cada vez menos
4. prep menos

less-developed adj **less-developed country** país m menos desarrollado

lessen ['lesən] vt & vi disminuir

lesser ['lesə(r)] adj menor ; **to a lesser extent** en menor grado

lesson ['lesən] n **a)** clase f ; [in book] lección f ; **Spanish lessons** clases de español **b)** REL lectura f

less-than adj **less-than sign** signo m inferior a

let [let] (pt & pp **let**) **1.** vt **a)** dejar, permitir ; **to let go of sth** soltar algo ; **to let sb know** avisar a algn ; Fig **to let oneself go** dejarse ir
b) [rent out] alquilar, Méx rentar ; **to let** [sign] se alquila
c) let alone ni mucho menos
2. v aux **let him wait** que espere ; **let me go!** ¡suéltame! ; **let's go!** ¡vamos!, ¡vámonos! ; **let's see** a ver

■ **let down** vt sep **a)** [lower] bajar ; [lengthen] alargar **b)** [deflate] desinflar **c)** [fail] fallar, defraudar

■ **let in** vt sep **a)** [admit] dejar entrar **b) to let oneself in for** meterse en

■ **let off** vt sep **a)** [bomb] hacer explotar ; [fireworks] hacer estallar **b)** [liquid, air] soltar **c)** Fam **to let sb off** [pardon] perdonar

■ **let on** vi Fam **don't let on** [reveal information] no se lo digas

■ **let out** vt sep **a)** [release] soltar ; [news] divulgar ; [secret] revelar **b)** [air, water] dejar salir **c)** [cry] soltar **d)** SEWING ensanchar

■ **let up** vi cesar, parar

letdown ['letdaʊn] n decepción f

lethal ['li:θəl] adj letal

lethargic [lɪ'θɑ:dʒɪk] adj aletargado(a)

letter ['letə(r)] n **a)** [of alphabet] letra f ; Fig **to the letter** al pie de la letra **b)** [written message] carta f ; Br **letter box** buzón m ; US **letter carrier** cartero(a) m,f ; COMM **letter of credit** carta de crédito

lettuce ['letɪs] n lechuga f

leukaemia [lu:'ki:mɪə] n leucemia f

level ['levəl] **1.** adj **a)** [flat] llano(a) ; [even] nivelado(a) ; [equal] igual, parejo(a) ; **a level spoonful of** una cucharada rasa de ; **to be level with** estar a nivel de ; Br **level crossing** paso m a nivel
b) [steady] estable ; [tone] uniforme
2. (pt & pp **levelled,** US pt & pp **leveled**) vt
a) nivelar, allanar
b) [building] arrasar
c) [stare, criticism] dirigir
3. n nivel m ; Br **AS level** examen opcional que cuenta para los A-levels ; **to be on a level with** estar al mismo nivel que
■ **level off, level out** vi estabilizarse
■ **level with** vt insep Fam ser franco(a) con

lever ['li:və(r), US 'levər] **1.** n palanca f
2. vt apalancar ; **to lever sth out** sacar algo con palanca

lewd [lu:d] adj [person] lascivo(a) ; [story] obsceno(a)

lift

liability [laɪə'bɪlɪtɪ] n a) JUR responsabilidad f b) [handicap] estorbo m c) FIN **liabilities** pasivo m

liable ['laɪəbəl] adj a) JUR responsable; [susceptible] sujeto(a); **to be liable for** ser responsable de b) **to be liable to do sth** ser propenso(a) a hacer algo; **it's liable to happen** es muy probable que (así) suceda

liaise [li:'eɪz] vi comunicarse (**with** con)

liaison [li:'eɪzɒn] n a) enlace m; **liaison officer** oficial mf de enlace b) [love affair] amorío m

liar ['laɪə(r)] n mentiroso(a) m,f, embustero(a) m,f

libel ['laɪbəl] **1.** n libelo m **2.** (pt & pp libelled, US pt & pp libeled) vt difamar, calumniar

liberal ['lɪbərəl] **1.** adj a) liberal; **Liberal Party** Partido m Liberal b) [abundant] abundante **2.** n POL Liberal liberal mf

liberate ['lɪbəreɪt] vt liberar; [prisoner etc] poner en libertad; **liberated woman** mujer liberada

liberation [lɪbə'reɪʃən] n liberación f

liberty ['lɪbətɪ] n libertad f; **to be at liberty to say sth** ser libre de decir algo; **to take liberties** tomarse libertades

Libra ['li:brə] n Libra m

librarian [laɪ'breərɪən] n bibliotecario(a) m,f

library ['laɪbrərɪ] n biblioteca f

Libya ['lɪbɪə] n Libia f

lice [laɪs] pl of **louse**

licence ['laɪsəns] n a) [permit] licencia f, permiso m; AUTO **licence number** matrícula f; US **licence plate** (placa f de la) matrícula b) [freedom] libertad f; [excessive freedom] libertinaje m

license ['laɪsəns] **1.** vt dar licencia a, autorizar **2.** n US = **licence**

lick [lɪk] **1.** vt lamer; **to lick one's lips** relamerse **2.** n lamedura f; Fam **a lick of paint** una mano de pintura

licorice ['lɪkərɪs] US n = **liquorice**

lid [lɪd] n a) [cover] tapa f b) [of eye] párpado m

lie¹ [laɪ] **1.** n mentira f **2.** vi mentir

lie² [laɪ] **1.** (pt lay, pp lain) vi a) [act] echarse, acostarse; [state] estar echado(a), estar acostado(a); [be buried] yacer b) [be situated] encontrarse, hallarse; **the valley lay before us** el valle se extendía ante nosotros c) [remain] quedarse **2.** n [position] situación f; [direction] orientación f ■ **lie about, lie around** vi [person] estar tumbado(a); [things] estar tirado(a) ■ **lie down** vi acostarse, echarse ■ **lie in** vi Br quedarse en la cama

lie-in ['laɪɪn] n Fam **to have a lie-in** levantarse tarde

lieu [lju:, lu:] n **in lieu of** en lugar de

lieutenant [Br lef'tenənt, US lu:'tenənt] n a) MIL teniente m b) [deputy, assistant] lugarteniente m

life [laɪf] (pl lives) n a) vida f; **to come to life** cobrar vida; **to take one's own life** suicidarse; Fam **how's life?** ¿qué tal?; **life belt** cinturón m salvavidas; **life imprisonment** cadena perpetua; **life insurance** seguro m de vida; **life jacket** chaleco m salvavidas; **life raft** lancha f salvavidas; **life style** estilo m de vida; **life story** biografía f b) [liveliness] vitalidad f

lifeboat ['laɪfbəʊt] n [on ship] bote m salvavidas; [on shore] lancha f de socorro

lifeguard ['laɪfgɑːd] n socorrista mf

lifelike ['laɪflaɪk] adj natural; [portrait] fiel

lifelong ['laɪflɒŋ] adj de toda la vida

life-saving adj **life-saving apparatus** aparatos mpl de salvamento; **life-saving vaccine** vacuna f que salva muchas vidas

life-size(d) ['laɪfsaɪz(d)] adj (de) tamaño natural

lifetime ['laɪftaɪm] n vida f; **in his lifetime** durante su vida; **it's the chance of a lifetime** es una ocasión única

lift [lɪft] **1.** vt a) levantar; [head etc] alzar; [pick up] coger b) [troops] transportar c) Fam [steal] birlar **2.** vi [clouds, mist] disiparse

lift-off

3. *n* **a)** *Br* [elevator] ascensor *m*
b) to give sb a lift llevar a algn en coche
c) *Fig* [boost] estímulo *m*
■ **lift up** *vt sep* levantar, alzar

lift-off ['lɪftɒf] *n* despegue *m*

ligament ['lɪgəmənt] *n* ligamento *m*

light¹ [laɪt] **1.** *n* **a)** luz *f*; *Fig* **in the light of** en vista de; *Fig* **to bring sth to light** sacar algo a la luz; *Fig* **to come to light** salir a la luz; **light bulb** bombilla *f*; **light switch** interruptor *m* de la luz; **light year** año *m* luz
b) [lamp] luz *f*, lámpara *f*; [traffic light] semáforo *m*; [headlight] faro *m*
c) [flame] lumbre *f*; **to set light to sth** prender fuego a algo; *Fam* **have you got a light?** ¿tiene fuego?
2. *(pt & pp* **lighted** *or* **lit)** *vt* **a)** [illuminate] iluminar, alumbrar
b) [ignite] encender
3. *adj* claro(a); [hair] rubio(a)
■ **light up 1.** *vt sep* iluminar, alumbrar **2.** *vi* **a)** iluminarse **b)** *Fam* encender un cigarrillo

light² [laɪt] **1.** *adj* ligero(a); [rain] fino(a); [breeze] suave; *Fig* [sentence etc] leve; *Fig* **to make light of sth** dar poca importancia a algo **2.** *adv* **to travel light** ir ligero(a) de equipaje

lighten¹ ['laɪtən] **1.** *vt* **a)** [colour] aclarar
b) [illuminate] iluminar **2.** *vi* aclararse

lighten² ['laɪtən] *vt* **a)** [weight] aligerar
b) *Fig* [mitigate] aliviar; [heart] alegrar

lighter ['laɪtə(r)] *n* (cigarette) lighter encendedor *m*, mechero *m*

light-hearted ['laɪthɑːtɪd] *adj* alegre

lighthouse ['laɪthaʊs] *n* faro *m*

lighting ['laɪtɪŋ] *n* **a)** [act] iluminación *f*
b) [system] alumbrado *m*

lightly ['laɪtlɪ] *adv* **a)** ligeramente **b) to get off lightly** salir casi indemne

lightning ['laɪtnɪŋ] *n* [flash] relámpago *m*; [stroke] rayo *m*; **lightning conductor** *or* **rod** pararrayos *m inv*; **lightning strike** huelga *f* relámpago

like¹ [laɪk] **1.** *adj* **a)** parecido(a), semejante
b) [equal] igual
2. *adv* **(as) like as not** a lo mejor
3. *prep* **a)** [similar to] como, parecido(a) a; [the same as] igual que; **it's not like her to do that** no es propio de ella hacer eso; **I've never seen anything like it** nunca he visto cosa igual; **like that** así; **people like that** ese tipo de gente; **what's he like?** ¿cómo es?
b) to feel like [want] tener ganas de; **I feel like a change** me apetece un cambio
4. *n* **brushes, combs and the like** cepillos, peines y cosas por el estilo

like² [laɪk] **1.** *vt* **a) do you like chocolate?** ¿te gusta el chocolate?; **he likes dancing** le gusta bailar; **she likes children** le gustan los niños
b) [want] querer; **whether you like it or not** quieras o no (quieras); **would you like a drink?** ¿te apetece tomar algo?
2. *vi* querer, gustar; **as you like** como quieras
3. *n* **a)** gusto *m*
b) likes preferencias *fpl*; **likes and dislikes** preferencias y aversiones
c) *Fam* **the likes of us / them** *etc* la gente como nosotros *etc*

likeable ['laɪkəbəl] *adj* simpático(a)

likelihood ['laɪklɪhʊd] *n* probabilidad *f*

likely ['laɪklɪ] **1.** *(compar* **likelier**, *superl* **likeliest)** *adj* probable; **he's likely to cause trouble** es probable que cause problemas; **where are you likely to be this afternoon?** ¿dónde piensas estar esta tarde? **2.** *adv* probablemente; **not likely!** ¡ni hablar!

liken ['laɪkən] *vt* comparar (**to** a *or* con)

likeness ['laɪknɪs] *n* **a)** semejanza *f*, parecido *m* **b)** [portrait] retrato *m*

likewise ['laɪkwaɪz] *adv* **a)** [also] también, asimismo **b)** [the same] lo mismo, igual

liking ['laɪkɪŋ] *n* [for thing] afición *f*; [for person] simpatía *f*; [for friend] cariño *m*; **to take a liking to sth** cogerle el gusto a algo; **to take a liking to sb** coger cariño a algn

lily ['lɪlɪ] n lirio m, azucena f; **lily of the valley** lirio de los valles

limb [lɪm] n miembro m; Fig **to be out on a limb** [in danger] estar en peligro; Br [isolated] estar aislado(a) ■ **limber up** ['lɪmbə(r)] vi SPORT entrar en calor; Fig prepararse (**for** para)

lime¹ [laɪm] n CHEM cal f

lime² [laɪm] n [fruit] lima f; [tree] limero m

limelight ['laɪmlaɪt] n Fig **to be in the limelight** estar en el candelero

limit ['lɪmɪt] **1.** n límite m; [maximum] máximo m; [minimum] mínimo m **2.** vt [restrict] limitar

limitation [lɪmɪ'teɪʃən] n limitación f

limited ['lɪmɪtɪd] adj limitado(a); **limited edition** edición limitada; Br **limited (liability) company** sociedad anónima

limousine ['lɪməziːn, lɪmə'ziːn] n limusina f

limp¹ [lɪmp] **1.** vi cojear **2.** n cojera f

limp² [lɪmp] adj a) [floppy] flojo(a) b) [weak] débil

line¹ [laɪn] n a) línea f; [straight] raya f b) [of writing] renglón m; [of poetry] verso m; THEAT **to learn one's lines** aprenderse el papel
c) [row] fila f; [of trees] hilera f; US [queue] cola f; Fig **to be in line (with)** coincidir (con); US **to stand in line** [queue] hacer cola; Fig **sth along these lines** algo por el estilo; **line dancing** baile m en línea (baile al ritmo de música country en el que los participantes se colocan en hileras y dan los mismos pasos)
d) [rope] cuerda f; [wire] cable m
e) TEL línea f; **hold the line!** ¡no cuelgue!
f) Br RAIL vía f
g) [range of goods] surtido m; **a new line** una nueva línea
h) **out of line** [remark, behaviour] fuera de lugar
■ **line up 1.** vt sep [arrange in rows] poner en fila **2.** vi [people] ponerse en fila; [troops] formar; [in queue] hacer cola

line² [laɪn] vt [pipe etc] revestir; SEWING forrar; Fam **to line one's pockets** forrarse

linen ['lɪnɪn] n a) [cloth] lino m b) [clothes] ropa f; [sheets etc] ropa blanca

liner ['laɪnə(r)] n transatlántico m

line-up ['laɪnʌp] n SPORT alineación f

linger ['lɪŋgə(r)] vi tardar; [dawdle] rezagarse; [smell, doubt] persistir; Fig [memory] perdurar

linguist ['lɪŋgwɪst] n lingüista mf; **he's a good linguist** se le dan bien los idiomas

linguistic [lɪŋ'gwɪstɪk] adj lingüístico(a)

linguistics [lɪŋ'gwɪstɪks] n sing lingüística f

lining ['laɪnɪŋ] n forro m

link [lɪŋk] **1.** n a) [of chain] eslabón m b) [connection] conexión f; Fig vínculo m; **rail link** enlace ferroviario c) COMPUT enlace m, vínculo m; **links to sth** enlaces mpl or vínculos mpl a algo d) **links** campo m de golf **2.** vt unir **3.** vi COMPUT tener un enlace or un vínculo; **to link to sth** enlazar or vincular a algo ■ **link up** vi unirse; [meet] encontrarse; [spaceships] acoplarse

lino ['laɪnəʊ] n Fam linóleo m

lint [lɪnt] n [for wounds] hilas fpl

lion ['laɪən] n león m

lip [lɪp] n a) labio m b) [of jug] pico m

lip-read ['lɪpriːd] vt & vi leer en los labios

lipstick ['lɪpstɪk] n lápiz m de labios

liqueur [lɪ'kjʊə(r)] n licor m

liquid ['lɪkwɪd] **1.** adj líquido(a) **2.** n líquido (m); US **dishwashing liquid** lavavajillas m inv

liquidate ['lɪkwɪdeɪt] vt liquidar

liquidize ['lɪkwɪdaɪz] vt licuar

liquidizer ['lɪkwɪdaɪzə(r)] n Br batidora f

liquor ['lɪkər] n US alcohol m, bebidas alcohólicas; **liquor store** tienda f de bebidas alcohólicas

liquorice ['lɪkərɪs] n regaliz m

lisp [lɪsp] **1.** n ceceo m **2.** vi cecear

list¹ [lɪst] **1.** n lista f; [catalogue] catálogo m **2.** vt [make a list of] hacer una lista de; [put on a list] poner en una lista; **it is not listed** no figura en la lista

list² [lɪst] **1.** n NAUT escora f **2.** vi NAUT escorar

listen ['lɪsən] vi escuchar; [pay attention] prestar atención ■ **listen out for** vt insep estar atento(a) a

listener ['lɪsənə(r)] n oyente mf

listless ['lɪstlɪs] adj apático(a)

lit [lɪt] pt & pp of **light**

liter ['liːtə(r)] US n = **litre**

literal ['lɪtərəl] adj literal

literally ['lɪtərəlɪ] adv literalmente

literary ['lɪtərərɪ] adj literario(a)

literate ['lɪtərɪt] adj alfabetizado(a)

literature ['lɪtərətʃə(r)] n a) literatura f b) Fam [documentation] folleto informativo

litigation [lɪtɪ'geɪʃən] n litigio m

litre ['liːtə(r)] n litro m

litter ['lɪtə(r)] **1.** n a) [rubbish] basura f; [papers] papeles mpl; **cat litter** arena f para gatos; **litter bin** papelera f b) [offspring] camada f **2.** vt ensuciar

little ['lɪtəl] **1.** adj a) pequeño(a); **a little dog** un perrito; **a little house** una casita; **little finger** (dedo m) meñique m b) [not much] poco(a); **a little cheese** un poco de queso; **a little money** un poco de dinero; **I speak a little French** hablo un poco de francés **2.** pron poco m; **a little** un poco; **save me a little** guárdame un poco **3.** adv poco; **I'm a little tired** estoy un poco cansado; **I walked on a little** seguí andando un poco; **little by little** poco a poco; **as little as possible** lo menos posible

live¹ [lɪv] **1.** vi vivir; **long live the King!** ¡viva el Rey! **2.** vt vivir; **to live an interesting life** vivir una vida interesante ■ **live down** vt sep conseguir que se olvide ■ **live off** vt insep vivir de ■ **live on 1.** vt insep [food, money] vivir de **2.** vi [memory] persistir ■ **live through** vt insep vivir durante ■ **live up to** vt insep [promises] cumplir con; **it didn't live up to expectations** no fue lo que se esperaba

live² [laɪv] adj a) [living] vivo(a) b) TV & RADIO en directo, en vivo c) [ammunition] real; [bomb] sin explotar; ELEC con corriente; Fam **he's a real live wire!** ¡éste no para nunca!

livelihood ['laɪvlɪhʊd] n sustento m

lively ['laɪvlɪ] (compar **livelier**, superl **liveliest**) adj [person] vivo(a); [place] animado(a); Fig [interest] entusiástico(a)

liver ['lɪvə(r)] n hígado m

lives [laɪvz] pl of **life**

livestock ['laɪvstɒk] n ganado m

livestream ['laɪvstriːm] n retransmisión f en directo en streaming

livid ['lɪvɪd] adj lívido(a); Fam [angry] furioso(a)

living ['lɪvɪŋ] **1.** adj vivo(a) **2.** n vida f; **living conditions** condiciones fpl de vida; **living expenses** dietas fpl; **to earn** or **make one's living** ganarse la vida; **living room** sala f de estar; **living standards** nivel m de vida; **living wage** sueldo mínimo

lizard ['lɪzəd] n [large] lagarto m; [small] lagartija f

load [ləʊd] **1.** n a) [burden, thing carried, ELEC & TECH] carga f; [weight] peso m b) Fam [large amount] **loads of**, **a load of** montones de, un montón de; **that's a load of rubbish** esp Br or **of bull** esp US ¡no son más que tonterías! **2.** vt [vehicle, goods etc & COMPUT] cargar; [DVD] poner; **to load sth/sb with** cargar algo/a algn con; **to load a gun/camera (with)** cargar un arma/una cámara (con); **to load the dice** trucar los dados **3.** vi a) [receive freight] cargar; **the ship is loading** están cargando el barco b) COMPUT [program] cargarse ■ **load down** vt sep cargar; **I'm loaded down with work** estoy cargado de trabajo; **he was loaded down with packages** iba cargado de paquetes ■ **load up** vi & vt sep cargar

loaded ['ləʊdɪd] *adj* **a)** cargado(a) **(with** de); *Fig* **a loaded question** una pregunta intencionada **b)** *Fam* **to be loaded** [rich] estar forrado(a)

loading ['ləʊdɪŋ] *n* [of lorry] carga *f*; **loading bay** zona *f* de carga y descarga

loaf[1] [ləʊf] *(pl* **loaves***) n* pan *m*; [French stick] barra *f* de pan; [sliced] pan de molde

loaf[2] [ləʊf] *vi* **to loaf (about** *or* **around)** holgazanear

loan [ləʊn] **1.** *n* préstamo *m*; FIN empréstito *m*; **on loan** prestado(a); [footballer] cedido(a) **2.** *vt* prestar

loathe [ləʊð] *vt* aborrecer, odiar

loaves [ləʊvz] *pl of* **loaf**

lobby ['lɒbɪ] **1.** *n* **a)** [hall] vestíbulo *m* **b)** [pressure group] grupo *m* de presión, lobby *m* **2.** *vt* presionar **3.** *vi* ejercer presiones

lobster ['lɒbstə(r)] *n* langosta *f*

local ['ləʊkəl] **1.** *adj* local; [person] del pueblo; MED **local anaesthetic** anestesia *f* local; TEL **local call** llamada urbana; **local government** gobierno *m* municipal **2.** *n Fam* **a) the locals** los vecinos **b)** *Br* [pub] bar *m* del barrio

locality [ləʊ'kælɪtɪ] *n* localidad *f*

localization, *Br* **localisation** [,ləʊkəlaɪ'zeɪʃn] *n* COMPUT localización *f*

locally ['ləʊkəlɪ] *adv* en *or* de la localidad

locate [ləʊ'keɪt] *vt* [situate] situar, ubicar; [find] localizar

location [ləʊ'keɪʃən] *n* **a)** lugar *m*, situación *f* **b)** CIN **location shots** exteriores *mpl*; **they're on location in Australia** están rodando en Australia

lock[1] ['lɒk] **1.** *n* **a)** [on door etc] cerradura *f*; [bolt] cerrojo *m*; [padlock] candado *m*
b) [on canal] esclusa *f*
2. *vt* cerrar con llave /cerrojo /candado
3. *vi* [door etc] cerrarse; [wheels] trabarse
■ **lock up** *vt sep* [house] cerrar; [jail] meter en la cárcel

lock[2] [lɒk] *n Liter* [of hair] mechón *m*

locker ['lɒkə(r)] *n* [cupboard] armario ropero; *US* **locker room** vestuarios *mpl*

locket ['lɒkɪt] *n* medallón *m*

locksmith ['lɒksmɪθ] *n* cerrajero *m*

locomotive [ləʊkə'məʊtɪv] *n* locomotora *f*

locust ['ləʊkəst] *n* langosta *f*

lodge [lɒdʒ] **1.** *n* [gamekeeper's] casa *f* del guarda; [porter's] portería *f*; [hunter's] refugio *m*
2. *vt* **a)** [accommodate] alojar
b) [complaint] presentar
3. *vi* **a)** [live] alojarse
b) [get stuck] meterse **(in** en)

lodger ['lɒdʒə(r)] *n* huésped(a) *m,f*

lodging ['lɒdʒɪŋ] *n* **a)** alojamiento *m*; **lodging house** casa *f* de huéspedes **b) lodgings** habitación *f* (de alquiler)

loft [lɒft] *n* desván *m*

log [lɒg] **1.** *n* **a)** tronco *m*; [for fuel] leño *m*; **log cabin** cabaña de troncos **b)** NAUT diario *m* de a bordo **2.** *vt* [record] registrar ■ **log in, log on** *vi* COMPUT iniciar sesión, conectarse ■ **log out, log off** *vi* COMPUT cerrar *or* finalizar sesión, desconectarse

logic ['lɒdʒɪk] *n* lógica *f*

logical ['lɒdʒɪkəl] *adj* lógico(a)

logistics [lə'dʒɪstɪks] *npl* logística *f*

loiter ['lɔɪtə(r)] *vi* [hang about] holgazanear; [lag behind] rezagarse; [prowl] merodear

loll [lɒl] *vi* [tongue, head] colgar ■ **loll about, loll around** *vi* repantigarse

lollipop ['lɒlɪpɒp] *n* piruleta *f*; *Br Fam* **lollipop lady /man** *persona encargada de ayudar a cruzar la calle a los colegiales*

lolly ['lɒlɪ] *n Fam* **a)** [sweet] piruleta *f*; **ice(d) lolly** polo *m* **b)** *Br Fam* [money] *Esp* pasta *f*, *Am* plata *f*

London ['lʌndən] *n* Londres

lone [ləʊn] *adj* [solitary] solitario(a); [single] solo(a)

loneliness ['ləʊnlɪnɪs] *n* soledad *f*

lonely ['ləʊnlɪ] *(compar* **lonelier,** *superl* **loneliest***) adj* solo(a), solitario(a)

long[1] [lɒŋ] **1.** *adj* **a)** [size] largo(a); **how long is the table?** ¿cuánto tiene de largo la mesa?; **it's 3 m long** tiene 3 m de largo; **long jump** salto *m* de longitud **b)** [time] mucho(a); **at long last** por fin; **how long is the film?** ¿cuánto tiempo dura la película?

2. *adv* mucho, mucho tiempo; **all day long** todo el día; **as long as the exhibition lasts** mientras dure la exposición; **as long as** *or* **so long as you don't mind** con tal de que no te importe; **before long** dentro de poco; **how long have you been here?** ¿cuánto tiempo llevas aquí?

long[2] [lɒŋ] *vi* añorar; **to long for** anhelar

long-distance ['lɒŋdɪstəns] *adj* de larga distancia; **long-distance call** conferencia interurbana; **long-distance runner** corredor(a) *m,f* de fondo

longing ['lɒŋɪŋ] *n* [desire] anhelo *m*; [nostalgia] nostalgia *f*

longitude ['lɒndʒɪtjuːd] *n* longitud *f*

long-range ['lɒŋreɪdʒ] *adj* [missile etc] de largo alcance; [weather forecast] de largo plazo

long-sighted [lɒŋ'saɪtɪd] *adj* **a)** MED présbita **b)** *Fig* previsor(a)

long-standing ['lɒŋstændɪŋ] *adj* antiguo(a), de mucho tiempo

long-term ['lɒŋtɜːm] *adj* a largo plazo

loo [luː] *n Br Fam* baño *m*, váter *m*

look [lʊk] **1.** *n* **a)** [glance] mirada *f*; **to take a look at** [peep] echar un vistazo a; [examine] examinar

b) [appearance] aspecto *m*, apariencia *f*; **I don't like the look of it** me da mala espina

c) [fashion] moda *f*

d) (good) looks belleza *f*

2. *vi* **a)** mirar, *Am* ver

b) [seem] parecer; **it looks delicious** tiene un aspecto buenísimo; **she looks like her father** [resembles] se parece a su padre

3. *vt* mirar

■ **look after** *vt insep* cuidar a, ocuparse de

■ **look at** *vt insep* mirar; *Fig* **whichever way you look at it** desde cualquier punto de vista

■ **look away** *vi* apartar la mirada

■ **look back** *vi* **a)** mirar hacia atrás; *Fig* **since then he has never looked back** desde entonces ha ido prosperando **b)** [remember] recordar

■ **look down** *vi Fig* **to look down on sth/sb** despreciar algo/a algn

■ **look for** *vt insep* buscar

■ **look forward to** *vt insep* esperar con ansia; **I look forward to hearing from you** [in letter] espero noticias suyas

■ **look into** *vt insep* examinar, investigar

■ **look on 1.** *vt insep* [consider] considerar **2.** *vi* quedarse mirando

■ **look onto** *vt insep* dar a

■ **look out** *vi* **a) the bedroom looks out onto the garden** el dormitorio da al jardín **b) look out!** [take care] ¡cuidado!, ¡ojo!

■ **look out for** *vt insep* [person] estar pendiente de; [new book] estar atento a la salida de

■ **look over** *vt sep* [examine] revisar; [place] inspeccionar

■ **look round 1.** *vi* mirar alrededor; [turn head] volver la cabeza **2.** *vt insep* [house, shop] ver

■ **look through** *vt insep* **a)** [window] mirar por **b)** [leaf through] hojear; [examine] revisar; [check] registrar

■ **look to** *vt insep* **a)** [take care of] velar por **b)** [turn to] recurrir a

■ **look up 1.** *vi* **a)** [glance upwards] alzar la vista **b)** *Fam* [improve] mejorar **2.** *vt sep* **a)** [look for] buscar **b)** [visit] ir a visitar

■ **look upon** *vt insep* considerar

■ **look up to** *vt insep* [person] respetar

lookout ['lʊkaʊt] *n* [person] centinela *mf*; [place] mirador *m*; **to be on the lookout for** estar al acecho de; *Fam* **that's his lookout!** ¡eso es asunto suyo!

lookup ['lʊkʌp] n COMPUT búsqueda f, consulta f

loom¹ [lu:m] n telar m

loom² [lu:m] vi alzarse; Fig [threaten] amenazar

loony ['lu:nɪ] (compar **loonier**, superl **looniest**) adj Fam loco(a)

loop [lu:p] **1.** n a) lazo m b) COMPUT bucle m **2.** vt a) encordar b) AVIAT **to loop the loop** rizar el rizo

loophole ['lu:phəʊl] n Fig escapatoria f

loose [lu:s] adj a) [not secure] flojo(a); [papers, hair, clothes] suelto(a); [tongue] desatado(a); [baggy] holgado(a); **to set sb loose** soltar a algn b) [not packaged] a granel; **loose change** suelto m c) [not exact] vago(a); [translation] libre d) [lax] relajado(a); **a loose woman** una mujer fácil

loosen ['lu:sən] **1.** vt aflojar; [belt] desabrochar; Fig [restrictions] flexibilizar **2.** vi [slacken] aflojarse

loot [lu:t] **1.** n botín m **2.** vt saquear

looting ['lu:tɪŋ] n saqueo m, pillaje m

lop [lɒp] vt podar ∎ **lop off** vt sep cortar

lopsided [lɒp'saɪdɪd] adj ladeado(a)

lord [lɔ:d] n a) señor m; [British peer] lord m; Br **the (House of) Lords** la cámara de los lores; **the Lord Mayor** el señor alcalde b) REL **the Lord** El Señor; **good Lord!** ¡Dios mío!; **the Lord's Prayer** el Padrenuestro c) [judge] señoría mf

lorry ['lɒrɪ] n Br camión m; **lorry driver** camionero(a) m,f; **lorry load** carga f

lose [lu:z] (pt & pp lost) **1.** vt perder; **to lose time** [clock] atrasarse **2.** vi perder; **to lose to sb** perder contra algn; **to lose out** salir perdiendo

loser ['lu:zə(r)] n perdedor(a) m,f

loss [lɒs] n pérdida f; **to make a loss** perder; Fig **to be at a loss for words** quedarse de una pieza; **to be at a loss what to do** no saber qué hacer

lost [lɒst] **1.** adj a) perdido(a); **to get lost** perderse; Fam **get lost!** ¡vete a la porra!; **lost property office**, US **lost and found department** oficina f de objetos perdidos b) [disoriented] desorientado(a); [distracted] distraído(a); **lost in thought** ensimismado(a) **2.** pt & pp of **lose**

lot [lɒt] n a) [fate] suerte f b) US [plot of land] parcela f c) [in an auction] lote m d) [everything] todo m; **he ate the lot** se lo comió todo e) **a lot of** [much] mucho(a); [many] muchos(as); **he feels a lot better** se encuentra mucho mejor; Fam **lots of** montones de, cantidad de

lotion ['ləʊʃən] n loción f

lottery ['lɒtərɪ] n lotería f; **lottery ticket** ≃ décimo m de lotería

loud [laʊd] **1.** adj a) [voice] alto(a); [noise] fuerte; [laugh] estrepitoso(a); [applause] clamoroso(a); [protests, party] ruidoso(a) b) [flashy] chillón(ona) c) [vulgar] hortera **2.** adv **to read / think out loud** leer / pensar en voz alta

loudspeaker [laʊd'spi:kə(r)] n altavoz m

lounge [laʊndʒ] **1.** n Br salón m, sala f de estar **2.** vi hacer el vago

louse [laʊs] (pl **lice**) n piojo m

lousy ['laʊzɪ] (compar **lousier**, superl **lousiest**) adj Fam fatal; **a lousy trick** una cochinada

lout [laʊt] n gamberro m

love [lʌv] **1.** n a) amor m (for por); [passion] pasión f (for por); **to be in love with sb** estar enamorado(a) de algn; **to fall in love** enamorarse; **to make love** hacer el amor; **(with) love (from) Mary** [in letter] un abrazo, Mary; **love affair** amorío m; **love life** vida f sentimental b) [person] amor m, cariño m; **my love** mi amor c) [in tennis] **forty love** cuarenta a cero **2.** vt [person] querer a, amar a; **he loves cooking / football** le encanta cocinar / el fútbol

lovely ['lʌvlɪ] (compar **lovelier**, superl **loveliest**) adj [charming] encantador(a); [beautiful] precioso(a), Am lindo(a); [delicious] riquísimo(a)

lover ['lʌvə(r)] n a) [sexual partner] amante mf b) [enthusiast] aficionado(a) m,f, amigo(a) m,f

loving ['lʌvɪŋ] adj cariñoso(a)

low 220

low¹ [ləʊ] **1.** *adj* **a)** bajo(a); [neckline] escotado(a)
b) [in quantity] bajo(a)
c) [poor] pobre
d) [battery] gastado(a); **low frequency** baja frecuencia
e) to feel low sentirse deprimido(a)
f) [reprehensible] malo(a)
2. *adv* bajo
3. *n* **a)** MET área *f* de baja presión
b) [low point] punto más bajo; **to reach an all-time low** tocar fondo

low² [ləʊ] *vi* [cow] mugir

lowdown ['ləʊdaʊn] *n Fam* pormenores *mpl*

low-energy *adj* de bajo consumo; **low-energy light bulb** bombilla *f* de bajo consumo

lower ['ləʊə(r)] **1.** *adj* (*compar of* **low¹**) inferior; TYP **lower case** minúscula *f*; **lower class** clase baja
2. *adv compar of* **low**
3. *vt* bajar; [flag] arriar; [reduce] reducir; [price] rebajar

low-income *adj* de bajos ingresos; **lower-income group** grupo *m* de ingresos más bajos

low-interest *adj* FIN [credit, loan] a bajo interés

lowly ['ləʊlɪ] (*compar* **lowlier**, *superl* **lowliest**) *adj* humilde

low-maintenance *adj* que da poco trabajo

low-octane *adj* de bajo octanaje

low-resolution *adj* de baja resolución

low-risk *adj* [investment, strategy] de bajo riesgo

low-voltage *adj* de bajo voltaje

loyal ['lɔɪəl] *adj* leal, fiel

loyalty ['lɔɪəltɪ] *n* lealtad *f*, fidelidad *f*; **loyalty card** tarjeta *f* de fidelidad

lozenge ['lɒzɪndʒ] *n* pastilla *f*

LP [el'piː] *n* (*abbr of* **long-playing record**) LP *m*

L-plate ['elpleɪt] *n Br* placa *f* de la "L"

LPR *US n* = lawful permanent resident

Ltd *Br* COMM (*abbr of* **limited**) S.L.

lubricate ['luːbrɪkeɪt] *vt* lubricar; [engine] engrasar

lucid ['luːsɪd] *adj* lúcido(a)

luck [lʌk] *n* suerte *f*; **bad luck!** ¡mala suerte!; **good luck!** ¡(buena) suerte!; **to be in luck** estar de suerte; **to be out of luck** no tener suerte; *Fig* **to push one's luck** tentar la suerte; *Fig* **to try one's luck** probar fortuna

luckily ['lʌkɪlɪ] *adv* por suerte, afortunadamente

lucky ['lʌkɪ] (*compar* **luckier**, *superl* **luckiest**) *adj* [person] afortunado(a); [day] de suerte; [move] oportuno(a); [charm] de la suerte; **to be lucky** tener suerte; **a lucky break** una oportunidad

lucrative ['luːkrətɪv] *adj* lucrativo(a)

ludicrous ['luːdɪkrəs] *adj* absurdo(a), ridículo(a)

luggage ['lʌgɪdʒ] *n* equipaje *m*; **luggage allowance** límite *m* de equipaje; **luggage rack** AUTO baca *f*; RAIL portaequipajes *m inv*

lukewarm ['luːkwɔːm] *adj* [water etc] tibio(a); *Fig* [reception etc] poco entusiasta

lull [lʌl] **1.** *n* [in storm] calma chicha; [in fighting] tregua *f* **2.** *vt* [cause to sleep] adormecer; **to lull sb into a false sense of security** infundir una falsa seguridad a algn

lullaby ['lʌləbaɪ] *n* canción *f* de cuna, nana *f*

lumber ['lʌmbə(r)] **1.** *n* **a)** *Br* [junk] trastos viejos **b)** *US* [wood] maderos *mpl* **2.** *vt Fam* cargar (**with de**)

lumberyard ['lʌmbəjɑːd] *n US* almacén *m* maderero, maderería *f*, *RP* barraca *f* maderera

luminous ['luːmɪnəs] *adj* luminoso(a)

lump [lʌmp] **1.** *n* [of coal etc] trozo *m*; [of sugar, earth] terrón *m*; [in sauce] grumo *m*; [swelling] bulto *m*; *Fam & Fig* [in throat] nudo *m*; **lump sum** cantidad *f* global **2.** *vt Fam* [endure] aguantar
■ **lump together** *vt sep* apelotonar

lumpy ['lʌmpɪ] *(compar* **lumpier**, *superl* **lumpiest***) adj* [bed] lleno(a) de bultos ; [sauce] grumoso(a)

lunar ['luːnə(r)] *adj* lunar

lunatic ['luːnətɪk] *adj & n* loco(a) *(m,f)*; **lunatic asylum** manicomio *m*

lunch [lʌntʃ] **1.** *n* comida *f*, almuerzo *m*; **lunch hour** hora *f* de comer **2.** *vi* comer, almorzar

luncheon ['lʌntʃən] *n Dated & Formal* almuerzo *m*; **luncheon voucher** vale *m* de comida ; **(pork) luncheon meat** carne *f* de cerdo troceada, chopped *m*

lung [lʌŋ] *n* pulmón *m*

lunge [lʌndʒ] **1.** *n* arremetida *f* **2.** *vi* **to lunge (forward)** arremeter; **to lunge (out) at sb** arremeter contra algn

lurch [lɜːtʃ] **1.** *n* **a)** [of vehicle] sacudida *f*; [of person] tambaleo *m* **b)** *Fam* **to leave sb in the lurch** dejar a algn en la cuneta **2.** *vi* [vehicle] dar sacudidas ; [person] tambalearse

lure [lʊə(r)] **1.** *n* [decoy] señuelo *m*; [bait] cebo *m*; *Fig* [charm] aliciente *m* **2.** *vt* atraer con engaños

lurid ['lʊərɪd] *adj* **a)** [gruesome] espeluznante ; [sensational] sensacionalista **b)** [gaudy] chillón(ona)

lurk [lɜːk] *vi* [lie in wait] estar al acecho ; [hide] esconderse

luscious ['lʌʃəs] *adj* [food] delicioso(a)

lush [lʌʃ] *adj* [vegetation] exuberante

lust [lʌst] **1.** *n* [sexual desire] lujuria *f*; [craving] ansia *f*; [greed] codicia *f* **2.** *vi* **to lust after sth/sb** codiciar algo / desear a algn

Luxembourg ['lʌksəmbɜːg] *n* Luxemburgo

luxurious [lʌgˈzjʊərɪəs] *adj* lujoso(a)

luxury ['lʌkʃərɪ] *n* lujo *m*; **luxury flat** piso *m* de lujo; **luxury hotel** hotel *m* de lujo

lying ['laɪɪŋ] **1.** *adj* mentiroso(a) **2.** *n* mentiras *fpl*

lynch [lɪntʃ] *vt* linchar

lyric ['lɪrɪk] **1.** *adj* lírico(a) **2.** *n* **a)** [poem] poema lírico **b)** **lyrics** [words of song] letra *f*

M

M, m [em] *n* [the letter] M, m *f*

m a) *(abbr of* **metre(s)***)* m **b)** *(abbr of* **million(s)***)* m

mac [mæk] *n* **a)** *Br Fam (abbr of* **mackintosh***)* [coat] impermeable *m* **b)** *(abbr of* **Macintosh***)* mac *m*

macabre [mə'kɑːbrə] *adj* macabro(a)

machine [mə'ʃiːn] **1.** *n* máquina *f*; **machine gun** ametralladora *f* **2.** *vt* trabajar a máquina

machinery [mə'ʃiːnərɪ] *n* [machines] maquinaria *f*; [workings of machine] mecanismo *m*

mackerel ['mækrəl] *(pl* **mackerel***)* n caballa *f*

mackintosh ['mækɪntɒʃ] *n* impermeable *m*

mad [mæd] *(compar* **madder**, *superl* **maddest***) adj* **a)** loco(a); [animal] furioso(a); [dog] rabioso(a); **to go mad** volverse loco(a); *Fam* **mad cow disease** el mal de las vacas locas **b)** [idea, plan] disparatado(a) **c)** *Fam* **to be mad about sth/sb** estar loco(a) por algo/algn **d)** *esp US Fam* **to be mad at sb** estar muy *esp Esp* enfadado(a) *or esp Am* enojado(a) con algn

madam ['mædəm] *n* señora *f*; **Dear Madam** [in letter] Muy señora mía, Estimada señora

made [meɪd] *pt & pp of* **make**

madly ['mædlɪ] *adv Fam* [extremely] terriblemente; **to be madly in love with sb** estar locamente enamorado(a) de algn

madman ['mædmən] *n* loco *m*

madness ['mædnɪs] *n* locura *f*

madrasah, madrassa, madrasa [mə'dræsə] *n* madrasa *f*

Madrid [mə'drɪd] *n* Madrid

magazine [mægə'ziːn] *n* **a)** [periodical] revista *f* **b)** [in rifle] recámara *f* **c)** MIL [storehouse] almacén *m*; [for explosives] polvorín *m*

magic ['mædʒɪk] **1.** *n* magia *f* **2.** *adj* **a)** mágico(a); **magic wand** varita mágica **b)** *Fam* [excellent] genial, *Esp* guay, *Am* salvo *RP* chévere, *Méx* padrísimo(a), *RP* bárbaro(a)

magician [mə'dʒɪʃən] *n* **a)** [wizard] mago(a) *m,f* **b)** [conjurer] prestidigitador(a) *m,f*

magistrate ['mædʒɪstreɪt] *n Br* juez *mf* de primera instancia; **magistrates' court** juzgado *m* de primera instancia

magnet ['mægnɪt] *n* imán *m*

magnetic [mæg'netɪk] *adj* magnético(a); *Fig* [personality] carismático(a); **magnetic tape** cinta magnetofónica

magnificent [mæg'nɪfɪsənt] *adj* magnífico(a)

magnify ['mægnɪfaɪ] *vt* **a)** [enlarge] aumentar **b)** *Fig* [exaggerate] exagerar

mahogany [mə'hɒgənɪ] **1.** *n* caoba *f* **2.** *adj* de caoba

maid [meɪd] *n* **a)** criada *f*, *Andes, RP* mucama *f* **b)** *Pej* **old maid** solterona *f*

maiden ['meɪdən] *adj* **a)** [unmarried] soltera *f*; **maiden name** apellido *m* de soltera **b)** [voyage, flight] inaugural

mail [meɪl] **1.** *n* correo *m*; **by mail** por correo; **mail order** venta *f* por correo **2.** *vt* [post] echar al buzón; [send] enviar por correo

mailbox ['meɪlbɒks] *n US* buzón *m*

mailing *n* COMM [posting] mailing *m*; **mailing list** lista *f* de direcciones *(para envío de publicidad)*; COMPUT lista *f* de correo *or* de distribución

maim [meɪm] *vt* lisiar

malignant

main [meɪn] **1.** adj [problem, door etc] principal; [square, mast, sail] mayor; [office] central; CULIN **main course** plato m principal; **main road** carretera f principal; US **Main Street** la Calle Mayor

2. n **a)** [pipe, wire] conducto m principal; **the mains** [water or gas system] la cañería maestra; ELEC la red eléctrica **b) in the main** por regla general

mainland ['meɪnlənd] n continente m

mainly ['meɪnlɪ] adv principalmente, sobre todo; [for the most part] en su mayoría

maintain [meɪn'teɪn] vt mantener; [conversation] sostener; [silence, appearances] guardar; [road, machine] conservar en buen estado

maintenance ['meɪntənəns] n **a)** [of car, equipment, roads] mantenimiento m **b)** [divorce allowance] pensión f

maize [meɪz] n maíz m, Andes, RP choclo m

majesty ['mædʒɪstɪ] n majestad f

major ['meɪdʒə(r)] **1.** adj **a)** principal, mayor; [contribution, operation] importante **b)** MUS mayor **2.** n **a)** MIL comandante m **b)** US UNIV especialidad f **3.** vi US UNIV **to major in** especializarse en

Majorca [mə'jɔːkə] n Mallorca

majority [mə'dʒɒrɪtɪ] n mayoría f; **to be in the majority** ser (la) mayoría

make [meɪk] (pt & pp made) **1.** vt **a)** [produce, prepare, perform] hacer; [manufacture] hacer, fabricar; [clothes, curtains] confeccionar; [meal] preparar; [payment] efectuar; [speech] pronunciar; [decision] tomar; [mistake] cometer; **to be made of** ser de; **to make a noise** hacer ruido

b) [render] poner, volver; [convert] convertir (**into** en); [appoint] nombrar; **he made it clear that ...** dejó claro que ...

c) [force, compel] obligar; [cause] causar; **to make do with sth** arreglárselas con algo

d) [earn] ganar; **to make a living** ganarse la vida

e) 7 and 5 make 12 7 y 5 son 12

f) [calculate, reckon] calcular; **I don't know what to make of it** no sé qué pensar de eso; **what time do you make it?** ¿qué hora tienes?

g) [achieve] alcanzar, conseguir

2. vi **a)** hacer; **to make sure of sth** asegurarse de algo

b) she made as if to leave hizo como si quisiera marcharse

3. n [brand] marca f

■ **make for** vt insep [move towards] dirigirse hacia

■ **make out 1.** vt sep **a)** [list, receipt] hacer; [cheque] extender **b)** [perceive] distinguir; [writing] descifrar **c)** [understand] entender **d)** [claim] pretender **2.** vi **how did you make out?** ¿qué tal te fue?

■ **make up 1.** vt sep **a)** [parcel, list] hacer; [prescription] preparar; [assemble] montar **b)** [story] inventar **c)** [apply cosmetics to] maquillar; [one's face] maquillarse **d)** [loss] compensar; [lost time] recuperar **e)** [constitute] componer **f) to make it up (with sb)** hacer las paces (con algn) **2.** vi maquillarse

■ **make up to** vt sep **to make it up to sb for sth** compensar a algn por algo

makeshift ['meɪkʃɪft] adj [improvised] improvisado(a); [temporary] provisional

make-up ['meɪkʌp] n **a)** [cosmetics] maquillaje m; **make-up remover** desmaquillador m **b)** [composition] composición f; [character] carácter m

malaria [mə'leərɪə] n malaria f

male [meɪl] **1.** adj [animal, plant] macho; [person] varón; [sex] masculino; Pej **male chauvinism** machismo m **2.** n [person] varón m; [animal, plant] macho m

malfunction [mæl'fʌŋkʃən] **1.** n Esp fallo m, Am falla f **2.** vi funcionar mal

malice ['mælɪs] n malicia f; JUR **with malice aforethought** con premeditación

malicious [mə'lɪʃəs] adj malévolo(a)

malignant [mə'lɪɡnənt] adj **a)** [person] malvado(a) **b)** MED maligno(a)

mall 224

mall [mɔːl] n US centro m comercial

mallrat ['mɔːlræt] n US joven que se pasa el tiempo en los centros comerciales

malnutrition [mælnjuːˈtrɪʃən] n desnutrición f

malt [mɔːlt] n malta f

malware ['mælweə(r)] n software m malicioso, programas mpl maliciosos

mammal ['mæməl] n mamífero m

man [mæn] **1.** (pl **men**) n **a)** hombre m; **old man** viejo m; **young man** joven m; Fig **the man in the street** el hombre de la calle **b)** [humanity] el hombre **c)** [husband] marido m; [partner] pareja f **2.** vt [boat, plane] tripular; [post] servir; **manned flight** vuelo tripulado

manage ['mænɪdʒ] **1.** vt a) [company, household] llevar; [money, affairs, person] manejar **b)** [succeed] conseguir; **to manage to do sth** lograr hacer algo **2.** vi [cope physically] poder; [esp financially] arreglárselas; **we're managing** vamos tirando

management ['mænɪdʒmənt] n dirección f

manager ['mænɪdʒə(r)] n **a)** [of company, bank] director(a) m,f; [head of department] jefe(a) m,f **b)** [of pop group etc] mánager m **c)** SPORT entrenador m

manageress [mænɪdʒəˈres] n [of shop, restaurant] encargada f; [of company] directora f

mandate ['mændeɪt] n mandato m

mane [meɪn] n [of horse] crin f; [of lion] melena f

maneuver [məˈnuːvər] US n, vt & vi = **manoeuvre**

manga ['mæŋɡə] n manga m

mangle¹ ['mæŋɡəl] n [for wringing] rodillo m

mangle² ['mæŋɡəl] vt [crush] aplastar; [destroy by cutting] despedazar

mango ['mæŋɡəʊ] (pl **mangoes**) n mango m

mania ['meɪnɪə] n manía f

maniac ['meɪnɪæk] n maníaco(a) m,f; **to drive like a maniac** Esp conducir or Am manejar como un loco

manicure ['mænɪkjʊə(r)] **1.** n manicura f **2.** vt **to manicure one's nails** hacerse la manicura

manifesto [mænɪˈfestəʊ] n programa m electoral

manipulate [məˈnɪpjʊleɪt] vt **a)** manipular **b)** Fig [accounts etc] falsificar

mankind [mænˈkaɪnd] n la humanidad, el género humano

man-made ['mænmeɪd] adj [lake] artificial; [fibres, fabric] sintético(a)

manner ['mænə(r)] n **a)** [way, method] manera f, modo m; **in this manner** de esta manera **b)** [way of behaving] forma f de ser **c)** Formal [type, class] clase f **d)** [etiquette] **(good) manners** buenos modales; **bad manners** falta f de educación

mannerism ['mænərɪzəm] n [gesture] gesto m; [affectation] amaneramiento m

manoeuvre [məˈnuːvə(r)] **1.** n maniobra f **2.** vt maniobrar; [person] manejar **3.** vi maniobrar

manpower ['mænpaʊə(r)] n mano f de obra

mansion ['mænʃən] n casa f grande; [in country] casa solariega

manslaughter ['mænslɔːtə(r)] n homicidio involuntario

mantelpiece ['mæntəlpiːs] n [shelf] repisa f de chimenea; [fireplace] chimenea f

manual ['mænjʊəl] adj & n manual (m)

manufacture [mænjʊˈfæktʃə(r)] **1.** vt fabricar **2.** n fabricación f

manufacturer [mænjʊˈfæktʃərə(r)] n fabricante mf

manure [məˈnjʊə(r)] n abono m, estiércol m

manuscript ['mænjʊskrɪpt] n manuscrito m

many ['menɪ] (compar **more**, superl **most**) **1.** adj mucho(a) / muchos(as); **a great many** muchísimos(as); **as many ... as** ... tantos(as) ... como ...; **how many days?** ¿cuántos días?; **too many** demasiados(as) **2.** pron muchos(as)

map [mæp] **1.** n [of country] mapa m; [of town, bus route] plano m **2.** vt trazar un mapa de ■ **map out** vt sep [route] trazar en un mapa; Fig [future etc] planear

maple ['meɪpəl] n arce m

marathon ['mærəθən] n maratón m

marble ['mɑːbəl] **1.** n **a)** [stone] mármol m **b)** [glass ball] canica f **2.** adj de mármol

march [mɑːtʃ] **1.** n **a)** MIL marcha f **b)** [demonstration] manifestación f **2.** vi **a)** marchar **b)** [demonstrate] manifestarse **3.** vt MIL hacer marchar

March [mɑːtʃ] n marzo m

mare [meə(r)] n yegua f

margarine [mɑːdʒəˈriːn] n margarina f

margin ['mɑːdʒɪn] n margen m; Fig **to win by a narrow margin** ganar por escaso margen

marijuana, marihuana [mærɪˈhwɑːnə] n marihuana f, marijuana f

marinate ['mærɪneɪt] vt adobar

marine [məˈriːn] **1.** adj marino(a) **2.** n marine mf, infante mf de marina, Am fusilero m naval

marital ['mærɪtəl] adj matrimonial; **marital status** estado m civil

mark[1] [mɑːk] **1.** n **a)** [left by blow etc] señal f; [stain] mancha f **b)** [sign, token] señal f; [indication] indicio m **c)** [in exam etc] nota f **2.** vt **a)** [stain] manchar **b)** [with tick, cross] señalar **c)** [exam] corregir; [student] dar notas a **d)** **mark my words** fíjate en lo que te digo ■ **mark out** vt sep **a)** [area] delimitar **b)** **to mark sb out for** destinar a algn a

mark[2] [mɑːk] n [unit of currency] marco m

marked [mɑːkt] adj [noticeable] marcado(a), acusado(a)

marker ['mɑːkə(r)] n **a)** [sign] indicador m **b)** [pen] rotulador m

market ['mɑːkɪt] **1.** n mercado m, CSur feria f, CAm, Méx tianguis m; **on the market** en venta; **market forces** tendencias fpl del mercado; **market price** precio m de mercado; **market research** estudio m de mercado **2.** vt [sell] poner en venta; [promote] promocionar

marketing ['mɑːkɪtɪŋ] n marketing m, mercadotecnia f

marketplace ['mɑːkɪtpleɪs] n mercado m

marmalade ['mɑːməleɪd] n mermelada f (de cítricos)

marriage ['mærɪdʒ] n [wedding] boda f, Andes matrimonio m, RP casamiento m; [institution, period, relationship] matrimonio m; **marriage bureau** agencia f matrimonial; **marriage certificate** certificado m de matrimonio

married ['mærɪd] adj casado(a); **to be married** estar or Am ser casado(a)

marrow ['mærəʊ] n **a)** (bone) **marrow** médula f **b)** Br (vegetable) **marrow** calabacín m

marry ['mærɪ] vt [take in marriage] casarse con; [give in marriage] casar (**to** con); [unite in marriage] casar; **to get married** casarse

marsh [mɑːʃ] n pantano m; **salt marsh** marisma f

marshal ['mɑːʃəl] **1.** n **a)** [army officer] mariscal m **b)** US [police chief] jefe(a) m,f de policía; [fire chief] jefe(a) m,f de bomberos; [police officer] policía mf **2.** (pt & pp **marshalled**, US pt & pp **marshaled**) vt **a)** [people, troops] dirigir **b)** [arguments, thoughts] poner en orden

martial ['mɑːʃəl] adj marcial; **martial arts** artes fpl marciales

martyr ['mɑːtə(r)] **1.** n mártir mf **2.** vt martirizar

marvel ['mɑːvəl] **1.** n maravilla f **2.** vi **to marvel at** maravillarse de

marvellous, US marvelous ['mɑːvələs] adj maravilloso(a)

Marxist ['mɑːksɪst] adj & n marxista (mf)

marzipan ['mɑːzɪpæn] n mazapán m

mascara [mæˈskɑːrə] n rímel m

masculine ['mæskjʊlɪn] adj masculino(a); [woman] hombruna

mash [mæʃ] **1.** n [for animals] afrecho m
2. vt **to mash (up)** machacar; **mashed
potatoes** puré m de Esp patatas or Am
papas

mask [mɑːsk] **1.** n máscara f; [of doctor,
dentist etc] mascarilla f **2.** vt enmas-
carar; Fig [conceal] ocultar (**from** de)

masochist ['mæsəkɪst] adj & n maso-
quista (mf)

mason ['meɪsən] n **a)** [builder] albañil m **b)** [freemason] masón m, franc-
masón m

mass¹ [mæs] n REL misa f; **to say mass**
decir misa

mass² [mæs] **1.** n **a)** masa f
b) [large quantity] montón m; [of
people] multitud f
c) the masses las masas
2. adj masivo(a); **mass media** medios mpl de comunicación (de masas);
mass production fabricación f en serie
3. vi [people] congregarse; MIL concentrarse

massacre ['mæsəkə(r)] **1.** n masacre f
2. vt masacrar

massage ['mæsɑːʒ, mə'sɑːdʒ] **1.** n masaje m **2.** vt **a)** dar masajes a **b)** Fig [figures]
amañar

massive ['mæsɪv] adj enorme; [heart
attack] grave

mass-produced adj fabricado(a)
en serie

mast [mɑːst] n **a)** NAUT mástil m
b) RADIO & TV torre f; **mobile phone
mast** antena f de telefonía móvil

master ['mɑːstə(r)] **1.** n **a)** [of dog, ser-
vant] amo m
b) Br [teacher] profesor m
c) UNIV **master's degree** ≃ máster m
d) [expert] maestro m
2. adj **a)** [main] original m; **master copy** original m; **mas-
ter key** llave f maestra
b) [expert] maestro(a)
3. vt **a)** [person, situation] dominar
b) [subject, skill] llegar a dominar

mastermind ['mɑːstəmaɪnd] **1.** n
[person] cerebro m **2.** vt ser el cerebro
de

masterpiece ['mɑːstəpiːs] n obra f
maestra

masturbate ['mæstəbeɪt] vi mastur-
barse

mat¹ [mæt] n [rug] alfombrilla f;
[doormat] felpudo m; [rush mat] estera f; SPORT colchoneta f

mat² [mæt] adj mate

match¹ [mætʃ] n fósforo m, Esp cerilla f,
Am cerillo m

match² [mætʃ] **1.** n **a)** SPORT partido m;
[in boxing] combate m
b) Fig **to meet one's match** [equal]
encontrar uno la horma de su zapato
2. vt **a)** [equal, be the equal of] igualar
b) [be in harmony with] armonizar;
they are well matched [teams] van
iguales; [couple] hacen buena pareja
c) [colours, clothes] hacer juego con;
[pair of socks, gloves] ser el compañero de
3. vi [harmonize] hacer juego

matchbox ['mætʃbɒks] n caja f de Esp
cerillas or Am cerillos

matching ['mætʃɪŋ] adj que hace juego

matchstick ['mætʃstɪk] n Esp cerilla f,
Am cerillo m

mate [meɪt] **1.** n **a)** [at school, work]
compañero(a) m,f, colega mf; Br, Austr
Fam [friend] amigo(a) m,f, Esp colega mf,
Méx cuate mf **b)** ZOOL [male] macho m;
[female] hembra f **c)** [assistant] ayudante mf **2.** vi ZOOL aparearse

material [mə'tɪərɪəl] **1.** n **a)** [substance]
materia f **b)** [cloth] tejido m, tela f
c) materials [ingredients, equipment]
materiales mpl **2.** adj **a)** substancial
b) [not spiritual] material

materialize [mə'tɪərɪəlaɪz] vi **a)** [hopes]
realizarse; [plan, idea] concretarse
b) [show up] presentarse

maternal [mə'tɜːnəl] adj maternal;
[uncle etc] materno(a)

maternity [mə'tɜːnɪtɪ] n maternidad f;
maternity dress vestido m premamá;
maternity hospital maternidad f

math [mæθ] US n = **maths**

mathematical [mæθə'mætɪkəl] *adj*
matemático(a)

mathematics [mæθə'mætɪks] *n sing*
matemáticas *fpl*

maths [mæθs] *n sing Br Fam* matemáticas *fpl*

matinée ['mætɪneɪ] *n* CIN sesión *f* de
tarde; THEAT función *f* de tarde

matrimony ['mætrɪmənɪ] *n* matrimonio *m*; [married life] vida *f* conyugal

matt, *US* **matte** [mæt] *adj* mate

matter ['mætə(r)] **1.** *n* **a)** [affair, question] asunto *m*; **as a matter of fact** en
realidad
b) [problem] **what's the matter?** ¿qué
pasa?
c) no matter what he does haga lo
que haga; **no matter where you go**
dondequiera que vayas; **no matter
how** como sea
d) [substance] materia *f*, sustancia *f*
e) [content] contenido *m*; [subject]
tema *m*
2. *vi* importar; **it doesn't matter** no
importa, da igual

matter-of-fact ['mætərəv'fækt] *adj*
[person] práctico(a); [account] realista;
[style] prosaico(a)

mattress ['mætrɪs] *n* colchón *f*; **air
mattress** colchón *m* inflable

mature [mə'tʃʊə(r)] **1.** *adj* maduro(a); FIN
vencido(a) **2.** *vi* madurar; FIN vencer
3. *vt* madurar

max [mæks] *adv Fam* como máximo
■ **max out** *vt sep US* **I maxed out my
credit card** he llegado al límite de mi
tarjeta de crédito

maximum ['mæksɪməm] **1.** *(pl* **maxima)**
n máximo *m* **2.** *adj* máximo(a)

may [meɪ] *(pt* **might)**

En el inglés hablado, y en el escrito en
estilo coloquial, la forma negativa **might
not** se transforma en **mightn't**. La forma
might have se transforma en **might've**.

v aux **a)** [expressing possibility] poder,
ser posible; **come what may** pase lo
que pase; **he may** *or* **might come** puede
que venga; **you may** *or* **might as well
stay** más vale que te quedes **b)** [permis-

sion] poder; **may I?** ¿me permite?; **you
may smoke** pueden fumar **c)** [wish]
ojalá (+ *subj)*; **may you always be
happy!** ¡ojalá seas siempre feliz!

May [meɪ] *n* mayo *m*; **May Day** el uno
de mayo

maybe ['meɪbiː] *adv* quizá(s), tal vez

mayonnaise [meɪə'neɪz] *n* mayonesa *f*,
mahonesa *f*

mayor [meə(r)] *n* [man] alcalde *m*;
[woman] alcaldesa *f*

maze [meɪz] *n* laberinto *m*

MBA [embiː'eɪ] *n* UNIV *(abbr of* **Master of
Business Administration)** MBA *m*,
máster *m* en administración de empresas

me [miː] *(unstressed* [mɪ]) *pers pron* **a)** [as
object] me; **he gave it to me** me lo dio;
listen to me escúchame; **she knows
me** me conoce **b)** [after prep] mí; **it's
for me** es para mí; **with me** conmigo
c) [emphatic] yo; **it's me** soy yo; **what
about me?** ¿y yo, qué?

meadow ['medəʊ] *n* prado *m*, pradera *f*

meagre, *US* **meager** ['miːgə(r)] *adj*
exiguo(a)

meal[1] [miːl] *n* [flour] harina *f*

meal[2] [miːl] *n* [food] comida *f*

mean[1] [miːn] *(pt & pp* **meant)** *vt* **a)** [signify] significar, querer decir; **what
do you mean by that?** ¿qué quieres
decir con eso? **b)** [intend] pensar, tener
la intención de; **I mean it** (te) lo digo en
serio; **she didn't mean to do it** lo hizo
sin querer **c)** [entail] suponer **d)** [refer
to] referirse a **e)** [destine] destinar (**for**
a *or* para)

mean[2] [miːn] *(compar* **meaner**, *superl*
meanest) *adj* **a)** [miserly] tacaño(a)
b) [unkind] malo(a); [petty]
mezquino(a); *US* [bad-tempered]
malhumorado(a); **to be mean to sb**
tratar mal a algn **c)** **it was no mean feat**
fue toda una hazaña

mean[3] [miːn] **1.** *adj* [average] medio(a)
2. *n* [average] promedio *m*; MATH media *f*

meaning ['miːnɪŋ] *n* sentido *m*, significado *m*

meaningful ['mi:nɪŋfʊl] *adj* sig-
nificativo(a)

meaningless ['mi:nɪŋlɪs] *adj* sin sentido

means [mi:nz] *n* **a)** (*sing or pl*) [method]
medio *m*, manera *f*; **by means of** por
medio de, mediante **b)** (*pl*) [resources,
wealth] medios *mpl* (de vida), recursos *mpl* (económicos) **c) by all means!**
¡por supuesto!

meant [ment] *pt & pp of* **mean**

meantime ['mi:ntaɪm] **1.** *adv* mientras
tanto **2.** *n* **in the meantime** mientras
tanto

meanwhile ['mi:nwaɪl] *adv* mientras
tanto

measles ['mi:zəlz] *n sing* sarampión *m*

measure ['meʒə(r)] **1.** *n* **a)** [action,
step] medida *f* **b)** [ruler] regla *f* **c) in
some measure** hasta cierto punto
d) MUS compás *m* **2.** *vt* [object, area]
medir; [person] tomar las medidas de
■ **measure up** *vi* **to measure up (to
sth)** estar a la altura (de algo)

measurement ['meʒəmənt] *n* medida *f*

meat [mi:t] *n* carne *f*; CULIN **meat pie**
empanada *f* de carne

Mecca ['mekə] *n* La Meca

mechanic [mɪ'kænɪk] *n* [person]
mecánico(a) *m,f*

mechanical [mɪ'kænɪkəl] *adj* mecá-
nico(a)

mechanics [mɪ'kænɪks] **1.** *n sing* [sci-
ence] mecánica *f* **2.** *npl* [technical as-
pects] mecanismo *m*

mechanism ['mekənɪzəm] *n* mecanismo *m*

medal ['medəl] *n* medalla *f*

medallion [mɪ'dæljən] *n* medallón *m*

meddle ['medəl] *vi* entrometerse (**in**
en); **to meddle with sth** manosear algo

media ['mi:dɪə] *npl* medios *mpl* de comunicación; **media coverage** cobertura
periodística; **media player** lector *m*
multimedia; **the new media** los nue-
vos medios; *Fam* **dead tree media**
medios *mpl* impresos

mediate ['mi:dɪeɪt] *vi* mediar

mediator ['mi:dɪeɪtə(r)] *n* media-
dor(a) *m,f*

medical ['medɪkəl] **1.** *adj* [treatment]
médico(a); [book] de medicina **2.** *n Fam*
reconocimiento médico

medication [medɪ'keɪʃən] *n* medicamento *m*, medicina *f*

medicine ['medɪsɪn] *n* [science] medicina *f*; [drugs etc] medicamento *m*

medieval [medɪ'i:vəl] *adj* medieval

mediocre [mi:dɪ'əʊkə(r)] *adj* mediocre

meditate ['medɪteɪt] *vi* meditar (**on**
sobre)

meditation [medɪ'teɪʃən] *n* medita-
ción *f*

Mediterranean [medɪtə'reɪnɪən] **1.** *adj*
mediterráneo(a) **2.** *n* **the Mediterranean** el Mediterráneo

medium ['mi:dɪəm] **1.** *adj* [average]
mediano(a); *Br* RADIO **medium wave**
onda media **2.** *n* **a)** (*pl* **media**) [means]
medio *m* **b)** (*pl* **mediums**) [spiritualist]
médium *mf*

meet [mi:t] (*pt & pp* **met**) **1.** *vt* **a)** [by
chance] encontrar, encontrarse con;
[by arrangement] reunirse con; [in
formal meeting] entrevistarse con
b) [get to know] conocer; **I'd like you to
meet my mother** quiero presentarte
a mi madre; **the first time I met him**
cuando lo conocí
c) [await arrival of] esperar; [collect]
ir a buscar
d) [danger] encontrar; [opponent] enfrentarse con
e) [satisfy] satisfacer; [obligations]
cumplir con
2. *vi* [by chance] encontrarse; [by
arrangement] reunirse; [formal meet-
ing] entrevistarse; [get to know each
other] conocerse; SPORT enfrentarse;
[join] unirse; [rivers] confluir
3. *n* [sports event] encuentro *m*; [in
athletics] reunión *f* atlética
■ **meet up** *vi* quedar; **to meet up with
sb** quedar con algn, encontrarse con
algn
■ **meet with** *vt insep* [difficulty] tropezar con; [loss] sufrir; [success] tener;
esp US [person] reunirse con

meeting ['miːtɪŋ] *n* [chance encounter] encuentro *m*; [prearranged] cita *f*; [formal] entrevista *f*; [of committee etc] reunión *f*; [of assembly] sesión *f*; [of shareholders] junta *f*; [rally] mitin *m*; SPORT encuentro *m*; [of rivers] confluencia *f*; **meeting place** lugar *m* de reunión

megabucks ['megəbʌks] *n Fam* pasta *f* (gansa); **her job pays megabucks** gana una pasta (gansa) en ese trabajo

megabyte ['megəbaɪt] *n* COMPUT megabyte *m*

megaphone ['megəfəʊn] *n* megáfono *m*

megastore ['megəstɔː(r)] *n* macrotienda *f*

mellow ['meləʊ] **1.** *adj* maduro(a); [wine] añejo(a); [colour, voice] suave; [person] apacible **2.** *vi* [fruit] madurar; [colour, voice] suavizarse

melody ['melədɪ] *n* melodía *f*

melon ['melən] *n* melón *m*

melt [melt] **1.** *vt* [metal] fundir; *Fig* [sb's heart] ablandar **2.** *vi* [snow] derretirse; [metal] fundirse; *Fig* ablandarse ∎ **melt away** *vi* [snow] derretirse; *Fig* [money] desaparecer; *Fig* [confidence] desvanecerse ∎ **melt down** *vt sep* [metal] fundir

member ['membə(r)] *n* miembro *mf*; [of a society] socio(a) *m,f*; [of party, union] afiliado(a) *m,f*; *US* **Member of Congress** congresista *mf*; *Br* **Member of Parliament** diputado(a) *m,f*

membership ['membəʃɪp] *n* [state] calidad *f* de socio; [entry] ingreso *m*; POL afiliación *f*; [number of members] número *m* de socios; **membership card** carnet *m* de socio

memento [məˈmentəʊ] *n* recuerdo *m*

memo ['meməʊ] *n* [official note] memorándum *m*; [personal note] nota *f*, apunte *m*

memoirs ['memwɑːz] *npl* memorias *fpl*

memorable ['memərəbəl] *adj* memorable

memorial [mɪˈmɔːrɪəl] **1.** *adj* [plaque etc] conmemorativo(a) **2.** *n* monumento conmemorativo

memorize ['meməraɪz] *vt* memorizar, aprender de memoria

memory ['memərɪ] *n* memoria *f*; [recollection] recuerdo *m*; COMPUT **memory module** módulo *m* de memoria

men [men] *pl of* **man**

menace ['menɪs] **1.** *n* [threat] amenaza *f*; [danger] peligro *m*; *Fam* [person] pesado(a) *m,f* **2.** *vt* amenazar

mend [mend] **1.** *vt* reparar, arreglar; [clothes] remendar; [socks etc] zurcir **2.** *vi* [ill person] reponerse **3.** *n* [patch] remiendo *m*; [darn] zurcido *m*

meningitis [ˌmenɪnˈdʒaɪtɪs] *n* meningitis *f inv*

menopause ['menəpɔːz] *n* menopausia *f*

menstruation [menstrʊˈeɪʃən] *n* menstruación *f*

menswear ['menzweə(r)] *n* ropa *f* de caballero *or* hombre

mental ['mentəl] *adj* **a)** mental; **mental home, mental hospital** hospital psiquiátrico; **mental illness** enfermedad *f* mental **b)** *Br Fam* [mad] pirado(a), *CSur* rayado(a)

mentality [menˈtælɪtɪ] *n* mentalidad *f*

mentally ['mentəlɪ] *adv* **mentally ill** enfermo(a) mental; **to be mentally handicapped** ser un(a) disminuido(a) psíquico(a)

mention ['menʃən] **1.** *n* mención *f* **2.** *vt* mencionar; **don't mention it!** ¡de nada!

menu ['menjuː] *n* **a)** [card] carta *f*; [fixed meal] menú *m*; **today's menu** menú del día **b)** COMPUT menú *m*; **help menu** menú *m* de ayuda

MEP [emiːˈpiː] *n* *(abbr of* **Member of the European Parliament***)* eurodiputado(a) *m,f*

merchandise ['mɜːtʃəndaɪz] *n* mercancías *fpl*, géneros *mpl*

merchant ['mɜːʃənt] n COMM & FIN comerciante mf; [retailer] detallista mf; **merchant bank** banco m comercial

merciless ['mɜːsɪlɪs] adj despiadado(a)

mercury ['mɜːkjʊrɪ] n mercurio m

mercy ['mɜːsɪ] n misericordia f, compasión f; **at the mercy of** a la merced de; **to have mercy on** tener compasión de

mere [mɪə(r)] adj mero(a), simple

merely ['mɪəlɪ] adv simplemente

merge [mɜːdʒ] **1.** vt [blend] unir (**with** con); COMM fusionar **2.** vi unirse; [roads] empalmar; COMM fusionarse

merger ['mɜːdʒə(r)] n COMM fusión f

merit ['merɪt] **1.** n [of person] mérito m; [of plan etc] ventaja f **2.** vt merecer, Am ameritar

merry ['merɪ] (compar **merrier**, superl **merriest**) adj [happy] alegre; Fam [slightly drunk] alegre, Esp piripi; **Merry Christmas!** ¡felices Navidades!

merry-go-round ['merɪɡəʊraʊnd] n tiovivo m, carrusel m, RP calesita f

mesh [meʃ] **1.** n TEXT malla f; TECH engranaje m; Fig red f **2.** vt TECH engranar

mesmerize ['mezməraɪz] vt hipnotizar

mess [mes] n **a)** [confusion] confusión f; [disorder] desorden m; **to be in a mess** [room etc] estar desordenado(a) **b)** [in life, affairs] lío m; **to get into a mess** meterse en un lío **c)** [dirt] suciedad f; Br **dog mess** caca f de perro; [referred to in official notices] deposiciones fpl caninas **d)** MIL [room] comedor m ■ **mess about, mess around** Fam **1.** vt sep fastidiar **2.** vi [act the fool] hacer el primo; [idle] gandulear; [kill time] pasar el rato ■ **mess about with** vt insep Fam [fiddle with] manosear; **to mess about with sb** tener un lío con algn ■ **mess up** vt sep Fam [make untidy] desordenar; [dirty] ensuciar; [spoil] estropear

message ['mesɪdʒ] n [communication] recado m; [of story etc] mensaje m; **bounce message** mensaje m rebotado; Fam **to get the message** comprender

messaging ['mesɪdʒɪŋ] n COMPUT mensajería f

messenger ['mesɪndʒə(r)] n mensajero(a) m,f

messy ['mesɪ] (compar **messier**, superl **messiest**) adj [untidy] desordenado(a); [confused] enredado(a); [dirty] sucio(a)

met [met] pt & pp of **meet**

metadata ['metədeɪtə] npl metadatos mpl

metal ['metəl] **1.** n metal m **2.** adj metálico(a)

metallic [mɪ'tælɪk] adj metálico(a); **metallic blue** azul metalizado

metaphor ['metəfə(r)] n metáfora f

meteor ['miːtɪə(r)] n bólido m

meter¹ ['miːtə(r)] **1.** n [measuring device] contador m **2.** vt [gas, electricity] medir (del consumo de)

meter² ['miːtər] US n = **metre**

method ['meθəd] n método m

methodical [mɪ'θɒdɪkəl] adj metódico(a)

meticulous [mə'tɪkjʊləs] adj meticuloso(a)

metre ['miːtə(r)] n metro m

metric ['metrɪk] adj métrico(a)

Mexican ['meksɪkən] adj & n mejicano(a) (m,f), mexicano(a) (m,f)

Mexico ['meksɪkəʊ] n Méjico, México

mice [maɪs] pl of **mouse**

microblog ['maɪkrəʊ,blɒɡ] n microblog m

microblogger ['maɪkrəʊ,blɒɡə(r)] n microblogero(a) m,f

microblogging ['maɪkrəʊ,blɒɡɪŋ] n microblogging m

microchip ['maɪkrəʊtʃɪp] n COMPUT microchip m

microphone ['maɪkrəfəʊn] n micrófono m

micropublishing ['maɪkrəʊ,pʌblɪʃɪŋ] n microedición f

microscope ['maɪkrəskəʊp] n microscopio m

microwave ['maɪkrəʊweɪv] *n* microonda *f*; **microwave (oven)** (horno *m*) microondas *m inv*

mid [mɪd] *adj* **(in) mid afternoon** a media tarde; **(in) mid April** a mediados de abril; **to be in one's mid thirties** tener unos treinta y cinco años

midday 1. [mɪd'deɪ] *n* mediodía *m* **2.** ['mɪddeɪ] *adj* de mediodía

middle ['mɪdəl] **1.** *adj* de en medio; **middle age** mediana edad; **the Middle Ages** la Edad Media; **the middle class** la clase media **2.** *n* **a)** centro *m*, medio *m*; **in the middle of** en medio de; **in the middle of winter** en pleno invierno; *Fam* **in the middle of nowhere** en el quinto pino **b)** *Fam* [waist] cintura *f*

middle-aged [mɪdəl'eɪdʒd] *adj* de mediana edad

middle-class [mɪdəl'klɑːs] *adj* de clase media

midget ['mɪdʒɪt] *n* enano(a) *m,f*

midnight ['mɪdnaɪt] *n* medianoche *f*

midst [mɪdst] *n* **in the midst of** en medio de

midway ['mɪdweɪ] *adv* a medio camino

midweek 1. [mɪd'wiːk] *adv* entre semana **2.** ['mɪdwiːk] *adj* de entre semana

midwife ['mɪdwaɪf] *n* comadrona *f*, partera *f*

might¹ [maɪt] *v aux see* **may**

might² [maɪt] *n Formal* fuerza *f*, poder *m*

mighty ['maɪtɪ] **1.** *(compar* **mightier**, *superl* **mightiest)** *adj* [strong] fuerte; [powerful] poderoso(a); [great] enorme **2.** *adv US Fam* un montón, *Esp* cantidad

migraine ['miːgreɪn, 'maɪgreɪn] *n* jaqueca *f*

migrant ['maɪgrənt] **1.** *adj* migratorio(a) **2.** *n* [person] emigrante *mf*; [bird] ave migratoria

migrate [maɪ'greɪt] *vi* emigrar

mike [maɪk] *n Fam* micro *m*

mild [maɪld] *adj* [person, character] apacible; [climate] templado(a); [punishment] leve; [tobacco, taste] suave

mile [maɪl] *n* milla *f*; *Fam* **miles better** muchísimo mejor

mileage ['maɪlɪdʒ] *n* kilometraje *m*

milestone ['maɪlstəʊn] *n* hito *m*

militant ['mɪlɪtənt] *adj* & *n* militante *(mf)*

military ['mɪlɪtərɪ] *adj* militar; **to do one's military service** hacer el servicio militar

milk [mɪlk] **1.** *n* leche *f*; **milk chocolate** chocolate *m* con leche; **milk shake** batido *m*, *Am* licuado *m* **2.** *vt* **a)** [cow, goat] ordeñar **b)** *Fam* **they milked him of all his money** le sangraron hasta el último centavo

milky ['mɪlkɪ] *(compar* **milkier**, *superl* **milkiest)** *adj* lechoso(a); [colour] pálido(a); **Milky Way** Vía Láctea

mill [mɪl] **1.** *n* [grinder] molino *m*; [for coffee] molinillo *m*; [factory] fábrica *f*; **cotton mill** hilandería *f* **2.** *vt* moler
■ **mill about**, **mill around** *vi* arremolinarse

milligram(me) ['mɪlɪgræm] *n* miligramo *m*

millimetre, *US* **millimeter** ['mɪlɪmiːtə(r)] *n* milímetro *m*

million ['mɪljən] *n* millón *m*

millionaire [mɪljə'neə(r)] *n* millonario(a) *m,f*

mime [maɪm] **1.** *n* [art] mímica *f*; [play] pantomima *f* **2.** *vt* representar con gestos

mimic ['mɪmɪk] **1.** *adj* & *n* mímico(a) *(m,f)* **2.** *vt* imitar

mince [mɪns] **1.** *n Br* [meat] *Esp*, *RP* carne, picada, *Am* carne molida; **mince pie** [containing meat] *especie de empanada de carne picada*; [containing fruit] *pastel navideño a base de fruta escarchada, frutos secos y especias* **2.** *vt Esp*, *RP* picar, *Am* moler

mincemeat ['mɪnsmiːt] *n* [meat] carne, *Esp*, *RP* picada *or Am* molida; [fruit] *relleno a base de fruta escarchada, frutos secos, especias, zumo de limón y grasa animal*

mincer ['mɪnsə(r)] *n Esp*, *RP* picadora *f*, *Am* moledora *f*

mind [maɪnd] **1.** n a) [intellect] mente f; [brain] cabeza f; **what kind of car do you have in mind?** ¿en qué clase de coche estás pensando?; **to lose one's mind** perder el juicio; **it slipped my mind** lo olvidé por completo
b) [opinion] **to be in two minds (about sth)** estar indeciso(a) (acerca de algo); **to my mind** a mi parecer
2. vt a) [child] cuidar; [house] vigilar; [be careful of] tener cuidado con; **mind the step!** ¡ojo con el escalón!; **mind your own business!** ¡no te metas donde no te llaman!
b) [object to] tener inconveniente en; **I wouldn't mind a cup of coffee** me vendría bien un café; **never mind** no importa
3. vi a) **mind you, he is fifty** ten en cuenta que tiene cincuenta años
b) [object] importar; **do you mind if I open the window?** ¿le importa que abra la ventana?

minder ['maɪndə(r)] n a) Br Fam [bodyguard] gorila m, Méx guarura m b) **(child** or **baby) minder** niñero(a) mf

mindless ['maɪndlɪs] adj [task] de autómata; [violence] injustificable

mind-numbing [-nʌmɪŋ] adj embrutecedor(a)

mindset ['maɪndset] n mentalidad f; **this is a dangerous mindset to be in** esa es una actitud peligrosa

mine¹ [maɪn] poss pron [one thing] (el) mío /(la) mía; [more than one] /(los) míos, (las) mías, lo mío; **a friend of mine** un amigo mío; **these gloves are mine** estos guantes son míos; **which is mine?** ¿cuál es el mío?

mine² [maɪn] **1.** n mina f; Fig **a mine of information** un pozo de información **2.** vt [coal etc] extraer; MIL minar

mineral ['mɪnərəl] **1.** adj mineral; **mineral water** agua f mineral **2.** n mineral m

mingle ['mɪŋgəl] vi mezclarse

miniature ['mɪnɪtʃə(r)] **1.** n miniatura f **2.** adj [railway] en miniatura; [camera, garden] diminuto(a)

mini-break n mini vacaciones fpl

minigolf ['mɪnɪgɒlf] n minigolf m

minimal ['mɪnɪməl] adj mínimo(a)

minimum ['mɪnɪməm] **1.** adj mínimo(a); **minimum charge** tarifa f mínima; **minimum wage** salario mínimo **2.** n mínimo m

mining ['maɪnɪŋ] **1.** n minería f, explotación f de minas; MIL & NAUT minado m **2.** adj minero(a)

mini-roundabout [mɪnɪ'raʊndəbaʊt] n Br mini rotonda f

minister ['mɪnɪstə(r)] **1.** n POL ministro(a) m,f; REL pastor(a) m,f **2.** vi **to minister to sb** atender a algn

ministry ['mɪnɪstrɪ] n POL ministerio m; REL sacerdocio m

minor ['maɪnə(r)] **1.** adj [lesser] menor; [unimportant] sin importancia; [role] secundario(a); MUS menor **2.** n JUR menor mf de edad

minority [maɪ'nɒrɪtɪ] n minoría f; **to be in the minority** ser (la) minoría; POL **minority party** partido minoritario

mint¹ [mɪnt] **1.** n FIN **the (Royal) Mint** ≈ la Casa de la Moneda, ≈ Esp la Fábrica Nacional de Moneda y Timbre **2.** vt [coin, words] acuñar

mint² [mɪnt] n BOT menta f; [sweet] pastilla f de menta

minus ['maɪnəs] **1.** prep **5 minus 3** 5 menos 3; **minus 10 degrees** 10 grados bajo cero
2. adj negativo(a)
3. n **minus (sign)** signo m (de) menos

minute¹ ['mɪnɪt] n a) minuto m; **at the last minute** a última hora; **just a minute** (espera) un momento; **this very minute** ahora mismo b) **minutes** [notes] acta f

minute² [maɪ'nju:t] adj [tiny] diminuto(a); [examination] minucioso(a)

miracle ['mɪrəkəl] n milagro m

miraculous [mɪ'rækjʊləs] adj milagroso(a)

mirror ['mɪrə(r)] **1.** n espejo m; Fig reflejo m; COMPUT **mirror site** sitio m espejo; **rear-view mirror** retrovisor m **2.** vt reflejar

misbehave [mɪsbɪ'heɪv] *vi* portarse mal

miscalculate [mɪs'kælkjʊleɪt] *vt* & *vi* calcular mal

miscarriage ['mɪskærɪʤ] *n* MED aborto *m* (espontáneo); **miscarriage of justice** error *m* judicial

miscellaneous [mɪsɪ'leɪnɪəs] *adj* variado(a); **miscellaneous expenses** gastos diversos

mischief ['mɪstʃɪf] *n* [naughtiness] travesura *f*; *Formal* [evil] malicia *f*; **to get up to mischief** hacer travesuras

mischievous ['mɪstʃɪvəs] *adj* [naughty] travieso(a); [playful] juguetón(ona); *Formal* [wicked] malicioso(a)

misconduct [mɪs'kɒndʌkt] *n* mala conducta

misdemeanour, *US* **misdemeanor** [mɪsdɪ'miːnə(r)] *n* [misdeed] fechoría *f*; JUR falta *m*

miser ['maɪzə(r)] *n* avaro(a) *m,f*

miserable ['mɪzərəbəl] *adj* [sad] triste; [unfortunate] desgraciado(a); [wretched] miserable

miserly ['maɪzəlɪ] *adj* avaro(a), tacaño(a)

misery ['mɪzərɪ] *n* [sadness] tristeza *f*; [wretchedness] desgracia *f*; [suffering] sufrimiento *m*; [poverty] miseria *f*; *Fam* [person] aguafiestas *mf*

misery-guts *adj Fam* amargado(a) *m,f*

misfit ['mɪsfɪt] *n* [person] inadaptado(a) *m,f*

misfortune [mɪs'fɔːtʃən] *n* desgracia *f*

misgiving [mɪs'gɪvɪŋ] *n* [doubt] recelo *m*; [fear] temor *m*

misguided [mɪs'gaɪdɪd] *adj* equivocado(a)

mishandle [mɪs'hændəl] *vt* llevar *or* manejar mal

mishap ['mɪshæp] *n* contratiempo *m*

misinform [mɪsɪn'fɔːm] *vt* informar mal

misinterpret [mɪsɪn'tɜːprɪt] *vt* interpretar mal

mislay [mɪs'leɪ] *vt* extraviar

mislead [mɪs'liːd] *vt* despistar; [deliberately] engañar

misleading [mɪs'liːdɪŋ] *adj* [erroneous] erróneo(a); [deliberately] engañoso(a)

mismanagement [mɪs'mænɪʤmənt] *n* mala administración *f*

misprint ['mɪsprɪnt] *n* errata *f*, error *m* de imprenta

miss¹ [mɪs] *n* señorita *f*

miss² [mɪs] **1.** *n* [throw etc] *Esp* fallo *m*, *Am* falla *f*; *Fam* **to give sth a miss** pasar de algo
2. *vt* **a)** [target] no acertar en; [shot, penalty] *Esp* fallar, *Am* errar
b) [train etc] perder; [opportunity] dejar pasar; **you have missed the point** no has captado la idea
c) [feel lack of] echar de menos, *esp Am* extrañar; **I miss you** te echo de menos, *esp Am* te extraño
3. *vi* [when throwing] fallar; [when shooting] errar
■ **miss out 1.** *vt sep* [omit] saltarse; [on purpose] pasar por alto **2.** *vt insep* **to miss out on** perderse

missile ['mɪsaɪl, *US* 'mɪsəl] *n* MIL misil *m*; [object thrown] proyectil *m*

missing ['mɪsɪŋ] *adj* [object] perdido(a); [person] desaparecido(a); [from meeting etc] ausente; **missing person** desaparecido(a) *m,f*; **three cups are missing** faltan tres tazas

mission ['mɪʃən] *n* misión *f*

missionary ['mɪʃənərɪ] *n* misionero(a) *m,f*

mist [mɪst] **1.** *n* neblina *f*; [thick] niebla *f*; [at sea] bruma *f* **2.** *vi* **to mist over** *or* **up** [countryside] cubrirse de neblina; [window etc] empañarse

mistake [mɪ'steɪk] **1.** *n* error *m*; **by mistake** por equivocación; **I hurt him by mistake** le golpeé sin querer; **to make a mistake** equivocarse, cometer un error **2.** (*pt* **mistook**, *pp* **mistaken**) *vt* [meaning] malentender; **to mistake Jack for Bill** confundir a Jack con Bill

mistaken [mɪ'steɪkən] *adj* equivocado(a), erróneo(a); **you are mistaken** estás equivocado(a)

mister ['mɪstə(r)] *n* señor *m*

mistletoe ['mɪsltəʊ] *n* muérdago *m*

mistreat [mɪs'tri:t] *vt* tratar mal

mistress ['mɪstrɪs] *n* [of house] señora *f*, ama *f*; [lover] amante *f*; SCH [primary school] maestra *f*; [secondary school] profesora *f*

mistrust [mɪs'trʌst] **1.** *n* recelo *m* **2.** *vt* desconfiar de

misty ['mɪstɪ] *(compar* mistier, *superl* mistiest) *adj* [day] de niebla; [window etc] empañado(a)

misunderstand [mɪsʌndə'stænd] *vt & vi* malentender

misunderstanding [mɪsʌndə'stændɪŋ] *n* malentendido *m*; [disagreement] desavenencia *f*

misuse 1. [mɪs'ju:s] *n* mal uso *m*; [of funds] malversación *f*; [of power] abuso *m* **2.** [mɪs'ju:z] *vt* emplear mal; [funds] malversar; [power] abusar de

mitten ['mɪtən] *n* manopla *f*; [fingerless] mitón *m*

mix [mɪks] **1.** *n* mezcla *f* **2.** *vt* mezclar **3.** *vi* [blend] mezclarse (**with** con); [go well together] ir bien juntos ■ **mix up** *vt sep* [confuse] confundir (**with** con); [papers] revolver; **to be mixed up in sth** estar involucrado(a) en algo

mixed [mɪkst] *adj* [assorted] surtido(a); [varied] variado(a); [school] mixto(a); [feelings] contradictorio(a)

mixer ['mɪksə(r)] *n* **a)** CULIN batidora *f*; **food mixer** batidora **b) to be a good mixer** [person] tener don de gentes

mixture ['mɪkstʃə(r)] *n* mezcla *f*

mix-up ['mɪksʌp] *n* Fam confusión *f*, lío *m*

mm *(abbr of* millimetre(s)) mm

moan [məʊn] **1.** *n* [groan] gemido *m*, quejido *m* **2.** *vi* [groan] gemir; [complain] quejarse (**about** de)

mob [mɒb] **1.** *n* multitud *f*; [riff-raff] gentuza *f*; **the mob** el populacho **2.** *vt* acosar

mobile ['məʊbaɪl, *US* 'məʊbəl] **1.** *adj* móvil; **mobile home** caravana *f*; **mobile phone** teléfono *m* móvil, *Am* teléfono *m* celular **2.** *n* **a)** [hanging ornament] móvil *m* **b)** *Fam* [mobile phone] móvil *m*, *Am* celular *m*

mobilize ['məʊbɪlaɪz] *vt* movilizar

mock [mɒk] **1.** *adj* [sympathy etc] fingido(a); [objects] de imitación **2.** *vt* [make fun of] burlarse de **3.** *vi* burlarse (**at** de)

mockery ['mɒkərɪ] *n* burla *f*

mod cons [ˌmɒd-] *npl (abbr of* modern conveniences) *Br Fam* **all mod cons** todo confort

model ['mɒdəl] **1.** *n* modelo *m*; [fashion model] modelo *mf*; **(scale) model** maqueta *f* **2.** *adj* [railway] en miniatura; [pupil] ejemplar; [school] modelo **3.** *vt* [clay etc] modelar; [clothes] presentar **4.** *vi* [make models] modelar; [work as model] trabajar de modelo

modem ['məʊdem] *n* COMPUT modem *m*

moderate¹ ['mɒdərɪt] **1.** *adj* moderado(a); [reasonable] razonable; [average] regular; [ability] mediocre **2.** *n* POL moderado(a) *m,f*

moderate² ['mɒdəreɪt] **1.** *vt* moderar **2.** *vi* moderarse; [wind] calmarse; [in debate] arbitrar

moderately ['mɒdərɪtlɪ] *adv* medianamente

moderation [mɒdə'reɪʃən] *n* moderación *f*; **in moderation** con moderación

modern ['mɒdən] *adj* moderno(a); [history] contemporáneo(a); **modern languages** lenguas modernas

modernize ['mɒdənaɪz] *vt* modernizar

modest ['mɒdɪst] *adj* modesto(a); [chaste] púdico(a); [price] módico(a); [success] discreto(a)

modification [mɒdɪfɪ'keɪʃən] *n* modificación *f*

modify ['mɒdɪfaɪ] *vt* modificar

moist [mɔɪst] *adj* húmedo(a)

moisten ['mɔɪsən] *vt* humedecer

moisture ['mɔɪstʃə(r)] *n* humedad *f*

moisturizer ['mɔɪstʃəraɪzə(r)] n crema f or leche f hidratante

mojo ['məʊdʒəʊ] n US Fam [energy] duende m

mold¹ [məʊld] US n = **mould**

mold² [məʊld] US n & vt = **mould**

moldy ['məʊldɪ] US adj = **mouldy**

mole¹ [məʊl] n [beauty spot] lunar m

mole² [məʊl] n [animal] topo m

molecule ['mɒlɪkjuːl] n molécula f

molest [mə'lest] vt importunar; [sexually assault] acosar (sexualmente)

mom [mɒm] n US Fam mamá f

moment ['məʊmənt] n momento m; **at the moment** en este momento; **for the moment** de momento; **in a moment** dentro de un momento; **at any moment** de un momento a otro

momentarily ['məʊməntərɪlɪ] adv momentáneamente; US [soon] dentro de poco

momentum [məʊ'mentəm] n PHYS momento m; [speed] velocidad f; Fig **to gather momentum** cobrar velocidad

mommy ['mɒmɪ] n US Fam mamá f

monarch ['mɒnək] n monarca m

monarchy ['mɒnəkɪ] n monarquía f

monastery ['mɒnəstərɪ] n monasterio m

Monday ['mʌndɪ] n lunes m

monetary ['mʌnɪtərɪ] adj monetario(a)

money ['mʌnɪ] n dinero m; [currency] moneda f; **to make money** ganar dinero; Fam **to make big money** hacer mucho dinero; Fam **advertising is where the big money is** en publicidad se hace mucho dinero; Fam **to earn big money** ganar mucho; Fam **you can earn big money selling carpets** se puede ganar mucho vendiendo alfombras

moneylender ['mʌnɪlendə(r)] n prestamista mf

mongrel ['mʌŋgrəl] n perro mestizo

monitor ['mɒnɪtə(r)] **1.** n [screen] monitor m; SCH delegado(a) m,f **2.** vt [check] controlar; [progress, events] seguir de cerca

monk [mʌŋk] n monje m

monkey ['mʌŋkɪ] n mono m; US **monkey bars** barras fpl trepadoras; Br **monkey nut** Esp cacahuete m, Am maní m, CAm, Méx cacahuate m

monologue, US **monolog** ['mɒnəlɒg] n monólogo m

monopolize [mə'nɒpəlaɪz] vt FIN monopolizar; [attention etc] acaparar

monopoly [mə'nɒpəlɪ] n monopolio m

monotonous [mə'nɒtənəs] adj monótono(a)

monster ['mɒnstə(r)] n monstruo m

monstrosity [mɒn'strɒsɪtɪ] n monstruosidad f

monstrous ['mɒnstrəs] adj [huge] enorme; [hideous] monstruoso(a); [outrageous] escandaloso(a)

month [mʌnθ] n mes m

monthly ['mʌnθlɪ] **1.** adj mensual; **monthly instalment** mensualidad f **2.** n [periodical] revista f mensual **3.** adv mensualmente, cada mes

monument ['mɒnjʊmənt] n monumento m

moo [muː] **1.** n mugido m **2.** vi mugir

mood [muːd] n humor m; **to be in a good / bad mood** estar de buen / mal humor; **to be in the mood for (doing) sth** estar de humor para (hacer) algo

moody ['muːdɪ] (compar **moodier**, superl **moodiest**) adj [changeable] de humor variable; [bad-tempered] malhumorado(a)

moon [muːn] n luna f; Fam **over the moon** en el séptimo cielo

moonlight ['muːnlaɪt] n luz f de la luna

moor¹ [mʊə(r)] n [heath] páramo m

moor² [mʊə(r)] vt NAUT amarrar

moose ['muːs] (pl **moose**) n alce m

mop [mɒp] **1.** n [for floor] fregona f **2.** vt fregar ■ **mop up** vt sep [liquids] enjugar; [enemy forces] acabar con

mope [məʊp] vi **to mope about** or **around** andar abatido(a)

moped ['məʊped] n ciclomotor m, vespa f

moral ['mɒrəl] **1.** *adj* moral **2.** *n* moraleja *f*; **morals** moral *f*, moralidad *f*

morale [mə'rɑːl] *n* moral *f*, estado *m* de ánimo

morality [mə'rælɪtɪ] *n* moralidad *f*

morbid ['mɔːbɪd] *adj* MED mórbido(a); [mind] morboso(a)

more [mɔː(r)] (*comp of* **much, many**) **1.** *adj* más; **is there any more tea?** ¿queda más té?; **I've no more money** no me queda más dinero; **more tourists** más turistas; **there are more and more cars on the roads** cada vez hay más coches en las carreteras
2. *pron* más; **how many more?** ¿cuántos más?; **many/much more** muchos(as)/mucho más; **more than a hundred** más de cien; **the more he has, the more he wants** cuanto más tiene más quiere; **and what is more** y lo que es más
3. *adv* más; **I won't do it any more** no lo volveré a hacer; **she doesn't live here any more** ya no vive aquí; **more and more difficult** cada vez más difícil; **more or less** más o menos

moreish ['mɔːrɪʃ] *adj Br Fam* irresistible, adictivo(a)

moreover [mɔː'rəʊvə(r)] *adv* además

morning ['mɔːnɪŋ] **1.** *n* mañana *f*; [before dawn] madrugada *f*; **in the morning** por la mañana; **on Monday mornings** los lunes por la mañana; **tomorrow morning** mañana por la mañana **2.** *adj* matutino(a)

mornings *adv* por las mañanas

Moroccan [mə'rɒkən] *adj* & *n* marroquí *(mf)*

Morocco [mə'rɒkəʊ] *n* Marruecos

morph [mɔːf] *vi* transformarse; **the car morphs into a robot** el coche se transforma en robot

mortal ['mɔːtəl] **1.** *adj* mortal **2.** *n* mortal *mf*

mortgage ['mɔːgɪdʒ] **1.** *n* hipoteca *f* **2.** *vt* hipotecar

mortuary ['mɔːtʃʊərɪ] *n* depósito *m* de cadáveres

mosaic [mə'zeɪɪk] *n* mosaico *m*

Moscow ['mɒskəʊ, *US* 'mɒskaʊ] *n* Moscú

mosey ['məʊzɪ] *vi US Fam* [amble] ir dando un paseo; **to mosey along** ir dando un paseo; **let's mosey over to the pond** vamos hasta el estanque dando un paseo

Moslem ['mɒzləm] *adj* & *n* musulmán(ana) *(m,f)*

mosque [mɒsk] *n* mezquita *f*

mosquito [mɒs'kiːtəʊ] *(pl* **mosquitoes)** *n* mosquito *m*, *Am* zancudo *m*; **mosquito net** mosquitero *m*

moss [mɒs] *n* musgo *m*

most [məʊst] **1.** (*superl of* **much, many**) *adj* **a)** [greatest in quantity etc] más; **this house suffered (the) most damage** esta casa fue la más afectada; **who made (the) most mistakes?** ¿quién cometió más errores?
b) [the majority of] la mayoría de, la mayor parte de; **most people** la mayoría de la gente
2. *pron* [greatest part] la mayor parte; [greatest number] lo máximo, lo más; [the majority of people] la mayoría; **at the (very) most** como máximo; **to make the most of sth** aprovechar algo al máximo
3. (*superl of* **much**) *adv* **a)** más; **the most intelligent student** el estudiante más inteligente; **what I like most** lo que más me gusta
b) [very] muy; **most of all** sobre todo

mostly ['məʊstlɪ] *adv* [chiefly] en su mayor parte; [generally] generalmente; [usually] normalmente

MOT [eməʊ'tiː] *n Br* (*abbr of* **Ministry of Transport**) **MOT test** inspección técnica de vehículos, ≃ *Esp* ITV, ≃ *RP* VTV *f*

motel [məʊ'tel] *n* motel *m*

moth [mɒθ] *n* mariposa nocturna; **clothes moth** polilla *f*

mother ['mʌðə(r)] **1.** *n* madre *f*; **Mother's Day** Día *m* de la Madre; **mother tongue** lengua materna **2.** *vt* cuidar maternalmente

motherhood ['mʌðəhʊd] *n* maternidad *f*

move

mother-in-law ['mʌðərɪnlɔː] n suegra f

mother-to-be [mʌðətə'biː] n futura madre

motion ['məʊʃən] **1.** n [movement] movimiento m; [gesture] ademán m; [proposal] moción f **2.** vt & vi hacer señas; **to motion (to) sb to do sth** hacer señas a algn para que haga algo

motivate ['məʊtɪveɪt] vt motivar

motivation [məʊtɪ'veɪʃən] n motivación f

motive ['məʊtɪv] **1.** adj [force] motriz **2.** n [reason] motivo m; JUR móvil m

motor ['məʊtə(r)] n [engine] motor m; Br Fam [car] coche m, Am carro m, CSur auto m; **motor home** autocaravana f, rulot f; **motor racing** carreras fpl de coches or Am carros or CSur autos

motorbike ['məʊtəbaɪk] n Fam motocicleta f, moto f

motorboat ['məʊtəbəʊt] n (lancha) motora f

motorcycle ['məʊtəsaɪkəl] n motocicleta f

motorcyclist ['məʊtəsaɪklɪst] n motociclista mf

motorist ['məʊtərɪst] n automovilista mf

motorway ['məʊtəweɪ] n Br autopista f

motto ['mɒtəʊ] n lema m

mould¹ [məʊld] n [fungus] moho m

mould² [məʊld] **1.** n molde m **2.** vt moldear; [clay] modelar

mouldy ['məʊldɪ] (compar **mouldier**, superl **mouldiest**) adj mohoso(a); **to go mouldy** enmohecerse

mound [maʊnd] n montón m; [small hill] montículo m

mount¹ [maʊnt] n monte m; **Mount Everest** (Monte) Everest m ■ **mount up** vi [accumulate] acumularse

mount² [maʊnt] **1.** n [horse] montura f; [support] soporte m, base f; [for photograph] marco m; [for jewel] engaste m **2.** vt [horse] subirse or montar a; [campaign] organizar; [photograph] enmarcar; [jewel] engastar

3. vi [go up] subir; [get on horse, bike] montar; [increase] subir

mountain ['maʊntɪn] **1.** n montaña f; Fig [pile] montón m **2.** adj de montaña, montañés(esa); **mountain range** sierra f, cordillera f

mountaineer [maʊntɪ'nɪə(r)] n montañero(a) m,f, alpinista mf, Am andinista mf

mountaineering [maʊntɪ'nɪərɪŋ] n montañismo m, alpinismo m, Am andinismo m

mountainous ['maʊntɪnəs] adj montañoso(a)

mourn [mɔːn] vt & vi **to mourn (for) sb** llorar la muerte de algn

mourning ['mɔːnɪŋ] n luto m; **in mourning** de luto

mouse [maʊs] (pl **mice**) n **a)** [animal] ratón m **b)** COMPUT Esp ratón m, Am mouse m

mousse [muːs] n CULIN mousse f; **(styling) mousse** [for hair] espuma f (moldeadora)

moustache [mə'stɑːʃ] n bigote m

mouth 1. [maʊθ] (pl **mouths** [maʊðz]) n **a)** boca f **b)** [of cave etc] entrada f; [of river] desembocadura f **2.** [maʊð] vt pronunciar; [insults] proferir

mouthful ['maʊθfʊl] n [of food] bocado m; [of drink] sorbo m

mouth organ ['maʊθɔːgən] n armónica f

mouthpiece ['maʊθpiːs] n MUS boquilla f; [of telephone] micrófono m; Fig [spokesman] portavoz m

mouthwash ['maʊθwɒʃ] n elixir m, enjuague m bucal

movable ['muːvəbəl] adj movible, móvil

move [muːv] **1.** n **a)** [movement] movimiento m; **to be on the move** estar en marcha; **we must make a move** debemos irnos ya; Fam **get a move on!** ¡date prisa!, Am ¡apúrate!
b) [in game] jugada f; [turn] turno m
c) [course of action] medida f
d) [to new home] mudanza f; [to new job] traslado m

2. *vt* **a)** mover; [furniture etc] cambiar de sitio; [transfer] trasladar; **to move house** mudarse (de casa)

b) [in game] mover

c) [motivate] inducir; [persuade] persuadir; **I won't be moved** no me harán cambiar de parecer

d) [affect emotionally] conmover

3. *vi* **a)** [change position] moverse, desplazarse; [change house] mudarse (de casa); [change post] trasladarse

b) [train etc] estar en marcha; **to start moving** ponerse en marcha

c) [leave] irse, marcharse

d) [in game] hacer una jugada

▪ **move about 1.** *vt sep* cambiar de sitio **2.** *vi* [be restless] ir y venir; [travel] viajar de un lugar a otro

▪ **move along 1.** *vt sep* [move forward] hacer avanzar; [keep moving] hacer circular **2.** *vi* [move forward] avanzar; [keep moving] circular; **move along!** [to person on bench] ¡haz sitio!

▪ **move around** *vt sep & vi* = **move about**

▪ **move away 1.** *vt sep* alejar, apartar (**from** de) **2.** *vi* [move aside] alejarse, apartarse; [leave] irse; [change house] mudarse (de casa)

▪ **move back 1.** *vt sep* [to original place] volver **2.** *vi* [withdraw] retirarse; [to original place] volver

▪ **move forward 1.** *vt sep* avanzar; [clock] adelantar **2.** *vi* avanzar, adelantarse

▪ **move in** *vi* [into new home] instalarse

▪ **move off** *vi* [go away] irse, marcharse; [train] salir

▪ **move on** *vi* [keep moving] circular; [go forward] avanzar; [time] transcurrir

▪ **move out** *vi* [leave] irse, marcharse; [leave house] mudarse

▪ **move over** *vi* correrse

▪ **move up** *vi* [go up] subir; *Fig* [be promoted] ser ascendido(a), ascender; [move along] correrse, hacer sitio

movement ['mu:vmənt] *n* **a)** movimiento *m*; [gesture] gesto *m*, ademán *m* **b)** [of goods] transporte *m*; [of employees] traslado *m* **c)** [of goods, capital] circulación *f*

movie ['mu:vɪ] *n* película *f*; **to go to the movies** ir al cine; **movie star** estrella *f* de cine; *US* **movie theater** cine *m*

moving ['mu:vɪŋ] *adj* [that moves] móvil; [car etc] en marcha; *Fig* [touching] conmovedor(a)

mow [məʊ] (*pt* mowed, *pp* mown [məʊn] *or* mowed) *vt* [lawn] cortar; [corn, wheat] segar; *Fig* **to mow down** segar

mower ['məʊə(r)] *n* cortacésped *m*

MP [em'pi:] *n Br* POL (*abbr of* **Member of Parliament**) diputado(a) *m,f*

MP3 [,empi:'θri:] *n* COMPUT (*abbr of* **moving picture experts group audio layer 3**) MP3 *m*; **MP3 player** lector *m* de MP3

MP4 *n* COMPUT (*abbr of* **moving picture experts group audio layer 4**) MP4 *m*; **MP4 player** lector *m* de MP4

mph [empi:'eɪtʃ] (*abbr of* **miles per hour**) millas *fpl* por hora

Mr ['mɪstə(r)] (*abbr of* **Mister**) Sr

Mrs ['mɪsɪz] (*abbr of* **Missus**) Sra

Ms [məz] *n* Sra / Srta

> **Ms** es el equivalente femenino de **Mr**, y se utiliza para dirigirse a una mujer sin precisar su estado civil.

much [mʌtʃ] (*compar* more, *superl* most) **1.** *adj* mucho(a); **as much ... as** tanto(a) ... como; **how much chocolate?** ¿cuánto chocolate?; **so much** tanto(a)

2. *adv* mucho; **as much as** tanto como; **as much as possible** todo lo posible; **how much?** ¿cuánto?; **how much is it?** ¿cuánto es?, ¿cuánto vale?; **much better** mucho mejor; **much more** mucho más; **thank you very much** muchísimas gracias; **too much** demasiado

3. *pron* mucho; **I thought as much** lo suponía; **much of the town was destroyed** gran parte de la ciudad quedó destruida; **much remains to be done** queda mucho por hacer

muck [mʌk] n [dirt] suciedad f; [mud] lodo m; Fig porquería f ■ **muck about**, **muck around** Br Fam **1.** vi [idle] perder el tiempo; [play the fool] hacer el tonto **2.** vt sep **to muck sb about** fastidiar a algn ■ **muck up** vt sep [dirty] ensuciar; Fig [spoil] echar a perder

mud [mʌd] n lodo m, barro m; [thick] fango m; Fig **to sling mud at sb** poner a algn por los suelos; **mud flat** marisma f

muddle ['mʌdəl] **1.** n desorden m; Fig [mix-up] embrollo m, lío m; **to get into a muddle** hacerse un lío **2.** vt confundir ■ **muddle through** vi arreglárselas, ingeniárselas ■ **muddle up** vt sep confundir

muddy ['mʌdɪ] (compar muddier, superl muddiest) adj [lane] fangoso(a); [hands] cubierto(a) de lodo; [liquid] turbio(a)

mudguard ['mʌdɡɑːd] n Br Esp, RP guardabarros m inv, Andes, CAm, Carib guardafango m, Méx salpicadera f

muffle ['mʌfəl] vt [sound] amortiguar; **to muffle (up)** [person] abrigar

mug¹ [mʌɡ] n [large cup] tazón m; [beer tankard] jarra f

mug² [mʌɡ] **1.** n Br Fam [gullible person] bobo(a) m,f, primo(a) m,f, Am zonzo(a) m,f; [face] jeta f **2.** vt atracar, asaltar

mugger ['mʌɡə(r)] n atracador(a) m,f

mule [mjuːl] n mulo(a) m,f

multicoloured, US **multicolored** ['mʌltɪkʌləd] adj multicolor

multifunction [ˌmʌltɪ'fʌŋkʃən] adj multifunción (inv)

multimedia [mʌltɪ'miːdɪə] **1.** n multimedia f. adj multimedia (inv)

multimillionaire [ˌmʌltɪmɪljə'neə(r)] n multimillonario(a) m,f

multiple ['mʌltɪpəl] **1.** adj múltiple; **multiple sclerosis** esclerosis f múltiple **2.** n múltiplo m

multiple-choice ['mʌltɪpl tʃɔɪs] adj **multiple-choice exam / question** multiplicación f, examen m / pregunta f (de) tipo test

multiplex ['mʌltɪpleks] n [cinema] cine m multisalas

multiplication [mʌltɪplɪ'keɪʃən] n multiplicación f; **multiplication sign** signo m de multiplicar

multiply ['mʌltɪplaɪ] **1.** vt multiplicar (**by** por) **2.** vi multiplicarse

multi-speed adj de varias velocidades

multistorey, US **multistory** [mʌltɪ'stɔːrɪ] adj [building] de varias plantas; **multistorey car park** estacionamiento m or Esp aparcamiento m or de varias plantas

multitask vi realizar varias tareas de forma simultánea

multitude ['mʌltɪtjuːd] n multitud f, muchedumbre f

mum¹ [mʌm] n Br Fam mamá f

mum² [mʌm] adj **to keep mum** no decir ni pío

mumble ['mʌmbəl] **1.** vi hablar entre dientes **2.** vt decir entre dientes

mummy¹ ['mʌmɪ] n Br Fam [mother] mamá f

mummy² ['mʌmɪ] n [body] momia f

mumps [mʌmps] n sing paperas fpl

munch [mʌntʃ] vt & vi mascar

municipal [mju:'nɪsɪpəl] adj municipal

mural ['mjʊərəl] adj & n mural (m)

murder ['mɜːdə(r)] **1.** n asesinato m, homicidio m **2.** vt asesinar

murderer ['mɜːdərə(r)] n asesino(a) m,f

murky ['mɜːkɪ] (compar murkier, superl murkiest) adj oscuro(a); [water] turbio(a)

murmur ['mɜːmə(r)] **1.** n murmullo m; [of traffic] ruido m; [complaint] queja f **2.** vt & vi murmurar

muscle ['mʌsəl] **1.** n músculo m **2.** vi Fam **to muscle in on sth** entrometerse en asuntos ajenos

muscular ['mʌskjʊlə(r)] adj [pain, tissue] muscular; [person] musculoso(a)

museum [mju:'zɪəm] n museo m

mushroom ['mʌʃruːm] **1.** n hongo m, Esp seta f; [button mushroom] champiñón m **2.** vi Fig crecer de la noche a la mañana

music ['mjuːzɪk] n música f; **music hall** teatro m de variedades; **music library** fonoteca f

musical ['mjuːzɪkəl] **1.** adj musical; **to be musical** estar dotado(a) para la música **2.** n musical m

musician [mjuːˈzɪʃən] n músico(a) m,f

Muslim ['mʊzlɪm] adj & n musulmán(ana) (m,f)

mussel ['mʌsəl] n mejillón m

must [mʌst] **1.** v aux **a)** [obligation] deber, tener que; **you must arrive on time** tienes que or debes llegar a la hora **b)** [probability] deber de; **he must be ill** debe de estar enfermo **2.** n Fam **to be a must** ser imprescindible

mustache ['mʌstæʃ] n US bigote m

mustard ['mʌstəd] n mostaza f

must-have n algo m indispensable

mustn't ['mʌsənt] = **must not**

must-see n **that film is a must-see** esta película hay que verla

musty ['mʌstɪ] (compar mustier, superl mustiest) adj que huele a cerrado or a humedad

mute ['mjuːt] **1.** adj mudo(a) **2.** n [person] mudo(a) m,f; MUS sordina f

mutiny ['mjuːtɪnɪ] **1.** n motín m **2.** vi amotinarse

mutter ['mʌtə(r)] **1.** n [mumble] murmullo m
2. vt murmurar, decir entre dientes
3. vi [angrily] refunfuñar

mutton ['mʌtən] n (carne f de) cordero m

mutual ['mjuːtʃʊəl] adj mutuo(a); [shared] común

mutually ['mjuːtʃʊəlɪ] adv mutuamente

muzzle ['mʌzəl] **1.** n [snout] hocico m; [for dog] bozal m; [of gun] boca f **2.** vt [dog] abozalar; Fig amordazar

my [maɪ] poss adj mi; **my cousins** mis primos; **my father** mi padre; **one of my friends** un amigo mío; **I washed my hair** me lavé el pelo; **I twisted my ankle** me torcí el tobillo

myself [maɪˈself] pers pron **a)** [reflexive] me; **I hurt myself** me hice daño **b)** [alone] yo solo(a); **I was by myself** estaba solo **c)** [emphatic] yo mismo(a) **d)** [after prep] mí (mismo(a))

mysterious [mɪˈstɪərɪəs] adj misterioso(a)

mystery ['mɪstərɪ] n misterio m

mystical ['mɪstɪkəl] adj místico(a)

mystify ['mɪstɪfaɪ] vt dejar perplejo(a)

myth [mɪθ] n mito m; **it's a complete myth** es pura fantasía

mythology [mɪˈθɒlədʒɪ] n mitología f

N

N, n [en] *n* [the letter] N, n *f*

N *(abbr of north)* N

nab [næb] *vt Fam* [catch] pescar, *Esp* trincar

nag [næg] **1.** *vt* fastidiar, dar la lata a; **to nag sb to do sth** fastidiar *or* dar la lata a algn para que haga algo **2.** *vi* quejarse

nail [neɪl] **1.** *n* **a)** [of finger, toe] uña *f*; **nail clippers** cortaúñas *m inv*; **nail polish** *or* **varnish** esmalte *m or* laca *f* de uñas; **nail polish remover, nail varnish remover** quitaesmaltes *m inv* **b)** [metal] clavo *m* **2.** *vt* **a)** clavar **b)** *Fam* [catch, trap] pillar, coger

naïve [naɪˈiːv] *adj* ingenuo(a)

naked [ˈneɪkɪd] *adj* desnudo(a); [flame] sin protección; **the naked truth** la pura verdad

name [neɪm] **1.** *n* **a)** nombre *m*; [surname] apellido *m*; **first name** nombre *m* de pila; **last name** apellido *m*; **what's your name?** ¿cómo te llamas?; **to call sb names** poner verde a algn **b)** [reputation] reputación *f*; **to make a name for oneself** hacerse famoso(a) **2.** *vt* **a)** llamar; **to name sb after** *or US* **for sb** poner a algn el nombre de algn **b)** [appoint] nombrar **c)** [refer to] mencionar

namely [ˈneɪmlɪ] *adv* a saber

nanny [ˈnænɪ] *n* niñera *f*

nap [næp] **1.** *n* [sleep] siesta *f*; **to have a nap** echar la *or* una siesta **2.** *vi Fig* **to catch sb napping** coger a algn desprevenido(a)

napkin [ˈnæpkɪn] *n* **(table) napkin** servilleta *f*

nappy [ˈnæpɪ] *n Br* pañal *m*

narrative [ˈnærətɪv] **1.** *n LITER* narrativa *f*; [story] narración *f* **2.** *adj* narrativo(a)

narrator [nəˈreɪtə(r)] *n* narrador(a) *m,f*

narrow [ˈnærəʊ] **1.** *adj* **a)** [passage, road etc] estrecho(a), angosto(a) **b)** [restricted] reducido(a); [sense] estricto(a); **to have a narrow escape** librarse por los pelos **2.** *vi* estrecharse ■ **narrow down 1.** *vt sep* reducir, limitar **2.** *vi* **narrow down to** reducirse a

narrowly [ˈnærəʊlɪ] *adv* **a)** [closely] de cerca **b)** [by a small margin] por poco

narrow-minded [ˈnærəʊˈmaɪndɪd] *adj* de miras estrechas

nasty [ˈnɑːstɪ] *(compar* **nastier,** *superl* **nastiest)** *adj* **a)** [person] desagradable; **to turn nasty** [weather, situation] ponerse feo(a) **b)** [unfriendly] antipático(a); [malicious] malintencionado(a); *Br Fam* **he's a nasty piece of work** es un asco de tío **c)** [illness, accident] grave

nation [ˈneɪʃən] *n* nación *f*

national [ˈnæʃnəl] **1.** *adj* nacional; **national anthem** himno *m* nacional; **national insurance** seguridad *f* social; *MIL* **national service** servicio *m* militar **2.** *n* súbdito(a) *m,f*

nationalist [ˈnæʃnəlɪst] *adj & n* nacionalista *(mf)*

nationality [næʃəˈnælɪtɪ] *n* nacionalidad *f*

nationalize [ˈnæʃnəlaɪz] *vt* nacionalizar

nationwide [ˈneɪʃənwaɪd] *adj* de ámbito nacional

native [ˈneɪtɪv] **1.** *adj* **a)** [place] natal; **native land** patria *f*; **native language** lengua materna **b)** [plant, animal] originario(a) **(to** de) **2.** *n* nativo(a) *m,f*, natural *mf*; [original inhabitant] indígena *mf*; **Native American** indio(a) americano(a)

NATO, Nato [ˈneɪtəʊ] *n (abbr of* **North Atlantic Treaty Organization)** OTAN *f*

natural [ˈnætʃərəl] **1.** *adj* **a)** natural **b)** [normal] normal; **it's only natural that …** es lógico que … **c)** [born] nato(a) **2.** *n* **a) she's a natural for the job** es la persona ideal para el trabajo **b)** MUS becuadro *m*

naturalize [ˈnætʃrəˈlaɪz] *vt Br* [person] naturalizar, nacionalizar

naturalized [ˈnætʃrəlaɪzd] *adj Br* [person] naturalizado(a), nacionalizado(a)

naturally [ˈnætʃərəlɪ] *adv* **a)** [of course] naturalmente **b)** [by nature] por naturaleza **c)** [in a relaxed manner] con naturalidad

nature [ˈneɪtʃə(r)] *n* **a)** naturaleza *f* **b)** [character] naturaleza *f*, carácter *m*; **by nature** por naturaleza; **human nature** la naturaleza humana **c)** [sort, kind] índole *f*, clase *f*

naught [nɔːt] *US n =* **nought**

naughty [ˈnɔːtɪ] *(compar* **naughtier**, *superl* **naughtiest)** *adj* **a)** [child] travieso(a) **b)** [joke, story] atrevido(a), picante

nausea [ˈnɔːzɪə] *n* MED [sickness] náusea *f*

nauseating [ˈnɔːzɪeɪtɪŋ] *adj* nauseabundo(a)

nautical [ˈnɔːtɪkəl] *adj* náutico(a); **nautical mile** milla marítima

naval [ˈneɪvəl] *adj* naval; **naval officer** oficial *mf* de marina; **naval power** potencia marítima *or* naval

navel [ˈneɪvəl] *n* ANAT ombligo *m*

navigate [ˈnævɪgeɪt] **1.** *vt* [river] navegar por; NAUT [ship] gobernar **2.** *vi* navegar; [in driving] indicar la dirección

navy [ˈneɪvɪ] *n* marina *f*; **navy blue** azul marino

Nazi [ˈnɑːtsɪ] *adj & n* nazi *(mf)*

NB, nb [enˈbiː] *(abbr of* **nota bene)** N.B.

dear MESSAGING *written abbr of* **no big**

near [nɪə(r)] **1.** *adj* [in space] cercano(a); [in time] próximo(a); **in the near future** en un futuro próximo
2. *adv* [in space] cerca; **that's near enough** (ya) vale, está bien
3. *prep* cerca de; **near the end of the film** hacia el final de la película
4. *vt* acercarse a

nearby [nɪəˈbaɪ] **1.** *adj* cercano(a) **2.** *adv* cerca

nearly [ˈnɪəlɪ] *adv* casi; **we haven't nearly enough** no alcanza ni con mucho

nearsighted [ˌnɪəˈsaɪtɪd] *adj US* miope

neat [niːt] *adj* **a)** [room, habits etc] ordenado(a); [handwriting] claro(a); [appearance] pulcro(a) **b)** [idea] ingenioso(a) **c)** [whisky etc] solo(a) **d)** *US Fam* [fine] chulísimo(a)

neatly [ˈniːtlɪ] *adv* **a)** [carefully] cuidadosamente **b)** [cleverly] hábilmente

necessarily [nesɪˈserəlɪ] *adv* necesariamente, por fuerza

necessary [ˈnesɪsərɪ] **1.** *adj* **a)** [essential] necesario(a); **if necessary** si es preciso **b)** [unavoidable] inevitable **2.** *n* **the necessary** lo necesario

necessity [nɪˈsesɪtɪ] *n* **a)** necesidad *f*; **out of necessity** por necesidad **b)** necessities [articles] necesidades *fpl*

neck [nek] *n* cuello *m*; [of animal] pescuezo *m*; **to stick one's neck out** arriesgarse

necklace [ˈneklɪs] *n* collar *m*

necktie [ˈnektaɪ] *n US* corbata *f*

nectarine [ˈnektəriːn] *n* nectarina *f*

need [niːd] **1.** *n* **a)** necesidad *f*; **there's no need for you to do that** no hace falta que hagas eso
b) [poverty] indigencia *f*; **to be in need** estar necesitado
2. *vt* **a)** necesitar; **I need to see him** tengo que verle; *Iron* **that's all I need** solo me faltaba eso
b) [action, solution etc] requerir, exigir
3. *v aux* tener que, deber; **need he go?** ¿tiene que ir?; **you needn't wait** no hace falta que esperes

Cuando se emplea como verbo modal solo existe una forma, y los auxiliares **do / does** no se usan : **he need only worry about himself ; need she go? ; it needn't matter.**

---

needle ['niːdəl] *n* **a)** [for sewing, knitting] aguja *f* **b)** BOT hoja *f*

needlessly ['niːdlɪslɪ] *adv* innecesariamente

needlework ['niːdəlwɜːk] *n* [sewing] costura *f* ; [embroidery] bordado *m*

needs *adv* **if needs must** si no hay más remedio

needy ['niːdɪ] *(compar* **needier**, *superl* **neediest)** *adj* necesitado(a)

negative ['negǝtɪv] **1.** *adj* negativo(a) **2.** *n* **a)** LING negación *f* **b)** PHOTO negativo *m*

negatory [nɪ'geɪtǝrɪ] *adj* US *Fam* negativo(a) ; **I guess that's negatory** supongo que eso quiere decir no ; **did you fix it? — negatory** ¿lo arreglaste? — negativo

neglect [nɪ'glekt] **1.** *vt* **a)** [child, duty etc] descuidar, desatender **b)** **to neglect to do sth** [omit to do] no hacer algo **2.** *n* dejadez *f*

negligent ['neglɪdʒənt] *adj* negligente, descuidado(a)

negligible ['neglɪdʒɪbəl] *adj* insignificante

negotiate [nɪ'gǝʊʃɪeɪt] **1.** *vt* **a)** [contract] negociar **b)** *Fig* [obstacle] salvar, franquear **2.** *vi* negociar

negotiation [nɪgǝʊʃɪ'eɪʃən] *n* negociación *f*

neigh [neɪ] **1.** *n* relincho *m* **2.** *vi* relinchar

neighbour, *US* **neighbor** ['neɪbǝ(r)] *n* vecino(a) *m,f* ; REL prójimo *m*

neighbourhood, *US* **neighborhood** ['neɪbǝhʊd] *n* [district] vecindad *f*, barrio *m* ; [people] vecindario *m*

neither ['naɪðǝ(r), 'niːðǝ(r)] **1.** *adj & pron* ninguno de los dos / ninguna de las dos **2.** *adv & conj* **a)** ni ; **neither ... nor** ni ...

ni b) tampoco ; **she was not there and neither was her sister** ella no estaba, ni su hermana tampoco

neon ['niːɒn] *n* neón *m* ; **neon light** luz *f* de neón

NE1 MESSAGING *written abbr of* **anyone**

nephew ['nefjuː] *n* sobrino *m*

nerd [nɜːd] *n* *Fam & Pej* petardo(a) *m,f* ; **computer nerd** obsesionado(a) *m,f* con la informática, nerd *mf*

nerve [nɜːv] *n* **a)** ANAT nervio *m* ; **to get on sb's nerves** poner los nervios de punta a algn **b)** [courage] valor *m* **c)** *Fam* [cheek] cara *f*, descaro *m* ; **what a nerve!** ¡qué cara!

nerve-racking ['nɜːvrækɪŋ] *adj* crispante, exasperante

nervous ['nɜːvǝs] *adj* **a)** nervioso(a) ; **nervous breakdown** depresión nerviosa **b)** [afraid] miedoso(a) **c)** [timid] tímido(a)

nest [nest] **1.** *n* ORNITH nido *m* ; [hen's] nidal *m* ; [animal's] madriguera *f* ; *Fig* **nest egg** ahorros *mpl* **2.** *vi* [birds] anidar

nestle ['nesǝl] **1.** *vt* recostar **2.** *vi* [settle comfortably] acomodarse

net¹ [net] *n* red *f* ; *Br* **net curtains** visillos *mpl*

net² [net] **1.** *adj* neto(a) ; **net weight** peso neto **2.** *vt* [earn] ganar neto

Netherlands ['neðǝlændz] *npl* **the Netherlands** los Países Bajos

nettle ['netǝl] **1.** *n* BOT ortiga *f* **2.** *vt* *Fam* irritar

network ['netwɜːk] **1.** *n* red *f* ; **social network** red *f* social **2.** *vi* [establish contacts] establecer contactos

neurotic [njʊ'rɒtɪk] *adj & n* neurótico(a) *(m,f)*

neuter ['njuːtǝ(r)] **1.** *adj* neutro(a) **2.** *n* LING neutro *m* **3.** *vt* [geld] castrar

neutral ['njuːtrǝl] **1.** *adj* neutro(a) ; POL **to remain neutral** permanecer neutral **2.** *n* AUTO punto muerto

neutralize ['njuːtrǝlaɪz] *vt* neutralizar

never ['nevǝ(r)] *adv* nunca, jamás ; **never again** nunca (ja)más ; *Fam* **never mind** da igual, no importa

never-ending ['nevər'endıŋ] *adj* sin fin, interminable

nevertheless [nevəðə'les] *adv* sin embargo, no obstante

new [njuː] *adj* nuevo(a); **as good as new** como nuevo; **new baby** recién nacido *m*; **new moon** luna nueva; **New Year** Año Nuevo; **New Year's Eve** Nochevieja *f*

NEway MESSAGING *written abbr of* anyway

newbie ['njuːbı] *n Fam & Pej* COMPUT cibernovato(a) *mf*, nuevito(a) *mf*, newbie *mf*

newborn ['njuːbɔːn] *adj* recién nacido(a)

newcomer ['njuːkʌmə(r)] *n* recién llegado(a) *m,f*; [to job etc] nuevo(a) *m,f*

newly ['njuːlı] *adv* recién, recientemente

newlywed ['njuːlıwed] *n* recién casado(a) *m,f*

news [njuːz] *n sing* noticias *fpl*; [TV programme] telediario *m*, *Am* noticiero *m*, *Andes, RP* noticioso *m*; **a piece of news** una noticia; **news agency** agencia *f* de información; *US* **news in brief** avance informativo; **news bulletin** boletín informativo; **news summary** avance informativo

newsagent ['njuːzeıdʒənt] *n Br* vendedor(a) *m,f* de periódicos

newsflash ['njuːzflæʃ] *n* noticia *f* de última hora

newsletter ['njuːzletə(r)] *n* hoja informativa

newspaper ['njuːzpeıpə(r)] *n* periódico *m*, diario *m*

newsreader ['njuːzriːdə(r)] *n* TV & RADIO presentador(a) *m,f* de los informativos

newsstand ['njuːzstænd] *n* quiosco *m* de prensa

New York *n* **a)** [city] **New York (City)** Nueva York **b)** [state] **New York (State)** el Estado *m* de Nueva York

next [nekst] **1.** *adj* **a)** [in place] de al lado

b) [in time] próximo(a); **the next day** el día siguiente; **next Friday** el viernes que viene; **next time** la próxima vez; **the week after next** dentro de dos semanas

c) [in order] siguiente, próximo(a); **next of kin** pariente *m* más cercano **2.** *adv* después, luego; **what shall we do next?** ¿qué hacemos ahora? **3.** *prep* **next to** al lado de, junto a; **next to nothing** casi nada

NHS [eneıtʃ'es] *n Br (abbr of* **National Health Service***) la sanidad pública británica*

nibble ['nıbəl] *vt & vi* mordisquear

Nicaragua [nıkə'rægjʊə] *n* Nicaragua *f*

Nicaraguan [nıkə'rægjʊən] *adj & n* nicaragüense *(mf)*

nice [naıs] *adj* **a)** [person] simpático(a), *Esp* majo(a), *RP* dulce; [thing] agradable; **nice and cool** fresquito(a); **to smell / taste nice** oler / saber bien **b)** [nice-looking] bonito(a), *Am* lindo(a) **c)** *Iron* menudo(a)

nicely ['naıslı] *adv* muy bien

niche [niːʃ] *n* **a)** hornacina *f*, nicho *m* **b)** *Fig* hueco *m*

nick [nık] **1.** *n* **a)** [notch] muesca *f*; [cut] herida pequeña; *Fam* **in the nick of time** en el momento preciso **b)** *Br Fam* [prison] cárcel *f*, *Esp* trullo *m*, *Andes, RP* cana *f*, *Méx* bote *m* **2.** *vt Br Fam* **a)** [steal] afanar, *Esp* mangar **b)** [arrest] detener, *Esp* trincar

nickel ['nıkəl] *n* **a)** níquel *m* **b)** *US* moneda *f* de 5 centavos

nickname ['nıkneım] **1.** *n* apodo *m* **2.** *vt* apodar

niece [niːs] *n* sobrina *f*

night [naıt] *n* noche *f*; **at night** de noche; **at twelve o'clock at night** a las doce de la noche; **last night** anoche; **night life** vida nocturna; **night school** escuela nocturna; **night shift** turno *m* de noche; *US* **night stand** *or* **table** mesita *f* or mesilla *f* de noche

nightclub ['naıtklʌb] *n* sala *f* de fiestas; [disco] discoteca *f*

nightdress ['naıtdres] *n* camisón *m*

nightfall ['naɪtfɔːl] n anochecer m

nightgown ['naɪtgaʊn] n camisón m

nightie ['naɪtɪ] n Fam camisón m

nightingale ['naɪtɪŋgeɪl] n ruiseñor m

nightmare ['naɪtmeə(r)] n pesadilla f

nights adv **a)** US [at night] por las noches **b)** Br [nightshift] **to work nights** trabajar de noche

night-time ['naɪttaɪm] n noche f; **at night-time** por la noche

nil [nɪl] n nada f; SPORT cero m; Br **two nil** dos a cero

Nile [naɪl] n **the Nile** el Nilo

nimble ['nɪmbəl] adj ágil, rápido(a)

nine [naɪn] adj & n nueve (m inv)

911 a) número de teléfono de urgencias en ciertos estados de Estados Unidos **b)** MESSAGING significa que se trata de algo urgente o que se la persona quiere que se pongan rápidamente en contacto con ella

nineteen [naɪn'tiːn] adj & n diecinueve (m inv)

ninety ['naɪntɪ] adj & n noventa (m inv)

ninth [naɪnθ] **1.** adj & n noveno(a) (m,f) **2.** n [fraction] noveno m

nip [nɪp] **1.** vt a) [pinch] pellizcar **b)** [bite] morder; **to nip sth in the bud** cortar algo de raíz **2.** n a) [pinch] pellizco m **b)** [bite] mordisco m

nipple ['nɪpəl] n a) ANAT [female] pezón m; [male] tetilla f **b)** US [on baby's bottle] tetilla f, tetina f

NITING MESSAGING written abbr of anything

nitrogen ['naɪtrədʒən] n CHEM nitrógeno m

Njoy MESSAGING written abbr of enjoy

no [nəʊ] **1.** adv no; **come here! — no!** ¡ven aquí! — ¡no!; **no longer** ya no; **no less than** no menos de **2.** adj ninguno(a); **she has no children** no tiene hijos; **I have no idea** no tengo (ni) idea; **it's no good** or **use** no vale la pena; AUTO **no parking** [sign] prohibido aparcar; Fam **no way!** ¡ni hablar! **3.** n no m; **to say no** decir que no

nobility [nəʊ'bɪlɪtɪ] n nobleza f

noble ['nəʊbəl] adj noble

nobody ['nəʊbədɪ] **1.** pron nadie; **there was nobody there** no había nadie; **nobody else** nadie más **2.** n nadie m; **he's a nobody** es un don nadie

no-brainer [nəʊ'breɪnə(r)] n US Fam **it's a no-brainer!** ¡es de cajón!

nod [nɒd] **1.** n [of greeting] saludo m (con la cabeza); [of agreement] señal f de asentimiento **2.** vi [greet] saludar con la cabeza; [agree] asentir con la cabeza **3.** vt **to nod one's head** inclinar la cabeza

■ **nod off** vi dormirse

no-fault adj US JUR **no-fault divorce** divorcio m de mutuo acuerdo; **no-fault insurance** seguro m a todo riesgo

no-frills [-'frɪlz] adj [service] mínimo(a), sin lujos; [airline] de bajo coste

no-holds-barred adj [report, documentary] sin restricciones

noise [nɔɪz] n ruido m; **to make a noise** hacer ruido

noisy ['nɔɪzɪ] (compar noisier, superl noisiest) adj ruidoso(a)

nominal ['nɒmɪnəl] adj nominal; [payment, rent] simbólico(a)

nominate ['nɒmɪneɪt] vt a) [propose] designar, proponer **b)** [appoint] nombrar

nomination [nɒmɪ'neɪʃən] n a) [proposal] propuesta f **b)** [appointment] nombramiento m

nondescript [Br 'nɒndɪskrɪpt, US nɒndɪ'skrɪpt] adj indescriptible; [uninteresting] soso(a)

none [nʌn] **1.** pron ninguno(a); **I know none of them** no conozco a ninguno de ellos; **none at all** nada en absoluto; **none other than ...** nada menos que... **2.** adv de ningún modo; **she's none the worse for it** no se ha visto afectada or perjudicada por ello; **none too soon** a buena hora

nonentity [nɒ'nentɪtɪ] n [person] cero m a la izquierda

nonetheless [nʌnðə'les] *adv* no obstante, sin embargo

nonexistent [nɒnɪg'zɪstənt] *adj* inexistente

nonfiction [nɒn'fɪkʃən] *n* no ficción *f*

nonsense ['nɒnsəns] *n* tonterías *fpl*, disparates *mpl*; **that's nonsense** eso es absurdo

nonsmoker [nɒn'sməʊkə(r)] *n* no fumador(a) *m,f*, persona *f* que no fuma

nonstop [nɒn'stɒp] **1.** *adj* sin parar; [train] directo(a) **2.** *adv* sin parar

noob [nu:b] *n Fam* novato(a) *m,f*

noodles ['nu:dəlz] *npl* CULIN fideos *mpl*

noon [nu:n] *n* mediodía *m*; **at noon** a mediodía

no one ['nəʊwʌn] *pron* nadie; **no one came** no vino nadie

No1 MESSAGING *written abbr of* **no one**

noose [nu:s] *n* lazo *m*; [hangman's] soga *f*

nor [nɔː(r)] *conj* ni, ni tampoco; **neither ... nor** ni ... ni; **neither you nor I** ni tú ni yo; **nor do I** (ni) yo tampoco

norm [nɔːm] *n* norma *f*

normal ['nɔːməl] *adj* normal

normally ['nɔːməlɪ] *adv* normalmente

north [nɔːθ] **1.** *n* norte *m*; **the North** el norte; **North America** América del Norte, Norteamérica; **North Korea** Corea del Norte; **North Pole** Polo *m* Norte
2. *adv* hacia el norte, al norte
3. *adj* del norte; **north wind** viento *m* del norte

northeast [nɔːθ'i:st] *n* nor(d)este *m*

northerly ['nɔːðəlɪ] *adj* norte, del norte

northern ['nɔːðən] *adj* del norte, septentrional; **northern hemisphere** hemisferio *m* norte; **Northern Ireland** Irlanda del Norte

northerner ['nɔːðənə(r)] *n* norteño(a) *m,f*

northward ['nɔːθwəd] *adj & adv* hacia el norte

northwest [nɔːθ'west] *n* noroeste *m*

Norway ['nɔːweɪ] *n* Noruega

Norwegian [nɔː'wiːdʒən] **1.** *adj* noruego(a) **2.** *n* **a)** [person] noruego(a) *m,f* **b)** [language] noruego *m*

nose [nəʊz] *n* **a)** nariz *f* **b)** [sense of smell] olfato *m* **c)** [of car, plane] morro *m* ■ **nose about, nose around** *vi* curiosear

nosebleed ['nəʊzbliːd] *n* hemorragia *f* nasal

no-smoking [nəʊ'sməʊkɪŋ] *adj* [carriage, area] de *or* para no fumadores; **no-smoking area** zona *f* de no fumadores

nostalgic [nɒ'stældʒɪk] *adj* nostálgico(a)

nostril ['nɒstrɪl] *n* ANAT orificio *m* nasal

no-strings *adj* **a)** *Fam* [contract, agreement] sin compromiso **b)** [relationship] sin ataduras; **looking for no-strings hookups** busca una relación sin ataduras

nosy ['nəʊzɪ] *(compar* nosier, *superl* nosiest) *adj Fam* entrometido(a)

not [nɒt] *adv* no; **he's not in today** hoy no está; **not at all** en absoluto; **thank you — not at all** gracias — no hay de qué; **not too well** bastante mal; *Fam* **not likely!** ¡ni hablar!

En el inglés hablado, y en el escrito en estilo coloquial, **not** se contrae después de verbos modales y auxiliares.

notable ['nəʊtəbəl] *adj* notable

notably ['nəʊtəblɪ] *adv* notablemente

notch [nɒtʃ] *n* muesca *f*; [cut] corte *m* ■ **notch up** *vt sep Fig* **to notch up a victory** apuntarse una victoria

note [nəʊt] **1.** *n* **a)** MUS nota *f* **b)** [on paper] nota *f* **c)** **to take note of** [notice] prestar atención a **d)** *esp Br* [banknote] billete *m* (de banco) **e)** **notes** apuntes *mpl*; **to take note** tomar apuntes **2.** *vt* **a)** [write down] apuntar, anotar **b)** [notice] notar, fijarse en

notebook ['nəʊtbʊk] *n* cuaderno *m*, libreta *f*; COMPUT *Esp* ordenador *m or Am* computadora *f* portátil, notebook *m*

noted ['nəʊtɪd] *adj* notable, célebre

notepad ['nəʊtpæd] *n* bloc *m* de notas

notepaper ['nəʊtpeɪpə(r)] n papel m de carta

not-for-profit adj US sin fines lucrativos

nothing ['nʌθɪŋ] **1.** n nada; **I saw nothing** no vi nada; **for nothing** [free of charge] gratis; **it's nothing** no es nada; **it's nothing to do with you** no tiene nada que ver contigo; **nothing else** nada más; Fam **nothing much** poca cosa **2.** adv **she looks nothing like her sister** no se parece en nada a su hermana

notice ['nəʊtɪs] **1.** n **a)** [warning] aviso m; **he gave a month's notice** presentó la dimisión con un mes de antelación; **at short notice** con poca antelación; **until further notice** hasta nuevo aviso; **without notice** sin previo aviso

b) [attention] atención f; **to take no notice of sth** no hacer caso de algo; **to take notice of sth** prestar atención a algo

c) [in newspaper etc] anuncio m

d) [sign] letrero m, aviso m **2.** vt darse cuenta de, notar

noticeable ['nəʊtɪsəbəl] adj que se nota, evidente

noticeboard ['nəʊtɪsbɔːd] n Br tablón m de anuncios

notification [nəʊtɪfɪ'keɪʃən] n aviso m

notify ['nəʊtɪfaɪ] vt avisar

notion ['nəʊʃən] n **a)** idea f, concepto m **b)** [whim] capricho m

notorious [nəʊ'tɔːrɪəs] adj Pej tristemente célebre

nought [nɔːt] n cero m

noun [naʊn] n nombre m, sustantivo m

nourishment ['nʌrɪʃmənt] n alimentación f, nutrición f

novel¹ ['nɒvəl] n novela f

novel² ['nɒvəl] adj original, novedoso(a)

novelist ['nɒvəlɪst] n novelista mf

novelty ['nɒvəltɪ] n novedad f

November [nəʊ'vembə(r)] n noviembre m

novice ['nɒvɪs] n **a)** [beginner] novato(a) m,f, principiante mf **b)** REL novicio(a) m,f

now [naʊ] **1.** adv **a)** [at this moment] ahora; **just now, right now** ahora mismo; **from now on** de ahora en adelante; **now and then, now and again** de vez en cuando **b)** [for events in past] entonces **c)** [at present, these days] actualmente, hoy (en) día **d)** [not related to time] **now (then)** ahora bien; **now, now!** ¡vamos!, ¡ya está bien! **2.** conj **now (that)** ahora que, ya que **3.** n **until now** hasta ahora; **he'll be home by now** ya habrá llegado a casa

nowadays ['naʊədeɪz] adv hoy (en) día, actualmente

nowhere ['nəʊweə(r)], US **noplace** ['nəʊpleɪs] adv en or a ninguna parte; **nowhere near** lejos de; **that will get you nowhere** eso no te servirá de nada; **it's nowhere near ready** no está preparado, ni mucho menos; **we're getting nowhere** no avanzamos

nozzle ['nɒzəl] n boca f, boquilla f

nuance ['njuːɑːns] n matiz m

nuclear ['njuːklɪə(r)] adj nuclear; **nuclear arms** armas fpl nucleares; **nuclear power** energía f nuclear; **nuclear power station** central f nuclear

nucleus ['njuːklɪəs] (pl **nuclei** ['njuːklɪaɪ]) n núcleo m

nude [njuːd] **1.** adj desnudo(a) **2.** n ART & PHOTO desnudo m; **in the nude** al desnudo

nudge [nʌdʒ] **1.** vt dar un codazo a **2.** n codazo m

nudist ['njuːdɪst] adj & n nudista (mf)

nufn (abbr of nothing) MESSAGING nd

nuisance ['njuːsəns] n **a)** molestia f, pesadez f; **what a nuisance!** ¡qué lata! **b)** [person] pesado(a) m,f

nuke [njuːk] Fam **1.** n arma f nuclear **2.** vt **a)** [bomb] atacar con armas nucleares **b)** [microwave] cocinar en el microondas

null [nʌl] *adj* nulo(a); **null and void** nulo y sin valor

numb [nʌm] **1.** *adj* [without feeling] entumecido(a); *Fig* paralizado(a); **numb with fear** paralizado de miedo **2.** *vt* [with cold] entumecer (de frío); [with anaesthetic] adormecer

number ['nʌmbə(r)] **1.** *n* a) [numeral & TEL] número *m*; TEL **number portability** portabilidad *f* numérica; TEL **have you got my number?** ¿tienes mi (número de) teléfono? b) [quantity] **a number of people** varias personas c) *Br* [of car] matrícula *f*; **number plate** (placa *f* de la) matrícula *f* d) *Br* **Number Ten** *residencia oficial del primer ministro británico* **2.** *vt* a) [put a number on] numerar b) [count] contar

numeral ['njuːmərəl] *n* número *m*, cifra *f*

numerous ['njuːmərəs] *adj* numeroso(a)

nun [nʌn] *n* monja *f*

nurse [nɜːs] **1.** *n* enfermero(a) *m,f* **2.** *vt* a) [look after] cuidar, atender b) [baby] acunar c) [suckle] amamantar d) *Fig* [grudge etc] guardar

nursery ['nɜːsərɪ] *n* a) [institution] guardería *f*; **nursery school** jardín *m* de infancia b) [in house] cuarto *m* de los niños; **nursery rhyme** poema *m* infantil c) [garden centre] vivero *m*

nursing ['nɜːsɪŋ] *n* **nursing home** *Br* [where children are born] maternidad *f*; [for old people, war veterans] residencia *f*

nut [nʌt] *n* a) [fruit] fruto seco b) *Fam* [head] coco *m* c) *Fam* [mad person] chiflado(a) *m,f*, *Esp* chalado(a) *m,f* d) TECH tuerca *f*

nutcase ['nʌtkeɪs] *n Fam* chiflado(a) *m,f*, *Esp* chalado(a) *m,f*

nutcracker ['nʌtkrækə(r)] *n* cascanueces *m inv*

nutmeg ['nʌtmeg] *n* nuez moscada

nutrition [njuːˈtrɪʃən] *n* nutrición *f*

nutritious [njuːˈtrɪʃəs] *adj* nutritivo(a), alimenticio(a)

nuts [nʌts] **1.** *adj Fam* chiflado(a), *Esp* majara; **to be nuts** estar chiflado(a) or majara **2.** *interj US Fam* ¡maldita sea!

nutshell ['nʌtʃel] *n* cáscara *f*; *Fig* **in a nutshell** en pocas palabras

nutty ['nʌtɪ] *(compar* **nuttier***, superl* **nuttiest)** *adj* a) [tasting of nuts] con sabor a frutos secos; [containing nuts] con frutos secos; **a nutty flavour** un sabor a frutos secos b) *Fam* [crazy] chiflado(a), *Esp* majara c) **as nutty as a fruitcake** como una regadera

nylon ['naɪlɒn] **1.** *n* a) nilón *m*, nailon *m* b) **nylons** medias *fpl* de nilón **2.** *adj* de nilón

NYPD [ˌenwaɪpiːˈdiː] *n (abbr of* **New York Police Department)** policía *f* de Nueva York

O, **o** [əʊ] *n* **a)** [the letter] O, o *f* **b)** MATH & TEL cero *m*

oaf [əʊf] *n* tarugo *m*, zote *m*

oak [əʊk] *n* roble *m*

OAP [əʊeɪ'piː] *n Br (abbr of old age pensioner)* pensionista *mf*, jubilado(a) *m,f*

oar [ɔː(r)] *n* remo *m*

oasis [əʊ'eɪsɪs] *(pl oases* [əʊ'eɪsiːz]*) n* oasis *m inv*

oat [əʊt] *n* avena *f*; **rolled oats** copos *mpl* de avena

oath [əʊθ] *(pl oaths* [əʊðz]*) n* **a)** JUR juramento *m*; **to take an oath** prestar juramento **b)** [swearword] palabrota *f*

obedience [ə'biːdɪəns] *n* obediencia *f*

obedient [ə'biːdɪənt] *adj* obediente

obese [əʊ'biːs] *adj* obeso(a)

obey [ə'beɪ] *vt* obedecer; [law] cumplir con

obituary [ə'bɪtjʊərɪ] *n* necrología *f*

object¹ ['ɒbdʒɪkt] *n* **a)** [thing] objeto *m* **b)** [aim, purpose] fin *m*, objetivo *m* **c)** [obstacle] inconveniente *m* **d)** LING complemento *m*

object² [əb'dʒekt] *vi* oponerse (**to** a); **do you object to my smoking?** ¿le molesta que fume?

objection [əb'dʒekʃən] *n* **a)** objeción *f* **b)** [drawback] inconveniente *m*; **provided there's no objection** si no hay inconveniente

objective [əb'dʒektɪv] **1.** *adj* objetivo(a) **2.** *n* objetivo *m*

obligation [ɒblɪ'geɪʃən] *n* obligación *f*; **to be under an obligation to sb** estarle muy agradecido(a) a algn

obligatory [ɒ'blɪgətərɪ] *adj* obligatorio(a)

oblige [ə'blaɪdʒ] *vt* **a)** [compel] obligar; **I'm obliged to do it** me veo obligado(a) a hacerlo **b)** [do a favour for] hacer un favor a **c) to be obliged** [grateful] estar agradecido(a)

obliging [ə'blaɪdʒɪŋ] *adj* solícito(a)

oblique [ə'bliːk] *adj* oblicuo(a), inclinado(a); *Fig* **an oblique reference** una alusión indirecta

oblivion [ə'blɪvɪən] *n* olvido *m*; **to sink into oblivion** caer en el olvido

oblivious [ə'blɪvɪəs] *adj* inconsciente

oblong ['ɒblɒŋ] **1.** *adj* oblongo(a) **2.** *n* rectángulo *m*

obnoxious [əb'nɒkʃəs] *adj* repugnante

oboe ['əʊbəʊ] *n* oboe *m*

obscene [əb'siːn] *adj* obsceno(a)

obscenity [əb'senɪtɪ] *n* obscenidad *f*

obscure [əb'skjʊə(r)] **1.** *adj* **a)** oscuro(a); [vague] vago(a) **b)** [author, poet etc] desconocido(a) **2.** *vt* [truth] ocultar

observant [əb'zɜːvənt] *adj* observador(a)

observation [ɒbzə'veɪʃən] *n* observación *f*; [surveillance] vigilancia *f*

observe [əb'zɜːv] *vt* **a)** observar; [in surveillance] vigilar **b)** [remark] advertir **c)** [obey] respetar

observer [əb'zɜːvə(r)] *n* observador(a) *m,f*

obsess [əb'ses] *vt* obsesionar; **to be obsessed (with** *or* **by)** estar obsesionado(a) (con)

obsession [əb'seʃən] *n* obsesión *f*

obsolete ['ɒbsəliːt, ɒbsə'liːt] *adj* obsoleto(a)

obstacle ['ɒbstəkəl] *n* obstáculo *m*; *Fig* impedimento *m*; **obstacle race** carrera *f* de obstáculos

obstinate ['ɒbstɪnɪt] *adj* **a)** [person] obstinado(a), terco(a) **b)** [pain] persistente

obstruct [əb'strʌkt] *vt* **a)** obstruir; [pipe etc] atascar; [view] tapar **b)** [hinder] estorbar; [progress] dificultar

obstruction [əb'strʌkʃən] *n* **a)** obstrucción *f* **b)** [hindrance] obstáculo *m*

obtain [əb'teɪn] *vt* obtener, conseguir

obvious ['ɒbvɪəs] *adj* obvio(a), evidente

obviously ['ɒbvɪəslɪ] *adv* evidentemente; **obviously!** ¡claro!, ¡por supuesto!

occasion [ə'keɪʒən] **1.** *n* **a)** ocasión *f*; **on occasion** de vez en cuando; **on the occasion of** con motivo de **b)** [event] acontecimiento *m* **c)** [cause] motivo *m* **2.** *vt Formal* ocasionar

occasional [ə'keɪʒənəl] *adj* esporádico(a), eventual

occasionally [ə'keɪʒənəlɪ] *adv* de vez en cuando

occupant ['ɒkjʊpənt] *n* ocupante *mf*; [tenant] inquilino(a) *m,f*

occupation [ɒkjʊ'peɪʃən] *n* **a)** [job, profession] profesión *f*, ocupación *f* **b)** [pastime] pasatiempo *m* **c)** [of building, house, country] ocupación *f*

occupier ['ɒkjʊpaɪə(r)] *n Br* ocupante *mf*; [tenant] inquilino(a) *m,f*

occupy ['ɒkjʊpaɪ] *vt* **a)** [live in] ocupar, habitar **b)** [time] pasar; **to occupy one's time in doing sth** dedicar su tiempo a hacer algo **c)** [building, factory etc in protest] tomar posesión de

occur [ə'kɜ:(r)] *vi* **a)** [event] suceder, acaecer; [change] producirse **b)** [be found] encontrarse **c)** **it occurred to me that ...** se me ocurrió que ...

occurrence [ə'kʌrəns] *n* suceso *m*, incidencia *f*

OCD *n* PSYCH (*abbr of* **obsessive-compulsive disorder**) TOC *m* (*trastorno obsesivo-compulsivo*)

ocean ['əʊʃən] *n* océano *m*

o'clock [ə'klɒk] *adv* (**it's) one o'clock** (es) la una; (**it's) two o'clock** (son) las dos

October [ɒk'təʊbə(r)] *n* octubre *m*

octopus ['ɒktəpəs] *n* pulpo *m*

odd [ɒd] **1.** *adj* **a)** [strange] raro(a), extraño(a) **b)** [occasional] esporádico(a); **odd job** trabajillo *m* **c)** **an odd number** [not even] un impar **d)** [unpaired] desparejado(a); **an odd sock** un calcetín suelto **2.** *adv* y pico; **twenty odd people** veinte y pico *or* y tantas personas

oddly ['ɒdlɪ] *adv* extrañamente; **oddly enough** por extraño que parezca

odds [ɒdz] *npl* **a)** [chances] probabilidades *fpl*; **the odds are that ...** lo más probable es que ... (+ *subj*) **b)** [in betting] puntos *mpl* de ventaja; **the odds are five to one** las apuestas están cinco a uno **c)** *Br* **makes no odds** da lo mismo **d)** **at odds with sb** [disagreeing] reñido(a) con algn **e)** **odds and ends** [small things] cositas *fpl*; [trinkets] chucherías *fpl*

odious ['əʊdɪəs] *adj* repugnante

odour, *US* **odor** ['əʊdə(r)] *n* olor *m*; [fragrance] perfume *m*

of [ɒv] (*unstressed* [əv]) *prep* de; **a friend of mine** un amigo mío; **a bottle of wine** una botella de vino; **a dress (made) of silk** un vestido de seda; **that's very kind of you** es usted muy amable; **there are four of us** somos cuatro; **two of them** dos de ellos; **south of** al sur de; **the 7th of November** el 7 de noviembre

off [ɒf] **1.** *prep* de; **she fell off her horse** se cayó del caballo; **a few kilometres off the coast** a unos kilómetros de la costa; **I'm off wine** he perdido el gusto al vino

2. *adv* **a)** **he turned off the radio** apagó la radio

b) [absent] fuera; **I have a day off** tengo un día libre; **to be off sick** estar de baja por enfermedad

c) [distant] **6 miles off** a 6 millas

d) **I'm off to London** me voy a Londres

e) **10 percent off** un descuento del 10 por ciento

f) **off and on** de vez en cuando

3. *adj* **a)** [gas etc] apagado(a); [water] cortado(a)

b) [cancelled] cancelado(a)

c) [low] bajo(a); [unsatisfactory] malo(a); **on the off chance** por si acaso; **the off season** la temporada baja

d) [gone bad - meat, fish] malo(a), pasado(a); [milk] agrio(a)

off-air *adj* fuera de antena

offence [ə'fens] *n* **a)** JUR delito *m* **b)** [insult] ofensa *f*; **to give offence** ofender; **to take offence at sth** ofenderse por algo **c)** MIL [attack] ofensiva *f*

offend [ə'fend] *vt* ofender

offender [ə'fendə(r)] *n* [criminal] delincuente *mf*

offense [ə'fens] *US n* = **offence**

offensive [ə'fensɪv] **1.** *adj* **a)** [insulting] ofensivo(a) **b)** [repulsive] repugnante **2.** *n* MIL ofensiva *f*; **to be on the offensive** estar a la ofensiva

offer ['ɒfə(r)] **1.** *vt* **a)** ofrecer; **to offer to do a job** ofrecerse para hacer un trabajo **b)** [propose] proponer **2.** *n* **a)** oferta *f*; [proposal] propuesta *f*; **offer of marriage** proposición *f* de matrimonio **b)** COMM **on offer** de oferta

offering ['ɒfərɪŋ] *n* **a)** ofrecimiento *m* **b)** REL ofrenda *f*

offhand 1. ['ɒf'hænd] *adj* [abrupt] brusco(a); [inconsiderate] descortés **2.** [ɒf'hænd] *adv* **I don't know offhand** así sin pensarlo, no lo sé

office ['ɒfɪs] *n* **a)** [room] despacho *m*; [building] oficina *f*; [of lawyer] despacho, bufete *m*; *US* [of doctor, dentist] consulta *f*; **office hours** horas *fpl* de oficina **b)** *Br* POL ministerio *m* **c)** *US* [federal agency] agencia *f* gubernamental **d)** [position] cargo *m* **e)** POL **to be in office** estar en el poder

officer ['ɒfɪsə(r)] *n* **a)** MIL oficial *mf* **b)** **(police) officer** agente *mf* de policía **c)** [government official] funcionario(a) *m,f* **d)** [of company, society] director(a) *m,f*

official [ə'fɪʃəl] **1.** *adj* oficial **2.** *n* funcionario(a) *m,f*

officially [ə'fɪʃəlɪ] *adv* oficialmente

off-licence ['ɒflaɪsəns] *n Br* tienda *f* de bebidas alcohólicas

off-line, offline ['ɒflaɪn] **1.** *adj* COMPUT desconectado(a) **2.** *adv* COMPUT sin estar conectado(a), fuera de línea

off-peak [ɒf'pi:k] *adj* [flight] de temporada baja; [rate] de fuera de las horas punta

off-putting ['ɒfputɪŋ] *adj Br Fam* desconcertante

off-road *adj* [driving] fuera de pista; **off-road vehicle** vehículo *m* todoterreno

offset [ɒf'set] *(pt & pp* offset*) vt* [balance out] compensar

offside 1. [ɒf'saɪd] *adv* FTBL fuera de juego **2.** ['ɒfsaɪd] *n* AUTO [with left-hand drive] lado derecho; [with right-hand drive] lado izquierdo

offspring ['ɒfsprɪŋ] *(pl* offspring*) n* [child] vástago *m*; [children] progenitura *f*

often ['ɒfən,'ɒftən] *adv* a menudo, con frecuencia; **every so often** de vez en cuando

oh [əʊ] *interj* ¡oh!, ¡ay!; **oh, my God!** ¡Dios mío!

OIC MESSAGING *written abbr of* **oh, I see**

oil [ɔɪl] **1.** *n* **a)** aceite *m*; **oil lamp** lámpara *f* de aceite, quinqué *m*; **olive oil** aceite de oliva **b)** [petroleum] petróleo *m*; **oil rig** plataforma petrolera; **oil slick** fuga *f* de petróleo, marea *f* negra; **oil tanker** [ship] petrolero *m*; [lorry] camión *m* cisterna; **oil well** pozo *m* petrolífero *or* de petróleo **c)** [painting] pintura *f* al óleo; **oil paint** óleo *m* **2.** *vt* engrasar

oilcan ['ɔɪlkæn] *n* aceitera *f*

oil-dependent *adj* petrodependiente

oilfield ['ɔɪlfi:ld] *n* yacimiento petrolífero

oily ['ɔɪlɪ] *(compar* oilier, *superl* oiliest*) adj* aceitoso(a), grasiento(a); [hair, skin] graso(a)

ointment ['ɔɪntmənt] *n* ungüento *m*, pomada *f*

O.K., okay [əʊ'keɪ] *Fam* **1.** *interj* de acuerdo, *Esp* vale, *Am* ok, *Méx* ándale **2.** *adj* bien; **is it O.K. if …?** ¿están bien si …? **3.** *vt* dar el visto bueno a

old [əʊld] **1.** *adj* **a)** viejo(a); **an old man** un anciano; **old age** vejez *f*; *Br* **old age pensioner** pensionista *mf*; *Br* **old**

boy [addressing sb] antiguo alumno; **old hand** veterano(a) *m,f*; **good old John!** ¡el bueno de John!; **how old are you?** ¿cuántos años tienes?; **she's five years old** tiene cinco años **b)** [former] antiguo(a) **c)** *Fam* [as intensifier] **any old** cualquier(a) **2.** *n* **the old** los ancianos *mpl*; **of old** de antaño

old-fashioned [ǝʊld'fæʃǝnd] *adj* [outdated] a la antigua; [unfashionable] anticuado(a), pasado(a) de moda

old-timer *n* **a)** [veteran] veterano(a) *m,f* **b)** *esp US* [old man] anciano *m,f*

olive ['ɒlɪv] *n* **a)** [tree] olivo *m* **b)** [fruit] aceituna *f*, oliva *f*

Olympic [ǝ'lɪmpɪk] **1.** *adj* olímpico(a); **Olympic Games** Juegos Olímpicos **2.** *npl* **the Olympics** las Olimpiadas

omelette, *US* **omelet** ['ɒmlɪt] *n* tortilla *f*; **Spanish omelette** tortilla española *or* de patatas *or Am* papas

omen ['ǝʊmen] *n* presagio *m*

OMG MESSAGING *written abbr of* **oh, my god**

ominous ['ɒmɪnǝs] *adj* de mal agüero

omission [ǝʊ'mɪʃǝn] *n* omisión *f*; *Fig* olvido *m*

omit [ǝʊ'mɪt] *vt* omitir; [accidentally] pasar por alto; [forget] olvidarse **(to** do)

on [ɒn] **1.** *prep* **a)** [location] sobre, encima de, en; **I hit him on the head** le di un golpe en la cabeza; **it's on the desk** está encima de *or* sobre el escritorio; **hanging on the wall** colgado de la pared; **on page 4** en la página 4
b) [alongside] en; **a town on the coast** un pueblo en la costa
c) [direction] en, a; **on the right** a la derecha; **on the way** en el camino
d) [time] **on 3 April** el 3 de abril; **on a sunny day** un día de sol; **on Monday** el lunes; **on Mondays** los lunes; **on time** a tiempo
e) en; **on TV/the radio** en la tele /radio; **on the phone** al teléfono
f) [at the time of] a; **on his arrival** a su llegada; **on learning of this** al conocer esto
g) [transport] en /a; **on foot** a pie

h) [state, process] en /de; **on holiday / business** de vacaciones /negocios
i) [regarding] sobre; **a lecture on numismatics** una conferencia sobre numismática
j) [against] contra; **an attack on** un ataque contra
2. *adv* **a)** [covering] encima, puesto; **she had a coat on** llevaba puesto un abrigo
b) *Fam* **have you anything on tonight?** ¿tienes algún plan para esta noche?
c) **and so on** y así sucesivamente; **he talks on and on** habla sin parar; **to work on** seguir trabajando
d) **from that day on** a partir de aquel día; **later on** más tarde
e) **on and off** de vez en cuando
3. *adj* *Fam* **a)** to be on [TV, radio, light] estar encendido(a) *or Am* prendido(a); [film, play] estar en cartelera
b) [definitely planned] previsto(a); **you're on!** ¡trato hecho!
c) *Br Fam* [acceptable] **that isn't on** eso no está bien

on-air *adj & adv* TV & RADIO en antena

on-camera *adj & adv* TV ante la cámara

once [wʌns] **1.** *adv* **a)** [one time] una vez; **once a week** una vez por semana; **once more** una vez más; **once or twice** un par de veces; *Fig* **once and for all** de una vez por todas **b)** [formerly] en otro tiempo; **once (upon a time) there was ...** érase una vez ... **c)** **at once** en seguida, inmediatamente **2.** *conj* una vez que (+ *subj*), en cuanto (+ *subj*)

once-only *adj* **a once-only offer** una oferta única

one [wʌn] **1.** *adj* **a)** un /una; **for one thing** primero; **you're the one person who knows** tú eres el único que lo sabe **b)** [indefinite] un /una; **he'll come back one day** un día volverá
2. *dem pron* **any one** cualquiera; **that one** ése /ésa; [distant] aquél /aquélla; **this one** éste /ésta; **the blue ones** los azules /las azules; **the one on the table** el /la que está encima de la mesa; **the ones that, the ones who** los /las que

3. *indef pron* **a)** uno(a) *m,f*; **one at a time** de uno en uno; **one by one** uno tras otro

b) [indefinite person] uno(a) *m,f*; **one has to fight** hay que luchar; **one hopes that will never happen** esperemos que no ocurra

c) one another el uno al otro; **they love one another** se aman

4. *n* [digit] uno *m*; **one hundred / thousand** cien /mil

one-armed *adj* **a)** [person] manco(a) **b)** *Br Fam* **one-armed bandit** (máquina *f*) tragaperras *finv*

1DAY MESSAGING *written abbr of* **one day**

one-off *adj Br Fam* [offer, event, product] único(a), aislado(a)

one-parent *adj* monoparental; **one-parent family** familia *f* monoparental

oneself [wʌn'self] *pron* **a)** [reflexive] uno(a) mismo(a) *m,f*, sí mismo(a) *m,f*; **to talk to oneself** hablar para sí **b)** [alone] uno(a) mismo(a) *m,f*; **by oneself** solo(a)

one-sided [wʌn'saɪdɪd] *adj* [bargain] desigual; [judgement] parcial; [decision] unilateral

one-size *adj* de talla única

one-to-one, *US* **one-on-one** *adj* [discussion] a solas, privado(a); **one-to-one tuition** clases *mpl* particulares

one-way ['wʌnweɪ] *adj* **a)** *US* [ticket] de ida *f* **b)** [street] de dirección única

ongoing ['ɒŋɡəʊɪŋ] *adj* **a)** [in progress] en curso, actual **b)** [developing] en desarrollo

onion ['ʌnjən] *n* cebolla *f*

on-line, **online** ['ɒnlaɪn] **1.** *adj* COMPUT & INTERNET en línea, por internet; **online banking** banca *f* en línea *or* por internet; **online community** comunidad *f* en línea; **online shopping** compras *fpl* por internet **2.** *adv* COMPUT en línea

onlooker ['ɒnlʊkə(r)] *n* espectador(a) *m,f*

only ['əʊnlɪ] **1.** *adj* único(a); **only son** hijo único

2. *adv* **a)** solamente, sólo *or* solo; **staff only** [sign] reservado al personal **b)** [not earlier than] apenas; **he has only just left** acaba de marcharse hace un momento; **only yesterday** ayer mismo

3. *conj* pero

onset ['ɒnset] *n* [start] comienzo *m*

onto ['ɒntʊ] (*unstressed* ['ɒntə]) *prep* sobre, encima de

on-trend *adj* que es la tendencia del momento

onward(s) ['ɒnwəd(z)] *adv* a partir de, en adelante; **from this time onward(s)** de ahora en adelante

opaque [əʊ'peɪk] *adj* opaco(a)

open ['əʊpən] **1.** *adj* **a)** abierto(a); **in the open air** al aire libre; **to be open with sb** ser sincero(a) con algn; **to keep an open mind** no tener prejuicios; **I am open to suggestions** acepto cualquier sugerencia; **open to criticism** susceptible a la crítica; AVIAT & RAIL **open ticket** billete *or* Am boleto abierto **b)** [opposition] manifiesto(a)

2. *vt* **a)** abrir; **to open fire** abrir fuego **b)** [exhibition etc] inaugurar; [negotiations, conversation] entablar

3. *vi* **a)** abrir, abrirse; **to open onto** [door, window] dar a **b)** [start] empezar; THEAT & CIN estrenarse

4. *n* **in the open** al aire libre

■ **open out 1.** *vt sep* abrir, desplegar **2.** *vi* [flowers] abrirse; [view] extenderse

■ **open up 1.** *vt sep* [market etc] abrir; [possibilities] crear **2.** *vi* **a)** abrirse; *Fam* **open up!** ¡abre la puerta! **b)** [start] empezar

opening ['əʊpənɪŋ] *n* **a)** [act] apertura *f*; **opening night** noche *f* de estreno; *Br* **opening time** [of pub] hora *f* de apertura **b)** [beginning] comienzo *m* **c)** [aperture] abertura *f*; [gap] brecha *f* **d)** COMM oportunidad *f* **e)** [vacancy] vacante *f*

openly ['əʊpənlɪ] *adv* abiertamente

open-minded [əupən'maɪndɪd] *adj* sin prejuicios

open-toe, open-toed [-təud] *adj* [shoe] abierto(a)

open-top *adj* descapotable

opera ['ɒpərə] *n* ópera *f*; **opera house** ópera, teatro *m* de la ópera

operate ['ɒpəreɪt] **1.** *vi* **a)** [function] funcionar **b)** MED operar; **to operate on sb for appendicitis** operar a algn de apendicitis **2.** *vt* **a)** [control] manejar **b)** [business] dirigir

operating ['ɒpəreɪtɪŋ] *adj* COMPUT **operating system** sistema *m* operativo

operation [ɒpə'reɪʃən] *n* **a)** [of machine] funcionamiento *m*; [by person] manejo *m* **b)** MIL maniobra *f* **c)** MED operación *f*, intervención quirúrgica; **to undergo an operation for** ser operado(a) de

operator ['ɒpəreɪtə(r)] *n* **a)** IND operario(a) *m,f* **b)** TEL operador(a) *m,f* **c)** [dealer] negociante *mf*, agente *mf*; **tour operator** agente de viajes

opinion [ə'pɪnjən] *n* opinión *f*; **in my opinion** en mi opinión, a mi juicio; **it's a matter of opinion** es cuestión de opiniones; **to have a high opinion of sb** tener buen concepto de algn; **opinion poll** encuesta *f*, sondeo *m*

opponent [ə'pəunənt] *n* adversario(a) *m,f*

opportunity [ɒpə'tju:nɪti] *n* **a)** oportunidad *f*, ocasión *f* **b)** [prospect] perspectiva *f*

oppose [ə'pəuz] *vt* oponerse a

opposed [ə'pəuzd] *adj* opuesto(a); **to be opposed to sth** estar en contra de algo; **as opposed to** comparado(a) con

opposing [ə'pəuzɪŋ] *adj* adversario(a)

opposite ['ɒpəzɪt] **1.** *adj* **a)** [facing] de enfrente; [page] contiguo(a) **b)** [contrary] opuesto(a), contrario(a); **in the opposite direction** en dirección contraria **2.** *n* **the opposite** lo contrario; **quite the opposite!** ¡al contrario! **3.** *prep* enfrente de, frente a **4.** *adv* enfrente

opposition [ɒpə'zɪʃən] *n* **a)** oposición *f*; **in opposition to** en contra de **b)** *Br* POL **the Opposition** la oposición

oppress [ə'pres] *vt* oprimir

oppression [ə'preʃən] *n* opresión *f*

oppressive [ə'presɪv] *adj* opresivo(a); [atmosphere] agobiante; [heat] sofocante

opt [ɒpt] *vi* optar; **to opt for** optar por; **to opt to do sth** optar por hacer algo ▪ **opt out** *vi* retirarse; **to opt out of doing sth** decidir no hacer algo

optical ['ɒptɪkəl] *adj* óptico(a)

optician [ɒp'tɪʃən] *n* óptico(a) *m,f*

optimism ['ɒptɪmɪzəm] *n* optimismo *m*

optimist ['ɒptɪmɪst] *n* optimista *mf*

optimistic [ɒptɪ'mɪstɪk] *adj* optimista

option ['ɒpʃən] *n* opción *f*; **I have no option** no tengo más remedio; **to keep one's options open** no comprometerse; **with the option of** con opción a

optional ['ɒpʃənəl] *adj* optativo(a), facultativo(a); SCH **optional subject** (asignatura *f*) optativa *f*

or [ɔ:(r)] (*unstressed* [ə(r)]) *conj* **a)** o; [before a word beginning with "o" or "ho"] u; **or else** si no, o bien; **whether you like it or not** tanto si te gusta como si no; **either a bun or a piece of cake** (o) una magdalena o un trozo de pastel **b)** [with negative] ni; **he can't read or write** no sabe leer ni escribir

oral ['ɔ:rəl, 'ɒrəl] **1.** *adj* oral **2.** *n* examen *m* oral

orange ['ɒrɪndʒ] **1.** *n* naranja *f*; **orange juice** *Esp* zumo *m* *or* *Am* jugo *m* de naranja **2.** *adj* de color naranja

orbit ['ɔ:bɪt] **1.** *n* ASTRON órbita *f* **2.** *vt* girar alrededor de **3.** *vi* girar

orchard ['ɔ:tʃəd] *n* huerto *m*

orchestra ['ɔ:kɪstrə] *n* orquesta *f*; US [in theatre] platea *f*

orchid ['ɔ:kɪd] *n* orquídea *f*

ordeal [ɔ:'di:l] *n* mala experiencia

order ['ɔ:də(r)] **1.** *n* **a)** [sequence] orden *m*; **to put in order** ordenar **b)** [condition] estado *m*; **out of order** [sign] averiado(a)

c) [peace] orden *m*; **to restore order** reestablecer el orden público
d) [command] orden *f*
e) COMM pedido *m*, encargo *m*; **order form** hoja *f* de pedido
f) REL orden *f*
g) in order that para que (+ *subj*), a fin de que (+ *subj*); **in order to** (+ *infin*) para (+ *infin*), a fin de (+ *infin*); **in the order of**, *US* **on the order of** del orden de
2. *vt* **a)** [command] ordenar, mandar; **to order sb to do sth** mandar a algn hacer algo
b) COMM pedir, encargar

■ **order about**, **order around** *vt sep* ordenar

orderly ['ɔːdəlɪ] *adj* [tidy etc] ordenado(a)

ordinance ['ɔːdɪnəns] *n Formal* [decree] ordenanza *f*, decreto *m*

ordinary ['ɔːdənrɪ] **1.** *adj* usual, normal; [average] corriente, común; **the ordinary citizen** el ciudadano de a pie **2.** *n* **the ordinary** lo corriente, lo normal; **out of the ordinary** fuera de lo común

organ ['ɔːgən] *n* MUS & ANAT órgano *m*

organic [ɔːˈgænɪk] *adj* orgánico(a); [farming, food] biológico(a), ecológico(a)

organism ['ɔːgənɪzəm] *n* organismo *m*

organization [ɔːgənaɪˈzeɪʃən] *n* organización *f*

organize ['ɔːgənaɪz] *vt* organizar

organizer ['ɔːgənaɪzə(r)] *n* organizador(a) *m,f*

orgasm ['ɔːgæzəm] *n* orgasmo *m*

Oriental [ɔːrɪˈentəl] *adj & n* oriental (*mf*)

orientate ['ɔːrɪənteɪt] *vt* orientar

origin ['ɒrɪdʒɪn] *n* origen *m*; **country of origin** país *m* natal *or* de origen

original [əˈrɪdʒɪnəl] **1.** *adj* **a)** original; [first] primero(a) **b)** [imaginative] original **2.** *n* original *m*

originally [əˈrɪdʒɪnəlɪ] *adv* **a)** [at first] en un principio **b)** [with imagination] con originalidad

originate [əˈrɪdʒɪneɪt] **1.** *vt* originar **2.** *vi* **to originate from** *or* **in** tener su origen en

ornament ['ɔːnəmənt] *n* ornamento *m*, adorno *m*

ornamental [ɔːnəˈmentəl] *adj* decorativo(a)

ornate [ɔːˈneɪt] *adj* vistoso(a)

orphan ['ɔːfən] **1.** *n* huérfano(a) *m,f* **2.** *vt* **she was orphaned** quedó huérfana

orthodox ['ɔːθədɒks] *adj* ortodoxo(a)

ostentatious [ɒstenˈteɪʃəs] *adj* ostentoso(a)

ostrich ['ɒstrɪtʃ] *n* avestruz *f*

other ['ʌðə(r)] **1.** *adj* **a)** otro(a); **every other day** cada dos días; **on the other hand** por otra parte; **other people have seen it** otros lo han visto; **the other four** los otros cuatro; **the other one** el otro / la otra; **the other thing** lo otro
b) he must be somewhere or other debe de estar en alguna parte
2. *pron* otro(a) *m,f*; **many others** otros muchos; **the others** los otros, los demás; **we see each other quite often** nos vemos con bastante frecuencia

otherwise ['ʌðəwaɪz] **1.** *adv* **a)** [if not] si no **b)** [differently] de otra manera **c)** [in other respects] por lo demás **2.** *adj* distinto(a)

ouch [aʊtʃ] *interj* [expressing pain] ¡ay!

ought [ɔːt]

En el inglés hablado, y en el escrito en estilo coloquial, la forma negativa **ought not** se transforma en **oughtn't**.

v aux **a)** [obligation] deber; **I thought I ought to tell you** creí que debía decírtelo; **she ought to do it** debería hacerlo
b) [vague desirability] tener que, deber; **you ought to see the exhibition** deberías ver la exposición
c) [expectation] **he ought to pass the exam** seguramente aprobará el examen; **that ought to do** con eso bastará

ounce [aʊns] *n* onza *f*

our [auə(r)] *poss adj* nuestro(a)

ours [auəz] *poss pron* **a)** [one thing] (el) nuestro /(la) nuestra; [more than one] (los) nuestros /(las) nuestras **b) a friend of ours** un amigo nuestro; **these books are ours** estos libros son nuestros; **which is ours?** ¿cuál es el nuestro?

ourselves [auə'selvz] *pers pron pl* **a)** [reflexive] nos; **we hurt ourselves** nos hicimos daño **b)** [alone] nosotros solos /nosotras solas; **we were by ourselves** estábamos solos **c)** [emphatic] nosotros mismos /nosotras mismas

out [aut] **1.** *adv* **a)** [outside, away] fuera; **to go out** salir **b) out of** [place, control, danger] fuera de; **to go out of the room** salir de la habitación; **out of date** [expired] caducado(a); [old-fashioned] pasado(a) de moda **c) out of** [cause, motive] por **d) out of** [made from] de **e) out of** [short of, without] sin **f) out of** [among] entre **2.** *adj* **a) the sun is out** ha salido el sol **b)** [unfashionable] pasado(a) de moda **c)** [fire] apagado(a) **d) she's out** [not in] ha salido, no está **e)** [inaccurate] equivocado(a); **to be out in one's calculations** equivocarse en los cálculos **f) before the week is out** antes de que acabe la semana **3.** *prep* [out of] por; **he jumped out of the window** saltó por la ventana

outbox [autbɒks] *n* [for e-mail] buzón *m* de salida

outbreak ['autbreik] *n* [of war] comienzo *m*; [of disease] brote *m*; [of violence] ola *f*; **at the outbreak of war** cuando estalló la guerra

outburst ['autbɜːst] *n* [of anger] arrebato *m*; [of generosity] arranque *m*

outcast ['autkɑːst] *n* marginado(a) *m,f*

outcome ['autkʌm] *n* resultado *m*

outcry ['autkraı] *n* **there was an outcry** hubo fuertes protestas

outdated [aut'deitid] *adj* anticuado(a), obsoleto(a)

outdo [aut'duː] *(pt* **outdid** [aut'dıd], *pp* **outdone** [aut'dʌn]) *vt* **to outdo sb** superar a algn

outdoor ['autdɔː(r)] *adj* **a)** al aire libre **b)** [clothes] de calle

outdoors [aut'dɔːz] *adv* fuera, al aire libre

outer ['autə(r)] *adj* exterior, externo(a)

outfit ['autfit] *n* **a)** [kit, equipment] equipo *m* **b)** [set of clothes] conjunto *m* **c)** *Fam* [group] grupo *m*

outgoing ['autgəuıŋ] **1.** *adj* **a)** [departing] saliente **b)** [sociable] extrovertido(a) **2.** *npl Br* **outgoings** gastos *mpl*

outgrow [aut'grəu] *(pt* **outgrew** [aut'gruː], *pp* **outgrown** [aut'grən]) *vt* **he's outgrowing all his clothes** toda la ropa se le está quedando pequeña; **she'll outgrow it** se le pasará con la edad

outing ['autıŋ] *n* excursión *f*

outlaw ['autlɔː] **1.** *n* proscrito(a) *m,f* **2.** *vt* prohibir

outlay ['autleı] *(pl* **outlays)** *n* [expense] desembolso *m*

outlet ['autlet] *n* **a)** [opening] salida *f* **b)** [for emotions] válvula *f* de escape **c)** COMM mercado *m*

outline ['autlaın] **1.** *n* **a)** [draft] bosquejo *m* **b)** [outer line] contorno *m*; [silhouette] perfil *m* **2.** *vt* **a)** [draw lines of] perfilar **b)** [summarize] resumir **c)** [describe roughly] trazar las líneas generales de

outlive [aut'lıv] *vt* sobrevivir a

outlook ['autluk] *n* **a)** [point of view] punto *m* de vista **b)** [prospect] perspectiva *f*; MET previsión *f*

outnumber [aut'nʌmbə(r)] *vt* exceder en número

out-of-doors *Br* **1.** *adv* = **outdoors** **2.** *adj* = **outdoor**

out-of-hand *adj US Fam* [extraordinary] gigantesco(a)

out-of-sync *adj* desincronizado(a)

out-of-the-box *adj* en cuanto se saca de la caja

out-of-town *adj* [shopping centre, retail park] de las afueras (de la ciudad)

outpatient ['aʊtpeɪʃənt] *n* paciente externo(a); **outpatients' department** clínica ambulatoria

output ['aʊtpʊt] *n* **a)** producción *f*; [of machine] rendimiento *m* **b)** ELEC potencia *f* **c)** COMPUT salida *f*

outrage ['aʊtreɪʤ] **1.** *n* ultraje *m*; **it's an outrage!** ¡es un escándalo! **2.** *vt* **to be outraged by sth** indignarse por algo

outrageous [aʊt'reɪʤəs] *adj* [behaviour] escandaloso(a); [clothes] extravagante; [price] exorbitante

outright 1. ['aʊtraɪt] *adj* [absolute] absoluto(a) **2.** [aʊt'raɪt] *adv* **a)** [completely] por completo **b)** [directly] directamente, sin reserva **c)** [immediately] en el acto

outset ['aʊtset] *n* comienzo *m*, principio *m*

outside 1. [aʊt'saɪd, 'aʊtsaɪd] *prep*
a) fuera de
b) [beyond] más allá de
c) [other than] aparte de
2. ['aʊtsaɪd] *adj* **a)** [exterior] exterior, externo(a)
b) [remote] remoto(a)
3. [aʊt'saɪd] *adv* fuera, afuera
4. [aʊt'saɪd, 'aʊtsaɪd] *n* exterior *m*; **on the outside** por fuera; *Fam* **at the outside** como mucho

outsider [aʊt'saɪdə(r)] *n* **a)** [stranger] extraño(a) *m,f*, forastero(a) *m,f* **b)** POL *candidato(a) con pocas posibilidades de ganar*

outsize(d) ['aʊtsaɪz(d)] *adj* **a)** [bigger than usual] desmedido(a) **b)** [clothes] de talla especial

outskirts ['aʊtskɜːts] *npl* afueras *fpl*

outspoken [aʊt'spəʊkən] *adj* directo(a), abierto(a)

outstanding [aʊt'stændɪŋ] *adj*
a) [exceptional] destacado(a)
b) [unpaid, unresolved] pendiente

outstretched [aʊt'stretʃt] *adj* extendido(a)

outward ['aʊtwəd] **1.** *adj* **a)** [external] exterior, externo(a) **b)** **the outward journey** el viaje de ida **2.** *adv* = **outwards**

outwards ['aʊtwədz] *adv* hacia (a)fuera

oval ['əʊvəl] **1.** *adj* oval, ovalado(a) **2.** *n* óvalo *m*

ovary ['əʊvərɪ] *n* ovario *m*

ovation [əʊ'veɪʃən] *n* ovación *f*

oven ['ʌvən] *n*
horno *m*; **oven fries** patatas *fpl* fritas para horno

over ['əʊvə(r)] **1.** *prep* **a)** [above, on top of] sobre, encima de, *Am* arriba de **b)** [across] al otro lado de; **the bridge over the river** el puente que cruza el río **c)** [during] durante **d)** [throughout] por **e)** [by the agency of] por; **over the phone** por teléfono **f)** [more than] más de; **men over twenty-five** hombres mayores de veinticinco años; **over and above** además de **g)** [recovered from] recuperado(a) de **2.** *adv* **a)** **over here / there** aquí / allí, *Am* acá / allá **b)** [throughout] por; **all over** por todas partes **c)** [more] más **d)** [again] otra vez; **over and over (again)** una y otra vez **e)** [in excess] de más **3.** *adj* [finished] acabado(a); **it's (all) over** se acabó

overall ['əʊvərɔːl] **1.** *adj* total, global **2.** *n Br* **overalls** [boiler suit] mono *m* (de trabajo), *Am* overol *m* **3.** [əʊvər'ɔːl] *adv* [on the whole] por lo general, en conjunto

overbearing [əʊvə'beərɪŋ] *adj* [domineering] dominante; [important] significativo(a)

overboard ['əʊvəbɔːd] *adv* por la borda; **man overboard!** ¡hombre al agua!; *Fam* **to go overboard** pasarse

overcast ['əʊvəkɑːst] *adj* nublado(a)

overcharge [əʊvə'tʃɑːʤ] *vt* **a)** [charge too much] cobrar demasiado **b)** [overload] sobrecargar

overcoat ['əʊvəkəʊt] *n* abrigo *m*

overcome [əʊvə'kʌm] *(pt* **overcame** [əʊvə'keɪm], *pp* **overcome)** *vt* **a)** [conquer] vencer; **overcome by grief** deshecho por el dolor **b)** [obstacle] superar

overcrowded [əʊvə'kraʊdɪd] *adj* [room] atestado(a) (de gente); [country] superpoblado(a)

overdo [əʊvə'du:] *(pt* **overdid** [əʊvə'dɪd], *pp* **overdone** [əʊvə'dʌn]) *vt* **a)** [carry too far] exagerar; **don't overdo it** no te pases **b)** CULIN cocer *or* asar demasiado

overdose ['əʊvədəʊs] *n* sobredosis *f*

overdraft ['əʊvədrɑːft] *n* giro *m* en descubierto; [amount] saldo *m* deudor

overdraw [əʊvə'drɔː] *(pt* **overdrew** [əʊvə'druː], *pp* **overdrawn** [əʊvə'drɔːn]) *vt* **to be overdrawn** tener la cuenta en descubierto

overdue [əʊvə'djuː] *adj* **to be overdue** [person, train] retrasarse, venir con retraso *or Am* demora; [bill] estar sin pagar

overestimate [əʊvər'estɪmeɪt] *vt* sobreestimar

overfish [,əʊvə'fɪʃ] *vt* [fishing ground] sobreexplotar

overfishing [,əʊvə(r)'fɪʃɪŋ] *n* sobrepesca *f*

overflow 1. [əʊvə'fləʊ] *vi* [river] desbordarse; [cup etc] derramarse **2.** ['əʊvəfləʊ] *n* [of river etc] desbordamiento *m*; **overflow pipe** cañería *f* de desagüe

overgrown [əʊvə'grəʊn] *adj* **a)** [with grass] cubierto(a) (de hierba) **b)** [in size] demasiado grande

overhaul 1. [əʊvə'hɔːl] *vt* revisar **2.** ['əʊvəhɔːl] *n* revisión *f* y reparación *f*

overhead 1. ['əʊvəhed] *adj* (por) encima de la cabeza; **overhead cable** cable aéreo; **overhead light** luz *f* de techo **2.** [əʊvə'hed] *adv* arriba, por encima de la cabeza **3.** *n* ['əʊvəhed] *US* = **overheads**

overheads ['əʊvəhedz] *npl Br* gastos *mpl* generales

overhear [əʊvə'hɪə(r)] *(pt & pp* **overheard** [əʊvə'hɜːd]) *vt* oír por casualidad

overheat [əʊvə'hiːt] *vi* recalentarse

overjoyed [əʊvə'dʒɔɪd] *adj* rebosante de alegría

overlap [əʊvə'læp] *vi* superponerse; *Fig* **our plans overlap** nuestros planes coinciden parcialmente

overleaf [əʊvə'liːf] *adv* al dorso

overload 1. [əʊvə'ləʊd] *vt* sobrecargar **2.** ['əʊvələʊd] *n* sobrecarga *f*

overlook [əʊvə'lʊk] *vt* **a)** [fail to notice] saltarse **b)** [ignore] no hacer caso de; **we'll overlook it this time** esta vez haremos la vista gorda **c)** [have a view of] dar a, tener vista a

overnight 1. [əʊvə'naɪt] *adv* **a)** [during the night] por la noche; **we stayed there overnight** pasamos la noche allí **b)** [suddenly] de la noche a la mañana **2.** ['əʊvənaɪt] *adj* [sudden] repentino(a)

overpowering [əʊvə'paʊərɪŋ] *adj* [emotion, heat] tremendo(a), desmesurado(a); [smell, taste] fortísimo(a), intensísimo(a)

overpriced [əʊvə'praɪst] *adj* excesivamente caro(a)

overrate [əʊvə'reɪt] *vt* sobreestimar, supervalorar

overreact [əʊvərɪ'ækt] *vi* reaccionar exageradamente

override [əʊvə'raɪd] *(pt* **overrode** [əʊvə'rəʊd], *pp* **overridden** [əʊvə'rɪdən]) *vt* **a)** [disregard] hacer caso omiso de **b)** [annul, cancel out] anular **c)** [be more important than] contar más que

overrule [əʊvə'ruːl] *vt* invalidar; JUR denegar

overseas 1. [əʊvə'siːz] *adv* en ultramar; **to live overseas** vivir en el extranjero **2.** ['əʊvəsiːz] *adj* de ultramar; [person] extranjero(a); [trade] exterior

oversee [əʊvə'siː] *(pt* **oversaw** [əʊvə'sɔː], *pp* **overseen** [əʊvə'siːn]) *vt* supervisar

overshadow [əʊvə'ʃædəʊ] *vt Fig* eclipsar

oversight ['əʊvəsaɪt] *n* descuido *m*

oversize(d) [,əʊvə'saɪz(d)] *adj* [very big] enorme, descomunal

oversleep [əʊvə'sliːp] *(pt & pp* **overslept** [əʊvə'slept]) *vi* quedarse dormido(a)

overstep [ˈəʊvəstep] *vt Fig* **to overstep the mark** pasarse de la raya

overstretched [ˈəʊvəˈstretʃt] *adj* [person] desbordado(a); [budget] muy ajustado(a)

overt [əʊˈvɜːt] *adj* patente

overtake [ˈəʊvəˈteɪk] *(pt* **overtook** [ˈəʊvəˈtʊk], *pp* **overtaken** [ˈəʊvəˈteɪkən]*) vt* **a)** *Br* AUTO adelantar **b)** [surpass] superar a **c)** [of night] sorprender

overthrow [ˈəʊvəˈθrəʊ] *(pt* **overthrew** [ˈəʊvəˈθruː], *pp* **overthrown** [ˈəʊvəˈθrəʊn]*) vt* [government] derribar

overtime [ˈəʊvətaɪm] *n* **a)** [work] horas *fpl* extra **b)** *US* prórroga *f*

overturn [ˈəʊvəˈtɜːn] *vt & vi* volcar

overweight [ˈəʊvəˈweɪt] *adj* demasiado pesado(a)

overwhelm [ˈəʊvəˈwelm] *vt* **a)** [defeat] aplastar; [overpower] abrumar; **I'm overwhelmed** estoy abrumado **b)** [with letters, work etc] inundar

overwhelming [ˈəʊvəˈwelmɪŋ] *adj* [defeat] aplastante; [desire etc] irresistible

overwork [ˈəʊvəˈwɜːk] **1.** *vi* trabajar demasiado **2.** *vt* [person] forzar; [excuse etc] abusar de

owe [əʊ] *vt* deber

owing [ˈəʊɪŋ] *adj* **owing to** debido a, a causa de

owl [aʊl] *n* **(short-eared) owl** búho *m*, *CAm, Méx* tecolote *m*; **(barn) owl** lechuza *f*

own [əʊn] **1.** *adj* propio(a); **it's his own fault** es culpa suya
2. *pron* **a) my own / your own / his own** *etc* lo mío / lo tuyo / lo suyo *etc*; *Fam* **to get one's own back** tomarse la revancha
b) on one's own [without help] uno(a) mismo(a); [alone] solo(a)
3. *vt* poseer, ser dueño(a) de
■ **own up** *vi* **to own up (to sth)** confesar (algo)

ownage [ˈəʊnɪdʒ] *n Fam* paliza *f*; **ownage!** ¡qué paliza!

owner [ˈəʊnə(r)] *n* propietario(a) *m,f*, dueño(a) *m,f*

ownership [ˈəʊnəʃɪp] *n* propiedad *f*, posesión *f*

ox [ɒks] *(pl* **oxen** [ˈɒksən]*) n* buey *m*

oxygen [ˈɒksɪdʒən] *n* oxígeno *m*; **oxygen mask** máscara *f* de oxígeno

oyster [ˈɔɪstə(r)] *n* ostra *f*

oz *(abbr of* **ounce(s)**) onza(s) *fpl*

ozone [ˈəʊzəʊn] *n* ozono *m*; **ozone layer** capa *f* de ozono

P

P, p [piː] *n* [the letter] P, p *f*

p a) *(pl* **pp)** *(abbr of* **page)** pág., p
b) [piː] *Br Fam (abbr of* **penny, pence)**
penique(s) *m(pl)*

pa [pɑː] *n US Fam* [dad] papá *m*

pace [peɪs] **1.** *n* [step] paso *m*; [speed]
ritmo *m*; **to keep pace with** seguir a;
Fig avanzar al mismo ritmo que; **to set
the pace** marcar el paso; *Fig* marcar la
pauta **2.** *vi* **to pace up and down** ir de
un lado a otro

pacemaker ['peɪsmeɪkə(r)] *n SPORT*
liebre *f*; *MED* marcapasos *m inv*

Pacific [pə'sɪfɪk] *adj* **the Pacific
(Ocean)** el (océano) Pacífico

pacifier ['pæsɪfaɪə(r)] *n US* [for baby]
chupete *m*

pacifist ['pæsɪfɪst] *adj & n* pacifista *(mf)*

pacify ['pæsɪfaɪ] *vt* [person] calmar;
[country] pacificar

pack¹ [pæk] **1.** *n* [parcel] paquete *m*;
[bundle] bulto *m*; *US* [of cigarettes] paquete *m*; *Br* [of playing cards] baraja *f*; [of
hounds] jauría *f*
2. *vt* **a)** [goods] embalar, envasar;
[in suitcase] poner; **to pack one's
suitcase** hacer la maleta *or Am* valija;
Fig marcharse
b) [fill] atestar
c) [press down] apretar
3. *vi* **a)** hacer las maletas; *Fam* **to send
sb packing** mandar a paseo a algn
b) [of people] apiñarse **(into** en)
■ **pack in 1.** *vt sep Fam* [stop] dejar;
pack it in! [stop annoying me] ¡ya vale!;
[shut up] ¡corta el rollo! **2.** *vi* averiarse
■ **pack off** *vt sep Fam* mandar
■ **pack up** *Fam* **1.** *vt sep* [give up] dejar
2. *vi* [stop working] dejarlo, parar de
trabajar; [machine etc] estropearse

pack² [pæk] *vt* [meeting] llenar de par-
tidarios

package ['pækɪdʒ] **1.** *n* **a)** [parcel] paquete *m*; [bundle] bulto *m* **b)** [of proposals
etc] paquete *m*; [agreement] acuerdo *m*;
package deal convenio *m* general;
package tour viaje *m* todo incluido
c) *COMPUT* paquete *m* de programas
2. *vt* [goods] envasar, embalar

packaging ['pækɪdʒɪŋ] *n* [for transport,
freight] embalaje *m*; [of product] envasado *m*

packed [pækt] *adj* **a)** [crowded]
abarrotado(a) **b) packed lunch** comida *f* preparada de casa *(para excursión,
trabajo, colegio)*

packet ['pækɪt] *n* **a)** [of tea, cigarettes]
paquete *m*; [bag] bolsa *f* **b)** *Fam* [lot of
money] **to make** *or* **earn a packet** ganar
una millonada *or Méx* un chorro de lana
or RP una ponchada de guita

packing ['pækɪŋ] *n* embalaje *m*; **packing case** caja *f* de embalar; **to do one's
packing** hacer las maletas

pact [pækt] *n* pacto *m*

pad¹ [pæd] **1.** *n* **a)** almohadilla *f*; [of
paper] bloc *m*, taco *m* **b) launch pad** plataforma *f* de lanzamiento **c)** *Fam* [flat]
casa *f*, *Esp* choza *f* **2.** *vt* [chair] acolchar
■ **pad out** *vt sep Fig* meter paja en

pad² [pæd] *vi* **to pad about** *or* **around**
andar silenciosamente

padded ['pædɪd] *adj* [envelope, jacket]
acolchado(a); **padded cell** celda *f*
acolchada

padding ['pædɪŋ] *n* [material] relleno *m*;
Fig [in speech etc] paja *f*

paddle¹ ['pædəl] **1.** *n* **a)** [oar] pala *f*; **paddle boat** *or* **steamer** vapor *m* de ruedas
b) *US* [for table tennis] pala *f*
2. *vt* [boat] remar con pala en
3. *vi* [in boat] remar con pala

paddle² ['pædəl] *vi* chapotear

paddling pool ['pædlɪŋpu:l] *n* [inflatable] piscina *for Méx* alberca *for RP* pileta *f* hinchable; [in park] piscina *f or Méx* alberca *for RP* pileta *f* para niños

padlock ['pædlɒk] **1.** *n* candado *m* **2.** *vt* cerrar con candado

paediatrician [pi:dɪə'trɪʃən] *n* pediatra *mf*

page¹ [peɪdʒ] *n* página *f*

page² [peɪdʒ] **1.** *n* [servant] paje *m*; [of knight] escudero *m*; [at club] botones *m inv* **2.** *vt* [call] avisar por megafonía

pager ['peɪdʒə(r)] *n* buscapersonas *m inv, Esp* busca *m, Méx* localizador *m, RP* radiomensaje *m*

page-turner *n Fam* libro *m* absorbente

paid [peɪd] **1.** *adj* pagado(a); *Fig* to put paid to sth acabar con algo **2.** *pt & pp of* **pay**

pain [peɪn] **1.** *n* a) dolor *m*; [grief] sufrimiento *m*; *Fam* he's a pain (in the neck) es un plomazo or pelmazo *or Méx* sangrón; on pain of death so pena de muerte b) to take pains over sth esmerarse en algo **2.** *vt* [grieve] dar pena a

painful ['peɪnful] *adj* doloroso(a); *Fam* [very bad] malísimo(a)

painkiller ['peɪnkɪlə(r)] *n* analgésico *m*

painless ['peɪnlɪs] *adj* sin dolor; *Fig* sin dificultades

painstaking ['peɪnzteɪkɪŋ] *adj* [person] concienzudo(a); [care, research] esmerado(a)

paint [peɪnt] **1.** *n* pintura *f* **2.** *vt* pintar; to paint sth white pintar algo de blanco **3.** *vi* pintar

paintball ['peɪntbɔ:l] *n* paintball *m*

paintbrush ['peɪntbrʌʃ] *n* ART pincel *m*; [for walls] brocha *f*

painter ['peɪntə(r)] *n* pintor(a) *m,f*

painting ['peɪntɪŋ] *n* cuadro *m*; [activity] pintura *f*

paintwork ['peɪntwɜ:k] *n* pintura *f*

pair [peə(r)] *n* [of gloves, shoes] par *m*; [of people, cards] pareja *f*; a pair of scissors unas tijeras; a pair of trousers un pantalón, unos pantalones

pajamas [pə'dʒæməz] *US npl* = **pyjamas**

Pakistan [pɑ:kɪ'stɑ:n] *n* Paquistán

Pakistani [pɑ:kɪ'stɑ:nɪ] *adj & n* paquistaní *(mf)*

pal [pæl] *n Fam* amiguete(a) *m,f, Esp* colega *mf*

palace ['pælɪs] *n* palacio *m*

pale¹ [peɪl] **1.** *adj* [skin] pálido(a); [colour] claro(a); [light] tenue; to turn pale palidecer **2.** *vi* palidecer

pale² [peɪl] *n Fig* to be beyond the pale ser inaceptable

pale-skinned *adj* de piel clara

Palestine ['pælɪstaɪn] *n* Palestina

Palestinian [pælɪ'stɪnɪən] *adj & n* palestino(a) *(m,f)*

palette ['pælɪt] *n* paleta *f*; palette knife espátula *f*

palm¹ [pɑ:m] *n* [tree] palmera *f*; [leaf] palma *f*; date palm palma datilera; Palm Sunday domingo *m* de Ramos

palm² [pɑ:m] *n* ANAT palma *f* ■ palm off *vt sep* to palm sth off on sb colocar or endosar algo a algn

palmtop COMPUT ordenador *m or Am* computadora *f* de bolsillo, miniordenador *m or Am* minicomputadora *f* portátil, palmtop *m*

pamper ['pæmpə(r)] *vt* mimar, consentir

pamphlet ['pæmflɪt] *n* folleto *m*

pan¹ [pæn] **1.** *n* a) [saucepan] cazuela *f*, cacerola *f* b) [of scales] platillo *m* c) *Br* [of lavatory] taza *f* **2.** *vt Fam* [criticize] vapulear, *Esp* poner por los suelos

pan² [pæn] *vi* CIN tomar vistas panorámicas

Panama ['pænəmɑ:] *n* Panamá; Panama Canal Canal *m* de Panamá

Panamanian [pænə'meɪnjən] *adj & n* panameño(a) *(m,f)*

pancake ['pænkeɪk] *n* crepe *f*

panda ['pændə] n panda m; Br **panda car** coche m or Am carro m or CSur auto m patrulla

pandemonium [pændɪ'məʊnɪəm] n alboroto m

pander ['pændə(r)] vi **to pander to** [person] complacer a; [wishes] acceder a

pane [peɪn] n **pane (of glass)** hoja m de vidrio or Esp cristal

panel ['pænəl] n **a)** [of wall] panel m; [flat surface] tabla f; [of instruments] tablero m; [of ceiling] artesón m **b)** [jury] jurado m; RADIO & TV concursantes mpl

panic ['pænɪk] **1.** n pánico m; **to get into a panic** ponerse histérico(a) **2.** vi aterrarse

panorama [pænə'rɑːmə] n panorama m

pansy ['pænzɪ] n BOT pensamiento m; Fam & Pej mariquita m

pant [pænt] **1.** n jadeo m **2.** vi jadear

pantomime ['pæntəmaɪm] n Br THEAT obra de teatro musical para niños basada en un cuento de hadas y representada en Navidad

pantry ['pæntrɪ] n despensa f

pants [pænts] npl **a)** Br [men's underwear] calzoncillos mpl, Chile fundillos mpl, Col pantaloncillos mpl, Méx calzones mpl, Méx chones mpl; [women's underwear] Esp bragas fpl, Chile, Col, Méx calzones mpl, RP bombacha f **b)** US [trousers] pantalones mpl

pantyhose ['pæntɪhəʊz] n US medias fpl, pantis mpl

paper ['peɪpə(r)] **1.** n **a)** papel m; Fig **on paper** en teoría; **writing paper** papel de escribir **b)** [exam] examen m; [essay] trabajo m (escrito) **c)** POL libro m **d)** [newspaper] periódico m; **the papers** la prensa; Br **free paper** periódico m gratuito **e)** papers [documents] documentos mpl **2.** vt empapelar

paperback ['peɪpəbæk] n libro m en rústica

paperclip ['peɪpəklɪp] n clip m, sujetapapeles m inv

paperweight ['peɪpəweɪt] n pisapapeles m inv

paperwork ['peɪpəwɜːk] n papeleo m

par [pɑː(r)] n [parity] igualdad f; [in golf] par m; Fig **it's par for the course** es lo normal en estos casos; Fig **to feel below par** estar en baja forma

paracetamol [pærə'siːtəmɒl] n paracetamol m

parachute ['pærəʃuːt] **1.** n paracaídas m inv **2.** vi **to parachute (down)** saltar or lanzarse en paracaídas

parade [pə'reɪd] **1.** n desfile m; MIL **to be on parade** pasar revista **2.** vt MIL hacer desfilar; Fig [flaunt] hacer alarde de **3.** vi [troops] pasar revista; [procession] desfilar

paradise ['pærədaɪs] n paraíso m

paradoxical [pærə'dɒksɪkəl] adj paradójico(a)

paraffin ['pærəfɪn] n parafina f; **liquid paraffin** aceite m de parafina; **paraffin lamp** lámpara f de petróleo

paraglider ['pærəglaɪdə(r)] n **a)** [person] parapentista mf **b)** [parachute] parapente m

paragraph ['pærəgrɑːf] n párrafo m

Paraguay ['pærəgwaɪ] n Paraguay m

Paraguayan [,pærə'gwaɪən] adj & n paraguayo(a) (m,f)

paralegal [pærə'liːgəl] n US ayudante mf de un abogado, RP procurador(ora) m,f

parallel ['pærəlel] **1.** adj paralelo(a) (**to** or **with** a); Fig comparable (**to** or **with** a) **2.** n GEOG paralelo m; GEOM paralela f; Fig paralelo **3.** vt Fig ser paralelo(a) a

Paralympics [,pærə'lɪmpɪks] npl **the Paralympics** los juegos mpl paralímpicos

paralyse ['pærəlaɪz] vt paralizar

paralysis [pə'rælɪsɪs] n parálisis f

paralyze ['pærəlaɪz] US vt = **paralyse**

paramedic [pærə'medɪk] n auxiliar mf sanitario(a)

paranoid ['pærənɔɪd] *adj* & *n* paranoico(a) *(m,f)*

paraphrase ['pærəfreɪz] *vt* parafrasear

parasite ['pærəsaɪt] *n* parásito *m*

parasol ['pærəsɒl] *n* sombrilla *f*

parcel ['pɑːsəl] **1.** *n* paquete *m*; **parcel bomb** paquete bomba **2.** *vt* **to parcel up** envolver, empaquetar

parched [pɑːtʃt] *adj* [land] reseco(a); [lips, mouth] seco(a); *Fig* **to be parched** estar muerto(a) de sed

pardon ['pɑːdən] **1.** *n* perdón *m*; JUR indulto *m*; **(I beg your) pardon?** ¿cómo (dice)? **2.** *vt* perdonar; JUR indultar; **pardon me!** ¡Usted perdone!

parental *adj* parental, paterno(a); US TV **parental advisory** aviso *m* parental

parents ['peərənts] *npl* padres

Paris ['pærɪs] *n* París

parish ['pærɪʃ] *n* parroquia *f*

Parisian [pə'rɪzɪən] *adj* & *n* parisino(a) *(m,f)*

park [pɑːk] **1.** *n* parque *m* **2.** *vt* estacionar, *Esp* aparcar

parking ['pɑːkɪŋ] *n* estacionamiento *m*, *Esp* aparcamiento *m*, *Col* parqueadero *m*; **no parking** [sign] prohibido estacionar *or Esp* aparcar, estacionamiento prohibido; *US* **parking lot** *Esp* aparcamiento *m*, *RP* playa *f* de estacionamiento, *Col* aparcadero *m*; **parking meter** parquímetro *m*; **parking space** estacionamiento *m*, sitio *m or* hueco *m* para estacionar

parliament ['pɑːləmənt] *n* parlamento *m*

parody ['pærədɪ] *n* parodia *f*

parole [pə'rəʊl] *n* JUR libertad *f* condicional; **on parole** en libertad bajo palabra

parrot ['pærət] *n* loro *m*, papagayo *m*

parsley ['pɑːslɪ] *n* perejil *m*

parsnip ['pɑːsnɪp] *n* chirivía *f*

parson ['pɑːsən] *n* cura *m*

part [pɑːt] **1.** *n* **a)** parte *f*; [piece] trozo *m*; [episode] capítulo *m*; TECH pieza *f*; **for the most part** en la mayor parte **b)** CIN & THEAT papel *m*; **to take part in sth** participar en algo **c)** [place] lugar *m*; **in these parts** por estos lugares **d)** **for my part** por mi parte; **to take sb's part** tomar partido por algn **e)** *US* [in hair] raya *f*, *Col, Méx, Ven* carrera *f* **2.** *adj* [partial] parcial **3.** *adv* [partly] en parte **4.** *vt* [separate] separar; **to part one's hair** hacerse raya *or Col, Méx, Ven* carrera (en el pelo) **5.** *vi* separarse; [say goodbye] despedirse

■ **part with** *vt insep* separarse de

partial ['pɑːʃəl] *adj* parcial; **to be partial to sth** ser aficionado(a) a algo

participant [pɑː'tɪsɪpənt] *n* participante *mf*; [in competition] concursante *mf*

participate [pɑː'tɪsɪpeɪt] *vi* participar (**in** en)

participation [pɑːtɪsɪ'peɪʃən] *n* participación *f*

particular [pə'tɪkjʊlə(r)] **1.** *adj* **a)** [special] particular, especial; **in this particular case** en este caso concreto; **that particular person** esa persona en particular **b)** [fussy] exigente **2.** *npl* **particulars** pormenores *mpl*; **to take down sb's particulars** anotar los datos personales de algn

particularly [pə'tɪkjʊlələɪ] *adv* particularmente, especialmente

parting ['pɑːtɪŋ] **1.** *n* [separation] separación *f*; [farewell] despedida *f*; *Br* [in hair] raya *f*, *Col, Méx, Ven* carrera *f* **2.** *adj* de despedida

partition [pɑː'tɪʃən] **1.** *n* [wall] tabique *m*; [of country] partición *f* **2.** *vt* dividir

partly ['pɑːtlɪ] *adv* en parte

partner ['pɑːtnə(r)] **1.** *n* compañero(a) *m,f*; [in dancing, tennis] pareja *f*; [husband] marido *m*; [wife] mujer *f*; COMM socio(a) *m,f*. **2.** *vt* acompañar

partnership ['pɑːtnəʃɪp] *n* a) [relationship] vida *f* en común; **civil partnership** *unión legal de parejas del mismo sexo* COMM sociedad *f*

partridge ['pɑːtrɪdʒ] *n* perdiz pardilla

part-time ['pɑːt'taɪm] **1.** *adj* [work etc] de tiempo parcial **2.** *adv* a tiempo parcial

party ['pɑːtɪ] **1.** *n* a) [celebration] fiesta *f*; *US* **bachelor party** despedida *f* de soltero *(removed example as it repeats translation)* b) [group] grupo *m* c) POL partido *m*; **party political broadcast** espacio *m* electoral **2.** *adj* de fiesta

partying ['pɑːtɪɪŋ] *n Fam* **she's a great one for partying** le encanta la fiesta

pass [pɑːs] **1.** *n* a) [of mountain] desfiladero *m*
b) [permit] permiso *m*; **bus pass** abono *m* de autobús
c) SPORT pase *m*
2. *vt* a) pasar; [overtake] adelantar
b) [exam, law] aprobar; JUR **to pass sentence** dictar sentencia
3. *vi* a) pasar; [procession] desfilar; [car] adelantar; [people] cruzarse; SPORT hacer un pase; **we passed on the stairs** nos cruzamos en la escalera
b) [in exam] aprobar
■ **pass as** *vt insep* pasar por
■ **pass away** *vi Euph* pasar a mejor vida
■ **pass by 1.** *vt sep* pasar de largo **2.** *vi* pasar
■ **pass for** *vt insep* pasar por
■ **pass off 1.** *vt sep* hacer pasar; **to pass oneself off as sth** hacerse pasar por algo **2.** *vi* [happen] transcurrir
■ **pass on 1.** *vt sep* [hand on] transmitir **2.** *vi Euph* pasar a mejor vida
■ **pass out** *vi* [faint] desmayarse; MIL graduarse
■ **pass over** *vt insep* a) [aircraft] volar por b) [disregard] pasar por alto

■ **pass up** *vt sep Fam* [opportunity] renunciar; [offer] rechazar

passable ['pɑːsəbəl] *adj* [road] transitable; [acceptable] pasable

passage ['pæsɪdʒ] *n* a) [alleyway] callejón *m*; [hallway] pasillo *m* b) [movement] tránsito *m*; NAUT travesía *f* c) MUS & LITER pasaje *m*

passenger ['pæsɪndʒə(r)] *n* pasajero(a) *m,f*; **passenger door** [of car] puerta *f* del pasajero

passer-by [pɑːsə'baɪ] *n* transeúnte *mf*

passing ['pɑːsɪŋ] **1.** *n* a) [of time] transcurso *m*; **in passing** de pasada b) [of law] aprobación *f* **2.** *adj* que pasa; [glance] rápido(a); [thought] pasajero(a)

passion ['pæʃən] *n* pasión *f*; **passion fruit** granadilla *f*

passionate ['pæʃənɪt] *adj* apasionado(a)

passive ['pæsɪv] *adj* pasivo(a)

passport ['pɑːspɔːt] *n* pasaporte *m*

password ['pɑːswɜːd] *n* contraseña *f*

past [pɑːst] **1.** *n* pasado *m*; **in the past** en el pasado; **to have a past** tener antecedentes
2. *adj* pasado(a); [former] anterior; **in the past weeks** en las últimas semanas
3. *adv* por delante; **to run past** pasar corriendo
4. *prep* [beyond] más allá de; [more than] más de; **he's past forty** pasa de los cuarenta (años); **it's five past ten** son las diez y cinco; *Fam* **to be past it** estar muy carroza

pasta ['pæstə] *n* pasta *f*, pastas *fpl*

paste [peɪst] **1.** *n* pasta *f*; [glue] engrudo *m* **2.** *vt* [stick] pegar; [put paste on] engomar

pastel ['pæstəl] *adj & n* pastel (*m*)

pasteurized ['pæstjəraɪzd] *adj* pasteurizado(a)

pastime ['pɑːstaɪm] *n* pasatiempo *m*

pastor ['pɑːstə(r)] *n* pastor *m*

pastry ['peɪstrɪ] n [dough] pasta f; [cake] pastel m, Col, CSur torta f

pasture ['pɑːstʃə(r)] n pasto m

pasty¹ ['pæstɪ] n CULIN empanada f, pastel m de carne

pasty² ['peɪstɪ] (compar **pastier**, superl **pastiest**) adj [complexion] pálido(a)

pat [pæt] **1.** n [caress] caricia f; [tap] palmadita f; Fig **to give sb a pat on the back** felicitar a algn **2.** vt acariciar; **to pat sb on the back** dar a algn una palmadita en la espalda

patch [pætʃ] n [of material] parche m; Br [of land] terreno m; [of colour, light] mancha f; Br Fam **to be going through a bad patch** estar pasando por una mala racha ■ **patch up** vt sep [wounded person] hacer una cura or Méx, RP curación de urgencia a; **to patch things up** [after argument] limar asperezas

patchwork ['pætʃwɜːk] **1.** n labor f de retales **2.** adj [quilt etc] hecho(a) con retales distintos

patchy ['pætʃɪ] (compar **patchier**, superl **patchiest**) adj [colour, performance] desigual; [knowledge] incompleto(a)

patent ['peɪtənt, Br 'peɪtənt] **1.** n COMM patente f **2.** adj [obvious] patente, evidente **3.** vt COMM patentar

patently [Br 'peɪtəntlɪ, US 'pætəntlɪ] adv **it is patently obvious** está clarísimo

paternal [pə'tɜːnəl] adj paternal; [grandmother etc] paterno(a)

path [pɑːθ] n camino m, sendero m; [route & COMPUT] ruta f; [of missile] trayectoria f

path-breaking adj revolucionario(a)

pathetic [pə'θetɪk] adj [pitiful] patético(a); Fam [hopeless] malísimo(a); **she was a pathetic sight** daba lástima verla

pathway ['pɑːθweɪ] n camino m, sendero m

patience ['peɪʃəns] n a) paciencia f; **to lose one's patience with sb** perder la paciencia con algn b) Br CARDS solitario m

patient ['peɪʃənt] **1.** adj paciente; **to be patient with sb** tener paciencia con algn **2.** n MED paciente mf

patio ['pætɪəʊ] n patio m

patriot ['pætrɪət, 'peɪtrɪət] n patriota mf

patriotic [pætrɪ'ɒtɪk] adj [person] patriota; [speech, act] patriótico(a)

patrol [pə'trəʊl] **1.** n patrulla f; **patrol car** coche m or Am carro m or CSur auto m patrulla **2.** vt patrullar por

patrolman [pə'trəʊlmən] n US policía m

patron ['peɪtrən] n a) [of charity] patrocinador(a) m,f; [of arts] mecenas m inv; **patron saint** (santo(a) m,f) patrón(ona) mf b) [customer] cliente mf habitual

patronize ['pætrənaɪz] vt a) [arts] fomentar; [shop] ser cliente habitual de; [club etc] frecuentar b) Pej [person] tratar con condescendencia

patter¹ ['pætə(r)] **1.** n [of rain] repiqueteo m; [of feet] pasito m **2.** vi [rain] repiquetear; [feet] hacer ruido sordo

patter² ['pætə(r)] n Fam labia f; [of salesman] discursillo preparado

pattern ['pætən] n SEWING patrón m; [design] dibujo m; [on material] estampado m; Fig [of behaviour] modelo m

paunch [pɔːntʃ] n barriga f, panza f, Chile guata f

pause [pɔːz] **1.** n pausa f; [silence] silencio m **2.** vi hacer una pausa; [be silent] callarse

pave [peɪv] vt pavimentar; [with stones] empedrar; Fig **to pave the way for sb / sth** preparar el terreno para algn / algo

pavement ['peɪvmənt] n a) Br [beside road] acera f, CSur vereda f, CAm, Méx banqueta f b) US [roadway] calzada f

pavilion [pə'vɪljən] n pabellón m; Br SPORT [changing rooms] vestuarios mpl

paving ['peɪvɪŋ] n [on road] pavimento m; [on floor] enlosado m; [with stones] empedrado m; **paving stone** losa f

paw [pɔː] **1.** n [foot] pata f; [of cat] garra f; [of lion] zarpa f **2.** vt [of lion] dar zarpazos a; Pej [of person] manosear, sobar

pawn¹ [pɔ:n] n [in chess] peón m; Fig **to be sb's pawn** ser el juguete de algn

pawn² [pɔ:n] vt empeñar

pawnbroker ['pɔ:nbrəʊkə(r)] n prestamista mf

pawnshop ['pɔ:nʃɒp] n casa f de empeños

pay [peɪ] (pt & pp **paid**) **1.** n [wages] paga f, sueldo m; **pay** Br **packet** or US **envelope** sobre m de la paga; **pay rise** aumento m del sueldo; **pay slip** nómina f
2. vt a) pagar; **to be** or **get paid** cobrar b) [attention] prestar; [homage] rendir; [visit] hacer; **to pay sb a compliment** halagar a algn c) [be profitable for] compensar
3. vi a) pagar; **to pay for sth** pagar (por) algo b) [be profitable] ser rentable
■ **pay back** vt sep reembolsar; Fig **to pay sb back** vengarse de algn
■ **pay in** vt sep [money] Esp ingresar, Am depositar
■ **pay off 1.** vt sep [debt] liquidar; [mortgage] cancelar **2.** vi [be successful] dar resultado
■ **pay out** vt sep [spend] gastar (**on** en)
■ **pay up** vi pagar

payable ['peɪəbəl] adj pagadero(a)

payment ['peɪmənt] n pago m; [of cheque] cobro m; **advance payment** anticipo m; **down payment** entrada f; **monthly payment** mensualidad f

paywall ['peɪwɔ:l] n muro m de pago, suscripción f por contenido; **the newspaper has put some of its best articles behind a paywall** algunos de los mejores artículos del periódico son de pago

PBJ US n = **peanut butter and jelly**

PC ['pi:'si:] **1.** n a) Br (abbr of **Police Constable**) agente mf de policía b) (abbr of **personal computer**) PC m **2.** adj (abbr of **politically correct**) políticamente correcto(a)

PDF n COMPUT (abbr of **portable document format**) PDF m

PE ['pi:'i:] n SCH (abbr of **physical education**) educación f física

pea [pi:] n guisante m, Am arveja f, Carib, Méx chícharo m

peace [pi:s] n paz f; [calm] tranquilidad f; **at** or **in peace** en paz; **peace and quiet** tranquilidad; **to make peace** hacer las paces; [countries] firmar la paz

peaceful ['pi:sfʊl] adj [demonstration] pacífico(a); [place] tranquilo(a)

peach [pi:tʃ] n melocotón m, Am durazno m

peacock ['pi:kɒk] n pavo m real

peak [pi:k] n [of cap] visera f; [of mountain] pico m; [summit] cima f; Fig cumbre f; **peak hours** horas fpl punta; **peak period** horas de mayor consumo; **peak season** temporada alta

peal [pi:l] n [of bells] repique m; **peal of thunder** trueno m; **peals of laughter** carcajadas fpl

peanut ['pi:nʌt] n cacahuete m, Andes, Carib, RP maní m, CAm, Méx cacahuate m; **peanut butter** mantequilla f or crema f de cacahuete or Andes, Carib, RP maní or CAm, Méx cacahuate

pear [peə(r)] n pera f

pearl [pɜ:l] n perla f

pear-shaped adj en forma de pera; **she's pear-shaped** es ancha de caderas; Fam **to go pear-shaped** salir mal; **everything went pear-shaped** todo salió mal

peasant ['pezənt] adj & n campesino(a) (m,f)

pebble ['pebəl] n guijarro m; [small] china f

pecan [Br 'pi:kən, US pɪ'kæn] n pacana f

peck [pek] **1.** n [of bird] picotazo m; Fam [kiss] besito m
2. vt [bird] picotear; Fam [kiss] dar un besito a
3. vi **to peck at one's food** picar la comida

peckish ['pekɪʃ] adj Br Fam **to be peckish** tener un poco de hambre or Esp gusa

peculiar [pɪ'kjuːlɪə(r)] *adj* [odd] extraño(a); [particular] característico(a)

pedal ['pedəl] **1.** *n* pedal *m* **2.** *vi* pedalear

pedantic [pɪ'dæntɪk] *adj* pedante

peddle ['pedəl] *vt & vi* COMM vender de puerta en puerta; **to peddle drugs** traficar con drogas

pedestal ['pedɪstəl] *n* pedestal *m*; *Fig* **to put sb on a pedestal** poner a algn sobre un pedestal

pedestrian [pɪ'destrɪən] **1.** *n* peatón(ona) *m,f*; **pedestrian crossing** paso *m* de peatones **2.** *adj Pej* prosaico(a)

pediatrician [piːdɪə'trɪʃən] *US n* = **paediatrician**

pedigree ['pedɪgriː] **1.** *n* linaje *m*; [family tree] árbol genealógico; [of animal] pedigrí *m* **2.** *adj* [animal] de raza

pee [piː] *Fam* **1.** *n* pis *m* **2.** *vi* hacer pis

peek [piːk] **1.** *n* ojeada *f* **2.** *vi* **to peek at sth** mirar algo a hurtadillas

peel [piːl] **1.** *n* piel *f*; [of orange, lemon] cáscara *f* **2.** *vt* [fruit] pelar **3.** *vi* [paint] desconcharse; [wallpaper] despegarse; [skin] pelarse

peeler ['piːlə(r)] *n* **potato peeler** pelapatatas *m inv*

peelings ['piːlɪŋz] *npl* peladuras *fpl*, mondaduras *fpl*

peep[1] [piːp] *n* [sound] pío *m*

peep[2] [piːp] **1.** *n* [glance] ojeada *f*; [furtive look] mirada furtiva **2.** *vi* **to peep at sth** echar una ojeada a algo; **to peep out from behind sth** dejarse ver detrás de algo

peer[1] [pɪə(r)] *n* [equal] igual *mf*; *Br* [noble] par *m*; **peer group** grupo parejo

peer[2] [pɪə(r)] *vi* mirar detenidamente; [shortsightedly] mirar con ojos de miope

peer-to-peer *adj* cliente a cliente

peeved [piːvd] *adj Fam* fastidiado(a), de mal humor

peg [peg] **1.** *n* clavija *f*; [for coat, hat] percha *f* **2.** *vt* [clothes] tender; [prices] fijar

pejorative [pɪ'dʒɒrətɪv] *adj* peyorativo(a)

pelican ['pelɪkən] *n* pelícano *m*; *Br* **pelican crossing** paso *m* de peatones

pelt[1] [pelt] *n* [skin] pellejo *m*

pelt[2] [pelt] **1.** *vt* **to pelt sb with sth** tirar algo a algn **2.** *vi Fam* **a) it was pelting (down)** [raining] diluviaba, *Esp* caían chuzos de punta **b) to pelt along** [rush] correr a toda prisa

pelvis ['pelvɪs] *n* pelvis *f*

pen[1] [pen] **1.** *n* [for writing] pluma *f* (estilográfica); [ballpoint] bolígrafo *m*, *Chile* lápiz *m* (de pasta), *Col, Ecuad, Ven* esferográfica *f*, *Méx* pluma *f*, *RP* birome *m*; *Fam* **pen pal** amigo(a) *m,f* por correspondencia **2.** *vt* escribir

pen[2] [pen] **1.** *n* [enclosure] corral *m*; [for sheep] redil *m*; [for children] corralito *m* **2.** *vt* **to pen in** acorralar

penal ['piːnəl] *adj* penal

penalize ['piːnəlaɪz] *vt* castigar; SPORT penalizar

penalty ['penəltɪ] *n* [punishment] pena *f*; SPORT castigo *m*; FTBL penalti *m*, *Am* penal *m*; **to pay the penalty for sth** cargar con las consecuencias de algo; **penalty area** área *f* de castigo

pence [pens] *pl of* **penny**

pencil ['pensəl] *n* lápiz *m*; **pencil case** estuche *m* de lápices; **pencil sharpener** sacapuntas *m inv*

pendant ['pendənt] *n* colgante *m*

pending ['pendɪŋ] **1.** *adj* pendiente **2.** *prep* a la espera de; **pending a decision** [until] hasta que se tome una decisión

pendulum ['pendjʊləm] *n* péndulo *m*

penetrate ['penɪtreɪt] **1.** *vt* penetrar; *Fig* adentrarse en **2.** *vi* atravesar; [get inside] penetrar

penguin ['peŋgwɪn] *n* pingüino *m*

penicillin [penɪ'sɪlɪn] *n* penicilina *f*

peninsula [pɪ'nɪnsjʊlə] *n* península *f*

penis ['piːnɪs] *n* pene *m*

penitentiary [penɪ'tenʃərɪ] *n US* cárcel *f*, penal *m*

penknife ['pennaɪf] n navaja f, corta-plumas m inv

penniless ['penɪlɪs] adj **to be penniless** estar sin un centavo or Esp duro

penny ['penɪ] (pl **pennies** or **pence**) n Br penique m; US centavo m

pension ['penʃən] n pensión f; **retirement pension** jubilación f

pensioner ['penʃənə(r)] n jubilado(a) m,f

pentagon ['pentəgən] n **a)** [shape] pentágono m **b)** US **the Pentagon** el Pentágono (sede del ministerio de la Defensa de Estados Unidos en Washington; el término designa también a las autoridades militares estadounidenses)

pent-up ['pentʌp] adj reprimido(a)

penultimate [pɪˈnʌltɪmɪt] adj penúltimo(a)

people ['piːpəl] npl a) gente f; [individuals] personas fpl; **many people** mucha gente; **old people's home** asilo m de ancianos; **people say that ...** se dice que ...; **some people** algunas personas **b)** [citizens] ciudadanos mpl; [inhabitants] habitantes mpl; **the people** el pueblo **c)** [nation] pueblo m, nación f

pepper ['pepə(r)] **1.** n [spice] pimienta f; [vegetable] pimiento m, Méx chile m, RP ají m, Col, Ven pimentón m; US **bell pepper** pimiento morrón; **black pepper** pimienta negra; Br **pepper pot** or US **shaker** pimentero m; **red / green pepper** pimiento rojo / verde; **pepper mill** molinillo m de pimienta **2.** vt Fig **peppered with** salpicado(a) de

pepperbox ['pepəbɒks] n US pimentero m

peppermint ['pepəmɪnt] n menta f; [sweet] pastilla f de menta

per [pɜː(r)] prep por; **five times per week** cinco veces a la semana; **per cent** por ciento; **per day / annum** al or por día / año; **per capita** per cápita

perceive [pəˈsiːv] vt [see] percibir

percentage [pəˈsentɪdʒ] n porcentaje m

perception [pəˈsepʃən] n percepción f

perceptive [pəˈseptɪv] adj perspicaz

perch¹ [pɜːtʃ] n [fish] perca f

perch² [pɜːtʃ] **1.** n [for bird] percha f **2.** vi [bird] posarse (**on en**)

percolator ['pɜːkəleɪtə(r)] n cafetera f

perennial [pəˈrenɪəl] adj BOT perenne

perfect 1. ['pɜːfɪkt] adj perfecto(a); **he's a perfect stranger to us** nos es totalmente desconocido; **perfect tense** tiempo perfecto **2.** [pəˈfekt] vt perfeccionar

perfection [pəˈfekʃən] n perfección f

perfectly ['pɜːfɪktlɪ] adv perfectamente; [absolutely] completamente

perforation [pɜːfəˈreɪʃən] n perforación f; [on stamps etc] perforado m

perform [pəˈfɔːm] **1.** vt [task] ejecutar, realizar; [piece of music] interpretar; THEAT representar **2.** vi [machine] funcionar; MUS interpretar; THEAT actuar

performance [pəˈfɔːməns] n [of task] ejecución f, realización f; MUS interpretación f; THEAT representación f; SPORT actuación f; [of machine etc] rendimiento m

performance-enhancing adj **performance-enhancing drug** potenciador m del rendimiento

performer [pəˈfɔːmə(r)] n MUS intérprete mf; THEAT actor m, actriz f

perfume ['pɜːfjuːm] n perfume m

perhaps [pəˈhæps, præps] adv tal vez, quizá(s), Am tal vez

peril ['perɪl] n [risk] riesgo m; [danger] peligro m

period ['pɪərɪəd] **1.** n **a)** período m; [stage] etapa f **b)** SCH clase f **c)** US [full stop] punto m **d)** [menstruation] regla f **2.** adj [dress, furniture] de época

periodical [pɪərɪˈɒdɪkəl] **1.** adj periódico(a) **2.** n revista f

periodically [pɪərɪˈɒdɪklɪ] adv de vez en cuando

peripheral [pəˈrɪfərəl] **1.** adj periférico(a) **2.** n COMPUT unidad periférica

perish ['perɪʃ] vi perecer; [material] echarse a perder

perishable ['perɪʃəbəl] *adj* perecedero(a)

perjury ['pɜːdʒərɪ] *n* perjurio *m*

perk [pɜːk] *n Br Fam* extra *m* ■ **perk up** *vi* [person] animarse ; [after illness] reponerse

perm [pɜːm] **1.** *n* permanente *f* **2.** *vt* **to have one's hair permed** hacerse la permanente

permanent ['pɜːmənənt] *adj* permanente ; [address, job] fijo(a)

permissible [pə'mɪsəbəl] *adj* admisible

permission [pə'mɪʃən] *n* permiso *m*

permissive [pə'mɪsɪv] *adj* permisivo(a)

permit 1. ['pɜːmɪt] *n* permiso *m* ; COMM licencia *f* **2.** [pə'mɪt] *vt* **to permit sb to do sth** permitir a algn hacer algo

perpendicular [pɜːpən'dɪkjʊlə(r)] **1.** *adj* perpendicular ; [cliff] vertical **2.** *n* perpendicular *f*

perpetrate ['pɜːpɪtreɪt] *vt* cometer

perpetrator ['pɜːpɪtreɪtə(r)] *n* autor(a) *m,f*

perpetual [pə'petʃʊəl] *adj* [noise] continuo(a) ; [arguing] interminable ; [snow] perpetuo(a)

perplex [pə'pleks] *vt* dejar perplejo(a)

persecute ['pɜːsɪkjuːt] *vt* perseguir ; [harass] acosar

persecution [pɜːsɪ'kjuːʃən] *n* persecución *f* ; [harassment] acoso *m*

perseverance [pɜːsɪ'vɪərəns] *n* perseverancia *f*

persevere [pɜːsɪ'vɪə(r)] *vi* perseverar

persist [pə'sɪst] *vi* empeñarse (**in** en)

persistent [pə'sɪstənt] *adj* [person] perseverante ; [smell etc] persistente ; [continual] constante

person ['pɜːsən] (*pl* **people**) *n* persona *f* ; [individual] individuo *m* ; **in person** en persona

personal ['pɜːsənəl] *adj* **a)** [private] personal ; [friend] íntimo(a) ; **personal computer** ordenador *m* personal, *Am* computadora *f* personal ; **personal column** anuncios *mpl* personales ; **personal details** [name, address] datos *mpl* personales ; **personal pronoun** pronombre *m* personal **b)** [in person] en persona ; **he will make a personal appearance** estará aquí en persona **c)** *Pej* [comment etc] indiscreto(a)

personality [pɜːsə'nælɪtɪ] *n* personalidad *f*

personally ['pɜːsənəlɪ] *adv* [for my part] personalmente ; [in person] en persona

personify [pɜː'sɒnɪfaɪ] *vt* personificar, encarnar

personnel [pɜːsə'nel] *n* personal *m*

perspective [pə'spektɪv] *n* perspectiva *f*

perspire [pə'spaɪə(r)] *vi* transpirar

persuade [pə'sweɪd] *vt* persuadir ; **to persuade sb to do sth** persuadir a algn para que haga algo

persuasion [pə'sweɪʒən] *n* persuasión *f* ; [opinion, belief] credo *m*

persuasive [pə'sweɪsɪv] *adj* persuasivo(a)

pertinent ['pɜːtɪnənt] *adj* [relevant] pertinente ; **pertinent to** relacionado(a) con, a propósito de

perturbing [pə'tɜːbɪŋ] *adj* inquietante

Peru [pə'ruː] *n* Perú

Peruvian [pə'ruːvjən] *adj* & *n* peruano(a) *(m,f)*

pervade [pɜː'veɪd] *vt* [of smell] penetrar ; [of light] difundirse por ; *Fig* [of influence] extenderse por

perverse [pə'vɜːs] *adj* [wicked] perverso(a) ; [contrary] contrario(a) a todo

perversion [*Br* pə'vɜːʃən, *US* pər'vɜːrʒən] *n* [sexual] perversión *f* ; [of justice, truth] desvirtuación *f*

pervert 1. ['pɜːvɜːt] *n* pervertido(a) *m,f* (sexual) **2.** [pə'vɜːt] *vt* pervertir ; [justice, truth] desvirtuar

pessimism ['pesɪmɪzəm] *n* pesimismo *m*

pessimist ['pesɪmɪst] *n* pesimista *mf*

pessimistic [pesɪ'mɪstɪk] *adj* pesimista

pest [pest] n a) ZOOL animal nocivo; BOT planta nociva b) Fam [person] pelma mf; [thing] lata f

pester ['pestə(r)] vt molestar, Esp incordiar

pesticide ['pestɪsaɪd] n pesticida m

pet [pet] 1. n a) animal doméstico b) [favourite] preferido(a) m,f; Fam cariño m
2. adj [favourite] preferido(a)
3. vt acariciar
4. vi Fam [sexually] Esp darse or pegarse el lote, Am manosearse

petal ['petəl] n pétalo m

peter ['pi:tə(r)] vi to peter out agotarse

petition [pɪ'tɪʃən] n petición f

petrify ['petrɪfaɪ] vt Liter petrificar; Fig they were petrified se quedaron de piedra

petrol ['petrəl] n Br gasolina f, RP nafta f; petrol can bidón m de gasolina or RP nafta; petrol pump surtidor m de gasolina or RP nafta; petrol station gasolinera f, estación f de servicio, Andes grifo m; petrol tank depósito m de gasolina, RP tanque m de nafta

petticoat ['petɪkəʊt] n enaguas fpl

petty ['petɪ] (compar pettier, superl pettiest) adj [trivial] insignificante; [small-minded] mezquino(a); petty cash dinero m para gastos pequeños; petty criminal pequeño(a) delincuente m,f; NAUT petty officer sargento m de marina

phantom ['fæntəm] adj & n fantasma (m)

pharmacist ['fɑ:məsɪst] n farmacéutico(a) m,f

pharmacy ['fɑ:məsɪ] n farmacia f

phase [feɪz] 1. n fase f 2. vt to phase sth in /out introducir /retirar algo progresivamente

PhD [pi:eɪtʃ'di:] n (abbr of Doctor of Philosophy) [person] Doctor(a) m,f en Filosofía

phenomenal [fɪ'nɒmɪnəl] adj fenomenal

phenomenon [fɪ'nɒmɪnən] (pl phenomena [fɪ'nɒmɪnə]) n fenómeno m

Philippines ['fɪlɪpi:nz] npl the Philippines las (Islas) Filipinas

philosopher [fɪ'lɒsəfə(r)] n filósofo(a) m,f

philosophical [fɪlə'sɒfɪkəl] adj filosófico(a)

philosophy [fɪ'lɒsəfɪ] n filosofía f

phishing ['fɪʃɪŋ] n COMPUT phishing m, fraude m por internet

phlegm [flem] n flema f

phobia ['fəʊbɪə] n fobia f

phone [fəʊn] n & vt = telephone

phonetic [fə'netɪk] 1. adj fonético(a) 2. n phonetics fonética f

phoney ['fəʊnɪ], **phony** (compar phonier, superl phoniest) 1. adj Fam [passport, address] falso(a); [person] farsante 2. n [person] farsante mf

photo ['fəʊtəʊ] n foto f

photocopier ['fəʊtəʊkɒpɪə(r)] n fotocopiadora f

photocopy ['fəʊtəʊkɒpɪ] 1. n fotocopia f 2. vt fotocopiar

photograph ['fəʊtəgrɑːf, 'fəʊtəgruːf] 1. n fotografía f; black and white / colour photograph fotografía en blanco y negro /en color 2. vt fotografiar

photographer [fə'tɒgrəfə(r)] n fotógrafo(a) m,f

photography [fə'tɒgrəfɪ] n fotografía f

phrase [freɪz] 1. n frase f; phrase book libro m de frases 2. vt expresar

physical ['fɪzɪkəl] adj físico(a); physical education educación física

physician [fɪ'zɪʃən] n médico(a) m,f

physics ['fɪzɪks] n sing física f

physiology [fɪzɪ'ɒlədʒɪ] n fisiología f

physiotherapist [fɪzɪəʊ'θerəpɪst] n fisioterapeuta mf

physique [fɪ'ziːk] n físico m

pianist ['pɪənɪst] n pianista mf

piano [pɪ'ænəʊ] n piano m

pick [pɪk] **1.** n a) [tool] pico m, piqueta f
b) **take your pick** [choice] elige el que
quieras
2. vt a) [choose] escoger; [team] seleccionar
b) [flowers, fruit] recoger, Esp coger
c) [scratch] hurgar; **to pick one's nose**
hurgarse la nariz
d) [lock] forzar
3. vi **to pick at one's food** comer sin
ganas
■ **pick off** vt sep a) [remove] quitar
b) [shoot] matar uno a uno
■ **pick on** vt insep [persecute] meterse con
■ **pick out** vt sep [choose] elegir;
[distinguish] distinguir; [identify]
identificar
■ **pick up 1.** vt sep a) [object on floor]
recoger, Esp coger; [telephone] descolgar; **to pick oneself up** levantarse; Fig
reponerse b) [collect] recoger; [shop-
ping, person] buscar; **to pick up speed**
ganar velocidad c) [acquire] conseguir;
[learn] aprender **2.** vi [improve] mejorarse, ir mejorando; [prices] subir

pickaxe, US **pickax** ['pɪkæks] n piqueta f

picket ['pɪkɪt] **1.** n piquete m; **picket
line** piquete **2.** vt piquetear **3.** vi hacer piquete

pickle ['pɪkəl] **1.** n a) Br [sauce] salsa agridulce a base de trocitos de fruta y verduras b) Fam [mess] lío m, apuro m **2.** vt
CULIN conservar en adobo o escabeche;
pickled onions cebollas fpl en vinagre

pickpocket ['pɪkpɒkɪt] n carterista mf

pick-up ['pɪkʌp] n Br **pick-up (arm)** [on
record player] brazo m; **pick-up (truck)**
camioneta f, furgoneta f

picnic ['pɪknɪk] **1.** n comida f de campo, picnic m **2.** vi hacer una comida de
campo

picture ['pɪktʃə(r)] **1.** n a) [painting] cuadro m; [drawing] dibujo m; [portrait]
retrato m; [photo] foto f; [illustra-
tion] ilustración f; **picture book** libro
ilustrado; **picture postcard** tarjeta f

postal b) TV imagen f; CIN película f;
Br **to go to the pictures** ir al cine **2.** vt
[imagine] imaginarse

picturesque [pɪktʃə'resk] adj pin-
toresco(a)

pie [paɪ] n [of fruit] tarta f, pastel m; [of
meat, fish] empanada f, pastel m, Col, CSur
torta f; [pasty] empanadilla f

piece [piːs] n a) [of food] pedazo m,
trozo m; [of paper] trozo; [part] pieza f; **a piece of advice** un consejo; **a
piece of news** una noticia; **to break
sth into pieces** hacer algo pedazos;
Fig **to go to pieces** perder el control
(de sí mismo) b) LITER & MUS obra f,
pieza f c) [coin] moneda f d) [in chess]
pieza f; [in draughts] ficha f ■ **piece
together** vt sep [facts] reconstruir;
[jigsaw] hacer

pier [pɪə(r)] n embarcadero m, muelle m;
[promenade] paseo de madera que entra
en el mar

pierce [pɪəs] vt perforar; [penetrate]
penetrar en

piercing ['pɪəsɪŋ] **1.** adj a) [sound,
look] penetrante b) [wind] cortante
2. n (body) **piercing** piercing m

pig [pɪg] n a) [animal] cerdo m b) Fam
[greedy person] comilón(ona) m,f,
glotón(ona) m,f, Am chacho m;
[unpleasant person] cerdo(a) m,f,
asqueroso(a) m,f, Am chancho m
c) Fam & Pej [policeman] Esp madero m,
Andes paco m, Méx tamarindo m, RP
cana m

pigeon ['pɪdʒɪn] n paloma f; CULIN &
SPORT pichón m

pigeonhole ['pɪdʒɪnhəʊl] n casilla f

pigment ['pɪgmənt] n pigmento m

pigsty ['pɪgstaɪ], US **pigpen** ['pɪgpen]
n pocilga f

pigtail ['pɪgteɪl] n trenza f; [bullfighter's]
coleta f

pile[1] [paɪl] **1.** n montón m **2.** vt amontonar **3.** vi Fam **to pile into** meterse atropelladamente en ■ **pile up 1.** vt sep
[things] amontonar; [riches, debts]
acumular **2.** vi amontonarse

pile² [paɪl] n [on carpet] pelo m; **thick pile** pelo largo

piles [paɪlz] npl MED almorranas fpl, hemorroides fpl

pile-up ['paɪlʌp] n AUTO choque m en cadena

pilgrim ['pɪlgrɪm] n peregrino(a) m,f

pilgrimage ['pɪlgrɪmɪʤ] n peregrinación f

pill [pɪl] n píldora f, pastilla f; **to be on the pill** estar tomando la píldora (anticonceptiva)

pillar ['pɪlə(r)] n pilar m, columna f; Br **pillar box** buzón m

pillow ['pɪləʊ] n almohada f

pillowcase ['pɪləʊkeɪs] n funda f de almohada

pilot ['paɪlət] **1.** n piloto m **2.** adj [trial] piloto (inv); **pilot light** piloto m; **pilot scheme** proyecto piloto **3.** vt pilotar

pimp [pɪmp] n proxeneta m, Esp chulo m, RP cafiolo m

pimple ['pɪmpəl] n grano m, espinilla f

pin [pɪn] **1.** n a) [for sewing] alfiler m; [bolt] clavija f; Br [of electric plug] clavija f; [in bowling] bolo m; [brooch, badge] pin m

b) Fam **pins and needles** hormigueo m; Fam **I've got pins and needles in my arm** tengo el brazo entumecido; US Fam & Fig **to be on pins and needles** estar sobre ascuas

2. vt [on board] clavar con chinchetas; [garment etc] sujetar con alfileres; **to pin sb against a wall** tener a algn contra una pared; Fig **to pin one's hopes on sth** poner sus esperanzas en algo; Fam **to pin a crime on sb** endosar un delito a algn

■ **pin down** vt sep Fig **to pin sb down** hacer que algn se comprometa

PIN n PIN (number) (número m) PIN m

pinball ['pɪnbɔːl] n flipper m, máquina f de petacos

pincers ['pɪnsəz] npl [on crab] pinzas fpl; [tool] tenazas fpl

pinch [pɪnʧ] **1.** n [nip] pellizco m; Fig Br **at** or US **in a pinch** en caso de apuro; **a pinch of salt** una pizca de sal **2.** vt pellizcar; Br Fam [steal] afanar, Esp levantar **3.** vi [shoes] apretar

pine¹ [paɪn] n [tree] pino m; **pine cone** piña f

pine² [paɪn] vi **to pine (away)** consumirse, morirse de pena; **to pine for sth/sb** echar de menos o añorar algo /a algn, Am extrañar algo /a algn

pineapple ['paɪnæpəl] n piña f, RP ananá m

pink [pɪŋk] **1.** n [colour] rosa m; BOT clavel m; **hot pink** rosa m fucsia **2.** adj [colour] rosa (inv); POL Fam rojillo(a); **hot pink** rosa fucsia (inv)

pinnacle ['pɪnəkəl] n [of building] pináculo m; [of mountain] cima f, pico m; Fig [of success] cumbre f

pinpoint ['pɪnpɔɪnt] vt señalar

pin-striped [-,straɪpt] adj de raya diplomática

pint [paɪnt] n pinta f; Br Fam **a pint (of beer)** una pinta (de cerveza)

pioneer [paɪə'nɪə(r)] **1.** n [settler] pionero(a) m,f; [forerunner] precursor(a) m,f **2.** vt ser pionero(a) en

pious ['paɪəs] adj piadoso(a), devoto(a); Pej beato(a)

pip¹ [pɪp] n [seed] pepita f

pip² [pɪp] n [sound] señal f (corta); [on dice] punto m

pipe [paɪp] **1.** n a) conducto m, tubería f; [of organ] caramillo m; Fam **the pipes** [bagpipes] la gaita b) [for smoking] pipa f; **pipe cleaner** limpiapipas m inv; Fig **pipe dream** sueño m imposible **2.** vt [water] llevar por tubería; [oil] transportar por oleoducto; **piped music** hilo m musical ■ **pipe down** vi Fam callarse ■ **pipe up** vi Fam hacerse oír

pipeline ['paɪplaɪn] n tubería f, cañería f; [for gas] gasoducto m; [for oil] oleoducto m

piping ['paɪpɪŋ] **1.** n [for water, gas etc] tubería f, cañería f **2.** adj **piping hot** bien caliente

pirate ['paɪrɪt] n pirata m; **pirate edition** edición f pirata; **pirate radio** emisora f pirata; **pirate ship** barco m pirata

Pisces ['paɪsiːz] n Piscis m inv

pissed [pɪst] adj v Fam a) Br [drunk] Esp, Méx pedo (inv), Col caído(a), RP en pedo b) US [angry] cabreado(a)

pistachio [pɪs'tɑːʃɪəʊ] n [nut] pistacho m

pistol ['pɪstəl] n pistola f

pit¹ [pɪt] **1.** n hoyo m; [large] hoya f; [coal mine] mina f de carbón; THEAT platea f; [in motor racing] foso m, box m **2.** vt to pit one's wits against sb medirse con algn

pit² [pɪt] n [of cherry] hueso m, pipo m, RP carozo m; US [of peach, plum] hueso, RP carozo m

pitch [pɪtʃ] **1.** vt a) [throw] lanzar, arrojar b) [tent] armar **2.** n a) MUS [of sound] tono m b) esp Br SPORT campo m, cancha f

pitcher ['pɪtʃə(r)] n [container] cántaro m, jarro m

pitfall ['pɪtfɔːl] n dificultad f, obstáculo m

pith [pɪθ] n [of orange] piel blanca; Fig meollo m

pitiful ['pɪtɪfʊl] adj [producing pity] lastimoso(a); [terrible] lamentable

pitiless ['pɪtɪlɪs] adj despiadado(a), implacable

pittance ['pɪtəns] n miseria f

pity ['pɪtɪ] **1.** n a) [compassion] compasión f, piedad f; to take pity on sb compadecerse de algn b) [shame] lástima f, pena f; what a pity! ¡qué pena!, ¡qué lástima! **2.** vt compadecerse de; I pity them me dan pena

pivot ['pɪvət] **1.** n pivote m **2.** vi girar sobre su eje

pixel ['pɪksl] n COMPUT pixel or píxel m

pixelate ['pɪksəleɪt], **pixelize** ['pɪksəlaɪz] vt pixelar, pixelizar

pixellated, US **pixelated** ['pɪksəleɪtɪd] adj COMPUT [image] pixelado(a), pixelizado(a)

pizza ['piːtsə] n pizza f; **pizza parlour** pizzería f

placard ['plækɑːd] n pancarta f

place [pleɪs] **1.** n a) [scheme] sitio m, lugar m; **all over the place** [everywhere] por todas partes; **in place of** en lugar de; **to be in / out of place** estar en / fuera de su sitio; **to take place** tener lugar
b) [seat] sitio m; [on bus] asiento m; [at university] plaza m; **to change places with sb** intercambiar el sitio con algn; **to take sb's place** sustituir a algn
c) [position on scale] posición f; [social position] rango m; **in the first place** en primer lugar
d) [house] casa f; [building] lugar m; **we're going to his place** vamos a su casa
2. vt a) poner, colocar; **to place an order with sb** hacer un pedido a algn
b) [face, person] recordar; [in job] colocar en un empleo

placid ['plæsɪd] adj apacible

plague [pleɪg] **1.** n [of insects] plaga f; MED peste f **2.** vt **to plague sb with requests** acosar a algn a peticiones

plaice [pleɪs] (pl **plaice**) n [fish] platija f

plain [pleɪn] **1.** adj a) [clear] claro(a), evidente; Fig **he likes plain speaking** le gusta hablar con franqueza b) [simple] sencillo(a); [chocolate] amargo(a); [flour] sin levadura; **in plain clothes** vestido(a) de paisano; **the plain truth** la verdad lisa y llana c) [unattractive] poco atractivo(a) **2.** n GEOG llanura f, llano m

plainly ['pleɪnlɪ] adv claramente; [simply] sencillamente; **to speak plainly** hablar con franqueza

plait [plæt] **1.** n trenza f **2.** vt trenzar

plan [plæn] **1.** n a) [scheme] plan m, proyecto m; [drawing] plano m
b) **plans** planes mpl; **have you any plans for tonight?** ¿tienes planes para esta noche?
2. vt a) [for future] planear, proyectar; [economy] planificar
b) [intend] pensar, tener la intención de; **it wasn't planned** no estaba previsto
3. vi hacer planes; **to plan on doing sth** tener la intención de hacer algo

plane¹ [pleɪn] **1.** *n* **a)** MATH plano *m*; *Fig* nivel *m* **b)** *Fam* AVIAT avión *m* **2.** *adj* GEOM plano(a) **3.** *vi* [glide] planear

plane² [pleɪn] **1.** *n* [tool] cepillo *m* **2.** *vt* cepillar

plane³ [pleɪn] *n* BOT **plane (tree)** plátano *m*

planet ['plænɪt] *n* planeta *m*

plank [plæŋk] *n* tabla *f*, tablón *m*

planned [plænd] *adj* [crime] premeditado(a); [economy] planificado(a), dirigido(a); [baby] deseado(a)

planning ['plænɪŋ] *n* planificación *f*; **family planning** planificación familiar; *Br* **planning permission** licencia *f* de obras

plant¹ [plɑːnt] **1.** *n* planta *f* **2.** *vt* [flowers] plantar; [seeds] sembrar; [bomb] colocar

plant² [plɑːnt] *n* [factory] planta *f*, fábrica *f*; [machinery] maquinaria *f*

plantation [plæn'teɪʃən] *n* plantación *f*

plaque [plæk] *n* placa *f*; [on teeth] sarro *m*

plasma *n* PHYS & MED plasma *m*; COMPUT **plasma screen** pantalla *f* de plasma; **plasma TV** televisión *f* con pantalla de plasma

plaster ['plɑːstə(r)] **1.** *n* CONSTR yeso *m*; MED escayola *f*; *Br* **(sticking) plaster** tirita® *f*, *Am* curita *f*; **plaster of Paris** yeso mate **2.** *vt* CONSTR enyesar; *Fig* [cover] cubrir (**with** de)

plastic ['plæstɪk] **1.** *n* plástico *m* **2.** *adj* [cup, bag] de plástico; **plastic surgery** cirugía plástica

plate [pleɪt] **1.** *n* **a)** plato *m* **b)** [sheet] placa *f*; **gold plate** chapa *f* de oro; **plate glass** vidrio cilindrado **c)** [in book] grabado *m*, lámina *f* **2.** *vt* chapar

plateau ['plætəʊ] *n* meseta *f*

platform ['plætfɔːm] *n* **a)** plataforma *f*; [stage] estrado *m*; [at meeting] tribuna *f* **b)** RAIL andén *m*; **platform ticket** billete *m* de andén **c)** POL [programme] programa *m*

platinum ['plætɪnəm] *n* platino *m*

plausible ['plɔːzəbəl] *adj* plausible

play [pleɪ] **1.** *vt* **a)** [game] jugar a; [team] jugar contra

b) [instrument, tune] tocar; **to play a CD** poner un CD

c) THEAT [part] hacer (el papel) de; [play] representar; *Fig* **to play a part in sth** participar en algo

2. *vi* **a)** [children] jugar (**with** con); [animals] juguetear

b) SPORT jugar; *Fig* **to play for time** tratar de ganar tiempo

c) [joke] bromear

d) MUS tocar; [instrument] sonar

3. *n* **a)** THEAT obra *f* de teatro

b) SPORT juego *m*

c) TECH & *Fig* [movement] juego *m*; **a play on words** un juego de palabras

■ **play about** *vi insep Br* [have fun - children] jugar; [frolic] enredar

■ **play about with** *vi insep* **a)** [fiddle with, tamper with] **to play about with sth** jugar con *or* juguetear con algo

b) [juggle - statistics, figures] jugar con; [consider - possibilities, alternatives] dar vueltas a **c)** *Fam* [trifle with] **to play about with sb** jugar con algn

■ **play along** *vi* **to play along (with sb)** seguir el juego (de algn)

■ **play around** *vi* [waste time] gandulear; [be unfaithful] tener líos

■ **play down** *vt sep* minimizar, quitar importancia a

■ **play on** *vt insep* [take advantage of] aprovecharse de; [nerves etc] exacerbar

■ **play up 1.** *vt sep* [annoy] dar la lata a, fastidiar **2.** *vi Br* [child, injury etc] dar guerra

playboy ['pleɪbɔɪ] *n* playboy *m*

player ['pleɪə(r)] *n* SPORT jugador(a) *m,f*; MUS músico(a) *m,f*; THEAT [man] actor *m*; [woman] actriz *f*

playful ['pleɪfʊl] *adj* juguetón(ona)

playground ['pleɪgraʊnd] *n* patio *m* de recreo

playgroup ['pleɪgruːp] *n* jardín *m* de infancia

playing ['pleɪɪŋ] n juego m; **playing card** carta f, naipe m; **playing field** campo m de deportes

playmate ['pleɪmeɪt] n compañero(a) m,f de juego

playtime ['pleɪtaɪm] n [at school] recreo m

playwright ['pleɪraɪt] n dramaturgo(a) m,f

PLC, **plc** [piːelˈsiː] n Br (abbr of **public limited company**) ≃ S.A.

plea [pliː] n a) [request] petición f, súplica f, Am pedido m; [excuse] pretexto m, disculpa f b) JUR alegato m

plead [pliːd] 1. vt a) JUR & Fig **to plead sb's cause** defender la causa de algn b) **to plead ignorance** [give as excuse] alegar ignorancia 2. vi a) [beg] rogar, suplicar; **to plead with sb to do sth** suplicar a algn que haga algo b) JUR **to plead guilty /not guilty** declararse culpable /inocente

pleasant ['plezənt] adj agradable

please [pliːz] 1. vt [give pleasure to] agradar, complacer; [satisfy] satisfacer; Fam **please yourself** como quieras 2. vi complacer; [give satisfaction] satisfacer; **easy /hard to please** poco / muy exigente 3. adv por favor; **may I? — please do** ¿me permite? — desde luego; **please do not smoke** [sign] se ruega no fumar; **yes, please** sí, por favor

pleased [pliːzd] adj [happy] contento(a); [satisfied] satisfecho(a); **pleased to meet you!** ¡encantado(a)!, ¡mucho gusto!; **to be pleased about sth** alegrarse de algo

pleasing ['pliːzɪŋ] adj [pleasant] agradable, grato(a); [satisfactory] satisfactorio(a)

pleasure ['pleʒə(r)] n placer m; **it's a pleasure to talk to him** da gusto hablar con él; **to take great pleasure in doing sth** disfrutar mucho haciendo algo; **with pleasure** con mucho gusto

pleat [pliːt] 1. n pliegue m 2. vt hacer pliegues en

pledge [pledʒ] 1. n promesa f; [token of love etc] señal f; [guarantee] prenda f 2. vt [promise] prometer; [pawn] empeñar

plentiful ['plentɪfʊl] adj abundante

plenty ['plentɪ] n abundancia f; **plenty of books** muchos libros; **plenty of time** tiempo de sobra; **we've got plenty** tenemos de sobra

pliers ['plaɪəz] npl alicates mpl, tenazas fpl

plight [plaɪt] n situación f grave

plimsolls ['plɪmsəlz] npl Br zapatos mpl de tenis

plod [plɒd] vi andar con paso pesado; Fig **to plod on** perseverar; Fig **to plod through a report** estudiar laboriosamente un informe

plonk[1] [plɒŋk] vt esp Br Fam dejar caer

plonk[2] [plɒŋk] n Br Fam [cheap wine] vino m peleón

plot[1] [plɒt] 1. n a) [conspiracy] complot m b) THEAT & LITER [story] argumento m, trama f 2. vt a) [course, route] trazar b) [scheme] fraguar 3. vi conspirar, tramar

plot[2] [plɒt] n AGR terreno m; [for building] solar m; **vegetable plot** campo m de hortalizas

plough [plaʊ] 1. n arado m 2. vt arar 3. vi **to plough into sth** chocar contra algo

PLS, **PLZ** MESSAGING (abbr of **please**) xfa

pluck [plʌk] 1. vt a) arrancar (**out of** de) b) [flowers] coger c) [chicken] desplumar d) [guitar] puntear 2. n [courage] valor m, ánimo m ■ **pluck up** vt sep **to pluck up courage** armarse de valor

plucky ['plʌkɪ] (compar **pluckier**, superl **pluckiest**) adj valiente

plug [plʌg] 1. n a) [in bath etc] tapón m b) ELEC enchufe m, clavija f; **two-/three-pin plug** clavija bipolar / tripolar

2. *vt* **a)** [hole] tapar **b)** *Fam* [publicize] dar publicidad a ; [idea etc] hacer hincapié en ■ **plug in** *vt sep & vi* enchufar

plug-and-play *adj* COMPUT de enchufar y usar

plughole ['plʌghəʊl] *n* desagüe *m*

plum [plʌm] **1.** *n* [fruit] ciruela *f* **2.** *adj* **a plum job** *Esp* un chollo *or Méx* churro (de trabajo), *RP* un laburazo

plumb [plʌm] **1.** *adv Fam* **plumb in the middle** justo en medio; *US* **he's plumb crazy** está completamente loco **2.** *vt Fig* **to plumb the depths** tocar fondo

plumber ['plʌmə(r)] *n* fontanero(a) *m,f*, *Méx*, *RP*, *Ven* plomero(a)

plumbing ['plʌmɪŋ] *n* [occupation] fontanería *f*, *Méx*, *RP*, *Ven* plomería *f*; [system] tuberías *fpl*, cañerías *fpl*

plummet ['plʌmɪt] *vi* [bird, plane] desplomarse, caer en picado *or Am* picada; *Fig* [prices] bajar vertiginosamente; [morale] caer a plomo

plump [plʌmp] *adj* [person] relleno(a); [baby] rechoncho(a) ■ **plump down** *vt sep* dejar caer ■ **plump for** *vt insep* optar por ■ **plump up** *vt sep* [cushions] ahuecar

plunder ['plʌndə(r)] **1.** *vt* saquear **2.** *n* [action] saqueo *m*, pillaje *m*; [loot] botín *m*

plunge [plʌndʒ] **1.** *vt* [immerse] sumergir; [thrust] arrojar
2. *vi* [dive] lanzarse, zambullirse; *Fig* [fall] caer, hundirse; [prices] desplomarse
3. *n* [dive] zambullida *f*; *Fig* [fall] desplome *m*; **to take the plunge** dar el paso decisivo

plural ['plʊərəl] *adj & n* plural (*m*)

plus [plʌs] **1.** *prep* más; **three plus four makes seven** tres más cuatro hacen siete **2.** *n* MATH signo *m* más; *Fig* [advantage] ventaja *f*

pluto [plu:təʊ] *vt US* relegar; **to be plutoed** ser relegado(a)

ply [plaɪ] **1.** *vt* **to ply one's trade** ejercer su oficio; **to ply sb with drinks** no parar de ofrecer copas a algn **2.** *vi* [ship] ir y venir; **to ply for hire** ir en busca de clientes

p.m. [piː'em] *(abbr of post meridiem)* después del mediodía; **at 2 p.m.** a las dos de la tarde

pneumonia [njuː'məʊnɪə] *n* pulmonía *f*

PO [piː'əʊ] *n (abbr of Post Office)* oficina *f* de correos; **PO Box** apartado *m* de correos, *CAm*, *Carib*, *Méx* casilla *f* postal, *Andes*, *RP* casilla de correos

poach[^1] [pəʊtʃ] *vt* **a) to poach fish /game** pescar /cazar furtivamente **b)** *Fam & Fig* [steal] birlar

poach[^2] [pəʊtʃ] *vt* CULIN [egg] escalfar; [fish] hervir

pocket ['pɒkɪt] **1.** *n* **a)** bolsillo *m*, *CAm*, *Méx*, *Perú* bolsa *f*; *Fig* **to be £10 in /out of pocket** salir ganando /perdiendo 10 libras; **pocket money** dinero *m* para gastos **b)** [of air] bolsa *f* **c)** [of resistance] foco *m* **2.** *vt* [money] embolsarse

pocketbook ['pɒkɪtbʊk] *n US* [wallet] cartera *f*; [handbag] *Esp* bolso *m*, *Col*, *CSur* cartera *f*, *Méx* bolsa *f*

podcast ['pɒdkæst] *n* COMPUT podcast *m*

po$bl MESSAGING *written abbr of* **possible**

poem ['pəʊɪm] *n* poema *m*

poet ['pəʊɪt] *n* poeta *mf*

poetic [pəʊ'etɪk] *adj* poético(a)

poetry ['pəʊɪtrɪ] *n* poesía *f*

poignant ['pɔɪnjənt] *adj* conmovedor(a)

point [pɔɪnt] **1.** *n* **a)** [sharp end] punta *f*
b) [place] punto *m*; *Fig* **point of no return** punto sin retorno
c) [quality] **good /bad point** cualidad buena /mala
d) [moment] **at that point** en aquel momento; **to be on the point of doing sth** estar a punto de hacer algo; **up to a point** hasta cierto punto, en cierto modo
e) [score] punto *m*, tanto *m*
f) [in argument] punto *m*; **I take your point** entiendo lo que quieres decir

g) [purpose] propósito *m*; **I don't see the point** no veo el sentido; **there's no point in going** no merece la pena ir; **to come to the point** llegar al meollo de la cuestión

h) [on scale] punto *m*; [in share index] entero *m*; **six point three** seis coma tres

i) GEOG punta *f*

j) points AUTO platinos *mpl*; RAIL agujas *fpl*

2. *vt* [way etc] señalar, indicar; **to point a gun at sb** apuntar a algn con una pistola

3. *vi* señalar, indicar; **to point at sth / sb** señalar algo / a algn con el dedo

■ **point out** *vt sep* indicar, señalar; [mention] hacer resaltar

point-blank ['pɔɪnt'blæŋk] **1.** *adj* a quemarropa; [refusal] rotundo(a) **2.** *adv* [shoot] a quemarropa; [refuse] rotundamente

pointed ['pɔɪntɪd] *adj* [sharp] puntiagudo(a); *Fig* [comment] intencionado(a); [cutting] mordaz

pointer ['pɔɪntə(r)] *n* **a)** [indicator] indicador *m*, aguja *f*; [for map] puntero *m* **b)** [dog] perro *m* de muestra **c)** COMPUT cursor *m*

pointless ['pɔɪntlɪs] *adj* sin sentido

poise [pɔɪz] **1.** *n* [bearing] porte *m*; [self-assurance] aplomo *m* **2.** *vt Fig* **to be poised to do sth** estar listo(a) para hacer algo

poison ['pɔɪzən] **1.** *n* veneno *m* **2.** *vt* envenenar

poisonous ['pɔɪzənəs] *adj* [plant, snake] venenoso(a); [gas] tóxico(a); *Fig* [rumour] pernicioso(a)

poke [pəʊk] *vt* [with finger or stick] dar con la punta del dedo / del bastón a; **to poke one's head out** asomar la cabeza; **to poke the fire** atizar el fuego ■ **poke about, poke around** *vi* fisgonear, hurgar ■ **poke out** *vt sep* [eye] sacar

poker¹ ['pəʊkə(r)] *n* [for fire] atizador *m*

poker² ['pəʊkə(r)] *n* CARDS póquer *m*

Poland ['pəʊlənd] *n* Polonia

polar ['pəʊlə(r)] *adj* polar; **polar bear** oso *m* polar; **polar bread** pan *m* polar

pole¹ [pəʊl] *n* palo *m*; **pole vault** salto *m* con pértiga

pole² [pəʊl] *n* GEOG polo *m*; *Fig* **to be poles apart** ser polos opuestos

Pole [pəʊl] *n* polaco(a) *m,f*

police [pə'liːs] **1.** *npl* policía *f*; **police car** coche *m or Am* carro *or CSur* auto de policía; *Br* **police constable** policía *m*; *US* **police department** jefatura *f* de policía; **police force** cuerpo *m* de policía; **police record** antecedentes *mpl* penales; **police state** estado *m* policial; **police station** comisaría *f* **2.** *vt* vigilar

policeman [pə'liːsmən] *n* policía *m*

policewoman [pə'liːswʊmən] *n* (mujer *f*) policía *f*

policy ['pɒlɪsɪ] *n* POL política *f*; [of company] norma *f*, principio *m*; INS póliza *f* (de seguros)

polio ['pəʊlɪəʊ] *n* poliomielitis *f*

polish ['pɒlɪʃ] **1.** *vt* pulir; [furniture] encerar; [shoes] limpiar; [silver] sacar brillo a **2.** *n* **a)** [for furniture] cera *f*; [for shoes] betún *m*; [for nails] esmalte *m* **b)** [shine] brillo *m*; *Fig* [refinement] refinamiento *m* ■ **polish off** *vt sep Fam* [work] despachar; [food] zamparse ■ **polish up** *vt sep Fig* perfeccionar

Polish ['pəʊlɪʃ] **1.** *adj* polaco(a) **2.** *n* **a) the Polish** los polacos **b)** [language] polaco *m*

polite [pə'laɪt] *adj* educado(a)

political [pə'lɪtɪkəl] *adj* político(a)

politician [pɒlɪ'tɪʃən] *n* político(a) *m,f*

politics ['pɒlɪtɪks] *n sing* política *f*

poll [pəʊl] **1.** *n* **a)** votación *f*; **the polls** las elecciones; **to go to the polls** acudir a las urnas **b)** [survey] encuesta *f* **2.** *vt* [votes] obtener

pollen ['pɒlən] *n* polen *m*

polling ['pəʊlɪŋ] *n* votación *f*; **polling booth** cabina *f* electoral; **polling station** colegio *m* electoral

pollute [pə'luːt] *vt* contaminar

pollution [pə'luːʃən] n contaminación f, polución f; **environmental pollution** contaminación ambiental

polo ['pəʊləʊ] n SPORT polo m; Br **polo neck (sweater)** suéter m or Esp jersey m or Col saco m or RP pulóver m de cuello alto or de cisne

polyester [pɒlɪ'estə(r)] n poliéster m

polythene [pɒlɪθiːn] n Br polietileno m

pompous ['pɒmpəs] adj [person] presumido(a); [speech] rimbombante

pond [pɒnd] n estanque m

ponder ['pɒndə(r)] **1.** vt considerar **2.** vi **to ponder over sth** meditar sobre algo

pong [pɒŋ] n Br Fam tufo m

pony ['pəʊnɪ] n poney m

ponyride ['pəʊnɪraɪd] n paseo m en pony

ponytail ['pəʊnɪteɪl] n cola f de caballo

poodle ['puːdəl] n caniche m

pool¹ [puːl] n [of water, oil etc] charco m; [pond] estanque m; [in river] pozo m; **(swimming) pool** piscina f, Méx alberca f, RP pileta f

pool² [puːl] **1.** n a) [common fund] fondo m común b) **typing pool** servicio m de mecanografía c) US [snooker] billar americano d) Br **the pools** las quinielas fpl, Arg el Prode, Col, CRica el totogol **2.** vt [funds] reunir; [ideas, resources] juntar

poor [pʊə(r)] **1.** adj pobre; [quality] malo(a); Fam **you poor thing!** ¡pobrecito! **2.** npl **the poor** los pobres

poorly ['pʊəlɪ] **1.** adv [badly] mal **2.** (compar **poorlier**, superl **poorliest**) adj [ill] mal, malo(a)

pop [pɒp] **1.** vt [burst] hacer reventar; [cork] hacer saltar
2. vi [burst] reventar; [cork] saltar; Fam **I'm just popping over to Ian's** voy un momento a casa de Ian
3. n a) [noise] pequeña explosión
b) Fam [drink] gaseosa f
c) US Fam [father] papá m
d) Fam MUS música f pop; **pop singer** cantante mf pop

■ **pop in** vi Fam entrar un momento, pasar

popcorn ['pɒpkɔːn] n palomitas fpl de maíz, RP pochoclo m

Pope [pəʊp] n **the Pope** el Papa

poplar ['pɒplə(r)] n álamo m

poppy ['pɒpɪ] n amapola f

Popsicle® ['pɒpsɪkəl] n US polo m

popular ['pɒpjʊlə(r)] adj popular; [fashionable] de moda; [common] corriente

popularity [pɒpjʊ'lærɪtɪ] n popularidad f

populate ['pɒpjʊleɪt] vt poblar

population [pɒpjʊ'leɪʃən] n población f; **the population explosion** la explosión demográfica

pop-up 1. adj a) [toaster] automático(a) b) [book] desplegable **2.** n COMPUT ventana f emergente

porcelain ['pɔːsəlɪn] n porcelana f

porch [pɔːtʃ] n Br [entrance] zaguán m; US [veranda] terraza f

pore¹ [pɔː(r)] vi **to pore over sth** leer or estudiar algo detenidamente

pore² [pɔː(r)] n ANAT poro m

pork [pɔːk] n (carne f de) cerdo m or Am chancho m

porky ['pɔːkɪ] (compar **porkier**, superl **porkiest**) **1.** adj Fam & Pej [fat] rechoncho(a) **2.** n Br Fam [lie] trola f

pornography [pɔː'nɒɡrəfɪ] n pornografía f

porridge ['pɒrɪdʒ] n gachas fpl de avena

port¹ [pɔːt] n [harbour & COMPUT] puerto m; **port of call** puerto de escala

port² [pɔːt] n NAUT & AVIAT babor m

port³ [pɔːt] n [wine] vino m de Oporto, oporto m

portable ['pɔːtəbəl] adj portátil

porter ['pɔːtə(r)] n [at station] mozo m de equipaje; esp Br [at hotel] portero(a) m,f, conserje mf; US [on train] mozo m

portfolio [pɔːt'fəʊlɪəʊ] n [file] carpeta f; [of artist, politician] cartera f

potent

porthole ['pɔːthəʊl] *n* portilla *f*

portion ['pɔːʃən] *n* [part, piece] parte *f*, porción *f*; [of food] ración *f* ■ **portion out** *vt sep* repartir

portrait ['pɔːtreɪt] *n* retrato *m*

portray [pɔː'treɪ] *vt* [paint portrait of] retratar; [describe] describir; THEAT representar

Portugal ['pɔːtjʊɡəl] *n* Portugal

Portuguese [pɔːtjʊ'ɡiːz] **1.** *adj* portugués(esa) **2.** *n* [person] portugués(esa) *m,f*; [language] portugués *m*

pose [pəʊz] **1.** *vt* [problem] plantear; [threat] representar **2.** *vi* [for painting] posar; *Pej* [behave affectedly] hacer pose; **to pose as** hacerse pasar por **3.** *n* [stance] postura *f*; *Pej* [affectation] pose *f*

posh [pɒʃ] *adj Br Fam* elegante, de lujo; [person, accent] *Esp* pijo(a), *Méx* fresa, *RP* (con)cheto(a)

position [pə'zɪʃən] **1.** *n* **a)** posición *f*; [location] situación *f*; [rank] rango *m*; **to be in a position to do sth** estar en condiciones de hacer algo **b)** [opinion] postura *f* **c)** [job] puesto *m* **2.** *vt* colocar

positive ['pɒzɪtɪv] *adj* positivo(a); [sign] favorable; [proof] incontrovertible; [sure] seguro(a); *Fam* [absolute] auténtico(a)

possess [pə'zes] *vt* poseer; [of fear] apoderarse de

possession [pə'zeʃən] *n* posesión *f*; **possessions** bienes *mpl*

possessive [pə'zesɪv] *adj* posesivo(a)

possibility [pɒsɪ'bɪlɪtɪ] *n* posibilidad *f*; **possibilities** [potential] potencial *m*

possible ['pɒsɪbəl] *adj* posible; **as much as possible** todo lo posible; **as often as possible** cuanto más mejor; **as soon as possible** cuanto antes

possibly ['pɒsɪblɪ] *adv* posiblemente; [perhaps] tal vez, quizás; **I can't possibly come** no puedo venir de ninguna manera

post¹ [pəʊst] **1.** *n* [of wood] poste *m* **2.** *vt* [affix] poner, pegar

post² [pəʊst] **1.** *n* [job] puesto *m*; *US* **trading post** factoría *f* **2.** *vt Br* [assign] destinar

post³ [pəʊst] *esp Br* **1.** *n* [mail] correo *m*; **by post** por correo; **post office** oficina *f* de correos; **Post Office Box** apartado *m* de correos **2.** *vt* [letter] echar al correo; **to post sth to sb** mandar algo por correo a algn

postage ['pəʊstɪdʒ] *n* franqueo *m*

postal ['pəʊstəl] *adj* postal, de correos; *Br* **postal code** código *m* postal; *Br* **postal order** giro *m* postal; **postal vote** voto *m* por correo

postbox ['pəʊstbɒks] *n Br* buzón *m* (de correos)

postcard ['pəʊstkɑːd] *n* (tarjeta *f*) postal *f*

postcode ['pəʊstkəʊd] *n Br* código *m* postal

poster ['pəʊstə(r)] *n* póster *m*; [advertising] cartel *m*

postgraduate [pəʊst'ɡrædjʊɪt] **1.** *n* posgraduado(a) *m,f* **2.** *adj* de posgraduado

posthumous ['pɒstjʊməs] *adj* póstumo(a)

postman ['pəʊstmən] *n Br* cartero *m*

postmark ['pəʊstmɑːk] *n* matasellos *m inv*

postmortem [pəʊst'mɔːtəm] *n* autopsia *f*

postpone [pəs'pəʊn] *vt* aplazar

posture ['pɒstʃə(r)] **1.** *n* postura *f*; [affected] pose *f* **2.** *vi* adoptar una pose

postwoman ['pəʊst,wʊmən] *(pl* **postwomen** ['wɪmɪn]*) n* cartera *f*

pot [pɒt] **1.** *n* [container] tarro *m*, pote *m*; [for cooking] olla *f*; [for flowers] maceta *f*; *Fam* **to go to pot** irse al garete *or Am* al diablo **2.** *vt* [plant] poner en una maceta

potato [pə'teɪtəʊ] *(pl* **potatoes***) n* patata *f*, *Am* papa *f*; **potato chips** patatas *fpl or Am* papas *fpl* fritas (de bolsa)

potent ['pəʊtənt] *adj* potente

potential [pə'tenʃəl] **1.** *adj* potencial, posible **2.** *n* potencial *m*

pothole ['pɒthəʊl] *n* GEOL cueva *f*; [in road] bache *m*

potsticker ['pɒtstɪkə(r)] *n US* CULIN empanaditas *fpl* chinas

potter[1] ['pɒtə(r)] *n* alfarero(a) *m,f*

potter[2] ['pɒtə(r)] *vi Br* **to potter about** *or* **around** entretenerse

pottery ['pɒtərɪ] *n* [craft, place] alfarería *f*; [objects] cerámica *f*

potty[1] ['pɒtɪ] *(compar* **pottier,** *superl* **pottiest)** *adj Br Fam* pirado(a), *Col* corrido(a), *CSur* rayado(a), *Méx* zafado(a)

potty[2] ['pɒtɪ] *n Fam* orinal *m*

pouch [paʊtʃ] *n* **a)** bolsa pequeña; [for ammunition] morral *m*; [for tobacco] petaca *f* **b)** ZOOL bolsa *f* abdominal

poultry ['pəʊltrɪ] *n* [live] aves *fpl* de corral; [food] pollos *mpl*

pounce [paʊns] *vi* **to pounce on** abalanzarse encima de

pound[1] [paʊnd] **1.** *vt* [strike] aporrear **2.** *vi* [heart] palpitar; [walk heavily] andar con paso pesado

pound[2] [paʊnd] *n* [money, weight] libra *f*

pound[3] [paʊnd] *n* [for dogs] perrera *f*; [for cars] depósito *m* de coches

pour [pɔː(r)] **1.** *vt* echar, verter; **to pour sb a drink** servirle una copa a algn **2.** *vi* correr, fluir; **it's pouring with rain** está lloviendo a cántaros ■ **pour out** *vt sep* echar, verter; *Fig* **to pour one's heart out to sb** desahogarse con algn

pout [paʊt] **1.** *vi* hacer pucheros **2.** *n* puchero *m*

poverty ['pɒvətɪ] *n* pobreza *f*

powder ['paʊdə(r)] **1.** *n* polvo *m*; **powder compact** polvera *f*; **powder keg** polvorín *m*; **powder puff** borla *f*; **powder room** baño *m or Esp* servicios *mpl or CSur* toilette *m* de señoras **2.** *vt* **to powder one's nose** ponerse polvos en la cara; *Euph* ir a los servicios *or* al tocador

powdered ['paʊdəd] *adj* [milk] en polvo; **powdered milk** leche *f* en polvo

power ['paʊə(r)] **1.** *n* **a)** fuerza *f*; [energy] energía *f*; ELEC **to cut off the power**

cortar la corriente; **power plant** central *f* eléctrica; *esp Br* **power point** enchufe *m*; **power station** central *or Andes, RP* usina *f* eléctrica; **solar power** energía *f* solar **b)** [ability] poder *m* **c)** [authority] poder *m*; [nation] potencia *f*; [influence] influencia *f*; **to be in power** estar en el poder **d)** TECH potencia *f*; [output] rendimiento *m* **2.** *vt* propulsar, impulsar

powerful ['paʊəfʊl] *adj* [strong] fuerte; [influential] poderoso(a); [remedy] eficaz; [engine, machine] potente; [emotion] fuerte; [speech] conmovedor(a)

powerless ['paʊəlɪs] *adj* impotente, ineficaz

PPL MESSAGING *written abbr of* **people**

PR [piː'ɑː(r)] *(abbr of* **public relations)** relaciones *fpl* públicas

practical ['præktɪkəl] *adj* práctico(a); [useful] útil; [sensible] adecuado(a)

practically ['præktɪkəlɪ] *adv* [almost] casi

practice ['præktɪs] **1.** *n* **a)** [habit] costumbre *f*
b) [exercise] práctica *f*; SPORT entrenamiento *m*; MUS ensayo *m*; **to be out of practice** no estar en forma
c) [way of doing sth] práctica *f*; **in practice** en la práctica; **to put sth into practice** poner algo en práctica
d) [of profession] ejercicio *m*
e) [place - of doctors] consultorio *m*; [of lawyers] bufete *m*
f) [clients - of doctors] pacientes *mpl*; [of lawyers] clientela *f*
2. *vt & vi US* = **practise**

practise ['præktɪs] **1.** *vt* practicar; [method] seguir; [principle] poner en práctica; MUS ensayar; [profession] ejercer **2.** *vi* practicar; SPORT entrenar; MUS ensayar; [doctor] practicar; [lawyer] ejercer

practitioner [præk'tɪʃənə(r)] *n Br* MED **general practitioner** médico(a) *m,f* de cabecera

pragmatic [præg'mætɪk] *adj* pragmático(a)

prairie ['preərɪ] *n* pradera *f*; *US* llanura *f*

praise [preız] **1.** n alabanza f **2.** vt alabar, elogiar

pram [præm] n Br cochecito m de niño

prank [præŋk] n broma f; [of child] travesura f

prawn [prɔ:n] n gamba f, Am camarón m; **prawn crackers** corteza f de gambas *(especie de corteza crujiente y ligera con sabor a marisco)*

pray [preı] vi rezar, orar

prayer [preə(r)] n rezo m, oración f; [entreaty] súplica f; **prayer book** misal m

preach [pri:tʃ] vi predicar

preacher ['pri:tʃə(r)] n predicador(a) m,f

precarious [prı'keərıəs] adj precario(a)

precaution [prı'kɔ:ʃən] n precaución f

precede [prı'si:d] vt preceder

precedent ['presıdənt] n precedente m

precinct ['pri:sıŋkt] n **a)** Br [area] **pedestrian / shopping precinct** zona f peatonal /comercial **b)** US [administrative, police division] distrito m; [police station] comisaría f (de policía)

precious ['preʃəs] **1.** adj precioso(a); **precious stones** piedras preciosas **2.** adv Fam **precious little /few** muy poco /pocos

precipice ['presıpıs] n precipicio m

precipitate 1. [prı'sıpıteıt] vt precipitar; Fig arrojar **2.** [prı'sıpıtət] adj precipitado(a)

precise [prı'saıs] adj preciso(a), exacto(a); [meticulous] meticuloso(a)

precisely [prı'saıslı] adv [exactly] precisamente, exactamente; **precisely!** ¡eso es!, ¡exacto!

precision [prı'sıʒən] n precisión f

preclude [prı'klu:d] vt excluir; [misunderstanding] evitar

precocious [prı'kəʊʃəs] adj precoz

preconceived [pri:kən'si:vd] adj preconcebido(a)

precondition [pri:kən'dıʃən] n condición previa

predator ['predətə(r)] n depredador m

predecessor ['pri:dısesə(r)] n antecesor(a) m,f

predicament [prı'dıkəmənt] n apuro m, aprieto m

predict [prı'dıkt] vt predecir, pronosticar

predictable [prı'dıktəbəl] adj previsible

prediction [prı'dıkʃən] n pronóstico m

predictive [prı'dıktıv] adj indicador(a), profético(a); TEL **predictive text(ing)** escritura f predictiva, T9 m

predispose [pri:dı'spəʊz] vt **to be predisposed to doing sth** estar predispuesto(a) a hacer algo

predominant [prı'dɒmınənt] adj predominante

predominate [prı'dɒmıneıt] vi predominar

pre-empt [prı'empt] vt adelantarse a

preface ['prefıs] **1.** n prefacio m **2.** vt prologar

prefect ['pri:fekt] n Br SCH monitor(a) m,f

prefer [prı'fɜ:(r)] vt preferir; **I prefer coffee to tea** prefiero el café al té

preferable ['prefərəbəl] adj preferible (to a)

preference ['prefərəns] n preferencia f; [priority] prioridad f; **to give preference to sth** dar prioridad a algo

prefix ['pri:fıks] n prefijo m

pregnancy ['pregnənsı] n embarazo m

pregnant ['pregnənt] adj [woman] embarazada; [animal] preñada; Fig **a pregnant pause** una pausa cargada de significado

prehistoric(al) [pri:hı'stɒrık(əl)] adj prehistórico(a)

pre-installed [,pri:ın'stɔ:ld] adj [software] preinstalado(a)

prejudge [pri:'dʒʌdʒ] vt prejuzgar

prejudice ['predʒʊdıs] **1.** n [bias] prejuicio m; [harm] perjuicio m **2.** vt [bias] predisponer; [harm] perjudicar

prejudiced

prejudiced ['predʒʊdɪst] *adj* parcial; **to be prejudiced against/in favour of** estar predispuesto(a) en contra/a favor de

preliminary [prɪ'lɪmɪnərɪ] **1.** *adj* preliminar; SPORT [round] eliminatorio(a) **2.** *n* **preliminaries** preliminares *mpl*

prelude ['prelju:d] *n* preludio *m*

premature [premə'tjʊə(r), 'prematjʊə(r)] *adj* prematuro(a)

premeditate [prɪ'medɪteɪt] *vt* [crime] premeditar

premier ['premjə(r)] **1.** *n* POL primer(a) ministro(a) *m,f* **2.** *adj* primer, primero(a)

premiere ['premɪeə(r)] *n* CIN estreno *m*

premises ['premɪsɪz] *npl* local *m*; **on the premises** en el local

premium ['pri:mɪəm] *n* COMM, FIN & IND prima *f*; **to be at a premium** tener sobreprecio; *Fig* estar muy solicitado(a); *Br* **premium bonds** *bonos numerados emitidos por el Gobierno británico, cuyo comprador entra en un sorteo mensual de premios en metálico*

premonition [premə'nɪʃən] *n* presentimiento *m*

preoccupied [pri:'ɒkjʊpaɪd] *adj* preocupado(a); **to be preoccupied with sth** preocuparse por algo

pre-owned *adj* usado(a)

prepaid [pri:'peɪd] *adj* con el porte pagado

preparation [prepə'reɪʃən] *n* preparación *f*; [plan] preparativo *m*

preparatory [prɪ'pærətərɪ] *adj* preparatorio(a), preliminar; **preparatory school** *Br* colegio privado para alumnos de entre 7 y 13 años; *US* escuela secundaria privada

prepare [prɪ'peə(r)] **1.** *vt* preparar **2.** *vi* prepararse (**for** para); **to prepare to do sth** prepararse *or Am* alistarse para hacer algo

prepared [prɪ'peəd] *adj* [ready] preparado(a); **to be prepared to do sth** [willing] estar dispuesto(a) a hacer algo

preposition [prepə'zɪʃən] *n* preposición *f*

preposterous [prɪ'pɒstərəs] *adj* absurdo(a), ridículo(a)

preppie, preppy ['prepɪ] *(pl* **preppies)** *US Fam* **1.** *n* he's a preppie es un pijo **2.** *adj* pijo(a)

prerequisite [pri:'rekwɪzɪt] *n* condición *f* previa

prerogative [prɪ'rɒgətɪv] *n* prerrogativa *f*

preschool [,pri:'sku:l] **1.** *adj* preescolar **2.** *n US* educación *f* infantil

preschool [pri:'sku:l] *adj* preescolar

prescribe [prɪ'skraɪb] *vt* [set down] prescribir; MED recetar; *Fig* [recommend] recomendar

prescription [prɪ'skrɪpʃən] *n* MED receta *f*

presence ['prezəns] *n* presencia *f*; [attendance] asistencia *f*; *Fig* **presence of mind** presencia de ánimo

present[1] ['prezənt] **1.** *adj* **a)** [in attendance] presente; LING **present tense** (tiempo *m*) presente *m*; **to be present at** estar presente en **b)** [current] actual **2.** *n* [time] presente *m*, actualidad *f*; **at present** actualmente; **for the present** de momento; **up to the present** hasta ahora

present[2] **1.** [prɪ'zent] *vt* **a)** [give as gift] regalar; [medals, prizes etc] entregar; **to present sb with sth** obsequiar a algn con algo **b)** [report etc] presentar; [opportunity] ofrecer; [problems] plantear **c)** [introduce - person, programme] presentar **2.** ['prezənt] *n* [gift] regalo *m*; [formal] obsequio *m*

presentable [prɪ'zentəbəl] *adj* presentable; **to make oneself presentable** arreglarse

presentation [prezən'teɪʃən] *n* **a)** presentación *f*; **presentation ceremony** ceremonia *f* de entrega **b)** RADIO & TV representación *f*

present-day ['prezəntdeɪ] *adj* actual, de hoy en día

presenter [prɪ'zentə(r)] *n* RADIO locutor(a) *m,f*; TV presentador(a) *m,f*

presently ['prezəntlɪ] *adv* [soon] dentro de poco; *US* [now] ahora

preservation [prezə'veɪʃən] *n* conservación *f*

preservative [prɪ'zɜːvətɪv] *n* conservante *m*

preserve [prɪ'zɜːv] **1.** *vt* **a)** [keep] mantener **b)** CULIN conservar **2.** *n* **a)** [hunting] coto *m* **b)** CULIN conserva *f*

preside [prɪ'zaɪd] *vi* presidir

presidency ['prezɪdənsɪ] *n* presidencia *f*

president ['prezɪdənt] *n* POL presidente(a) *m,f*; *US* COMM director(a) *m,f*, gerente *mf*; **President's Day** el tercer lunes de febrero, día de fiesta en Estados Unidos en el que se conmemoran los cumpleaños de los presidentes Washington y Lincoln

presidential [prezɪ'denʃəl] *adj* presidencial

press [pres] **1.** *vt* **a)** apretar; [button] pulsar; [grapes] pisar; [trousers etc] planchar **b)** [urge] presionar; **to press sb to do sth** acosar a algn para que haga algo **2.** *vi* **a)** [push] apretar; **to press against sb/sth** apretarse contra algn/algo; **to press (down) on sth** hacer presión sobre algo **b)** [be urgent] **time is pressing** el tiempo apremia **3.** *n* **a)** [machine] prensa *f*; **to go to press** [newspaper] entrar en prensa **b)** PRESS **the press** la prensa; **press agency** agencia *f* de prensa; **press conference** rueda *f* de prensa ■ **press on** *vi* seguir adelante

pressed [prest] *adj* **to be (hard) pressed for** andar escaso(a) de; **I'd be hard pressed to do it** me costaría mucho hacerlo

pressing ['presɪŋ] *adj* apremiante, urgente

press-up ['presʌp] *n Br* flexión *f* (de brazos)

pressure ['preʃə(r)] *n* presión *f*; MED & MET **high/low pressure** altas/bajas presiones; **pressure cooker** olla *f* a presión; **pressure gauge** manómetro *m*; *Fig* **to bring pressure (to bear) on sb** ejercer presión sobre algn

pressurize ['preʃəraɪz] *vt Fig* presionar; **pressurized cabin** cabina presurizada

prestige [pre'stiːʒ] *n* prestigio *m*

prestigious [pres'tɪdʒəs] *adj* prestigioso(a)

presumably [prɪ'zjuːməblɪ] *adv* es de suponer que

presume [prɪ'zjuːm] **1.** *vt* suponer, presumir **2.** *vi* [suppose] suponer; **we presume so/not** suponemos que sí/no

presumption [prɪ'zʌmpʃən] *n* **a)** [supposition] suposición *f* **b)** [boldness] osadía *f*; [conceit] presunción *f*

pretence [prɪ'tens] *n* **a)** [deception] fingimiento *m*; **false pretences** estafa *f*; **under the pretence of** so pretexto de **b)** [claim] pretensión *f*

pretend [prɪ'tend] **1.** *vt* [feign] fingir, aparentar; [claim] pretender **2.** *vi* [feign] fingir

pretense [prɪ'tens] *US n* = **pretence**

pretentious [prɪ'tenʃəs] *adj* presuntuoso(a), pretencioso(a)

pretext ['priːtekst] *n* pretexto *m*; **on the pretext of** so pretexto de

pretty ['prɪtɪ] **1.** *(compar* **prettier,** *superl* **prettiest)** *adj* bonito(a), *Am* lindo(a) **2.** *adv Fam* bastante; **pretty much the same** más o menos lo mismo

prevail [prɪ'veɪl] *vi* **a)** predominar **b)** [win through] prevalecer **c) to prevail upon** *or* **on sb to do sth** [persuade] persuadir *or* convencer a algn para que haga algo

prevailing [prɪ'veɪlɪŋ] *adj* [wind] predominante; [opinion] general; [condition, fashion] actual

prevent [prɪ'vent] *vt* impedir; [accident] evitar; [illness] prevenir; **to prevent sb from doing sth** impedir a algn hacer algo; **to prevent sth from happening** evitar que pase algo

prevention [prɪ'venʃən] *n* prevención *f*

preview ['priːvjuː] n [of film etc] preestreno m

previous ['priːvɪəs] **1.** adj anterior, previo(a); **previous conviction** antecedente m penal **2.** adv **previous to going** antes de ir

previously ['priːvɪəslɪ] adv anteriormente, previamente

prey [preɪ] **1.** n presa f; Fig víctima f **2.** vi **to prey on** alimentarse de

price [praɪs] **1.** n precio m; **what price is that coat?** ¿cuánto cuesta el abrigo?; **price bracket** gama f de precios; **price bubble** burbuja f de precios; **price increase** alza f or aumento m de precios; **price list** lista f de precios; **price tag** etiqueta f **2.** vt [put price on] poner un precio a; [value] valorar

priceless ['praɪslɪs] adj que no tiene precio

pricey ['praɪsɪ] adj Fam carillo(a)

prick [prɪk] **1.** vt picar; **to prick one's finger** pincharse el dedo; Fig **to prick up one's ears** aguzar el oído **2.** n **a)** [with pin] pinchazo m **b)** Vulg [penis] Esp polla f, Am verga f, Méx pito m, RP pija f **c)** Vulg [person] Esp gilipollas mf inv, Am pendejo(a) m,f, RP forro m

prickly ['prɪklɪ] (compar **pricklier**, superl **prickliest**) adj espinoso(a); Fig [touchy] enojadizo(a); **prickly heat** sarpullido por causa del calor; **prickly pear** higo chumbo, Am tuna f

pride [praɪd] **1.** n orgullo m; [arrogance] soberbia f; **to take pride in sth** enorgullecerse de algo **2.** vt **to pride oneself on** enorgullecerse de

priest [priːst] n sacerdote m, cura m

prim [prɪm] (compar **primmer**, superl **primmest**) adj **prim (and proper)** remilgado(a)

primarily ['praɪmərɪlɪ] adv ante todo

primary ['praɪmərɪ] **1.** adj fundamental, principal; **of primary importance** primordial; **primary colour** color primario; **primary education/school** enseñanza/escuela primaria **2.** n US POL (elección f) primaria f

prime [praɪm] **1.** adj **a)** principal; [major] primordial; **Prime Minister** primer(a) ministro(a) m,f **b)** [first-rate] de primera; **prime number** número primo **2.** n **in the prime of life** en la flor de la vida **3.** vt [pump, engine] cebar; [surface] imprimar; Fig [prepare] preparar

primer[1] ['praɪmə(r)] n [textbook] cartilla f

primer[2] ['praɪmə(r)] n [paint] imprimación f

primitive ['prɪmɪtɪv] adj primitivo(a); [method, tool] rudimentario(a)

prince [prɪns] n príncipe m; **Prince Charming** Príncipe Azul

princess [prɪn'ses] n princesa f

principal ['prɪnsɪpəl] **1.** adj principal **2.** n SCH director(a) m,f; THEAT [in play] protagonista mf principal

principle ['prɪnsɪpəl] n principio m; **in principle** en principio; **on principle** por principio

print [prɪnt] **1.** vt **a)** imprimir; [publish] publicar; Fig grabar; **printed matter** impresos mpl **b)** [write] escribir con letra de imprenta **2.** n **a)** [of hand, foot] huella f **b)** [written text] letra f; **out of print** agotado(a) **c)** TEXT estampado m **d)** ART grabado m; PHOTO copia f ■ **print out** vt sep COMPUT imprimir

printer ['prɪntə(r)] n [person] impresor(a) m,f; [machine] impresora f

printing ['prɪntɪŋ] n [industry] imprenta f; [process] impresión f; [print run] tirada f; **printing press** prensa f

print-out ['prɪntaʊt] n COMPUT impresión f; [copy] copia impresa

prior ['praɪə(r)] adj previo(a), anterior; **prior to leaving** antes de salir

priority [praɪ'ɒrɪtɪ] n prioridad f

prison ['prɪzən] n cárcel f, prisión f

prisoner ['prɪzənə(r)] n preso(a) m,f; **to hold sb prisoner** detener a algn; **prisoner of war** prisionero(a) m,f de guerra

privacy ['praɪvəsɪ, 'prɪvəsɪ] n intimidad f

private ['praɪvɪt] **1.** adj privado(a); [secretary] particular; [matter] personal;

[letter] confidencial; **one's private life** la vida privada de uno; **private** [notice - on road] carretera privada; [on gate] propiedad privada; [on envelope] confidencial; **private detective,** *Fam* **private eye** detective *mf* privado(a); **private school** escuela privada **2.** *n* MIL soldado raso

privately ['praɪvɪtlɪ] *adv* en privado; [personally] personalmente

privatize ['praɪvɪtaɪz] *vt* privatizar

privilege ['prɪvɪlɪdʒ] *n* privilegio *m*

privileged ['prɪvɪlɪdʒd] *adj* privilegiado(a)

prize [praɪz] **1.** *n* premio *m* **2.** *adj* [first-class] de primera (categoría *or* clase) **3.** *vt* [value] apreciar, valorar

prizewinner ['praɪzwɪnə(r)] *n* premiado(a) *m,f*

pro¹ [prəʊ] *n* pro *m*; **the pros and cons of an issue** los pros y los contras de una cuestión

pro² [prəʊ] *n Fam* profesional *mf*, *Méx* profesionista *mf*

probability [prɒbə'bɪlɪtɪ] *n* probabilidad *f*

probable ['prɒbəbəl] *adj* probable

probably ['prɒbəblɪ] *adv* probablemente

probation [prə'beɪʃən] *n* JUR **to be on probation** estar en libertad condicional; **to be on two months' probation** [at work] trabajar dos meses de prueba

probe [prəʊb] **1.** *n* sonda *f*; [investigation] sondeo *m* **2.** *vt* MED sondar; [investigate] investigar ▪ **probe into** *vt insep* investigar

problem ['prɒbləm] *n* problema *m*

problematic(al) [prɒblə'mætɪk(əl)] *adj* problemático(a); **it's problematic(al)** tiene sus problemas

problem-free *adj* sin problemas

procedure [prə'si:dʒə(r)] *n* procedimiento *m*; [legal, business] gestión *f*, trámite *m*

proceed [prə'si:d] *vi* seguir, proceder; **to proceed to do sth** ponerse a hacer algo; **to proceed to the next matter** pasar a la siguiente cuestión

proceedings [prə'si:dɪŋz] *npl* [of meeting] actas *fpl*; [measures] medidas *fpl*; JUR proceso *m*

proceeds ['prəʊsi:dz] *npl* ganancias *fpl*

process ['prəʊses] **1.** *n* proceso *m*; [method] método *m*, sistema *m*; **in the process of** en vías de **2.** *vt* [information] tramitar; [food] tratar; COMPUT procesar

procession [prə'seʃən] *n* desfile *m*; REL procesión *f*

processor ['prəʊsesə(r)] *n* COMPUT procesador *m*

proclaim [prə'kleɪm] *vt* proclamar, declarar

prod [prɒd] *vt* [with stick etc] golpear; [push] empujar

prodigy ['prɒdɪdʒɪ] *n* prodigio *m*

produce 1. [prə'dju:s] *vt* **a)** producir; IND fabricar **b)** THEAT dirigir; RADIO & TV realizar; CIN producir **c)** [give birth to] dar a luz a **d)** [document] enseñar; [bring out] sacar **2.** ['prɒdju:s] *n* productos *mpl*; **produce of Spain** producto *m* de España

producer [prə'dju:sə(r)] *n* **a)** productor(a) *m,f*; IND fabricante *mf* **b)** THEAT director(a) *m,f* de escena; RADIO & TV realizador(a) *m,f*; CIN productor(a) *m,f*

product ['prɒdʌkt] *n* producto *m*

production [prə'dʌkʃən] *n* **a)** producción *f*; IND fabricación *f* **b)** THEAT representación *f*; RADIO & TV realización *f*; CIN producción *f*; **production line** cadena *f* de montaje

productive [prə'dʌktɪv] *adj* productivo(a)

productivity [prɒdʌk'tɪvɪtɪ] *n* productividad *f*

profession [prə'feʃən] *n* profesión *f*

professional [prə'feʃənəl] **1.** *adj* profesional ; [soldier] de profesión ; [polished] de gran calidad **2.** *n* profesional *mf*

professor [prə'fesə(r)] *n Br* UNIV catedrático(a) *m,f* ; *US* profesor(a) *m,f*

proficient [prə'fɪʃənt] *adj* [in language] experto(a) ; [in skill] hábil

profile ['prəʊfaɪl] *n* perfil *m* ; **in profile** de perfil

profit ['prɒfɪt] **1.** *n* **a)** beneficio *m*, ganancia *f* ; **to make a profit on** sacar beneficios de **b)** *Formal* [benefit] provecho *m* **2.** *vi Fig* sacar provecho ; **to profit from** aprovecharse de

profitable ['prɒfɪtəbəl] *adj* COMM rentable ; *Fig* [worthwhile] provechoso(a)

profound [prə'faʊnd] *adj* profundo(a)

programme ['prəʊgræm], *US* **program 1.** *n* [gen & COMPUT] programa *m* ; [plan] plan *m* **2.** *vt* **a)** [plan] planear, planificar **b)** COMPUT programar

programmer ['prəʊgræmə(r)] *n* programador(a) *m,f*

progress 1. ['prəʊgres] *n* progreso *m* ; [development] desarrollo *m* ; MED mejora *f* ; **to make progress** hacer progresos ; **in progress** en curso **2.** [prəʊ'gres] *vi* avanzar ; [develop] desarrollar ; [improve] hacer progresos ; MED mejorar

progressive [prə'gresɪv] *adj* [increasing] progresivo(a) ; POL progresista

prohibit [prə'hɪbɪt] *vt* prohibir ; **to prohibit sb from doing sth** prohibir a algn hacer algo

prohibitive [prə'hɪbɪtɪv] *adj* prohibitivo(a)

project 1. ['prɒdʒekt] *n* proyecto *m* ; [plan] plan *m* ; SCH trabajo *m* ; *US* **(housing) project** urbanización con viviendas de protección oficial **2.** [prə'dʒekt] *vt* proyectar, planear **3.** [prə'dʒekt] *vi* [stick out] sobresalir

projector [prə'dʒektə(r)] *n* CIN proyector *m*

prolific [prə'lɪfɪk] *adj* prolífico(a)

prologue ['prəʊlɒg] *n* prólogo *m*

prolong [prə'lɒŋ] *vt* prolongar

prom [prɒm] *n Br Fam* [seafront] paseo marítimo ; *Br* [concert] concierto sinfónico en que parte del público está de pie ; *US* [school dance] baile de fin de curso

promenade [prɒmə'nɑːd] **1.** *n Br* [at seaside] paseo marítimo **2.** *vi* pasearse

prominent ['prɒmɪnənt] *adj* [standing out] saliente ; *Fig* [important] importante ; [famous] eminente

promiscuous [prə'mɪskjʊəs] *adj* promiscuo(a)

promise ['prɒmɪs] **1.** *n* promesa *f* ; **to show promise** ser prometedor(a) **2.** *vt* & *vi* prometer

promising ['prɒmɪsɪŋ] *adj* prometedor(a)

promote [prə'məʊt] *vt* ascender ; [product] promocionar ; [ideas] fomentar ; FTBL **they've been promoted** han subido

promotion [prə'məʊʃən] *n* [in rank] promoción *f*, ascenso *m* ; [of product] promoción ; [of arts etc] fomento *m*

prompt ['prɒmpt] **1.** *adj* [quick] rápido(a) ; [punctual] puntual **2.** *adv* **at two o'clock prompt** a las dos en punto **3.** *vt* **a)** [motivate] incitar ; **to prompt sb to do sth** instar a algn a hacer algo **b)** [actor] apuntar

promptly [prɒmptlɪ] *adv* [quickly] rápidamente ; [punctually] puntualmente

prone [prəʊn] *adj* **a) to be prone to do sth** ser propenso(a) a hacer algo **b)** *Formal* [face down] boca abajo

pronoun ['prəʊnaʊn] *n* pronombre *m*

pronounce [prə'naʊns] **1.** *vt* pronunciar ; *Formal* [declare] declarar **2.** *vi Formal* **to pronounce on sth** opinar sobre algo

pronunciation [prənʌnsɪ'eɪʃən] *n* pronunciación *f*

proof [pruːf] **1.** *n* prueba *f* **2.** *adj* **a)** [secure] a prueba de **b) this rum is 70 per cent proof** este ron tiene 70 grados **3.** *vt* impermeabilizar

prop¹ [prɒp] **1.** n [support] puntal m; Fig sostén m **2.** vt [support] apoyar; Fig sostener ∎ **prop up** vt sep apoyar

prop² [prɒp] n Fam THEAT accesorio m

propaganda [prɒpə'gændə] n propaganda f

propel [prə'pel] vt propulsar

propeller [prə'pelə(r)] n hélice f

proper ['prɒpə(r)] adj **a)** adecuado(a), correcto(a); **the proper time** el momento oportuno **b)** [real] real, auténtico(a); [actual, exact] propiamente dicho(a) **c)** [characteristic] propio(a); LING **proper noun** nombre propio

properly ['prɒpəlɪ] adv [suitably, correctly, decently] correctamente; **it wasn't properly closed** no estaba bien cerrado(a); **she refused, quite properly** se negó, y con razón

property ['prɒpətɪ] n **a)** [quality] propiedad f **b)** [possession] propiedad f, posesión f; **personal property** bienes mpl; **public property** dominio público **c)** [estate] finca f

prophecy ['prɒfɪsɪ] n profecía f

prophet ['prɒfɪt] n profeta mf

proportion [prə'pɔːʃən] n proporción f; [part, quantity] parte f; **in proportion to** or **with** en proporción a

proportional [prə'pɔːʃənəl] adj proporcional (**to** a); POL **proportional representation** representación f proporcional

proportionate [prə'pɔːʃənɪt] adj proporcional

proposal [prə'pəʊzəl] n propuesta f; [suggestion] sugerencia f; **proposal of marriage** propuesta de matrimonio

propose [prə'pəʊz] **1.** vt proponer; [suggest] sugerir; Formal [intend] tener la intención de **2.** vi declararse

proposition [prɒpə'zɪʃən] n propuesta f; MATH proposición f

proprietor [prə'praɪətə(r)] n propietario(a) m,f

prose [prəʊz] n LITER prosa f; SCH texto m para traducir

prosecute ['prɒsɪkjuːt] vt procesar

prosecution [prɒsɪ'kjuːʃən] n [action] proceso m, juicio m; **the prosecution** la acusación

prospect **1.** ['prɒspekt] n [outlook] perspectiva f; [hope] esperanza f; **the job has prospects** es un trabajo con porvenir
2. [prə'spekt] vt explorar
3. [prə'spekt] vi **to prospect for gold / oil** buscar oro / petróleo

prospective [prə'spektɪv] adj [future] futuro(a); [possible] eventual, probable

prospectus [prə'spektəs] n prospecto m

prosper ['prɒspə(r)] vi prosperar

prosperity [prɒ'sperɪtɪ] n prosperidad f

prosperous ['prɒspərəs] adj próspero(a)

prostitute ['prɒstɪtjuːt] n prostituta f

protagonist [prəʊ'tægənɪst] n protagonista mf

protect [prə'tekt] vt proteger; [interests etc] salvaguardar; **to protect sb from sth** proteger a algn de algo

protection [prə'tekʃən] n protección f

protective [prə'tektɪv] adj protector(a)

protein ['prəʊtiːn] n proteína f

protest **1.** ['prəʊtest] n protesta f; [complaint] queja f **2.** [prə'test] vt US protestar en contra de **3.** [prə'test] vi Br protestar

Protestant ['prɒtɪstənt] adj & n protestante (mf)

protester [prə'testə(r)] n manifestante mf

protracted [prə'træktɪd] adj prolongado(a)

proud [praʊd] adj orgulloso(a); [arrogant] soberbio(a)

prove [pruːv] vt **a)** probar, demostrar; MATH comprobar; **to prove oneself** dar pruebas de valor **b)** **it proved to be disastrous** [turned out] resultó ser desastroso(a)

proverb ['prɒvɜːb] n refrán m, proverbio m

provide [prə'vaɪd] **1.** vt proporcionar; [supplies] suministrar, proveer **2.** vi proveer; **to provide for sb** mantener a algn

provided [prə'vaɪdɪd] conj **provided (that)** con tal de que

provider [prə'vaɪdə(r)] n **a)** [gen] proveedor(a) m,f; **she's the family's sole provider** ella es el único sostén de la familia **b)** COMPUT proveedor m

providing [prə'vaɪdɪŋ] conj = **provided**

province ['prɒvɪns] n provincia f; Fig [field of knowledge] campo m

provincial [prə'vɪnʃəl] **1.** adj provincial; Pej provinciano(a) **2.** n Pej [person] provinciano(a) m,f

provision [prə'vɪʒən] n provisión f; [supply] suministro m; **provisions** [food] provisiones fpl, víveres mpl

provisional [prə'vɪʒənəl] adj provisional

provocative [prə'vɒkətɪv] adj provocador(a); [flirtatious] provocativo(a)

provoke [prə'vəʊk] vt provocar

prowl [praʊl] **1.** n merodeo m; **to be on the prowl** merodear, rondar **2.** vi merodear; Fam **to prowl about** or **around** rondar

proxy ['prɒksɪ] n JUR [power] poderes mpl; [person] apoderado(a) m,f; **by proxy** por poderes

PRT MESSAGING (abbr of **party**) fsta

prudent ['pruːdənt] adj prudente

prudish ['pruːdɪʃ] adj remilgado(a)

prune¹ [pruːn] n ciruela pasa

prune² [pruːn] vt [roses etc] podar; Fig acortar

pry [praɪ] vi curiosear, husmear; **to pry into sb's affairs** meterse en asuntos ajenos

PS, ps [piː'es] (abbr of **postscript**) P.S., P.D.

pseudonym ['sjuːdənɪm] n (p)seudónimo m

psychiatric [saɪkɪ'ætrɪk] adj psiquiátrico(a)

psychiatrist [saɪ'kaɪətrɪst] n psiquiatra mf

psychiatry [saɪ'kaɪətrɪ] n psiquiatría f

psychic ['saɪkɪk] **1.** adj psíquico(a) **2.** n médium mf

psychoanalysis [saɪkəʊə'nælɪsɪs] n psicoanálisis f

psychological [saɪkə'lɒdʒɪkəl] adj psicológico(a)

psychologist [saɪ'kɒlədʒɪst] n psicólogo(a) m,f

psychology [saɪ'kɒlədʒɪ] n psicología f

psychopath ['saɪkəʊpæθ] n psicópata mf

PTB MESSAGING written abbr of **please text back**

PTO, pto [piːtiː'əʊ] (abbr of **please turn over**) sigue

pub [pʌb] n Br Fam bar m, pub m

puberty ['pjuːbətɪ] n pubertad f

public ['pʌblɪk] **1.** adj público(a); **to make sth public** hacer público algo; COMM **to go public** [company] salir a Bolsa; **public company** empresa pública; Br **public convenience** servicios mpl or Esp aseos mpl públicos; **public holiday** día f festivo or Am feriado; Br **public house** pub m, taberna f; Br **public limited company** sociedad anónima; **public opinion** opinión pública; **public property** [land, etc] bien m público; Br **public prosecutor** fiscal m; **public relations** relaciones públicas; **public school** Br colegio privado; US colegio público; **public transport** transporte público **2.** n **the public** el público; **in public** en público

publication [pʌblɪ'keɪʃən] n publicación f

publicity [pʌ'blɪsɪtɪ] n publicidad f

publicize ['pʌblɪsaɪz] vt [make public] hacer público(a); [advertise] hacer publicidad a

publish ['pʌblɪʃ] vt publicar, editar

publisher ['pʌblɪʃə(r)] n [person] editor(a) m,f; [firm] (casa f) editorial f

pudding ['pʊdɪŋ] n CULIN pudín m; Br [dessert] postre m; **Christmas pudding** pudín a base de frutos secos típico de Navidad; **pudding basin** cuenco m; **steamed pudding** budín m

puddle ['pʌdəl] n charco m

Puerto Rico [ˌpwɜːtəʊˈriːkəʊ] n Puerto Rico m

puff [pʌf] **1.** n [of wind] racha f; [of smoke] nube f; **puff pastry** pasta f de hojaldre
2. vi [person] jadear, resoplar; [train] echar humo; **to puff on a cigarette** dar chupadas or Esp caladas or Am pitadas a un cigarrillo
3. vt [cigarette] dar una calada a
■ **puff up** vi hincharse

puke [pjuːk] Fam vi echar la papa, devolver

pull [pʊl] **1.** n a) [act of pulling] tirón m, Am salvo RP jalón m; **to give sth a pull** dar un tirón or Am salvo RP jalón a algo b) [attraction] atracción f; [influence] enchufe m
2. vt a) [tug] dar un tirón or Am salvo RP jalón a; **to pull the trigger** apretar el gatillo; **to pull to pieces** hacer pedazos; Fig poner algo por los suelos; Fig **to pull sb's leg** tomar el pelo a algn b) [draw] tirar, arrastrar c) [draw out] sacar d) Fam [people] atraer
3. vi [drag] tirar, Am salvo RP jalar
■ **pull apart** vt sep desmontar; Fig [criticize] poner por los suelos
■ **pull down** vt sep [building] derribar
■ **pull in 1.** vt sep [crowds] atraer **2.** vi [train] entrar en la estación; [stop] parar
■ **pull off 1.** vt sep Fam [carry out] llevar a cabo **2.** vi [vehicle] arrancar
■ **pull out 1.** vt sep [withdraw] retirar **2.** vi AUTO **to pull out to overtake** salir para adelantar
■ **pull over** vi [driver] parar en, Esp el arcén or Méx el acotamiento or RP la banquina

■ **pull through** vi reponerse, restablecerse
■ **pull together** vt sep **to pull oneself together** calmarse
■ **pull up 1.** vt sep a) [uproot] desarraigar b) [chair] acercar **2.** vi [stop] pararse

pullover ['pʊləʊvə(r)] n suéter m, Esp jersey m, RP pulóver m

pulp [pʌlp] n [of paper, wood] pasta f; [of fruit] pulpa f

pulse¹ [pʌls] n ANAT pulso m

pulse² [pʌls] n BOT & CULIN legumbre f

pump¹ [pʌmp] **1.** n a) bomba f b) [gas, petrol station] surtidor m; **pump prices** precios mpl en surtidor **2.** vt bombear; **to pump sth in/out** meter / sacar algo con una bomba ■ **pump out** vt sep [empty] vaciar ■ **pump up** vt sep [tyre] inflar

pump² [pʌmp] n Br [shoe] zapatilla f

pumped [pʌmpt] adj US Fam excitado(a), emocionado(a)

pumpkin ['pʌmpkɪn] n calabaza f, Andes, RP zapallo m, Col, Carib ahuyama f

pun [pʌn] n juego m de palabras

punch¹ [pʌntʃ] **1.** n [for making holes] perforadora f; [for tickets] taladradora f; [for leather etc] punzón m **2.** vt [make hole in] perforar; [ticket] picar; [leather] punzar

punch² [pʌntʃ] **1.** n [blow] puñetazo m; [in boxing] pegada f; Fig **it lacks punch** le falta fuerza; **punch line** remate m (de un chiste) **2.** vt [with fist] dar un puñetazo a

punch³ [pʌntʃ] n [drink] ponche m

punctual ['pʌŋktjʊəl] adj puntual

punctuation [pʌŋktjʊˈeɪʃən] n puntuación f

puncture ['pʌŋktʃə(r)] **1.** n pinchazo m, Guat, Méx ponchadura f **2.** vt [tyre] pinchar, Guat, Méx ponchar

pungent ['pʌndʒənt] adj [smell] acre; [taste] fuerte

punish ['pʌnɪʃ] vt castigar

punishment ['pʌnɪʃmənt] n castigo m

punk [pʌŋk] *n Fam* **a)** punk *mf*; **punk music** música *f* punk **b)** *US* mamón *m*

punter ['pʌntə(r)] *n* [gambler] jugador(a) *m,f*; [customer] cliente *mf*

puny ['pju:nɪ] (*compar* **punier**, *superl* **puniest**) *adj* enclenque, endeble

pup [pʌp] *n* [young dog] cachorro *m*

pupil¹ ['pju:pəl] *n* SCH alumno(a) *m,f*

pupil² ['pju:pəl] *n* ANAT pupila *f*

puppet ['pʌpɪt] *n* títere *m*

puppy ['pʌpɪ] *n* cachorro(a) *m,f*, perrito *m*

purchase ['pɜ:tʃɪs] **1.** *n* compra *f* **2.** *vt* comprar; **purchasing power** poder adquisitivo

purchaser ['pɜ:tʃɪsə(r)] *n* comprador(a) *m,f*

pure [pjʊə(r)] *adj* puro(a)

purée ['pjʊəreɪ] *n* puré *m*

purely [pjʊəlɪ] *adv* simplemente

purge [pɜ:dʒ] **1.** *n* purga *f* **2.** *vt* purgar

purify ['pjʊərɪfaɪ] *vt* purificar

puritanical [pjʊərɪ'tænɪkəl] *adj* puritano(a)

purity ['pjʊərɪtɪ] *n* pureza *f*

purple ['pɜ:pəl] *adj* morado(a), purpúreo(a); **to go purple (in the face)** ponerse morado(a)

purpose ['pɜ:pəs] *n* **a)** propósito *m*, intención *f*; **on purpose** a propósito **b)** [use] utilidad *f*

purr [pɜ:(r)] *vi* [cat] ronronear; [engine] zumbar

purse [pɜ:s] **1.** *n Br* [for coins] monedero *m*; *US* [bag] *Esp* bolso *m*, *Col, CSur* cartera *f*, *Méx* bolsa *f*; [prize money] premio *m* en metálico **2.** *vt* **to purse one's lips** apretarse los labios

pursue [pə'sju:] *vt* [criminal] perseguir; [person] seguir; [pleasure] buscar; [career] ejercer

pursuit [pə'sju:t] *n* [of criminal] persecución *f*; [of animal] caza *f*; [of pleasure] búsqueda *f*; [pastime] pasatiempo *m*

push [pʊʃ] **1.** *n* empujón *m*, *CAm, Méx* aventón *m*; *Fig* [drive] brío *m*, dinamismo *m*

2. *vt* **a)** empujar; [button] pulsar, apretar; **to push one's finger into a hole** meter el dedo en un agujero

b) *Fig* [pressurize] instar; [harass] acosar; *Fam* **to be (hard) pushed for time** estar apurado(a) *or RP* corto de tiempo **c)** *Fam* [product] promover; **to push drugs** pasar droga

3. *vi* empujar

■ **push aside** *vt sep* [object] apartar

■ **push in** *vi* colarse

■ **push off** *vi* [in boat] desatracar; *Fam* **push off!** ¡lárgate!

■ **push on** *vi* [continue] seguir adelante

■ **push through** *vt sep* abrirse paso entre

pushchair ['pʊʃtʃeə(r)] *n Br* sillita *f* (de ruedas)

push-up ['pʊʃʌp] *n* flexión *f* (de brazos)

pushy ['pʊʃɪ] (*compar* **pushier**, *superl* **pushiest**) *adj Fam* agresivo(a)

puss [pʊs], **pussy** ['pʊsɪ] *n Fam* minino *m*

put [pʊt] (*pt & pp* **put**) **1.** *vt* **a)** poner; [place] colocar; [insert] meter; **to put to bed** acostar a; **to put a picture up on the wall** colgar un cuadro en la pared **b)** [present] presentar, exponer; **to put a question to sb** hacer una pregunta a algn

c) [express] expresar, decir; **to put sth simply** explicar algo de manera sencilla

d) [estimate] calcular

e) [money] ingresar; [invest] invertir

2. *vi* NAUT **to put to sea** zarpar

3. *adv* **to stay put** quedarse quieto(a)

■ **put about** *vt sep* [rumour] hacer correr

■ **put across** *vt sep* [idea etc] comunicar

■ **put aside** *vt sep* [money] ahorrar; [time] reservar

pyramid

■ **put away** *vt sep* [tidy away] recoger; *Fam* [eat] zamparse; [save money] ahorrar

■ **put back** *vt sep* [postpone] aplazar; **to put the clock back** retrasar la hora

■ **put by** *vt sep* [money] ahorrar

■ **put down** *vt sep* [set down] dejar; [suppress] sofocar; [humiliate] humillar; [criticize] criticar; [animal] provocar la muerte de; [write down] apuntar

■ **put down to** *vt sep* achacar a

■ **put forward** *vt sep* [theory] exponer; [proposal] hacer; **to put one's name forward for sth** presentarse como candidato(a) para algo

■ **put in 1.** *vt sep* [install] instalar; [complaint, request] presentar; [time] pasar **2.** *vi* NAUT hacer escala (**at** en)

■ **put off** *vt sep* [postpone] aplazar; **to put sb off doing sth** quitarle *or Am* sacarle a algn las ganas de hacer algo

■ **put on** *vt sep* [clothes] poner, ponerse; [show] montar; [concert] dar; [switch on - radio] poner; [light] encender, *Am* prender; [water, gas] abrir; **to put on weight** aumentar de peso; **to put on the brakes** frenar; *Fig* **to put on a straight face** poner cara de serio(a)

■ **put out** *vt sep* [light, fire] apagar; [place outside] sacar; [extend - arm] extender; [tongue] sacar; [hand] tender; [spread - rumour] hacer correr; [annoy] molestar; [inconvenience] incordiar; [anger] **to be put out by sth** enojarse por algo

■ **put through** *vt sep* TEL **put me through to Pat, please** póngame con Pat, por favor

■ **put together** *vt sep* [join] unir, reunir; [assemble] armar, montar

■ **put up** *vt sep* [raise] levantar, subir; [picture] colocar; [curtains] colgar; [building] construir; [tent] armar; [prices] subir, aumentar; [accommodate] alojar, hospedar; **to put up a fight** ofrecer resistencia

■ **put up to** *vt sep* **to put sb up to sth** incitar a algn a hacer algo

■ **put up with** *vt insep* aguantar, soportar

puzzle ['pʌzəl] **1.** *n* rompecabezas *m inv*; [crossword] crucigrama *m*; *Fig* [mystery] misterio *m* **2.** *vt* dejar perplejo(a); **to be puzzled about sth** no entender algo ■ **puzzle over** *vt insep* **to puzzle over sth** dar vueltas a algo (en la cabeza)

PVC [pi:vi:'si:] *n (abbr of* **polyvinyl chloride***)* PVC *m*

pwn [pəʊn] *v Fam* dar una paliza a *(durante un juego de internet)*

pyjamas [pə'dʒɑːməz] *npl* pijama *m*, *Am* piyama *m or f*

pylon ['paɪlən] *n* torre *f* (de conducción eléctrica)

pyramid ['pɪrəmɪd] *n* pirámide *f*

Q

Q, q [kjuː] *n* [the letter] Q, q *f*

QPSA? MESSAGING *written abbr of* **qué pasa?**

quack [kwæk] **1.** *n* **a)** [of duck] graznido *m* **b)** *Br Fam, Pej or Hum* [doctor] matasanos *m inv* **2.** *vi* graznar

quad *n* **quad bike** (moto *f*) quad *m*

quadruple [ˈkwɒdrʊpəl, kwɒˈdruːpəl] **1.** *n* cuádruplo *m* **2.** *adj* cuádruple **3.** *vt* cuadruplicar **4.** *vi* cuadruplicarse

quaint [kweɪnt] *adj* [picturesque] pintoresco(a); [original] singular

quake [kweɪk] **1.** *vi* temblar **2.** *n Fam* temblor *m* de tierra

Quaker [ˈkweɪkə(r)] *n* cuáquero(a) *m,f*

qualification [kwɒlɪfɪˈkeɪʃən] *n* **a)** [ability] aptitud *f* **b)** [requirement] requisito *m* **c)** [diploma etc] título *m* **d)** [reservation] reserva *f*

qualified [ˈkwɒlɪfaɪd] *adj* **a)** capacitado(a); **qualified teacher** profesor titulado **b)** [modified] **qualified approval** aprobación *f* condicional

qualify [ˈkwɒlɪfaɪ] **1.** *vt* **a)** [entitle] capacitar **b)** [modify] modificar; [statement] matizar; LING calificar **2.** *vi* **a)** **to qualify as** [doctor etc] sacar el título de; **when did you qualify?** ¿cuándo terminaste la carrera? **b)** [in competition] quedar clasificado(a)

quality [ˈkwɒlɪtɪ] *n* **a)** [excellence] calidad *f*; **quality control** control *m* de calidad; *Br* **quality newspapers** prensa *f* no sensacionalista **b)** [attribute] cualidad *f*

qualm [kwɑːm] *n* **a)** [scruple] escrúpulo *m*, reparo *m* **b)** [pang of nausea] náusea *f*

quantity [ˈkwɒntɪtɪ] *n* cantidad *f*

quarantine [ˈkwɒrəntiːn] *n* cuarentena *f*

quarrel [ˈkwɒrəl] **1.** *n* [argument] riña *f*, pelea *f*; [disagreement] desacuerdo *m* **2.** *vi* [argue] pelearse, reñir; **to quarrel with sth** discrepar de algo

quarry¹ [ˈkwɒrɪ] **1.** *n* MINING cantera *f* **2.** *vt* MINING extraer

quarry² [ˈkwɒrɪ] *n* presa *f*

quart [kwɔːt] *n* [measurement] *cuarto de galón* (*Br* = 1,13 *l*; *US* = 0,94 *l*)

quarter [ˈkwɔːtə(r)] **1.** *n* **a)** cuarto *m*, cuarta parte; **a quarter of an hour** un cuarto de hora

b) *Br* **it's a quarter to three**, *US* **it's a quarter of three** son las tres menos cuarto; **it's a quarter past** *Br* *or US* **after six** son las seis y cuarto **c)** *US* [coin] cuarto *m* (de dólar) **d)** [district] barrio *m* **e)** [of moon] cuarto *m* **f)** **quarters** [lodgings] alojamiento *m* **g)** *US* MUS **quarter note** negra *f* **2.** *vt* **a)** [cut into quarters] dividir en cuartos **b)** [accommodate] alojar

quarterback [ˈkwɔːtəbæk] *n US* quarterback *m*, *Méx* mariscal *m* de campo

quarterfinal [ˈkwɔːtəfaɪnəl] *n* SPORT cuarto *m* de final

quarterly [ˈkwɔːtəlɪ] **1.** *adj* trimestral **2.** *n* publicación *f* trimestral **3.** *adv* trimestralmente

quartet(te) [kwɔːˈtet] *n* cuarteto *m*

quartz [kwɔːts] *n* cuarzo *m*; **quartz watch** reloj *m* de cuarzo

quash [kwɒʃ] *vt* JUR anular; [uprising] aplastar

quay(side) [ˈkiː(saɪd)] *n* muelle *m*

queasy ['kwi:zɪ] *(compar* queasier, *superl* queasiest) *adj* to feel queasy [ill] tener náuseas

queen [kwi:n] *n* a) reina *f* b) *Fam & Pej* loca *f*, marica *m*

queer [kwɪə(r)] **1.** *adj* [strange] extraño(a), raro(a) **2.** *n Fam & Pej* marica *m*, maricón *m*

quench [kwentʃ] *vt* apagar

query ['kwɪərɪ] **1.** *n* [question] pregunta *f* **2.** *vt* [ask questions about] preguntar acerca de ; [have doubts about] poner en duda

quest [kwest] *n Liter* búsqueda *f*

question ['kwestʃən] **1.** *n* pregunta *f*; **question mark** signo *m* de interrogación ; *Fig* interrogante *m*; **to ask sb a question** hacer una pregunta a algn; **he did it without question** lo hizo sin rechistar; **to call sth into question** poner algo en duda; **that's out of the question!** ¡ni hablar!; **the... in question** le /la /los /las... en cuestión **2.** *vt* [ask questions of] hacer preguntas a ; [interrogate] interrogar ; [query] poner en duda

questionable ['kwestʃənəbəl] *adj* [doubtful] dudoso(a) ; [debatable] discutible

questionnaire [kwestʃə'neə(r)] *n* cuestionario *m*

queue [kju:] *Br* **1.** *n* cola *f* **2.** *vi* to queue (up) hacer cola

quiche [ki:ʃ] *n* quiche *m or f*

quick [kwɪk] **1.** *adj* a) [fast] rápido(a) ; a quick look un vistazo ; a quick snack un bocado ; be quick! ¡date prisa!, *Am* ¡apúrate! b) [clever] espabilado(a) ; [wit] agudo(a) c) she has a quick temper se enfada con nada **2.** *adv Fam* rápido, rápidamente

quick-drying *adj* [paint, concrete] de secado rápido

quicken ['kwɪkən] **1.** *vt* acelerar ; to quicken one's pace acelerar el paso **2.** *vi* [speed up] acelerarse

quickfire ['kwɪkfaɪə(r)] *adj* he directed quickfire questions at me me ametralló a preguntas ; a series of quickfire questions una ráfaga de preguntas

quickie ['kwɪkɪ] *n Fam* [gen] uno *m* rápido

quickly ['kwɪklɪ] *adv* rápidamente, de prisa

quicksand ['kwɪksænd] *n* arenas *fpl* movedizas

quick-setting *adj* [cement] de endurecimiento rápido ; [jelly] de cuajado rápido

quid [kwɪd] *(pl* quid) *n Br Fam* [pound] libra *f*

quiet ['kwaɪət] **1.** *n* a) [silence] silencio *m* b) [calm] tranquilidad *f* **2.** *adj* a) [silent] silencioso(a) ; [street] tranquilo(a) ; **keep quiet!** ¡silencio! b) [calm] tranquilo(a) c) [person] reservado(a) d) [not showy - clothes] sobrio(a) ; [colours] apagado(a) **3.** *vt US* calmar **4.** *vi US* calmarse
■ **quiet down 1.** *vt sep* calmar, tranquilizar **2.** *vi* calmarse

quieten ['kwaɪətən] **1.** *vt* [silence] callar ; [calm] calmar **2.** *vi* [silence] callarse ; [calm] calmarse ■ **quieten down** *Br* **1.** *vt sep* calmar **2.** *vi* calmarse

quietly ['kwaɪətlɪ] *adv* a) [silently] silenciosamente ; **he spoke quietly** habló en voz baja b) [calmly] tranquilamente c) [discreetly] discretamente

quilt [kwɪlt] **1.** *n* edredón *m* **2.** *vt* acolchar

quip [kwɪp] **1.** *n* salida *f* ; [joke] chiste *m* **2.** *vi* bromear

quit [kwɪt] *(pt & pp* quitted *or* quit) **1.** *vt* a) [leave] dejar, abandonar b) COMPUT salir ; **to quit an application** salir de un programa c) **quit making that noise!** ¡deja de hacer ese ruido! **2.** *vi* a) [go] irse ; [give up] dimitir b) [cease] dejar de hacer algo c) COMPUT salir **3.** *adj* **let's call it quits** dejémoslo estar

quite [kwaɪt] *adv* **a)** [entirely] totalmente; **she's quite right** tiene toda la razón **b)** [rather] bastante; **quite a while** un buen rato; **that's quite enough!** ¡ya está bien!; **it's quite something** es increíble **c)** [exactly] exactamente; **quite (so)!** ¡en efecto!, ¡exacto!

quiver¹ [ˈkwɪvə(r)] *vi* temblar

quiver² [ˈkwɪvə(r)] *n* [for arrows] aljaba *f*, carcaj *m*

quiz [kwɪz] **1.** *n* RADIO & TV **quiz show** concurso *m* **2.** *vt* hacer preguntas a

quota [ˈkwəʊtə] *n* **a)** [proportional share] cuota *f*, parte *f* **b)** [prescribed amount, number] cupo *m*

quotation [kwəʊˈteɪʃən] *n* **a)** LITER cita *f*; **quotation marks** comillas *fpl* **b)** FIN cotización *f*

quote [kwəʊt] **1.** *vt* **a)** [cite] citar **b)** COMM **to quote a price** dar un presupuesto **c)** FIN cotizar **2.** *n* **a)** LITER cita *f* **b)** COMM presupuesto *m*

R

R, r [ɑː(r)] *n* [the letter] R, r *f*

rabbi ['ræbaɪ] *n* rabí *m*, rabino *m*

rabbit ['ræbɪt] **1.** *n* conejo(a) *m,f*; **rabbit hutch** conejera *f* **2.** *vi Fam* **to rabbit (on)** enrollarse

rabies ['reɪbiːz] *n* rabia *f*

raccoon [rə'kuːn] *n* mapache *m*

race¹ [reɪs] **1.** *n* **a)** SPORT carrera *f*; **race bike** moto *f* de carreras
b) *Br* **the races** las carreras (de caballos)
2. *vt* **a)** **I'll race you!** ¡te echo una carrera!
b) [car, horse] hacer correr
c) [engine] acelerar
3. *vi* [go quickly] correr; [pulse] acelerarse

race² [reɪs] *n* [people] raza *f*

racecourse ['reɪskɔːs] *n Br* hipódromo *m*

racehorse ['reɪshɔːs] *n* caballo *m* de carreras

racetrack ['reɪstræk] *n* [for cars, people, bikes] pista *f*; *US* [for horses] hipódromo *m*

racial ['reɪʃəl] *adj* racial

racing ['reɪsɪŋ] **1.** *n* carreras *fpl* **2.** *adj* de carreras; **racing bicycle** bicicleta *f* de carreras; **racing car** coche *m or Am* carro *m or CSur* auto *m* de carreras

racism ['reɪsɪzəm] *n* racismo *m*

racist ['reɪsɪst] *adj & n* racista (*mf*)

rack [ræk] **1.** *n* **a)** [shelf] estante *m*; [for clothes] percha *f*; **dish rack** escurreplatos *m inv*; **luggage rack** portaequipajes *m inv*; **roof rack** baca *f* **b)** [for torture] potro *m* **2.** *vt Liter* [torment] atormentar; *Fam & Fig* **to rack one's brains** devanarse los sesos

racket¹ ['rækɪt] *n* **a)** [din] estruendo *m*, *Esp* jaleo *m* **b)** [swindle] timo *m*; [shady business] chanchullo *m*

racket² ['rækɪt] *n* SPORT raqueta *f*

radar ['reɪdɑː(r)] *n* radar *m*; **radar speed check** control *m* por radar

radiant ['reɪdɪənt] *adj* radiante, resplandeciente

radiate ['reɪdɪeɪt] *vt* irradiar; *Fig* **she radiated happiness** rebosaba de alegría

radiation [reɪdɪ'eɪʃən] *n* radiación *f*

radiator ['reɪdɪeɪtə(r)] *n* radiador *m*

radical ['rædɪkəl] *adj* radical

radio ['reɪdɪəʊ] *n* radio *f*; **on the radio** en *or* por la radio; **radio station** emisora *f* (de radio)

radioactive [reɪdɪəʊ'æktɪv] *adj* radiactivo(a)

radish ['rædɪʃ] *n* rábano *m*

radius ['reɪdɪəs] *n* radio *m*; **within a radius of** en un radio de

RAF [ɑːreɪ'ef] *n Br (abbr of Royal Air Force)* fuerzas aéreas británicas

raffle ['ræfəl] **1.** *n* rifa *f* **2.** *vt* rifar

raft [rɑːft] *n* balsa *f*

rag [ræg] *n* **a)** [torn piece] harapo *m* **b)** [for cleaning] trapo *m* **c)** *Fam* **rags** [clothes] trapos *mpl* **d)** *Pej* PRESS periodicucho *m*

rage [reɪdʒ] **1.** *n* **a)** [fury] cólera *f* **b)** *Fam* **it's all the rage** hace furor **2.** *vi* **a)** [person] rabiar, estar furioso(a) **b)** *Fig* [storm, sea] rugir; [wind] bramar

ragged ['rægɪd] *adj* **a)** [clothes] hecho(a) jirones **b)** [person] harapiento(a) **c)** [edge] mellado(a) **d)** *Fig* [uneven] desigual

ragtop ['rægtɒp] *n US Fam* AUTO descapotable *m*

raid [reɪd] **1.** n MIL incursión f; [by police] redada f; [robbery etc] atraco m **2.** vt MIL hacer una incursión en; [police] hacer una redada en; [rob] asaltar; Fam **to raid the larder** vaciar la despensa

rail [reɪl] n **a)** barra f **b)** [railing] baranda f, Esp barandilla f **c)** RAIL carril f; **by rail** [send sth] por ferrocarril; [travel] en tren

railing ['reɪlɪŋ] n (usu pl) verja f

railroad ['reɪlrəʊd] n US ferrocarril m

railway ['reɪlweɪ] n Br ferrocarril m; **railway line, railway track** vía férrea; **railway station** estación f de ferrocarril

rain [reɪn] **1.** n lluvia f; **in the rain** bajo la lluvia **2.** vi llover; **it's raining** llueve

rainbow ['reɪnbəʊ] n arco m iris

raincoat ['reɪnkəʊt] n impermeable m

rainfall ['reɪnfɔːl] n [falling of rain] precipitación f; [amount] pluviosidad f

rainforest ['reɪnfɒrɪst] n selva f tropical

rainy ['reɪnɪ] (compar rainier, superl rainiest) adj lluvioso(a)

raise [reɪz] **1.** n US aumento m (de sueldo) **2.** vt **a)** levantar; [glass] brindar; [voice] subir **b)** [prices] aumentar **c)** [money, help] reunir **d)** [issue] plantear **e)** [crops, children] criar **f)** [standards] mejorar

raisin ['reɪzən] n pasa f

rake¹ [reɪk] **1.** n [garden tool] rastrillo m; [for fire] hurgón m **2.** vt [leaves] rastrillar; [fire] hurgar; [with machine gun] barrer

rake² [reɪk] n [dissolute man] calavera m, libertino m

rally ['rælɪ] **1.** n **a)** [gathering] reunión f; POL mitin m **b)** AUTO rallye m **c)** [in tennis] jugada f **2.** vt [support] reunir **3.** vi recuperarse ▪ **rally round** vi formar una piña

ram [ræm] **1.** n **a)** ZOOL carnero m **b)** TECH maza f **2.** vt **a)** [drive into place] hincar; [cram] embutir; Fam **to ram sth home** hacer algo patente **b)** [crash into] chocar con

ramble ['ræmbəl] **1.** n [walk] caminata f **2.** vi **a)** [walk] hacer una excursión a pie **b)** Fig [digress] divagar

rambler ['ræmblə(r)] n **a)** [person] excursionista mf **b)** BOT rosal m trepador

rambling ['ræmblɪŋ] adj **a)** [incoherent] incoherente **b)** [house] laberíntico(a) **c)** BOT trepador(a)

ramp [ræmp] n **a)** rampa f; **access ramp** rampa f de acceso **b)** [to plane] escalerilla f

rampant ['ræmpənt] adj incontrolado(a); **corruption is rampant** la corrupción está muy extendida

ran [ræn] pt of **run**

ranch [rɑːntʃ] n US rancho m, hacienda f

rancid ['rænsɪd] adj rancio(a)

random ['rændəm] **1.** n **at random** al azar **2.** adj fortuito(a); **random selection** selección hecha al azar

rang [ræŋ] pt of **ring**

range [reɪndʒ] **1.** n **a)** [of mountains] cordillera f, sierra f **b)** US [open land] pradera f **c)** [choice] surtido m; [of products] gama f **d) firing range** campo m de tiro **e)** [of missile] alcance m; **at close range** de cerca **f)** [cooker] fogón m, cocina f or Col, Méx, Ven estufa f de carbón **2.** vi [extend] extenderse (**to** hasta); **prices range from £5 to £20** los precios oscilan entre 5 y 20 libras

rank¹ [ræŋk] **1.** n **a)** MIL [row] fila f; **the ranks** los soldados rasos **b)** [position in army] graduación f; [in society] rango m **c)** Br **(taxi) rank** parada f de taxis **2.** vt [classify] clasificar **3.** vi [figure] figurar; **to rank above / below sb** figurar por encima /debajo de algn; **to rank with** estar al mismo nivel que

rank² [ræŋk] adj Formal [foul-smelling] fétido(a)

-ranking suff **high-ranking** de alto rango; **low-ranking** de bajo rango

ransack ['rænsæk] vt [plunder] saquear; [rummage in] registrar

ransom ['rænsəm] n rescate m; **to hold sb to ransom** pedir rescate por algn; Fig poner a algn entre la espada y la pared

rant [rænt] vi vociferar; Fam **to rant and rave** pegar gritos

rap [ræp] **1.** n a) [blow] golpe m seco; [on door] golpecito m b) MUS rap **2.** vt & vi [knock] golpear

rape¹ [reɪp] **1.** n JUR violación f **2.** vt JUR violar

rape² [reɪp] n BOT colza f

rapid ['ræpɪd] **1.** adj rápido(a) **2.** n **rapids** [in river] rápidos mpl

rapist ['reɪpɪst] n violador(a) m,f

rare¹ [reə(r)] adj raro(a), poco común

rare² [reə(r)] adj [steak] poco hecho(a)

rarely ['reəlɪ] adv raras veces

raring ['reərɪŋ] adj Fam **to be raring to do sth** morirse de ganas de hacer algo

rarity ['reərɪtɪ] n rareza f

rascal ['rɑːskəl] n granuja mf

rash¹ [ræʃ] n a) MED erupción f, sarpullido m b) Fig [of robberies etc] racha f

rash² [ræʃ] adj [reckless] impetuoso(a); [words, actions] precipitado(a), imprudente

rasher ['ræʃə(r)] n Br **rasher (of bacon)** loncha f de tocino or Esp beicon

raspberry ['rɑːzbərɪ] n frambuesa f

rat [ræt] n a) [animal] rata f; **rat poison** raticida m b) US Fam [informer] soplón(ona) m,f, chivato(a) m,f

rate [reɪt] **1.** n a) [ratio] índice m, tasa f; **at any rate** [at least] al menos; [anyway] en cualquier caso
b) [cost] precio m; FIN [of interest, exchange] tipo m, tasa f
c) **at the rate of** [speed] a la velocidad de; [quantity] a razón de
d) Br **(business) rates** impuestos mpl municipales (para empresas) **2.** vt a) [estimate] estimar
b) [evaluate] tasar
c) [consider] considerar

rather ['rɑːðə(r)] adv a) [quite] más bien, bastante; [very much so] muy b) [more accurately] mejor dicho; **rather than** [instead of] en vez de; [more than] más que c) **she would rather stay here** [prefer to] prefiere quedarse aquí

ratify ['rætɪfaɪ] vt ratificar

rating ['reɪtɪŋ] n a) [valuation] tasación f; [score] valoración f b) TV **(programme) ratings** índice m de audiencia c) NAUT marinero m sin graduación

ratio ['reɪʃɪəʊ] n razón f; **in the ratio of** a razón de

ration ['ræʃən] **1.** n a) [allowance] ración f b) **rations** víveres mpl **2.** vt racionar

rational ['ræʃənəl] adj racional

rationalize ['ræʃənəlaɪz] vt racionalizar

rattle ['rætəl] **1.** n a) [of train, cart] traqueteo m; [of metal] repiqueteo m; [of glass] tintineo m
b) [toy] sonajero m; [instrument] carraca f
2. vt a) [keys etc] hacer sonar
b) Fam [unsettle] poner nervioso(a)
3. vi sonar; [metal] repiquetear; [glass] tintinear

raucous ['rɔːkəs] adj estridente

rave [reɪv] **1.** vi a) [be delirious] delirar
b) [be angry] enfurecerse (at con) c) Fam [show enthusiasm] entusiasmarse (about por) **2.** n Fam **rave review** crítica f muy favorable

raven ['reɪvən] n cuervo m

ravenous ['rævənəs] adj **I'm ravenous** tengo un hambre que no veo

ravine [rə'viːn] n barranco m

raving ['reɪvɪŋ] n Fam **raving mad** loco(a) de atar

raw [rɔː] adj a) [uncooked] crudo(a)
b) [not processed] bruto(a); **raw material** materia prima c) [emotion] instintivo(a) d) **raw deal** trato injusto
e) US [inexperienced] novato(a)

ray¹ [reɪ] n rayo m; Fig **ray of hope** rayo de esperanza

ray² [reɪ] n [fish] raya f

rayon ['reɪɒn] n rayón m

razor ['reɪzə(r)] n [for shaving] maquinilla f de afeitar; **razor blade** hoja f de afeitar

Rd (abbr of Road) calle f, c /

re [ri:] prep respecto a, con referencia a

reach [ri:tʃ] **1.** vt a) [arrive at] llegar a b) [contact] localizar **2.** vi alcanzar; **to reach for sth** (tratar de) alcanzar algo; **to reach out** extender la mano **3.** n alcance m; **out of reach** fuera del alcance; **within reach** al alcance

react [rɪ'ækt] vi reaccionar

reaction [rɪ'ækʃən] n reacción f

reactionary [rɪ'ækʃənərɪ] n & adj reaccionario(a) (m,f)

reactor [rɪ'æktə(r)] n reactor m

read [ri:d] (pt & pp read [red]) **1.** vt a) leer b) Br UNIV estudiar c) [of dial] marcar; [of signpost, text] decir **2.** vi leer ■ **read out** vt sep leer en voz alta

readable ['ri:dəbəl] adj a) [interesting] interesante b) [legible] legible

reader ['ri:də(r)] n a) lector(a) m,f b) [book] libro m de lectura c) Br UNIV profesor(a) m,f adjunto(a)

readily ['redɪlɪ] adv a) [easily] fácilmente; **readily available** disponible en el acto b) [willingly] de buena gana

reading ['ri:dɪŋ] n a) lectura f; **reading light** lámpara f para leer b) Fig interpretación f c) [of laws, bill] presentación f

ready ['redɪ] adj a) [prepared] listo(a), preparado(a); **ready, steady, go!** ¡preparados, listos, ya! b) **ready to** [about to] a punto de c) [to hand] a mano; **ready cash** dinero m en efectivo d) [willing] dispuesto(a)

ready-made ['redɪ'meɪd] adj confeccionado(a); [food] preparado(a)

real [rɪəl] adj a) real, verdadero(a); Fam **for real** de veras b) [genuine] auténtico(a); **real leather** piel legítima c) US COMM **real estate** bienes mpl inmuebles; **real estate agent** agente inmobiliario

realistic ['rɪəlɪstɪk] adj realista

reality [rɪ'ælɪtɪ] n realidad f; **reality TV** telerrealidad f; **in reality** en realidad

realization [rɪəlaɪ'zeɪʃən] n a) [understanding] comprensión f b) [of plan, assets] realización f

realize ['rɪəlaɪz] vt a) [become aware of] darse cuenta de b) [assets, plan] realizar

really ['rɪəlɪ] adv verdaderamente, realmente; **I really don't know** no lo sé de verdad; **really?** ¿de veras?

realtor ['rɪəltə(r)] n US agente mf inmobiliario(a)

reap [ri:p] vt AGR cosechar; Fig **to reap the benefits** llevarse los beneficios

reappear [ri:ə'pɪə(r)] vi reaparecer

rear¹ [rɪə(r)] **1.** n a) [back part] parte f de atrás b) Fam [buttocks] trasero m **2.** adj trasero(a); **rear entrance** puerta f de atrás

rear² [rɪə(r)] **1.** vt a) [breed, raise] criar b) [lift up] levantar **2.** vi **to rear up** [horse] encabritarse

rearrange [ri:ə'reɪndʒ] vt a) [furniture] colocar de otra manera b) [appointment] fijar otra fecha para

rear-view ['rɪəvju:] adj **rear-view mirror** (espejo m) retrovisor m

reason ['ri:zən] **1.** n a) motivo m, razón f; **for no reason** sin razón; **for some reason** por algún motivo b) [good sense] razón f; **it stands to reason** es lógico; **to listen to reason** atender a razones, Am atender razones **2.** vi a) **to reason with sb** convencer a algn b) [argue, work out] razonar

reasonable ['ri:zənəbəl] adj a) [fair] razonable b) [sensible] sensato(a) c) [average] regular

reasonably ['ri:zənəblɪ] adv [fairly] bastante

reasoning ['ri:zənɪŋ] n razonamiento m

reassure [ri:ə'ʃʊə(r)] vt a) [comfort] tranquilizar b) [restore confidence] dar confianza a

reassuring [ri:ə'ʃʊərɪŋ] adj consolador(a)

rebate ['ri:beɪt] n devolución f; **tax rebate** devolución fiscal

rebel 1. ['rebəl] adj & n rebelde (mf) **2.** [rɪ'bel] vi rebelarse, sublevarse (**against** contra)

rebellion [rɪ'beljən] n rebelión f

reboot [,ri:'bu:t] vi COMPUT reiniciar, reinicializar, resetear

rebound 1. ['ri:baʊnd] n [of ball] rebote m; Fig **on the rebound** de rebote **2.** [rɪ'baʊnd] vi [ball] rebotar

rebuild [ri:'bɪld] vt reconstruir

rebuke [rɪ'bju:k] **1.** n reproche m **2.** vt reprochar

recall [rɪ'kɔ:l] vt **a)** [soldiers, products] hacer volver; [ambassador] retirar **b)** [remember] recordar

recap 1. [ri:'kæp] vt & vi resumir; **to recap** en resumen **2.** ['ri:kæp] n recapitulación f

recede [rɪ'si:d] vi retroceder; **to have a receding hairline** tener entradas

receipt [rɪ'si:t] n **a)** [act] recepción f; **to acknowledge receipt of sth** acusar recibo de algo **b)** COMM [paper] recibo m **c) receipts** [takings] recaudación f

receive [rɪ'si:v] vt **a)** recibir **b)** JUR [stolen goods] ocultar **c)** [welcome] acoger **d)** TV & RADIO captar

receiver [rɪ'si:və(r)] n **a)** [person] receptor(a) m,f **b)** JUR [of stolen goods] perista mf **c)** [of telephone] auricular m, RP, Ven tubo m

recent ['ri:sənt] adj reciente; **in recent years** en los últimos años

recently ['ri:səntlɪ] adv hace poco, recientemente

reception [rɪ'sepʃən] n **a)** [welcome] recibimiento m **b)** [party] recepción f; **wedding reception** banquete m de boda or Andes matrimonio or RP casamiento **c) reception (desk)** recepción f **d)** RADIO & TV recepción f

receptionist [rɪ'sepʃənɪst] n recepcionista mf

receptive [rɪ'septɪv] adj receptivo(a)

recess ['ri:ses, rɪ'ses] n **a)** [in a wall] hueco m **b)** [secret place] escondrijo m **c)** US SCH recreo m; POL período m de vacaciones

recession [rɪ'seʃən] n recesión f

recharge [ri:'tʃɑ:dʒ] vt [battery] recargar

recipe ['resɪpɪ] n CULIN receta f; Fig fórmula f

recipient [rɪ'sɪpɪənt] n receptor(a) m,f; [of letter] destinatario(a) m,f

reciprocate [rɪ'sɪprəkeɪt] **1.** vt [favour etc] devolver **2.** vi hacer lo mismo

recital [rɪ'saɪtəl] n recital m

recite [rɪ'saɪt] vt & vi recitar

reckless ['reklɪs] adj [unwise] imprudente; [fearless] temerario(a)

reckon ['rekən] vt & vi **a)** [calculate] calcular; [count] contar **b)** Fam [think] creer; [consider] considerar ■ **reckon on** vt insep contar con

reckoning ['rekənɪŋ] n cálculo m; **by my reckoning ...** según mis cálculos ...; Fig **day of reckoning** día m del juicio final

reclaim [rɪ'kleɪm] vt **a)** [recover] recuperar; [demand back] reclamar **b)** [marshland etc] convertir

recline [rɪ'klaɪn] vi recostarse, reclinarse

recliner [rɪ'klaɪnə(r)] n [for sunbathing] tumbona f; [armchair] sillón m reclinable

recluse [rɪ'klu:s] n solitario(a) m,f

recognition [rekəg'nɪʃən] n reconocimiento m; [appreciation] apreciación f; **changed beyond all recognition** irreconocible

recognizable [rekəg'naɪzəbəl] adj reconocible

recognize ['rekəgnaɪz] vt reconocer

recoil 1. ['ri:kɔɪl] n [of gun] culatazo m; [of spring] aflojamiento m **2.** [rɪ'kɔɪl] vi **a)** [gun] dar un culatazo; [spring] aflojarse **b)** [in fear] espantarse

recollect [rekə'lekt] vt recordar

recollection [rekə'lekʃən] n recuerdo m

recommend [rekə'mend] vt recomendar

recommendation [rekəmen'deɪʃən] n recomendación f

recommended adj recomendado(a); **recommended daily allowance** or **intake** consumo m diario recomendado

reconcile ['rekənsaɪl] vt [two people] reconciliar; [two ideas] conciliar; **to reconcile oneself to** resignarse a

reconsider [ri:kən'sɪdə(r)] vt reconsiderar

reconstruct [ri:kən'strʌkt] vt reconstruir

record 1. ['rekɔːd] n a) [written account] registro m; [file] documento m; [account] relación f; [of meeting] actas fpl; **to keep sth on record** dejar constancia escrita de algo; **(police) record** antecedentes mpl penales; **off the record** confidencialmente b) MUS [vinyl disc] disco m; **record player** tocadiscos m inv c) [best achievement & SPORT] récord m d) **records** archivos fpl; **public records office** archivo m nacional **2.** ['rekɔːd] adj récord (inv) **3.** [rɪ'kɔːd] vt a) [relate] hacer constar; [note down] anotar, apuntar b) [music, TV programme] grabar

recorded [rɪ'kɔːdɪd] adj Br **recorded delivery** correo certificado; **recorded message** mensaje grabado

recorder [rɪ'kɔːdə(r)] n a) [person] registrador(a) m, f; JUR magistrado(a) m, f b) MUS flauta f

recording [rɪ'kɔːdɪŋ] n [registering] registro m; [recorded music, message etc] grabación f

recount [rɪ'kaʊnt] vt [tell] contar

recourse [rɪ'kɔːs] n **to have recourse to** recurrir a

recover [rɪ'kʌvə(r)] **1.** vt [items, lost time] recuperar; [consciousness] recobrar **2.** vi [from illness etc] reponerse

recovery [rɪ'kʌvərɪ] n a) [retrieval] recuperación f b) [from illness] restablecimiento m

re-create [ri:krɪ'eɪt] vt recrear

recreation [rekrɪ'eɪʃən] n a) diversión f b) SCH [playtime] recreo m

recrimination [rɪkrɪmɪ'neɪʃən] n reproche m

recruit [rɪ'kruːt] **1.** n recluta m **2.** vt [soldiers] reclutar; [workers] contratar

rectangle ['rektæŋgəl] n rectángulo m

rectangular [rek'tæŋjʊlə(r)] adj rectangular

rectify ['rektɪfaɪ] vt rectificar

rector ['rektə(r)] n a) REL párroco m b) Scot SCH director(a) m, f

recuperate [rɪ'kuːpəreɪt] vi reponerse

recur [rɪ'kɜː(r)] vi repetirse

recycle [ri:'saɪkəl] vt reciclar; COMPUT **recycle bin** papelera f de reciclaje

red [red] **1.** (compar **redder**, superl **reddest**) adj rojo(a); **red light** semáforo m en rojo; **red wine** vino tinto; **to go red** ponerse colorado(a); **to have red hair** ser pelirrojo(a); Fig **red herring** truco m para despistar; Fam **to roll out the red carpet for sb** recibir a algn con todos los honores; **Red Cross** Cruz Roja; **Red Indian** piel roja mf; **Red Riding Hood** Caperucita Roja; **Red Sea** Mar Rojo; **red tape** papeleo m
2. n a) [colour] rojo m
b) FIN **to be in the red** estar en números rojos

redcurrant ['redkʌrənt] n grosella roja

redeem [rɪ'diːm] vt a) [regain] recobrar; [voucher] canjear b) [debt] amortizar c) [film, novel etc] salvar d) REL redimir; Fig **to redeem oneself** redimirse

red-handed [red'hændɪd] adj **he was caught red-handed** lo Esp cogieron or Am agarraron con las manos en la masa

redhead ['redhed] n pelirrojo(a) m, f

red-hot [red'hɒt] adj a) candente; **red-hot news** noticia(s) f(pl) de última hora b) Fam [passionate] ardiente

redirect [ri:dɪ'rekt] vt a) [funds] redistribuir b) [letter] remitir a la nueva dirección

redo [ri:'duː] (pt **redid** [ri:'dɪd], pp **redone** [ri:'dʌn]) vt rehacer

reduce [rɪ'dju:s] *vt* **a)** reducir **b)** [in rank] degradar **c)** CULIN [sauce] espesar **d)** MED recomponer

reduction [rɪ'dʌkʃən] *n* reducción *f*; COMM [in purchase price] descuento *m*, rebaja *f*

redundancy [rɪ'dʌndənsɪ] *n Br* [dismissal] despido *m*

redundant [rɪ'dʌndənt] *adj* **a)** [superfluous] redundante **b)** *Br* IND **to be made redundant** perder el empleo; **to make sb redundant** despedir a algn

reed [ri:d] *n* **a)** BOT caña *f* **b)** MUS caramillo *m*

reef [ri:f] *n* arrecife *m*

reek [ri:k] **1.** *n* tufo *m* **2.** *vi* apestar

reel [ri:l] **1.** *n* **a)** [spool] bobina *f*, carrete *m* **b)** *Scot* MUS danza *f* tradicional **2.** *vi* [stagger] tambalearse

ref [ref] *n* **a)** *Fam* SPORT árbitro *m* **b)** COMM (*abbr of* **reference**) ref

refectory [rɪ'fektərɪ] *n* refectorio *m*

refer [rɪ'fɜ:(r)] **1.** *vt* mandar, enviar; **to refer a matter to a tribunal** remitir un asunto a un tribunal **2.** *vi* **a)** [allude] referirse, aludir (**to** a) **b)** **to refer to** [consult] consultar

referee [refə'ri:] **1.** *n* **a)** SPORT árbitro(a) *m,f* **b)** *Br* [for job application] garante *mf* **2.** *vt* SPORT arbitrar

reference ['refərəns] *n* **a)** referencia *f*; **with reference to** referente a, con referencia a; **reference book** libro *m* de consulta; **reference library** biblioteca *f* de consulta **b)** *Br* [from employer] informe *m*, referencia *f*

referendum [refə'rendəm] *n* referéndum *m*

refill 1. ['ri:fɪl] *n* **a)** [replacement] recambio *m*, carga *f* **b)** *Fam* [drink] otra copa **2.** [ri:'fɪl] *vt* rellenar

refine [rɪ'faɪn] *vt* refinar

refined [rɪ'faɪnd] *adj* refinado(a)

refinement [rɪ'faɪnmənt] *n* refinamiento *m*

reflect [rɪ'flekt] **1.** *vt* [light, attitude] reflejar **2.** *vi* [think] reflexionar; **to reflect on sth** meditar sobre algo

reflection [rɪ'flekʃən] *n* **a)** [indication, mirror image] reflejo *m* **b)** [thought] reflexión *f*; **on reflection** pensándolo bien **c)** [criticism] crítica *f*

reflector [rɪ'flektə(r)] *n* [of vehicle] catafaro *m*

reflex ['ri:fleks] *n* reflejo *m*

reflexive [rɪ'fleksɪv] *adj* reflexivo(a)

reform [rɪ'fɔ:m] **1.** *n* reforma *f*; **reform school** reformatorio *m* **2.** *vt* reformar

refrain [rɪ'freɪn] **1.** *n* MUS estribillo *m*; *Fig* lema *m* **2.** *vi* abstenerse (**from** de)

refresh [rɪ'freʃ] *vt* refrescar

refreshing [rɪ'freʃɪŋ] *adj* refrescante; **a refreshing change** un cambio muy agradable

refreshment [rɪ'freʃmənt] *n* refresco *m*

refrigerator [rɪ'frɪdʒəreɪtə(r)] *n* nevera *f*, frigorífico *m*, *Andes* frigider *m*, *RP* heladera *f*

refuel [ri:'fju:əl] *vt & vi* repostar

refuge ['refju:dʒ] *n* refugio *m*, cobijo *m*; **to take refuge** refugiarse

refugee [refjʊ'dʒi:] *n* refugiado(a) *m,f*

refund 1. ['ri:fʌnd] *n* reembolso *m* **2.** [rɪ'fʌnd] *vt* reembolsar, devolver

refurbish [ˌri:'fɜ:bɪʃ] *vt* remodelar, renovar

refusal [rɪ'fju:zəl] *n* negativa *f*; **to have first refusal on sth** tener la primera opción en algo

refuse[1] [rɪ'fju:z] **1.** *vt* rechazar; **to refuse sb sth** negar algo a algn **2.** *vi* negarse

refuse[2] ['refju:s] *n* basura *f*; **refuse collector** basurero *m*

regain [rɪ'geɪn] *vt* recuperar; [consciousness] recobrar

regard [rɪ'gɑ:d] **1.** *n* **a)** [concern] consideración *f*, respeto *m*; **with regard to** respecto a **b)** [esteem] estima *f* **c)** **regards** [good wishes] saludos *mpl*, *CAm, Col, Ecuad* saludes *fpl*; **give him my regards** dale recuerdos de mi parte **2.** *vt* **a)** [consider] considerar **b)** **as regards** [regarding] respecto a

regarding [rɪ'gɑːdɪŋ] *prep* respecto a

regardless [rɪ'gɑːdlɪs] **1.** *prep* regardless of sin tener en cuenta; **regardless of the outcome** pase lo que pase **2.** *adv* a toda costa

regime [reɪ'ʒiːm] *n* régimen *m*

regiment ['reʤɪmənt] **1.** *n* regimiento *m* **2.** *vt* regimentar

region ['riːʤən] *n* **a)** región *f* **b) in the region of** aproximadamente

regional ['riːʤənəl] *adj* regional

register ['reʤɪstə(r)] **1.** *n* registro *m* **2.** *vt* **a)** [record] registrar **b)** [letter] certificar **c)** [show] mostrar **3.** *vi* [for course] inscribirse; UNIV matricularse

registered ['reʤɪstəd] *adj* certificado(a); Br **registered letter** carta certificada; **registered trademark** marca registrada

registration [reʤɪ'streɪʃən] *n* inscripción *f*; UNIV matrícula *f*; Br AUTO **registration number** matrícula *f*

registry ['reʤɪstrɪ] *n* registro *m*; **to get married in a registry office** casarse por lo civil; Br **registry office** registro civil

regret [rɪ'gret] **1.** *n* [remorse] remordimiento *m*; [sadness] pesar *m*; **regrets** [excuses] excusas *fpl*; **to have no regrets** no arrepentirse de nada **2.** *vt* arrepentirse de, lamentar

regrettable [rɪ'gretəbəl] *adj* lamentable

regular ['regjʊlə(r)] **1.** *adj* **a)** regular **b)** [usual] normal **c)** [staff] permanente **d)** [frequent] frecuente **e) regular army** tropas *fpl* regulares **f)** US Fam **a regular guy** un tío legal, Am un tipo derecho **2.** *n* [customer] cliente *mf* habitual

regularly ['regjʊləlɪ] *adv* con regularidad

regulate ['regjʊleɪt] *vt* regular

regulation [regjʊ'leɪʃən] **1.** *n* **a)** [control] regulación *f* **b)** [rule] regla *f* **2.** *adj* reglamentario(a)

rehearsal [rɪ'hɜːsəl] *n* ensayo *m*

rehearse [rɪ'hɜːs] *vt & vi* ensayar

reign [reɪn] **1.** *n* reinado *m* **2.** *vi* reinar

reimburse [riːɪm'bɜːs] *vt* reembolsar

reindeer ['reɪndɪə(r)] *n* reno *m*

reinforce [riːɪn'fɔːs] *vt* [strengthen] reforzar; [support] apoyar; **reinforced concrete** hormigón *or* Am concreto armado

reinforcement [riːɪn'fɔːsmənt] *n* **a)** refuerzo *m*; CONSTR armazón *m* **b)** MIL **reinforcements** refuerzos *mpl*

reinstall [riːɪn'stɔːl] *vt* COMPUT reinstalar

reinstate [riːɪn'steɪt] *vt* [to job] reincorporar

reissue [riː'ɪʃuː] **1.** *n* [of book] reedición *f*; [of film] reestreno *m* **2.** *vt* [book, CD] reeditar; [film] reestrenar

reject 1. ['riːʤekt] *n* **a)** desecho *m* **b)** COMM **rejects** artículos defectuosos **2.** [rɪ'ʤekt] *vt* rechazar

rejection [rɪ'ʤekʃən] *n* rechazo *m*

rejoice [rɪ'ʤɔɪs] *vi* regocijarse (**at** *or* **over** de)

rejuvenate [rɪ'ʤuːvɪneɪt] *vt* rejuvenecer; Fig revitalizar

relapse [rɪ'læps] **1.** *n* **a)** MED recaída *f*; **to have a relapse** sufrir una recaída **b)** [into crime, alcoholism] reincidencia *f* **2.** *vi* recaer

relate [rɪ'leɪt] **1.** *vt* **a)** [connect] relacionar **b)** [tell] relatar **2.** *vi* relacionarse

related [rɪ'leɪtɪd] *adj* **a)** [linked] relacionado(a) (**to** con) **b) to be related to sb** ser pariente de algn

relation [rɪ'leɪʃən] *n* **a)** [link] relación *f*; **in** *or* **with relation to** respecto a; **it bears no relation to what we said** no tiene nada que ver con lo que dijimos **b)** [member of family] pariente(a) *m,f*

relationship [rɪ'leɪʃənʃɪp] *n* **a)** [link] relación *f* **b)** [between people] relaciones *fpl*; **to have a good / bad relationship with sb** llevarse bien / mal con algn

relative ['relətɪv] **1.** *n* pariente *mf* **2.** *adj* relativo(a)

relatively ['relətɪvlɪ] *adv* relativamente

relax [rɪ'læks] **1.** *vt* [muscles, rules] relajar **2.** *vi* relajarse

relaxation [riːlækˈseɪʃən] n **a)** [rest] descanso m, relajación f **b)** [of rules] relajación f **c)** [pastime] distracción f

relaxed [rɪˈlækst] adj relajado(a); [peaceful] tranquilo(a)

relaxing [rɪˈlæksɪŋ] adj relajante

relay 1. [ˈriːleɪ] n a) relevo m; **relay (race)** carrera f de relevos **b)** RADIO & TV retransmisión f **2.** [rɪˈleɪ] vt **a)** [pass on] difundir **b)** RADIO & TV retransmitir

release [rɪˈliːs] **1.** n **a)** [of prisoner] liberación f, puesta f en libertad; [of gas] escape m **b)** COMM puesta f en venta **c)** CIN estreno m **d)** [record] disco m **2.** vt **a)** [let go] soltar; [prisoner] poner en libertad; [gas] despedir **b)** COMM poner en venta **c)** CIN estrenar **d)** [record] editar

relegate [ˈrelɪgeɪt] vt **a)** relegar **b)** Br FTBL **to be relegated** bajar a una división inferior

relent [rɪˈlent] vi ceder; [storm] aplacarse

relentless [rɪˈlentlɪs] adj implacable

relevance [ˈreləvəns] n pertinencia f

relevant [ˈreləvənt] adj pertinente (**to** a); **it is not relevant** no viene al caso

reliability [rɪlaɪəˈbɪlɪti] n **a)** [of person] formalidad f **b)** [of car, machine] fiabilidad f, Am confiabilidad f

reliable [rɪˈlaɪəbəl] adj [person, machine] fiable, Am confiable; **a reliable car** un coche seguro; **a reliable source** una fuente fidedigna

relic [ˈrelɪk] n **a)** REL reliquia f **b)** [reminder of past] vestigio m

relief [rɪˈliːf] n **a)** alivio m **b)** [help] auxilio m, ayuda f; US **to be on relief** cobrar un subsidio **c)** ART & GEOG relieve m

relieve [rɪˈliːv] vt **a)** aliviar; [monotony] romper **b)** [take over from] relevar **c)** Euph **to relieve oneself** hacer sus necesidades **d) to relieve sb of sth** coger algo a algn

religion [rɪˈlɪdʒən] n religión f

religious [rɪˈlɪdʒəs] adj religioso(a)

relinquish [rɪˈlɪŋkwɪʃ] vt renunciar a; **to relinquish one's hold on sth** soltar algo

relish [ˈrelɪʃ] **1.** n **a)** [enjoyment] deleite m **b)** CULIN condimento m **2.** vt agradar

reluctant [rɪˈlʌktənt] adj reacio(a); **to be reluctant to do sth** estar poco dispuesto(a) a hacer algo

rely [rɪˈlaɪ] vi contar (**on** con), confiar (**on** en)

remain [rɪˈmeɪn] **1.** vi **a)** [stay] permanecer, quedarse **b)** [be left] quedar; **it remains to be seen** está por ver **2.** npl **remains** restos mpl

remainder [rɪˈmeɪndə(r)] n resto m

remaining [rɪˈmeɪnɪŋ] adj restante

remark [rɪˈmɑːk] **1.** n comentario m **2.** vt comentar, observar

remarkable [rɪˈmɑːkəbəl] adj extraordinario(a); [strange] curioso(a)

remedy [ˈremɪdɪ] **1.** n remedio m **2.** vt remediar

remember [rɪˈmembə(r)] **1.** vt **a)** acordarse de, recordar **b)** **remember me to your mother** dale recuerdos a tu madre **2.** vi acordarse, recordar; **I don't remember** no me acuerdo

remembrance n Formal & Liter [memory] recuerdo m; Br **Remembrance Day** or **Sunday** día m de homenaje a los caídos (en las dos guerras mundiales)

remind [rɪˈmaɪnd] vt recordar; **remind me to do it** recuérdame que lo haga; **she reminds me of your sister** me recuerda a tu hermana; **that reminds me** ahora que me acuerdo

reminder [rɪˈmaɪndə(r)] n recordatorio m, aviso m

reminisce [remɪˈnɪs] vi rememorar

reminiscent [remɪˈnɪsənt] adj Formal nostálgico(a); **to be reminiscent of** recordar

remittance [rɪˈmɪtəns] n **a)** [sending] envío m **b)** [payment] giro m, pago m

remorse [rɪˈmɔːs] n remordimiento m

remorseless [rɪˈmɔːslɪs] adj despiadado(a)

remote [rɪˈməʊt] adj **a)** [far away] remoto(a); **remote control** mando m a distancia **b)** [isolated] aislado(a)

c) [possibility] remoto(a) ; **I haven't the remotest idea** no tengo la más mínima idea

remotely [rɪ'məʊtlɪ] *adv* **a)** [vaguely] vagamente **b)** [distantly] en lugar aislado

removable [rɪ'muːvəbəl] *adj* [detachable] que se puede quitar

removal [rɪ'muːvəl] *n* **a)** [moving house] mudanza *f*; **removal van** camión *m* de mudanzas **b)** [of stain etc] eliminación *f*

remove [rɪ'muːv] *vt* **a)** [move] quitar, *Am* sacar; **to remove one's make-up** desmaquillarse; **to remove one's name from a list** tachar su nombre de una lista **b)** [from office] despedir

rendezvous ['rɒndɪvuː] **1.** *n* **a)** [meeting] cita *f* **b)** [place] lugar *m* de reunión **2.** *vi* reunirse

renew [rɪ'njuː] *vt* [contract etc] renovar; [talks etc] reanudar; **with renewed vigour** con renovadas fuerzas

renounce [rɪ'naʊns] *vt Formal* renunciar

renovate ['renəveɪt] *vt* renovar, hacer reformas en

renowned [rɪ'naʊnd] *adj* renombrado(a)

rent [rent] **1.** *n* **a)** [for building, car, TV] alquiler *m* **b)** [for land] arriendo *m* **2.** *vt* **a)** [building, car, TV] alquilar, *Méx* rentar **b)** [land] arrendar

rental ['rentəl] *n* [of house etc] alquiler *m*

reorganize [riːˈɔːgənaɪz] *vt* reorganizar

repair [rɪ'peə(r)] **1.** *n* reparación *f*, arreglo *m*; **in good / bad repair** en buen / mal estado **2.** *vt* **a)** arreglar; [car] reparar; [clothes] remendar **b)** [make amends for] reparar

repay [riːˈpeɪ] *(pt & pp repaid) vt* devolver; **to repay a debt** liquidar una deuda; **to repay a kindness** devolver un favor

repayment [riːˈpeɪmənt] *n* pago *m*

repeal [rɪ'piːl] **1.** *n* JUR revocación *f* **2.** *vt* JUR revocar

repeat [rɪ'piːt] **1.** *vt* repetir; **to repeat oneself** repetirse **2.** *n* [repetition] repetición *f*; TV reposición *f*

repeated [rɪ'piːtɪd] *adj* repetido(a)

repeatedly [rɪ'piːtɪdlɪ] *adv* repetidas veces

repel [rɪ'pel] *vt* **a)** [fight off] repeler **b)** [disgust] repugnar

repellent [rɪ'pelənt] **1.** *adj* repelente; **water-repellent** impermeable **2.** *n* (insect) **repellent** loción *f* / spray *m* anti-insectos

repent [rɪ'pent] *vt & vi* arrepentirse (de)

repercussion [riːpəˈkʌʃən] *n* [usu pl] repercusión *f*

repertoire ['repətwɑː(r)] *n* repertorio *m*

repetition [repɪ'tɪʃən] *n* repetición *f*

repetitive [rɪ'petɪtɪv] *adj* repetitivo(a)

replace [rɪ'pleɪs] *vt* **a)** [put back] volver a poner en su sitio **b)** [substitute for] sustituir, reemplazar

replacement [rɪ'pleɪsmənt] *n* **a)** [returning] reemplazo *m* **b)** [person] sustituto(a) *m,f* **c)** [part] pieza *f* de recambio

replay ['riːpleɪ] *n* repetición *f*

replica ['replɪkə] *n* réplica *f*

reply [rɪ'plaɪ] **1.** *n* respuesta *f*, contestación *f* **2.** *vi* responder, contestar

report [rɪ'pɔːt] **1.** *n* **a)** informe *m*, *Andes, CAm, Méx, Ven* reporte *m* ; *Br* **school report** informe escolar **b)** [piece of news] noticia *f* **c)** PRESS, RADIO & TV reportaje *m* **2.** *vt* **a)** **it is reported that ...** se dice que ... **b)** [tell authorities about] denunciar **c)** PRESS hacer un reportaje sobre **3.** *vi* **a)** [of committee member etc] hacer un informe **b)** PRESS hacer un reportaje **c)** [for duty etc] presentarse

reported [rɪ'pɔːtɪd] *adj* **reported speech** estilo indirecto

reporter [rɪ'pɔːtə(r)] *n* periodista *mf*

represent [reprɪ'zent] *vt* representar

representation [reprɪzen'teɪʃən] *n* **a)** representación *f* **b)** *Formal* **representations** queja *f*

representative [reprɪ'zentətɪv] **1.** *adj* representativo(a) **2.** *n* **a)** representante *mf* **b)** *US* POL diputado(a) *m,f*

repress [rɪ'pres] *vt* reprimir, contener

repressive [rɪ'presɪv] *adj* represivo(a)

reprieve [rɪ'priːv] **1.** *n* **a)** JUR indulto *m* **b)** *Fig* alivio *m* **2.** *vt* JUR indultar

reprimand ['reprɪmɑːnd] **1.** *n* reprimenda *f* **2.** *vt* reprender

reprint 1. ['riːprɪnt] *n* reimpresión *f* **2.** [riː'prɪnt] *vt* reimprimir

reprisal [rɪ'praɪzəl] *n* represalia *f*

reproach [rɪ'prəʊtʃ] **1.** *n* reproche *m*; **beyond reproach** intachable **2.** *vt* reprochar

reproduce [riː'prə'djuːs] **1.** *vt* reproducir **2.** *vi* reproducirse

reproduction [riː'prə'dʌkʃən] *n* reproducción *f*

reptile ['reptaɪl] *n* reptil *m*

republic [rɪ'pʌblɪk] *n* república *f*

republican [rɪ'pʌblɪkən] *adj* & *n* republicano(a) *(m,f)*; *US* POL **Republican Party** Partido Republicano

repugnant [rɪ'pʌgnənt] *adj* repugnante

repulsive [rɪ'pʌlsɪv] *adj* repulsivo(a)

reputable ['repjʊtəbəl] *adj* [company etc] acreditado(a); [person, products] de toda confianza

reputation [repjʊ'teɪʃən] *n* reputación *f*

reputed [rɪ'pjuːtɪd] *adj* supuesto(a); **to be reputed to be** ser considerado(a) como

request [rɪ'kwest] **1.** *n* petición *f*, solicitud *f*, *Am* pedido *m*; **available on request** disponible a petición de los interesados; *Br* **request stop** [for bus] parada *f* discrecional **2.** *vt* pedir, solicitar

require [rɪ'kwaɪə(r)] *vt* **a)** [need] necesitar, requerir **b)** [demand] exigir

requirement [rɪ'kwaɪəmənt] *n* **a)** [need] necesidad *f* **b)** [demand] requisito *m*

requisite ['rekwɪzɪt] *Formal* **1.** *adj* requerido(a) **2.** *n* requisito *m*

rescue ['reskjuː] **1.** *n* rescate *m*; **rescue team** equipo *m* de rescate **2.** *vt* rescatar

research [rɪ'sɜːtʃ] **1.** *n* investigación *f*; **Research and Development** Investigación más Desarrollo **2.** *vt* & *vi* investigar

researcher [rɪ'sɜːtʃə(r)] *n* investigador(a) *m,f*

resemblance [rɪ'zembləns] *n* semejanza *f*

resemble [rɪ'zembəl] *vt* parecerse a

resent [rɪ'zent] *vt* ofenderse por

resentment [rɪ'zentmənt] *n* resentimiento *m*

reservation [rezə'veɪʃən] *n* reserva *f*, *Am* reservación *f*

reserve [rɪ'zɜːv] **1.** *n* **a)** reserva *f*; **to keep sth in reserve** guardar algo de reserva **b)** SPORT suplente *mf* **c)** MIL **reserves** reservas *fpl* **2.** *vt* reservar

reserved [rɪ'zɜːvd] *adj* reservado(a)

reservoir ['rezəvwɑː(r)] *n* embalse *m*, pantano *m*; *Fig* reserva *f*

reset [riː'set] *(pt & pp* reset*)* *vt* **a)** [clock, watch] ajustar; [meter, controls] poner a cero **b)** COMPUT reiniciar, reinicializar, resetear

reshuffle [riː'ʃʌfəl] *n* POL remodelación *f*

reside [rɪ'zaɪd] *vi* *Formal* residir

residence ['rezɪdəns] *n* *Formal* [home] residencia *f*; [address] domicilio *m*; [period of time] permanencia *f*

resident ['rezɪdənt] *adj* & *n* residente *(mf)*; *US* MED *médico que ha cumplido la residencia y prosigue con su especialización*; **to be resident in** estar domiciliado(a) en

residential [rezɪ'denʃəl] *adj* residencial

resign [rɪ'zaɪn] **1.** *vt* **a)** [give up] dimitir **b) to resign oneself to sth** resignarse a algo **2.** *vi* [from job] dimitir

resignation [ˌrezɪɡ'neɪʃən] n a) [from a job] dimisión f b) [acceptance] resignación f

resilient [rɪ'zɪlɪənt] adj [strong] resistente

resist [rɪ'zɪst] 1. vt a) [not yield to] resistir b) [oppose] oponerse a 2. vi resistir

resistance [rɪ'zɪstəns] n resistencia f

resistant [rɪ'zɪstənt] adj to be resistant to sth [change, suggestion] mostrarse remiso(a) a aceptar algo, mostrar resistencia a algo ; [disease] ser resistente a algo

resit [riː'sɪt] vt Br [exam] volver a presentarse a

resolute ['rezəluːt] adj resuelto(a), decidido(a)

resolution [rezə'luːʃən] n resolución f

resolve [rɪ'zɒlv] 1. n resolución f 2. vt resolver; to resolve to do resolverse a hacer 3. vi resolverse

resort [rɪ'zɔːt] 1. n a) [place] lugar m de vacaciones; tourist resort centro turístico b) [recourse] recurso m; as a last resort como último recurso 2. vi recurrir (to a)

resounding [rɪ'zaʊndɪŋ] adj a resounding failure un fracaso total; a resounding success un éxito rotundo

resource [rɪ'sɔːs] n recurso m

resourceful [rɪ'sɔːsful] adj ingenioso(a)

respect [rɪ'spekt] 1. n a) [deference] respeto m; to pay one's respects to sb presentar sus respetos a algn b) [relation, reference] respecto m; in that respect a ese respecto; with respect to con referencia a 2. vt respetar

respectable [rɪ'spektəbəl] adj respetable; [clothes] decente

respective [rɪ'spektɪv] adj respectivo(a)

respond [rɪ'spɒnd] vi responder

response [rɪ'spɒns] n a) [reply] respuesta f b) [reaction] reacción f

responsibility [rɪspɒnsə'bɪlɪtɪ] n responsabilidad f

responsible [rɪ'spɒnsəbəl] adj responsable (for de); to be responsible to sb tener que dar cuentas a algn

responsive [rɪ'spɒnsɪv] adj sensible

rest¹ [rest] 1. n a) [break] descanso m; US rest room baño m, Esp servicios mpl, CSur toilette m

b) [peace] tranquilidad f; at rest [object] inmóvil

c) [support] apoyo m

2. vt a) descansar

b) [lean] apoyar; to rest a ladder against a wall apoyar una escalera contra una pared

3. vi a) descansar

b) [be calm] quedarse tranquilo(a)

c) it doesn't rest with me no depende de mí

rest² [rest] n the rest [remainder] el resto, lo demás; the rest of the girls las demás chicas

restaurant ['restərɒnt] n restaurante m; Br RAIL restaurant car coche m restaurante

restful ['restful] adj relajante

restless ['restlɪs] adj agitado(a), inquieto(a)

restore [rɪ'stɔː(r)] vt a) [give back] devolver b) [re-establish] restablecer c) [building etc] restaurar

restrain [rɪ'streɪn] vt contener; to restrain one's anger reprimir la cólera; to restrain oneself contenerse

restrained [rɪ'streɪnd] adj [person] moderado(a); [emotion] contenido(a)

restraint [rɪ'streɪnt] n a) [restriction] restricción f; [hindrance] traba f b) [moderation] moderación f

restrict [rɪ'strɪkt] vt restringir, limitar

restriction [rɪ'strɪkʃən] n restricción f, limitación f

result [rɪ'zʌlt] 1. n a) resultado m b) [consequence] consecuencia f; as a result of como consecuencia de 2. vi a) resultar; to result from resultar de b) to result in causar

resume [rɪˈzjuːm] **1.** vt [journey, work, conversation] reanudar ; [control] reasumir **2.** vi recomenzar

résumé [ˈrezjʊmeɪ] n a) [summary] resumen m b) US [curriculum vitae] currículum (vitae) m

resurrection [rezəˈrekʃən] n resurrección f

resuscitate [rɪˈsʌsɪteɪt] vt MED reanimar

retail [ˈriːteɪl] **1.** n venta f al por menor, Am menoreo m ; **retail outlet** punto m de venta ; Br **retail park** centro m comercial ; **retail price** precio m de venta al público ; Br **retail price index** Índice m de Precios al Consumo ; Fam **to do some retail therapy** ir de compras para levantar el ánimo **2.** vt vender al por menor **3.** vi venderse al por menor **4.** adv al por menor

retailer [ˈriːteɪlə(r)] n detallista mf

retain [rɪˈteɪn] vt a) [heat] conservar ; [personal effects] guardar b) [water] retener c) [facts, information] recordar

retaliate [rɪˈtælɪeɪt] vi tomar represalias (**against** contra)

retaliation [rɪtælɪˈeɪʃən] n represalias fpl ; **in retaliation** en represalia

retch [retʃ] vi tener náuseas

reticent [ˈretɪsənt] adj reticente

retire [rɪˈtaɪə(r)] **1.** vt jubilar **2.** vi a) [stop working] jubilarse b) [from race] retirarse ; **to retire for the night** irse a la cama, acostarse

retired [rɪˈtaɪəd] adj jubilado(a)

retirement [rɪˈtaɪəmənt] n jubilación f

retrace [riːˈtreɪs] vt [recall] reconstruir ; **to retrace one's steps** volver sobre sus pasos

retract [rɪˈtrækt] **1.** vt a) [claws] retraer ; [landing gear] replegar b) [statement] retirar **2.** vi a) [claws] retraerse ; [landing gear] replegarse b) Formal retractarse

retreat [rɪˈtriːt] **1.** n a) MIL retirada f b) [shelter] refugio m c) REL retiro m **2.** vi retirarse (**from** de)

retribution [retrɪˈbjuːʃən] n represalias fpl

retrieve [rɪˈtriːv] vt a) [recover & COMPUT] recuperar ; [of dog] cobrar b) [rescue] salvar

retrospect [ˈretrəʊspekt] n **in retrospect** retrospectivamente

retrospective [retrəʊˈspektɪv] **1.** adj retrospectivo(a) **2.** n ART (exposición f) retrospectiva f

return [rɪˈtɜːn] **1.** n a) [of person] regreso m, vuelta f ; **by return of post** a vuelta de correo ; **in return for** a cambio de ; **many happy returns!** ¡felicidades! ; **return match** partido m de vuelta ; Br **return (ticket)** billete m de ida y vuelta b) [of sth borrowed, stolen] devolución f c) [profit] beneficio m, ganancia f d) [interest] interés m **2.** vt [give back] devolver ; **return to sender** [on envelope] devuélvase al remitente ; **to return sb's love** corresponder al amor de algn **3.** vi a) [come or go back] volver, regresar b) [reappear] reaparecer

retweet [ˈriːtwiːt] **1.** vi retuitear **2.** n retuit m

reunion [riːˈjuːnjən] n reunión f

reunite [riːjuːˈnaɪt] vt **to be reunited with** [after separation] reunirse con

reuse [riːˈjuːz] vt volver a utilizar, reutilizar

revamp [ˌriːˈvæmp] vt Fam renovar, modernizar

reveal [rɪˈviːl] vt [make known] revelar ; [show] dejar ver

revealing [rɪˈviːlɪŋ] adj revelador(a)

revel [ˈrevəl] vi disfrutar (**in** con) ; **to revel in doing sth** gozar muchísimo haciendo algo

revelation [revəˈleɪʃən] n revelación f

revenge [rɪˈvendʒ] n venganza f ; **to take revenge on sb for sth** vengarse de algo en algn

revenue ['revɪnjuː] n renta f

reverence ['revərəns] n reverencia f

reversal [rɪ'vɜːsəl] n a) [of order] inversión f b) [of attitude, policy] cambio m total c) JUR revocación f

reverse [rɪ'vɜːs] 1. adj inverso(a) 2. n a) quite the reverse todo lo contrario b) [other side - of cloth] revés m; [of coin] cruz f; [of page] dorso m c) AUTO **reverse gear** marcha f atrás 3. vt a) [order] invertir b) [turn round] volver del revés c) [change] cambiar totalmente d) BrTEL **to reverse the charges** poner una conferencia a cobro revertido 4. vi AUTO dar marcha atrás

revert [rɪ'vɜːt] vi volver (to a)

review [rɪ'vjuː] 1. n a) [examination] examen m b) PRESS crítica f, reseña f c) [magazine] revista f 2. vt a) [examine] examinar b) MIL **to review the troops** pasar revista a las tropas c) [book etc] hacer una crítica de

reviewer [rɪ'vjuːə(r)] n crítico(a) m,f

revise [rɪ'vaɪz] vt a) [look over] revisar; Br [at school] repasar b) [change] modificar

revision [rɪ'vɪʒən] n a) revisión f; Br [at school] repaso m b) [change] modificación f

revival [rɪ'vaɪvəl] n a) [of interest] renacimiento m; [of economy, industry] reactivación f; [of a country] resurgimiento m b) THEAT reestreno m c) MED reanimación f

revive [rɪ'vaɪv] 1. vt a) [interest] renovar; [a law] restablecer; [economy, industry] reactivar; [hopes] despertar b) THEAT reestrenar c) MED reanimar 2. vi a) [interest, hopes] renacer b) MED volver en sí

revolt [rɪ'vəʊlt] 1. n rebelión f, sublevación f 2. vi rebelarse, sublevarse 3. vt repugnar, dar asco a

revolting [rɪ'vəʊltɪŋ] adj repugnante

revolution [revə'luːʃən] n revolución f

revolutionary [revə'luːʃənərɪ] adj & n revolucionario(a) (m,f)

revolve [rɪ'vɒlv] 1. vi girar; Fig **to revolve around** girar en torno a 2. vt hacer girar

revolver [rɪ'vɒlvə(r)] n revólver m

revolving [rɪ'vɒlvɪŋ] adj giratorio(a)

revulsion [rɪ'vʌlʃən] n repulsión f

reward [rɪ'wɔːd] 1. n recompensa f 2. vt recompensar

rewarding [rɪ'wɔːdɪŋ] adj provechoso(a)

rewind [riː'waɪnd] (pt & pp rewound [riː'waʊnd]) vt [tape, film] rebobinar

RGDS MESSAGING written abbr of **regards**

rhetoric ['retərɪk] n retórica f

rhetorical [rɪ'tɒrɪkəl] adj retórico(a)

rheumatism ['ruːmətɪzəm] n reuma m

rhinoceros [raɪ'nɒsərəs] n rinoceronte m

rhubarb ['ruːbɑːb] n ruibarbo m

rhyme [raɪm] 1. n rima f; [poem] poema m 2. vi rimar

rhythm ['rɪðəm] n ritmo m

rib [rɪb] n ANAT costilla f; **rib cage** caja torácica

ribbon ['rɪbən] n cinta f; [in hair etc] lazo m; **torn to ribbons** hecho(a) jirones

rice [raɪs] n arroz m; **rice pudding** arroz con leche

rich [rɪtʃ] 1. adj [person, food] rico(a); [soil] fértil; [voice] sonoro(a); [colour] vivo(a) 2. npl **the rich** los ricos

riches ['rɪtʃɪz] npl riquezas fpl

rid [rɪd] (pt & pp rid) vt librar; **to get rid of sth** deshacerse de algo; **to rid oneself of** librarse de

ridden ['rɪdən] pp of **ride**

riddle¹ ['rɪdəl] n a) [puzzle] acertijo m, adivinanza f b) [mystery] enigma m

riddle² ['rɪdəl] vt [with bullets] acribillar

ride [raɪd] (pt rode, pp ridden) 1. n paseo m, vuelta f; **a short bus ride** un corto trayecto en autobús; Fam **to take sb for a ride** tomar el pelo a algn

2. *vt* [bicycle, horse] montar en; **can you ride a bicycle?** ¿sabes montar *or Am* andar en bicicleta?

3. *vi* **a)** [on horse] montar *or Am* andar a caballo

b) [travel - in bus, train etc] viajar

■ **ride out** *vt sep* sobrevivir; **to ride out the storm** capear el temporal

rider ['raɪdə(r)] *n* [of horse - man] jinete *m*; [woman] amazona *f*; [of bicycle] ciclista *mf*; [of motorbike] motociclista *mf*

ridge [rɪdʒ] *n* [crest of a hill] cresta *f*; [hillock] loma *f*; [of roof] caballete *m*; MET área *m*

ridicule ['rɪdɪkjuːl] **1.** *n* burla *f* **2.** *vt* burlarse de

ridiculous [rɪ'dɪkjʊləs] *adj* ridículo(a)

riding ['raɪdɪŋ] *n* equitación *f*; **riding breeches** pantalones *mpl* de montar; **riding school** escuela hípica

rife [raɪf] *adj* abundante; **rumour is rife that ...** corre la voz de que ...; **to be rife with** abundar en

riffraff ['rɪfræf] *n Fam* chusma *f*, gentuza *f*

rifle[1] ['raɪfəl] *n* fusil *m*, rifle *m*; **rifle range** campo *m* de tiro

rifle[2] ['raɪfəl] *vt* desvalijar

rift [rɪft] *n* **a)** GEOL falla *f* **b)** *Fig* [in friendship] ruptura *f*; POL [in party] escisión *f*; [quarrel] desavenencia *f*

rig [rɪg] **1.** *n* **a)** NAUT aparejo *m* **b)** (oil) **rig** [onshore] torre *f* de perforación; [offshore] plataforma petrolífera **2.** *vt Pej* amañar ■ **rig out** *vt sep Fam* ataviar ■ **rig up** *vt sep* improvisar, *Esp* apañar

right [raɪt] **1.** *adj* **a)** [not left] derecho(a)

b) [correct] correcto(a); [time] exacto(a); **to be right (about)** tener razón (en); **right?** ¿vale?

c) [morally correct] bien (*inv*); **to be right to do sth** hacer bien en hacer algo

d) [true] cierto(a)

e) [appropriate] adecuado(a); **the right time** el momento oportuno

f) [proper] apropiado(a)

g) *Fam* [healthy] bien

h) *Br Fam* [complete] auténtico(a)

i) right angle ángulo recto

2. *n* **a)** [right side] derecha *f*

b) [right hand] mano derecha

c) [moral correctness] bien *m*; **right and wrong** el bien y el mal; **to be in the right** tener razón

d) POL **the Right** la derecha

e) [lawful claim] derecho *m*; **in one's own right** por derecho propio; **right of way** [across land] derecho de paso; [on roads] prioridad *f*

f) rights derechos *mpl*; **I know my rights** conozco mis derechos; **by rights** en justicia

3. *adv* **a)** [correctly] bien; **it's just right** es justo lo que hace falta

b) [to the right] a la derecha; **right and left** a diestro y siniestro

c) [emphatic use] directamente; **go right on** sigue recto; **right at the top** en todo lo alto; **right away** [immediately] en seguida, inmediatamente, *CAm, Méx* ahorita; **right down/up** hasta arriba/abajo; **right here** aquí mismo; **right in the middle** justo en medio; **right now** ahora mismo; **go right to the end of the street** vaya hasta el final de la calle

4. *interj* ¡de acuerdo!, ¡vale!

5. *vt* **a)** [injustice, wrong] reparar, corregir

b) [ship] enderezar

right-click 1. *vt* COMPUT hacer clic derecho en **2.** *vi* COMPUT hacer clic derecho

rightful ['raɪtfʊl] *adj* legítimo(a)

right-hand ['raɪthænd] *adj* derecho(a); **right-hand drive** conducción *f* por la derecha; **right-hand side** lado derecho; *Fam* **right-hand man** brazo derecho

right-handed [raɪt'hændɪd] *adj* [person] que usa la mano derecha; [tool] para la mano derecha

rightly ['raɪtlɪ] *adv* debidamente; **and rightly so** y con razón

right-wing ['raɪtwɪŋ] *adj* de derechas, derechista

rigid ['rɪdʒɪd] *adj* rígido(a)

rigorous ['rɪgərəs] *adj* riguroso(a)

rim [rɪm] n [edge] borde m; [of wheel] llanta f; [of spectacles] montura f

rind [raɪnd] n [of fruit, cheese] corteza f

ring¹ [rɪŋ] (pt **rang**, pp **rung**) **1. n a)** [sound of bell] toque m; [of doorbell, alarm clock] timbre m
b) TEL llamada f
2. vt a) [bell] tocar; Fig **it rings a bell** me suena
b) Br [on phone] llamar (por teléfono) a, RP hablar a
3. vi a) [bell, phone etc] sonar
b) my ears are ringing tengo un pitido en los oídos
c) TEL llamar
■ **ring back** vt sep Br TEL volver a llamar
■ **ring off** vi Br TEL colgar
■ **ring out** vi resonar
■ **ring up** vt sep Br TEL llamar (por teléfono) a, RP hablar a

ring² [rɪŋ] **1. n a)** [metal hoop] aro m; **curtain ring** anilla f; **ring binder** archivador m or carpeta f de anillas, RP bibliorato m **b)** [for finger] anillo m, sortija f **c)** [circle] círculo m; Br **ring road** carretera f de circunvalación **d)** [group of people] corro m; [of spies] red f; [of thieves] banda f **e)** [arena] pista f; [for boxing] cuadrilátero m; [for bullfights] ruedo m **2. vt** [surround] rodear

ringing [ˈrɪŋɪŋ] n [of bell] toque m, repique m; [in ears] pitido m

ringleader [ˈrɪŋliːdə(r)] n cabecilla mf

ringtone [ˈrɪŋtəʊn] n melodía f

rink [rɪŋk] n pista f; **ice rink** pista de hielo

rinse [rɪns] **1. n** to give sth a rinse enjuagar or Esp aclarar algo **2. vt** [clothes, dishes] enjuagar, Esp aclarar; **to rinse one's hands** enjuagarse las manos

riot [ˈraɪət] **1. n a)** disturbio m, motín m; **to run riot** desmandarse; **riot police** policía f antidisturbios **b)** Fig [of colour] profusión f **2. vi** amotinarse

rioter [ˈraɪətə(r)] n amotinado(a) m,f

rip [rɪp] **1. n** [tear] rasgón m **2. vt** rasgar, rajar; **to rip one's trousers** rajarse los pantalones **3. vi** rasgarse, rajarse ■ **rip off** vt sep Fam **to rip sb off** clavar or Esp timar a algn ■ **rip up** vt sep hacer pedacitos

ripe [raɪp] adj **a)** maduro(a) **b)** [ready] listo(a); **the time is ripe** es el momento oportuno

ripen [ˈraɪpən] vt & vi madurar

rip-off [ˈrɪpɒf] n Fam timo m, Col, RP cagada f

ripped [rɪpt] adj US Fam **to be ripped, to have a ripped body** ser todo músculo

rise [raɪz] **1. n a)** [of slope, hill] cuesta f
b) [of waters] crecida f
c) [in prices, temperature] subida f; Br **(pay) rise** aumento m (de sueldo)
d) to give rise to ocasionar
2. (pt **rose**, pp **risen** [ˈrɪzən]) vi **a)** [land etc] elevarse
b) [waters] crecer; [river] nacer; [tide] subir; [wind] levantarse
c) [sun, moon] salir
d) [voice] alzarse
e) [in rank] ascender
f) [prices, temperature] subir; [wages] aumentar
g) [curtain] subir
h) [from bed] levantarse
i) [stand up] levantarse; Fig [city, building] erguirse
■ **rise above** vt insep estar por encima de
■ **rise up** vi [rebel] sublevarse

rising [ˈraɪzɪŋ] **1. adj** [sun] naciente; [tide] creciente; [prices] en aumento; **rising damp** humedad f **2. n a)** [of sun] salida f **b)** [rebellion] levantamiento m

risk [rɪsk] **1. n** riesgo m; **at risk** en peligro; **at your own risk** por su cuenta y riesgo; **to take risks** arriesgarse **2. vt** arriesgar; **I'll risk it** correré el riesgo

risky [ˈrɪskɪ] (compar **riskier**, superl **riskiest**) adj arriesgado(a)

rite [raɪt] n rito m; **the last rites** la extremaunción

ritual [ˈrɪtjʊəl] adj & n ritual (m)

rival [ˈraɪvəl] **1. adj** & n rival (mf) **2. vt** rivalizar con

rivalry [ˈraɪvəlrɪ] n rivalidad f

river ['rɪvə(r)] n río m; **down/up river** río abajo /arriba

riveting ['rɪvɪtɪŋ] adj Fig fascinante

RLR MESSAGING written abbr of **earlier**

rly MESSAGING written abbr of **really**

RMB MESSAGING written abbr of **ring my bell**

road [rəʊd] n a) carretera f; Br A/B road carretera nacional /secundaria; **main road** carretera principal; **road accident** accidente m de tráfico; **road safety** seguridad f vial; **road sign** señal f de tráfico; US **road trip** [short] vuelta f en coche; [longer] viaje m en coche; **road** Br **works** or US **work** obras fpl **b)** [street] calle f **c)** [way] camino m

roadblock ['rəʊdblɒk] n control m policial

roadside ['rəʊdsaɪd] n borde m de la carretera; **roadside restaurant/café** restaurante m /cafetería f de carretera

roam [rəʊm] **1.** vt vagar por, rondar **2.** vi vagar

roar [rɔː(r)] **1.** n [of lion] rugido m; [of bull, sea, wind] bramido m; [of crowd] clamor m **2.** vi [lion, crowd] rugir; [bull, sea, wind] bramar; [crowd] clamar; Fig **to roar with laughter** reírse a carcajadas

roaring ['rɔːrɪŋ] adj **a roaring success** un éxito clamoroso; **to do a roaring trade** hacer un negocio redondo

roast [rəʊst] **1.** adj [meat] asado(a); **roast beef** rosbif m **2.** n CULIN asado m **3.** vt [meat] asar; [coffee, nuts] tostar **4.** vi asarse

rob [rɒb] vt robar; [bank] atracar

robber ['rɒbə(r)] n ladrón(ona) m,f; **bank robber** atracador(a) m,f

robbery ['rɒbərɪ] n robo m

robe [rəʊb] n [ceremonial] toga f; [dressing gown] bata f

robin ['rɒbɪn] n petirrojo m

robot ['rəʊbɒt] n robot m

robust [rəʊ'bʌst] adj [sturdy] robusto(a)

rock [rɒk] **1.** n a) roca f; Fig **on the rocks** [marriage] a punto de fracasar; [whisky] con hielo **b)** US [stone] piedra f **c)** Br [sweet] **stick of rock** barra de caramelo de menta que se vende sobre todo en localidades costeras y lleva el nombre del lugar impreso **d)** MUS música f rock; **rock and roll** rock and roll m **2.** vt a) [chair] mecer; [baby] acunar **b)** [shake] hacer temblar; Fig [shock] conmover **3.** vi a) [move to and fro] mecerse **b)** [shake] vibrar

rocket ['rɒkɪt] **1.** n cohete m; **rocket launcher** lanzacohetes m inv **2.** vi Fam [prices] dispararse

rocky ['rɒkɪ] (compar **rockier**, superl **rockiest**) adj rocoso(a); Fam & Fig [unsteady] inseguro(a); **the Rocky Mountains** las Montañas Rocosas

rod [rɒd] n [of metal] barra f; [stick] vara f; **fishing rod** caña f de pescar

rode [rəʊd] pt of **ride**

rodent ['rəʊdənt] n roedor m

ROFL MESSAGING written abbr of **rolling on the floor laughing**

ROFLOL MESSAGING written abbr of **rolling on the floor laughing out loud**

rogue [rəʊg] n granuja m

role, **rôle** [rəʊl] n papel m; **to play a role** desempeñar un papel

roll [rəʊl] **1.** n a) [of paper, film] rollo m **b)** [bread] panecillo m, Méx bolillo m **c)** [list of names] lista f, nómina f **d)** [of drum] redoble m; [of thunder] fragor m **2.** vt a) [ball] hacer rodar **b)** [cigarette] liar **c)** [push] empujar **3.** vi a) [ball] rodar **b)** [animal] revolcarse **c)** [ship] balancearse **d)** [drum] redoblar; [thunder] retumbar

▪ **roll about**, **roll around** vi rodar (de acá para allá)

▪ **roll by** vi [years] pasar

■ **roll in** *vi Fam* **a)** [arrive] llegar **b)** [money] llegar a raudales

■ **roll out 1.** *vi insep* salir; **to roll out of bed** [person] salir de la cama **2.** *vt sep* **a)** [ball] hacer rodar; [pastry] extender (con el rodillo) **b)** [produce speech] soltar **c)** [product, offer] sacar

■ **roll over** *vi* dar una vuelta

■ **roll up 1.** *vt sep* enrollar; [blinds] subir; **to roll up one's sleeves** (ar)remangarse **2.** *vi Fam* [arrive] llegar

roller ['rəʊlə(r)] *n* **a)** TECH rodillo *m*; **roller blades** patines *mpl* en línea; **roller coaster** montaña rusa; **roller skates** patines *mpl* (de ruedas) **b)** [large wave] ola *f* grande **c)** [for hair] rulo *m*, *Chile* tubo *m*, *RP* rulero *m*

ROM [rɒm] *n* COMPUT (*abbr of* **read-only memory**) ROM *f*

Roman ['rəʊmən] *adj & n* romano(a) *(m,f)*; **Roman Catholic** católico(a) *m,f* (romano(a)); **Roman law** derecho romano; **Roman numerals** números romanos

romance [rəʊ'mæns] **1.** *n* **a)** [tale] novela romántica **b)** [love affair] aventura amorosa **c)** [romantic quality] lo romántico **2.** *vi* fantasear

Romania [rə'meɪnɪə] *n* Rumanía

Romanian [rə'meɪnɪən] **1.** *adj* rumano(a) **2.** *n* [person] rumano(a) *m,f*; [language] rumano *m*

romantic [rəʊ'mæntɪk] *adj & n* romántico(a) *(m,f)*

romp [rɒmp] **1.** *n* jugueteo *m* **2.** *vi* juguetear

rompers ['rɒmpəz] *npl* pelele *m*

roof [ru:f] **1.** *n* **a)** [of building] tejado *m*; *Fam & Fig* **to go through the roof** [prices] estar por las nubes; [with anger] subirse por las paredes **b)** AUTO techo *m*; **roof rack** baca *f* **c)** [of mouth] cielo *m* **2.** *vt* techar

rooftop ['ru:ftɒp] *n* tejado *m*; *Fig* **to shout sth from the rooftops** proclamar algo a los cuatro vientos

room [ru:m] *n* **a)** [in house] habitación *f*, cuarto *m*; [in hotel] habitación *f*; [bedroom] dormitorio *m*, *Am* cuarto *m*, *CAm, Col, Méx* recámara *f*; **single room** habitación individual; **room fragrance** fragancia *f* para el hogar; **room service** servicio *m* de habitaciones **b)** [space] sitio *m*, espacio *m*, *Am* lugar *m*, *Andes* campo *m*; **to make room (for sb)** hacer sitio *or Am* lugar *or Andes* campo (para *or a* algn)

roomie ['ru:mɪ] *n US Fam* compañero(a) *m,f* de habitación

roommate ['ru:mmeɪt] *n* compañero(a) *m,f* de habitación

roomy ['ru:mɪ] (*compar* **roomier**, *superl* **roomiest**) *adj* amplio(a)

roost [ru:st] **1.** *n* palo *m*, percha *f*; **(hen) roost** gallinero *m*; *Fig* **to rule the roost** llevar la batuta **2.** *vi* posarse

rooster ['ru:stə(r)] *n esp US* gallo *m*

root¹ [ru:t] **1.** *n* raíz *f*; **to take root** echar raíces **2.** *vt* arraigar **3.** *vi* arraigar ■ **root out**, **root up** *vt sep* arrancar de raíz

root² [ru:t] *vi* [search] buscar; **to root about** *or* **around for sth** hurgar en busca de algo

root³ [ru:t] *vi Fam* **to root for a team** animar a un equipo

rope [rəʊp] **1.** *n* **a)** [thin] cuerda *f*; [thick] soga *f*; NAUT cabo *m* **b)** *Fam & Fig* **to know the ropes** estar al tanto **2.** *vt* [package] atar; [climbers] encordar ■ **rope in** *vt sep Fam* enganchar ■ **rope off** *vt sep* acordonar

rosary ['rəʊzərɪ] *n* rosario *m*

rose¹ [rəʊz] *pt of* **rise**

rose² [rəʊz] *n* **a)** BOT rosa *f*; **rose bed** rosaleda *f*; **rose bush** rosal *m* **b)** [colour] rosa *m* **c)** [of watering can] alcachofa *f*

rosette [rəʊ'zet] *n* [of ribbons] escarapela *f*

roster ['rɒstə(r)] *n* lista *f*

rosy ['rəʊzɪ] (*compar* **rosier**, *superl* **rosiest**) *adj* **a)** [complexion] sonrosado(a) **b)** *Fig* [future] prometedor(a)

rot [rɒt] **1.** *n* **a)** [decay] putrefacción *f*; **dry rot** putrefacción de la madera **b)** *Br*

Fam [nonsense] sandeces *fpl*, *Am* pendejadas *fpl* **2.** *vt* pudrir ■ **rot away** *vi* pudrirse

rota ['rəutə] *n Br* lista *f*

rotate [rəu'teɪt] **1.** *vt* **a)** [revolve] hacer girar **b)** [jobs, crops] alternar **2.** *vi* [revolve] girar

rotation [rəu'teɪʃən] *n* rotación *f*

rotten ['rɒtən] *adj* **a)** [decayed] podrido(a); [tooth] picado(a) **b)** *Fam* [very bad] malísimo(a); *Fam* **I feel rotten** me siento *Esp* fatal *or Am* pésimo

rough [rʌf] **1.** *adj* **a)** [surface, skin] áspero(a); [terrain] accidentado(a); [sea] agitado(a); [weather] tempestuoso(a)
b) [violent] violento(a)
c) [wine] áspero(a)
d) *Fam* **to feel rough** encontrarse fatal; **to have a rough time** pasarlo mal
e) [approximate] aproximado(a); **rough copy, rough draft** borrador *m*; **rough sketch** bosquejo *m*
f) [harsh] severo(a)
2. *adv* duramente; *Fam & Fig* **to sleep rough** dormir a la intemperie *or Am* al raso
3. *n* **a)** GOLF rough *m*
b) [undetailed form] **in rough** en borrador
4. *vt Fam* **to rough it** apañarse como uno(a) pueda; **we had to rough it** nos las arreglamos *or Esp* apañamos como pudimos
■ **rough up** *vt sep Fam* [person] dar una paliza a

roughen ['rʌfən] *vt* poner áspero(a)

roughly ['rʌflɪ] *adv* **a)** [crudely] toscamente **b)** [clumsily] torpemente **c)** [not gently] bruscamente **d)** [approximately] aproximadamente

round [raund] **1.** *adj* redondo(a); **round trip** viaje *m* de ida y vuelta
2. *n* **a)** [series] serie *f*; **round of talks** ronda *f* de negociaciones
b) [of ammunition] cartucho *m*; [salvo] salva *f*
c) [of drinks] ronda *f*, *Am* vuelta *f*
d) [in golf] partido *m*

e) [in boxing] round *m*
f) [in a competition] eliminatoria *f*
3. *adv* **all year round** durante todo el año; **to invite sb round** invitar a algn a casa
4. *prep* alrededor de; **round here** por aquí; **it's just round the corner** está a la vuelta de la esquina, *RP* queda a la vuelta
5. *vt* [turn] dar la vuelta a
■ **round off** *vt sep* acabar, concluir
■ **round on** *vt insep* [attack] atacar
■ **round up** *vt sep* [cattle] acorralar, rodear; [people] reunir

roundabout ['raundəbaut] **1.** *n* **a)** *Br* [merry-go-round] tiovivo *m*, carrusel *m*, *RP* calesita *f* **b)** [for cars] rotonda *f*, *Esp* glorieta *f* **2.** *adj* indirecto(a)

rounders ['raundəz] *n Br* juego parecido al béisbol

rouse [rauz] *vt* despertar; [stir up] suscitar

route [ru:t] **1.** *n* **a)** ruta *f*; [of bus] línea *f*; NAUT derrota *f*; *Fig* camino *m*; **route map** mapa *m* de carreteras **b)** *US* **Route** ≃ carretera *f* nacional **2.** *vt* encaminar

router ['ru:tə, *US* 'rautə(r)] *n* COMPUT enrutador *m*, direccionador *m*, router *m*

routine [ru:'ti:n] **1.** *n* **a)** rutina *f* **b)** THEAT número *m* **2.** *adj* rutinario(a)

row¹ [rəu] *n* fila *f*, hilera *f*; *US* **row house** casa *f* adosada; *Fig* **three times in a row** tres veces seguidas

row² [rəu] *vt & vi* [in a boat] remar

row³ [rau] **1.** *n* **a)** [quarrel] pelea *f*, bronca *f* **b)** [noise] jaleo *m*; [protest] escándalo *m* **2.** *vi* pelearse

rowdy ['raudɪ] **1.** *(compar* **rowdier**, *superl* **rowdiest)** *adj* **a)** [noisy] ruidoso(a); [disorderly] alborotador(a) **b)** [quarrelsome] camorrista **2.** *n* camorrista *mf*

rowing ['rəuɪŋ] *n* remo *m*; *esp Br* **rowing boat** bote *m* de remos

royal ['rɔɪəl] **1.** *adj* real; **royal blue** azul marino; **the Royal Air Force** el ejército *m* del aire británico; **the Royal Family** la Familia Real **2.** *npl* **the Royals** los miembros de la Familia Real

royalty ['rɔɪəltɪ] *n* a) [royal persons] miembro(s) *m(pl)* de la Familia Real b) **royalties** derechos *mpl* de autor

rub [rʌb] **1.** *n* to give sth a rub frotar algo **2.** *vt* frotar; [hard] restregar; [massage] friccionar **3.** *vi* rozar (**against** contra) ■ **rub down** *vt sep* rotar; [horse] almohazar; [surface] raspar ■ **rub in** *vt sep* a) [cream etc] frotar con b) *Fam* **don't rub it in** no me lo refriegues ■ **rub off 1.** *vt sep* [erase] borrar **2.** *vi Fig* **to rub off on sb** influir en algn ■ **rub out** *vt sep* borrar

rubber[1] ['rʌbə(r)] *n* a) [substance] goma *f*, *Am* hule *m*; **rubber band** goma; **rubber stamp** tampón *m* b) *Br* [eraser] goma *f* (de borrar) c) *Fam* [condom] goma *f*, *Méx* impermeable *m*, *RP* forro *m*

rubber[2] ['rʌbə(r)] *n* [in bridge] rubber *m*

rubbish ['rʌbɪʃ] *n* a) *Br* [refuse] basura *f*; *Br* **rubbish bin** cubo *m or Am* bote *m* de la basura; **rubbish dump** *or* **tip** vertedero *m* b) *Fam* [worthless thing] birria *f* c) *Fam* [nonsense] tonterías *fpl*

rubble ['rʌbəl] *n* escombros *mpl*

ruby ['ru:bɪ] *n* rubí *m*

rucksack ['rʌksæk] *n* mochila *f*

rudder ['rʌdə(r)] *n* timón *m*

rude [ru:d] *adj* a) [impolite] maleducado(a); [foul-mouthed] grosero(a); **don't be rude to your mother** no le faltes al respeto a tu madre b) [abrupt] a **rude awakening** un despertar repentino

rug [rʌg] *n* alfombra *f*, alfombrilla *f*

rugby ['rʌgbɪ] *n* rugby *m*; **rugby league** rugby a trece; **rugby union** rugby a quince

rugged ['rʌgɪd] *adj* a) [terrain] accidentado(a) b) [features] marcado(a) c) [character] vigoroso(a)

rugrat ['rʌgræt] *n US Fam* [child] renacuajo(a) *m,f*

ruin ['ru:ɪn] **1.** *n* a) ruina *f* b) **ruins** ruinas *fpl*, restos *mpl*; **in ruins** en ruinas **2.** *vt* arruinar; [spoil] estropear

ruined ['ru:ɪnd] *adj* [building] en ruinas

rule [ru:l] **1.** *n* a) regla *f*, norma *f*; **to work to rule** hacer una huelga de celo; **as a rule** por regla general b) [government] dominio *m*; [of monarch] reinado *m*; **rule of law** imperio *m* de la ley **2.** *vt & vi* a) [govern] gobernar; [of monarch] reinar b) [decide] decidir; [decree] decretar c) [draw] tirar ■ **rule out** *vt sep* descartar

ruler ['ru:lə(r)] *n* a) dirigente *mf*; [monarch] soberano(a) *m,f* b) [for measuring] regla *f*

ruling ['ru:lɪŋ] **1.** *adj* [in charge] dirigente; *Fig* [predominant] predominante; **the ruling party** el partido en el poder **2.** *n* JUR fallo *m*

rum [rʌm] *n* ron *m*

Rumania [ru:'meɪnɪə] *n* = **Romania**

rumble ['rʌmbəl] **1.** *n* a) ruido sordo; [of thunder] estruendo *m* b) [of stomach] ruido *m* **2.** *vi* a) hacer un ruido sordo; [thunder] retumbar b) [stomach etc] hacer ruidos

rummage ['rʌmɪdʒ] *vi* revolver (**through** en); *US* **rummage sale** [in store] *venta de productos discontinuados o sin salida en un almacén*; [for charity] rastrillo benéfico

rumour, *US* rumor ['ru:mə(r)] **1.** *n* rumor *m*; **rumour has it that …** se dice que … **2.** *vt* **it is rumoured that** se rumorea que

rump [rʌmp] *n* [of animal] ancas *fpl*; *Fam & Hum* [of person] trasero *m*; **rump steak** filete *m* de lomo

run [rʌn] (*pt* ran, *pp* run) **1.** *n* a) carrera *f*; **on the run** fugado(a); **to go for a run** hacer footing; *Fig* **in the long run** a largo plazo b) [trip] paseo *m*, vuelta *f* c) [sequence] serie *f* d) [in stocking] carrera *f* **2.** *vt* a) correr; **to run a race** correr en una carrera b) [drive] llevar c) [house, business] llevar; [company] dirigir; [organize] organizar d) [fingers] pasar e) COMPUT **to run a program** ejecutar un programa

3. *vi* **a)** correr

b) [colour] desteñirse

c) [water, river] correr; **to leave the tap running** dejar el grifo abierto; *Fam* **your nose is running** se te caen los mocos

d) [machine] funcionar (**on** con)

e) POL **to run for president** presentarse como candidato a la presidencia

f) [range] oscilar (**between** entre)

g) shyness runs in the family la timidez le viene de familia

■ **run about** *vi* corretear

■ **run across** *vt insep* [meet] tropezar con

■ **run away** *vi* fugarse; [horse] desbocarse

■ **run down 1.** *vt insep* [stairs] bajar corriendo **2.** *vt sep* **a)** [in car] atropellar **b)** [criticize] criticar **3.** *vi* [battery] agotarse; [clock] pararse

■ **run in** *vt sep* AUTO rodar

■ **run into** *vt insep* **a)** [room] entrar corriendo en **b)** [people, problems] tropezar con **c)** [crash into] chocar contra

■ **run off 1.** *vt sep* [print] tirar **2.** *vi* escaparse

■ **run on 1.** *vt sep* TYP enlazar **2.** *vi* [meeting] continuar

■ **run out** *vi* **a)** [exit] salir corriendo **b)** [come to an end] agotarse; [of contract] vencer; **to run out of** quedarse sin

■ **run over 1.** *vt sep* [in car] atropellar **2.** *vt insep* [rehearse] ensayar **3.** *vi* [overflow] rebosar

■ **run through** *vt insep* **a)** [of river] pasar por **b)** [read quickly] echar un vistazo a **c)** [rehearse] ensayar

■ **run up** *vt sep* **a)** [flag] izar **b)** [debts] acumular

■ **run up against** *vt insep* tropezar con

runaway ['rʌnəweɪ] **1.** *n* fugitivo(a) *m,f* **2.** *adj* [person] huido(a); [horse] desbocado(a); [vehicle] incontrolado(a); [inflation] galopante; [success] clamoroso(a)

rundown ['rʌndaʊn] *n* [report] resumen *m*, informe *m*

run-down *adj* **a)** [building] descuidado(a) **b)** [person] débil, flojo(a)

rung[1] [rʌŋ] *pp of* **ring**

rung[2] [rʌŋ] *n* [of ladder] escalón *m*, peldaño *m*

runner ['rʌnə(r)] *n* **a)** [person] corredor(a) *m,f* **b)** *Br* **runner bean** *Esp* judía *f* verde, *Bol, RP* chaucha *f*, *Méx* ejote *m*

runner-up [rʌnər'ʌp] *n* subcampeón(ona) *m,f*

running ['rʌnɪŋ] **1.** *n* **a)** he likes running le gusta correr; *Fig* **to be in the running for sth** tener posibilidades de conseguir algo **b)** [of company] dirección *f* **c)** [of machine] funcionamiento *m* **2.** *adj* **a) running commentary** comentario *m* en directo; **running costs** costos *mpl* de mantenimiento; POL **running mate** candidato *m* a la vicepresidencia; **running water** agua *f* corriente **b) three weeks running** tres semanas seguidas

runny ['rʌnɪ] *(compar* runnier, *superl* runniest) *adj* **a) running** blando(a); [egg] crudo(a); [butter] derretido(a); [nose] que moquea

runway ['rʌnweɪ] *n* AVIAT pista *f* (de aterrizaje y despegue *or Am* decolaje)

RUOK? MESSAGING *(abbr of* **are you OK?)** tas OK?

rupture ['rʌptʃə(r)] **1.** *n* **a)** MED hernia *f* **b)** *Fig* ruptura *f* **2.** *vt* **a) to rupture oneself** herniarse **b)** [break] romper

rural ['rʊərəl] *adj* rural

ruse [ruːz] *n* ardid *m*, astucia *f*

rush[1] [rʌʃ] *n* BOT junco *m*

rush[2] [rʌʃ] **1.** *n* **a)** [hurry] prisa *f*, *Am* apuro *m*; **the rush hour** *Esp* la hora punta, *Am* la hora pico **b)** [demand] demanda *f* **2.** *vt* **a)** [task] hacer de prisa; [person] meter prisa a; **to rush sb to hospital** llevar a algn urgentemente al hospital **b)** [attack] abalanzarse sobre; MIL tomar por asalto **3.** *vi* [go quickly] precipitarse

■ **rush about** *vi* correr de un lado a otro

■ **rush into** *vt insep Fig* to rush into sth hacer algo sin pensarlo bien
■ **rush off** *vi* irse corriendo

rusk [rʌsk] *n galleta dura para niños*

Russia ['rʌʃə] *n* Rusia

Russian ['rʌʃən] **1.** *adj* ruso(a) **2.** *n* **a)** [person] ruso(a) *m,f* **b)** [language] ruso *m*

rust [rʌst] **1.** *n* **a)** [substance] herrumbre *f* **b)** [colour] pardo rojizo **2.** *vt* oxidar **3.** *vi* oxidarse

rustic ['rʌstɪk] *adj* rústico(a)

rustle ['rʌsəl] **1.** *n* crujido *m* **2.** *vt* [papers etc] hacer crujir **3.** *vi* [steal cattle] robar ganado

rusty ['rʌstɪ] *(compar* rustier, *superl* rustiest) *adj* oxidado(a); *Fam & Fig* my French is a bit rusty tengo el francés un poco oxidado

rut [rʌt] *n* **a)** [furrow] surco *m*; [groove] ranura *f* **b)** *Fig* to be in a rut ser esclavo de la rutina **c)** ZOOL celo *m*

ruthless ['ruːθlɪs] *adj* despiadado(a)

RV [ɑːˈviː] *n US (abbr of* recreational vehicle) autocaravana *f,* casa *for* coche *m* caravana

rye [raɪ] *n* centeno *m*; **rye bread** pan *m* de centeno; **rye grass** ballica *f; US* **rye (whiskey)** whisky *m* de centeno

S

S, **s** [es] n [the letter] S, s f

S (abbr of **south**) S

Sabbath ['sæbəθ] n **the Sabbath** el Sabbat

sabotage ['sæbəta:ʒ] **1.** n sabotaje m **2.** vt sabotear

sack [sæk] **1.** n a) [bag] saco m b) Fam **to get the sack** ser despedido(a); Fam **to give sb the sack** despedir a algn **2.** vt a) Fam despedir b) MIL saquear

sacred ['seɪkrɪd] adj sagrado(a)

sacrifice ['sækrɪfaɪs] **1.** n sacrificio m **2.** vt sacrificar

sad [sæd] (compar **sadder**, superl **saddest**) adj triste; **how sad!** ¡qué pena!

sadden ['sædən] vt entristecer

saddle ['sædəl] **1.** n [for horse] silla f (de montar); [of bicycle etc] sillín m **2.** vt [horse] ensillar; Fam **to saddle sb with sth** encajar or Esp, Méx encasquetar algo a algn

sadistic [sə'dɪstɪk] adj sádico(a)

sadly ['sædlɪ] adv [to reply, smile] tristemente; **sadly, this is so** así es, por desgracia

sadness ['sædnɪs] n tristeza f

safari [sə'fɑːrɪ] n safari m; **safari park** reserva f

safe [seɪf] **1.** adj a) [unharmed] ileso(a); [out of danger] a salvo; **safe and sound** sano(a) y salvo(a) b) [not dangerous] inocuo(a) c) [secure, sure] seguro(a) d) [driver] prudente **2.** n [for money etc] caja f fuerte

safeguard ['seɪfgɑːd] **1.** n [protection] salvaguarda f; [guarantee] garantía f **2.** vt proteger, salvaguardar

safely ['seɪflɪ] adv a) con toda seguridad b) **to arrive safely** llegar sin incidentes

safety ['seɪftɪ] n seguridad f; **safety first!** ¡la seguridad ante todo!; **safety belt** cinturón m de seguridad; **safety lock** cierre f de seguridad; **safety net** red f de protección; **safety pin** imperdible m, Am alfiler m de gancho, CAm, Méx seguro m

sag [sæg] vi a) [roof] hundirse; [wall] pandear; [wood, iron] combarse; [flesh] colgar b) Fig [spirits] flaquear

saga ['sɑːgə] n [story] saga f; Fig **a saga of corruption** una historia interminable de corrupción

Sagittarius [sædʒɪ'teərɪəs] n Sagitario m

Sahara [sə'hɑːrə] n **the Sahara** el Sahara

said [sed] **1.** adj dicho(a) **2.** pt & pp of **say**

sail [seɪl] **1.** n a) [canvas] vela f; **to set sail** zarpar b) [trip] paseo m en barco **2.** vt [ship] gobernar; Liter navegar **3.** vi a) ir en barco b) [set sail] zarpar

■ **sail through** vt insep Fam **he sailed through university** en la universidad todo le fue sobre ruedas

sailboat ['seɪlbəʊt] n US velero m

sailing ['seɪlɪŋ] n navegación f; [yachting] vela f; Fam **it's all plain sailing** es todo coser y cantar; Br **sailing boat** (barco m) velero m; **sailing ship** barco m de vela

sailor ['seɪlə(r)] n marinero m

saint [seɪnt] n santo(a) m,f; (before all masculine names except those beginning **Do** or **To**) San; [before feminine names] Santa; **Saint Dominic** Santo Domingo; **Saint Helen** Santa Elena; **Saint John** San Juan; **All Saints' Day** Día m de Todos los Santos

sake [seɪk] n **for the sake of** por (el bien de); **for your own sake** por tu propio bien

salad ['sæləd] n ensalada f; **potato salad** ensalada de patatas or Am papas; **salad bowl** ensaladera f; Br **salad cream** salsa f tipo mahonesa; **salad dressing** aderezo m or Esp aliño m para la ensalada

salami [sə'lɑːmɪ] n salami m, Am salame m

salary ['sælərɪ] n salario m, sueldo m

sale [seɪl] n **a)** venta f; **for** or **on sale** en venta; US **garage sale** mercadillo en casa de un particular; **sales department** departamento m comercial; **sales manager** jefe(a) m,f de ventas; US **sales slip** tícket m de compra; **sales tax** impuesto m de venta **b)** [at low prices] rebajas fpl

salesclerk ['seɪlzklɜːrk] n US dependiente(a) m,f

salesman ['seɪlzmən] n **a)** vendedor m; [in shop] dependiente m **b)** [commercial traveller] representante m

saleswoman ['seɪlzwʊmən] n **a)** vendedora f; [in shop] dependienta f **b)** [commercial traveller] representante f

salmon ['sæmən] **1.** n salmón m **2.** adj (de color) salmón

salon ['sælɒn] n salón m

saloon [sə'luːn] n **a)** [on ship] cámara f **b)** US [bar] taberna f, bar m; Br **saloon (bar)** bar de lujo **c)** Br [car] turismo m

salt [sɔːlt] **1.** n sal f; Fig **to take sth with a pinch of salt** creer algo con reservas; **bath salts** sales de baño; **smelling salts** sales aromáticas **2.** adj salado(a) **3.** vt **a)** [cure] salar **b)** [add salt to] echar sal a

saltcellar ['sɔːltselə(r)], US **saltshaker** ['sɔːltʃeɪkər] n salero m

saltwater ['sɔːltwɔːtər] **1.** n agua f de mar **2.** adj de agua salada

salty ['sɔːltɪ] (compar **saltier**, superl **saltiest**) adj salado(a)

salute [sə'luːt] **1.** n [greeting] saludo m **2.** vt **a)** MIL saludar **b)** Fig [achievement etc] aplaudir **3.** vi MIL saludar

salvage ['sælvɪdʒ] **1.** n **a)** [of ship etc] salvamento m, rescate m **b)** [objects recovered] objetos recuperados **c)** JUR derecho m de salvamento **2.** vt [from ship etc] rescatar

salvation [sæl'veɪʃən] n salvación f; **Salvation Army** Ejército m de Salvación

same [seɪm] **1.** adj mismo(a); **at that very same moment** en ese mismísimo momento; **at the same time** [simultaneously] al mismo tiempo; [however] sin embargo; **in the same way** del mismo modo; **the two cars are the same** los dos coches son iguales **2.** pron **the same** el mismo / la misma / lo mismo; Fam **the same here** lo mismo digo yo; Fam **the same to you!** ¡igualmente! **3.** adv del mismo modo, igual; **all the same, just the same** sin embargo, aun así; **it's all the same to me** (a mí) me da igual or lo mismo

sample ['sɑːmpəl] **1.** n muestra f **2.** vt [wines] catar; [dish] probar

sanatorium, US **sanitorium** (pl **sanitoriums** or **sanitoria** [-rɪə]) [sænə'tɔːrɪəm] n sanatorio m

sanction ['sæŋkʃən] **1.** n **a)** [authorization] permiso m **b)** [penalty] sanción f **c)** POL **sanctions** sanciones fpl **2.** vt sancionar

sanctuary ['sæŋktjʊərɪ] n **a)** REL santuario m **b)** POL asilo m **c)** [for birds, animals] reserva f

sand [sænd] **1.** n arena f; **sand castle** castillo m de arena; **sand dune** duna f **2.** vt **to sand (down)** lijar

sandal ['sændəl] n sandalia f, Andes, CAm ojota f, Méx guarache m

sandpit ['sændpɪt], US **sandbox** ['sændbɒks] n recinto m de arena

sandwich ['sænwɪdʒ, 'sænwɪtʃ] **1.** n [with sliced bread] sándwich m; [with French bread] Esp bocadillo m, Am sándwich m, CSur sándwiche m, Méx torta f; SCH **sandwich course** curso teórico-práctico

2. *vt* intercalar; **it was sandwiched between two lorries** quedó encajonado entre dos camiones

sandy ['sændɪ] *(compar* **sandier,** *superl* **sandiest)** *adj* **a)** [earth, beach] arenoso(a) **b)** [hair] rubio(a) rojizo(a)

sane [seɪn] *adj* [not mad] cuerdo(a) ; [sensible] sensato(a)

sang [sæŋ] *pt of* **sing**

sanitary ['sænɪtərɪ] *adj* sanitario(a) ; [hygienic] higiénico(a) ; **sanitary** *Br* **towel** *or US* **napkin** compresa *f, Am* toalla *f* higiénica

sanitation [sænɪ'teɪʃən] *n* sanidad *f* (pública) ; [plumbing] sistema *m* de saneamiento

sanity ['sænɪtɪ] *n* cordura *f*, juicio *m* ; [good sense] sensatez *f*

sank [sæŋk] *pt of* **sink**

Santa (Claus) ['sæntə(ˌklɔːz)] *n* Papá *m* Noel

sap¹ [sæp] *n* BOT savia *f*

sap² [sæp] *vt* [undermine] minar ; *Fig* agotar

sapphire ['sæfaɪə(r)] *n* zafiro *m*

sarcastic [sɑːˈkæstɪk] *adj* sarcástico(a)

sardine [sɑːˈdiːn] *n* sardina *f*

Sardinia [sɑːˈdɪnɪə] *n* Cerdeña *f*

SARS ['sɑːz] *n (abbr of* **severe acute respiratory syndrome)** SRAS *m (síndrome respiratorio agudo severo)*

sat [sæt] *pt & pp of* **sit**

SAT [sæt] *n* **a)** *(abbr of* **Standard Assessment Test)** *evaluación de los alumnos de 7, 11 y 14 años en Inglaterra* **b)** *(abbr of* **Scholastic Aptitude Test)** *examen de entrada a la universidad en Estados Unidos*

satchel ['sætʃəl] *n* cartera *f* de colegial

satellite ['sætəlaɪt] *n* satélite *m* ; **satellite dish (aerial)** antena parabólica

satin ['sætɪn] *n* satén *m* ; **satin finish** (acabado *m*) satinado *m*

satire ['sætaɪə(r)] *n* sátira *f*

satirical [səˈtɪrɪkəl] *adj* satírico(a)

satisfaction [sætɪsˈfækʃən] *n* satisfacción *f*

satisfactory [sætɪsˈfæktərɪ] *adj* satisfactorio(a)

satisfy ['sætɪsfaɪ] *vt* **a)** satisfacer **b)** [fulfil] cumplir con **c)** [convince] convencer

satisfying ['sætɪsfaɪɪŋ] *adj* satisfactorio(a) ; [pleasing] agradable ; [meal] que llena

satnav ['sætnæv] *n* GPS *m*

saturate ['sætʃəreɪt] *vt* saturar **(with** de)

Saturday ['sætədɪ] *n* sábado *m*; **Saturday girl** dependienta *f* para los sábados

sauce [sɔːs] *n* **a)** salsa *f* **b)** *Br Fam* [impudence] descaro *m*

saucepan ['sɔːspən] *n* cacerola *f* ; [large] olla *f*

saucer ['sɔːsə(r)] *n* platillo *m*

Saudi Arabia ['saʊdɪəˈreɪbɪə] *n* Arabia Saudí

sauna ['sɔːnə] *n* sauna *f, Am* sauna *m or f*

saunter ['sɔːntə(r)] **1.** *n* paseo **2.** *vi* pasearse

sausage ['sɒsɪdʒ] *n* [raw] salchicha *f* ; [cured] salchichón *m* ; [spicy] chorizo *m* ; *Fam* **sausage dog** perro *m* salchicha ; *Br* **sausage roll** empanada *f* de carne

savage ['sævɪdʒ] **1.** *adj* **a)** [ferocious] feroz ; [cruel] cruel ; [violent] salvaje **b)** [primitive] salvaje **2.** *n* salvaje *mf* **3.** *vt* [attack] embestir ; *Fig* [criticize] criticar despiadadamente

save [seɪv] **1.** *vt* **a)** [rescue] salvar, rescatar ; *Fig* **to save face** salvar las apariencias
b) [put by] guardar ; [money, energy, time] ahorrar ; [food] almacenar ; **it saved him a lot of trouble** le evitó muchos problemas
c) COMPUT guardar
2. *vi* **a)** **to save (up)** ahorrar
b) **to save on paper** [economize] ahorrar papel
3. *n* FTBL parada *f*
4. *prep Liter* salvo, excepto

saving ['seɪvɪŋ] *n* **a)** [of time, money] ahorro *m* **b)** **savings** ahorros *mpl* ; **savings account** cuenta *f* de ahorros

saviour, *US* **savior** ['seɪvjə(r)] *n* salvador(a) *m,f*

savour, US **savor** ['seɪvə(r)] **1.** n sabor m, gusto m **2.** vi saborear

savoury, US **savory** ['seɪvərɪ] adj [tasty] sabroso(a); [salted] salado(a); [spicy] picante

saw¹ [sɔː] (pt sawed, pp sawed or sawn [sɔːn]) **1.** n [tool] sierra f **2.** vt & vi serrar
■ **saw up** vt sep serrar (**into** en)

saw² [sɔː] pt of **see**

sawdust ['sɔːdʌst] n (a) serrín m

saxophone ['sæksəfəʊn] n saxofón m

say [seɪ] **1.** (pt & pp said) vt **a)** decir; **it goes without saying that ...** huelga decir que ...; **it is said that ...** se dice que ...; **not to say ...** por no decir ...; **that is to say** es decir; **to say yes/no** decir que sí/no; Fam **I say!** ¡oiga!; **what does the sign say?** ¿qué pone en el letrero? **b)** [think] pensar
c) shall we say Friday then? ¿quedamos el viernes, pues?
2. n **I have no say in the matter** no tengo ni voz ni voto en el asunto; **to have one's say** dar su opinión

saying ['seɪɪŋ] n refrán m, dicho m

scab [skæb] n **a)** MED costra f **b)** Fam esquirol mf, Am rompehuelgas mf inv

scaffolding ['skæfəldɪŋ] n CONSTR andamio

scald [skɔːld] **1.** n escaldadura f **2.** vt escaldar

scale¹ [skeɪl] n [of fish, on skin] escama f; [in boiler] incrustaciones fpl
■ **scale down** vt sep [drawing] reducir a escala; [production] reducir

scale² [skeɪl] **1.** n **a)** escala f; **on a large scale** a gran escala; **to scale** a escala; **scale model** maqueta f **b)** [extent] alcance m **c)** MUS escala f **2.** vt [climb] escalar

scales [skeɪlz] npl **(pair of) scales** [shop, kitchen] balanza f; [bathroom] báscula f

scalp [skælp] **1.** n cuero cabelludo **2.** vt arrancar el cuero cabelludo a

scamper ['skæmpə(r)] vi corretear

scampi ['skæmpɪ] n gambas empanadas

scan [skæn] **1.** vt **a)** [scrutinize] escrutar; [horizon] otear **b)** [glance at] ojear **c)** [of radar] explorar **d)** COMPUT escanear **2.** n MED exploración ultrasónica; [in gynaecology etc] ecografía f

scandal ['skændəl] n **a)** escándalo m; **what a scandal!** ¡qué vergüenza! **b)** [gossip] chismorreo m, Esp cotilleo m

scandalous ['skændələs] adj escandaloso(a)

Scandinavia [skændɪ'neɪvɪə] n Escandinavia

Scandinavian [skændɪ'neɪvɪən] adj & n escandinavo(a) (m,f)

scanner ['skænə(r)] n MED & COMPUT escáner m

scanty ['skæntɪ] (compar **scantier**, superl **scantiest**) adj escaso(a); [meal] insuficiente; [clothes] ligero(a)

scapegoat ['skeɪpgəʊt] n chivo expiatorio

scar [skɑː(r)] n cicatriz f

scarce [skeəs] adj escaso(a); Fig **to make oneself scarce** largarse

scarcely ['skeəslɪ] adv apenas

scare [skeə(r)] **1.** n [fright] susto m; [widespread alarm] pánico m; **bomb scare** amenaza f de bomba; **scare story** historia f alarmista **2.** vt asustar; Fam **to be scared stiff** estar muerto(a) de miedo ■ **scare away**, **scare off** vt sep ahuyentar

scarf [skɑːf] (pl **scarfs** or **scarves** [skɑːvz]) n [long, woollen] bufanda f; [square] pañuelo m; [silk] fular m

scarlet ['skɑːlɪt] **1.** adj escarlata **2.** n escarlata f; **scarlet fever** escarlatina f

scary ['skeərɪ] adj Fam [noise, situation] aterrador(a), espantoso(a); [film, book] de miedo

scathing ['skeɪðɪŋ] adj mordaz, cáustico(a)

scatter ['skætə(r)] **1.** vt **a)** [papers etc] esparcir, desparramar **b)** [crowd] dispersar **2.** vi dispersarse

scatterbrain ['skætəbreɪn] n cabeza f de chorlito, despistado(a) m,f

scavenger ['skævɪndʒə(r)] *n* **a)** [person] rebuscador(a) *m,f*, trapero *m* **b)** [animal] animal *m* carroñero

scenario [sɪ'nɑːrɪəʊ] *n* **a)** CIN guión *m* **b)** [situation] situación *f* hipotética

scene [siːn] *n* **a)** THEAT, CIN & TV escena *f* **b)** [place] lugar *m*, escenario *m* **c) to make a scene** [fuss] hacer una escena, *Esp* montar un número

scenery ['siːnərɪ] *n* **a)** [landscape] paisaje *m* **b)** THEAT decorado *m*

scenic ['siːnɪk] *adj* [picturesque] pintoresco(a)

scent [sent] **1.** *n* **a)** [smell] olor *m*; [of food] aroma *m* **b)** [perfume] perfume *m* **c)** [in hunting] pista *f* **2.** *vt* [add perfume to] perfumar; [smell] olfatear; *Fig* presentir

sceptic ['skeptɪk] *n* escéptico(a) *m,f*

sceptical ['skeptɪkəl] *adj* escéptico(a)

schedule ['ʃedjuːl, *US* 'skedʒʊəl] **1.** *n* **a)** [plan, agenda] programa *m*; [timetable] horario *m*; **on schedule** a la hora (prevista); **to be behind schedule** llevar retraso **b)** [list] lista *f*; [inventory] inventario *m* **2.** *vt* [plan] programar, fijar

scheduled ['ʃedjuːld, *US* 'skedʒʊəld] *adj* previsto(a), fijo(a); **scheduled flight** vuelo regular

scheme [skiːm] **1.** *n* **a)** [plan] plan *m*; [project] proyecto *m*; [idea] idea *f*; **colour scheme** combinación *f* de colores **b)** [plot] intriga *f*; [trick] ardid *m* **2.** *vi* [plot] tramar, intrigar

schizophrenic [skɪtsəʊ'frenɪk] *adj* & *n* esquizofrénico(a) *(m,f)*

schmuck [ʃmʌk] *n US Fam* lelo(a) *m,f*

scholar ['skɒlə(r)] *n* [learned person] erudito(a) *m,f*; [pupil] alumno(a) *m,f*

scholarly ['skɒləlɪ] *adj* erudito(a)

scholarship ['skɒləʃɪp] *n* **a)** [learning] erudición *f* **b)** [grant] beca *f*; **scholarship holder** becario(a) *m,f*

school [skuːl] **1.** *n* **a)** [for children - up to 14] colegio *m*, escuela *f*; [from 14 to 18] instituto *m*; **middle school** *Br* escuela *para niños de ocho a doce años*; *US* escuela *para niños de once a catorce años*; **school**

friend amigo(a) *m,f* del colegio; **school year** año *m* escolar **b)** *US* [university] universidad *f* **c)** [university department] facultad *f* **d)** [group of artists] escuela *f* **2.** *vt* [teach] enseñar; [train] formar

schoolboy ['skuːlbɔɪ] *n* alumno *m*

schoolchild ['skuːltʃaɪld] *n* alumno(a) *m,f*

schoolgirl ['skuːlgɜːl] *n* alumna *f*

schoolteacher ['skuːltiːtʃə(r)] *n* profesor(a) *m,f*; [primary school] maestro(a) *m,f*

schtum [ʃtʊm] *adj Br Fam* **to keep schtum** no decir ni pío

science ['saɪəns] *n* ciencia *f*; [school subject] ciencias; **science fiction** ciencia-ficción *f*

scientific [saɪən'tɪfɪk] *adj* científico(a)

scientist ['saɪəntɪst] *n* científico(a) *m,f*

sci-fi [ˌsaɪ'faɪ] *n (abbr of science fiction) Fam* ciencia *f* ficción

scissors ['sɪzəz] *npl* tijeras *fpl*; **a pair of scissors** unas tijeras

scoff¹ [skɒf] *vi* [mock] mofarse (**at** de)

scoff² [skɒf] *vt Br Fam* [eat] zamparse

scold [skəʊld] *vt* regañar, reñir

scone [skəʊn, skɒn] *n* bollo *m*, pastelito *m*

scoop [skuːp] *n* **a)** [for flour] pala *f*; [for ice cream] cucharón *m*; [amount] palada *f*, cucharada *f* **b)** PRESS exclusiva *f* ∎ **scoop out** *vt sep* [flour etc] sacar con pala; [water - from boat] achicar ∎ **scoop up** *vt sep* recoger

scooter ['skuːtə(r)] *n* [child's] patinete *m*; [adult's] Vespa® *f*

scope [skəʊp] *n* **a)** [range] alcance *m*; [of undertaking] ámbito *m* **b)** [freedom] libertad *f*

scorch [skɔːtʃ] *vt* [singe] chamuscar

scorching ['skɔːtʃɪŋ] *adj Fam* abrasador(a)

score [skɔː(r)] **1.** *n* **a)** SPORT tanteo *m*; CARDS & GOLF puntuación *f*; [result] resultado *m*
b) on that score a ese respecto
c) [twenty] veintena *f*

d) MUS [of opera] partitura *f*; [of film] música *f*
2. *vt* **a)** [goal] marcar; [points] conseguir
b) [wood] hacer una muesca en; [paper] rayar
3. *vi* **a)** SPORT marcar un tanto; FTBL marcar un gol
b) *Fam* ligar (**with** con)
■ **score out** *vt sep* [word etc] tachar

scoreboard ['skɔːbɔːd] *n* marcador *m*

scorn [skɔːn] **1.** *n* desprecio *m* **2.** *vt* despreciar

scornful ['skɔːnfʊl] *adj* desdeñoso(a)

Scorpio ['skɔːpɪəʊ] *n* Escorpio *m*, Escorpión *m*

scorpion ['skɔːpɪən] *n* alacrán *m*, escorpión *m*

Scot [skɒt] *n* escocés(esa) *m,f*

Scotch [skɒtʃ] **1.** *adj* escocés(esa); *US* **Scotch tape®** cinta adhesiva, *Esp* celo® *m*, *CAm*, *Méx* Durex® *m* **2.** *n* [whisky] whisky *m* escocés

Scotland ['skɒtlənd] *n* Escocia

Scotsman ['skɒtsmən] *n* escocés *m*

Scotswoman ['skɒtswʊmən] *n* escocesa *f*

Scottish ['skɒtɪʃ] *adj* escocés(esa)

scoundrel ['skaʊndrəl] *n* sinvergüenza *mf*, canalla *m*

scour¹ [skaʊə(r)] *vt* [clean] fregar, restregar

scour² [skaʊə(r)] *vt* [search - countryside] rastrear; [building] registrar

scout [skaʊt] **1.** *n* MIL explorador(a) *m,f*; SPORT & CIN cazatalentos *m inv*; **boy scout** boy *m* scout **2.** *vi* MIL reconocer el terreno; **to scout around for sth** andar en busca de algo

scowl [skaʊl] **1.** *vi* fruncir el ceño; **to scowl at sb** mirar a algn con ceño **2.** *n* ceño *m*

scram [skræm] *(pt & pp* **scrammed***) vi Fam* largarse, *Esp*, *RP* pirarse; **scram!** ¡largo!

scramble ['skræmbəl] **1.** *vi* trepar; **to scramble for** pelearse por; **to scramble up a tree** trepar a un árbol

2. *vt* **a)** CULIN **scrambled eggs** huevos revueltos
b) RADIO & TEL [message] codificar; [broadcast] interferir
3. *n* [climb] subida *f*; *Fig* **it's going to be a scramble** [rush] va a ser muy apresurado

scrap¹ [skræp] **1.** *n* **a)** [small piece] pedazo *m*; **there isn't a scrap of truth in it** no tiene ni un ápice de verdad; **scrap (metal)** chatarra *f*; **scrap dealer** or **merchant** chatarrero(a) *m,f*; **scrap paper** papel *m* de borrador; **scrap yard** [for cars] cementerio *m* de coches **b)** **scraps** restos *mpl*; [of food] sobras *fpl* **2.** *vt* [discard] desechar; *Fig* [idea] descartar

scrap² [skræp] *Fam* **1.** *n* [fight] pelea *f* **2.** *vi* pelearse (**with** con)

scrapbook ['skræpbʊk] *n* álbum *m* de recortes

scrape [skreɪp] **1.** *vt* [paint, wood] raspar; [knee] arañarse, hacerse un rasguño en **2.** *vi* [make noise] chirriar; [rub] rozar **3.** *n Fam* [trouble] lío *m* ■ **scrape through** *vi Fam* [exam] aprobar por los pelos ■ **scrape together** *vt sep* reunir a duras penas

scratch [skrætʃ] **1.** *n* **a)** [on skin,] arañazo *m*, rasguño *m*; [on glass, paint, record] raya *f*
b) [noise] chirrido *m*
c) *Fig* **to be up to scratch** dar la talla; **to do sth from scratch** hacer algo a partir de cero; **to start from scratch** partir de cero
2. *adj* **scratch team** equipo improvisado
3. *vt* **a)** [with nail, claw] arañar, rasguñar; [paintwork] rayar
b) [to relieve itching] rascarse
c) SPORT [cancel] suspender
4. *vi* rascar; [person] rascarse

scratchcard ['skrætʃkɑːd] *n* tarjeta *f* de rasca y gana, boleto *m* de lotería instantánea, *Am* raspadito *m*

scream [skri:m] **1.** *n* chillido *m*; **screams of laughter** carcajadas *fpl* **2.** *vt* [insults etc] gritar **3.** *vi* chillar; **to scream at sb** chillar a algn

screech [skri:tʃ] **1.** *n* [of person] chillido *m*; [of tyres, brakes] chirrido *m* **2.** *vi* [person] chillar; [tyres] chirriar

screen [skri:n] **1.** *n* **a)** [movable partition] biombo *m* **b)** *Fig* cortina *f* **c)** CIN, TV & COMPUT pantalla *f* **2.** *vt* **a)** [protect] proteger; [conceal] tapar **b)** [candidates] seleccionar **c)** [show-film] proyectar; [for first time] estrenar **d)** MED examinar

screenager ['skri:neɪdʒə(r)] *n* joven *mf* adicto(a) al ordenador

screw [skru:] **1.** *n* **a)** [for fastening] tornillo *m* **b)** [propeller] hélice *f* **2.** *vt* **a)** [fix with screws] atornillar; **to screw sth down** *or* **in** *or* **on** fijar algo con tornillos; **to screw sth to sth** atornillar algo a algo **b)** *Vulg Esp* follar, *Am* coger; **screw you!** ¡que te den por culo! **3.** *vi* [bolt, lid] enroscarse ■ **screw up** *vt sep* **a)** [piece of paper] arrugar **b)** [eyes] apretar; [face] torcer **c)** *v Fam* [ruin] jorobar, joder

screwdriver ['skru:draɪvə(r)] *n* destornillador *m*, *Am* desatornillador *m*

scribble ['skrɪbəl] **1.** *n* garabatos *mpl* **2.** *vt* [message etc] garabatear **3.** *vi* hacer garabatos

script [skrɪpt] *n* **a)** [writing] escritura *f*; [handwriting] letra *f*; TYP letra cursiva **b)** [in exam] escrito *m* **c)** CIN guión *m*

scroll [skrəʊl] **1.** *n* **a)** rollo *m* de pergamino **b)** COMPUT barra *f* or botón *m* de desplazamiento, scroll *m* **2.** *vt* COMPUT desplazarse (por la pantalla)

scrounge [skraʊndʒ] *Fam* **1.** *vi* gorrear, *Esp* gorronear; **to scrounge (around) for** buscar; **to scrounge off sb** vivir a costa de algn **2.** *vt* gorrear, *Esp* gorronear

scrub¹ [skrʌb] *n* [undergrowth] maleza *f*

scrub² [skrʌb] **1.** *vt* **a)** frotar **b)** *Fam* [cancel] borrar **2.** *n* [cleaning] fregado *m*

scruff [skrʌf] *n* pescuezo *m*, cogote *m*

scruffy ['skrʌfɪ] *(compar* **scruffier***, superl* **scruffiest)** *adj Fam* desaliñado(a)

scrum [skrʌm] *n* melé *f*, *Am* scrum *f*; **scrum half** medio (de) melé *mf*

scrupulous ['skru:pjʊləs] *adj* escrupuloso(a)

scrutinize ['skru:tɪnaɪz] *vt* escudriñar

scuba diving ['sku:bədaɪvɪŋ] *n* buceo *m* or submarinismo *m* con botellas de oxígeno

scuffle ['skʌfəl] **1.** *n* pelea *f* **2.** *vi* pelearse (**with** con)

sculptor ['skʌlptə(r)] *n* escultor(a) *m,f*

sculpture ['skʌlptʃə(r)] *n* escultura *f*

scum [skʌm] *n* **a)** [on liquid] espuma *f* **b)** *Fig* escoria *f*

scurry ['skʌrɪ] *vi* [run] corretear; [hurry] apresurarse; **to scurry away** *or* **off** escabullirse

sea [si:] *n* mar *m or f*; **by the sea** a orillas del mar; **out at sea** en alta mar; **to go by sea** ir en barco; **to put to sea** zarpar; *Fig* **to be all at sea** estar desorientado(a); **sea breeze** brisa marina; *Fig* **sea change** metamorfosis *f*; **sea level** nivel *m* del mar; **sea lion** león marino; **sea water** agua *f* de mar

seafood ['si:fu:d] *n* marisco *m*, *Am* mariscos *mpl*

seafront ['si:frʌnt] *n* paseo marítimo

seagull ['si:gʌl] *n* gaviota *f*

seal¹ [si:l] *n* ZOOL foca *f*

seal² [si:l] **1.** *n* **a)** [official stamp] sello *m* **b)** [airtight closure] cierre hermético; [on bottle] precinto *m* **2.** *vt* **a)** [with official stamp] sellar; [with wax] lacrar **b)** [close] cerrar; [make airtight] cerrar herméticamente **c)** [determine] **this sealed his fate** esto decidió su destino ■ **seal off** *vt sep* [pipe etc] cerrar; [area] acordonar

sealable ['si:lɪbl] *adj* precintable

seam [si:m] *n* **a)** SEWING costura *f*; TECH juntura *f*; *Fam* **to be bursting at the seams** [room] rebosar de gente **b)** GEOL & MINING veta *f*, filón *m*

seamless ['si:mlɪs] *adj* **a)** [stocking] sin costuras; [metal tube] de una pieza **b)** *Fig* [transition, changeover] perfecto(a)

search [sɜːʧ] **1.** *vt* [files etc] buscar en; [building, suitcase] registrar; [person] cachear; [one's conscience] examinar **2.** *vi* buscar; **to search through** registrar **3.** *n* búsqueda *f*; [of building etc] registro *m*; [of person] cacheo *m*; **in search of** en busca de; COMPUT **search engine** motor *m* de búsqueda; **search party** equipo *m* de salvamento; **search result** resultado *m* de búsqueda; **search warrant** orden *f* de registro

searchlight ['sɜːʧlaɪt] *n* reflector *m*

seashell ['siːʃel] *n* concha marina

seashore ['siːʃɔː(r)] *n* [beach] playa *f*

seasick ['siːsɪk] *adj* mareado(a); **to get seasick** marearse

seaside ['siːsaɪd] *n* playa *f*, costa *f*; **seaside resort** lugar *m* de vacaciones junto al mar; **seaside town** pueblo costero

season¹ ['siːzən] *n* época *f*; [of year] estación *f*; [for sport etc] temporada *f*; **the busy season** la temporada alta; **the rainy season** la estación de lluvias; **in season** [fruit] en sazón; [animal] en celo; *Br* **season ticket** abono *m*

season² ['siːzən] *vt* CULIN sazonar

seasonal ['siːzənəl] *adj* estacional

seasoning ['siːzənɪŋ] *n* condimento *m*, aderezo *m*

seat [siːt] **1.** *n* **a)** asiento *m*; [place] plaza *f*; CIN & THEAT localidad *f*; AUTO **seat belt** cinturón *m* de seguridad **b)** PARL escaño *m* **2.** *vt* **a)** [guests etc] sentar **b)** [accommodate] tener cabida para

seating ['siːtɪŋ] *n* asientos *mpl*

seawater *n* **seawater therapy** talasoterapia *f*

seaweed ['siːwiːd] *n* alga *f* (marina)

secluded [sɪ'kluːdɪd] *adj* retirado(a), apartado(a)

second¹ ['sekənd] **1.** *adj* segundo(a); **every second day** cada dos días; **it's the second highest mountain** es la segunda montaña más alta; **on second thought(s)** ... pensándolo bien

...; **to have second thoughts about sth** dudar de algo; **to settle for second best** conformarse con lo que hay **2.** *n* **a)** [in series] segundo(a) *m,f*; **Charles the Second** Carlos Segundo; **the second of October** el dos de octubre **b)** AUTO [gear] segunda *f* **c)** COMM **seconds** artículos defectuosos **3.** *vt* [motion] apoyar **4.** *adv* **to come second** terminar en segundo lugar

second² ['sekənd] *n* [time] segundo *m*; *Fam* **in a second** enseguida; *Fam* **just a second!** ¡un momentito!; **second hand** [of watch, clock] segundero *m*

secondary ['sekəndərɪ] *adj* secundario(a); *Br* **secondary school** escuela secundaria

second-class ['sekənd'klɑːs] **1.** *adj* *Br* [ticket, carriage] de segunda (clase) **2.** *adv* **to travel second-class** viajar en segunda

second-hand ['sekənd'hænd] *adj* & *adv* de segunda mano

secondly ['sekəndlɪ] *adv* en segundo lugar

second-rate ['sekənd'reɪt] *adj* de segunda categoría

secrecy ['siːkrəsɪ] *n* secreto *m*; **in secrecy** en secreto

secret ['siːkrɪt] **1.** *adj* secreto(a); **to keep sth secret** mantener algo en secreto; **secret ballot** votación secreta **2.** *n* secreto *m*; *Fig* clave *f*; **in secret** en secreto; **to keep a secret** guardar un secreto

secretarial [sekrɪ'teərɪəl] *adj* de secretario(a)

secretary ['sekrətrɪ] *n* secretario(a) *m,f*; **Secretary of State** *Br* ministro(a) *m,f* con cartera, *US* ministro(a) *m,f* de Asuntos Exteriores

secretive ['siːkrɪtɪv] *adj* reservado(a)

secretly ['siːkrɪtlɪ] *adv* en secreto

sect [sekt] *n* secta *f*

section ['sekʃən] n a) [part] sección f, parte f; [of law] artículo m; [of community] sector m; [of orchestra, department] sección b) [cut] corte m

sector ['sektə(r)] n sector m

secular ['sekjʊlə(r)] adj [school, teaching] laico(a); [music, art] profano(a); [priest] seglar, secular

secure [sɪ'kjʊə(r)] **1.** adj seguro(a); [window, door] bien cerrado(a); [ladder etc] firme **2.** vt a) [make safe] asegurar b) [fix - rope, knot] sujetar, fijar; [object to floor] afianzar; [window, door] cerrar bien c) [obtain] conseguir, obtener

security [sɪ'kjʊərɪtɪ] n a) seguridad f; **security check(point)** control m de seguridad; **security gate** [at airport] control m de seguridad b) FIN [for loan] fianza f c) FIN **securities** valores mpl

sedan [sɪ'dæn] n a) HIST **sedan chair** silla f de manos b) US AUTO turismo m

sedative ['sedətɪv] adj & n sedante (m)

seduce [sɪ'djuːs] vt seducir

seductive [sɪ'dʌktɪv] adj seductor(a)

see¹ [siː] (pt saw, pp seen) vt & vi a) ver; **let's see** a ver; **see page 10** véase la página 10; **to see the world** recorrer el mundo; **see you (later) / soon!** ¡hasta luego / pronto! b) [meet with] ver, tener cita con; **they are seeing each other** [couple] salen juntos c) [understand] entender; **as far as I can see** por lo visto; **I see ya ved o) to see sb home** acompañar a algn a casa ■ **see about** vt insep [deal with] ocuparse de ■ **see off** vt sep [say goodbye to] despedirse de ■ **see out** vt sep a) [show out] acompañar hasta la puerta b) [survive] sobrevivir ■ **see through 1.** vt insep Fam **to see through sb** verle el plumero a algn **2.** vt sep a) **I'll see you through** puedes contar con mi ayuda; **£20 should see me through** con 20 libras me las apaño b) **to see sth through** [carry out] llevar algo a cabo ■ **see to** vt insep [deal with] ocuparse de

see² [siː] n REL sede f; **the Holy See** la Santa Sede

seed [siːd] **1.** n a) BOT semilla f; [of fruit] pepita f; **to go to seed** [plant] granar;

Fig [person] descuidarse b) [in tennis - player] cabeza mf de serie **2.** vt a) [sow with seed] sembrar b) [grapes] despepitar c) [in tennis] preseleccionar

seedy ['siːdɪ] (compar **seedier**, superl **seediest**) adj Fam [bar etc] sórdido(a); [clothes] raído(a); [appearance] desaseado(a)

seeing ['siːɪŋ] conj **seeing that** visto que, dado que

seek [siːk] (pt & pp sought) **1.** vt a) [look for] buscar b) [advice, help] solicitar **2.** vt buscar; **to seek to do sth** procurar hacer algo ■ **seek after** vt insep buscar; **much sought after** [person] muy solicitado(a); [thing] muy cotizado(a)

seem [siːm] vi parecer; **I seem to remember his name was Colin** creo recordar que su nombre era Colin; **it seems to me that** me parece que; **so it seems** eso parece

seemingly ['siːmɪŋlɪ] adv aparentemente, según parece

seen [siːn] pp of **see**

seep [siːp] vi **to seep through / into / out** filtrarse por / en / de

seesaw ['siːsɔː] **1.** n balancín m, subibaja m **2.** vi a) columpiarse, balancearse b) Fig vacilar, oscilar

see-through ['siːθruː] adj transparente

segment ['segmənt] n segmento m; [of orange] gajo m

segregate ['segrɪgeɪt] vt segregar (**from** de)

segregation [segrɪ'geɪʃən] n segregación f

seize [siːz] vt [grab] agarrar, Esp coger; JUR [property, drugs] incautar; [assets] secuestrar; [territory] tomar; [arrest] detener; **to seize an opportunity** aprovechar una ocasión; **to seize power** hacerse con el poder ■ **seize on** vt insep [chance] agarrar; [idea] aferrarse a ■ **seize up** vi agarrotarse

seizure ['siːʒə(r)] n a) JUR [of property, drugs] incautación f; [of newspaper] secuestro m; [arrest] detención f b) MED ataque m (de apoplejía)

seldom ['seldəm] *adv* rara vez, raramente

select [sɪ'lekt] **1.** *vt* [thing] escoger, elegir; [team] seleccionar **2.** *adj* selecto(a)

selection [sɪ'lekʃən] *n* [choosing] elección *f*; [people or things chosen] selección *f*; [range] surtido *m*

selective [sɪ'lektɪv] *adj* selectivo(a)

self [self] (*pl* **selves**) *n* uno(a) mismo(a), sí mismo(a); **the self** [in psychology] el yo

self-addressed envelope ['selfə'drest'envələup] *n* sobre *m* dirigido a uno mismo

self-assured [selfə'ʃuəd] *adj* seguro(a) de sí mismo(a)

self-belief *n* confianza *f* en sí mismo(a); **to have self-belief** creer en sí mismo(a)

self-catering [self'keɪtərɪŋ] *adj* sin servicio de comida

self-centred, *US* **self-centered** [self'sentəd] *adj* egocéntrico(a)

self-checkout *n* caja *f* automática, caja *f* autoservicio

self-confidence [self'kɒnfɪdəns] *n* confianza *f* en sí mismo(a)

self-confident [self'kɒnfɪdənt] *adj* seguro(a) de sí mismo(a)

self-conscious [self'kɒnʃəs] *adj* cohibido(a)

self-control [selfkən'trəul] *n* autocontrol *m*

self-defence, *US* **self-defense** [selfdɪ'fens] *n* autodefensa *f*

self-discipline [self'dɪsɪplɪn] *n* autodisciplina *f*

self-employed [selfɪm'plɔɪd] *adj* [worker] autónomo(a)

self-esteem [selfɪ'sti:m] *n* amor propio, autoestima *f*

self-evident [self'evɪdənt] *adj* evidente, patente

self-indulgent [selfɪn'dʌldʒənt] *adj* inmoderado(a)

self-injury *n* automutilación *f*

self-interest [self'ɪntrɪst] *n* egoísmo *m*

selfish ['selfɪʃ] *adj* egoísta

selfishness ['selfɪʃnɪs] *n* egoísmo *m*

selfless ['selflɪs] *adj* desinteresado(a)

self-loathing *n* desprecio *m* de uno(a) mismo(a)

self-obsessed *adj* egocéntrico(a)

self-pity [self'pɪtɪ] *n* autocompasión *f*

self-portrait [self'pɔ:treɪt] *n* autorretrato *m*

self-raising ['selfreɪzɪŋ] *adj* **self-raising flour** *Esp* harina *f* con levadura, *Am* harina *f* con polvos de hornear, *RP* harina *f* leudante

self-respect [selfrɪ'spekt] *n* amor propio, dignidad *f*

self-righteous [self'raɪtʃəs] *adj* santurrón(ona)

self-rising ['selfraɪzɪŋ] *US n* = **self-raising**

self-sacrifice [self'sækrɪfaɪs] *n* abnegación *f*

self-satisfaction *n* autosatisfacción

self-satisfied [self'sætɪsfaɪd] *adj* satisfecho(a) de sí mismo(a)

self-service [self's3:vɪs] **1.** *n* [in shop etc] autoservicio *m* **2.** *adj* de autoservicio

self-taught [self'tɔ:t] *adj* autodidacta

sell [sel] (*pt & pp* **sold**) **1.** *vt* vender **2.** *vi* venderse; **this record is selling well** este disco se vende bien **3.** *n* **hard/soft sell** [in advertising] publicidad agresiva/discreta
■ **sell off** *vt sep* vender; [goods] liquidar
■ **sell out 1.** *vi* **to sell out to the enemy** claudicar ante el enemigo **2.** *vt sep* COMM **we're sold out of sugar** se nos ha agotado el azúcar; THEAT **sold out** [sign] agotadas las localidades

sell-by date ['selbaɪdeɪt] *n* COMM fecha *f* límite de venta

seller ['selə(r)] *n* vendedor(a) *m,f*

Sellotape® ['seləteɪp] **1.** *n* *Br* cinta adhesiva, *Esp* celo *m*, *CAm*, *Méx* Durex® *m* **2.** *vt* pegar *or* fijar con celo

semen ['si:men] *n* semen *m*

sentimental

semester [sɪ'mestə(r)] n semestre m

semi- ['semɪ] pref semi-

semicircle ['semɪsɜ:kəl] n semicírcu-
lo m

semicolon [semɪ'kəʊlən] n punto y
coma m

semidetached [semɪdɪ'tætʃt] Br **1.** adj
adosado(a) **2.** n chalé adosado, casa
adosada

semifinal [semɪ'faɪnəl] n semifinal f

seminar ['semɪnɑ:(r)] n seminario m

semi-skimmed [-skɪmd] adj [milk]
semidesnatado(a)

semolina [semə'li:nə] n sémola f

senate ['senɪt] n **a)** POL senado m **b)** UNIV
claustro m

senator ['senətə(r)] n senador(a) m,f

send [send] (pt & pp sent) **1.** vt **a)** [letter]
enviar, mandar; [radio signal] transmi-
tir; [rocket, ball] lanzar; **he was sent
to prison** lo mandaron a la cárcel; **to
send sth flying** tirar algo **b) to send sb
mad** [cause to become] volver loco(a) a
algn **2.** vi **to send for sb** mandar llamar a algn; **to send for sth** encargar
algo ▪ **send away 1.** vt sep [dismiss]
despedir **2.** vi **to send away for sth**
escribir pidiendo algo ▪ **send back**
vt sep [goods etc] devolver; [person]
hacer volver ▪ **send in** vt sep [appli-
cation etc] mandar; [troops] enviar
▪ **send off** vt sep **a)** [letter etc] enviar;
[goods] despachar **b)** FTBL [player] expulsar ▪ **send on** vt sep [luggage -
ahead] facturar; [later] mandar (más
tarde) ▪ **send out** vt sep **a)** [person]
echar **b)** [invitations] enviar **c)** [emit]
emitir▪ **send up** vt sep **a)** hacer subir;
[rocket] lanzar; [smoke] echar **b)** Br Fam
[parody] parodiar, remedar

sender ['sendə(r)] n remitente mf

senile ['si:naɪl] adj senil

senior ['si:njə(r)] **1.** adj **a)** [in age] mayor;
William Armstrong Senior William
Armstrong padre; **senior citizen**
jubilado(a) m,f; US **senior high school**
≃ instituto m **b)** [in rank] superior;
[with longer service] más antiguo(a);
MIL **senior officer** oficial mf de alta graduación **2.** n **a) she's three years my
senior** [in age] me lleva tres años **b)** US
SCH estudiante mf del último curso

sensation [sen'seɪʃən] n sensación f; **to
be a sensation** ser un éxito; **to cause
a sensation** causar sensación

sensational [sen'seɪʃənəl] adj [mar-
vellous] sensacional; [exaggerated]
sensacionalista

sense [sens] **1.** n **a)** [faculty] sentido m;
[feeling] sensación f; **sense of direction / humour** sentido m de la orientación / del humor **b)** [wisdom] sentido m común, juicio m; **common sense**
sentido común **c)** [meaning] sentido m;
[of word] significado m; **in a sense** en
cierto sentido; **it doesn't make sense**
no tiene sentido **d) to come to one's
senses** recobrar el juicio **2.** vt sentir,
percatarse de

senseless ['senslɪs] adj **a)** [absurd]
insensato(a), absurdo(a) **b)** [uncon-
scious] sin conocimiento

sensibility [sensɪ'bɪlɪtɪ] n **a)** [sensiti-
vity] sensibilidad f **b) sensibilities**
susceptibilidad f

sensible ['sensɪbəl] adj **a)** [wise]
sensato(a) **b)** [choice] acertado(a)
c) [clothes, shoes] práctico(a),
cómodo(a)

sensitive ['sensɪtɪv] adj **a)** [person]
sensible; [touchy] susceptible **b)** [skin]
delicado(a); [document] confidencial

sensitivity [sensɪ'tɪvɪtɪ] n sensibilidad f

sensual ['sensjʊəl] adj sensual

sensuous ['sensjʊəs] adj sensual

sent [sent] pt & pp of **send**

sentence ['sentəns] **1.** n **a)** frase f; LING
oración f **b)** JUR sentencia f; **to pass
sentence on sb** imponer una pena a
algn; **life sentence** cadena perpetua
2. vt JUR condenar

sentiment ['sentɪmənt] n **a)** [sentimen-
tality] sensiblería f **b)** [feeling] sentimiento m **c)** [opinion] opinión f

sentimental [sentɪ'mentəl] adj sentimental

separate 1. ['sepəreɪt] *vt* separar (**from** de) ; [divide] dividir (**into** en) ; [distinguish] distinguir
2. ['sepəreɪt] *vi* separarse
3. ['sepərɪt] *adj* separado(a) ; [different] distinto(a) ; [entrance] particular
4. *npl* **separates** ['sepərɪts] [clothes] piezas *fpl*

separately ['sepərətlɪ] *adv* por separado

separation [sepə'reɪʃən] *n* separación *f*

September [sep'tembə(r)] *n* se(p)tiembre *m*

septic ['septɪk] *adj* séptico(a) ; **to become septic** [wound] infectarse; **septic tank** fosa séptica

sequel ['si:kwəl] *n* secuela *f*; [of film etc] continuación *f*

sequence ['si:kwəns] *n* a) [order] secuencia *f*, orden *m* b) [series] serie *f*, sucesión *f*; CIN **film sequence** secuencia *f*

serenade [serɪ'neɪd] *n* serenata *f*

serene [sɪ'ri:n] *adj* sereno(a), tranquilo(a)

sergeant ['sɑ:dʒənt] *n* MIL sargento *mf*; [of police] ≃ oficial *mf* de policía; **sergeant major** sargento *mf* mayor

serial ['sɪərɪəl] *n* a) RADIO & TV serial *m*; [soap opera] radionovela *f*, telenovela *f* b) **serial number** número *m* de serie

serialize ['sɪərɪəlaɪz] *vt* [in newspaper, magazine] publicar por entregas; [on TV] emitir en forma de serial

series ['sɪəri:z] (*pl* **series**) *n* serie *f*; [of books] colección *f*; [of concerts, lectures] ciclo *m*

serious ['sɪərɪəs] *adj* a) [solemn, earnest] serio(a) ; **I am serious** hablo en serio b) [causing concern] grave

seriously ['sɪərɪəslɪ] *adv* a) [in earnest] en serio b) [dangerously, severely] gravemente

sermon ['s3:mən] *n* sermón *m*

servant ['s3:vənt] *n* [domestic] criado(a) *m,f*; *Fig* servidor(a) *m,f*

serve [s3:v] **1.** *vt* a) servir
b) [customer] atender a
c) [in tennis] servir

d) **it serves him right** bien merecido lo tiene
2. *vi* a) servir; **to serve on a committee** ser miembro de una comisión
b) [in tennis] servir
3. *n* [in tennis] servicio *m*
■ **serve out**, **serve up** *vt sep* servir

server ['s3:və(r)] *n* COMPUT servidor *m*

service ['s3:vɪs] **1.** *n* a) servicio *m*; **at your service!** ¡a sus órdenes!; **service (charge)** included servicio incluido; **service area** área *m* de servicio; **service industry** sector *m* de servicios; **service station** estación *f* de servicio b) MIL **the Services** las Fuerzas Armadas c) [maintenance] revisión *f* d) REL oficio *m*; [mass] misa *f* e) [in tennis] servicio *m* **2.** *vt* [car, machine] revisar

serviceman ['s3:vɪsmən] *n* militar *m*

serviette [s3:vɪ'et] *n Br* servilleta *f*

servile ['s3:vaɪl] *adj* servil

serving ['s3:vɪŋ] *n* [portion] ración *f*; **serving spoon** cuchara *f* de servir

session ['seʃən] *n* a) sesión *f*; **to be in session** estar reunido(a) ; [Parliament, court] celebrar una sesión b) SCH [academic year] año académico

set¹ [set] (*pt & pp* **set**) **1.** *vt* a) [put, place] poner, colocar; [trap] poner (**for** para); **the novel is set in Moscow** la novela se desarrolla en Moscú; **to set fire to sth** prender fuego a algo; **to set sb free** poner en libertad a algn
b) [time, price] fijar; [record] establecer; **to set one's watch** poner el reloj en hora
c) [bone] encajar
d) [arrange] arreglar; **he set the words to music** puso música a la letra; **to set the table** poner la mesa
e) [exam, homework] poner; [example] dar; [precedent] sentar
2. *vi* a) [sun, moon] ponerse
b) [jelly, jam] cuajar; [cement] fraguar; [bone] encajarse
c) **to set to** [begin] ponerse a
3. *n* CIN [stage] plató *m*; THEAT escenario *m*; [scenery] decorado *m*

4. *adj* **a)** [task, idea] fijo(a) ; [date, time] señalado(a) ; [opinion] inflexible ; **set phrase** frase hecha ; **to be set on doing sth** estar empeñado(a) en hacer algo **b)** [ready] listo(a)

■ **set about** *vt insep* **a)** [begin] empezar **b)** [attack] agredir

■ **set aside** *vt sep* [time, money] reservar ; [differences] dejar de lado

■ **set back** *vt sep* **a)** [delay] retrasar ; [hinder] entorpecer **b)** *Fam* [cost] costar

■ **set down** *vt sep* [luggage etc] dejar (en el suelo) ; *Br* [passengers] dejar

■ **set in** *vi* [winter, rain] comenzar ; **panic set in** cundió el pánico

■ **set off 1.** *vi* [depart] salir **2.** *vt sep* **a)** [bomb] hacer estallar ; [burglar alarm] hacer sonar ; [reaction] desencadenar **b)** [enhance] hacer resaltar

■ **set out 1.** *vi* **a)** [depart] salir ; **to set out for ...** partir hacia ... **b) to set out to do sth** proponerse hacer algo **2.** *vt sep* [arrange] disponer ; [present] presentar

■ **set up 1.** *vt sep* **a)** [position] colocar ; [statue, camp] levantar ; [tent, stall] montar **b)** [business etc] establecer ; *Fam* montar ; [committee] constituir ; *Fam* **you've been set up!** ¡te han timado! **2.** *vi* establecerse

set² [set] *n* **a)** [series] serie *f* ; [of golf clubs etc] juego *m* ; [of tools] estuche *m* ; [of books] colección *f* ; [of teeth] dentadura *f* ; **chess set** juego de ajedrez ; **set of cutlery** cubertería *f* **b)** [of people] grupo *m* ; *Pej* [clique] camarilla *f* **c)** MATH conjunto *m* **d)** [in tennis] set *m* **e)** **TV set** televisor *m*

setback ['setbæk] *n* revés *m*, contratiempo *m*

SETE MESSAGING *written abbr of* **smiling ear to ear**

settee [se'tiː] *n* sofá *m*

setting ['setɪŋ] *n* **a)** [background] marco *m* ; [of novel, film] escenario *m* **b)** [of jewel] engaste *m*

settle ['setəl] **1.** *vt* **a)** [put in position] colocar

b) [decide on] acordar ; [date, price] fijar ; [problem] resolver ; [differences] arreglar

c) [debt] pagar

d) [nerves] calmar ; [stomach] asentar

e) [establish - person] instalar

2. *vi* **a)** [bird, insect] posarse ; [dust] depositarse ; [liquid] asentarse ; **to settle into an armchair** acomodarse en un sillón

b) [put down roots] afincarse ; [in a colony] asentarse

c) [child, nerves] calmarse

d) [pay] pagar ; **to settle out of court** llegar a un acuerdo amistoso

■ **settle down** *vi* **a)** [put down roots] instalarse ; [marry] casarse **b) to settle down to work** ponerse a trabajar **c)** [child] calmarse ; [situation] normalizarse

■ **settle for** *vt insep* conformarse con

■ **settle in** *vi* [move in] instalarse ; [become adapted] adaptarse

■ **settle with** *vt sep* [pay debt to] ajustar cuentas con

settlement ['setəlmənt] *n* **a)** [agreement] acuerdo *m* **b)** [of debt] pago *m* **c)** [colony] asentamiento *m* ; [village] poblado *m*

settler ['setlə(r)] *n* colono *m*

setup ['setʌp] *n* [system] sistema *m* ; [situation] situación *f* ; *Fam* montaje *m*

seven ['sevən] *adj & n* siete (*m inv*)

7K MESSAGING *written abbr of* **sick**

seventeen [sevən'tiːn] *adj & n* diecisiete (*m inv*), diez y siete (*m inv*)

seventeenth [sevən'tiːnθ] **1.** *adj & n* decimoséptimo(a) (*m,f*) **2.** *n* [fraction] decimoséptima parte

seventh ['sevənθ] **1.** *adj & n* séptimo(a) (*m,f*) **2.** *n* [fraction] séptimo *m*

seventy ['sevəntɪ] *adj & n* setenta (*m inv*)

sever ['sevə(r)] *vt* [cut] cortar ; *Fig* [relations] romper

several ['sevərəl] **1.** *adj* **a)** [more than a few] varios(as) **b)** [different] distintos(as) **2.** *pron* algunos(as)

severe [sɪ'vɪə(r)] *adj* severo(a) ; [climate, blow] duro(a) ; [illness, loss] grave ; [pain] intenso(a)

sew [səʊ] *(pt sewed, pp sewed or sewn) vt & vi* coser ■ **sew up** *vt sep* [stitch together] coser ; [mend] remendar

sewage ['su:ɪʤ] *n* aguas *fpl* residuales

sewer ['su:ə(r)] *n* alcantarilla *f*, cloaca *f*

sewing ['səʊɪŋ] *n* costura *f*; **sewing machine** máquina *f* de coser

sewn [səʊn] *pp of* **sew**

sex [seks] *n* sexo *m*; **sex education** educación *f* sexual; **to have sex with sb** tener relaciones sexuales con algn; **sex appeal** sex-appeal *m*; **sex offender** agresor(a) *m,f* sexual

sexist ['seksɪst] *adj & n* sexista *(mf)*

sexting ['sekstɪŋ] *n US* envío de SMS de carácter sexual

sexual ['seksjʊəl] *adj* sexual

sexuality [seksjʊ'ælɪtɪ] *n* sexualidad *f*

sexy ['seksɪ] *(compar* **sexier**, *superl* **sexiest)** *adj Fam* sexi, erótico(a)

shack [ʃæk] *n* casucha *f*, *Esp* chabola *f*, *CSur, Ven* rancho *m*

shade [ʃeɪd] **1.** *n* **a)** [shadow] sombra *f*; **in the shade** a la sombra **b)** [eyeshade] visera *f*; [lampshade] pantalla *f*; *US* [blind] persiana *f* **c)** [of colour] tono *m*, matiz *m*; *Fig* [of meaning] matiz *m* **d)** *Fam* **shades** gafas *fpl* or *Am* anteojos *mpl* de sol **2.** *vt* [from sun] proteger contra el sol

shadow ['ʃædəʊ] **1.** *n* **a)** [shade] sombra *f* **b)** *Br* **the Shadow Cabinet** el gabinete de la oposición **2.** *vt Fig* seguir la pista a

shady ['ʃeɪdɪ] *(compar* **shadier**, *superl* **shadiest)** *adj* [place] a la sombra ; [suspicious - person] sospechoso(a) ; [deal] turbio(a)

shaft [ʃɑːft] *n* **a)** [of tool, golf club] mango *m* **b)** TECH eje *m* **c)** [of mine] pozo *m* ; [of lift, elevator] hueco *m* **d)** [beam of light] rayo *m*

shaggy ['ʃægɪ] *(compar* **shaggier**, *superl* **shaggiest)** *adj* [hairy] peludo(a) ; [long-haired] melenudo(a) ; [beard] desgreñado(a)

shake [ʃeɪk] *(pt* **shook**, *pp* **shaken) 1.** *n* sacudida *f*

2. *vt* [carpet etc] sacudir ; [bottle] agitar ; [dice] mover ; [building] hacer temblar ; **the news shook him** la noticia le conmocionó ; **to shake hands with sb** estrechar la mano a algn ; **to shake one's head** negar con la cabeza **3.** *vi* [person, building] temblar ; **to shake with cold** tiritar de frío

■ **shake off** *vt sep* **a)** [dust etc] sacudirse **b)** *Fig* [bad habit] librarse de ; [cough, cold] quitarse or *Am* de encima ; [pursuer] dar esquinazo a

■ **shake up** *vt sep Fig* [shock] trastornar ; [reorganize] reorganizar

shaken ['ʃeɪkən] *pp of* **shake**

shaky ['ʃeɪkɪ] *(compar* **shakier**, *superl* **shakiest)** *adj* **a)** [building, table] tambaleante, poco firme ; [hand, voice] tembloroso(a) **b)** [health, position] débil ; [argument, team] flojo(a)

shall [ʃæl] *(unstressed* [ʃəl])

En inglés hablado, y en el escrito en estilo coloquial, el verbo **shall** se contrae de manera que **I/you/he** etc **shall** se transforman en **I'll/you'll/he'll** etc. La forma negativa **shall not** se transforma en **shan't**.

v aux **a)** [used to form future tense - first person only] **I shall** or **I'll buy it** lo compraré ; **I shall not** or **I shan't say anything** no diré nada **b)** [used to form questions - usu first person] **shall I close the door?** ¿cierro la puerta? ; **shall I mend it for you?** ¿quieres que te lo repare? ; **shall we go?** ¿nos vamos? **c)** [emphatic, command, threat - all persons] **we shall overcome** venceremos ; **you shall leave immediately** te irás enseguida

shallow ['ʃæləʊ] *adj* poco profundo(a) ; *Fig* superficial

sham [ʃæm] **1.** *adj* falso(a) ; [illness etc] fingido(a) **2.** *n* **a)** [pretence] engaño *m*, farsa *f* **b)** [person] fantoche *m* **3.** *vt* fingir, simular **4.** *vi* fingir

shambles ['ʃæmbəlz] *n sing* confusión *f*; **the performance was a shambles** la función fue un desastre

shame [ʃeɪm] **1.** *n* a) vergüenza *f*, *Am salvo RP* pena *f*; **to put to shame** [far outdo] eclipsar, sobrepasar **b)** [pity] pena *f*, lástima *f*; **what a shame!** ¡qué pena!, ¡qué lástima! **2.** *vt* avergonzar, *Am salvo RP* apenar; [disgrace] deshonrar

shameful [ˈʃeɪmfʊl] *adj* vergonzoso(a)

shameless [ˈʃeɪmlɪs] *adj* desvergonzado(a)

shampoo [ʃæmˈpuː] **1.** *n* champú *m* **2.** *vt* lavar con champú; **to shampoo one's hair** lavarse el pelo

shan't [ʃɑːnt] = **shall not**

shape [ʃeɪp] **1.** *n* a) [form] forma *f*; [shadow] silueta *m*; **to take shape** tomar forma **b)** **in good / bad shape** [condition] en buen / mal estado; **to be in good shape** [health] estar en forma **2.** *vt* dar forma a; [clay] modelar; [stone] tallar; [character] formar; [destiny] determinar; **star-shaped** con forma de estrella **3.** *vi* (*also* **shape up**) tomar forma; **to shape up well** [events] tomar buen cariz; [person] hacer progresos

shapeless [ˈʃeɪplɪs] *adj* amorfo(a), informe

shapely [ˈʃeɪplɪ] (*compar* **shapelier,** *superl* **shapeliest**) *adj* escultural

share [ʃeə(r)] **1.** *n* a) [portion] parte *f* **b)** FIN acción *f*; **share index** índice *m* de la Bolsa; **share prices** cotizaciones *fpl* **2.** *vt* a) [divide] dividir **b)** [have in common] compartir **3.** *vi* compartir
■ **share out** *vt sep* repartir

shareholder [ˈʃeəhəʊldə(r)] *n* accionista *mf*

shark [ʃɑːk] *n* a) [fish] tiburón *m* **b)** *Fam* [swindler] estafador(a) *m,f*; **loan shark** usurero(a) *m,f*

sharp [ʃɑːp] **1.** *adj* a) [razor, knife] afilado(a), *Am* filoso(a); [needle, pencil] puntiagudo(a) **b)** [bend] cerrado(a) **c)** [contrast] marcado(a) **d)** [clever] listo(a); [quick-witted] avispado(a); [cunning] astuto(a) **e)** [pain, cry] agudo(a) **f)** [sour] acre

g) [temper] arisco(a); [tone] seco(a)
h) MUS sostenido(a)
2. *adv* **at two o'clock sharp** [exactly] a las dos en punto
3. *n* MUS sostenido *m*

sharpen [ˈʃɑːpən] *vt* a) [knife] afilar; [pencil] sacar punta a **b)** *Fig* [desire, intelligence] agudizar

Sharpie® [ˈʃɑːpɪ] *n* US marcador *m* permanente

sharply [ˈʃɑːplɪ] *adv* a) [abruptly] bruscamente **b)** [clearly] marcadamente

shat [ʃæt] *pt & pp of* **shit**

shatter [ˈʃætə(r)] **1.** *vt* hacer añicos; [nerves] destrozar; [hopes] frustrar **2.** *vi* hacerse añicos

shattered [ˈʃætəd] *adj Fam* **to be shattered** [stunned] quedarse destrozado(a); *Br* [exhausted] estar rendido(a), *Méx* estar camotes

shave [ʃeɪv] (*pt* **shaved**, *pp* **shaved** *or* **shaven** [ˈʃeɪvən]) **1.** *n* afeitado *m*; **to have a shave** afeitarse; *Fig* **to have a close shave** escaparse por los pelos **2.** *vt* [person] afeitar; [wood] cepillar **3.** *vi* afeitarse

shaver [ˈʃeɪvə(r)] *n* **(electric) shaver** máquina *f* de afeitar

shaving [ˈʃeɪvɪŋ] *n* a) [of wood] viruta *f* **b)** **shaving brush** brocha *f* de afeitar; **shaving cream** crema *f* de afeitar; **shaving foam** espuma *f* de afeitar

shawl [ʃɔːl] *n* chal *m*, *Am* rebozo *m*

she [ʃiː] *pers pron* ella (*usually omitted in Spanish, except for contrast*)

sheaf [ʃiːf] (*pl* **sheaves**) *n* AGR gavilla *f*; [of arrows] haz *m*; [of papers, banknotes] fajo *m*

shear [ʃɪə(r)] (*pt* **sheared**, *pp* **shorn** *or* **sheared**) **1.** *vt* [sheep] esquilar; **to shear off** cortar **2.** *vi* esquilar ovejas

sheath [ʃiːθ] *n* a) [for sword] vaina *f*; [for knife, scissors] funda *f* **b)** [contraceptive] preservativo *m*

shed¹ [ʃed] *n* [in garden] cobertizo *m*; [for cattle] establo *m*; [in factory] nave *f*, *Andes, Carib, RP* galpón *m*; **bike shed** cobertizo *m* para bicicletas

shed² [ʃed] (pt & pp **shed**) vt **a)** [clothes] despojarse de ; [unwanted thing] deshacerse de; **the snake shed its skin** la serpiente mudó de piel **b)** [blood, tears] derramar

sheep [ʃiːp] (pl **sheep**) n oveja f

sheepdog [ˈʃiːpdɒg] n perro m pastor

sheepish [ˈʃiːpɪʃ] adj avergonzado(a)

sheepskin [ˈʃiːpskɪn] n piel f de carnero

sheer [ʃɪə(r)] adj **a)** [utter] total, puro(a) **b)** [cliff] escarpado(a) ; [drop] vertical **c)** [stockings, cloth] fino(a)

sheet [ʃiːt] n **a)** [on bed] sábana f **b)** [of paper] hoja f ; [of tin, glass, plastic] lámina f ; [of ice] capa f

shelf [ʃelf] (pl **shelves**) n [on bookcase] estante m ; [in cupboard] tabla f ; **shelves** estantería f

shell [ʃel] **1.** n **a)** [of egg, nut] cáscara f ; [of pea] vaina f ; [of tortoise etc] caparazón m ; [of snail etc] concha f **b)** [of building] armazón m **c)** [mortar etc] obús m, proyectil m ; [cartridge] cartucho m; **shell shock** neurosis f de guerra **2.** vt **a)** [peas] desvainar ; [nuts] pelar **b)** MIL bombardear

shellfish [ˈʃelfɪʃ] (pl **shellfish**) n marisco m, mariscos mpl

shelter [ˈʃeltə(r)] **1.** n **a)** [protection] abrigo m, amparo m ; **to take shelter (from)** refugiarse (de) **b)** [place] refugio m ; [for homeless] asilo m; **bus shelter** marquesina f **2.** vt **a)** [protect] abrigar, proteger **b)** [take into one's home] ocultar **3.** vi refugiarse

sheltered [ˈʃeltəd] adj [place] abrigado(a) ; **to lead a sheltered life** vivir apartado(a) del mundo

shelve [ʃelv] vt Fig [postpone] dar carpetazo a

shelving [ˈʃelvɪŋ] n estanterías fpl

shepherd [ˈʃepəd] **1.** n pastor m ; **shepherd's pie** pastel de carne picada con puré de patatas or (Am) papas **2.** vt Fig **to shepherd sb in** hacer entrar a algn

sheriff [ˈʃerɪf] n Br representante de la Corona ; Scot ≃ juez mf de primera instancia ; US sheriff m

sherry [ˈʃerɪ] n jerez m

shield [ʃiːld] **1.** n **a)** escudo m ; [of policeman] placa f **b)** [on machinery] blindaje m **2.** vt proteger (**from** de)

shift [ʃɪft] **1.** n **a)** [change] cambio m ; US AUTO (gear) **shift** cambio de velocidades

b) [period of work, group of workers] turno m; **to be on the day shift** hacer el turno de día

2. vt [change] cambiar ; [move] cambiar de sitio, trasladar

3. vi [move] moverse ; [change place] cambiar de sitio ; [opinion] cambiar ; [wind] cambiar de dirección

shiftwork [ˈʃɪftwɜːk] n trabajo m por turnos

shifty [ˈʃɪftɪ] (compar **shiftier**, superl **shiftiest**) adj [look] furtivo(a) ; [person] sospechoso(a)

shimmer [ˈʃɪmə(r)] **1.** vi relucir ; [shine] brillar **2.** n luz trémula, reflejo trémulo ; [shining] brillo m

shin [ʃɪn] n espinilla f, RP canilla f; **shin pad** espinillera f, RP canillera f

shine [ʃaɪn] (pt & pp **shone**) **1.** vi **a)** [light] brillar ; [metal] relucir

b) Fig [excel] sobresalir (**at** en)

2. vt **a)** [lamp] dirigir

b) (pt & pp **shined**) [polish] sacar brillo a ; [shoes] limpiar

3. n brillo m, lustre m

shiny [ˈʃaɪnɪ] (compar **shinier**, superl **shiniest**) adj brillante

ship [ʃɪp] **1.** n barco m, buque m **2.** vt **a)** [take on board] embarcar **b)** [transport] transportar (en barco) ; [send] enviar, mandar

shipment [ˈʃɪpmənt] n **a)** [act] transporte m **b)** [load] consignación f, envío m

shipping [ˈʃɪpɪŋ] n **a)** [ships] barcos mpl ; **shipping lane** vía f de navegación **b)** [loading] embarque m ; [transporting] transporte m (en barco); **shipping company** compañía naviera

shipwreck [ˈʃɪprek] **1.** n naufragio m **2.** vt **to be shipwrecked** naufragar

shipyard ['ʃɪpjɑːd] n astillero m

shirk [ʃɜːk] **1.** vt [duty] faltar a ; [problem] eludir **2.** vi gandulear

shirt [ʃɜːt] n camisa f; **in shirt sleeves** en mangas de camisa; Fam **keep your shirt on!** ¡no te sulfures!

shit [ʃɪt] Vulg **1.** n [excrement] mierda f; [mess] porquería f, mierda f; **to** Br**have or** US**take a shit** cagar **2.** (pt & pp shitted or shat) vt **to shit oneself** [defecate] cagarse (encima) ; [be scared] cagarse or Esp jiñarse de miedo

shiver ['ʃɪvə(r)] **1.** vi [with cold] tiritar ; [with fear] temblar, estremecerse **2.** n [with cold, fear] escalofrío m

shoal [ʃəʊl] n [of fish] banco m

shock [ʃɒk] **1.** n a) [jolt] choque m; **shock absorber** amortiguador m; **shock resistant** resistente a los golpes ; **shock wave** onda expansiva **b)** [upset] conmoción f; [scare] susto m **c)** MED shock m **2.** vt [upset] conmover ; [startle] sobresaltar ; [scandalize] escandalizar

shock-horror adj Fam [story, headline] sensacionalista

shocking ['ʃɒkɪŋ] adj a) [causing horror] espantoso(a) ; Fam [very bad] horroroso(a) **b)** [disgraceful] escandaloso(a) **c)** **shocking pink** rosa chillón

shoddy ['ʃɒdɪ] (compar shoddier, superl shoddiest) adj [goods] de mala calidad ; [work] chapucero(a)

shoe [ʃuː] **1.** n a) zapato m ; [for horse] herradura f; **brake shoe** zapata f; **shoe polish** betún m ; **shoe repair (shop)** remiendo m de zapatos ; **shoe shop,** US**shoe store** zapatería f **b)** **shoes** calzado m **2.** (pt & pp shod [ʃɒd]) vt [horse] herrar

shoelace ['ʃuːleɪs] n cordón m (de zapatos)

shone [ʃɒn, US ʃəʊn] pt & pp of **shine**

shoo [ʃuː] **1.** interj ¡fuera! **2.** vt **to shoo (away)** espantar

shook [ʃʊk] pt of **shake**

shoot [ʃuːt] (pt & pp shot) **1.** n BOT retoño m ; [of vine] sarmiento m **2.** vt

a) pegar un tiro a ; [kill] matar ; [execute] fusilar ; [hunt] cazar ; **to shoot dead** matar a tiros **b)** [missile, glance] lanzar ; [bullet, ball] disparar **c)** [film] rodar, filmar ; PHOTO fotografiar **3.** vi a) [with gun] disparar (**at sb** a algn) ; **to shoot at a target** tirar al blanco ; FTBL **to shoot at the goal** chutar a puerta **b)** **to shoot past** or **by** pasar flechado(a) ▪ **shoot down** vt sep [aircraft] derribar ▪ **shoot out** vi [person] salir disparado(a) ; [water] brotar ; [flames] salir ▪ **shoot up** vi a) [flames] salir ; [water] brotar ; [prices] dispararse **b)** Fam [inject drugs] pincharse, Esp chutarse

shoot-em-up n videojuego m violento

shooting ['ʃuːtɪŋ] **1.** n a) [shots] tiros mpl ; [murder] asesinato m ; [hunting] caza f; **shooting star** estrella f fugaz **b)** [of film] rodaje m **2.** adj [pain] punzante

shop [ʃɒp] **1.** n a) tienda f; [large store] almacén m; **cyber shop** cibertienda f; US **number shop** ≃ despacho m de lotería ; **shop assistant** dependiente(a) m,f; **shop window** escaparate m, Am vidriera f, Am vitrina f **b)** [workshop] taller m ; **shop floor** [place] planta f; [workers] obreros mpl; **shop steward** enlace mf sindical **2.** vi hacer compras ; **to go shopping** ir de compras

shopkeeper ['ʃɒpkiːpə(r)] n tendero(a) m,f

shoplifter ['ʃɒplɪftə(r)] n ladrón(ona) m,f (de tiendas)

shoplifting ['ʃɒplɪftɪŋ] n hurtos mpl (en comercios)

shopper ['ʃɒpə(r)] n comprador(a) m,f

shopping ['ʃɒpɪŋ] n [purchases] compra fpl, Am compras fpl; **shopping bag / basket** bolsa f / cesta f de la compra ; **shopping centre** or **precinct** or US **mall** or US **plaza** centro m comercial ; TV **shopping channel** canal m de compras, teletienda f; **shopping trolley** or US **cart** carrito m (de la compra) ; **to go on a shopping spree** salir a comprar a lo loco

shopsoiled ['ʃɒpsɔɪld], US **shopworn** ['ʃɒpwɔːn] adj deteriorado(a) (en la tienda)

shore [ʃɔː(r)] n [of sea, lake] orilla f; US [beach] playa f; [coast] costa f; **to go on shore** desembarcar

---

short [ʃɔːt] **1.** adj **a)** [physically] corto(a); [person] bajo(a), Méx chaparro(a), RP petiso(a); **in the short term** a corto plazo; **short circuit** cortocircuito m; **short cut** atajo m; **short story** relato corto, cuento m; **short wave** onda corta

b) [brief] corto(a), breve; **"Bob" is short for "Robert"** "Bob" es el diminutivo de "Robert"; **in short** en pocas palabras

c) to be short of breath faltarle a uno la respiración; **to be short of food** andar escaso(a) de comida

2. adv **a) to pull up short** pararse en seco

b) to cut short [holiday] interrumpir; [meeting] suspender; **we're running short of coffee** se nos está acabando el café

c) short of [except] excepto, menos

shortage ['ʃɔːtɪdʒ] n escasez f

shortbread ['ʃɔːtbred] n mantecado m

short-circuit [ʃɔːt'sɜːkɪt] **1.** vt provocar un cortocircuito en **2.** vi tener un cortocircuito

shortcomings ['ʃɔːtkʌmɪŋz] npl defectos mpl

shorten ['ʃɔːtən] vt [skirt, visit] acortar; [word] abreviar; [text] resumir

shorthand ['ʃɔːthænd] n taquigrafía f; Br **shorthand typist** taquimecanógrafo(a) m,f

shortly ['ʃɔːtlɪ] adv [soon] dentro de poco; **shortly after** poco después

shorts [ʃɔːts] npl **a)** pantalones mpl cortos; **a pair of shorts** un pantalón corto **b)** US [underpants] calzoncillos mpl

short-sighted [ʃɔːt'saɪtɪd] adj [person] miope; Fig [plan etc] sin visión de futuro

short-staffed [-'stɑːft] adj **to be short-staffed** ir falto(a) de personal

short-term [ʃɔːt'tɜːm] adj a corto plazo

shot¹ [ʃɒt] n **a)** [act, sound] tiro m, disparo m **b)** [pellets] perdigones mpl **c)** [person] tirador(a) m,f **d)** FTBL [kick] tiro m (a puerta); [in billiards, cricket, golf] golpe m **e)** [attempt] tentativa f; **to have a shot at sth** intentar hacer algo **f)** [injection] inyección f; Fam pinchazo m **g)** [drink] trago m **h)** PHOTO foto f; CIN toma f

shot² [ʃɒt] pt & pp of **shoot**

shotgun ['ʃɒtgʌn] n escopeta f

---

should [ʃʊd] (unstressed [ʃəd])

En el inglés hablado, y en el escrito en estilo coloquial, la forma negativa **should not** se transforma en **shouldn't**.

v aux **a)** [duty] deber; **all employees should wear helmets** todos los empleados deben llevar casco; **he should have been an architect** debería haber sido arquitecto

b) [probability] deber de; **he should have finished by now** ya debe de haber acabado; **this should be interesting** esto promete ser interesante

c) [conditional use] **if anything strange should happen** si pasara algo raro

d) I should like to ask a question quisiera hacer una pregunta

shoulder ['ʃəʊldə(r)] **1.** n **a)** hombro m; **shoulder blade** omóplato m; **shoulder strap** [of garment] tirante m, CSur bretel m; [of bag] correa f; Br AUTO **hard shoulder** arcén m, Andes berma f, Méx acotamiento m, RP banquina f, Ven hombrillo m **b)** CULIN paletilla f **c)** US AUTO arcén m, Andes berma f, Méx acotamiento m, RP banquina f, Ven hombrillo m **2.** vt Fig [responsibilities] cargar con

shout [ʃaʊt] **1.** n grito m **2.** vt gritar **3.** vi gritar; **to shout at sb** gritar a algn ▪ **shout down** vt sep abuchear

shouting ['ʃaʊtɪŋ] n gritos mpl, vocerío m

shove [ʃʌv] **1.** n Fam empujón m **2.** vt empujar; **to shove sth into one's pocket** meterse algo en el bolsillo a empellones

3. *vi* empujar; [jostle] dar empellones ■ **shove off** *vi Fam* largarse ■ **shove up** *vi Fam* [move along] correrse

shovel ['ʃʌvəl] **1.** *n* pala *f*; **mechanical shovel** excavadora *f* **2.** *vt* mover con pala *or* a paladas

show [ʃəʊ] *(pt* showed, *pp* shown *or* showed) **1.** *vt* **a)** [ticket etc] mostrar; [painting etc] exponer; [film] poner **b)** [display] demostrar **c)** [explain] explicar **d)** [temperature, way etc] indicar **e)** [prove] llevar **f)** [conduct] llevar; **to show sb in** hacer pasar a algn; **to show sb to the door** acompañar a algn hasta la puerta **2.** *vi* [be visible] notarse **3.** *n* **a)** [display] demostración *f* **b)** [outward appearance] apariencia *f* **c)** [exhibition] exposición *f*; *Br* **show flat** piso *m* piloto; **on show** expuesto(a) **d)** THEAT [entertainment] espectáculo *m*; [performance] función *f*; RADIO & TV programa *m*; **show business** *or Fam* **biz** el mundo del espectáculo ■ **show off 1.** *vt sep* **a)** [highlight] hacer resaltar **b)** *Fam* [flaunt] hacer alarde de **2.** *vi Fam* farolear ■ **show up 1.** *vt sep* **a)** [reveal] sacar a luz; [highlight] hacer resaltar **b)** *Fam* [embarrass] dejar en evidencia **2.** *vi* **a)** [stand out] destacarse **b)** *Fam* [arrive] aparecer

showcase ['ʃəʊkeɪs] *n* vitrina *f*

showdown ['ʃəʊdaʊn] *n* enfrentamiento *m*

shower ['ʃaʊə(r)] **1.** *n* **a)** [rain] chubasco *m*, chaparrón *m* **b)** *Fig* [of stones, insults] lluvia *f* **c)** [bath] ducha *f*, *Col, Méx, Ven* regadera *f*; **shower room** baño *m* con ducha; **to have a shower** ducharse **2.** *vt* **a)** [spray] rociar **b)** *Fig* **to shower gifts/praise on sb** colmar a algn de regalos/elogios **3.** *vi* ducharse

showery ['ʃaʊərɪ] *adj* lluvioso(a)

shown [ʃəʊn] *pp of* show

show-off ['ʃəʊɒf] *n Fam* fanfarrón(ona) *m,f*, *Esp* fantasma *mf*

show-stopping *adj* sensacional

showy ['ʃəʊɪ] *(compar* showier, *superl* showiest) *adj* llamativo(a)

shrank [ʃræŋk] *pt of* shrink

shred [ʃred] **1.** *n* triza *f*; [of cloth] jirón *m*; [of paper] tira *f* **2.** *vt* [paper] hacer trizas; [vegetables] rallar

shrewd [ʃruːd] *adj* astuto(a); [clear-sighted] perspicaz; [wise] sabio(a); [decision] acertado(a)

shriek [ʃriːk] **1.** *n* chillido *m*; **shrieks of laughter** carcajadas *fpl* **2.** *vi* chillar

shrill [ʃrɪl] *adj* agudo(a), estridente

shrimp [ʃrɪmp] *n Br* camarón *m*, quisquilla *f*; *US* [prawn] gamba *f*

shrine [ʃraɪn] *n* [tomb] sepulcro *m*; [chapel] capilla *f*; [holy place] lugar sagrado

shrink [ʃrɪŋk] *(pt* shrank, *pp* shrunk) **1.** *vt* encoger **2.** *vi* **a)** [clothes] encoger(se) **b)** [savings] disminuir **c) to shrink (back)** echarse atrás; **to shrink from doing sth** no tener valor para hacer algo **3.** *n Fam* [psychiatrist] psiquiatra *mf*

shrivel ['ʃrɪvəl] **1.** *vt* **to shrivel (up)** encoger; [plant] secar; [skin] arrugar **2.** *vi* encogerse; [plant] secarse; [skin] arrugarse

shroud [ʃraʊd] **1.** *n* REL sudario *m* **2.** *vt* *Fig* envolver

shrub [ʃrʌb] *n* arbusto *m*

shrug [ʃrʌg] **1.** *vt* **to shrug one's shoulders** encogerse de hombros **2.** *vi* encogerse de hombros **3.** *n* encogimiento *m* de hombros ■ **shrug off** *vt sep* no dejarse desanimar por

shrunk [ʃrʌŋk] *pp of* shrink

shrunken ['ʃrʌŋkən] *adj* encogido(a)

shudder ['ʃʌdə(r)] **1.** *n* **a)** escalofrío *m*, estremecimiento *m* **b)** [of machinery] sacudida *f* **2.** *vi* **a)** [person] estremecerse **b)** [machinery] dar sacudidas

shuffle [ˈʃʌfəl] **1.** vt a) [feet] arrastrar **b)** [papers etc] revolver; [cards] barajar **2.** vi a) [walk] andar arrastrando los pies **b)** CARDS barajar

shun [ʃʌn] vt [person] esquivar; [responsibility] rehuir

shut [ʃʌt] (pt & pp **shut**) **1.** vt cerrar **2.** vi cerrarse **3.** adj cerrado(a) ■ **shut down 1.** vt sep a) [factory] cerrar **b)** COMPUT apagar **2.** vi [factory] cerrar ■ **shut off** vt sep [gas, water etc] cortar ■ **shut out** vt sep a) [lock out] dejar fuera **b)** [exclude] excluir ■ **shut up 1.** vt sep a) [close] cerrar **b)** [imprison] encerrar **c)** Fam [silence] callar **2.** vi Fam [keep quiet] callarse

shutter [ˈʃʌtə(r)] n a) [on window] contraventana f, postigo m **b)** PHOTO obturador m

shuttle [ˈʃʌtəl] **1.** n a) [in weaving] lanzadera f **b)** AVIAT puente aéreo; **(space) shuttle** transbordador m espacial **2.** vi ir y venir

shy [ʃaɪ] **1.** (compar **shyer** or **shier**, superl **shyest** or **shiest**) adj [timid] tímido(a), Am salvo RP penoso(a); [reserved] reservado(a) **2.** vi [horse] espantarse (at de); Fig **to shy away from doing sth** negarse a hacer algo

Sicily [ˈsɪsɪlɪ] n Sicilia

sick [sɪk] adj a) [ill] enfermo(a); **sick leave** baja f por enfermedad; **sick pay** subsidio m de enfermedad **b) to feel sick** [about to vomit] tener ganas de devolver; **to be sick** devolver **c)** Fam [fed up] harto(a) **d)** Fam [mind, joke] morboso(a); **sick humour** humor negro

sicken [ˈsɪkən] **1.** vt [make ill] poner enfermo; [revolt] dar asco a **2.** vi [fall ill] enfermar

sickening [ˈsɪkənɪŋ] adj nauseabundo(a); [revolting] repugnante; [horrifying] escalofriante

sickly [ˈsɪklɪ] (compar **sicklier**, superl **sickliest**) adj a) [person] enfermizo(a) **b)** [taste] empalagoso(a) **c)** [smile] forzado(a)

sickness [ˈsɪknɪs] n a) [illness] enfermedad f **b)** [nausea] náuseas fpl

side [saɪd] **1.** n a) lado m; [of coin etc] cara f; [of hill] ladera f; AUTO **blind side** ángulo m muerto

b) [of body] costado m; [of animal] ijar m; **by my side** a mi lado; **side by side** juntos

c) [edge] borde m; [of lake, river] orilla f

d) Fig [aspect] aspecto m

e) [team] equipo m; POL partido m; **she's on our side** está de nuestro lado; **to take sides with sb** ponerse de parte de algn; **side effect** efecto secundario; **side entrance** entrada f lateral; **side street** calle f lateral

2. vi **to side with sb** ponerse de parte de algn

sideboard [ˈsaɪdbɔːd] n aparador m

sideburns [ˈsaɪdbɜːnz], Br **sideboards** [ˈsaɪdbɔːdz] npl patillas fpl

sidelight [ˈsaɪdlaɪt] n AUTO luz f lateral, piloto m

sideline [ˈsaɪdlaɪn] n a) SPORT línea f de banda **b)** COMM [product] línea suplementaria; [job] empleo suplementario

sidestep [ˈsaɪdstep] vt [issue] esquivar

sidetrack [ˈsaɪdtræk] vt Fig [person] despistar

sidewalk [ˈsaɪdwɔːk] n US acera f, CSur vereda f, CAm, Méx banqueta f

sideways [ˈsaɪdweɪz] **1.** adj [movement] lateral; [look] de reojo **2.** adv de lado

siding [ˈsaɪdɪŋ] n [on railway] apartadero m; [connected at only one end to main track] vía f muerta

siege [siːdʒ] n sitio m, cerco m; **to lay siege to** sitiar

sieve [sɪv] **1.** n [fine] tamiz m; [coarse] criba f **2.** vt [fine] tamizar; [coarse] cribar

sift [sɪft] vt [sieve] tamizar; Fig **to sift through** examinar cuidadosamente

sigh [saɪ] **1.** vi suspirar **2.** n suspiro m

sight [saɪt] **1.** n a) [faculty] vista f; **at first sight** a primera vista; **to catch sight of** divisar; **to know by sight** conocer de vista; **to lose sight of sth/sb** perder algo/a algn de vista **b)** [range of vision] vista f; **within sight** a la vista; **to come into sight** aparecer **c)** [spectacle] espectáculo *m* **d)** [on gun] mira *f*; *Fig* **to set one's sights on** tener la mira puesta en **e) the sights** [of city] los lugares de interés **2.** *vt* ver; [land] divisar

sight-read *(pt & pp* **sight-read** [-red]*)vi & vt* MUS repentizar

sightseeing ['saɪtsiːɪŋ] *n* turismo *m*; **to go sightseeing** hacer turismo

sign [saɪn] **1.** *n* **a)** [symbol] signo *m*; **sign language** lenguaje *m* de signos; TYP & COMPUT **at sign** arroba *f* **b)** [gesture] gesto *m*, seña *f*; [signal] señal *f* **c)** [indication] señal *f*; [trace] rastro *m*, huella *f* **d)** [notice] anuncio *m*; [board] letrero *m* **2.** *vt* **a)** [letter etc] firmar **b)** FTBL fichar **3.** *vi* firmar

■ **sign off** *vi insep* **a)** RADIO & TV despedir la emisión **b)** [in letter] **I'll sign off now** ya me despido

■ **sign on** *vi Br* [worker] firmar un contrato; *Br Fam* registrarse para recibir el seguro de desempleo, *Esp* apuntarse al paro; [regularly] ir a firmar *or Esp* sellar

■ **sign up 1.** *vt sep* [soldier] reclutar; [worker] contratar **2.** *vi* [soldier] alistarse; [worker] firmar un contrato

signal ['sɪgnəl] **1.** *n* señal *f*; RADIO & TV sintonía *f*; RAIL **signal box** garita *f* de señales **2.** *vt* **a)** [message] transmitir por señales **b)** [direction etc] indicar **3.** *vi* [with hands] hacer señales; [in car] señalar

signature ['sɪgnɪtʃə(r)] *n* [name] firma *f*; **digital signature** firma *f* digital; RADIO & TV **signature tune** sintonía *f*

significance [sɪg'nɪfɪkəns] *n* [meaning] significado *m*; [importance] importancia *f*

significant [sɪg'nɪfɪkənt] *adj* [meaningful] significativo(a); [important] importante

significantly [sɪg'nɪfɪkəntlɪ] *adv* [markedly] sensiblemente

signify ['sɪgnɪfaɪ] *vt* **a)** [mean] significar **b)** [show, make known] indicar

signpost ['saɪnpəʊst] *n* poste *m* indicador

silence ['saɪləns] **1.** *n* silencio *m* **2.** *vt* acallar; [engine] silenciar

silent ['saɪlənt] *adj* silencioso(a); [not talkative] callado(a); [film] mudo(a); **be silent!** ¡cállate!; **to remain silent** guardar silencio

silently ['saɪləntlɪ] *adv* silenciosamente

silhouette [sɪluː'et] *n* silueta *f*

silicon ['sɪlɪkən] *n* silicio *m*; **silicon chip** chip *m* (de silicio)

silk [sɪlk] **1.** *n* seda *f* **2.** *adj* de seda

silky ['sɪlkɪ] *(compar* **silkier,** *superl* **silkiest) adj** [cloth] sedoso(a); [voice etc] aterciopelado(a)

sill [sɪl] *n* [of window] alféizar *m*

silly ['sɪlɪ] *(compar* **sillier,** *superl* **silliest) adj** tonto(a)

silver ['sɪlvə(r)] **1.** *n* **a)** [metal] plata *f* **b)** *Br* [coins] monedas *fpl* plateadas *(de entre 5 y 50 peniques)* **c)** [tableware] vajilla *f* de plata **2.** *adj* de plata; **silver foil** [tinfoil] papel *m* de aluminio; *Br* **silver paper** papel de plata; **silver wedding** bodas *fpl* de plata

silver-plated [sɪlvə'pleɪtɪd] *adj* plateado(a)

similar ['sɪmɪlə(r)] *adj* parecido(a), semejante **(to** a); **to be similar** parecerse

similarity [sɪmɪ'lærɪtɪ] *n* semejanza *f*

similarly ['sɪmɪləlɪ] *adv* **a)** [as well] igualmente **b)** [likewise] del mismo modo, asimismo

simmer ['sɪmə(r)] **1.** *vt* cocer a fuego lento **2.** *vi* cocerse a fuego lento ■ **simmer down** *vi Fam* calmarse

simple ['sɪmpəl] *adj* **a)** sencillo(a); **simple interest** interés *m* simple **b)** [natural] natural **c)** [foolish] simple; [naïve] ingenuo(a); [dim] de pocas luces

simplicity [sɪm'plɪsɪtɪ] *n* **a)** sencillez *f* **b)** [naïveté] ingenuidad *f*

simplify ['sɪmplɪfaɪ] *vt* simplificar

simply ['sɪmplɪ] *adv* **a)** [plainly] sencillamente **b)** [only] simplemente, solamente, sólo, solo

simulate ['sɪmjʊleɪt] *vt* simular

simultaneous [sıməl'teınıəs] *adj* simultáneo(a)

sin [sın] **1.** *n* pecado *m* **2.** *vi* pecar

---

since [sıns] **1.** *adv* **(ever) since** desde entonces ; **long since** hace mucho tiempo ; **it has since come out that ...** desde entonces se ha sabido que ... **2.** *prep* desde ; **she has been living here since 1975** vive aquí desde 1975 **3.** *conj* a) [time] desde que ; **how long is it since you last saw him?** ¿cuánto tiempo hace que lo viste por última vez?
b) [because, as] ya que, puesto que

---

sincere [sın'sıə(r)] *adj* sincero(a)

sincerely [sın'sıəlı] *adv* sinceramente ; **Yours sincerely** [in letter] (le saluda) atentamente

sincerity [sın'serıtı] *n* sinceridad *f*

sinful ['sınful] *adj* [person] pecador(a) ; [act, thought] pecaminoso(a) ; *Fig* [waste etc] escandaloso(a)

sing [sıŋ] *(pt* sang, *pp* sung) **1.** *vt* cantar **2.** *vi* [person, bird] cantar ; [kettle, bullets] silbar

singe [sındʒ] *vt* chamuscar

singer ['sıŋə(r)] *n* cantante *mf*

singing ['sıŋıŋ] *n* [art] canto *m* ; [songs] canciones *fpl* ; [of kettle] silbido *m*

single ['sıŋgəl] **1.** *adj* a) [solitary] solo(a) **b)** [only one] único(a) **c)** [not double] sencillo(a) ; **single bed / room** cama *f* / habitación *f* individual **d)** [unmarried] soltero(a) ; **single mother** *or* **mum** madre *f* soltera **2.** *n* a) *Br* RAIL billete *m or Am* boleto *m or Am* pasaje *m* sencillo *or* de ida **b)** [record] single *m* **c)** SPORT **singles** individuales *mpl* ■ **single out** *vt sep* [choose] escoger ; [distinguish] distinguir

single-handed ['sıŋgəl'hændıd] *adj & adv* sin ayuda

single-minded ['sıŋgəl'maındıd] *adj* resuelto(a)

single-use *adj* de un único uso

singly ['sıŋglı] *adv* [individually] por separado ; [one by one] uno por uno

singular ['sıŋgjulə(r)] **1.** *adj* a) LING singular **b)** *Formal* [outstanding] excepcional **c)** *Formal* [unique] único(a) **2.** *n* LING singular *m*

sinister ['sınıstə(r)] *adj* siniestro(a)

sink[1] [sıŋk] *n* [in kitchen] fregadero *m* ; [in bathroom] lavabo *m*, *Am* lavamanos *m inv*

sink[2] [sıŋk] *(pt* sank, *pp* sunk) **1.** *vt* a) [ship] hundir, echar a pique ; *Fig* [hopes] acabar con **b)** [hole, well] cavar ; [post, knife, teeth] hincar **2.** *vi* a) [ship] hundirse **b)** *Fig* **my heart sank** se me cayó el alma a los pies **c)** [sun] ponerse **d) to sink to one's knees** hincarse de rodillas ■ **sink in** *vi* [penetrate] penetrar ; *Fig* **it hasn't sunk in yet** todavía no me he / se ha *etc* hecho a la idea

sinner ['sınə(r)] *n* pecador(a) *m,f*

sinus ['saınəs] *n* seno *m* (nasal)

sip [sıp] **1.** *n* sorbo *m* **2.** *vt* sorber, beber a sorbos

siphon ['saıfən] *n* sifón *m* ■ **siphon off** *vt sep* [liquid] sacar con sifón ; *Fig* [funds, traffic] desviar

sir [sɜː(r)] *n Formal* a) señor *m* ; **yes, sir** sí, señor **b)** [title] sir ; **Sir Walter Raleigh** Sir Walter Raleigh

siren ['saırən] *n* sirena *f*

sister ['sıstə(r)] *n* a) [relation] hermana *f* **b)** *Br* MED enfermera *f* jefe **c)** REL hermana *f* ; [before name] sor

sister-in-law ['sıstərınlɔː] *n* cuñada *f*

sit [sıt] *(pt & pp* sat) **1.** *vt* a) [child etc] sentar **(in / on** en**) b)** *Br* [exam] presentarse a **2.** *vi* a) [action] sentarse **b)** [be seated] estar sentado(a) **c)** [object] estar ; [be situated] hallarse ; [person] quedarse **d)** [assembly] reunirse ■ **sit back** *vi* recostarse ■ **sit down** *vi* sentarse ■ **sit in on** *vt insep* asistir sin participar a ■ **sit out** *vt sep* aguantar hasta el final ■ **sit through** *vt insep* aguantar ■ **sit up** *vi* a) incorporarse **b)** [stay up late] quedarse levantado(a)

sitcom ['sıtkɒm] *n Fam* telecomedia *f*

site [saıt] **1.** *n* a) [area] lugar *m* ; **building site** solar *m* ; [under construction] obra *f*

b) [location] situación *f*; **nuclear testing site** zona *f* de pruebas nucleares **2.** *vt* situar

sitting ['sɪtɪŋ] **1.** *n* [of committee] sesión *f*; [in canteen] turno *m* **2.** *adj Br* **sitting room** sala *f* de estar

situated ['sɪtjʊeɪtɪd] *adj* situado(a), ubicado(a)

situation [sɪtjʊ'eɪʃən] *n* **a)** situación *f* **b)** [job] puesto *m*; *Br* **situations vacant** [in newspaper] ofertas de trabajo

six [sɪks] *adj & n* seis (*m inv*)

sixteen [sɪks'ti:n] *adj & n* dieciséis (*m inv*), diez y seis (*m inv*)

sixteenth [sɪks'ti:nθ] **1.** *adj & n* decimosexto(a) (*m,f*) **2.** *n* [fraction] dieciseisavo *m*

sixth [sɪksθ] **1.** *adj* sexto(a); *Br* SCH **the sixth form** *últimos dos cursos del bachillerato británico previos a los estudios superiores*; *Br* SCH **sixth former** *estudiante de los dos últimos cursos del bachillerato británico* **2.** *n* **a)** [in series] sexto(a) *m,f* **b)** [fraction] sexto *m*, sexta parte

sixty ['sɪkstɪ] *adj & n* sesenta (*m inv*)

size [saɪz] *n* tamaño *m*; [of garment] talla *f*; [of shoes] número *m*; [of person] estatura *f*; [scope] alcance *m*; **what size do you take?** [garment] ¿qué talla tienes?; [shoes] ¿qué número calzas? ▪ **size up** *vt sep* [person] juzgar; [situation, problem] evaluar

sizzle ['sɪzəl] *vi* chisporrotear

skanky ['skæŋkɪ] *adj US Fam* asqueroso(a)

skate[1] [skeɪt] **1.** *n* patín *m* **2.** *vi* patinar

skate[2] [skeɪt] *n* [fish] raya *f*

skateboard ['skeɪtbɔːd] *n* monopatín *m*, *RP* skate *m*

skater ['skeɪtə(r)] *n* patinador(a) *m,f*

skating ['skeɪtɪŋ] *n* patinaje *m*; **skating rink** pista *f* de patinaje

skeleton ['skelɪtən] **1.** *n* **a)** esqueleto *m* **b)** [of building] armazón *m* **c)** [outline] esquema *m* **2.** *adj* [staff, service] reducido(a); **skeleton key** llave maestra

skeptic ['skeptɪk] *US n* = **sceptic**

skeptical ['skeptɪkəl] *US adj* = **sceptical**

sketch [sketʃ] **1.** *n* **a)** [preliminary drawing] bosquejo *m*, esbozo *m*; [drawing] dibujo *m*; [outline] esquema *m*; [rough draft] boceto *m* **b)** THEAT & TV sketch *m* **2.** *vt* [draw] dibujar; [preliminary drawing] bosquejar, esbozar

sketchy ['sketʃɪ] *(compar* **sketchier**, *superl* **sketchiest)** *adj* [incomplete] incompleto(a); [not detailed] vago(a)

skewer ['skjʊə(r)] *n* pincho *m*, broqueta *f*

ski [ski:] **1.** *n* esquí *m* **2.** *adj* de esquí; **ski boots** botas *fpl* de esquiar; **ski jump** [action] salto *m* con esquís; **ski lift** telesquí *m*; [with seats] telesilla *f*; **ski pants** pantalón *m* de esquiar; **ski resort** estación *f* de esquí; **ski stick** *or* **pole** bastón *m* de esquiar **3.** *vi* esquiar; **to go skiing** ir a esquiar

skid [skɪd] **1.** *n* patinazo *m* **2.** *vi* patinar

skier ['ski:ə(r)] *n* esquiador(a) *m,f*

skiing ['ski:ɪŋ] *n* esquí *m*

skilful ['skɪlfʊl] *adj* hábil, diestro(a)

skill [skɪl] *n* **a)** [ability] habilidad *f*, destreza *f*; [talent] don *m*; SCH **key skill** competencia *f* de base **b)** [technique] técnica *f*

skilled [skɪld] *adj* **a)** [dextrous] hábil, diestro(a); [expert] experto(a) **b)** [worker] cualificado(a)

skillful ['skɪlfʊl] *US adj* = **skilful**

skim [skɪm] **1.** *vt* **a)** [milk] *Esp* quitar la nata a, *Am* sacar la crema a; **skim** *or* **skimmed milk** leche desnatada **b)** [brush against] rozar; **to skim the ground** [bird, plane] volar a ras de suelo **2.** *vi Fig* **to skim through a book** hojear un libro

skimpy ['skɪmpɪ] *(compar* **skimpier**, *superl* **skimpiest)** *adj* [shorts] muy corto(a); [meal] escaso(a)

skin [skɪn] **1.** *n* **a)** piel *f*; [of face] cutis *m*; [complexion] tez *f* **b)** [of fruit] piel *f*; [of lemon] cáscara *f*; [peeling] mondadura *f* **c)** [of sausage] pellejo *m* **2.** *vt* **a)** [animal] despellejar **b)** [graze] arañar

skinny ['skɪnɪ] *(compar* **skinnier,** *superl* **skinniest)** *adj Fam* flaco(a)

skip¹ [skɪp] **1.** *n* [jump] salto *m*, brinco *m* **2.** *vi* [jump] saltar, brincar; [with rope] saltar a la cuerda *or Esp* comba; *Fig* **to skip over sth** saltarse algo **3.** *vt Fig* saltarse

skip² [skɪp] *n Br* [for rubbish] contenedor *m*

skirt [skɜːt] **1.** *n* falda *f*, *CSur* pollera *f* **2.** *vt* [town etc] rodear; [coast] bordear; *Fig* [problem] esquivar

skittle ['skɪtəl] *n* **a)** [pin] bolo *m* **b)** **skittles** [game] (juego *m* de los) bolos *mpl*, boliche *m*

skull [skʌl] *n* ANAT cráneo *m*; *Fam* calavera *f*

skunk [skʌŋk] *n* mofeta *f*

sky [skaɪ] *n* cielo *m*; **sky blue** azul *m* celeste

skydiving ['skaɪdaɪvɪŋ] *n* caída *f* libre (en paracaídas)

skylight ['skaɪlaɪt] *n* tragaluz *m*, claraboya *f*

skyline ['skaɪlaɪn] *n* [of city] perfil *m*

skyscraper ['skaɪskreɪpə(r)] *n* rascacielos *m inv*

slack [slæk] **1.** *adj* **a)** [not taut] flojo(a) **b)** [lax] descuidado(a); [lazy] vago(a) **c)** [market] flojo(a); **business is slack** hay poco negocio **2.** *n* [in rope] parte floja

slacken ['slækən] **1.** *vt* **a)** [rope] aflojar **b)** [speed] reducir **2.** *vi* **a)** [rope] aflojarse; [wind] amainar **b)** [trade] aflojar ▪ **slacken off** *vi* disminuirse

slam [slæm] **1.** *n* [of door] portazo *m* **2.** *vt* [bang] cerrar de golpe; **to slam sth down on the table** soltar algo sobre la mesa de un palmetazo; **to slam the door** dar un portazo; **to slam on the brakes** dar un frenazo **3.** *vi* [door] cerrarse de golpe

slander ['slɑːndə(r)] **1.** *n* difamación *f*, calumnia *f* **2.** *vt* difamar, calumniar

slang [slæŋ] *n* argot *m*

slant [slɑːnt] **1.** *n* **a)** inclinación *f*; [slope] pendiente *f* **b)** *Fig* [point of view] punto *m* de vista **2.** *vt Fig* [problem etc] enfocar subjetivamente **3.** *vi* inclinarse

slap [slæp] **1.** *n* palmada *f*; [in face] bofetada *f* **2.** *adv Fam* **he ran slap into the fence** se dio de lleno contra la valla; **slap in the middle of ...** justo en medio de ... **3.** *vt* pegar con la mano; [hit in face] dar una bofetada a; **to slap sb on the back** dar a algn una palmada en la espalda

slapdash [slæp'dæʃ] *adj Fam* descuidado(a); [work] chapucero(a)

slapstick ['slæpstɪk] *n* bufonadas *fpl*, payasadas *fpl*

slash [slæʃ] **1.** *n Fam* TYP barra oblicua; COMPUT **forward slash** barra *f* oblicua **2.** *vt* **a)** [with knife] acuchillar; [with sword] dar un tajo a **b)** *Fig* [prices] rebajar

slate [sleɪt] **1.** *n* pizarra *f*; *Fig* **to wipe the slate clean** hacer borrón y cuenta nueva **2.** *vt Fam* vapulear, *Esp* poner por los suelos, *Méx* viborear

slaughter ['slɔːtə(r)] **1.** *n* [of animals] matanza *f*; [of people] carnicería *f* **2.** *vt* [animals] matar; [people] matar brutalmente; [in large numbers] masacrar

slave [sleɪv] **1.** *n* esclavo(a) *m,f*; **slave trade** trata *f* de esclavos **2.** *vi* **to slave (away)** dar el callo

slavery ['sleɪvərɪ] *n* esclavitud *f*

sleazebag ['sliːzbæg], **sleazeball** ['sliːzbɔːl] *n Fam* [despicable person] sinvergüenza *mf*

sleazy ['sliːzɪ] *(compar* **sleazier,** *superl* **sleaziest)** *adj* sórdido(a)

sledge [sledʒ] *n Br* trineo *m*

sledgehammer ['sledʒhæmə(r)] *n* almádena *f*

sleek [sliːk] *adj* [hair] lustroso(a); [appearance] impecable

sleep [sliːp] **1.** *n* sueño *m*; **to go to sleep** dormirse; *Fig* **to send to sleep** (hacer) dormir; **my foot has gone to sleep** se me ha dormido el pie **2.** *(pt & pp* **slept)** *vi* dormir; **to sleep like a log** dormir como un lirón ▪ **sleep in** *vi Br* [oversleep] quedarse dormido(a); [have a lie-in] quedarse en la cama ∎ **sleep with** *vt insep Fam* **to sleep with sb** acostarse con algn

sleeper ['sli:pə(r)] *n* **a)** [person] durmiente *mf*; **to be a heavy sleeper** tener el sueño pesado **b)** *Br* RAIL [on track] traviesa *f* **c)** RAIL [coach] coche-cama *m*; [berth] litera *f*

sleeping ['sli:pɪŋ] *adj* **sleeping bag** saco *m* de dormir, *Col, Méx* sleeping *m* (bag), *RP* bolsa *f* de dormir; **Sleeping Beauty** la Bella Durmiente; **sleeping car** coche-cama *m*; *Br* COMM **sleeping partner** socio(a) *m,f* comanditario(a); **sleeping pill** somnífero *m*

sleepy ['sli:pɪ] *(compar* **sleepier,** *superl* **sleepiest)** *adj* soñoliento(a); **to be** or **feel sleepy** tener sueño

sleet [sli:t] **1.** *n* aguanieve *f* **2.** *vi* **it's sleeting** cae aguanieve

sleeve [sli:v] *n* [of garment] manga *f*; [of record] funda *f*

sleigh [sleɪ] *n* trineo *m*; **sleigh bell** cascabel *m*

slender ['slendə(r)] *adj* **a)** [thin] delgado(a) **b)** *Fig* [hope, chance] remoto(a)

slept [slept] *pt & pp of* **sleep**

slice [slaɪs] **1.** *n* **a)** [of bread] rebanada *f*; [of ham] loncha *f*; [of beef etc] tajada *f*; [of lemon etc] rodaja *f*; [of cake] trozo *m* **b)** [utensil] pala *f* **2.** *vt* [food] cortar a rebanadas / lonchas / tajadas / rodajas; [divide] partir

slick [slɪk] **1.** *adj* **a)** [programme, show] logrado(a) **b)** [skilful] hábil, mañoso(a) **2.** *n* **(oil) slick** marea negra

slide [slaɪd] *(pt & pp* **slid** [slɪd]*)* **1.** *n* **a)** [act] resbalón *m* **b)** [in prices etc] baja *f* **c)** [in playground] tobogán *m* **d)** PHOTO diapositiva *f*; **slide projector** proyector *m* de diapositivas **e)** *Br* [for hair] pasador *m* **2.** *vt* deslizar; [furniture] correr **3.** *vi* [on purpose] deslizarse; [slip] resbalar

sliding ['slaɪdɪŋ] *adj* [door, window] corredizo(a); FIN **sliding scale** escala *f* móvil

slight [slaɪt] **1.** *adj* **a)** [small] pequeño(a); **not in the slightest** en absoluto **b)** [build] menudo(a); [slim] delgado(a); [frail] delicado(a) **c)** [trivial] leve **2.** *n* [affront] desaire *m* **3.** *vt* **a)** [scorn] despreciar **b)** [snub] desairar

slightly ['slaɪtlɪ] *adv* [a little] ligeramente, algo

slim [slɪm] **1.** *(compar* **slimmer,** *superl* **slimmest)** *adj* **a)** [person] delgado(a) **b)** *Fig* [resources] escaso(a); [hope, chance] remoto(a) **2.** *vi* adelgazar

slime [slaɪm] *n* [mud] lodo *m*, cieno *m*; [of snail] baba *f*

slimeball ['slaɪmbɔ:l] *US v Fam n* = **sleazebag**

slimy ['slaɪmɪ] *(compar* **slimier,** *superl* **slimiest)** *adj* **a)** [muddy] lodoso(a); [snail] baboso(a) **b)** *Fig* [person] zalamero(a)

sling [slɪŋ] **1.** *n* **a)** [catapult] honda *f*; [child's] tirador *m* **b)** MED cabestrillo *m* **2.** *(pt & pp* **slung)** *vt* [throw] tirar

slip [slɪp] **1.** *n* **a)** [slide] resbalón *m* **b)** [mistake] error *m*; [moral] desliz *m*; **a slip of the tongue** un lapsus linguae **c)** [of paper] trocito *m* **2.** *vi* **a)** [slide] resbalar **b)** MED dislocarse; **slipped disc** vértebra dislocada **c)** [move quickly] ir de prisa **d)** [standards etc] deteriorarse **3.** *vt* **a)** [slide] dar a escondidas **b) it slipped my memory** se me fue de la cabeza

∎ **slip away** *vi* [person] escabullirse

∎ **slip off** *vt sep* [clothes] quitarse rápidamente

∎ **slip on** *vt sep* [clothes] ponerse rápidamente

∎ **slip out** *vi* **a)** [leave] salir **b)** *Fig* **the secret slipped out** se le escapó el secreto

∎ **slip up** *vi Fam* [blunder] cometer un desliz

slipper ['slɪpə(r)] *n* zapatilla *f*

slippery ['slɪpərɪ] *adj* resbaladizo(a)

slippy ['slɪpɪ] *(compar* **slippier,** *superl* **slippiest)** *adj* resbaladizo(a)

slit [slɪt] **1.** n [opening] hendidura f; [cut] corte m, raja f **2.** (pt & pp **slit**) vt cortar, rajar

slob [slɒb] n Fam [untidy person] cerdo(a) m,f, Esp guarro(a) m,f; [lazy person] dejado(a) m,f, tirado(a) m,f

slog [slɒg] Fam **1.** n it was a bit of a slog fue un aburrimiento or Esp tostonazo (de trabajo); **it's a long slog** [walk] hay un buen trecho or Esp una buena tirada **2.** vi [work hard] trabajar como un /una negro(a), Esp dar el callo

slogan ['sləʊgən] n (e)slogan m, lema m

slop [slɒp] **1.** vi to slop (over) derramarse; **to slop about** chapotear **2.** vt derramar

slope [sləʊp] **1.** n [incline] cuesta f, pendiente f; [up] subida f; [down] bajada f; [of mountain] ladera f; [of roof] vertiente f **2.** vi inclinarse; **to slope up/down** subir /bajar en pendiente ■ **slope off** vi Br Fam escabullirse

sloping ['sləʊpɪŋ] adj inclinado(a)

sloppy ['slɒpɪ] (compar **sloppier**, superl **sloppiest**) adj Fam descuidado(a); [work] chapucero(a); [appearance] desaliñado(a)

slot [slɒt] **1.** n **a)** [for coin] ranura f; [opening] rendija f; **slot machine** [for gambling] (máquina f) tragaperras f inv; [vending machine] distribuidor automático **b)** RADIO & TV espacio m **2.** vt [place] meter; [put in] introducir **3.** vi to slot in or together encajar

slouch [slaʊtʃ] vi andar or sentarse con los hombros caídos

Slovenia [slə'viːnjə] n Eslovenia f

slow [sləʊ] **1.** adj **a)** lento(a); **in slow motion** a cámara lenta; **to be slow to do sth** tardar or Am demorar en hacer algo
b) [clock] atrasado(a)
c) [stupid] lento(a), torpe
2. adv despacio, lentamente
3. vt [car] reducir la marcha de; [progress] retrasar
4. vi to slow down or up ir más despacio; [in car] reducir la velocidad

slow-cook vt cocinar a fuego lento

slowly ['sləʊlɪ] adv despacio, lentamente

slug [slʌg] **1.** n **a)** ZOOL babosa f **b)** US Fam [bullet] posta f **c)** Fam [blow] porrazo m **2.** vt Fam [hit] aporrear

sluggish ['slʌgɪʃ] adj **a)** [river, engine] lento(a); COMM flojo(a) **b)** [lazy] perezoso(a)

slum [slʌm] n [district] barrio m bajo; [on outskirts] arrabal m, suburbio m; [house] tugurio m

slump [slʌmp] **1.** n **a)** [drop in sales etc] bajón m **b)** [economic depression] crisis económica **2.** vi **a)** [sales etc] caer de repente; [prices] desplomarse; [the economy] hundirse; Fig [morale] hundirse **b)** [fall] caer

slung [slʌŋ] pt & pp of **sling**

slur [slɜː(r)] **1.** n [stigma] mancha f; [slanderous remark] calumnia f **2.** vt [word] tragarse

slush [slʌʃ] n **a)** [snow] aguanieve f **b)** Fam [sentimentality] sentimentalismo m **c)** POL US Fam **slush fund** fondos mpl para corrupción, Esp corruptelas fpl

slut [slʌt] n v Fam & Peja) [untidy woman] marrana f, Esp guarra f **b)** [whore] fulana f

sly [slaɪ] (compar **slyer** or **slier**, superl **slyest** or **sliest**) adj **a)** [cunning] astuto(a) **b)** [secretive] furtivo(a) **c)** [mischievous] travieso(a) **d)** [underhand] malicioso(a)

smack¹ [smæk] **1.** n **a)** [slap] bofetada f **b)** [sharp sound] ruido sonoro **2.** vt **a)** [slap] dar una bofetada a **b)** [hit] golpear; Fig to smack one's lips relamerse

smack² [smæk] vi Fig to smack of oler a

small [smɔːl] **1.** adj **a)** pequeño(a), Am chico(a); Br small ads pequeños anuncios mpl; Fig small print letra pequeña **b)** [in height] bajo(a) **c)** [scant] escaso(a); **small change** cambio m, suelto m, Am vuelto m **d)** [minor] insignificante; **small businessmen** pequeños comerciantes; **small talk** charloteo m **e)** [increase] ligero(a) **2.** n small of the back región f lumbar

small-minded [smɔːl'maɪndɪd] *adj* mezquino(a)

smallpox ['smɔːlpɒks] *n* viruela *f*

smart [smɑːt] **1.** *adj* **a)** [elegant] elegante **b)** [clever] listo(a), inteligente; *Fam* **smart alec(k)** sabelotodo *mf*, listillo(a) *m,f*, *Méx, RP* vivo(a) *m,f* **c)** [quick] rápido(a); [pace] ligero(a) **2.** *vi* **a)** [sting] picar, escocer **b)** *Fig* sufrir

smarten ['smɑːtən] **1.** *vt* **to smarten (up)** arreglar **2.** *vi* **to smarten (oneself) up** arreglarse

smartly ['smɑːtlɪ] *adv* **a)** [elegantly] elegantemente **b)** [quickly] rápidamente, con rapidez

smartphone ['smɑːtfəʊn] *n* smartphone *m*; **the smartphone market** el mercado de los smartphones

smash [smæʃ] **1.** *n* **a)** [loud noise] estrépito *m*; [collision] choque violento **b)** [in tennis] smash *m* **2.** *vt* **a)** [break] romper; [shatter] hacer pedazos; [crush] aplastar **b)** [destroy] destrozar; [defeat] aplastar **c)** [record] fulminar **3.** *vi* [break] romperse; [shatter] hacerse pedazos; [crash] estrellarse; [in tennis] hacer un mate
■ **smash up** *vt sep Fam* [car] hacer pedazos; [place] destrozar

smashing ['smæʃɪŋ] *adj Br Fam* genial, *Méx* padre, *RP* bárbaro(a)

smattering ['smætərɪŋ] *n* **he had a smattering of French** hablaba un poquito de francés

smear [smɪə(r)] **1.** *n* **a)** [smudge] mancha *f*; **smear (test)** citología *f* **b)** *Fig* [defamation] calumnia *f*. *vt* **a)** [butter etc] untar; [grease] embadurnar **b)** [make dirty] manchar **c)** *Fig* [defame] calumniar, difamar

smell [smel] (*pt & pp* smelled *or* smelt) **1.** *n* **a)** [sense] olfato *m* **b)** [odour] olor *m* **2.** *vt* oler; *Fig* olfatear **3.** *vi* oler (**of** a); **it smells good / like lavender** huele bien / a lavanda; **he smelt of whisky** olía a whisky

smelly ['smelɪ] (*compar* smellier, *superl* smelliest) *adj Fam* maloliente, apestoso(a)

smelt¹ [smelt] *vt* [ore] fundir

smelt² [smelt] *pt & pp of* smell

smile [smaɪl] **1.** *n* sonrisa *f* **2.** *vi* sonreír; **to smile at sb** sonreír a algn; **to smile at sth** reírse de algo

smirk [smɜːk] **1.** *n* [conceited] sonrisa satisfecha; [foolish] sonrisa boba **2.** *vi* [conceitedly] sonreír con satisfacción; [foolishly] sonreír bobamente

smoke [sməʊk] **1.** *n* humo *m*; **smoke alarm** detector *m* de humos; **smoke bomb** bomba *f* de humo; **smoke screen** cortina *f* de humo **2.** *vi* fumar; [chimney etc] echar humo **3.** *vt* **a)** [tobacco] fumar; **to smoke a pipe** fumar en pipa **b)** [fish, meat] ahumar

smoker ['sməʊkə(r)] *n* **a)** [person] fumador(a) *m,f* **b)** RAIL vagón *m* de fumadores

smoking ['sməʊkɪŋ] *n* **'no smoking'** 'prohibido fumar'

smoky ['sməʊkɪ] (*compar* smokier, *superl* smokiest) *adj* **a)** [chimney] humeante; [room] lleno(a) de humo; [atmosphere] cargado(a) (de humo); [taste] ahumado(a) **b)** [colour] ahumado(a)

smooth [smuːð] **1.** *adj* **a)** [surface] liso(a); [skin] suave; [road] llano(a) **b)** [beer, wine] suave **c)** [flowing] fluido(a) **d)** [flight] tranquilo(a); [transition] sin problemas **e)** *Pej* [slick] zalamero(a) **2.** *vt* **a)** [hair etc] alisar **b)** [plane down] limar ■ **smooth out** *vt sep* [creases] alisar; *Fig* [difficulties] allanar; [problems] resolver ■ **smooth over** *vt sep Fig* **to smooth things over** limar asperezas

smoothie ['smuːðɪ] *n* CULIN batido *m* de frutas (*en ocasiones con yogur o leche*)

smoothly ['smuːðlɪ] *adv* sobre ruedas

smother ['smʌðə(r)] *vt* **a)** [asphyxiate] asfixiar; [suffocate] sofocar **b)** *Fig* [cover] cubrir (**with** de)

smoulder ['sməʊldə(r)] *vi* [fire] arder sin llama; *Fig* [passions] arder; **smouldering hatred** odio latente

SMS [ˌesemˈes] n (abbr of **short message service**) SMS m

smudge [smʌdʒ] **1.** n [stain] mancha f; [of ink] borrón m **2.** vt manchar; [piece of writing] emborronar

smug [smʌg] (compar **smugger**, superl **smuggest**) adj engreído(a)

smuggle ['smʌgəl] vt pasar de contrabando

smuggler ['smʌglə(r)] n contrabandista mf

smuggling ['smʌgəlɪŋ] n contrabando m

snack [snæk] n tentempié m, Esp piscolabis m inv, Méx botana f; **snack bar** cafetería f

snacking ['snækɪŋ] n el picar entre comidas; **is snacking healthy?** ¿es sano picar entre comidas?

snag [snæg] **1.** n [difficulty] pega f, problemilla m **2.** vt [clothing] enganchar

snail [sneɪl] n caracol m; Fam COMPUT **snail mail** correo m ordinario or común

snake [sneɪk] n [big] serpiente f; [small] culebra f

snap [snæp] **1.** n **a)** [noise] ruido seco; [of branch, fingers] chasquido m
b) [bite] mordisco m
c) PHOTO (foto f) instantánea f
2. adj [sudden] repentino(a)
3. vt **a)** [branch etc] partir (en dos)
b) [make noise] **to snap one's fingers** chasquear los dedos; **to snap sth shut** cerrar algo de golpe
c) PHOTO sacar una foto de
4. vi **a)** [break] romperse
b) [make noise] hacer un ruido seco
c) [whip] chasquear; **to snap shut** cerrarse de golpe
d) to snap at sb [dog] intentar morder a algn; Fam [person] hablar en mal tono a algn
■ **snap off 1.** vt sep [branch etc] arrancar **2.** vi [branch etc] separarse
■ **snap up** vt sep Fam **to snap up a bargain** llevarse una ganga

snarky ['snɑːkɪ] adj Fam mordaz

snarl¹ [snɑːl] **1.** n gruñido m **2.** vi gruñir

snarl² [snɑːl] **1.** n [in wool] maraña f
2. vt **to snarl (up)** [wool] enmarañar; [traffic] atascar; [plans] enredar

snatch [snætʃ] **1.** n **a)** Fam [theft] robo m; **bag snatch** tirón m **b)** [fragment] fragmentos mpl **2.** vt **a)** [grab] arrebatar **b)** Fam [steal] robar; [kidnap] secuestrar
3. vi **to snatch at sth** intentar agarrar or Esp coger algo

sneak [sniːk] (pt & pp **sneaked**, US pt & pp **snuck**) **1.** n Br Fam Esp chivato(a) m,f, Méx hocicón(ona) m,f, RP buchón(ona) m,f
2. vt **to sneak sth out of a place** sacar algo de un lugar a escondidas
3. vi **a) to sneak off** escabullirse; **to sneak in /out** entrar /salir a hurtadillas
b) Fam **to sneak on sb** [tell tales] ir con cuentos, Esp chivarse

sneaker ['sniːkə(r)] n US playera f

sneer [snɪə(r)] vi **to sneer at** hacer un gesto de desprecio a

sneeze [sniːz] **1.** n estornudo m **2.** vi estornudar

snickerdoodle ['snɪkəduːdl] n US CULIN galleta de canela

sniff [snɪf] **1.** n [by person] aspiración f; [by dog] husmeo m **2.** vt [flower etc] oler; [suspiciously] husmear; [snuff etc] aspirar; [glue] esnifar **3.** vi aspirar por la nariz

snigger ['snɪgə(r)] **1.** n risa disimulada **2.** vi reír disimuladamente; **to snigger at sth** burlarse de algo

snip [snɪp] **1.** n **a)** [cut] tijeretada f; [small piece] recorte m **b)** Br Fam [bargain] Esp chollo m, Am regalo m **2.** vt cortar a tijeretazos

snivel ['snɪvəl] vi lloriquear

snob [snɒb] n (e)snob mf

snobbish ['snɒbɪʃ] adj (e)snob

snooker ['snuːkə(r)] n snooker m, billar m ruso

snoop [snuːp] vi fisgonear, Esp fisgar

snooze [snuːz] Fam **1.** n Esp siestecilla f, Am siestita f **2.** vi echarse una Esp siestecilla or Am siestita

snore [snɔ:(r)] **1.** *n* ronquido *m* **2.** *vi* roncar

snoring ['snɔ:rɪŋ] *n* ronquidos *mpl*

snorkel ['snɔ:kəl] *n* [of swimmer] tubo *m* de respiración ; [of submarine] esnórquel *m*

snorkelling, *US* **snorkeling** ['snɔ:klɪŋ] *n* **to go snorkelling** bucear con tubo

snort [snɔ:t] **1.** *n* resoplido *m* **2.** *vi* resoplar

snot [snɒt] *n Fam* mocos *mpl*

snout [snaʊt] *n* [of animal, gun etc] morro *m*

snow [snəʊ] **1.** *n* nieve *f*; **snow shower** nevada *f* **2.** *vi* nevar; **it's snowing** está nevando **3.** *vt Fig* **to be snowed under with work** estar agobiado(a) de trabajo

snowball ['snəʊbɔ:l] **1.** *n* bola *f* de nieve **2.** *vi Fig* aumentar rápidamente

snowdrop ['snəʊdrɒp] *n* campanilla *f* de invierno

snowflake ['snəʊfleɪk] *n* copo *m* de nieve

snowman ['snəʊmæn] *n* hombre *m* de nieve

snowplough, *US* **snowplow** ['snəʊplaʊ] *n* quitanieves *m inv*

snowshoe ['snəʊʃu:] *n* raqueta *f* (de nieve)

snowstorm ['snəʊstɔ:m] *n* nevasca *f*

snub [snʌb] **1.** *n* [of person] desaire *m* ; [of offer] rechazo *m* **2.** *vt* [person] desairar ; [offer] rechazar

snuck [snʌk] *US pt & pp of* **sneak**

snug [snʌg] *(compar* **snugger**, *superl* **snuggest)** *adj* **a)** [cosy] cómodo(a) **b)** [tightfitting] ajustado(a)

snuggle ['snʌgəl] *vi* **to snuggle down in bed** acurrucarse en la cama; **to snuggle up to sb** arrimarse a algn

so [səʊ] **1.** *adv* **a)** [to such an extent] tanto; **he was so tired that …** estaba tan cansado que …; **it's so long since …** hace tanto tiempo que …; *Fam* **so long!** ¡hasta luego!

b) [degree] tanto ; **a week or so** una semana más o menos ; **we loved her so (much)** la queríamos tanto ; *Fam* **he's ever so handsome!** ¡es tan guapo!
c) [thus, in this way] así, de esta manera ; **and so on, and so forth** y así sucesivamente ; **if so** en este caso ; **I think/hope so** creo /espero que sí ; **I told you so** ya te lo dije ; **so far** hasta ahora *or* allí ; **so they say** eso dicen
d) [also] **I'm going to Spain – so am I** voy a España – yo también
2. *conj* **a)** [expresses result] así que ; **so you like England, do you?** ¿así que te gusta Inglaterra, pues? ; *Fam* **so what?** ¿y qué?
b) [expresses purpose] para que ; **I'll put the key here so (that) everyone can see it** pongo la llave aquí para que todos la vean

---

soak [səʊk] **1.** *vt* [washing, food] remojar ; [cotton, wool] empapar **(in** en) **2.** *vi* [washing, food] estar en remojo ▪ **soak in** *vi* penetrar ▪ **soak up** *vt sep* absorber

soaking ['səʊkɪŋ] *adj* [object] empapado(a) ; [person] calado(a) hasta los huesos

soap [səʊp] **1.** *n* **a)** jabón *m*; **soap flakes** jabón en escamas; **soap powder** jabón en polvo **b)** *TV* **soap opera** culebrón *m* **2.** *vt* enjabonar

soapsuds ['səʊpsʌdz] *npl* espuma *f* (de jabón)

soar [sɔ:(r)] *vi* [bird, plane] remontar el vuelo ; *Fig* [skyscraper] elevarse ; [hopes, prices] aumentar

sob [sɒb] **1.** *n* sollozo *m* **2.** *vi* sollozar

sober ['səʊbə(r)] *adj* [not drunk, moderate] sobrio(a) ; [sensible] sensato(a) ; [serious] serio(a) ; [colour] discreto(a) ▪ **sober up** *vi* **he sobered up** se le pasó la borrachera

so-called [-kɔ:ld] *adj* [misleadingly named] mal llamado(a)

soccer ['sɒkə(r)] *n* fútbol *m*

sociable ['səʊʃəbəl] *adj* [gregarious] sociable ; [friendly] amistoso(a)

social ['səʊʃəl] *adj* social ; **social class** clase *f* social; **social climber**

arribista *mf*; **Social Democrat** socialdemócrata; *US* **social insurance** seguro *m* social; **social media** medios *mpl* sociales; **social network** red *f* social; **social networking** redes *fpl* sociales; **social security** seguridad *f* social; **the social services** los servicios sociales; **social welfare** or **work** asistencia *f* social; **social worker** asistente(a) *m,f* social

socialist ['səʊʃəlɪst] *adj & n* socialista *(mf)*

socialize ['səʊʃəlaɪz] **1.** *vi* alternar, mezclarse con la gente **2.** *vt* socializar

socially *adv* socialmente; **socially responsible** socialmente responsable; **socially responsible investment** (*SRI*) inversión *f* socialmente responsable (*ISR*)

society [sə'saɪətɪ] **1.** *n* a) sociedad *f*; **the consumer society** la sociedad de consumo; **(high) society** la alta sociedad **b)** [club] asociación *f* **c)** [companionship] compañía *f* **2.** *adj* de sociedad; **society column** ecos *mpl* de sociedad

sociology [səʊsɪ'ɒlədʒɪ] *n* sociología *f*

sock [sɒk] *n* calcetín *m*, *CSur* zoquete *m*

socket ['sɒkɪt] *n* a) [of eye] cuenca *f* **b)** ELEC enchufe *m*

soda ['səʊdə] *n* a) CHEM sosa *f*; **baking soda** bicarbonato sódico **b)** **soda water** soda *f* **c)** *US* [fizzy drink] gaseosa *f*

sofa ['səʊfə] *n* sofá *m*; **sofa bed** sofá cama

soft [sɒft] *adj* a) [not hard] blando(a); **soft drinks** refrescos *mpl*; **soft drugs** drogas blandas; **soft toy** muñeco *m* de peluche **b)** [skin, colour, hair, light, music] suave; [breeze, steps] ligero(a) **c)** [lenient] permisivo(a) **d)** [voice] bajo(a)

softball ['sɒftbɔːl] *n juego parecido al béisbol jugado en un campo más pequeño y con una pelota más blanda*

soften ['sɒfən] **1.** *vt* [leather, heart] ablandar; [skin] suavizar; *Fig* [blow] amortiguar **2.** *vi* [leather, heart] ablandarse; [skin] suavizarse

softly ['sɒftlɪ] *adv* [gently] suavemente; [quietly] silenciosamente

software ['sɒftweə(r)] *n* COMPUT software *m*; **software licence** licencia *f* de software; **software package** paquete *m*

soggy ['sɒgɪ] *(compar* **soggier***, superl* **soggiest***) adj* empapado(a); [bread] pastoso(a)

soil [sɔɪl] **1.** *n* [earth] tierra *f* **2.** *vt* [dirty] ensuciar; *Fig* [reputation] manchar

solar ['səʊlə(r)] *adj* solar

sold [səʊld] *pt & pp of* **sell**

soldier ['səʊldʒə(r)] *n* soldado *m*; [officer] militar *m*; **toy soldier** soldadito *m* de plomo ■ **soldier on** *vi Fig* continuar contra viento y marea

sole¹ [səʊl] *n* [of foot] planta *f*; [of shoe, sock] suela *f*

sole² [səʊl] *n* [fish] lenguado *m*

sole³ [səʊl] *adj* [only] único(a)

solely ['səʊllɪ] *adv* únicamente

solemn ['sɒləm] *adj* solemne

solicitor [sə'lɪsɪtə(r)] *n* abogado(a) *m,f*; [for wills] notario(a) *m,f*

solid ['sɒlɪd] **1.** *adj* a) [not liquid] sólido(a); [firm] firme **b)** [not hollow, pure-metal] macizo(a) **c)** [of strong material] resistente **2.** *n* sólido *m*

solidarity [sɒlɪ'dærɪtɪ] *n* solidaridad *f*

solitary ['sɒlɪtərɪ] *adj* a) [alone] solitario(a); [secluded] apartado(a) **b)** [only] solo(a)

solitude ['sɒlɪtjuːd] *n* soledad *f*

solo ['səʊləʊ] **1.** *n* solo *m* **2.** *adj* **solo parent** [father] padre *m* soltero; [mother] madre *f* soltera

soloist ['səʊləʊɪst] *n* solista *mf*

soluble ['sɒljʊbəl] *adj* soluble

solution [sə'luːʃən] *n* solución *f*

solve [sɒlv] *vt* resolver, solucionar

solvent ['sɒlvənt] *adj & n* solvente (*m*)

sombre, *US* **somber** ['sɒmbə(r)] *adj* [dark] sombrío(a); [gloomy] lúgubre; [pessimistic] pesimista

some [sʌm] **1.** *adj* a) [with plural nouns] unos(as), algunos(as); [several] varios(as) ; [a few] unos(as) cuantos(as) ; **there were some roses** había unas rosas ; **some more peas** más guisantes

b) [with singular nouns] algún /alguna; [a little] un poco de ; **there's some wine left** queda un poco de vino ; **would you like some coffee?** ¿quiere café?

c) [certain] cierto(a), alguno(a) ; **to some extent** hasta cierto punto ; **some people say that ...** algunas personas dicen que ...

d) [unspecified] algún /alguna ; **for some reason or other** por una razón o por otra ; **some day** algún día

e) [quite a lot of] bastante ; **some years ago** hace algunos años

2. *pron* **a)** [people] algunos(as), unos(as) ; **some go by bus and some by train** unos van en autobús y otros en tren

b) [objects] algunos(as) ; [a few] unos(as) cuantos(as) ; [a little] algo, un poco ; [certain ones] algunos(as)

3. *adv* **some thirty cars** unos treinta coches

---

somebody ['sʌmbədɪ] *pron* alguien ; **somebody else** otro(a)

somehow ['sʌmhaʊ] *adv* **a)** [in some way] de alguna forma **b)** [for some reason] por alguna razón

someone ['sʌmwʌn] *pron* = **somebody**

someplace ['sʌmpleɪs] *US adv* = **somewhere**

somersault ['sʌməsɔːlt] **1.** *n* voltereta *f* ; [by acrobat etc] salto *m* mortal ; [by car] vuelta *f* de campana **2.** *vi* dar volteretas ; [acrobat etc] dar un salto mortal ; [car] dar una vuelta de campana

something ['sʌmθɪŋ] *pron & n* algo ; **something to eat /drink** algo de comer /beber ; **are you drunk or something?** ¿estás borracho o qué? ; **something must be done** hay que hacer algo ; **she has a certain something** tiene un no sé qué ; **is something the matter?** ¿le pasa algo? ; **something else** otra cosa ; **something of the kind** algo por el estilo

sometime ['sʌmtaɪm] *adv* algún día ; **sometime last week** un día de la semana pasada ; **sometime next year** durante el año que viene

sometimes ['sʌmtaɪmz] *adv* a veces, de vez en cuando

somewhat ['sʌmwɒt] *adv Formal* algo, un tanto

somewhere ['sʌmweə(r)] *adv* **a)** [in some place] en alguna parte ; [to some place] a alguna parte ; **somewhere else** [in some other place] en otra parte ; [to some other place] a otra parte ; **somewhere or other** no sé dónde **b) somewhere in the region of** [approximately] más o menos

son [sʌn] *n* hijo *m* ; **eldest /youngest son** hijo mayor /menor

song [sɒŋ] *n* canción *f* ; [of bird] canto *m*

son-in-law ['sʌnɪnlɔː] *n* yerno *m*

soon [suːn] *adv* **a)** [within a short time] pronto, dentro de poco ; [quickly] rápidamente ; **soon after midnight** poco después de medianoche ; **soon afterwards** poco después **b) as soon as I arrived** en cuanto llegué ; **as soon as possible** cuanto antes **c)** [preference] **I would just as soon stay at home** prefiero quedarme en casa

soot [sʊt] *n* hollín *m*

soothe [suːð] *vt* [calm] tranquilizar ; [pain] aliviar

sophisticated [sə'fɪstɪkeɪtɪd] *adj* sofisticado(a)

sophomore ['sɒfəmɔː(r)] *n US* [in high school, university] estudiante *mf* de segundo

sopping ['sɒpɪŋ] *adj Fam* **sopping (wet)** como una sopa

soppy ['sɒpɪ] *(compar* **soppier**, *superl* **soppiest)** *adj Fam* sensiblero(a), *Esp* ñoño(a)

soprano [sə'prɑːnəʊ] *n* soprano *mf*

sordid ['sɔːdɪd] *adj* sórdido(a)

sore [sɔː(r)] **1.** *adj* **a)** dolorido(a) ; **to have a sore throat** tener dolor de garganta **b)** *Fam* [annoyed] *esp Esp* enfadado(a), enojado(a) **(about** por) ; **to feel sore about sth** estar resentido(a) por algo **2.** *n* llaga *f*

sorrow ['sɒrəʊ] n pena f, dolor m

sorry ['sɒrɪ] **1.** (compar **sorrier**, superl **sorriest**) adj a) **I feel very sorry for her** me da mucha pena b) [pitiful] triste c) **to be sorry (about sth)** sentir (algo); **I'm sorry I'm late** siento llegar tarde **2.** interj a) [apology] ¡perdón! b) Br [for repetition] ¿cómo?

sort [sɔ:t] **1.** n a) [kind] clase f, tipo m; [brand] marca f; **it's a sort of teapot** es una especie de tetera b) **he is a musician of sorts** tiene algo de músico; **there's an office of sorts** hay una especie de despacho c) **sort of** en cierto modo **2.** vt [classify] clasificar ∎ **sort out** vt sep a) [classify] clasificar; [put in order] ordenar b) [problem] arreglar, solucionar

so-so ['səʊsəʊ] adv Fam así así, regular

sought [sɔ:t] pt & pp of **seek**

soul [səʊl] n a) alma f b) **he's a good soul** [person] es muy buena persona c) MUS (música f) soul m

sound¹ [saʊnd] **1.** n sonido m; [noise] ruido m; **sound effects** efectos sonoros **2.** vt [bell, trumpet] tocar; **to sound the alarm** dar la señal de alarma **3.** vi a) [trumpet, bell, alarm] sonar b) [give an impression] parecer; **it sounds interesting** parece interesante ∎ **sound out** vt sep sondear

sound² [saʊnd] **1.** adj a) [healthy] sano(a); [in good condition] en buen estado b) [safe, dependable] seguro(a); [correct] acertado(a); [logical] lógico(a) c) [basis etc] sólido(a) d) [sleep] profundo(a) **2.** adv **to be sound asleep** estar profundamente dormido(a)

sound³ [saʊnd] vt NAUT & MED sondar

sound⁴ [saʊnd] n GEOG estrecho m

soundly ['saʊndlɪ] adv a) [logically] razonablemente b) [solidly] sólidamente c) **to sleep soundly** dormir profundamente

soundproof ['saʊndpru:f] adj insonorizado(a)

soundtrack ['saʊndtræk] n banda sonora

soup [su:p] n sopa f; [thin, clear] caldo m; **Fam in the soup** en un apuro; **soup dish** plato hondo; **soup spoon** cuchara f sopera

sour [saʊə(r)] adj a) [fruit, wine] agrio(a); [milk] cortado(a); **to go sour** [milk] cortarse; [wine] agriarse; Fig [situation] empeorar b) Fig [person] amargado(a)

source [sɔ:s] n fuente f; [of infection] foco m

south [saʊθ] **1.** n sur m; **the Deep South** [in the US] el Sur profundo (Alabama, Florida, Georgia, Luisiana, Misisipi, Carolina del Sur y la zona este de Texas); **in the south of England** en el sur de Inglaterra; **to the south of York** al sur de York
2. adj del sur; **South America** Sudamérica; **South American** sudamericano(a) (m,f); **South Africa** Sudáfrica; **South African** sudafricano(a) (m,f); **South Korea** Corea del Sur; **South Pole** Polo m Sur
3. adv [location] al sur; [direction] hacia el sur

southeast [saʊθ'i:st] **1.** n sudeste m **2.** adv [location] al sudeste; [direction] hacia el sudeste

southern ['sʌðən] adj del sur, meridional; **Southern Europe** Europa del Sur; **the southern hemisphere** el hemisferio sur

southerner ['sʌðənə(r)] n sureño(a) m,f

southward ['saʊθwəd] adj & adv hacia el sur

southwest [saʊθ'west] **1.** n suroeste m **2.** adj suroeste **3.** adv [location] al suroeste; [direction] hacia el suroeste

souvenir [su:və'nɪə(r)] n recuerdo m, souvenir m

sovereign ['sɒvrɪn] **1.** n a) [monarch] soberano(a) m,f b) HIST [coin] soberano m **2.** adj soberano(a)

sovereignty ['sɒvrəntɪ] n soberanía f

sow¹ [səʊ] (pt sowed, pp sowed or sown [səʊn]) vt sembrar

sow² [saʊ] n ZOOL cerda f, puerca f, Am chancha f

soya ['sɔɪə] *n* soja *f*; **soya bean** semilla *f* de soja

space [speɪs] **1.** *n* **a)** espacio *m*; COMPUT **disk space** espacio *m* en disco; **space age** era *f* espacial; **space shuttle** transbordador *m* espacial; **space station** estación *f* espacial **b)** [room] sitio *m*; **in a confined space** en un espacio reducido **2.** *vt* (*also* **space out**) espaciar, separar

spaceship ['speɪsʃɪp] *n* nave *f* espacial

spacious ['speɪʃəs] *adj* espacioso(a), amplio(a)

spade¹ [speɪd] *n* [for digging] pala *f*

spade² [speɪd] *n* CARDS pica *f*

spaghetti [spə'getɪ] *n* espaguetis *mpl*

Spain [speɪn] *n* España

span [spæn] **1.** *n* [of wing] envergadura *f*; [of hand] palmo *m*; [of arch] luz *f*; [of road] tramo *m*; [of time] lapso *m*; **life span** vida *f* **2.** *vt* [river etc] extenderse sobre, atravesar; [period of time etc] abarcar **3.** *pt of* **spin**

Spaniard ['spænjəd] *n* español(a) *m,f*

Spanish ['spænɪʃ] **1.** *adj* español(a) **2.** *n* **a) the Spanish** los españoles **b)** [language] español *m*, castellano *m*

Spanish-American *adj* hispanoamericano(a)

spank [spæŋk] *vt* zurrar

spanner ['spænə(r)] *n* Br llave *f* plana (*herramienta*); Fam **to throw a spanner in the works** estropear los planes

spare [speə(r)] **1.** *vt* **a)** [do without] prescindir de; **I can't spare the time** no tengo tiempo
b) [begrudge] escatimar
c) [show mercy to] perdonar
d) spare me the details ahórrate los detalles
2. *adj* [left over] sobrante; [surplus] de sobra, de más; **spare part** (pieza *f* de) recambio *m*; **spare room** cuarto *m* de los invitados; **spare wheel** rueda *f* de recambio *or* RP auxilio, Méx llanta *f* de refacción
3. *n* AUTO (pieza *f* de) recambio *m*

sparingly ['speərɪŋlɪ] *adv* en poca cantidad

spark [spɑːk] **1.** *n* chispa *f*; AUTO **spark plug** bujía *f* **2.** *vi* echar chispas ▪ **spark off** *vt sep* desatar

sparkle ['spɑːkəl] **1.** *vi* [diamond, glass] centellear, destellar; [eyes] brillar **2.** *n* [of diamond, glass] centelleo *m*, destello *m*; [of eyes] brillo *m*

sparkling ['spɑːklɪŋ] *adj* **a)** [diamond, glass] centelleante; [eyes] brillante; **sparkling wine** vino espumoso **b)** Fig [person, conversation] vivaz

sparrow ['spærəʊ] *n* gorrión *m*

sparse [spɑːs] *adj* [thin] escaso(a); [scattered] esparcido(a); [hair] ralo(a)

spasm ['spæzəm] *n* **a)** MED espasmo *m*; [of coughing] acceso *m* **b)** [of anger, activity] arrebato *m*

spat [spæt] *pt & pp of* **spit**

spate [speɪt] *n* **a)** [of letters] avalancha *f*; [of words] torrente *m*; [of accidents] racha *f* **b)** Br [river] desbordamiento *m*; **to be in full spate** estar crecido(a)

spatter ['spætə(r)] *vt* salpicar (**with** de)

speak [spiːk] (*pt* **spoke**, *pp* **spoken**) **1.** *vt*
a) [utter] decir; **to speak the truth** decir la verdad
b) [language] hablar
2. *vi* **a)** [gen] hablar, *esp Am* conversar, Méx platicar; **roughly speaking** a grandes rasgos; **so to speak** por así decirlo; **speaking of …** a propósito de …; **to speak to sb** hablar *or esp Am* conversar *or* Méx platicar con algn
b) [make a speech] pronunciar un discurso; [take the floor] tomar la palabra
c) TEL hablar; **speaking!** ¡al habla!; **who's speaking, please?** ¿de parte de quién?
▪ **speak for** *vt insep* [person, group] hablar en nombre de; **it speaks for itself** es evidente
▪ **speak out** *vi* **to speak out against sth** denunciar algo
▪ **speak up** *vi* hablar más fuerte; Fig **to speak up for sb** intervenir a favor de algn

speaker ['spiːkə(r)] n **a)** [in dialogue] interlocutor(a) m,f; [at conference] conferenciante mf, Am conferencista mf; **(public) speaker** orador(a) m,f **b)** [of language] hablante mf **c)** [loudspeaker] altavoz m, Am altoparlante m, Méx bocina f

spear [spɪə(r)] n lanza f; [javelin] jabalina f; [harpoon] arpón m

special ['speʃəl] **1.** adj especial; [specific] específico(a); [exceptional] extraordinario(a); **special delivery** envío m urgente; **special effects** efectos mpl especiales; **special needs children** niños con dificultades de aprendizaje **2.** n RADIO & TV programa m especial

specialist ['speʃəlɪst] n especialista mf

speciality [speʃɪˈælɪtɪ] n esp Br especialidad f

specialize ['speʃəlaɪz] vi especializarse **(in** en)

specially ['speʃəlɪ] adv [specifically] especialmente; [on purpose] a propósito

specialty ['speʃəltɪ] US n = **speciality**

species ['spiːʃiːz] (pl species) n especie f

specific [spɪˈsɪfɪk] adj específico(a); [definite] concreto(a); [precise] preciso(a); **to be specific** concretar

specifically [spɪˈsɪfɪklɪ] adv [exactly] específicamente; [expressly] expresamente; [namely] en concreto

specifications [spesɪfɪˈkeɪʃənz] npl [of machine] especificaciones fpl or características fpl técnicas

specify ['spesɪfaɪ] vt especificar, precisar

specimen ['spesɪmɪn] n [sample] muestra f; [example] ejemplar m; **urine/tissue specimen** espécimen de orina/tejido

speck [spek] n [of dust] mota f; [stain] manchita f; [small trace] pizca f

specs [speks] npl Fam [spectacles] gafas fpl, Am lentes mpl, Am anteojos mpl

spectacle ['spektəkəl] n **a)** [display] espectáculo m **b) spectacles** [glasses] gafas fpl, Am lentes mpl, Am anteojos mpl

spectacular [spekˈtækjʊlə(r)] **1.** adj espectacular, impresionante **2.** n CIN & TV (gran) espectáculo m

spectator [spekˈteɪtə(r)] n espectador(a) m,f

spectre, US **specter** ['spektə(r)] n espectro m, fantasma m

spectrum ['spektrəm] n espectro m

speculate ['spekjʊleɪt] vi especular

speculation [spekjʊˈleɪʃən] n especulación f

sped [sped] pt & pp of **speed**

speech [spiːtʃ] n **a)** [faculty] habla f; [pronunciation] pronunciación f; **freedom of speech** libertad f de expresión **b)** [address] discurso m; **to give a speech** pronunciar un discurso **c)** LING **part of speech** parte f de la oración

speechless ['spiːtʃlɪs] adj mudo(a), boquiabierto(a)

speed [spiːd] **1.** n velocidad f; [rapidity] rapidez f; **at top speed** a toda velocidad; **speed bump** badén m, resalto m; **speed camera** radar m; **speed dating** citas fpl rápidas, speed dating m; **speed limit** límite m de velocidad **2.** vi **a)** (pt & pp sped) [go fast] ir corriendo; [hurry] apresurarse; **to speed along** [car etc] ir a toda velocidad; **to speed past** pasar volando **b)** (pt & pp speeded) [exceed speed limit] conducir con exceso de velocidad ▪ **speed up 1.** vt sep acelerar; [person] meter prisa a **2.** vi [person] darse prisa, Am apurarse

speedboat ['spiːdbəʊt] n lancha rápida

speedometer [spɪˈdɒmɪtə(r)] n velocímetro m

speedy ['spiːdɪ] (compar speedier, superl speediest) adj veloz, rápido(a)

spell[1] [spel] (pt & pp spelt or spelled) **1.** vt [letter by letter] deletrear; Fig [denote] significar; **how do you spell your name?** ¿cómo se escribe su nombre? **2.** vi **she can't spell** comete faltas de ortografía ▪ **spell out** vt sep Fig explicar con detalle

spell[2] [spel] n [magical] hechizo m, encanto m

spell³ [spel] *n* **a)** [period] período *m*; [short period] rato *m*; MET **cold spell** ola *f* de frío **b)** [shift] turno *m*

spell-checker ['speltʃekə(r)] *n* COMPUT corrector *m* ortográfico

spelling ['spelɪŋ] *n* ortografía *f*

spelt [spelt] *pt & pp of* **spell**

spend [spend] *(pt & pp spent) vt* **a)** [money] gastar (**on** en) **b)** [time] pasar; **to spend time on sth** dedicar tiempo a algo

spending ['spendɪŋ] *n* gastos *mpl*; **spending money** dinero *m* de bolsillo; **spending power** poder adquisitivo

spent [spent] **1.** *adj* gastado(a) **2.** *pt & pp of* **spend**

sperm [spɜːm] *n* esperma *m*; **sperm bank** banco *m* de esperma; **sperm whale** cachalote *m*

sphere [sfɪə(r)] *n* esfera *f*

spice [spaɪs] **1.** *n* **a)** especia *f* **b)** *Fig* sal *f* **2.** *vt* **a)** CULIN sazonar **b) to spice (up)** [story etc] salpimentar

spicy ['spaɪsɪ] *(compar* **spicier**, *superl* **spiciest) adj* **a)** CULIN sazonado(a); [hot] picante **b)** *Fig* [story etc] picante

spider ['spaɪdə(r)] *n* araña *f*; *Br* **spider's** *or US* **spider web** telaraña *f*

spike¹ [spaɪk] *n* [sharp point] punta *f*; [metal rod] pincho *m*; [on railing] barrote *m*; SPORT [on shoes] clavo *m*

spike² [spaɪk] *n* BOT espiga *f*

spiky ['spaɪkɪ] *(compar* **spikier**, *superl* **spikiest) adj* puntiagudo(a); [hairstyle] de punta

spill [spɪl] *(pt & pp* **spilled** *or* **spilt** [spɪlt]) **1.** *vt* derramar **2.** *vi* [liquid] derramarse ■ **spill over** *vi* desbordarse

spin [spɪn] *(pt* **span** *or* **spun**, *pp* **spun**) **1.** *vt* **a)** [wheel etc] hacer girar; [washing] centrifugar **b)** [cotton, wool] hilar; [spider's web] tejer **2.** *vi* [wheel etc] girar; AVIAT caer en barrena; AUTO patinar **3.** *n* **a)** [turn] vuelta *f*, giro *m* **b)** SPORT efecto *m* **c)** *Br* **to go for a spin** [ride] dar una vuelta

d) POL **spin doctor** asesor(a) *m,f* político(a) *(para dar buena prensa a un partido o político)*

spinach ['spɪnɪtʃ] *n* espinacas *fpl*

spin-dryer [spɪn'draɪə(r)] *n* secador centrífugo

spine [spaɪn] *n* **a)** ANAT columna *f* vertebral, espinazo *m*; [of book] lomo *m* **b)** ZOOL púa *f*; BOT espina *f*

spinster ['spɪnstə(r)] *n* soltera *f*

spiral ['spaɪərəl] **1.** *n* espiral *f* **2.** *adj* en espiral; **spiral staircase** escalera *f* de caracol

spire ['spaɪə(r)] *n* [of church] aguja *f*

spirit¹ ['spɪrɪt] *n* **a)** [soul] espíritu *m*, alma *f*; [ghost] fantasma *m* **b)** [attitude] espíritu *m*; [mood] humor *m* **c)** [courage] valor *m*; [liveliness] ánimo *m*; [vitality] vigor *m* **d)** **spirits** [mood] humor *m*; **to be in good spirits** estar de buen humor

spirit² ['spɪrɪt] *n* **a)** CHEM alcohol *m*; **spirit level** nivel *m* de aire **b) spirits** [alcoholic drinks] licores *mpl*

spiritual ['spɪrɪtjʊəl] *adj* espiritual

spit¹ [spɪt] *(pt & pp* **spat**) **1.** *vt* escupir **2.** *vi* escupir; *Fam* **he's the spitting image of his father** es el vivo retrato de su padre **3.** *n* [saliva] saliva *f*

spit² [spɪt] *n* CULIN asador *m*

spite [spaɪt] **1.** *n* **a)** [ill will] rencor *m*, ojeriza *f* **b)** **in spite of** a pesar de, pese a; **in spite of the fact that** a pesar de que, pese a que **2.** *vt* [annoy] fastidiar

spiteful ['spaɪtfʊl] *adj* [person] rencoroso(a); [remark] malévolo(a); [tongue] viperino(a)

splash [splæʃ] **1.** *vt* salpicar **2.** *vi* **a) to splash (about)** [in water] chapotear **b)** [water etc] salpicar **3.** *n* **a)** [noise] chapoteo *m* **b)** [spray] salpicadura *f*; *Fig* [of colour] mancha *f* ■ **splash out** *vi Fam* tirar la casa por la ventana

splendid ['splendɪd] *adj* espléndido(a)

splendour, *US* **splendor** ['splendə(r)] *n* esplendor *m*

splint [splɪnt] *n* tablilla *f*

splinter ['splɪntə(r)] **1.** n [wood] astilla f; [bone, stone] esquirla f; [glass] fragmento m; **splinter group** grupo m disidente **2.** vi **a)** [wood etc] astillarse **b)** POL escindirse

split [splɪt] (pt & pp **split**) **1.** n [crack] grieta f, hendidura f; [tear] desgarrón m; Fig [division] cisma m; POL escisión f **2.** adj partido(a); **in a split second** en una fracción de segundo **3.** vt **a)** [crack] agrietar; [cut] partir; [tear] rajar; [atom] desintegrar **b)** [divide] dividir **c)** [share out] repartir **d)** POL escindir **4.** vi **a)** [crack] agrietarse; [into two parts] partirse; [garment] rajarse **b)** [divide] dividirse **c)** POL escindirse

■ **split up 1.** vt sep [break up] partir; [divide up] dividir; [share out] repartir **2.** vi [couple] separarse

spoil [spɔɪl] (pt & pp **spoiled** or **spoilt**) **1.** vt **a)** [ruin] estropear, echar a perder **b)** [child] mimar a; **to be spoilt for choice** tener demasiadas cosas para elegir **2.** vi [food] estropearse

spoilt [spɔɪlt] **1.** adj **a)** [food, merchandise] estropeado(a) **b)** [child] mimado(a) **2.** pt & pp of **spoil**

spoke¹ [spəʊk] pt of **speak**

spoke² [spəʊk] n [of wheel] radio m, rayo m

spoken ['spəʊkən] pp of **speak**

spokesman ['spəʊksmən] n portavoz m

spokeswoman ['spəʊkswʊmən] n portavoz f

sponge [spʌndʒ] **1.** n esponja f; Fig **to throw in the sponge** arrojar la toalla; Br **sponge cake** bizcocho m **2.** vt [wash] lavar con esponja **3.** vi Fam vivir de gorra ■ **sponge off, sponge on** vt insep vivir a costa de

sponger ['spʌndʒə(r)] n Fam gorrero(a) m,f, Esp, Méx gorrón(ona) m,f, RP garronero(a) m,f

sponsor ['spɒnsə(r)] **1.** vt patrocinar; FIN avalar; [support] respaldar **2.** n patrocinador(a) m,f; FIN avalador(a) m,f

sponsorship ['spɒnsəʃɪp] n patrocinio m; FIN aval m; [support] respaldo m

spontaneous [spɒn'teɪnɪəs] adj espontáneo(a)

spooky ['spu:kɪ] (compar **spookier**, superl **spookiest**) adj Fam espeluznante

spoon [spu:n] **1.** n cuchara f; [small] cucharita f **2.** vt sacar con cuchara; [serve] servir con cuchara

spoonful ['spu:nfʊl] n cucharada f

sport [spɔ:t] **1.** n **a)** deporte m; **extreme sport** deporte m extremo **b)** Fam **he's a good sport** es buena persona; **be a sport!** ¡sé amable! **2.** vt [display] lucir

sports [spɔ:ts] adj **sports car** coche m or Am carro m or CSur auto m deportivo; **sports centre** polideportivo m; Br **sports jacket** chaqueta f or Am saco m de sport

sportsman ['spɔ:tsmən] n deportista m

sportswear ['spɔ:tsweə(r)] n ropa f de deporte

sportswoman ['spɔ:tswʊmən] n deportista f

spot [spɒt] **1.** n **a)** [dot] punto m; [on fabric] lunar m **b)** [stain] mancha f **c)** [pimple] grano m **d)** [place] sitio m, lugar m; **on the spot** [person] allí, presente; **to be in a tight spot** estar en un apuro; **to put sb on the spot** poner a algn en un aprieto **e)** Br Fam [small amount - of rain, wine] gota f; **a spot of bother** una problemilla **2.** vt [notice] darse cuenta de, notar; [see] ver

spotless ['spɒtlɪs] adj [very clean] impecable; Fig [reputation etc] intachable

spotlight ['spɒtlaɪt] n foco m; AUTO faro m auxiliar; Fig **to be in the spotlight** ser objeto de la atención pública

spotty ['spɒtɪ] (compar **spottier**, superl **spottiest**) adj Pej con granos

spouse [spaʊs] n cónyuge mf

spout [spaʊt] **1.** n [of jug] pico m ; [of teapot] pitorro m **2.** vt Fam [nonsense] soltar **3.** vi **to spout out/up** [liquid] brotar

sprain [spreɪn] **1.** n esguince m **2.** vt torcer ; **to sprain one's ankle** torcerse el tobillo

sprang [spræŋ] pt of **spring**

spray[1] [spreɪ] **1.** n **a)** [of water] rociada f ; [from sea] espuma f ; [from aerosol] pulverización f **b)** [aerosol] spray m ; [for plants] pulverizador m ; **spray can** aerosol m **2.** vt [water] rociar ; [insecticide, perfume] pulverizar

spray[2] [spreɪ] n [of flowers] ramita f

spread [spred] (pt & pp **spread**) **1.** n
a) extensión f ; [of ideas] difusión f ; [of disease, fire] propagación f ; [of terrorism] generalización f
b) [for bread] pasta f ; **cheese spread** queso m para untar
c) Fam [large meal] banquetazo m
2. vt **a)** [unfold] desplegar ; [lay out] extender
b) [butter etc] untar
c) [news] difundir ; [rumour] hacer correr ; [disease, fire] propagar ; [panic] sembrar
3. vi **a)** [stretch out] extenderse ; [unfold] desplegarse
b) [news] difundirse ; [rumour] correr ; [disease] propagarse

spreadsheet ['spredʃiːt] n COMPUT hoja f de cálculo

spree [spriː] n juerga f ; **to go on a spree** ir de juerga

spring[1] [sprɪŋ] **1.** n [season] primavera f **2.** adj primaveral ; **spring onion** cebolleta f, RP cebolla f de verdeo ; **spring roll** rollo m de primavera, RP arrollado m de primavera

spring[2] [sprɪŋ] (pt **sprang**, pp **sprung**) **1.** n **a)** [of water] manantial m, fuente f **b)** [of watch etc] resorte m ; [of mattress] muelle m ; AUTO ballesta f **2.** vi **a)** [jump] saltar ; **the lid sprang open** la tapa se abrió de golpe **b)** [appear] aparecer (de repente) **3.** vt **a)** **to spring a leak** hacer agua **b)** Fig [news, surprise] dar de golpe

■ **spring up** vi aparecer ; [plants] brotar ; [buildings] elevarse ; [problems] surgir

springboard ['sprɪŋbɔːd] n trampolín m

springtime ['sprɪŋtaɪm] n primavera f

sprinkle ['sprɪŋkəl] vt [with water] rociar (**with** de) ; [with sugar] espolvorear (**with** de)

sprint [sprɪnt] **1.** n esprint m **2.** vi esprintar

sprout [spraʊt] **1.** vi [bud] brotar ; Fig crecer rápidamente **2.** n (**Brussels**) **sprouts** coles fpl or CSur repollitos mpl de Bruselas

spruce [spruːs] adj pulcro(a) ■ **spruce up** vt sep acicalar

sprung [sprʌŋ] pp of **spring**

spun [spʌn] pt & pp of **spin**

spur [spɜː(r)] **1.** n **a)** espuela f **b)** Fig [stimulus] acicate m ; **on the spur of the moment** sin pensarlo **2.** vt **a)** [horse] espolear **b)** Fig incitar

spurt [spɜːt] **1.** n **a)** [of liquid] chorro m **b)** Fig [of activity etc] racha f ; [effort] esfuerzo m **2.** vi **a)** [liquid] chorrear **b)** [make an effort] hacer un último esfuerzo ; [accelerate] acelerar

spy [spaɪ] **1.** n espía mf **2.** vt Formal [see] divisar **3.** vi espiar (**on** a)

spying ['spaɪɪŋ] n espionaje m

squabble ['skwɒbəl] **1.** n riña f, pelea f **2.** vi reñir, pelearse (**over** or **about** por)

squad [skwɒd] n MIL pelotón m ; [of police] brigada f ; SPORT equipo m ; **drugs squad** brigada antidroga

squalid ['skwɒlɪd] adj [very dirty] asqueroso(a) ; [poor] miserable ; [motive] vil

squalor ['skwɒlə(r)] n [dirtiness] mugre f ; [poverty] miseria f

squander ['skwɒndə(r)] vt [money] derrochar, despilfarrar ; [time] desperdiciar

square [skweə(r)] **1.** n **a)** cuadro m ; [on chessboard, crossword] casilla f **b)** [in town] plaza f **c)** MATH cuadrado m

2. *adj* **a)** [in shape] cuadrado(a)
b) MATH [metre, root] cuadrado(a)
c) a square meal una buena comida
d) [old-fashioned] carroza ; [conservative] carca
3. *vt* **a)** MATH elevar al cuadrado
b) [settle] arreglar
4. *vi* [agree] cuadrar (**with** con)

squash[1] [skwɒʃ] **1.** *n Br* [drink] **orange / lemon** (bebida *f* a base de) concentrado *m* de naranja / limón **2.** *vt* [crush] aplastar **3.** *vi* aplastarse

squash[2] [skwɒʃ] *n* SPORT squash *m*

squash[3] [skwɒʃ] *n US* [vegetable] calabacín *m*

squat [skwɒt] **1.** *adj* [person] rechoncho(a) **2.** *vi* **a)** [crouch] agacharse, sentarse en cuclillas **b)** [in building] ocupar ilegalmente **3.** *n Br* [illegally occupied dwelling] casa *f* ocupada *(ilegalmente)*

squawk [skwɔːk] **1.** *n* graznido *m* **2.** *vi* graznar

squeak [skwiːk] **1.** *n* [of mouse] chillido *m* ; [of hinge, wheel] chirrido *m* ; [of shoes] crujido *m* **2.** *vi* [mouse] chillar ; [hinge, wheel] chirriar, rechinar ; [shoes] crujir

squeal [skwiːl] **1.** *n* [of animal, person] chillido *m* **2.** *vi* **a)** [animal, person] chillar **b)** *Fam* [inform] chivarse

squeamish ['skwiːmɪʃ] *adj* muy sensible

squeeze [skwiːz] **1.** *vt* apretar ; [lemon etc] exprimir ; [sponge] estrujar ; **to squeeze paste out of a tube** sacar pasta de un tubo apretando **2.** *vi* **to squeeze in** apretujarse **3.** *n* **a)** [pressure] estrujón *m* ; **a squeeze of lemon** unas gotas de limón **b)** [of hand] apretón *m* ; [hug] abrazo *m* ; [crush] apiñamiento *m* ; **credit squeeze** reducción *f* de créditos

squid [skwɪd] *n* calamar *m* ; [small] chipirón *m*

squint [skwɪnt] **1.** *n* **a)** bizquera *f* ; **to have a squint** ser bizco(a) **b)** *Br* [quick look] ojeada *f*, vistazo *m* **2.** *vi* **a)** ser bizco(a) **b) to squint at sth** [glance]

echar un vistazo a algo ; [with eyes half-closed] mirar algo con los ojos entrecerrados

squirm [skwɜːm] *vi* retorcerse ; [with embarrassment] ruborizarse, avergonzarse, *Am* apenarse

squirrel ['skwɪrəl] *n* ardilla *f*

squirt [skwɜːt] **1.** *n* [of liquid] chorro *m* **2.** *vt* lanzar a chorro **3.** *vi* **to squirt out** salir a chorros

Sry MESSAGING *(abbr of* **sorry***)* xdon

St a) *(abbr of* **Saint***)* S. / Sto. / Sta. **b)** *(abbr of* **Street***)* c /

stab [stæb] **1.** *n* [with knife] puñalada *f* ; [of pain] punzada *f* **2.** *vt* apuñalar

stability [stə'bɪlɪtɪ] *n* estabilidad *f*

stabilize ['steɪbɪlaɪz] **1.** *vt* estabilizar **2.** *vi* estabilizarse

stable[1] ['steɪbəl] *adj* estable

stable[2] ['steɪbəl] *n* cuadra *f*, caballeriza *f*

stack [stæk] **1.** *n* [pile] montón *m* ; *Fam* **he's got stacks of money** está forrado **2.** *vt* [pile up] amontonar, apilar ; *Fig* **the odds are stacked against us** todo está en contra nuestra

stackable ['stækəbəl] *adj* apilable

stadium ['steɪdɪəm] *n* estadio *m*

staff [stɑːf] **1.** *n* **a)** [personnel] personal *m* ; MIL estado mayor ; **staff meeting** claustro *m* ; *Br* **staff nurse** enfermera cualificada **b)** [stick] bastón *m* ; [of shepherd] cayado *m* **2.** *vt* proveer de personal

stag [stæg] *n* ciervo *m*, venado *m* ; *Fam* **stag party** despedida *f* de soltero

stage [steɪdʒ] **1.** *n* **a)** [platform] plataforma *f* **b)** [in theatre] escenario *m* ; **stage door** entrada *f* de artistas ; **stage fright** miedo escénico ; **stage manager** director(a) *m,f* de escena **c)** [phase - of development, journey, rocket] etapa *f* ; [of road, pipeline] tramo *m* ; **at this stage of the negotiations** a estas alturas de las negociaciones ; **in stages** por etapas **2.** *vt* **a)** [play] poner en escena, montar **b)** [arrange] organizar ; [carry out] llevar a cabo

stagger ['stægə(r)] **1.** *vi* tambalearse **2.** *vt* **a)** [amaze] asombrar **b)** [hours, work] escalonar

stagnant ['stægnənt] *adj* estancado(a)

stain [stem] **1.** *n* **a)** mancha *f*; **stain remover** quitamanchas *m inv* **b)** [dye] tinte *m* **2.** *vt* **a)** manchar **b)** [dye] teñir **3.** *vi* mancharse

stained [stemd] *adj* **stained glass window** vidriera *f* de colores

stainless ['stemlɪs] *adj* [steel] inoxidable

stair [steə(r)] *n* escalón *m*, peldaño *m*; **stairs** escalera *f*

staircase ['steəkeɪs] *n* escalera *f*

stake¹ [steɪk] **1.** *n* [stick] estaca *f*; [for plant] rodrigón *m*; [post] poste *m* **2.** *vt* **to stake (out)** cercar con estacas

stake² [steɪk] **1.** *n* **a)** [bet] apuesta *f*; **the issue at stake** el tema en cuestión; **to be at stake** [at risk] estar en juego **b)** [investment] interés *m* **2.** *vt* [bet] apostar; [invest] invertir; **to stake a claim to sth** reivindicar algo

stale [steɪl] *adj* [food] pasado(a); [bread] duro(a)

stalemate ['steɪlmeɪt] *n* [in chess] tablas *fpl*; *Fig* **to reach stalemate** llegar a un punto muerto

stalk¹ [stɔːk] *n* [of plant] tallo *m*; [of fruit] rabo *m*

stalk² [stɔːk] **1.** *vt* [of hunter] cazar al acecho; [of animal] acechar **2.** *vi* **he stalked out of the room** salió *esp Esp* enfadado *or esp Am* enojado de la habitación

stalker ['stɔːkə(r)] *n* acosador(a) *m,f* (que persigue a su víctima de forma obsesiva), acechador(a) *mf*

stall¹ [stɔːl] **1.** *n* **a)** [in market] puesto *m*; [at fair] caseta *f* **b)** [stable] establo *m*; [stable compartment] casilla *f* de establo **c)** *Br* CIN & THEAT **the stalls** el patio de butacas **2.** *vt* [hold off] retener **3.** *vi* AUTO pararse, *Esp* calarse; AVIAT perder velocidad

stall² [stɔːl] *vi* **to stall (for time)** intentar ganar tiempo

stamina ['stæmɪnə] *n* resistencia *f*

stammer ['stæmə(r)] **1.** *n* tartamudeo *m* **2.** *vi* tartamudear

stamp [stæmp] **1.** *n* **a)** [postage stamp] sello *m*, *Am* estampilla *f*, *CAm, Méx* timbre *m*; **stamp collector** filatelista *mf*; **stamp** *Br* **duty** *or US* **tax** póliza *f* (impuesto de transmisiones patrimoniales) **b)** [rubber stamp] tampón *m*; [for metals] cuño *m* **c)** [with foot] patada *f* **2.** *vt* **a)** [with postage stamp] poner el sello a; *Br* **stamped addressed envelope**, *US* **self-addressed stamped envelope** sobre franqueado con la dirección del remitente **b)** [with rubber stamp] sellar **c)** **to stamp one's feet** patear; [in dancing] zapatear **3.** *vi* patear
■ **stamp out** *vt sep Fig* [racism etc] acabar con; [rebellion] sofocar

stampede [stæm'piːd] **1.** *n* estampida *f*; *Fig* [rush] desbandada *f* **2.** *vi* desbandarse; *Fig* [rush] precipitarse

stamping-ground ['stæmpɪŋgraʊnd] *n Fam* lugar *m* predilecto

stance [stæns] *n* postura *f*

stand [stænd] (*pt & pp* **stood**) **1.** *n* **a)** [position] posición *f*, postura *f*; **to make a stand** resistir **b)** [of lamp, sculpture] pie *m* **c)** [market stall] puesto *m*; [at fair] caseta *f*; [at exhibition] stand *m* **d)** [platform] plataforma *f*; [in stadium] gradas *fpl*, *Esp* graderío *m*; *US* [witness box] estrado *m* **2.** *vt* **a)** [place] poner, colocar **b)** [tolerate] aguantar, soportar **3.** *vi* **a)** [be upright] estar de pie *or Am* parado(a); [get up] levantarse; [remain upright] quedarse de pie *or Am* parado(a); **stand still!** ¡estáte quieto(a)! **b)** [be situated] estar, encontrarse **c)** [remain valid] seguir vigente **d)** **as things stand** tal como están las cosas **e)** POL presentarse
■ **stand back** *vi* [allow sb to pass] abrir paso

■ **stand by 1.** *vi* a) [do nothing] quedarse sin hacer nada b) [be ready] estar listo(a) **2.** *vt insep* [person] apoyar a ; [promise] cumplir con ; [decision] atenerse a

■ **stand down** *vi Fig* retirarse

■ **stand for** *vt insep* a) [mean] significar b) [represent] representar c) [tolerate] aguantar

■ **stand in** *vi* sustituir

■ **stand in for** *vt insep* sustituir

■ **stand out** *vi* [mountain etc] destacarse (**against** contra) ; *Fig* [person] destacar

■ **stand up** *vi* [get up] ponerse de pie, *Am* pararse ; [be standing] estar de pie, *Fig* it will stand up to wear and tear es muy resistente ; *Fig* to stand up for sb defender a algn ; *Fig* to stand up to sb hacer frente a algn

standard ['stændəd] **1.** *n* a) [level] nivel *m* ; **standard of living** nivel de vida b) [criterion] criterio *m* c) [norm] norma *f*, estándar *m* **2.** *adj* normal, estándar ; **standard lamp** lámpara *f* de pie

standardize ['stændədaɪz] *vt* normalizar

standby ['stændbaɪ] *n* a) [thing] recurso *m* b) [person] suplente *mf* ; **to be on standby** MIL estar de retén ; AVIAT estar en la lista de espera ; **standby ticket** billete *m* sin reserva

stand-in ['stændɪn] *n* suplente *mf* ; CIN doble *mf*

standing ['stændɪŋ] **1.** *adj* a) [not sitting] de pie ; [upright] recto(a) ; **to give sb a standing ovation** ovacionar a algn de pie ; **there was standing room only** no quedaban asientos b) [committee] permanente ; [invitation] permanente ; **standing charges** gastos *mpl* fijos ; *Br* **standing order** pago *m* fijo **2.** *n* a) [social position] rango *m* b) [duration] duración *f* ; [in job] antigüedad *f*

standpoint ['stændpɔɪnt] *n* punto *m* de vista

standstill ['stændstɪl] *n* at a standstill [car, traffic] parado(a) ; [industry]

paralizado(a) ; **to come to a standstill** [car, traffic] pararse ; [industry] paralizarse

stank [stæŋk] *pt of* **stink**

staple¹ ['steɪpəl] **1.** *n* [fastener] grapa *f*, *Chile* corchete *m*, *RP* ganchito *m* **2.** *vt* grapar

staple² ['steɪpəl] **1.** *adj* [food] básico(a) ; [product] de primera necesidad **2.** *n* [food] alimento básico

stapler ['steɪplə(r)] *n* grapadora *f*, *Am* engrapadora *f*, *Chile* corchetera *f*, *RP* abrochadora *f*

star [stɑː(r)] **1.** *n* estrella *f* **2.** *adj* estelar **3.** *vt* CIN tener como protagonista a **4.** *vi* CIN **to star in a movie** protagonizar una película

starboard ['stɑːbəd] *n* estribor *m*

starch [stɑːtʃ] **1.** *n* almidón *m* **2.** *vt* almidonar

stare [steə(r)] **1.** *n* mirada fija **2.** *vi* mirar fijamente

stark [stɑːk] *adj* [landscape] desolado(a) ; [décor] austero(a) ; **the stark truth** la dura realidad ; **stark poverty** la miseria

start [stɑːt] **1.** *n* a) [beginning] principio *m*, comienzo *m* ; [of race] salida *f* ; **for a start** para empezar ; **from the start** desde el principio ; **to make a fresh start** volver a empezar b) [advantage] ventaja *f* c) [jump] sobresalto *m* **2.** *vt* a) [begin] empezar, comenzar ; **to start doing sth** empezar a hacer algo b) [cause] causar, provocar c) [found] fundar ; **to start a business** montar un negocio d) [set in motion] arrancar **3.** *vi* a) [begin] empezar, comenzar ; [engine] arrancar ; **starting from Monday** a partir del lunes b) [take fright] asustarse, sobresaltarse

■ **start off** *vi* a) [begin] empezar, comenzar ; **to start off by / with** empezar por / con b) [leave] salir, ponerse en camino

■ **start up 1.** *vt sep* [engine] arrancar **2.** *vi* empezar ; [car] arrancar

starter ['stɑːtə(r)] n a) SPORT [official] juez mf de salida ; [competitor] competidor(a) m,f b) AUTO motor m de arranque c) CULIN entrada f

starting ['stɑːtɪŋ] n **starting block** taco m de salida ; **starting point** punto m de partida ; **starting post** línea f de salida

startle ['stɑːtəl] vt asustar

starvation [stɑːˈveɪʃən] n hambre f

starve [stɑːv] **1.** vt privar de comida ; Fig **he was starved of affection** fue privado de cariño **2.** vi pasar hambre ; **to starve to death** morirse de hambre

state [steɪt] **1.** n a) estado m ; **state of emergency** estado de emergencia ; **state of mind** estado de ánimo ; **to be in no fit state to do sth** no estar en condiciones de hacer algo **b) the States** los Estados Unidos ; US **blue state** estado m demócrata ; US **red state** estado m republicano ; US **state highway** ≃ carretera f nacional ; US **State Department** Departamento m de Estado (Ministerio de Asuntos or (Am) Relaciones Exteriores estadounidense) **2.** adj a) POL estatal ; **state education** enseñanza pública ; **state ownership** propiedad f del Estado ; **state pension** pensión f del estado **b)** [ceremonial] de gala ; **state visit** visita f oficial **3.** vt declarar, afirmar ; [case] exponer ; [problem] plantear

statement ['steɪtmənt] n a) declaración f ; **official statement** comunicado m oficial ; JUR **to make a statement** prestar declaración **b)** FIN estado m de cuenta ; **monthly statement** balance m mensual

state-run adj del estado

statesman ['steɪtsmən] n estadista m

static ['stætɪk] **1.** adj estático(a) **2.** n RADIO ruido m

station ['steɪʃən] **1.** n a) estación f ; US **station wagon** camioneta f **b)** [position] puesto m **c)** [social standing] rango m **2.** vt [place] colocar ; MIL apostar

stationary ['steɪʃənərɪ] adj [not moving] inmóvil ; [unchanging] estacionario(a)

stationer ['steɪʃənə(r)] n papelero(a) m,f ; **stationer's (shop)** papelería f

stationery ['steɪʃənərɪ] n [paper] papel m de escribir ; [pens, ink etc] artículos mpl de escritorio

statistic [stəˈtɪstɪk] n estadística f

statue ['stætjuː] n estatua f

stature ['stætʃə(r)] n [physical build] estatura f ; [reputation] talla f, estatura f

status ['steɪtəs] n estado m ; **social status** estatus m ; COMPUT **status bar** barra f de estado ; **status symbol** signo m de prestigio ; **status quo** status quo m

stave [steɪv] n MUS pentagrama m
■ **stave off** vt sep [repel] rechazar ; [avoid] evitar ; [delay] aplazar

stay¹ [steɪ] **1.** n Esp, Méx estancia f, Am estadía f
2. vi a) [remain] quedarse, permanecer **b)** [reside temporarily] alojarse ; **she's staying with us for a few days** ha venido a pasar unos días con nosotros
3. vt Fig **to stay the course** aguantar hasta el final ; **staying power** resistencia f
■ **stay in** vi quedarse en casa
■ **stay on** vi quedarse
■ **stay out** vi **to stay out all night** no volver a casa en toda la noche
■ **stay up** vi no acostarse

stay² [steɪ] n [rope] estay m, viento m

steadily ['stedɪlɪ] adv [improve] constantemente ; [walk] con paso seguro ; [gaze] fijamente ; [rain, work] sin parar

steady ['stedɪ] **1.** (compar **steadier**, superl **steadiest**) adj firme, seguro(a) ; [gaze] fijo(a) ; [prices] estable ; [demand, speed] constante ; [pace] regular ; [worker] aplicado(a) ; **steady job** empleo fijo
2. vt [table etc] estabilizar ; [nerves] calmar
3. vi [market] estabilizarse

steak [steɪk] n filete m, bistec m, RP bife m

steal [stiːl] (*pt* stole, *pp* stolen) **1.** *vt* robar; **to steal a glance at sth** echar una mirada furtiva a algo; **to steal the show** llevarse todos los aplausos **2.** *vi* a) [rob] robar
b) [move quietly] moverse con sigilo; **to steal away** escabullirse

stealthy ['stelθɪ] (*compar* stealthier, *superl* stealthiest) *adj* sigiloso(a), furtivo(a)

steam [stiːm] **1.** *n* vapor *m*; *Fam* **to let off steam** desahogarse; **steam engine** máquina *f* de vapor **3.** *vt* CULIN cocer al vapor **3.** *vi* [give off steam] echar vapor; [bowl of soup etc] humear ▪ **steam up** *vi* [window etc] empañarse

steamer ['stiːmə(r)] *n* NAUT vapor *m*

steel [stiːl] **1.** *n* acero *m*; **steel industry** industria siderúrgica **2.** *vt* *Fig* **to steel oneself to do sth** armarse de valor para hacer algo

steep¹ [stiːp] *adj* [hill etc] empinado(a); *Fig* [price, increase] excesivo(a)

steep² [stiːp] *vt* [washing] remojar; [food] poner en remojo

steeple ['stiːpəl] *n* aguja *f*

steer [stɪə(r)] **1.** *vt* dirigir; [car] conducir, *Am* manejar; [ship] gobernar **2.** *vi* [car] conducir, *Am* manejar; *Fig* **to steer clear of sth** evitar algo

steering ['stɪərɪŋ] *n* dirección *f*; **assisted steering** dirección asistida; **steering wheel** volante *m*, *Andes* timón *m*

stem [stem] **1.** *n* a) [of plant] tallo *m*; [of glass] pie *m*; [of pipe] tubo *m* **b)** [of word] raíz *f* **2.** *vi* **to stem from** derivarse de **3.** *vt* [blood] restañar; [flood, attack] contener

stench [stentʃ] *n* hedor *m*

step [step] **1.** *n* a) paso *m*; [sound] paso, pisada *f*; **step by step** poco a poco **b)** [measure] medida *f*; **a step in the right direction** un paso acertado **c)** [stair] peldaño *m*, escalón *m* **d)** steps escalera *f* **2.** *vi* dar un paso; **step this way, please** haga el favor de pasar por aquí; **to step aside** apartarse ▪ **step**

down *vi* dimitir ▪ **step forward** *vi* [volunteer] ofrecerse ▪ **step in** *vi* intervenir ▪ **step up** *vt sep* aumentar

stepdaughter ['stepdɔːtə(r)] *n* hijastra *f*

stepfather ['stepfɑːðə(r)] *n* padrastro *m*

stepladder ['steplædə(r)] *n* escalera *f* de tijera

stepmother ['stepmʌðə(r)] *n* madrastra *f*

stepson ['stepsʌn] *n* hijastro *m*

stereo ['sterɪəʊ] **1.** *n* estéreo *m* **2.** *adj* estereo(fónico(a))

stereotype ['sterɪətaɪp] *n* estereotipo *m*

sterile ['steraɪl] *adj* [barren] estéril

sterilize ['sterɪlaɪz] *vt* esterilizar

sterling ['stɜːlɪŋ] **1.** *n* libras *fpl* esterlinas; **sterling silver** plata *f* de ley; **the pound sterling** la libra esterlina **2.** *adj* [person, quality] excelente

stern¹ [stɜːn] *adj* [severe] severo(a)

stern² [stɜːn] *n* NAUT popa *f*

steroid ['sterɔɪd] *n* esteroide *m*

stethoscope ['steθəskəʊp] *n* estetoscopio *m*

stew [stjuː] **1.** *n* estofado *m*, cocido *m* **2.** *vt* [meat] guisar, estofar; [fruit] cocer

steward ['stjʊəd] *n* [on estate] administrador *m*; [on ship] camarero *m*; [on plane] auxiliar *m* de vuelo; **air steward** auxiliar *m* de vuelo

stewardess ['stjʊədɪs] *n* [on ship] camarera *f*; [on plane] auxiliar *f* de vuelo, azafata *f*, *Am* aeromoza *f*; *Dated* **air stewardess** auxiliar *f* de vuelo, azafata *f*, *Am* aeromoza *f*

stick¹ [stɪk] *n* a) palo *m*; [walking stick] bastón *m*; [of dynamite] cartucho *m*; **memory stick** memoria *f* USB, lápiz *m* de memoria; *Br Fam* **to give sb stick** dar caña a algn **b)** *Fam* **to live in the sticks** vivir en el quinto infierno *or Esp* pino

stick² [stɪk] (*pt & pp* stuck) **1.** *vt* a) [push] meter; [knife] clavar; **he stuck his head out of the window** asomó la cabeza por la ventana **b)** *Fam* [put] meter **c)** [with glue etc] pegar **d)** *Fam* [tolerate] soportar, aguantar **2.** *vi* **a)** [become attached] pegarse **b)** [window, drawer] atrancarse ; [machine part] encasquillarse ▪ **stick at** *vt insep* perseverar en ▪ **stick by** *vt insep* [friend] ser fiel a ; [promise] cumplir con ▪ **stick out 1.** *vi* [project] sobresalir ; [be noticeable] resaltar **2.** *vt sep* [tongue] sacar ; *Fig* **to stick one's neck out** jugarse el tipo ▪ **stick to** *vt insep* [principles] atenerse a ▪ **stick up 1.** *vi* [project] sobresalir ; [hair] ponerse de punta **2.** *vt sep* **a)** [poster] fijar **b)** [hand etc] levantar ▪ **stick up for** *vt insep* defender

sticker ['stɪkə(r)] *n* [label] etiqueta adhesiva ; [with slogan] pegatina *f*

sticky ['stɪkɪ] *(compar* stickier, *superl* stickiest) *adj* pegajoso(a) ; [label] engomado(a) ; [weather] bochornoso(a) ; *Fam* [situation] difícil

stiff [stɪf] **1.** *adj* **a)** rígido(a), tieso(a) ; [collar, lock] duro(a) ; [joint] entumecido(a) ; [machine part] atascado(a) ; **to have a stiff neck** tener tortícolis **b)** *Fig* [test] difícil ; [punishment] severo(a) ; [price] excesivo(a) ; [drink] fuerte ; [person - unnatural] estirado(a) **2.** *n Fam* [corpse] fiambre *m*

stiffen ['stɪfən] **1.** *vt* [fabric] reforzar ; [collar] almidonar ; *Fig* [resistance] fortalecer **2.** *vi* [person] ponerse tieso(a) ; [joints] entumecerse ; *Fig* [resistance] fortalecerse

stifle ['staɪfəl] **1.** *vt* sofocar ; [yawn] reprimir **2.** *vi* ahogarse, sofocarse

stigma ['stɪgmə] *n* estigma *m*

stiletto [stɪ'letəʊ] *(pl* **stilettos)** *n* **a)** [shoe] zapato *m* de tacón *or Am* taco *m* de aguja **b)** [dagger] estilete *m* **c)** **stilettos** tacones *mpl or Am* tacos *mpl* de aguja

still [stɪl] **1.** *adv* **a)** [up to this time] todavía, aún, *Am* siempre **b)** *(with compar adj & adv)* [even] aún ; **still colder** aún más frío **c)** [nonetheless] no obstante, con todo **d)** [however] sin embargo **e)** [motionless] quieto ; **to stand still** no moverse **2.** *adj* [calm] tranquilo(a) ; [peaceful] sosegado(a) ; [silent] silencioso(a) ; [motionless] inmóvil ; *ART* **still life** naturaleza muerta

stilt [stɪlt] *n* **a)** [for walking] zanco *m* **b)** [in architecture] poste *m*, pilote *m*

stilted ['stɪltɪd] *adj* afectado(a)

stimulant ['stɪmjʊlənt] *n* estimulante *m*

stimulate ['stɪmjʊleɪt] *vt* estimular

stimulus ['stɪmjʊləs] *(pl* **stimuli** ['stɪmjʊlaɪ]*) n* estímulo *m* ; *Fig* incentivo *m*

sting [stɪŋ] *(pt & pp* **stung) 1.** *n* [part of bee, wasp] aguijón *m* ; [wound] picadura *f* ; [burning] escozor *m* ; *Fig* [of remorse] punzada *f* ; *Fig* [of remark] sarcasmo *m* **2.** *vt* picar ; *Fig* [conscience] remorder ; *Fig* [remark] herir en lo vivo **3.** *vi* picar

stingy ['stɪndʒɪ] *(compar* stingier, *superl* stingiest) *adj Fam* [person] tacaño(a) ; [amount] escaso(a) ; **to be stingy with** escatimar

stink [stɪŋk] **1.** *n* peste *m*, hedor *m* **2.** *(pt* **stank** *or* **stunk,** *pp* **stunk)** *vi* apestar, heder (**of** a)

stipulate ['stɪpjʊleɪt] *vt* estipular

stir [stɜː(r)] **1.** *n Fig* revuelo *m* **2.** *vt* **a)** [liquid] remover **b)** [move] agitar **c)** *Fig* [curiosity, interest] despertar ; [anger] provocar **3.** *vi* [move] rebullirse ▪ **stir up** *vt sep Fig* [memories, curiosity] despertar ; [passions] excitar ; [anger] provocar ; [revolt] fomentar

stirrup ['stɪrəp] *n* estribo *m*

stitch [stɪtʃ] **1.** *n* **a)** SEWING puntada *f* ; [in knitting] punto *m* ; MED punto (de sutura) ; *Fam* **we were in stitches** nos tronchábamos de risa **b)** [pain] punzada *f* **2.** *vt* SEWING coser ; MED suturar, dar puntos a

stock [stɒk] **1.** *n* **a)** [supply] reserva *f* ; COMM [goods] existencias *fpl*, stock *m* ; [selection] surtido *m* ; **out of stock** agotado(a) ; **to have sth in stock** tener existencias de algo ; *Fig* **to take stock of** evaluar

b) FIN capital *m* social ; **stocks and shares** acciones *fpl*, valores *mpl* ; **Stock Exchange** Bolsa *f* (de valores) ; **stock market** bolsa

c) CULIN caldo *m* ; **stock cube** cubito *m* de caldo

d) [descent] estirpe *f*

2. *adj* [excuse, response] de siempre ; [phrase] gastado(a)

3. *vt* **a)** [have in stock] tener existencias de

b) [provide] abastecer, surtir (**with** de) ; [cupboard] llenar (**with** de)

■ **stock up** *vi* abastecerse (**on** *or* **with** de)

stockbroker ['stɒkbrəʊkə(r)] *n* corredor(a) *m,f* de Bolsa

stockholder ['stɒk,həʊldə(r)] *n US* accionista *mf*, inversor(a) *m,f*, inversionista *mf*

stocking ['stɒkɪŋ] *n* [for woman] media *f*

stockpile ['stɒkpaɪl] **1.** *n* reservas *fpl* **2.** *vt* almacenar ; [accumulate] acumular

stocky ['stɒkɪ] *(compar* **stockier***, superl* **stockiest)** *adj* [squat] rechoncho(a) ; [heavily built] fornido(a)

stodgy ['stɒdʒɪ] *(compar* **stodgier***, superl* **stodgiest)** *adj* [food] indigesto(a) ; *Fig* [book, person] pesado(a)

stoked [stəkd] *adj US Fam* **to be stoked about sth** [excited] estar ilusionado(a) con algo

stole¹ [stəʊl] *pt of* **steal**

stole² [stəʊl] *n* estola *f*

stolen ['stəʊlən] *pp of* **steal**

stomach ['stʌmək] **1.** *n* estómago *m* ; **stomach ache** dolor *m* de estómago ; **stomach upset** trastorno gástrico **2.** *vt Fig* aguantar

stone [stəʊn] **1.** *n* **a)** piedra *f* ; [on grave] lápida *f* **b)** [of fruit] hueso *m*, *RP* carozo *m* **c)** *Br* [weight] = 6,348 kg **2.** *adj* de piedra

stone-cold [stəʊn'kəʊld] *adj* helado(a)

stoned [stəʊnd] *adj Fam* [drugged] colocado(a) ; [drunk] como una cuba

stone-deaf [stəʊn'def] *adj* sordo(a) como una tapia

stony ['stəʊnɪ] *(compar* **stonier***, superl* **stoniest)** *adj* [ground] pedregoso(a) ; *Fig* [look, silence] glacial

stood [stʊd] *pt & pp of* **stand**

stool [stuːl] *n* **a)** [seat] taburete *m* **b)** MED heces *fpl*

stoop [stuːp] *vi* **a)** [have a stoop] andar encorvado(a) **b)** [bend] **to stoop down** inclinarse, agacharse **c)** *Fig* **to stoop to** rebajarse a ; **he wouldn't stoop so low** no se rebajaría tanto

stop [stɒp] **1.** *n* **a)** [halt] parada *f*, alto *m* ; **to come to a stop** pararse ; **to put a stop to sth** poner fin a algo

b) [break] pausa *f* ; [for refuelling etc] escala *f*

c) [for bus, tram] parada *f*

d) [punctuation mark] punto *m*

2. *vt* **a)** parar ; [conversation] interrumpir ; [pain, abuse etc] poner fin a

b) [payments] suspender ; [cheque] anular

c) **to stop doing sth** dejar de hacer algo ; **stop it!** ¡basta ya!

d) [prevent] evitar ; **to stop sb from doing sth** impedir a algn hacer algo

3. *vi* **a)** [person, moving vehicle] pararse, detenerse

b) [cease] acabarse, terminar

■ **stop by** *vi Fam* visitar

■ **stop off** *vi* pararse un rato

■ **stop over** *vi* [spend the night] pasar la noche ; [for refuelling etc] hacer escala

■ **stop up** *vt sep* [hole] tapar

stop-and-search *n* registros *mpl* policiales *(en la calle)*

stopover ['stɒpəʊvə(r)] *n* parada *f* ; AVIAT escala *f*

stoppage ['stɒpɪdʒ] *n* **a)** [of game, payments] suspensión *f* ; [of work] paro *m* ; [strike] huelga *f* ; [deduction] deducción *f* **b)** [blockage] obstrucción *f*

stopper ['stɒpə(r)] *n* tapón *m*

stopwatch ['stɒpwɒtʃ] *n* cronómetro *m*

storage ['stɔːrɪdʒ] *n* **a)** almacenaje *m*, almacenamiento *m* ; **storage battery** acumulador *m* ; **storage heater** placa *f* acumuladora ; **storage room** trastero *m* **b)** COMPUT almacenamiento *m*

store [stɔː(r)] **1.** *n* **a)** [stock] provisión *f* **b)** **stores** víveres *mpl* **c)** [warehouse] almacén *m* **d)** *esp US* [shop] tienda *f* ; **department store** gran almacén *m*

2. *vt* **a)** [furniture, computer data] almacenar; [keep] guardar **b) to store (up)** acumular

storekeeper ['stɔ:ki:pə(r)] *n US* tendero(a) *m,f*

storeroom ['stɔ:ru:m] *n* despensa *f*

storey ['stɔ:rɪ] *n* piso *m*

stork [stɔ:k] *n* cigüeña *f*

storm [stɔ:m] **1.** *n* tormenta *f*; [with wind] vendaval *m*; *Fig* [uproar] revuelo *m*; *Fig* **she has taken New York by storm** ha cautivado a todo Nueva York **2.** *vt* tomar por asalto **3.** *vi* [with rage] echar pestes

stormy ['stɔ:mɪ] *(compar* **stormier**, *superl* **stormiest)** *adj* [weather] tormentoso(a); *Fig* [discussion] acalorado(a); [relationship] tempestuoso(a)

story[1] ['stɔ:rɪ] *n* historia *f*; [tale, account] relato *m*; [article] artículo *m*; [plot] trama *f*; [joke] chiste *m*; [rumour] rumor *m*; **it's a long story** sería largo de contar; **tall story** cuento chino

story[2] ['stɔ:rɪ] *US n* = **storey**

storytelling ['stɔ:rɪ,telɪŋ] *n* **a)** [art] cuentacuentos *m inv*; **to be good at storytelling** saber contar historias **b)** *Euph* [telling lies] cuentos *mpl*

stout [staʊt] **1.** *adj* **a)** [fat] gordo(a), corpulento(a) **b)** [strong] fuerte **c)** [brave] valiente; [determined] firme **2.** *n* [beer] cerveza negra

stove [stəʊv] *n* **a)** [for heating] estufa *f* **b)** [cooker] cocina *f*, *Col, Méx, Ven* estufa *f*

stow [stəʊ] *vt* **a)** [cargo] estibar **b)** [put away] guardar ■ **stow away** *vi* [on ship, plane] viajar de polizón

stowaway ['stəʊəweɪ] *n* polizón *mf*

straight [streɪt] **1.** *adj* **a)** [not bent] recto(a), derecho(a); [hair] liso(a) **b)** [honest] honrado(a); [answer] sincero(a); [refusal] rotundo(a) **2.** *adv* **a)** [in a straight line] en línea recta **b)** [directly] directamente, derecho; **keep straight ahead** sigue todo recto; **straight out** sin rodeos **c)** [immediately] **straight away** en seguida; **straight off** inmediatamente

straighten ['streɪtən] *vt* [sth bent] enderezar, poner derecho(a); [tie, picture] poner bien; [hair] alisar ■ **straighten out** *vt sep* [problem] resolver

straight-faced *adj* con la cara seria

straightforward [streɪt'fɔ:wəd] *adj* **a)** [honest] honrado(a); [sincere] franco(a) **b)** *Br* [simple] sencillo(a)

strain[1] [streɪn] **1.** *vt* **a)** [rope etc] estirar; *Fig* crear tensiones en **b)** *MED* torcer(se); [eyes, voice] forzar; [heart] cansar **c)** [liquid] filtrar; [vegetables, tea] colar **2.** *vi* [pull] tirar (**at** de) **3.** *n* **a)** tensión *f*; [effort] esfuerzo *m* **b)** [exhaustion] agotamiento *m* **c)** *MED* torcedura *f* **d)** *MUS* **strains** son *m*

strain[2] [streɪn] *n* **a)** [breed] raza *f* **b)** [streak] vena *f*

strained ['streɪnd] *adj* **a)** [muscle] torcido(a); [eyes] cansado(a); [voice] forzado(a) **b)** [atmosphere] tenso(a)

strainer ['streɪnə(r)] *n* colador *m*

strait [streɪt] *n* **a)** *GEOG* estrecho *m* **b)** *(usu pl)* [difficulty] aprieto *m*; **in dire straits** en un gran aprieto

strand[1] [strænd] *vt* *Fig* [person] abandonar; **to leave stranded** dejar plantado(a)

strand[2] [strænd] *n* [of thread] hebra *f*; [of hair] pelo *m*

strange [streɪndʒ] *adj* **a)** [unknown] desconocido(a); [unfamiliar] nuevo(a) **b)** [odd] raro(a), extraño(a)

stranger ['streɪndʒə(r)] *n* [unknown person] desconocido(a) *m,f*; [outsider] forastero(a) *m,f*

strangle ['stræŋgəl] *vt* estrangular

strap [stræp] **1.** *n* [of leather] correa *f*; [on bag] bandolera *f*; [on dress, bra] tirante *m*, *Am* bretel *m* **2.** *vt* atar con correa

strategic [strə'ti:dʒɪk] *adj* estratégico(a)

strategy ['strætɪdʒɪ] *n* estrategia *f*

straw [strɔ:] *n* **a)** paja *f*; *Fig* **to clutch at straws** agarrarse a un clavo ardiente;

Fam **that's the last straw!** ¡eso ya es el colmo! **b)** [for drinking] pajita *f, Méx* popote *m*

strawberry ['strɔ:bərɪ] *n* fresa *f, CSur* frutilla *f*

stray [streɪ] **1.** *vi* [from path] desviarse; [get lost] extraviarse **2.** *n* animal extraviado **3.** *adj* [bullet] perdido(a); [animal] callejero(a)

streak [stri:k] **1.** *n* **a)** [line] raya *f*; **streak of lightning** rayo *m* **b)** [in hair] reflejo *m* **c)** *Fig* [of genius etc] vena *f*; *Fig* [of luck] racha *f* **2.** *vt* rayar (**with** de) **3.** *vi* **to streak past** pasar como un rayo

stream [stri:m] **1.** *n* **a)** [small river] arroyo *m*, riachuelo *m* **b)** [of water, air] flujo *m*; [of blood] chorro *m*; [of light] raudal *m* **c)** [of people] oleada *f*; [of cars] alud *m*; [of complaints, abuse] torrente *m*, alud *m* **d)** *Br* SCH nivel *m* de aptitud **2.** *vi* **a)** [liquid] salir a chorros, chorrear; [light] entrar a raudales **b)** [people, cars] afluir; **to stream in / out / past** entrar / salir / pasar ininterrumpidamente **3.** *vt* **a)** COMPUT [music, news] descargar *or Fam* bajar en streaming **b)** *Br* SCH dividir por niveles de aptitud

streamer ['stri:mə(r)] *n* [paper ribbon] serpentina *f*

streaming ['stri:mɪŋ] **1.** *n* **a)** *Br* SCH división *f* por niveles de aptitud **b)** COMPUT streaming *m* **2.** *adj* [surface, window] chorreante; *Br* **I've got a streaming cold** tengo un catarro muy fuerte

streamlined ['stri:mlaɪnd] *adj* **a)** [car] aerodinámico(a) **b)** [system, method] racionalizado(a)

street [stri:t] *n* calle *f*; **the man in the street** el hombre de la calle; **street map** *or* **plan** (plano *m*) callejero *m*

streetcar ['stri:tkɑ:(r)] *n US* tranvía *m*

strength [streŋθ] *n* **a)** fuerza *f*; [of rope etc] resistencia *f*; [of emotion, colour] intensidad *f*; [of alcohol] graduación *f* **b)** [power] poder *m* **c)** [ability] punto *m* fuerte

strengthen ['streŋθən] **1.** *vt* **a)** reforzar; [character] fortalecer **b)** [intensify] intensificar **2.** *vi* **a)** [gen] reforzarse **b)** [intensify] intensificarse

strenuous ['strenjʊəs] *adj* **a)** [denial] enérgico(a); [effort, life] intenso(a) **b)** [exhausting] fatigoso(a), cansado(a)

stress [stres] **1.** *n* **a)** TECH tensión *f* **b)** MED estrés *m* **c)** [emphasis] hincapié *m*; [on word] acento *m* **2.** *vt* [emphasize] subrayar; [word] acentuar

stress-buster *n Fam* eliminador *m* de estrés

stressful ['stresfʊl] *adj* estresante

stress-related *adj* relacionado(a) con el estrés

stretch [stretʃ] **1.** *vt* [elastic] estirar; [wings] desplegar
2. *vi* [elastic] estirarse; *Fig* **my money won't stretch to it** mi dinero no me llegará para eso
3. *n* **a)** [length] trecho *m*, tramo *m*
b) [of land] extensión *f*; [of time] intervalo *m*
■ **stretch out 1.** *vt sep* [arm, hand] alargar; [legs] estirar **2.** *vi* **a)** [person] estirarse **b)** [countryside, years etc] extenderse

stretcher ['stretʃə(r)] *n* camilla *f*

stricken ['strɪkən] *adj* [with grief] afligido(a); [with illness] aquejado(a); [by disaster etc] afectado(a); [damaged] dañado(a)

strict [strɪkt] *adj* **a)** estricto(a) **b)** [absolute] absoluto(a)

strictly ['strɪktlɪ] *adv* **a)** [categorically] terminantemente **b)** [precisely] estrictamente; **strictly speaking** en sentido estricto

stride [straɪd] **1.** *n* zancada *f*, tranco *m*; *Fig* [progress] progresos *mpl* **2.** (*pt* **strode**, *pp* **stridden** ['strɪdən]) *vi* **to stride (along)** andar a zancadas

strike [straɪk] (*pt & pp* **struck**) **1.** *vt* **a)** [hit] pegar, golpear
b) [collide with] chocar contra; [of bullet, lightning] alcanzar
c) [match] encender, *Am* prender

d) the clock struck three el reloj dio las tres

e) [oil, gold] descubrir

f) [impress] impresionar; **it strikes me…** me parece…

2. *vi* **a)** [attack] atacar; [disaster] sobrevenir

b) [clock] dar la hora

c) [workers] declararse en huelga

3. *n* **a)** [by workers] huelga *f*; **to call a strike** convocar una huelga

b) MIL ataque *m*

■ **strike back** *vi* devolver el golpe

■ **strike down** *vt sep* fulminar, abatir

■ **strike out 1.** *vt sep* [cross out] tachar **2.** *vi* **to strike out at sb** arremeter contra algn

■ **strike up** *vt insep* **a)** [friendship] trabar; [conversation] entablar **b)** [tune] empezar a tocar

striker ['straɪkə(r)] *n* **a)** [worker] huelguista *mf* **b)** *Fam* FTBL marcador(a) *m,f*

striking ['straɪkɪŋ] *adj* [eye-catching] llamativo(a); [noticeable] notable; [impressive] impresionante

string [strɪŋ] **1.** *n* **a)** [cord] cuerda *f*; *Fig* **to pull strings for sb** enchufar a algn; **string bean** judía *f* verde, *Bol, RP* chaucha *f*, *CAm* ejote *m*, *Col, Cuba* habichuela *f*, *Chile* poroto *m* verde, *Ven* vainita *f* **b)** [of events] cadena *f*; [of flies] sarta *f* **c)** [of racket, guitar] cuerda *f*; MUS **the strings** los instrumentos de cuerda **2.** *(pt & pp* **strung)** *vt* **a)** [beads] ensartar **b)** [racket etc] encordar **c)** [beans] quitar la hebra a

stringed [strɪŋd] *adj* [instrument] de cuerda

stringent ['strɪndʒənt] *adj* severo(a), estricto(a)

strip¹ [strɪp] **1.** *vt* **a)** [person] desnudar; [bed] quitar la ropa de; [paint] rascar, quitar, *Am* sacar **b)** TECH **to strip (down)** desmontar **2.** *vi* [undress] desnudarse; [perform striptease] hacer un striptease ■ **strip off 1.** *vt sep* quitar, *Am* sacar **2.** *vi* [undress] desnudarse

strip² [strɪp] *n* tira *f*; [of land] franja *f*; [of metal] fleje *m*; *Br* **football strip** indu-

mentaria *f*; **strip cartoon** historieta *f*; **strip lighting** alumbrado *m* fluorescente; **to tear sb off a strip** echar una bronca a algn

stripe [straɪp] *n* raya *f*; MIL galón *m*

striped [straɪpt] *adj* rayado(a), a rayas

strive [straɪv] *(pt* **strove**, *pp* **striven** ['strɪvən]*) vi* **to strive to do sth** esforzarse por hacer algo

strode [strəʊd] *pt of* **stride**

stroke [strəʊk] **1.** *n* **a) a stroke of luck** un golpe de suerte **b)** [of pen] trazo *m*; [of brush] pincelada *f* **c)** [caress] caricia *f* **d)** MED apoplejía *f* **2.** *vt* acariciar

stroll [strəʊl] **1.** *vi* dar un paseo **2.** *n* paseo *m*

stroller ['strəʊlə(r)] *n US* [for baby] cochecito *m*

strong [strɒŋ] **1.** *adj* **a)** fuerte **b)** [durable] sólido(a) **c)** [firm, resolute] firme **d)** [colour] intenso(a); [light] brillante **2.** *adv* fuerte; **to be going strong** [business] ir fuerte; [elderly person] conservarse bien

strove [strəʊv] *pt of* **strive**

struck [strʌk] *pt & pp of* **strike**

structure ['strʌktʃə(r)] *n* estructura *f*; [constructed thing] construcción *f*; [building] edificio *m*

struggle ['strʌɡəl] **1.** *vi* luchar **2.** *n* lucha *f*; [physical fight] pelea *f*

strung [strʌŋ] *pt & pp of* **string**

strut [strʌt] *vi* pavonearse

stub [stʌb] **1.** *n* [of cigarette] colilla *f*; [of pencil] cabo *m*; [of cheque] matriz *f* **2.** *vt* **a)** [strike] golpear **b) to stub (out)** apagar

stubble ['stʌbəl] *n* [in field] rastrojo *m*; [on chin] barba *f* de tres días

stubborn ['stʌbən] *adj* **a)** terco(a), testarudo(a) **b)** [stain] difícil **c)** [refusal] rotundo(a)

stuck [stʌk] *pt & pp of* **stick**

stuck-up [stʌk'ʌp] *adj Fam* creído(a)

stud¹ [stʌd] **1.** *n* [on clothing] tachón *m*; [on football boots] *Esp* taco *m*,

RP tapón m; [on shirt] botonadura f
2. vt [decorate] tachonar (**with** de); Fig
[dot, cover] salpicar (**with** de)

stud² [stʌd] n [horse] semental m

student ['stjuːdənt] n estudiante mf;
student teacher profesor(a) m,f en
prácticas

studio ['stjuːdɪəʊ] n TV & CIN estudio m;
[artist's] taller m; **studio (apartment
or Br flat)** estudio

studious ['stjuːdɪəs] adj estudioso(a)

study ['stʌdɪ] **1.** vt estudiar; [facts etc]
examinar, investigar; [behaviour] observar **2.** vi estudiar; **to study to be a
doctor** estudiar para médico **3.** n a) estudio m; **study group** grupo m de trabajo **b)** [room] despacho m, estudio m

stuff [stʌf] **1.** vt a) [container] llenar
(**with** de); CULIN rellenar (**with** con or de
); [animal] disecar **b)** [cram] atiborrar
(**with** de) **2.** n Fam a) [substance] cosa f
b) [things] cosas fpl

stuffed [stʌft] adj **stuffed shirt** petulante, estirado(a); **he's a real stuffed
shirt** es muy estirado

stuffing ['stʌfɪŋ] n CULIN relleno m

stuffy ['stʌfɪ] (compar **stuffier**, superl **stuffi-
est**) adj a) [room] mal ventilado(a);
[atmosphere] cargado(a) **b)** [pompous]
estirado(a); [narrow-minded] de miras
estrechas

stumble ['stʌmbəl] vi tropezar, dar un
traspié; Fig **to stumble across** or **on** or
upon tropezar or dar con

stump [stʌmp] **1.** n a) [of pencil] cabo m;
[of tree] tocón m; [of arm, leg] muñón m
b) [in cricket] estaca f **2.** vt [puzzle]
confundir; **to be stumped** estar
perplejo(a)

stumpy ['stʌmpɪ] (compar **stump-
ier**, superl **stumpiest**) adj [person]
achaparrado(a)

stun [stʌn] vt [of blow] aturdir; Fig [of
news etc] sorprender

stung [stʌŋ] pt & pp of **sting**

stunk [stʌŋk] pt & pp of **stink**

stunned [stʌnd] adj a) [knocked out]
sin sentido **b)** Fig atónito(a)

stunning ['stʌnɪŋ] adj [blow] duro(a);
[news] sorprendente; Fam [woman,
outfit] fenomenal

stunt¹ [stʌnt] vt [growth] atrofiar

stunt² [stʌnt] n a) AVIAT acrobacia f
b) publicity stunt truco publicitario
c) CIN escena peligrosa; **stunt man**
doble m

stupid ['stjuːpɪd] adj estúpido(a), imbécil

stupidity [stjuː'pɪdɪtɪ] n estupidez f

sturdy ['stɜːdɪ] (compar **sturdier**, superl
sturdiest) adj robusto(a), fuerte; [re-
sistance] enérgico(a)

stutter ['stʌtə(r)] **1.** vi tartamudear **2.** n
tartamudeo m

sty [staɪ] n [pen] pocilga f

style [staɪl] **1.** n a) estilo m; [of dress] modelo m **b)** [fashion] moda f **c)** **to live in
style** [elegance] vivir a lo grande **2.** vt
[hair] marcar

stylish ['staɪlɪʃ] adj con estilo

sub- [sʌb] pref sub-

subconscious [sʌb'kɒnʃəs] **1.** adj subconsciente **2.** n the subconscious el
subconsciente

subdue [səb'djuː] vt a) [nation, people]
sojuzgar **b)** [feelings] dominar
c) [colour, light] atenuar

subject **1.** ['sʌbdʒɪkt] n a) [citizen]
súbdito m
b) [topic] tema m; **subject matter** materia f; [contents] contenido m
c) SCH asignatura f
d) LING sujeto m
2. ['sʌbdʒɪkt] adj **subject to** [law, tax]
sujeto(a) a; [conditional upon] previo(a)
3. [səb'dʒekt] vt someter

subjective [səb'dʒektɪv] adj sub-
jetivo(a)

subjunctive [səb'dʒʌŋktɪv] **1.** adj
subjuntivo(a) **2.** n subjuntivo m

sublime [sə'blaɪm] adj sublime

submarine ['sʌbməriːn] n submarino m

submerge [səb'mɜːdʒ] vt sumergir;
[flood] inundar; Fig **submerged in ...**
sumido(a) en ...

submissive [səb'mɪsɪv] *adj* sumiso(a)

submit [səb'mɪt] **1.** *vt* **a)** [present] presentar **b)** [subject] someter (**to** a) **2.** *vi* [surrender] rendirse

subordinate [sə'bɔːdɪnɪt] *adj* & *n* subordinado(a) (*m,f*)

subprime ['sʌbpraɪm] *n* US FIN **subprime (loan** *or* **mortgage)** subprime *m* (*hipoteca de alto riesgo*)

subscribe [səb'skraɪb] *vi* [magazine] suscribirse (**to** a) ; [opinion, theory] adherirse (**to** a)

subscriber [səb'skraɪbə(r)] *n* abonado(a) *m,f*

subscription [səb'skrɪpʃən] *n* [to magazine] suscripción *f* ; [to club] cuota *f*

subsequent ['sʌbsɪkwənt] *adj* subsiguiente

subside [səb'saɪd] *vi* [land] hundirse ; [floodwater] bajar ; [wind, anger] amainar

subsidence [səb'saɪdəns] *n* [of land] hundimiento *m* ; [of floodwater] bajada *f* ; [of wind] amaine *m*

subsidiary [sʌb'sɪdɪərɪ] **1.** *adj* [role] secundario(a) **2.** *n* COMM sucursal *f*, filial *f*

subsidize ['sʌbsɪdaɪz] *vt* subvencionar

subsidy ['sʌbsɪdɪ] *n* subvención *f*

substance ['sʌbstəns] *n* **a)** sustancia *f* **b)** [essence] esencia *f* **c) a woman of substance** [wealth] una mujer acaudalada

substantial [səb'stænʃəl] *adj* **a)** [solid] sólido(a) **b)** [sum, loss] importante ; [difference, improvement] notable ; [meal] abundante

substitute ['sʌbstɪtjuːt] **1.** *vt* sustituir ; **to substitute X for Y** sustituir X por Y **2.** *n* [person] suplente *mf* ; [thing] sucedáneo *m*

substitution [sʌbstɪ'tjuːʃən] *n* sustitución *f* ; SPORT sustitución *f*, cambio *m*

subtext ['sʌbˌtekst] *n* mensaje *m* subyacente

subtitle ['sʌbtaɪtəl] *n* subtítulo *m*

subtle ['sʌtəl] *adj* sutil ; [taste] delicado(a) ; [remark] ingenioso(a) ; [irony] fino(a)

subtotal ['sʌbtəʊtəl] *n* subtotal *m*

subtract [səb'trækt] *vt* restar

subtraction [səb'trækʃən] *n* resta *f*

suburb ['sʌbɜːb] *n* barrio periférico ; **the suburbs** las afueras

suburban [sə'bɜːbən] *adj* suburbano(a)

suburbia [sə'bɜːbɪə] *n* barrios residenciales periféricos

subversive [səb'vɜːsɪv] *adj* & *n* subversivo(a) (*m,f*)

subway ['sʌbweɪ] *n* **a)** *Br* [underpass] paso subterráneo **b)** *US* [underground railway] metro *m*, *RP* subte *m*

succeed [sək'siːd] **1.** *vi* **a)** [person] tener éxito ; [plan] salir bien ; **to succeed in doing sth** conseguir hacer algo **b)** [follow after] suceder ; **to succeed to** [throne] suceder a **2.** *vt* [monarch] suceder a

success [sək'ses] *n* éxito *m*

successful [sək'sesfʊl] *adj* de éxito, exitoso(a) ; [business] próspero(a) ; [marriage] feliz ; **to be successful in doing sth** lograr hacer algo

successfully [sək'sesfʊlɪ] *adv* con éxito

succession [sək'seʃən] *n* sucesión *f*, serie *f* ; **in succession** sucesivamente

successive [sək'sesɪv] *adj* sucesivo(a), consecutivo(a)

successor [sək'sesə(r)] *n* sucesor(a) *m,f*

succumb [sə'kʌm] *vi* sucumbir (**to** a)

such [sʌtʃ] **1.** *adj* **a)** [of that sort] tal, semejante ; **artists such as Monet** artistas como Monet ; **at such and such a time** a tal hora ; **in such a way that** de tal manera que **b)** [so much, so great] tanto(a) ; **he's always in such a hurry** siempre anda con tanta prisa ; **she was in such pain** sufría tanto **2.** *adv* [so very] tan ; **it's such a long time ago** hace tanto tiempo ; **she's such a clever woman** es una mujer tan inteligente ; **such a lot of books** tantos libros ; **we had such good weather** hizo un tiempo tan bueno

suck [sʌk] **1.** vt [by pump] aspirar; [liquid] sorber; [lollipop, blood] chupar **2.** vi [person] chupar; [baby] mamar ■ **suck in** vt sep [of whirlpool] tragar

suckle ['sʌkəl] vt [mother] amamantar

suction ['sʌkʃən] n succión f

sudden ['sʌdən] adj a) [hurried] súbito(a), repentino(a) b) [unexpected] imprevisto(a) c) [abrupt] brusco(a); **all of a sudden** de repente

suddenly ['sʌdənlɪ] adv de repente

suds [sʌdz] npl espuma f de jabón, jabonaduras fpl

sue [su:, sju:] **1.** vt JUR demandar **2.** vi JUR presentar una demanda; **to sue for divorce** solicitar el divorcio

suede [sweɪd] n ante m, gamuza f; [for gloves] cabritilla f

suffer ['sʌfə(r)] **1.** vt a) sufrir b) [tolerate] aguantar, soportar **2.** vi sufrir; **to suffer from** sufrir de

sufferer ['sʌfərə(r)] n MED enfermo(a) m,f

suffering ['sʌfərɪŋ] n [affliction] sufrimiento m; [pain, torment] dolor m

sufficient [sə'fɪʃənt] adj suficiente, bastante

sufficiently [sə'fɪʃəntlɪ] adv suficientemente, bastante

suffix ['sʌfɪks] n LING sufijo m

suffocate ['sʌfəkeɪt] **1.** vt asfixiar **2.** vi asfixiarse

sugar ['ʃʊgə(r)] **1.** n azúcar m or f; Br **caster sugar** azúcar m or f extrafino(a); **sugar beet** remolacha f (azucarera), Méx betabel m (azucarero); **sugar bowl** azucarero m; **sugar cane** caña f de azúcar **2.** vt azucarar, echar azúcar a

suggest [sə'dʒest] vt a) [propose] sugerir b) [advise] aconsejar c) [indicate, imply] indicar

suggestion [sə'dʒestʃən] n a) [proposal] sugerencia f b) [trace] sombra f; [small amount] toque m

suggestive [sə'dʒestɪv] adj a) [reminiscent, thought-provoking] sugerente b) [remark] insinuante

suicide ['sju:ɪsaɪd] n suicidio m

suit [su:t, sju:t] **1.** n a) [clothes] traje m, Andes, RP terno m b) JUR pleito m, demanda f c) CARDS palo m **2.** vt a) [be convenient, appropriate to] venir bien a, convenir b) [be right, appropriate for] ir bien a; [clothes, hairstyle] favorecer a, sentar bien a; **red really suits you** el rojo te favorece mucho; **they are well suited** están hechos el uno para el otro c) [please] **suit yourself!** ¡como quieras! **3.** vi would some time next week **suit?** ¿le vendría bien la semana que viene? ■ **suit up** vi insep [dress-diver, pilot, astronaut, etc] ponerse el traje

suitable ['sju:təbəl] adj [convenient] conveniente; [appropriate] adecuado(a); **the most suitable woman for the job** la mujer más indicada para el puesto

suitcase ['su:tkeɪs] n maleta f, Méx petaca f, RP valija f

suite [swi:t] n a) [of furniture] juego m b) [of hotel rooms, music] suite f

sulk [sʌlk] vi enfurruñarse

sullen ['sʌlən] adj hosco(a); [sky] plomizo(a)

sultana [sʌl'tɑ:nə] n esp Br [raisin] pasa f de Esmirna

sum [sʌm] n a) [arithmetic problem, amount] suma f b) [total amount] total m; [of money] importe m ■ **sum up** **1.** vt sep resumir **2.** vi resumir; **to sum up ...** en resumidas cuentas ...

summarize ['sʌməraɪz] vt & vi resumir

summary ['sʌmərɪ] **1.** n resumen m **2.** adj sumario(a)

summer ['sʌmə(r)] **1.** n verano m **2.** adj [holiday etc] de verano; [weather] veraniego(a); [resort] de veraneo

summertime ['sʌmətaɪm] n verano m

summit ['sʌmɪt] n a) [of mountain] cima f, cumbre f b) POL summit (meeting) cumbre f

summon ['sʌmən] vt a) [meeting, person] convocar b) [aid] pedir c) JUR citar ■ **summon up** vt sep [resources] reunir; **to summon up one's courage** armarse de valor

summons ['sʌmənz] **1.** *n sing* **a)** [call] llamada *f*, llamamiento *m* **b)** JUR citación *f* judicial **2.** *vt* JUR citar

SUM1 MESSAGING *written abbr of* **someone**

sumptuous ['sʌmptjʊəs] *adj* suntuoso(a)

sun [sʌn] **1.** *n* sol *m*; **sun cream** crema *f* solar **2.** *vt* **to sun oneself** tomar el sol

sunbathe ['sʌnbeɪð] *vi* tomar el sol

sunburn ['sʌnbɜːn] *n* [burn] quemadura *f* de sol

sunburnt ['sʌnbɜːnt] *adj* [burnt] quemado(a) por el sol; [tanned] bronceado(a)

Sunday ['sʌndɪ] *n* domingo *m inv*; **Sunday newspaper** periódico *m* del domingo; **Sunday school** catequesis *f*

sundial ['sʌndaɪəl] *n* reloj *m* de sol

sunflower ['sʌnflaʊə(r)] *n* girasol *m*

sung [sʌŋ] *pp of* **sing**

sunglasses ['sʌnglɑːsɪz] *npl* gafas *fpl* *or Am* anteojos de sol

sunk [sʌŋk] *pp of* **sink**

sunlamp ['sʌnlæmp] *n* lámpara *f* solar

sunlight ['sʌnlaɪt] *n* sol *m*, luz *f* del sol

sunny ['sʌnɪ] *(compar* **sunnier**, *superl* **sunniest**) *adj* **a)** [day] de sol; [place] soleado(a); **it is sunny** hace sol **b)** *Fig* [smile, disposition] alegre; [future] prometedor(a)

sunrise ['sʌnraɪz] *n* salida *f* del sol

sunroof ['sʌnruːf] *n* AUTO techo corredizo

sunset ['sʌnset] *n* puesta *f* del sol

sunshade ['sʌnʃeɪd] *n* sombrilla *f*

sunshine ['sʌnʃaɪn] *n* sol *m*, luz *f* del sol

sunstroke ['sʌnstrəʊk] *n* insolación *f*

suntan ['sʌntæn] *n* bronceado *m*; **suntan oil** crema protectora; **suntan lotion** (aceite *m*) bronceador *m*

sup [sʌp] *interj US Fam (abbr of* **what's up?)** ¿qué pasa?

super ['suːpə(r)] *adj Fam* genial, *Am* salvo *RP* chévere, *Méx* padre, *RP* bárbaro(a)

super- ['suːpə(r)] *pref* super-, sobre-

superb [sʊ'pɜːb] *adj* espléndido(a)

superficial [suːpə'fɪʃəl] *adj* superficial

superfluous [suː'pɜːfluəs] *adj* sobrante, superfluo(a); **to be superfluous** sobrar

superintendent [suːpərɪn'tendənt] *n* **a)** [police officer - in UK] comisario(a) *m,f*; [in US] comisario(a) *m,f* jefe **b)** *US* [of apartment building] portero(a) *m,f*

superior [suː'pɪərɪə(r)] **1.** *adj* **a)** superior **b)** [haughty] altivo(a) **2.** *n* superior(a) *m,f*

superiority [suːpɪərɪ'ɒrɪtɪ] *n* superioridad *f*

superlative [suː'pɜːlətɪv] **1.** *adj* superlativo(a) **2.** *n* LING superlativo *m*

supermarket ['suːpəmɑːkɪt] *n* supermercado *m*

supermodel ['suːpəmɒdl] *n* top model *f*

supernatural [suːpə'næt[ərəl] **1.** *adj* sobrenatural **2.** *n* **the supernatural** lo sobrenatural

superpower ['suːpəpaʊə(r)] *n* POL superpotencia *f*

supersize ['suːpəsaɪz] **1.** *adj* gigante **2.** *vt* aumentar (de forma considerable) el tamaño de; **the company has supersized itself** la empresa ha aumentado de tamaño de forma considerable

supersonic [suːpə'sɒnɪk] *adj* supersónico(a)

superstition [suːpə'stɪʃən] *n* superstición *f*

superstitious [suːpə'stɪʃəs] *adj* supersticioso(a)

supervise ['suːpəvaɪz] *vt* supervisar; [watch over] vigilar

supervisor ['suːpəvaɪzə(r)] *n* supervisor(a) *m,f*

supper ['sʌpə(r)] *n* cena *f*; **to have supper** cenar

supple ['sʌpəl] *adj* flexible

supplement 1. ['sʌplɪmənt] *n* suplemento *m* **2.** ['sʌplɪment] *vt* complementar

supplementary [sʌplɪ'mentərɪ] *adj* adicional

supplier [sə'plaɪə(r)] n suministrador(a) m,f; COMM proveedor(a) m,f

supply [sə'plaɪ] **1.** n a) suministro m; COMM provisión f; [stock] surtido m; **supply and demand** oferta f y demanda **b) supplies** [food] víveres mpl; MIL pertrechos mpl **2.** vt a) [provide] suministrar **b)** [with provisions] aprovisionar **c)** [information] facilitar **d)** COMM surtir

support [sə'pɔ:t] **1.** n a) [moral] apoyo m **b)** [funding] ayuda f económica **c)** COMPUT ayuda f **2.** vt a) [weight etc] sostener **b)** Fig [back] apoyar; [substantiate] respaldar **c)** SPORT ser (hincha) de **d)** [sustain] mantener; [feed] alimentar

supporter [sə'pɔ:tə(r)] n POL partidario(a) m,f; SPORT hincha mf

supportive [sə'pɔ:tɪv] adj **he was supportive** apoyó mucho, fue muy comprensivo

suppose [sə'pəʊz] vt suponer; [presume] creer; **I suppose not /so** supongo que no /sí; **you're not supposed to smoke in here** no está permitido fumar aquí dentro; **you're supposed to be in bed** deberías estar acostado(a) ya

suppress [sə'pres] vt suprimir; [feelings, laugh etc] contener; [news, truth] callar; [revolt] sofocar

supreme [sʊ'pri:m] adj supremo(a); **with supreme indifference** con total indiferencia; US JUR **Supreme Court** Tribunal m Supremo, Am Corte f Suprema

surcharge ['sɜ:tʃɑ:dʒ] n recargo m

sure [ʃʊə(r)] **1.** adj a) seguro(a); **I'm sure (that) ...** estoy seguro(a) de que ...; **make sure that it's ready** asegúrate de que esté listo; **sure of oneself** seguro(a) de sí mismo(a) **b)** Fam **sure thing!** ¡claro!; US **it sure is cold** qué frío que hace **2.** adv a) [of course] claro; **sure enough** efectivamente **b)** [certainly] seguro; **for sure** seguro

surely ['ʃʊəlɪ] adv [without a doubt] sin duda; **surely not!** ¡no puede ser!

surf [sɜ:f] **1.** n [waves] oleaje m; [foam] espuma f **2.** vt COMPUT **to surf the Net** navegar por internet **3.** vi SPORT hacer surf

surface ['sɜ:fɪs] **1.** n superficie f; [of road] firme m
2. adj superficial; **surface area** área f de la superficie; **by surface mail** por vía terrestre or marítima
3. vt [road] revestir
4. vi [submarine etc] salir a la superficie; Fam [wake up] levantarse

surfboard ['sɜ:fbɔ:d] n tabla f de surf

surfing ['sɜ:fɪŋ] n surf m, surfing m

surge [sɜ:dʒ] **1.** n a) [growth] alza f **b)** [of sea, sympathy] oleada f; Fig [of anger, energy] arranque m **2.** vi **to surge forward** [people] avanzar en tropel

surgeon ['sɜ:dʒən] n cirujano(a) m,f

surgery ['sɜ:dʒərɪ] n a) [operation] cirugía f **b)** Br [consulting room] consultorio m; **surgery hours** horas fpl de consulta

surgical ['sɜ:dʒɪkəl] adj quirúrgico(a); **surgical spirit** alcohol m de 90°

surly ['sɜ:lɪ] (compar **surlier**, superl **surliest**) adj [bad-tempered] hosco(a), malhumorado(a); [rude] maleducado(a)

surname ['sɜ:neɪm] n apellido m

surpass [sɜ:'pɑ:s] vt superar

surplus ['sɜ:pləs] **1.** n [of goods] excedente m; [of budget] superávit m **2.** adj excedente

surprise [sə'praɪz] **1.** n sorpresa f; **to take sb by surprise** Esp coger or Am agarrar desprevenido(a) a algn **2.** adj [visit] inesperado(a); **surprise attack** ataque m sorpresa **3.** vt [astonish] sorprender; **I'm not surprised that ...** no me extraña que ...

surprising [sə'praɪzɪŋ] adj sorprendente

surrender [sə'rendə(r)] **1.** n MIL rendición f; [of weapons] entrega f; INS rescate m
2. vt MIL rendir; [right] renunciar a
3. vi [give in] rendirse

surrogate ['sʌrəgɪt] *n Formal* sustituto(a) *m,f*; **surrogate mother** madre *f* de alquiler

surround [sə'raʊnd] **1.** *n* marco *m*, borde *m* **2.** *vt* rodear

surrounding [sə'raʊndɪŋ] **1.** *adj* circundante **2.** *npl* **surroundings** [of place] alrededores *mpl*, cercanías *fpl*

surveillance [sɜː'veɪləns] *n* vigilancia *f*

survey 1. ['sɜːveɪ] *n* **a)** [of building] inspección *f*; [of land] reconocimiento *m* **b)** [of trends etc] encuesta *f* **c)** [overall view] panorama *m* **2.** [sə'veɪ] *vt* **a)** [building] inspeccionar; [land] medir **b)** [trends etc] hacer una encuesta sobre **c)** [look at] contemplar

surveyor [sə'veɪə(r)] *n* agrimensor(a) *m,f*; **quantity surveyor** aparejador(a) *m,f*

survival [sə'vaɪvəl] *n* supervivencia *f*

survive [sə'vaɪv] **1.** *vi* sobrevivir; [remain] perdurar **2.** *vt* sobrevivir a

survivor [sə'vaɪvə(r)] *n* superviviente *mf*

susceptible [sə'septəbəl] *adj* [to attack] susceptible (**to** a); [to illness] propenso(a) (**to** a)

suspect 1. ['sʌspekt] *adj* [dubious] sospechoso(a) **2.** ['sʌspekt] *n* sospechoso(a) *m,f* **3.** [sə'spekt] *vt* **a)** [person] sospechar (**of** de); [plot, motives] recelar de **b)** [think likely] imaginar, creer

suspend [sə'spend] *vt* suspender; [pupil] expulsar por un tiempo

suspenders [sə'spendəz] *npl* **a)** *Br* [for stockings] liguero *m* **b)** *US* [for trousers] tirantes *mpl*

suspense [sə'spens] *n* [uncertainty] incertidumbre *f*; [in movie] *Esp* suspense *m*, *Am* suspenso *m*; **to keep sb in suspense** mantener a algn en la incertidumbre

suspicion [sə'spɪʃən] *n* **a)** sospecha *f*; [mistrust] recelo *m*; [doubt] duda *f* **b)** [trace] pizca *f*

suspicious [sə'spɪʃəs] *adj* **a)** [arousing suspicion] sospechoso(a) **b)** [distrustful] receloso(a); **to be suspicious of sb** desconfiar de algn

sustain [sə'steɪn] *vt* **a)** sostener **b)** [nourish] sustentar **c)** JUR [objection] admitir **d)** [injury etc] sufrir

sustainability [sə,steɪnə'bɪlɪtɪ] *n* sostenibilidad *f*

sustainable [səs'teɪnəbl] *adj* sostenible; **sustainable resources** recursos *mpl* sostenibles

SUV *n* AUTO *(abbr of* sport utility vehicle*)* 4x4 *m*

swagger ['swægə(r)] **1.** *n* pavoneo *m* **2.** *vi* pavonearse

swallow¹ ['swɒləʊ] **1.** *n* [of drink, food] trago *m* **2.** *vt* **a)** [drink, food] tragar **b)** *Fig* [believe] tragarse **3.** *vi* tragar ■ **swallow up** *vt sep Fig* **a)** [engulf] tragar **b)** [eat up] consumir

swallow² ['swɒləʊ] *n* ORNITH golondrina *f*

swam [swæm] *pt of* **swim**

swamp [swɒmp] **1.** *n* ciénaga *f* **2.** *vt* **a)** [boat] hundir **b)** *Fig* inundar (**with** or **by** de)

swan [swɒn] **1.** *n* cisne *m* **2.** *vi Fam* **to swan around** pavonearse; **to swan around doing nothing** hacer el vago

swanky ['swæŋkɪ] *(compar* swankier, *superl* swankiest*) adj Fam* pijo(a)

swap [swɒp] **1.** *n Fam* intercambio *m* **2.** *vt* cambiar ■ **swap round**, **swap over** *vt sep* [switch] cambiar

swarm [swɔːm] **1.** *n* enjambre *m* **2.** *vi* [bees] enjambrar; *Fig* **Neath was swarming with tourists** Neath estaba lleno de turistas

swat [swɒt] *vt* aplastar

sway [sweɪ] **1.** *n* **a)** [movement] balanceo *m* **b)** **to hold sway over sb** dominar a algn **2.** *vi* **a)** [swing] balancearse, mecerse **b)** [totter] tambalearse **3.** *vt Fig* [persuade] convencer

swear [sweə(r)] *(pt* swore, *pp* sworn*)* **1.** *vt* [vow] jurar; **to swear an oath** prestar juramento **2.** *vi* **a)** [formally] jurar, prestar juramento **b)** [curse] soltar tacos, decir palabrotas; [blaspheme] jurar; **to swear at sb** echar pestes contra algn

swearing ['sweərɪŋ] n [use of swear words] palabrotas fpl

swearword ['sweəwɜːd] n palabrota f

sweat [swet] **1.** n [perspiration] sudor m; Fam [hard work] trabajo duro **2.** vi [perspire] sudar; Fig [work hard] sudar la gota gorda **3.** vt Fam **to sweat it out** aguantar

sweater ['swetə(r)] n suéter m, Esp jersey m, RP pulóver m

sweatshirt ['swetʃɜːt] n sudadera f, Col, RP buzo m

Swede [swiːd] n [person] sueco(a) m,f

Sweden ['swiːdən] n Suecia

Swedish ['swiːdɪʃ] **1.** adj sueco(a) **2.** n **a)** [language] sueco m **b)** the Swedish los suecos

sweep [swiːp] (pt & pp swept) **1.** n **a)** [with broom] barrido m, Am barrida f **b)** (chimney) sweep deshollinador(a) m,f **2.** vt [floor etc] barrer **3.** vi **a)** [with broom] barrer **b)** to sweep in /out /past entrar /salir / pasar rápidamente ▪ **sweep aside** vt sep apartar bruscamente; Fig [objections] rechazar ▪ **sweep away** vt sep **a)** [dust] barrer **b)** [of storm] arrastrar ▪ **sweep up** vi barrer

sweeping ['swiːpɪŋ] adj **a)** [broad] amplio(a); **a sweeping statement** una declaración demasiado general **b)** [victory] aplastante **c)** [reforms, changes etc] radical

sweet [swiːt] **1.** adj **a)** dulce; [sugary] azucarado(a); **to have a sweet tooth** ser goloso(a); **sweet pea** guisante m de olor; **sweet shop** confitería f **b)** [pleasant] agradable; [smell] fragante; [sound] melodioso(a) **c)** [person, animal] encantador(a) **2.** n **a)** Br [confectionery] dulce m; (boiled) sweet caramelo m **b)** [dessert] postre m

sweetcorn ['swiːtkɔːn] n maíz tierno, Andes, RP choclo m, Méx elote m

sweeten ['swiːtən] vt **a)** [tea etc] azucarar **b)** Fig [temper] aplacar; **to sweeten the pill** suavizar el golpe

sweetheart ['swiːthɑːt] n **a)** [boyfriend] novio m; [girlfriend] novia f **b)** [dear, love] cariño m, amor m

sweetie ['swiːtɪ] n Fam **a)** [darling] cariño m; **he's a real sweetie** es un encanto **b)** Br (baby talk) [sweet] chuche m

sweet-tempered adj apacible

swell [swel] **1.** n [of sea] marejada f, oleaje m **2.** adj US Fam genial, Méx padre, RP bárbaro(a) **3.** (pt swelled, pp swollen) vi [part of body] hincharse; [river] subir ▪ **swell up** vi hincharse

swelling ['swelɪŋ] n hinchazón f; MED tumefacción f

swept [swept] pt & pp of **sweep**

swerve [swɜːv] **1.** n **a)** [by car] viraje m **b)** SPORT [by player] regate m **2.** vi **a)** [car] dar un viraje brusco **b)** SPORT [player] dar un regate

swift [swɪft] **1.** adj rápido(a), veloz **2.** n ORNITH vencejo m (común) ▪ **swill out** vt sep enjuagar, Esp aclarar

swim [swɪm] (pt swam, pp swum) **1.** vi nadar; **to go swimming** ir a nadar; Fam **my head is swimming** la cabeza me da vueltas **2.** vt [the Channel] pasar a nado **3.** n baño m; **swim briefs** bañador m (masculino); **to go for a swim** ir a nadar or bañarse

swimmer ['swɪmə(r)] n nadador(a) m,f

swimming ['swɪmɪŋ] n natación f; **swimming cap** gorro m de baño; **swimming costume** traje m de baño, bañador m, Ecuad, Perú, RP malla f; **swimming pool** piscina f, Méx alberca f, RP pileta f; **swimming trunks** Esp bañador m (de hombre) Ecuad, Perú, RP malla f (de hombre)

swindle ['swɪndəl] **1.** n estafa f **2.** vt estafar

swindler ['swɪndlə(r)] n estafador(a) m,f

swine [swaɪn] n **a)** (pl swine) [pig] cerdo m, puerco m, Am chancho m **b)** (pl swines) Fam [person] canalla mf, cochino(a) m,f

swing [swɪŋ] (pt & pp swung) **1.** n **a)** balanceo m, vaivén m; Fig [in votes etc] viraje m **b)** [in golf] swing m

c) [plaything] columpio *m*
d) [rhythm] ritmo *m*; **in full swing** en plena marcha
2. *vi* **a)** [move to and fro] balancearse; [arms, legs] menearse; [on swing] columpiarse
b) [turn] girar; **he swung round** dio media vuelta
3. *vt* [cause to move to and fro] balancear; [arms, legs] menear

swipe [swaɪp] **1.** *n* **a)** golpe *m* **b) swipe card** tarjeta *f* magnética **2.** *vt* **a)** [hit] dar un tortazo a **b)** *Fam* [steal] afanar, birlar

swirl [swɜ:l] **1.** *n* remolino *m*; [of cream, smoke] voluta *f* **2.** *vi* arremolinarse

Swiss [swɪs] **1.** *adj* suizo(a) **2.** (*pl* **Swiss**) *n* [person] suizo(a) *m,f*; **the Swiss** los suizos

switch [swɪtʃ] **1.** *n* **a)** ELEC interruptor *m* **b)** [changeover] cambio repentino; [exchange] intercambio *m* **c)** *US* RAIL agujas *fpl* **2.** *vt* **a)** [jobs, direction] cambiar de **b)** [allegiance] cambiar (**to** por); [attention] desviar (**to** hacia) ■ **switch off** *vt sep* apagar ■ **switch on** *vt sep* encender, *Am* prender ■ **switch over** *vi* cambiar (**to** a)

switchboard ['swɪtʃbɔ:d] *n* centralita *f*, *Am* conmutador *m*

Switzerland ['swɪtsələnd] *n* Suiza

swivel ['swɪvəl] **1.** *n* **swivel chair** silla giratoria **2.** *vt & vi* girar

swollen ['swəʊlən] **1.** *adj* [ankle, face] hinchado(a); [river, lake] crecido(a) **2.** *pp of* **swell**

swoop [swu:p] **1.** *n* **a)** [of bird] calada *f*; [of plane] (vuelo *m* en) picado **b)** [by police] redada *f* **2.** *vi* **a)** [plane, bird] volar en picado *or Am* picada **b)** [police] hacer una redada

swop [swɒp] *n & vt* = **swap**

sword [sɔ:d] *n* espada *f*

swore [swɔ:(r)] *pt of* **swear**

sworn [swɔ:n] **1.** *adj* jurado(a) **2.** *pp of* **swear**

swot [swɒt] *vi Br Fam* matarse estudiando, *Esp* empollar, *RP* tragar (**for** para)

swum [swʌm] *pp of* **swim**

swung [swʌŋ] *pt & pp of* **swing**

sycamore ['sɪkəmɔ:(r)] *n* **a)** *Br* sicomoro *m* **b)** *US* [plane tree] plátano *m*

syllable ['sɪləbəl] *n* sílaba *f*

syllabus ['sɪləbəs] *n* programa *m* de estudios

symbol ['sɪmbəl] *n* símbolo *m*

symbolic [sɪm'bɒlɪk] *adj* simbólico(a)

symmetry ['sɪmɪtrɪ] *n* simetría *f*

sympathetic [sɪmpə'θetɪk] *adj* **a)** [showing pity] compasivo(a) **b)** [understanding] comprensivo(a); [kind] amable

sympathize ['sɪmpəθaɪz] *vi* **a)** [show pity] compadecerse (**with** de) **b)** [understand] comprender

sympathy ['sɪmpəθɪ] *n* **a)** [pity] compasión *f* **b)** [condolences] pésame *m*; **letter of sympathy** pésame; **to express one's sympathy** dar el pésame **c)** [understanding] comprensión *f*

symphony ['sɪmfənɪ] *n* sinfonía *f*

symptom ['sɪmptəm] *n* síntoma *m*

synagogue ['sɪnəgɒg] *n* sinagoga *f*

synchronize ['sɪŋkrənaɪz] *vt* sincronizar

syndicate ['sɪndɪkɪt] *n* corporación *f*; **newspaper syndicate** sindicato periodístico

syndrome ['sɪndrəʊm] *n* síndrome *m*; MED **Down's syndrome** síndrome *m* de Down

synonym ['sɪnənɪm] *n* sinónimo *m*

synonymous [sɪ'nɒnɪməs] *adj* sinónimo(a) (**with** de)

synthetic [sɪn'θetɪk] *adj* sintético(a)

syringe [sɪ'rɪndʒ] *n* jeringa *f*, jeringuilla *f*

syrup ['sɪrəp] *n* jarabe *m*, almíbar *m*

SYS MESSAGING (*abbr of* **see you soon**) ta prnt

system ['sɪstəm] *n* sistema *m*; *Fam* **the system** el orden establecido; **solar system** sistema *m* solar; COMPUT **systems analyst** analista *mf* de sistemas

systematic [sɪstɪ'mætɪk] *adj* sistemático(a)

T

T, t [tiː] *n* [the letter] T, t *f*

ta [tɑː] *interj Br Fam* gracias

tab [tæb] *n* **a)** [flap] lengüeta *f*; [label] etiqueta *f*; *Fam* **to keep tabs on sb** vigilar a algn **b)** *US Fam* [bill] cuenta *f*

table ['teɪbəl] **1.** *n* **a)** mesa *f*; **to lay** *or* **set the table** poner la mesa; **table lamp** lámpara *f* de mesa; **table mat** salvamanteles *m inv*; **table tennis** ping-pong® *m*, tenis *m* de mesa; **table wine** vino *m* de mesa **b)** [of figures] tabla *f*, cuadro *m*; **table of contents** índice *m* de materias **2.** *vt* [motion, proposal] *Br* presentar; *US* posponer

tablecloth ['teɪbəlklɒθ] *n* mantel *m*

tablespoon ['teɪbəlspuːn] *n* cucharón *m*

tablespoonful ['teɪbəlspuːnfʊl] *n* cucharada *f* grande

tablet ['tæblɪt] *n* **a)** MED pastilla *f* **b)** [of stone] lápida *f* **c)** COMPUT **tablet (computer)** tableta *f*, tablet *f*

tabloid ['tæblɔɪd] *n* periódico *m* de pequeño formato; **tabloid press** prensa sensacionalista

taboo [tə'buː] *adj & n* tabú *(m)*

tack [tæk] **1.** *n* **a)** [small nail] tachuela *f* **b)** SEWING hilván *m* **c)** NAUT amura *f*; [distance] bordada *f*; *Fig* **to change tack** cambiar de rumbo **2.** *vt* **a) to tack sth down** clavar algo con tachuelas **b)** SEWING hilvanar **3.** *vi* NAUT virar de bordo

■ **tack on** *vt sep* [add] añadir

tackle ['tækəl] **1.** *n* **a)** [equipment] aparejos *mpl*; **fishing tackle** aparejos de pescar **b)** [challenge] [in football] entrada *f*; [in rugby, American football] placaje *m*, *Am* tackle *m* **2.** *vt* agarrar; [task] emprender; [problem] abordar; [in football] entrar a; [in rugby, American football] hacer un placaje a, *Am* tacklear

tacky¹ ['tækɪ] *(compar* **tackier**, *superl* **tackiest)** *adj* pegajoso(a)

tacky² ['tækɪ] *adj Fam* [tasteless] chabacano(a), ordinario(a)

tact [tækt] *n* tacto *m*, diplomacia *f*

tactful ['tæktfʊl] *adj* diplomático(a)

tactic ['tæktɪk] *n* táctica *f*; **tactics** táctica *f*

tactical ['tæktɪkəl] *adj* táctico(a)

tactless ['tæktlɪs] *adj* [person] poco diplomático(a); [question] indiscreto(a)

TAFN MESSAGING *written abbr of* **that's all for now**

tag [tæg] **1.** *n* **a)** [label] etiqueta *f* **b)** [saying] coletilla *f* **2.** *vt* COMPUT etiquetar

■ **tag along** *vi Fam* pegarse ■ **tag on** *vt sep* [add to end] añadir

tagging ['tægɪŋ] *n* COMPUT etiquetado *m*

tail [teɪl] **1.** *n* **a)** cola *f*; **tail end** cola *f* **b)** [of shirt] faldón *m*; **to wear tails** ir de frac; **tail coat** frac *m* **c) tails** [of coin] cruz *f*, *Andes, Ven* sello *m*, *Méx* sol *m*, *RP* ceca *f* **2.** *vt Fam* [follow] seguir de cerca ■ **tail away**, **tail off** *vi* desvanecerse

tailback ['teɪlbæk] *n Br* caravana *f*

tail-light ['teɪllaɪt] *n* AUTO faro *m* trasero

tailor ['teɪlə(r)] **1.** *n* sastre *m*; **tailor's (shop)** sastrería *f* **2.** *vt* [suit] confeccionar; *Fig* adaptar

tailor-made *adj Fig* a medida

take [teɪk] *(pt* **took**, *pp* **taken)** *vt* **a)** tomar, coger, *Am* agarrar; **to take an opportunity** aprovechar una oportunidad; **to take hold of sth** agarrar algo;

to take sth from one's pocket sacarse algo del bolsillo; **take your time!** ¡tómate el tiempo que quieras!; **to take a bath** bañarse; **to take care (of oneself)** cuidarse; **is this seat taken?** ¿está ocupado este asiento?; **to take a decision** tomar una decisión; **to take a liking / dislike to sb** tomar cariño /antipatía a algn; **to take a photograph** sacar una fotografía; **take the first road on the left** coja la primera a la izquierda; **to take the train** coger el tren

b) [accept] aceptar

c) [win] ganar; [prize] llevarse

d) [eat, drink] tomar; **to take drugs** drogarse

e) she's taking (a degree in) law estudia derecho; **to take an exam (in …)** examinarse (de …)

f) [person to a place] llevar

g) [endure] aguantar

h) [consider] considerar

i) I take it that … supongo que …

j) [require] requerir; **it takes an hour to get there** se tarda una hora en llegar hasta allí

k) to be taken ill enfermar

■ **take after** vt insep parecerse a

■ **take apart** vt sep [machine] desmontar

■ **take away** vt sep **a)** [carry off] llevarse **b)** to take sth away from sb quitar or Am sacar algo a algn **c)** MATH restar

■ **take back** vt sep **a)** [give back] devolver; [receive back] recuperar **b)** [withdraw] retractarse

■ **take down** vt sep **a)** [lower] bajar **b)** [demolish] derribar **c)** [write] apuntar

■ **take in** vt sep **a)** [shelter, lodge] alojar, acoger **b)** SEWING meter **c)** [include] abarcar **d)** [understand] entender **e)** [deceive] engañar

■ **take off 1.** vt sep **a)** quitar, Am sacar; **he took off his jacket** se quitó or Am se sacó la chaqueta **b)** [lead or carry away] llevarse **c)** [deduct] descontar **d)** [imitate] imitar burlonamente **2.** vi [plane] despegar, Am decolar

■ **take on** vt sep **a)** [undertake] encargarse de **b)** [acquire] tomar **c)** [employ] contratar **d)** [compete with] competir con

■ **take out** vt sep sacar, quitar; **he's taking me out to dinner** me ha invitado a cenar fuera

■ **take over 1.** vt sep COMM & POL tomar posesión de **2.** vi to take over from sb relevar a algn

■ **take to** vt insep [become fond of] coger cariño a; **to take to drink** darse a la bebida

■ **take up** vt sep **a)** SEWING acortar **b)** [accept] aceptar; [adopt] adoptar **c)** I've taken up the piano / French he empezado a tocar el piano /a aprender francés **d)** [occupy] ocupar

■ **take up on** vt sep [accept] **to take sb up on an offer** aceptar la oferta de algn

takeaway ['teɪkəweɪ] Br **1.** n [food] comida f para llevar; [restaurant] restaurante m que vende comida para llevar **2.** adj [food] para llevar

taken ['teɪkən] pp of **take**

takeoff ['teɪkɒf] n **a)** [plane, economy] despegue m, Am decolaje m **b)** [imitation] imitación burlona

takeover ['teɪkəʊvə(r)] n COMM absorción f; **military takeover** golpe m militar; **takeover bid** oferta pública de adquisición, OPA f

taking ['teɪkɪŋ] **1.** adj atractivo(a) **2.** n **a)** [of city, power, blood, sample] toma f; [of criminal] arresto m **b)** Br COMM **takings** recaudación f

talc [tælk] n talco m

tale [teɪl] n cuento m; **to tell tales** contar chismes

talent ['tælənt] n talento m

talented ['tæləntɪd] adj dotado(a)

talk [tɔːk] **1.** vi hablar, CAm, Méx platicar; [chat] charlar; [gossip] chismorrear; **talk radio** tertulia f radiofónica **2.** vt **to talk nonsense** decir tonterías; **to talk sense** hablar con sentido común; **to talk shop** hablar del trabajo

3. *n* **a)** [conversation] conversación *f*, *CAm, Méx* plática *f*

b) [words] palabras *fpl*; **he's all talk** no hace más que hablar

c) [rumour] rumor *m*; [gossip] chismes *mpl*

d) [lecture] charla *f*

■ **talk into** *vt sep* **to talk sb into sth** convencer a algn para que haga algo

■ **talk out of** *vt sep* **to talk sb out of sth** disuadir a algn de que haga algo

■ **talk over** *vt sep* discutir

talkative ['tɔːkətɪv] *adj* hablador(a)

talking ['tɔːkɪŋ] **1.** *n* conversación *f*; **he did all the talking** él se encargó de hablar **2.** *adj* [film] sonoro(a); [bird] que habla

tall [tɔːl] *adj* alto(a); **a tree 10 m tall** un árbol de 10 m (de alto); **how tall are you?** ¿cuánto mides?; *Fig* **that's a tall order** eso es mucho pedir

tally ['tælɪ] **1.** *vi* **to tally with sth** corresponderse con algo **2.** *n* COMM apunte *m*; **to keep a tally of** llevar la cuenta de

tambourine [tæmbə'riːn] *n* pandereta *f*

tame [teɪm] **1.** *adj* **a)** [animal] domado(a); [by nature] manso(a); [person] dócil **b)** [style] soso(a) **2.** *vt* domar

tamper ['tæmpə(r)] *vi* **to tamper with** [text] adulterar; [records, an entry] falsificar; [lock] intentar forzar

tampon ['tæmpɒn] *n* tampón *m*

tan [tæn] **1.** *n* **a)** [colour] marrón rojizo **b)** [of skin] bronceado *m*, *Esp* moreno *m* **2.** *adj* [colour] marrón rojizo **3.** *vt* **a)** [leather] curtir **b)** [skin] broncear **4.** *vi* ponerse moreno(a)

tangerine [tændʒə'riːn] *n* clementina *f*

tangible ['tændʒəbəl] *adj* tangible

tangle ['tæŋgəl] *n* [of thread] maraña *f*; *Fig* lío *m*; *Fig* **to get into a tangle** hacerse un lío

tangled ['tæŋgəld] *adj* enredado(a), enmarañado(a)

tank [tæŋk] *n* **a)** [container] depósito *m* **b)** MIL tanque *m*

tanker ['tæŋkə(r)] *n* NAUT tanque *m*; [for oil] petrolero *m*; AUTO camión *m* cisterna

tantrum ['tæntrəm] *n* rabieta *f*

tap¹ [tæp] **1.** *vt* golpear suavemente; [with hand] dar una palmadita a **2.** *vi* **to tap at the door** llamar suavemente a la puerta **3.** *n* golpecito *m*; **tap dancing** claqué *m*

tap² [tæp] *n Br* [for water] grifo *m*, *Chile, Col, Méx* llave *f*, *RP* canilla *f*; *Fig* **funds on tap** fondos *mpl* disponibles

tape [teɪp] **1.** *n* **a)** [strip] cinta *f*; **sticky tape** cinta adhesiva; **tape measure** cinta métrica **b)** [for recording] cinta *f* (magnetofónica); **tape recorder** magnetófono *m*, cassette *m*; **tape recording** grabación *f* **2.** *vt* **a)** pegar (con cinta adhesiva); *Fig* **I've got him / it taped** lo tengo controlado **b)** [record] grabar (en cinta)

taper ['teɪpə(r)] **1.** *vi* estrecharse; [to a point] afilarse **2.** *n* [candle] vela *f* ■ **taper off** *vi* ir disminuyendo

tapestry ['tæpɪstrɪ] *n* tapiz *m*

tar [tɑː(r)] *n* alquitrán *m*

tardy ['tɑːdɪ] (*compar* **tardier**, *superl* **tardiest**) **1.** *adj* **a)** US SCH con retraso escolar **b)** *Formal & Liter* [late] tardío(a) **c)** *Formal & Liter* [slow] lento(a) **2.** *n US* SCH alumno(a) *m,f* con retraso escolar

target ['tɑːgɪt] *n* **a)** [object aimed at] blanco *m*; **target practice** tiro *m* al blanco **b)** [purpose] meta *f*

tariff ['tærɪf] *n* tarifa *f*, arancel *m*

tarmac® ['tɑːmæk] **1.** *n* **a)** [substance] alquitrán *m* **b)** AVIAT pista *f* de aterrizaje **2.** *vt* alquitranar

tarnish ['tɑːnɪʃ] *vt* deslustrar

tart¹ [tɑːt] *n Br* CULIN tarta *f*

tart² [tɑːt] *adj* [taste] ácido(a), agrio(a)

tart³ [tɑːt] *Fam* **1.** *n* fulana *f*, *Méx* piruja *f* **2.** *vt Br* **to tart oneself up** emperifollarse

tartan ['tɑːtən] *n* tartán *m*

tase [teiz] *vt* **to tase sb** usar una pistola Taser® contra algn

taser ['teizə(r)] *n* (pistola *f*) Taser® *m*

task [tɑːsk] *n* tarea *f*; **to take sb to task** reprender a algn; MIL **task force** destacamento *m* (de fuerzas)

taste [teist] **1.** *n* **a)** [sense] gusto *m*; [flavour] sabor *m*; **it has a burnt taste** sabe a quemado **b)** [sample - of food] bocado *m*; [of drink] trago *m* **c)** [liking] afición *f*; **to have a taste for sth** gustarle a uno algo **d) in bad taste** de mal gusto; **to have (good) taste** tener (buen) gusto **2.** *vt* [sample] probar **3.** *vi* **to taste of sth** saber a algo

tasteful ['teistful] *adj* de buen gusto

tasteless ['teistlis] *adj* **a)** [food] soso(a) **b)** [in bad taste] de mal gusto

tasty ['teisti] *(compar* **tastier,** *superl* **tastiest)** *adj* sabroso(a)

tatters ['tætəz] *npl* **in tatters** hecho(a) jirones

tattoo¹ [tæ'tuː] *n* MIL retreta *f*

tattoo² [tæ'tuː] **1.** *vt* tatuar **2.** *n* [mark] tatuaje *m*

tatty ['tæti] *(compar* **tattier,** *superl* **tattiest)** *adj Fam* ajado(a), *Esp* sobado(a)

taught [tɔːt] *pt & pp of* **teach**

taunt [tɔːnt] **1.** *vt* **to taunt sb with sth** echar algo en cara a algn **2.** *n* pulla *f*

Taurus ['tɔːrəs] *n* Tauro *m*

taut [tɔːt] *adj* tenso(a), tirante

tax [tæks] **1.** *n* impuesto *m*; **green tax** impuesto *m* ecológico; **tax free** exento(a) de impuestos; **tax collector** recaudador(a) *m,f* (de impuestos); **tax evasion** evasión *f* fiscal; **tax return** declaración *f* de renta **2.** *vt* **a)** gravar **b)** [patience etc] poner a prueba

taxable ['tæksəbəl] *adj* imponible

taxation [tæk'seiʃən] *n* impuestos *mpl*

taxi ['tæksi] **1.** *n* taxi *m*; **taxi driver** taxista *mf*; **taxi** *Br* **rank** *or US* **stand** parada *f* de taxis **2.** *vi* [aircraft] rodar por la pista

taxpayer ['tækspeiə(r)] *n* contribuyente *mf*

TB *n* **a)** = **tuberculosis b)** = **text back**

tea [tiː] *n* **a)** té *m*; **tea bag** bolsita *f* de té; **tea break** descanso *m*; *Br* **tea cosy** cubretetera *f*; **tea leaf** hoja *f* de té; **tea service** *or* **set** juego *m* de té; **tea towel** trapo *m* or paño *m* (de cocina), *RP* repasador *m* **b)** [snack] merienda *f*; **(high) tea** merienda-cena *f*

teach [tiːtʃ] *(pt & pp* **taught)** **1.** *vt* enseñar; [subject] dar clases de; **to teach sb (how) to do sth** enseñar a algn a hacer algo; *US* **to teach school** ser profesor(a) **2.** *vi* dar clases, ser profesor(a)

teacher ['tiːtʃə(r)] *n* profesor(a) *m,f*; [in primary school] maestro(a) *m,f*

teaching ['tiːtʃiŋ] *n* enseñanza *f*

teacup ['tiːkʌp] *n* taza *f* de té

team [tiːm] *n* equipo *m*; [of oxen] yunta *f*

teamwork ['tiːmwɜːk] *n* trabajo *m* en equipo

teapot ['tiːpɒt] *n* tetera *f*

tear¹ [tiə(r)] *n* lágrima *f*; **to be in tears** estar llorando; **tear gas** gas *m* lacrimógeno

tear² [teə(r)] *(pt* **tore,** *pp* **torn) 1.** *vt* **a)** rajar, desgarrar **b) to tear sth out of sb's hands** arrancarle algo de las manos a algn **2.** *vi* **a)** [cloth] rajarse **b) to tear along** ir a toda velocidad **3.** *n* desgarrón *m*; [in clothes] rasgón *m* ▪ **tear down** *vt sep* derribar ▪ **tear off** *vt sep* arrancar ▪ **tear out** *vt sep* arrancar ▪ **tear up** *vt sep* **a)** romper, hacer pedazos **b)** [uproot] arrancar de raíz

tearoom ['tiːruːm] *Br n* = **teashop**

tease [tiːz] **1.** *vt* tomar el pelo a **2.** *n* bromista *mf*

teashop ['tiːʃɒp] *n Br* salón *m* de té

teaspoon ['tiːspuːn] *n* cucharilla *f*

teaspoonful ['tiːspuːnful] *n* cucharadita *f*

teatime ['tiːtaim] *n esp Br* hora *f* del té

technical ['teknikəl] *adj* técnico(a); *Br* **technical college** instituto *m* de formación profesional

technician [tek'niʃən] *n* técnico(a) *m,f*

technique [tek'niːk] *n* técnica *f*

technological [teknə'lɒdʒɪkəl] *adj* tecnológico(a)

technology [tek'nɒlədʒɪ] *n* tecnología *f*

tedious ['tiːdɪəs] *adj* tedioso(a), aburrido(a)

teem [tiːm] *vi* **to teem with** rebosar de; *Fam* **it was teeming down** llovía a cántaros

teen [tiːn] *adj Fam* [fashion, music] adolescente; [problems] de adolescentes

teenage ['tiːneɪdʒ] *adj* adolescente

teenager ['tiːneɪdʒə(r)] *n* adolescente *mf*

teens [tiːnz] *npl* adolescencia *f*

teeshirt ['tiːʃɜːt] *n* camiseta *f*, *Méx* playera, *RP* remera *f*

teeth [tiːθ] *pl of* **tooth**

teethe [tiːð] *vi* echar los dientes

teetotaller [tiː'təʊtələ(r)] *n* abstemio(a) *m,f*

TEFL ['tefl] *n (abbr of* **teaching English as a foreign language)** enseñanza del inglés como lengua extranjera

telecommunications ['telɪkəmjuː- nɪ'keɪʃənz] *n sing* telecomunicaciones *fpl*

telegram ['telɪgræm] *n* telegrama *m*

telegraph ['telɪɡrɑːf] **1.** *n* telégrafo *m*; **telegraph pole** poste telegráfico **2.** *vt & vi* telegrafiar

telephone ['telɪfəʊn] **1.** *n* teléfono *m*; **telephone banking** telebanca *f*; *Br* **telephone booth** *or* **box** cabina *f* (telefónica); **telephone call** llamada telefónica, *Am* llamado telefónico; **telephone directory** guía telefónica, *Am* directorio *m* de teléfonos; **telephone number** número *m* de teléfono **2.** *vt* telefonear, llamar por teléfono a, *Am* hablar por teléfono a

telescope ['telɪskəʊp] **1.** *n* telescopio *m* **2.** *vi* plegarse (como un catalejo) **3.** *vt* plegar

televise ['telɪvaɪz] *vt* televisar

television ['telɪvɪʒən] *n* televisión *f*; **television programme** programa *m* de televisión; **television (set)** televisor *m*

telex ['teleks] **1.** *n* télex *m* **2.** *vt* enviar por télex

tell [tel] *(pt & pp* **told) 1.** *vt* **a)** [say] decir; [relate] contar; [inform] comunicar; **to tell lies** mentir; **to tell sb about sth** contarle algo a algn

b) [order] mandar; **to tell sb to do sth** decir a algn que haga algo

c) [distinguish] distinguir; **to know how to tell the time** saber decir la hora **2.** *vi* **a)** [reveal] reflejar

b) who can tell? [know] ¿quién sabe?

c) [have effect] notarse; **the pressure is telling on her** está acusando la presión

■ **tell apart** *vt sep* distinguir

■ **tell off** *vt sep Fam* [scold] **to tell sb off (for)** echar una reprimenda *or Esp* bronca a algn (por)

telling-off *(pl* **tellings-off)** *n Fam* rapapolvo *m*

telltale ['telteɪl] *n* acusica *mf*, *Esp* chivato(a) *m,f*; **telltale signs** señales reveladoras

telly ['telɪ] *n Br Fam* **the telly** la tele

temper ['tempə(r)] **1.** *n* **a)** [mood] humor *m*; **to keep one's temper** no perder la calma; **to lose one's temper** perder los estribos **b)** [temperament] to **have a bad temper** tener (mal) genio **2.** *vt* [in metallurgy] templar; *Fig* suavizar

temperament ['tempərəmənt] *n* temperamento *m*

temperate ['tempərɪt] *adj* **a)** mesurado(a) **b)** [climate] templado(a)

temperature ['temprɪtʃə(r)] *n* temperatura *f*; **to have a temperature** tener fiebre

temple¹ ['tempəl] *n* ARCHIT templo *m*

temple² ['tempəl] *n* ANAT sien *f*

tempo ['tempəʊ] *n* tempo *m*

temporary ['tempərərɪ] *adj* temporal, *Am* temporario(a); [office, arrangement, repairs] provisional, *Am* temporario(a)

tempt [tempt] *vt* tentar; **to tempt providence** tentar la suerte; **to tempt sb to do sth** incitar a algn a hacer algo

temptation [temp'teɪʃən] *n* tentación *f*

tempting ['temptɪŋ] *adj* tentador(a)

ten [ten] *adj* & *n* diez (*m inv*)

tenacious [tɪˈneɪʃəs] *adj* tenaz

tenancy [ˈtenənsɪ] *n* [of house] alquiler *m*; [of land] arrendamiento *m*

tenant [ˈtenənt] *n* [of house] inquilino(a) *m,f*; [of farm] arrendatario(a) *m,f*

tend¹ [tend] *vi* [be inclined] tender, tener tendencia (**to** a)

tend² [tend] *vt* [care for] cuidar

tendency [ˈtendənsɪ] *n* tendencia *f*

tender¹ [ˈtendə(r)] *adj* [affectionate] cariñoso(a); [compassionate] compasivo(a); [meat] tierno(a)

tender² [ˈtendə(r)] **1.** *vt* ofrecer; **to tender one's resignation** presentar la dimisión **2.** *vi* COMM **to tender for** sacar a concurso **3.** *n* **a)** COMM oferta *f* **b) legal tender** moneda *f* de curso legal

tenement [ˈtenɪmənt] *n* **tenement (building)** bloque *m* de apartamentos *or Esp* pisos *or Arg* departamentos

tennis [ˈtenɪs] *n* tenis *m*; **tennis ball** pelota *f* de tenis; **tennis court** pista *f* de tenis; **tennis player** tenista *mf*; **tennis racket** raqueta *f* de tenis; **tennis shoe** zapatilla *f* de tenis

tenor [ˈtenə(r)] *n* MUS tenor *m*

10Q MESSAGING (*abbr of* **thank you**) asias

tense¹ [tens] *adj* tenso(a)

tense² [tens] *n* LING tiempo *m*

tension [ˈtenʃən] *n* tensión *f*

tent [tent] *n* tienda *f* de campaña, *Am* carpa *f*; **tent peg** estaca *f*

tentative [ˈtentətɪv] *adj* **a)** [not definite] de prueba **b)** [hesitant] indeciso(a)

tenth [tenθ] **1.** *adj* & *n* décimo(a) (*m,f*) **2.** *n* [fraction] décimo *m*

tenuous [ˈtenjʊəs] *adj* **a)** tenue **b)** [argument] flojo(a)

tepid [ˈtepɪd] *adj* tibio(a)

term [tɜːm] **1.** *n* **a)** [period] período *m*; SCH trimestre *m*; **term of office** mandato *m*, legislatura *f*; **in the long/short term** a largo/corto plazo **b)** [word] término *m*; *Fig* **in terms of money** en cuanto al dinero **c) terms** [conditions] condiciones *fpl*; **to come to terms with**

hacerse a la idea de **d) to be on good/bad terms with sb** tener buenas/malas relaciones con algn **2.** *vt* calificar de

terminal [ˈtɜːmɪnəl] **1.** *adj* terminal; **terminal cancer** cáncer incurable **2.** *n* terminal *f*

terminate [ˈtɜːmɪneɪt] **1.** *vt* terminar; **to terminate a pregnancy** abortar **2.** *vi* terminarse

terminus [ˈtɜːmɪnəs] (*pl* **termini** [ˈtɜːmɪnaɪ]) *n* terminal *m*

terrace [ˈterəs] *n* **a)** AGR bancal *m* **b)** *Br* [of houses] hilera *f* de casas **c)** [patio] terraza *f* **d)** *Br* FTBL **the terraces** las gradas

terrain [təˈreɪn] *n* terreno *m*

terrestrial [tɪˈrestrɪəl] *adj* terrestre

terrible [ˈterəbəl] *adj* horrible, terrible

terribly [ˈterəblɪ] *adv* tremendamente mal, *Esp* fatal

terrier [ˈterɪə(r)] *n* terrier *m*

terrific [təˈrɪfɪk] *adj* **a)** *Fam* [excellent] estupendo, genial **b)** [extreme] tremendo(a)

terrify [ˈterɪfaɪ] *vt* aterrorizar

terrifying [ˈterɪfaɪɪŋ] *adj* aterrador(a)

territory [ˈterɪtərɪ] *n* territorio *m*

terror [ˈterə(r)] *n* terror *m*; **terror attack** atentado *m* terrorista

terrorism [ˈterərɪzəm] *n* terrorismo *m*

terrorist [ˈterərɪst] *adj* & *n* terrorista (*mf*)

terrorize [ˈterəraɪz] *vt* aterrorizar

test [test] **1.** *vt* probar, someter a una prueba; [analyse] analizar; MED hacer un análisis de **2.** *n* prueba *f*, examen *m*; **test match** partido *m* internacional; **test pilot** piloto *m* de pruebas; **test tube** probeta *f*; **test-tube baby** niño *m* probeta

testament [ˈtestəmənt] *n* testamento *m*; **Old/New Testament** Antiguo/Nuevo Testamento

testicle [ˈtestɪkəl] *n* testículo *m*

testify [ˈtestɪfaɪ] **1.** *vt* declarar **2.** *vi Fig* **to testify to sth** atestiguar algo

testimony [ˈtestɪmənɪ] *n* testimonio *m*, declaración *f*

tetanus ['tetənəs] *n* tétano(s) *m inv*

tether ['teðə(r)] **1.** *n* ronzal *m*; *Fig* to be at the end of one's tether estar hasta la coronilla **2.** *vt* [animal] atar

text [tekst] **1.** *n* texto *m*; TEL **text message** mensaje *m* (de texto) **2.** *vt* [send text message to] enviar un mensaje de texto a

textbook ['tekstbʊk] *n* libro *m* de texto

textile ['tekstaɪl] **1.** *n* tejido *m* **2.** *adj* textil

texting ['tekstɪŋ] *n* TEL & COMPUT envío *m* de SMS

texture ['tekstʃə(r)] *n* textura *f*

Thames [temz] *n* **the Thames** el Támesis

than [ðæn] (*unstressed* [ðən]) *conj* que; [with numbers] de; **he's older than me** es mayor que yo; **I have more / less than you** tengo más /menos que tú; **more interesting than we thought** más interesante de lo que creíamos; **more than once** más de una vez; **more than ten people** más de diez personas

thank [θæŋk] *vt* agradecer a; **thank you** gracias

thankful ['θæŋkfʊl] *adj* agradecido(a)

thanks [θæŋks] *npl* gracias *fpl*; **no thanks** no gracias; **many thanks** muchas gracias; **thanks for phoning** gracias por llamar; **thanks to** gracias a

Thanksgiving [θæŋks'gɪvɪŋ] *n US* **Thanksgiving Day** Día *m* de Acción de Gracias

that [ðæt] (*unstressed* [ðət]) **1.** (*pl* **those**) *dem pron* **a)** ése *m*, ésa *f*; [further away] aquél *m*, aquélla *f*; **this one is new but that is old** éste es nuevo pero ése es viejo
b) [indefinite] eso; [remote] aquello; **after that** después de eso; **like that** así; **that's right** eso es; **that's where I live** allí vivo yo; **what's that?** ¿qué es eso?; **who's that?** ¿quién es?
c) [with relative] el /la; **all those I saw** todos los que vi
2. (*pl* **those**) *dem adj* [masculine] ese; [feminine] esa; [further away - mas-

culine] aquel; [feminine] aquella; **at that time** en aquella época; **that book** ese /aquel libro; **that one** ése /aquél
3. *rel pron* **a)** [subject, direct object] que; **all (that) you said** todo lo que dijiste; **the letter (that) I sent you** la carta que te envié
b) [governed by preposition] que, el /la que, los /las que, el /la cual, los /las cuales; **the car (that) they came in** el coche en el que vinieron
c) [when] que, en que; **the moment (that) you arrived** el momento en que llegaste

El pronombre relativo **that** puede omitirse salvo cuando es sujeto de la oración subordinada.

4. *conj* que; **he said (that) he would come** dijo que vendría

La conjunción **that** se puede omitir cuando introduce una oración subordinada.

5. *adv* así de, tanto, tan; **I don't think it can be that old** no creo que sea tan viejo; **we haven't got that much money** no tenemos tanto dinero

thatched [θætʃt] *adj* cubierto(a) con paja; **thatched cottage** casita *f* con techo de paja; **thatched roof** techo *m* de paja

thaw [θɔː] **1.** *vt* [snow] derretir; [food, freezer] descongelar **2.** *vi* descongelarse; [snow] derretirse **3.** *n* deshielo *m*

the [ðə] (*before vowel sound* [ðɪ], *emphatic* [ðiː]) **1.** *def art* **a)** el /la, *pl* los /las; **at / to the** al /a la, *pl* a los /a las; **of or from the** del /de la, *pl* de los /de las; **the Alps** los Alpes
b) [omitted] **George the Sixth** Jorge Sexto
c) [by the day] al día; **by the dozen** a docenas
d) [with adjectives used as nouns] **the elderly** los ancianos
2. *adv* **the more the merrier** cuantos más mejor; **the sooner the better** cuanto antes mejor

theatre, *US* **theater** ['θɪətə(r)] *n* teatro *m*

theatrical [θɪ'ætrɪkəl] *adj* teatral

theft [θeft] *n* robo *m*; **petty theft** hurto *m*

their [ðeə(r)] *poss adj* [one thing] su; [various things] sus

theirs [ðeəz] *poss pron* (el) suyo /(la) suya, *pl* (los) suyos /(las) suyas

them [ðem] (*unstressed* [ðəm]) *pers pron pl* **a)** [direct object] los /las; [indirect object] les; **I know them** los / las conozco; **I shall tell them so** se lo diré (a ellos /ellas); **it's them!** ¡son ellos!; **speak to them** hábleles **b)** [with preposition] ellos /ellas; **walk in front of them** camine delante de ellos; **they took the keys away with them** se llevaron las llaves; **both of them, the two of them** los dos; **neither of them** ninguno de los dos; **none of them** ninguno de ellos

theme [θiːm] *n* tema *m*; **theme tune** sintonía *f*

themselves [ðəm'selvz] *pers pron pl* [as subject] ellos mismos /ellas mismas; [as direct or indirect object] se; [after a preposition] sí mismos /sí mismas; **they did it by themselves** lo hicieron ellos solos

then [ðen] **1.** *adv* **a)** [at that time] entonces; **since then** desde entonces; **there and then** en el acto; **till then** hasta entonces

b) [next, afterwards] luego

c) [anyway] de todas formas

d) [in that case] entonces; **go then** pues vete

e) then and there allí mismo, en el acto **2.** *conj* entonces

3. *adj* **the then president** el entonces presidente

---

theoretic(al) [θɪə'retɪk(əl)] *adj* teórico(a)

theory ['θɪərɪ] *n* teoría *f*

therapeutic [θerə'pjuːtɪk] *adj also Fig* terapéutico(a)

therapy ['θerəpɪ] *n* terapia *f*

there [ðeə(r)] (*unstressed* [ðə(r)]) **1.** *adv* **a)** [referring to place] allí, allá; [nearer speaker] ahí; **I'm going there next**

week voy allí la semana que viene; **there it is** ahí está; **here and there** aquí y allí; **in there** ahí dentro; **there again** por otra parte; **there and then** allí mismo, en el acto; **it's six kilometres there and back** son seis kilómetros de ida y vuelta **b)** [in existence, available] ahí; **is anybody there?** ¿hay alguien ahí?; **is John there, please?** [when telephoning] ¿está John? **c)** [emphatic] **hello** *or* **hi there!** ¡hola!; **that man there** aquel hombre; **there you go again!** ¡ya estamos otra vez!; **we're getting there** ya está, casi **2.** *pron* **a)** [indicating existence of sth] **there is /are…** hay…; **there's someone at the door** hay alguien a la puerta; **there must be some mistake** tiene que haber un error; **there were six of us** éramos seis **b)** [in respect] **there's the difficulty** ahí está la dificultad **3.** *interj* **so there!** ¡ea!; **there, I knew he'd turn up** ¿lo ves? ya sabía yo que aparecería; **there, there** vamos, vamos

thereabouts ['ðeərəbaʊts], *US* **thereabout** ['ðeərəbaʊt] *adv* **in Cambridge or thereabouts** en Cambridge o por allí cerca; **at four o'clock or thereabouts** a las cuatro o así

thereby ['ðeəbaɪ] *adv* por eso *or* ello

therefore ['ðeəfɔː(r)] *adv* por lo tanto, por eso

thermometer [θə'mɒmɪtə(r)] *n* termómetro *m*

Thermos® ['θɜːməs] *n* **Thermos**® **(flask)** termo *m*

thermostat ['θɜːməstæt] *n* termostato *m*

these [ðiːz] **1.** *dem adj pl* estos(as) **2.** *dem pron pl* éstos(as); *see* **this**

thesis ['θiːsɪs] (*pl* **theses** ['θiːsiːz]) *n* tesis *f inv*

they [ðeɪ] *pron pl* **a)** ellos /ellas (*usually omitted in Spanish, except for contrast*); **they are dancing** están bailando; **they are rich** son ricos **b)** [stressed] **they alone** ellos solos; **they themselves told me** me lo dijeron ellos mismos **c)** [with relative] los / las **d)** [indefinite] **that's what they say** eso es lo que se dice; **they say that …** se dice que …

thick [θɪk] **1.** *adj* **a)** [book etc] grueso(a); **a wall 2 m thick** un muro de 2 m de espesor **b)** [dense] espeso(a) **c)** *Fam* [stupid] tonto(a) **2.** *adv* densamente **3.** *n* **to be in the thick of it** estar metido(a) de lleno

thicken ['θɪkən] **1.** *vt* espesar **2.** *vi* espesarse; *Fig* [plot] complicarse

thickness ['θɪknɪs] *n* [of wall etc] espesor *m*; [of wire, lips] grueso *m*; [of liquid, woodland] espesura *f*

thief [θi:f] *(pl* **thieves** [θi:vz]*) n* ladrón(ona) *m,f*

thigh [θaɪ] *n* muslo *m*

thimble ['θɪmbəl] *n* dedal *m*

thin [θɪn] **1.** *(compar* **thinner,** *superl* **thinnest) adj* **a)** delgado(a); **a thin slice** una loncha fina **b)** [hair, vegetation] ralo(a); [liquid] claro(a); [population] escaso(a) **c)** *Fig* [voice] débil; **a thin excuse** un pobre pretexto **2.** *vt* **to thin (down)** [paint] diluir

thing [θɪŋ] *n* **a)** cosa *f*; **for one thing** en primer lugar; **the thing is ...** resulta que ...; **what with one thing and another** entre unas cosas y otras **b) poor little thing!** ¡pobrecito(a)! **c) things** cosas *fpl*; **my things** [clothing] mi ropa *f*; [possessions] mis cosas *fpl*; **as things are** tal como están las cosas; *Fam* **how are things?** [life, situation] ¿qué tal van las cosas?

think [θɪŋk] *(pt & pp* **thought) 1.** *vt* **a)** [believe] pensar, creer; **I think so/not** creo que sí/no
b) I thought as much yo me lo imaginaba **2.** *vi* **a)** pensar **(of** *or* **about** en); **give me time to think** dame tiempo para reflexionar; **to think ahead** prevenir **b)** [have as opinion] opinar, pensar; **to think highly of sb** apreciar a algn; **what do you think?** ¿a ti qué te parece? **c) just think!** ¡imagínate!

■ **think out** *vt sep* meditar; **a carefully thought-out answer** una respuesta razonada

■ **think over** *vt sep* reflexionar; **we'll have to think it over** lo tendremos que pensar

■ **think up** *vt sep* imaginar, idear

thinly ['θɪnlɪ] *adv* poco, ligeramente

third [θɜ:d] **1.** *adj* tercero(a); [before masculine singular noun] tercer; **(on) the third of March** el tres de marzo; **the Third World** el Tercer Mundo; **third party insurance** seguro *m* a terceros **2.** *n* **a)** [in series] tercero(a) *m,f* **b)** [fraction] tercio *m*, tercera parte

third-generation *adj* COMPUT & TEL de tercera generación

thirdly ['θɜ:dlɪ] *adv* en tercer lugar

thirst [θɜ:st] *n* sed *f*

thirst-quenching [-kwentʃɪŋ] *adj* que quita la sed

thirsty ['θɜ:stɪ] *(compar* **thirstier,** *superl* **thirstiest) adj** sediento(a); **to be thirsty** tener sed

thirteen [θɜ:'ti:n] *adj & n* trece *(m inv)*

thirteenth [θɜ:'ti:nθ] **1.** *adj & n* decimotercero(a) *(m,f)* **2.** *n* [fraction] decimotercera parte

thirtieth ['θɜ:tɪɪθ] **1.** *adj & n* trigésimo(a) *(m,f)* **2.** *n* [fraction] trigésima parte

thirty ['θɜ:tɪ] *adj & n* treinta *(m inv)*

this [ðɪs] **1.** *(pl* **these)** *dem adj* [masculine] este; [feminine] esta; **this book/these books** este libro/estos libros; **this one** éste/ésta
2. *(pl* **these)** *dem pron* **a)** [indefinite] esto; **it was like this** fue así
b) [place] **this is where we met** fue aquí donde nos conocimos
c) [time] **it should have come before this** debería haber llegado ya
d) [introduction] **this is Mr Álvarez** le presento al Sr. Álvarez; [specific person or thing] éste *m*, ésta *f*; **I prefer these to those** me gustan más éstos que aquéllos
3. *adv* **he got this far** llegó hasta aquí; **this small/big** así de pequeño/grande

thistle ['θɪsəl] *n* cardo *m*

thorn [θɔ:n] *n* espina *f*

thorough ['θʌrə] *adj* [careful] minucioso(a); [work] concienzudo(a);

[knowledge] profundo(a); **to carry out a thorough enquiry into a matter** investigar a fondo un asunto

thoroughfare [ˈθʌrəfeə(r)] n [road] carretera f; [street] calle f

thoroughly [ˈθʌrəlɪ] adv [carefully] a fondo; [wholly] completamente

those [ðəʊz] **1.** dem pron pl ésos(as); [remote] aquéllos(as); **those who** los que / las que **2.** dem adj pl esos(as); [remote] aquellos(as); see **that**

though [ðəʊ] **1.** conj a) aunque; **strange though it may seem** por (muy) extraño que parezca b) **as though** como si; **it looks as though he's gone** parece que se ha ido **2.** adv sin embargo

thought [θɔːt] **1.** n a) [act of thinking] pensamiento m; **what a tempting thought!** ¡qué idea más tentadora! b) [reflection] reflexión f c) **it's the thought that counts** [intention] lo que cuenta es la intención **2.** pt & pp of **think**

thoughtful [ˈθɔːtfʊl] adj [pensive] pensativo(a); [considerate] atento(a)

thoughtless [ˈθɔːtlɪs] adj [person] desconsiderado(a); [action] irreflexivo(a)

thousand [ˈθaʊzənd] adj & n mil (m); **thousands of people** miles de personas

thrash [θræʃ] **1.** vt dar una paliza a **2.** vi **to thrash about** or **around** agitarse ▪ **thrash out** vt sep discutir a fondo

thrashing [ˈθræʃɪŋ] n [beating, defeat] paliza f

thread [θred] **1.** n a) hilo m; **length of thread** hebra f b) [of screw] rosca f **2.** vt a) [needle] enhebrar b) **to thread one's way (through)** colarse (por)

threat [θret] n amenaza f

threaten [ˈθretən] vt amenazar; **to threaten to do sth** amenazar con hacer algo

threatening [ˈθretənɪŋ] adj amenazador(a)

three [θriː] adj & n tres (m inv)

three-course adj [meal] de tres platos

threshold [ˈθreʃəʊld] n umbral m; Fig **to be on the threshold of** estar a las puertas or en los umbrales de

threw [θruː] pt of **throw**

thrifty [ˈθrɪftɪ] (compar **thriftier**, superl **thriftiest**) adj económico(a), ahorrador(a)

thrill [θrɪl] **1.** n a) [excitement] emoción f b) [quiver] estremecimiento m **2.** vt [excite] emocionar; [audience] entusiasmar

thriller [ˈθrɪlə(r)] n thriller m

thrilling [ˈθrɪlɪŋ] adj emocionante

thrive [θraɪv] (pt **thrived** or **throve**, pp **thrived** or **thriven** [ˈθrɪvən]) vi a) [person] rebosar de salud b) Fig [business] prosperar; **he thrives on it** le viene de maravilla

thriving [ˈθraɪvɪŋ] adj Fig próspero(a)

throat [θrəʊt] n garganta f

throb [θrɒb] **1.** n [of heart] latido m; [of machine] zumbido m **2.** vi [heart] latir; [machine] zumbar; **my head is throbbing** me va a estallar la cabeza

throne [θrəʊn] n trono m

throttle [ˈθrɒtəl] **1.** n **throttle (valve)** [of engine] válvula reguladora **2.** vt [person] estrangular ▪ **throttle back** vt sep [engine] desacelerar

through [θruː] **1.** prep a) [place] a través de, por; **to look through the window** mirar por la ventana
b) [time] a lo largo de; **all through his life** durante toda su vida; US **Tuesday through Thursday** desde el martes hasta el jueves inclusive
c) [by means of] por, mediante; **I learnt of it through Jack** me enteré por Jack
d) [because of] a or por causa de; **through ignorance** por ignorancia
2. adj **a through train** un tren directo; **through traffic** tránsito m
3. adv a) [from one side to the other] de un lado a otro; **to let sb through** dejar pasar a algn; Fig **socialist / French through and through** socialista / francés por los cuatro costados
b) **I'm through with him** he terminado con él

c) TEL **to get through to sb** comunicar con algn

throughout [θruː'aʊt] **1.** *prep* por todo(a); **throughout the year** durante todo el año **2.** *adv* [place] en todas partes; [time] todo el tiempo

throw [θrəʊ] **1.** (*pt* threw, *pp* thrown) *vt* **a)** tirar, *Am* aventar; [to the ground] derribar; [rider] desmontar; *Fig* **he threw a fit** le dio un ataque; *Fig* **to throw a party** dar una fiesta **b)** [disconcert] desconcertar **2.** *n* tiro *m*, lanzamiento *m*; [in wrestling] derribo *m* ▪ **throw away** *vt sep* [rubbish] tirar, *Am* botar; [money] malgastar; [opportunity] perder ▪ **throw in** *vt sep* **a)** tirar; SPORT sacar de banda; *Fig* **to throw in the towel** arrojar la toalla **b)** [include] añadir; [in deal] incluir (gratis) ▪ **throw off** *vt sep* [person, thing] deshacerse de; [clothes] quitarse ▪ **throw out** *vt sep* [rubbish] tirar; [person] echar ▪ **throw up 1.** *vt sep* **a)** lanzar al aire **b)** CONSTR construir rápidamente **2.** *vi* *Fam* vomitar, devolver

thrown [θrəʊn] *pp of* **throw**

thrush [θrʌʃ] *n* ORNITH tordo *m*, zorzal *m*

thrust [θrʌst] **1.** (*pt & pp* thrust) *vt* empujar con fuerza; **he thrust a letter into my hand** me puso una carta violentamente en la mano **2.** *n* [push] empujón *m*; AVIAT & PHYS empuje *m*

thud [θʌd] *n* ruido sordo

thug [θʌg] *n* [lout] gamberro *m*; [criminal] criminal *m*

thumb [θʌm] **1.** *n* pulgar *m* **2.** *vt* **a)** manosear **b) to thumb a lift** hacer autostop, *CAm, Méx, Perú* pedir aventón ▪ **thumb through** *vt insep* [book] hojear

thump [θʌmp] **1.** *n* **a)** [sound] ruido sordo **b)** [blow] golpazo *m*; *Fam* torta *f* **2.** *vt* golpear **3.** *vi* **a) to thump on the table** golpear la mesa **b)** [heart] latir ruidosamente

thunder ['θʌndə(r)] **1.** *n* trueno *m*; **thunder of applause** estruendo *m* de aplausos **2.** *vi* tronar

thunderstorm ['θʌndəstɔːm] *n* tormenta *f*

Thursday ['θɜːzdɪ] *n* jueves *m*

thus [ðʌs] *adv* así, de esta manera; **and thus ...** así que ...

Thx, THX, Thnx MESSAGING *(abbr of* thanks*)* asias

thyme [taɪm] *n* tomillo *m*

tic [tɪk] *n* tic *m*

tick¹ [tɪk] **1.** *n* **a)** [sound] tic-tac *m* **b)** *Br Fam* **I'll do it in a tick** ahora mismo lo hago **c)** [mark] marca *f* de visto bueno **2.** *vi* hacer tic-tac **3.** *vt* marcar ▪ **tick off** *vt sep* **a)** [mark] marcar **b)** *Br Fam* [reprimand] regañar ▪ **tick over** *vi* AUTO funcionar al ralentí

tick² [tɪk] *n* **a)** [insect] garrapata *f* **b) tick box** casilla *f*

ticket ['tɪkɪt] *n* **a)** [for train, plane, lottery] billete *m*, *Am* boleto *m*; [for theatre, cinema] entrada *f*, *Col, Méx* boleto; **ticket collector** revisor(a) *m,f*; **ticket office** taquilla *f*, *Am* boletería *f*; *Fam* **to be a hot ticket** tener mucha demanda **b)** [receipt] recibo *m* **c)** [label] etiqueta *f* **d)** AUTO multa *f*

tickle ['tɪkəl] **1.** *vt* hacer cosquillas a **2.** *vi* hacer cosquillas **3.** *n* cosquillas *fpl*

ticklish ['tɪklɪʃ] *adj* **to be ticklish** tener cosquillas

tick-tack-toe [tɪktæk'təʊ] *n* *US* tres en raya *m*

tide [taɪd] *n* **a)** marea *f*; **high / low tide** marea alta / baja **b)** *Fig* [of events] curso *m*; **the tide has turned** han cambiado las cosas; **to go against the tide** ir contra corriente

tidy ['taɪdɪ] **1.** (*compar* tidier, *superl* tidiest) *adj* **a)** [room, habits] ordenado(a) **b)** [appearance] arreglado(a) **2.** *vt* arreglar; **to tidy away** poner en su sitio **3.** *vi* **to tidy (up)** ordenar las cosas

tie [taɪ] **1.** *vt* [shoelaces etc] atar; **to tie a knot** hacer un nudo **2.** *vi* SPORT empatar (**with** con) **3.** *n* **a)** [bond] lazo *m*, vínculo *m* **b)** *Fig* [hindrance] atadura *f* **c)** [clothing] corbata *f* **d)** SPORT [match] partido *m*; [draw] empate *m* ▪ **tie down** *vt sep* sujetar; *Fig* **to be tied down** estar atado(a); *Fig* **to tie sb down to a promise** obligar a algn a cumplir una promesa ▪ **tie up** *vt sep* **a)** [parcel, dog] atar **b)** [deal] concluir **c)** [capital] inmovilizar; *Fig* **I'm tied up just now** de momento estoy muy ocupado(a)

tier [tɪə(r)] *n* [of seats] fila *f*; [in stadium] grada *f*; **four-tier cake** pastel *m* de cuatro pisos

tiger ['taɪgə(r)] *n* tigre *m*

tight [taɪt] **1.** *adj* **a)** apretado(a); [clothing] ajustado(a); [seal] hermético(a); **my shoes are too tight** me aprietan los zapatos
b) [scarce] escaso(a); **money's a bit tight** estamos escasos de dinero
c) [mean] agarrado(a)
d) *Fam* [drunk] alegre, *Esp* piripi
2. *adv* estrechamente; [seal] herméticamente; **hold tight** agárrate fuerte; **shut tight** bien cerrado(a); **to sit tight** no moverse de su sitio

tighten ['taɪtən] **1.** *vt* [screw] apretar; [rope] tensar; *Fig* **to tighten (up) restrictions** intensificar las restricciones **2.** *vi* apretarse; [cable] tensarse

tightrope ['taɪtrəʊp] *n* cuerda floja; **tightrope walker** funámbulo(a) *m,f*

tights [taɪts] *npl* [woollen] leotardos *mpl*, *Col* medias *fpl* veladas, *RP* cancanes *mpl*; *Br* [nylon, silk] medias *fpl*, pantis *mpl*

tile [taɪl] **1.** *n* [of roof] teja *f*; [glazed] azulejo *m*; [for floor] baldosa *f* **2.** *vt* [roof] tejar; [wall] poner azulejos en, *Esp* alicatar; [floor] embaldosar

till¹ [tɪl] *n* [for cash] caja *f*

till² [tɪl] *vt* [field] labrar, cultivar

till³ [tɪl] **1.** *prep* hasta; **from morning till night** de la mañana a la noche; **till then** hasta entonces **2.** *conj* hasta que

tilt [tɪlt] **1.** *n* **a)** [angle] inclinación *f* **b)** **(at) full tilt** [speed] a toda velocidad **2.** *vi* **to tilt over** volcarse; **to tilt (up)** inclinarse **3.** *vt* inclinar

timber ['tɪmbə(r)] *n* [wood] madera *f* (de construcción); [trees] árboles *mpl*; **(piece of) timber** viga *f*

time [taɪm] **1.** *n* **a)** tiempo *m*; **all the time** todo el tiempo; **I haven't seen him for a long time** hace mucho (tiempo) que no lo veo; **for the time being** por el momento; **in a short time** en poco tiempo; **in no time** en un abrir y cerrar de ojos; **in time** a tiempo; **in three weeks' time** dentro de tres semanas; **to take one's time over sth** hacer algo con calma; **time bomb** bomba *f* de relojería; **time limit** límite *m* de tiempo; [for payment etc] plazo *m*; **time waster** vago(a) *m,f*; '**no time wasters please'** 'por favor, abstenerse curiosos'; **time zone** huso horario
b) [era] época *f*, tiempos *mpl*; **to be behind the times** tener ideas anticuadas
c) [point in time] momento *m*; **at that time** (en aquel) entonces; **at the same time** al mismo tiempo; **at times** a veces; **from time to time** de vez en cuando
d) [time of day] hora *f*; **on time** puntualmente; **what's the time?** ¿qué hora es?
e) **time of year** época *f* del año
f) **to have a good/bad time** pasarlo bien/mal
g) [occasion] vez *f*; **four at a time** cuatro a la vez; **next time** la próxima vez; **time after time** una y otra vez
h) [in multiplication] **three times four** tres (multiplicado) por cuatro; **four times as big** cuatro veces más grande
i) *MUS* compás *m*; **in time** al compás
2. *vt* **a)** [speech] calcular la duración de; *SPORT* [race] cronometrar
b) [choose the time of] escoger el momento oportuno para

timeline ['taɪmlaɪn] *n* línea *f* cronológica

timely ['taɪmlɪ] (*compar* **timelier**, *superl* **timeliest**) *adj* oportuno(a)

timer ['taɪmə(r)] *n* [device] temporizador *m*

timeshare *n* multipropiedad *f*

timespan ['taɪmspæn] *n* plazo *m*

timetable ['taɪmteɪbəl] *n* horario *m*

timid ['tɪmɪd] *adj* tímido(a)

timing ['taɪmɪŋ] *n* **a)** [timeliness] oportunidad *f*; [coordination] coordinación *f*; **your timing was wrong** no calculaste bien **b)** *SPORT* cronometraje *m*

tin [tɪn] **1.** *n* **a)** [metal] estaño *m*; **tin plate** hojalata *f* **b)** *esp Br* [container] lata *f*, *Am* tarro *m* **2.** *vt* enlatar; **tinned food** conservas *fpl*

tinfoil ['tɪnfɔɪl] *n* papel *m* de estaño

tinge [tɪndʒ] **1.** *n* tinte *m*, matiz *m* **2.** *vt* teñir

tingle ['tɪŋgəl] *vi* **my feet are tingling** siento un hormigueo en los pies

tinker ['tɪŋkə(r)] **1.** *n Pej* calderero(a) *mf* **2.** *vi* **stop tinkering with the radio** deja de toquetear la radio

tinkle ['tɪŋkəl] *vi* tintinear

tinsel ['tɪnsəl] *n* oropel *m*

tint [tɪnt] **1.** *n* tinte *m*, matiz *m* **2.** *vt* teñir; **to tint one's hair** teñirse el pelo

tiny ['taɪnɪ] (*compar* **tinier**, *superl* **tiniest**) *adj* pequeñito(a); **a tiny bit** un poquitín

tip¹ [tɪp] **1.** *n* [end] punta *f*; [of cigarette] colilla *f*; **it's on the tip of my tongue** lo tengo en la punta de la lengua **2.** *vt* poner cantera a; **tipped with steel** con punta de acero ∎ **tip off** *vt sep* [police] dar el chivatazo a ∎ **tip over 1.** *vt sep* volcar **2.** *vi* volcarse

tip² [tɪp] **1.** *n* **a)** [gratuity] propina *f* **b)** [advice] consejo *m* **c)** SPORT [racing] pronóstico *m* **2.** *vt* **a)** dar una propina a **b)** SPORT pronosticar

tip³ [tɪp] **1.** *n Br* **rubbish tip** vertedero *m* **2.** *vt* inclinar; *Br* [rubbish] verter **3.** *vi* **to tip (up)** ladearse; [cart] bascular

tipsy ['tɪpsɪ] (*compar* **tipsier**, *superl* **tipsiest**) *adj* contentillo(a)

tiptoe ['tɪptəʊ] **1.** *vi* caminar *or Esp* andar de puntillas; **to tiptoe in/out** entrar/salir de puntillas **2.** *n* **on tiptoe** de puntillas

tire¹ [taɪə(r)] *US n* = **tyre**

tire² [taɪə(r)] **1.** *vt* cansar; **to tire sb out** agotar a algn **2.** *vi* cansarse; **to tire of doing sth** cansarse de hacer algo

tired ['taɪəd] *adj* cansado(a); **tired out** rendido(a); **to be tired** estar cansado(a); **to be tired of sth** estar harto(a) de algo

tiredness ['taɪədnɪs] *n* [fatigue] cansancio *m*, fatiga *f*

tireless ['taɪəlɪs] *adj* incansable

tiresome ['taɪəsəm] *adj* pesado(a)

tiring ['taɪərɪŋ] *adj* agotador(a)

tissue ['tɪʃuː, 'tɪsjuː] *n* **a)** BIOL tejido *m* **b)** TEXT tisú *m*; **tissue paper** papel *m* de seda **c)** [handkerchief] pañuelo *m* de papel, kleenex® *m*

titbit ['tɪtbɪt] *n* tentempié *m*, refrigerio *m*

title ['taɪtəl] *n* **a)** título *m*; CIN **credit titles** ficha técnica; **title page** portada *f*; **title role** papel *m* principal **b)** JUR título *m*

titter ['tɪtə(r)] **1.** *vi* reírse nerviosamente; [foolishly] reírse tontamente **2.** *n* risa ahogada; [foolish] risilla tonta

Tks MESSAGING (*abbr of* **thanks**) asias

TMB MESSAGING *written abbr of* **text me back**

to [tuː] (*unstressed before vowels* [tʊ], *before consonants* [tə]) **1.** *prep* **a)** [with place] a; [expressing direction] hacia; **he went to France/Japan** fue a Francia/Japón; **I'm going to Mary's** voy a casa de Mary; **it is 30 miles to London** Londres está a 30 millas; **the train to Madrid** el tren de Madrid; **to the east** hacia el este; **to the right** a la derecha

b) [time] a; **from two to four** de dos a cuatro; *Br* **it's ten to (six)** son (las seis) menos diez, *Am salvo RP* faltan diez (para las seis)

c) [as far as] hasta; **accurate to a millimetre** exacto(a) hasta el milímetro

d) [with indirect object] **he gave it to his cousin** se lo dio a su primo

e) [towards a person] **he was very kind to me** se portó muy bien conmigo

f) [of] de; **adviser to the president** consejero *m* del presidente

g) **to come to sb's assistance** acudir en ayuda de algn; **to everyone's surprise** para sorpresa de todos

h) **to the best of my knowledge** que yo sepa

i) [compared to] **that's nothing to what I've seen** eso no es nada en comparación con lo que he visto yo

j) [in proportion] **one house to the square kilometre** una casa por kilómetro cuadrado; **six votes to four** seis votos contra cuatro

2. *with infin* **a)** (*with simple infinitives* **to** *is not translated but is shown by the verb endings*) **to buy** comprar; **to come** venir

b) [in order to] para; [with verbs of motion or purpose] a, por; **he did it to help me** lo hizo para ayudarme; **he stopped to talk** se detuvo a hablar

c) *various verbs followed by dependent infinitives take particular prepositions* **a, de, en, por, con, para** *etc and others take no preposition; see the entry of the verb in question*

d) (*with adj and infin*) a, de; **difficult to do** difícil de hacer; **too hot to drink** demasiado caliente para bebérselo

e) [with noun and infin] **the first to complain** el primero en quejarse; **to have a great deal to do** tener mucho que hacer

f) [with verbs of ordering, wishing etc] **he asked me to do it** me pidió que lo hiciera

g) [replacing infin] **go if you want to** váyase si quiere

3. *adv* **to go to and fro** ir y venir; **to push the door to** encajar la puerta

toad [təʊd] *n* sapo *m*

toadstool ['təʊdstuːl] *n Esp* seta *f* venenosa, *Am* hongo *m* (venenoso)

toast¹ [təʊst] **1.** *n* CULIN pan tostado; **a slice of toast** una tostada **2.** *vt* CULIN tostar

toast² [təʊst] **1.** *n* [drink] brindis *m* inv; **to drink a toast to** brindar por **2.** *vt* brindar por

toaster ['təʊstə(r)] *n* tostador *m* (de pan)

toastie ['təʊstɪ] *n Fam* sándwich *m* caliente

toasty ['təʊstɪ] *Fam* **1.** *adj US* [warm] **it's toasty in here** se está calentito aquí **2.** *n* [sandwich] = **toastie**

tobacco [təˈbækəʊ] *n* tabaco *m*

tobacconist [təˈbækənɪst] *n Br* estanquero(a) *m,f*; *Br* **tobacconist's (shop)** estanco *m*, *CSur* quiosco *m*, *Méx* estanquillo *m*

toboggan [təˈbɒgən] *n* tobogán *m*

today [təˈdeɪ] **1.** *n* hoy *m* **2.** *adv* hoy; [nowadays] hoy en día; **a week today** justo dentro de una semana

toddler ['tɒdlə(r)] *n* niño(a) *m,f* que empieza a andar; **the toddlers** los pequeñitos

to-do *adj* **to-do list** lista *f* de tareas

toe [təʊ] **1.** *n* dedo *m* del pie; **big toe** dedo gordo **2.** *vt* **to toe the line** conformarse

TOEFL ['təʊfl] *n* (*abbr of* Test of English as a Foreign Language) *examen de inglés reconocido internacionalmente por instituciones oficiales y centros educativos*

toffee ['tɒfɪ] *n* caramelo *m*

together [təˈgeðə(r)] *adv* junto, juntos(as); **all together** todos juntos; **together with** junto con; **to bring together** reunir

toggle *n* **toggle switch** ELEC conmutador *m* de palanca; COMPUT tecla *f* de cambio de modo

toil [tɔɪl] **1.** *n* trabajo duro **2.** *vi* afanarse, trabajar (duro); **to toil up a hill** subir penosamente una cuesta

toilet ['tɔɪlɪt] *n* **a)** *Br* [in house] cuarto *m* de baño, retrete *m*; [in public place] aseos *mpl*, servicio(s) *m(pl)*, *CSur* toilette *f*; **toilet facilities** aseos *mpl*, servicio(s) *m(pl)*, *CSur* toilette *f*; **toilet paper** *or* **tissue** papel higiénico; **toilet roll** rollo *m* de papel higiénico **b)** [washing etc] aseo *m* (personal); **toilet bag** neceser *m*; **toilet soap** jabón *m* de tocador

toiletries ['tɔɪlɪtrɪz] *npl* artículos *mpl* de aseo

token ['təʊkən] **1.** *n* **a)** [sign] señal *f*; **as a token of respect** en señal de respeto **b)** COMM vale *m*; **book token** vale para comprar libros **2.** *adj* simbólico(a)

told [təʊld] *pt & pp of* **tell**

tolerable ['tɒlərəbəl] *adj* tolerable

tolerance ['tɒlərəns] *n* tolerancia *f*

tolerant ['tɒlərənt] *adj* tolerante

tolerate ['tɒləreɪt] *vt* tolerar

toll¹ [təʊl] **1.** *vt* tocar **2.** *vi* doblar

toll² [təʊl] n a) [charge] peaje m, Méx cuota f b) [loss] pérdidas fpl; **the death toll** el número de víctimas mortales

tomato [tə'mɑːtəʊ, US tə'meɪtəʊ] (pl **tomatoes**) n tomate m, Méx jitomate m

tomb [tuːm] n tumba f, sepulcro m

tombstone ['tuːmstəʊn] n lápida f sepulcral

tomorrow [tə'mɒrəʊ] **1.** n mañana m; **the day after tomorrow** pasado mañana; **tomorrow night** mañana por la noche **2.** adv mañana; **see you tomorrow!** ¡hasta mañana!; **tomorrow week** dentro de ocho días a partir de mañana

ton [tʌn] n tonelada f; Fam **tons of** montones de

tone [təʊn] **1.** n tono m **2.** vi **to tone (in) with sth** armonizar con algo ■ **tone down** vt sep atenuar

tongs [tɒŋz] npl [for sugar, hair] tenacillas fpl; **(fire) tongs** tenazas fpl

tongue [tʌŋ] n a) lengua f; Fig **to say sth tongue in cheek** decir algo con la boca pequeña; Fig **tongue twister** trabalenguas m inv b) [of shoe] lengüeta f; [of bell] badajo m

tonic ['tɒnɪk] **1.** n a) MED tónico m b) [drink] tónica f **2.** adj tónico(a)

tonight [tə'naɪt] adv & n esta noche

tonne [tʌn] n = **ton**

tonsil ['tɒnsəl] n amígdala f; **to have one's tonsils out** ser operado(a) de las amígdalas

tonsillitis [tɒnsɪ'laɪtɪs] n amigdalitis f

too [tuː] adv a) [besides] además b) [also] también c) [excessively] demasiado; **too much money** demasiado dinero; **£10 too much** 10 libras de más; **too frequently** con demasiada frecuencia; **too old** demasiado viejo

took [tʊk] pt of **take**

tool [tuːl] n [utensil] herramienta f; **tool box** caja f de herramientas

tooth [tuːθ] (pl **teeth**) n a) diente m; [molar] muela f; Fig **to fight tooth and nail** luchar a brazo partido b) [of saw] diente m; [of comb] púa f

toothache ['tuːθeɪk] n dolor m de muelas

toothbrush ['tuːθbrʌʃ] n cepillo m de dientes

toothpaste ['tuːθpeɪst] n pasta dentífrica

top¹ [tɒp] **1.** n a) [upper part] parte f de arriba; [of hill] cumbre f, cima f; [of tree] copa f; **from top to bottom** de arriba abajo; **on top of** encima de; Fig **on top of it all ...** para colmo ...; **top copy** original m; **top hat** sombrero m de copa b) [surface] superficie f c) [of list etc] cabeza f d) [of bottle etc] tapa f, tapón m e) [garment] camiseta f f) [best] lo mejor **2.** adj a) [part] superior, de arriba; **the top floor** el último piso b) [highest] más alto(a); Br AUTO **top gear** directa f c) [best] mejor **3.** vt a) [place on top of] coronar; Fig **and to top it all** y para colmo b) THEAT **to top the bill** encabezar el reparto ■ **top up**, US **top off** vt sep [glass] rellenar; [mobile] recargar; **to top up the petrol tank** llenar el depósito

top² [tɒp] n [toy] peonza f

topic ['tɒpɪk] n tema m

topical ['tɒpɪkəl] adj de actualidad

topple ['tɒpəl] **1.** vi [building] venirse abajo; **to topple (over)** volcarse **2.** vt volcar; Fig [government] derrocar

top-quality adj de calidad superior

top-secret ['tɒp'siːkrɪt] adj de alto secreto

topsy-turvy ['tɒpsɪ'tɜːvɪ] adj & adv al revés; [in confusion] en desorden, patas arriba

top-up n **top-up card** tarjeta f de recarga

torch [tɔːtʃ] n Br [electric] linterna f

tore [tɔː(r)] pt of **tear**

torment 1. [tɔː'ment] vt atormentar **2.** ['tɔːment] n tormento m, suplicio m

torn [tɔːn] pp of **tear**

tornado [tɔː'neɪdəʊ] n tornado m

torpedo [tɔː'piːdəʊ] n torpedo m

torrent ['tɒrənt] n torrente m

tortoise ['tɔːtəs] n tortuga f (de tierra)

tortuous ['tɔːtjʊəs] adj [path] tortuoso(a); [explanation] enrevesado(a)

torture ['tɔːtʃə(r)] **1.** vt torturar; Fig atormentar **2.** n tortura f; Fig tormento m

Tory ['tɔːrɪ] adj & n Br POL conservador(a) (m,f)

toss [tɒs] **1.** vt a) [ball] tirar; **to toss a coin** echar a cara o cruz, Méx echar a águila o sol, RP echar a cara o seca **b)** [throw about] sacudir
2. vi a) **to toss about** agitarse; **to toss and turn** dar vueltas en la cama **b)** SPORT **to toss (up)** sortear
3. n a) [of ball] lanzamiento m; [of coin] sorteo m (a cara o cruz) **b)** [of head] sacudida f

tot¹ [tɒt] n a) **(tiny) tot** [child] nene(a) m,f **b)** [of whisky etc] trago m

tot² [tɒt] vt Br **to tot up** sumar

total ['təʊtəl] **1.** n total m; [in bill] importe m; **grand total** suma f total
2. adj total
3. vt sumar
4. vi **to total up to** ascender a

totally ['təʊtəlɪ] adv totalmente

totter ['tɒtə(r)] vi tambalearse

touch [tʌtʃ] **1.** vt a) tocar; Fig **to touch on a subject** tocar un tema **b)** [equal] igualar **c)** [move] conmover
2. vi tocarse
3. n a) toque m **b)** [sense of touch] tacto m **c)** [contact] contacto m; **to be /get / keep in touch with sb** estar /ponerse /mantenerse en contacto con algn **d)** [small amount] pizca f
■ **touch down** vi [plane] aterrizar
■ **touch off** vt sep desencadenar
■ **touch up** vt sep [picture] retocar

touchdown ['tʌtʃdaʊn] n a) [of plane] aterrizaje m; [of space capsule] amerizaje m **b)** [in American football] ensayo m

touched [tʌtʃt] adj a) [moved] emocionado(a) **b)** Fam [crazy] Esp tocado(a) del ala, Am zafado(a)

touching ['tʌtʃɪŋ] adj conmovedor(a)

touchpad ['tʌtʃpæd] n panel m táctil; **touchpad mouse** ratón m táctil

touch-sensitive adj táctil

touchy ['tʌtʃɪ] (compar **touchier**, superl **touchiest**) adj Fam [person] susceptible; [subject] delicado(a)

tough [tʌf] **1.** adj [material, competitor etc] fuerte, resistente; [test, criminal, meat] duro(a); [punishment] severo(a); [problem] difícil **2.** n [person] matón m

toughen ['tʌfən] vt endurecer

toupee ['tuːpeɪ] n tupé m

tour [tʊə(r)] **1.** n a) [journey] viaje m; **audio tour** audioguía f; **package tour** viaje organizado; **tour guide** [person] guía mf **b)** [of monument etc] visita f; [of city] recorrido turístico **c)** SPORT & THEAT gira f; **on tour** de gira **2.** vt a) [country] viajar por **b)** [building] visitar **c)** THEAT estar de gira en **3.** vi estar de viaje

tourism ['tʊərɪzəm] n turismo m

tourist ['tʊərɪst] n turista mf; **tourist attraction** atracción f turística; **tourist centre** centro m de información turística; AVIAT **tourist class** clase f turista

tournament ['tʊənəmənt] n torneo m

tout [taʊt] **1.** vt COMM tratar de vender; Br [tickets] revender **2.** vi salir a la caza y captura de compradores **3.** n COMM gancho m

tow [təʊ] **1.** n **to take a car in tow** remolcar un coche; US **tow truck** grúa f **2.** vt remolcar

towards [tə'wɔːdz, tɔːdz] prep a) [direction, time] hacia **b)** [with regard to] hacia, (para) con; **our duty towards others** nuestro deber para con los demás; **what is your attitude towards religion?** ¿cuál es su actitud respecto a la religión?

towel ['taʊəl] **1.** *n* toalla *f*; **hand towel** toallita *f*; **towel** Br**rail** *or* US**bar** toallero *m* **2.** *vt* **to towel dry** secar con una toalla

tower ['taʊə(r)] **1.** *n* torre *f* **2.** *vi* **to tower over** *or* **above sth** dominar algo

town [taʊn] *n* ciudad *f*; [small] pueblo *m*; **to go into town** ir al centro; *Fam* **to go to town** tirar la casa por la ventana; *Br* **town council** ayuntamiento *m*; **town councillor** concejal(a) *m,f*; **town hall** ayuntamiento *m*; **town house** casa *f* adosada (*urbana*); **town planning** urbanismo *m*

toxic ['tɒksɪk] *adj* tóxico(a); **toxic waste** residuos *mpl* tóxicos

toy [tɔɪ] **1.** *n* juguete *m* **2.** *vi* **to toy with an idea** acariciar una idea; **to toy with one's food** comer sin gana

T+ MESSAGING *written abbr of* **think positive**

trace [treɪs] **1.** *n* **a)** [sign] indicio *m*, vestigio *m* **b)** [tracks] huella(s) *f(pl)* **2.** *vt* **a)** [drawing] calcar **b)** [plan] bosquejar **c)** [locate] seguir la pista de

tracing ['treɪsɪŋ] *n* **tracing paper** papel *m* de calco

track [træk] **1.** *n* **a)** [trail] huellas *fpl*, pista *f*; **to keep / lose track of sb** no perder / perder de vista a algn
b) [pathway] camino *m*; **to be on the right / wrong track** ir por el buen / mal camino
c) SPORT pista *f*; [for motor racing] circuito *m*; *Fig* **track record** historial *m*
d) RAIL vía *f*; *Fig* **he has a one-track mind** tiene una única obsesión
e) [on record, CD] canción *f*
f) US SCH *cada una de las divisiones del alumnado en grupos por niveles de aptitud*
2. *vt* seguir la pista de; [with radar] seguir la trayectoria de
■ **track down** *vt sep* [locate] localizar

tracksuit ['træksuːt] *n Esp* chándal *m*, *Méx* pants *m*, *RP* jogging *m*

tractor ['træktə(r)] *n* tractor *m*

trade [treɪd] **1.** *n* **a)** [profession] oficio *m*; **by trade** de oficio
b) COMM comercio *m*; **fair trade** comercio *m* justo; **trade name** nombre *m* comercial; **trade union** sindicato *m*; **trade unionist** sindicalista *mf*; **it's good for trade** es bueno para los negocios; **the building trade** (la industria de) la construcción
2. *vi* comerciar (**in** en)
3. *vt* **to trade sth for sth** trocar algo por algo
■ **trade in** *vt sep* dar como entrada

trademark ['treɪdmɑːk] *n* marca *f* (de fábrica); **registered trademark** marca registrada

trader ['treɪdə(r)] *n* comerciante *mf*

tradesman ['treɪdzmən] *n* [shopkeeper] tendero *m*

trading ['treɪdɪŋ] *n* comercio *m*; *Br* **trading estate** polígono *m* industrial; **trading hours** horario *fpl* comercial

tradition [trə'dɪʃən] *n* tradición *f*

traditional [trə'dɪʃənəl] *adj* tradicional

traffic ['træfɪk] **1.** *n* **a)** tráfico *m*, circulación *f*; US **traffic circle** rotonda *f*; **traffic island** isleta *f*; **traffic jam** atasco *m*; **traffic lights** semáforo *m*; *Br* **traffic warden** ≃ guardia *mf* urbano(a)
b) [trade] tráfico *m* **2.** (*pt & pp* **trafficked**) *vi* **to traffic in drugs** traficar con droga

trafficker ['træfɪkə(r)] *n* traficante *mf*

trafficking ['træfɪkɪŋ] *n* tráfico *m*; **human trafficking** tráfico de seres humanos

tragedy ['trædʒɪdɪ] *n* tragedia *f*

tragic ['trædʒɪk] *adj* trágico(a)

trail [treɪl] **1.** *vt* **a)** [drag] arrastrar **b)** [follow] rastrear **2.** *vi* **a)** [drag] arrastrarse **b)** **to trail behind** rezagarse **3.** *n* **a)** [track] pista *f*, rastro *m* **b)** [path] senda *f*, camino *m* **c)** [of smoke] estela *f*

trailer ['treɪlə(r)] *n* **a)** AUTO remolque *m* **b)** US AUTO [caravan] caravana *f* **c)** CIN trailer *m*, avance *m*

train [treɪn] **1.** *n* **a)** RAIL tren *m*; **train station** estación *f* de tren; **boat train** tren *que enlaza con un barco* **b)** [of vehicles] convoy *m*; [of followers] séquito *m*; [of events] serie *f* **c)** [of dress] cola *f* **2.** *vt* **a)** [teach] formar; SPORT entrenar; [animal] amaestrar; [voice etc] educar **b)** [gun] apuntar (**on** a); [camera] enfocar (**on** a) **3.** *vi* prepararse; SPORT entrenarse

trainee [treɪˈniː] *n* aprendiz(a) *m,f*

trainer [ˈtreɪnə(r)] *n* **a)** SPORT entrenador(a) *m,f*; [of dogs] amaestrador(a) *m,f*; [of lions] domador(a) *m,f* **b)** Br **trainers** [shoes] zapatillas *fpl* de deporte

training [ˈtreɪnɪŋ] *n* [instruction] formación *f*; SPORT entrenamiento *m*; [of animals] amaestramiento *m*; [of lions] doma *f*; **training course** curso *m* or cursillo *m* de formación; **to go into training** empezar el entrenamiento; **vocational training** formación profesional

trait [treɪt] *n* rasgo *m*

traitor [ˈtreɪtə(r)] *n* traidor(a) *m,f*

tram [træm], **tramcar** [ˈtræmkɑː(r)] *n* Br tranvía *m*

tramp [træmp] **1.** *vi* **a)** [travel on foot] caminar **b)** [walk heavily] andar con pasos pesados **2.** *n* [person] vagabundo(a) *m,f*; *Pej* **she's a tramp** es una fulana or Méx reventada

trample [ˈtræmpəl] *vt* **to trample down the grass** pisotear la hierba; **to trample sth underfoot** pisotear algo

trampoline [ˈtræmpəliːn] *n* cama elástica

trance [trɑːns] *n* trance *m*

tranquillizer [ˈtræŋkwɪlaɪzə(r)] *n* tranquilizante *m*

transaction [trænˈzækʃən] *n* [procedure] tramitación *f*; [deal] transacción *f*

transatlantic [trænzətˈlæntɪk] *adj* transatlántico(a)

transcend [trænˈsend] *vt* trascender

transcript [ˈtrænskrɪpt] *n* **a)** transcripción *f* **b)** US SCH expediente *m*

transfer 1. [trænsˈfɜː(r)] *vt* trasladar; [funds] trasferir; JUR ceder; FTBL traspasar; US RAIL hacer transbordo

2. [ˈtrænsfɜː(r)] *n* **a)** traslado *m*; [of funds] trasferencia *f*; JUR cesión *f*; FTBL traspaso *m* **b)** [picture, design] calcomanía *f* **c)** US RAIL transbordo *m*

transform [trænsˈfɔːm] *vt* trasformar

transformation [trænsfəˈmeɪʃən] *n* trasformación *f*

transformer [trænsˈfɔːmə(r)] *n* ELEC transformador *m*

transfusion [trænsˈfjuːʒən] *n* MED transfusión *f* (de sangre)

transit [ˈtrænzɪt] *n* tránsito *m*; **in transit** de tránsito

transition [trænˈzɪʃən] *n* transición *f*

transitive [ˈtrænzɪtɪv] *adj* transitivo(a)

translate [trænsˈleɪt] *vt* traducir

translation [trænsˈleɪʃən] *n* traducción *f*

translator [trænsˈleɪtə(r)] *n* traductor(a) *m,f*

transmission [trænzˈmɪʃən] *n* transmisión *f*

transmit [trænzˈmɪt] *vt* transmitir

transmitter [trænzˈmɪtə(r)] *n* RADIO [set] transmisor *m*; RADIO & TV [station] emisora *f*

transparent [trænsˈpærənt] *adj* transparente

transpire [trænˈspaɪə(r)] *vi* [happen] ocurrir; **it transpired that ...** ocurrió que ...

transplant 1. [trænsˈplɑːnt] *vt* trasplantar **2.** [ˈtrænsplɑːnt] *n* trasplante *m*

transport 1. [trænsˈpɔːt] *vt* transportar **2.** [ˈtrænspɔːt] *n* transporte *m*; **transport aircraft/ship** avión *m* / buque *m* de transporte; Br **transport café** bar *m* de carretera

transvestite [trænzˈvestaɪt] *n* Fam travestido(a) *m,f*, Esp travestí *mf*

trap [træp] **1.** *n* trampa *f*; **trap door** trampilla *f*; THEAT escotillón *m* **2.** *vt* atrapar

trash [træʃ] *n* [inferior goods] bazofia *f*; US [rubbish] basura *f*; *Fig* **to talk a lot of trash** decir tonterías; US **trash can** cubo *m* de la basura; US **trash collector** basurero(a) *m,f*

trashed [træʃt] *adj US Fam* [drunk] pedo (*inv*); **to get trashed** ponerse pedo

trashy ['træʃɪ] (*compar* **trashier**, *superl* **trashiest**) *adj Fam* de pacotilla, *Esp* cutre, *Méx* gacho(a)

traumatic [trɔː'mætɪk] *adj* traumático(a)

travel ['trævəl] **1.** *vi* a) viajar; **to travel through** recorrer b) [vehicle, electric current] ir; *Fig* [news] propagarse **2.** *vt* recorrer **3.** *n* viajar m; **travel agency** agencia f de viajes; **travel documents** documentación f para el viaje

traveller, *US* **traveler** ['trævələ(r)] *n* viajero(a) m,f; **traveller's** *Br* **cheque** or *US* **check** cheque m de viaje

travelling, *US* **traveling** ['trævəlɪŋ] **1.** *adj* [salesman] ambulante **2.** *n* viajes *mpl*, (el) viajar m; **I'm fond of travelling** me gusta viajar; **travelling expenses** gastos *mpl* de viaje

travel-size(d) *adj* [shampoo etc] de viaje

travesty ['trævɪstɪ] *n* parodia f burda

tray [treɪ] *n* [for food] bandeja f; [for letters] cesta f (*para la correspondencia*)

treacherous ['tretʃərəs] *adj* a) [person] traidor(a); [action] traicionero(a) b) [dangerous] peligroso(a)

treachery ['tretʃərɪ] *n* traición f

treacle ['triːkəl] *n Br* melaza f

tread [tred] (*pt* **trod**, *pp* **trod** or **trodden**) **1.** *vi* pisar; **to tread on** pisar **2.** *vt* a) [step on] pisar b) **to tread water** mantenerse a flote verticalmente **3.** *n* a) [step] paso m; [sound] ruido m de pasos b) [of tyre] banda f de rodadura

treadmill ['tredmɪl] *n* a) [fitness] tapiz m rodante, cinta f de footing b) *Fig* [dull routine] rutina f

treason ['triːzən] *n* traición f

treasure ['treʒə(r)] **1.** *n* tesoro m **2.** *vt* [keep] guardar como oro en paño; [value] apreciar muchísimo

treasurer ['treʒərə(r)] *n* tesorero(a) m,f

treat [triːt] **1.** *n* a) [present] regalo m b) [pleasure] placer m **2.** *vt* a) tratar; **to**

treat badly maltratar b) [regard] considerar c) **he treated them to dinner** les invitó a cenar

treatment ['triːtmənt] *n* a) [of person] trato m b) [of subject, of patient] tratamiento m

treaty ['triːtɪ] *n* tratado m

treble ['trebəl] **1.** *adj* a) [triple] triple b) MUS **treble clef** clave f de sol; **treble voice** voz f triple **2.** *vt* triplicar **3.** *vi* triplicarse

tree [triː] *n* a) [plant] árbol m; **apple / cherry tree** manzano m / cerezo m b) COMPUT árbol m, arborescencia f

trek [trek] **1.** *n* [journey] viaje m (largo y difícil); *Fam* [walk] caminata f **2.** *vi* hacer un viaje largo y difícil; *Fam* [walk] ir caminando

trekking ['trekɪŋ] *n* senderismo m

tremble ['trembəl] *vi* temblar, estremecerse

tremendous [trɪ'mendəs] *adj* [huge] enorme; [success] arrollador(a); [shock etc] tremendo(a); *Fam* [marvellous] estupendo(a)

trench [trentʃ] *n* a) [ditch] zanja f; MIL trinchera f b) **trench coat** trinchera f

trend [trend] **1.** *n* [tendency] tendencia f; [fashion] moda f **2.** *vi* tender (**to** or **towards** hacia)

trendy ['trendɪ] (*compar* **trendier**, *superl* **trendiest**) *adj Fam* [person] modernillo(a) m,f, *RP* modernoso(a) m,f; [clothes] a la última

trespass ['trespəs] *vi* entrar sin autorización

trial ['traɪəl] *n* a) JUR proceso m, juicio m b) [test] prueba f; **on trial** a prueba; **by trial and error** a fuerza de equivocarse c) **trials** [competition] concurso m d) **trials** [suffering] sufrimiento m; **trials and tribulations** tribulaciones *fpl*

triangle ['traɪæŋgəl] *n* triángulo m

triangular [traɪ'æŋgjʊlə(r)] *adj* triangular

tribe [traɪb] *n* tribu f

tribunal [traɪ'bjuːnəl] *n* tribunal m

tribute ['trɪbjuːt] *n* **a)** [payment] tributo *m* **b)** [mark of respect] homenaje *m*; **to pay tribute to** rendir homenaje a

trick [trɪk] **1.** *n* **a)** [ruse] ardid *m*; [dishonest] engaño *m*; [in question] trampa *f*
b) [practical joke] broma *f*; **to play a trick on sb** gastarle una broma a algn; [malicious] jugar una mala pasada a algn
c) [of magic, knack] truco *m*
d) CARDS baza *f*
2. *vt* engañar; **to trick sb out of sth** quitar *or Am* sacarle algo a algn a base de engaños

trickle ['trɪkəl] **1.** *vi* discurrir; [water] gotear **2.** *n* hilo *m*

tricky ['trɪkɪ] *(compar* **trickier**, *super* **trickiest)** *adj* [person] astuto(a); [situation, mechanism] delicado(a)

tricycle ['traɪsɪkəl] *n* triciclo *m*

trifle ['traɪfəl] **1.** *n* **a)** [insignificant thing] bagatela *f* **b)** Br CULIN *postre de bizcocho, gelatina, frutas y (Esp) nata or (Am) crema de leche* **2.** *vi* **to trifle with** tomar a la ligera

trifling ['traɪflɪŋ] *adj* insignificante, trivial

trigger ['trɪɡə(r)] **1.** *n* [of gun] gatillo *m*; [of mechanism] disparador *m* **2.** *vt* **to trigger (off)** desencadenar

trilogy ['trɪlədʒɪ] *n* trilogía *f*

trim [trɪm] **1.** *(compar* **trimmer**, *super* **trimmest)** *adj* [neat] aseado(a) **2.** *vt* **a)** [cut] recortar; *Fig* [expenses] disminuir
b) [decorate] adornar **3.** *n* **a)** [condition] estado *m*; NAUT asiento *m* **b)** [cut] recorte *m*

trinket ['trɪŋkɪt] *n* baratija *f*

trio ['triːəʊ] *n* trío *m*

trip [trɪp] **1.** *n* **a)** [journey] viaje *m*; [excursion] excursión *f*; **to go on a trip** ir de excursión
b) *Fam* **to be on a trip** [on drugs] estar colocado(a)
2. *vi* **a) to trip (up)** [stumble] tropezar (**over** con); *Fig* [err] equivocarse
b) to trip along ir con paso ligero

3. *vt* **to trip sb (up)** poner la zancadilla a algn; *Fig* coger *or* pillar a algn

triple ['trɪpəl] **1.** *adj* triple **2.** *vt* triplicar **3.** *vi* triplicarse

triplet ['trɪplɪt] *n* trillizo(a) *m,f*

triplicate ['trɪplɪkɪt] *adj* **in triplicate** por triplicado

tripod ['traɪpɒd] *n* trípode *m*

triumph ['traɪəmf] **1.** *n* triunfo *m* **2.** *vi* triunfar

triumphant [traɪˈʌmfənt] *adj* triunfante

trivial ['trɪvɪəl] *adj* trivial, banal

trod [trɒd] *pt & pp of* **tread**

trodden ['trɒdən] *pp of* **tread**

trolley ['trɒlɪ] *n Br* carro *m*; *Br* **trolley case** maleta *f* con ruedas

trombone [trɒmˈbəʊn] *n* trombón *m*

troop [truːp] **1.** *n* **a)** [of people] grupo *m*
b) MIL **troops** tropas *fpl* **2.** *vi* **to troop in/out/off** entrar/salir/marcharse en tropel

trooper ['truːpə(r)] *n* **a)** [soldier] soldado *m (de caballería o división acorazada)*
b) *US* [policeman] policía *mf*

trophy ['trəʊfɪ] *n* trofeo *m*

tropic ['trɒpɪk] *n* trópico *m*

tropical ['trɒpɪkəl] *adj* tropical

trot [trɒt] **1.** *vi* trotar **2.** *n* trote *m*; **to go at a trot** ir al trote; *Br Fam* **on the trot** [in succession] seguidos(as)

trouble ['trʌbəl] **1.** *n* **a)** [misfortune] desgracia *f*
b) [problems] problemas *mpl*; **to be in trouble** estar en un lío; **to cause sb trouble** ocasionar problemas a algn; **to get sb out of trouble** sacar a algn de un apuro; **the trouble is that ...** lo que pasa es que ...
c) [effort] esfuerzo *m*; **it's no trouble** no es ninguna molestia; **it's not worth the trouble** no merece la pena; **to take the trouble to do sth** molestarse en hacer algo
d) [conflict] conflicto *m*
e) MED enfermedad *f*; **to have liver trouble** tener problemas de hígado

2. *vt* **a)** [affect] afligir; [worry] preocupar; **that doesn't trouble him at all** eso le tiene sin cuidado
b) [bother] molestar
3. *vi* molestarse

troublemaker ['trʌbəlmeɪkə(r)] *n* alborotador(a) *m,f*

troublesome ['trʌbəlsəm] *adj* molesto(a)

trough [trɒf] *n* **a)** **(drinking) trough** abrevadero *m*; **(feeding) trough** pesebre *m* **b)** [of wave] seno *m* **c)** GEOG & MET depresión *f*

trousers ['traʊzəz] *npl* pantalón *m*, pantalones *mpl*; **combat trousers** pantalones *mpl* de camuflaje

trout [traʊt] *n* trucha *f*

trowel ['traʊəl] *n* **a)** [builder's] palustre *m* **b)** [for gardening] desplantador *m*

truant ['truːənt] *n Br* **to play truant** faltar a clase, *Esp* hacer novillos, *Méx* irse de pinta

truce [truːs] *n* tregua *f*

truck¹ [trʌk] *n* **a)** *Br* RAIL vagón *m* **b)** AUTO camión *m*; **truck driver** camionero(a) *m,f*, *CAm*, *Méx* trailero(a) *m,f*

truck² [trʌk] *n* **a)** **to have no truck with** no estar dispuesto a tolerar **b)** *US* verduras *fpl*; **truck farm** huerta *f*; **truck farmer** hortelano(a) *m,f*; **truck farming** cultivo *m* de hortalizas

trucker ['trʌkə(r)] *n US* [lorry driver] camionero(a) *m,f*, *CAm*, *Méx* trailero(a) *m,f*

trudge [trʌdʒ] *vi* caminar con dificultad

true [truː] *(compar* **truer**, *superl* **truest)** *adj* **a)** verdadero(a); **it's true that ...** es verdad que ...; **to come true** cumplirse, hacerse realidad **b)** [faithful] fiel **c)** [aim] acertado(a)

truly ['truːlɪ] *adv* **a)** de verdad; **really and truly?** ¿de veras? **b)** [faithfully] fielmente; **yours truly** atentamente

trump [trʌmp] **1.** *n* CARDS triunfo *m* **2.** *vt* CARDS fallar

trumpet ['trʌmpɪt] *n* trompeta *f*

truncheon ['trʌntʃən] *n Br* porra *f* (de policía)

trunk [trʌŋk] *n* **a)** [of tree, body] tronco *m* **b)** [of elephant] trompa *f* **c)** [luggage] baúl *m* **d)** *Br* TEL **trunk call** llamada *for Am* llamado *m* de larga distancia, *Esp* conferencia *f*; **trunk road** carretera *f* principal **e)** *US* [of car] maletero *m*, *CAm*, *Méx* cajuela *f*, *RP* baúl *m*

trust [trʌst] **1.** *n* **a)** confianza *f*; **breach of trust** abuso *m* de confianza **b)** JUR fideicomiso *m* **c)** FIN trust *m* **2.** *vt* **a)** [hope] esperar **b)** [rely upon] fiarse de; **to trust sb with sth** confiar algo a algn **3.** *vi* confiar **(in** en)

trusted ['trʌstɪd] *adj* de fiar

trustworthy ['trʌstwɜːðɪ] *adj* [person] de confianza, *Am* confiable; [information] fidedigno(a), *Am* confiable

truth [truːθ] *n* verdad *f*; **to tell the truth** decir la verdad

truthful ['truːθfʊl] *adj* [person] veraz, sincero(a); [testimony] verídico(a)

try [traɪ] *(pt & pp* **tried)** **1.** *vt* **a)** [attempt] intentar; **to try to do sth** tratar de *or* intentar hacer algo
b) [test] probar, ensayar; **to try sb's patience** poner a prueba la paciencia de algn
c) JUR juzgar
2. *vi* intentar
3. *n* **a)** [attempt] tentativa *f*, intento *m*
b) SPORT ensayo *m*
■ **try on** *vt sep* [dress] probarse
■ **try out** *vt sep* probar

trying ['traɪɪŋ] *adj* [person] molesto(a), pesado(a); **to have a trying time** pasar un mal rato

T-shirt ['tiːʃɜːt] *n* camiseta *f*, *Méx* playera, *RP* remera *f*

T2Go MESSAGING *written abbr of* **time to go**

TTYL, TTYL8R MESSAGING *(abbr of* **talk to you later)** hl, ta luego

tub [tʌb] *n* **a)** [container] tina *f*, cuba *f* **b)** [bath] bañera *f*, *Am* tina *f*, *Am* bañadera *f*

tuba ['tjuːbə] *n* tuba *f*

turn

tube [tju:b] *n* a) tubo *m*; ANAT conducto *m*; [of bicycle] cámara *f* (de aire) b) *Br Fam* **the tube** [underground] el metro, *RP* el subte

tuberculosis [tjʊbɜːkjʊˈləʊsɪs] *n* tuberculosis *f*

tuck [tʌk] **1.** *vt* **to tuck sb in** arropar a algn; **to tuck one's shirt into one's trousers** meterse la camisa por dentro (de los pantalones) **2.** *n* SEWING pliegue *m* ▪ **tuck in** *vi Fam* devorar

Tuesday [ˈtjuːzdɪ] *n* martes *m*

tuft [tʌft] *n* [of hair] mechón *m*

tug [tʌg] **1.** *vt* [pull at] tirar de; [haul along] arrastrar; NAUT remolcar **2.** *n* a) [pull] tirón *m*; **tug of war** [game] lucha *f* de la cuerda; *Fig* lucha encarnizada b) NAUT remolcador *m*

tuition [tjuːˈɪʃən] *n* instrucción *f*; **private tuition** clases *fpl* particulares; **tuition fees** honorarios *mpl*

T2ul MESSAGING *(abbr of* **talk to you later***)* hl, ta luego

TUL MESSAGING *written abbr of* **tell you later**

tulip [ˈtjuːlɪp] *n* tulipán *m*

tumble [ˈtʌmbəl] **1.** *vi* [person] caerse; [acrobat] dar volteretas; [building] venirse abajo **2.** *vt* volcar **3.** *n* a) caída *f* b) **tumble dryer** secadora *f*

tumble-drier *n* secadora *f*

tumbler [ˈtʌmblə(r)] *n* vaso *m*

tummy [ˈtʌmɪ] *n Fam* barriga *f*, *Chile* guata *f*

tumour, US **tumor** [ˈtjuːmə(r)] *n* tumor *m*

tuna [ˈtjuːnə] *n* atún *m*, bonito *m*

tune [tjuːn] **1.** *n* a) [melody] melodía *f*; *Fig* **to change one's tune** cambiar de tono
b) MUS tono *m*; **in /out of tune** afinado /desafinado; **to sing out of tune** desafinar
2. *vt* MUS afinar
3. *vi* RADIO & TV **to tune in to a station** sintonizar una emisora
▪ **tune up** *vi* afinar los instrumentos

tuner [ˈtjuːnə(r)] *n* a) [of pianos] afinador(a) *m,f* b) RADIO & TV [knob] sintonizador *m*

Tunisia [tjuːˈnɪzɪə] *n* Túnez

tunnel [ˈtʌnəl] **1.** *n* túnel *m*; MINING galería *f* **2.** *vt* **to tunnel through** abrir un túnel a través de

turban [ˈtɜːbən] *n* turbante *m*

turbulent [ˈtɜːbjʊlənt] *adj* turbulento(a)

turf [tɜːf] *n* a) [grass] césped *m*; [peat] turba *f* b) *Br* **turf accountant** [in horse racing] corredor(a) *m,f* de apuestas ▪ **turf out** *vt sep Br Fam* **to turf sb out** poner a algn de patitas en la calle

Turk [tɜːk] *n* turco(a) *m,f*

turkey [ˈtɜːkɪ] *n* a) pavo *m*, *Méx* guajolote *m* b) *Slang* **cold turkey** mono *m*; **to go cold turkey** [stop taking drugs] dejar las drogas de golpe; [suffer withdrawal symptoms] tener el mono

Turkey [ˈtɜːkɪ] *n* Turquía

Turkish [ˈtɜːkɪʃ] **1.** *adj* turco(a) **2.** *n* [language] turco *m*

turmoil [ˈtɜːmɔɪl] *n* confusión *f*

turn [tɜːn] **1.** *vt* a) volver; [rotate] girar, hacer girar; **to turn sth inside out** volver algo del revés; **to turn a page** volver una hoja; **to turn one's head/gaze** volver la cabeza /mirada (**towards** hacia); **to turn the corner** doblar *or Am* voltear la esquina
b) [change] transformar (**into** en)
c) [on lathe] tornear
2. *vi* a) [rotate] girar
b) [turn round] volverse, dar la vuelta; **to turn to sb** volverse hacia algn; *Fig* [for help] acudir a algn; **to turn upside down** volcarse; *Fig* **to turn on sb** volverse contra algn
c) [become] volverse; **the milk has turned sour** la leche se ha cortado
3. *n* a) [of wheel] vuelta *f*; **done to a turn** [meat] en su punto
b) [change of direction] cambio *m* de dirección; [in road] curva *f*; **left /right turn** giro *m* a la izquierda /derecha; *US* AUTO **turn signal** intermitente *m*, *Col, Ecuad, Méx* direccional *m or f*
c) **to do sb a good turn** hacer un favor a algn

d) MED ataque *m*

e) [in game, queue] turno *m*, vez *f*; **it's your turn** te toca a ti; **to take turns (at doing sth),** *Br* **to take it in turns to do sth** turnarse para hacer algo

f) THEAT número *m*

g) turn of phrase giro *m*

■ **turn around** *vt sep* = **turn round**

■ **turn aside 1.** *vt sep* desviar **2.** *vi* desviarse

■ **turn away 1.** *vt sep* [person] rechazar **2.** *vi* volver la cabeza

■ **turn back 1.** *vt sep* [person] hacer retroceder; [clock] retrasar **2.** *vi* volverse

■ **turn down** *vt sep* **a)** [gas, radio etc] bajar **b)** [reject] rechazar **c)** [fold] doblar

■ **turn in** *Fam* **1.** *vt sep* [person] entregar a la policía **2.** *vi* acostarse

■ **turn off 1.** *vt insep* [road, path] salir de **2.** *vt sep* [electricity] desconectar; [radio, TV, engine, gas] apagar; [water] cerrar **3.** *vi* desviarse

■ **turn on 1.** *vt sep* **a)** [electricity, radio, TV] encender, *Am* prender; [tap, gas] abrir; [engine, machine] poner en marcha; **to turn the light on** encender la luz **b)** *Fam* [excite sexually] excitar; *Fam* **it turns me on** me excita **2.** *vt insep* [attack] volverse contra

■ **turn out 1.** *vt sep* **a)** [extinguish] apagar **b)** [eject] echar; [empty] vaciar **c)** [produce] producir **2.** *vi* **a)** [attend] asistir **b)** **it turns out that ...** resulta que ...; **things have turned out well** las cosas han salido bien

■ **turn over 1.** *vt sep* [turn upside down] poner al revés; [page] dar la vuelta a **2.** *vi* volverse

■ **turn round,** *US* **turn around 1.** *vt sep* **a)** [reverse] volver, dar la vuelta a **b)** [wheel, head] girar **2.** *vi* **a)** [rotate] girar, dar vueltas **b)** [person] darse la vuelta

■ **turn up 1.** *vt sep* **a)** [collar] levantar; **to turn up one's shirt sleeves** arremangarse; **turned-up nose** nariz respingona **b)** RADIO & TV subir **2.** *vi* **a)** *Fig*

something is sure to turn up algo saldrá **b)** [arrive] llegar, presentarse **c)** [attend] asistir

turned [tɜːnd] *adj* [milk] costado(a)

turning ['tɜːnɪŋ] *n* **a)** *Fig* **turning point** punto decisivo **b)** [in road] salida *f*

turnip ['tɜːnɪp] *n* nabo *m*

turnout ['tɜːnaʊt] *n* asistencia *f*

turnover ['tɜːnəʊvə(r)] *n* COMM [sales] facturación *f*; [of goods] movimiento *m*

turnpike ['tɜːnpaɪk] *n* US autopista *f* de peaje

turntable ['tɜːnteɪbəl] *n* [for record] plato *m* (giratorio)

turn-up ['tɜːnʌp] *n* *Br* [of trousers] vuelta *f*

turquoise ['tɜːkwɔɪz] **1.** *n* [colour, stone] turquesa *f* **2.** *adj* **turquoise (blue)** azul turquesa

turret ['tʌrɪt] *n* torrecilla *f*

turtle ['tɜːtəl] *n* *Br* tortuga *f*; *US* [tortoise] tortuga *f*

tusk [tʌsk] *n* colmillo *m*

tussle ['tʌsəl] *n* pelea *f*, lucha *f*

tutor ['tjuːtə(r)] *n* *Br* UNIV tutor(a) *m,f*; **private tutor** profesor(a) *m,f* particular

tutorial [tjuːˈtɔːrɪəl] *n* *Br* UNIV tutoría *f*, seminario *m*

tuxedo [tʌkˈsiːdəʊ] *n* US smoking *m*

TV [tiːˈviː] *n (abbr of* **television***)* televisión *f*

tweeps [twiːps] *npl* *Fam* my tweeps mis seguidores *mpl* en Twitter®

Tweet® [twiːt] *n* tuit *m*

tweezers ['twiːzəz] *npl* pinzas *fpl*

twelfth [twelfθ] **1.** *adj* & *n* duodécimo(a) *(m,f)* **2.** *n* [fraction] duodécimo *m*

twelve [twelv] *adj* & *n* doce *(m inv)*

twentieth ['twentɪɪθ] **1.** *adj* & *n* vigésimo(a) *(m,f)* **2.** *n* [fraction] vigésimo *m*

twenty ['twentɪ] *adj* & *n* veinte *(m inv)*

twenty-four /seven *adv* *Fam* las veinticuatro horas del día

twice [twaɪs] *adv* dos veces; **he's twice as old as I am** tiene el doble de años que yo

twiddle ['twɪdəl] **1.** *vt* dar vueltas a; **to twiddle one's thumbs** estar mano sobre mano **2.** *vi* **to twiddle with sth** juguetear con algo

twig¹ [twɪg] *n* ramilla *f*

twig² [twɪg] *vi Br Fam* darse cuenta

twilight ['twaɪlaɪt] *n* crepúsculo *m*

twin [twɪn] **1.** *n* mellizo(a) *m,f*; **identical twins** gemelos (idénticos); **twin brother/sister** hermano gemelo / hermana gemela; **twin beds** camas *fpl* gemelas; **twin pack** pack *m* doble **2.** *vt* hermanar

twine [twaɪn] **1.** *n* bramante *m* **2.** *vt* entretejer **3.** *vi* **to twine round sth** enroscarse alrededor de algo

twinge [twɪndʒ] *n* [of pain] punzada *f*; *Fig* **twinge of conscience** remordimiento *m*

twinkle ['twɪŋkəl] *vi* [stars] centellear; [eyes] brillar

twirl [twɜ:l] **1.** *vt* girar rápidamente **2.** *vi* [spin] girar rápidamente; [dancer] piruetear **3.** *n* [movement] giro rápido; [of dancer] pirueta *f*

twist [twɪst] **1.** *vt* torcer; [sense] tergiversar; **to twist one's ankle** torcerse el tobillo **2.** *vi* [smoke] formar volutas; [path] serpentear **3.** *n* **a)** [of yarn] torzal *m* **b)** [movement] torsión *f*; MED torcedura *f* **c)** [in road] vuelta *f* **d)** [dance] twist *m*

twit [twɪt] *n Br Fam* lerdo(a) *m,f*, *Esp* memo(a) *m,f*

twitch [twɪtʃ] **1.** *vt* dar un tirón a **2.** *vi* crisparse; **his face twitches** tiene un tic en la cara

twitter ['twɪtə(r)] **1.** *vi* gorjear **2.** *n* gorjeo *m*

two [tu:] **1.** *adj* dos (*inv*); *Fig* **to be in** *or* **of two minds about sth** estar indeciso(a) respecto a algo **2.** *n* dos *m inv*; *Fig* **to put two and two together** atar cabos

2 MESSAGING **a)** *written abbr of* **to b)** *written abbr of* **too**

2DAY MESSAGING *written abbr of* **today**

2d4 MESSAGING *written abbr of* **to die for**

two-faced ['tu:'feɪst] *adj* hipócrita

twofold ['tu:fəʊld] *adj* doble

2L8 MESSAGING *written abbr of* **too late**

2MORO MESSAGING *(abbr of* **tomorrow)** mñn

2NITE MESSAGING *written abbr of* **tonight**

tycoon [taɪ'ku:n] *n* magnate *m*

type [taɪp] **1.** *n* **a)** [kind] tipo *m*, clase *f*; [brand] marca *f*; [of car] modelo *m* **b)** TYP carácter *m*; [print] caracteres *mpl* **2.** *vt & vi* [with typewriter] escribir a máquina; [with word processor] escribir en *Esp* el ordenador *or Am* la computadora

typewriter ['taɪpraɪtə(r)] *n* máquina *f* de escribir

typhoid ['taɪfɔɪd] *n* **typhoid (fever)** fiebre tifoidea

typhoon [taɪ'fu:n] *n* tifón *m*

typical ['tɪpɪkəl] *adj* típico(a)

typing ['taɪpɪŋ] *n* mecanografía *f*

typist ['taɪpɪst] *n* mecanógrafo(a) *m,f*

tyrant ['taɪrənt] *n* tirano(a) *m,f*

tyre [taɪə(r)] *n* neumático *m*, *Am* llanta *f*; **tyre pressure** presión *f* de los neumáticos

TYVM MESSAGING *written abbr of* **mxs asias**

U

U, u [ju:] *n* [the letter] U, u *f*

U [ju:] *adj* [film] ≃ (apta) para todos los públicos

ugh [ʌx] *interj* ¡uf!, ¡puf!

ugly ['ʌglɪ] *(compar* **uglier,** *superl* **ugliest)** *adj* feo(a); [situation] desagradable; *Fig* **ugly duckling** patito feo

UHF *n (abbr of* **ultra high frequency)** UHF

UK [ju:'keɪ] *n (abbr of* **United Kingdom)** Reino *m* Unido

ulcer ['ʌlsə(r)] *n* [sore] llaga *f*; [internal] úlcera *f*

ultimate ['ʌltɪmɪt] *adj* **a)** [final] último(a); [aim] final **b)** [basic] esencial

ultimately ['ʌltɪmɪtlɪ] *adv* **a)** [finally] finalmente **b)** [basically] en el fondo

ultimatum [ʌltɪ'meɪtəm] *n* ultimátum *m*

ultramodern [,ʌltrə'mɒdən] *adj* ultramoderno(a)

ultraviolet [ʌltrə'vaɪəlɪt] *adj* ultravioleta

umbrella [ʌm'brelə] *n* paraguas *m inv*, *Col* sombrilla *f*

umpire ['ʌmpaɪə(r)] **1.** *n* árbitro *m* **2.** *vt* arbitrar

umpteen [ʌmp'ti:n] *adj Fam* la tira de, muchísimos(as)

umpteenth [ʌmp'ti:nθ] *adj* enésimo(a)

UN [ju:'en] *n (abbr of* **United Nations (Organization))** ONU *f*

unable [ʌn'eɪbəl] *adj* incapaz; **to be unable to do sth/anything** no poder hacer algo/nada

unacceptable [ʌnək'septəbəl] *adj* inaceptable

unaccompanied [ʌnə'kʌmpənɪd] *adj* solo(a)

unaccustomed [ʌnə'kʌstəmd] *adj* **he's unaccustomed to this climate** no está muy acostumbrado a este clima

unanimous [ju:'nænɪməs] *adj* unánime

unarmed [ʌn'ɑ:md] *adj* desarmado(a)

unassuming [ʌnə'sju:mɪŋ] *adj* sin pretensiones

unattainable [ʌnə'teɪnəbəl] *adj* inalcanzable

unattended [ʌnə'tendɪd] *adj* [counter etc] desatendido(a); **to leave a child unattended** dejar a un niño solo

unattractive [ʌnə'træktɪv] *adj* poco atractivo(a)

unauthorized [ʌn'ɔ:θəraɪzd] *adj* **a)** [person] no autorizado(a) **b)** [trade etc] ilícito(a), ilegal

unavailable [ʌnə'veɪləbəl] *adj* **to be unavailable** no estar disponible

unavoidable [ʌnə'vɔɪdəbəl] *adj* inevitable; [accident] imprevisible

unaware [ʌnə'weə(r)] *adj* **to be unaware of sth** ignorar algo

unawares [ʌnə'weəz] *adv* **a)** [unexpectedly] desprevenido(a) **b)** [without knowing] inconscientemente

unbalanced [ʌn'bælənst] *adj* desequilibrado(a)

unbearable [ʌn'beərəbəl] *adj* insoportable

unbeatable [ʌn'bi:təbəl] *adj* [team] invencible; [price, quality] inmejorable

unbelievable [ʌnbɪ'li:vəbəl] *adj* increíble

unbia(s)sed [ʌn'baɪəst] *adj* imparcial

unblock [ʌn'blɒk] *vt* [sink, pipe] desatascar

unborn [ʌn'bɔ:n] *adj* sin nacer, nonato(a)

unbreakable [ʌn'breɪkəbəl] *adj* irrompible ; *Fig* inquebrantable

unbroken [ʌn'brəʊkən] *adj* **a)** [whole] intacto(a) **b)** [uninterrupted] continuo(a) **c)** [record] imbatido(a)

unbutton [ʌn'bʌtən] *vt* desabrochar

uncanny [ʌn'kænɪ] *adj* misterioso(a), extraño(a)

uncertain [ʌn'sɜːtən] *adj* **a)** [not certain] incierto(a) ; [doubtful] dudoso(a) ; **in no uncertain terms** claramente **b)** [hesitant] indeciso(a)

uncertainty [ʌn'sɜːtəntɪ] *n* incertidumbre *f*

unchanged [ʌn'tʃeɪndʒd] *adj* igual

uncheck [ʌn'tʃek] *vt* [box] desmarcar

uncle ['ʌŋkəl] *n* tío *m*

unclear [ʌn'klɪə(r)] *adj* poco claro(a)

uncomfortable [ʌn'kʌmftəbəl] *adj* incómodo(a) ; **to make things uncomfortable for** complicarle la vida a

uncommon [ʌn'kɒmən] *adj* **a)** [rare] poco común ; [unusual] extraordinario(a) **b)** [excessive] excesivo(a)

uncompromising [ʌn'kɒmprəmaɪzɪŋ] *adj* intransigente ; **uncompromising honesty** sinceridad absoluta

unconditional [ʌnkən'dɪʃənəl] *adj* incondicional ; **unconditional refusal** negativa rotunda

unconnected [ʌnkə'nektɪd] *adj* no relacionado(a)

unconscious [ʌn'kɒnʃəs] **1.** *adj* **a)** inconsciente (**of** de) **b)** [unintentional] involuntario(a) **2.** *n* **the unconscious** el inconsciente

unconstitutional [ʌnkɒnstɪ'tjuːʃənəl] *adj* inconstitucional, anticonstitucional

uncontrollable [ʌnkən'trəʊləbəl] *adj* incontrolable ; [desire] irresistible

unconventional [ʌnkən'venʃənəl] *adj* poco convencional, original

unconvincing [ʌnkən'vɪnsɪŋ] *adj* poco convincente

uncooperative [ʌnkəʊ'ɒpərətɪv] *adj* poco cooperativo(a)

uncouth [ʌn'kuːθ] *adj* [rude] grosero(a)

uncover [ʌn'kʌvə(r)] *vt* destapar ; *Fig* descubrir

undecided [ʌndɪ'saɪdɪd] *adj* **a)** [person] indeciso(a) **b)** [issue] pendiente ; **it's still undecided** está aún por decidir

undeniable [ʌndɪ'naɪəbəl] *adj* innegable

under ['ʌndə(r)] **1.** *prep* **a)** debajo de, bajo, *Am* abajo de ; **under the sun** bajo el sol
b) [less than] menos de ; **incomes under £1,000** ingresos inferiores a 1.000 libras ; **under age** menor de edad
c) [of rank] de rango inferior a
d) **under Caesar** bajo César
e) [subject to] bajo ; **under arrest** detenido(a) ; **under cover** a cubierto ; **under the circumstances** dadas las circunstancias ; *Fig* **I was under the impression that …** tenía la impresión de que …
f) [according to] según, conforme a
2. *adv* abajo, debajo

undercharge [ʌndə'tʃɑːdʒ] *vt* cobrar menos de lo debido

underclothes ['ʌndəkləʊðz] *npl* ropa *f* interior

undercooked [ʌndər'kʊkt] *adj* poco cocinado(a)

undercover [ʌndə'kʌvə(r)] *adj* secreto(a)

undercut [ʌndə'kʌt] (*pt* & *pp* **undercut**) *vt* COMM vender más barato que

underdeveloped [ʌndədɪ'veləpt] *adj* subdesarrollado(a)

underdog ['ʌndədɒg] *n* desvalido(a) *m,f*

underestimate [ʌndər'estɪmeɪt] *vt* infravalorar

underfoot [ʌndə'fʊt] *adv* en el suelo

undergo [ʌndə'gəʊ] (*pt* **underwent**, *pp* **undergone** [ʌndə'gɒn]) *vt* experimentar ; [change] sufrir ; [test etc] pasar por

undergraduate [ʌndə'grædjʊɪt] *n* estudiante *mf* universitario(a)

underground 1. ['ʌndəgraʊnd] *adj* subterráneo(a) ; *Fig* clandestino(a)
2. ['ʌndəgraʊnd] *n* **a)** POL movimiento clandestino

b) *Br* the **underground** [train] el metro, *RP* el subte
3. [ʌndə'graund] *adv Fig* **to go underground** pasar a la clandestinidad

undergrowth ['ʌndəgrəʊθ] *n* maleza *f*

underhand 1. ['ʌndəhænd] *adj* [method] ilícito(a) ; [person] solapado(a) **2.** [ʌndə'hænd] *adv* bajo cuerda

underline [ʌndə'laɪn] *vt* subrayar

underlying [ʌndə'laɪɪŋ] *adj* [basic] fundamental

undermine [ʌndə'maɪn] *vt* socavar, minar

underneath [ʌndə'niːθ] **1.** *prep* debajo de, bajo
2. *adv* abajo, debajo
3. *adj* de abajo
4. *n* parte *f* inferior

underpaid [ʌndə'peɪd] *adj* mal pagado(a)

underpants ['ʌndəpænts] *npl* calzoncillos *mpl*, *Chile* fundillos *mpl*, *Méx* calzones *mpl*

underpass ['ʌndəpɑːs] *n* paso subterráneo

underprivileged [ʌndə'prɪvɪlɪdʒd] **1.** *adj* desfavorecido(a) **2.** *npl* **the underprivileged** los menos favorecidos

underrate [ʌndə'reɪt] *vt* subestimar, infravalorar

underside ['ʌndəsaɪd] *n* parte *f* inferior

understand [ʌndə'stænd] *(pt & pp* **understood)** *vt & vi* **a)** [comprehend] entender, comprender; **do I make myself understood?** ¿me explico? **b)** [assume, believe] entender; **she gave me to understand that ...** me dio a entender que ... **c)** [hear] tener entendido **d) to understand one another** entenderse

understandable [ʌndə'stændəbəl] *adj* comprensible

understanding [ʌndə'stændɪŋ] **1.** *n* **a)** [intellectual grasp] entendimiento *m*, comprensión *f* **b)** [interpretation] intepretación *f* **c)** [agreement] acuerdo *m* **d) on the understanding that ...** a condición de que ... **2.** *adj* comprensivo(a)

understatement [ʌndə'steɪtmənt] *n* **to make an understatement** minimizar, subestimar; **to say that the boy is rather clever is an understatement** decir que el chico es bastante listo es quedarse corto

understood [ʌndə'stʊd] **1.** *adj* **a) I wish it to be understood that ...** que conste que ... **b)** [agreed on] convenido(a) **c)** [implied] sobreentendido(a) **2.** *pt & pp of* **understand**

undertake [ʌndə'teɪk] *(pt* **undertook**, *pp* **undertaken** [ʌndə'teɪkən]*) vt* **a)** [responsibility] asumir; [task, job] encargarse de **b)** [promise] comprometerse a

undertaker ['ʌndəteɪkə(r)] *n* empresario(a) *m,f* de pompas fúnebres; **undertaker's** funeraria *f*

undertaking [ʌndə'teɪkɪŋ] *n* **a)** [task] empresa *f* **b)** [promise] compromiso *m*

undertone ['ʌndətəʊn] *n* **in an undertone** en voz baja

undertook [ʌndə'tʊk] *pt of* **undertake**

underwater [ʌndə'wɔːtə(r)] **1.** *adj* submarino(a) **2.** *adv* bajo el agua

underwear ['ʌndəweə(r)] *n* ropa *f* interior

underwent [ʌndə'went] *pt of* **undergo**

undesirable [ʌndɪ'zaɪrəbəl] *adj & n* indeseable *(mf)*

undisclosed [ˌʌndɪs'kləʊzd] *adj* no revelado(a)

undiscovered [ʌndɪ'skʌvəd] *adj* sin descubrir

undisputed [ʌndɪ'spjuːtɪd] *adj* [unchallenged] incontestable ; [unquestionable] indiscutible

undo [ʌn'duː] *(pt* **undid**, *pp* **undone**) *vt* **a)** deshacer ; [button] desabrochar **b)** [put right] enmendar

undoing [ʌn'duːɪŋ] *n* perdición *f*

undone¹ [ʌn'dʌn] *adj* [unfinished] inacabado(a)

undone² [ʌn'dʌn] **1.** *adj* [knot etc] deshecho(a) ; **to come undone**

[shoelace] desatarse ; [button, blouse] desabrocharse ; [necklace etc] soltarse **2.** *pp of* **undo**

undoubted [ʌn'dautɪd] *adj* indudable

undress [ʌn'dres] **1.** *vt* desnudar **2.** *vi* desnudarse

undue [ʌn'djuː] *adj* **a)** [excessive] excesivo(a) **b)** [improper] indebido(a)

unduly [ʌn'djuːlɪ] *adv* excesivamente

unearthly [ʌn'ɜːθlɪ] *adj* **a)** [being] sobrenatural **b)** *Fam* [din] espantoso(a) ; **at an unearthly hour** a una hora intempestiva

uneasy [ʌn'iːzɪ] *adj* **a)** [worried] preocupado(a) ; [disturbing] inquietante **b)** [uncomfortable] incómodo(a)

uneconomic(al) [ʌniːkə'nɒmɪk(əl)] *adj* poco económico(a)

uneducated [ʌn'edjukeɪtɪd] *adj* inculto(a)

unemployed [ʌnɪm'plɔɪd] **1.** *adj* desempleado(a), *Esp* parado(a), *Am* desocupado(a) ; **to be unemployed** estar desempleado(a) *or Esp* en (el) paro *or Am* desocupado(a) **2.** *npl* **the unemployed** los desempleados, *Esp* los parados, *Am* los desocupados

unemployment [ʌnɪm'plɔɪmənt] *n* desempleo *m*, *Esp* paro *m*, *Am* desocupación *f*; **unemployment benefit**, *US* **unemployment compensation** subsidio *m* de desempleo *or Am* de desocupación

unequal [ʌn'iːkwəl] *adj* desigual

uneven [ʌn'iːvən] *adj* **a)** [not level] desigual ; [bumpy] accidentado(a) **b)** [variable] irregular

uneventful [ʌnɪ'ventful] *adj* sin acontecimientos

unexpected [ʌnɪk'spektɪd] *adj* [unhoped for] inesperado(a) ; [event] imprevisto(a)

unexplained [ʌnɪks'pleɪnd] *adj* inexplicado(a)

unexplored [ˌʌnɪk'splɔːd] *adj* inexplorado(a)

unfair [ʌn'feə(r)] *adj* injusto(a) ; SPORT sucio(a)

unfaithful [ʌn'feɪθful] *adj* [friend] desleal ; [husband, wife] infiel

unfamiliar [ʌnfə'mɪljə(r)] *adj* [unknown] desconocido(a) ; [not conversant] no familiarizado(a) (**with** con)

unfashionable [ʌn'fæʃənəbəl] *adj* pasado(a) de moda ; [ideas etc] poco popular

unfasten [ʌn'fɑːsən] *vt* [knot] desatar ; [clothing, belt] desabrochar

unfavourable, *US* **unfavorable** [ʌn'feɪvərəbəl] *adj* desfavorable ; [criticism] adverso(a) ; [winds] contrario(a)

unfilled [ʌn'fɪld] *adj* [post, vacancy] por cubrir

unfinished [ʌn'fɪnɪʃt] *adj* inacabado(a) ; **unfinished business** un asunto pendiente

unfit [ʌn'fɪt] *adj* **a)** [thing] inadecuado(a) ; [person] no apto(a) (**for** para) **b)** [incompetent] incompetente **c)** [physically] incapacitado(a) ; **to be unfit** no estar en forma

unfold [ʌn'fəʊld] **1.** *vt* **a)** [sheet] desdoblar ; [newspaper] abrir **b)** [plan, secret] revelar **2.** *vi* **a)** [open up] abrirse ; [landscape] extenderse **b)** [plot] desarrollarse **c)** [secret] descubrirse

unforeseeable [ʌnfə'siːəbəl] *adj* imprevisible

unforeseen [ʌnfɔː'siːn] *adj* imprevisto(a)

unforgettable [ʌnfə'getəbəl] *adj* inolvidable

unforgivable [ʌnfə'gɪvəbəl] *adj* imperdonable

unfortunate [ʌn'fɔːtʃənɪt] *adj* [person, event] desgraciado(a) ; [remark] desafortunado(a) ; **how unfortunate!** ¡qué mala suerte!

unfortunately [ʌn'fɔːtʃənɪtlɪ] *adv* desgraciadamente, por desgracia

unfounded [ʌn'faundɪd] *adj* infundado(a)

unfriend [un'frend] *vt* INTERNET [in social network] **to unfriend sb** borrar a algn de la lista de amigos

unfriendly [ʌn'frendlɪ] *(compar* un-friendlier, *superl* **unfriendliest)** *adj* antipático(a), poco amistoso(a)

unfulfilled [ʌnfʊl'fɪld] *adj* **to feel unful-filled** sentirse insatisfecho(a)

unfurnished [ʌn'fɜːnɪʃt] *adj* sin amue-blar

ungainly [ʌn'geɪnlɪ] *adj* [gait] desgarbado(a)

ungrateful [ʌn'greɪtfʊl] *adj* [person] desagradecido(a); [task] ingrato(a)

unhappy [ʌn'hæpɪ] *(compar* unhappi-er, *superl* **unhappiest)** *adj* **a)** [sad] triste **b)** [wretched] desgraciado(a), infeliz; [unfortunate] desafortunado(a)

unharmed [ʌn'hɑːmd] *adj* ileso(a), indemne

unhealthy [ʌn'helθɪ] *(compar* un-healthier, *superl* **unhealthiest)** *adj* **a)** [ill] enfermizo(a) **b)** [unwholesome] malsano(a)

unhelpful [ʌn'helpfʊl] *adj* [person] poco servicial; [criticism, advice] poco constructivo(a)

unhurt [ʌn'hɜːt] *adj* ileso(a), indemne

unhygienic [ʌnhaɪ'dʒiːnɪk] *adj* antihigiénico(a)

uniform ['juːnɪfɔːm] *adj & n* unifor-me *(m)*

unify ['juːnɪfaɪ] *vt* unificar

unilateral [juːnɪ'lætərəl] *adj* unilateral

unimaginative [ʌnɪ'mædʒɪnətɪv] *adj* **to be unimaginative** [person] tener poca imaginación; [book, choice] ser muy poco original, no tener originalidad

unimportant [ʌnɪm'pɔːtənt] *adj* poco importante

uninhabited [ʌnɪn'hæbɪtɪd] *adj* despoblado(a)

uninhibited [ʌnɪn'hɪbɪtɪd] *adj* sin in-hibición

uninspiring [ʌnɪn'spaɪərɪŋ] *adj* que no inspira

unintelligible [ʌnɪn'telɪdʒəbəl] *adj* ininteligible, incomprensible

unintended [ʌnɪn'tendɪd] *adj* involuntario(a)

unintentional [ʌnɪn'tenʃənəl] *adj* involuntario(a)

uninterested [ʌn'ɪntərestɪd] *adj* poco interesado(a)

uninteresting [ʌn'ɪntrɪstɪŋ] *adj* poco interesante

uninterrupted [ʌnɪntə'rʌptɪd] *adj* ininterrumpido(a)

union ['juːnjən] **1.** *n* **a)** unión *f*; **civil union** unión civil **b)** [organization] sindicato *m* **c)** *US* **the Union** los Esta-dos Unidos; *Br* **Union Jack** bandera *f* del Reino Unido **2.** *adj* sindical

unique [juː'niːk] *adj* único(a)

unison ['juːnɪsən] *n* MUS unisonancia *f*; *Fig* [harmony] armonía *f*; **in unison** al unísono

unit ['juːnɪt] *n* **a)** unidad *f*; **monetary unit** unidad monetaria; *Br* FIN **unit trust** sociedad *f* de inversiones **b)** [piece of furniture] módulo *m*; **kitchen unit** mueble *m* de cocina **c)** TECH grupo *m* **d)** [department] servicio *m* **e)** [team] equipo *m*

unite [juː'naɪt] **1.** *vt* unir **2.** *vi* unirse

unity ['juːnɪtɪ] *n* unidad *f*; [harmony] armonía *f*

universal [juːnɪ'vɜːsəl] *adj* universal

universe ['juːnɪvɜːs] *n* universo *m*

university [juːnɪ'vɜːsɪtɪ] **1.** *n* universi-dad *f* **2.** *adj* universitario(a)

unjust [ʌn'dʒʌst] *adj* injusto(a)

unkind [ʌn'kaɪnd] *adj* [not nice] poco amable; [cruel] despiadado(a)

unknowingly [ʌn'nəʊɪŋlɪ] *adv* incons-cientemente, inadvertidamente

unknown [ʌn'nəʊn] **1.** *adj* des-conocido(a); **unknown quantity** incóg-nita *f* **2.** *n* **the unknown** lo desconocido

unlawful [ʌn'lɔːfʊl] *adj* [not legal] ilegal

unleaded [ʌn'ledɪd] *adj* **unleaded** *Br* **petrol** *or US* **gasoline** gasolina *f or RP* nafta *f* sin plomo

unleaded [ˌʌn'ledɪd] **1.** *adj* sin plomo **2.** *n Fam* [petrol] gasolina *f* sin plomo

unleash [ʌn'liːʃ] *vt* **a)** [dog] soltar **b)** *Fig* [release] liberar; [provoke] desenca-denar

unless [ʌn'les] *conj* a menos que, a no ser que

unlike [ʌn'laɪk] **1.** *adj* diferente, distinto(a) **2.** *prep* a diferencia de

unlikely [ʌn'laɪklɪ] *adj* **a)** [improbable] poco probable **b)** [unusual] raro(a)

unlimited [ʌn'lɪmɪtɪd] *adj* ilimitado(a)

unload [ʌn'ləʊd] *vt & vi* descargar

unlock [ʌn'lɒk] *vt* abrir (con llave)

unlucky [ʌn'lʌkɪ] *(compar* **unluckier**, *superl* **unluckiest)** *adj* [unfortunate] desgraciado(a); **to be unlucky** [person] tener mala suerte; [thing] traer mala suerte

unmade ['ʌnmeɪd] *adj* [bed] deshecho(a), sin hacer

unmanageable [ʌn'mænɪdʒəbəl] *adj* [people] ingobernable; [child, hair] incontrolable

unmarried [ʌn'mærɪd] *adj* soltero(a)

unmistakable [ʌnmɪs'teɪkəbəl] *adj* inconfundible

unmoved [ʌn'muːvd] *adv* **to watch / listen unmoved** observar /escuchar impertérrito(a)

unnatural [ʌn'nætʃərəl] *adj* **a)** [against nature] antinatural; [abnormal] anormal **b)** [affected] afectado(a)

unnecessary [ʌn'nesɪsərɪ] *adj* innecesario(a), inútil; **it's unnecessary to add that ...** sobra añadir que ...

unnoticed [ʌn'nəʊtɪst] *adj* desapercibido(a); **to let sth pass unnoticed** pasar algo por alto

UNO *n (abbr of* **United Nations Organization)** ONU *f (Organización de las Naciones Unidas)*

unoccupied [ʌn'ɒkjʊpaɪd] *adj* [house] desocupado(a); [seat] libre

unofficial [ʌnə'fɪʃəl] *adj* no oficial; IND **unofficial strike** huelga *f* no apoyada por los sindicatos

unorthodox [ʌn'ɔ:θədɒks] *adj* **a)** [behaviour etc] poco ortodoxo(a) **b)** REL heterodoxo(a)

unpack [ʌn'pæk] **1.** *vt* [boxes] desembalar; [suitcase] deshacer, *Am* desempacar **2.** *vi* deshacer la(s) maleta(s)

unpaid [ʌn'peɪd] *adj* **a)** [work, volunteer] no retribuido(a) **b)** [bill, debt] impagado(a)

unparalleled [ʌn'pærəleld] *adj* **a)** [in quality] incomparable **b)** [without precedent] sin precedente

unpleasant [ʌn'plezənt] *adj* desagradable (**to** con)

unplug [ʌn'plʌg] *vt* desenchufar

unpopular [ʌn'pɒpjʊlə(r)] *adj* impopular; **to make oneself unpopular** ganarse la antipatía de todos

unprecedented [ʌn'presɪdentɪd] *adj* sin precedente

unpredictable [ʌnprɪ'dɪktəbəl] *adj* imprevisible

unprepared [ʌnprɪ'peəd] *adj* [speech etc] improvisado(a); [person] desprevenido(a)

unprofessional [ʌnprə'feʃənəl] *adj* [unethical] poco profesional; [substandard] de aficionado(a)

unpublished [ʌn'pʌblɪʃt] *adj* inédito(a)

unqualified [ʌn'kwɒlɪfaɪd] *adj* **a)** [without qualification] sin título; [incompetent] incompetente **b)** [unconditional] incondicional; [denial] rotundo(a); [endorsement] sin reserva; [success] total

unquestionable [ʌn'kwestʃənəbəl] *adj* indiscutible

unravel [ʌn'rævəl] **1.** *vt* desenmarañar **2.** *vi* desenmarañarse

unrealistic [ʌnrɪə'lɪstɪk] *adj* poco realista

unreasonable [ʌn'ri:zənəbəl] *adj* poco razonable; [demands] desmedido(a); [prices] exorbitante; [hour] inoportuno(a)

unrecognizable [ʌnrekəg'naɪzəbl] *adj* irreconocible

unrelated [ʌnrɪ'leɪtɪd] *adj* [not connected] no relacionado(a)

unrelenting [ʌnrɪ'lentɪŋ] *adj* [behaviour] implacable; [struggle] encarnizado(a)

unreliable [ʌnrɪˈlaɪəbəl] adj a) [person] de poca confianza b) [information] que no es de fiar ; [machine] poco fiable

unrepentant [ʌnrɪˈpentənt] adj impenitente

unrest [ʌnˈrest] n [social etc] malestar m ; **political unrest** agitación política

unroll [ʌnˈrəʊl] vt desenrollar

unruly [ʌnˈruːlɪ] (compar unrulier, superl unruliest) adj a) [child] revoltoso(a) b) [hair] rebelde

unsafe [ʌnˈseɪf] adj [dangerous] peligroso(a) ; [risky] inseguro(a) ; **to feel unsafe** sentirse expuesto(a)

unsaid [ʌnˈsed] adj **it's better left unsaid** más vale no decir nada ; **much was left unsaid** quedó mucho por decir

unsatisfactory [ʌnsætɪsˈfæktərɪ] adj insatisfactorio(a) ; **it's most unsatisfactory** deja mucho que desear

unscrew [ʌnˈskruː] vt destornillar

unscrupulous [ʌnˈskruːpjʊləs] adj sin escrúpulos

unseemly [ʌnˈsiːmlɪ] adj impropio(a)

unseen [ʌnˈsiːn] **1.** adj invisible ; [unnoticed] inadvertido(a) **2.** n Br SCH texto no trabajado en clase

unselfish [ʌnˈselfɪʃ] adj desinteresado(a)

unsettle [ʌnˈsetəl] vt perturbar

unshaven [ʌnˈʃeɪvən] adj sin afeitar

unsightly [ʌnˈsaɪtlɪ] adj feo(a), desagradable

unskilled [ʌnˈskɪld] adj [worker] no cualificado(a) ; [work] no especializado(a)

unsociable [ʌnˈsəʊʃəbəl] adj insociable, huraño(a)

unsophisticated [ʌnsəˈfɪstɪkeɪtɪd] adj a) [naïve] ingenuo(a) b) [simple] poco sofisticado(a)

unspeakable [ʌnˈspiːkəbəl] adj a) indecible b) Fig [evil] atroz

unspent [ʌnˈspent] **1.** adj no gastado(a) **2.** adv **the money went unspent** el dinero no se gastó

unstable [ʌnˈsteɪbəl] adj inestable

unsteady [ʌnˈstedɪ] adj [not firm] inestable ; [table, chair] cojo(a) ; [hand, voice] tembloroso(a)

unstuck [ʌnˈstʌk] adj **to come unstuck** despegarse ; Fig venirse abajo

unsuccessful [ʌnsəkˈsesfʊl] adj a) [fruitless] fracasado(a) ; [useless] vano(a) b) [businessman etc] fracasado(a) ; [candidate] derrotado(a) ; **to be unsuccessful at sth** no tener éxito con algo

unsuitable [ʌnˈsuːtəbəl] adj a) [person] no apto(a) b) [thing] inadecuado(a) ; [remark] inoportuno(a) ; [time] inconveniente

unsuited [ʌnˈsuːtɪd] adj a) [person] no apto(a) ; [thing] impropio(a) (**to** para) b) [incompatible] incompatible

unsupervised [ʌnˈsuːpəvaɪzd] adj sin supervisar ; **'unsupervised minors not admitted'** 'no se admiten menores sin la supervisión de un adulto'

unsure [ʌnˈʃʊə(r)] adj poco seguro(a)

unsustainable [ˌʌnsəˈsteɪnəbl] adj insostenible

untangle [ʌnˈtæŋgəl] vt desenredar, desenmarañar

unthinkable [ʌnˈθɪŋkəbəl] adj impensable, inconcebible

untidy [ʌnˈtaɪdɪ] (compar untidier, superl untidiest) adj [room, person] desordenado(a) ; [hair] despeinado(a) ; [appearance] desaseado(a)

untie [ʌnˈtaɪ] vt desatar ; [free] soltar

until [ʌnˈtɪl] **1.** conj hasta que ; **she worked until she collapsed** trabajó hasta desfallecer ; **until she gets back** hasta que vuelva **2.** prep hasta ; **until now** hasta ahora ; **until ten o'clock** hasta las diez ; **not until Monday** hasta el lunes no

untold [ʌnˈtəʊld] adj a) [indescribable] indecible b) Fig [loss, wealth] incalculable c) [not told] sin contar

untoward [ʌntəˈwɔːd] adj a) [unfortunate] desafortunado(a) b) [adverse] adverso(a)

untrue [ʌn'tru:] *adj* **a)** [false] falso(a) **b)** [unfaithful] infiel **c)** [inexact] inexacto(a)

untruthful [ʌn'tru:θful] *adj* [person] embustero(a), mentiroso(a); [story, reply] falso(a)

unused [ʌn'ju:zd] *adj* **a)** [car] sin usar; [flat etc] sin estrenar; [stamp] sin matar **b)** [not in use] que ya no se utiliza **c)** [ʌn'ju:st] [unaccustomed] desacostumbrado(a) (**to** a)

unusual [ʌn'ju:ʒʊəl] *adj* [rare] insólito(a), poco común; [original] original; [exceptional] excepcional

unusually [ʌn'ju:ʒʊəlɪ] *adv* excepcionalmente

unveil [ʌn'veɪl] *vt* descubrir

unwanted [ʌn'wɒntɪd] *adj* [attentions, baby] no deseado(a); [clothes, trinkets] desechado(a)

unwarranted [ʌn'wɒrəntɪd] *adj* injustificado(a); [remark] gratuito(a)

unwelcome [ʌn'welkəm] *adj* [visitor] molesto(a); [visit] inoportuno(a); *Fig* [news etc] desagradable

unwell [ʌn'wel] *adj* malo(a), indispuesto(a)

unwieldy [ʌn'wi:ldɪ] *adj* [difficult to handle] poco manejable; [clumsy] torpe

unwilling [ʌn'wɪlɪŋ] *adj* **to be unwilling to do sth** no estar dispuesto a hacer algo

unwind [ʌn'waɪnd] (*pt & pp* **unwound**) **1.** *vt* desenrollar **2.** *vi* **a)** desenrollarse **b)** [relax] relajarse

unwise [ʌn'waɪz] *adj* imprudente, desaconsejable

unwitting [ʌn'wɪtɪŋ] *adj* involuntario(a)

unworthy [ʌn'wɜːðɪ] *adj* indigno(a)

unwound [ʌn'waʊnd] *pt & pp of* **unwind**

unwrap [ʌn'ræp] *vt* [gift] desenvolver; [package] deshacer

unzip [ʌnzɪp] (*pt & pp* **unzipped**) *vt* abrir la cremallera *or Am* el cierre de

up [ʌp] **1.** *prep* **a)** [movement] to climb **up the mountain** escalar la montaña; **to walk up the street** caminar *or Esp* andar por la calle

b) [position] en lo alto de; **further up the street** más adelante (en la misma calle); **halfway up the ladder** a mitad de la escalera

2. *adv* **a)** [upwards] arriba, hacia arriba; [position] arriba; **from £10 up** de 10 libras para arriba; **halfway up** a medio camino; **right up (to the top)** hasta arriba (del todo); **this side up** [sign] este lado hacia arriba

b) the moon is up ha salido la luna

c) [towards] hacia; **to come** *or* **go up to sb** acercarse a algn; **to walk up and down** ir de un lado a otro

d) [in, to] **he's up in Yorkshire** está en Yorkshire

e) it's up for discussion se está discutiendo; **up for sale** en venta

f) *Fam* **something's up** pasa algo; **what's up (with you)?** ¿qué pasa (contigo)?

g) up to [as far as, until] hasta; **I can spend up to £5** puedo gastar un máximo de 5 libras; **up to here** hasta aquí; **up to now** hasta ahora

h) to be up to [depend on] depender de; [be capable of] estar a la altura de

i) he's up to sth está tramando algo

3. *adj* **a)** [out of bed] levantado(a)

b) [finished] terminado(a); **time's up** (ya) es la hora

4. *vt Fam* aumentar

5. *n Fig* **ups and downs** altibajos *mpl*

upbringing ['ʌpbrɪŋɪŋ] *n* educación *f*

upcoming ['ʌp,kʌmɪŋ] *adj* [event] próximo(a); [book, film] de próxima aparición; **'upcoming attractions'** 'próximamente'

update [ʌp'deɪt] *vt* actualizar, poner al día

upgrade 1. [ʌp'greɪd] *vt* **a)** [promote] ascender **b)** [improve] mejorar la calidad de **c)** COMPUT [software, hardware] actualizar **2.** ['ʌpgreɪd] *n* COMPUT actualización *f*

upheaval [ʌp'hi:vəl] *n* trastorno *m*

uphill 1. ['ʌphɪl] *adj* ascendente ; *Fig* arduo(a) **2.** [ʌp'hɪl] *adv* cuesta arriba

uphold [ʌp'həʊld] (*pt & pp* **upheld** [ʌp'held]) *vt* sostener

upholstery [ʌp'həʊlstərɪ] *n* tapizado *m*, tapicería *f*

upkeep ['ʌpkiːp] *n* mantenimiento *m*

upload ['ʌpləʊd] **1.** *n* COMPUT carga *f*, *Fam* subida *f* **2.** *vt* COMPUT cargar, *Fam* subir, *Fam* colgar **3.** *vi* COMPUT cargarse

upon [ə'pɒn] *prep Formal* en, sobre ; **once upon a time …** érase una vez … ; **upon my word** (mi) palabra de honor

upper ['ʌpə(r)] **1.** *adj* **a)** [position] superior ; **upper storey** piso de arriba ; *Fig* **to have the upper hand** llevar la delantera **b)** [in rank] alto(a) ; **the upper class** la clase alta ; **the Upper House** la Cámara Alta **2.** *n* [of shoe] pala *f*

uppermost ['ʌpəməʊst] *adj* más alto(a) ; *Fig* **it was uppermost in my mind** era lo que me preocupaba más

upright ['ʌpraɪt] **1.** *adj* **a)** [vertical] vertical **b)** [honest] honrado(a) **2.** *adv* derecho **3.** *n* FTBL [post] poste *m*

uprising ['ʌpraɪzɪŋ] *n* sublevación *f*

uproar ['ʌprɔː(r)] *n* tumulto *m*, alboroto *m*

uproot [ʌp'ruːt] *vt* [plant] arrancar de raíz

upset 1. [ʌp'set] (*pt & pp* **upset**) *vt* **a)** [overturn] volcar ; [spill] derramar **b)** [shock] trastornar ; [worry] preocupar ; [displease] disgustar **c)** [spoil] desbaratar **d)** [make ill] sentar mal a **2.** [ʌp'set] *adj* [shocked] alterado(a) ; [displeased] disgustado(a) ; **to have an upset stomach** sentirse mal del estómago **3.** ['ʌpset] *n* **a)** [reversal] revés *m* **b)** SPORT resultado inesperado

upshot ['ʌpʃɒt] *n* resultado *m*

upside ['ʌpsaɪd] *n* **upside down** al revés

upstairs [ʌp'steəz] **1.** *adv* al piso de arriba ; **she lives upstairs** vive en el piso de arriba **2.** *n* piso *m* de arriba

uptight [ʌp'taɪt] *adj Fam* nervioso(a)

uptown ['ʌptaʊn] *US* **1.** *adj* [area] residencial **2.** *n* barrio *m* residencial

upward ['ʌpwəd] *adj* ascendente

upward(s) ['ʌpwəd(z)] *adv* hacia arriba ; **from ten (years) upward(s)** a partir de los diez años ; *Fam* **upward(s) of** algo más de

urban ['ɜːbən] *adj* urbano(a)

urge [ɜːdʒ] **1.** *vt* **a)** instar ; [plead] exhortar **b)** [advocate] preconizar ; **to urge that sth should be done** insistir en que se haga algo **2.** *n* impulso *m* ■ **urge on** *vt sep* animar a

urgency ['ɜːdʒənsɪ] *n* urgencia *f*

urgent ['ɜːdʒənt] *adj* urgente ; [need, tone] apremiante

urinate ['jʊərɪneɪt] *vi* orinar

urine ['jʊərɪn] *n* orina *f*

urn [ɜːn] *n* **a)** urna *f* **b)** **tea urn** tetera *f* grande

Uruguay ['jʊərəɡwaɪ] *n* Uruguay *m*

Uruguayan [ˌjʊərə'ɡwaɪən] *adj & n* uruguayo(a) *(m,f)*

us [ʌs] (*unstressed* [əs]) *pers pron* **a)** [as object] nos ; **let's forget it** olvidémoslo **b)** [after prep] nosotros(as) ; **both of us** nosotros dos ; **he's one of us** es de los nuestros **c)** [after verb "to be"] nosotros(as) ; **she wouldn't believe it was us** no creía que fuéramos nosotros **d)** *Fam* me ; **give us a kiss!** ¡dame un beso!

USA [juːes'eɪ] *n (abbr of* **United States of America***)* EE.UU. *mpl*

usage ['juːsɪdʒ] *n* **a)** [habit, custom] costumbre *f* **b)** LING uso *m*

USB *n* COMPUT USB *m* ; **USB key** *or* **pen** memoria *f* USB, lápiz *m* de memoria

use 1. [juːz] *vt* **a)** emplear, utilizar ; **what is it used for?** ¿para qué sirve? ; **to use force** hacer uso de la fuerza **b)** [consume] consumir, gastar **c)** [take unfair advantage of] aprovecharse de **2.** *v aux* **used to** ['juːstə] soler, acostumbrar ; **where did you use to live?** ¿dónde vivías (antes)?

Como verbo auxiliar, aparece siempre en la forma **used to**. Se traduce al español por el verbo principal en pretérito imperfecto, o por el pretérito imperfecto de **soler** más infinitivo.

3. [ju:s] *n* **a)** uso *m*, empleo *m*; [handling] manejo *m*; **directions for use** modo de empleo; **in use** en uso; **not in use** [on lift] no funciona; **to make (good) use of sth** aprovechar algo; **to put to good use** sacar partido de **b)** [application] aplicación *f* **c)** [usefulness] utilidad *f*; **what's the use?** ¿para qué?; *Fam* **it's no use crying** no sirve de nada llorar; **to be of use** servir

■ **use up** *vt sep* acabar

use-by date ['ju:zbaɪdeɪt] *n* COMM fecha *f* de caducidad

used *adj* **a)** [ju:zd] [second-hand] usado(a) **b)** [ju:st] **to be used to** estar acostumbrado(a) a

useful ['ju:sfʊl] *adj* útil; [practical] práctico(a); *Br* **to come in useful** venir bien

useless ['ju:slɪs] *adj* inútil

user ['ju:zə(r)] *n* **a)** usuario(a) *m,f*; **Internet user** internauta *mf*; COMPUT **user ID** *or* **name** nombre *m* de usuario; **user profile** perfil *m* de usuario **b)** *Fam* [of drugs] drogadicto(a) *m,f*

user-friendly [ju:zə'frendlɪ] *adj* COMPUT de fácil manejo

USPS *n (abbr of* **United States Postal Service***) servicio de correos estadounidense*

usual ['ju:ʒəl] **1.** *adj* corriente, normal; **as usual** como siempre; **at the usual hour** a la hora habitual; **earlier than usual** más pronto que de costumbre **2.** *n* lo habitual; **out of the usual** fuera de lo común

usually ['ju:ʒəlɪ] *adv* normalmente

usurp [ju:'zɜ:p] *vt* usurpar

utensil [ju:'tensəl] *n* utensilio *m*; **kitchen utensils** batería *f* de cocina

uterus ['ju:tərəs] *(pl* **uteri** [-raɪ] *or* **uteruses** [-rəsi:z]*) n* útero *m*

utility [ju:'tɪlɪtɪ] *n* **a)** utilidad *f*; **utility room** cuarto *m* de planchar; [for storage] trascocina *f* **b)** **(public) utility** empresa *f* de servicio público **c)** COMPUT utilidad *f*

utilize ['ju:tɪlaɪz] *vt* utilizar

utmost ['ʌtməʊst] **1.** *adj* sumo(a); **of the utmost importance** de suma importancia **2.** *n* máximo *m*; **to do** *or* **try one's utmost** hacer todo lo posible; **to the utmost** al máximo, a más no poder

utter¹ ['ʌtə(r)] *vt* [words] pronunciar; [sigh] dar; [cry, threat] lanzar

utter² ['ʌtə(r)] *adj* total, completo(a)

utterly ['ʌtəlɪ] *adv* completamente, totalmente

U-turn ['ju:tɜ:n] *n* cambio *m* de sentido; POL giro *m* de 180 grados

U2 MESSAGING *written abbr of* **you too**

V

V, v [viː] *n* [the letter] V, v *f*

V *(abbr of* **volt(s))** V

vacancy ['veɪkənsɪ] *n* a) [job] vacante *f* b) [room] habitación *f* libre; **no vacancies** [sign] completo

vacant ['veɪkənt] *adj* a) [empty] vacío(a) b) [job] vacante; *Br* **situations vacant** [in newspaper] ofertas de trabajo c) [free, not in use] libre

vacate [vəˈkeɪt] *vt* [flat] desalojar

vacation [vəˈkeɪʃən] **1.** *n US*, *Br* UNIV vacaciones *fpl*; **on vacation** de vacaciones **2.** *vi US* pasar las vacaciones (**in/at** en)

vaccinate ['væksɪneɪt] *vt* vacunar

vaccination [væksɪˈneɪʃən] *n* MED vacunación *f*

vaccine ['væksiːn] *n* vacuna *f*

vacuum ['vækjʊəm] **1.** *n* vacío *m*; **vacuum cleaner** aspiradora *f*; *Br* **vacuum flask** termo *m* **2.** *vt* [carpet, room] pasar la aspiradora por

vagina [vəˈdʒaɪnə] *n* vagina *f*

vague [veɪg] *adj* [imprecise] vago(a), impreciso(a); [indistinct] borroso(a)

vain [veɪn] *adj* a) [proud] vanidoso(a), presumido(a) b) [hopeless] vano(a); **in vain** en vano

valentine ['væləntaɪn] *n* a) [card] tarjeta que se manda el Día de los Enamorados b) [sweetheart] novio(a) *m,f*

valid ['vælɪd] *adj* válido(a); **no longer valid** caducado(a)

validate ['vælɪdeɪt] *vt* validar

valley ['vælɪ] *n* valle *m*

valuable ['væljʊəbəl] **1.** *adj* valioso(a), de valor **2.** *npl* **valuables** objetos *mpl* de valor

valuation [væljʊˈeɪʃən] *n* a) [act] valoración *f* b) [price] valor *m*

value ['væljuː] **1.** *n* valor *m*; **to get good value for money** sacarle jugo al dinero; *Br* **value-added tax** impuesto *m* sobre el valor añadido *or Am* agregado **2.** *vt* valorar

valve [vælv] *n* a) ANAT & TECH válvula *f* b) RADIO lámpara *f*

van [væn] *n* a) AUTO furgoneta *f* b) *Br* RAIL furgón *m*

vandal ['vændəl] *n* vándalo(a) *m,f*, *Esp* gamberro(a) *m,f*

vandalism ['vændəlɪzəm] *n* vandalismo *m*, *Esp* gamberrismo *m*

vandalize ['vændəlaɪz] *vt* destruir, destrozar

vanilla [vəˈnɪlə] *n* vainilla *f*

vanish ['vænɪʃ] *vi* desaparecer

vanity ['vænɪtɪ] *n* vanidad *f*; **vanity bag** *or* **case** neceser *m*

vapour ['veɪpə(r)] *n* vapor *m*; [on windowpane] vaho *m*; **vapour trail** estela *f* de humo

variable ['veərɪəbəl] *adj & n* variable (*f*)

variant ['veərɪənt] *n* variante *f*

variation [veərɪˈeɪʃən] *n* variación *f*

varied ['veərɪd] *adj* variado(a), diverso(a)

variety [vəˈraɪɪtɪ] *n* a) [diversity] variedad *f*; [assortment] surtido *m*; **for a variety of reasons** por razones diversas b) **variety show** espectáculo *m* de variedades

various ['veərɪəs] *adj* diversos(as), varios(as)

varnish ['vɑːnɪʃ] **1.** *n* barniz *m*; *Br* **nail varnish** esmalte *m* de uñas **2.** *vt* barnizar; *Br* [nails] esmaltar

vary ['veərɪ] *vi* variar; **prices vary from £2 to £4** los precios oscilan entre 2 y 4 libras; **to vary in size** variar de tamaño

vase [Br vɑːz, US veɪs] n jarrón m

vast [vɑːst] adj vasto(a) ; [majority] inmenso(a)

vat [væt] n cuba f, tina f

VAT [viːeɪˈtiː, væt] n Br (abbr of **value-added tax)** IVA m

Vatican [ˈvætɪkən] n the Vatican el Vaticano

vault¹ [vɔːlt] n bóveda f ; [for wine] bodega f ; [tomb] cripta f ; [of bank] cámara acorazada, Am bóveda f de seguridad

vault² [vɔːlt] **1.** vt & vi saltar **2.** n salto m

VBG MESSAGING written abbr of **very big grin**

VCR [viːsiːˈɑː(r)] n (abbr of **video cassette recorder)** (aparato m de) vídeo m or Am video m

VDU [viːdiːˈjuː] n (abbr of **visual display unit)** monitor m

veal [viːl] n ternera f

veer [vɪə(r)] vi [ship] virar ; [car] girar

vegan [ˈviːgən] n vegetariano(a) m,f (vegetariano estricto que no come ningún producto de origen animal)

vegetable [ˈvedʒtəbəl] n [food] verdura f, hortaliza f ; **vegetable garden** huerta f, huerto m

vegetarian [vedʒɪˈteərɪən] adj & n vegetariano(a) (m,f)

vegetation [vedʒɪˈteɪʃən] n vegetación f

vehicle [ˈviːɪkəl] n vehículo m

veil [veɪl] **1.** n velo m **2.** vt velar

vein [veɪn] n vena f

velvet [ˈvelvɪt] n terciopelo m

vending [ˈvendɪŋ] n **vending machine** máquina expendedora

vendor [ˈvendɔː(r)] n vendedor(a) m,f

veneer [vɪˈnɪə(r)] n **a)** [covering] chapa f **b)** Fig apariencia f

Venezuela [venɪzˈweɪlə] n Venezuela m

Venezuelan [venɪzˈweɪlən] adj & n venezolano(a) (m,f)

vengeance [ˈvendʒəns] n venganza f ; Fam it was raining with a vengeance llovía con ganas

venison [ˈvenɪsən] n carne f de venado

venom [ˈvenəm] n veneno m

vent [vent] **1.** n **a)** [opening] abertura f, orificio m ; [grille] rejilla f de ventilación ; **air vent** respiradero m **b)** [of volcano] chimenea f **2.** vt Fig [feelings] descargar

ventilate [ˈventɪleɪt] vt ventilar

ventilation [ventɪˈleɪʃən] n ventilación f

ventriloquist [venˈtrɪləkwɪst] n ventrílocuo(a) m,f

venture [ˈventʃə(r)] **1.** vt arriesgar, aventurar ; **he didn't venture to ask** no se atrevió a preguntarlo **2.** vi arriesgarse ; **to venture out of doors** atreverse a salir **3.** n empresa arriesgada, aventura f ; COMM **business / joint venture** empresa comercial / colectiva

venue [ˈvenjuː] n **a)** [meeting place] lugar m de reunión **b)** [for concert etc] local m

veranda(h) [vəˈrændə] n porche m, terraza f

verb [vɜːb] n verbo m

verbal [ˈvɜːbəl] adj verbal

verdict [ˈvɜːdɪkt] n **a)** JUR veredicto m, fallo m **b)** [opinion] opinión f, juicio m

verge [vɜːdʒ] **1.** n **a)** [margin] borde m ; Fig **on the verge of** al borde de ; Fig **to be on the verge of doing sth** estar a punto de hacer algo **b)** Br [of road] arcén m, Andes berma f, Méx acotamiento m, RP banquina f, Ven hombrillo m **2.** vi rayar (**on** en)

verify [ˈverɪfaɪ] vt verificar, comprobar

vermin [ˈvɜːmɪn] npl **a)** [animals] bichos mpl, sabandijas fpl **b)** Fig gentuza f

versatile [ˈvɜːsətaɪl] adj [person] polifacético(a) ; [object] versátil

verse [vɜːs] n **a)** [stanza] estrofa f **b)** [poetry] versos mpl, poesía f **c)** [of song] copla f **d)** [of Bible] versículo m

versed [vɜːst] adj **to be (well) versed in** ser (muy) versado en

version [ˈvɜːʃən, ˈvɜːʒən] n **a)** versión f ; **stage version** adaptación f teatral **b)** AUTO modelo m

versus [ˈvɜːsəs] prep contra

vertical ['vɜːtɪkəl] adj & n vertical (f)

very ['verɪ] **1.** adv **a)** [extremely] muy; **to be very hungry** tener mucha hambre; **very much** muchísimo; **very well** muy bien

b) [emphatic] **at the very latest** como máximo; **at the very least** como mínimo; **the very first / last** el primero / último de todos; **the very same day** el mismo día

2. adj **a) at the very end / beginning** al final / principio de todo

b) [precise] **at this very moment** en este mismo momento; **her very words** sus palabras exactas

c) [mere] **the very thought of it!** ¡solo con pensarlo!

vessel ['vesəl] n **a)** [container] vasija f **b)** NAUT buque m, nave f **c)** ANAT & BOT vaso m

vest [vest] **1.** n **a)** Br [undershirt] camiseta f de tirantes or Am breteles **b)** US chaleco m **2.** vt JUR **by the power vested in me ...** por los poderes que se me han conferido ...

vested ['vestɪd] adj JUR & FIN **vested interests** derechos adquiridos; Fig intereses mpl personales

vestige ['vestɪdʒ] n vestigio m

vet [vet] **1.** n veterinario(a) m,f **2.** vt Br someter a investigación, examinar

veteran ['vetərən] n **a)** veterano(a) m,f **b)** US **(war) veteran** excombatiente mf

veto ['viːtəʊ] (pl **vetoes**) **1.** n veto m **2.** vt POL vetar; [suggestion etc] descartar

VGA n (abbr of **video graphics array / adapter**) COMPUT VGA m

via ['vaɪə] prep por, vía

viable ['vaɪəbəl] adj viable, factible

viaduct ['vaɪədʌkt] n viaducto m

vibrant ['vaɪbrənt] adj **a)** [sound] vibrante **b)** Fig [personality] vital; [city] animado(a)

vibrate [vaɪ'breɪt] vi vibrar (**with** de)

vibration [vaɪ'breɪʃən] n vibración f

vicar ['vɪkə(r)] n párroco m

vice¹ [vaɪs] n vicio m

vice² [vaɪs] n Br [tool] torno m de banco

vice- [vaɪs] pref vice-; **vice--chancellor** rector(a) m,f; **vice--president** vicepresidente(a) m,f

vice versa [vaɪsɪ'vɜːsə] adv viceversa

vicious ['vɪʃəs] adj [violent] violento(a); [malicious] malintencionado(a); [cruel] cruel; **vicious circle** círculo vicioso

victim ['vɪktɪm] n víctima f

victimize ['vɪktɪmaɪz] vt perseguir, tratar injustamente

victorious [vɪk'tɔːrɪəs] adj victorioso(a)

victory ['vɪktərɪ] n victoria f

vidcast ['vɪdkɑːst] n vidcast m

video ['vɪdɪəʊ] n vídeo m, Am video m; TEL **video call** videollamada f; **video camera** cámara f de vídeo or Am video; **video cassette** cinta f de vídeo or Am video; **video (cassette) recorder** (aparato m de) vídeo m or Am video; **video game** videojuego m; **video projector** videoproyector m; **video tape** cinta f de vídeo or Am video

videocast ['vɪdɪəʊkɑːst] n vídeocast m

video-tape ['vɪdɪəʊteɪp] vt grabar (en vídeo or Am video)

vie [vaɪ] vi competir (**against** or **with** con)

view [vjuː] **1.** n **a)** [sight] vista f, panorama m; **on view** a la vista; **to come into view** aparecer; Fig **in view of the fact that ...** dado que ...

b) [opinion] opinión f; **point of view** punto m de vista

c) [aim] fin m; **with a view to** con la intención de

2. vt **a)** [look at] mirar; [house etc] visitar

b) [consider] contemplar; [topic, problem] enfocar

viewer ['vjuːə(r)] n **a)** TV televidente mf **b)** PHOTO visionador m

viewfinder ['vjuːfaɪndə(r)] n visor m

viewpoint ['vjuːpɔɪnt] n punto m de vista

vigilant ['vɪdʒɪlənt] adj alerta

vigorous ['vɪgərəs] adj vigoroso(a), enérgico(a)

vile [vaɪl] *adj* **a)** [evil] vil, infame **b)** [disgusting] repugnante **c)** *Fam* [awful] horrible

villa ['vɪlə] *n* **a)** [in country] casa *f* de campo **b)** *Br* chalet *m*

village ['vɪlɪdʒ] *n* [small] aldea *f*; [larger] pueblo *m*

villager ['vɪlɪdʒə(r)] *n* aldeano(a) *m,f*

villain ['vɪlən] *n* villano(a) *m,f*; CIN & THEAT malo(a) *m,f*

vindicate ['vɪndɪkeɪt] *vt* justificar, vindicar

vindictive [vɪn'dɪktɪv] *adj* vengativo(a)

vine [vaɪn] *n* vid *f*; [climbing] parra *f*

vinegar ['vɪnɪgə(r)] *n* vinagre *m*

vineyard ['vɪnjəd] *n* viña *f*, viñedo *m*

vintage ['vɪntɪdʒ] **1.** *n* **a)** [crop, year] cosecha *f* **b)** [season] vendimia *f* **c)** [era] era *f* **2.** *adj* **a)** [wine] añejo(a) **b)** [classic] clásico(a); **vintage car** coche *m* de época

violate ['vaɪəleɪt] *vt* violar

violence ['vaɪələns] *n* violencia *f*

violent ['vaɪələnt] *adj* **a)** violento(a) **b)** [intense] intenso(a)

violet ['vaɪəlɪt] **1.** *n* **a)** BOT violeta *f* **b)** [colour] violeta *m* **2.** *adj* violeta

violin [vaɪə'lɪn] *n* violín *m*

violinist [vaɪə'lɪnɪst] *n* violinista *mf*

VIP [viːaɪ'piː] *n Fam (abbr of* **very important person***)* personaje *m* muy importante

viper ['vaɪpə(r)] *n* víbora *f*

viral *adj* viral; **viral video** vídeo *m* viral

virgin ['vɜːdʒɪn] **1.** *n* virgen *f*; **the Virgin Mary** la Virgen María; **to be a virgin** ser virgen **2.** *adj* virgen

Virgo ['vɜːgəʊ] *n* virgo *m*

virile ['vɪraɪl] *adj* viril

virtual ['vɜːtjʊəl] *adj* virtual; COMPUT **virtual reality** realidad *f* virtual

virtually ['vɜːtjʊəlɪ] *adv* [almost] prácticamente

virtue ['vɜːtjuː] *n* virtud *f*; **by virtue of** en virtud de

virtuous ['vɜːtjʊəs] *adj* virtuoso(a)

virus ['vaɪrəs] *n* virus *m inv*; COMPUT **virus check** detección *f* de virus

virus-free *adj* COMPUT sin virus

visa ['viːzə] *n* visado *m*, *Am* visa *f*

visibility [vɪzɪ'bɪlɪtɪ] *n* visibilidad *f*

visible ['vɪzɪbəl] *adj* visible

vision ['vɪʒən] *n* **a)** visión *f* **b)** [eyesight] vista *f*

visit ['vɪzɪt] **1.** *vt* **a)** [person] visitar, hacer una visita a **b)** [place] visitar, ir a **2.** *n* visita *f*; **to pay sb a visit** hacerle una visita a algn

visitor ['vɪzɪtə(r)] *n* **a)** [guest] invitado(a) *m,f*; **we've got visitors** tenemos visita **b)** [in hotel] cliente(a) *m,f* **c)** [tourist] turista *mf*

visor ['vaɪzə(r)] *n* visera *f*

visual ['vɪʒʊəl] *adj* visual; **visual aids** medios *mpl* visuales

visualize ['vɪʒʊəlaɪz] *vt* **a)** [imagine] imaginar(se) **b)** [foresee] prever

vital ['vaɪtəl] *adj* **a)** [lively] enérgico(a) **b)** [essential] fundamental **c)** [decisive] decisivo(a); *Fam* **vital statistics** medidas *fpl* del cuerpo de la mujer **d)** MED [function, sign] vital

vitality [vaɪ'tælɪtɪ] *n* vitalidad *f*

vitamin ['vɪtəmɪn, *US* 'vaɪtəmɪn] *n* vitamina *f*

vivacious [vɪ'veɪʃəs] *adj* vivaz

vivid ['vɪvɪd] *adj* **a)** [bright, lively] vivo(a), intenso(a) **b)** [graphic] gráfico(a)

vocabulary [və'kæbjʊlərɪ] *n* vocabulario *m*

vocal ['vəʊkəl] *adj* vocal; **vocal cords** cuerdas *fpl* vocales

vocation [vəʊ'keɪʃən] *n* vocación *f*

vocational [vəʊ'keɪʃənəl] *adj* profesional; **vocational training** formación *f* profesional

vociferous [vəʊ'sɪfərəs] *adj* **a)** [protest] enérgico(a) **b)** [noisy] clamoroso(a)

vodka ['vɒdkə] *n* vodka *m*

vogue [vəʊg] *n* boga *f*, moda *f*; **in vogue** de moda

voice [vɔɪs] **1.** *n* voz *f*; TEL **voice dialling** marcación *f* vocal; COMPUT **voice mail**

buzón *m* de voz; **to lose one's voice** quedarse afónico; **to send / receive voice mail** dejar / recibir un mensaje en el buzón de voz; *Fig* **at the top of one's voice** a voz en grito **2.** *vt* **a)** [express] manifestar **b)** LING sonorizar

void [vɔɪd] **1.** *adj* **a)** void of sin **b)** JUR nulo(a), inválido(a) **2.** *n* vacío *m*

volatile ['vɒlətaɪl] *adj* volátil

volcano [vɒl'keɪnəʊ] *(pl* **volcanoes***) n* volcán *m*

volley ['vɒlɪ] **1.** *n* **a)** [of shots] descarga *f* **b)** *Fig* [of stones, insults] lluvia *f* **c)** [in tennis, football] volea *f* **2.** *vt* [in tennis, football] volear

volleyball ['vɒlɪbɔːl] *n* voleibol *m*

volt [vəʊlt] *n* voltio *m*

voltage ['vəʊltɪdʒ] *n* voltaje *m*

volume ['vɒljuːm] *n* **a)** volumen *m* **b)** [book] volumen *m*, tomo *m*; *Fig* **to speak volumes** decirlo todo

voluntary ['vɒləntərɪ] *adj* voluntario(a); **voluntary organization** organización benéfica

volunteer [vɒlən'tɪə(r)] **1.** *n* voluntario(a) *m,f* **2.** *vt* [help etc] ofrecer **3.** *vi* **a)** ofrecerse **(for** para) **b)** MIL alistarse como voluntario

vomit ['vɒmɪt] **1.** *vt* & *vi* vomitar **2.** *n* vómito *m*

vote [vəʊt] **1.** *n* voto *m*; [voting] votación *f*; **vote of confidence** voto de confianza; **to take a vote on sth** someter algo a votacíon; **to have the vote** tener derecho al voto **2.** *vt* **a)** votar **b)** [elect] elegir **c)** *Fam* proponer **3.** *vi* votar; **to vote for sb** votar a algn

voter ['vəʊtə(r)] *n* votante *mf*

voting ['vəʊtɪŋ] *n* votación *f*

vouch [vaʊtʃ] *vi* **to vouch for sth / sb** responder de algo / por algn

voucher ['vaʊtʃə(r)] *n Br* vale *m*

vow [vaʊ] **1.** *n* voto *m* **2.** *vt* jurar

vowel ['vaʊəl] *n* vocal *f*

voyage ['vɔɪɪdʒ] *n* viaje *m*; [crossing] travesía *f*; **to go on a voyage** hacer un viaje (en barco)

vulgar ['vʌlgə(r)] *adj* [coarse] vulgar, ordinario(a); [in poor taste] de mal gusto

vulnerable ['vʌlnərəbəl] *adj* vulnerable

vulture ['vʌltʃə(r)] *n* buitre *m*

W

W, w ['dʌbəlju:] *n* [the letter] W, w *f*

W **a)** *(abbr of* **west)** O **b)** *(abbr of* **watt(s)**) W

W@ MESSAGING *(abbr of* **what)** q, k

WABOL MESSAGING *written abbr of* **with a bit of luck**

wacko ['wækəʊ] *(pl* **wackos)** *n & adj Fam* pirado(a) *m,f*

wad [wɒd] *n* [of paper] taco *m*; [of cotton wool] bolita *f*; [of banknotes] fajo *m*

waddle ['wɒdəl] *vi* caminar *or* andar como un pato

wade [weɪd] *vi* caminar por el agua; **to wade across a river** vadear un río ■ **wade through** *vt insep* hacer con dificultad; **I'm wading through the book** me cuesta mucho terminar el libro

wafer ['weɪfə(r)] *n* barquillo *m*; REL hostia *f*

waffle¹ ['wɒfəl] *n* [food] *Esp* gofre *m*, *Am* wafle *m*

waffle² ['wɒfəl] *Br Fam* **1.** *vi* meter mucha paja; **to waffle on** parlotear **2.** *n* paja *f*

waft [wɑ:ft, wɒft] **1.** *vt* llevar por el aire **2.** *vi* flotar (por *or* en el aire)

wag [wæg] **1.** *vt* menear **2.** *vi* [tail] menearse

wage [weɪdʒ] **1.** *n* (*also* **wages**) salario *m*, sueldo *m*; **wage earner** asalariado(a) *m,f*; **wage freeze** congelación *f* salarial **2.** *vt* [campaign] realizar (**against** contra); **to wage war (on)** hacer la guerra (a)

wager ['weɪdʒə(r)] **1.** *n* apuesta *f* **2.** *vt* apostar

waggle ['wægəl] **1.** *vt* menear **2.** *vi* menearse

wa(g)gon ['wægən] *n* [horse-drawn] carro *m*; *Br* RAIL vagón *m*

wail [weɪl] **1.** *n* lamento *m*, gemido *m* **2.** *vi* [person] lamentar, gemir

waist [weɪst] *n* ANAT cintura *f*; SEWING talle *m*

waistcoat ['weɪstkəʊt] *n Br* chaleco *m*

wait [weɪt] **1.** *n* espera *f*; [delay] demora *f*; **to lie in wait** estar al acecho **2.** *vi* **a)** esperar, aguardar; **I can't wait to see her** me muero de ganas de verla; **while you wait** en el acto; **to keep sb waiting** hacer esperar a algn **b)** *Br* **to wait at table** servir la mesa ■ **wait about**, **wait around** *vi* esperar ■ **wait on** *vt insep* servir

waiter ['weɪtə(r)] *n* camarero *m*, *Andes*, *RP* mozo *m*, *Chile*, *Ven* mesonero *m*, *Col*, *Guat*, *Méx*, *Salv* mesero *m*

waiting ['weɪtɪŋ] *n* **no waiting** [sign] prohibido aparcar; **waiting list** lista *f* de espera; **waiting room** sala *f* de espera

waitlist ['weɪtlɪst] *vt US* poner en lista de espera; **I'm waitlisted for the next flight** estoy en lista de espera para el próximo vuelo

waitress ['weɪtrɪs] *n* camarera *f*, *Andes*, *RP* moza *f*, *Chile*, *Ven* mesonera *f*, *Col*, *Guat*, *Méx*, *Salv* mesera *f*

wake¹ [weɪk] *(pt* **woke**, *pp* **woken)** **1.** *vt* **to wake sb (up)** despertar a algn **2.** *vi* **to wake (up)** despertar(se) **3.** *n* [for dead] velatorio *m*, *Am* velorio *m*

wake² [weɪk] *n* [in water] estela *f*; *Fig* **in the wake of** tras

wake-up *n* **wake-up call** servicio *m* despertador

Wales [weɪlz] *n* (el país de) Gales

walk [wɔːk] **1.** *n* **a)** [long] caminata *m*; [short] paseo *m*; **to go for a walk** dar un paseo; **to take the dog for a walk** sacar a pasear al perro

b) [gait] andares *mpl*, modo *m* de caminar or *Esp* andar

c) people from all walks of life gente *f* de toda condición

2. *vt* **a) we walked her home** la acompañamos a casa

b) [dog] pasear

3. *vi* **a)** caminar, *Esp* andar

b) [go on foot] ir andando

■ **walk away** *vi* irse (caminando or *Esp* andando); *Fig* **to walk away with a prize** llevarse un premio

■ **walk into** *vt insep* **a)** [place] entrar en; *Fig* [trap] caer en **b)** [bump into] chocarse contra

■ **walk out** *vi* salir; IND declararse en huelga; **to walk out on sb** abandonar a algn

■ **walk up** *vi* **to walk up to sb** abordar a algn

walker ['wɔːkə(r)] *n* paseante *mf*; SPORT marchador(a) *m,f*

walking ['wɔːkɪŋ] **1.** *n* caminar *m*, *Esp* andar *m*; [hiking] excursionismo *m* **2.** *adj* **at walking pace** a paso de marcha; **walking shoes** zapatos *mpl* de andar; **walking stick** bastón *m*

Walkman® ['wɔːkmən] *(pl* **Walkmans)** *n* walkman® *m*

walk-up *US* **1.** *adj* [apartment, building] sin ascensor **2.** *n* [apartment] piso *m* sin ascensor; [office] oficina *f* sin ascensor; [building] edificio *m* sin ascensor

wall [wɔːl] *n* **a)** [freestanding, exterior] muro *m*; *Fig* **to have one's back to the wall** estar entre la espada y la pared; **garden wall** tapia *f* **b)** [interior] pared *f* **c)** FTBL barrera *f* ■ **wall up** *vt sep* [door, fireplace] tabicar

wallet ['wɒlɪt] *n* cartera *f*

wallpaper ['wɔːlpeɪpə(r)] **1.** *n* papel pintado **2.** *vt* empapelar

walnut ['wɔːlnʌt] *n* nuez *f*; [tree, wood] nogal *m*

walrus ['wɔːlrəs] *n* morsa *f*

waltz [wɔːls] **1.** *n* vals *m* **2.** *vi* bailar un vals

wan [wɒn] *adj* pálido(a)

wand [wɒnd] *n* **(magic) wand** varita *f* (mágica)

wander ['wɒndə(r)] **1.** *vt* **to wander the streets** vagar por las calles **2.** *vi* **a)** [aimlessly] vagar, errar; **to wander about** deambular; **to wander in/out** entrar/salir sin prisas **b)** [stray] desviarse; [mind] divagar

wangle ['wæŋgəl] *vt Fam* agenciarse

want [wɒnt] **1.** *n* **a)** [lack] falta *f*; **for want of** por falta de **b)** [poverty] miseria *f* **2.** *vt* **a)** [desire] querer, desear; **to want to do sth** querer hacer algo **b)** *Fam* [need] necesitar; **the grass wants cutting** hace falta cortar el césped **c)** [seek] buscar; **you're wanted on the phone** te llaman al teléfono ■ **want for** *vt insep* carecer de; **to want for nothing** tenerlo todo

wanted [wɒntɪd] *adj* [on police poster] se busca; **wanted, a good cook** [advertisement] se necesita buen cocinero

WAN2 MESSAGING *written abbr of* **want to**

war [wɔː(r)] *n* guerra *f*; **to be at war (with)** estar en guerra (con); *Fig* **to declare/ wage war on** declarar/hacer la guerra a; **war crime** crimen *m* de guerra

ward [wɔːd] *n* **a)** [of hospital] sala *f* **b)** JUR pupilo(a) *m,f*; **ward of court** pupilo(a) bajo tutela judicial **c)** *Br* POL distrito *m* electoral ■ **ward off** *vt sep* [blow] parar, desviar; [attack] rechazar; [danger] evitar; [illness] prevenir

warden ['wɔːdən] *n* **a)** [of institution, hostel] guardián(ana) *m,f*; **game warden** guardia *m* de coto **b)** *US* [of prison] director(a) *m,f*, alcaide(esa) *m,f*

wardrobe ['wɔːdrəʊb] *n* **a)** armario *m*, ropero *m* **b)** [clothes] guardarropa *m* **c)** THEAT vestuario *m*

warehouse ['weəhaʊs] *n* almacén *m*

wares [weəz] *npl* mercancías *fpl*

warfare ['wɔːfeə(r)] *n* guerra *f*

warm [wɔːm] **1.** *adj* **a)** [water] tibio(a); [hands] caliente; [climate] cálido(a); **a warm day** un día de calor; **I am warm**

tengo calor; **it is (very) warm today** hoy hace (mucho) calor; **warm clothing** ropa f de abrigo **b)** [welcome, applause] cálido(a) **2.** vt calentar; Fig alegrar **3.** vi calentarse; **to warm to sb** cogerle simpatía a algn ■ **warm up 1.** vt sep **a)** calentar; [soup] (re)calentar **b)** [audience] animar **2.** vi **a)** calentarse; [food] (re)calentarse; [person] entrar en calor **b)** [athlete] hacer ejercicios de calentamiento **c)** Fig [audience, party] animarse

warmth [wɔ:mθ] n [heat] calor m; Fig cordialidad f

warn [wɔ:n] vt avisar (**of** de), advertir (**about/against** sobre/contra); **he warned me not to go** me advirtió que no fuera; **to warn sb that** advertir a algn que

warning ['wɔ:nɪŋ] **1.** adj **warning light** piloto m; **warning sign** señal f de aviso **2.** n **a)** [of danger] advertencia f, aviso m **b)** [replacing punishment] amonestación f **c)** [notice] aviso m; **without warning** sin previo aviso

warp [wɔ:p] **1.** vt **a)** [wood] alabear, combar **b)** Fig [mind] pervertir **2.** vi alabearse, combarse

warrant ['wɒrənt] **1.** n **a)** JUR orden f judicial; **death warrant** sentencia f de muerte **b)** [authorization note] cédula f; COMM bono m **2.** vt **a)** [justify] justificar **b)** [guarantee] garantizar

warranty ['wɒrəntɪ] n COMM garantía f

warren ['wɒrən] n conejera f; Fig laberinto m

warrior ['wɒrɪə(r)] n guerrero(a) m,f

wart [wɔ:t] n verruga f

wartime ['wɔ:taɪm] n tiempos mpl de guerra

wary ['weərɪ] (comparwarier, superlwariest) adj cauteloso(a); **to be wary of doing sth** dudar en hacer algo; **to be wary of sb/sth** recelar de algn/algo

was [wɒz] pt of **be**

wash [wɒʃ] **1.** n **a)** lavado m; **to have a wash** lavarse **b)** [of ship] estela f;

[sound] chapoteo m **2.** vt **a)** lavar; [dishes] fregar; **to wash one's hair** lavarse el pelo **b)** [of sea, river] arrastrar **3.** vi **a)** [person] lavarse; [do the laundry] hacer la colada **b)** [lap] batir ■ **wash away** vt sep [of sea] llevarse; [traces] borrar ■ **wash off** vi lavar, quitar or Am sacar lavando ■ **wash out 1.** vt sep **a)** [stain] quitar lavando **b)** [bottle] enjuagar **2.** vi quitarse lavando ■ **wash up 1.** vt sep Br [dishes] fregar **2.** vi **a)** Br fregar los platos **b)** US lavarse rápidamente

washable ['wɒʃəbəl] adj lavable

washbasin ['wɒʃbeɪsən], US **washbowl** ['wɒʃbəʊl] n lavabo m, Am lavamanos m inv

washcloth ['wɒʃklɒθ] n US manopla f

washer ['wɒʃə(r)] n [on tap] zapata f, junta f

washing ['wɒʃɪŋ] n [action] lavado m; [of clothes] colada f; **(dirty) washing** ropa sucia; **to do the washing** hacer la colada; **washing line** tendedero m; **washing machine** lavadora f, RP lavarropas m inv; **washing powder** detergente m

washing-up [wɒʃɪŋˈʌp] n Br **a)** [action] fregado m; **washing-up bowl** palangana for Esp barreño m para lavar los platos; **washing-up liquid** (detergente m) lavavajillas m inv **b)** [dishes] platos mpl (para fregar)

wasp [wɒsp] n avispa f

waste [weɪst] **1.** adj **a)** [unwanted] desechado(a); **waste products** productos mpl de desecho **b)** [ground] baldío(a) **2.** n **a)** [unnecessary use] desperdicio m; [of resources, effort, money] derroche m; [of time] pérdida f; **to go to waste** echarse a perder **b)** [leftovers] desperdicios mpl; [rubbish] basura f; **radioactive waste** desechos mpl radiactivos; Br **waste disposal unit** trituradora f (de desperdicios); **waste carrier** transportador m de residuos; **waste management** gestión f de los residuos; **waste pipe** tubo m de desagüe

3. *vt* [squander] desperdiciar, malgastar; [resources] derrochar; [money] despilfarrar; [time] perder

■ **waste away** *vi* consumirse

wasteful ['weistful] *adj* derrochador(a)

wastepaper [weist'peipǝ(r)] *n* **wastepaper basket** *or* **bin** papelera *f*, *Méx* bote *m*

watch [wɒtʃ] **1.** *n* a) [lookout] vigilancia *f*; **to keep a close watch on sth/sb** vigilar algo/a algn muy atentamente **b)** MIL [body] guardia *f*; [individual] centinela *m*; **to be on watch** estar de guardia **c)** [timepiece] reloj *m*; **watch strap** correa *f* de reloj **2.** *vt* a) [observe] mirar, observar **b)** [keep an eye on] vigilar; [with suspicion] acechar **c)** [be careful of] tener cuidado con; *Fig* **to watch one's step** ir con pies de plomo **3.** *vi* [look] mirar, observar; **watch out!** ¡cuidado!

■ **watch out for** *vt insep* [be careful of] tener cuidado con

watchdog ['wɒtʃdɒg] *n* perro *m* guardián; *Fig* guardián(ana) *m,f*

watchful ['wɒtʃful] *adj* vigilante

watchstrap ['wɒtʃstræp] *n Br* correa *f* (de reloj)

water ['wɔːtǝ(r)]. **1.** *n* a) agua *f*; **water bottle** cantimplora *f*; **water lily** nenúfar *m*; **water main** conducción *f* de aguas; **water polo** water polo *m*; **water ski** esquí *m* acuático; **water sports** deportes acuáticos; **water tank** depósito *m* de agua **b)** **to pass water** orinar **2.** *vt* [plants] regar **3.** *vi* **my eyes are watering** me lloran los ojos; **it made my mouth water** se me hizo la boca agua ■ **water down** *vt sep* [drink] aguar

watercolour, *US* **watercolor** ['wɔːtǝkʌlǝ(r)] *n* acuarela *f*

watercress ['wɔːtǝkres] *n* berro *m*

waterfall ['wɔːtǝfɔːl] *n* cascada *f*; [very big] catarata *f*

watering ['wɔːtǝrɪŋ] *n* [of plants] riego *m*; **watering can** regadera *f*; **watering place** abrevadero *m*

watermelon ['wɔːtǝmelǝn] *n* sandía *f*

waterpark ['wɔːtǝpɑːk] *n* parque *m* acuático

waterproof ['wɔːtǝpruːf] **1.** *adj* [material] impermeable; [watch] sumergible **2.** *n* [coat] impermeable *m*

waterside ['wɔːtǝsaɪd] **1.** *adj* junto a la orilla, ribereño(a) **2.** *n* **the waterside** la orilla, la ribera

water-ski *vi* hacer esquí acuático

watertight ['wɔːtǝtaɪt] *adj* hermético(a)

watery ['wɔːtǝrɪ] *adj* a) [soup] aguado(a); [coffee] flojo(a) **b)** [eyes] lacrimoso(a) **c)** [pale] pálido(a)

watt [wɒt] *n* vatio *m*

wave [weɪv] **1.** *n* a) [at sea] ola *f*; **wave farm** granja *f* de olas, planta *f* undimotriz; **wave pool** piscina *f* de olas **b)** [in hair & RADIO] onda *f* **c)** *Fig* [of anger, strikes etc] oleada *f* **d)** [gesture] saludo *m* con la mano **2.** *vt* a) [brandish] blandir **b)** [hair] ondular **3.** *vi* a) agitar el brazo; **she waved (to me)** [greeting] me saludó con la mano; [goodbye] se despidió (de mí) con la mano; [signal] me hizo señas con la mano **b)** [flag] ondear; [corn] ondular

wavefile ['weɪvfaɪl] *n* COMPUT archivo *m* WAVE

wavelength ['weɪvleŋθ] *n* longitud *f* de onda

waver ['weɪvǝ(r)] *vi* [hesitate] vacilar (**between** entre); [voice] temblar; [courage] flaquear

wavy ['weɪvɪ] *(compar* **wavier**, *superl* **waviest)** *adj* ondulado(a)

wax¹ [wæks] **1.** *n* cera *f* **2.** *vt* encerar

wax² [wæks] *vi* a) [moon] crecer **b)** **to wax lyrical** exaltarse

way [weɪ] **1.** *n* a) [route] camino *m*; [road] vía *f*, camino; **on the way here** de camino hacia aquí; **out of the way**

apartado(a); **to ask the way** preguntar el camino; **to go the wrong way** ir por el camino equivocado; **to lose one's way** perderse; **which is the way to the station?** ¿por dónde se va a la estación?; **way in** entrada *f*; **way out** salida *f*; **on the way back** en el viaje de regreso; **on the way up/down** en la subida / bajada; **you're in the way** estás estorbando; **(get) out of the way!** ¡quítate de en medio!; **there's a wall in the way** hay un muro en medio; **to give way** ceder; AUTO ceder el paso

b) [direction] dirección *f*; **which way did he go?** ¿por dónde se fue?; **that way** por allá

c) [distance] distancia *f*; **a long way off** lejos; *Fig* **we've come a long way** hemos hecho grandes progresos

d) to get under way [travellers, work] ponerse en marcha; [meeting, match] empezar

e) [means, method] método *m*, manera *f*; **I'll do it my way** lo haré a mi manera

f) [manner] modo *m*, manera *f*; **in a friendly way** de modo amistoso; *Fam* **no way!** ¡ni hablar!; **she has a way with children** tiene un don para los niños; **either way** en cualquier caso; **in a way** en cierto sentido

g) [custom] hábito *m*, costumbre *f*; **to be set in one's ways** tener costumbres arraigadas

h) [state] estado *m*; **leave it the way it is** déjalo tal como está; **he is in a bad way** está bastante mal

i) by the way a propósito

2. *adv Fam* mucho, muy; **way back in 1940** allá en 1940

---

wayward ['weɪwəd] *adj* rebelde; [capricious] caprichoso(a)

WB MESSAGING **a)** *written abbr of* **welcome back b)** *written abbr of* **write back**

WBS MESSAGING *written abbr of* **write back soon**

WC [dʌblju:'si:] *n* (*abbr of* **water closet**) váter *m*, WC *m*

WDYT MESSAGING *written abbr of* **what do you think?**

we [wi:] *pers pron* nosotros(as) (*usually omitted in Spanish, except for contrast*)

weak [wi:k] *adj* débil; [argument, excuse] pobre; [team, piece of work, tea] flojo(a)

weaken ['wi:kən] **1.** *vt* debilitar; [argument] quitar fuerza a **2.** *vi* **a)** debilitarse **b)** [concede ground] ceder

weakness ['wi:knɪs] *n* debilidad *f*; [character flaw] punto flaco

wealth [welθ] *n* riqueza *f*; *Fig* abundancia *f*

wealthy ['welθɪ] (*compar* **wealthier**, *superl* **wealthiest**) *adj* rico(a)

weapon ['wepən] *n* arma *f*

---

wear [weə(r)] (*pt* **wore**, *pp* **worn**) **1.** *vt* **a)** [clothes] llevar puesto, vestir; [shoes] llevar puestos, calzar; **he wears glasses** lleva gafas; **to wear black** vestirse de negro

b) [erode] desgastar

2. *vi* **to wear (thin/smooth)** desgastarse (con el roce)

3. *n* **a)** ropa *f*; **leisure wear** ropa de sport

b) [use - clothes] uso *m*

c) [deterioration] desgaste *m*; **normal wear and tear** desgaste natural

■ **wear away 1.** *vt sep* erosionar **2.** *vi* [stone etc] erosionarse; [inscription] borrarse

■ **wear down 1.** *vt sep* [heels] desgastar; *Fig* **to wear sb down** vencer la resistencia de algn **2.** *vi* desgastarse

■ **wear off** *vi* [effect, pain] pasar, desaparecer

■ **wear out 1.** *vt sep* gastar; *Fig* agotar **2.** *vi* gastarse

---

weary ['wɪərɪ] **1.** (*compar* **wearier**, *superl* **weariest**) *adj* **a)** [tired] cansado(a) **b)** [fed up] harto(a) **2.** *vt* cansar **3.** *vi* cansarse (**of** de)

weather ['weðə(r)] **1.** *n* tiempo *m*; **the weather is fine** hace buen tiempo; *Fig* **to feel under the weather** no encontrarse bien; **weather chart** mapa meteorológico; **weather forecast** parte meteorológico; **weather girl** presentadora *f* del tiempo; **weather**

man presentador *m or* hombre *m* del tiempo **2.** *vt Fig* [crisis] aguantar; *Fig* **to weather the storm** capear el temporal

weave [wi:v] *(pt* **wove**, *pp* **woven**) **1.** *n* tejido *m* **2.** *vt* **a)** TEXT tejer **b)** [intertwine] entretejer **c)** [intrigues] tramar **3.** *vi* [person, road] zigzaguear

web [web] *n* **a)** [of spider] telaraña *f* **b)** [of lies] sarta *f* **c)** INTERNET **the Web** la Web; **web access** acceso *m* a internet; **web address** dirección *f* de internet; **web administrator** administrador(a) *m,f* de páginas web; **web browser** navegador *m*, explorador *m*, browser *m*; **web designer** diseñador(a) *m,f* (de páginas) web; **web developer** desarrollador(a) *m,f* web; **web feed** fuente *f* web; **web host** alojador *m* web; **web hosting** alojamiento *m* de páginas web; **web page** página *f* web; **web site** página *f* web, sitio *m* web; **web space** espacio *m* web; **web user** internauta *mf*

webcam ['webkæm] *n* cámara *f* web

webcast ['webkɑ:st] **1.** *n* COMPUT webcast *m* **2.** *vt* COMPUT difundir en la Red

webcasting ['webkɑ:stɪŋ] *n* COMPUT webcasting *m*

weblog ['weblɒg] *n* COMPUT bitácora *f*, weblog *m*

webphone ['webfəʊn] *n* teléfono *m* web

website ['websaɪt] *n* página *f* web, sitio *m* web

webzine ['webzi:n] *n* COMPUT webzine *m*

wed [wed] *(pt & pp* **wed** *or* **wedded**) *vt Liter* casarse con

wedding ['wedɪŋ] *n* boda *f*, *Andes* matrimonio *m*, *RP* casamiento *m*; **wedding cake** tarta *f or* pastel *m* de boda; **wedding day** día *m* de la boda; **wedding dress** traje *m* de novia; **wedding present** regalo *m* de boda; **wedding ring** alianza *f*

wedge [wedʒ] **1.** *n* **a)** cuña *f*; [for table leg] calce *m* **b)** [of cake, cheese] trozo *m* grande **2.** *vt* calzar; **to be wedged tight** [object] estar completamente atrancado(a)

Wednesday ['wenzdɪ] *n* miércoles *m*

wee¹ [wi:] *adj esp Scot* pequeñito(a)

wee² [wi:] *Br Fam* **1.** *n* pipí *m* **2.** *vi* hacer pipí

weed [wi:d] **1.** *n* BOT mala hierba **2.** *vt* **a)** [garden] escardar **b)** *Fig* **to weed out** eliminar **3.** *vi* escardar

weedkiller ['wi:dkɪlə(r)] *n* herbicida *m*

week [wi:k] *n* semana *f*; **a week (ago) today/yesterday** hoy hace /ayer hizo una semana; **a week today** justo dentro de una semana; **last /next week** la semana pasada /que viene; **once a week** una vez por semana; **week in, week out** semana tras semana

weekday ['wi:kdeɪ] *n* día *m* laborable

weekend [wi:k'end] *n* fin *m* de semana

weekly ['wi:klɪ] **1.** *adj* semanal **2.** *adv* semanalmente; **twice weekly** dos veces por semana **3.** *n* PRESS semanario *m*

weep [wi:p] *(pt & pp* **wept**) **1.** *vi* llorar; **to weep for sb** llorar la muerte de algn **2.** *vt* [tears] derramar

weigh [weɪ] **1.** *vt* **a)** pesar **b)** *Fig* [consider] ponderar **c)** **to weigh anchor** levar anclas **2.** *vi* **a)** pesar **b)** *Fig* [influence] influir ■ **weigh down** *vt sep* sobrecargar ■ **weigh in** *vi* **a)** SPORT pesarse **b)** *Fam* [join in] intervenir ■ **weigh up** *vt sep* [matter] evaluar; [person] formar una opinión sobre; **to weigh up the pros and cons** sopesar los pros y los contras

weight [weɪt] *n* **a)** peso *m*; **to lose weight** adelgazar; **to put on weight** subir de peso **b)** [of clock, scales] pesa *f* **c)** *Fig* **that's a weight off my mind** eso me quita *or Am* saca un peso de encima

W8 MESSAGING *written abbr of* **wait**

W84M MESSAGING *written abbr of* **wait for me**

weightlifting ['weɪtlɪftɪŋ] *n* halterofilia *f*, levantamiento *m* de pesos

W8N MESSAGING *written abbr of* **waiting**

weighty ['weɪtɪ] *(compar* **weightier**, *superl* **weightiest**) *adj* pesado(a); *Fig* [problem, matter] importante, grave; [argument] de peso

weird [wɪəd] *adj* raro(a), extraño(a)

welcome ['welkəm] **1.** *adj* [person] bienvenido(a); [news] grato(a); [change] oportuno(a); **to make sb welcome** acoger a algn calurosamente; **you're welcome!** ¡no hay de qué! **2.** *n* [greeting] bienvenida *f* **3.** *vt* acoger; [more formally] darle la bienvenida a; [news] acoger con agrado; [decision] aplaudir

welfare ['welfeə(r)] *n* **a)** [well-being] bienestar *m*; **animal/child welfare** protección *f* de animales/de menores; **welfare state** estado *m* del bienestar; **welfare work** asistencia *f* social; **welfare worker** asistente *mf* social **b)** *US* [social security] seguridad *f* social

well¹ [wel] *n* **a)** pozo *m* **b)** [of staircase, lift] hueco *m* **c)** [of court, hall] hemiciclo *m* ▪ **well up** *vi* brotar

well² [wel] **1.** *adj* **a)** [healthy] bien; **to get well** reponerse
b) [satisfactory] bien; **all is well** todo va bien; **it's just as well** menos mal
2. *(compar* **better,** *superl* **best)** *adv*
a) [properly] bien; **he has done well (for himself)** ha prosperado; **she did well in the exam** el examen le fue bien; **well done!** ¡muy bien!
b) [thoroughly] bien; CULIN **well done** muy hecho(a)
c) he's well over thirty tiene treinta años bien cumplidos; **well after six o'clock** mucho después de las seis
d) [easily, with good reason] **he couldn't very well say no** difícilmente podía decir que no; **I may well do that** puede que haga eso
e) as well también; **as well as** así como; **children as well as adults** tanto niños como adultos
3. *interj* **a)** [surprise] ¡bueno!, ¡vaya!; **well I never!** ¡no me digas!
b) [agreement, interrogation, resignation] bueno; **very well** bueno; **well? ** ¿y bien?
c) [doubt] pues; **well, I don't know** pues no sé
d) [resumption] **well, as I was saying** pues (bien), como iba diciendo

well-behaved ['welbɪheɪvd] *adj* [child] formal, educado(a)

well-being ['welbiːɪŋ] *n* bienestar *m*

well-built ['welbɪlt] *adj* [building etc] de construcción sólida; [person] fornido(a)

well-informed ['welɪnfɔːmd] *adj* bien informado(a)

wellingtons ['welɪŋtənz] *npl Br* botas *fpl* de agua *or* goma *or Méx, Ven* caucho

well-known ['welnəʊn] *adj* (bien) conocido(a)

well-meaning [wel'miːnɪŋ] *adj* bien intencionado(a)

wellness ['welnɪs] *n* bienestar *m*; **wellness centre** centro *m* de bienestar

well-off [wel'ɒf] *adj* [rich] acomodado(a)

well-prepared *adj* bien preparado(a)

well-respected *adj* respetado(a)

well-stocked [-stɒkt] *adj* [shop] bien provisto(a)

well-to-do [weltə'duː] *adj* acomodado(a)

Welsh [welʃ] **1.** *adj* galés(esa); **Welsh rarebit** *tostada con queso fundido* **2.** *n* **a)** [language] galés *m* **b) the Welsh** los galeses

Welshman ['welʃmən] *n* galés *m*

Welshwoman ['welʃwʊmən] *n* galesa *f*

went [went] *pt of* **go**

wept [wept] *pt & pp of* **weep**

were [wɜː(r)] *(unstressed* [wə(r)]*) pt of* **be**

west [west] **1.** *n* oeste *m*, occidente *m*; **in/to the west** al oeste; POL **the West** los países occidentales **2.** *adj* del oeste, occidental; **the West Indies** las Antillas; **West Indian** antillano(a) **3.** *adv* al oeste, hacia el oeste

western ['westən] **1.** *adj* del oeste, occidental; **Western Europe** Europa Occidental **2.** *n* CIN western *m*, película *f* del oeste

westward ['westwəd] *adj* **in a westward direction** hacia el oeste

westwards ['westwədz] *adv* hacia el oeste

wet [wet] **1.** *(compar* **wetter,** *superl* **wettest)** *adj* **a)** mojado(a); [slightly] húmedo(a);

Fig **wet blanket** aguafiestas *mf inv*; **wet paint** [sign] recién pintado; **wet through** [person] calado(a) hasta los huesos; [thing] empapado(a) **b)** [rainy] lluvioso(a) **c)** *Br Fam* [person] soso(a) **2.** (*pt & pp* **wet**) *vt* mojar; **to wet oneself** orinarse

W4u MESSAGING *written abbr of* **waiting for you**

whack [wæk] **1.** *vt* [hit hard] dar un porrazo o *Méx* madrazo a **2.** *n* **a)** [blow] porrazo *m*, *Méx* madrazo *m* **b)** *Fam* [share] parte *f*, porción *f*

whale [weɪl] *n* ballena *f*

whassup [wɒˈsʌp] *interj US Fam* [hello, what's going on] ¿qué pasa?

what [wɒt] (*unstressed* [wət]) **1.** *adj* **a)** [direct question] qué; **what (sort of) bird is that?** ¿qué tipo de ave es ésa?; **what good is that?** ¿para qué sirve eso? **b)** [indirect question] qué; **ask her what colour she likes** pregúntale qué color le gusta

2. *pron* **a)** [direct question] qué; **what about your father?** ¿y tu padre (qué)?; **what about going tomorrow?** ¿qué te parece si vamos mañana?; **what did it cost?** ¿cuánto costó?; **what did you do that for?** ¿por qué hiciste eso?; **what (did you say)?** ¿cómo?; **what is happening?** ¿qué pasa?; **what is it?** [definition] ¿qué es?; [what's the matter] ¿qué pasa?; **what's this for?** ¿para qué sirve esto?

b) [indirect question] qué, lo que; **he asked me what I thought** me preguntó lo que pensaba; **I didn't know what to say** no sabía qué decir

c) **guess what!** ¿sabes qué?; **it's just what I need** es exactamente lo que necesito

d) [in exclamations] **what a goal!** ¡qué *or* vaya golazo!; **what a lovely picture!** ¡qué cuadro más bonito!

3. *interj* [surprise, indignation] ¡cómo!; **what, no dessert?** ¿cómo, no hay postre?

whatever [wɒtˈevə(r)] (*unstressed* [wətˈevə(r)]) **1.** *adj* **a)** [any] cualquiera que; **at whatever time you like** a la hora que quieras; **of whatever colour** no importa de qué color

b) [with negative] **nothing whatever** nada en absoluto

2. *pron* **a)** [what] **whatever happened?** ¿qué pasó?

b) [anything, all that] (todo) lo que; **do whatever you like** haz lo que quieras

c) [no matter what] **don't tell him, whatever you do** no se te ocurra decírselo; **whatever (else) you find** cualquier (otra) cosa que encuentres

whatsoever [wɒtsəʊˈevə(r)] *adj* **anything whatsoever** cualquier cosa; **nothing whatsoever** nada en absoluto

wheat [wiːt] *n* trigo *m*; **wheat germ** germen *m* de trigo

wheedle [ˈwiːdəl] *vt* **to wheedle sb into doing sth** engatusar a algn para que haga algo; **to wheedle sth out of sb** sonsacar algo a algn halagándole

wheel [wiːl] **1.** *n* rueda *f* **2.** *vt* [bicycle] empujar **3.** *vi* **a)** [bird] revolotear **b)** **to wheel round** girar sobre los talones

wheelbarrow [ˈwiːlbærəʊ] *n* carretilla *f*

wheelchair [ˈwiːltʃeə(r)] *n* silla *f* de ruedas

wheeze [wiːz] *vi* respirar con dificultad, resollar

when [wen] **1.** *adv* **a)** [direct question] cuándo; **since when?** ¿desde cuándo?; **when did he arrive?** ¿cuándo llegó? **b)** [indirect question] cuándo; **tell me when to go** dime cuándo debo irme **c)** [on which] cuando, en que; **the days when I work** los días en que trabajo **2.** *conj* **a)** cuando; **I'll tell you when she comes** se lo diré cuando llegue **b)** [whenever] cuando **c)** [given that, if] si **d)** [although] aunque

whenever [wenˈevə(r)] **1.** *conj* [when] cuando; [every time] siempre que **2.** *adv* **whenever that might be** sea cuando sea

where [weə(r)] *adv* **a)** [direct question] dónde; [direction] adónde; **where are you going?** ¿adónde vas?; **where did we go wrong?** ¿en qué nos equivocamos?; **where do you come from?** ¿de dónde es usted?
b) [indirect question] dónde; [direction] adónde; **tell me where you went** dime adónde fuiste
c) [at, in which] donde; [direction] adonde, a donde
d) [when] cuando

whereabouts 1. [weərə'baʊts] *adv* **whereabouts do you live?** ¿por dónde vives? **2.** ['weərəbaʊts] *n* paradero *m*

whereas [weər'æz] *conj* **a)** [but, while] mientras que **b)** JUR considerando que

whereby [weə'baɪ] *adv* por el/la/lo cual

wherever [weər'evə(r)] **1.** *conj* dondequiera que; **I'll find him wherever he is** le encontraré dondequiera que esté; **sit wherever you like** siéntate donde quieras **2.** *adv* [direct question] adónde

whether ['weðə(r)] *conj* **a)** [if] si; **I don't know whether it is true** no sé si es verdad; **I doubt whether he'll win** dudo que gane **b)** **whether he comes or not** venga o no

which [wɪtʃ] **1.** *adj* **a)** [direct question] qué; **which colour do you prefer?** ¿qué color prefieres?; **which one?** ¿cuál?; **which way?** ¿por dónde?
b) [indirect question] qué; **tell me which dress you like** dime qué vestido te gusta
c) by which time y para entonces; **in which case** en cuyo caso
2. *pron* **a)** [direct question] cuál/cuáles; **which of you did it?** ¿quién de vosotros lo hizo?
b) [indirect question] cuál/cuáles; **I don't know which I'd rather have** no sé cuál prefiero
c) [defining relative] que; [after preposition] que, el/la cual, los/las cuales, el/la que, los/las que; **here are the books (which) I have read** aquí están los libros que he leído; **the accident (which) I told you about** el accidente del que te hablé; **the car in which he was travelling** el coche en (el) que viajaba; **this is the one (which) I like** éste es el que me gusta
d) [non-defining relative] el/la cual, los/las cuales; **I played three sets, all of which I lost** jugué tres sets, todos los cuales perdí
e) [referring to a clause] lo cual, lo que; **he won, which made me very happy** ganó, lo cual o lo que me alegró mucho

whichever [wɪtʃ'evə(r)] **1.** *adj* el/la que, cualquiera que; **I'll take whichever books you don't want** tomaré los libros que no quieras **2.** *pron* el/la que

while [waɪl] **1.** *n* **a)** [length of time] rato *m*, tiempo *m*; **in a little while** dentro de poco; **once in a while** de vez en cuando **b)** **it's not worth your while staying** no merece la pena que te quedes **2.** *conj* **a)** [time] mientras; **he fell asleep while driving** se durmió mientras conducía **b)** [although] aunque **c)** [whereas] mientras que ■ **while away** *vt sep* **to while away the time** pasar el rato

whilst [waɪlst] *Br conj* = **while**

whim [wɪm] *n* capricho *m*, antojo *m*

whimper ['wɪmpə(r)] **1.** *n* quejido *m* **2.** *vi* lloriquear

whine [waɪn] *vi* **a)** [child] lloriquear; [with pain] dar quejidos **b)** [complain] quejarse **c)** [engine] chirriar

whip [wɪp] **1.** *n* **a)** [for punishment] látigo *m*; [for riding] fusta *f* **b)** Br POL oficial encargado(a) de la disciplina de un partido **2.** *vt* **a)** [as punishment] azotar; [horse] fustigar **b)** CULIN batir; **whipped cream** *Esp* nata montada, *Am* crema batida **c)** *Fam* [steal] mangar ■ **whip away** *vt sep* arrebatar ■ **whip up** *vt sep* [passions, enthusiasm] avivar; [support] incrementar

whirl [wɜːl] **1.** *n* giro *m*; *Fig* torbellino *m* **2.** *vt* **to whirl sth round** dar vueltas a *or* hacer girar algo **3.** *vi* **to whirl round** girar con rapidez; [leaves etc] arremolinarse

whirlpool ['wɜːlpuːl] *n* remolino *m*

whirlwind [ˈwɜːlwɪnd] *n* torbellino *m*

whirr [wɜː(r)] *vi* zumbar, runrunear

whisk [wɪsk] **1.** *n* CULIN batidor *m*; [electric] batidora *f* **2.** *vt* CULIN batir
■ **whisk away, whisk off** *vt sep* quitar bruscamente, llevarse de repente

whiskers [ˈwɪskəz] *npl* [of person] patillas *fpl*; [of cat] bigotes *mpl*

whisky, *US* **whiskey** [ˈwɪskɪ] *n* whisky *m*

whisper [ˈwɪspə(r)] **1.** *n* a) [sound] susurro *m* b) [rumour] rumor *m* **2.** *vt* decir en voz baja **3.** *vi* susurrar

whistle [ˈwɪsəl] **1.** *n* a) [instrument] pito *m* b) [sound] silbido *m*, pitido *m* **2.** *vt* [tune] silbar **3.** *vi* [person, kettle, wind] silbar; [train] pitar

white [waɪt] **1.** *adj* blanco(a); **to go white** [face] palidecer; [hair] encanecer; **white coffee** café *m* con leche; **white hair** pelo cano; *Fig* **a white lie** una mentira piadosa; **white sauce** bechamel *f*, *Col, CSur* salsa *f* blanca **2.** *n* a) [colour, person, of eye] blanco *m* b) [of egg] clara *f*

whitewash [ˈwaɪtwɒʃ] **1.** *n* a) cal *f* b) *Fig* [cover-up] encubrimiento *m* c) *Fig* [defeat] paliza *f* **2.** *vt* a) [wall] enjalbegar, blanquear b) *Fig* encubrir

whiz(z) [wɪz] *vi* a) [sound] silbar b) **to whiz(z) past** pasar volando; *Fam* **whiz(z) kid** joven *mf* dinámico(a) y emprendedor(a)

who [huː] *pron* a) [direct question] quién /quiénes; **who are they?** ¿quiénes son?; **who is it?** ¿quién es? b) [indirect question] quién; **I don't know who did it** no sé quién lo hizo c) [defining relative] que; **those who don't know** los que no saben d) [non-defining relative] quien /quienes, el /la cual, los /las cuales; **Elena's mother, who is very rich ...** la madre de Elena, la cual es muy rica ...

whoever [huːˈevə(r)] *pron* a) quienquiera que; **give it to whoever you like** dáselo a quien quieras; **whoever said that is a fool** el que dijo eso es un tonto; **whoever you are** quienquiera que seas b) [direct question] **whoever told you that?** ¿quién te dijo eso?

whole [həʊl] **1.** *adj* a) [entire] entero(a), íntegro(a); **a whole week** una semana entera; **he took the whole lot** se los llevó todos; **whole grain** [bread, flour] integral b) [in one piece] intacto(a) **2.** *n* a) [single unit] todo *m*, conjunto *m*; **as a whole** en su totalidad b) [all] totalidad *f*; **the whole of London** todo Londres c) **on the whole** en general

wholemeal [ˈhəʊlmiːl] *adj* *Br* integral

wholesale [ˈhəʊlseɪl] **1.** *n* COMM compraventa *f* al por mayor, *Am* mayoreo *m* **2.** *adj* COMM al por mayor; *Fig* total **3.** *adv* al por mayor; *Fig* en su totalidad

wholesome [ˈhəʊlsəm] *adj* sano(a)

wholly [ˈhəʊllɪ] *adv* enteramente, completamente

whom [huːm] *pron* *Formal* a) [direct question - accusative] a quién; **whom did you talk to?** ¿con quién hablaste?; **of / from whom?** [after preposition] ¿de quién?; **to whom are you referring?** ¿a quién te refieres? b) [rel] [accusative] que, a quien /a quienes; **those whom I have seen** aquéllos a quienes he visto c) [rel] [after preposition] quien / quienes, el /la cual, los /las cuales; **my brothers, both of whom are miners** mis hermanos, que son mineros los dos

En la actualidad, solo aparece en contextos formales. **Whom** se puede sustituir por **who** en todos los casos salvo cuando va después de preposición.

whooping cough [ˈhuːpɪŋkɒf] *n* tos ferina

whore [hɔː(r)] *n v Fam & Pej* puta *f*

whose [huːz] **1.** *pron* a) [direct question] de quién /de quiénes; **whose are these gloves?** ¿de quién son estos guantes?; **whose is this?** ¿de quién es esto? b) [indirect question] de quién /de quiénes; **I don't know whose these coats are** no sé de quién son estos abrigos c) [rel] cuyo(s) /cuya(s); **the man whose children we saw** el hombre a cuyos hijos vimos

2. *adj* whose car/house is this? ¿de quién es este coche/esta casa?

why [waɪ] **1.** *adv* por qué; [for what purpose] para qué; **why did you do that?** ¿por qué hiciste eso?; **why not go to bed?** ¿por qué no te acuestas?; **I don't know why he did it** no sé por qué lo hizo **2.** *interj* **a)** [fancy that!] ¡toma!, ¡vaya!; **why, it's David!** ¡si es David! **b)** [protest, assertion] sí, vamos

wick [wɪk] *n* mecha *f*

wicked [ˈwɪkɪd] *adj* **a)** malvado(a) **b)** *Fam* malísimo(a); [temper] de perros

wicker [ˈwɪkə(r)] **1.** *n* mimbre *m* **2.** *adj* de mimbre

wicket [ˈwɪkɪt] *n* [in cricket - stumps] palos *mpl*

wide [waɪd] **1.** *adj* **a)** [road, trousers] ancho(a); [gap, interval] grande; **it is 10 m wide** tiene 10 m de ancho **b)** [area, knowledge, support, range] amplio(a); **wide interests** intereses muy diversos **c)** [off target] desviado(a) **2.** *adv* **to open one's eyes wide** abrir los ojos de par en par; **wide awake** completamente despierto(a); **wide open** abierto(a) de par en par

widely [ˈwaɪdlɪ] *adv* [travel etc] extensamente; [believed] generalmente; **he is widely known** es muy conocido

widen [ˈwaɪdən] **1.** *vt* ensanchar; [interests] ampliar **2.** *vi* ensancharse

widescreen [ˈwaɪdskriːn] *adj* CIN en cinemascope, de pantalla ancha; **widescreen TV** televisor *m* panorámico *or* de pantalla panorámica

widespread [ˈwaɪdspred] *adj* [unrest, belief] general; [damage] extenso(a); **to become widespread** generalizarse

widow [ˈwɪdəʊ] *n* viuda *f*

widower [ˈwɪdəʊə(r)] *n* viudo *m*

width [wɪdθ] *n* **a)** anchura *f* **b)** [of material, swimming pool] ancho *m*

wield [wiːld] *vt* [weapon] blandir; *Fig* [power] ejercer

wife [waɪf] *(pl* **wives)** *n* mujer *f*, esposa *f*

WiFi [ˈwaɪfaɪ] *n* COMPUT *(abbr of* **wireless fidelity)** wifi *m inv*, wi-fi *m inv*; **Wifi hotspot** punto *m* de acceso wifi

wig [wɪg] *n* peluca *f*

wiggle [ˈwɪgəl] **1.** *vt* [finger etc] menear; **to wiggle one's hips** contonearse **2.** *vi* menearse

wild [waɪld] **1.** *adj* **a)** [animal, tribe] salvaje; **wild beast** fiera *f* **b)** [plant] silvestre **c)** [landscape] agreste; **the Wild West** el Salvaje Oeste **d)** [temperament, behaviour] alocado(a); [appearance] desordenado(a); [passions etc] desenfrenado(a); [laughter, thoughts] loco(a); [applause] fervoroso(a); *Fam & Fig* **she is wild about him/about tennis** está loca por él/por el tenis **2.** *adv Fig* **to run wild** [children] desmandarse **3.** *n* **in the wild** en el estado salvaje

wilderness [ˈwɪldənɪs] *n* desierto *m*

wildlife [ˈwaɪldlaɪf] *n* fauna *f*; **wildlife park** parque *m* natural

wildly [ˈwaɪldlɪ] *adv* **a)** [rush round etc] como un(a) loco(a); [shoot] sin apuntar; [hit out] a tontas y a locas **b)** **wildly enthusiastic** loco(a) de entusiasmo; **wildly inaccurate** totalmente erróneo(a)

wilful, *US* **wilfull** [ˈwɪlfʊl] *adj* **a)** [stubborn] terco(a) **b)** JUR premeditado(a)

will[1] [wɪl] **1.** *n* **a)** voluntad *f*; **good/ill will** buena/mala voluntad; **of my own free will** por mi propia voluntad **b)** JUR [testament] testamento *m*; **to make one's will** hacer testamento **2.** *vt* **fate willed that ...** el destino quiso que ...

will[2] [wɪl]

En el inglés hablado, y en el escrito en estilo coloquial, el verbo **will** se contrae de manera que **I/you/he** *etc* **will** se transforman en **I'll, you'll, he'll** *etc*. La forma negativa **will not** se transforma en **won't**.

v aux **a)** [future - esp 2nd & 3rd person] **they'll come** vendrán; **will he be there? — yes, he will** ¿estará allí?

— sí(, estará); **you'll tell him, won't you?** se lo dirás, ¿verdad?; **she won't do it** no lo hará

b) [command] **you will be here at eleven!** ¡debes estar aquí a las once!

c) [future perfect] **they'll have finished by tomorrow** habrán terminado para mañana

d) [willingness] **I won't have it!** ¡no lo permito!; **won't you sit down?** ¿quiere sentarse?

e) [custom] **accidents will happen** siempre habrá accidentes

f) [persistence] **if you will go out without a coat …** si te empeñas en salir sin abrigo …

willing ['wɪlɪŋ] *adj* [obliging] complaciente; **to be willing to do sth** estar dispuesto(a) a hacer algo

willingly ['wɪlɪŋlɪ] *adv* de buena gana

willingness ['wɪlɪŋnɪs] *n* buena voluntad

willow ['wɪləʊ] *n* **willow (tree)** sauce *m*; **weeping willow** sauce *m* llorón

willpower ['wɪlpaʊə(r)] *n* (fuerza *f* de) voluntad *f*

wilt [wɪlt] *vi* marchitarse

win [wɪn] (*pt & pp* **won**) **1.** *n* victoria *f* **2.** *vt* **a)** ganar; [prize] llevarse; [victory] conseguir

b) *Fig* [sympathy, friendship] ganarse; [praise] cosechar; **to win sb's love** conquistar a algn

3. *vi* ganar

■ **win back** *vt sep* recuperar

■ **win over** *vt sep* [to cause, idea] atraer (**to** a); [voters, support] ganarse

■ **win through** *vi* conseguir triunfar

wince [wɪns] *vi* tener un rictus de dolor

winch [wɪntʃ] *n* cigüeña *f*, torno *m*

wind¹ [wɪnd] **1.** *n* **a)** viento *m*; *Fig* **to get wind of sth** olerse algo; **wind farm** parque eólico **b)** [breath] aliento *m*; **to get one's second wind** recobrar el aliento **c)** MED flato *m*, gases *mpl* **d)** **wind instrument** instrumento *m* de viento **2.** *vt* **to be winded** quedarse sin aliento

wind² [waɪnd] (*pt & pp* **wound**) **1.** *vt* **a)** [on to a reel] enrollar **b)** **to wind on / back** [film, tape] avanzar / rebobinar **c)** [clock] dar cuerda a **2.** *vi* [road, river] serpentear ■ **wind down 1.** *vt sep* [window] bajar **2.** *vi Fam* [person] relajarse ■ **wind up 1.** *vt sep* **a)** [roll up] enrollar **b)** [business etc] cerrar; [debate] clausurar **c)** [clock] dar cuerda a **2.** *vi* [meeting] terminar

windfall ['wɪndfɔːl] *n Fig* ganancia inesperada

winding ['waɪndɪŋ] *adj* [road, river] sinuoso(a); [staircase] de caracol

windmill ['wɪndmɪl] *n* molino *m* (de viento)

window ['wɪndəʊ] *n* [of building & COMPUT] ventana *f*; [of vehicle, ticket office etc] ventanilla *f*; **(shop) window** escaparate *m*, *Am* vidriera *f*, *Chile, Col, Méx* vitrina *f*; **to clean the windows** limpiar los cristales; **window box** jardinera *f*; **window cleaner** limpiacristales *mf inv*

windowpane ['wɪndəʊpeɪn] *n* vidrio *m* or *Esp* cristal *m* (de ventana)

window-shopping ['wɪndəʊʃɒpɪŋ] *n* **to go window-shopping** ir a mirar escaparates

windowsill ['wɪndəʊsɪl] *n* alféizar *m*

windscreen ['wɪndskriːn], *US* **windshield** ['wɪndiːld] *n* parabrisas *m inv*; **windscreen wiper** limpiaparabrisas *m inv*

windsurfing ['wɪndsɜːfɪŋ] *n* **to go windsurfing** ir a hacer windsurf or tabla a vela

windy ['wɪndɪ] (*compar* **windier**, *superl* **windiest**) *adj* [weather] ventoso(a); [place] desprotegido(a) del viento; **it is very windy today** hoy hace mucho viento

wine [waɪn] *n* vino *m*; **wine cellar** bodega *f*; **wine list** lista *f* de vinos; **wine merchant** vinatero(a) *m,f*; **wine tasting** cata *f* de vinos; **wine vinegar** vinagre *m* de vino

wineglass ['waɪnglɑːs] *n* copa *f* (para vino)

wing [wɪŋ] *n* **a)** ORNITH & AVIAT ala *f* **b)** [of building] ala *f* **c)** *Br* AUTO aleta *f*; **wing mirror** retrovisor *m* lateral **d)** THEAT **(in the) wings** (entre) bastidores *mpl* **e)** FTBL banda *f* **f)** POL ala *f*; **the left wing** la izquierda

wink [wɪŋk] **1.** *n* guiño *m* **2.** *vi* **a)** [person] guiñar (el ojo) **b)** [light] parpadear

winner ['wɪnə(r)] *n* ganador(a) *m,f*

winning ['wɪnɪŋ] *adj* [person, team] ganador(a); [number] premiado(a); [goal] decisivo(a); **winning post** meta *f*

winter ['wɪntə(r)] **1.** *n* invierno *m* **2.** *adj* de invierno; **winter sports** deportes *mpl* de invierno **3.** *vi* invernar

win-win *adj* **it's a win-win situation** es una situación en la que todos ganan

wipe [waɪp] *vt* limpiar; **to wipe one's brow** enjugarse la frente; **to wipe one's feet/nose** limpiarse los pies / las narices ■ **wipe away** *vt sep* [tear] enjugar ■ **wipe off** *vt sep* quitar frotando; **to wipe sth off the blackboard/the tape** borrar algo de la pizarra / de la cinta ■ **wipe out** *vt sep* **a)** [erase] borrar **b)** [army] aniquilar; [species etc] exterminar ■ **wipe up** *vt sep* limpiar

wiper ['waɪpə(r)] *n* AUTO limpiaparabrisas *m inv*

wire [waɪə(r)] **1.** *n* **a)** alambre *m*; ELEC cable *m*; TEL hilo; **wire cutters** cizalla *f* **b)** [telegram] telegrama *m* **2.** *vt* **a)** **to wire (up) a house** poner la instalación eléctrica de una casa; **to wire (up) an appliance to the mains** conectar un aparato a la toma eléctrica **b)** [information] enviar por telegrama

wiring ['waɪərɪŋ] *n* [network] cableado *m*; [action] instalación *f* del cableado

wisdom ['wɪzdəm] *n* **a)** [learning] sabiduría *f*, saber *m* **b)** [good sense - of person] cordura *f*; [of action] sensatez *f* **c) wisdom tooth** muela *f* del juicio

wise [waɪz] *adj* **a)** sabio(a); **a wise man** un sabio **b)** [remark] juicioso(a); [decision] acertado(a); **it would be wise to keep quiet** sería prudente callarse

wish [wɪʃ] **1.** *n* **a)** [desire] deseo *m* (**for** de); **to make a wish** pedir un deseo

b) best wishes felicitaciones *fpl*; **give your mother my best wishes** salude a su madre de mi parte; **with best wishes, Peter** [at end of letter] saludos cordiales, Peter

2. *vt* **a)** [want] querer, desear; **I wish I could stay longer** me gustaría poder quedarme más tiempo; **I wish you had told me!** ¡ojalá me lo hubieras dicho! **b) to wish sb goodnight** darle las buenas noches a algn; **to wish sb well** desearle a algn mucha suerte

3. *vi* [want] desear; **as you wish** como quieras; **to wish for sth** desear algo

wishful ['wɪʃful] *adj* **it's wishful thinking** es hacerse ilusiones

wisp [wɪsp] *n* [of wool, hair] mechón *m*; [of smoke] voluta *f*

wistful ['wɪstful] *adj* melancólico(a)

wit [wɪt] *n* **a)** (often *pl*) [intelligence] inteligencia *f*; *Fig* **to be at one's wits' end** estar para volverse loco(a); *Fam* & *Fig* **to have one's wits about one** ser despabilado(a) **b)** [humour] ingenio *m*

witch [wɪtʃ] *n* bruja *f*; *Fig* **witch hunt** caza *f* de brujas

with [wɪð, wɪθ] *prep* con; **do you have any money with you?** ¿traes dinero?; **the man with the glasses** el hombre de las gafas; **he went with me/you** fue conmigo / contigo; **with all his faults, I admire him** le admiro con todos sus defectos; **with your permission** con su permiso; **we're all with you** [support] todos estamos contigo; **you're not with me, are you?** [understand] no me entiendes, ¿verdad?; **to fill a vase with water** llenar un jarrón de agua; **it is made with butter** está hecho con mantequilla; **to be paralysed with fear** estar paralizado(a) de miedo

withdraw [wɪð'drɔ:] (*pt* withdrew, *pp* withdrawn) **1.** *vt* **a)** retirar, sacar; **to withdraw money from the bank** sacar dinero del banco **b)** [go back on] retirar; [statement] retractarse de; [plan, claim] renunciar a **2.** *vi* **a)** retirarse **b)** [drop out] renunciar

withdrawal [wɪðˈdrɔːəl] *n* retirada *f*; [of statement] retractación *f*; [of complaint, plan] renuncia *f*; **withdrawal symptoms** síndrome *m* de abstinencia

withdrawn [wɪðˈdrɔːn] **1.** *adj* [person] introvertido(a) **2.** *pp of* **withdraw**

withdrew [wɪðˈdruː] *pt of* **withdraw**

withhold [wɪðˈhəʊld] *(pt & pp* **withheld** [wɪðˈheld]*)vt* [money] retener; [decision] aplazar; [consent] negar; [information] ocultar

within [wɪˈðɪn] **1.** *prep* **a)** [inside] dentro de **b)** [range] **the house is within walking distance** se puede ir andando a la casa; **situated within 5 km of the town** situado(a) a menos de 5 km de la ciudad; **within sight of the sea** con vistas al mar **c)** [time] **they arrived within a few days of each other** llegaron con pocos días de diferencia; **within the next five years** durante los cinco próximos años **2.** *adv* dentro; **from within** desde dentro

without [wɪˈðaʊt] *prep* sin; **he did it without my knowing** lo hizo sin que lo supiera yo; *Fig* **to do** o **go without sth** [voluntarily] prescindir de algo; [forcibly] pasar(se) sin algo

withstand [wɪðˈstænd] *(pt & pp* **withstood** [wɪðˈstʊd]*) vt* resistir a; [pain] aguantar

witness [ˈwɪtnɪs] **1.** *n* **a)** [person] testigo *mf*; **witness box**, *US* **witness stand** barra *f* de los testigos **b)** [evidence] **to bear witness to sth** dar fe de algo **2.** *vt* **a)** [see] presenciar, ser testigo de **b)** *Fig* [notice] notar **c)** *JUR* **to witness a document** firmar un documento como testigo

wittily [ˈwɪtɪlɪ] *adv* ingeniosamente

witty [ˈwɪtɪ] *(compar* **wittier,** *superl* **wittiest)adj** ingenioso(a), agudo(a)

wives [waɪvz] *pl of* **wife**

wizard [ˈwɪzəd] *n* hechicero *m*, mago *m*

WKND MESSAGING *(abbr of* **weekend)** we

WMD *npl (abbr of* **weapons of mass destruction)** ADM *fpl*

wobble [ˈwɒbəl] *vi* [table, ladder etc] tambalearse; [jelly] temblar

wobbly [ˈwɒblɪ] *adj* [chair, table] cojo(a); [shelf, ladder] tambaleante

woe [wəʊ] *n Liter* infortunio *m*; **woe betide you if I catch you!** ¡ay de ti si te cojo!

woke [wəʊk] *pt of* **wake**

woken [ˈwəʊkən] *pp of* **wake**

wolf [wʊlf] *(pl* **wolves** [wʊlvz]*)n* lobo *m*; *Fig* **a wolf in sheep's clothing** un lobo con piel de cordero

woman [ˈwʊmən] *(pl* **women)***n* mujer *f*; **old woman** vieja *f*; *Fam* **women's libber** feminista *mf*; *Fam* **women's lib** movimiento *m* feminista; **women's rights** derechos *mpl* de la mujer

womb [wuːm] *n* matriz *f*, útero *m*

women [ˈwɪmɪn] *pl of* **woman**

won [wʌn] *pt & pp of* **win**

wonder [ˈwʌndə(r)] **1.** *n* **a)** [miracle] milagro *m*; **no wonder he hasn't come** no es de extrañar que no haya venido **b)** [amazement] admiración *f*, asombro *m*; **boy wonder** pequeño genio *m* **2.** *vt* **a)** [be surprised] sorprenderse **b)** [ask oneself] preguntarse; **I wonder why** ¿por qué será? **3.** *vi* **a)** [marvel] maravillarse; **to wonder at sth** admirarse de algo **b)** **it makes you wonder** [reflect] te da que pensar

wonderful [ˈwʌndəfʊl] *adj* maravilloso(a)

won't [wəʊnt] = **will not**

wood [wʊd] *n* **a)** [forest] bosque *m* **b)** [material] madera *f*; [for fire] leña *f*

wooden [ˈwʊdən] *adj* **a)** de madera; **wooden spoon/leg** cuchara *f*/pata *f* de palo **b)** *Fig* rígido(a); [acting] sin expresión

woodwork [ˈwʊdwɜːk] *n* **a)** [craft] carpintería *f* **b)** [of building] maderaje *m*

woodworm [ˈwʊdwɜːm] *n* carcoma *f*

wool [wʊl] **1.** *n* lana *f*; *Fig* **to pull the wool over sb's eyes** embaucar o dar el pego a algn **2.** *adj* de lana

woollen, *US* **woolen** [ˈwʊlən] **1.** *adj* **a)** de lana **b)** [industry] lanero(a) **2.** *npl* **woollens** géneros *mpl* de lana o de punto

word [wɜːd] **1.** *n* **a)** [spoken, written] palabra *f*; **in other words ...** es decir ..., o sea ...; *Fig* **a word of advice** un consejo; *Fig* **I'd like a word with you** quiero hablar contigo un momento; *Fig* **she didn't say it in so many words** no lo dijo de modo tan explícito; **in the words of the poet ...** como dice el poeta ...; *Fig* **word for word** palabra por palabra; **word processing** tratamiento *m* de textos; **word processor** procesador *m* de textos **b)** *Fig* [message] mensaje *m*; **by word of mouth** de palabra; **is there any word from him?** ¿hay noticias de él?; **to send word** mandar recado **c)** *Fig* [promise] palabra *f*; **he's a man of his word** es hombre de palabra **2.** *vt* [express] formular; **a badly worded letter** una carta mal redactada

wording [ˈwɜːdɪŋ] *n* expresión *f*; **I changed the wording slightly** cambié algunas palabras

wordy [ˈwɜːdɪ] *adj* verboso(a)

wore [wɔː(r)] *pt of* **wear**

work [wɜːk] **1.** *n* **a)** trabajo *m*; **his work in the field of physics** su labor en el campo de la física; **it's hard work** cuesta trabajo **b)** [employment] trabajo *m*, empleo *m*; **work permit** permiso *m* de trabajo; **to be out of work** no tener trabajo, *Esp* estar parado(a) **c)** [action] obra *f*, acción *f*; **keep up the good work!** ¡que siga así! **d)** a work of art una obra de arte **e)** **works** [construction] obras *fpl*; **public works** obras (públicas) **f)** **works** [machinery] mecanismo *m* **g)** *Br* **works** [factory] fábrica *f*; [mechanism] mecanismo *m*; [digging, building] obras *fpl* **2.** *vt* **a)** [drive] hacer trabajar; **to work one's way up in a firm** trabajarse el ascenso en una empresa **b)** [machine] manejar **c)** [miracles, changes] operar, hacer **d)** [land] cultivar **e)** [wood, metal etc] trabajar **3.** *vi* **a)** trabajar (**on** *or* **at** en); **to work as a gardener** trabajar de jardinero **b)** [machine] funcionar; **it works on gas** funciona con gas **c)** [drug] surtir efecto; [system] funcionar bien; [plan, trick] salir bien **d)** [operate] obrar; **to**

work loose soltarse; **we have no data to work on** no tenemos datos en que basarnos ■ **work off** *vt sep* [fat] eliminar trabajando; [anger] desahogar ■ **work out 1.** *vt sep* **a)** [plan] idear; [itinerary] planear; [details] desarrollar **b)** [problem] solucionar; [solution] encontrar; [amount] calcular; **I can't work out how he did it** no me explico cómo lo hizo **2.** *vi* **a)** **things didn't work out for her** las cosas no le salieron bien **b)** **it works out at five each** sale a cinco cada uno **c)** SPORT hacer ejercicio ■ **work through** *vi* penetrar (**to** hasta) ■ **work up** *vt sep* [excite] acalorar; **to get worked up** excitarse

workaholic [wɜːkəˈhɒlɪk] *n Fam* adicto(a) *m,f* al trabajo

worker [ˈwɜːkə(r)] *n* trabajador(a) *m,f*; [manual] obrero(a) *m,f*

workforce [ˈwɜːkfɔːs] *n* mano *f* de obra

working [ˈwɜːkɪŋ] **1.** *adj* **a)** [population, capital] activo(a); **working class** clase obrera; **working man** obrero *m* **b)** [clothes, conditions, hours] de trabajo; **working day** día *m* laborable; [number of hours] jornada *f* laboral; *Br* **working week** semana *f* laboral **c)** [majority] suficiente; **working knowledge** conocimientos básicos **d)** **it is in working order** funciona **2.** *n* **workings** [mechanics] funcionamiento *m*; MINING explotación *f*

workload [ˈwɜːkləʊd] *n* cantidad *f* de trabajo

workman [ˈwɜːkmən] *n* [manual] obrero *m*

workmanship [ˈwɜːkmənʃɪp] *n* [appearance] acabado *m*; [skill] habilidad *f*, arte *m*; **a fine piece of workmanship** un trabajo excelente

workplace [ˈwɜːkpleɪs] *n* lugar *m* de trabajo

workshop [ˈwɜːkʃɒp] *n* taller *m*

workspace [ˈwɜːkspeɪs] *n* COMPUT área *f* or espacio *m* de trabajo

workstation [ˈwɜːkˌsteɪʃn] *n* COMPUT puesto *m* de trabajo

worktop [ˈwɜːktɒp] *n Br* encimera *f*

workweek *n US* semana *f* laboral

world [wɜːld] *n* mundo *m*; **the best in the world** el mejor del mundo; FTBL **the World Cup** los Mundiales; **world record** récord *m* mundial; **world war** guerra *f* mundial

worldly ['wɜːldlɪ] *adj* mundano(a)

worldwide ['wɜːldwaɪd] *adj* mundial

worm [wɜːm] **1.** *n* a) [animal & COMPUT] gusano *m*; **(earth) worm** lombriz *f* (de tierra) b) MED **worms** lombrices *fpl* **2.** *vt* **to worm a secret out of sb** sonsacarle un secreto a algn

worn [wɔːn] **1.** *adj* gastado(a), usado(a) **2.** *pp of* **wear**

worn-out ['wɔːnaʊt] *adj* [thing] gastado(a); [person] rendido(a), agotado(a)

worried ['wʌrɪd] *adj* inquieto(a), preocupado(a)

worry ['wʌrɪ] **1.** *vt* a) preocupar, inquietar; **it doesn't worry me** me trae sin cuidado b) [pester] molestar **2.** *vi* preocuparse (**about** por); **don't worry** no te preocupes **3.** *n* [state] inquietud *f*; [cause] preocupación *f*

worrying ['wʌrɪɪŋ] *adj* inquietante, preocupante

worse [wɜːs] **1.** (*compar of* **bad**) *adj* peor; **he gets worse and worse** va de mal en peor; **to get worse** empeorar; *Fam* **worse luck!** ¡mala suerte! **2.** *n* **a change for the worse** un empeoramiento; *Fig* **to take a turn for the worse** empeorar **3.** (*compar of* **badly**) *adv* peor; **worse than ever** peor que nunca

worsen ['wɜːsən] *vt* & *vi* empeorar

worship ['wɜːʃɪp] **1.** *vt* adorar **2.** *n* a) adoración *f* b) [ceremony] culto *m* c) *Br* **his Worship the Mayor** el señor alcalde; JUR **Your Worship** señoría

worst [wɜːst] **1.** (*superl of* **bad**) *adj* peor; **the worst part about it is that ...** lo peor es que ... **2.** *n* a) [person] el / la peor, los / las peores b) **the worst of the storm is over** ya ha pasado lo peor de la tormenta

3. (*superl of* **badly**) *adv* peor; **at (the) worst** en el peor de los casos; *Fig* **to come off worst** salir perdiendo

worth [wɜːθ] **1.** *adj* a) **to be worth £3** valer 3 libras; **a house worth £50,000** una casa que vale 50.000 libras b) [deserving of] merecedor(a) de; **a book worth reading** un libro que merece la pena leer; **for what it's worth** por si sirve de algo; **it's worth your while**, **it's worth it** vale *or* merece la pena; **it's worth mentioning** es digno de mención **2.** *n* a) [in money] valor *m*; **£5 worth of petrol** gasolina por valor de 5 libras b) [of person] valía *f*

worthless ['wɜːθlɪs] *adj* sin valor; [person] despreciable

worthwhile [wɜːθ'waɪl] *adj* valioso(a), que vale la pena

worthy ['wɜːðɪ] (*compar* **worthier**, *superl* **worthiest**) *adj* a) [deserving] digno(a) (**of** de); [winner, cause] justo(a) b) [citizen] respetable; [effort, motives, action] loable

would [wʊd] (*unstressed* [wəd])

En el inglés hablado, y en el escrito en estilo coloquial, el verbo **would** se contrae de manera que **I** / **you** / **he** *etc* **would** se transforman en **I'd**, **you'd**, **he'd** *etc*. La forma negativa **would not** se transforma en **wouldn't**.

v aux a) [conditional] **I would go if I had time** iría si tuviera tiempo; **he would have won but for that** habría ganado si no hubiera sido por eso b) [reported speech] **he said that he would come** dijo que vendría c) [willingness] **the car wouldn't start** el coche no arrancaba; **would you do me a favour?** ¿me haces un favor? d) [wishing] **I'd rather go home** preferiría ir a casa; **would you like a cigarette?** ¿quiere un cigarrillo? e) [custom] **we would go for walks** solíamos dar un paseo

wound¹ [waʊnd] *pt* & *pp of* **wind**

wound² [wuːnd] **1.** *n* herida *f* **2.** *vt* herir

wove [wəʊv] *pt of* **weave**

woven ['wəʊvən] *pp of* **weave**

wow [waʊ] *interj Fam* ¡hala!, *RP* ¡uau!

wrap [ræp] **1.** *vt* **to wrap (up)** envolver; **he wrapped his arms around her** la estrechó entre sus brazos **2.** *vi Fam* **wrap up well** abrígate **3.** *n* [shawl] chal *m*; [cape] capa *f*

wrapped [ræpt] *adj* [bread, cheese] envuelto(a)

wrapper ['ræpə(r)] *n* [of sweet] envoltorio *m*; [of book] sobrecubierta *f*

wrapping ['ræpɪŋ] *n* **wrapping paper** papel *m* de envolver

wreath [riːθ] *(pl* **wreaths** [riːðz, riːθs]*) n* [of flowers] corona *f*; **laurel wreath** corona de laurel

wreck [rek] **1.** *n* **a)** NAUT naufragio *m*; [ship] barco naufragado **b)** [of car, plane] restos *mpl*; [of building] ruinas *fpl* **c)** *Fig* [person] ruina *f* **2.** *vt* **a)** [ship] hacer naufragar **b)** [car, machine] destrozar **c)** *Fig* [health, life] arruinar; [plans, hopes] desbaratar; [chances] echar a perder

wreckage ['rekɪʤ] *n* [of ship, car, plane] restos *mpl*; [of building] ruinas *fpl*

wrench [renʧ] **1.** *n* **a)** [pull] tirón *m* **b)** MED torcedura *f* **c)** [tool] *Br* llave inglesa; *US* llave **2.** *vt* **to wrench oneself free** soltarse de un tirón; **to wrench sth off sb** arrebatar algo a algn; **to wrench sth off/open** quitar/abrir algo de un tirón

wrestle ['resəl] *vi* luchar

wrestler ['reslə(r)] *n* luchador(a) *m,f*

wrestling ['reslɪŋ] *n* lucha *f*

wretched ['reʧɪd] *adj* **a)** desdichado(a); [conditions] deplorable; *Fam* [bad, poor] horrible **b)** **I feel wretched** [ill] me siento fatal **c)** [contemptible] despreciable **d)** *Fam* [damned] maldito(a), condenado(a)

wriggle ['rɪgəl] **1.** *vt* menear **2.** *vi* **to wriggle (about)** [worm] serpentear; [restless child] moverse nerviosamente; **to wriggle free** escapar deslizándose

wring [rɪŋ] *(pt & pp* **wrung***) vt* **a)** [clothes] escurrir; [hands] retorcer **b)** *Fig* [extract] arrancar, sacar

wrinkle ['rɪŋkəl] **1.** *n* arruga *f* **2.** *vt* arrugar **3.** *vi* arrugarse

wrist [rɪst] *n* muñeca *f*

wristwatch ['rɪstwɒʧ] *n* reloj *m* de pulsera

write [raɪt] *(pt* **wrote***, pp* **written***) * **1.** *vt* escribir; [article] redactar; [cheque] extender **2.** *vi* escribir (**about** sobre); **to write for a paper** colaborar en un periódico ▪ **write back** *vi* contestar ▪ **write down** *vt sep* poner por escrito; [note] apuntar ▪ **write in** *vi* escribir ▪ **write off 1.** *vt sep* [debt] condonar; [car] destrozar **2.** *vi* **to write off for sth** pedir algo por escrito ▪ **write out** *vt sep* [cheque, recipe] extender ▪ **write up** *vt sep* [notes] redactar; [diary, journal] poner al día

writer ['raɪtə(r)] *n* [by profession] escritor(a) *m,f*; [of book, letter] autor(a) *m,f*

writing ['raɪtɪŋ] *n* **a)** [script] escritura *f*; [handwriting] letra *f*; **in writing** por escrito **b)** **writings** escritos *mpl* **c)** [action] escritura *f*; **writing desk** escritorio *m*

written ['rɪtən] *pp of* **write**

w r o n g [rɒŋ] **1.** *adj* **a)** [person] equivocado(a); **to be wrong** no tener razón; **you're wrong in thinking that ...** te equivocas si piensas que ... **b)** [answer, way] incorrecto(a), equivocado(a); **my watch is wrong** mi reloj anda mal; **to go the wrong way** equivocarse de camino; TEL **I've got the wrong number** me he confundido de número **c)** [unsuitable] impropio(a), inadecuado(a); [time] inoportuno(a); **to say the wrong thing** decir algo inoportuno **d)** [immoral etc] malo(a); **what's wrong with smoking?** ¿qué tiene de malo fumar? **e)** **something's wrong** hay algo que no está bien; **what's wrong (with you)?** ¿qué (te) pasa? **2.** *adv* mal, incorrectamente; **to get it wrong** equivocarse; *Fam* **to go wrong** [plan] fallar, salir mal **3.** *n* **a)** [evil, bad action] mal *m* **b)** [injustice] injusticia *f*; [offence] agravio *m*; **the rights and wrongs of a matter** lo justo y lo injusto de un asunto **c) to be in the**

wrong [be to blame] tener la culpa **4.** *vt* [treat unfairly] ser injusto(a) con ; [offend] agraviar

wrongly ['rɒŋlɪ] *adv* **a)** [incorrectly] incorrectamente **b)** [mistakenly] equivocadamente **c)** [unjustly] injustamente

wrote [rəʊt] *pt of* **write**

wrung [rʌŋ] *pt & pp of* **wring**

wry [raɪ] *(compar* **wrier** *or* **wryer**, *superl* **wriest** *or* **wryest)** *adj* sardónico(a)

WTG MESSAGING *written abbr of* **way to go**

WTF MESSAGING *written abbr of* **what the fuck**

WTH MESSAGING *written abbr of* **what the hell**

wuss [wʌs] *n Fam* **a)** [physically] debilucho(a) *m,f* **b)** [lacking character] blandengue *mf*

WUWH MESSAGING *written abbr of* **wish you were here**

WWW *n (abbr of* **World Wide Web***)* WWW *m*

X

X, **x** [eks] *n* [the letter] X, x *f*

xenophobia [zenə'fəʊbɪə] *n* xenofobia *f*

Xerox® ['zɪərɒks] **1.** *n* fotocopia *f*, xerocopia *f* **2.** *vt* fotocopiar

XLNT MESSAGING *written abbr of* **excellent**

Xmas ['krɪsməs, 'eksməs] *n (abbr of* **Christmas***)* Navidad *f*

XML [ˌeksem'el] *n* COMPUT *(abbr of* **Extensible Markup Language***)* XML *m*

XO MESSAGING *(abbr of* **kiss and a hug***)* bss

X-ray ['eksreɪ] **1.** *n* [radiation] rayo *m* X; [picture] radiografía *f*; **to have an X-ray** hacerse una radiografía **2.** *vt* radiografiar

xylophone ['zaɪləfəʊn] *n* xilófono *m*, xilofón *m*

Y

Y, y [waɪ] *n* [the letter] Y, y *f*

yacht [jɒt] *n* yate *m*; **yacht club** club náutico

yard¹ [jɑːd] *n* [measure] yarda *f (aprox 0,914 m)*

yard² [jɑːd] *n* patio *m*; *US* jardín *m*

yardman [ˈjɑːdmæn] *n US* jardinero *m*

yarn [jɑːn] *n* **a)** SEWING hilo *m* **b)** [story] historia *f*, cuento *m*; **to spin a yarn** [lie] inventarse una historia

yawn [jɔːn] **1.** *vi* bostezar **2.** *n* bostezo *m*

year [jɪə(r)] *n* **a)** año *m*; **all year round** durante todo el año; **last year** el año pasado; **next year** el año que viene; **year in, year out** año tras año; **I'm ten years old** tengo diez años **b)** SCH curso *m*; **first-year student** estudiante *mf* de primero; SCH & UNIV **gap year** año que muchos jóvenes utilizan para viajar por el mundo o trabajar cuando terminan la educación secundaria y antes de ingresar a la universidad; **I spent my gap year in Australia** pasé un año en Australia antes de ir a la universidad

yearly [ˈjɪəlɪ] **1.** *adj* anual **2.** *adv* anualmente, cada año

yearn [jɜːn] *vi* **to yearn for sth** anhelar algo

yeast [jiːst] *n* levadura *f*

yell [jel] **1.** *vi* gritar **2.** *n* grito *m*, alarido *m*

yellow [ˈjeləʊ] **1.** *adj* amarillo(a); TEL **Yellow Pages®** páginas amarillas **2.** *n* amarillo *m*

yenta [ˈjentə] *n US Fam* [gossip] cotilla *mf*, chismoso(a) *m,f*; **she's a yenta** es una cotilla, es una chismosa

yes [jes] **1.** *adv* sí; **you said yes** dijiste que sí **2.** *n* sí *m*

yesterday [ˈjestədeɪ] *adv* & *n* ayer *m*; **the day before yesterday** anteayer; **yesterday morning** ayer por la mañana

yet [jet] **1.** *adv* **a)** not yet aún no, todavía no; **as yet** hasta ahora; **I haven't eaten yet** no he comido todavía **b)** [in questions] ya; **has he arrived yet?** ¿ha venido ya? **c)** [even] más; **yet again** otra vez; **yet more** todavía más **d)** [eventually] todavía, aún; **he'll win yet** todavía puede ganar **2.** *conj* sin embargo

yield [jiːld] **1.** *n* **a)** rendimiento *m* **b)** AGR cosecha *f* **c)** FIN beneficio *m* **2.** *vt* producir; AGR dar; [money] producir **3.** *vi* **a)** [surrender, break] ceder **b)** *US* AUTO ceder el paso

yikes [jaɪks] *interj* ¡caray!

yoga [ˈjəʊgə] *n* yoga *m*

yog(h)urt [ˈjɒgət] *n* yogur *m*

yolk [jəʊk] *n* yema *f*

yolo [ˈjəʊləʊ] *interj Fam (abbr of you only live once)* solo se vive una vez

yonks [jɒŋks] *n Br Fam* **I haven't been there for yonks** hace siglos que no voy allí

you [juː] (*unstressed* [jʊ])

In Spanish, the formal form **usted** takes a third person singular verb and **ustedes** takes a third person plural verb. In many Latin American countries, **ustedes** is the standard form of the second person plural and is not considered formal.

pers pron **a)** (*usually omitted in Spanish, except for contrast*) [subject - singular] tú, *esp RP* vos, *Formal* usted; [pl] *Esp* vosotros(as), *Am or Formal* ustedes; **have you got it?** [singular] ¿lo tienes tú?, *Formal* ¿lo tiene usted?; [pl] *Esp* ¿lo tenéis vosotros?, *Am or Formal* ¿lo tienen ustedes?

youth

b) [direct object - singular] te, *Formal* lo(la); [pl] *Esp* os, *Am* or *Formal* los(las); **I can understand your son but not you** [singular] a tu hijo lo entiendo, pero a ti no, *Formal* a su hijo lo entiendo, pero a usted no; [pl] *Esp* a vuestro hijo lo entiendo, pero a vosotros no, *Am* or *Formal* a su hijo lo entiendo, pero a ustedes no
c) [indirect object - singular] te, *Formal* le; [pl] *Esp* os, *Am* or *Formal* les; **I gave you the book** [singular] te di el libro, *Formal* le di el libro; [pl] *Esp* os di el libro, *Am* or *Formal* les di el libro; **I told you** [singular] te lo dije, *Formal* se lo dije; [pl] *Esp* os lo dije, *Am* or *Formal* se lo dije
d) [after preposition - singular] ti, *Formal* usted; [pl] *Esp* vosotros(as), *Am* or *Formal* ustedes
e) [impers] **you don't do that kind of thing** esas cosas no se hacen

young [jʌŋ] **1.** *adj* [age] joven; [brother etc] pequeño(a); **young lady** señorita *f*; **young man** joven *m* **2.** *npl* **a)** [people] **the young** los jóvenes, la juventud **b)** [animals] crías *fpl*

youngster ['jʌŋstə(r)] *n* muchacho(a) *m,f*

your [jɔː(r)] (unstressed [jə(r)]) *poss adj*
a) [of one person] tu, *Formal* su; **your house** tu/su casa; **your books** tus/sus libros
b) [of more than one person] *Esp* vuestro(a), *Am* or *Formal* su; **your house** *Esp* vuestra casa, *Am* or *Formal* su casa; **your books** *Esp* vuestros libros, *Am* or *Formal* sus libros
c) [for parts of body, clothes - translated by definite article] **did you hit your head?** ¿te has or *Formal* se ha dado un golpe en la cabeza?
d) [impersonal] **smoking is bad for your health** el tabaco perjudica la salud

yours [jɔːz]

In Spanish, the forms **tuyo(a), suyo(a)** and **vuestro(a)** require a definite article in the singular and in the plural when they are the subject of the phrase.

poss pron **a)** [of one person - singular] tuyo(a) *m,f*, *Formal* suyo(a) *m,f*; [pl] tuyos(as) *m,fpl*, *Formal* suyos(as) *m,fpl*; **my house is big but yours is bigger** mi casa es grande, pero la tuya/suya es mayor; **this book is yours** este libro es tuyo/suyo; **these books are yours** estos libros son tuyos/suyos; **yours (sincerely/faithfully)** atentamente
b) [of more than one person - singular] *Esp* vuestro(a), *Am* or *Formal* suyo(a); [pl] *Esp* vuestros(as), *Am* or *Formal* suyos(as); **this book is yours** este libro es vuestro/suyo; **these books are yours** estos libros son vuestros/suyos

yourself [jɔː'self] *pron* **a)** [reflexive] te, *Formal* se; **have you hurt yourself?** ¿te has hecho daño?; *Formal* ¿se ha hecho daño? **b)** [emphatic] tú mismo *m*, tú misma *f*, *Formal* usted mismo *m*, usted misma *f*; **you told me yourself** me lo dijiste tú mismo, *Formal* me lo dijo usted mismo **c)** [after preposition] ti, *Formal* usted; **did you do this by yourself?** ¿lo has hecho tú solo?, *Formal* ¿lo ha hecho usted solo?; **do you live by yourself?** ¿vives solo?, *Formal* ¿vive solo?

yourselves [jɔː'selvz] *pron* **a)** [reflexive] *Esp* os, *Am* or *Formal* se; **have you hurt yourselves?** *Esp* ¿os habéis hecho daño?, *Am* or *Formal* ¿se han hecho daño?
b) [emphatic] *Esp* vosotros(as) mismos(as), *Am* or *Formal* ustedes mismos(as); **did you do all the work yourselves?** *Esp* ¿habéis hecho todo el trabajo vosotros solos?, *Am* or *Formal* ¿han hecho todo el trabajo ustedes solos?
c) [after preposition] *Esp* vosotros(as), *Am* or *Formal* ustedes; **did you do this by yourselves?** *Esp* ¿lo habéis hecho vosotros solos?, *Am* or *Formal* ¿lo han hecho ustedes solos?; **did you buy it for yourselves?** *Esp* ¿os lo habéis comprado para vosotros?, *Am* or *Formal* ¿se lo han comprado para ustedes?

youth [juːθ] *n* **a)** juventud *f* **b)** [young man] joven *m*; **youth club** club *m* juvenil; **youth hostel** albergue *m* juvenil

youthful [ˈjuːθfʊl] *adj* juvenil, joven

YouTube® [ˈjuːˌtjuːb] **1.** *n* INTERNET YouTube® *m* **2.** *v* INTERNET colgar en YouTube®

Yugoslavia [ˌjuːgəˈslɑːvɪə] *n* Yugoslavia *f*; **the former Yugoslavia** la antigua Yugoslavia

yuppie [ˈjʌpɪ] *n* yupi *mf*; **a yuppie restaurant** un restaurante de yupis

Z

Z, z [zed, *US* ziː] *n* [the letter] Z, z *f*

zany ['zeɪnɪ] *(compar* **zanier**, *superl* **zaniest)** *adj Fam* **a)** [mad] *Esp* chiflado(a), *Am* zafado(a), *RP* rayado(a) **b)** [eccentric] estrafalario(a)

zeal [ziːl] *n* [enthusiasm] entusiasmo *m*

zealous ['zeləs] *adj* [enthusiastic] entusiasta

zebra ['ziːbrə, 'zebrə] *n* cebra *f*; *Br* **zebra crossing** paso *m* de cebra

zero ['zɪərəʊ] *n* cero *m*; **zero hour** hora *f* cero

zero-carbon *adj* cero carbono, con cero emisiones netas

zest [zest] *n* [eagerness] entusiasmo *m*

zigzag ['zɪgzæg] **1.** *n* zigzag *m* **2.** *vi* zigzaguear

zinc [zɪŋk] *n* cinc *m*, zinc *m*

zinger ['zɪŋə(r)] *n US Fam* **a)** [pointed remark] pulla *f* **b)** [impressive thing] **it was a real zinger** fue impresionante; **a real zinger of a black eye** un ojo morado impresionante

zip [zɪp] **1.** *n* **a)** *Br* **zip (fastener)** cremallera *f*, *Am* cierre *m* **b)** *Fam* brío *m*; *US* **zip code** código *m* postal **2.** *vi* cerrarse con cremallera ▪ **zip by** *vi* pasar como un rayo ▪ **zip up** *vt sep* cerrar la cremallera *or Am* el cierre de; **to zip sb up** cerrar la cremallera *or Am* el cierre a algn

zipper ['zɪpə(r)] *n US* cremallera *f*, *Am* cierre *m*

zit [zɪt] *n Fam* grano *m*

zodiac ['zəʊdɪæk] *n* zodiaco *m*, zodíaco *m*

zone [zəʊn] **1.** *n* zona *f* **2.** *vt* dividir en zonas

zoo [zuː] *n* zoo *m*

zoom [zuːm] **1.** *n* **a)** [buzz] zumbido *m* **b)** **zoom lens** zoom *m*, teleobjetivo *m* **2.** *vi* **a)** [buzz] zumbar **b)** **to zoom past** pasar volando ▪ **zoom in** *vi* [camera] acercarse rápidamente

zucchini [zuːˈkiːnɪ] *n US* calabacín *m*, *CSur* zapallito *m*

Supplement

Spanish Verb Conjugations

Models for regular verbs

TOMAR to take

INDICATIVE

PRESENT	FUTURE	CONDITIONAL
1. tomo	tomaré	tomaría
2. tomas	tomarás	tomarías
3. toma	tomará	tomaría
1. tomamos	tomaremos	tomaríamos
2. tomáis	tomaréis	tomaríais
3. toman	tomarán	tomarían

IMPERFECT	PRETERITE	PERFECT
1. tomaba	tomé	he tomado
2. tomabas	tomaste	has tomado
3. tomaba	tomó	ha tomado
1. tomábamos	tomamos	hemos tomado
2. tomabais	tomasteis	habéis tomado
3. tomaban	tomaron	han tomado

FUTURE PERFECT	CONDITIONAL PERFECT	PLUPERFECT
1. habré tomado	habría tomado	había tomado
2. habrás tomado	habrías tomado	habías tomado
3. habrá tomado	habría tomado	había tomado
1. habremos tomado	habríamos tomado	habíamos tomado
2. habréis tomado	habríais tomado	habíais tomado
3. habrán tomado	habrían tomado	habían tomado

SUBJUNCTIVE

PRESENT	IMPERFECT	PERFECT/PLUPERFECT
1. tome	tom-ara/ase	haya/hubiera* tomado
2. tomes	tom-aras/ases	hayas/hubieras tomado
3. tome	tom-ara/ase	haya/hubiera tomado

* the alternative form 'hubiese' etc is also possible.

1. tomemos	tom-áramos/ásemos	hayamos/hubiéramos tomado
2. toméis	tom-arais/aseis	hayáis/hubierais tomado
3. tomen	tom-aran/asen	hayan/hubieran tomado

IMPERATIVE

(tú) toma
(Vd) tome
(nosotros) tomemos
(vosotros) tomad
(Vds) tomen

INFINITIVE

PRESENT
tomar

PERFECT
haber tomado

PARTICIPLE

PRESENT
tomando

PAST
tomado

COMER to eat

INDICATIVE

PRESENT	FUTURE	CONDITIONAL
1. como	comeré	comería
2. comes	comerás	comerías
3. come	comerá	comería
1. comemos	comeremos	comeríamos
2. coméis	comeréis	comeríais
3. comen	comerán	comerían

IMPERFECT	PRETERITE	PERFECT
1. comía	comí	he comido
2. comías	comiste	has comido
3. comía	comió	ha comido
1. comíamos	comimos	hemos comido
2. comíais	comisteis	habéis comido
3. comían	comieron	han comido

FUTURE PERFECT	CONDITIONAL PERFECT	PLUPERFECT
1. habré comido	habría comido	había comido
2. habrás comido	habrías comido	habías comido
3. habrá comido	habría comido	había comido
1. habremos comido	habríamos comido	habíamos comido
2. habréis comido	habríais comido	habíais comido
3. habrán comido	habrían comido	habían comido

SUBJUNCTIVE

PRESENT	IMPERFECT	PERFECT/PLUPERFECT
1. coma	com-iera/iese	haya/hubiera* comido
2. comas	com-ieras/ieses	hayas/hubieras comido
3. coma	com-iera/iese	haya/hubiera comido
1. comamos	com-iéramos/iésemos	hayamos/hubiéramos comido
2. comáis	com-ierais/ieseis	hayáis/hubierais comido
3. coman	com-ieran/iesen	hayan/hubieran comido

* the alternative form 'hubiese' etc is also possible

IMPERATIVE

(tú) come
(Vd) coma
(nosotros) comamos
(vosotros) comed
(Vds) coman

INFINITIVE

PRESENT
comer

PERFECT
haber comido

PARTICIPLE

PRESENT
comiendo

PAST
comido

PARTIR to leave

INDICATIVE

PRESENT	FUTURE	CONDITIONAL
1. parto	partiré	partiría
2. partes	partirás	partirías
3. parte	partirá	partiría
1. partimos	partiremos	partiríamos
2. partís	partiréis	partiríais
3. parten	partirán	partirían

IMPERFECT	PRETERITE	PERFECT
1. partía	partí	he partido
2. partías	partiste	has partido
3. partía	partió	ha partido
1. partíamos	partimos	hemos partido
2. partíais	partisteis	habéis partido
3. partían	partieron	han partido

FUTURE PERFECT	**CONDITIONAL PERFECT**	**PLUPERFECT**
1. habré partido	habría partido	había partido
2. habrás partido	habrías partido	habías partido
3. habrá partido	habría partido	había partido
1. habremos partido	habríamos partido	habíamos partido
2. habréis partido	habríais partido	habíais partido
3. habrán partido	habrían partido	habían partido

SUBJUNCTIVE

PRESENT	**IMPERFECT**	**PERFECT/PLUPERFECT**
parta	parti-era/ese	haya/hubiera* partido
partas	parti-eras/eses	hayas/hubieras partido
parta	parti-era/ese	haya/hubiera partido
partamos	parti-éramos/ésemos	hayamos/hubiéramos partido
partáis	parti-erais/eseis	hayáis/hubierais partido
partan	parti-eran/esen	hayan/hubieran partido

* the alternative form 'hubiese' etc is also possible

IMPERATIVE

(tú) parte
(Vd) parta
(nosotros) partamos
(vosotros) partid
(Vds) partan

INFINITIVE

PRESENT
partir

PERFECT
haber partido

PARTICIPLE

PRESENT
partiendo

PAST
partido

Models for irregular verbs

[1] pensar PRES pienso, piensas, piensa, pensamos, pensáis, piensan; **PRES SUBJ** piense, pienses, piense, pensemos, penséis, piensen; **IMPERAT** piensa, piense, pensemos, pensad, piensen

[2] contar PRES cuento, cuentas, cuenta, contamos, contáis, cuentan; **PRES SUBJ** cuente, cuentes, cuente, contemos, contéis, cuenten; **IMPERAT** cuenta, cuente, contemos, contad, cuenten

[3] perder PRES pierdo, pierdes, pierde, perdemos, perdéis, pierden; **PRES SUBJ** pierda, pierdas, pierda, perdamos, perdáis, pierdan; **IMPERAT** pierde, pierda, perdamos, perded, pierdan

[4] morder PRES muerdo, muerdes, muerde, mordemos, mordéis, muerden; **PRES SUBJ** muerda, muerdas, muerda, mordamos, mordáis, muerdan; **IMPERAT** muerde, muerda, mordamos, morded, muerdan

[5] sentir PRES siento, sientes, siente, sentimos, sentís, sienten; **PRES SUBJ** sienta, sientas, sienta, sintamos, sintáis, sientan; **PRES P** sintiendo; **IMPERAT** siente, sienta, sintamos, sentid, sientan

[6] vestir PRES visto, vistes, viste, vestimos, vestís, visten; **PRES SUBJ** vista, vistas, vista, vistamos, vistáis, vistan; **PRES P** vistiendo; **IMPERAT** viste, vista, vistamos, vestid, vistan

[7] dormir PRES duermo, duermes, duerme, dormimos, dormís, duermen; **PRES SUBJ** duerma, duermas, duerma, durmamos, durmáis, duerman; **PRES P** durmiendo; **IMPERAT** duerme, duerma, durmamos, dormid, duerman

[8] andar PRET anduve, anduviste, anduvo, anduvimos, anduvisteis, anduvieron; **IMPERF SUBJ** anduviera/anduviese

[9] caber PRES quepo, cabes, cabe, cabemos, cabéis, caben; **PRES SUBJ** quepa, quepas, quepa, quepamos, quepáis, quepan; **FUT** cabré; **COND** cabría; **PRET** cupe, cupiste, cupo, cupimos, cupisteis, cupieron; **IMPERF SUBJ** cupiera/cupiese; **IMPERAT** cabe, quepa, quepamos, cabed, quepan

[10] conducir PRES conduzco, conduces, conduce, conducimos, conducís, conducen; **PRES SUBJ** conduzca, conduzcas, conduzca, conduzcamos, conduzcáis, conduzcan; **PRET** conduje, condujiste, condujo, condujimos, condujisteis, condujeron; **IMPERF SUBJ** condujera/condujese; **IMPERAT** conduce, conduzca, conduzcamos, conducid, conduzcan

[11] dar PRES doy, das, da, damos, dais, dan; **PRES SUBJ** dé, des, dé, demos, deis, den; **PRET** di, diste, dio, dimos, disteis, dieron; **IMPERF SUBJ** diera/diese; **IMPERAT** da, dé, demos, dad, den

[12] decir PRES digo, dices, dice, decimos, decís, dicen; **PRES SUBJ** diga, digas, diga, digamos, digáis, digan; **FUT** diré; **COND** diría; **PRET** dije, dijiste, dijo, dijimos, dijisteis, dijeron; **IMPERF SUBJ** dijera/dijese; **PRES P** diciendo; **PP** dicho; **IMPERAT** di, diga, digamos, decid, digan

[13] **ESTAR** to be

INDICATIVE

PRESENT	**FUTURE**	**CONDITIONAL**
1. estoy	estaré	estaría
2. estás	estarás	estarías
3. está	estará	estaría
1. estamos	estaremos	estaríamos
2. estáis	estaréis	estaríais
3. están	estarán	estarían

IMPERFECT	**PRETERITE**	**PERFECT**
1. estaba	estuve	he estado
2. estabas	estuviste	has estado
3. estaba	estuvo	ha estado
1. estábamos	estuvimos	hemos estado
2. estabais	estuvisteis	habéis estado
3. estaban	estuvieron	han estado

FUTURE PERFECT	**CONDITIONAL PERFECT**	**PLUPERFECT**
1. habré estado	habría estado	había estado
2. habrás estado	habrías estado	habías estado
3. habrá estado	habría estado	había estado
1. habremos estado	habríamos estado	habíamos estado
2. habréis estado	habríais estado	habíais estado
3. habrán estado	habrían estado	habían estado

SUBJUNCTIVE

PRESENT	**IMPERFECT**	**PERFECT/PLUPERFECT**
1. esté	estuv-iera/iese	haya/hubiera* estado
2. estés	estuv-ieras/ieses	hayas/hubieras estado
3. esté	estuv-iera/iese	haya/hubiera estado
1. estemos	estuv-iéramos/iésemos	hayamos/hubiéramos estado
2. estéis	estuv-ierais/ieseis	hayáis/hubierais estado
3. estén	estuv-ieran/iesen	hayan/hubieran estado

IMPERATIVE

(tú) está
(Vd) esté
(nosotros) estemos
(vosotros) estad
(Vds) estén

INFINITIVE

PRESENT
estar

PERFECT
haber estado

PARTICIPLE

PRESENT
estando

PAST
estado

* the alternative form 'hubiese' etc is also possible

[14] HABER to have (*auxiliary*)

INDICATIVE

PRESENT	FUTURE	CONDITIONAL
1. he	habré	habría
2. has	habrás	habrías
3. ha/hay*	habrá	habría
1. hemos	habremos	habríamos
2. habéis	habréis	habríais
3. han	habrán	habrían

IMPERFECT	PRETERITE	PERFECT
1. había	hube	
2. habías	hubiste	
3. había	hubo	ha habido*
1. habíamos	hubimos	
2. habíais	hubisteis	
3. habían	hubieron	

FUTURE PERFECT	CONDITIONAL PERFECT	PLUPERFECT
1.		
2.		
3. habrá habido*	habría habido*	había habido*
1.		
2.		
3.		

SUBJUNCTIVE

PRESENT	IMPERFECT	PERFECT/PLUPERFECT
1. haya	hub-iera/iese	
2. hayas	hub-ieras/ieses	
3. haya	hub-iera/iese	haya/hubiera** habido*
1. hayamos	hub-iéramos/iésemos	
2. hayáis	hub-ierais/ieseis	
3. hayan	hub-ieran/iesen	

INFINITIVE

PRESENT
haber
PERFECT
haber habido*

PARTICIPLE

PRESENT
habiendo
PAST
habido

* 'haber' is an auxiliary verb used with the participle of another verb to form compound tenses (eg he bebido – I have drunk). 'Hay' means 'there is/are' and all third person singular forms in their respective tenses have this meaning. The forms highlighted with an asterisk are used only for this latter construction.

** the alternative form 'hubiese' is also possible.

Spanish Verb Conjugations

[15] hacer PRES hago, haces, hace, hacemos, hacéis, hacen; **PRES SUBJ** haga, hagas, haga, hagamos, hagáis, hagan; **FUT** haré; **COND** haría; **PRET** hice, hiciste, hizo, hicimos, hicisteis, hicieron; **IMPERF SUBJ** hiciera/hiciese; **PP** hecho; **IMPERAT** haz, haga, hagamos, haced, hagan

[16] ir PRES voy, vas, va, vamos, vais, van; **PRES SUBJ** vaya, vayas, vaya, vayamos, vayáis, vayan; **IMPERF** iba, ibas, iba, íbamos, ibais, iban; **PRET** fui, fuiste, fue, fuimos, fuisteis, fueron; **IMPERF SUBJ** fuera/fuese; **PRES P** yendo; **IMPERAT** ve, vaya, vamos, id, vayan

[17] oír PRES oigo, oyes, oye, oímos, oís, oyen; **PRES SUBJ** oiga, oigas, oiga, oigamos, oigáis, oigan; **PRET** oí, oíste, oyó, oímos, oísteis, oyeron; **IMPERF SUBJ** oyera/oyese; **PRES P** oyendo; **PP** oído; **IMPERAT** oye, oiga, oigamos, oíd, oigan

[18] poder PRES puedo, puedes, puede, podemos, podéis, pueden; **PRES SUBJ** pueda, puedas, pueda, podamos, podáis, puedan; **FUT** podré; **COND** podría; **PRET** pude, pudiste, pudo, pudimos, pudisteis, pudieron; **IMPERF SUBJ** pudiera/pudiese; **PRES P** pudiendo; **IMPERAT** puede, pueda, podamos, poded, puedan

[19] poner PRES pongo, pones, pone, ponemos, ponéis, ponen; **PRES SUBJ** ponga, pongas, ponga, pongamos, pongáis, pongan; **FUT** pondré; **PRET** puse, pusiste, puso, pusimos, pusisteis, pusieron; **IMPERF SUBJ** pusiera/pusiese; **PP** puesto; **IMPERAT** pon, ponga, pongamos, poned, pongan

[20] querer PRES quiero, quieres, quiere, queremos, queréis, quieren; **PRES SUBJ** quiera, quieras, quiera, queramos, queráis, quieran; **FUT** querré; **COND** querría; **PRET** quise, quisiste, quiso, quisimos, quisisteis, quisieron; **IMPERF SUBJ** quisiera/quisiese; **IMPERAT** quiere, quiera, queramos, quered, quieran

[21] saber PRES sé, sabes, sabe, sabemos, sabéis, saben; **PRES SUBJ** sepa, sepas, sepa, sepamos, sepáis, sepan; **FUT** sabré; **COND** sabría; **PRET** supe, supiste, supo, supimos, supisteis, supieron; **IMPERF SUBJ** supiera/supiese; **IMPERAT** sabe, sepa, sepamos, sabed, sepan

[22] salir PRES salgo, sales, sale, salimos, salís, salen; **PRES SUBJ** salga, salgas, salga, salgamos, salgáis, salgan; **FUT** saldré; **COND** saldría; **IMPERAT** sal, salga, salgamos, salid, salgan

[23] ser PRES soy, eres, es, somos, sois, son; **PRES SUBJ** sea, seas, sea, seamos, seáis, sean; **IMPERF** era, eras, era, éramos, erais, eran; **PRET** fui, fuiste, fue, fuimos, fuisteis, fueron; **IMPERF SUBJ** fuera/fuese; **IMPERAT** sé, sea, seamos, sed, sean

[24] tener PRES tengo, tienes, tiene, tenemos, tenéis, tienen; **PRES SUBJ** tenga, tengas, tenga, tengamos, tengáis, tengan; **FUT** tendré; **COND** tendría; **PRET** tuve, tuviste, tuvo, tuvimos, tuvisteis, tuvieron; **IMPERF SUBJ** tuviera/tuviese; **IMPERAT** ten, tenga, tengamos, tened, tengan

[25] traer PRES traigo, traes, trae, traemos, traéis, traen; **PRES SUBJ** traiga, traigas, traiga, traigamos, traigáis, traigan; **PRET** traje, trajiste, trajo, trajimos, trajisteis, trajeron; **IMPERF SUBJ** trajera/trajese; **IMPERAT** trae, traiga, traigamos, traed, traigan

[26] valer PRES valgo, vales, vale, valemos, valéis, valen; **PRES SUBJ** valga, valgas, valga, valgamos, valgáis, valgan; **FUT** valdré; **COND** valdría; **IMPERAT** vale, valga, valemos, valed, valgan

[27] venir PRES vengo, vienes, viene, venimos, venís, vienen; **PRES SUBJ** venga, vengas, venga, vengamos, vengáis, vengan; **FUT** vendré; **COND** vendría; **PRET** vine, viniste, vino, vinimos, vinisteis, vinieron; **IMPERF SUBJ** viniera/viniese; **PRES P** viniendo; **IMPERAT** ven, venga, vengamos, venid, vengan

[28] ver PRES veo, ves, ve, vemos, veis, ven; **PRES SUBJ** vea, veas, vea, veamos, veáis, vean; **IMPERF** veía, veías, veía, veíamos, veíais, veían; **PRET** vi, viste, vio, vimos, visteis, vieron; **IMPERF SUBJ** viera/viese; **IMPERAT** ve, vea, veamos, ved, vean

[29] desviar PRES desvío, desvías, desvía, desviamos, desviáis, desvían; **PRES SUBJ** desvíe, desvíes, desvíe, desviemos, desviéis, desvíen; **IMPERAT** desvía, desvíe, desviemos, desviéis, desvíen

[30] continuar PRES continúo, continúas, continúa, continuamos, continuáis, continúan; **PRES SUBJ** continúe, continúes, continúe, continuemos, continuéis, continúen; **IMPERAT** continúa, continúe, continuemos, continuad, continúen

[31] adquirir PRES adquiero, adquieres, adquiere, adquirimos, adquirís, adquieren; **PRES SUBJ** adquiera, adquieras, adquiera, adquiramos, adquiráis, adquieran; **IMPERAT** adquiere, adquiera, adquiramos, adquirid, adquieran

[32] jugar PRES juego, juegas, juega, jugamos, jugáis, juegan; **PRES SUBJ** juegue, juegues, juegue, juguemos, juguéis, jueguen; **IMPERAT** juega, juegue, juguemos, jugad, jueguen

[33] agradecer PRES agradezco, agradeces, agradece, agradecemos, agradecéis, agradecen; **PRES SUBJ** agradezca, agradezcas, agradezca, agradezcamos, agradezcáis, agradezcan; **IMPERAT** agradece, agradezca, agradezcamos, agradeced, agradezcan

[34] conocer PRES conozco, conoces, conoce, conocemos, conocéis, conocen; **PRES SUBJ** conozca, conozcas, conozca, conozcamos, conozcáis, conozcan; **IMPERAT** conoce, conozca, conozcamos, conoced, conozcan

[35] lucir PRES luzco, luces, luce, lucimos, lucís, lucen; **PRES SUBJ** luzca, luzcas, luzca, luzcamos, luzcáis, luzcan; **IMPERAT** luce, luzca, luzcamos, lucid, luzcan

[36] leer PRET leí, leíste, leyó, leímos, leísteis, leyeron; **IMPERF SUBJ** leyera/leyese; **PRES P** leyendo; **PP** leído; **IMPERAT** lee, lea, leamos, leed, lean

[37] huir PRES huyo, huyes, huye, huimos, huís, huyen; **PRES SUBJ** huya, huyas, huya, huyamos, huyáis, huyan; **PRET** huí, huiste, huyó, huimos, huisteis, huyeron; **IMPERF SUBJ** huyera/huyese; **PRES P** huyendo; **PP** huido; **IMPERAT** huye, huya, huyamos, huid, huyan

[38] roer PRES roo/roigo/royo, roes, roe, roemos, roéis, roen; **PRES SUBJ** roa/roiga/roya, roas, roa, roamos, roáis, roan; **PRET** roí, roíste, royó, roímos, roísteis, royeron; **IMPERF SUBJ** royera/royese; **PRES P** royendo; **PP** roído; **IMPERAT** roe, roa, roamos, roed, roan

[39] caer PRES caigo, caes, cae, caemos, caéis, caen; **PRES SUBJ** caiga, caigas, caiga, caigamos, caigáis, caigan; **PRES P** cayendo; **PP** caído; **IMPERAT** cae, caiga, caigamos, caed, caigan

[40] cazar PRET cacé, cazaste, cazó, cazamos, cazasteis, cazaron; **PRES SUBJ** cace, caces, cace, cacemos, cacéis, cacen

[41] cocer PRES cuezo, cueces, cuece, cocemos, cocéis, cuecen; **PRES SUBJ** cueza, cuezas, cueza, cozamos, cozáis, cuezan; **IMPERAT** cuece, cueza, cozamos, coced, cuezan

[42] llegar PRET llegué, llegaste, llegó, llegamos, llegasteis, llegaron; **PRES SUBJ** llegue, llegues, llegue, lleguemos, lleguéis, lleguen

[43] cambiar PRES cambio, cambias, cambia, cambiamos, cambiáis, cambian; **PRES SUBJ** cambie, cambies, cambie, cambiemos, cambiéis, cambien; **IMPERAT** cambia, cambie, cambiemos, cambiad, cambien

[44] sacar PRET saqué, sacaste, sacó, sacamos, sacasteis, sacaron; **PRES SUBJ** saque, saques, saque, saquemos, saquéis, saquen; **IMPERAT** saca, saque, saquemos, sacad, saquen

[45] averiguar PRET averigüé, averiguaste, averiguó, averiguamos, averiguasteis, averiguaron; **PRES SUBJ** averigüe, averigües, averigüe, averigüemos, averigüéis, averigüen; **IMPERAT** averigua, averigüe, averigüemos, averiguad, averigüen

[46] asir PRES asgo, ases, ase, asimos, asís, asen; **PRES SUBJ** asga, asgas, asga, asgamos, asgáis, asgan; **IMPERAT** ase, asga, asgamos, asid, asgan

[47] adecuar PRES adecuo/adecúo, adecuas/adecúas, adecua/adecúa, adecuamos, adecuáis, adecuan/adecúan; **PRES SUBJ** adecue/adecúe, adecues/adecúes, adecue/adecúe, adecuemos, adecuéis, adecuen/adecúen; **IMPERAT** adecua/adecúa, adecue/adecúe, adecuemos, adecuad, adecuen/adecúen

[48] delinquir PRES delinco, delinques, delinque, delinquimos, delinquís, delinquen; **PRES SUBJ** delinca, delincas, delinca, delincamos, delincáis, delincan; **IMPERAT** delinque, delinca, delincamos, delinquid, delincan

[49] mecer PRES mezo, meces, mece, mecemos, mecéis, mecen; **PRES SUBJ** meza, mezas, meza, mezamos, mezáis, mezan; **IMPERAT** mece, meza, mezamos, meced, mezan

[50] errar PRES yerro, yerras, yerra, erramos, erráis, yerran; **PRES SUBJ** yerre, yerres, yerre, erremos, erréis, yerren; **IMPERAT** yerra, yerre, erremos, errad, yerren

[51] comenzar PRES comienzo, comienzas, comienza, comenzamos, comenzáis, comienzan; **PRES SUBJ** comience, comiences, comience, comencemos, comencéis, comiencen; **IMPERAT** comienza, comience, comencemos, comenzad, comiencen

[52] zurcir PRES zurzo, zurces, zurce, zurcimos, zurcís, zurcen; **PRES SUBJ** zurza, zurzas, zurza, zurzamos, zurzáis, zurzan; **IMPERAT** zurce, zurza, zurzamos, zurcid, zurzan

[53] proteger PRES protejo, proteges, protege, protegemos, protegéis, protegen; **PRES SUBJ** proteja, protejas, proteja, protejamos, protejáis, protejan; **IMPERAT** protege, proteja, protejamos, proteged, protejan

[54] discernir PRES discierno, disciernes, discierne, discernimos, discernís, disciernen; **PRES SUBJ** discierna, disciernas, discierna, discernamos, discernáis, disciernan; **IMPERAT** discierne, discierna, discernamos, discernid, disciernan

[55] erguir PRES irgo/yergo, irgues/yergues, irgue/yergue, erguimos, erguís, irguen/yerguen; **PRET** erguí, erguiste, irguió, erguimos, erguisteis, irguieron; **PRES SUBJ** irga/yerga, irgas/yergas, irga/yerga, irgamos/yergamos, irgáis/yergáis, irgan/yergan; **IMPERF SUBJ** irguiera/irguiese; **IMPERAT** irgue/yergue, irga/yerga, irgamos/yergamos, erguid, irgan/yergan

[56] reír PRES río, ríes, ríe, reímos, reís, ríen; **PRET** reí, reíste, rió, reímos, reísteis, rieron; **PRES SUBJ** ría, rías, ría, riamos, riáis, rían; **IMPERF SUBJ** riera/riese; **IMPERAT** ríe, ría, riamos, reíd, rían

[57] dirigir PRES dirijo, diriges, dirige, dirigimos, dirigís, dirigen; **PRES SUBJ** dirija, dirijas, dirija, dirijamos, dirijáis, dirijan; **IMPERAT** dirige, dirija, dirijamos, dirigid, dirijan

[58] regir PRES rijo, riges, rige, regimos, regís, rigen; **PRES SUBJ** rija, rijas, rija, rijamos, rijáis, rijan; **IMPERAT** rige, rija, rijamos, regid, rijan

[59] distinguir PRES distingo, distingues, distingue, distinguimos, distinguís, distinguen; **PRES SUBJ** distinga, distingas, distinga, distingamos, distingáis, distingan; **IMPERAT** distingue, distinga, distingamos, distinguid, distingan

[60] nacer PRES nazco, naces, nace, nacemos, nacéis, nacen; **PRES SUBJ** nazca, nazcas, nazca, nazcamos, nazcáis, nazcan; **IMPERAT** nace, nazca, nazcamos, naced, nazcan

[61] yacer PRES yazco/yazgo/yago, yaces, yace, yacemos, yacéis, yacen; **PRES SUBJ** yazca/yazga/yaga; **IMPERAT** yace/yaz, yazca/yazga/yaga, yazcamos/yazgamos/yagamos, yaced, yazcan/yazgan/yagan

[62] argüir PRES arguyo, arguyes, arguye, argüimos, argüís, arguyen; **PRET** argüí, argüiste, arguyó, argüimos, argüisteis, arguyeron; **PRES SUBJ** arguya, arguyas, arguya, arguyamos, arguyáis, arguyan; **IMPERF SUBJ** arguyera/arguyese; **IMPERAT** arguye, arguya, arguyamos, argüid, arguyan

[63] avergonzar PRES avergüenzo, avergüenzas, avergüenza, avergonzamos, avergonzáis, avergüenzan; **PRET** avergoncé, avergonzaste, avergonzó, avergonzamos, avergonzasteis, avergonzaron; **PRES SUBJ** avergüence, avergüences, avergüence, avergoncemos, avergoncéis, avergüencen; **IMPERAT** avergüenza, avergüence, avergoncemos, avergonzad, avergüencen

[64] trocar PRES trueco, truecas, trueca, trocamos, trocáis, truecan; **PRET** troqué, trocaste, trocó, trocamos, trocasteis, trocaron; **PRES SUBJ** trueque, trueques, trueque, troquemos, troquéis, truequen; **IMPERAT** trueca, trueque, troquemos, trocad, truequen

[65] oler PRES huelo, hueles, huele, olemos, oléis, huelen; **PRES SUBJ** huela, huelas, huela, olamos, oláis, huelan; **IMPERAT** huele, huela, olamos, oled, huelan

Verbos irregulares ingleses

INFINITIVE	PAST SIMPLE	PAST PARTICIPLE
arise	arose	arisen
awake	awoke	awoken
be	was, were	been
bear	bore	borne
beat	beat	beaten
become	became	become
begin	began	begun
bend	bent	bent
bet	bet, betted	bet, betted
bid (offer)	bid	bid
bind	bound	bound
bite	bit	bitten
bleed	bled	bled
blow	blew	blown
break	broke	broken
breed	bred	bred
bring	brought	brought
broadcast	broadcast	broadcast
build	built	built
burn	burnt, burned	burnt, burned
burst	burst	burst
buy	bought	bought
cast	cast	cast
catch	caught	caught
choose	chose	chosen
cling	clung	clung
come	came	come
cost	cost	cost
creep	crept	crept
cut	cut	cut
deal	dealt	dealt
dig	dug	dug
dive	dove	dived
do	did	done
draw	drew	drawn
dream	dreamt, dreamed	dreamt, dreamed
drink	drank	drunk
drive	drove	driven
eat	ate	eaten
fall	fell	fallen
feed	fed	fed
feel	felt	felt
fight	fought	fought
find	found	found
flee	fled	fled

INFINITIVE	PAST SIMPLE	PAST PARTICIPLE
fling	flung	flung
fly	flew	flown
forbid	forbad(e)	forbidden
forecast	forecast	forecast
foresee	foresaw	foreseen
forget	forgot	forgotten
forgive	forgave	forgiven
freeze	froze	frozen
get	got	gotten
give	gave	given
go	went	gone
grind	ground	ground
grow	grew	grown
hang	hung, hanged	hung, hanged
have	had	had
hear	heard	heard
hide	hid	hidden
hit	hit	hit
hold	held	held
hurt	hurt	hurt
keep	kept	kept
kneel	knelt	knelt
know	knew	known
lay	laid	laid
lead	led	led
lean	leant, leaned	leant, leaned
leap	leapt, leaped	leapt, leaped
learn	learnt, learned	learnt, learned
leave	left	left
lend	lent	lent
let	let	let
lie	lay	lain
light	lit, lighted	lit, lighted
lose	lost	lost
make	made	made
mean	meant	meant
meet	met	met
mislay	mislaid	mislaid
mislead	misled	misled
mistake	mistood	mistaken
misunderstand	misunderstood	misunderstood
mow	mowed	mown, mowed
outdo	outdid	outdone
overcome	overcame	overcome
overdo	overdid	overdone
overtake	overtook	overtaken
pay	paid	paid
put	put	put
quit	quit	quit
read	read	read
redo	redid	redone

INFINITIVE	PAST SIMPLE	PAST PARTICIPLE
rend	rent	rent
rewind	rewound	rewound
ride	rode	ridden
ring	rang	rung
rise	rose	risen
run	ran	run
saw	sawed	sawn, sawed
say	said	said
see	saw	seen
seek	sought	sought
sell	sold	sold
send	sent	sent
set	set	set
sew	sewed	sewn, sewed
shake	shook	shaken
shear	sheared	shorn, sheared
shed	shed	shed
shine	shone	shone
shoot	shot	shot
show	showed	shown, showed
shrink	shrank, shrunk	shrunk
shut	shut	shut
sing	sang	sung
sink	sank	sunk
sit	sat	sat
sleep	slept	slept
slide	slid	slid
sling	slung	slung
slink	slunk	slunk
slit	slit	slit
smell	smelt, smelled	smelt, smelled
sneak	sneaked, *US* snuck	sneaked, *US* snuck
sow	sowed	sown, sowed
speak	spoke	spoken
speed	sped, speeded	sped, speeded
spell	spelt, spelled	spelt, spelled
spend	spent	spent
spill	spilt, spilled	spilt, spilled
spin	spun	spun
spit	spat	spat
split	split	split
spoil	spoilt, spoiled	spoilt, spoiled
spread	spread	spread
spring	sprang	sprung
stand	stood	stood
steal	stole	stolen
stick	stuck	stuck
sting	stung	stung
stink	stank	stunk
stride	strode	stridden
strike	struck	struck

INFINITIVE	PAST SIMPLE	PAST PARTICIPLE
string	strung	strung
strive	strove	striven
swear	swore	sworn
sweep	swept	swept
swell	swelled	swollen
swim	swam	swum
swing	swung	swung
take	took	taken
teach	taught	taught
tear	tore	torn
tell	told	told
think	thought	thought
thrive	thrived, throve	thrived, thriven
throw	threw	thrown
thrust	thrust	thrust
tread	trod	trodden
undergo	underwent	undergone
understand	understood	understood
undertake	undertook	undertaken
undo	undid	undone
upset	upset	upset
wake	woke	woken
wear	wore	worn
weave	wove	woven
weep	wept	wept
wet	wet	wet
win	won	won
wind	wound	wound
withdraw	withdrew	withdrawn
withhold	withheld	withheld
wring	wrung	wrung
write	wrote	written

Conversation Guide
I. The Basics

Spanish has two separate sets of words to translate "you", "your", "yours", and "yourself". **Tú**, **te**, **tu/tus**, and **el tuyo** etc all correspond to the **tú** form of the verb, used when speaking to one person you know well (such as a friend or relative) or to someone younger (in parts of South America and in most of Central America, the pronoun **vos** is used in these informal contexts). **Usted**, **suyo/suyos**, and **el suyo** etc correspond to the **usted** form of the verb, and are used when speaking to one person you do not know well. If in doubt as to whether to call someone **tú** or **usted**, it is always safer to use the **usted** form. A Spanish-speaking person may invite you to use the less formal **tú** form by saying, "Puedes tutearme". All translations in this guide use formal **usted**, except in those examples where the context clearly indicates an informal situation.

Ustedes, **suyo/suyos**, and **el suyo** etc correspond to the **ustedes** form of the verb, and are used when speaking to more than one person. **Ustedes** is both formal and informal use in Latin America, but only formal in Spain. When speaking informally to more than one person in Spain, **vosotros**, **vuestro/vuestros**, and **el vuestro** etc are used, with the corresponding **vosotros** form of the verb.

good evening buenas noches	**OK** OK
good morning/afternoon buenos días/buenas tardes	**please** por favor
	see you later hasta luego
good night buenas noches	**see you on Monday** hasta el lunes
goodbye adiós	**see you soon** hasta pronto
hello hola	**see you tomorrow** hasta mañana
hi hola	**thank you** gracias
no no	**yes** sí
no, thank you no, gracias	**yes, please** sí, por favor

1) Meeting someone you know

How are you?
¿Cómo está?

Hi, how are you doing?
Hola, ¿cómo le va?

Good evening, how are you?
Buenas noches, ¿cómo le va?

Very good, thank you. And you?
Muy bien, gracias. ¿Y usted?

Fine, and you?
Bien, ¿y a usted?

Not too bad.
Bien.

Not very well, I have the flu.
No demasiado bien, tengo gripe or (*Méx*) gripa.

How are your parents/children?   **They're doing well, thanks.**
¿Cómo están tus papás/hijos?   Están bien, gracias.

2) Introducing yourself and meeting people you don't know

Name:

What's your name?   **My name is John.**
¿Cómo se llama?   Me llamo John.

Let me introduce you to my brother Steve. And this is my cousin Rachel.
Le presento a mi hermano Steve. Y ella es mi prima Rachel.

Hi, I'm Peter, Anna's colleague.
Hola, yo soy Peter, un compañero de Anna.

I'm sorry, I've forgotten your name.
Discúlpeme, no me acuerdo de su nombre.

Pleased to meet you.
Encantado de conocerla.

Age:

How old are you?   **I'm 12/24/45 years old.**
¿Qué edad tiene?   Tengo doce/veinticuatro/cuarenta y
cinco años.

What's your date of birth?   **I was born in 19 ...**
¿Cuál es su fecha de nacimiento?   Nací en mil novecientos ...

Nationality:

What country are you from?   **I'm from the United States.**
¿De qué país es usted?   Soy de Estados Unidos.

What's your nationality?   **I'm American.**
¿Cuál es su nacionalidad?   Soy estadounidense.

Where do you live?   **I live in New York.**
¿Dónde vive?   Vivo en Nueva York.

I come from a little rural town in Montana.
Soy de un pueblito rural de Montana.

Occupation:

What do you do?   **I'm still in high school.**
¿A qué te dedicas?   Todavía estoy en la secundaria.

I'm a student/a teacher/a doctor.   **I'm retired.**
Soy estudiante/profesor/médico.   Soy/Estoy jubilado.

I work in a bank.
Trabajo en un banco.

I work in the export department of a computer hardware company.
Trabajo en el departamento de exportaciones de una empresa de informática.

Family:

Do you have any brothers and sisters?
¿Tiene hermanos?

I have two brothers and one sister.
Tengo dos hermanos y una hermana.

I'm an only child.
Soy hijo único.

I have an older brother.
Tengo un hermano mayor.

I have a younger sister.
Tengo una hermana menor.

I have two little sisters.
Tengo dos hermanitas.

Are you married?
¿Es casado?

I'm single/separated/divorced.
Soy soltero/separado/divorciado.

Do you have any children?
¿Tiene hijos?

I have one son/daughter.
Tengo un hijo/una hija.

3) Likes and dislikes

I like skiing/swimming/playing basketball.
Me gusta esquiar/nadar/jugar al básquetbol.

I'm fond of classical music.
Me gusta (mucho) la música clásica.

I love movies.
Me encanta ir al cine.

I like/love playing chess/pool.
Me gusta/Me encanta jugar al ajedrez/al billar.

What's your favorite band/book?
¿Cuál es tu grupo/libro favorito?

I prefer reading/shopping.
Prefiero leer/ir de compras.

I prefer coffee to tea.
Prefiero el café al té.

I prefer football to basketball.
Prefiero el fútbol americano al básquetbol.

Did you enjoy the movie?
¿Te gustó la película?

I really liked it/didn't like it.
Me gustó mucho/No me gustó.

I liked/didn't like the ending.
Me gustó/No me gustó el final.

I don't like going to the opera.
No me gusta ir a la ópera.

I don't like that at all.
No me gusta nada.

I hate cheese.
Odio el queso.

I can't stand this kind of music.
No soporto este tipo de música.

This book is (really) awful.
Este libro es (realmente) horrible.

4) Expressing surprise and interest

No, you're kidding! Are you sure?
¡No puede ser! ¿Estás seguro?

Really?
¿En serio?

You're kidding?
¡Estás bromeando!

Are you pulling my leg?
¿Me estás tomando el pelo?

What a coincidence/a surprise!
¡Qué coincidencia/sorpresa!

Really? I'm a doctor too!
¿En serio? ¡Yo también soy médico!

That's strange.
¡Qué raro!

It's really interesting/fascinating/ amazing.
Es realmente interesante/fascinante/ increíble.

5) Expressing disappointment

What a shame!
¡Qué lástima!

It's too bad it's raining.
Es una lástima que esté lloviendo. (subjuntivo)

What a pity he couldn't come!
¡Qué lástima que no haya podido venir! (subjuntivo)

The concert has been canceled, how disappointing!
El concierto se canceló. ¡Qué lástima!

6) Saying thank you and expressing gratitude

Thank you.
Gracias.

Thank you very much.
Muchas gracias.

Thank you, that's really nice.
Gracias, es muy amable.

Thank you, but you shouldn't have!
Gracias, ¡no se hubiera molestado!

It's very kind of you.
Muy amable.

I'd like that very much.
Me gustaría mucho.

Thanks for your help/for helping me.
Gracias por su ayuda/por ayudarme.

To which the other person may reply:

De nada.
You're welcome.

Por favor, no hay de qué.
Please, don't mention it.

7) Apologizing

Sorry, it was an accident!
¡Perdón, no fue a propósito!

I'm (really) sorry.
Lo siento (de verdad).

I'm sorry I'm late.
Discúlpeme por el atraso.

I'm sorry to bother you, but ...
Disculpe que lo moleste, pero ...

I apologize.	**Excuse me.**
Discúlpeme.	Perdón.

Sorry for interrupting the conversation.
Perdón por interrumpir la conversación.

Sorry, it's my fault.	**I'm sorry but it's not my fault.**
Perdón, es mi culpa.	Discúlpeme, pero no es mi culpa.

I'm afraid I won't be able to come.
Temo que no podré ir.

That's very kind of you but unfortunately I'm not free that day.
Es muy amable de su parte pero lamentablemente voy a estar ocupado
  ese día.

To which the other person may reply:

No es nada.
It doesn't matter.

No se preocupe.
Don't worry about it.

8) Congratulations and compliments

Congratulations!	**I wish you lots of happiness.**
¡Felicitaciones!	Les deseo lo mejor.
I'm very happy for you!	**It's great/wonderful/beautiful!**
¡Me alegro por usted!	¡Es excelente/maravilloso/hermoso!
It was very good/delicious.	**I had a great time.**
Estaba muy rico/delicioso.	Me divertí mucho.
The party was a big success.	
La fiesta fue un éxito.	

9) Making suggestions and expressing desires

Do you want to go?	**Would you like to go to a**
¿Quiere ir?	**restaurant?**
	¿Le gustaría ir a un restaurante?
How about going to the museum?	**How about a pizza?**
¿Y si vamos al museo?	¿Qué tal una pizza?
I think we should meet at seven.	**Let's meet outside the restaurant.**
Podríamos encontrarnos a las siete.	Nos vemos en la puerta del
	restaurante.
I want to go back to the apartment.	**I don't want to go to the swimming**
Quiero volver al apartamento.	**pool.**
	No quiero ir a la alberca.

Conversation Guide

I feel like going to the movies.
Quiero ir al cine.

I don't feel like watching TV.
No tengo ganas de mirar televisión.

I wouldn't mind going to the theater.
Me gustaría ir al teatro.

I'd rather stay at home/do something else.
Preferiría quedarme en casa/hacer alguna otra cosa.

I'd like to go to Spain next year.
Me gustaría ir a España el año que viene.

I wish I was on vacation.
Ojalá estuviera de vacaciones.

I don't mind.
Me da lo mismo.

I have no preference.
No tengo preferencia.

10) Making requests

Can we have more bread, please?
¿Podría traernos más pan, por favor?

Could you please make a little less noise?
¿Podría hacer un poco menos de ruido?

Could I have a glass of water?
¿Podría traerme un vaso de agua?

Could I make a phone call?
¿Puedo hacer una llamada?

Can I open the window?
¿Puedo abrir la ventana?

Could you lend me ...?
¿Podría prestarme ...?

Can I borrow ...?
¿Podría prestarme ...?

Would it be possible to go?
¿Se puede ir?

Do you mind if I smoke?
¿Le molesta si fumo?

Would you be able to give me a ride?
¿Podría llevarme?

11) Expressing an opinion

What do you think?
¿Qué le parece?

What's your opinion?
¿Qué opina?

I think/I don't think that's a very good idea.
Creo que es una muy buena idea./No creo que sea muy buena idea.

I think we should go.
Creo que deberíamos ir.

I think she's very pretty.
Me parece muy bonita.

In my opinion, he shouldn't have said that.
En mi opinión, no debió haber dicho eso.

I agree/don't agree with you.
Estoy/No estoy de acuerdo con usted.

I've changed my mind.
Cambié de opinión.

I'm sure they'll win.
Estoy seguro de que van a ganar.

I totally agree with him.
Estoy totalmente de acuerdo con él.

I disagree.
No estoy de acuerdo.

You're (absolutely) right.
Tiene (toda la) razón.

No, not at all/absolutely not.
No, en absoluto.

Of course not!
¡Por supuesto que no!

You're mistaken.
Se equivoca.

You're wrong.
Está equivocado.

That's true/not true.
Es verdad./No es verdad.

Nonsense!
¡Qué disparate!

12) Having problems understanding Spanish

Could you speak more slowly?
¿Podría hablar más despacio?

Can you repeat that, please?
¿Podría repetir, por favor?

I don't understand this expression.
No entiendo esta expresión.

I understand a little.
Entiendo un poquito.

I don't understand a word of that.
No entiendo ni una palabra.

I didn't understand.
No entendí.

I can understand Spanish but I can't speak it.
Entiendo español, pero no sé hablarlo.

I speak hardly any Spanish.
Casi no hablo español.

**I have trouble understanding/
speaking.**
Me cuesta entender/hablar.

Do you speak English?
¿Habla inglés?

Pardon?/What?/Eh?
¿Perdón?/¿Qué?/¿Eh?

What's it called?
¿Cómo se llama esto?

How do you say ... in Spanish?
¿Cómo se dice ... en español?

How do you spell it/pronounce it?
¿Cómo se escribe/pronuncia?

Could you write it down?
¿Podría escribírmelo?

What does it mean?
¿Qué quiere decir?

What's that?
¿Qué es eso?

What's happening?
¿Qué pasa?

II. Vacations in Mexico

1) Traveling and using public transportation

Traveling by plane:

Where is the Mexicana check-in desk?
¿En dónde está la ventanilla de Mexicana?

What time does boarding start?
¿A qué hora es el abordaje?

I'd like to confirm my return flight.
Quisiera confirmar mi vuelo de
  regreso.

I'd like a window seat/an aisle seat.
Quisiera un asiento en la ventana/
  el pasillo.

One of my suitcases is missing.
Me falta una maleta.

I'd like to report the loss of my luggage/my hand luggage.
Quisiera reportar la pérdida de mis maletas/mi maleta de mano.

The plane was two hours late and I've missed my connection.
El avión se atrasó dos horas y perdí la conexión.

Traveling by train:

I'd like to reserve a ticket, please.
Quisiera reservar un pasaje, por favor.

What are the reduced fares?
¿Cuáles son las tarifas rebajadas?

How much is a ticket to ...?
¿Cuánto cuesta el pasaje a ...?

Are there any tickets left for ...?
¿Quedan pasajes a ...?

No smoking (section), please.
Sección de no fumar, por favor.

Do you have a timetable, please?
¿Tiene los horarios, por favor?

When is the next train to Los Mochis?
¿A qué hora sale el próximo tren a
  Los Mochis?

Is there an earlier/a later one?
¿Hay alguno más temprano/tarde?

**What platform does the train for ...
leave from?**
¿De qué plataforma sale el tren a ...?

I've missed the last train.
Perdí el último tren.

On the subway:

Where can I buy tickets?
¿Dónde puedo comprar boletos?

Does this line go to Chapultepec?
¿Esta línea para en Chapultepec?

Can I have a map of the subway?
¿Podría darme un mapa del metro?

What time is the last subway train?
¿A qué hora pasa el último metro?

Which line do I take to get to ...?
¿Qué línea tengo que tomar para
  ir a ...?

Traveling by bus:

Where can I get a bus to ...?
¿Dónde puedo tomar el camión a ...?

Is this the right stop for ...?
¿Es esta la parada del camión ...?

Does the bus for the airport leave from here?
¿El camión al aeropuerto sale de aquí?

Where is the bus station?
¿Dónde está la central camionera?

Renting a car:

I'd like to rent a car for a week.
Quisiera rentar un carro por una semana.

How much is the deposit?
¿Cuánto es el depósito?

I'd like to take out comprehensive insurance.
Quisiera contratar un seguro cobertura total.

I'd like an automatic/a stickshift.
Quisiera un carro automático/con cambios.

On the road:

Where can I find a gas station/a repair shop?
¿Dónde hay una gasolinería/un taller de reparaciones?

I've broken down.
Tengo una falla mecánica.

I have a flat tire. Where can I park?
Se me ponchó una llanta. ¿Dónde puedo estacionarme?

It won't start; the battery's dead.
No arranca, se descargó la batería.

I have a problem with the brakes/ the light indicators.
Tengo un problema con los frenos/ las luces.

Taking a cab:

I'd like to reserve a taxi for 8 o'clock.
Quisiera reservar un taxi para las 8 en punto.

Is this cab for hire?
¿Está libre?

How much will it cost to go to the airport?
¿Cuánto costaría ir hasta al aeropuerto?

I'd like to go to the train station.
Quisiera ir a la estación de trenes.

Could you take me to this address, please?
¿Podría llevarme a esta dirección, por favor?

You can drop me off here, thanks.
Déjeme aquí, por favor.

Asking for directions:

Excuse me, where is ..., please?
Perdón, ¿dónde queda ..., por favor?

I'm looking for ...
Estoy buscando ...

Conversation Guide

Could you tell me how to get to ...?
¿Podría decirme cómo llego a ...?

I'm lost.
Estoy perdido.

Which way is it to ...?
¿Cuál es el camino para llegar a ...?

Is it far/near?
¿Está lejos/cerca?

How can I get to the station?
¿Cómo llego a la estación?

Can you show me the way?
¿Podría mostrarme el camino?

Could you show me on the map?
¿Podría mostrármelo en el mapa?

Understanding the person you asked for help:

Es la segunda calle a la derecha/
a la izquierda.
**It's the second street on the right/
on the left.**

Tome la próxima salida.
Take the next exit.

Siga derecho hasta el semáforo.
Keep going straight on until you get to the (traffic) lights.

2) Renting accommodations

Staying in a hotel or a B&B:

Do you have any rooms available?
¿Tiene alguna habitación libre?

It's for a couple and two children.
Es para un matrimonio y dos niños.

I'd like to reserve a room for tomorrow night, please.
Quisiera reservar una habitación para mañana en la noche, por favor.

I've reserved three single/double rooms over the phone, in the name of ...
Reservé por teléfono tres habitaciones para una persona/dobles, a
nombre de ...

Would it be possible to stay another night/to add an extra bed?
¿Podríamos quedarnos otra noche/agregar una cama?

Can I see the room?
¿Puedo ver la habitación?

How much is a room with its own bathroom?
¿Cuánto cuesta una habitación con baño privado?

Do you take credit cards?
¿Aceptan tarjetas de crédito?

We're planning to stay for two nights.
Pensamos quedarnos dos noches.

Is breakfast included?
¿El desayuno está incluido?

The key for room 12, please.
La llave de la habitación doce,
por favor.

The outlet for razors isn't working.
El enchufe para la afeitadora no
funciona.

We don't have towels/toilet paper.
No tenemos toallas/papel higiénico.

Could you wake me up at seven o'clock?
¿Podría despertarme a las siete en punto?

Understanding the receptionist:

No, lo siento, no tenemos lugar.
No, I'm sorry, we're full.

¿Podría llenar esta forma?
Could you fill out this form?

El check-out es al mediodía.
Check-out time is noon.

El desayuno se sirve entre las siete y media y las nueve.
Breakfast is served between 7:30 and 9.

Renting an apartment or a bungalow:

I'm looking for something to rent close to the center of town
Estoy buscando departamento para rentar cerca del centro.

Is it completely furnished?
¿Está totalmente amueblado?

Is there a washing machine?
¿Hay lavadora?

Where do I pick up/leave the keys?
¿Dónde entrego/retiro las llaves?

Where is the electricity meter?
¿Dónde está el contador de la luz?

Where do I take the garbage out?
¿Dónde se saca la basura?

Are there any spare ...?
¿Hay ... de recambio?

I'm sorry, I can't find/I've broken the ...
Lo siento, no encuentro/se me rompió el ...

There's no hot water.
No hay agua caliente.

Camping:

Is there a campsite near here?
¿Hay algún lugar para acampar aquí cerca?

I'd like a space for one tent for two days.
Quiero un lugar para una tienda de campaña por dos días.

We want to rent a trailer.
Queremos rentar una casa rodante.

Where are the showers?
¿Dónde quedan las regaderas?

Is there a swimming pool/a night club/a tennis court in the campsite?
¿Hay alberca/discoteca/cancha de tenis en el campamento?

How much is it a day/per person/per tent?
¿Cuánto cuesta por día/persona/tienda de campaña?

3) Visiting

I'd like some information on ...
Quisiera información sobre ...

What is there to see/visit in the area?
¿Qué hay para ver/visitar en la región?

Is it open on Sundays?
¿Está abierto los domingos?

Is it free?
¿Es gratis?

How much does it cost to get in?
¿Cuánto cuesta la entrada?

Are there any discounts for young people?
¿Hay descuento para jóvenes?

How long does the tour last?
¿Cuánto dura la visita?

When is the next guided tour?
¿A qué hora es la próxima visita guiada?

Is this ticket valid for the exhibition too?
¿El boleto también sirve para la exposición?

Are there many hiking paths here?
¿Hay muchos senderos para caminatas por aquí?

4) Inquiring about the weather for the next few days

Do you know what the weather's going to be like this weekend?
¿Sabe cómo va a estar el tiempo el fin de semana?

What's the weather forecast for tomorrow?
¿Cuál es el pronóstico del tiempo para mañana?

Understanding the answer:

Han anunciado lluvias/tormentas.
They've forecast rain/storms.

Va a llover/nevar.
It's going to rain/to snow.

Va a hacer frío/calor/un calor sofocante.
It's going to be cold/hot/stiflingly hot.

Parece que va a estar bonito mañana.
The weather should be good tomorrow.

Lamentablemente prevén mal tiempo.
I'm afraid they're forecasting bad weather.

Va a haber neblina/heladas.
It's going to be foggy/icy.

Va a estar soleado, igual que hoy.
It will be sunny, like today.

Va a haber viento/mucho viento.
It's going to be windy/very windy.

Va a hacer 30° C a la sombra/ menos 2.
It's going to be 86° F in the shade/ minus 2.

Va a refrescar/entibiar.
It's going to get colder/warmer.

III. Going out

1) Going for a drink

Do you want to go for a drink?
¿Quiere ir a tomar una copa?

Let's go for a coffee.
Vamos a tomar un café.

Excuse me, please!
(to call the waiter)
¡Disculpe!

What are you having?
¿Qué va a tomar?

I'll buy you a drink. What would you like?
Lo invito con una copa. ¿Qué quiere tomar?

It's on me!
¡Yo invito!

Could I have a beer?
Una cerveza, por favor.

I'd like a glass of dry white wine.
Quisiera un vaso de vino blanco seco.

I'll have a Coke® with/without ice, please.
Voy a tomar una Coca-Cola® con/sin hielo, por favor.

A coffee and a glass of water, please.
Un café y un vaso de agua, por favor.

Something non-alcoholic.
Algo sin alcohol.

I'll have the same.
Lo mismo para mí.

I'll have the same again.
Voy a tomar otra vez lo mismo.

To your health!
¡Salud!

Could you bring me an ashtray?
¿Podría traerme un cenicero?

We can go to a club afterwards.
Podemos ir a una discoteca después.

2) Going to the restaurant

Reserving a table:

Hello, I'd like to reserve a table for two for tomorrow night, around 8 o'clock.
Hola, quisiera reservar una mesa para dos, para mañana en la noche, alrededor de las ocho.

I've reserved a table in the name of ...
Tengo una mesa reservada a nombre de ...

A table for four, please.
Una mesa para cuatro, por favor.

You don't have a table available before then?
¿No tiene ninguna mesa libre más temprano?

Conversation Guide

Understanding the waiter:

¿Para qué hora?
For what time?

¿A las ocho y media le queda bien?
Would 8:30 suit you?

Buenos días, ¿van a comer?
Hello, will you be eating?

¿Para cuántas personas?
For how many people?

¿Tiene reserva? ¿A nombre de quién?
Have you reserved a table?
  What's the name?

¿Fumar o no fumar?
Smoking or no-smoking?

Ordering food:

Could you bring me the menu/the wine list/the dessert menu, please?
¿Me podría traer la carta/la carta de vinos/la carta de postres, por favor?

What do you recommend?
¿Qué nos recomienda?

Do you have vegetarian dishes?
¿Tiene platos vegetarianos?

What's today's special?
¿Cuál es la especialidad de hoy?

I'll take that, then.
Voy a pedir eso entonces.

We'll both have the set menu.
Plato del día para los dos.

Where is the restroom, please?
¿Dónde es el tocador, por favor?

This isn't what I ordered, I asked for …
Esto no es lo que pedí, yo había pedido …

Could we have another jug of water/some more bread, please?
¿Podría traernos otra jarra de agua/un poco más de pan, por favor?

Understanding the waiter:

¿Ya eligieron?
Are you ready to order?

¿Y para beber?
And what would you like to drink?

¿Quieren algún postre?
Would you like a dessert?

¡Buen provecho!
Enjoy your meal!

Commenting on the food:

It's delicious.
Está delicioso.

It was really good.
Estaba muy rico.

It's very greasy/too spicy.
Está demasiado grasoso/picante.

It doesn't have enough salt.
Le falta sal.

Asking for the check:

Could I have the check, please?
La cuenta, por favor.

I think there's a mistake in the check.
Creo que hay un error en la cuenta.

Is the tip included?
¿Está incluida la propina?

We're all paying together.
Vamos a pagar todo junto.

3) Arranging to meet someone

What are you doing tonight?
¿Qué planes tiene para esta noche?

Do you have anything planned?
¿Tiene planes para esta noche?

How about going to the movies?
¿Qué te parece si vamos al cine?

When do you want to meet? And where?
¿A qué hora nos encontramos? ¿Y en dónde?

We can meet in front of the movie theater.
Podemos encontrarnos en la puerta del cine.

I'll meet you later, I need to stop by the hotel first.
Los veré más tarde, necesito hacer una parada en el hotel primero.

4) Going to see movies, shows, and concerts

I'd like three tickets for ...
Quisiera tres entradas para ...

Are there any discounts for students?
¿Hay descuento para estudiantes?

What time does the program/movie start?
¿A qué hora es la función/la película?

How long is the movie?
¿Cuánto dura la película?

Is the movie in the original language?
¿Esta película está en versión original?

It's out next week.
Se estrena la semana que viene.

I'd like to go to a show.
Me gustaría ir a ver un espectáculo.

Do we have to reserve in advance?
¿Hay que reservar con anticipación?

Do we have good seats?
¿Tenemos buenas localidades?

Will we be able to see the stage?
¿Se ve bien el escenario?

Are there any free/open-air concerts?
¿Hay conciertos gratis/al aire libre?

What kind of music is it?
¿Qué tipo de música es?

Understanding the clerk in the box office:

No hay más entradas para esta función.
This showing is sold out.

Las entradas están agotadas hasta ...
It's sold out until ...

El espectáculo dura una hora y media, incluyendo el intervalo.
The performance lasts for an hour and a half, including the intermission.

IV. Stores, Banks, and Post Offices

1) Buying food

Is there a supermarket/market nearby?
¿Hay algún supermercado/mercado por aquí cerca?

Where can I find a grocery store that stays open late?
¿Dónde puedo encontrar una tienda que esté abierta hasta tarde?

I'm looking for the frozen foods/dairy products aisle.
Busco la sección de productos congelados/lácteos.

I'd like five slices of ham/a little piece of that cheese.
Quisiera cinco rebanadas de jamón/un pedacito de ese queso.

It's for four people.
Es para cuatro personas.

A kilo of potatoes, please.
Un kilo de papas, por favor.

A little more/less, please.
Un poco más/menos, por favor.

Could I taste it?
¿Puedo probarlo?

That's everything, thanks.
Nada más, gracias.

Could I have a (plastic) bag?
¿Podría darme una bolsa (de plástico)?

Paying:

Where can I pay?
¿Dónde se paga?

How much do I owe you?
¿Cuánto le debo?

Can I pay by Visa®?
¿Puedo pagar con tarjeta Visa®?

I'll pay cash.
Voy a pagar en efectivo.

You've made a mistake with my change.
Se equivocó con el cambio.

Sorry, I don't have any change.
Lo siento, no tengo cambio.

Could you give me change, please?
¿Podría darme cambio, por favor?

Could I have a receipt?
¿Podría darme un recibo?

Understanding the clerk:

¿Algo más?
Is there anything else?

¿Cómo va a pagar?
How would you like to pay?

¿No tiene nada de cambio?
Don't you have any change?

Puede marcar su clave.
You can type in your number.

2) Buying clothes

I'm looking for the men's/children's department.
Busco la sección de hombres/niños.

No thanks, I'm only looking.
No gracias, sólo estoy mirando.

I'd like to try on the one in the window.
Quisiera probarme el que está en la vidriera.

Can I try it on?
¿Puedo probármelo?

Do you have it in another color/in red?
¿Lo tiene en otro color/en rojo?

I need a bigger/smaller size.
Necesito una talla más grande/ más pequeña.

Yes, that's fine, I'll take them.
Sí, está bien, me los llevo.

I'd like a jacket/a pair of pants/ a shirt.
Quisiera una chaqueta/un pantalón/una camisa.

Where are the dressing rooms?
¿Dónde quedan los probadores?

I take a size 8.
Calzo del número ocho en Estados Unidos.

It's too small/large.
Es demasiado pequeño/grande.

The skirt is too short/long.
La falda es demasiado corta/larga.

I'll think about it.
Voy a pensarlo.

Understanding the clerk:

¿Buenos días, qué se les ofrece?
Hello, can I help you?

¿Qué talla usa?
What's your size?

No nos queda ninguno en esa talla.
We don't have any left in this size.

Podemos encargarlo/ajustarlo.
We can order it/do alterations.

¿Qué es lo que buscan?
Are you looking for something?

Sólo lo tenemos en azul o negro.
We only have it in blue or black.

Le queda bien.
It really suits/fits you.

3) Buying presents and souvenirs

I'm looking for a present to take back.
Busco un regalo para llevar a casa.

I'd like something easy to transport.
Quisiera algo fácil de transportar.

It's for a little four-year-old girl.
Es para una niñita de cuatro años.

Does it keep well?
¿Se conserva bien?

It's a present; can you gift-wrap it for me?
Es para regalar; ¿podría envolvérmelo?

4) Going to the bank

Are banks open on Saturdays?
¿Los bancos abren los sábados?

I'm looking for an ATM.
Estoy buscando un cajero automático.

Where can I change money?
¿Dónde puedo cambiar dinero?

I'd like to change $80.
Quisiera cambiar ochenta dólares.

What commission do you charge?
¿Cuánto es la comisión?

Can I have $300 in cash?
¿Podría darme trescientos dólares en efectivo?

I'd like to transfer some money.
Quisiera hacer un giro.

I'm waiting for a money order.
Estoy esperando una orden de pago.

The ATM has swallowed my card.
El cajero automático se tragó mi tarjeta.

I'd like to report the loss of my credit cards.
Quisiera informar el extravío de mis tarjetas de crédito.

5) Going to the post office

Is there a mailbox near here?
¿Hay un buzón cerca de aquí?

Where can I find a post office?
¿Dónde puedo encontrar una oficina de correos?

Is the post office open on Saturdays?
¿El correo está abierto los sábados?

What time does the post office close?
¿A qué hora cierra el correo?

I'd like five stamps for the United States.
Quisiera cinco estampillas para Estados Unidos.

I'd like to send this letter/postcard/package to New York.
Quisiera enviar esta carta/postal/este paquete a Nueva York.

I'd like to send it by registered mail.
Quisiera enviarla certificada.

How much is a stamp for Spain?
¿Cuánto cuesta una estampilla para España?

How long will it take to get there?
¿Cuánto tiempo tarda en llegar?

Where can I buy envelopes?
¿Dónde puedo comprar sobres?

Is there any mail for me?
¿Hay correo para mí?

Did I receive any mail?
¿Llegó algo para mí en el correo?

V. Expressions of time

1) The date

Note that in Spanish, months and days are masculine and do not have a capital letter. Cardinal numbers (e.g. *dos*, *tres*, etc.) are used for the dates of the month except the first.

What's today's date?
¿Qué fecha es hoy?

What day is it today?
¿Qué día es hoy?

It's Tuesday, May first.
Es martes primero de mayo.

It's November second/third, 2005.
Es dos/tres de noviembre de 2005.

Today is September fifteenth.
Hoy es quince de septiembre.

I was born in 1962/1985.
Nací en 1962/1985.

I wrote to you on March twenty-second.
Le escribí el veintidós de marzo.

This store is open on Sunday mornings.
Esta tienda abre los domingos en la mañana.

I've been there before, several years ago. I think it was in 1996.
Estuve ahí hace unos años. Creo que fue en 1996.

I spent a month in Spain a few years ago.
Pasé un mes en España hace algunos años.

I came last year at the same time/in 2002.
Estuve aquí el año pasado, en la misma época/en 2002.

Understanding:

Fue construido a mediados del siglo XVII.
It was built in the middle of the 17th century.

Sale cada dos semanas/dos veces por mes.
It comes out once every two weeks/twice a month.

La gente sale sobre todo el fin de semana, pero muy poco entre semana.
People go out mainly on the weekend, but very rarely during the week.

¿Hasta cuándo se queda?
How long are you staying?

¿Se va dentro de dos días?
Are you leaving in two days?

Tómelo tres veces por día/hora.
Take it three times a day/an hour.

Conversation Guide

2) The time

The 24-hour clock is commonly used in Spanish (e.g. 2:35 p.m. = 14h35 = *tres menos veincitinco* or *catorce treinta y cinco*). In Mexico it is commonly said: *veinticinco para las tres* or *dos y treinta y cinco*.

I'm on time/early/late.
Estoy a tiempo/adelantado/atrasado.

It's very early/late.
Es muy temprano/tarde.

Excuse me, do you have the time, please?
Disculpe, ¿me dice la hora, por favor?

What time is it?
¿Qué hora es?

It's three o'clock exactly.
Son las tres en punto.

It's almost one o'clock.
Es casi la una.

It's ten after one/ten to one.
Es la una y diez/una menos diez, (*Méx*) diez para la una.

It's a quarter after one/to one.
Es la una y cuarto/una menos cuarto, (*Méx*) cuarto para la una.

It's one-thirty.
Es la una y media.

It's noon/midnight.
Son las doce del mediodía/de la noche.

It's eleven-forty.
Son las once cuarenta.

It's twenty after twelve.
Son las doce y veinte.

I arrived around two o'clock.
Llegué alrededor de las dos en punto.

It's two (o'clock) in the afternoon.
Son las dos de la tarde.

I have an appointment at 8 a.m./ 8 p.m.
Tengo una cita a las ocho de la mañana/a ocho de la noche.

It was eight (o'clock) in the morning/ in the evening.
Eran las ocho de la mañana/de la noche.

Are you free in the morning? Does 10:30 suit you?
¿Está libre en la mañana? ¿Le viene bien a las diez y media?

I've been waiting for two hours/ since 3 p.m.
Hace dos horas que estoy esperando./ Estoy esperando desde las tres de la tarde.

I waited for twenty minutes.
Esperé veinte minutos.

The train was fifteen minutes late.
El tren llegó quince minutos tarde.

I got home an hour ago.
Volví a casa hace una hora.

Do you want to meet in half an hour?
¿Nos encontramos dentro de media hora?

I'll be back in a quarter of an hour.
Vuelvo dentro de quince minutos.

It lasts for around three quarters of an hour/an hour and a half.
Dura alrededor de tres cuartos de hora/de una hora y media.

There's a three-hour time difference between ... and ...
Hay tres horas de diferencia entre ... y ...

I don't have time to take a nap in the afternoon.
No tengo tiempo de dormir la siesta.

I'm in a hurry, come on, hurry up!
Estoy apurado, vamos, ¡apúrese!

VI. Using the telephone

When giving their telephone numbers, Spanish-speakers say the first three numbers together and the rest, two by two: 409 37 58: cuatrocientos nueve, treinta y siete, cincuenta y ocho. In large cities (due to the many digits in phone numbers), Mexicans say the telephone numbers two by two. When it comes to cellphones, which start with 044, people usually say: *cero cuarenta y cuatro*, and after that, the numbers are said two by two.

1) Calling from a pay phone

Where can I buy a phone card?
¿Dónde puedo comprar una tarjeta de teléfono/telefónica?

Do you know if there's a card-/coin-operated pay phone near here?
¿Sabe si hay un teléfono público de tarjeta/monedas por aquí?

Could you give me change of ... to make a phone call?
¿Podría darme cambio de ...? Es para hacer una llamada.

I'd like to make a collect call.
Quisiera hacer una llamada por cobrar.

2) Asking for information from the operator or switchboard

Could you put me through to information, please?
¿Podría comunicarme con información, por favor?

I'm trying to get a number in Monterrey.
Estoy intentando conseguir un número en Monterrey.

Could you give me the number for ..., please?
¿Podría darme el número de ..., por favor?

What's the country code for Chile?
¿Cuál es el código de Chile?

How do I get an outside line?
¿Cómo hago una llamada al exterior?

Conversation Guide

3) Answering the telephone

When the phone is ringing:

I'll get it!
¡Yo contesto!

Can you get it, please?
¿Puedes contestar, por favor?

When you pick up the phone:

Hello?
¿Bueno?

Hello, Helen Smith speaking
Hola, habla Helen Smith.

4) Confirming you are the person to whom the caller wishes to speak

Yes, it's me.
Sí, soy yo.

This is he/she.
Es él/ella mismo(a).

How can I help you?
¿En qué puedo servirle?

What can I do for you?
¿Qué puedo hacer por usted?

5) Asking to speak to someone

Hi María. This is Sharon here. Is Pedro there?
Buenos días María. Habla Sharon. ¿Está Pedro por ahí?

Can/could I speak to Esteban, please? It's David.
¿Puedo/podría hablar con Esteban, por favor? De parte de David.

To which the other person may reply

Un momento, por favor. Voy a buscarlo.
Just a moment, please. I'll get him for you.

No corte, se lo paso.
Hold on, I'll just hand you over to him.

Lo siento, pero no está aquí en este momento.
I'm sorry but he's not in right now.

Ha salido. Estará de vuelta en media hora.
He's gone out. He'll be back in half an hour.

6) Asking to speak to someone in a company or institution

Hello, I'd like to speak to Mr. Flores, this is Tim Clark.
Hola, quisiera hablar con el señor Flores, de parte de Tim Clark.

Could you put me through to the sales manager, please?
¿Podría comunicarme con el gerente de ventas, por favor?

Could you put me through to extension 321, please?
¿Podría comunicarme a la extensión trescientos veintiuno.

Phrases used by a receptionist or secretary taking a call

Mudanzas García, buen día/buenas tardes.
Good morning/afternoon, Mudanzas García.

¿De parte de quién?
Who's calling?/Who should I say is calling?

No corte, ya le paso.
One moment, I'll put you through.

Da ocupado.
The line's busy.

No contestan.
There's no answer.

Le diré que llamó.
I'll tell him you called.

Está en otra llamada, ¿quiere esperar?
He's on another call, would you like to hold?

Lo siento, está en reunión/ de vacaciones.
I'm sorry, he's in a meeting/ on vacation.

¿Quiere que le dé algún mensaje?
Would you like me to give him a message?

¿Quiere dejarle un mensaje?
Would you like to leave a message?

7) Leaving a message for someone

Just tell him I called, thanks. I'll try again later.
Sólo dígale que llamé, gracias. Volveré a intentarlo más tarde.

Could you tell her that I called? Thank you.
¿Podría decirle que llamé? Gracias.

Could you tell him I'll call back later? Do you know when I'll be able to reach him/when he'll be back?
¿Podría decirle que volveré a llamar más tarde? ¿Sabe cuándo puedo encontrarlo/cuándo estará de vuelta?

Could you ask her to call me back today? She can reach me at ...
¿Podría pedirle que me llame hoy? Me encuentra en el ...

Do you have a pen and paper?
¿Tiene papel y lápiz?

My name is ... and my phone number is ...
Mi nombre es ... y mi número es ...

8) Stating the reason for one's call

Hi Jorge, it's James. I just wanted to know if you had any plans for this evening.
Hola Jorge, habla James. Sólo quería saber si tenías planes para esta noche.

Hello, Lucía? It's me, Peter. Are you free to go to the movies on Saturday?
Hola, ¿Lucía? Soy yo, Peter. ¿Estás libre para ir al cine el sábado?

Conversation Guide

Hello, is this Mr. Tapia? ... Hi. This is Frank Simpson. I'm calling about the ad in ...
Hola, ¿es la casa del señor Tapia? ... Buen día. Me llamo Frank Simpson. Lo llamo por el aviso publicado en ...

I'm calling to inform you that I still haven't received my itemized phone bill.
Lo llamo para informarle que todavía no he recibido la factura de teléfono detallada.

I'm just calling to let you know I'll be a bit late.
Lo llamo para avisarle que voy a llegar un poquito atrasado.

I'd like to make an appointment for next Monday.
Quisiera hacer una cita para el próximo lunes.

9) Understanding recorded messages

- *On someone's answering machine:*

Hola. Usted se ha comunicado con Rafael y Gracia. No estamos en casa en este momento, pero puede dejar un mensaje y lo llamaremos en cuanto volvamos.
Hello, you've reached Rafael and Gracia. We're not available right now, but please leave us a message and we'll return your call as soon as we can.

Por favor, deje su mensaje después de la señal.
Please leave a message after the tone.

- *When you are asked to follow instructions:*

Apriete la tecla numeral/asterisco.
Press the hash/star key.

- *If you are put through to an answering machine, the usual recorded message while waiting is:*

Por favor espere mientras conectamos su llamada.
Please hold while we connect your call.

- *If you have to leave a message, you will hear the following standard set of sentences:*

Usted se ha comunicado con ... No podemos responder a su llamado. Por favor, deje su nombre y número de teléfono después de la señal y lo llamaremos lo antes posible. Gracias.
You've reached... We're unable to take your call right now. Please leave your name and number after the beep and we'll get back to you as soon as we can. Thank you.

- *If you have dialed a number that doesn't exist, you will hear:*

El número que usted marcó no existe.
The number you have dialed has not been recognized.

10) Leaving a message on an answering machine

Hi, it's Kate. I see you're not at home. Oh well … I'll call back later. Bye!
Hola, habla Kate. Por lo visto no estás en casa. Bueno … volveré a llamar más tarde. Bye.

Hello, it's me again. It's just to tell you there are some traffic delays, but I see you've already left. Too bad.
Hola, soy yo otra vez. Sólo quería decirte que hay varios embotellamientos en el camino. Pero por lo visto ya has salido. Qué pena.

Hello, it's David McLean here. Can you contact me on my cell phone whenever you get this message? The number's 07712 745 792. Thank you.
Buen día, habla David McLean. ¿Podría por favor llamarme al celular cuando reciba este mensaje? Mi número es cero setenta y siete, doce, setenta y cuatro, cincuenta y siete, noventa y dos. Gracias.

Hello, this is Kim Thomas from Double Page bookstore. I'm calling to tell you that the book you ordered has arrived.
Buen día, habla Kim Thomas de la librería Double Page. Llamo para decirle que el libro que encargó ya ha llegado.

11) Ending the conversation

Thank you, goodbye.
Gracias, adiós.

Thanks a lot. Bye.
Gracias. Bye.

Thanks for your help, bye.
Gracias por tu ayuda, bye.

Thank you for calling.
Gracias por llamar.

Sorry, but I've got to hang up. My mom needs the phone. Can I call you back later?
Disculpa, pero tengo que cortar. Mi madre precisa el teléfono. ¿Te puedo llamar más tarde?

I've got to go.
Tengo que cortar.

We'll talk soon, OK?
Nos hablamos pronto, ¿ok?

We'll talk again, OK?
Nos hablamos, ¿ok?

12) Cell phones

Do you have a cellphone number?
¿Tiene un número de celular?

I've run out of minutes.
Se me terminaron los minutos.

The signal's very bad.
La señal es muy mala.

I can't get any reception here.
No capto llamadas aquí.

Do you know where I can get a new phone card for my cellphone?
¿Sabe dónde puedo comprar una tarjeta para mi celular?

Can I plug my cellphone in here to recharge it? The battery's dead.
¿Puedo conectar mi celular aquí para recargarlo? Estoy sin batería.

Conversation Guide

Is there an outlet so that I can recharge my cellphone?
¿Hay un enchufe por aquí, para recargar mi celular?

Did you get my text message?
¿Ha recibido mi mensaje?

I forgot my charger.
Me olvidé del cargador.

13) Problems

I'm sorry, I must have dialed the wrong number.
Perdón, debo haber marcado el número equivocado.

Sorry to have bothered you.
Siento haberlo molestado.

You've dialed the wrong number.
Marcó un número equivocado.

You've got the wrong number.
Se equivocó de número.

Could you say that again more slowly?
¿Podría repetir lo que dijo, pero más despacio?

I can barely hear you. Could you speak up?
Lo oigo muy mal. ¿Podría hablar más fuerte?

I'm sorry, I didn't really understand. Could you spell it?
Discúlpeme, no entendí bien. ¿Cómo se deletrea?

Hello, can you hear me?
Hola, ¿me oye?

We got cut off.
Se cortó.

Hold on, we're going to be cut off, I need to put some more change in.
Espera, se va a cortar, tengo que poner más monedas.

I can't reach him.
No logro comunicarme.

I keep getting a busy signal.
Da siempre ocupado.

I don't have many minutes left on my card.
No me quedan muchos minutos en la tarjeta.

A

a

a combines with the article **el** to form the contraction **al** (e.g. **al centro** to the centre).

prep **a)** [dirección] to; **ir a Colombia** to go to Colombia; **llegar a Valencia** to arrive in Valencia; **subir al tren** to get on the train; **vete a casa** go home **b)** [lugar] at, on; **a la derecha** on the right; **a la entrada** at the entrance; **a lo lejos** in the distance; **a mi lado** at o by my side, next to me; **al sol** in the sun; **a la mesa** at (the) table **c)** [tiempo] at; **a las doce** at twelve o'clock; **a los sesenta años** at the age of sixty; **a los tres meses/la media hora** three months/half an hour later; **al principio** at first **d)** [distancia] away; **a 100 km de aquí** 100 km from here **e)** [manera] **a la inglesa** (in the) English fashion o manner o style; **escrito a máquina** typed, typewritten; **a mano** by hand **f)** [proporción] **a 90 km por hora** at 90 km an hour; **a dos euros el kilo** two euros a kilo; **tres veces a la semana** three times a week **g)** DEP **ganar cuatro a dos** to win four (to) two **h)** [complemento indirecto] to; [procedencia] from; **díselo a Javier** tell Javier; **te lo di a ti** I gave it to you; **saludé a tu tía** I said hello to your aunt **i)** *Fam* **ir a por algn/algo** to go and fetch sb/sth **j)** [verbo + 'a' + infinitivo] to; **aprender a nadar** to learn (how) to swim; **fueron a ayudarle** they went to help him **k)** [nombre + 'a' + infinitivo] **distancia a recorrer** distance to be covered **l)** **a no ser por ...** if it were not for ...; **a no ser que** unless; **a ver** let's see; **¡a comer!** lunch/dinner, *etc* is ready!

abad *nm* abbot

abadía *nf* abbey

abajeño, -a *nm, f Am* lowlander

abajo **1.** *adv* **a)** [en una casa] downstairs; **el piso de abajo** the downstairs flat; **la vecina de abajo** the downstairs *Br* neighbour o *US* neighbor; **el estante de abajo** the shelf below; **la tienda de abajo** the shop below us **b)** [dirección] down, downwards; **ahí/aquí abajo** down there/here; **la parte de abajo** the bottom (part); **más abajo** further down; **hacia abajo** down, downwards; **calle abajo** down the street; **echar algo abajo** to knock sth down; **venirse abajo** [edificio] to fall down; *Fig* [proyecto] to fall through **2.** *interj* **¡abajo la censura!** down with censorship! **3.** *prep Am* **abajo de** under

abalanzarse *vpr* to rush forward

abalear *vt Andes, CAm, Ven* to shoot at

abandonado, -a *adj* **a)** abandoned; **tiene a su familia muy abandonada** he takes absolutely no interest in his family **b)** [desaseado] untidy, unkempt

abandonar 1. *vt* **a)** [lugar] to leave, to quit; [persona, cosa] to abandon; [proyecto, plan] to give up **b)** DEP [carrera] to drop out of **2. abandonarse** *vpr* to let oneself go

abandono *nm* **a)** [acción] abandoning, desertion **b)** [de proyecto, idea] giving up **c)** [descuido] neglect

abanicarse *vpr* to fan oneself

abanico *nm* **a)** fan **b)** [gama] range; **un amplio abanico de posibilidades** a wide range of possibilities

abarcar [44] *vt* [incluir] to cover

abarrotado, -a *adj* packed, crammed (**de** with)

abarrotería *nf CAm, Méx* grocer's (shop), grocery store

abarrotero, -a *nm, f CAm, Méx* grocer

abarrotes *nmpl Andes, CAm, Méx* **a)** [mercancías] groceries **b) tienda de abarrotes** grocer's (shop), grocery store

abastecer [33] **1.** *vt* to supply **2. abastecerse** *vpr* **abastecerse de** to be supplied with

abastecimiento *nm* supply, provision

abatible *adj* folding, collapsible; **asiento abatible** reclining seat

abatido, -a *adj* downcast

abatir 1. *vt* **a)** [derribar] to knock down, to pull down **b)** [matar] to kill; **abatir a tiros** to shoot down **c)** [desanimar] to depress, to dishearten **2. abatirse** *vpr* [desanimarse] to lose heart, to become depressed

abdicar [44] *vt & vi* to abdicate

abdomen *nm* abdomen

abdominales *nmpl* sit-ups

abecedario *nm* alphabet

abeja *nf* bee; **abeja reina** queen bee

abejorro *nm* bumblebee

aberración *nf* aberration

abertura *nf* [hueco] opening, gap; [grieta] crack, slit

abertzale *adj & nmf Espradical Basque* nationalist

abeto *nm* BOT fir (tree); **abeto rojo** spruce

abiertamente *adv* [declarar, criticar, apoyar] openly; [sonreír] widely

abierto, -a 1. *pp de* **abrir 2.** *adj* **a)** open; [grifo] (turned) on; **abierto de par en par** wide open **b)** [persona] openminded

abismo *nm* abyss; *Fig* **al borde del abismo** on the brink of ruin; *Fig* **entre ellos media un abismo** they are worlds apart

ablandar 1. *vt* to soften **2. ablandarse** *vpr* **a)** to soften, to go soft **b)** *Fig* [persona] to mellow

abnegado, -a *adj* self-sacrificing

abochornado, -a *adj* embarrassed

abofetear *vt* to slap

abogado, -a *nm, f Br* lawyer, *US* attorney; [en tribunal supremo] lawyer, *Br* barrister; **abogado de oficio** legal aid lawyer; **abogado defensor** counsel for the defence; **abogado del diablo** devil's advocate; **abogado laboralista** union lawyer

abolición *nf* abolition

abolir *vt* to abolish

abollar *vt* to dent

abonable *adj* payable

abonado, -a 1. *nm, f* [a revista] subscriber; [a teléfono, de gas] customer **2.** *adj* FIN [pagado] paid; **abonado en cuenta** credited

abonar 1. *vt* **a)** AGRIC to fertilize **b)** [pagar] to pay (for) **c)** [subscribir] to subscribe **2. abonarse** *vpr* to subscribe (**a** to)

abonero, -a *nm, f Méx* hawker, street trader

abono *nm* **a)** AGRIC [producto] fertilizer; [estiércol] manure **b)** [pago] payment **c)** [a revista etc] subscription; [billete] season ticket **d)** *Méx* [plazo] instalment; **pagar en abonos** to pay by instalments

abordar *vt* [persona] to approach; [barco] to board; **abordar un asunto** to tackle a subject

aborrecer [33] *vt* to detest, to loathe

abortar 1. *vi* [involuntariamente] to miscarry, to have a miscarriage; [intencionadamente] to abort, to have an abortion **2.** *vt* to abort

abortivo, -a *adj* abortive

aborto *nm* miscarriage; [provocado] abortion

abotargado, -a *adj* **a)** [hinchado] bloated **b)** [alelado] dazed

abrasador, -a *adj* scorching

abrasar 1. *vt* & *vi* to scorch **2. abrasarse** *vpr* to burn

abrazadera *nf* clamp

abrazar [40] **1.** *vt* to embrace, to hug; *Fig* [doctrina] to embrace **2. abrazarse** *vpr* **abrazarse a algn** to embrace sb; **se abrazaron** they embraced each other

abrazo *nm* embrace, hug; **un abrazo, abrazos** [en carta] best wishes

abreboca *nm Am* appetizer

abrebotellas *nm inv* bottle opener

abrecartas *nm inv* letter-opener, paperknife

abrefácil *adj inv* easy-open

abrelatas *nm inv* can opener, *Br* tin-opener

abreviar [43] **1.** *vt* to shorten; [texto] to abridge; [palabra] to abbreviate **2.** *vi* to be quick o brief; **para abreviar** to cut a long story short

abreviatura *nf* abbreviation

abridor *nm* [de latas, botellas] (can-) opener, *Br* (tin-)opener

abrigado, -a *adj* [persona] wrapped up

abrigar [42] *vt* **a)** to keep warm; **esta chaqueta abriga mucho** this cardigan is very warm **b)** [proteger] to protect, to shelter **c)** [esperanza] to cherish; [duda] to have, to harbour

abrigo *nm* **a)** [prenda] coat, overcoat; **ropa de abrigo** warm clothes **b) al abrigo de** protected o sheltered from

abril *nm* April

abrillantador *nm* polish

abrillantar *vt* to polish

abrir¹ *nm* **en un abrir y cerrar de ojos** in the twinkling of an eye

abrir² *(pp abierto)* **1.** *vi* to open **2.** *vt* **a)** to open; [cremallera] to undo **b)** [gas, grifo] to turn on **c)** *JUR* **abrir (un) expediente** to start proceedings **3. abrirse** *vpr* **a)** to open; *Fig* **abrirse paso** to make one's way **b)** *Fam* **¡me abro!** I'm off!

abrochar 1. *vt* [botones] to do up; [camisa] to button (up); [cinturón] to fasten; [zapatos] to tie up; [cremallera] to do up **2. abrocharse** *vpr* = **abrochar**

abrumado, -a *adj* overwhelmed

abrumador, -a *adj* overwhelming

abrumar *vt* to overwhelm, to crush; **tantos problemas me abruman** all these problems are getting on top of me

abrupto, -a *adj* **a)** [terreno] steep, abrupt **b)** *Fig* abrupt, sudden

ABS *nm (abr de* **anti-lock braking system)** ABS *(anti-lock braking system)*

ábside *nm* ARQUIT apse

absolución *nf* **a)** REL absolution **b)** JUR acquittal

absolutamente *adv* absolutely, completely; **absolutamente nada** nothing at all

absoluto, -a *adj* absolute; **en absoluto** not at all, by no means

absolver [4] *(pp absuelto) vt* **a)** REL to absolve **b)** JUR to acquit

absorbente *adj* **a)** [papel] absorbent **b)** *Fig* absorbing, engrossing

absorber *vt* to absorb

absorto, -a *adj* absorbed, engrossed **(en** in)

abstemio, -a 1. *adj* teetotal, abstemious **2.** *nm, f* teetotaller

abstención *nf* abstention

abstenerse [24] *vpr* to abstain **(de** from); [privarse] to refrain **(de** from)

abstinencia *nf* abstinence; **síndrome de abstinencia** withdrawal symptoms

abstracto, -a *adj* abstract

absuelto, -a *pp de* **absolver**

absurdo, -a 1. *adj* absurd **2.** *nm* absurdity, absurd thing

abuelo *nm* **a)** grandfather; *Fam* grandad, grandpa; *Fig* old man **b) abuelos** grandparents

abultado, -a *adj* bulky, big

abultar 1. *vi* to be bulky; **abulta mucho** it takes up a lot of space **2.** *vt* to exaggerate

abundancia *nf* abundance, plenty; *Fig* **nadar en la abundancia** to be rolling in money

abundante *adj* abundant, plentiful

aburguesamiento *nm* [de sociedad] embourgeoisement; [de zona] gentrification

aburrido, -a *adj* a) **ser aburrido** to be boring b) **estar aburrido** to be bored; **estar aburrido de** [harto] to be tired of

aburrimiento *nm* boredom; **¡qué aburrimiento!** how boring!, what a bore!

aburrir 1. *vt* to bore **2. aburrirse** *vpr* to get bored; **aburrirse como una ostra** to be bored stiff

abusado, -a *adj Méx Fam* smart, sharp

abusar *vi* a) [propasarse] to go too far b) **abusar de** [situación, persona] to take (unfair) advantage of; [poder, amabilidad] to abuse; **abusar de la bebida/del tabaco** to drink/smoke too much o to excess; JUR **abusar de un niño/una mujer** to abuse a child/woman

abusivo, -a *adj* [precio] exorbitant

abuso *nm* abuse

ac SMS *written abbr of* **hace**

a. C. *(abr de* **antes de Cristo***)* BC

a/c *(abr de* **a cuenta***)* on account

acá *adv* a) [lugar] here, over here; **más acá** nearer; **¡ven acá!** come here! b) **de entonces acá** since then

acabar 1. *vt* to finish (off); [completar] to complete
2. *vi* a) to finish, to end; **acabar bien** to have a happy ending; **acabar con algo** [terminarlo] to finish sth; [romperlo] to break sth
b) **acabar de ...** to have just ...; **acaba de entrar** he has just come in; **no acaba de convencerme** I'm not quite convinced
c) **acabaron casándose** o **por casarse** they ended up getting married

3. acabarse *vpr* to finish, to come to an end; **se nos acabó la gasolina** we ran out of *Br* petrol o *US* gas; *Fam* **¡se acabó!** that's that!

academia *nf* academy; **academia de idiomas** language school

académico, -a *adj* & *nm, f* academic

acallar *vt* a) [persona, ruido] *Br* to quieten down, *US* to quiet down b) *Fig* [críticas, protestas, rumores] to silence

acaloradamente *adv* heatedly, passionately

acalorado, -a *adj* a) hot b) *Fig* [excitado] worked up, excited; [debate etc] heated, angry

acalorarse *vpr* a) to get warm o hot b) *Fig* to get excited o worked up

acampada *nf* camping; **ir de acampada** to go camping; **zona de acampada** camp site, *US* campground

acampanado, -a *adj* bell-shaped; [prendas] flared

acampar *vi* to camp

acantilado *nm* cliff

acaparar *vt* a) [productos] to hoard; [el mercado] to corner b) *Fig* to monopolize

acápite *nm* a) *Am* [párrafo] paragraph b) *CAm* [título] title

acariciar [43] *vt* to caress; [pelo, animal] to stroke; [esperanza] to cherish

acartonado, -a *adj* a) [papel, tejido] cardboardy b) *Fam* [piel] wizened

acaso *adv* perhaps, maybe; **¿acaso no te lo dije?** did I not tell you, by any chance?; **por si acaso** just in case; **si acaso viene ...** if he should come ...

acatarrado, -a *adj* **estar acatarrado** to have a cold

acatarrarse *vpr* to catch a cold

acaudalado, -a *adj* rich, wealthy

acceder *vi* **acceder a** [consentir] to accede to, to consent to; [tener acceso] to gain admittance to; INFORM to access

accesible *adj* accessible; [persona] approachable

acceso *nm* **a)** [entrada] access, entry; INFORM **acceso al azar, acceso directo** random access; UNIV **prueba de acceso** entrance examination; **acceso a Internet** Internet access **b)** [carretera] approach, access **c)** MED & *Fig* fit

accesorio, -a *adj & nm* accessory

accidentado, -a 1. *adj* [terreno] uneven, hilly; [viaje, vida] eventful **2.** *nm, f* casualty, accident victim

accidental *adj* accidental; **un encuentro accidental** a chance meeting

accidente *nm* **a)** accident; **por accidente** by chance; **accidente laboral** industrial accident **b)** GEOGR **accidentes geográficos** geographical features

acción *nf* **a)** action; [acto] act; **poner en acción** to put into action; **ponerse en acción** to go into action; **campo de acción** field of action; **película de acción** adventure movie *o Br* film **b)** FIN share

acechar *vt* to lie in wait for; **un grave peligro nos acecha** great danger awaits us

aceite *nm* oil; **aceite de girasol / maíz / oliva** sunflower / corn / olive oil

aceitera *nf* **a)** oilcan **b) aceiteras** cruet

aceitero, -a *adj* oil-producing; **una región aceitera** an oil-producing region

aceitoso, -a *adj* oily

aceituna *nf* olive; **aceituna rellena** stuffed olive

acelerador *nm* AUTO accelerator

acelerar *vt* to accelerate

acelga *nf* chard

acento *nm* **a)** accent; [de palabra] stress **b)** [énfasis] stress, emphasis

acentuar [30] **1.** *vt* **a)** to stress **b)** *Fig* to emphasize, to stress **2. acentuarse** *vpr Fig* to become more pronounced *o* noticeable

aceptable *adj* acceptable

aceptación *nf* **a)** acceptance **b) tener poca aceptación** to have little success, not to be popular

aceptar *vt* to accept

acequia *nf* irrigation ditch *o* channel

acera *nf Br* pavement, *US* sidewalk; *Fam & Despec* **ser de la acera de enfrente** to be gay *o* queer

acerca *adv* **acerca de** about

acercamiento *nm* bringing together, coming together; POL rapprochement

acercar [44] **1.** *vt* to bring near *o* nearer, to bring (over); *Fig* to bring together; **¿te acerco a casa?** can I give you a *Br* lift *o US* ride home? **2. acercarse** *vpr* **a) acercarse (a)** to approach **b)** [ir] to go; [venir] to come

acero *nm* steel; **acero inoxidable** stainless steel

acertado, -a *adj* **a)** [solución] right, correct; [decisión] wise **b) no estuviste muy acertado al decir eso** it wasn't very wise of you to say that

acertar [1] **1.** *vt* [pregunta] to get right; [adivinar] to guess correctly; **acertar las quinielas** to win the pools **2.** *vi* to be right; **acertó con la calle que buscaba** she found the street she was looking for

acertijo *nm* riddle

achacable *adj* imputable; **achacable a** attributable to

achacar *vt* **achacar algo a** to attribute sth to

achicharrado, -a *adj* **a)** [quemado] burnt to a crisp **b)** [acalorado] **estar achicharrado** to be baking *o* boiling

achicharrante *adj* scorching

achicharrarse *vpr* [quemarse] to burn; *Fig* [de calor] to bake

achinado, -a *adj* **a)** [ojos] slanting **b)** *RP* [aindiado] Indian-looking

achispado, -a *adj Fam* tipsy

acholado, -a *adj Bol, Chile, Perú Despec* [mestizo-físicamente] Indian-looking; [culturalmente] *who has adopted Indian ways*

achuchar *vt Fam* **a)** [abrazar] to squeeze **b)** [estrujar] to wring out **c)** *Fig* [presionar] to lean on

ácido, -a 1. *adj* [sabor] sharp, tart ; QUÍM acidic ; *Fig* [tono] harsh **2.** *nm* QUÍM acid

acierto *nm* [buena decisión] good choice *o* idea ; **con gran acierto** very wisely

aclamar *vt* to acclaim

aclarar 1. *vt* **a)** [explicar] to clarify, to explain ; [color] to lighten, to make lighter **b)** *Esp* [enjuagar] to rinse **2.** *v impers* METEOR to clear (up) **3. aclararse** *vpr* **a)** [decidirse] to make up one's mind ; [entender] to understand **b)** METEOR to clear (up)

aclimatación *nf Br* acclimatization, *US* acclimation

aclimatar 1. *vt Br* to acclimatize, *US* to acclimate (**a** to) **2. aclimatarse** *vpr Fig* **aclimatarse a algo** to get used to sth

acogedor, -a *adj* cosy, warm

acoger [53] **1.** *vt* **a)** [recibir] to receive ; [a invitado] to welcome **b)** [persona desvalida] to take in **2. acogerse** *vpr Fig* **acogerse a** to take refuge in ; [amnistía] to avail oneself of ; **acogerse a la ley** to have recourse to the law

acogida *nf* reception, welcome

acojonar *Vulg* **1.** *vt Esp* **a)** [asustar] to scare the shit out of **b)** [impresionar] to amaze **2.** *vi* **a)** [asustar] to be freaky **b)** [impresionar] to be amazing **3. acojonarse** *vpr* to freak out, to be shit-scared

acomodado, -a *adj* well-off, well-to-do

acomodador, -a *nm, f* usher, *f* usherette

acomodar 1. *vt* **a)** [alojar] to lodge, to accommodate **b)** [en cine etc] to find a place for **2. acomodarse** *vpr* **a)** to make oneself comfortable **b)** [adaptarse] to adapt

acompañado, -a *adj* accompanied

acompañamiento *nm* CULIN & MÚS accompaniment

acompañante 1. *nmf* companion **2.** *adj* accompanying

acompañar *vt* **a)** to accompany ; **le acompañó hasta la puerta** she saw him to the door ; **me acompañó al médico** he came with me to see the doctor ; **¿te acompaño a casa?** can I walk you home? ; *Formal* **le acompaño en el sentimiento** my condolences **b)** [adjuntar] to enclose

acomplejado, -a *adj* **estar acomplejado** to have a complex (**por** about)

acondicionado, -a *adj* **aire acondicionado** air conditioning

acondicionador *nm* conditioner

acondicionar *vt* to prepare, to set up ; [mejorar] to improve ; [cabello] to condition

acongojado, -a *adj* [preocupado] distressed, worried sick ; [apenado] very upset

aconsejable *adj* advisable

aconsejar *vt* to advise

acontecer [33] *v impers* to happen, to take place

acontecimiento *nm* event

acoplar 1. *vt* **a)** to fit (together), to join **b)** TÉC to couple, to connect **2. acoplarse** *vpr* [nave espacial] to dock

acordado, -a *adj* agreed ; **según lo acordado** as agreed

acordar [2] **1.** *vt* to agree ; [decidir] to decide **2. acordarse** *vpr* to remember ; **no me acuerdo (de Silvia)** I can't remember (Silvia)

acorde 1. *adj* in agreement **2.** *nm* MÚS chord

acordeón *nm* **a)** [instrument] accordion **b)** *Col, Méx Fam* [en examen] crib

acortar *vt* to shorten ; **acortar distancias** to cut down the distance

acosar *vt* to harass ; *Fig* **acosar a algn a preguntas** to bombard sb with questions

acoso *nm* harassment ; **acoso sexual** sexual harassment

acostado, -a *adj* [tumbado] lying down ; [en la cama] in bed

acostar [2] **1.** *vt* to put to bed **2. acostarse** *vpr* **a)** to go to bed **b)** *Fam* **acostarse con algn** to sleep with sb, to go to bed with sb

acostumbrar 1. *vi* **acostumbrar a** [soler] to be in the habit of **2.** *vt* **acostumbrar a algn a algo** [habituar] to get sb used to sth **3. acostumbrarse** *vpr* [habituarse] **acostumbrarse a algo** to get used to sth

acotamiento *nm Méx* [arcén] *Br* hard shoulder, *US* shoulder

acreditado *adj* **a)** [médico, abogado] distinguished; [marca] reputable **b)** [embajador, representante] accredited

acreditar *vt* **a)** to be a credit to **b)** [probar] to prove **c)** [embajador] to accredit **d)** FIN to credit

acrílico, -a *adj* acrylic

acriollarse *vpr Am* to adopt local ways

acristalado, -a *adj* glazed

acrobacia *nf* acrobatics (*sing*)

acróbata *nmf* acrobat

acta *nf* **a)** [de reunión] minutes, record **b)** [certificado] certificate, official document; **acta notarial** affidavit; **Acta Única (Europea)** Single European Act

Takes the masculine articles **el** and **un**

actitud *nf* attitude

activar *vt* **a)** to activate **b)** [avivar] to liven up

actividad *nf* activity

activo, -a 1. *adj* active; **en activo** on active service **2.** *nm* FIN assets

acto *nm* **a)** act, action; **acto sexual** sexual intercourse; **en el acto** at once; **acto seguido** immediately afterwards; MIL **en acto de servicio** in action; **hacer acto de presencia** to put in an appearance **b)** [ceremonia] ceremony **c)** TEATRO act

actor *nm* actor; **actor principal** *o* **primer actor** lead (actor); **actor secundario** *o* **de reparto** supporting actor

actriz *nf* actress; **actriz principal** *o* **primera actriz** lead (actress); **actriz secundaria** *o* **de reparto** supporting actress

actuación *nf* **a)** performance **b)** [intervención] intervention, action

actual *adj* current, present; [al día] up-to-date; **un tema muy actual** a very topical subject

actualidad *nf* **a)** present time; **en la actualidad** at present; **estar de actualidad** to be fashionable; **temas de actualidad** topical subjects **b)** [hechos] current affairs

actualizar [40] *vt* to update, to bring up to date; INFORM [software, hardware] to upgrade

actualmente *adv* [hoy en día] nowadays, these days; [ahora] at the moment, at present

actuar [30] *vi* **a)** to act; **actuar como** *o* **de** to act as **b)** CINE & TEATRO to perform, to act

acuarela *nf* watercolour

Acuario *nm* Aquarium

acuático, -a *adj* aquatic; **esquí acuático** water-skiing

acudir *vi* [ir] to go; [venir] to come, to arrive; **nadie acudió en su ayuda** nobody came to help him; **no sé dónde acudir** I don't know where to turn

acueducto *nm* aqueduct

acuerdo *nm* agreement; **¡de acuerdo!** all right!, O.K.!; **de acuerdo con** in accordance with; **de común acuerdo** by common consent; **estar de acuerdo en algo** to agree on sth; **ponerse de acuerdo** to agree; **acuerdo marco** framework agreement

acumulación *nf* accumulation

acumular 1. *vt* to accumulate **2. acumularse** *vpr* **a)** to accumulate, to build up **b)** [gente] to crowd

acupuntura *nf* acupuncture

acusación *nf* **a)** accusation **b)** JUR charge

acusado, -a 1. *nm, f* accused, defendant **2.** *adj* [marcado] marked, noticeable

acusar 1. *vt* **a)** to accuse (**de** of); JUR to charge (**de** with) **b)** [golpe etc] to feel; *Fig* **su cara acusaba el cansancio** his face showed his exhaustion **c)** COM **acusar recibo** to acknowledge receipt **2. acusarse** *vpr* **a)** [acentuarse] to become more pronounced **b)** *Fig* [notarse] to show

acústica *nf* acoustics (*sing*)

adaptable *adj* adaptable

adaptación *nf* adaptation

adaptador *nm* adapter

adaptar 1. *vt* **a)** to adapt **b)** [ajustar] to adjust **2. adaptarse** *vpr* to adapt oneself (**a** to)

adecuación *nf* adaptation

adecuado, -a *adj* appropriate, suitable

adecuar [47] *vt* to adapt

a. de J.C. *(abr de* **antes de Jesucristo)** BC

adelantado, -a *adj* **a)** advanced; [desarrollado] developed; [precoz] precocious **b)** [reloj] fast **c) pagar por adelantado** to pay in advance

adelantamiento *nm* overtaking; **hacer un adelantamiento** to overtake

adelantar 1. *vt* **a)** to move *o* bring forward; [reloj] to put forward; *Fig* to advance **b)** AUTO to overtake **c)** [fecha] to bring forward; *Fig* **adelantar (los) acontecimientos** to get ahead of oneself **2.** *vi* **a)** to advance **b)** [progresar] to make progress **c)** [reloj] to be fast **3. adelantarse** *vpr* **a)** [ir delante] to go ahead **b)** [reloj] to gain, to be fast **c) el verano se ha adelantado** we are having an early summer

adelante 1. *adv* forward; **más adelante** [lugar] further on; [tiempo] later; **seguir adelante** to keep going, to carry on; **llevar adelante un plan** to carry out a plan **2.** *interj* **¡adelante!** come in!

adelanto *nm* **a)** advance; [progreso] progress **b) el reloj lleva diez minutos de adelanto** the watch is ten minutes fast **c)** [de dinero] advance payment

adelgazar [40] *vi* to slim, to lose weight

además *adv* moreover, furthermore; **además, no lo he visto nunca** what's more, I've never seen him; **además de él** besides him

adentro 1. *adv* [dentro] inside; **mar adentro** out to sea; **tierra adentro** inland **2.** *nmpl* **decir algo para sus adentros** to say sth to oneself

adherente *adj* adhesive, sticky

adherir [5] **1.** *vt* to stick on **2. adherirse** *vpr* **adherirse a** to adhere to; [partido] to join

adhesión *nf* adhesion; [a partido] joining; [a teoría] adherence

adhesivo, -a *adj & nm* adhesive

adicción *nf* addiction; **crear adicción** to be addictive

adición *nf* addition

adicional *adj* additional

adictivo, -a *adj* addictive

adicto, -a 1. *nm, f* addict **2.** *adj* addicted (**a** to)

adiós 1. *interj* goodbye; *Fam* bye-bye; [al cruzarse] hello **2.** *nm* goodbye

adivinación *nf* [predicción] prediction, divination; [adivinanza] guessing

adivinanza *nf* riddle, puzzle

adivinar *vt* to guess; **adivinar el pensamiento de algn** to read sb's mind

adivino, -a *nm, f* fortune-teller

adjetivo, -a 1. *nm* adjective **2.** *adj* adjectival

adjuntar *vt* to enclose

adjunto, -a 1. *adj* **a)** [unido] attached; **adjunto le remito...** please find attached... **b)** [auxiliar] assistant; **director adjunto** assistant director **2.** *nm, f* [auxiliar] assistant **3.** *nm* INFORM attachment

administración *nf* **a)** [gobierno] **la Administración** *Br* the Government, *US* the Administration; POL **admi-**

nistración central central government; **administración pública** civil service **b)** [de empresa] administration, management **c)** [oficina] (branch) office; *Esp* **administración de loterías** *lottery-ticket selling business in Spain*

administrar 1. *vt* **a)** to administer **b)** [dirigir] to run, to manage **2. administrarse** *vpr* to manage one's own money

administrativo, -a 1. *adj* administrative **2.** *nm, f* [funcionario] official

admiración *nf* **a)** admiration; **causar admiración** to impress **b)** LING *Br* exclamation mark, *US* exclamation point

admirar 1. *vt* **a)** to admire **b)** [sorprender] to amaze, to astonish **2. admirarse** *vpr* to be amazed, to be astonished

admisible *adj* admissible, acceptable

admitir *vt* **a)** to admit, to let in **b)** [aceptar] to accept; **no se admiten cheques** [en letrero] no cheques accepted **c)** [tolerar] to allow **d)** [reconocer] to admit, to acknowledge; **admito que mentí** I admit that I lied

admón. *(abr de* **administración***)* admin.

ADN *(abr de* **ácido desoxirribonucleico***) nm* DNA

adobado, -a *adj* **a)** [alimentos] marinated **b)** [pieles] tanned

adobe *nm* adobe

adoctrinamiento *nm* indoctrination

adolescencia *nf* adolescence

adolescente *adj & nmf* adolescent

adonde *adv* where

adónde *adv interr* where (to)?

adopción *nf* adoption

adoptar *vt* to adopt

adoptivo, -a *adj* [hijo] adopted; [padres] adoptive; *Fig* **país adoptivo** country of adoption

adoquín *nm* cobble, paving stone

adorable *adj* adorable

adoración *nf* adoration; **sentir adoración por algn** to worship sb

adorar *vt* **a)** REL to worship **b)** *Fig* to adore

adormecido, -a *adj* **a)** [persona] sleepy **b)** [pierna, brazo] numb

adormilado, -a *adj* dopey, half asleep

adornar *vt* to adorn, to decorate

adorno *nm* decoration, adornment; **de adorno** decorative

a2, a10 SMS *written abbr of* **adiós**

adosado, -a 1. *adj* adjacent; [casa, chalet] semi-detached *(two houses together)*, terraced *(more than two houses in a row)*; [pared] party; **un garage adosado a la casa** a garage attached to the house **2.** *nm* semi-detached house *(two houses together)*, terraced house *(more than two houses in a row)*

adquirir [31] *vt* to acquire; [comprar] to purchase

adquisición *nf* acquisition; [compra] buy, purchase

adquisitivo, -a *adj* **poder adquisitivo** purchasing power

adrede *adv* deliberately, on purpose

ADSL *nm (abr de* **asymmetric digital subscriber line***)* INFORM & TELECOM ADSL

aduana *nf* customs

aduanero, -a 1. *adj* customs **2.** *nm, f* customs officer

adulterio *nm* adultery

adúltero, -a 1. *adj* adulterous **2.** *nm, f* [hombre] adulterer; [mujer] adulteress

adulto, -a *adj & nm, f* adult

adverbio *nm* adverb

adversario, -a 1. *nm, f* adversary, opponent **2.** *adj* opposing

adverso, -a *adj* adverse

advertencia *nf* warning

advertir [5] *vt* **a)** to warn; [informar] to inform, to advise; *Fam* **te advierto que yo tampoco lo vi** mind you, I didn't see it either **b)** [notar] to realize, to notice

adyuvante *adj & nm* adjuvant

aéreo, -a *adj* **a)** aerial **b)** AVIACIÓN air; **tráfico aéreo** air traffic; COM **por vía aérea** by air

aeróbic *nm* aerobics (*sing*)

aerocarril *nm Arg, PRico, Urug* cable car

aerogenerador *nm* wind turbine

aeromodelismo *nm* aeroplane modelling

aeromozo, -a *nm, f Am* air steward, f air hostess

aeronave *nf* airship

aeropuerto *nm* airport

aerosol *nm* aerosol

afán *nm* **a)** [esfuerzo] effort **b)** [celo] zeal

afanador, -a *nm, f* **a)** *Méx* [empleado] (office) cleaner **b)** *Méx, RP Fam* [ladrón] crook, thief

afección *nf* disease

afectado, -a *adj* affected

afectar *vt* afectar a to affect; **le afectó mucho** she was deeply affected; **nos afecta a todos** it concerns all of us

afectivo *adj* [emocional] emotional; **tener problemas afectivos** to have emotional problems

afecto *nm* affection; **tomarle afecto a algn** to become fond of sb

afectuoso, -a *adj* affectionate

afeitado *nm* shave

afeitar 1. *vt* to shave **2. afeitarse** *vpr* = **afeitar**

afeminado, -a *adj* effeminate

aferrarse *vpr* aferrarse a to cling to

afiche *nm Am* poster

afición *nf* **a)** liking; **tiene afición por la música** he is fond of music **b)** DEP **la afición** the fans

aficionado, -a 1. *nm, f* **a)** enthusiast; **un aficionado a la música** a music lover **b)** [no profesional] amateur **2.** *adj* **a)** keen, fond; **ser aficionado a algo** to be fond of sth **b)** [no profesional] amateur

aficionarse *vpr* to become fond (**a** of), to take a liking (**a** to)

afiebrarse *vpr Am* to get a temperature

afilado, -a *adj* sharp

afilar *vt* to sharpen

afiliado, -a *nm, f* member

afiliarse [43] *vpr* to become a member

afín *adj* [semejante] kindred, similar; [relacionado] related

afinar *vt* **a)** [puntería] to sharpen **b)** [instrumento] to tune

afinidad *nf* affinity

afirmación *nf* affirmation; **afirmaciones** [declaración] statement

afirmar 1. *vt* **a)** [aseverar] to state, to declare **b)** [afianzar] to strengthen, to reinforce **2. afirmarse** *vpr* afirmarse **en** to steady o.s. on

afirmativo, -a *adj* affirmative; **en caso afirmativo ...** if the answer is yes ...

afligir [57] **1.** *vt* to afflict **2. afligirse** *vpr* to grieve, to be distressed

aflojar 1. *vt* to loosen **2.** *vi* [viento etc] to weaken, to grow weak **3. aflojarse** *vpr* to come o work loose; [rueda] to go down

afluencia *nf* inflow, influx; **gran afluencia de público** great numbers of people

afluente *nm* tributary

afónico, -a *adj* estar afónico to have lost one's voice

aforo *nm* [capacidad] seating capacity

afortunadamente *adv* fortunately, luckily

afortunado, -a *adj* fortunate; **las Islas Afortunadas** the Canaries

afrentar *vt* **a)** [deshonrar, avergonzar] *Br* to dishonour, *US* to dishonor **b)** [agraviar, ofender] to affront, to insult

África *n* Africa

africano, -a *adj & nm, f* African

afrodisíaco, -a *adj & nm* aphrodisiac

afrutado, -a *adj* fruity

afta *nf* aphtha

aftershave, **after shave** *nm* aftershave

aftersun *adj inv* aftersun

afuera 1. *adv* outside; **la parte de afuera** the outside; **más afuera** further out; **salir afuera** to come o go out **2.** *nfpl* **afueras** outskirts

afuerita *adv Am Fam* outside

afusilar *vt Am Fam* to shoot

agachar 1. *vt* to lower **2. agacharse** *vpr* to duck

agarradera *nf* **a)** *Am* [mango - alargado] handle; [redondo] knob **b)** *Bol, Col, Méx, PRico* [abrazadera] hook, bracket

agarrar 1. *vt* **a)** to grasp, to seize; **agárralo fuerte** hold it tight **b)** *Am* [tomar] to take; **agarrar un taxi** to take a taxi **c)** *Fam* [pillar] to catch; **agarrar una borrachera** to get drunk o pissed **2. agarrarse** *vpr* to hold on; **agarraos bien** hold tight

agarrotado, -a *adj* **a)** [rígido] stiff **b)** [mecanismo, motor] seized up

agazapado, -a *adj* crouched

agazaparse *vpr* [para acechar, atacar] to crouch (*before attacking*)

agencia *nf* agency; [sucursal] branch; **agencia de viajes** travel agency; **agencia de seguros** insurance agency; **agencia inmobiliaria** *Br* estate agent's, *US* real estate office

agenda *nf* diary

agente *nmf* agent; **agente de policía** [hombre] policeman; [mujer] policewoman; **agente de bolsa** stockbroker; **agente de seguros** insurance broker

ágil *adj* agile

agilidad *nf* agility

agitación *nf* [intranquilidad] restlessness; [social, político] unrest

agitado, -a *adj* agitated; [persona] anxious; [mar] rough; **una vida muy agitada** a very hectic life

agitar 1. *vt* [botella] to shake; [multitud] to agitate **2. agitarse** *vpr* [persona] to become agitated; [mar] to become rough

aglomerado *nm* chipboard

agnosticismo *nm* agnosticism

agnóstico, -a *adj & nm, f* agnostic

agobiado, -a *adj Fig* **agobiado de problemas** snowed under with problems; *Fig* **agobiado de trabajo** up to one's eyes in work

agobiar [43] **1.** *vt* to overwhelm **2. agobiarse** *vpr* [con problemas] to be over-anxious; [por el calor] to suffocate

agosto *nm* August; *Fam* **hacer agosto** to make a packet

agotado, -a *adj* **a)** [cansado] exhausted, worn out **b)** COM sold out; [existencias] exhausted; [libro] out of print

agotador, -a *adj* exhausting

agotamiento *nm* exhaustion

agotar 1. *vt* **a)** [cansar] to exhaust, to wear out **b)** [acabar] to exhaust, to use up (completely) **2. agotarse** *vpr* **a)** [acabarse] to run out, to be used up; COM to be sold out **b)** [persona] to become exhausted o tired out

agradable *adj* pleasant

agradar *vi* to please; **no me agrada** I don't like it

agradecer [33] *vt* **a)** [dar las gracias] to thank for; **les agradezco su atención** (I) thank you for your attention; **te lo agradezco mucho** thank you very much **b)** [estar agradecido] to be grateful to; **te agradecería que vinieras** I'd be grateful if you'd come **c)** [uso impers] **siempre se agradece un descanso** a rest is always welcome

agradecido, -a *adj* grateful; **le estoy muy agradecido** I am very grateful to you

agradecimiento *nm* gratitude

agravamiento *nm* aggravation

agredir *vt* to assault

agregado, -a 1. *adj* EDUC **profesor agregado** [escuela] secondary school teacher ; UNIV assistant teacher **2.** *nm*, *f* POL attaché

agregar [42] **1.** *vt* **a)** [añadir] to add **b)** [destinar] to appoint **2. agregarse** *vpr* **agregarse a** to join

agresión *nf* aggression

agresivo, -a *adj* aggressive

agresor, -a 1. *nm*, *f* aggressor, attacker **2.** *adj* attacking

agreste *adj* [abrupto, rocoso] rough, rugged ; Fig [basto, rudo] coarse, uncouth

agrícola *adj* agricultural

agricultor, -a *nm*, *f* farmer

agricultura *nf* agriculture; **agricultura biológica** o **ecológica** organic farming

agridulce *adj* bittersweet

agrietado, -a *adj* **a)** [muro] cracked **b)** [labios, manos] chapped

agringarse [42] *vpr Am Despec* to become like a North American or European

agrio, -a 1. *adj* sour **2.** *nmpl* **agrios** citrus fruits

agrocarburante *nm* agrofuel

agroindustrial *adj* agro-industrial

agrupación *nf* association

agrupar 1. *vt* to group **2. agruparse** *vpr* **a)** [congregarse] to group together, to form a group **b)** [asociarse] to associate

agua *nf* water; **agua potable** drinking water; **agua corriente / del grifo** running / tap water; **agua dulce / salada** fresh / salt water; **agua mineral sin / con gas** still / fizzy o sparkling mineral water; **agua de colonia** (eau de) cologne; Fig **estar con el agua al cuello** to be up to one's neck in it; **aguas jurisdiccionales** territorial waters; **aguas residuales** sewage

Takes the masculine articles **el** and **un**

aguacate *nm* [árbol] avocado ; [fruto] avocado (pear)

aguacero *nm* shower, downpour

aguafiestas *nmf inv* spoilsport, wet blanket

aguamala *nf Carib, Col, Ecuad, Méx* jellyfish

aguamiel *nm* o *nf* **a)** Am [bebida] water mixed with honey or cane syrup **b)** Carib, Méx [jugo] maguey juice

aguanieve *nf* sleet

aguantar 1. *vt* **a)** [soportar] to tolerate; **no lo aguanto más** I can't stand it any longer **b)** [sostener] to support, to hold; **aguanta esto** hold this **c)** **aguanta la respiración** hold your breath **2. aguantarse** *vpr* **a)** [contenerse] to keep back ; [lágrimas] to hold back ; **no pude aguantarme la risa** I couldn't help laughing **b)** [resignarse] to resign oneself

aguardar 1. *vt* to await **2.** *vi* to wait

aguardiente *nm* liquor, brandy

aguarrás *nm* turpentine

aguatero, -a *nm*, *f Am* water seller

aguaviva *nf RP* jellyfish

agudeza *nf* **a)** sharpness ; [del dolor] acuteness **b)** Fig [ingenio] witticism, witty saying

agudización *nf* **a)** [de mente] sharpening **b)** [de situación] worsening

agudo, -a *adj* [dolor] acute ; [voz] high-pitched ; [sonido] treble, high ; Fig [ingenioso] witty ; Fig [sentido] sharp, keen

águila *nf* **a)** eagle ; **águila real** golden eagle **b)** Méx [de moneda] heads; **¿águila o sol?** heads or tails?

Takes the masculine articles **el** and **un**

aguinaldo *nm* tip given at Christmas, Br Christmas box; **pedir el aguinaldo** to go carol singing

agüita *nf Chile* (herbal) tea

aguja *nf* **a)** needle ; [de reloj] hand ; [de tocadiscos] stylus **b)** ARQUIT spire **c)** FERROC point, US switch

agujerear *vt* to make holes in

agujero *nm* **a)** hole ; **agujero negro** black hole **b)** ECON deficit, shortfall

agujetas *nfpl* a) *Esp* [en los músculos] stiffness; **tener agujetas** to be stiff b) *Méx* shoelaces

ahí *adv* there; **ahí está** there he /she / it is; *Am* **ahí no más** just there; **ve por ahí** go that way; **está por ahí** it's over there; **setenta o por ahí** seventy or thereabouts; **de ahí** hence

ahijado, -a *nm, f* godchild; [niño] godson; [niña] goddaughter; **ahijados** godchildren

ahogado, -a 1. *adj* a) [en líquido] drowned; **morir ahogado** to drown b) [asfixiado] suffocated **2.** *nm, f* drowned person

ahogar [42] **1.** *vt* a) [en líquido] to drown b) [asfixiar] to suffocate **2. ahogarse** *vpr* a) [en líquido] to drown, to be drowned; *Fig* **ahogarse en un vaso de agua** to make a mountain out of a molehill b) [asfixiarse] to suffocate c) [motor] to be flooded

ahora 1. *adv* a) [en este momento] now; **ahora mismo** right now; **de ahora en adelante** from now on; **por ahora** for the time being b) **ahora voy** I'm coming; **ahora vuelvo** I'll be back in a minute c) **hasta ahora** [hasta el momento] until now, so far; [hasta luego] see you later **2.** *conj* **ahora bien** [sin embargo] however; [y bueno] well then

ahorcar [44] **1.** *vt* to hang **2. ahorcarse** *vpr* to hang oneself

ahorita, ahoritica *adv Am salvo RP Fam* a) [en el presente] (right) now; **ahorita voy** I'm just coming b) [pronto] in a second c) [hace poco] just now, a few minutes ago

ahorrar 1. *vt* to save **2. ahorrarse** *vpr* **ahórrate los comentarios** keep your comments to yourself

ahorro *nm* a) saving; **ahorro energético** energy saving b) **ahorros** savings; FIN **caja de ahorros** savings bank

ahuecar [44] *vt* a) to hollow out; *Fam* **ahuecar el ala** to clear off, to beat it b) [voz] to deepen

ahuevado, -a *adj CAm, Ecuad, Perú Fam* [tonto] **estar ahuevado con algo** to be bowled over by sth

ahumado, -a *adj* [cristal, jamón] smoked; [bacon] smoky; **salmón ahumado** smoked salmon

aimara, aimará 1. *adj & nmf* Aymara (Indian) **2.** *nm* [idioma] Aymara

airbag ['erβaɣ, air'βaɣ] *(pl* **airbags)** *nm* airbag

aire *nm* a) air; **aire acondicionado** air conditioning; **al aire** [hacia arriba] into the air; [al descubierto] uncovered; **al aire libre** in the open air; **en el aire** [pendiente] in the air; RADIO on the air; **saltar por los aires** to blow up; **tomar el aire** to get some fresh air; **necesito un cambio de aires** I need a change of scene
b) [viento] wind; **hace aire** it's windy
c) [aspecto] air, appearance
d) **él va a su aire** he goes his own sweet way
e) **darse aires** to put on airs

airear *vt* [ropa, lugar] to air; *Fig* [asunto] to publicize

airoso, -a *adj* graceful, elegant; *Fig* **salir airoso de una situación** to come out of a situation with flying colours

aislado, -a *adj* a) isolated b) TÉC insulated

aislamiento *nm* a) isolation b) TÉC insulation

aislante 1. *adj* **cinta aislante** insulating tape **2.** *nm* insulator

aislar *vt* a) to isolate b) TÉC to insulate

ajado, -a *adj* old

ajedrez *nm* a) [juego] chess b) [piezas y tablero] chess set

ajeno, -a *adj* belonging to other people; **los bienes ajenos** other people's goods; **por causas ajenas a nuestra voluntad** for reasons beyond our control

ajete *nm Esp* young garlic

ajetreado, -a *adj* a) [persona] very busy b) [vida, día, ritmo] hectic

ajetreo *nm* activity, hard work, bustle

ají *(pl* **ajís** *o* **ajíes)** *nm Andes, RP* a) [pimiento] chilli (pepper) b) [salsa] *sauce made from oil, vinegar, garlic and chilli*

ajiaceite *nm* garlic mayonnaise

ajiaco *nm* a) *Andes, Carib* [estofado] *chilli-based stew* b) *Méx* [estofado con ajo] *tripe stew flavoured with garlic*

ajillo *nm* CULIN **al ajillo** fried with garlic

ajo *nm* garlic; **cabeza / diente de ajo** head / clove of garlic; *Fam* **estar en el ajo** to be in on it

ajonjolí *(pl* **ajonjolís** *o* **ajonjolíes)** *nm* sesame

ajuar *nm* [de novia] trousseau

ajustable *adj* adjustable

ajustado, -a *adj* tight

ajustar *vt* a) to adjust b) [apretar] to tighten c) FIN [cuenta] to settle; *Fig* **ajustarle las cuentas a algn** to settle a score with sb

ajusticiar *vt* to execute

al *(contracción de* **a** *+* **el)** a) *ver* **a** b) [+ infinitivo] **al salir** on leaving; **está al caer** it's about to happen; **al parecer** apparently

ala **1.** *nf* a) wing; *Fig* **cortarle las alas a algn** to clip sb's wings; DEP **ala delta** hang glider b) [de sombrero] brim **2.** *nmf* DEP winger

Alá *n* Allah

alabanza *nf* praise

alabar *vt* to praise

alabastro *nm* alabaster

alacena *nf* (food) cupboard

alambrar *vt* to fence with wire

alambre *nm* wire; **alambre de púas** barbed wire

alameda *nf* a) poplar grove b) [paseo] avenue, boulevard

álamo *nm* poplar

alardear *vi* to brag, to boast; **alardear de rico** *o* **de riqueza** to flaunt one's wealth

alargado, -a *adj* elongated

alargar [42] **1.** *vt* a) to lengthen; [estirar] to stretch; **ella alargó la mano para cogerlo** she stretched out her hand to get it b) [prolongar] to prolong, to extend c) [dar] to pass, to hand over; **alárgame ese jersey** can you pass me that sweater? **2. alargarse** *vpr* a) to get longer b) [prolongarse] to go on c) **¿puedes alargarme a casa?** can you give me a lift home?

alarma *nf* alarm; **la alarma saltó** the alarm went off; **falsa alarma** false alarm; **señal de alarma** alarm (signal)

alarmante *adj* alarming

alarmar 1. *vt* to alarm **2. alarmarse** *vpr* to be alarmed

alarmista *adj* & *nmf* alarmist

alba *nf* dawn, daybreak

albañil *nm* bricklayer

albañilería *nf* building, bricklaying *(spcializing in laying bricks)*

albarán *nm Esp* COM delivery note, despatch note

albarda *nf* packsaddle

albaricoque *nm Esp* apricot

albatros *nm inv* albatross

albedrío *nm* will; **libre albedrío** free will

alberca *nf* a) [depósito] water tank b) *Col, Méx* [piscina] swimming pool

albergar [42] **1.** *vt* [alojar] to house, to accommodate; *Fig* [sentimientos] to cherish, to harbour **2. albergarse** *vpr* to stay

albergue *nm* hostel; **albergue juvenil** youth hostel

alberguista *nmf Br* youth hosteller, *US* youth hosteler

albóndiga *nf* meatball

albornoz *nm* bathrobe

alborotado, -a *adj* a) worked up, agitated b) [desordenado] untidy, messy c) [mar] rough; [tiempo] stormy

alborotar 1. *vt* a) [agitar] to agitate, to work up b) [desordenar] to make untidy, to turn upside down **2.** *vi* to kick up a racket **3. alborotarse** *vpr* **a)** to get excited o worked up **b)** [mar] to get rough; [tiempo] to get stormy

alboroto *nm* **a)** [jaleo] din, racket **b)** [desorden] disturbance, uproar

alborozado, -a *adj* jubilant

albufera *nf* lagoon

álbum *nm* album

alcachofa *nf* **a)** BOT artichoke **b)** *Esp* [de regadera] rose, sprinkler; [de ducha] shower head

alcalde *nm* mayor

alcaldía *nf* **a)** [cargo] mayorship **b)** [oficina] mayor's office

alcalino, -a *adj* alkaline

alcance *nm* **a)** reach; **al alcance de cualquiera** within everybody's reach; **dar alcance a** to catch up with; **fuera del alcance de los niños** out of the reach of children **b)** *Fig* scope; [de noticia] importance

alcanfor *nm* camphor

alcantarilla *nf* sewer; [boca] drain

alcanzar [40] **1.** *vt* **a)** to reach; [persona] to catch up with; **la producción alcanza dos mil unidades** production is up to two thousand units **b) alcánzame la sal** [pasar] pass me the salt **c)** [conseguir] to attain, to achieve **2.** *vi* [ser suficiente] to be sufficient; **con un kilo no alcanza para todos** one kilo won't be enough for all of us

alcaparra *nf* [fruto] caper; [planta] caper bush

alcaucil *nm* *RP* artichoke

alcayata *nf* hook

alcázar *nm* **a)** [fortaleza] fortress, citadel **b)** [castillo] castle, palace

alcoba *nf* bedroom

alcohol *nm* alcohol

alcohólico, -a *adj & nm, f* alcoholic

alcoholímetro, alcohómetro *nm* Breathalyzer®

alcoholismo *nm* alcoholism

alcoholizado, -a *adj & nm, f* alcoholic

alcoholizarse *vpr* to become an alcoholic

alcohómetro *nm pp de* **alcoholímetro**

alcornoque *nm* cork oak

aldea *nf* village

aldeano, -a 1. *adj* village **2.** *nm, f* villager

alebrestarse *vpr* **a)** [enojarse] to get annoyed o angry **b)** *Méx* [alborotarse, entusiasmarse] to get excited **c)** *Méx, Col* [ponerse nervioso] to get nervous, to get worked up **d)** *Méx, Ven* [rebelarse, indisciplinarse] to rebel

alegar 1. *vt* [motivos] to cite; [pruebas, argumentos] to give, to put forward **2.** *vi* **a)** *Am* [aducir] to claim **b)** [quejarse] to complain

alegrar 1. *vt* **a)** [complacer] to make happy o glad; **me alegra que se lo hayas dicho** I am glad you told her **b)** *Fig* [avivar] to enliven, to brighten up **2. alegrarse** *vpr* to be glad, to be happy; **me alegro de verte** I am pleased to see you; **me alegro por ti** I am happy for you

alegre *adj* **a)** [contento] happy, glad **b)** [color] bright; [música] lively; [lugar] pleasant, cheerful **c)** *Fig* [borracho] tipsy, merry

alegremente *adv* [con alegría] happily, joyfully; [irreflexivamente] blithely

alegría *nf* joy, happiness

alejado, -a *adj* **a)** [lugar] remote **b)** [persona] estranged

alejar 1. *vt* to move further away **2. alejarse** *vpr* to go away, to move away; **no te alejes de mí** keep close to me

alemán, -ana 1. *adj & nm, f* German **2.** *nm* [idioma] German

Alemania *n* Germany; **Alemania del Este / Oeste** East / West Germany; **Alemania Occidental / Oriental** West / East Germany

alentar *vt* to encourage

alergeno, alérgeno nm allergen

alergia nf allergy

alérgico, -a adj allergic

alergista nmf allergist

alergólogo, -a nm, f allergist

alero nm eaves

alerta nf & adj alert; **estar en estado de alerta** to be (on the) alert

aleta nf [de pez] fin; [de foca, de nadador] flipper

aletear vi **a)** [pez] to flap its fins **b)** [ave] to flap its wings

alevín nm [pescado] young fish; Fig [principiante] beginner

alfabético, -a adj alphabetic

alfabetización nf teaching to read and write; **campaña de alfabetización** literacy campaign

alfabetizar vt [personas] to teach to read and write

alfabeto nm alphabet

alfajor nm RP biscuit or cookie with a sweet filling

alfarero, -a nm, f potter

alférez nm second lieutenant

alfil nm bishop

alfiler nm pin; [broche] pin, brooch; [de corbata] tiepin; [para tender] peg; Andes, RP, Ven **alfiler de gancho** [imperdible] safety pin

alfombra nf rug; [moqueta] carpet

alfombrilla nf **a)** [alfombra pequeña] rug **b)** [del baño] bath mat **c)** INFORM **alfombrilla de** o **para ratón** Br mouse mat, US mouse pad

alga nf alga; [marina] seaweed

Takes the masculine articles **el** and **un**

álgebra nf algebra

Takes the masculine articles **el** and **un**

algo **1.** pron indef **a)** [afirmativo] something; [interrogativo] anything; **algo así** something like that; **¿algo más?** anything else?; **por algo será** there must be a reason for it; Fam **algo es algo** it's better than nothing

b) [cantidad indeterminada] some; **¿queda algo de pastel?** is there any cake left?

2. adv [un poco] quite, somewhat; **se siente algo mejor** she's feeling a bit better

algodón nm cotton; **algodón (hidrófilo)** Br cotton wool, US absorbent cotton; **algodón de azúcar** Br candy floss, US cotton candy

algoritmo nm INFORM algorithm

alguien pron indef **a)** [afirmativo] somebody, someone; **he visto a alguien en el jardín** I saw someone in the garden **b)** [interrogativo] anybody, anyone; **¿alguien conoce la respuesta?** (does) anyone know the answer?

alguno, -a **1.** adj **a)** [delante de nombre - afirmativo] some; [interrogativo] any; **algunos días** some days; **algunas veces** some times; **¿has tomado alguna medicina?** have you taken any medicine?; **¿le has visto alguna vez?** have you ever seen him?

b) [después de nombre] not at all; **no vino persona alguna** nobody came

algún is used instead of **alguno** before masculine singular nouns (e.g. **algún día** some day)

2. pron indef **a)** someone, somebody; **alguno dirá que ...** someone might say that ...; **alguno que otro** some **b)** algunos, -as some (people)

alhaja nf jewel

aliado, -a **1.** adj allied **2.** nm, f los Aliados the Allies

alianza nf **a)** [pacto] alliance **b)** [anillo] wedding ring

aliarse [29] vpr to become allies, to form an alliance

alicates nmpl pliers

aliciente nm **a)** [atractivo] lure, charm **b)** [incentivo] incentive

aliento nm **a)** breath; **sin aliento** breathless **b)** [ánimo] encouragement

aligerar 1. *vt* [acelerar] to speed up; **aligerar el paso** to quicken one's pace **2.** *vi Fam* ¡**aligera!** hurry up!

alijo *nm* haul; **un alijo de drogas** a consignment of drugs

alimentación *nf* a) [comida] food b) [acción] feeding c) TÉC supply d) INFORM power supply; **alimentación de papel** paper feeder

alimentar 1. *vt* a) [dar alimento] to feed; [ser nutritivo] to be nutritious b) *Fig* [sentimientos] to nourish c) INFORM to feed; TÉC to supply **2. alimentarse** *vpr* **alimentarse con** o **de** to live on

alimenticio, -a *adj* nutritious; **productos alimenticios** food products, foodstuffs; **valor alimenticio** nutritional value

alimento *nm* a) [comida] food b) *Fig* **tiene poco alimento** it is not very nourishing

alinear 1. *vt* to align, to line up **2. alinearse** *vpr* to line up

aliñar *vt* to season, to flavour; [ensalada] to dress

aliño *nm* seasoning, dressing

alioli *nm* garlic mayonnaise

aliscafo, alíscafo *nm RP* hydrofoil

alistar 1. *vt* MIL to recruit, enlist **2. alistarse** *vpr* a) MIL to enlist, to enrol b) *Am* [prepararse] to get ready

alivianar 1. *vt* a) *Am* [ayudar] to help b) *Méx* [reconfortar] to comfort **2. alivianarse** *vpr Am* [descansar] to rest, to take a load off

aliviar [43] **1.** *vt* [dolor] to soothe, to relieve; [carga] to lighten, to make lighter **2. aliviarse** *vpr* [dolor] to diminish, to get better

alivio *nm* relief

allá *adv* a) [lugar alejado] there, over there; **allá abajo / arriba** down / up there; ¡**allá voy!** here I go!; **más allá** further on; **más allá de** beyond; **el más allá** the afterlife b) [tiempo] **allá por los años veinte** back in the twenties c) **allá tú** that's your problem

allegado, -a 1. *adj* close **2.** *nm, f* close friend

allí *adv* there, over there; **allí abajo / arriba** down / up there; **de allí para acá** back and forth; **por allí** [movimiento] that way; [posición] over there

alma *nf* soul; **no había ni un alma** there was not a soul

Takes the masculine articles **el** and **un**

almacén *nm* a) [local] warehouse; [habitación] storeroom b) COM **(grandes) almacenes** department store (*sing*) c) *Andes, RP* [de alimentos] grocer's (shop), grocery store d) *CAm* [de ropa] clothes shop

almacenar *vt* to store

almacenero, -a *nm, f Andes, RP* grocer

almanaque *nm* calendar

almeja *nf* clam; *muy Fam* pussy

almenas *nfpl* battlements

almendra *nf* almond; **almendra garapiñada** sugared almond

almendrado 1. *adj* almond-shaped; **ojos almendrados** almond eyes **2.** *nm* CULIN almond paste

almendro *nm* almond tree

almíbar *nm* syrup

almidón *nm* starch

almidonado, -a 1. *adj* starched **2.** *nm* starching

almidonar *vt* to starch

almirante *nm* admiral

almohada *nf* pillow; *Fam* **consultarlo con la almohada** to sleep on it

almohadilla *nf* (small) cushion

almorrana *nf Fam* pile

almorzar [2] **1.** *vi* to have lunch **2.** *vt* to have for lunch

almuerzo *nm* lunch

aló *interj Andes, Carib* [al teléfono] hello!

alocado, -a *adj* thoughtless, rash

alojado, -a *nm, f Andes, Méx* guest

alojamiento *nm* accommodation; **dar alojamiento** to accommodate

alojar 1. *vt* to accommodate **2. alojarse** *vpr* to stay

alondra *nf* lark; **alondra común** skylark

alpargata *nf* canvas sandal, espadrille

Alpes *n pl* **los Alpes** the Alps

alpinismo *nm* mountaineering, climbing

alpinista *nmf* mountaineer, climber

alpino, -a *adj* Alpine; **esquí alpino** downhill skiing

alpiste *nm* **a)** [planta] canary grass **b)** [semilla] birdseed

alquilar *vt* to hire; [pisos, casas] to rent; **se alquila** [en letrero] to let

alquiler *nm* **a)** [de pisos, casas] renting; **alquiler de coches** *Br* car hire, *US* car rental; **de alquiler** [pisos, casas] to let, rented; [coche] for hire; [televisión] for rent **b)** [precio] hire, rental; [de pisos, casas] rent

alquitrán *nm* tar

alrededor 1. *adv* [lugar] round, around; **mira alrededor** look around; **alrededor de la mesa** round the table; **alrededor de las dos** around two o'clock; **alrededor de quince** about fifteen **2.** *nmpl* **alrededores** surrounding area; **en los alrededores de Murcia** in the area round Murcia

Alsacia *n* Alsace

alta *nf* dar de *o* el alta [a un enfermo] to discharge from hospital

Takes the masculine articles **el** and **un**

altamente *adv* extremely; **altamente satisfechos** extremely satisfied

altar *nm* altar

altavoz *nm* loudspeaker

alteración *nf* **a)** [cambio] alteration **b)** [alboroto] quarrel, row; **alteración del orden público** disturbance of the peace **c)** [excitación] agitation

alterar 1. *vt* to alter, to change; **alterar el orden público** to disturb the peace **2. alterarse** *vpr* **a)** [cambiar] to change **b)** [inquietarse] to be upset **c)** [alimentos] to go off

altercado *nm* quarrel, argument

altermundialista *nmf* alterglobalist

alternar 1. *vt* to alternate **2.** *vi* [relacionarse] to meet people, to socialize **3. alternarse** *vpr* to alternate

alternativa *nf* alternative

alternativamente *adv* **a)** [con alternancia] alternately **b)** [como segunda opción] alternatively

alterno, -a *adj* alternate; **días alternos** alternate days

alteza *nf* Highness; **Su Alteza Real** His / Her Royal Highness

altibajos *nmpl Fig* ups and downs

altillo *nm* **a)** [desván] attic, loft **b)** *Esp* [armario] *small storage cupboard above head height, usually above another cupboard*

altiplano *nm* high plateau

altitud *nf* altitude

altivo, -a *adj* arrogant, haughty

alto¹, a 1. *adj* [persona, árbol, edificio] tall; [montaña, techo, presión] high; [sonido] loud; *Fig* [precio, tecnología] high; [tono] high-pitched; **los pisos altos** the top floors; **en lo alto** at the top; **alta sociedad** high society; **clase alta** upper class; **en voz alta** aloud, in a loud voice; **a altas horas de la noche** late at night **2.** *adv* **a)** [arriba] high, high up **b)** [en voz fuerte] loud, loudly; **pon la radio más alta** turn the radio up; **¡habla más alto!** speak up!; **pasar por alto** not to notice, to overlook **3.** *nm* **a)** [altura] height; **¿cuánto tiene de alto?** how tall / high is it?; *Fig* **por todo lo alto** in a grand way **b)** [elevación] hill **c)** MÚS alto

alto² 1. *nm* **a)** [interrupción] stop, break **b)** MIL halt; **dar el alto** to order to halt; **un alto el fuego** a cease-fire **2.** *interj* ¡alto! stop!, halt!

altoparlante *nm Am* loudspeaker

altramuz *nm* lupin

altruismo *nm* altruism

altruista 1. *adj* altruistic **2.** *nmf* altruist

altura *nf* **a)** height; **de 10 m de altura** 10 m high **b)** [nivel] level; **a la misma altura** on the same level; GEOGR on the same latitude; **a la altura del cine** by the cinema; *Fig* **estar a la altura de las circunstancias** to meet the challenge; *Fig* **no está a su altura** he does not measure up to him; *Fig* **a estas alturas** at this stage **c)** REL **alturas** heaven

alubia *nf* bean

alucinación *nf* hallucination

alucinar 1. *vt* to hallucinate; *Fig* [encantar] to fascinate **2.** *vi Fam* to be amazed, to be spaced out

alud *nm* avalanche

aludido, -a *adj Fig* **darse por aludido** to take it personally

aludir *vi* to allude to, to mention

alumbrado, -a 1. *adj* lit **2.** *nm* ELEC lighting; **alumbrado público** street lighting

alumbrar 1. *vt* [iluminar] to light, to illuminate **2.** *vi* [parir] to give birth

aluminio *nm Br* aluminium, *US* aluminum

alumno, -a *nm, f* **a)** [de colegio] pupil; **alumno externo** day pupil; **alumno interno** boarder **b)** UNIV student

alusión *nf* allusion, mention

alverja *nf Am* pea

alza *nf* **a)** rise; **en alza** rising; **jugar al alza** [bolsa] to bull the market **b)** MIL sight

Takes the masculine articles **el** and **un**

alzar [40] **1.** *vt* to raise, to lift; **alzar el vuelo** to take off; **alzar los ojos / la vista** to look up; **álzate el cuello** turn your collar up **2.** **alzarse** *vpr* **a)** [levantarse] to get up, to rise **b)** [rebelarse] to rise, to rebel **c)** **alzarse con la victoria** to win, to be victorious

Alzheimer *n* Alzheimer's (disease)

a.m. *adv* a.m.

amabilidad *nf* kindness; *Formal* **tenga la amabilidad de esperar** would you be so kind as to wait?

amable *adj* kind, nice; *Formal* **¿sería usted tan amable de ayudarme?** would you be so kind as to help us?

amaestrado *adj* [animal] trained; [en circo] performing

amaestrar *vt* to train; [domar] to tame

amamantar *vt* to breast-feed; ZOOL to suckle

amancay *nm Andes* golden hurricane lily

amanecer [33] **1.** *v impers* to dawn; **¿a qué hora amanece?** when does it get light?; **amaneció lluvioso** it was rainy at daybreak
2. *vi* **amanecimos en Finlandia** we were in Finland at daybreak; **amaneció muy enfermo** he woke up feeling very ill
3. *nm* dawn, daybreak; **al amanecer** at dawn

amanerado, -a *adj* mannered, affected

amansar *vt* **a)** to tame **b)** *Fig* [apaciguar] to tame, to calm

amante *nmf* lover; **amante del arte** art lover

amapola *nf* poppy

amar 1. *vt* to love **2.** **amarse** *vpr* to love each other

amargado, -a 1. *adj* [rencoroso] embittered, bitter; *Fam* [agobiado] pissed off; **estoy amargado con los exámenes** I'm pissed off with the exams **2.** *nm, f* bitter person

amargar [42] **1.** *vt* to make bitter; *Fig* to embitter, to sour **2.** **amargarse** *vpr Fig* to become embittered o bitter; **no te amargues por eso** don't let that make you bitter

amargo, -a *adj* bitter

amargoso, -a *adj Am* bitter

amarillear 1. *vt* to turn yellow **2.** *vi* to (turn) yellow

amarillo, -a *adj* & *nm* yellow; **prensa amarilla** gutter press

amarilloso, -a *adj Col, Méx, Ven* yellowish

amarradero *nm* **a)** [poste] bollard **b)** NÁUT [para barco] mooring

amarrar *vt* [atar] to tie (up), to bind; NÁUT to moor, to tie up

amarre *nm* NÁUT mooring

amarrete, -a *adj Andes, RP Fam* mean, tight

amasar *vt* **a)** CULIN to knead **b)** *Fig* [fortuna] to amass

amasiato *nm CAm, Chile, Méx* [concubinato] cohabitation, common-law marriage

amasio, -a *nm, f CAm, Méx* live-in lover, common-law partner

amateur [ama'ter] (*pl* **amateurs**) *adj* & *nmf* amateur

amazona *nf* **a)** [jinete] horsewoman **b)** [en mitología] Amazon

Amazonas *n* **el Amazonas** the Amazon

amazónico, -a *adj* Amazonian

ámbar *nm* amber

ambición *nf* ambition

ambicioso, -a 1. *adj* ambitious **2.** *nm, f* ambitious person

ambientador *nm* air freshener

ambiental *adj* environmental

ambientalista *nmf* environmentalist

ambiente 1. *nm* **a)** [gen] environment; *Fig* [medio] environment, milieu **b)** *Andes, RP* [habitación] room **2.** *adj* environmental; **temperatura ambiente** room temperature

ambigüedad *nf* ambiguity

ambiguo, -a *adj* ambiguous

ámbito *nm* field, sphere; **empresa de ámbito nacional** nationwide company

ambos, -as *adj pl Formal* both; **por ambos lados** on both sides

ambulancia *nf* ambulance

ambulante *adj* travelling, mobile; **biblioteca ambulante** mobile library

ambulatorio *nm* surgery, clinic

amén[1] *nm* amen

amén[2] *adv* **amén de** in addition to

amenaza *nf* threat

amenazador, -a *adj* threatening

amenazante *adj* threatening

amenazar [40] *vt* to threaten; **amenazar de muerte a algn** to threaten to kill sb

amenizar [40] *vt* to liven up

ameno, -a *adj* entertaining

América *n* America; **América Central / del Norte / del Sur** Central / North / South America

americana *nf* [prenda] jacket

americano, -a *adj* & *nm, f* American

ameritar *vt Am* to deserve

ametralladora *nf* machine gun

ametrallar *vt* to machine-gun

amígdala *nf* tonsil

amigo, -a 1. *nm, f* friend; **hacerse amigo de** to make friends with; **hacerse amigos** to become friends; **son muy amigos** they are very good friends **2.** *adj* [aficionado] fond (**de** of)

amistad *nf* **a)** friendship **b) amistades** friends

amnesia *nf* amnesia

amnistía *nf* amnesty

amo *nm* **a)** [dueño] owner **b)** [señor] master

amodorrarse *vpr* to get drowsy

amolarse *vpr Am Fam* to lump it

amoldar 1. *vt* to adapt, to adjust **2. amoldarse** *vpr* to adapt oneself

amoniaco, amoníaco *nm* ammonia

amontonar 1. *vt* to pile up, to heap up **2. amontonarse** *vpr* to pile up, to heap up; [gente] to crowd together

amor *nm* **a)** love; **hacer el amor** to make love; **amor propio** self-esteem; **¡por el amor de Dios!** for God's sake! **b) amores** loves

amordazar [40] *vt* [perro] to muzzle ; [persona] to gag

amoroso, -a *adj* loving, affectionate

amortiguador *nm* AUTO shock absorber

amortiguar [45] *vt* [golpe] to cushion ; [ruido] to muffle ; [luz] to subdue

amostazarse *vpr Andes, CAm* to go red, to be embarrassed

amparar 1. *vt* to protect **2. ampararse** *vpr* to seek refuge

amparo *nm* protection, shelter ; **al amparo de la ley** under the protection of the law

ampliación *nf* enlargement ; [de plazo, casa] extension

ampliamente *adv* **a)** [de manera amplia] easily **b)** [mucho] totally

ampliar [29] *vt* to enlarge ; [casa, plazo] to extend

amplificador *nm* amplifier

amplio, -a *adj* large, roomy ; [ancho] wide, broad ; **en el sentido más amplio de la palabra** in the broadest sense of the word

amplitud *nf* **a)** spaciousness ; **amplitud de miras** broad-mindedness **b)** [de espacio] room, space **c)** FÍS amplitude

ampolla *nf* **a)** MED blister ; *Fig* **levantar ampollas** to raise people's hackles **b)** [de medicina] ampoule

amr SMS *written abbr of* **amor**

amueblado, -a 1. *adj* [piso] furnished **2.** *nm* furniture

amueblar *vt* to furnish

amuermar 1. *vt Esp Fam* [aburrir] to bore **2. amuermarse** *vpr Fam* **a)** [atontarse] to zombify **b)** *Esp* [aburrirse] to get bored stiff

amuleto *nm* amulet ; **amuleto de la suerte** lucky charm

amurallar *vt* to wall, to fortify

analfabetismo *nm* illiteracy

analfabeto, -a *nm, f* illiterate

analgésico, -a *adj & nm* analgesic

análisis *nm inv* analysis ; **análisis de sangre** blood test

analista *nmf* MED, INFORM & FIN analyst ; **analista programador** computer analyst and programmer

analítico, -a *adj* analytical

analizar [40] *vt* to analyse

analogía *nf* analogy

analógico, -a *adj* **a)** [análogo] analogical **b)** INFORM & TECNOL analogue

análogo, -a *adj* analogous, similar

ananá *nm* pineapple

ananás *nm inv* pineapple

anaranjado, -a *adj & nm* orange

anarquía *nf* anarchy

anárquico, -a *adj* anarchic

anarquista *adj & nmf* anarchist

anatomía *nf* anatomy

anatómico, -a *adj* anatomical

anca *nf* haunch ; **ancas de rana** frogs' legs

> Takes the masculine articles **el** and **un**

ancho, -a 1. *adj* wide, broad ; **a lo ancho** breadthwise ; **te está muy ancho** it's too big for you **2.** *nm* **a)** [anchura] width, breadth ; **2 m de ancho** 2 m wide ; **¿qué ancho tiene?** how wide is it? **b)** COST width **3.** *nfpl Esp Fam* **a mis** *o* **tus anchas** at ease, comfortable

anchoa *nf* anchovy

anchura *nf* width, breadth

anciano, -a 1. *adj* very old **2.** *nm, f* old person ; **los ancianos** old people

ancla *nf* anchor

> Takes the masculine articles **el** and **un**

anda *interj* ¡anda! [¡vamos!, ¡por favor!] come on! ; [sorpresa, desilusión] no!, you're joking! ; **¡anda ya!** [incredulidad] you've gotta be kidding!, you're joking, aren't you?

andador *nm* baby walker

ándale *interj CAm, Méx Fam* come on!

Andalucía *n* Andalusia

andaluz, -a *adj* & *nm, f* Andalusian

andamio *nm* scaffold

andar¹ *nm* andar o andares (*nmpl*) walk, gait

andar² [8] **1.** *vi* **a)** *esp Esp* [caminar] to walk
b) [coche etc] to move; **este coche anda despacio** this car goes very slowly
c) [funcionar] to work; **esto no anda** this doesn't work
d) *Fam* anda por los cuarenta he's about forty; **anda siempre diciendo que …** he's always saying that …; **¿cómo andamos de tiempo?** how are we off for time?; **tu bolso debe andar por ahí** your bag must be over there somewhere
2. *vt* [recorrer] to walk
3. amuermarse *vpr* [obrar] **andarse con cuidado / misterios** to be careful / secretive

ándele *interj CAm, Méx Fam* come on!

andén *nm* **a)** [en estación] platform **b)** *Andes, CAm* [acera] *Br* pavement, *US* sidewalk **c)** *Andes* [bancal de tierra] terrace

Andes *nmpl* Andes

andinismo *nm Am* mountaineering, mountain climbing

andinista *nmf Am* mountaineer, mountain climber

andino, -a *adj* & *nm, f* Andean

anécdota *nf* anecdote

anecdótico, -a *adj* anecdotal

anemia *nf* anaemia

anémico, -a 1. *adj* anaemic **2.** *nm, f* anaemia sufferer

anestesia *nf* anaesthesia

anestesista *nmf* anaesthetist

anexo, -a 1. *adj* attached, joined (**a** to) **2.** *nm* appendix

anfetamina *nf* amphetamine

anfibio, -a 1. *adj* amphibious **2.** *nm* amphibian

anfiteatro *nm* **a)** amphitheatre **b)** CINE & TEATRO gallery

anfitrión, -ona *nm, f* host, *f* hostess

ánfora *nf* amphora

ángel *nm* **a)** angel; **ángel de la guarda** guardian angel **b)** *Am* [micrófono] hand-held microphone

angelical, angélico, -a *adj* angelic

angina *nf* angina; **tener anginas** to have tonsillitis; MED **angina de pecho** angina pectoris

anglosajón, -ona *adj* & *nm, f* Anglo-Saxon

anguila *nf* eel; **anguila de mar** conger eel

angula *nf* elver

angular *adj* angular; FOTO **(objetivo) gran angular** wide-angle lens; **piedra angular** cornerstone

ángulo *nm* angle; [rincón] corner

angustia *nf* anguish

angustiado, -a *adj* anguished, distressed

angustiar [43] *vt* to distress

angustioso, -a *adj* distressing

anhelar *vt* to long for, to yearn for

anhelo *nm* longing, yearning

anidar *vi* to nest

anilla *nf* **a)** ring; **carpeta de anillas** ring-binder **b)** DEP **anillas** rings

anillo *nm* ring; **anillo de boda** wedding ring

ánima *nf* soul

Takes the masculine articles **el** and **un**

animación *nf* [diversión] entertainment

animadamente *adv* animatedly, in a lively way

animado, -a *adj* [fiesta etc] lively

animal 1. *nm* animal; *Fig* [basto] brute; [necio] dunce **2.** *adj* animal

animar 1. *vt* **a)** [alentar] to encourage **b)** [alegrar - persona] to cheer up; [fiesta, bar] to liven up, to brighten up **2. animarse** *vpr* **a)** [persona] to cheer up; [fiesta, reunión] to brighten up **b) ¿te animas a venir?** do you fancy coming along?

ánimo *nm* **a)** [espíritu] spirit; **estado de ánimo** frame *o* state of mind **b) con ánimo de** [intención] with the intention of **c)** [valor, coraje] courage; **dar ánimos a** to encourage; **¡ánimo!** cheer up!

aniñado, -a *adj* childlike; *Despec* childish

aniquilar *vt* to annihilate

anís *nm* **a)** [bebida] anisette **b)** [grano] aniseed

aniversario *nm* anniversary

ano *nm* anus

anoche *adv* last night; [por la tarde] yesterday evening; **antes de anoche** the night before last

anochecer [33] **1.** *v impers* to get dark; **cuando anochece** at nightfall, at dusk **2.** *vi* to be somewhere at dusk; **anochecimos en Cuenca** we were in Cuenca at dusk **3.** *nm* nightfall, dusk

anomalía *nf* anomaly

anómalo, -a *adj* anomalous

anón *nm Am* sugar apple

anonimato *nm* anonymity; **permanecer en el anonimato** to remain anonymous *o* nameless

anónimo, -a 1. *adj* **a)** [desconocido] anonymous **b)** COM **sociedad anónima** public liability company, *US* incorporated company **2.** *nm* [carta] anonymous letter

anorak *(pl* **anoraks)** *nm* anorak

anorexia *nf* MED anorexia

anoréxico, -a *adj & nm, f* MED anorexic

anotar 1. *vt* **a)** to annotate **b)** [apuntar] to take down, to make a note of **2. anotarse** *vpr RP* [en curso] to enrol (**en** for); [para actividad] to sign up (**en** for)

ansia *nf* **a)** [deseo] longing, yearning **b)** [ansiedad] anxiety **c)** MED sick feeling

ansiedad *nf* anxiety; **con ansiedad** anxiously

ansioso, -a *adj* **a)** [deseoso] eager (**por** for) **b)** [avaricioso] greedy

antártico, -a 1. *adj* Antarctic **2.** *nm* **el Antártico** the Antarctic

ante¹ *nm* **a)** ZOOL elk, moose **b)** [piel] suede

ante² *prep* **a)** before, in the presence of; JUR **ante notario** in the presence of a notary; **ante todo** most of all **b)** [en vista de] faced with, in view of; **ante la crisis energética** faced with the energy crisis

anteanoche *adv* the night before last

anteayer *adv* the day before yesterday

antebrazo *nm* forearm

antecedente 1. *adj* previous **2.** *nm* antecedent **3.** *nmpl* **a) antecedentes** [historial] record; JUR **antecedentes penales** criminal record **b)** *Fig* **poner en antecedentes** to put in the picture

anteceder *vt* to precede, to go before

antecesor, -a *nm, f* **a)** [en un cargo] predecessor **b)** [antepasado] ancestor

antelación *nf* notice; **con poca antelación** at short notice; **con un mes de antelación** a month beforehand, with a month's notice

antemano *adv* **de antemano** beforehand, in advance

antena *nf* **a)** RADIO & TV aerial; **antena parabólica** satellite dish; **en antena** on the air **b)** ZOOL antenna, feeler

anteojo *nm* **a)** telescope **b) anteojos** [binoculares] binoculars; *Am* [gafas] spectacles, glasses

antepasado, -a *nm, f* ancestor

antepenúltimo, -a *adj* antepenultimate; **el capítulo antepenúltimo** the last chapter but two

anterior *adj* **a)** previous; **el día anterior** the day before **b)** [delantero] front; **parte anterior** front part

anteriormente *adv* previously, before

antes *adv* **a)** [tiempo] before; **antes de las tres** before three o'clock; **mucho antes** long before; **la noche antes** the night before; **cuanto antes** as soon as possible **b)** [antaño] in the past; **antes llovía más** it used to rain more in the past **c)** [lugar] before; **antes del semáforo** before the traffic lights **d)** **antes prefiero hacerlo yo** I'd rather do it myself; **antes (bien)** on the contrary

antesala *nf* antechamber, anteroom; *Fig* **en la antesala de** on the eve of

antiabortista **1.** *adj* anti-abortion, pro-life **2.** *nmf* anti-abortion o pro-life campaigner

antiarrugas *adj inv* anti-wrinkle

antibiótico, -a *adj & nm* antibiotic

anticatarral *nm* cold remedy

anticiclón *nm* anticyclone, high pressure area

anticiclónico, -a *adj* high-pressure

anticipadamente *adv* in advance; **pagar anticipadamente** to pay in advance; **jubilarse anticipadamente** to take early retirement

anticipado, -a *adj* brought forward; **elecciones anticipadas** early elections; **gracias anticipadas** thanks in advance; COM **por anticipado** in advance

anticipar **1.** *vt* [acontecimiento] to bring forward; [dinero] to pay in advance; **no anticipemos acontecimientos** we'll cross that bridge when we come to it
2. anticiparse *vpr* **a)** [adelantarse] to beat to it; **iba a decírtelo, pero él se me anticipó** I was going to tell you, but he beat me to it
b) [llegar pronto] to arrive early; *Fig* **anticiparse a su tiempo** to be ahead of one's time

anticipo *nm* [adelanto] advance; **pedir un anticipo** to ask for an advance (on one's wages)

anticonceptivo, -a *adj & nm* contraceptive

anticuado, -a *adj* antiquated

anticuario, -a *nm, f* antique dealer

anticucho *nm Andes* [brocheta] kebab

anticuerpo *nm* antibody

antidepresivo, -a **1.** *adj* antidepressant **2.** *nm* antidepressant (drug)

antidolor *adj inv* **un tratamiento antidolor** a treatment to help with the pain

antier *adv Am Fam* the day before yesterday

antifaz *nm* mask

antiguamente *adv* [hace mucho] long ago; [previamente] formerly

antigüedad *nf* **a)** [período histórico] antiquity; **en la antigüedad** in olden days, in former times **b)** [en cargo] seniority **c)** **tienda de antigüedades** antique shop

antiguo, -a *adj* **a)** old, ancient **b)** [pasado de moda] old-fashioned **c)** [en cargo] senior **d)** [anterior] former

antihistamínico, -a *adj & nm* antihistamine

antiinflamatorio, -a **1.** *adj* anti-inflammatory **2.** *nm* anti-inflammatory drug

Antillas *nfpl* **las Antillas** the West Indies, the Antilles

antílope *nm* antelope

antinuclear *adj* antinuclear; [refugio] nuclear

antipatía *nf* antipathy, dislike; **tener antipatía a** to dislike

antipático, -a *adj* unpleasant; **Pedro me es antipático** I don't like Pedro

antirracista *adj & nmf* antiracist

antirrobo **1.** *adj inv* antitheft; **alarma antirrobo** burglar alarm; [para coche] car alarm **2.** *nm* [para coche] car alarm; [para casa] burglar alarm

antisemitismo *nm* anti-Semitism

antiséptico, -a *adj & nm* antiseptic

antitabaco *adj inv* antismoking

antitranspirante **1.** *adj* antiperspirant **2.** *nm* antiperspirant (deodorant)

antivirus *nm inv* INFORM antivirus (program)

antojitos *nmpl Ecuad, Méx* snacks, appetizers

antojo *nm* **a)** [capricho] whim, caprice; [de embarazada] craving; **a su antojo** in one's own way, as one pleases **b)** [en la piel] birthmark

antología *nf* anthology

antónimo *nm* antonym

antorcha *nf* torch

antro *nm* dump, hole; *Fig* **antro de perdición** den of vice

anual *adj* annual; **ingresos anuales** yearly income

anualizar *vt* to annualize

anuario *nm* yearbook

anular¹ *nm* ring finger

anular² *vt* **a)** COM [pedido] to cancel; DEP [gol] to disallow; [matrimonio] to annul; JUR [ley] to repeal **b)** INFORM to delete

anunciar [43] **1.** *vt* **a)** [producto etc] to advertise **b)** [avisar] to announce **2. anunciarse** *vpr* to advertise oneself; **anunciarse en un periódico** to put an advert in a newspaper

anuncio *nm* **a)** [comercial] advertisement, advert, ad **b)** [aviso] announcement **c)** [cartel] notice, poster

añadidura *nf* addition; **por añadidura** besides, on top of everything else

añadir *vt* to add (**a** to)

añicos *nmpl* smithereens; **hacer añicos** to smash to smithereens

año *nm* **a)** year; **el año pasado** last year; **el año que viene** next year; **hace años** a long time ago, years ago; **los años noventa** the nineties; **todo el año** all the year (round); **año luz** light year **b)** **¿cuántos años tienes? — tengo 17 (años)** how old are you? — I'm 17 (years old); **¿cuántos años vas a cumplir?** how old will you be?; **tiene seis años** he's six years old; **entrado en años** getting on

añoranza *nf* longing, yearning

añorar *vt* [pasado] to long for, to yearn for; [país] to feel homesick for, to miss

anzuelo *nm* (fish) hook

aora SMS *written abbr of* **ahora**

aorta *nf* ANAT aorta

apabullante *adj Fam* staggering

apache *adj* & *nmf* Apache

apachurrar *vt Fam* to squash, to crush

apacible *adj* mild, calm

apadrinar *vt* **a)** [en bautizo] to act as godfather to; [en boda] to be best man for **b)** [artista] to sponsor

apagado, -a *adj* **a)** [luz, cigarro] out **b)** [color] dull; [voz] sad; [mirada] expressionless, lifeless; [carácter, persona] spiritless

apagar [42] *vt* [fuego] to put out; [luz, tele etc] to turn off, to switch off; [color] to soften; [sed] to quench

apagón *nm* power cut, blackout

apaisado, -a *adj* **a)** oblong **b)** [papel] landscape

apalabrar *vt* [concertar] to make a verbal agreement on

apalancado, -a *adj Esp Fam* **se pasó la tarde apalancado delante del televisor** he spent the afternoon lounging in front of the television

apalancar 1. *vt* [para abrir] to prise; [para mover] to lever **2. apalancarse** *vpr Esp Fam* [apoltronarse] to plonk oneself; **se apalancó en el sofá y no se movió de allí** he plonked himself on the sofa and didn't move from there

apañado, -a *adj Fam* [hábil, mañoso] clever, resourceful; **estar apañado** to have had it; **¡estamos apañados!** we've had it!

apañar 1. *vt* to mend, to fix **2. apañárselas** *vpr Esp* [arreglarse] to cope, to manage; **apañárselas (para hacer algo)** to manage (to do sth); *Méx* **apañarse con** [robar] to make off with, to steal

apapachado, -a *adj Méx Fam* cuddled

apapachar *vt Méx Fam* [mimar] to cuddle; [consentir] to spoil

apapacho nm Méx Fam [mimo] cuddle

aparador nm [mueble] sideboard; [de tienda] shop window

aparato nm a) (piece of) apparatus; [dispositivo] device; [instrumento] instrument; **aparato de radio/televisión** radio/television set; **aparato digestivo** digestive system; **aparato eléctrico** thunder and lightning b) TEL **¿quién está al aparato?** who's speaking? c) [ostentación] display

aparcacoches nmf inv valet parking

aparcamiento nm Esp [parking] Br car park, US parking lot; [hueco] parking place

aparcar [44] vt Esp to park

aparearse vpr to mate

aparecer [33] 1. vi a) to appear; **no aparece en mi lista** he is not on my list b) to turn up, to show up; **¿apareció el dinero?** did the money turn up?; **no apareció nadie** nobody turned up 2. **aparecerse** vpr a) [Virgen etc] to appear b) Am Fam [presentarse] to turn up

aparejador, -a nm, f quantity surveyor

aparejar vt a) [caballo] to harness b) [emparejar] to pair off

aparejo nm a) [equipo] equipment b) [de caballo] harness

aparentar 1. vt a) [fingir] to affect b) [tener aspecto] to look; **no aparenta esa edad** she doesn't look that age 2. vi to show off

aparente adj a) apparent; **sin motivo aparente** for no apparent reason b) Fam [conveniente] suitable

aparentemente adv apparently

aparición nf a) appearance b) [visión] apparition

apariencia nf appearance; **en apariencia** apparently; Fig **guardar las apariencias** to keep up appearances

apartado, -a 1. adj [lugar] remote, isolated; **mantente apartado de él** keep away from him 2. nm a) [párrafo] section, paragraph b) **apartado de correos** Post Office Box

apartamento nm esp Am [en edificio] Br flat, US apartment; Esp [más pequeño] apartment

apartar 1. vt a) [alejar] to move away, to remove; **apartar la mirada** to look away b) [guardar] to put aside 2. vi **¡aparta!** move out of the way! 3. **apartarse** vpr [alejarse] to move over, to move away; **apártate de en medio** move out of the way

aparte 1. adv a) aside; **ponlo aparte** put it aside; **modestia/bromas aparte** modesty/joking apart b) **eso hay que pagarlo aparte** [separadamente] you have to pay for that separately c) **aparte de eso** [además] besides that; [excepto] apart from that d) **eso es caso aparte** that's completely different 2. nm a) TEATRO aside b) LING **punto y aparte** full stop, new paragraph

apasionado, -a 1. adj passionate; **apasionado de la música** very fond of music 2. nm, f enthusiast

apasionante adj exciting

apasionar vt to excite, to thrill; **le apasiona el jazz** he is mad about jazz

apdo. (abr de **apartado**) PO Box

apechugar [42] vi **apechugar con** to shoulder

apego nm love, affection; **tener apego a** to be attached to

apellidarse vpr to have as a surname, to be called

apellido nm surname; **apellido de soltera** maiden name

apenado, -a adj a) [entristecido] sad b) Am salvo RP [avergonzado] embarrassed; **está muy apenado por lo que hizo** he's very embarrassed about what he did

apenar 1. vt to sadden 2. **apenarse** vpr a) [entristecerse] to be saddened b) Am salvo RP [avergonzarse] to be embarrassed

apenas adv a) [casi no] hardly, scarcely; **apenas come** he hardly eats anything; **apenas (si) hay nieve** there is hardly any snow **b)** [tan pronto como] scarcely; **apenas llegó, sonó el teléfono** no sooner had he arrived than the phone rang

apéndice *nm* appendix

apendicitis *nf inv* appendicitis

aperitivo *nm* [bebida] apéritif; [comida] appetizer

apertura *nf* **a)** [comienzo] opening **b)** POL liberalization

apesadumbrado, -a *adj* regretful, distressed

apestar 1. *vi* to stink (**a** of) **2.** *vt* to infect with the plague

apetecer [33] **1.** *vi Esp* ¿te apetece un café? do you fancy a coffee?; ¿qué te apetece para cenar? what would you like for supper?; me apetece salir I feel like going out; hoy no me apetece salir I don't feel like going out today; ¿te apetece ir al cine? do you fancy going to the cinema? **2.** *vt* tenían todo cuanto apetecían they had everything they could wish for

apetecible *adj* tempting, inviting

apetito *nm* appetite; **tengo mucho apetito** I'm really hungry

apetitoso, -a *adj* appetizing, tempting; [comida] delicious, tasty

apicultura *nf* beekeeping, apiculture

apiñado, -a *adj* [apretado] packed, crammed

apiñarse *vpr* to crowd together

apio *nm* celery

apisonadora *nf* roadroller, steamroller

aplanar *vt* to level

aplastar *vt* **a)** to flatten, to squash **b)** *Fig* [vencer] to crush

aplaudir *vt* **a)** to clap, to applaud **b)** *Fig* to applaud

aplauso *nm* applause

aplazar [40] *vt* to postpone, to adjourn; FIN [pago] to defer

aplicación *nf* application

aplicado, -a *adj* hard-working

aplicar [44] **1.** *vt* to apply **2. aplicarse** *vpr* **a)** [esforzarse] to apply oneself, to work hard **b)** [norma, ley] to apply, to be applicable

aplique *nm* wall light, wall lamp

aplomo *nm* aplomb

apocado, -a *adj* timid

apoderarse *vpr* to take possession (**de** of), to seize; *Fig* el miedo se apoderó de ella she was seized by fear

apodo *nm* nickname

apogeo *nm* height; **estar en pleno apogeo** [fama etc] to be at its height

aportación *nf* contribution

aportar 1. *vt* to contribute **2.** *vi* NÁUT to reach port

aporte *nm* contribution; **aporte vitamínico** vitamin content

aposta *adv Esp* on purpose, intentionally

apostar¹ [2] **1.** *vt* to bet; **te apuesto una cena a que no viene** I bet you a dinner that he won't come **2.** *vi* to bet (**por** on); **apostar a los caballos** to bet on horses; **apuesto a que sí viene** I bet she will come **3. apostarse** *vpr* to bet; **me apuesto lo que quieras** I bet you anything

apostar² *vt* [situar] to post, to station

apóstol *nm* apostle

apóstrofo *nm* apostrophe

apoyabrazos *nm inv* armrest

apoyar 1. *vt* **a)** to lean **b)** [causa] to support **2. apoyarse** *vpr* **a)** apoyarse en to lean on; **apóyate en mi brazo** take my arm **b)** apoyarse en [opinión] to be based on, to rest on

apoyo *nm* support

apreciable *adj* appreciable, noticeable

apreciación *nf* appreciation

apreciado, -a *adj* [querido] esteemed, highly regarded

apreciar [43] **1.** *vt* **a)** to appreciate **b)** [percibir] to notice, to see **2. apreciarse** *vpr* to be noticeable

aprecio nm regard, esteem; **tener aprecio a algn** to be fond of sb

apremiar [43] vi to be urgent; **el tiempo apremia** time is at a premium

aprender vt to learn; **así aprenderás** that'll teach you

aprendiz, -a nm, f apprentice, trainee

aprendizaje nm a) learning b) [instrucción] apprenticeship, traineeship

aprensión nf apprehension

aprensivo, -a adj apprehensive

apresuradamente adv a) [con rapidez] hurriedly b) [con precipitación] hastily

apresurado, -a adj [persona] in a hurry; [cosa] hurried

apresurar 1. vt [paso etc] to speed up **2. apresurarse** vpr to hurry up

apretado, -a adj a) [ropa, cordón] tight; **íbamos todos apretados en el coche** we were all squashed together in the car b) [día, agenda] busy

apretar [1] **1.** vt [botón] to press; [nudo, tornillo] to tighten; **apretar el gatillo** to pull the trigger; **me aprietan las botas** these boots are too tight for me **2.** vi **apretaba el calor** it was really hot **3. apretarse** vpr to squeeze together, to cram together; Fig **apretarse el cinturón** to tighten one's belt

apretujar 1. vt to squeeze, to crush **2. apretujarse** vpr to squeeze together, to cram together

aprisa adv quickly

aprobado nm EDUC pass

aprobar [2] vt a) [autorizar] to approve b) [estar de acuerdo con] to approve of c) EDUC to pass d) POL [ley] to pass

aprontar 1. vt [preparar] to quickly prepare o get ready **2. aprontarse** vpr RP [prepararse] to get ready

apropiado, -a adj suitable, appropriate

apropiarse [43] vpr to appropriate

aprovechado, -a adj a) mal aprovechado [recurso, tiempo] wasted; bien aprovechado put to good use b) [espacio] well-planned c) [egoísta] self-seeking

aprovechar 1. vt a) to make good use of, to make the most of; **aprovechamos bien la tarde** we've done lots of things this afternoon b) [recursos etc] to take advantage of; **aprovechar la ocasión** to seize the opportunity **2.** vi **¡que aproveche!** enjoy your meal!, bon appétit! **3. aprovecharse** vpr to use to one's advantage, to take advantage; **aprovecharse de algn** to take advantage of sb; **aprovecharse de algo** to make the most of sth

aproximación nf a) approximation b) [en lotería] consolation prize

aproximadamente adv approximately, roughly

aproximar 1. vt to bring o put nearer **2. aproximarse** vpr **aproximarse (a)** to approach

aproximativo, -a adj approximate

apto, -a adj a) [apropiado] suitable, appropriate; CINE **apto para todos los públicos** Br U, US G b) [capacitado] capable, able c) EDUC passed

apuesta nf bet, wager

apuesto, -a adj good-looking; [hombre] handsome

apunado, -a adj Andes **estar apunado** to have altitude sickness

apunarse vpr Andes to get altitude sickness

apuntador, -a nm, f TEATRO prompter

apuntar 1. vt a) [con arma] to aim b) [señalar] to point out c) [anotar] to note down, to make a note of d) [indicar] to indicate, to suggest; **todo parece apuntar a ...** everything seems to point to ... **2.** vi **cuando apunta el día** when day breaks

3. apuntarse *vpr* **a)** [en una lista] to put one's name down
b) *Fam* **¿te apuntas?** are you game?; **me apunto** count me in

apunte *nm* [usu pl] note; **tomar apuntes** to take notes

apuñalar *vt* to stab

apurar 1. *vt* **a)** [terminar] to finish off, to end **b)** [preocupar] to worry **2. apurarse** *vpr* **a)** *Esp, Méx* [preocuparse] to worry, to get worried; **no te apures** don't worry **b)** [darse prisa] to rush, to hurry, to pester; **apúrate** get a move on

apuro *nm* **a)** [situación difícil] tight spot, fix, jam; **estar en un apuro** to be in a tight spot **b)** [escasez de dinero] hardship; **pasar apuros** to be hard up **c)** [vergüenza] embarrassment; **¡qué apuro!** how embarrassing!

aquel, -ella *(mpl* **aquellos,** *fpl* **aquellas)** *adj demos* **a)** that; **aquel niño** that boy **b)** **aquellos, -as** those; **aquellas niñas** those girls

aquél, -élla *(mpl* **aquéllos,** *fpl* **aquéllas)** *pron demos m, f* **a)** that one; [el anterior] the former; **aquél/aquélla ... éste/ésta** the former ... the latter **b)** **todo aquél que** anyone who, whoever **c)** **aquéllos, -as** those; [los anteriores] the former

aquello *pron neutro m* that, it

aquellos, -as *adj demos pl ver* **aquel**

aquéllos, -as *pron demos m, fpl ver* **aquél**

aquí *adv* **a)** [lugar] here; **aquí arriba/fuera** up/out here; **aquí está** here it is; **aquí mismo** right here; **de aquí para allá** up and down, to and fro; **hasta aquí** this far; **por aquí, por favor** this way please; **está por aquí** it's around here somewhere **b)** [tiempo] **de aquí en adelante** from now on; **de aquí a junio** between now and June; **hasta aquí** up till now

árabe 1. *adj* [de Arabia] Arab **2.** *nmf* [persona] Arab **3.** *nm* [idioma] Arabic

Arabia *n* Arabia; **Arabia Saudí** Saudi Arabia

arácnido *nm* ZOOL **a)** arachnid **b)** **arácnidos** arachnids

arado *nm* plough

arandela *nf* TÉC washer; [anilla] ring

araña *nf* **a)** spider **b)** [lámpara] chandelier

arañar *vt* to scratch

arañazo *nm* scratch

arar *vt* to plough

araucano, -a 1. *adj & nm, f* Araucanian **2.** *nm* [idioma] Araucanian

arbitrar *vt* **a)** to arbitrate **b)** DEP to referee; TENIS to umpire

árbitro, -a *nm, f* **a)** DEP referee; [de tenis] umpire **b)** [mediador] arbitrator

árbol *nm* **a)** BOT tree **b)** TÉC shaft **c)** NÁUT mast **d)** [gráfico] tree (diagram); **árbol genealógico** family o genealogical tree

arbusto *nm* bush, shrub

arca *nf* **a)** chest **b)** [para caudales] strongbox, safe; **arcas públicas** Treasury

Takes the masculine articles **el** and **un**

arcada *nf* **a)** arcade; [de puente] arch **b)** [náusea] retching

arcaico, -a *adj* archaic

arcángel *nm* archangel

arcén *nm* *Esp* [en carretera] *Br* hard shoulder, *US* shoulder

archipiélago *nm* archipelago

archivador *nm* filing cabinet

archivar *vt* **a)** [documento etc] to file (away) **b)** [caso, asunto] to shelve **c)** INFORM to save

archivo *nm* **a)** file **b)** [archivador] filing cabinet **c)** **archivos** archives **d)** INFORM file; **archivo adjunto** attachment

arcilla *nf* clay

arco *nm* **a)** ARQUIT arch **b)** MAT & ELEC arc **c)** [de violín] bow **d)** [para flechas] bow; **tiro con arco** archery **e)** **arco iris** rainbow **f)** *esp Am* DEP [portería] goal, goalmouth

arder *vi* to burn; *Fam* **la conversación está que arde** the conversation is really heating up; **Juan está que arde** Juan is really fuming

ardiente *adj* **a)** [encendido] burning; **capilla ardiente** chapel of rest **b)** *Fig* [fervoroso] eager

ardilla *nf* squirrel

área *nf* **a)** area; DEP penalty area **b)** [medida] are *(100 square metres)*

Takes the masculine articles **el** and **un**

arena *nf* **a)** sand; **playa de arena** sandy beach **b)** TAUROM bullring

arenoso, -a *adj* sandy

arenque *nm* herring; CULIN **arenque ahumado** kipper

arepa *nf Carib, Col* pancake made of maize flour

arequipe *nm Col* sweet caramelized milk used in desserts

arete *nm Andes, Méx* [pendiente] earring; *Esp* [en forma de aro] hoop earring

argan *nm* argan; **aceite de argan** argan oil

Argelia *n* Algeria

Argentina *n* Argentina

argentino, -a *adj & nm, f* Argentinian, Argentine

argolla *nf* **a)** [aro] (large) ring **b)** *Andes, Méx* [alianza] wedding ring **c)** *Carib* [pendiente] hoop earring

argot *(pl argots) nm* [popular] slang; [técnico] jargon

argüende *nm Méx Fam* **a)** [chisme] gossip **b)** [fiesta] party, *Br* rave-up

argüir [62] *vt* **a)** [deducir] to deduce **b)** [argumentar] to argue

argumentar 1. *vt* [alegar] to argue **2.** *vi* [discutir] to argue

argumento *nm* **a)** LITER & TEATRO [trama] plot **b)** [razonamiento] argument

aria *nf* [de ópera] aria

árido, -a *adj* arid; *Fig* dry

Aries *nm* Aries

arista *nf* edge

aristocracia *nf* aristocracy

aristócrata *nmf* aristocrat

aritmética *nf* arithmetic

arlequín *nm* harlequin

arma *nf* weapon; **arma blanca** knife; **arma de fuego** firearm; **arma homicida** murder weapon; **arma nuclear** nuclear weapon; *Fig* **arma de doble filo** double-edged sword

Takes the masculine articles **el** and **un**

armada *nf* navy

armadillo *nm* armadillo

armadura *nf* **a)** [armazón] frame **b)** HIST suit of armour

armamento *nm* armaments; **armamento nuclear** nuclear weapons

armar 1. *vt* **a)** [tropa, soldado] to arm **b)** [piezas] to fit o put together, to assemble **c)** *Fam* **armaron un escándalo** they created a scandal **2. armarse** *vpr* to arm oneself; *Fig* **armarse de paciencia** to summon up one's patience; *Fig* **armarse de valor** to pluck up courage; *Fam* **se armó la gorda** all hell broke loose

armario *nm* [para ropa] wardrobe; [de cocina] cupboard; **armario empotrado** built-in wardrobe o cupboard

armazón *nm* frame; [de madera] timberwork; ARQUIT shell

armisticio *nm* armistice

armonía *nf* harmony

armónica *nf* harmonica, mouth organ

armonioso, -a *adj* harmonious

armonizar [40] *vt & vi* to harmonize

aro *nm* **a)** [gen] hoop; *Fam* **pasar por el aro** to knuckle under **b)** *Am* [pendiente] earring; [en forma de aro] hoop earring **c)** *Ven* [alianza] wedding ring **d)** *Col* [montura] rim **e)** *Bol* [anillo] ring

aroma *nm* aroma; [de vino] bouquet

aromaterapia *nf* aromatherapy

aromatizante *nm Br* flavouring, *US* flavoring

arpa *nf* harp

> Takes the masculine articles **el** and **un**

arquear 1. *vt* **a)** [cuerpo, brazos, piernas] to bend; [cejas] to raise; [espalda] to arch **b)** *Am* COM to calculate **2. arquearse** *vpr* [por el peso] to bow, to sag

arqueología *nf* archaeology

arqueólogo, -a *nm, f* archaeologist

arquero, -a *nm, f* **a)** [tirador] archer **b)** *Am* [portero de fútbol] goalkeeper

arquitecto, -a *nm, f* architect

arquitectónico, -a *adj* architectural

arquitectura *nf* architecture

arrabalero, -a 1. *adj* **a)** [del arrabal] suburban **b)** *Esp* [grosero, mal educado] vulgar, *Br* common; [barriobajero] *Despec* plebby; [lenguaje] vulgar, *Br* common **2.** *nm, f Esp* **a)** [grosero, mal educado] vulgar person, *Br* common person **b)** [barriobajero] pleb

arraigado, -a *adj* deep-rooted

arraigar [42] *vi* to take root

arrancar [44] **1.** *vt* **a)** [planta] to uproot, to pull up; **arrancar de raíz** to uproot
b) [extraer] to pull o tear off o out; [diente, pelo] to pull out; *Fig* [confesión etc] to extract; **arranca una hoja del cuaderno** tear a page out of the notebook **c)** [coche, motor] to start; INFORM to boot
2. *vi* **a)** AUTO & TÉC to start; INFORM to boot (up)
b) [empezar] to begin; **arrancar a llorar** to burst out crying

---

arranchar *vt Andes, CAm* to stay with

arranque *nm* **a)** AUTO & TÉC starting **b)** [comienzo] start **c)** *Fam* [arrebato] outburst, fit

arrastrar 1. *vt* to pull (along), to drag (along); **vas arrastrando el vestido** your dress is trailing on the ground; **lo arrastró la corriente** he was swept away by the current **2. arrastrarse** *vpr* to drag oneself; *Fig* [humillarse] to crawl

arrastre *nm* **a)** pulling, dragging; *Esp Fam* **estar para el arrastre** to have had it **b) (pesca de) arrastre** trawling **c)** *RP Fam* **tener arrastre** to have a lot of influence

arrebatar 1. *vt* [coger] to snatch, to seize; *Fig* [cautivar] to captivate, to fascinate **2. arrebatarse** *vpr* [enfurecerse] to become furious; [exaltarse] to get carried away

arrebato *nm* outburst, fit

arrecharse *vpr Am Fam* to get really annoyed

arreglar 1. *vt* **a)** to arrange; [habitación] to tidy; [papeles] to put in order **b)** [reparar] to repair, to fix **c)** [solucionar] to sort (out) **d)** [vestir] to get ready **e)** MÚS to arrange **f)** *Fam* [como amenaza] **¡ya te arreglaré!** I'll sort you out! **2.** *vi Am* [quedar] **arreglé de ir al cine con Juan el sábado** I've arranged to go and see a movie with John on Saturday; **¿cómo vas a la fiesta? — ya arreglé con Silvia** how are you getting to the party? — I've already made arrangements with Sylvia **3. arreglarse** *vpr* **a)** [vestirse] to get ready **b)** [apañarse] *Fam* **arreglárselas** to manage; **saber arreglárselas** to know how to look after oneself, to manage perfectly well **c)** [reconciliarse] to make up

arreglo *nm* **a)** arrangement; [acuerdo] compromise **b)** [reparación] repair; **no tiene arreglo** it is beyond repair; *Fam* **¡no tienes arreglo!** you're hopeless! **c)** *Formal* **con arreglo a** in accordance with

arrendar *vt* to rent; *Am* **se arrienda** [en letrero] to rent

arrendatario, -a *nm, f* leaseholder, lessee; [inquilino] tenant

arreos *nmpl* **a)** [de caballería] harness, trappings **b)** [adornos] adornments

arrepentirse [5] *vpr* **arrepentirse de** to regret; REL to repent

arrestar *vt* to arrest, to detain; [encarcelar] to put in prison

arriba 1. *adv* up; [encima] on the top; **ahí arriba** up there; **la vecina de arriba** the upstairs *Br* neighbour o *US* neighbor; **el estante de arriba** the top shelf; **de arriba abajo** from top to bottom; *Fam* **mirar a algn de arriba abajo** to look sb up and down; **desde arriba** from above; **hacia arriba** upwards; **de un millón para arriba** from one million upwards; **más arriba** higher up, further up; **arriba del todo** right on o at the top; **la parte de arriba** the top (part); **vive arriba** he lives upstairs; **véase más arriba** see above **2.** *interj* get up!, up you get!; **¡arriba la República!** long live the Republic!; **¡arriba las manos!** hands up! **3.** *prep Am* **arriba (de)** on top of; **¿dónde has dejado el libro? — creo que arriba de la mesa** where have you put the book? — I think I left it on top of the table

arribeño, -a *Am* **1.** *adj* highland **2.** *nm, f* highlander

arriesgado, -a *adj* **a)** [peligroso] risky **b)** [temerario] fearless, daring

arriesgar [42] **1.** *vt* to risk **2. arriesgarse** *vpr* to risk; **se arriesga demasiado** he's taking too many risks

arrimar 1. *vt* to move closer, to bring near o nearer; *Fam* **arrimar el hombro** to lend a hand **2. arrimarse** *vpr* to move o get close, to come near o nearer

arroba *nm* INFORM at, @ sign

arrodillarse *vpr* to kneel down

arrogancia *nf* arrogance

arrogante *adj* arrogant

arrojar 1. *vt* **a)** [tirar] to throw, to fling **b)** COM [saldo] to show **2. arrojarse** *vpr* to throw oneself, to fling oneself

arroyo *nm* brook, stream

arroz *nm* rice; **arroz con leche** rice pudding

arruga *nf* [en la piel] wrinkle; [en la ropa] crease

arrugar [42] **1.** *vt* [piel] to wrinkle; [ropa] to crease; [papel] to crumple (up) **2. arrugarse** *vpr* [piel] to wrinkle; [ropa] to crease

arruinado, -a *adj* ruined

arruinar 1. *vt* to ruin **2. arruinarse** *vpr* to be ruined

arrumar *vt Am* to pile up

arrume *nm Am* pile, heap

arsenal *nm* **a)** *Esp* [de barcos] shipyard **b)** [de armas] arsenal

arsénico *nm* arsenic

arte *nm o nf* **a)** art; **bellas artes** fine arts; *Fam* **por amor al arte** for the love of it **b)** [habilidad] skill

Takes the masculine articles **el** and **un**

artefacto *nm* device; **artefacto explosivo** explosive device

arteria *nf* artery; [carretera] highway

artesanado *nm* **a)** [profesión] craft industry **b)** [profesionales] artisans (*pl*)

artesanal *adj* handmade

artesanalmente *adv* **fabricado artesanalmente** artisanally-made

artesanía *nf* **a)** [cualidad] craftsmanship **b)** [objetos] crafts, handicrafts

artesano, -a 1. *nm, f* craftsman, f craftswoman **2.** *adj* handmade

ártico, -a 1. *adj* arctic; **el océano Ártico** the Arctic Ocean **2.** *nm* **el Ártico** the Arctic

articulación *nf* **a)** ANAT joint, articulation **b)** TÉC joint

articulado, -a *adj* [tren etc] articulated

articular *vt* to articulate

articulista *nmf* feature writer

artículo *nm* article; **artículo de fondo** leader (article)

artificial *adj* artificial; TEXT man-made o synthetic

artificio *nm* **a)** artifice; **fuego de artificio** firework **b)** [artimaña] ruse

artista *nmf* artist; **artista de cine** movie o *Br* film star

artístico, -a *adj* artistic

arveja *nf RP* pea

arzobispo *nm* archbishop

as *nm* ace

asa *nf* handle

Takes the masculine articles **el** and **un**

asado, -a 1. *adj* CULIN roast; **pollo asado** roast chicken; *Fig* **asado de calor** roasting, boiling hot **2.** *nm* CULIN roast; *Col, CSur* [barbacoa] barbecue

asador *nm* **a)** [aparato] roaster **b)** [restaurante] grill, grillroom

asalariado, -a 1. *adj* salaried **2.** *nm, f* wage earner, salaried worker

asaltar *vt* to assault, to attack; [banco] to rob; *Fig* to assail

asalto *nm* **a)** assault, attack; **asalto a un banco** bank robbery **b)** [en boxeo] round

asamblea *nf* meeting; **asamblea general** general meeting

asar 1. *vt* to roast **2. asarse** *vpr Fig* to be roasting, to be boiling hot

ascendencia *nf* ancestry, ancestors; **de ascendencia escocesa** of Scottish descent

ascendente 1. *adj* rising **2.** *nm* [en astrología] ascendant

ascender [3] **1.** *vt* [en un cargo] to promote **2.** *vi* **a)** to move upward; [temperatura] to rise; **la factura asciende a ...** the bill adds up to ... **b)** [al trono] to ascend **c)** [de categoría] to be promoted

ascendiente *nmf* ancestor

ascenso *nm* promotion; [subida] rise

ascensor *nm Br* lift, *US* elevator

asco *nm* disgust, repugnance; **me da asco** it makes me (feel) sick; **¡qué asco!** how disgusting o revolting!

ascua *nf* ember; *Fig* **en ascuas** on tenterhooks

Takes the masculine articles **el** and **un**

asdc SMS *written abbr of* **al salir de clase**

aseado, -a *adj* tidy, neat

asear 1. *vt* to clean, to tidy up **2. asearse** *vpr* to wash, to get washed

asegurado, -a *adj* **a)** insured **b)** [indudable] secure

asegurar 1. *vt* **a)** to insure **b)** [garantizar] **me aseguró que ...** he assured me that ...; **asegurar el éxito de un proyecto** to ensure the success of a project **c)** [cuerda] to fasten **2. asegurarse** *vpr* **a)** to make sure; **asegurarse de que ...** to make sure that ... **b)** SEGUROS to insure oneself

asentir [5] *vi* to assent, to agree; **asentir con la cabeza** to nod

aseo *nm* **a)** [limpieza] cleanliness, tidiness **b)** *Esp* [habitación] bathroom; **aseos** *Br* toilets, *US* restroom

aséptico, -a *adj* MED aseptic; *Fig* [indiferente] detached

asequible *adj* affordable; [comprensible] easy to understand; [alcanzable] attainable

asesinar *vt* to murder; [rey, ministro] to assassinate

asesinato *nm* murder; [de rey, ministro] assassination

asesino, -a 1. *adj* murderous **2.** *nm, f* killer; [hombre] murderer; [mujer] murderess; POL assassin; **asesino en serie** serial killer

asesor, -a 1. *nm, f* adviser; **asesor fiscal** tax adviser **2.** *adj* advisory

asesorar 1. *vt* **a)** to advise, to give (professional) advice to **b)** COM to act as consultant to **2. asesorarse** *vpr* to consult

asesoría *nf* consultant's office

asfaltado, -a 1. *adj* asphalt **2.** *nm* [acción] asphalting, surfacing; [asfalto] asphalt, (road) surface

asfaltar *vt* to asphalt, to surface

asfalto *nm* asphalt

asfixia *nf* asphyxiation, suffocation

asfixiante *adj* asphyxiating, suffocating; *Fam* **hace un calor asfixiante** it's stifling

asfixiar [43] **1.** *vt* to asphyxiate, to suffocate **2. asfixiarse** *vpr* = **asfixiar**

así 1. *adv* **a)** [de esta manera] like this o that, this way, thus; **ponlo así** put it this way; **así es** that's right; **así de grande /alto** this big /tall; **era así de**

largo it was this long; **algo así** something like this o that; **¿no es así?** isn't that so o right?; **así así** so-so; **así es / era / fue como** this is / was how; **y así sucesivamente** and so on (and so forth) **b) a las seis o así** around six o'clock; **diez años o así** ten years more or less **c) así como** [igual que] as well as; [del mismo modo] the same as **d) aun así** and despite that **e) así pues** so, therefore; **así que ... so ... f) así y todo** even so, despite that **g)** *Am Fam* **así no más** o **nomás** [regular] so-so; [de repente] just like that **2.** *adj inv* [como éste] like this **3.** *conj* **a)** [de modo que] so; **así (es) que** so; **estoy enferma así que no voy** I'm sick so I'm not going **b)** *Am* [aunque] even if; **te encontraré, así tenga que buscar bajo las piedras** I'll find you, even if I have to search high and low

Asia *n* Asia; **Asia Menor** Asia Minor

asias SMS *(abr de* **gracias)** Thx, THX, Thnx, Tks

asiático, -a *adj* & *nm, f* Asian

asiento *nm* **a)** seat; **asiento trasero / delantero** back / front seat; **tome asiento** take a seat **b)** [poso] sediment **c)** FIN entry

asignatura *nf* subject; **asignatura pendiente** failed subject

asilado, -a *nm, f* refugee

asilo *nm* asylum; **asilo de ancianos** old people's home; POL **asilo político** political asylum

asimilación *nf* assimilation

asimilar *vt* to assimilate

asir [46] **1.** *vt* to grasp, to take hold of **2. asirse** *vpr también Fig* to cling (**a** to)

asistencia *nf* **a)** [presencia] attendance; **falta de asistencia** absence **b) asistencia médica / técnica** medical / technical assistance **c)** [público] audience, public

asistente *nmf* **a)** [ayudante] assistant, helper; **asistente social** social worker **b)** [presente] person present; **los asistentes** [el público] the audience

asistido, -a *adj* AUTO & INFORM assisted; **asistido por ordenador** computer-aided

asistir 1. *vt* to assist, to help **2.** *vi* **asistir (a)** to attend, to be present (at)

asma *nf* asthma

Takes the masculine articles **el** and **un**

asmático, -a *adj* & *nm, f* asthmatic

asno *nm* donkey, ass

asociación *nf* association

asociar [43] **1.** *vt* to associate **2. asociarse** *vpr* **a)** to be associated **b)** COM to become partners

asolar [2] *vt* to devastate, to destroy

asomar 1. *vt* to put out, to stick out; **asomó la cabeza por la ventana** he put his head out of the window **2.** *vi* to appear **3. asomarse** *vpr* **a)** to lean out; **asomarse a la ventana** to lean out of the window **b)** [entrar] to pop in; [salir] to pop out

asombrar 1. *vt* to amaze, to astonish **2. asombrarse** *vpr* to be astonished; **asombrarse de algo** to be amazed at sth

asombro *nm* amazement, astonishment

asorocharse *vpr Andes* **a)** [por la altitud] to get altitude sickness **b)** [sonrojarse] to blush

aspa *nf* **a)** [de molino] arm; [de ventilador] blade **b)** [cruz] cross

Takes the masculine articles **el** and **un**

aspecto *nm* **a)** look, appearance **b)** [de un asunto] aspect

aspereza *nf* roughness; *Fig* **limar asperezas** to smooth things over

áspero, -a *adj* rough; *Fig* [carácter] surly

aspirador *nm* vacuum cleaner, *Br* Hoover®

aspiradora *nf* vacuum cleaner, *Br* Hoover®

aspirar 1. *vt* **a)** [respirar] to inhale, to breathe in **b)** TÉC [absorber] to suck in, to draw in **2.** *vi Fig* **aspirar a algo** to aspire after sth

aspirina *nf* aspirin

asqueado, -a *adj* disgusted; **estar asqueado de (hacer) algo** to have had enough of (doing) sth

asquear *vt* to disgust, to make sick

asquerosidad *nf* filthy o revolting thing; **¡que asquerosidad!** how revolting!

asqueroso, -a 1. *adj* [sucio] filthy; [desagradable] revolting, disgusting **2.** *nm, f* filthy o revolting person

asta *nf* **a)** [de bandera] staff, pole; **a media asta** at half-mast **b)** ZOOL [cuerno] horn

Takes the masculine articles **el** and **un**

asterisco *nm* asterisk

astillero *nm* shipyard

astro *nm* star

astrología *nf* astrology

astrólogo, -a *nm, f* astrologer

astronauta *nmf* astronaut

astronomía *nf* astronomy

astronómico, -a *adj* astronomical

astrónomo, -a *nm, f* astronomer

astuto, -a *adj* astute, shrewd

asumir *vt* to assume

asunto *nm* **a)** subject; **no es asunto tuyo** it's none of your business **b) Asuntos Exteriores** Foreign Affairs

asustar 1. *vt* to frighten, to scare **2. asustarse** *vpr* to be frightened, to be scared

atacar [44] *vt* to attack, to assault; *Fig* **me ataca los nervios** he gets on my nerves

atajo *nm* **a)** [camino corto, medio rápido] short cut **b)** *Esp Despec* [panda] bunch **c)** INFORM **atajo de teclado** shortcut key

ataque *nm* **a)** attack, assault; **ataque aéreo** air raid **b)** MED fit; **ataque**

cardíaco o **al corazón** heart attack; **ataque de nervios /tos** fit of hysterics /coughing

atar 1. *vt* **a)** to tie; *Fig* **atar cabos** to put two and two together; *Fam* **loco de atar** as mad as a hatter **b)** *Fig* to tie down **2. atarse** *vpr Fig* to get tied up; **átate los zapatos** do your shoes up

atardecer [33] **1.** *v impers* to get o grow dark **2.** *nm* evening, dusk

atareado, -a *adj* busy

atascado, -a *adj* **a)** [tubería] blocked (up) **b)** [mecanismo] jammed

atascar 1. *vt* to block **2. atascarse** *vpr* **a)** [tubería] to block up, to get blocked up **b)** [mecanismo] to jam

atasco *nm* traffic jam

ataúd *nm* coffin

ate *nm Méx* quince jelly

ateísmo *nm* atheism

atemorizar *vt* to scare

atención 1. *nf* **a)** attention; **llamar la atención** to attract attention; **prestar /poner atención** to pay attention (**a** to) **b) atenciones** (care and) attention **2.** *interj* attention!

atender [3] **1.** *vt* to attend to; [petición] to agree to **2.** *vi* [alumno] to pay attention (**a** to)

atentado *nm* attack; **atentado terrorista** terrorist attack

atentamente *adv* **le saluda atentamente** [en carta] yours sincerely o faithfully

atento, -a *adj* **a)** attentive; **estar atento a** to be mindful o aware of **b)** [amable] thoughtful, considerate; **atentos saludos de** [en carta] yours faithfully

ateo, -a 1. *adj* atheistic **2.** *nm, f* atheist

aterciopelado, -a *adj* velvety

aterrado, -a *adj* terrified

aterrizaje *nm* AVIACIÓN landing; **aterrizaje forzoso** forced landing

aterrizar [40] *vi* to land

aterrorizar [40] **1.** *vt* to terrify; MIL & POL to terrorize **2. aterrorizarse** *vpr* to be terrified

atestado¹, -a *adj* packed, crammed; **estaba atestado de gente** it was full of people

atestado² *nm* JUR affidavit, statement; **atestados** testimonials

atestiguar [45] *vt* a) JUR to testify to b) *Fig* to vouch for

ático *nm* [piso] *attic (Br) flat o (US) apartment, usually with a roof terrace*; [desván] attic

atinar *vi* to get it right; **atinar a hacer algo** to succeed in doing sth; **atinar al blanco** to hit the target; **atinó con la solución** he found the solution

atingencia *nf* a) *Am, CAm, Chile, Méx* [relación] connection b) *Chile, Méx* [adecuación] appropriateness; **la Cámara está estudiando la atingencia de esa ley** the House is investigating whether the law is appropriate o acceptable c) *Méx* [tino] good sense

atípico, -a *adj* atypical

atizar [40] *vt* a) [fuego] to poke, to stir b) [sospechas, discordias] to fan c) *Esp* [persona] **me atizó bien fuerte** [un golpe] he hit me really hard; [una paliza] he gave me a good hiding

atlántico, -a **1.** *adj* Atlantic **2.** *nm* **el (océano) Atlántico** the Atlantic (Ocean)

atlas *nm inv* atlas

atleta *nmf* athlete

atlético, -a *adj* athletic

atletismo *nm* athletics (*sing*)

atmósfera *nf* atmosphere

atmosférico, -a *adj* atmospheric

atole, atol *nm CAm, Méx* thick hot drink made of corn meal

atolondrar **1.** *vt* to confuse, to bewilder **2. atolondrarse** *vpr* to be confused, to be bewildered

atómico, -a *adj* atomic

átomo *nm* atom

atónito, -a *adj* amazed, astonished

atontado, -a *adj* a) [tonto] silly, foolish b) [aturdido] bewildered, amazed

atorarse *vpr* a) [atragantarse] to choke (**con** on) b) *Am* [atascarse] to get stuck c) *Am* [meterse en un lío] to get into a mess

atormentar *vt* to torment

atorón *nm Méx* traffic jam

atorrante **1.** *adj RP Fam* [holgazán] lazy **2.** *nmf* tramp, *US* bum

atracador, -a *nm, f* [de banco] (bank) robber; [en la calle] attacker, mugger

atracar [44] **1.** *vt* to hold up; [persona] to rob **2.** *vi* NÁUT to come alongside, to tie up **3. atracarse** *vpr* [de comida] to stuff oneself (**de** with), to gorge oneself (**de** on)

atracción *nf* attraction; **parque de atracciones** funfair

atraco *nm* hold-up, robbery; **atraco a mano armada** armed robbery

atractivo, -a **1.** *adj* attractive, appealing **2.** *nm* attraction, appeal

atraer [25] *vt* to attract

atragantarse *vpr* to choke (**con** on), to swallow the wrong way; *Fig* **esa chica se me ha atragantado** I can't stand that girl

atrapar *vt* to catch

atrás **1.** *adv* a) [lugar] at the back, behind; **hacia/para atrás** backwards; **puerta de atrás** back o rear door; *Fig* **echarse atrás** to back out b) [tiempo] previously, in the past, ago; **un año atrás** a year ago; **venir de muy atrás** to go o date back a long time **2.** *prep Am* **atrás de** behind; **el perchero está atrás de la puerta** the coat rack is behind the door; **una atrás de otra** one after the other

atrasado, -a *adj* late, slow; [pago] overdue; [reloj] slow; [país] backward; PRENSA **número atrasado** back number

atrasar **1.** *vt* to put back **2.** *vi* [reloj] to be slow **3. atrasarse** *vpr* a) to remain o stay behind, to lag behind b) [tren] to be late

atraso *nm* a) delay b) [de país] backwardness c) FIN **atrasos** arrears

atravesar [1] **1.** *vt* **a)** [calle] to cross **b)** [muro] to pierce, to go through **c)** [poner a través] to lay across, to put across, to put crosswise **2. atravesarse** *vpr* to get in the way; *Fig* **se me ha atravesado Luis** I can't stand Luis

atreverse *vpr* to dare; **atreverse a hacer algo** to dare to do sth

atrevido, -a *adj* **a)** [osado] daring, bold **b)** [insolente] insolent, impudent **c)** [ropa etc] daring, risqué

atribución *nf* **a)** [imputación] attribution **b)** [competencia] responsibility, duty

atribuir [37] **1.** *vt* to attribute, to ascribe **2. atribuirse** *vpr* to assume

atributo *nm* [gen & INFORM] attribute

atrio *nm* **a)** [pórtico] portico **b)** [patio interior] atrium

atropellar *vt* to knock down, to run over

atropello *nm* **a)** AUTO knocking down, running over **b)** [abuso] abuse

ATS *nmf (abr de* **ayudante técnico sanitario)** *Esp* qualified nurse

atún *nm* tuna, tunny

audaz *adj* audacious, bold

audiencia *nf* **a)** [público] audience; TV & RADIO **horas de máxima audiencia** prime time; **índice de audiencia** viewing figures, ratings; **récord de audiencia** record viewing figures **b)** [entrevista] audience **c)** JUR court hearing

audífono *nm* **a)** hearing aid **b)** **audífonos** *Am* [auriculares] earphones; [cascos] headphones

audio 1. *adj inv* [material, archivo, libro] audio **2.** *nm* sound

audiovisual *adj* audio-visual

auditivo, -a 1. *adj* auditory; **comprensión auditiva** listening comprehension **2.** *nm* receiver

auditor *nm* FIN auditor

auditoría *nf* **a)** FIN [profesión] auditing **b)** [despacho] auditor's, auditing company **c)** [balance] audit; **auditoría externa / interna** external / internal audit

auditorio *nm* **a)** [público] audience **b)** [sala] auditorium, hall

auge *nm* peak; ECON boom; *Fig* **estar en auge** to be thriving o booming

aula *nf* [en colegio] classroom; UNIV lecture room; **aula magna** amphitheatre

Takes the masculine articles **el** and **un**.

aullar *vt* to howl, to yell

aullido *nm* howl, yell

aumentar 1. *vt* to increase; [precios] to put up; [producción] to step up; FOTO to enlarge; ÓPT to magnify **2.** *vi* [precios] to go up, to rise; [valor] to appreciate **3. aumentarse** *vpr* to increase, to be on the increase

aumento *nm* increase; ÓPT magnification; **aumento de precios** rise in prices; **ir en aumento** to be on the increase

aun *adv* even; **aun así** even so, even then; **aun más** even more

aún *adv* still; [en negativas] yet; **aún está aquí** he's still here; **ella no ha venido aún** she hasn't come yet

aunque *conj* although, though; [enfático] even if, even though; **aunque no vengas** even if you don't come

aúpa 1. *adj Fam* **de aúpa** [tremendo] total; **tenía un miedo de aúpa** I was totally scared; **hace un frío de aúpa** it's freezing cold; **se dio un golpe de aúpa** he had a hell of a blow **2.** *interj Esp Fam* **a)** [¡levántate!] up you get! **b)** [¡viva!] **¡aúpa el Atlético!** come on Atlético!

au pair *(pl* **au pairs)** *nmf inv* au pair

aureola *nf* halo

auricular *nm* **a)** TEL receiver **b)** **auriculares** earphones, headphones

auscultación *nf* auscultation

ausencia *nf* absence

ausente 1. *adj* absent **2.** *nmf* absentee

austeridad *nf* austerity

austero, -a *adj* austere

Australia *n* Australia

australiano, -a *adj & nm, f* Australian

Austria *n* Austria

austríaco, -a *adj* & *nm, f* Austrian

Austrias *n* los Austrias [dinastía] the Habsburgs

autenticación *nf* [gen & INFORM] authentification

autenticar *vt* INFORM to authenticate

autenticidad *nf* authenticity

auténtico, -a *adj* authentic

autentificación *vt* INFORM authentification

autentificar *vt* INFORM to authenticate

auto¹ *nm* esp CSur [coche] car

auto² *nm* JUR decree, writ; **autos** [pleito] papers, documents

autoabastecerse *vpr* to supply o.s., to be self-sufficient; **autoabastecerse de** to be self-sufficient in

autoaprendizaje *nm* self-learning, self-study; **materiales de autoaprendizaje** self-study materials

autobiografía *nf* autobiography

autobronceador, -a 1. *adj* [crema, producto] self-tanning **2.** *nm* self-tanner, self-tanning lotion, self-tanning cream

autobús *nm* bus

autocar *nm* Esp bus, Br coach

autocarril *nm* Am type of bus that travels along rails

autocontrol *nm* self-control

autóctono, -a *adj* indigenous

autodestruirse *vpr* to self-destruct

autodominio *nm* self-control

autoedición *nf* INFORM desktop publishing, DTP

autoempleo *nm* self-employment

autoempresario, -a *nm, f* self-employed businessman, self-employed businesswoman

autoescuela *nf* driving school, school of motoring

autogobernarse *vpr* to self-govern

autógrafo *nm* autograph

automático, -a *adj* automatic

automoción *nf* **a)** [facultad, condición] transport **b)** [transporte] **medio de automoción** mode of transport; **la industria de la automoción** the automotive industry, Br the car industry

automóvil *nm* Br car, US automobile

automovilismo *nm* motoring

automovilista *nmf* motorist

autonomía *nf* **a)** autonomy **b)** [región] autonomous region

autonómico, -a *adj* autonomous, self-governing; **elecciones autonómicas** elections for the autonomous parliament; **televisión autonómica** regional television

autónomo, -a *adj* autonomous

autopista *nf* Br motorway, US freeway; INFORM **autopista de la información** information superhighway

autoproclamarse *vpr* to declare o.s.

autopsia *nf* autopsy, postmortem

autor, -a *nm, f* author, f authoress; [de crimen] perpetrator

autoría *nf* [de obra] authorship; [de crimen] perpetration

autoridad *nf* authority

autoritario, -a *adj* authoritarian

autorización *nf* authorization; **dar autorización a algn (para hacer algo)** to authorize sb (to do sth)

autorizado, -a *adj* authoritative, official

autorizar [40] *vt* to authorize

autorregulación *nf* self-regulation

autorretrato *nm* self-portrait

autoservicio *nm* **a)** [tienda] self-service; **ser autoservicio** to be self-service **b)** [restaurante] self-service restaurant

autostop *nm* hitch-hiking; **hacer autostop** to hitch-hike

autostopista *nmf* hitch-hiker

autosuficiente *adj* self-sufficient

autosugestionarse *vpr* to autosuggest, to use autosuggestion

autovía *nf Br* dual carriageway, *US* divided highway

auxiliar [43] **1.** *adj* & *nmf* auxiliary, assistant **2.** *vt* to help, to assist

auxilio *nm* help, assistance; **primeros auxilios** first aid

auyama *nf Carib, Col* pumpkin

Av. *nf (abr de* **Avenida***)* Ave

aval *nm* COM & FIN endorsement

avalancha *nf* avalanche

avalar *vt* to guarantee, to endorse

avalista *nmf* guarantor

avance *nm* **a)** advance **b)** FIN advance payment **c)** TV **avance informativo** news summary, *US* news in brief

avanzada *nf* **a)** MIL advance party **b)** *Am* **de avanzada** cutting-edge; **tecnología de avanzada** cutting-edge technology

avanzado, -a *adj* advanced; **de avanzada edad** advanced in years

avanzar [40] *vt* to advance

avaricioso, -a *adj* greedy

avaro, -a 1. *adj* avaricious, miserly **2.** *nm, f* miser

avatar *nm* **a)** REL & INFORM avatar **b)** [vicisitud] **avatares** ups and downs, *Formal* vicissitudes

Avda. = **Av.**

ave *nf* bird; **aves de corral** poultry; **ave de rapiña** bird of prey

Takes the masculine articles **el** and **un**.

AVE *nf (abr de* **Alta Velocidad Española***)* High Speed Train

avellana *nf* hazelnut

avellano *nm* hazelnut tree

avena *nf* oats

avenida *nf* avenue

avenir 1. *vt* to reconcile, to bring together **2. avenirse** *vpr* [ponerse de acuerdo] to agree on, to come to an agreement on; **avenirse a** [acceder] to agree to

aventar [1] **1.** *vt* **a)** AGRIC to winnow **b)** [el fuego] to fan **c)** *Andes, CAm, Méx Fam* [tirar] to throw; **le aventé una bofetada** I slapped him **d)** *CAm, Méx, Perú* [empujar] to push, to shove **2. aventarse** *vpr Méx* **a)** [tirarse] to throw oneself **b)** [atreverse] **aventarse a hacer algo** to dare to do sth

aventón *nm CAm, Méx, Perú* **dar aventón a algn** to give sb a ride; **pedir aventón** to hitch a ride

aventura *nf* **a)** adventure **b)** [amorosa] (love) affair

aventurarse *vpr* to venture

aventurero, -a 1. *adj* **a)** [persona, espíritu] adventurous **b)** *Cuba* [maíz, arroz] out-of-season **2.** *nm, f* aventurer

avergonzado, -a *adj* ashamed

avergonzar [63] **1.** *vt* to shame **2. avergonzarse** *vpr* to be ashamed (**de** of)

avería *nf* breakdown

averiado, -a *adj* out of order; [coche] broken down

averiar [29] **1.** *vt* to break **2. averiarse** *vpr* [estropearse] to malfunction, to go wrong; [coche] to break down

averiguar [45] *vt* to ascertain

aversión *nf* aversion

avestruz *nm* ostrich

aviación *nf* **a)** aviation; **accidente de aviación** plane crash; **aviación civil** civil aviation **b)** MIL air force

aviador, -a *nm, f* aviator, flier; MIL [piloto] air force pilot

avión[1] *nm* aircraft, *Br* aeroplane, *US* airplane; **viajar en avión** to fly, to go by plane; **por avión** [en carta] airmail

avión[2] *nm* ORNIT martin

avioneta *nf* light aircraft o plane

avisar *vt* **a)** [informar] to inform; **avísame cuando hayas acabado** let me know when you finish **b)** [advertir] to warn; **ya te avisé** I warned you **c)** [llamar] to call for; **avisar a la policía** to notify the police; **avisar al médico** to send for the doctor

aviso *nm* **a)** notice; [advertencia] warning; [nota] note; **hasta nuevo aviso** until further notice; **sin previo aviso**

without notice **b) estar sobre aviso** to know what's going on, be in on it **c)** *Am* [anuncio] advertisement; **aviso clasificado** classified advertisement

avispa *nf* wasp

avituallamiento *nm* provisioning

avituallar *vt* to provide with food

axila *nf* armpit, axilla

ay *interj* [dolor] ouch!

ayer 1. *adv* yesterday; **ayer por la mañana / por la tarde** yesterday morning / afternoon; **ayer por la noche** last night; **antes de ayer** the day before yesterday **2.** *nm* **el ayer** yesteryear

aymara 1. *adj* & *nmf* Aymara (Indian) **2.** *nm* [idioma] Aymara

ayuda *nf* help, assistance; **ir en ayuda de algn** to come to sb's assistance; **ayuda al desarrollo** development aid

ayudante *nmf* assistant; MED **ayudante técnico-sanitario** nurse

ayudar 1. *vt* to help; **¿en qué puedo ayudarle?** (how) can I help you? **2. ayudarse** *vpr* **a)** [unos a otros] to help **b) ayudarse de** to use, to make use of

ayunar *vi* to fast

ayuntamiento *nm* [institución] *Br* town council, *US* city council; [edificio] *Br* town hall, *US* city hall

azada *nf* hoe

azafata *nf* **a)** AVIACIÓN air stewardess, *Br* air hostess **b)** [de congresos] stewardess; [de concurso] hostess

azafate *nm CAm, Carib, Méx, Perú* tray

azafrán *nm* saffron

azar *nm* chance; **por azar** by chance; **al azar** at random; **juegos de azar** games of chance; **los azares de la vida** the ups and downs of life

azotea *nf* flat roof

azúcar *nm o nf* sugar

azucarado, -a *adj* sweetened

azucarera *nf* [fábrica] sugar refinery; [recipiente] sugar bowl

azucena *nf* white lily

azufre *nm* sulphur

azul *adj* & *nm* blue; **azul celeste** sky blue; **azul marino** navy blue; **azul turquesa** turquoise; **sangre azul** blue blood

azulado, -a *adj* bluish

azulejo *nm* (glazed) tile

B

b SMS *written abbr of* **bien**

baba *nf* dribble; *Fig* **se le caía la baba** he was delighted

babero *nm* bib

babor *nm* NÁUT port, port side

babosa *nf* slug

babosada *nf CAm, Méx Fam* [disparate] daft thing; **¡no digas babosadas!** don't talk *Br* rubbish *o US* bull!

baboso, -a *Fam* **1.** *adj* **a)** [despreciable] slimy **b)** *Am* [tonto] daft, stupid **2.** *nm, f* **a)** [persona despreciable] creep **b)** *Am* [tonto] twit, idiot

babucha *nf* **a)** [calzado] Moroccan slipper, babouche **b)** *Arg, Urug* **a babucha** on one's back

baca *nf* AUTO roof rack

bacalao *nm* [pez] cod

bacán 1. *adj Cuba, Perú* cool, wicked **2.** *nm Cuba* toff; **como un bacán** like a real gentleman

bachata *nm Cuba, PRico* party; **estar de bachata** to party, to have a good time

bachillerato *nm academically orientated Spanish secondary school course for pupils aged 14-17*

bacinica *nf Am* chamber pot, potty

bacon *nm Esp* bacon

bádminton *nm* badminton

bafle, baffle ['bafle] *nm* loudspeaker

bahía *nf* bay

bailable *adj* danceable

bailar *vt & vi* to dance; *Fig* **bailar al son que le tocan** to toe the line; *Fam* **¡que me quiten lo baila(d)o!** but at least I had a good time!

bailarín, -ina *nm, f* dancer; [clásico] ballet dancer

baile *nm* **a)** [danza] dance **b)** [fiesta popular] dance; [formal] ball; **baile de disfraces** fancy dress ball

baja *nf* **a)** [descenso] drop, fall; FIN **jugar a la baja** to bear the market
b) [cese] **dar de baja a algn** [en una empresa] to lay sb off; [en un club, sindicato] to expel sb; **darse de baja (de)** [dimitir] to resign (from); [salirse] to drop out (of)
c) [permiso - por enfermedad] sick leave; **estar/darse de baja** to be on / take sick leave; **baja por maternidad** maternity leave
d) MIL loss, casualty; **bajas civiles** civilian casualties

bajada *nf* **a)** [descenso] descent **b)** [cuesta] slope **c)** **bajada de bandera** [de taxi] minimum fare

bajar 1. *vt* **a)** to come / go down; **bajar la escalera** to come / go downstairs
b) [descender] to bring / get / take down; [volumen] to turn down; [voz, telón] to lower; [precios etc] to reduce, to cut; [persiana] to let down; [cabeza] to bow o lower
c) INFORM [fichero] to download
2. *vi* **a)** to go / come down
b) [apearse] to get off; [de un coche] to get out (**de** of)
c) [disminuir] to fall, to drop
3. bajarse *vpr* **a)** to come / go down
b) [apearse] to get off; [de un coche] to get out (**de** of)

bajativo *nm Andes, RP* [licor] digestive liqueur; [tisana] herbal tea

bajial *nm Méx, Perú* lowland

bajío *nm* **a)** sandbank **b)** [terreno bajo] lowland

bajo, -a 1. *adj* low; [persona] short; [sonido] faint, soft; **en voz baja** in a low voice; **planta baja** ground floor; **de baja calidad** of poor quality; **la clase baja** the lower class
2. *nm* a) MÚS bass
b) [planta baja - piso] *Br* ground floor flat, *US* first floor apartment
3. *adv* low; [hablar] quietly
4. *prep* under, underneath; **bajo cero** below zero; **bajo tierra** underground; **bajo la lluvia** in the rain

bala *nf* bullet; *Fig* **como una bala** like a shot

balacear *vt Am* to shoot

balacera *nf Am* shoot-out

balada *nf* ballad

balance *nm* a) FIN balance sheet; **balance ecológico** ecological balance; *Fig* **hacer balance de una situación** to take stock of a situation b) [resultado] outcome

balanceo *nm* a) rocking, swinging; [de barco, avión] rolling b) *Am* AUTO wheel balance

balancín *nm* a) [mecedora] rocking chair; [en el jardín] swing hammock b) [columpio] seesaw

balanza *nf* scales; *Fig* **estar en la balanza** to be in the balance o in danger; **balanza comercial** balance of trade; **balanza de pagos** balance of payments

balar *vi* to bleat

balboa *nm* balboa

balcón *nm* balcony

balde¹ *nm* pail, bucket

balde² *loc adv* a) **de balde** [gratis] free b) **en balde** [en vano] in vain

baldosa *nf* (ceramic) floor tile; [para pavimentar] flagstone, paving stone

balear 1. *vt Am* [disparar] to shoot
2. *adj* Balearic

Baleares *n pl* **las (Islas) Baleares** the Balearic Islands

baleo *nm Am* shoot-out

balido *nm* bleating, bleat

baliza *nf* a) [para barcos] buoy; [para aviones] beacon b) *RP* [señal] warning triangle

ballena *nf* whale

ballet [ba'le] *(pl* **ballets***)* *nm* ballet

balneario *nm* spa, health resort

balón *nm* a) ball, football; *Fig* **balón de oxígeno** boost b) [bombona] gas cylinder

baloncesto *nm* basketball

balonmano *nm* handball

balonvolea *nm* volleyball

balsa *nf* a) NÁUT raft b) *Fig* **como una balsa de aceite** very quiet

balsámico, -a *adj* a) [tranquilizante] soothing; **una pastilla balsámica** a soothing pastille b) [de bálsamo] balsamic; **vinagre balsámico** balsamic vinegar

bálsamo *nm* balsam, balm

balsero, -a *nm, f* boat person, especially Cuban, who tries to cross into the US illegally

bambú *(pl* **bambúes** *o* **bambús***)* *nm* bamboo

banana *nf* banana

banca *nf* a) [asiento] bench b) COM & FIN (the) banks; [actividad] banking; **banca electrónica** electronic banking c) [en juegos] bank

banco *nm* a) bench b) COM, FIN, INFORM & MED bank; **Banco Mundial** World Bank c) **banco de arena** sandbank d) [de peces] shoal, school e) GEOL layer

banda *nf* a) MÚS band b) CINE **banda sonora** soundtrack c) [de pájaros] flock d) [cinta] sash e) [lado] side; FÚT **línea de banda** touchline; **saque de banda** throw-in

bandeja *nf* tray; *Fig* **servir algo a algn en bandeja** to hand sth to sb on a plate

bandera *nf* flag; **bandera azul** [en playa] blue flag

banderazo *nm* a) DEP [señal de salida] starting signal; [señal de llegada] *Br* chequered flag, *US* checkered flag b) *Méx, Ven* [en taxi] minimum fare

banderilla nf **a)** TAUROM banderilla *(barbed dart thrust into bull's back)* **b)** Esp [aperitivo] *hors d'œuvre of pickles and olives on a cocktail stick*

banderín nf pennant, small flag

bandido nm bandit, outlaw

bando[1] nm **a)** JUR [edicto] edict, proclamation **b) bandos** banns

bando[2] nm faction, side; **pasarse al otro bando** to go over to the other side, to change side

banjo ['banjo] nm banjo

banner ['baner] nm INFORM banner; **banner publicitario** banner (ad)

banquero, -a nm, f banker

banqueta nf **a)** [asiento] stool **b)** [para los pies] foot-stool **c)** CAm, Méx [acera] Br pavement, US sidewalk

banquina nf RP [arcén] Br hard shoulder, US shoulder

bañadera nf **a)** Arg [bañera] bath **b)** RP [vehículo] *old-fashioned school bus*

bañado nm Bol, RP [terreno] marshy area

bañador nm Esp [de mujer] swimsuit; [de hombre] swimming trunks

bañar 1. vt **a)** to bath **b)** [cubrir] to coat, cover; **bañar en oro** to gold plate **2. bañarse** vpr [en baño] to have o take a bath; [en mar, piscina] to go for a swim; Am [ducharse] to have a shower

bañera nf bath, bathtub

bañista nmf bather, swimmer

baño nm **a)** bath; **tomar un baño** to have o take a bath; Fig **darse un baño de sol** to sunbathe; **baño de sangre** bloodbath; **baño María** bain-marie **b)** [de oro etc] coat; [de chocolate etc] coating, covering **c)** [cuarto de aseo] bathroom; [servicios] Br toilet, US bathroom **d)** [establecimiento] **baños** thermal baths

bar nm bar, pub

baraja nf Br pack o US deck (of cards)

barajar vt [cartas] to shuffle; Fig [nombres, cifras] to juggle with

baranda, Esp **barandilla** nf [de escalera] handrail, banister; [de balcón] handrail

barata nf Méx [saldo] sale

baratero, -a nm, f Am ≃ Br pound shop, ≃ US dime store

baratija nf trinket, knick-knack

barato, -a 1. adj cheap **2.** adv cheaply

barba nf **a)** ANAT chin **b)** [pelo] beard; Esp **2 euros por barba** 2 euros a head

barbacoa nf barbecue

barbaridad nf **a)** atrocity **b)** [disparate] piece of nonsense; **no digas barbaridades** don't talk nonsense **c) una barbaridad** a lot; **costar una barbaridad** to cost a fortune

barbarie nf savagery, cruelty

bárbaro, -a 1. adj **a)** HIST barbarian **b)** [cruel] barbaric, barbarous **c)** Fam [enorme] massive **d)** RP Fam [estupendo] tremendous, terrific **2.** nm, f HIST barbarian

barbería nf barber's (shop)

barbero nm barber

barbilla nf chin

barbudo, -a adj with a heavy beard

barca nf small boat

Barça nm DEP Barça (Catalan name of the Barcelona football team)

barcaza nf lighter

Barcelona n Barcelona

barcelonés, -esa 1. adj of / from Barcelona **2.** nm, f person from Barcelona

barco nm boat, ship; **barco de pasajeros** liner; **barco de vapor** steamer

barítono nm baritone

barman (pl **barmans**) nm barman

barniz nm **a)** [en madera] varnish; [en cerámica] glaze **b)** Fig veneer

barnizado, -a adj [madera] varnished; [cerámica] glazed

barnizar [40] vt [madera] to varnish; [cerámica] to glaze

barómetro nm barometer

barquillo nm wafer

barra *nf* **a)** bar; **barra de pan** French loaf, baguette; **barra de labios** lipstick **b)** [mostrador] bar; **barra americana** *bar where hostesses chat with clients* **c)** DEP **barra fija** horizontal bar; **barras paralelas** parallel bars **d)** INFORM slash **e)** *Andes, RP Fam* [de amigos] gang; **barra brava** *group of violent soccer supporters*

barraca *nf* **a)** [caseta] shack, hut **b)** [en Valencia y Murcia] thatched farmhouse

barranco *nm* [despeñadero] cliff, precipice; [torrentera] gully, ravine

barranquismo *nm* canyoning

barrendero, -a *nm, f* sweeper, street sweeper

barreño *nm Esp* washing-up bowl

barrer 1. *vt* to sweep **2.** *vi* [en elecciones] to win by a landslide

barrera *nf* barrier

barriada *nf* **a)** [barrio popular] neighbourhood, area **b)** *Am* [barrio de chabolas] shanty town

barriga *nf* belly; *Fam* tummy

barril *nm* barrel; **cerveza de barril** draught beer

barrio *nm* area, district, *US* neighborhood; **barrio chino** [de chinos] Chinatown; *Esp* [de prostitución] red-light district; **barrio ecológico** eco-friendly community; **el Barrio Gótico** the Gothic Quarter; **barrios bajos** slums; **del barrio** local; *Esp Fam* **irse al otro barrio** to kick the bucket; *Esp Fam* **mandar a algn al otro barrio** to take sb out

barro *nm* **a)** [lodo] mud **b)** [arcilla] clay; **objetos de barro** earthenware

barroco, -a *adj* baroque

bártulos *nmpl Fam* things, bits and pieces

barullo *nm* [alboroto] row, din; [confusión] confusion

basar 1. *vt* to base (en on) **2. basarse** *vpr* [teoría, película] **basarse en** to be based on; **¿en qué te basas para decir eso?** what grounds do you have for saying that?

basca *nf Esp Fam* people, crowd

báscula *nf* scales; [para camiones] weighbridge

base *nf* **a)** base; **sueldo base** minimum wage; INFORM **base de datos** database **b)** [de argumento, teoría] basis; **en base a** on the basis of; **a base de estudiar** by studying; **a base de productos naturales** using natural products **c)** [de partido] grass roots; **miembro de base** rank and file member **d)** [nociones] grounding

básicamente *adv* basically

básico, -a *adj* basic

básquet, básquetbol *nmf Am* basketball

basquetbolista *nmf Am* basketball player

basta *interj* that's enough!; **¡basta de chistes/tonterías!** that's enough jokes/of this nonsense!

bastante 1. *adj* **a)** [suficiente] enough; **bastante tiempo/comida** enough time/food; **bastantes platos** enough plates
b) [abundante] quite a lot of; **hace bastante calor/frío** it's quite hot/cold; **bastantes amigos** quite a lot of friends
2. *adv* **a)** [suficiente] enough; **con esto hay bastante** that is enough; **no soy lo bastante rico (como) para …** I am not rich enough to …
b) [considerablemente] fairly, quite; **me gusta bastante** I quite like it; **vamos bastante al cine** we go to the cinema quite o fairly often

bastar 1. *vi* to be sufficient o enough, to suffice; **basta con tres** three will be enough; **¡basta de tonterías!** enough of this nonsense!; **basta con tocarlo para que se abra** you only have to touch it and it opens; **¡basta (ya)!** that's enough!, that will do! **2. bastarse** *vpr* **bastarse a sí mismo** to be self-sufficient, to rely only on oneself

bastardo, -a *adj & nm, f* bastard

bastidor *nm* **a)** [armazón] frame **b)** TEATRO **bastidores** wings; *Fig* **entre bastidores** behind the scenes

basto, -a *adj* [cosa] rough, coarse; [persona] coarse, uncouth

bastón *nm* stick, walking stick

bastoncillo *nm* [para oídos] *Br* cotton bud, *US* cotton swab, *US* Q-Tip®

basura *nf Br* rubbish, *US* garbage, *US* trash

basurero *nm* **a)** [persona] *Br* dustman, *US* garbage man **b)** [lugar] *Br* rubbish tip o dump, *US* garbage dump

bata *nf* [para casa] dressing gown; [de médico etc] white coat; [de científico] lab coat; *Am* **bata de baño** bathrobe

batacazo *nm* **a)** [golpe] bump, bang; **los resultados representan un nuevo batacazo para el partido** the results are another blow for the party **b)** *CSur Fam* [triunfo inesperado] surprise victory

batalla *nf* battle; **librar batalla** to do o join battle; **batalla campal** pitched battle

batata *nf* sweet potato

batería 1. *nf* **a)** battery **b)** MÚS drums **c) batería de cocina** pots and pans, set of pans **2.** *nmf* drummer

batido, -a 1. *adj* **a)** CULIN whipped **b)** DEP **tierra batida** clay **2.** *nm* milk shake

batidora *nf* [eléctrica] mixer

batín *nm* short dressing gown

batir 1. *vt* **a)** to beat **b)** [huevo] to beat; [nata] to whip, to whisk **c)** [récord] to break **d)** [en caza] to beat **2. batirse** *vpr* to fight

batuta *nf* MÚS baton; *Fig* **llevar la batuta** to be in charge

baúl *nm* **a)** [cofre] trunk **b)** *Arg, Col* [maletero] *Br* boot, *US* trunk

bautismo *nm* baptism, christening

bautizar [40] *vt* to baptize, to christen; [vino] to water down

bautizo *nm* baptism, christening

baya *nf* berry

bayeta *nf* floorcloth

bayoneta *nf* bayonet

baza *nf* **a)** [en naipes] trick **b)** [ventaja] advantage **c) meter baza en** to stick one's oar in

bazar *nm* bazaar

bb SMS *written abbr of* **bebé**

bbr SMS *written abbr of* **beber**

be *nf* **a)** *Esp* [letra] name of the letter "b" **b)** *Am* **be alta** o **grande** o **larga** b (to distinguish from "v")

beato, -a *adj* [piadoso] devout; *Despec* prudish, sanctimonious

bebe, -a *nm, f Am Fam* baby

bebé *nm* baby; **bebé probeta** test-tube baby

bebedero *nm* **a)** [recipiente] trough **b)** [abrevadero] watering hole **c)** *Méx, RP* [fuente] drinking fountain

beber *vt & vi* to drink

bebida *nf* drink; **darse a la bebida** to take to drink

bebido, -a *adj* drunk

beca *nf* grant

becario, -a *nm, f* grant holder

becerro *nm* calf

bechamel *nf* bechamel; **salsa bechamel** bechamel sauce, white sauce

bedel *nm* beadle

begonia *nf* begonia

beicon *nm* bacon

beige *adj & nm inv* beige

Beijing, Pekín *n* Peking

béisbol *nm* baseball

belén *nm* nativity scene, crib

belga *adj & nmf* Belgian

Bélgica *n* Belgium

bélico, -a *adj* warlike, bellicose; [preparativos etc] war; **material bélico** armaments

belleza *nf* beauty

bello, -a *adj* beautiful

bellota *nf* BOT acorn; *Fig* **animal de bellota** blockhead

bencina *nf Chile* [gasolina] *Br* petrol, *US* gas

bencinera *nf Chile Br* petrol station, *US* gas station

bendecir [12] *vt* to bless; **bendecir la mesa** to say grace; **¡Dios te bendiga!** God bless you!

bendición *nf* blessing

bendito, -a 1. *adj* blessed; [maldito] damned **2.** *nm, f* [bonachón] good sort, kind soul; [tontorrón] simple soul

beneficencia *nf* beneficence, charity

beneficiar [43] **1.** *vt* to benefit **2. beneficiarse** *vpr* **beneficiarse de** o **con algo** to profit from o by sth

beneficio *nm* **a)** COM & FIN profit **b)** [bien] benefit; **en beneficio propio** in one's own interest; **un concierto a beneficio de …** a concert in aid of …

benéfico, -a *adj* charitable

benevolencia *nf* benevolence

benevolente, benévolo, -a *adj* benevolent

bengala *nf* flare

berberecho *nm* (common) cockle

berenjena *nf* Br aubergine, US eggplant

berma *nf* Andes [arcén] Br hard shoulder, US shoulder

bermudas *nmpl* o *nfpl* Bermuda shorts

Bermudas *nfpl* las (Islas) Bermudas Bermuda

berrinche *nm* Fam tantrum; Esp **coger** o **hacer un berrinche** to have a fit, to fly off the handle

berza *nf* cabbage

besar 1. *vt* to kiss **2. besarse** *vpr* to kiss

beso *nm* kiss; Esp Fam **beso de tornillo** French kiss

bestia 1. *nf* beast, animal; **bestia de carga** beast of burden **2.** *nmf* Fam & Fig brute, beast **3.** *adj* Fig brutish, boorish; **a lo bestia** rudely

besugo *nm* **a)** [pez] sea bream **b)** Esp [persona] idiot, half-wit

betabel *nf* Méx Br beetroot, US beet

betarraga *nf* Andes Br beetroot, US beet

betún *nm* [para el calzado] shoe polish; QUÍM bitumen

biberón *nm* baby's bottle, feeding bottle

Biblia *nf* Bible

bibliografía *nf* bibliography

bibliorato *nm* RP lever arch file

biblioteca *nf* **a)** [institución] library; **biblioteca ambulante** mobile library **b)** Chile, Perú, RP [mueble] bookcase

bibliotecario, -a *nm, f* librarian

bicarbonato *nm* bicarbonate; **bicarbonato sódico** bicarbonate of soda

bíceps *nm inv* biceps

bicho *nm* **a)** bug, insect; **¿qué bicho le ha picado?** Br what's up with him?, US what's eating him? **b)** TAUROM bull **c)** Fam **todo bicho viviente** every living soul; **un bicho raro** a weirdo, an oddball

bici *nf* Fam bike

bicicleta *nf* bicycle; **montar en bicicleta** to ride a bicycle

bicicross *nm* cyclo-cross

bicitaxi *nm* cycle taxi

bicolor *adj* two-coloured; POL **gobierno bicolor** two-party government

bidé *nm* bidet

bidón *nm* drum

bien¹ 1. *adv* **a)** [correctamente] well; **habla bien (el) inglés** she speaks English well; **responder bien** to answer correctly; **hiciste bien en decírmelo** you were right to tell me; **las cosas le van bien** things are going well for him; **¡bien!** good!, great!; **¡muy bien!** excellent, first class!; **¡qué bien!** great!, fantastic!
b) [de salud] well; **sentirse/encontrarse/estar bien** to feel well
c) vivir bien to be comfortably off; **¡está bien!** [¡de acuerdo!] fine!, all right!; **¡ya está bien!** that's (quite) enough!; **aquí se está muy bien** it's really nice here; **esta falda te sienta bien** this skirt suits you; Fam **ese libro está muy bien** that book is very good
d) [intensificador] very, quite; **bien temprano** very early, nice and early; **bien caliente** pretty hot; **bien es verdad que …** it's quite clear that …

e) más bien rather, a little

f) bien podía haberme avisado she might have let me know

2. *conj* **ahora bien** now, now then; **o bien** or, or else; **bien…o bien…** either… or…; **no bien** as soon as; **no bien llegó…** no sooner had she arrived than…; **si bien** although, even if

3. *adj inv* **la gente bien** the wealthy, the upper classes

bien² *nm* **a)** [bondad] good; **el bien y el mal** good and evil; **un hombre / familia de bien** a good man / family **b)** [bienestar] **por el bien de** for the good of; **lo hace por tu bien** he does it for your sake **c) bienes** goods; **bienes de equipo** capital goods; **bienes inmuebles** real estate, *US* real property; **bienes de consumo** consumer goods

bienal *nf* biennial exhibition

bienestar *nm* [personal] well-being, contentment; [comodidad] ease, comfort; **la sociedad del bienestar** the affluent society

bienvenida *nf* welcome; **dar la bienvenida a algn** to welcome sb

bienvenido, -a *adj* welcome

bife *nm Andes, RP* **a)** [bistec] steak; **bife ancho** entrecote **b)** [bofetada] slap

bifocal *adj* bifocal; **gafas bifocales** bifocals

bigote *nm* [de persona] moustache; (*usu pl*) [de animal] whiskers

bigotudo, -a *adj* with a big moustache

bigudí (*pl* **bigudí** o **bigudíes**) *nm* curler

bilingüe *adj* bilingual

billar *nm* **a)** [juego] billiards (*sing*); **billar americano** pool; **billar ruso** snooker **b)** [mesa] billiard table

billete *nm* **a)** *Esp* [transporte] ticket; *Am* **billete chico** *Br* small denomination note, *US* small denomination bill; **billete de ida** [en avión] one-way (ticket); **billete de ida y vuelta** *Br* return (ticket), *US* round-trip (ticket) **b)** [de banco] *Br* note, *US* bill; **un billete de cinco euros** a five euro note

billetera *nf* wallet, *US* billfold

billetero *nm* = **billetera**

billón *nm* trillion

bingo *nm* **a)** [juego] bingo **b)** [sala] bingo hall

biodegradable *adj* biodegradable

biodiversidad *nf* biodiversity

biografía *nf* biography

biográfico, -a *adj* biographical

biología *nf* biology

biométrico, -a *adj* biometric; **pasaporte biométrico** biometric passport

biopsia *nf* biopsy

bioquímica *nf* biochemistry

biotecnología *nf* biotechnology

biquini *nm* bikini

birlar *vt Fam* to pinch, *Br* to nick

birome *nf RP* Biro®, ballpoint (pen)

birra *nf Fam* beer, *US* brew

birria *nf Fam* rubbish

bisabuelo *nm* great-grandfather; **bisabuelos** great-grandparents

bisexual *adj & nmf* bisexual

bisnieto, -a *nm, f* great-grandson, *f* great-granddaughter; **mis bisnietos** my great-grandchildren

bisonte *nm* bison, American buffalo

bistec (*pl* **bistecs**) *nm* steak

bisturí (*pl* **bisturíes**) *nm* scalpel

bisutería *nf* imitation jewellery

bit (*pl* **bits**) *nm* INFORM bit

bíter *nm* bitters

bizco, -a 1. *adj* cross-eyed **2.** *nm, f* cross-eyed person

bizcocho *nm* sponge cake

blanca *nf Esp* **estar sin blanca** to be flat broke

blanco¹, a 1. *adj* white; [tez] fair **2.** *nm, f* [hombre] white man; [mujer] white woman; **los blancos** whites

blanco² *nm* **a)** [color] white **b)** [hueco] blank; **dejó la hoja en blanco** he left the page blank; **votos en blanco** blank votes; *Fig* **pasar la noche en blanco** to have a sleepless night; **me quedé en blanco** my mind went blank **c)** [dia-

na] target; **dar en el blanco** to hit the
target; *Fig* **ser el blanco de todas las
miradas** to be the centre of attention

blando, -a *adj* soft

blanquear *vt* **a)** to whiten **b)** [encalar]
to whitewash **c)** [dinero] to launder

blanquillo *nm* **a)** *CAm, Méx* [huevo] egg
b) *Andes* [melocotón] white peach

blaugrana *adj & nmf* Catalan term
used to refer to the Barcelona football
team based on the colour of their shirt

blindado, -a *adj* MIL armoured, ar-
mour-plated; [antibalas] bullet-proof;
coche blindado bullet-proof car; **puerta blindada** reinforced door,
security door

blindar *vt* to armour-plate

bloc *(pl* **blocs***)* *nm* pad; **bloc de notas**
notepad

blog *nm* blog

bloguero, -a *nm, f* *Fam* blogger

bloque *nm* **a)** [gen & INFORM] block;
en bloque en bloc; **bloque de pisos**
Br (block of) flats, *US* apartment block
b) POL bloc; **el bloque comunista** the
Communist Bloc

bloquear *vt* **a)** to block **b)** MIL to blockade

bloqueo *nm* blockade; DEP block

blúmer *(pl* **blúmers** *o* **blúmeres***)* *nm*
CAm, Carib panties, *Br* knickers

blusa *nf* blouse

bluyín *nm* *Andes, Ven* jeans

bluyines *nmpl* *Andes, Ven* jeans

bobada *nf* nonsense; **decir bobadas**
to talk nonsense

bobina *nf* **a)** reel **b)** ELEC coil

bobo, -a **1.** *adj* [tonto] stupid, silly;
[ingenuo] naïve **2.** *nm, f* fool

boca *nf* **a)** mouth; **boca abajo** face
downward; **boca arriba** face upward;
Fam **¡cierra la boca!** shut up!; *Fam* **con la
boca abierta** open-mouthed; *Fam* **se le
hizo la boca agua** his mouth watered;
el boca a boca kiss of life, mouth-to-
mouth resuscitation **b)** boca del me-

tro *Br* tube *o* underground entrance,
US subway entrance; **boca de riego**
hydrant

bocacalle *nf* entrance to a street

bocadillo *nm* **a)** *Esp* [con pan] filled roll
(made with a baguette),; **un bocadillo
de jamón / tortilla** a ham /an omelette
sandwich **b)** [de cómic] balloon

bocadito *nm* *RP* canapé

bocado *nm* **a)** [mordedura] bite **b)** [de
caballo] bit

bocata *nm* *Esp Fam* filled roll *(made with
a baguette)*

boceto *nm* ARTE sketch, outline; [es-
quema] outline, plan

bochorno *nm* **a)** [tiempo] sultry *o* close
weather; [calor sofocante] stifling heat
b) *Fig* [vergüenza] shame, embarrassment

bochornoso, -a *adj* **a)** [tiempo] sultry,
close, muggy; [calor] stifling **b)** *Fig* [ver-
gonzoso] shameful, embarrassing

bocina *nf* horn; **tocar la bocina** to
blow *o* sound one's horn

bocón, -ona *nm, f* *Am Fam* [boca-
zas] **ser bocón** to be a bigmouth *o*
blabbermouth

boda *nf* wedding, marriage; **bodas de
plata** silver wedding

bodega *nf* **a)** wine cellar; [tienda]
wine shop **b)** NÁUT hold **c)** *Méx* [alma-
cén] warehouse **d)** *CAm, Carib* [colmado]
small grocery store

bodegón *nm* still life

bodrio *nm* *Fam* **un bodrio** *Br* rubbish,
US trash

bofetada *nf* slap on the face; **dar una
bofetada** *o* **un bofetada a algn** to slap
sb's face

bofetón *nm* = **bofetada**

bofia *nf* *Esp Fam* **la bofia** the cops *(pl)*

bogavante *nm* lobster

bohemio, -a **1.** *adj* **a)** [aspecto, vida,
barrio] bohemian **b)** [de Bohemia] Bohemian **2.** *nm, f* **a)** [artista, vividor]
bohemian **b)** [de Bohemia] Bohemian

bohío *nm* *Carib* hut, cabin

boicot *(pl* **boicots***)* *nm* boycott

boicotear vt to boycott

bóiler nm Méx boiler

boina nf beret

bola nf a) ball; [canica] marble; **bola de nieve** snowball; Am **dar en bola** to succeed, to hit the nail on the head; Esp Fam **ir a mi/tu/su bola** to do what you like; **en el instituto él siempre iba a su bola** he always did what the hell he liked at school; Esp Fam **no dar pie con bola** to be unable to do anything right; Esp Fam **no rascar** o **tocar bola** not to lift a finger b) Fam [mentira] fib, lie; **meter bolas** to tell fibs c) [rumor] rumour; **corre la bola por ahí de que te has echado novio** they say you've got yourself a boyfriend

bolear vt Méx [sacar brillo] to shine, to polish

bolera nf bowling alley

bolería nf Méx shoeshine store

bolero nm bolero

boleta nf a) Cuba, Méx, RP [para votar] ballot, voting slip b) CSur [comprobante - de venta, de depósito bancario] receipt c) CAm, CSur [multa] parking ticket d) Méx [de calificaciones] Br (school) report, US report card

boletería nf Am [de cine, teatro] box office; [de estación] ticket office

boletero, -a nm, f Am box office attendant

boletín nm bulletin; **Boletín Oficial del Estado** Official Gazette

boleto nm a) [de lotería, rifa] ticket b) [para transporte] ticket; Am **boleto de ida y vuelta** return (ticket); Méx **boleto redondo** return (ticket) c) Col, Méx [para espectáculo] ticket d) Méx Fam **¡trae el pan, de boleto!** hurry up with the bread!

boli nm Esp Fam pen, Biro®

boliche nm a) [juego] bowling b) [bola] jack c) [lugar] bowling alley d) CSur Fam [bar] cheap bar; [tienda] small-town store

bolígrafo nm ballpoint (pen), Br Biro®

bolillo nm a) [en costura] bobbin b) Méx [panecillo] bread roll

bolita nf CSur [bola] marble; **jugar a las bolitas** to play marbles

Bolivia n Bolivia

boliviano, -a adj & nm, f Bolivian

bollera nf Fam & Despec dyke

bollería nf a) [tienda] cake shop b) [productos] cakes

bollo nm a) CULIN bun, bread roll b) [abolladura] dent

bolo¹ nm [pieza] skittle, pin; **bolos** [juego] (ten-pin) bowling

bolo², -a nm, f CAm Fam [borracho] boozer

bolsa¹ nf bag; CAm, Méx [de mano] Br handbag, US purse; AVIACIÓN **bolsa de aire** air pocket; **bolsa de deportes** sports bag; **bolsa de la compra** shopping bag; **bolsa de viaje** travel bag

bolsa² nf FIN Stock Exchange; **jugar a la bolsa** to play the market

bolsillo nm [en prenda] pocket; **de bolsillo** pocket, pocket-size; **libro de bolsillo** paperback; **lo pagó de su bolsillo** he paid for it out of his own pocket

bolsista nmf CAm, Méx pickpocket

bolso nm a) Esp [de mujer] Br handbag, US purse b) [de viaje] bag

boludear vi RP Vulg a) [hacer tonterías] to mess about b) [decir tonterías] to talk rubbish c) [perder el tiempo] to waste one's time

boludez nf RP a) Vulg [tontería] **¡son boludeces!** that's just bollocks! b) muy Fam [pereza] laziness

boludo, -a nm, f RP Vulg [estúpido] Br prat, US jerk

bomba¹ nf pump; Chile, Ecuad, Ven [gasolinera] Br petrol station, US gas station; **bomba de aire** air pump; **bomba de incendios** fire engine; Chile, Ecuad, Ven **bomba (de gasolina)** [surtidor] Br petrol pump, US gas pump

bomba² nf bomb; **bomba atómica/de hidrógeno/de neutrones** atomic/hydrogen/neutron bomb; **bomba de relojería** time bomb; **bomba fétida** stink bomb; Fam **noticia bomba** shattering piece of news; Esp Fam **pasarlo bomba** to have a whale of a time

bombacha *nf RP* [braga] *Br* knickers, *US* panties; **bombachas** [pantalones] *loose trousers worn by cowboys*

bombardear *vt* to bomb, to shell; **bombardear a algn a preguntas** to bombard sb with questions

bombardeo *nm* bombing, bombardment

bombero, -a *nm, f* **a)** [de incendios] firefighter; [hombre] fireman; [mujer] firewoman; **cuerpo de bomberos** *Br* fire brigade, *US* fire department; **parque de bomberos** fire station **b)** *Ven* [de gasolinera] *Br* petrol-pump *o US* gas-pump attendant

bombilla *nf Esp* (light) bulb; **bombilla de ahorro de energía** energy saving bulb, low energy bulb

bombillo *nm CAm, Carib, Col, Méx* (light) bulb

bombita *nf RP* light bulb

bombo *nm* **a)** *MÚS* bass drum; *Fig* **a bombo y platillo(s)** with a great song and dance; *Fam* **darse bombo** to blow one's own trumpet **b)** [de sorteo] lottery drum

bombón *nm* chocolate

bombona *nf* cylinder; **bombona de butano** butane gas cylinder

bonanza *nf* **a)** *NÁUT* [tiempo] fair weather; [mar] calm at sea **b)** *Fig* [prosperidad] prosperity

bondad *nf* goodness; *Formal* **tenga la bondad de esperar** please be so kind as to wait

bondadoso, -a *adj* kind, good-natured

boniato *nm Esp, Cuba, Urug* sweet potato

bonificación *nf* bonus

bonificar [44] *vt* COM to give a bonus to

bonito, a **1.** *adj* pretty, nice **2.** *adv Am* **a)** [bien] well; **baila muy bonito** she dances really well, she's a really good dancer **b)** [mucho] a lot, really; **ha crecido bonito** he's grown a lot, he's really grown **3.** *nm* [pez] tuna

bono *nm* **a)** [vale] voucher **b)** FIN bond, debenture; **bonos del tesoro** *o* **del Estado** Treasury bonds

bonobús *nm Esp* multiple-journey bus ticket

bonoloto *nm* Spanish state-run lottery

bonotrén *nm* train pass

bonsái *nm* bonsai

boñiga *nf* cowpat

boquerón *nm* anchovy

boquete *nm* hole

boquilla *nf* **a)** [de cigarro] tip; [de pipa] mouthpiece; **decir algo de boquilla** to pay lip service to sth **b)** MÚS mouthpiece **c)** [orificio] opening

Borbón *n* [dinastía] Bourbon; **los Borbones** the Bourbons

borbotón *nm* bubbling

borda *nf* NÁUT gunwale; **arrojar** *o* **echar por la borda** to throw overboard; **fuera borda** [motor] outboard motor

bordado, -a **1.** *adj* embroidered; *Esp* **el examen me salió bordado** I made a good job of that exam **2.** *nm* embroidery

bordar *vt* **a)** to embroider **b)** *Fig* to do excellently

borde¹ *nm* [de mesa, camino] edge; COST hem, edge; [de vasija] rim, brim; **al borde de** on the brink of, on the verge of; **al borde del mar** at the seaside

borde² *Esp Fam* **1.** *adj* [antipático] **ser borde** to be *Br* a ratbag *o US* an s.o.b. **2.** *nmf* [antipático] *Br* ratbag, *US* s.o.b., stroppy person

bordear *vt* to go round the edge of, to skirt

bordillo *nm Br* kerb, *US* curb

bordo *nm* **a bordo** on board; **subir a bordo** to go on board

bordó *adj inv RP* burgundy

borla *nf* tassel

borra *nf* **a)** [pelusa] fluff **b)** [poso] sediment, dregs

borrachera *nf* [embriaguez] drunkenness; **agarrarse** *o* **cogerse una borrachera** to get drunk

borracho, -a 1. adj **a)** [bebido] drunk; **estar borracho** to be drunk **b)** [bizcocho] with rum **2.** nm, f drunkard, drunk

borrador nm **a)** [escrito] rough copy, first draft **b)** [croquis] rough o preliminary sketch **c)** [para pizarra] board duster

borrar 1. vt **a)** [con goma] Br to rub out, US to erase; [pizarra] to clean **b)** INFORM to delete **2. borrarse** vpr [de un club etc] to drop out, to withdraw

borrasca nf area of low pressure

borrón nm blot, smudge

borroso, -a adj blurred; **veo borroso** I can't see clearly, everything's blurred

boscoso, -a adj wooded

bosque nm wood

bostezar [40] vi to yawn

bostezo nm yawn

bota nf **a)** boot; Fig **ponerse las botas** to make a killing **b)** [de vino] wineskin

botana nf Méx snack, appetizer

botánica nf botany

botar 1. vi **a)** Esp [saltar] to jump **b)** [pelota] to bounce **2.** vt **a)** [barco] to launch **b)** [pelota] to bounce **c)** Am salvo RP [tirar] to throw away; **bótalo a la basura** throw it away **3. botarse** vpr Am [tirarse] to jump; **botarse al río** to jump into the river

bote nm **a)** [envase - tarro] jar; Esp [lata] tin, can; [de champú, pastillas] bottle; Am **bote de la basura** Br rubbish bin, US garbage can; **bote de humo** smoke canister
b) [barca] boat; **bote salvavidas** lifeboat; **bote de remos** rowing boat
c) [propinas] tips; **para el bote** as a tip
d) [salto] jump; **dar botes** [saltar] to jump up and down; [tren, coche] to bump up and down; **pegar un bote** [de susto] to jump, to give a start
e) [de pelota] bounce; **dar botes** to bounce
f) [expresiones] Esp **chupar del bote** to feather one's nest; Esp **tener en el bote a algn** to have sb eating out of one's hand

botella nf **a)** bottle **b)** Cuba [autoestop] **dar botella a algn** to give sb a ride o esp Br lift; **hacer botella** to hitch-hike

botellín nm small bottle

botijo nm earthenware pitcher (with spout and handle)

botín¹ nm [de un robo] loot, booty

botín² nm [calzado] ankle boot

botiquín nm **a)** medicine chest o cabinet; [portátil] first-aid kit **b)** [enfermería] first-aid post

botón nm button; **pulsar el botón** to press the button; **botón de muestra** sample

bouquet [bu'ke] (pl **bouquets**) nm bouquet

boutique [bu'tik] nf boutique

bóveda nf vault

bovino, -a adj bovine; **ganado bovino** cattle

box nm **a)** [de caballo] stall **b)** [de coches] pit **c)** Am [boxeo] boxing

boxear vi to box

boxeo nm boxing

boxer nm [prenda] boxers (pl)

boya nf **a)** NÁUT buoy **b)** [corcho] float

bozal nm **a)** [para perro] muzzle **b)** Am [cabestro] halter

braga nf Esp Br knickers, US panties

bragueta nf [de pantalón etc] Br flies, US zipper

bramar vi to low, to bellow

brandy (pl **brandies**) nm brandy

brasa nf ember, red-hot coal; **a la brasa** barbecued

brasero nm brazier

brasier, brassier nm Am bra

Brasil n Brazil

brasileño, -a, RP **brasilero, -a** adj & nm, f Brazilian

brassier nm = **brasier**

bravo, -a 1. adj **a)** [valiente] brave, courageous **b)** [feroz] fierce, ferocious; **un toro bravo** a fighting bull **c)** [mar] rough, stormy **d)** Méx **a la brava** any old how; **hizo la tarea a la brava**

he did his homework without putting any effort into it **2.** *nm* [aplauso] **bravos** cheers, applause **3.** *interj* ¡bravo! well done!, bravo!

braza *nf* **a)** [medida] fathom **b)** *Esp* [en natación] breaststroke; **nadar a braza** to do the breaststroke

brazalete *nm* **a)** [insignia] armband **b)** [pulsera] bracelet

brazo *nm* **a)** arm; [de animal] foreleg; [de sillón, tocadiscos] arm; **brazo de gitano** *Br* Swiss roll, *US* jelly roll; **en brazos** in one's arms; **ir del brazo** to walk arm in arm; *Fig* **con los brazos abiertos** with open arms; *Fig* **no dar su brazo a torcer** not to give in, stand firm; **quedarse** *o* **estarse con los brazos cruzados** to just stand there doing nothing **b)** **brazo de mar** inlet

brebaje *nm* concoction, brew

brecha *nf* [en muro] opening, gap; *MIL & Fig* breach; *Fig* **estar siempre en la brecha** to be always in the thick of things

brécol *nm* broccoli

bretel *nm CSur* strap; **un vestido sin breteles** a strapless dress

breva *nf* **a)** [fruta] early fig **b)** *Esp Fam* ¡no caerá esa breva! some chance (of that happening)!

breve *adj* brief; **en breve, en breves momentos** shortly, soon; **en breves palabras** in short

brevedad *nf* briefness; [concisión] brevity; **con la mayor brevedad posible** as soon as possible

brevet *nm Chile* [de avión] pilot's licence; *Bol, Ecuad, Perú* [de automóvil] *Br* driving licence, *US* driver's license; *RP* [de velero] sailor's licence

brezo *nm* heather

bricolaje *nm Br* DIY, do-it-yourself, *US* home improvement

bricolajear *vt Fam* to DIY

brida *nf* **a)** [rienda] rein, bridle **b)** *TÉC* flange

brigada 1. *nf* **a)** *MIL* brigade **b)** [de policías] squad; **brigada antiterrorista** anti-terrorist squad **2.** *nm MIL* sergeant major

brillante 1. *adj* brilliant **2.** *nm* diamond

brillantina *nf* brilliantine

brillar *vi* [resplandecer] to shine; [ojos, joyas] to sparkle; [lentejuelas etc] to glitter; **brillar por su ausencia** to be conspicuous by one's absence

brillo *nm* [resplandor] shine; [del sol, de la luna] brightness; [de lentejuelas etc] glittering; [del cabello, tela] sheen; [de color] brilliance; [de pantalla] brightness; [de zapatos] shine; **sacar brillo a** to shine, to polish

brilloso, -a *adj Am* shining

brindar 1. *vi* to drink a toast; **brindar por algn / algo** to drink to sb / sth **2.** *vt* **a)** [oportunidad] to offer, to provide **b)** *TAUROM* to dedicate (**a** to) **3. brindarse** *vpr* to offer (**a** to), to volunteer (**a** to)

brindis *nm inv* **a)** toast **b)** *TAUROM* dedication (of the bull)

brío *nm* energy

brisa *nf* breeze; **brisa marina** sea breeze

británico, -a 1. *adj* British; **las Islas Británicas** the British Isles **2.** *nm, f* Briton; **los británicos** the British

brizna *nf* [de hierba] blade; [de carne] string

broca *nf* TÉC bit

brocha *nf* [para pintar] paintbrush; **brocha de afeitar** shaving brush

broche *nm* **a)** [joya] brooch; *Fig* **poner el broche de oro** to finish with a flourish **b)** [de vestido] fastener

brocheta *nf* CULIN shish kebab; [aguja] skewer

brócoli, bróculi *nm* broccoli

broma *nf* [chiste] joke; **bromas aparte** joking apart; **en broma** as a joke; ¡ni en broma! not on your life!; **broma pesada** practical joke; **gastar una broma** to play a joke

bromear *vi* to joke

bromista 1. *adj* fond of joking o playing jokes **2.** *nmf* joker, prankster

bronca *nf* a) [jaleo] row; **armar (una) bronca** to kick up a row b) *Esp* [crítica] scolding, telling-off; **echar una bronca a algn** to bawl sb out c) *RP Fam* [rabia] **me da bronca** it hacks me off; **el jefe le tiene bronca** the boss can't stand him

bronce *nm* bronze

bronceado, -a 1. *adj* suntanned, tanned **2.** *nm* suntan, tan

bronceador, -a 1. *adj* **leche bronceadora** suntan cream **2.** *nm* suntan cream o lotion

broncearse *vpr* to get a tan o a suntan

bronco, -a *adj* a) [material] rough b) [voz] gruff, rough c) [tos] hacking d) [sonido] harsh e) *Fig* [persona, modales] rough

bronquio *nm* bronchial tube

bronquitis *nf inv* bronchitis

brotar *vi* [planta] to sprout; [agua] to spring, to gush; [lágrimas] to well up; [epidemia] to break out

brote *nm* a) BOT [renuevo] bud, shoot; [de agua] gushing b) [de epidemia, violencia] outbreak

bruja *nf* witch, sorceress

brujería *nf* witchcraft, sorcery

brujo, -a 1. *nm* wizard, sorcerer **2.** *adj Méx Fam* broke; **estar brujo** to be broke

brújula *nf* compass

brusco, -a *adj* a) [persona] brusque, abrupt b) [repentino] sudden, sharp

Bruselas *n* Brussels

brusquedad *nf* brusqueness, abruptness

brutal *adj* brutal

brutalidad *nf* brutality

bruto, -a 1. *adj* a) [necio] stupid, thick; [grosero] coarse, uncouth b) FIN gross; **peso bruto** gross weight c) **un diamante en bruto** an uncut diamond **2.** *nm, f* blockhead, brute

bs, bss SMS *written abbr of* **besos**

b7s SMS *written abbr of* **besitos**

bucear *vi* to swim under water

buche *nm* maw; [de ave] craw; *Fam* [estómago] belly, stomach

bucle *nm* a) curl, ringlet b) [de carretera] *Br* hairpin bend, *US* hairpin turn c) INFORM loop

bucólico, -a *adj* a) [campestre] **un paisaje bucólico** a charmingly rural landscape b) LITER bucolic

Buda *n* Buddha

buena *nf* a) *Irón* **librarse de una buena** to get off scot-free b) **¡buenas!** [saludos] hello!; **de buenas a primeras** suddenly, all at once; **por las buenas** willingly

---

bueno, -a

> **buen** is used instead of **bueno** before masculine singular nouns (e.g. **buen hombre** good man). The comparative form of **bueno** is **mejor** (better), and the superlative form is **el mejor** (masculine) or **la mejor** (feminine) (the best).

1. *adj* a) good; **un alumno muy bueno** a very good pupil; **una buena película** a good movie o *Br* film
b) [amable] (*con* **ser**) good, kind; **el bueno de Carlos** good old Carlos; **es muy buena persona** he's a very kind soul
c) [sano] (*con* **estar**) well, in good health
d) [tiempo] good; **hoy hace buen tiempo** it's fine today; **mañana hará bueno** it will be fine o a nice day tomorrow
e) [conveniente] good; **no es bueno comer tanto** it's not good for you to eat so much
f) [considerable] considerable; **un buen número de** a good number of
g) [grande] good, big; **un buen trozo de pastel** a nice o good big piece of cake
h) *Fam* [atractivo] gorgeous, sexy; **Rosa está muy buena** Rosa's a bit of all right!; **una tía buena** a good-looking girl
i) *Irón* fine, real, proper; **¡en buen lío te has metido!** that's a fine mess you've got yourself into!
j) [locuciones] **un susto de los buenos** a real fright; *Irón* **¡estaría bueno!** I should jolly well hope not!; *Am* **¡qué**

bueno! great!, excellent!; **¡qué bueno que terminaste las clases!** that's great that you've finished your lessons! **2.** *interj* **a)** [vale] all right, OK **b)** [expresa sorpresa] hey! **c)** *Col, Méx* [al teléfono] hello

buey *(pl* **bueyes***)nm* ox, bullock

búfalo, -a *nm, f* buffalo

bufanda *nf* scarf

bufé *nm* buffet; **bufé libre** self-service buffet meal

bufete *nm* [despacho de abogado] lawyer's office

buffet *(pl* **buffets***)nm* = **bufé**

buhardilla *nf* attic, garret

búho *nm* owl; **búho real** eagle owl

buitre *nm* vulture

bujía *nf* **a)** AUTO spark plug **b)** FÍS candlepower

bula *nf* [documento] (papal) bull

bulbo *nm* bulb

bulerías *nfpl* popular Andalusian song and dance

bulevar *nm* boulevard

Bulgaria *n* Bulgaria

búlgaro, -a *adj & nm, f* Bulgarian

bulimia *nf* MED bulimia

bulímico, -a *adj & nm, f* MED bulimic; **trastorno bulímico** bulimic episode

bulín *nm* RP Fam [picadero] bachelor pad

bulla *nf* Fam **a)** [ruido] racket, uproar; **armar bulla** to kick up a racket **b)** Esp [prisa] **meter bulla a algn** to hurry sb up

bullicio *nm* [de ciudad, mercado] hustle and bustle; [de multitud] hubbub

bullicioso, -a 1. *adj* **a)** [agitado - reunión, multitud] noisy; [calle, mercado] busy, bustling **b)** [inquieto] rowdy, boisterous **2.** *nm, f* boisterous person

bulto *nm* **a)** [cosa indistinta] shape, form **b)** [maleta, caja] piece of luggage **c)** MED lump **d) hacer mucho bulto** to be very bulky; Fam **escurrir el bulto** to pass the buck

bumerán *nm* boomerang

bungalow [bunga'lo] *(pl* **bungalows***) nm* bungalow

búnker *nm* **a)** [refugio] bunker **b)** Esp POL reactionary forces

buñuelo *nm* doughnut

BUP *nm (abr de* **Bachillerato Unificado Polivalente***) formerly, academically orientated Spanish secondary school course for pupils aged 14-17*

buque *nm* ship; **buque de guerra** warship; **buque de pasajeros** liner, passenger ship; **buque insignia** flagship

burbuja *nf* bubble; **hacer burbujas** to bubble, make bubbles

burdel *nm* brothel

burger *(pl* **burgers***),* **búrguer** *(pl* **búrguers***) nm* Fam burger bar, fast-food restaurant

burgués, -esa *adj & nm, f* bourgeois

burguesía *nf* bourgeoisie

burla *nf* gibe, jeer; **hacer burla de algo / algn** to make fun of sth / sb; **hacer burla a algn** to stick one's tongue out at sb

burlar 1. *vt* **a)** [engañar] to deceive **b)** [eludir] to dodge, to evade **2. burlarse** *vpr* to make fun (**de** of), to laugh (**de** at)

buró *nm* **a)** POL executive committee **b)** [escritorio] bureau, desk **c)** Méx [mesa de noche] bedside table

burrada *nf* [comentario] stupid o foolish remark; [hecho] stupid o foolish act

burrito *nm* Méx CULIN burrito

burro, -a 1. *adj* Fam **a)** [necio] stupid, dumb **b)** [obstinado] stubborn **2.** *nm, f* **a)** donkey, ass; **burro de carga** dogsbody, drudge; Fam & Fig **bajarse del burro** to climb o back down; Fam **no ver tres en un burro** to be as blind as a bat **b)** Fam [estúpido] dimwit, blockhead

bus *nm* AUTO & INFORM bus

buscador, -a 1. *nm, f* [en general] hunter; **buscador de oro** gold prospector **2.** *nm* INFORM [en Internet] search engine

buscar [44] **1.** *vt* **a)** to look o search for; **buscar una palabra en el diccionario** to look up a word in the dictionary **b)** INFORM to search **c)** **ir a buscar algo** to go and get sth, to fetch sth; **fue a buscarme a la estación** she picked me up at the station **2. buscarse** *vpr Fam* **buscarse la vida** to try and earn one's living; *Fam* **te la estás buscando** you're asking for it; **se busca** [en anuncios] wanted

buseta *nf Col, CRica, Ecuad, Ven* minibus

busto *nm* bust

butaca *nf* **a)** [sillón] armchair, easy chair **b)** CINE & TEATRO seat; **butaca de platea** o **patio** seat in the stalls

butano *nm* butane; **(gas) butano** butane gas

butifarra *nf* sausage

buzo *nm* **a)** [persona] diver **b)** *Arg* [sudadera] sweatshirt **c)** *Col, Urug* [jersey] sweater, *Br* jumper

buzón *nm* post box, *Br* letter box, *US* mailbox; INFORM [de correo electrónico] (electronic) mailbox; **echar una carta al buzón** to *Br* post o *US* mail a letter; **buzón de voz** voice mail

buzz *nm* INTERNET buzz

byte ['bait] *nm* INFORM byte

C

C SMS *written abbr of* **se**; *written abbr of* **sé**

c / a) *(abr de* **calle)** St, Rd **b)** *(abr de* **cargo)** cargo, freight **c)** *(abr de* **cuenta)** a /c

cabal 1. *adj* **a)** [exacto] exact, precise **b)** [honesto] honest, upright **2.** *nmpl Fam* **no está en sus cabales** he's not in his right mind

cabalgar [42] *vt & vi* to ride

cabalgata *nf* cavalcade; **la cabalgata de los Reyes Magos** the procession of the Three Wise Men

caballa *nf* mackerel

caballería *nf* **a)** [cabalgadura] mount, steed **b)** MIL cavalry

caballero *nm* **a)** gentleman; **¿qué desea, caballero?** can I help you, sir?; **ropa de caballero** menswear **b)** HIST knight **c) caballeros** [en letrero] gents

caballete *nm* **a)** [de pintor] easel **b)** TÉC trestle **c)** [de nariz] bridge

caballito *nm* **a) caballito de mar** seahorse **b) caballitos** merry-go-round, *US* carousel

caballo *nm* **a)** horse; **a caballo** on horseback; **montar a caballo** to ride; *Fig* **a caballo entre** ... halfway between ... **b)** TÉC **caballo de vapor** horsepower **c)** [pieza de ajedrez] knight **d)** NAIPES queen **e)** *Fam* [heroína] horse, smack

cabaña *nf* cabin

cabaret *(pl* **cabarets)** *nm* cabaret

cabecear 1. *vi* to nod **2.** *vt* DEP to head

cabecera *nf* **a)** [de fila, mesa] head; [de cama] headboard **b)** *Esp* [de texto] heading; [de periódico] masthead

cabecilla *nmf* leader

cabellera *nf* head of hair

cabello *nm* **a)** hair **b)** CULIN **cabello de ángel** *sweet made of gourd and syrup*

caber [9] *vi* **a)** to fit, to be (able to be) contained; **cabe en el maletero** it fits in the boot; **¿cabemos todos?** is there room for all of us?; **en este coche / jarro caben** ... this car / jug holds ...; **no caber en sí de** [alegría etc] to be beside oneself with; **no cabe por la puerta** it won't go through the door; **no me cabe en la cabeza** I can't understand it; **no cabe duda** there is no doubt; **cabe la posibilidad de que** ... there is a possibility o chance that ...

b) [ser posible] **dentro de lo que cabe** [dentro de lo posible] under the circumstances; [después de todo] all things considered

c) [ser necesario] **cabe señalar que** ... we should point out that ...

d) MAT **doce entre cuatro caben a tres** four into twelve goes three (times)

cabestrillo *nm* sling

cabeza 1. *nf* head; **cabeza de ajo** garlic bulb; **cabeza de turco** scapegoat; **el cabeza de familia** the head of the family; **alzar** o **levantar cabeza** to turn the corner, to get back on one's feet; *Fig* **a la cabeza de** at the front o top of; **en cabeza** in the lead; *Fig* **estar mal de la cabeza** to be a mental case; *Esp Fam* **llevar de cabeza a algn** to drive sb mad; **perder la cabeza** to go mad; *Méx* **quebrarse la cabeza** to rack one's brains; **romperse la cabeza** to rack one's brains; **por cabeza** a head, per person; **sentar la cabeza** to settle down **2.** *nm* **cabeza rapada** skinhead

cabezada *nf* **a)** [golpe] butt, blow on the head **b)** *Fam* **echar una cabezada** to have a snooze; **dar cabezadas** to nod

cabida *nf* capacity; **dar cabida a** to leave room for

cabina *nf* cabin; **cabina telefónica** [con puerta] *Br* phone box, *US* phone booth

cabinero, -a *nm, f Col* flight attendant

cable *nm* cable; *Fam* **echarle un cable a algn** to give sb a hand

cableado *nm* wiring

cabo *nm* a) [extremo] end; **al cabo de** after; **de cabo a rabo** from start to finish b) MIL corporal; [policía] sergeant c) NÁUT rope, cable; *Fig* **atar cabos** to put two and two together; *Fig* **no dejar ningún cabo suelto** to leave no loose ends d) GEOGR cape; **Ciudad del Cabo** Cape Town; **Cabo Verde** Cape Verde

cabra *nf* goat; *Fam* **estar como una cabra** to be off one's head

cabré *indic futuro ver* **caber**

cabreado, -a *adj muy Fam* **cabreado con** really annoyed with

cabrear *muy Fam* **1.** *vt* to make angry, *Br* to piss off **2. cabrearse** *vpr* to get, *Br* pissed off o *US* pissed

cabreo *nm muy Fam* rage, fit; **agarrar** o *Esp* **coger un cabreo** to get really *Br* narked o *US* pissed

cabrito *nm* ZOOL kid

cabro, -a *nm, f Chile Fam* kid

cabrón, -ona 1. *adj Vulg* [para insultar] bloody **2.** *nm, f* a) *Vulg* bastard, *f* bitch, *US* asshole b) *Méx muy Fam* [individuo] guy, *f* girl **3.** *nm Vulg* [cornudo] cuckold

cabronada *nf Vulg* dirty trick

cabuya *nf* a) [planta] agave b) [fibra] hemp fibre c) *CAm, Col, Ven* [cuerda] rope

caca *nf Fam Br* poo, *US* poop

cacahuete, *CAm, Méx* **cacahuate** *nm* peanut, *US* groundnut

cacao *nm* a) BOT cacao b) [polvo, bebida] cocoa c) *Fam* [lío] mess

cacarear 1. *vi* [gallina] to cluck **2.** *vt Fig* to boast about

cacería *nf* a) [actividad] hunting, shooting b) [partida] hunt, shoot

cacerola *nf* saucepan

cachaco, -a *Col* **1.** *adj* from Bogotá **2.** *nm, f* native or inhabitant of Bogotá

cachalote *nm* sperm whale

cachar *vt Am Fam* a) [sorprender] to surprise b) [atrapar] to catch

cacharro *nm* a) earthenware pot o jar b) *Fam* [cosa] thing, piece of junk c) **cacharros** [de cocina] pots and pans

cachear *vt* to frisk, to search

cachemir *nm* cashmere

cachemira *nf* = **cachemir**

cachetada *nf* slap

cachete *nm* a) [bofetada] slap b) *Am* [mejilla] cheek

cachila *nf RP* [automóvil] vintage car

cachimba *nf* a) [pipa] pipe b) *RP* [pozo] well

cachivache *nm Fam* thing, knick-knack

cacho¹ *nm Fam* [pedazo] bit, piece; *Esp* ¡**cacho tonto!** you idiot!

cacho² *nm* a) *Andes, Ven* [asta] horn b) *Andes, Guat, Ven* [cuento] story; **no me vengan a contar cachos, que sé lo que pasó** don't start telling me stories, I know what happened c) *Andes, Guat, Ven* [burla] joke

cachondearse *vpr Esp Fam* **cachondearse de algn** to make a fool out of sb, *Br* to take the mickey out of sb

cachondeo *nm Esp Fam* **estar de cachondeo** [divertirse] to be having a great time; [bromear] to be having a laugh, to be joking around; **ser un cachondeo** to be a laugh; **tomarse algo a cachondeo** to take sth as a joke

cachondo, -a 1. *adj* a) *Esp Fam* [divertido, gracioso] **ser cachondo** to be funny b) *Esp, Méx muy Fam* [excitado sexualmente] **estar cachondo** to be horny; **ponerse cachondo** to get randy o turned on **2.** *nm, f* a) [gracioso] gas b) [excitado] horny devil

cachorro, -a *nm, f* [de perro] pup, puppy; [de gato] kitten; [de otros animales] cub, baby

cacique *nm* [jefe] local boss

cacto *nm* BOT cactus

cactus *nm inv* = **cacto**

cada *adj* [de dos] each; [de varios] each, every; **cada día** every day; **cada dos días** every second day; **cada vez más** more and more; **¿cada cuánto?** how often?; **cada dos por tres** every other minute; **cuatro de cada diez** four out of (every) ten; **¡tienes cada cosa!** you come up with some fine ideas!

cadáver *nm* [de persona] corpse, (dead) body; [de animal] body, carcass; **ingresar cadáver** to be dead on arrival

cadena *nf* a) chain; [correa de perro] lead, leash b) TV channel c) INDUST line; **cadena de montaje** assembly line; **trabajo en cadena** assembly line work d) GEOGR **cadena montañosa** mountain range e) JUR **cadena perpetua** life imprisonment f) AUTO **cadenas** tyre chains

cadencia *nf* rhythm; MÚS cadenza

cadera *nf* hip

cadete 1. *nm* [en ejército] cadet 2. *nm, f RP* [chico de los recados] office junior

caducado, -a *adj* expired

caducar [44] *vi* to expire

caducidad *nf* expiry; **fecha de caducidad** [en alimento, medicamento] use-by date

caduco, -a *adj* a) BOT deciduous b) [anticuado] out-of-date

caer [39] 1. *vi* a) to fall; **dejar caer** to drop; *Fig* **está al caer** [llegar] he'll arrive any minute now; [ocurrir] it's on the way b) [fecha] to be; **su cumpleaños cae en sábado** his birthday falls on a Saturday c) [entender] to understand, to see; **ya caigo** I get it; **no caí** I didn't twig d) *Esp* [estar, quedar] **cae cerca de aquí** it's not far from here e) **me cae bien/mal** I like/don't like her 2. **caerse** *vpr* to fall (down); **me caí de la moto** I fell off the motorbike; **se le cayó el pañuelo** she dropped her handkerchief

café *nm* a) coffee; **café con leche** white coffe; *Esp* **café solo**, *Andes*, *Ven* **café tinto** black coffee b) [cafetería] café

cafeína *nf* caffeine

cafetera *nf* coffee-maker

cafetería *nf* snack bar, coffee bar; FERROC buffet car

cafiche *nm Andes Fam* [proxeneta] pimp

cagar [42] *Fam* 1. *vi* to shit, to crap 2. **cagarse** *vpr* to crap oneself; **cagarse de miedo** to be shit-scared

caída *nf* a) fall; [de pelo, diente] loss b) [de precios] drop c) POL downfall, collapse

caído, -a 1. *adj* fallen 2. *nmpl* **los caídos** the fallen

caimán *nm* alligator

caja *nf* a) box; **caja fuerte** safe; *Fam* TV **la caja tonta** the box, *Br* the telly, *US* the boob tube b) [de leche etc] carton c) [de embalaje] crate, case; **una caja de cerveza** a crate of beer d) FIN [en tienda] cash desk; [en banco] cashier's desk e) AUTO **caja de cambios** gearbox f) *Esp* [entidad financiera] **caja de ahorros** savings bank g) [féretro] coffin

cajero, -a *nm, f* cashier; **cajero automático** cash point, cash dispenser

cajetilla *nf* packet, pack

cajón *nm* a) [en un mueble] drawer; *Fig* **cajón de sastre** jumble; *Fam* **de cajón** obvious, self-evident b) [caja grande] crate, chest

cajuela *nf CAm*, *Méx* [maletero] *Br* boot, *US* trunk

cal[1] *nf* lime; *Fig* **a cal y canto** hermetically; *Fam* **una de cal y otra de arena** six of one and half a dozen of the other

cal[2] (*abr de* **caloría**) cal

cala *nf* a) GEOGR creek, cove b) NÁUT hold

calabacín *nm* a) BOT [pequeño] *Br* courgette, *US* zucchini b) [grande] *Br* marrow, *US* squash

calabaza *nf* pumpkin, gourd

calabozo *nm* a) [prisión] jail, prison b) [celda] cell

calada *nf Esp Fam* [de cigarrillo] drag, puff

calamar *nm* squid *inv*; CULIN **calamares a la romana** squid fried in batter

calambre *nm* a) ELEC [descarga] electric shock; **ese cable da calambre** that wire is live b) [en músculo] cramp

calamidad *nf* calamity

calar 1. *vt* **a)** [mojar] to soak, to drench **b)** [agujerear] to pierce, to penetrate **2.** *vi* **a)** [prenda] to let in water **b)** NÁUT to draw **3. calarse** *vpr* **a)** [prenda, techo] to let in water; [mojarse] to get soaked **b)** [el sombrero] to pull down **c)** *Esp* [motor] to stall

calavera 1. *nf* **a)** [cráneo] skull **b)** *Méx* AUTO **calaveras** tail lights **2.** *nm* tearaway

calcar [44] *vt* **a)** [un dibujo] to trace **b)** *Fig* [imitar] to copy, to imitate

calcetín *nm* sock

calcio *nm* calcium

calcomanía *nf* transfer

calculador, -a *adj también Fig* calculating

calculadora *nf* calculator

calcular *vt* **a)** MAT to calculate **b)** [evaluar] to (make an) estimate **c)** [suponer] to figure, to guess

cálculo *nm* **a)** calculation; **según mis cálculos** by my reckoning **b)** MED gallstone **c)** MAT calculus

caldear *vt* to heat up

caldera *nf* **a)** [industrial] boiler; [olla] cauldron **b)** *Urug* [hervidor] kettle

calderilla *nf* small change

caldo *nm* stock, broth; **caldo de cultivo** culture medium; *Fig* breeding ground

calefacción *nf* heating; **calefacción central** central heating

calefaccionar *vt CSur* [calentar] to heat (up), to warm (up)

calefactor *nm* heater

calefón *nm CSur* [calentador] water heater

calendario *nm* calendar

calentador *nm* heater

calentamiento *nm* DEP warm-up

calentar [1] **1.** *vt* **a)** [agua, horno] to heat; [comida, habitación] to warm up; *Fig* **no me calientes la cabeza** don't bug me **b)** *Fam* [pegar] to smack **c)** *Fam* [excitar] to arouse (sexually), to turn

on **2. calentarse** *vpr* **a)** to get hot o warm, to heat up **b)** *Fig* **se calentaron los ánimos** people became very excited

calesita *nf RP* merry-go-round, *US* carousel

calibración *nf* calibration

calibrar *vt* to gauge, to bore

calibre *nm* **a)** [de arma] calibre **b)** *Fig* [importancia] importance

calidad *nf* **a)** quality; **de primera calidad** first-class; **un vino de calidad** good-quality wine **b)** **en calidad de** as

cálido, -a *adj* warm; **una cálida acogida** a warm welcome

caliente *adj* **a)** hot **b)** *Fig* [debate] heated; **en caliente** in the heat of the moment **c)** *Fam* [cachondo] hot, randy

calificación *nf* **a)** qualification **b)** EDUC *Br* mark, *US* grade

calificar [44] *vt* **a)** to describe (**de** as); **le calificó de inmoral** he called him immoral **b)** [examen] to mark, to grade

caligrafía *nf* calligraphy; [modo de escribir] handwriting

calimocho *nm Esp* calimocho (*red wine and coke cocktail*)

cáliz *nm* chalice

callado, -a *adj* quiet; **te lo tenías muy callado** you were keeping that quiet

callar 1. *vi* **a)** [dejar de hablar] to stop talking; **¡calla!** be quiet!, *Fam* shut up! **b)** [no hablar] to keep quiet, to say nothing **2.** *vt* [noticia] not to mention, to keep to oneself **3. callarse** *vpr* to stop talking, to be quiet; **¡cállate!** shut up!

calle *nf* **a)** street, road; **calle de dirección única** one-way street; **calle mayor** *Br* high street, *US* main street; **el hombre de la calle** the man in the street; **dejar a algn en la calle** o **echar a algn a la calle** to throw sb out (on the street) **b)** *Esp* DEP [en pista de atletismo, piscina] lane

calleja *nf* narrow street

callejero, -a 1. *nm* [mapa] street directory **2.** *adj* street ; **gato callejero** alley cat

callejón *nm* back alley o street ; **callejón sin salida** cul-de-sac, dead end

callejuela *nf* narrow street, lane

callo *nm* a) MED callus, corn ; *Fam* **dar el callo** to slog b) *Esp* CULIN **callos** tripe

calma *nf* a) calm ; **¡calma!** calm down! ; **en calma** calm ; **tómatelo con calma** take it easy b) METEOR calm weather ; **calma chicha** dead calm

calmante *nm* painkiller

calmar 1. *vt* [persona] to calm (down) ; [dolor] to soothe, to relieve **2. calmarse** *vpr* a) [persona] to calm down b) [dolor, viento] to ease off

calor *nm* a) heat ; **hace calor** it's hot ; **tengo calor** I'm hot ; **entrar en calor** to warm up b) *Fig* [afecto] warmth

caloría *nf* calorie

calote *nm* *RP Fam* swindle

calumnia *nf* a) calumny b) JUR slander

calumniador, -a 1. *adj* slanderous **2.** *nm, f* slanderer

calumniar [43] *vt* a) to calumniate b) JUR to slander

calumnioso, -a *adj* [de palabra] slanderous ; [por escrito] libellous

caluroso, -a *adj* hot ; [acogida etc] warm

calva *nf* bald patch

calvario *nm* [vía crucis] Calvary, Stations of the Cross ; *Fig* [sufrimiento] ordeal

calvicie *nf* baldness

calvo, -a 1. *adj* bald ; **ni tanto ni tan calvo** neither one extreme nor the other **2.** *nm* bald man

calzada *nf* road (surface), *US* pavement

calzado *nm* shoes, footwear

calzador *nm* shoehorn

calzar [40] **1.** *vt* a) [poner calzado] to put shoes on ; **¿qué número calzas?** what size do you take? b) [mueble] to wedge **2. calzarse** *vpr* **calzarse los zapatos** to put on one's shoes

calzón *nm* a) *Esp* DEP shorts b) *Andes, Méx, RP* [bragas] panties, *Br* knickers ; **un calzón, unos calzones** a pair of panties o *Br* knickers c) *Bol, Méx* **calzones** [calzoncillos] *Br* underpants, *US* shorts

calzoncillos *nmpl* [slip] briefs, *Br* (under)pants, *US* shorts ; [bóxer] boxer shorts

calzoneta *nm* *CAm* swimming trunks

cama *nf* bed ; **cama doble / individual** double / single bed ; **cama turca** couch ; **estar en** o **guardar cama** to be confined to bed ; *Am Fam* **estar** o **quedar de cama** *Br* to be knackered, to be dead tired ; **hacer la cama** to make the bed ; **irse a la cama** to go to bed

camaleón *nm* chameleon

cámara 1. *nf* a) [aparato] camera ; **a cámara lenta** in slow motion b) POL Chamber, House ; **Cámara Alta / Baja** Upper / Lower House c) AUTO inner tube d) [habitación] room, chamber ; **cámara de gas** gas chamber ; **cámara frigorífica** cold-storage room ; **música de cámara** chamber music **2.** *nmf* cameraman, *f* camerawoman

camarada *nmf* comrade

camarero, -a *nm, f* a) [de restaurante] waiter, *f* waitress ; [tras la barra] barman, *f* barmaid b) [de avión] flight attendant

camarista *nf* *Méx* [en hotel] chambermaid

camarón *nm* *Br* shrimp, *US* prawn

camarote *nm* cabin

camarotero *nm* *Am* cabin steward (on cruise liners)

camastro *nm* ramshackle bed

camba *Bol Fam* **1.** *adj* of / from the forested lowland region of Bolivia **2.** *nmf* person from the forested lowland region of Bolivia

cambalache *nm* *RP* [tienda] junk shop

cambiar [43] **1.** *vt* a) to change ; **cambiar algo de sitio** to move sth b) [intercambiar] to swap, to exchange c) [dinero] to change

2. *vi* to change; **cambiar de casa** to move (house); **cambiar de idea** to change one's mind; **cambiar de trabajo** to get another job; **cambiar de velocidad** to change gear

3. cambiarse *vpr* **a)** [de ropa] to change (clothes) **b)** [de casa] to move (house)

---

cambio *nm* **a)** change; [de impresiones] exchange; **cambio de planes** change of plans; **un cambio en la opinión pública** a shift in public opinion; *Fig* **a cambio de** in exchange for; **en cambio** on the other hand **b)** [dinero] change; **¿tienes cambio de cinco euros?** have you got change for five euros? **c)** FIN [de divisas] exchange; [de acciones] price; **libre cambio** free trade **d)** AUTO gear change; **cambio automático** automatic transmission

cambur *nm Ven* [plátano] banana

camello, -a 1. *nm, f* camel **2.** *nm Fam* [traficante de drogas] (drug) pusher

camellón *nm Col, Méx* [en avenida] *Br* central reservation, *US* median (strip)

camembert ['kamember] (*pl* **camemberts**) *nm* camembert

camerino *nm* dressing room

camilla *nf* **a)** stretcher **b)** **mesa camilla** *small round table under which a heater is placed*

camillero, -a *nm, f* stretcher-bearer

caminante *nmf* walker

caminar 1. *vi* to walk **2.** *vt* to cover, to travel; **caminaron 10 km** they walked for 10 km

caminata *nf* long walk; DEP **caminata nórdica** Nordic walking

camino *nm* **a)** [ruta] route, way; **ir camino de** to be going to; **ponerse en camino** to set off; *Fig* **ir por buen/mal camino** to be on the right/wrong track; **abrirse camino** to break through; **a medio camino** half-way; **en el camino a, de camino a** on the way to; **estar en camino** to be on the way; **nos coge o pilla de camino** it is on the way **b)** [vía] path, track **c)** [modo] way

camión *nm* **a)** truck, *Br* lorry; **camión cisterna** tanker; **camión de la basura** *Br* dustcart, *US* garbage truck; **camión frigorífico** refrigerated truck **b)** *CAm, Méx* [autobús] bus

camionero, -a *nm, f Br* lorry driver, *US* trucker

camioneta *nf* van

camisa *nf* shirt; **en mangas de camisa** in one's shirtsleeves; **camisa de fuerza** straitjacket

camisería *nf* [tienda] shirt shop, outfitter's

camisero, -a *nm, f* [persona] shirtmaker

camiseta *nf* **a)** [ropa interior] *Br* vest, *US* undershirt **b)** [de manga corta] T-shirt **c)** DEP [de tirantes] vest; [con mangas] shirt; **sudar la camiseta** to run oneself into the ground

camisola *nf* **a)** [prenda interior] camisole **b)** DEP sports shirt

camisón *nm* nightdress, *Fam* nightie

camomila *nf* camomile

camorra *nf Fam* trouble

camote *nm* **a)** *Andes, CAm, Méx* [batata] sweet potato; [bulbo] tuber, bulb **b)** *Méx Fam* [complicación] mess; **meterse en un camote** to get into a mess o pickle

campamento *nm* camp

campana *nf* bell; **pantalones de campana** bell-bottom trousers

campanario *nm* belfry, bell tower

campaña *nf* **a)** campaign; **campaña electoral** election campaign; **campaña publicitaria** advertising campaign **b)** MIL campaign; **hospital/ambulancia de campaña** field hospital/ambulance **c)** *RP* [campo] countryside

campechano, -a *adj* unpretentious

campeón, -ona *nm, f* champion; **campeón mundial** world champion

campeonato *nm* championship; **un tonto de campeonato** an utter idiot

campera *nf* **a)** *Esp* [bota] cowboy boot **b)** *RP* [chaqueta] jacket

campero, -a *adj* country; **bota campera** cowboy boot

campesino, **-a** *nm, f* countryman, *f* countrywoman

campestre *adj* rural

cámping *(pl* **cámpings***) nm* campsite, *US* campground; **hacer** *o* **ir de cámping** to go camping

campista *nmf* camper

campo *nm* **a)** country, countryside; **a campo través** cross-country; **jugar en campo contrario** to play away; **trabaja (en) el campo** he works (on) the land; **trabajo de campo** fieldwork **b)** [parcela] field **c)** FÍS & FOTO field **d)** [ámbito] field; **campo de acción** field of action; MIL **campo de batalla** battlefield; **campo de concentración** concentration camp; **campo de trabajo** [para prisioneros] *Br* labour camp, *US* labor camp; **campo visual** field of vision **e)** *Esp* DEP [de fútbol] pitch; [de golf] course **f)** *RP* [hacienda] farm, ranch **g)** *Andes* [sitio] room, space

campus *nm inv* campus

camuflar *vt* to camouflage

cana *nf* [gris] grey hair; [blanca] white hair; **tener canas** to have grey hair; *Fam* **echar una cana al aire** to let one's hair down

Canadá *n* Canada

canadiense *adj & nmf* Canadian

canal *nf* **a)** [artificial] canal; [natural] channel; **Canal de la Mancha** English Channel **b)** TV, ELEC & INFORM channel

canalla **1.** *nm* swine, rotter **2.** *nf* riff-raff, mob

canapé *nm* **a)** CULIN canapé **b)** [sofá] couch, sofa

Canarias *nfpl* **las (islas) Canarias** the Canary Islands, the Canaries

canario, **-a** **1.** *adj & nm, f* Canarian **2.** *nm* ORNIT canary

canasta *nf* basket

canastilla *nf* small basket; [de un bebé] layette

cancán *nm* frilly petticoat; *RP* **cancanes** [leotardos] *Br* tights, *US* pantyhose *(pl)*

cancela *nf* wrought-iron gate

cancelación *nf* cancellation

cancelar *vt* **a)** [acto etc] to cancel **b)** [deuda] to pay off **c)** *Chile, Ven* [compra] to pay for

cáncer *nm* cancer; **cáncer de pulmón/mama** lung/breast cancer

Cáncer *nm* Cancer

cancerígeno, **-a** *adj* carcinogenic

cancha *nf* DEP [de tenis] court; *Am* **cancha de césped** grass court

canciller *nm* chancellor

cancillería *nf* [de asuntos exteriores] foreign ministry

canción *nf* song

cancionero *nm* songbook

candado *nm* padlock

candela *nf* fire

candelabro *nm* candelabrum

candidato, **-a** *nm, f* candidate; [a un puesto] applicant

candidatura *nf* **a)** [lista] list of candidates **b)** **presentar su candidatura** to submit one's application

candil *nm* oil lamp; *Méx* [candelabro] chandelier

candilejas *nfpl* TEATRO footlights

canela *nf* cinnamon

canelones *nmpl* CULIN cannelloni

cangrejo *nm* [de mar] crab; [de río] freshwater crayfish

canguro **1.** *nm* kangaroo **2.** *nmf Esp Fam* baby-sitter

caníbal *adj & nmf* cannibal

canica *nf* marble

canijo, **-a** *adj Fam* puny, weak

canilla *nf* **a)** *Fam* [espinilla] shinbone **b)** *RP* [grifo] *Br* tap, *US* faucet **c)** *Méx* [fuerza] strength

canillera *nf Am* [temblor de piernas] **tenía canillera** his legs were trembling *o* shaking

canillita *nm RP* newspaper vendor

canje *nm* exchange

canjeable *adj* exchangeable

canjear *vt* to exchange

cano, **-a** *adj* [pelo, barba] white

canoa *nf* canoe

canon *nm* **a)** canon, norm **b)** MÚS & REL canon **c)** COM royalty

canónico, -a *adj* canonical; JUR **derecho canónico** canon law

canoso, -a *adj* [de pelo blanco] white-haired; [de pelo gris] grey-haired; [pelo] white, grey

cansado, -a *adj* **a)** [agotado] tired, weary; **estar cansado** to be tired **b) ser cansado** [pesado] to be boring o tiresome

cansador, -a *adj* Andes, RP [que cansa] tiring; [que aburre] boring

cansancio *nm* tiredness, weariness; *Fam* **estoy muerto de cansancio** I'm on my last legs

cansar 1. *vt* to tire **2.** *vi* to be tiring **3. cansarse** *vpr* to get tired; **se cansó de esperar** he got fed up (with) waiting

cantábrico, -a *adj* Cantabrian; **Mar Cantábrico** Bay of Biscay

cantaleta *nf Am* **la misma cantaleta** the same old story

cantante 1. *nmf* singer **2.** *adj* singing; **llevar la voz cantante** to rule the roost

cantaor, -a *nm, f* flamenco singer

cantar¹ *vt & vi* **a)** MÚS to sing; *Fig* **en menos que canta un gallo** in a flash **b)** *Fam* [confesar] to sing, to spill the beans **c)** *Esp muy Fam* [apestar] to stink

cantar² *nm* LITER song; *Fam* **¡eso es otro cantar!** that's a totally different thing!

cántaro *nm* pitcher; *Fig* **llover a cántaros** to rain cats and dogs

cantautor, -a *nm, f* singer-songwriter

cante *nm* **a)** [canto] singing; **cante hondo** o **jondo** *traditional gipsy flamenco song* **b)** *Esp Fam* **dar el cante** to attract attention

cantegril *nm Urug* shanty town

cantera *nf* **a)** [de piedra] quarry **b)** *Fig* FÚT young players

cantero *nm* **a)** [masón] stonemason **b)** *Cuba, RP* [parterre] flowerbed

cantidad 1. *nf* quantity; [de dinero] amount, sum; **en cantidad** a lot; *Fam* **cantidad de gente** thousands of people **2.** *adv Esp Fam* a lot; **me gusta cantidad** I really like it a lot

cantimplora *nf* water bottle

cantina *nf* canteen

canto¹ *nm* **a)** [arte] singing **b)** [canción] song

canto² *nm* [borde] edge; **de canto** on its side

canto³ *nm* [guijarro] pebble, stone; **canto rodado** [grande] boulder; [pequeño] pebble

canturrear *vi* to hum, to croon

canutas *nfpl Esp Fam* **pasarlas canutas** to go through a tough time

caña *nf* **a)** *Esp* [de cerveza] small glass of beer **b)** BOT reed; [tallo] cane, stem; **caña de azúcar** sugar cane **c)** [de pescar] rod **d)** *Fam* **darle caña al coche** to go at full speed **e)** *Andes, Cuba, RP* [aguardiente] caña *(type of rum made using sugar cane spirit)*

cáñamo *nm* hemp

cañaveral *nm* reedbed

cañería *nf* (piece of) piping; **cañerías** plumbing

cañero, -a *nm, f Am* [trabajador] sugar plantation worker; [propietario] sugar plantation owner

caño *nm* [tubo] tube; [tubería] pipe

cañón *nm* **a)** cannon; *Fig* **estar siempre al pie del cañón** to be always ready for a fight **b)** [de fusil] barrel **c)** GEOGR canyon

cañonazo *nm* gunshot

caoba *nf* mahogany

caos *nm inv* chaos

caótico, -a *adj* chaotic

capa *nf* **a)** [prenda] cloak, cape; **de capa caída** low-spirited **b)** [de pintura] layer, coat; CULIN coating **c)** GEOL stratum, layer

capacidad *nf* **a)** [cabida] capacity **b)** [aptitud] capacity, ability

capacitador, -a *adj & nm, f Am* [entrenador] trainer

caparazón *nm* shell

capataz, -a *nm, f* foreman, *f* fore-woman

capaz 1. *adj* capable, able; **ser capaz de hacer algo** [tener la habilidad de] to be able to do sth; [atreverse a] to dare to do sth; **si se entera es capaz de despedirle** if he finds out he could quite easily sack him **2.** *adv Andes, RP Fam* [tal vez] maybe

capazo *nm* large wicker basket

capellán *nm* chaplain

capicúa *adj* **número capicúa** reversible number; **palabra capicúa** palindrome

capilar *adj* hair; **loción capilar** hair lotion

capilla *nf* chapel; **capilla ardiente** chapel of rest

capital 1. *nf* capital
2. *nm* FIN capital; **capital activo** *o* **social** working *o* share capital
3. *adj* capital, main; **de importancia capital** of capital importance; **pena capital** capital punishment

capitalismo *nm* capitalism

capitalista *adj* & *nmf* capitalist

capitán, -ana *nm, f* captain; **capitán general** *Br* field marshal, *US* general of the army

capitanía *nf* a) MIL [empleo] captaincy b) [oficina] military headquarters; **capitanía general** Captaincy General

capitel *nm* ARQUIT capital

capítulo *nm* a) [de libro] chapter b) *Fig* **dentro del capítulo de ...** [tema] under the heading of ...

capó *nm* AUTO *Br* bonnet, *US* hood

capón *nm* rap on the head with the knuckles

capota *nf* AUTO *Br* convertible roof, *US* convertible top

capote *nm* a) TAUROM cape b) MIL greatcoat

capricho *nm* a) [antojo] whim, caprice b) MÚS caprice, capriccio

caprichoso, -a *adj* whimsical

Capricornio *nm* Capricorn

cápsula *nf* capsule

captar *vt* a) [ondas] to receive, to pick up b) [comprender] to understand, to grasp c) [interés etc] to attract

capturar *vt* [criminal] to capture; [cazar, pescar] to catch; MIL to seize

capucha *nf* hood

capuchino *nm* [café] cappuccino

capullo 1. *nm* a) [de insecto] cocoon
b) [de flor] bud
c) *Esp Vulg* [glande] head
2. *nm, f Esp muy Fam* [persona despreciable] jerk, *Br* dickhead

cara 1. *nf* a) face; **cara a cara** face to face; **cara a la pared** facing the wall; **decir algo a algn a la** *o* **en cara** to say sth to sb to their face; **me daba el sol de cara** I had the sun in my eyes; **poner mala cara** to pull a long face; **tener buena/mala cara** to look good/bad; *Fig* **cara de circunstancias** serious look; *Fig* **dar la cara** to face the consequences (of one's acts); *Fig* **dar la cara por algn** to stand up for sb; *Fig* **(de) cara a** with a view to; *Fig* **echarle a algn algo en cara** to reproach sb for sth b) [lado] side; [de moneda] right side; **¿cara o cruz?** heads or tails?; **echar algo a cara o cruz** to toss (a coin) for sth, *US* to flip (a coin) for sth c) *Fam* [desfachatez] cheek, nerve; **¡qué cara (más dura) tienes!** what a cheek you've got! **2.** *nm Fam* [desvergonzado] cheeky person

carabela *nf* caravel

carabina *nf* a) [arma] carbine, rifle b) [persona] chaperon

carabinero *nm* a) [marisco] scarlet shrimp *(type of large red prawn)* b) *Chile* [policía] military policeman

caracol 1. *nm* a) [de tierra] snail; *Am* shell b) [rizo] kiss-curl **2.** *interj* **¡caracoles!** good heavens!

caracola *nf* conch

caracolada *nf* CULIN *stew made with snails*

carácter *(pl* **caracteres)** *nm* a) [temperamento] character; **de mucho ca-**

rácter with a strong character; **tener buen / mal carácter** to be good-natured / bad-tempered **b)** *Fig* [índole] nature; **con carácter de invitado** as a guest **c)** IMPR character

característica *nf* characteristic

característico, -a *adj* characteristic

caracterizar [40] *vt* to characterize

caradura *nmf Fam* cheeky devil; **¡qué caradura eres!** you're so cheeky!

carajillo *nm Fam* coffee with a dash of brandy

caramba *interj Fam* [sorpresa] good heavens!, *Br* blimey!, *US* jeez!; [enfado] for heaven's sake!

carambola *nf Br* cannon, *US* carom

caramelo *nm* **a)** [dulce] *Br* (boiled) sweet, *US* candy **b)** [azúcar quemado] caramel; CULIN **a punto de caramelo** syrupy

caraota *nf Ven* bean

carátula *nf* **a)** [cubierta] cover **b)** [máscara] mask

caravana *nf* **a)** [vehículo] *Br* caravan, *US* trailer **b)** [de tráfico] *Br* tailback, *US* backup **c)** *Urug* [aro, pendiente] earring

caray *interj* [sorpresa] good heavens!, *Br* blimey!, *US* jeez!; [enfado] for heaven's sake!

carbón *nm* coal; **carbón vegetal** charcoal; **carbón mineral** coal

carboncillo *nm* charcoal

carbono *nm* carbon

carburador *nm* carburettor

carburante *nm* fuel

carcajada *nf* guffaw

cárcel *nf* prison, jail

carcoma *nf* woodworm

cardenal *nm* **a)** REL cardinal **b)** MED bruise

cardiaco, -a, cardíaco, -a 1. *adj* cardiac, heart; **ataque cardiaco** heart attack **2.** *nm, f* person with a heart condition

cardinal *adj* cardinal; **punto / número cardinal** cardinal point / number

cardiólogo, -a *nm, f* cardiologist

cardo *nm* [con espinas] thistle

carecer [33] *vi* **carecer de** to lack

carencia *nf* lack (**de** of)

careta *nf* mask; **careta antigás** gas mask

carey *nm* tortoiseshell

carga *nf* **a)** [acción] loading **b)** [cosa cargada] load; [de avión, barco] cargo, freight; *Fig* **carga afectiva** emotional content **c)** FIN [gasto] debit; **carga fiscal** tax charge **d)** *Fig* [obligación] burden **e)** MIL & ELEC charge

cargado, -a *adj* **a)** loaded **b)** [bebida] strong; **un café cargado** a strong coffee **c)** [ambiente] heavy; **atmósfera cargada** stuffy atmosphere **d)** *Fig* burdened; **cargado de deudas** up to one's eyes in debt **e)** ELEC charged

cargador *nm* **a)** [de arma] chamber **b)** [persona] loader; **cargador de muelle** docker, stevedore **c)** [de baterías] charger

cargar [42] **1.** *vt* **a)** to load; [mechero, pluma] to fill; [batería] to charge; *Fig* **cargar las culpas a algn** to put the blame on sb
b) COM to charge; **cárguelo a mi cuenta** charge it to my account
c) INFORM [fichero] to load *(via a server)* **2.** *vi* **a)** **cargar con** [llevar] to carry; *Fig* **cargar con la responsabilidad** to take the responsibility; *Fig* **cargar con las consecuencias** to suffer the consequences
b) MIL **cargar contra** to charge
3. cargarse *vpr* **a)** *Esp Fam* **te la vas a cargar** you're asking for trouble and you're going to get it
b) *Fam* [estropear] to smash, to ruin
c) *Fam* [matar] to kill, to bump off

cargo *nm* **a)** [puesto] post, position; **alto cargo** [puesto] top job, high ranking position; [persona] top person **b)** **estar al cargo de** to be in charge of; **correr a cargo de** [gastos] to be met by; **hacerse cargo de** to take charge of; **hazte cargo de mi situación** please try to understand my situation **c)** FIN charge, debit; **con cargo a mi cuenta** charged to my account **d)** JUR charge, accusation

cargosear *vt CSur* to annoy, to pester

cargoso, -a *adj CSur* annoying

carguero *nm* [barco] cargo

cariado, -a *adj* decayed

Caribe 1. *adj* **el mar Caribe** the Caribbean (Sea) **2.** *nm* **el Caribe** [mar] the Caribbean (Sea); [región] the Caribbean

caribeño, -a 1. *adj* Caribbean **2.** *nm, f* person from the Caribbean

caricatura *nf* caricature

caricia *nf* caress, stroke

caridad *nf* charity

caries *nf inv* decay, caries

cariño *nm* **a)** [amor] affection; **coger / tener cariño a algo / algn** to grow / to be fond of sth /sb; **con cariño** [en carta] love **b)** [apelativo] dear, love, *US* honey **c)** [abrazo] cuddle

cariñoso, -a *adj* loving, affectionate

carisma *nm* charisma

caritativo, -a *adj* charitable

cariz *nm* look

carmín *nm* (de color) carmín carmine; **carmín (de labios)** lipstick

carnal 1. *adj* **a)** [de la carne] carnal **b)** [pariente] first; **primo carnal** first cousin **2.** *nm Méx Fam* [amigo] *Br* mate, *US* buddy

carnaval *nm* carnival

carne *nf* **a)** flesh; *Fam* **ser de carne y hueso** to be only human; *Fig* **carne de cañón** cannon fodder; **carne de gallina** goosepimples; **carne viva** raw flesh **b)** [alimento] meat; **carne de cerdo / cordero / ternera / vaca** pork / lamb / veal / beef; *Esp, RP* **carne picada** [de ternera] mincemeat; [de cerdo] pork **c)** [de fruta] pulp

carné *nm* card; **carné de conducir** *Br* driving licence, *US* driver's license; **carné de identidad** identity card; **carné de socio** membership card

carnear *vt* **a)** *Andes, RP* [sacrificar] to slaughter, to butcher **b)** *Chile* [engañar] to deceive, to take in

carnero *nm* ram; CULIN mutton

carnicería *nf* **a)** butcher's (shop) **b)** *Fig* [masacre] slaughter

carnicero, -a *nm, f* butcher

carnitas *nfpl Méx* small pieces of braised pork

caro, -a 1. *adj* expensive, dear **2.** *adv* **salir caro** to cost a lot; **te costará caro** [amenaza] you'll pay dearly for this

carozo *nm RP* [de fruta, aceituna] stone, *US* pit

carpa *nf* **a)** [pez] carp **b)** [de circo] big top; [en parque, la calle] marquee **c)** *Am* [de tienda de campaña] tent

carpeta *nf* file, folder

carpintería *nf* **a)** [oficio] carpentry; **carpintería metálica** metalwork **b)** [taller] carpenter's (shop)

carpintero, -a *nm, f* carpenter

carrera *nf* **a)** run; **a la carrera** in a hurry **b)** [competición] race; **carrera contra reloj** race against the clock; **carrera de coches** rally, meeting; **echar una carrera a algn** to race sb; **carrera de armamentos** arms race **c)** [estudios] university course; **hacer la carrera de derecho / físicas** to study law / physics (at university) **d)** [profesión] career, profession **e)** [en medias] *Br* ladder, *US* run

carrerilla *nf* **tomar** *o Esp* **coger carrerilla** to take a run; **de carrerilla** [de corrido] on the trot; [de memoria] by heart; **decir algo de carrerilla** to reel sth off

carreta *nf* cart

carrete *nm* [de hilo] reel; [de película] spool; [de cable] coil

carretera *nf* road; **carretera de acceso** access road; [en autopista] slip road; **carretera de circunvalación** *Br* ring road, *US* beltway; **carretera comarcal** minor road; *Méx* **carretera de cuota** toll road; **carretera nacional** ≃ *Br* A road, ≃ *US* state highway

carretero, -a *adj Am* road; **un accidente carretero** a road accident; **el tránsito carretero** the road traffic

carretilla *nf* wheelbarrow

carril *nm* **a)** FERROC rail **b)** AUTO lane

carriola *nf* **a)** [cama] truckle bed **b)** *Méx* [coche de bebé] *Br* pram, *US* baby carriage

carrito *nm* **a)** [para el equipaje] (small) wheeled suitcase, cabin case **b)** [en un supermercado] **carrito (de la compra)** *Br* (shopping) trolley, *US* (shopping) cart

carro *nm* **a)** [carreta] cart; *Fam* **¡para el carro!** hang on a minute! **b)** MIL **carro de combate** tank **c)** [de máquina de escribir] carriage **d)** *Am salvo RP* [automóvil] car **e)** *Méx* [vagón] car; **carro comedor** dining car, *Br* buffet car

carrocería *nf* AUTO bodywork

carromato *nm* [carro] wagon

carroña *nf* carrion

carroza 1. *nf* **a)** [coche de caballos] coach, carriage **b)** [de carnaval] float **2.** *nmf Fam* old fogey

carruaje *nm* carriage, coach

carrusel *nm* [tiovivo] merry-go-round, *US* carousel

carta *nf* **a)** [escrito] letter **b)** [menú] menu; **a la carta** à la carte; **carta de vinos** wine list **c)** NAIPES card; **echar las cartas a algn** to tell sb's fortune **d)** GEOGR [mapa] chart **e)** *Fig* **tomar cartas en un asunto** to take part in an affair

cartabón *nm* set square

cartearse *vpr* to correspond (**con** with), to exchange letters (**con** with)

cartel *nm* poster; **pegar o fijar carteles** to put o stick up bills

cartelera *nf* billboard, *Br* hoarding; PRENSA **cartelera de espectáculos** entertainments section o page

cartera *nf* **a)** [de bolsillo] wallet, *US* billfold **b)** [para documentos] briefcase; [de colegial] satchel, schoolbag **c)** POL [ministerio] portfolio **d)** COM portfolio; **cartera de clientes** client portfolio, client list; **cartera de pedidos** order book **e)** *Andes, RP* [bolso] *Br* handbag, *US* purse

carterista *nm* pickpocket

cartero, -a *nm, f Br* postman, *f* postwoman, *US* mailman, *f* mailwoman

cartilla *nf* **a)** [libreta] book; **cartilla de ahorros** savings book **b)** [libro] first reader; *Fam* **leerle la cartilla a algn** to tell sb off

cartón *nm* **a)** [material] card, cardboard; **cartón piedra** papier mâché **b)** [de cigarrillos] carton

cartuchera *nf* [para cartuchos] cartridge clip

cartucho *nm* **a)** [de balas] cartridge **b)** [de papel] cone

cartulina *nf* card

casa *nf* **a)** [edificio] house; **casa adosada** terraced house; **casa de campo** country house; **casa consistorial** ≃ town hall; *Am* **casa de gobierno** presidential palace; **casa de huéspedes** *Br* guesthouse, *US* rooming house; **casa piloto** *Br* show home, *US* model home; **casa real** [palacio] palace; **casa de socorro** first-aid post; **casa unifamiliar** family home *(for one family)*; **echar o tirar la casa por la ventana** [derrochar] to spare no expense, to go to town **b)** [hogar] home; **vete a casa** go home; **en casa de Daniel** at Daniel's; **de andar por casa** everyday **c)** [empresa] company, firm; **casa matriz / principal** head / central office **d)** [familia] family; **casa real** the royal family

casadero, -a *adj* of marrying age

casado, -a 1. *adj* married **2.** *nm, f* married person; **los recién casados** the newlyweds

casamiento *nm* marriage; [boda] wedding

casar¹ 1. *vt* to marry **2.** *vi* to match, to go o fit together **3. casarse** *vpr* to marry, to get married; **casarse por la iglesia / por lo civil** to get married in church / in a registry office

casar² *vt* JUR to annul, to quash

cascabel nm bell

cascada nf waterfall, cascade

cascado, -a adj a) [hecho en casa] Esp Fam [estropeado] bust, Br clapped-out; [persona, ropa] worn-out b) [ronco] rasping

cascanueces nm inv nutcracker

cascar [44] **1.** vt a) to crack b) Fam **cascarla** to kick the bucket, to snuff it **2.** vi Esp Fam [hablar] to witter on **3. cascarse** vpr to crack

cáscara nf shell; [de fruta] skin, peel; [de grano] husk

casco nm a) [para la cabeza] helmet b) [de caballo] hoof c) Esp, Méx [envase] empty bottle d) **casco urbano** city centre e) [de barco] hull f) **cascos** [auriculares] headphones; **los cascos azules** [tropas] Blue Helmets (UN peacekeeping force)

caserío nm country house

casero, -a 1. adj a) [hecho en casa] home-made b) [persona] home-loving **2.** nm, f [dueño] landlord, f landlady

caseta nf hut, booth; [de feria, exposición] stand, stall; Méx **caseta de cobro** tollbooth; Méx **caseta telefónica** phone box, US phone booth

casete 1. nm [magnetófono] cassette player o recorder **2.** nf [cinta] cassette (tape)

casi adv almost, nearly; **casi mil personas** almost one thousand people; **casi ni me acuerdo** I can hardly remember it; **casi nunca** hardly ever; **casi nadie** hardly anyone; **casi me caigo** I almost fell

casilla nf a) [de caja, armario] compartment; [para cartas] pigeonhole; Andes, RP **casilla de correos** PO Box; CAm, Carib, Méx **casilla postal** PO Box b) [recuadro] box c) Fig **sacar a algn de sus casillas** to drive sb mad

casillero nm pigeonholes

casino nm casino

caso nm case; **el caso es que ...** the fact o thing is that ...; **el caso Mattei** the Mattei affair; **(en) caso contrario** otherwise; **en caso de necesidad** if need be; **en cualquier caso** in any case; **en el mejor / peor de los casos** at best / worst; **en ese caso** in such a case; **en todo caso** in any case; **en un caso extremo, en último caso** as a last resort; **hacer caso a o de algn** to pay attention to sb; **hacer caso omiso de** to take no notice of; **no venir al caso** to be beside the point; **pongamos por caso** let's say

casona nf pile

caspa nf dandruff

casquería nf a) [tienda] tripe shop b) [producto] offal

casquete nm a) [de bala] case, shell b) GEOGR **casquete polar** polar cap

casquillo nm [de bala] case

casta nf a) [linaje] lineage, descent b) [animales] breed; **de casta** thoroughbred, purebred c) [división social] caste

castaña nf chestnut; Fig **sacarle a algn las castañas del fuego** to save sb's bacon

castaño, -a 1. adj chestnut-brown; [pelo, ojos] brown, dark **2.** nm BOT chestnut

castañuela nf castanet

castellano, -a 1. adj & nm, f Castilian **2.** nm [idioma] Spanish, Castilian

castidad nf chastity

castigar [42] vt a) to punish b) [dañar] to harm, to ruin c) JUR & DEP to penalize

castigo nm punishment; JUR penalty; DEP **área de castigo** penalty area

castillo nm castle

casting nm casting

castizo, -a adj pure, authentic

casto, -a adj chaste

castor nm beaver

castrante adj emasculating

castrar vt to castrate

casualidad nf chance, coincidence; **de o por casualidad** by chance; **dio la casualidad que ...** it so happened that ...; **¿tienes un lápiz, por casualidad?** do you happen to have a pencil?; **¡qué casualidad!** what a coincidence!

casualmente adv as it happens

catacumbas *nfpl* catacombs

catalán, -ana 1. *adj* & *nm, f* Catalan **2.** *nm* [idioma] Catalan

catálogo *nm* catalogue

Cataluña *n* Catalonia

catamarán *nm* catamaran

catar *vt* to taste

catarata *nf* **a)** waterfall **b)** MED cataract

catarro *nm* (common) cold

catástrofe *nf* catastrophe

catastrófico, -a *adj* catastrophic

catavinos *nmf inv* wine taster

cateado, -a *Esp Fam* **1.** *adj* failed **2.** *nm, f* person who fails

catear 1. *vt* **a)** *Esp Fam* [alumno, candidato] to fail; **el profe de ciencias ha cateado a toda la clase** the science teacher has failed the whole class **b)** *Esp Fam* [asignatura, prueba] to fail, *US* to flunk; **ha cateado inglés** he's failed English **c)** *Am* [casa] to search **2.** *vi Esp Fam* [suspender] to fail

catecismo *nm* catechism

cátedra *nf* (professorial) chair; **le han dado la cátedra** they have appointed him professor

catedral *nf* cathedral

catedrático, -a *nm, f* **a)** EDUC & UNIV professor **b)** [de instituto] head of department

categoría *nf* category; *Fig* class; **de categoría** [persona] important; [vino etc] quality

catequesis *nf inv* catechism lesson, ≃ Sunday school

cateto, -a *nm, f Despec* yokel, bumpkin

catire, -a *adj Carib* [rubio] blond, *f* blonde

catolicismo *nm* Catholicism

católico, -a *adj* & *nm, f* Catholic

catorce *adj* & *nm inv* fourteen

catre *nm Fam* camp bed, *US* cot

cauce *nm* **a)** [de un río] bed **b)** *Fig* [canal] channel; **cauces oficiales** official channels

caucho *nm* **a)** [sustancia] rubber **b)** *Ven* [impermeable] *Br* mac, *US* slicker **c)** *Ven* [neumático] tyre

caudal *nm* **a)** [de un río] flow **b)** [riqueza] wealth, riches

caudaloso, -a *adj* [río] plentiful

caudillo *nm* leader, head

causa *nf* **a)** cause; **a o por causa de** because of **b)** [ideal] cause **c)** JUR [caso] case; [juicio] trial

causante 1. *adj* causal, causing **2.** *nmf* **el causante del incendio** the person who caused the fire

causar *vt* to cause, to bring about; **me causa un gran placer** it gives me great pleasure; **causar buena / mala impresión** to make a good / bad impression

cáustico, -a *adj* caustic

cautela *nf* caution

cautivador, -a 1. *adj* captivating, enchanting **2.** *nm, f* charmer

cautivar *vt* **a)** to capture, to take prisoner **b)** *Fig* [fascinar] to captivate

cautiverio *nm* captivity

cautividad *nf* captivity

cautivo, -a *adj* & *nm, f* captive

cauto, -a *adj* cautious, wary

cava 1. *nf* [bodega] wine cellar **2.** *nm* [vino espumoso] cava, champagne

cavar *vt* to dig

caverna *nf* cave; **hombre de las cavernas** caveman

caviar *nm* caviar

cavidad *nf* cavity

cavilar *vt* to ponder

cayuco *nf* [canoa] kayak; [de inmigrantes] *boat used by sub-Saharan immigrants attempting to reach the Canaries illegally*

caza 1. *nf* **a)** hunting; **ir de caza** to go hunting; **caza furtiva** poaching **b)** [animales] game; **caza mayor / menor** big / small game **c)** *Fig* [persecución] hunt; **caza de brujas** witch hunt **2.** *nm* AVIACIÓN fighter, fighter plane

cazabe *nm Am* cassava bread

cazador, -a nm, f hunter; **cazador furtivo** poacher

cazadora nf (waist-length) jacket

cazar [40] vt to hunt; Fam **cazarlas al vuelo** to be quick on the uptake

cazatalentos nmf inv [de ejecutivos] headhunter; [de artistas, deportistas] talent scout

cazo nm a) [cacerola] saucepan b) [cucharón] ladle

cazuela nf saucepan; [guiso] casserole, stew; **a la cazuela** stewed

cazurro, -a 1. adj [bruto] stupid **2.** nm, f [bruto] idiot, fool

c /c (abr de **cuenta corriente**) c/a

CD (pl **CDs**) nm (abr de **compact disc**) CD; **CD interactivo** interactive CD

CD-ROM ['θeδe'rrom] (pl **CD-ROMs**) nm CD-ROM

cebar 1. vt a) [animal] to fatten; [persona] to feed up b) [anzuelo] to bait c) [fuego, caldera] to stoke, to fuel; [máquina, arma] to prime d) RP [mate] to prepare, to brew **2. cebarse** vpr **cebarse con** [ensañarse] to delight in tormenting

cebiche, ceviche nm Am ceviche (raw fish dish marinated in lemon and onion)

cebo nm bait

cebolla nf onion

cebolleta nf Br spring onion, US scallion

cebra nf zebra; **paso de cebra** Br zebra crossing, US crosswalk

cecear vi to lisp

cecina nf Am dried, salted meat

ceder 1. vt to give, to hand over; AUTO **ceder el paso** to give way **2.** vi a) [cuerda, cable] to give way b) [lluvia, calor] to diminish, to slacken c) [consentir] to give in

cedro nm cedar

cédula nf a) document, certificate; Am **cédula de identidad** identity card b) COM & FIN bond, certificate, warrant

cegato, -a Fam **1.** adj short-sighted **2.** nm, f short-sighted person

ceguera nf blindness

ceja nf eyebrow

celda nf cell; **celda de castigo** punishment cell

celebración nf a) [festejo] celebration b) [de juicio etc] holding

celebrar 1. vt a) to celebrate; **celebro que todo saliera bien** I'm glad everything went well b) [reunión, juicio, elecciones] to hold c) [triunfo] to laud **2. celebrarse** vpr to take place, to be held

célebre adj famous, well-known

celebridad nf a) celebrity, fame b) [persona] celebrity

celeste 1. adj a) [de cielo] celestial b) [color] sky-blue **2.** nm sky blue

celestial adj celestial, heavenly

celo nm a) [esmero] zeal b) **en celo** [macho] in rut; [hembra] Br on heat, US in heat c) **celos** jealousy; **tener celos (de algn)** to be jealous (of sb)

celofán nm cellophane®

celoso, -a adj a) jealous b) [cumplidor] conscientious

célula nf cell

celular 1. adj a) cellular b) **coche celular** police van c) Am **teléfono celular** mobile phone, cellphone **2.** nm Am mobile (phone), cellphone

celulitis nf inv cellulitis

cementerio nm cemetery, graveyard; **cementerio de coches** scrapyard

cemento nm cement; **cemento armado** reinforced cement

cena nf evening meal; [antes de acostarse] supper; **la Última Cena** the Last Supper

cenador, cenadero nm Br arbour, US arbor

cenar 1. vi to have supper o dinner **2.** vt to have for supper o dinner

cencerro nm cowbell

cenefa nf [de ropa] edging, trimming; [de suelo, techo] ornamental border, frieze

cenicero nm ashtray

ceniza nf ash

censar *vt* to take a census of

censo *nm* census; *Esp* **censo electoral** electoral roll

censor *nm* censor

censura *nf* a) censorship b) POL **moción de censura** vote of no confidence

censurar *vt* a) [libro, película] to censor b) [criticar] to censure, to criticize

centena *nf* hundred; **una centena de …** a hundred …

centenar *nm* hundred; **un centenar de …** a hundred …; **a centenares** by the hundred

centenario *nm* centenary, hundredth anniversary

centeno *nm* rye

centésimo, -a *adj & nm, f* hundredth

centígrado, -a *adj* centigrade

centímetro *nm* centimetre

céntimo *nm* cent

centinela *nm* sentry

centollo *nm* spider crab

centrado, -a *adj* a) centred b) [equilibrado] balanced

central 1. *adj* central **2.** *nf* a) ELEC **central nuclear / térmica** nuclear / coal-fired power station b) [oficina principal] head office

centralismo *nm* centralism

centralita *nf* TEL switchboard

centralizado, -a *adj* centralized

centrar 1. *vt* a) to centre b) [esfuerzos, atención] to concentrate, to centre (**en** on) **2. centrarse** *vpr* a) to be centred o based b) **centrarse en** [concentrarse] to concentrate on

céntrico, -a *adj* centrally situated; **zona céntrica** centrally situated area

centrifugado *nm* [de ropa] spin-drying

centrifugar [42] *vt* to centrifuge; [ropa] to spin-dry

centro *nm* a) middle, centre; **centro de la ciudad** town o city centre b) [establecimiento] institution, centre; **centro comercial** shopping centre o US mall

Centroamérica *n* Central America

centroamericano, -a 1. *adj* Central American **2.** *nm, f* native or inhabitant of Central America

centuria *nf* century

ceñido, -a *adj* tight-fitting, clinging

ceñirse [6] *vpr* a) [atenerse, limitarse] to limit oneself, to stick (**a** to); **ceñirse al tema** to keep to the subject b) **ceñirse a** [prenda] to cling to

ceño *nm* scowl, frown; **con el ceño fruncido** frowning

cepa *nf* a) [de vid] vine b) *Fig* **vasco de pura cepa** [origen] Basque through and through

cepillar 1. *vt* a) to brush b) [en carpintería] to plane (down) c) *Fam* [robar] to pinch **2. cepillarse** *vpr* a) [con cepillo] to brush b) *Fam* [matar] to do in c) *muy Fam* to lay

cepillo *nm* brush; [en carpintería] plane; **cepillo de dientes** toothbrush; **cepillo del pelo** hairbrush

cepo *nm* a) [para cazar] trap b) AUTO clamp

cera *nf* wax; [de abeja] beeswax

cerámica *nf* ceramics (*sing*)

ceramista *nmf* potter

cerca¹ *adv* a) near, close; **ven más cerca** come closer; **ya estamos cerca** we are almost there b) **cerca de** [al lado de] near, close to; **el colegio está cerca de mi casa** the school is near my house c) **cerca de** [casi] nearly, around; **cerca de cien personas** about one hundred people d) **de cerca** closely; **lo vi muy de cerca** I saw it close up

cerca² *nf* fence, wall

cercanía *nf* a) proximity, nearness b) **cercanías** outskirts, suburbs; **(tren de) cercanías** suburban train

cercano, -a *adj* nearby; **el Cercano Oriente** the Near East

cercar [44] *vt* a) [tapiar] to fence, to enclose b) [rodear] to surround

cerco *nm* a) circle, ring b) MIL [sitio] siege; **poner cerco (a una ciudad)** to besiege (a town)

cerda *nf* **a)** ZOOL sow **b)** [pelo] bristle; **cepillo de cerda** bristle brush

cerdo *nm* **a)** pig **b)** [carne] pork **c)** *Fam* pig, arsehole

cereal *nm* cereal

cerebro *nm* brain; *Fig* [inteligencia] brains

ceremonia *nf* ceremony

ceremonioso, -a *adj* ceremonious, formal; *Despec* pompous, stiff

cereza *nf* cherry

cerezo *nm* cherry tree

cerilla *nf Esp* match

cerillo *nm CAm, Ecuad, Méx* match

cero *nm* zero; DEP Br nil, US zero; *Fig* **partir de cero** to start from scratch; *Fig* **ser un cero a la izquierda** to be useless o a good-for-nothing

cerquillo *nm Am* Br fringe, US bangs

cerrado, -a *adj* **a)** closed, shut; **a puerta cerrada** behind closed doors **b)** [reservado] reserved; [intransigente] uncompromising, unyielding; *Fam* [torpe] thick; [acento] broad; [curva] tight, sharp **c)** [barba] bushy

cerradura *nf* lock

cerrajería *nf* **a)** [oficio] locksmithery **b)** [local] locksmith's (shop)

cerrajero, -a *nm, f* locksmith

cerrar [1] **1.** *vt* to shut, to close; [grifo, gas] to turn off; [luz] to turn off, to switch off; [cremallera] to do up; [negocio] to close down; [cuenta] to close; [carta] to seal; [puños] to clench; **cerrar con llave** to lock; **cerrar el paso a algn** to block sb's way; *Fam* **cerrar el pico** to shut one's trap
2. *vi* to close, to shut
3. cerrarse *vpr* to close, to shut; *Fam* **cerrarse en banda** to stick to one's guns

cerro *nm* hill

cerrojo *nm* bolt; **echar el cerrojo (de una puerta)** to bolt (a door)

certamen *nm* competition, contest

certeza *nf* certainty; **saber (algo) con certeza** to be certain (of sth); **tener la certeza de que ...** to be sure o certain that ...

certidumbre *nf* certainty

certificado, -a 1. *adj* **a)** certified **b)** [correo] registered **2.** *nm* certificate

certificar [44] *vt* **a)** to certify **b)** [carta] to register

cervecería *nf* **a)** [bar] pub, bar **b)** [fábrica] brewery

cerveza *nf* beer; **cerveza de barril** draught beer; **cerveza dorada** o **ligera** lager; **cerveza negra** stout

cesante *adj* [destituido] dismissed, sacked; *CSur, Méx* [parado] unemployed

cesantear *vt Am* [empleado] to dismiss; [contrato] to terminate

cesar 1. *vi* **cesar (de)** to stop, to cease; **sin cesar** incessantly **2.** *vt* [empleado] to dismiss, Br to sack

cesárea *nf* Caesarean (section)

cese *nm* **a)** cessation, suspension **b)** [despido] dismissal

cesión *nf* cession, transfer; JUR **cesión de bienes** surrender of property

césped *nm* lawn, grass

cesta *nf* **a)** basket; **cesta de Navidad** Christmas hamper **b)** COM & INFORM **'añadir a la cesta'** Br 'add to basket', US 'add to cart'

cesto *nm* basket

cetro *nm* sceptre

ceviche *nm* = **cebiche**

chabacano, -a 1. *adj* cheap **2.** *nm Méx* [fruto] apricot; [árbol] apricot tree

chabola *nf Esp* shack; **barrio de chabolas** shanty town

chacarero, -a *nm, f Andes, RP* farmer

chacha *nf* maid

cháchara *nf* **a)** *Fam* small talk, chinwag; **estar de cháchara** to have a yap **b)** *Méx Fig* **chácharas** [baratijas] knicknacks, trinkets

chacinería *nf* charcuterie

chacolí *nm* light wine from the Basque Country

chacra *nf Andes, RP* farm

chafar *vt* **a)** *Fam* [plan etc] to ruin, to spoil **b)** [aplastar] to squash, to flatten

chagra *Am* **1.** *nmf* peasant **2.** *nf* small farm

chal *nm* shawl

chalado, -a *adj Fam* crazy, nuts (**por** about)

chalé *nm* villa

chaleco *nm Br* waistcoat, *US* vest; [de punto] sleeveless pullover; **chaleco antibalas** bullet-proof vest; **chaleco salvavidas** life jacket

chalet = **chalé**

chalupa *nf* **a)** [embarcación] boat, launch **b)** *Méx* [torta] *small tortilla with a raised rim to contain a filling*

chamaco, -a *nm, f Méx Fam* **a)** [muchacho] kid **b)** [pareja] boyfriend, *f* girlfriend

chamba *nf CAm, Méx, Perú, Ven Fam* [trabajo] job

chambón, -ona *nm, f Am Fam* sloppy *o* shoddy worker

champa *nf CAm* [tienda de campaña] tent

champán, champaña *nm o nf* champagne

champiñón *nm* mushroom

champú *(pl* **champú** *o* **champúes)** *nm* shampoo

chamuscado, -a *adj* [pelo, plumas] singed; [tela, papel] scorched; [tostada] burnt

chamuscar [44] *vt* to singe, to scorch

chamusquina *nf* singeing, scorching; *Fam* **esto me huele a chamusquina** there's something fishy going on here

chance 1. *nm o nf Am* [ocasión] opportunity, chance; **a la primera chance** at the first opportunity; **dar una chance a algn** to give sb a chance **2.** *adv Méx* maybe; **chance sí, chance no** maybe, maybe not

chanchada *nf Am* **a)** [porquería] ¡**no hagas chanchadas!** stop that, don't be disgusting! **b)** *Fam* [jugarreta] dirty trick

chancho, -a 1. *adj Am* [sucio] filthy **2.** *nm, f Am* **a)** [animal] pig, *f* sow **b)** [persona] (filthy) pig

chancla *nf Br* flip-flop, *US, Austr* thong

chanclo *nm* [zueco] clog; [de goma] overshoe, galosh

chándal *(pl* **chandals)** *nm Esp* tracksuit

changa *nf Bol, RP* [trabajo temporal] odd job

changador *nm RP* [cargador] porter

changarro *nm Méx* [tienda] small shop; [puesto] stand

chanquete *nm* whitebait

chantaje *nm* blackmail; **hacer chantaje a algn** to blackmail sb

chantajista *nmf* blackmailer

chapa *nf* **a)** [de metal] sheet; [de madera] panel-board **b)** [tapón] bottle top, cap **c)** [de adorno] badge **d)** *RP* [de matrícula] *Br* number plate, *US* license plate **e)** *Col, Cuba, Méx* [cerradura] lock

chapado, -a *adj* [metal] plated; **chapado en oro** gold-plated; *Fig* **chapado a la antigua** old-fashioned

chapar 1. *vt* [recubrir - con metal] to plate; [con madera] to veneer **2.** *vi Esp muy Fam* [cerrar] to shut, to close

chaparro, -a 1. *adj* squat **2.** *nm, f* shorty ■ **chaparro** *nm* **a)** oak shrub **b)** *Méx* [chico] kid

chaparrón *nm* downpour, heavy shower

chapopote *nm Carib, Méx* bitumen, pitch

chapoteo *nm* [ruido] splashing

chapucería *nf* botch (job)

chapucero, -a *adj* [trabajo] slapdash, shoddy; [persona] bungling

chapulín *nm CAm, Méx* [saltamontes] grasshopper

chapuza *nf* **a)** [trabajo mal hecho] shoddy piece of work **b)** [trabajo ocasional] odd job

chaqué *nm* morning coat

chaqueta *nf* jacket; POL **cambiar de chaqueta** to change sides

chaquetilla *nf* short jacket

chaquetón *nm* heavy jacket, short coat

charca *nf* pond, pool

charco *nm* puddle

charcutería *nf* delicatessen

charla *nf* [conversación] talk, chat; [conferencia] informal lecture *o* address; INFORM chat

charlar *vi* to talk, to chat; INFORM to chat

charlatán, -ana 1. *adj* [parlanchín] talkative; [chismoso] gossipy **2.** *nm, f* **a)** [parlanchín] chatterbox; [chismoso] gossip; [bocazas] bigmouth **b)** [embaucador] trickster, charmer

charol *nm* **a)** [piel] patent leather; **zapatos de charol** patent leather shoes **b)** *Andes* [bandeja] tray

charola *nf Bol, CAm, Méx* tray

charque, charqui *nm Andes, RP* jerked *o* salted beef

charro, -a 1. *adj* **a)** *Esp* [salmantino] Salamancan **b)** [recargado] gaudy, showy **c)** *Méx* [líder sindical] *in league with the bosses* **2.** *nm, f* **a)** *Esp* [salmantino] Salamancan **b)** *Méx* [jinete] horseman, *f* horsewoman

chárter *adj inv* **(vuelo) chárter** charter (flight)

chasca *nf Andes* [greña] mop of hair

chasco *nm Fam* disappointment; **llevarse un chasco** to be disappointed

chasis *nm inv* chassis

chatarra *nf* scrap (metal), scrap iron; *Fam* junk

chatarrero, -a *nm, f* scrap (metal) dealer

chateador, -a *nm, f Fam* INTERNET chatroom user

chateo *nm Fam* **a)** INTERNET chat **b)** [bebida] *Esp* **ir de chateo** to go for a drink

chato, -a 1. *adj* **a)** [nariz] snub (*before noun*); [persona] snub-nosed **b)** [objeto] flat, flattened **c)** *PRico, RP Fam* [sin ambiciones] commonplace; **una vida chata** a humdrum existence **2.** *nm, f Fam* [apelativo] lovely, darling; **¡chata!** [piropo] hi gorgeous! **3.** *nm Esp Fam* small glass of wine

chau, chaucito *interj Am Fam* bye!, see you!

chaucha 1. *adj RP Fam* dull, boring **2.** *nf* **a)** *Bol, RP* green bean **b)** *Andes* [patata] early potato

chaucito *interj* = **chau**

chava *nf Am Fam* girl, *Fam* chick

chaveta *nf* **a)** [clavija] cotter pin **b)** *Fam* [cabeza] nut, head; **perder la chaveta** [volverse loco] to go off one's rocker **c)** *Andes* [navaja] penknife

chavo, -a *Fam* **1.** *nm, f Méx* **a)** [chico] guy; [chica] girl **b)** [novio] boyfriend; [novia] girlfriend **2.** *nm* [dinero] **no tener un chavo** to be broke

che *interj RP Fam* **¿qué hacés, che?, ¿cómo andás, che?** hey, how's it going, then?; **che, ¡vení para acá!** hey, over here, you!

checar *vt Andes, CAm, Méx* **a)** [comprobar] to check, to verify **b)** [vigilar] to check up on

chef [tʃef] (*pl* **chefs**) *nm* chef

chele, -a *CAm* **1.** *adj* [rubio] blond, *f* blonde; [de piel blanca] fair-skinned **2.** *nmf* [rubio] blond, *f* blonde; [de piel blanca] fair-skinned person

chelo, -a *adj Méx* blond, *f* blonde

cheque *nm Br* cheque, *US* check; **cheque al portador** cheque payable to bearer; **cheque de viaje** *o* **(de) viajero** traveller's cheque

chequear *vt* **a)** MED **chequear a algn** to give sb a check up **b)** [comprobar] to check, to verify

chequeo *nm* [comprobación] check; MED checkup; AUTO service

chequera *nf Br* chequebook, *US* checkbook

chévere *adj Am salvo RP Fam* great, fantastic

chic *adj inv* chic, elegant

chicha¹ *nf* **a)** *Esp Fam* [para comer] meat **b)** *Esp Fam* [de persona] flesh; **tiene po-**

cas chichas [está flaco] he's as thin as a rake **c)** [bebida alcohólica] *alcoholic drink made from fermented maize* **d)** [bebida refrescante] *thick, sweet drink made from rice, condensed milk and vanilla*

chicha² *adj inv* NÁUT **calma chicha** dead calm

chícharo *nm* CAm, Méx pea

chicharra *nf* a) [insecto] cicada **b)** Méx [timbre] electric buzzer

chiche 1. *adj* Andes, RP very easy **2.** *nm* a) Andes, RP Fam [juguete] toy **b)** Andes, RP [joya] piece of Br jewellery o US jewelry; [baratija] trinket **c)** Am Fam [chuchería] treat, snack **d)** CAm, Méx muy Fam [pecho] tit

chichón *nm* bump, lump

chicle *nm* chewing gum

chico, -a 1. *nm, f* [muchacho] boy, lad; [muchacha] girl **2.** *adj* small, little

chicote *nm* Am whip

chiflado, -a *adj* Fam mad, crazy **(por** about)

chiflar *vt* a) [silbar] to hiss (at), to boo (at) **b)** Fam **le chiflan las motos** he's really into motorbikes

chiflido *nm* whistling

chigüín, -a *nm* CAm Fam kid

chilango, -a Méx Fam **1.** *adj* of /from Mexico City **2.** *nm, f* person from Mexico City

chile *nm* CAm, Méx CULIN chilli

Chile *n* Chile

chileno, -a *adj & nm, f* Chilean

chillar *vi* [persona] to scream, to shriek; [ratón] to squeak; [frenos] to screech, to squeal; [puerta] to creak, to squeak

chillido *nm* [de persona] scream, shriek; [de ratón] squeak; [de frenos] screech, squeal; [de puerta] creaking, squeaking

chillón, -ona *adj* a) [voz] shrill, high-pitched; [sonido] harsh, strident **b)** [color] loud, gaudy

chilote *nm* Méx alcoholic drink made from pulque, chillies, and garlic

chilpotle *nm* Méx smoked or pickled jalapeño chile

chimbo, -a *adj* Col, Ven Fam a) [de mala calidad] crap, useless **b)** [complicado] screwed-up

chimenea *nf* a) [hogar abierto] fireplace, hearth **b)** [conducto] chimney; [de barco] funnel, stack

chimichurri *nm* RP barbecue sauce made from garlic, parsley, oregano and vinegar

chimpancé *nm* chimpanzee

china *nf* a) [piedra] pebble, small stone; Fam **tocarle a uno la china** to get the short straw **b)** Fam [droga] lump, piece **c)** Am [campesina] country girl **d)** Am Despec [criada] servant

China *n* China

chinampa *nf* Méx man-made island for growing flowers, fruit and vegetables, in Xochimilco near Mexico City

chinche *nf* bedbug; Fam **caer como chinches** to drop like flies

chincheta *nf* Br drawing pin, US thumbtack

chinchín 1. *nm* a) [ruido] clink **b)** Fam [brindis] toast **2.** *interj* cheers!, (to) your (good) health!

chinchulín *nm* Andes, RP [plato] piece of sheep or cow intestine, plaited and then roasted

chingada *nf* Méx muy Fam a) [fastidio] crap **b)** ¡**vete a la chingada!** piss off!, fuck off!

chingado, -a *adj* Esp, Méx muy Fam [estropeado] bust, Br knackered

chingana *nf* Andes Fam cheap bar or café

chingar [42] **1.** *vt* a) Esp, Méx muy Fam [estropear] to bust, Br to knacker **b)** Esp, Méx muy Fam [molestar] **chingar a algn** to piss sb off, to get up sb's nose **c)** Esp, Méx Vulg [copular] to fuck; Méx ¡**chinga tu madre!** fuck you! **2.** *vi* Esp, Méx Vulg [copular] to screw, to fuck; ¡**chíngale!** shit! **3. chingarse** *vpr* Méx muy Fam a) [estropearse] **se nos chingó la fiesta** the party was ruined

b) [beber mucho] **nos chingamos todas las botellas** we downed all the bottles
c) [comer] to eat, Br Fam to scoff

chingón, -ona adj Am Fam great

chinita nf Am ladybird, US ladybug

chino¹ nm [piedra] pebble, stone

chino², a 1. adj **a)** [de China] Chinese **b)** Am [mestizo] of mixed ancestry **c)** [rizado] curly **2.** nm, f **a)** [de China] Chinese man, f Chinese woman **b)** Am [mestizo] person of mixed ancestry **c)** Am [indio] American Indian **3.** nm **a)** [idioma] Chinese; Fam **eso me suena a chino** it's all Greek to me **b)** Am [rizo] curl

chip (pl **chips**) nm INFORM chip

chipirón nm baby squid

Chipre n Cyprus

chiquear vt Méx to flatter

chiqueo nm Méx Fam show of affection; **hacerle chiqueos a algn** to kiss and cuddle sb

chiquito, -a 1. adj very small **2.** nm, f Am [niño] little boy, f little girl **3.** nm Esp [de vino] small glass of wine

chirimoya nf custard apple

chiripá (pl **chiripaes**) nm Bol, CSur garment worn by gauchos over trousers

chirona nf Esp Fam & Jerga [prisión] Br nick, US can; **en chirona** Br in the nick, US in the can

chisme nm **a)** [habladuría] piece of gossip **b)** Fam [trasto] knick-knack; [cosa] thing

chismoso, -a 1. adj gossipy **2.** nm, f gossip

chispa nf **a)** spark; **echar chispas** to fume **b)** Fam [un poco] bit, tiny amount **c)** Fam [agudeza] wit, sparkle; [viveza] liveliness **d)** Fam **chispas** (inv) [electricista] electrician, Br Fam sparky **e)** Méx **¡chispas!** yikes!

chiste nm joke; **contar un chiste** to tell a joke; **chiste verde** blue joke, dirty joke

chistorra nf type of cured pork sausage typical of Aragon and Navarre

chistoso, -a adj [persona] funny, witty; [anécdota] funny, amusing

chivar 1. vt Fam **a)** Esp [contar] to tell **b)** Am [fastidiar] to annoy **2. chivarse** vpr Esp Fam **a)** [entre niños] to tell, Br to split (**de** on) **b)** [entre delincuentes, adultos] to squeal, Br to grass (**de** on)

chivatazo nm Esp Fam tip-off; **dar el chivatazo** to squeal, Br to grass

chivato, -a 1. adj & nm, f Esp Fam **a)** [delincuente] informer, Br grass, US rat **b)** [niño] telltale, US tattletale **2.** nm **a)** [luz] warning light **b)** [alarma] beeper **c)** Am Fam [pez gordo] big shot

chivito nm **a)** Arg [carne] roast kid **b)** Urug steak sandwich (containing cheese and salad)

chocar [44] **1.** vi **a)** [topar] to crash, to collide; **chocar con** o **contra** to run into, to collide with **b)** [en discusión] to clash **2.** vt **a)** to knock; [la mano] to shake; Fam **¡chócala!, ¡choca esos cinco!** shake (on it)!, put it there! **b)** [sorprender] to surprise

chocho, -a 1. adj [senil] senile; **viejo chocho** old dodderer **2.** nm **a)** [altramuz] lupin **b)** Esp, Méx Vulg [vulva] Br fanny, US beaver

choclo nm Andes, RP maize, US corn

choco nm [sepia] cuttlefish

chocolatada nf hot chocolate party

chocolate nm **a)** chocolate; **chocolate con leche** milk chocolate **b)** Esp Fam [droga] dope

chocolatería nf **a)** [fábrica] chocolate factory **b)** [establecimiento] café where drinking chocolate is served

chocolatina nf bar of chocolate, chocolate bar

chófer, Am chofer nm chauffeur

chollo nm Esp Fam [ganga] bargain

cholo, -a Am **1.** adj mixed-race **2.** nm, f mixed-race person

chomba nf **a)** Arg polo shirt **b)** Chile, Perú [suéter] sweater

chompa nf Andes sweater, pullover

chompipe nm CAm, Méx turkey

chongo nm Méx **a)** [moño] bun **b)** chongos zamoranos [dulce] *Mexican dessert made from milk curds, served in syrup*

chonta nf CAm, Perú *type of palm tree*

chop, chopp (pl chops o chopps) nm CSur **a)** [jarra] beer mug **b)** [cerveza] (mug of) beer

chopo nm poplar

choque nm **a)** [impact; [de coches etc] crash, collision; **choque frontal** head-on collision; **choque múltiple** pile-up **b)** Fig [contienda] clash

chorbo, -a nm, f Esp Fam guy, f chick

chorizo, a 1. adj Fam [ladrón] thieving **2.** nm, f **a)** Esp Fam [ladrón] thief; [carterista] pickpocket **b)** Am [bobo] twit **3.** nm **a)** [embutido] chorizo (spicy Spanish sausage) **b)** CSur [material] daub

choro nm Andes mussel

chorra 1. nmf muy Fam [tonto] idiot; **es un chorra** he's an idiot **2.** nf Esp muy Fam [suerte] luck; **tener chorra** to be lucky

chorrada nf Esp Fam **decir una chorrada** to say something stupid; **chorradas** Br rubbish, US garbage

chorrear vi to drip, to trickle; Fam **chorrear de sudor** to pour with sweat; Fam **tengo el abrigo chorreando** my coat is dripping wet

chorro 1. nm **a)** [de líquido] jet, stream; **salir a chorros** to flood out **b)** TÉC jet **c)** Fig [de luz, gente, dinero] stream **2.** adv Méx Fam loads; **me gusta chorro** I love it

choto nm, f **a)** [cabrito] kid, young goat; Fam **estar como una chota** to be crazy, to be off one's rocker **b)** [ternero] calf

choza nf hut, shack

christmas nm inv Christmas card

chubasco nm heavy shower, downpour

chubasquero nm raincoat, Br mac

chúcaro, -a adj Andes, CAm, RP **a)** [animal] wild **b)** Fam [persona] **ser chúcaro** to be shy o withdrawn

chuchería nf Fam Br sweet, US candy

chucho nm Fam **a)** [perro] mutt, dog **b)** RP [susto] fright; **un chucho de frío** a shiver

chueco, -a 1. adj Am [torcido] twisted; [patizambo] bowlegged; Méx, Ven Fam [cojo] lame **2.** nm, f Am [patizambo] bowlegged person; Méx, Ven Fam [cojo] lame person

chufa nf groundnut

chuleta nf **a)** [de carne] chop; **chuleta de cerdo** pork chop **b)** Esp, Ven Fam [en exámenes] crib note

chullo nm Andes woollen cap

chulo, -a Fam **1.** nm, f Esp show-off **2.** nm [proxeneta] pimp **3.** adj Esp, Méx Fam [bonito] cool, Br top, US neat

chumbera nf prickly pear cactus

chuño nm Andes, RP potato starch

chupachús (pl chupachuses) nm Esp lollipop

chupado, -a adj **a)** [flaco] skinny, thin **b)** Fam **está chupado** it's dead easy

chupamedias nmf inv Andes, RP, Ven Fam toady

chupar **1.** vt **a)** to suck **b)** [lamer] to lick **c)** [absorber] to soak up, to absorb **2.** vi to suck **3. chuparse** vpr **a)** **está para chuparse los dedos** it's really mouthwatering **b)** Esp Fam to put up with; **nos chupamos toda la película** we sat through the whole film

chupe nm **a)** Andes, Arg [comida] stew **b)** Méx, RP Fam [bebida] booze

chupete nm Br dummy, US pacifier

chupito nm shot

churrasco nm barbecued meat

churrasquería nf restaurant serving chargrilled meats

churrería nf fritter shop

churro nm **a)** dough formed into sticks or rings, fried in oil and covered in sugar **b)** Fam [chapuza] mess

churruscar 1. *vt* to grill until crisp **2. churruscarse** *vpr* to frazzle, to burn to a crisp

chusma *nf* rabble, mob

chutar 1. *vi* **a)** DEP [a gol] to shoot **b)** *Esp Fam* [funcionar] to work; **¡y vas que chutas!** and then you're well away! **2. chutarse** *vpr Esp Fam* [drogas] to shoot up

chute *nm* **a)** DEP shot **b)** *Esp Fam* [drogas] fix

Cía., cía. *(abr de* **compañía)** Co

cibercafé *nm* INFORM Internet cafe, cybercafe

cicatriz *nf* scar

cicatrizar [40] *vt & vi* MED to heal

ciclismo *nm* cycling

ciclista 1. *adj* cycling **2.** *nmf* cyclist

ciclo *nm* cycle; [de conferencias etc] course, series

ciclomotor *nm* moped

ciclón *nm* cyclone

cicloturismo *nm* cycle tourism

ciclovía *nf Am* bike lane, *Br* cycle lane

ciego, -a 1. *adj* **a)** [invidente] blind; **a ciegas** blindly **b)** *Esp Fam* [borracho] blind drunk, *Br* pissed; [de droga] stoned **2.** *nm, f* blind person; **los ciegos** the blind

cielo *nm* **a)** sky **b)** REL heaven; *Fig* **caído del cielo** [oportuno] heaven-sent; [inesperado] out of the blue; **¡cielo santo!** good heavens! **c)** ARQUIT **cielo raso** ceiling **d) cielo de la boca** roof of the mouth

ciempiés *nm inv* centipede

cien *adj & nm inv* hundred; **cien libras** a o one hundred pounds; **cien por cien** one hundred percent

ciencia *nf* **a)** science; *Fig* **saber algo a ciencia cierta** to know sth for certain; **ciencia ficción** science fiction; **ciencia infusa** intuition; **ciencias ocultas** the occult **b)** [conocimiento] knowledge

100pre SMS *(abr de* **siempre)** Alwz

científico, -a 1. *adj* scientific **2.** *nm, f* scientist

cientista *nmf CSur* **cientista social** social scientist

ciento *adj* hundred; **ciento tres** one hundred and three; **por ciento** percent

cierre *nm* **a)** [acción] closing, shutting; [de fábrica] shutdown; TV close-down; **cierre patronal** lockout **b)** [de bolso] clasp; [de puerta] catch; [prenda] fastener; **cierre de seguridad** safety lock; **cierre centralizado** central locking **c)** *Andes, Méx, RP* [cremallera] *Br* zip (fastener), *US* zipper; *Andes, Méx* **cierre relámpago** *Br* zip (fastener), *US* zipper

ciertamente *adv* certainly

cierto, -a 1. *adj* **a)** [verdadero] true; [seguro] certain; **estar en lo cierto** to be right; **lo cierto es que ...** the fact is that ...; **por cierto** by the way **b)** [algún] certain; **ciertas personas** certain o some people **2.** *adv* certainly

ciervo, -a *nm, f* deer; [macho] stag; [hembra] doe, hind

cifra *nf* **a)** [número] figure, number **b)** [código] cipher, code

cigala *nf* Norway lobster, scampi

cigarra *nf* cicada

cigarrería *nf Am* tobacconist

cigarrillo *nm* cigarette

cigarro *nm* **a)** [puro] cigar **b)** [cigarrillo] cigarette

cigüeña *nf* **a)** ORNIT stork **b)** TÉC crank

cilindrada *nf* AUTO cylinder capacity

cilíndrico, -a *adj* cylindrical

cilindro *nm* cylinder

cima *nf* summit

cimborio, cimborrio *nm* dome

cimientos *nmpl* foundations; **echar** o **poner los cimientos** to lay the foundations

cinco *adj & nm inv* five

cincuenta *adj & nm inv* fifty

cine *nm* **a)** [local] cinema, *US* movie theater **b)** [arte] cinema; **cine mudo** silent movies o *Br* films; **cine sonoro** talking pictures, talkies

cineasta *nmf* movie maker o director, *Br* film maker o director

cinematografía *nf* cinematography, *Br* film-making

cinematográfico, -a *adj* movie, *Br* film; **la industria cinematográfica** the movie *o Br* film industry

cínico, -a *adj* shameless **2.** *nm, f* shameless person; **es un cínico** he's shameless, he has no shame

cinismo *nm* shamelessness

cinta *nf* **a)** [tira] band, strip; [para adornar] ribbon; COST braid, edging **b)** TÉC & MÚS tape; **cinta adhesiva** adhevise tape, sticky tape; **cinta aislante** insulating tape; *Am* **cinta durex**® *Br* Sellotape®, Scotch tape®; **cinta magnética** *o* **magnetofónica** magnetic tape; **cinta métrica** tape measure; **cinta (transportadora)** conveyor belt; [de personas] travelator; **cinta de vídeo** video tape **c)** CINE movie, *Br* film **d)** INFORM tape

cintura *nf* waist

cinturón *nm* belt; *Fig* **apretarse el cinturón** to tighten one's belt; **cinturón de seguridad** safety belt; *Am* **cinturón de miseria** *slum or shanty town area round a large city*

cipote¹ *nm* **a)** *Fam* [bobo] dimwit, moron **b)** *Vulg* [pene] prick, cock

cipote², a *nm, f CAm* kid

ciprés *nm* cypress

circo *nm* circus

circuito *nm* circuit

circulación *nf* **a)** circulation **b)** AUTO [tráfico] traffic

circular 1. *adj & nf* circular **2.** *vi* [moverse] to circulate; [líquido] to flow; [tren, autobús] to run; *Fig* [rumor] to go round; **circule por la izquierda** [en letrero] keep to the left

círculo *nm* circle; *Fig* **círculo vicioso** vicious circle

circunferencia *nf* circumference

circunscribir *vt* **a)** [limitar] to restrict, to confine **b)** GEOM to circumscribe

circunscrito, -a 1. *pp de* **circunscribir 2.** *adj* **a)** [limitado] confined **b)** GEOM circumscribed

circunstancia *nf* circumstance; **en estas circunstancias …** under the circumstances …

circunstancial *adj* circumstantial

cirio *nm* wax candle; *Fam & Fig* **ser /montar un cirio** to be / create a commotion

cirrosis *nf inv* cirrhosis

ciruela *nf* plum; **ciruela claudia** greengage; **ciruela pasa** prune

ciruelo *nm* plum tree

cirugía *nf* surgery; **cirugía estética** *o* **plástica** plastic surgery

cirujano, -a *nm, f* surgeon

cisco *nm* **a)** [carbón] slack **b)** *Fam* [alboroto] ruckus **c)** *Fam* **hecho cisco** [persona] shattered; [cosa] smashed to bits

cisma *nm* **a)** REL schism **b)** POL split

cisne *nm* swan

cisterna *nf* cistern, tank

cita *nf* **a)** appointment; **darse cita** to come together **b)** [amorosa] date **c)** [mención] quotation

citación *nf* JUR citation, summons (*sing*)

citar 1. *vt* **a)** [dar cita] to arrange to meet, to make an appointment with **b)** [mencionar] to quote **c)** JUR to summons **2. citarse** *vpr* to arrange to meet, to make a date (**con** with)

cítrico, -a 1. *adj* citric, citrus **2.** *nmpl* **cítricos** citrus fruits

ciudad *nf* town; [capital] city; *Méx* **ciudad perdida** shanty town

ciudadanía *nf* citizenship

ciudadano, -a 1. *nm, f* citizen; **el ciudadano de a pie** the man in the street **2.** *adj* civic

cívico, -a *adj* civic

civil 1. *adj* **a)** civil; **matrimonio civil** civil marriage **b)** MIL civilian **2.** *nm* member of the Guardia Civil

civilización *nf* civilization

civilizado, -a *adj* civilized

civismo *nm* **a)** [urbanidad] public-spiritedness **b)** [cortesía] civility

cl *(abr de* **centilitro***)* cl

clan *nm* clan

clara *nf* a) [de huevo] white b) *Esp Fam* [bebida] shandy

claraboya *nf* skylight

clarear *vi* a) [amanecer] to dawn b) [despejar] to clear up c) [transparentar] to wear thin, to become transparent

claridad *nf* a) [luz] light, brightness b) [inteligibilidad] clarity; **con claridad** clearly

clarinete *nm* clarinet

clarividencia *nf* far-sightedness, perception

claro, **-a 1.** *adj* a) clear; **dejar algo claro** to make sth clear b) [líquido, salsa] thin c) [color] light **2.** *interj* of course!; **¡claro que no!** of course not!; **¡claro que sí!** certainly! **3.** *nm* a) [espacio] gap, space; [en un bosque] clearing b) METEOR bright spell **4.** *adv* clearly

clase *nf* a) [grupo] class; **clase alta / media** upper / middle class; **clases pasivas** pensioners; **primera / segunda clase** first / second class b) [tipo] kind, sort; **toda clase de ...** all kinds of ... c) EDUC [curso] class; [aula] classroom; **clase particular** private class o lesson d) [estilo] class; **tener clase** to have class

clásico, **-a 1.** *adj* classical; [típico] classic; [en el vestir] classic **2.** *nm* a) [autor, obra] classic b) *Am* DEP big game, final; **hoy se juega el clásico** it's the final today

clasificación *nf* a) classification; DEP league table b) [para campeonato, concurso] qualification

clasificado *nm* *Am* small ad

clasificador, **-a 1.** *adj* classifying **2.** *nm* [mueble] filing cabinet

clasificar [44] **1.** *vt* to classify, to class **2. clasificarse** *vpr* DEP to qualify

claudicar [44] *vi* to give in

claustro *nm* a) ARQUIT cloister b) [reunión] ≃ staff meeting, *US* faculty meeting

claustrofobia *nf* claustrophobia

claustrofóbico, **-a** *adj* claustrophobic

cláusula *nf* clause

clausura *nf* a) [cierre] closure; **ceremonia de clausura** closing ceremony b) REL enclosure

clausurar *vt* to close

clavadista *nmf* *CAm, Méx* diver

clavado, **-a** *adj* a) [con clavos] nailed b) [a la medida] just right c) [parecido] almost identical; **ser clavado a algn** to be the spitting image of sb

clavar 1. *vt* a) to nail; [clavo] to bang o hammer in; [estaca] to drive in b) *Fam* [timar] to sting o fleece **2. clavarse** *vpr* **clavarse una astilla** to get a splinter

clave 1. *nf* key; **la palabra clave** the key word **2.** *nm* harpsichord

clavel *nm* carnation

clavícula *nf* collarbone

clavija *nf* TÉC jack

clavo *nm* a) nail; *Fig* **dar en el clavo** to hit the nail on the head b) BOT clove

claxon *nm* horn; **tocar el claxon** to sound the horn

cleptomanía *nf* kleptomania

clericó *nm* *RP* drink made of white wine and fruit

clérigo *nm* priest

clero *nm* clergy

clic *(pl* **clics)** *nm* INFORM click; **clic derecho / izquierdo** right / left click; **hacer clic** to click; **hacer doble clic** to double-click

cliché *nm* a) *Fig* [tópico] cliché b) FOTO negative c) IMPR plate

click = clic

cliente *nmf* customer, client

clima *nm* climate

climático, **-a** *adj* climatic

climatizado, **-a** *adj* air-conditioned

climatología *nf* a) [tiempo] climate b) [ciencia] climatology

clímax *nm inv* climax

clínica *nf* clinic

clínico, -a *adj* clinical

clip *(pl* **clips)** *nm* clip

cloaca *nf* sewer, drain

cloro *nm* chlorine

clorofila *nf* chlorophyll

clóset *(pl* **clósets)** *nm Am* fitted cupboard, *US* closet

club *(pl* **clubs** *o* **clubes)** *nm* club; **club náutico** yacht club

cm *(abr de* **centímetro(s))** cm

coacción *nf* coercion

coaccionar *vt* to coerce

coach ['koutʃ] *(pl* **coachs)** *nmf* coach

coartada *nf* alibi

coba *nf Esp, Méx Fam* [halago] flattery; **dar coba a algn** [adular] to suck up *o* crawl to sb; [aplacar] to soft-soap sb

cobarde 1. *adj* cowardly **2.** *nmf* coward

cobardía *nf* cowardice

cobertizo *nm* shed, shack

cobija *nf Am* [manta] blanket

cobijar 1. *vt* to shelter **2. cobijarse** *vpr* to take shelter

cobra *nf* cobra

cobrador, -a *nm, f* a) [de autobús] conductor, *f* conductress b) [de luz, agua etc] collector

cobrar 1. *vt* a) [dinero] to charge; [cheque] to cash; [salario] to earn; **¿me cobra?** how much is that? b) *Fig* [fuerza] to gain, to get; **cobrar ánimos** to take courage *o* heart; **cobrar importancia** to become important **2.** *vi Fam* to catch it **3. cobrarse** *vpr* **¿se cobra?** [al pagar] how much is that?

cobre *nm* copper

cobro *nm* [pago] collecting; [de cheque] cashing; TEL **llamada a cobro revertido** *Br* reverse-charge call, *US* collect call

coca *nf* a) BOT coca b) *Fam* [droga] cocaine, coke

cocaína *nf* cocaine

cocainómano, -a *nm, f* cocaine addict

cocalero, -a *Bol, Perú* **1.** *adj* región cocalera coca-producing area; **productor cocalero** coca farmer *o* producer **2.** *nm, f* coca farmer *o* producer

cocción *nf* cooking; [en agua] boiling; [en horno] baking

cocear *vi* to kick

cocedor *nm* boiler

cocer [41] **1.** *vt* to cook; [hervir] to boil; [hornear] to bake **2.** *vi* [hervir] to boil **3. cocerse** *vpr* a) [comida] to cook; [hervir] to boil; [hornear] to bake b) [tramarse] to be going on

cochayuyo *nm Chile, Perú* seaweed

coche *nm* a) car, *US* automobile; **en coche** by car; **coche de carreras** racing car; **coche de bomberos** fire engine, *US* fire truck; **coche fúnebre** hearse b) FERROC coach, *Br* carriage, *US* car; **coche cama** sleeping car, sleeper c) [de caballos] carriage

cochecito *nm* [de niño] *Br* pram, *US* baby carriage

cochera *nf* [de autobuses, tranvías] depot; *Am* [de coches] garage

cochinillo *nm* suckling pig

cochino, -a 1. *nm, f* a) pig, *f* sow b) *Fam* [persona] filthy person, pig **2.** *adj* [sucio] filthy, disgusting

cocido *nm* stew

cocina *nf* a) kitchen b) [aparato] cooker, stove; **cocina eléctrica / de gas** electric / gas cooker c) [arte] cooking; **cocina casera** home cooking; **cocina española** Spanish cooking *o* cuisine

cocinar *vt & vi* to cook

cocinero, -a *nm, f* cook

cocinilla *nf* camping stove

coco¹ *nm* coconut; *Fam* [cabeza] nut; **comerle el coco a algn** to brainwash sb; **comerse el coco** to get obsessed

coco² *nm Fam* [fantasma] bogeyman

cocodrilo *nm* crocodile

cocoliche *nm RP Fam* pidgin Spanish spoken by Italian immigrants

cocotero *nm* coconut palm

cóctel *nm* cocktail; *CAm* **cóctel de frutas** fruit cocktail; **cóctel Molotov** Molotov cocktail

coctelera *nf* cocktail shaker

coctelería *nf* cocktail bar

codazo *nm* **a)** [señal] nudge with one's elbow **b)** [golpe] blow with one's elbow

codiciar [43] *vt* to covet

codificado, -a *adj* [emisión de TV] scrambled

codificar *vt* **a)** [gen & INFORM] to code **b)** [ley] to codify

código *nm* code; **código de circulación** highway code; **código postal** *Br* postcode, postal code, *US* zip code

codo *nm* elbow; *Fig* **codo con codo** side by side; *Fam* **hablar por los codos** to talk nonstop

codorniz *nf* quail

coeficiente *nm* **a)** coefficient **b)** [grado] rate; **coeficiente intelectual** intelligence quotient

coetáneo, -a *adj & nm, f* contemporary

coexistencia *nf* coexistence

coexistir *vi* to coexist

cofia *nf* bonnet

cofradía *nf* [hermandad] brotherhood; [asociación] association

cofre *nm* [arca] trunk, chest; [para joyas] box, casket

coger [53] **1.** *vt* **a)** to take; [del suelo] to pick (up); [fruta, flores] to pick; [asir] to seize, take hold of; [bus, tren] to take, catch; [pelota, ladrón, resfriado] to catch; [entender] to grasp; [costumbre] to pick up; [velocidad, fuerza] to gather; [atropellar] to run over, knock down **b)** *Am Vulg* to screw, to fuck **2.** *vi Fam* **cogió y se fue** he upped and left **3. cogerse** *vpr* [agarrarse] to hold on

cogida *nf* goring

cogollo *nm* [de lechuga] heart

cogote *nm Esp* nape o back of the neck

cohabitar *vi* to live together, to cohabit

coherencia *nf* coherence

coherente *adj* coherent

cohesionar *vt* to bring cohesion to

cohete *nm* rocket; **cohete espacial** space rocket

COI *nm (abr de* Comité Olímpico Internacional) DEP IOC

coima *nf Andes, RP Fam* bribe, *Br* backhander

coincidencia *nf* coincidence

coincidir *vi* **a)** to coincide **b)** [concordar] to agree; **todos coincidieron en señalar que** everyone agreed that **c)** [encontrarse] to meet by chance

coito *nm* coitus, intercourse

cojear *vi* [persona] to limp, to hobble; [mueble] to wobble

cojín *nm* cushion

cojo, -a 1. *adj* [persona] lame; [mueble] rickety **2.** *nm, f* lame person

cojón *nm Esp Vulg* ball; **de cojones** [estupendo] *Br* bloody o *US* goddamn brilliant; [pésimo] *Br* bloody o *US* goddamn awful

cojonudo, -a *adj Esp muy Fam Br* bloody o *US* goddamn brilliant

cojudez *nf Andes muy Fam* **¡qué cojudez!** [acto] what a *Br* bloody o *US* goddamn stupid thing to do!; [dicho] what a *Br* bloody o *US* goddamn stupid thing to say!

cojudo, -a *adj Andes muy Fam Br* bloody o *US* goddamn stupid

col *nf* cabbage; **col de Bruselas** Brussels sprout

cola *nf* **a)** [de animal] tail; [de vestido] train; [de pelo] ponytail; **a la cola** at the back o rear; *Fam* **traer cola** to have consequences **b)** [fila] *Br* queue, *US* line; **hacer cola** *Br* to queue (up), *US* to stand in line **c)** [pegamento] glue

colaboración *nf* **a)** collaboration **b)** PRENSA contribution

colaborador, -a 1. *nm, f* **a)** collaborator **b)** PRENSA contributor **2.** *adj* collaborating

colaborar *vi* to collaborate, to co-operate

colaborativo, -a *adj* collaborative

colada *nf Esp* wash, laundry; **hacer la colada** to do the washing o laundry

colado, -a *adj* **a)** [líquido] strained **b)** *Fam* [enamorado] **estar colado por algn** to have a crush on sb

colador *nm* colander, sieve; [de té, café] strainer

colar [2] **1.** *vt* **a)** [líquido] to strain, to filter
b) [por agujero] to slip
2. *vi Fam* **esa mentira no cuela** that lie won't wash
3. colarse *vpr* **a)** to slip in; [a fiesta] to gatecrash; [en una cola] *Br* to jump the queue, *US* to cut in line
b) *Fam* [pasarse] to go too far

colcha *nf* bedspread

colchón *nm* **a)** [de cama] mattress **b)** INFORM buffer

colchoneta *nf* air bed

colear 1. *vi* **a)** [animal] to wag its tail **b)** *Fig* [asunto, problema] **el asunto todavía colea** the issue isn't quite resolved yet **2.** *vt Col, Méx Fam* [fastidiar] to annoy **3. colearse** *vpr Arg, Ven* to skid about

colección *nf* collection

coleccionar *vt* to collect

coleccionismo *nm* collecting

coleccionista *nmf* collector

colecta *nf* collection

colectar *vt* **a)** [dinero] to collect **b)** [plantas, frutos] to pick

colectivo, -a 1. *adj* collective **2.** *nm* **a)** [asociación] association **b)** *Andes* [taxi] collective taxi *(with a fixed rate and travelling a fixed route)* **c)** *Arg, Bol* [autobús] bus

colega *nmf* **a)** [compañero profesional] colleague, *US* co-worker **b)** *Esp Fam* [amigo] pal, *Br* mate, *US* buddy

colegiado, -a *nm, f* DEP referee

colegial, -a 1. *adj* [escolar] school **2.** *nm, f* [alumno] schoolboy; [alumna] schoolgirl; **los colegiales** the schoolchildren

colegio *nm* **a)** [escuela] school; **colegio privado** private school, *Br* public o independent school **b)** [profesional] association, college; **colegio de abogados** the Bar; POL **colegio electoral** electoral college **c)** *Esp* **colegio mayor** hall of residence

cólera[1] *nf* anger, rage

cólera[2] *nm* MED cholera

colérico, -a *adj* furious

colesterol *nm* cholesterol

coleta *nf* pigtail, ponytail; *Fig* **cortarse la coleta** to retire

colgador *nm* [percha] hanger, coat-hanger; [gancho] hook

colgar [2] **1.** *vt* **a)** to hang (up); [colada] to hang (out)
b) [ahorcar] to hang
2. *vi* **a)** to hang (**de** from); *Fig* **colgar de un hilo** to hang by a thread
b) TEL to hang up
3. colgarse *vpr* [ahorcarse] to hang oneself

coliflor *nf* cauliflower

colilla *nf* (cigarette) end o butt

colimba *nf Arg Fam* military service

colina *nf* hill

colirio *nm* eye-drops

colitis *nf* colitis

colla *Bol* **1.** *adj* of /from the altiplano **2.** *nmf* indigenous person from the altiplano

collage *nm* collage

collar *nm* **a)** [adorno] necklace **b)** [de perro] collar

collarín *nm* surgical collar

colmado, -a *adj* full, filled; [cuchrada] heaped

colmar *vt* **a)** to fill (right up); [vaso, copa] to fill to the brim; *Fig* to shower (**de** with) **b)** [ambiciones] to fulfil, to satisfy

colmena *nf* beehive

colmillo *nm* eye o canine tooth; ZOOL [de carnívoro] fang; [de jabalí, elefante] tusk

colmo *nm* height; **el colmo de** the height of; **¡eso es el colmo!** that's the last straw!; **para colmo** to top it all

colocación *nf* a) [acto] positioning b) [disposición] layout c) [empleo] job, employment

colocado, -a *adj* a) [empleado] employed b) *Fam* [drogado] high

colocar [44] **1.** *vt* a) to place, to put b) FIN [invertir] to invest c) [emplear] to give work to **2. colocarse** *vpr* a) [situarse] to put oneself b) [emplearse] to take a job (**de** as) c) *Fam* [drogarse] to get high

Colombia *n* Colombia

colombiano, -a *adj & nm, f* Colombian

colonia¹ *nf* colony; [campamento] summer camp; *Méx* [barrio] district

colonia² *nf* [perfume] cologne

coloniaje *nm Am* a) [época] *period of Spanish colonialism in the American continent* b) [gobierno] colonial government

colonización *nf* colonization

colonizar [40] *vt* to colonize

colono *nm* settler, colonist

coloquial *adj* colloquial

coloquio *nm* discussion, colloquium

color *nm* colour; CINE & FOTO **en color** in colour; **de colores** multicoloured; **persona de color** coloured person

coloración *nf* colouration

colorado, -a **1.** *adj* red; **ponerse colorado** to blush **2.** *nm* red

colorante *nm* colouring

colorete *nm* rouge

colorido *nm* colour

colosal *adj* colossal

columna *nf* column; ANAT **columna vertebral** vertebral column, spinal column

columpiar [43] **1.** *vt* to swing **2. columpiarse** *vpr* to swing

columpio *nm* swing

coma¹ *nf* a) LING & MÚS comma b) MAT point; **tres coma cinco** three point five

coma² *nm* MED coma

comadre *nf* a) [madrina] *godmother of one's child, or mother of one's godchild* b) *Fam* [amiga] *Br* mate, *US* buddy

comadreja *nf* weasel

comadrona *nf* midwife

comal *nm CAm, Méx flat clay or metal dish used for baking "tortillas"*

comandante *nm* a) MIL commander, commanding officer b) AVIACIÓN captain

comando *nm* a) MIL commando b) INFORM command

comarca *nf* region

comba *nf Esp* a) [juego] skipping; **jugar a la comba** *Br* to skip, *US* to jump rope b) [cuerda] *Br* skipping rope, *US* jump rope

combate *nm* combat; [en boxeo] fight; MIL battle; **fuera de combate** out for the count; [eliminado] out of action

combatir 1. *vt* to combat **2.** *vi* **combatir contra** to fight against

combinación *nf* a) combination b) [prenda] slip c) INFORM **combinación de teclas** keyboard shortcuts

combinado, -a 1. *adj* combined **2.** *nm* a) [cóctel] cocktail b) DEP line-up

combinar 1. *vt* to combine **2. combinarse** *vpr* = **combinar**

combustible 1. *nm* fuel **2.** *adj* combustible

combustión *nf* combustion

comecocos *nm inv* a) *Fam* [para convencer] **este panfleto es un comecocos** this pamphlet is designed to brainwash you b) *Fam* [cosa difícil de comprender] mind-bending problem o puzzle c) [juego] pac-man®

comedia *nf* comedy

comediante, -a *nm, f* [hombre] actor; [mujer] actress

comedor *nm* dining room

comensal *nmf* companion at table

comentar *vt* comentar algo con algn to talk sth over with sb; **me han comentado que ...** I've been told that ...

comentario *nm* a) comment, remark; [crítica] commentary; **sin comentario** no comment b) **comentarios** [cotilleos] gossip

comentarista *nmf* commentator

comenzar [51] *vt* & *vi* to begin, to start; **comenzó a llover** it started raining o to rain; **comenzó diciendo que ...** he started by saying that ...

comer **1.** *vt* a) [alimentos] to eat, b) [en juegos] to take, to capture **2.** *vi* [ingerir alimentos] to eat; *Esp*, *Méx* [al mediodía] to have lunch; **dar de comer a algn** to feed sb **3. comerse** *vpr* a) to eat b) *Fig* [saltarse] to skip

comercial **1.** *adj* commercial; [zona, calle] shopping; **centro comercial** shopping mall, *Br* shopping centre **2.** *nmf* [vendedor, representante] salesman, *f* saleswoman **3.** *nm Am* [anuncio] commercial, *Br* advert

comercializar [40] *vt* to market

comerciante *nmf* merchant

comerciar [43] *vi* to trade; **comercia con oro** he trades in gold

comercio *nm* a) commerce, trade; **comercio exterior** foreign trade; INFORM **comercio electrónico** e-commerce; **comercio justo** fair trade b) [tienda] shop

comestible **1.** *adj* edible **2.** *nmpl* **comestibles** food, foodstuff(s); **tienda de comestibles** grocer's shop, *US* grocery store

cometa **1.** *nm* ASTRON comet **2.** *nf* [juguete] kite

cometer *vt* [error, falta] to make; [delito, crimen] to commit

cometido *nm* a) [tarea] task, assignment b) [deber] duty; **cumplir su cometido** to do one's duty

cómic *(pl* **cómics)** *nm* comic

comicios *nmpl* elections

cómico, -a 1. *adj* a) comical, funny b) TEATRO **actor cómico** comedian **2.** *nm*, *f* comic; [hombre] comedian; [mujer] comedienne

comida *nf* a) [alimento] food b) [almuerzo, cena] meal; *Esp*, *Méx* [al mediodía] lunch

comienzo *nm* beginning, start; **a comienzos de** at the beginning of; **dar comienzo (a algo)** to begin o start (sth)

comillas *nfpl* inverted commas; **entre comillas** in inverted commas

comilón, -ona 1. *adj* greedy, gluttonous **2.** *nm*, *f* big eater, glutton

comilona *nf Fam* blowout, *Br* slap-up meal

comino *nm* cumin, cummin; *Fam* **me importa un comino** I don't give a damn (about it)

comisaría *nf* police station, *US* precinct, *US* station house

comisario *nm* a) [de policía] *Br* superintendent, *US* captain b) [delegado] commissioner; **comisario europeo** European Commissioner

comisión *nf* a) COM [retribución] commission; **a** o **con comisión** on a commission basis b) [comité] committee; **la Comisión Europea** the European Commission

comisura *nf* corner *(of mouth, eyes)*

comité *nm* committee

comitiva *nf* suite, retinue

como 1. *adv* a) [manera] **me gusta como cantas** I like the way you sing; **dilo como quieras** say it however you like

b) [comparación] like; **habla como su padre** he talks like his father; **blanco como la nieve** as white as snow; *Am* **como ser** like; **frutas exóticas como ser mangostinos** exotic fruits like mangosteens

c) [según] as; **como decíamos ayer** as we were saying yesterday

d) [en calidad de] as; **como presidente** as president; **lo compré como recuerdo** I bought it as a souvenir

e) [aproximadamente] about ; **como unos diez** about ten

2. *conj* **a)** *Esp* (+ *subjuntivo*) [si] if ; **como no estudies vas a suspender** if you don't study hard, you'll fail

b) [porque] as, since ; **como no venías me marché** as you didn't come, I left

c) como que [que] that ; **le pareció como que lloraban** he thought that they were crying ; **como quiera que** [de cualquier modo que] however ; **como quiera que sea** however ; **como si** as if ; **como si nada** *o* **tal cosa** as if nothing had happened

---

cómo 1. *adv* **a)** ¿cómo? [¿perdón?] what? **b)** [interrogativo] how ; ¿cómo estás? how are you? ; ¿cómo lo sabes? how do you know? ; ¿cómo es de grande / ancho? how big / wide is it? ; *Esp* ¿a cómo están los tomates? how much are the tomatoes? ; ¿cómo es que no viniste a la fiesta? [por qué] how come you didn't come to the party? **c)** [exclamativo] how ; ¡cómo has crecido! you've really grown a lot! ; ¡cómo no! but of course! **2.** *nm* el cómo y el porqué the whys and wherefores

cómoda *nf* chest of drawers

comodidad *nf* **a)** comfort **b)** [conveniencia] convenience

comodín *nm* NAIPES joker

cómodo, -a *adj* **a)** comfortable ; **ponerse cómodo** to make oneself comfortable **b)** [útil] handy, convenient

comodón, -ona 1. *adj* [amante de la comodidad] comfort-loving ; [vago] laid-back ; **no seas comodón** don't be so lazy **2.** *nm, f* [amante de la comodidad] comfort-lover ; [vago] laid-back person

compa *nmf Fam* pal, *Br* mate, *US* buddy

compact ['kompak] *nm inv* CD, compact disc

compacto, -a *adj* compact ; **disco compacto** compact disc, CD

compadecer [33] **1.** *vt* to feel sorry for, to pity **2. compadecerse** *vpr* to have *o* take pity (**de** on)

compadre *nm* **a)** [padrino] *godfather of one's child, or father of one's godchild* **b)** *Fam* [amigo] *Br* mate, *US* buddy

compadrear *vi RP* to brag, to boast

compadreo *nm* [amistad] friendship

compaginar *vt* to combine

compañerismo *nm* companionship, comradeship

compañero, -a *nm, f* companion ; **compañero de colegio** school friend ; *Esp* **compañero de piso** *Br* flatmate, *US* roommate ; **compañero sentimental** partner

compañía *nf* company ; **hacer compañía (a algn)** to keep (sb) company ; **compañía de seguros / de teatro** insurance / theatre company

comparación *nf* comparison ; **en comparación** comparatively ; **en comparación con** compared to ; **sin comparación** beyond compare

comparar *vt* to compare (**con** with)

comparsa *nf* band of revellers

compartido, -a *adj* shared

compartimento, compartimiento *nm* compartment ; **compartimento de primera / segunda clase** first- / second-class compartment

compartir *vt* to share ; **se comparte piso** flat share available

compás *nm* **a)** TÉC (pair of) compasses **b)** NÁUT compass **c)** MÚS [división] time ; [intervalo] beat ; [ritmo] rhythm ; **compás de espera** MÚS bar rest ; *Fig* [pausa] delay ; **al compás de** in time to

compasión *nf* compassion, pity ; **tener compasión (de algn)** to feel sorry (for sb)

compasivo, -a *adj* compassionate

compatible *adj* [gen & INFORM] compatible

compatriota *nmf* compatriot, fellow countryman, *f* fellow countrywoman

compay *nm Cuba Fam Br* mate, *US* buddy

compenetrado, -a *adj* **estar muy compenetrados** to be really close

compenetrarse *vpr* to get along well

compensación *nf* compensation

compensar 1. *vt* [pérdida, error] to make up for; [indemnizar] to compensate (for) **2.** *vi* to be worthwhile; **este trabajo no compensa** this job's not worth my while

competencia *nf* **a)** [rivalidad, empresas rivales] competition **b)** [capacidad] competence **c)** [incumbencia] field, province; **no es de mi competencia** it's not up to me

competente *adj* competent

competición *nf* competition, contest

competir [6] *vi* to compete (**con/en/por** with o against/in/for)

competitivo, -a *adj* competitive

compilar *vt* [gen & INFORM] to compile; [información] to gather

complacer [60] **1.** *vt* to please; *Formal* **me complace presentarles a …** it gives me great pleasure to introduce to you… **2. complacerse** *vpr* to delight (**en** in), to take pleasure (**en** in)

complaciente *adj* obliging

complejidad *nf* complexity

complejo, -a *adj* & *nm* complex

complementar 1. *vt* to complement **2. complementarse** *vpr* to complement (each other), to be complementary to (each other)

complementario, -a *adj* complementary

complemento *nm* complement; LING object

completamente *adv* completely

completar *vt* to complete

completo, -a *adj* **a)** [terminado] complete; **por completo** completely **b)** [lleno] full; **al completo** full up to capacity

complexión *nf* build; **de complexión fuerte** well-built

complicación *nf* complication

complicado, -a *adj* **a)** [complejo] complicated **b)** [implicado] involved

complicar [44] **1.** *vt* **a)** to complicate **b) complicar en** [involucrar] to involve in **2. complicarse** *vpr* to get complicated; **complicarse la vida** to make life difficult for oneself

cómplice *nmf* accomplice

complot *(pl* **complots)** *nm* conspiracy, plot

componente 1. *adj* component **2.** *nm* **a)** [pieza] component; [ingrediente] ingredient **b)** [persona] member

componer [19] *(pp* **compuesto)** **1.** *vt* **a)** [formar] to compose, to make up **b)** MÚS & LITER to compose **c)** [reparar] to mend, to repair **2. componerse** *vpr* **a) componerse de** [consistir] to be made up of, to consist of **b)** [arreglarse] to dress up **c)** *Fam* **componérselas** to manage **d)** *Am* [de enfermedad] to get better

comportamiento *nm* behaviour

comportar 1. *vt* to entail, to involve **2. comportarse** *vpr* to behave; **comportarse mal** to misbehave

composición *nf* composition

compositor, -a *nm, f* composer

compostelano, -a 1. *adj* from Santiago de Compostela **2.** *nm, f* native or inhabitant of Santiago de Compostela

compostura *nf* composure

compota *nf* compote

compra *nf* [acción] buying; [cosa comprada] purchase, buy; **hace** *Esp* **la compra** o *Am* **las compras** to do the shopping; **ir de compras** to go shopping

comprador, -a *nm, f* purchaser, buyer

comprar *vt* **a)** to buy **b)** *Fig* [sobornar] to bribe, to buy off

comprender *vt* **a)** [entender] to understand; **se comprende** it's understandable **b)** [contener] to comprise, to include

comprensible *adj* understandable

comprensión *nf* understanding

comprensivo, -a *adj* understanding

compresa *nf* **a)** [para mujer] sanitary *Br* towel o *US* napkin **b)** MED compress

compresor, -a 1. *adj* compressing **2.** *nm* compressor

comprimido, -a 1. *nm* FARM tablet **2.** *adj* compressed; **escopeta de aire comprimido** air rifle

comprimir *vt* to compress

comprobación *nf* checking

comprobar [2] *vt* to check

comprometer 1. *vt* **a)** [arriesgar] to compromise, to jeopardize **b)** [obligar] to compel, to force **2. comprometerse** *vpr* **a)** comprometerse a hacer algo to undertake to do sth **b)** [novios] to become engaged

comprometido, -a *adj* **a)** [situación] difficult **b)** [para casarse] engaged

compromiso *nm* **a)** [obligación] obligation, commitment; **sin compromiso** without obligation; **por compromiso** out of a sense of duty **b) poner (a algn) en un compromiso** to put (sb) in a difficult o embarrassing situation **c)** [acuerdo] agreement; *Formal* **compromiso matrimonial** engagement; **soltero y sin compromiso** single and unattached

compuerta *nf* floodgate, sluicegate

compuesto, -a 1. *adj* **a)** compound **b) compuesto de** composed of **2.** *nm* compound

compungido, -a *adj* [arrepentido] remorseful; [triste] sorrowful, sad

computación *nf* **a)** [cálculo] computation **b)** *Am* [ciencia] ICT *(Information and Communications Technology)*

computacional *adj* computer

computador *nm* computer

computadora *nf* computer

comulgar [42] *vi* **a)** to receive Holy Communion **b)** *Fig* **no comulgo con sus ideas** I don't share his ideas

común 1. *adj* **a)** common; **de común acuerdo** by common consent; **hacer algo en común** to do sth jointly; **poco común** unusual; **por lo común** generally **b)** [compartido] shared, communal; **amigos comunes** mutual friends **2.** *nm* Br POL **los Comunes** the Commons

comuna *nf* **a)** [colectividad] commune **b)** *Am* [municipalidad] municipality

comunero, -a *nm, f Perú, Méx* [indígena] *member of an indigenous village community*

comunicación *nf* **a)** communication; **ponerse en comunicación (con algn)** to get in touch (with sb) **b)** [comunicado] communication; **comunicación oficial** communiqué **c)** TEL connection; **se nos cortó la comunicación** we were cut off **d)** [unión] link, connection

comunicado, -a 1. *adj* **una zona bien comunicada** a well-served zone; **dos ciudades bien comunicadas** two towns with good connections (between them) **2.** *nm* communiqué; **comunicado de prensa** press release

comunicador, -a *nm, f* communicator

comunicar [44] **1.** *vt* to communicate; **comuníquenoslo lo antes posible** let us know as soon as possible
2. *vi* **a)** to communicate
b) *Esp* TEL *Br* to be engaged, *US* to be busy; **está comunicando** it's *Br* engaged o *US* busy
3. comunicarse *vpr* to communicate

comunicativo, -a *adj* communicative

comunidad *nf* community; **Comunidad Autónoma** autonomous region; **Comunidad Europea** European Community; **Comunidad de Estados Independientes** Commonwealth of Independent States

comunión *nf* communion

comunismo *nm* communism

comunista *adj & nmf* communist

comunitario, -a *adj* **a)** of o relating to the community **b)** [de UE] of o relating to the EU; **la política agraria comunitaria** the common agricultural policy

con *prep* **a)** with; **córtalo con las tijeras** cut it with the scissors; **voy cómodo con este jersey** I'm comfortable in this sweater
b) [compañía] with; **vine con mi hermana** I came with my sister
c) [contenido] with; **con ese frío / niebla** in that cold / fog; **estar con (la) gripe** to have the flu
d) [contenido] with; **una bolsa con dinero** a bag (full) of money

e) [relación] to ; **habló con todos** he spoke to everybody ; **sé amable con ella** be nice to her

f) [+ infinitivo] **con llamar será suficiente** it will be enough just to phone **g)** [+ que + subjuntivo] **bastará con que lo esboces** a general idea will do **h) con tal (de) que ...** provided that ...; **con todo (y eso)** even so

conato *nm* attempt ; **conato de asesinato** attempted murder

cóncavo, -a *adj* concave

concebir [6] **1.** *vt* **a)** [plan, hijo] to conceive **b)** [entender] to understand **2.** *vi* [mujer] to become pregnant, to conceive

conceder *vt* to grant ; [premio] to award

concejal, -a *nm, f* town councillor

concentración *nf* concentration ; [de manifestantes] gathering ; [de coches, motos] rally ; [de equipo] base

concentrado *nm* concentrate

concentrar 1. *vt* to concentrate **2. concentrarse** *vpr* **a)** [mentalmente] to concentrate (**en** on) **b)** [reunirse] to gather

concepción *nf* conception

concepto *nm* **a)** [idea] concept ; **tener buen / mal concepto de** to have a good / a bad opinion of ; **bajo** *o* **por ningún concepto** under no circumstances **b) en concepto de** under the heading of **c)** [en factura] item

concernir [54] *v impers* **a)** [afectar] to concern ; **en lo que a mí concierne** as far as I am concerned ; **en lo que concierne a** with regard / respect to **b)** [corresponder] to be up to

concertación *nf* compromise, agreement

concertado, -a *adj* **a)** [precio] agreed **b)** *Esp* [escuela] private school (*which receives a state grant*)

concertar [1] **1.** *vt* **a)** [cita] to arrange ; [precio] to agree on ; [acuerdo] to reach **b)** [una acción etc] to plan, to co-ordinate **2.** *vi* to agree, to tally

concesión *nf* **a)** concession **b)** [de un premio, contrato] awarding

concesionario, -a *nm, f* dealer

concha *nf* **a)** ZOOL [caparazón] shell ; [carey] tortoiseshell **b)** *Andes, RP Vulg* [vulva] cunt **c)** *Ven* [de árbol] bark ; [de fruta] peel, rind ; [de pan] crust ; [de huevo] shell **d)** *Am Vulg* **concha de su madre** bastard, *f* bitch

concheto, -a *RP Fam* **1.** *adj* posh **2.** *nm, f* rich kid

conchudo, -a *nm, f* **a)** *Andes, Méx, Ven Fam* [desfachatado] **ser bien conchudo** to have a real nerve, *Vulg* to have balls **b)** *Andes, Méx, Ven Fam* [cómodo] lazybones, layabout **c)** *Perú, RP muy Fam* jerk, *Br* dickhead

conciencia *nf* **a)** conscience ; **tener la conciencia tranquila** to have a clear conscience **b)** [conocimiento] consciousness, awareness ; **a conciencia** conscientiously ; **tener / tomar conciencia (de algo)** to be / to become aware (of sth)

concienciar [43], *Am* **concientizar** [40] **1.** *vt* to make aware (**de** of) **2. concienciarse** *vpr* to become aware (**de** of)

concientizarse *Am vpr* = **concienciarse**

concienzudo, -a *adj* conscientious

concierto *nm* **a)** MÚS concert ; [composición] concerto **b)** [acuerdo] agreement

conciliación *nf* [en un litigio] reconciliation ; [en un conflicto laboral] conciliation

conciliar [43] *vt* to reconcile ; **conciliar el sueño** to get to sleep

concisión *nf* conciseness

conciso, -a *adj* concise

concluir [37] *vt* to conclude

conclusión *nf* conclusion ; **sacar una conclusión** to draw a conclusion

concomerse *vpr* **concomerse de** [envidia, remordimiento] to be eaten up with ; [impaciencia] to be itching with

concordancia *nf* [gen & LING] agreement

concordar [2] **1.** *vi* to agree; **esto no concuerda con lo que dijo ayer** this doesn't fit in with what he said yesterday **2.** *vt* to bring into agreement

concordia *nf* concord

concretar *vt* [precisar] to specify, to state explicitly; [fecha, hora] to fix

concreto, -a 1. *adj* a) [preciso, real] concrete b) [particular] specific; **en concreto** specifically; **en el caso concreto de ...** in the specific case of ... **2.** *nm Am* [hormigón] concrete; **concreto armado** reinforced concrete

concubina *nf* concubine

concurrencia *nf* a) [de dos cosas] concurrence b) [público] audience

concurrente 1. *adj* concurrent **2.** *nmf* person present

concurrido, -a *adj* crowded, busy

concursante *nmf* a) contestant, competitor b) [para un empleo] candidate

concursar *vi* to compete, to take part

concurso *nm* a) [competición] competition; [de belleza etc] contest; TV quiz show; **presentar (una obra) a concurso** to invite tenders (for a piece of work) b) *Formal* [ayuda] help

condado *nm* [territorio] county

condal *adj* of o relating to a count; **la Ciudad Condal** Barcelona

conde *nm* count

condecoración *nf* decoration

condena *nf* a) JUR sentence b) [desaprobación] condemnation, disapproval

condenado, -a 1. *adj* a) JUR convicted; **condenado a muerte** condemned to death b) REL or *Fam* damned; **condenado al fracaso** doomed to failure **2.** *nm, f* a) JUR convicted person; [a muerte] condemned person b) REL damned person

condenar 1. *vt* a) JUR to convict, to find guilty; **condenar a algn a muerte** to condemn sb to death b) [desaprobar] to condemn **2. condenarse** *vpr* REL to be damned

condensación *nf* condensation

condensar 1. *vt* to condense **2. condensarse** *vpr* to condense

condición *nf* a) condition; **en buenas /malas condiciones** in good / bad condition; **condiciones de trabajo** working conditions; **con la condición de que ...** on the condition that ... b) [manera de ser] nature, character c) **en su condición de director** [calidad] in his capacity as director

condicional *adj* conditional

condimentar *vt* to season, to flavour

condimento *nm* seasoning, flavouring

condominio *nm Am* [edificio] *Br* block of flats, *US* condominium

conducción *nf* a) *Esp* [de vehículo] driving b) [por tubería] piping; [por cable] wiring

conducir [10] **1.** *vt* [coche] to drive; [electricidad] to conduct **2.** *vi* a) AUTO to drive; **permiso de conducir** *Br* driving licence, *US* driver's license b) [camino, actitud] to lead; **eso no conduce a nada** this leads nowhere

conducta *nf* behaviour, conduct; **mala conducta** misbehaviour, misconduct

conducto *nm* a) [tubería] pipe; *Fig* **por conductos oficiales** through official channels b) ANAT duct, canal

conductor, -a 1. *nm, f* AUTO driver **2.** *nm* ELEC conductor

conectado, -a *adj* a) ELEC connected, plugged in b) INFORM connected

conectar *vt* a) to connect up b) ELEC to plug in, to switch on

conejera *nf* [madriguera] (rabbit) warren; [conejar] rabbit hutch

conejo *nm* rabbit

conexión *nf* connection

confección *nf* a) COST dressmaking, tailoring b) [de un plan etc] making, making up

confederación *nf* confederation

conferencia *nf* a) lecture; **dar una conferencia (sobre algo)** to give a lec-

confundir

ture (on sth) **b) conferencia de prensa**
press conference **c)** TEL long-distance
call

conferenciante *nmf* lecturer

conferencista *nmf* Am lecturer

confesar [1] **1.** *vt* to confess, to admit;
[crimen] to own up to; REL [pecados]
to confess
2. *vi* JUR to own up
3. confesarse *vpr* to confess; **confesar culpable** to admit one's guilt;
REL to go to confession

confesión *nf* confession, admission;
REL confession

confesionario *nm* REL confessional

confesor *nm* confessor

confeti (*pl* **confetis**) *nm* confetti

confiado, -a *adj* **a)** [seguro] self-confident **b)** [crédulo] gullible, unsuspecting

confianza *nf* **a)** [seguridad] confidence; **tener confianza en uno mismo**
to be self-confident **b) de confianza**
reliable **c) tener confianza con algn**
to be on intimate terms with sb; **con
toda confianza** in all confidence; **tomarse (demasiadas) confianzas** to
take liberties

confiar [29] **1.** *vt* [entregar] to entrust;
[información, secreto] to confide
2. *vi* **confiar en** to trust; **confío en ella**
I trust her; **no confíes en su ayuda**
don't count on his help
3. confiarse *vpr* to confide (**en o a** in);
confiarse demasiado to be over-con-
fident

confidencia *nf* confidence

confidencial *adj* confidential

confidencialidad *nf* confidentiality

confidente, -a *nm, f* **a)** [hombre]
confidant; [mujer] confidante **b)** [de
la policía] informer

configuración *nf* [gen & INFORM]
configuration

configurar *vt* **a)** [formar] to shape, to
form **b)** INFORM to configure

confirmación *nf* confirmation

confirmar *vt* to confirm; **la excepción confirma la regla** the exception
proves the rule

confiscar [44] *vt* to confiscate

confitado, -a *adj* candied; **frutas
confitadas** crystallized fruit

confite *nm* Br sweet, US candy

confitería *nf* **a)** [tienda] confectioner's
b) RP [café] café

confitura *nf* preserve, jam

conflictivo, -a *adj* [asunto] controversial; [época] unsettled; **niño conflictivo** problem child

conflicto *nm* conflict; **conflicto laboral** industrial dispute

confluencia *nf* confluence

confluir [37] *vi* to converge; [caminos,
ríos] to meet, to come together

conformar 1. *vt* to shape **2. conformarse** *vpr* to resign oneself, to
be content

conforme 1. *adj* **a)** [satisfecho] satisfied; **conforme** agreed, all right; **no
estoy conforme** I don't agree **b) conforme a** in accordance o keeping with
2. *conj* **a)** [según, como] as; **conforme
lo vi / lo oí** as I saw / heard it **b)** [a medida que] as; **la policía los detenía
conforme iban saliendo** the police
were arresting them as they came out

conformidad *nf* **a)** approval, consent
b) en conformidad con in conformity with

conformismo *nm* conformity

conformista *adj & nmf* conformist

confort (*pl* **conforts**) *nm* comfort; **todo
confort** [en anuncio] all mod cons

confortable *adj* comfortable

confrontación *nf* **a)** [enfrentamien-
to] confrontation **b)** [comparación]
contrast

confundido, -a *adj* **a)** [confuso] confused **b)** [equivocado] **estar confundido** to be mistaken

confundir 1. *vt* **a)** to confuse (**con**
with); **confundir a una persona
con otra** to mistake somebody for
somebody else

b) [persona] to mislead
c) [turbar] to confound
2. confundirse *vpr* **a)** [equivocarse] to be mistaken; TEL **se ha confundido** you've got the wrong number
b) [mezclarse] to mingle; **se confundió entre el gentío** he disappeared into the crowd

---

confusión *nf* confusion

confuso, -a *adj* **a)** confused; [formas, recuerdo] blurred, vague **b)** [mezclado] mixed up

congelación *nf* **a)** freezing **b)** FIN freeze; **congelación salarial** wage freeze **c)** MED frostbite

congelado, -a 1. *adj* frozen; MED frostbitten **2.** *nmpl* **congelados** frozen food

congelador *nm* freezer

congelar 1. *vt* to freeze **2. congelarse** *vpr* **a)** to freeze; *Fam* **me estoy congelando** I'm freezing **b)** MED to get o become frostbitten

congeniar [43] *vi* to get on (**con** with)

congénito, -a *adj* congenital

congestión *nf* congestion; MED **congestión cerebral** stroke

congestionado, -a *adj* congested

conglomerado *nm* conglomerate

congregar [42] **1.** *vt* to congregate, to assemble **2. congregarse** *vpr* = **congregar**

congresista *nmf* member of a congress

congreso *nm* congress, conference; POL **Congreso de los Diputados** *lower house of Spanish Parliament,* ≃ *Br* House of Commons, ≃ *US* House of Representatives

conjetura *nf* conjecture; **por conjetura** by guesswork

conjugación *nf* conjugation

conjugar [42] **1.** *vt* to conjugate; *Fig* [planes, opiniones] to combine **2. conjugarse** *vpr* **a)** GRAM to conjugate **b)** *Fig* [elementos] to join together, to combine

conjunción *nf* conjunction

conjuntivitis *nf inv* conjunctivitis

conjunto, -a 1. *nm* **a)** [grupo] collection, group **b)** [todo] whole; **de conjunto** overall; **en conjunto** on the whole **c)** MÚS [pop] group, band **d)** [prenda] outfit, ensemble **e)** MAT set **f)** DEP team **2.** *adj* joint

conmemoración *nf* commemoration

conmemorar *vt* to commemorate

conmigo *pron pers* with me; **vino conmigo** he came with me; **él habló conmigo** he talked to me

conmoción *nf* commotion, shock; **conmoción cerebral** concussion

conmover [4] *vt* to touch, to move

conmutador *nm* **a)** ELEC switch **b)** *Am* TEL switchboard

connotado, a *adj Am* distinguished

cono *nm* cone; **Cono Sur** *Chile, Argentina, Paraguay and Uruguay*

conocer [34] **1.** *vt* **a)** to know; **dar (algo/algn) a conocer** to make (sth/sb) known **b)** [a una persona] to meet **c)** [reconocer] to recognize; **te conocí por la voz** I recognized you by your voice **2. conocerse** *vpr* [dos personas] to know each other; [por primera vez] to meet

conocido, -a 1. *adj* known; [famoso] well-known **2.** *nm, f* acquaintance

conocimiento *nm* **a)** knowledge; **con conocimiento de causa** with full knowledge of the facts **b)** [conciencia] consciousness; **perder/recobrar el conocimiento** to lose/regain consciousness **c)** **conocimientos** knowledge

conque *conj* so

conquista *nf* conquest

conquistador, -a *nm, f* conqueror

conquistar *vt* [país, ciudad] to conquer; *Fig* [puesto, título] to win; [a una persona] to win over

consagrado, -a *adj* **a)** REL consecrated **b)** [dedicado] dedicated **c)** [reconocido] recognized, established

consagrar 1. *vt* **a)** REL to consecrate **b)** [artista] to confirm **c)** [tiempo, vida] to devote **2. consagrarse** *vpr* **a) consagrarse a** [dedicarse] to devote oneself to, to dedicate oneself to **b)** [lograr fama] to establish oneself

consciente *adj* **a)** conscious, aware; **ser consciente de algo** to be aware of sth **b)** MED conscious

conscripto *nm Andes, Arg* conscript

consecuencia *nf* **a)** consequence; **a** *o* **como consecuencia de** as a consequence *o* result of; **en consecuencia** therefore; **tener** *o* **traer (malas) consecuencias** to have (ill) effects; **sacar como** *o* **en consecuencia** to come to a conclusion **b)** [coherencia] consistency; **actuar en consecuencia** to be consistent

consecuente *adj* consistent

consecutivo, -a *adj* consecutive; **tres días consecutivos** three days in a row

conseguir [6] *vt* **a)** to get, to obtain; [objetivo] to achieve **b) conseguí terminar** I managed to finish

consejo *nm* **a)** [recomendación] advice; **un consejo** a piece of advice **b)** [junta] council; **consejo de ministros** cabinet; [reunión] cabinet meeting; **consejo de administración** board of directors; **consejo de guerra** court martial

consenso *nm* consensus

consentido, -a *adj* spoiled

consentir [5] **1.** *vt* **a)** [tolerar] to allow, to permit; **no consientas que haga eso** don't allow him to do that **b)** [mimar] to spoil **2.** *vi* to consent; **consentir en** to agree to

conserje *nm* [de colegio, ministerio] doorman, *Br* porter; [de bloque de viviendas] *Br* caretaker, *US* superintendent, *US* supervisor

conserjería *nf* [de colegio, ministerio] porter's lodge; [de bloque de viviendas] *Br* caretaker's office, *US* superintendent's *o* supervisor's office

conserva *nf* canned food, *Br* tinned food

conservador, -a 1. *adj & nm, f* conservative; POL Conservative **2.** *nm* [de museo] curator

conservante *nm* preservative

conservar 1. *vt* to conserve, to preserve; [mantener] to keep up, to maintain; [alimentos] to preserve **2. conservarse** *vpr* **a)** [tradición etc] to survive **b) conservarse bien** [persona] to age well

conservatorio *nm* conservatory

considerable *adj* considerable

consideración *nf* **a)** consideration; **tomar algo en consideración** to take sth into account **b)** [respeto] regard **c) de consideración** important, considerable; **herido de consideración** seriously injured

considerar *vt* to consider; **lo considero imposible** I think it's impossible

consigna *nf* **a)** [para maletas] *Br* left-luggage office, *US* checkroom **b)** MIL orders, instructions

consigo¹ *pron pers* **a)** [tercera persona - hombre] with him; [mujer] with her; [cosa, animal] with it; [plural] with them; [usted] with you **b) hablar consigo mismo** to speak to oneself

consigo² *indic pres de* **conseguir**

consiguiente *adj* resulting, consequent; **por consiguiente** therefore, consequently

consistencia *nf* **a)** consistency **b)** [de argumento] soundness

consistente *adj* **a)** [firme] firm, solid **b)** [teoría] sound **c) consistente en** consisting of

consistir *vi* to consist (**en** of); **el secreto consiste en tener paciencia** the secret lies in being patient

consistorio *nm* town *o US* city council

consola *nf* [tablero de mandos] console table; INFORM console; **consola de videojuegos** games console

consolar [2] **1.** *vt* to console, to comfort **2. consolarse** *vpr* to console oneself, to take comfort (**con** from)

consolidación *nf* consolidation

consolidar 1. *vt* to consolidate **2. consolidarse** *vpr* = **consolidar**

consomé *nm* clear soup, consommé

consonante *adj* & *nf* consonant

consorcio *nm* consortium

consorte 1. *adj* **príncipe consorte** prince consort **2.** *nmf* [cónyuge] partner, spouse

conspiración *nf* conspiracy, plot

conspirar *vi* to conspire, to plot

constancia *nf* a) constancy, perseverance b) [testimonio] proof, evidence; **dejar constancia de algo** to put sth on record

constante 1. *adj* constant; [persona] steadfast **2.** *nf* constant feature; MAT constant

constantemente *adv* constantly

constar *vi* a) [figurar] to figure, to be included (**en** in); **constar en acta** to be on record b) **me consta que ...** I am absolutely certain that ... c) **constar de** to be made up of, to consist of

constatación *nf* verification

constatar *vt* [observar] to observe, to notice; [comprobar] to verify

constelación *nf* constellation

constipado, -a 1. *adj* **estar constipado** to have a cold *o* a chill **2.** *nm* cold, chill

constiparse *vpr* to catch a cold *o* a chill

constitución *nf* constitution

constitucional *adj* constitutional

constituir [37] **1.** *vt* a) [formar] to constitute; **estar constituido por** to consist of b) [suponer] to represent c) [fundar] to constitute, to set up **2. constituirse** *vpr* **constituirse en** to set oneself up as

construcción *nf* a) construction; [sector] the building industry; **en construcción** under construction b) [edificio] building

constructivo, -a *adj* constructive

constructor, -a 1. *nm, f* builder **2.** *adj* **empresa constructora** builders, construction company

construir [37] *vt* to build, to manufacture

consuelo *nm* consolation

cónsul *nmf* consul

consulado *nm* consulate

consulta *nf* a) consultation; **obra de consulta** reference book b) [despacho de médico] *Br* surgery, *US* office; **horas de consulta** surgery hours

consultar *vt* to consult, to seek advice (**con** from); [libro] to look up

consultor, -a 1. *adj* consulting **2.** *nm, f* consultant

consultorio *nm* a) [de un médico] *Br* surgery, *US* office b) PRENSA problem page, advice column

consumición *nf* a) consumption b) [bebida] drink

consumidor, -a 1. *nm, f* consumer **2.** *adj* consuming

consumir 1. *vt* to consume **2. consumirse** *vpr* [al hervir] to boil away; *Fig* [persona] to waste away

consumismo *nm* consumerism

consumo *nm* consumption; **bienes de consumo** consumer goods; **sociedad de consumo** consumer society

contabilidad *nf* a) COM [profesión] accountancy b) [de empresa, sociedad] accounting, bookkeeping

contable *nmf Esp* accountant

contacto *nm* a) contact; AUTO ignition; **perder el contacto** to lose touch; **ponerse en contacto** to get in touch b) **contactos** [amistades] contacts; *Esp* PRENSA personals, personal ads

contado, -a 1. *adj* a) [raro] few; **contadas veces, en contadas ocasiones** rarely b) [enumerado] listed, counted **2.** *nm* a) *Am* [plazo] instalment, *US* installment b) **pagar al contado** to pay cash

contador, -a 1. *nm, f Am* [persona] accountant; **contador público** *Br* chartered accountant, *US* certified public accountant **2.** *nm* [aparato] meter; **contador de agua** water meter

contagiar [43] **1.** *vt* MED to pass on **2. contagiarse** *vpr* **a)** [persona] to get infected **b)** [enfermedad] to be contagious

contagio *nm* contagion

contagioso, -a *adj* contagious; *Fam* [risa] infectious

container *(pl* containers*) nm* [para mercancías] container

contaminación *nf* contamination; [del aire] pollution

contaminado, -a *adj* [alimento] contaminated; [medio ambiente] polluted

contaminar *vt* to contaminate; [aire, agua] to pollute

---

contar [2] **1.** *vt* **a)** [sumar] to count **b)** [narrar] to tell **2.** *vi* **a)** to count **b) contar con** [confiar en] to count on; [tener] to have **3. contarse** *vpr Fam* **¿qué te cuentas?** how's it going?

---

contemplación *nf* **a)** [meditación] contemplation **b)** [consideración] **contemplaciones** consideration; **tratar a algn sin contemplaciones** not to take sb's feelings into account; **nos echaron sin contemplaciones** they threw us out unceremoniously

contemplar *vt* to contemplate; [considerar] to consider; [estipular] to stipulate

contemporáneo, -a *adj* & *nm, f* contemporary

contenedor *nm* container

contener [24] **1.** *vt* **a)** to contain **b)** [pasiones etc] to restrain, to hold back **2. contenerse** *vpr* to control oneself, to hold (oneself) back

contenido *nm* content, contents

contentar 1. *vt* **a)** [satisfacer] to please **b)** [alegrar] to cheer up **2. contentarse** *vpr* **a)** [conformarse] to make do (**con** with), to be satisfied (**con** with) **b)** [alegrarse] to cheer up

contento, -a *adj* happy, pleased (**con** with)

contestación *nf* answer; **dar contestación** to answer

contestador *nm* **contestador automático** answering machine

contestar *vt* **a)** to answer **b)** *Fam* [replicar] to answer back

contexto *nm* context

contienda *nf* [competición, combate] competition; [guerra] conflict

contigo *pron pers* with you

contiguo, -a *adj* contiguous (**a** to), adjoining

continental *adj* continental

continente *nm* **a)** GEOGR continent **b)** [compostura] countenance

continuación *nf* continuation; **a continuación** next

continuamente *adv* continuously

continuar [30] *vt* & *vi* to continue, to carry on (with); **continúa en Francia** he's still in France; **continuará** to be continued

continuo, -a 1. *adj* **a)** continuous; AUTO **línea continua** solid white line **b)** [reiterado] continual, constant **2.** *nm* continuum

contorno *nm* **a)** outline **b) contornos** surroundings, environment

contra 1. *prep* against; **en contra de** against **2.** *nm* **los pros y los contras** the pros and cons

contrabajo *nm* double bass

contrabandista *nmf* smuggler; **contrabandista de armas** gunrunner

contrabando *nm* smuggling; **contrabando de armas** gunrunning; **pasar algo de contrabando** to smuggle sth in

contracorriente 1. *nf* crosscurrent **2.** *adv* **ir (a) contracorriente** to go against the tide

contractura *nf* contraction

contradecir [12] *(pp* contradicho*) vt* to contradict

contradicción *nf* contradiction

contradictorio, -a *adj* contradictory

contraer [25] **1.** *vt* to contract; **contraer matrimonio con algn** to marry sb **2. contraerse** *vpr* to contract

contraindicado, -a *adj* **está contraindicado beber alcohol durante el embarazo** alcohol should be avoided during pregnancy

contralor *nm Am* [en institución, empresa] comptroller

contraloría *nf Am* [oficina] comptroller's office

contraluz *nm* view against the light; **a contraluz** against the light

contramano ▪ **a contramano** *loc adv* **el coche venía a contramano** the car was driving on the wrong side of the road, the car was driving the wrong way up the road

contraoferta *nf* counteroffer

contrapartida *nf* **en contrapartida** in return

contrapelo ▪ **a contrapelo** *loc adv* [acariciar] the wrong way; **su intervención iba a contrapelo del resto** his remarks went against the general opinion; **vivir a contrapelo** to have an unconventional lifestyle

contrapeso *nm* counterweight

contrariar [29] *vt* **a)** [oponerse a] to oppose, to go against **b)** [disgustar] to upset

contrario, -a 1. *adj* **a)** opposite; **lo contrario de** the opposite of; **en el lado / sentido contrario** on the other side / in the other direction; **al contrario, por el contrario** on the contrary; **de lo contrario** otherwise; **todo lo contrario** quite the opposite **b)** [perjudicial] contrary (**a** to) **2.** *nm, f* opponent, rival **3.** *nf* **llevar la contraria** to be contrary

contraseña *nf* password

contrastar *vt* to contrast (**con** with)

contraste *nm* **a)** contrast **b)** [en oro, plata] hallmark

contratar *vt* to hire, to engage

contratiempo *nm* setback, hitch

contrato *nm* contract; **contrato de trabajo** work contract; **contrato de alquiler** lease, leasing agreement; **contrato basura** short-term contract with poor conditions

contribuidor, -a *nm, f* contributor

contribuir [37] **1.** *vt* to contribute (**a** to) **2.** *vi* **a)** to contribute **b)** [pagar impuestos] to pay taxes

contributivo, -a *adj* contributive

contrincante *nmf* rival, opponent

control *nm* **a)** control; **control a distancia** remote control **b)** [inspección] check; [de policía etc] checkpoint

controlador, -a 1. *nm, f* controller; **controlador aéreo** air-traffic controller **2.** *nm* INFORM controller

controlar 1. *vt* **a)** to control **b)** [comprobar] to check **2. controlarse** *vpr* to control oneself

controvertido, a *adj* controversial

contusión *nf* contusion, bruise

conuco *nm Carib* [parcela] small plot of land

conurbano *nm RP* suburbs (*pl*)

convalidar *vt* to validate; [documento] to ratify

convencer [49] *vt* to convince; **convencer a algn de algo** to convince sb about sth

convención *nf* convention

convencional *adj* conventional

conveniente *adj* **a)** [oportuno] convenient; [aconsejable] advisable **b)** [precio] good, fair

convenio *nm* agreement; **convenio laboral** agreement on salary and conditions

convenir [27] *vt & vi* **a)** [acordar] to agree; **convenir una fecha** to agree on a date; **sueldo a convenir** salary negotiable; **convenir en** to agree on **b)** [ser oportuno] to suit, to be good for; **conviene recordar que …** it's as well to remember that …

convento *nm* [de monjas] convent; [de monjes] monastery

conversación *nf* conversation

conversada *nf Am Fam* chat

conversar *vi* to converse, to talk

convertir [54] **1.** *vt* to change, to convert **2. convertirse** *vpr* **a)** **convertirse en** to turn into, to become **b)** REL to be converted (**a** to)

convicción *nf* conviction; **tengo la convicción de que ...** I am convinced that ...

convidado, -a *adj & nm, f* guest

convidar *vt* to invite

convincente *adj* convincing

convite *nm* reception

convivencia *nf* life together; *Fig* coexistence

convivir *vi* to live together; *Fig* to coexist (**con** with)

convocar [44] *vt* to summon; [reunión, elecciones] to call

convocatoria *nf* **a)** [a huelga etc] call **b)** EDUC diet

convulsión *nf* MED convulsion; [agitación social] upheaval

convulsivo, -a *adj* MED convulsive

cónyuge *nmf* spouse; **cónyuges** married couple, husband and wife

coña *nf Esp muy Fam* **dar la coña** to be a pain in the neck, to get on sb's nerves; **está de coña** she's just pissing around; **pasárselo de coña** to have a brilliant time

coñac (*pl* **coñacs**) *nm* brandy, cognac

coñazo *nm Esp muy Fam* pain, drag; **dar el coñazo** to be a real pain

coño *esp Esp Vulg* **1.** *nm* cunt, twat **2.** *interj* [enfado] for fuck's sake!

cooperar *vi* to co-operate (**con** with)

cooperativa *nf* co-operative

coordinación *nf* co-ordination

coordinar *vt* to co-ordinate

copa *nf* **a)** glass; **tomar una copa** to have a drink **b)** [de árbol] top **c)** DEP cup **d)** NAIPES **copas** hearts

copado, -a *adj RP Fam* great

copeo *nm Fam* boozing; **ir de copeo** to go out boozing

copete *nm* **a)** [de ave] crest **b)** [de pelo] tuft **c)** **de alto copete** high-society, *Br* posh

copetín *nm RP* **a)** [bebida] aperitif **b)** [comida] appetizer

copia *nf* copy; INFORM **copia de seguridad** backup; INFORM **hacer una copia de seguridad de algo** to back up sth

copiar [43] *vt* to copy

copiloto *nm* AVIACIÓN co-pilot; AUTO co-driver

copioso, -a *adj* abundant, copious

copla *nf* verse, couplet

copo *nm* flake; [de nieve] snowflake; **copos de maíz** cornflakes

copyright [,kopi'rait] *nm* copyright

coquetear *vi* to flirt (**con** with)

coqueteo *nm* flirting

coqueto, -a 1. *adj* coquettish **2.** *nm, f* flirt

coraje *nm* **a)** [valor] courage **b)** [ira] anger, annoyance; *Fig* **dar coraje a algn** to infuriate sb; **¡qué coraje!** how maddening!

coral¹ *nm* ZOOL coral

coral² *nf* MÚS choral, chorale

coraza *nf* armour; *Fig* protection

corazón *nm* **a)** heart; *Fig* **de (todo) corazón** in all sincerity; **romper** *o* **partir el corazón a algn** to break sb's heart; *Fig* **tener buen corazón** to be kind-hearted **b)** [parte central] heart; [de fruta] core **c)** NAIPES **corazones** hearts

corbata *nf* tie, *US* necktie; **con corbata** wearing a tie

corchea *nf* MÚS *Br* quaver, *US* eighth note

corchete *nm* **a)** IMPR square bracket **b)** COST hook and eye

corcho *nm* cork; [de pesca] float

cordel *nm* rope, cord

cordero, -a *nm, f* lamb

cordial *adj* cordial, warm

cordillera *nf* mountain chain *o* range; *RP* **la Cordillera** the Andes

cordillerano, -a *RP* **1.** *adj* Andean **2.** *nm, f* person from the Andes

cordón nm a) string; [de zapatos] shoelace; ANAT **cordón umbilical** umbilical cord; **cordón policial** police cordon b) CSur, Cuba [de la vereda] Br kerb, US curb

Corea n Korea; **Corea del Norte / Sur** North / South Korea

coreografía nf choreography

corista 1. nmf [en coro] chorus singer 2. nf [en cabaret] chorus girl

cornada nf TAUROM goring

cornamenta nf a) [de toro] horns; [de ciervo] antlers b) Fam & Fig [de marido engañado] cuckold's horns

córnea nf cornea

corneja nf crow

córner (pl **córners**) nm DEP corner (kick); **sacar un córner** to take a corner

cornete nm a) ANAT turbinate bone b) [helado] cornet, cone

cornflakes® ['konfleiks] nmpl Corn Flakes®

cornisa nf cornice

coro nm MÚS choir; TEATRO chorus; Fig **a coro** all together

corona nf a) crown b) [de flores etc] wreath, garland; **corona funeraria** funeral wreath

coronar vt to crown

coronel nm colonel

coronilla nf crown of the head; Fam **estar hasta la coronilla (de)** to be fed up (with)

corpiño nm [vestido] bodice; Arg [sostén] bra

corporal adj corporal; **castigo corporal** corporal punishment; **olor corporal** body odour, BO

corpulento, -a adj corpulent, stout

corpus nm corpus

corral nm farmyard, US corral; [de casa] courtyard

corralón nm Méx car pound

correa nf a) [tira] strap; [de reloj] watchstrap; [de pantalón] belt; [de perro] lead, leash b) TÉC belt

corrección nf a) [rectificación] correction b) [urbanidad] courtesy, politeness

correcto, -a adj a) [sin errores] correct b) [educado] polite, courteous (**con** to); [conducta] proper

corredor, -a nm, f a) DEP runner b) FIN **corredor de bolsa** stockbroker

corregir [58] 1. vt to correct 2. **corregirse** vpr to mend one's ways

correo nm a) Br post, US mail; **correo aéreo** airmail; **correo basura** junk mail, spam; **correo certificado** registered Br post o US mail; **correo comercial** junk mail; INFORM **correo electrónico** electronic mail, e-mail; INFORM **me envió un correo (electrónico)** [un mensaje] she e-mailed me, she sent me an e-mail; **echar algo al correo** to Br post o US mail sth; **por correo** by Br post o US mail b) Am [organismo] **el Correo** the mail, Br the post c) Esp **Correos** [institución] the post office

correr 1. vi a) to run; [coche] to go fast; [conductor] to drive fast; [viento] to blow; Fig **no corras, habla más despacio** don't rush, speak slower; **correr prisa** to be urgent
b) **correr con los gastos** to foot the bill; **corre a mi cargo** I'll take care of it 2. vt a) [cortina] to draw; [cerrojo] to close; [aventura etc] to have; **correr el riesgo** o **peligro** to run the risk
b) [mover] to pull up, to draw up
3. **correrse** vpr a) [moverse] to move over
b) Fam **correrse una juerga** to go on a spree
c) Andes, Esp muy Fam [tener un orgasmo] to come

correspondencia nf a) correspondence b) FERROC connection

corresponder 1. vi a) to correspond (**a** to; **con** with)
b) [incumbir] to concern, to be incumbent upon; **esta tarea te corresponde a ti** it's your job to do this
c) [pertenecer] to belong; **me dieron lo que me correspondía** they gave me my share

2. corresponderse *vpr* **a)** [ajustarse] to correspond
b) [dos cosas] to tally; **no se corresponde con la descripción** it does not match the description
c) [dos personas] to love each other

correspondiente *adj* corresponding (**a** to)

corresponsal *nmf* correspondent

corrida *nf* **corrida (de toros)** bullfight

corriente 1. *adj* **a)** [común] common
b) [agua] running
c) [mes, año] current, present; **el diez del corriente** the tenth of this month
d) FIN [cuenta] current
e) estar al corriente to be up to date
2. *nf* **a)** current, stream; *Fig* **ir** *o* **navegar contra corriente** to go against the tide; *Fam* **seguirle** *o* **llevarle la corriente a algn** to humour sb; ELEC **corriente eléctrica** (electric) current
b) [de aire] *Br* draught, *US* draft
c) [tendencia] trend, current

corro *nm* **a)** circle, ring **b)** [juego] ring-a-ring-a-roses

corromper 1. *vt* **a)** [pudrir] to turn bad, to rot **b)** [pervertir] to corrupt, to pervert **2. corromperse** *vpr* **a)** [pudrirse] to go bad, to rot **b)** [pervertirse] to become corrupted

corrupción *nf* **a)** [putrefacción] rot, decay **b)** *Fig* corruption; JUR **corrupción de menores** corruption of minors

corsé *nm* corset

corsetería *nf* ladies' underwear shop

cortacésped *nm o nf* lawnmower

cortado, -a 1. *adj* **a)** cut (up) **b)** [leche] sour **c)** [labios] chapped **d)** *Fam* [tímido] shy **2.** *nm* small coffee with a dash of milk

cortante *adj* **a)** [afilado] sharp **b)** *Fig* [tajante - frase, estilo] cutting; [viento] biting; [frío] bitter

cortar 1. *vt* **a)** to cut; [carne] to carve; [árbol] to cut down; *Fam* **cortar por lo**
sano to take drastic measures; *Fam* **cortó con su novio** she split up with her boyfriend
b) [piel] to chap, to crack
c) [luz, teléfono] to cut off
d) [paso, carretera] to block
e) INFORM to cut; **cortar y pegar** to cut and paste
2. cortarse *vpr* **a)** [herirse] to cut oneself
b) **cortarse el pelo** to have one's hair cut
c) [leche etc] to curdle
d) TEL **se cortó la comunicación** we were cut off
e) *Fam* [aturdirse] to become all shy

cortaúñas *nm inv* nail clippers

corte¹ *nm* **a)** cut; **corte de pelo** haircut; TV **corte publicitario** commercial break; **corte de mangas** ≃ V-sign
b) [sección] section; **corte transversal** cross-section **c)** *Fam* rebuff; **dar un corte a algn** to cut sb dead

corte² *nf* **a)** [real] court **b)** *Esp* **las Cortes** (Spanish) Parliament

cortés *(pl* **corteses)** *adj* courteous, polite

cortesía *nf* courtesy, politeness

corteza *nf* [de árbol] bark; [de queso] rind; [de pan] crust

cortijo *nm* Andalusian farm *o* farmhouse

cortina *nf* curtain; **cortina de humo** smoke screen

corto, -a 1. *adj* **a)** [distancia, tiempo] short; *Fam* **corto de luces** dim-witted; **corto de vista** short-sighted; AUTO **luz corta** dipped headlights
b) *Fam* **quedarse corto** [calcular mal] to underestimate **c)** [apocado] timid, shy **2.** *nm* **a)** CINE short (movie *o Br* film)
b) *Am* **cortos** trailer

cortometraje *nm* short (movie *o Br* film)

cosa *nf* **a)** thing; **no he visto cosa igual** I've never seen anything like it; **no ser gran cosa** not to be up to much **b)** [asunto] matter, business; **eso es cosa tuya** that's your business o affair; **eso es otra cosa** that's different **c) hace cosa de una hora** about an hour ago

coscorrón nm knock o blow on the head

cosecha nf a) AGRIC harvest, crop b) [año del vino] vintage

cosechar vt to harvest, to gather (in)

coser vt a) to sew; Fam **es coser y cantar** it's a piece of cake b) MED to stitch up

cosmopolita adj & nmf cosmopolitan

cosmos nm inv cosmos

coso nm a) TAUROM bullring b) CSur Fam [objeto] whatnot, thing; **¿para qué sirve ese coso?** [en aparato] what's this thing o thingumajig for?

cosquillas nfpl tickling; **hacer cosquillas a algn** to tickle sb; **tener cosquillas** to be ticklish

cosquilleo nm tickling

costa¹ nf coast; [litoral] coastline; [playa] beach, seaside

costa² nf a **costa de** at the expense of; **a toda costa** at all costs, at any price; **vive a costa mía** he lives off me

costado nm side; **de costado** sideways; **es catalana por los cuatro costados** she's Catalan through and through

costanera nf CSur promenade

costar [2] vi a) to cost; **¿cuánto cuesta?** how much is it?; **costar barato / caro** to be cheap /expensive b) Fig **te va a costar caro** you'll pay dearly for this; **costar trabajo o mucho** to be hard; **me cuesta hablar francés** I find it difficult to speak French; **cueste lo que cueste** at any cost

Costa Rica n Costa Rica

costarricense adj & nmf Costa Rican

costarriqueño, -a adj & nm, f Costa Rican

coste nm Esp cost; **coste de la vida** cost of living; **a precio de coste** (at) cost price; **de bajo coste** [producto, viaje] low-cost; **compañías aéreas de bajo coste** low-cost airlines

costera nf Méx [paseo] promenade (along the seafront)

costero, -a 1. adj coastal; **ciudad costera** seaside town **2.** nm, f Am [habitante] coastal dweller **3.** nm [carretera] coastal road

costilla nf a) ANAT rib b) CULIN cutlet

costo¹ nm cost

costo² nm Esp Fam [hachís] dope, shit, stuff

costoso, -a adj costly, expensive

costra nf crust; MED scab

costumbre nf a) [hábito] habit; **como de costumbre** as usual; **tengo la costumbre de levantarme temprano** I usually get up early; **tenía la costumbre de ...** he used to ... b) [tradición] custom

costura nf a) sewing b) [confección] dressmaking; **alta costura** haute couture c) [línea de puntadas] seam

costurera nf seamstress

costurero nm sewing basket

cota nf GEOGR height above sea level; Fig rating

cotejar vt to compare

cotidiano, -a adj daily; **vida cotidiana** everyday life

cotilla Fam **1.** adj Esp **es muy cotilla** she's a real gossip **2.** nmf Esp [persona] gossip; **eres un cotilla** you love a bit of gossip

cotilleo nm Esp Fam gossip

cotillón nm party on New Year's Eve or 5th of January

cotización nf a) FIN (market) price, quotation b) [cuota] membership fees, subscription

cotizar [40] **1.** vt FIN to quote **2.** vi to pay national insurance **3. cotizarse** vpr FIN **cotizarse a** to sell at

coto nm a) enclosure, reserve; **coto de caza** game reserve b) **poner coto a** to put a stop to

cotorra nf parrot; Fig [persona] chatterbox

country nm (abr de countries) Arg luxury suburban housing development

coyote *nm* **a)** [mamífero] coyote **b)** *Méx Fam* [guía] *guide who helps people cross the border illegally from Mexico into the US*

coyuntura *nf* **a)** ANAT articulation, joint **b)** *Fig* [circunstancia] juncture; **la coyuntura económica** the economic situation

coz *nf* kick; **dar una coz** to kick

cráneo *nm* cranium, skull

crápula 1. *nm* debauched man, wastrel; **es un crápula** he's debauched, he leads a debauched existence **2.** *nf* debauched woman **3.** *nmf Am* [mala persona] scumbag

cráter *nm* crater

creación *nf* creation

creador, -a *nm, f* creator

crear *vt* to create

creatividad *nf* creativity

creativo, -a *adj* creative

crecer [33] *vi* **a)** to grow; **crecer en importancia** to become more important **b)** [al tricotar] to increase

crecimiento *nm* growth

credencial *adj* credential; **(cartas) credenciales** credentials

crédito *nm* **a)** COM & FIN credit **b)** [confianza] belief; **dar crédito a** to believe

credo *nm* creed

creencia *nf* belief

creer [36] **1.** *vt* **a)** to believe **b)** [pensar] to think; **creo que no** I don't think so; **creo que sí** I think so; **ya lo creo** I should think so **2.** *vi* to believe; **creer en** to believe in **3. creerse** *vpr* **a)** to consider oneself to be; **¿qué te has creído?** what o who do you think you are? **b) no me lo creo** I can't believe it

creído, -a 1. *adj* arrogant, vain **2.** *nm, f* bighead

crema *nf* cream

cremallera *nf Br* zip (fastener), *US* zipper

crepe *nm* crêpe, pancake

cresta *nf* **a)** crest; [de gallo] comb **b)** [de punk] mohican

cretino, -a 1. *adj* stupid, cretinous **2.** *nm, f* cretin

creyente *nmf* believer; **no creyente** non-believer

cría *nf* **a)** [cachorro] young **b)** [crianza] breeding, raising

criadero *nm* nursery

criadilla *nf* CULIN bull's testicle

criado, -a 1. *adj* **mal criado** spoilt **2.** *nm, f* servant

crianza *nf* [de animales] breeding; *Fig* **vinos de crianza** vintage wines

criar [29] *vt* **a)** [animales] to breed, to raise; [niños] to bring up, to rear **b)** [producir] to have, to grow

criatura *nf* **a)** (living) creature **b)** [crío] baby, child

crimen *nm* murder; **crimen de guerra** war crime

criminal *nmf & adj* criminal

criminólogo, -a *nm, f* criminologist

crío, -a 1. *nm Fam* kid **2.** *adj* babyish

criollo, -a *adj & nm, f* Creole

criptografía *nf* cryptography

críquet *nm* cricket

crisis *nf inv* **a)** crisis **b)** [ataque] fit, attack; **crisis nerviosa** nervous breakdown

crispado, a *adj* tense

cristal *nm* **a)** crystal; **cristal de roca** rock crystal **b)** *Esp* [vidrio] glass; [de gafas] lens; [de ventana] (window) pane

cristalería *nf* [conjunto] glassware; [vasos] glasses

cristalero *nm Am* [de tienda] display case; [escaparate] shop window

cristalino, -a *adj* crystal clear

cristianismo *nm* Christianity

cristiano, -a *adj & nm, f* Christian

Cristo *nm* Christ

criterio *nm* **a)** [pauta] criterion **b)** [opinión] opinion **c)** [discernimiento] discretion; **lo dejo a tu criterio** I'll leave it up to you

crítica *nf* a) criticism b) PRENSA review; **tener buena crítica** to get good reviews c) [conjunto de críticos] critics

criticar [44] **1.** *vt* to criticize **2.** *vi* [murmurar] to gossip

crítico, -a 1. *adj* critical **2.** *nm, f* critic

croar *vi* to croak

crocanti *nm* nut brittle

croissant [krwa'san] *(pl* **croissants***)* *nm* croissant

croissantería [krwasante'ria] *nf* shop selling filled croissants

crol *nm* crawl

cromo *nm* a) [metal] chromium, chrome b) *Esp* [estampa] picture card

crónica *nf* a) account, chronicle b) PRENSA feature, article

cronometrar *vt* to time

cronómetro *nm* stopwatch

croqueta *nf* croquette

croquis *nm inv* sketch

cross *nm inv* DEP [carrera] cross-country race; [deporte] cross-country (running)

cruce *nm* a) crossing; [de carreteras] crossroads; [de razas] crossbreeding b) TEL crossed line

crucero *nm* NÁUT cruise; [barco] cruiser

crucial *adj* crucial

crucificar *vt* [en una cruz] to crucify; *Fig* [atormentar] to torment

crucifijo *nm* crucifix

crucigrama *nm* crossword (puzzle)

crudo, -a 1. *adj* a) raw; [comida] underdone; *Fam & Fig* **lo veo muy crudo** it doesn't look too good b) [clima] harsh c) [color] cream **2.** *nm* [petróleo] crude

cruel *adj* cruel

crueldad *nf* cruelty; *Fig* [del clima] severity

crujido *nm* [de puerta] creak, creaking; [de dientes] grinding

crujiente *adj* crunchy

crustáceo *nm* crustacean

cruz *nf* a) cross; **Cruz Roja** Red Cross; **cruz gamada** swastika b) **¿cara o cruz?** ≈ heads or tails?

cruza *nf Am* cross, crossbreed

cruzada *nf* crusade

cruzar [40] **1.** *vt* a) to cross
b) [palabras, miradas] to exchange
c) [animal, planta] to cross, to crossbreed
2. *vi* [atravesar] to cross
3. cruzarse *vpr* to cross; **cruzarse con algn** to pass sb

cta. *(abr de* **cuenta***)* COM a/c

cta. cte. *(abr de* **cuenta corriente***)* COM c/a

cte. *(abr de* **corriente***)* inst.

cuaderno *nm* notebook

cuadra *nf* a) [establo] stable b) *Am* [en calle] block c) *Perú* [recibidor] reception room

cuadrado, -a 1. *adj* a) GEOM square
b) [complexión física] broad, stocky
c) *Fig* [mente] rigid **2.** *nm* a) GEOM square
b) MAT square; **elevar (un número) al cuadrado** to square (a number)

cuadrangular 1. *adj* quadrangular
2. *nm Am* DEP [en béisbol] quadrangular tournament

cuadrar 1. *vt* a) MAT to square b) *Andes* [aparcar] to park **2.** *vi* [coincidir] to square, agree **(con** with); [sumas, cifras] to tally **3. cuadrarse** *vpr* [soldado] to stand to attention

cuadriculado, -a *adj* **papel cuadriculado** square paper

cuadrilla *nf* [equipo] gang, team; MIL squad; TAUROM bullfighter's team

cuadro *nm* a) GEOM square; **tela a cuadros** checked cloth b) ARTE painting, picture c) TEATRO scene d) ELEC & TÉC panel; **cuadro de mandos** control panel e) [gráfico] chart, graph

cuajada *nf* curd

cual 1. *pron relat* a) *(precedido de artículo)* [persona - sujeto] who; [objeto] whom b) [cosa] which **2.** *pron* a) **tal cual** exactly as b) *Literario* [comparativo] such as, like

cuál 1. *pron interr* which (one)?, what?; **¿cuál quieres?** which one do you want? **2.** *adj interr* which **3.** *loc adv* **a cuál más tonto** each more stupid than the other

cualidad *nf* quality

cualificado, -a *adj* qualified

cualquier *adj indef* any; **cualquier cosa** anything; **en cualquier momento** at any moment o time

cualquiera *(pl* **cualesquiera)**

Note that **cualquier** is used before singular nouns (e.g. **cualquier hombre** any man).

1. *adj indef* a) [indefinido] any; **un profesor cualquiera** any teacher b) [corriente] ordinary **2.** *pron indef* a) [persona] anybody; **cualquiera te lo puede decir** anybody can tell you b) [cosa, animal] anyone c) **cualquiera que sea** whatever it is **3.** *nmf Fig* **ser un cualquiera** to be a nobody; **es una cualquiera** she's a tart

cuando 1. *adv* [de tiempo] when; **cuando más** at the most; **cuando menos** at least; **de cuando en cuando, de vez en cuando** from time to time **2.** *conj* a) [temporal] when; **cuando quieras** whenever you want; **cuando vengas** when you come b) [condicional - si] if c) [concesiva - aunque] **(aun) cuando** even if **3.** *prep* during, at the time of; **cuando la guerra** during the war; **cuando niño** as a child

cuándo 1. *adv interr* a) when?; **¿cuándo vienes?** when are you coming?; **¿desde cuándo?** since when?; **¿para cuándo lo quieres?** when do you want it for? b) *Am* **los empleados se quejan de los sueldos bajos — ¡cuándo no!** the workers are complaining about low wages — there's a surprise! **2.** *nm* **el cómo y el cuándo** the whys and the wherefores; **ignora**

el cómo y el cuándo de la operación he doesn't know any of the details of the operation

cuantía *nf* quantity, amount

cuanto, -a 1. *adj* all; **gasta cuanto dinero gana** he spends all the money o as much as he earns; **unas cuantas niñas** a few girls **2.** *pron relat* as much as; **coma cuanto quiera** eat as much as you want; **regala todo cuanto tiene** he gives away everything he's got **3.** *pron indef pl* **unos cuantos** a few **4.** *adv* a) [tiempo] **cuanto antes** as soon as possible; **en cuanto** as soon as b) [cantidad] **cuanto más ... más** the more ... the more; **cuanto más lo miro, más me gusta** the more I look at it, the more I like it; **cuantas más personas (haya) mejor** the more the merrier c) **en cuanto a** with respect to, regarding; **en cuanto a Juan** as for Juan, as far as Juan is concerned

cuánto, -a 1. *adj & pron interr* [sing] how much?; [pl] how many?; **¿cuántas veces?** how many times?; **¿cuánto es?** how much is it? **2.** *adv* how, how much; **¡cuánta gente hay!** what a lot of people there are!

cuarenta *adj & nm inv* forty; *Fam* **cantarle a algn las cuarenta** to give sb a piece of one's mind

cuaresma *nf* Lent

cuartel *nm* MIL barracks; **cuartel general** headquarters; *Fig* **no dar cuartel** to give no quarter

cuartelazo *nm* military uprising, revolt

cuarteto *nm* quartet

cuartilla *nf* sheet of paper

cuarto, -a 1. *nm* a) [habitación] room; **cuarto de baño** bathroom; **cuarto de estar** living room b) [cuarta parte] quarter; **cuarto de hora** quarter of an hour; *DEP* **cuartos de final** quarter finals c) *Fam* **cuartos** [dinero] dough, money d) **tres cuartos** [abrigo] car coat **2.** *adj & nm, f* fourth

cuarzo *nm* quartz

cuate *nmf CAm, Ecuad, Méx Fam* **a)** [amigo] pal, *US* buddy **b)** [persona - hombre] guy, *Br* bloke ; [mujer] woman

cuatro 1. *adj & nm inv* four **2.** *nm Fam* a few ; **cayeron cuatro gotas** it rained a little bit

cuatrocientos, -as *adj & nm* four hundred

Cuba *n* Cuba

cubalibre *nm* rum / gin and coke

cubano, -a *adj & nm, f* Cuban

cubertería *nf* cutlery

cubeta *nf* [cuba pequeña] bucket, pail ; [de barómetro] bulb ; FOTO tray

cúbico, -a *adj* cubic ; MAT **raíz cúbica** cube root

cubierta *nf* **a)** cover **b)** [de rueda] tyre **c)** NÁUT deck **d)** [techo] roof

cubierto, -a 1. *adj* **a)** covered ; [piscina] indoors ; [cielo] overcast **b)** [trabajo, plaza] filled **2.** *nm* **a)** [en la mesa] place setting **b)** **cubiertos** cutlery

cubitera *nf* **a)** [bandeja] ice tray **b)** [cubo] ice bucket

cubito *nm* little cube ; **cubito de hielo** ice cube

cúbito *nm* ANAT ulna

cubo *nm* **a)** bucket ; **cubo de la basura** *Br* rubbish bin, *US* garbage can **b)** MAT cube **c)** [de rueda] hub

cubrir *(pp* cubierto*)* **1.** *vt* to cover **2. cubrirse** *vpr* [cielo] to become overcast

cucaracha *nf* cockroach

cuchara *nf* spoon

cucharada *nf* spoonful ; **cucharada rasa / colmada** level / heaped spoonful

cucharilla *nf* teaspoon ; **cucharilla de café** coffee spoon

cucharón *nm* ladle

cucheta *nf Am* bunk

cuchilla *nf* blade ; **cuchilla de afeitar** razor blade

cuchillo *nm* knife

cuclillas *nfpl* **en cuclillas** squatting ; **ponerse en cuclillas** to squat (down)

cucufato, -a *nm, f CSur Fam* nut

cucurucho *nm* **a)** [para helado] cornet **b)** [de papel] paper cone

cuello *nm* **a)** [de persona, animal, botella] neck **b)** [de prendas] collar

cuenca *nf* **a)** GEOGR basin **b)** [de los ojos] socket

cuenco *nm* earthenware bowl

cuenta *nf* **a)** [factura] bill ; [en restaurante] *Br* bill, *US* check
b) FIN [de banco] account ; **cuenta corriente** *Br* current account, *US* checking account
c) [cálculo] count ; **cuenta atrás** countdown ; **hacer** *o* **echar cuentas** to do sums, to do some calculations, to work out the cost
d) [de collar] bead
e) INFORM account ; **cuenta de correo (electrónico)** e-mail account
f) [locuciones] **caer en la cuenta, darse cuenta** to realize ; **dar cuenta** to report ; **tener en cuenta** to take into account ; **más sillas de la cuenta** too many chairs ; **en resumidas cuentas** in short ; **pedir cuentas** to ask for an explanation ; **trabajar por cuenta propia** to be self-employed

cuentagotas *nm inv* dropper

cuentakilómetros *nm inv* [distancia] ≃ *Br* mileometer, ≃ *US* odometer ; [velocidad] speedometer

cuento *nm* story ; LITER short story ; **cuento chino** tall story ; **cuento de hadas** fairy story ; *Am Fam* **cuento del tío** confidence game, *Br* con trick ; **contar un cuento** to tell a story ; *Fig* **eso no viene a cuento** that's beside the point ; **tener (mucho) cuento** to know how to put it on, *Br* to play up

cuerda *nf* **a)** [cordel] rope ; *Fig* **bajo cuerda** dishonestly ; **cuerda floja** tightrope ; **cuerdas vocales** vocal cords **b)** [de instrumento] string **c)** [del reloj] spring ; **dar cuerda al reloj** to wind up a watch

cueriza *nf Andes Fam* beating, leathering

cuerno *nm* horn ; [de ciervo] antler ; *Fam* **¡vete al cuerno!** get lost! ; *Fam* **ponerle cuernos a algn** to be unfaithful to sb

cuero *nm* **a)** leather ; **chaqueta de cuero** leather jacket **b) cuero cabelludo** scalp ; *Fam* **en cueros (vivos)** (stark) naked

cuerpo *nm* **a)** body ; **de cuerpo entero** full-length ; *Fig* **tomar cuerpo** to take shape **b)** [cadáver] corpse ; **de cuerpo presente** lying in state **c)** [parte] section, part **d)** [grupo] corps, force ; **cuerpo de bomberos** *Br* fire brigade, *US* fire department ; **cuerpo diplomático** diplomatic corps

cuervo *nm* raven

cuesta **1.** *nf* slope ; **cuesta abajo** downhill ; **cuesta arriba** uphill **2.** *loc adv* **a cuestas** on one's back o shoulders

cuestión *nf* **a)** [asunto] matter, question ; **es cuestión de vida o muerte** it's a matter of life or death ; **en cuestión de unas horas** in just a few hours **b)** [pregunta] question

cuestionamiento *nm* questioning

cuestionario *nm* questionnaire

cueva *nf* cave

cuico, -a *nm, f Méx Fam* [policía] cop

cuidado **1.** *nm* **a)** care ; **con cuidado** carefully ; **tener cuidado** to be careful ; **estar al cuidado de** [cosa] to be in charge of ; [persona] to look after ; **me trae sin cuidado** I couldn't care less ; *MED* **cuidados intensivos** intensive care **2.** *interj* look out!, watch out! ; **¡cuidado con lo que dices!** watch what you say! ; **¡cuidado con el escalón!** mind the step!

cuidadoso, -a *adj* careful

cuidar **1.** *vt* to care for, to look after ; **cuidar de que todo salga bien** to make sure that everything goes all right ; **cuidar los detalles** to pay attention to details **2. cuidarse** *vpr* **cuídate** look after yourself

cuitlacoche *nm CAm, Méx* corn smut *(edible fungus which grows on maize)*

culata *nf* **a)** [de arma] butt **b)** *AUTO* cylinder head

culebra *nf* snake

culebrón *nm Esp Fam* soap opera

culo *nm* **a)** *Am Fam* [nalgas] *Br* bum, *US* butt ; *Esp Vulg* **¡vete a tomar por culo!** fuck off! **b)** [de recipiente] bottom

culpa *nf* **a)** blame ; **echar la culpa a algn** to put the blame on sb ; **fue culpa mía** it was my fault ; **por tu culpa** because of you **b)** [culpabilidad] guilt

culpabilidad *nf* guilt, culpability

culpable **1.** *nmf* offender, culprit **2.** *adj* guilty ; *JUR* **declararse culpable** to plead guilty

culpar *vt* to blame ; **culpar a algn de un delito** to accuse sb of an offence

cultivar *vt* **a)** to cultivate **b)** *BIOL* to culture

cultivo *nm* **a)** cultivation ; [planta] crop **b)** *BIOL* culture

culto, -a **1.** *adj* educated ; [palabra] learned **2.** *nm* cult ; *REL* worship

cultura *nf* culture

cultural *adj* cultural

culturismo *nm* body building

cumbre *nf* **a)** [de montaña] summit, top ; **(conferencia) cumbre** summit conference **b)** *Fig* [culminación] pinnacle

cumpleaños *nm inv* birthday ; **¡feliz cumpleaños!** happy birthday!

cumplido, -a **1.** *adj* **a)** completed ; [plazo] expired ; **misión cumplida** mission accomplished **b)** [cortés] polite **2.** *nm* compliment

cumplir **1.** *vt* **a)** to carry out, to fulfil ; [deseo] to fulfil ; [promesa] to keep ; [sentencia] to serve

b) ayer cumplí veinte años I was twenty (years old) yesterday

2. *vi* **a)** [plazo] to expire, to end

b) cumplir con el deber to do one's duty

3. cumplirse *vpr* **a)** [deseo, sueño] to be fulfilled, to come true

b) [plazo] to expire

cúmulo *nm* pile, load

cuna *nf* a) cot b) *Fig* [origen] cradle

cundir *vi* a) [propagarse] to spread b) *Esp* [dar de sí - comida, reservas] to go a long way; [trabajo, estudio] to go well; **me cundió mucho el tiempo** I got a lot done

cuneta *nf* [de la carretera] gutter; **quedarse en la cuneta** to be left behind

cuña *nf* a) [pieza] wedge; **cuña publicitaria** commercial break b) *Andes, RP Fam* [enchufe] **tener cuña** to have friends in high places

cuñado, -a *nm, f* [hombre] brother-in-law; [mujer] sister-in-law

cuota *nf* a) [de club etc] membership fees *pl*, dues *pl* b) *Am* [plazo] instalment; **comprar en cuotas** to buy on *Br* hire purchase o *US* an installment plan c) [porción] quota, share d) *Méx* [importe] toll; **autopista de cuota** toll motorway, *US* turnpike

cuplé *nm* popular song

cupo *nm* ceiling; MIL **excedente de cupo** exempt from military service

cupón *nm* coupon, voucher

cúpula *nf* dome, cupola; [líderes] leadership

cura 1. *nm* REL priest **2.** *nf* MED cure; *Fig* **no tiene cura** there's no remedy

curandero, -a *nm, f* quack

curar 1. *vt* a) [sanar] to cure; [herida] to dress; [enfermedad] to treat b) [carne, pescado] to cure **2.** *vi* [sanar] to recover, to get well; [herida] to heal up **3. curarse** *vpr* to recover, to get well; [herida] to heal up; **curar en salud** to make sure

curcuncho, -a *adj Andes Fam* hunchbacked

curiosidad *nf* curiosity; **tener curiosidad de** to be curious about

curioso, -a 1. *adj* a) [indiscreto] curious, inquisitive b) [extraño] strange, odd; **lo curioso es que ...** the strange thing is that ... c) [limpio] neat, tidy **2.** *nm, f* a) [mirón] onlooker b) [chismoso] nosy-parker, busybody

curita *nf Am* [para heridas] *Br* (sticking) plaster, *US* Band-aid®

currante *Esp Fam* **1.** *adj* hard-working **2.** *nmf* worker

currar *vi Esp Fam* to work

curre, currele, currelo *nm pp de* **curro**

currículum (vitae) [ku'rrikulum ('bite)] *(pl* **currícula** o **currículums (vitae))** *nm* curriculum vitae, *Br* CV, *US* résumé

curro, curre, currele, currelo *nm Esp Fam* [tarea, empleo, lugar] work

curry *nm* curry; **pollo al curry** chicken curry

cursi *adj* [vestido, canción] tacky, *Br* naff; [modales, persona] affected

cursillo *nm* short course; **cursillo de reciclaje** refresher course

curso *nm* a) [año académico] year; [clase] class b) *Fig* **año /mes en curso** current year /month; **en el curso de** during c) [de acontecimientos, río] course d) FIN **moneda de curso legal** legal tender

cursor *nm* INFORM cursor

curtiembre *nf Andes, RP* tannery

curva *nf* a) curve b) [en carretera] bend; **curva cerrada** sharp bend

curvado, -a *adj* [forma] curved; [espalda] bent

custodia *nf* custody

cutis *nm inv* complexion

cutre *adj Esp Fam* [sórdido] shabby, dingy

cuyo, -a *pron relat* [de persona] whose; [de cosa] of which; **en cuyo caso** in which case

D

d SMS *written abbr of* **de**

D. *(abr de* **don)** Mr

dado¹, a *adj* **a)** given; **en un momento dado** at a certain point **b) ser dado a** to be given to **c) dado que** since, given that

dado² *nm* die, dice

daga *nf* dagger

dalia *nf* dahlia

dama *nf* **a)** [señora] lady **b)** [en damas] king **c) damas** [juego] *Br* draughts, *US* checkers

damasco *nm* **a)** [tela] damask **b)** *Andes, RP* [albaricoque] apricot

danés, -esa 1. *adj* Danish **2.** *nm, f* [persona] Dane **3.** *nm* **a)** [idioma] Danish **b) gran danés** [perro] Great Dane

danza *nf* dancing; [baile] dance

dañado, -a *adj* damaged

dañar *vt* [cosa] to damage; [persona] to hurt, to harm

danzar [40] *vt & vi* to dance

dañino, -a *adj* harmful, damaging (**para** to)

daño *nm* [a cosa] damage; [a persona - físico] hurt; [perjuicio] harm; **se hizo daño en la pierna** he hurt his leg; JUR **daños y perjuicios** (legal) damages

dar [11] **1.** *vt* **a)** to give; [recado, recuerdos] to pass on, to give; [noticia] to tell **b)** [mano de pintura, cera] to apply, to put on **c)** [película] to show, to screen; [fiesta] to throw, to give **d)** [cosecha] to produce, to yield; [fruto, flores] to bear; [beneficio, interés] to give, to yield **e)** [bofetada etc] to deal; **dar a algn en la cabeza** to hit sb on the head **f) dale a la luz** switch the light on; **dar la mano a algn** to shake hands with sb; **dar los buenos días / las buenas noches a algn** to say good morning / good evening to sb; **me da lo mismo, me da igual** it's all the same to me; **¿qué más da?** what difference does it make? **g)** [hora] to strike; **ya han dado las nueve** it's gone nine (o'clock) **h) dar de comer a** to feed **i) dar a conocer** [noticia] to release; **dar a entender a algn que ...** to give sb to understand that ... **j) dar por** [considerar] to assume, to consider; **lo dieron por muerto** he was assumed dead, he was given up for dead; **dar por descontado / sabido** to take for granted, to assume

2. *vi* **a) me dio un ataque de tos / risa** I had a coughing fit / an attack of the giggles **b) dar a** [ventana, habitación] to look out onto, to overlook; [puerta] to open onto, to lead to **c) dar con** [persona] to come across; **dar con la solución** to hit upon the solution **d) dar de sí** [ropa] to stretch, to give **e) dar en** to hit; **el sol me daba en los ojos** the sun was (shining) in my eyes **f) dar para** to be enough o sufficient for; **el presupuesto no da para más** the budget will not stretch any further **g) le dio por nadar** he took it into his head to go swimming **h) dar que hablar** to set people talking; **el suceso dio que pensar** the incident gave people food for thought

3. darse *vpr* **a) se dio un caso extraño** something strange happened **b)** [hallarse] to be found, to exist **c) darse a** to take to; **se dio a la bebida** he took to drink

d) darse con o **contra** to bump o crash into

e) dárselas de to consider oneself

f) darse por satisfecho to feel satisfied; **darse por vencido** to give in

g) se le da bien / mal el francés she's good / bad at French

---

dardo nm dart

dátil nm date

dato nm a) piece of information; **datos personales** personal details b) INFORM **datos** data; **datos de acceso** login details

d.C. (abr de **después de Cristo**) AD

dcha. (abr de **derecha**) rt.

dcr SMS written abbr of **decir**

d2 SMS written abbr of **dedos**

de

de combines with the article **el** to form the contraction **del** (e.g. **del hombre** of the man).

prep a) [pertenencia] of; **el título de la novela** the title of the novel; **el coche / hermano de Sofía** Sofía's car / brother; **las bicicletas de los niños** the boys' bicycles

b) [procedencia] from; **de Madrid a Valencia** from Madrid to Valencia; **soy de Palencia** I'm from o I come from Palencia

c) [descripción] **el niño de ojos azules** the boy with blue eyes; **el señor de la chaqueta** the man in the jacket; **un reloj de oro** a gold watch; **un joven de veinte años** a young man of twenty

d) [contenido] of; **un saco de patatas** a sack of potatoes

e) [oficio] as; **trabaja de secretaria** she's working as a secretary

f) [acerca de] about; **curso de informática** computer course

g) [tiempo] **a las tres de la tarde** at three in the afternoon; **de día** by day; **de noche** at night; **de lunes a jueves** from Monday to Thursday; **de pequeño** as a child; **de año en año** year in year out

h) [precio] at; **patatas de 30 céntimos el kilo** potatoes at 30 cents a kilo

i) **una avenida de 3 km** an avenue 3 km long; **una botella de litro** a litre bottle

j) [con superlativo] in; **el más largo de España** the longest in Spain

k) [causa] with, because of; **llorar de alegría** to cry with joy; **morir de hambre** to die of hunger

l) [condicional] **de haber llegado antes** if he had arrived before; **de no ser así** if that wasn't o weren't the case

---

debajo adv underneath, below; **el mío es el de debajo** mine is the one below; **está debajo de la mesa** it's under the table; **por debajo de lo normal** below normal; **salió por debajo del coche** he came out from under the car

debate nm debate

debatir 1. vt to debate **2. debatirse** vpr to struggle; **debatirse entre la vida y la muerte** to fight for one's life

deber¹ nm a) duty; **cumplir con su deber** to do one's duty b) EDUC **deberes** homework

deber² **1.** vt [dinero, explicación] to owe

2. vi a) [obligación] must; **debe (de) comer** he must eat; **la factura debe pagarse mañana** the bill must be paid tomorrow

b) [consejo] **deberías visitar a tus padres** you ought to visit your parents; **no debiste hacerlo** you shouldn't have done it

c) [suposición] **deben de estar fuera** they must be out

3. deberse vpr **deberse a** to be due to; **esto se debe a la falta de agua** this is due to lack of water

---

debido, -a adj a) due; **a su debido tiempo** in due course; **con el debido respeto** with due respect b) [adecuado] proper; **más de lo debido** too much; **tomaron las debidas precauciones** they took the proper precautions; **como es debido** properly c) **debido a** because of, due to; **debido a que** because of the fact that

débil adj weak; [luz] dim; **punto débil** weak spot

debilidad *nf* weakness; *Fig* **tener debilidad por** [persona] to have a soft spot for; [cosa] to have a weakness for

debilitar 1. *vt* to weaken, to debilitate **2. debilitarse** *vpr* to weaken, to grow weak

debut (*pl* **debuts**) *nm* début, debut

década *nf* decade; **en la década de los noventa** during the nineties

decadencia *nf* decadence

decadente *adj* & *nmf* decadent

decaer [39] *vi* to deteriorate

decaído, -a *adj* down

decano, -a *nm, f* UNIV dean

decena *nf* (about) ten; **una decena de veces** (about) ten times; **por decenas** in tens

decente *adj* decent; [decoroso] modest

decepción *nf* disappointment

decepcionado, -a *adj* disappointed

decepcionante *adj* disappointing

decepcionar *vt* to disappoint

decidido, -a *adj* determined, resolute

decidir 1. *vt* & *vi* to decide **2. decidirse** *vpr* to make up one's mind; **decidirse a hacer algo** to make up one's mind to do sth; **decidirse por algo** to decide on sth

decimal *adj* & *nm* decimal; **el sistema métrico decimal** the decimal system

décimo, -a 1. *adj* & *nm, f* tenth **2.** *nm* **a)** [parte] tenth **b)** [billete de lotería] tenth part of a lottery ticket

decir¹ *nm* saying

decir² [12] (*pp* **dicho**) **1.** *vt* **a)** to say; **dice que no quiere venir** he says he doesn't want to come
b) **decir una mentira/la verdad** to tell a lie/the truth
c) *Esp* **¿diga?, ¿dígame?** [al teléfono] hello?
d) **¿qué me dices del nuevo jefe?** what do you think of the new boss?

e) [sugerir] to mean; **¿qué te dice el cuadro?** what does the picture mean to you?; **esta película no me dice nada** this film doesn't appeal to me
f) **querer decir** to mean
g) [locuciones] **es decir** that is (to say); **por así decirlo** as it were, so to speak; **digamos** let's say; **digo yo** in my opinion; **el qué dirán** what people say; **ni que decir tiene** needless to say; **¡no me digas!** really!; *Esp* **¡y que lo digas!** you can say that again!
2. decirse *vpr* **¿cómo se dice "mesa" en inglés?** how do you say "mesa" in English?; **se dice que ...** they say that ...

decisión *nf* **a)** decision; **tomar una decisión** to take *o* make a decision **b)** [resolución] determination; **con decisión** decisively

declaración *nf* **a)** declaration; **declaración de (la) renta** tax declaration *o* return **b)** [afirmación] statement; **hacer declaraciones** to comment **c)** JUR **prestar declaración** to give evidence

declarado, -a *adj* [manifiesto] open, professed; **es un homosexual declarado** he is openly gay; **hay un odio declarado entre ellos** there is open hostility between them

declarar 1. *vt* **a)** to declare; **declarar la guerra a** to declare war on
b) [afirmar] to state
c) JUR **declarar culpable/inocente a algn** to find sb guilty/not guilty
2. *vi* **a)** to declare
b) JUR to testify
3. declararse *vpr* **a)** **declararse a favor/en contra de** to declare oneself in favour of/against; **declararse en huelga** to go on strike; **declararse a algn** to declare one's love for sb
b) [guerra, incendio] to start, to break out
c) JUR **declararse culpable** to plead guilty

declinar *vt* & *vi* to decline
decolaje *nm Am* take-off
decolar *vi Am* to take off

decoloración *nf* discolouration; [del pelo] bleaching

decoración *nf* decoration

decorado *nm* scenery, set

decorar *vt* to decorate

decretar *vt* to decree

decreto *nm* decree; **decreto-ley** decree, *Br* order in council

dedal *nm* thimble

dedicación *nf* dedication

dedicar [44] **1.** *vt* to dedicate; [tiempo, esfuerzos] to devote (**a** to) **2. dedicarse** *vpr* ¿**a qué se dedica V** dedicar? what do you do for a living?; **los fines de semana ella se dedica a pescar** at weekends she spends her time fishing

dedo *nm* [de la mano] finger; [del pie] toe; **dedo anular / corazón / índice / meñique** ring / middle / index / little finger; **dedo pulgar, dedo gordo** thumb; **hacer dedo** to hitch-hike; *Fig* **elegir a algn a dedo** to handpick sb

deducción *nf* deduction

deducir [10] **1.** *vt* a) to deduce, to infer b) COM to deduct **2. deducirse** *vpr* **de aquí se deduce que ...** from this it follows that ...

defecar [44] *vi* to defecate

defecto *nm* defect, fault; **defecto físico** physical defect

defender [3] **1.** *vt* to defend (**de** from); **defender del frío / viento** to shelter from the cold / wind **2. defenderse** *vpr* a) to defend oneself b) *Fam* **se defiende en francés** he can get by in French

defensa 1. *nf* defence; **en defensa propia, en legítima defensa** in self-defence; **salir en defensa de algn** to come out in defence of sb **2.** *nm* DEP defender, back

defensor, -a *nm, f* defender; **abogado defensor** counsel for the defence; *Esp* **defensor del pueblo** ombudsman

deficiencia *nf* deficiency, shortcoming; **deficiencia mental** mental deficiency; **deficiencia renal** kidney failure

deficiente 1. *adj* deficient **2.** *nmf* **deficiente mental** mentally retarded person **3.** *nm* EDUC fail

déficit *(pl* **déficits***) nm* deficit; [carencia] shortage

definición *nf* definition; **por definición** by definition

definir *vt* to define

definitivo, -a *adj* definitive; **en definitiva** in short

deformación *nf* deformation

deformado, -a *adj* deformed

deformar 1. *vt* to deform, to put out of shape; [cara] to disfigure; *Fig* [la verdad, una imagen] to distort **2. deformarse** *vpr* to go out of shape, to become distorted

defraudador, -a *nm, f* defrauder

defraudar *vt* a) [decepcionar] to disappoint b) [al fisco] to defraud, to cheat; **defraudar a Hacienda** to evade taxes

defunción *nf Formal* decease, demise

degenerado, -a *adj & nm, f* degenerate

degenerar *vi* to degenerate

degustación *nf* tasting

dejadez *nf* slovenliness

dejar 1. *vt* a) to leave; **déjame en paz** leave me alone

b) *Esp* [prestar] **dejar algo a algn** to lend sb sth, to lend sth to sb

c) [abandonar] to give up; **dejé el tabaco y la bebida** I gave up smoking and drinking

d) [permitir] to let, to allow; **dejar entrar / salir** to let in / out; **dejar caer** to drop

e) [omitir] to leave out, to omit

f) [+ adj] to make; **dejar triste** to make sad; **dejar preocupado / sorprendido** to worry / surprise

g) [posponer] **dejaron el viaje para el verano** they put the trip off until the summer

2. *v aux* **dejar de** [+ infinitivo] to stop, to give up; **dejó de fumar el año pa-**

sado he gave up smoking last year; **no deja de llamarme** she's always phoning me up

3. dejarse *vpr* **a) me he dejado las llaves dentro** I've left the keys inside **b)** [locuciones] **dejarse barba** to grow a beard; **dejarse caer** to flop down; **dejarse llevar por** to be influenced by

del (*contracción de* **de** + **el**) *ver* **de**

delantal *nm* apron

delante *adv* **a)** in front; **la entrada de delante** the front entrance **b) delante de** in front of; [en serie] ahead of **c) por delante** in front; **se lo lleva todo por delante** he destroys everything in his path; **tiene toda la vida por delante** he has his whole life ahead of him

delantera *nf* **a)** [ventaja] lead; **tomar la delantera** take the lead **b)** FÚT forward line, forwards

delantero, -a 1. *adj* front **2.** *nm* FÚT forward; **delantero centro** centre forward

delatar *vt* **a)** to inform against **b)** *Fig* to give away

delegación *nf* **a)** [acto, delegados] delegation **b)** [sucursal] local office; *Esp* **Delegación del Gobierno** *office representing central government in each province*; *Esp* **Delegación de Hacienda** *head tax office (in each province)* **c)** *Chile, Ecuad, Méx* [distrito municipal] municipal district

delegado, -a *nm, f* **a)** delegate; **delegado de Hacienda** chief tax inspector **b)** COM representative

delegar [42] *vt* to delegate (**en** to)

deletrear *vt* to spell (out)

delfín *nm* dolphin

delgado, -a *adj* slim; [capa] fine

deliberado, -a *adj* deliberate

deliberar *vi* to deliberate (on), to consider

delicadeza *nf* **a)** [finura] delicacy, daintiness **b)** [tacto] tactfulness; **falta de delicadeza** tactlessness

delicado, -a *adj* **a)** delicate **b)** [exigente] fussy, hard to please **c)** [sensible] hypersensitive

delicia *nf* delight; **hacer las delicias de algn** to delight sb

delicioso, -a *adj* [comida] delicious; [agradable] delightful

delimitación *nf* delimitation

delincuencia *nf* delinquency

delincuente *adj* & *nmf* delinquent; **delincuente juvenil** juvenile delinquent

delinquir [48] *vi* to commit a crime

delirante *adj* delirious

delirar *vi* to be delirious

delirio *nm* delirium; **delirios de grandeza** delusions of grandeur

delito *nm* crime, offence

delta *nm* delta; **ala delta** hang-glider

demanda *nf* **a)** JUR lawsuit **b)** COM demand

demandar *vt* to sue

demarcar *vt* to demarcate

demás 1. *adj* **los /las demás** the rest of; **la demás gente** the rest of the people **2.** *pron* **lo /los /las demás** the rest; **por lo demás** otherwise, apart from that; **y demás** etcetera

demasiado, -a 1. *adj* [singular] too much; [plural] too many; **hay demasiada comida** there is too much food; **quieres demasiadas cosas** you want too many things **2.** *adv* too (much); **es demasiado grande /caro** it is too big / dear; **fumas /trabajas demasiado** you smoke /work too much

demencia *nf* dementia, insanity

demente 1. *adj* insane, mad **2.** *nmf* mental patient

democracia *nf* democracy

demócrata 1. *adj* democratic **2.** *nmf* democrat

democrático, -a *adj* democratic

demoledor, -a *adj* *Fig* devastating

demoler [4] *vt* to demolish

demonio *nm* devil, demon ; *Fam* ¿cómo/dónde demonios ...? how/ where the hell ...? ; *Fam* ¡demonio(s)! hell!, damn! ; *Fam* ¡demonio de niño! you little devil!

demora *nf* delay

demorar 1. *vt* a) [retrasar] to delay, hold up
b) [tardar] demoraron 3 días en pintar la casa it took them three days to paint the house
2. *vi Am* [tardar] ¡no demores! don't be late! ; este quitamanchas demora en actuar this stain remover takes a while to work
3. demorarse *vpr* a) [retrasarse] to be delayed, be held up
b) [detenerse] to dally
c) *esp Am* [retrasarse] to be late ; no se demoren don't be late
d) *Am* [tardar en] to take (too) long

demostración *nf* demonstration ; una demostración de fuerza/afecto a show of strength, affection

demostrar [2] *vt* a) [mostrar] to show, to demonstrate b) [evidenciar] to prove

dengue *nm* a) MED dengue b) *Fam* fussiness

denominación *nf* denomination ; denominación de origen [vinos] *guarantee of region of origin*

densidad *nf* [gen & INFORM] density ; alta/doble densidad [disquete] high/ double density ; densidad de población population density

denso, -a *adj* dense

dentadura *nf* teeth, set of teeth ; dentadura postiza false teeth, dentures

dentífrico, -a 1. *adj* pasta/crema dentífrica toothpaste 2. *nm* toothpaste

dentista *nmf* dentist

dentistería *nf CAm, Col, Ecuad, Ven* [consultorio] dentist's, dental surgery

dentro *adv* a) [en el interior] inside ; aquí dentro in here ; por dentro (on the) inside ; por dentro está triste deep down (inside) he feels sad b) dentro de [lugar] inside c) dentro de poco shortly, soon ; dentro de un mes in a month's time ; dentro de lo que cabe all things considered

denuncia *nf* [a la policía] report ; presentar una denuncia to make a formal complaint ; [por un delito] to report a crime

denunciante *nmf* person who reports a crime

denunciar [43] *vt* a) [delito] to report (a to) b) [criticar] to denounce

departamento *nm* a) department b) FERROC compartment c) [territorial] province, district d) *Arg* [piso] *Br* flat, *US* apartment

dependencia *nf* a) dependence (de on) b) dependencias premises

depender *vi* to depend (de on) ; [económicamente] to be dependent (de on)

dependiente 1. *adj* dependent (de on) 2. *nm Br* shop o sales assistant, *US* salesclerk

depiladora *nf* epilator

depilar *vt* to remove the hair from ; [cejas] to pluck

depilatorio, -a *adj & nm* depilatory ; crema depilatoria hair-remover, hair-removing cream

deportar *vt* to deport

deporte *nm* sport ; hacer deporte to practise sports ; deporte de aventura adventure sport

deportista 1. *nmf* [hombre] sportsman ; [mujer] sportswoman 2. *adj* sporty

deportivo, -a 1. *adj* sports ; club/chaqueta deportivo sports club/jacket 2. *nm* AUTO sports car

depositar 1. *vt* a) FIN to deposit b) [colocar] to place, to put 2. depositarse *vpr* to settle

depósito *nm* a) FIN deposit ; en depósito on deposit b) [de agua, gasolina] tank c) [de basuras] rubbish tip o dump ; depósito de cadáveres mortuary, morgue

depresión *nf* depression; **depresión nerviosa** nervous breakdown

depresivo, -a *adj* depressive

depresor, -a *adj* depressant

deprimido, -a *adj* depressed

deprimir 1. *vt* to depress **2. deprimirse** *vpr* to get depressed

deprisa *adv* quickly

depuradora *nf* purifier

depurar *vt* a) [agua] to purify b) [partido] to purge c) [estilo] to refine

derecha *nf* a) [mano] right hand b) [lugar] right, right-hand side; **a la derecha** too on the right, on the right-hand side c) POL **la derecha** the right; *Esp* **ser de derechas** to be right-wing

derecho, -a 1. *adj* a) [de la derecha] right
b) [recto] upright, straight
2. *nm* a) [privilegio] right; **derechos civiles/humanos** civil/human rights; **tener derecho a** to be entitled to, to have the right to; **estar en su derecho** to be within one's rights; **no hay derecho** it's not fair
b) JUR law; **derecho penal/político** criminal/constitutional law
c) COM **derechos** duties; **derechos de autor** royalties; **derechos de matrícula** enrolment fees
3. *adv* **siga todo derecho** go straight ahead

derivar 1. *vt* to divert; [conversación] to steer **2.** *vi* a) to drift b) **derivar de** to derive from **3. derivarse** *vpr* a) **derivarse de** [proceder] to result o stem from b) LING **derivarse de** to be derived from

dermoprotector *adj* skin-protecting

derramar 1. *vt* to spill; [lágrimas] to shed **2. derramarse** *vpr* to spill

derrame *nm* MED discharge; **derrame cerebral** brain haemorrhage

derrapar *vi* to skid

derrape *nm* skid

derretir [6] **1.** *vt* to melt; [hielo, nieve] to thaw **2. derretirse** *vpr* = **derretir**

derribar *vt* a) [edificio] to pull down, to knock down b) [avión] to shoot down c) [gobierno] to bring down

derrocar *vt* to topple

derrochar *vt* to waste, to squander

derroche *nm* a) [de dinero, energía] waste, squandering b) [abundancia] profusion, abundance

derrota *nf* a) defeat b) NÁUT (ship's) course

derrotado, -a *adj & nm, f* defeated

derrotar *vt* to defeat, to beat

derruir *vt* to demolish

derrumbar 1. *vt* [edificio] to knock down, to pull down **2. derrumbarse** *vpr* to collapse, to fall down; [techo] to fall in, to cave in

desabrochar 1. *vt* to undo **2. desabrocharse** *vpr* a) **desabróchate la camisa** undo your shirt b) [prenda] to come undone

desacompasado, -a *adj pp de* **descompasado**

desacreditar *vt* a) [desprestigiar] to discredit, to bring into discredit b) [criticar] to disparage

desacuerdo *nm* disagreement

desafiar [29] *vt* to challenge

desafinar 1. *vi* to sing out of tune; [instrumento] to play out of tune **2.** *vt* to put out of tune **3. desafinarse** *vpr* to go out of tune

desafío *nm* challenge

desafortunado, -a *adj* unlucky, unfortunate

desagradable *adj* unpleasant, disagreeable

desagradecido, -a 1. *adj* ungrateful **2.** *nm, f* ungrateful person

desagüe *nm* [vaciado] drain; [cañería] waste pipe, drainpipe

desahogarse [42] *vpr* to let off steam; **se desahogó de su depresión** he got his depression out of his system

desaire *nm* slight, rebuff

desajuste nm upset; **desajuste económico** economic imbalance; **un desajuste de horarios** clashing timetables

desaladora nf desalination plant

desalar vt [pescado] to soak (to remove the salt from); [agua del mar] to desalinate

desalentador, -a adj disheartening

desalinizadora nf desalination plant

desaliñado, -a adj scruffy, untidy

desalojar vt a) [inquilino] to evict; [público] to move on; [lugar] to evacuate b) [abandonar] to move out of, to abandon

desamparado, -a 1. adj [persona] helpless, unprotected; [lugar] abandoned, forsaken **2.** nm, f helpless o abandoned person

desangrarse vpr to lose (a lot of) blood

desanimar 1. vt to discourage, to dishearten **2. desanimarse** vpr to lose heart, to get discouraged

desaparecer [33] vi to disappear

desaparecido, -a 1. adj missing **2.** nm, f missing person

desaparición nf disappearance

desapercibido, -a adj a) [inadvertido] unnoticed; **pasar desapercibido** to go unnoticed b) [desprevenido] unprepared

desaprovechar vt [dinero, tiempo] to waste; **desaprovechar una ocasión** to fail to make the most of an opportunity

desarmado, -a adj unarmed

desarmador nm Méx [herramienta] screwdriver

desarraigado, -a adj rootless

desarraigar vt a) [planta, persona, pueblo] to uproot b) [vicio, costumbre] to eradicate

desarrollado, -a adj developed; **país desarrollado** developed country

desarrollador, -a nm, f INFORM (software) developer

desarrollar 1. vt to develop **2. desarrollarse** vpr a) [persona, enfermedad] to develop b) [tener lugar] to take place

desarrollo nm development; **países en vías de desarrollo** developing countries

desasosegado, -a adj restless

desasosiego nm restlessness

desastre nm disaster; **eres un desastre** you're just hopeless

desatado, -a adj a) [nudo] undone b) Fam [persona, sentimiento] wild, out of control

desatar 1. vt to untie, to undo; [provocar] to unleash **2. desatarse** vpr a) [zapato, cordón] to come undone b) [tormenta] to break; [pasión] to run wild

desatascador nm plunger

desatino nm blunder

desatornillar vt to unscrew

desavenencia nf disagreement

desavenido, -a adj **estar desavenido con algn** to be on bad terms with sb

desaventajado, -a adj a) [inferior] disadvantaged b) [poco ventajoso] disadvantageous

desayunar 1. vi to have breakfast; Formal to breakfast **2.** vt to have for breakfast

desayuno nm breakfast

desbarajuste nm confusion, disorder

desbaratar vt to ruin, to wreck; [jersey] to unravel

desbloquear vt a) [mecanismo, carretera] to clear b) [país] to lift the blockade from

desbocar vi **desbocar en** [río] to flow into; [calle, camino] to join, to lead into

desbolado, -a RP Fam **1.** adj messy, untidy **2.** nm, f untidy person

desbolarse vpr RP Fam to undress, to strip

desbole *nm RP Fam* mess, chaos

desbordado, -a *adj* overflowing

desbordante *adj* overflowing

desbordar 1. *vt* to overflow; *Fig* to overwhelm **2.** *vi* to overflow (**de** with) **3. desbordarse** *vpr* to overflow, to flood

descabellado, -a *adj* crazy, wild

descacharrado, -a *adj pp de* **escacharrado**

descacharrarse *vpr pp de* **escacharrarse**

descafeinado, -a *adj* **a)** [café] decaffeinated **b)** *Fig* watered-down, diluted

descalcificar *vt* [huesos] to decalcify

descalificar [44] *vt* to disqualify

descalzarse [40] *vpr* to take one's shoes off

descalzo, -a *adj* barefoot

descaminado, -a *adj* **ir descaminado** to be lost

descampado *nm* waste ground

descansado, -a *adj* **a)** [trabajo, vida] easy **b)** [aspecto, rostro] rested, refreshed

descansar *vi* **a)** to rest, to have a rest; [corto tiempo] to take a break **b)** *Euf* **que en paz descanse** may he/she rest in peace

descansillo *nm* landing

descanso *nm* **a)** rest, break; **un día de descanso** a day off **b)** [en cine] intermission; [en teatro] *Br* interval, *US* intermission; DEP half-time, interval **c)** [alivio] relief **d)** [rellano] landing

descapotable *adj & nm* convertible

descarado, -a 1. *adj* **a)** [insolente] cheeky, insolent; [desvergonzado] shameless **b)** *Esp Fam* **descarado que sí/no** [por supuesto] of course/course not **2.** *nm, f* cheeky person

descarga *nf* **a)** unloading **b)** ELEC & MIL discharge **c)** INFORM download

descargar [42] **1.** *vt* **a)** [mercancías, camión, barco] to unload **b)** [disparar] to fire; [golpe] to deal **c)** ELEC to discharge

d) INFORM [fichero] to download **2.** *vi* [tormenta] to burst **3. descargarse** *vpr* [batería] to go flat

descaro *nm* cheek, nerve; **¡qué descaro!** what a cheek!

descarriarse *vpr* **a)** [ganado] to get lost **b)** [moralmente] to lose one's way

descarrilar *vi* to go off the rails, to be derailed

descartable *adj Am* [objeto] disposable

descartar 1. *vt* to rule out **2. descartarse** *vpr* NAIPES to discard cards; **me descarté de un cinco** I got rid of a five

descendencia *nf* descendants; **morir sin descendencia** to die without issue

descender [3] **1.** *vi* **a)** [temperatura, nivel] to fall, to drop **b)** **descender de** to descend from **2.** *vt* to lower

descendiente *adj & nmf* descendant

descenso *nm* **a)** descent; [de temperatura] fall, drop **b)** DEP relegation

descifrar *vt* to decipher; [mensaje] to decode; [misterio] to solve; [motivos, causas] to figure out

descolgar [2] **1.** *vt* [teléfono] to pick up; [cuadro, cortinas] to take down **2. descolgarse** *vpr* to let oneself down, to slide down

descolorido, -a *adj* faded

descompasado, -a, desacompasado, -a *adj* excessive

descompensado, -a *adj* unbalanced

descomponer [19] *(pp* **descompuesto**) **1.** *vt* **a)** to break down **b)** [corromper] to rot, to decompose **2. descomponerse** *vpr* **a)** [corromperse] to rot, to decompose **b)** [ponerse nervioso] to lose one's cool **c)** *Am* [averiarse] to break down **d)** *Am* [tiempo atmosférico] to turn nasty

descomposición *nf* **a)** [de carne] decomposition, rotting; [de país] disintegration **b)** QUÍM breakdown **c)** *Esp* [diarrea] diarrhoea

descompostura *nf* **a)** *Am* [malestar] unpleasant o nasty turn **b)** *Méx*, *RP* [avería] breakdown

descompuesto, -a *adj* **a)** [podrido] rotten, decomposed **b)** [furioso] furious

desconcertado, -a *adj* disconcerted

desconcertante *adj* disconcerting

desconcertar [1] **1.** *vt* to disconcert **2. desconcertarse** *vpr* to be bewildered, to be puzzled

desconectado, -a *adj* disconnected

desconexión *nf* **a)** [de aparato, alarma] disconnection, unplugging; [de línea telefónica] disconnection **b)** [falta de relación] disconnect

desconfianza *nf* distrust, mistrust

desconfiar [29] *vi* **desconfiar (de)** to distrust, to mistrust

descongelar *vt* [nevera] to defrost; [créditos] to unfreeze

descongestionante *nm* decongestant

descongestionar *vt* to clear, to decongest

desconocer [34] *vt* not to know, to be unaware of

desconocido, -a **1.** *adj* unknown; [irreconocible] unrecognizable **2.** *nm* **lo desconocido** the unknown **3.** *nm, f* stranger

desconocimiento *nm* ignorance, lack of knowledge

desconsiderado, -a **1.** *adj* inconsiderate, thoughtless **2.** *nm, f* inconsiderate o thoughtless person

desconsolado, -a *adj* disconsolate, grief-stricken

desconsuelo *nm* grief, sorrow

descontar [2] *vt* **a)** to deduct **b)** *DEP* [tiempo] to add on

descontrolado, -a *adj* uncontrolled

descorchador *nm* corkscrew

descrédito *nm* disrepute, discredit

describir *(pp* **descrito)** *vt* to describe

descripción *nf* description

descrito, -a *pp de* **describir**

descuartizar [40] *vt* to cut up, to cut into pieces

descubierto, -a **1.** *adj* open, uncovered; **a cielo descubierto** in the open **2.** *nm* **a)** FIN overdraft **b) al descubierto** in the open; **poner al descubierto** to uncover, to bring out into the open

descubrimiento *nm* discovery

descubrir *(pp* **descubierto)** *vt* to discover; [conspiración] to uncover; [placa] to unveil

descuento *nm* discount

descuidado, -a *adj* **a)** [desaseado] untidy, neglected **b)** [negligente] careless, negligent **c)** [desprevenido] off one's guard

descuidar **1.** *vt* to neglect, to overlook
2. *vi* **descuida, voy yo** don't worry, I'll go
3. descuidarse *vpr* [despistarse] to be careless; **como te descuides, llegarás tarde** if you don't watch out, you'll be late

descuido *nm* **a)** oversight, mistake; **por descuido** inadvertently, by mistake **b)** [negligencia] negligence, carelessness

desde *adv* **a)** [tiempo] since; **desde ahora** from now on; **desde el lunes / entonces** since Monday / then; **espero desde hace media hora** I've been waiting for half an hour; **no lo he visto desde hace un año** I haven't seen him for a year **b)** [lugar] from; **desde arriba / abajo** from above / below **c) desde luego** of course **d) desde que** ever since; **desde que lo conozco** ever since I've known him

desdén *nm* disdain

desdentado, -a *adj* toothless

desdicha *nf* misfortune; **por desdicha** unfortunately

desdoblar *vt* to unfold

desear *vt* **a)** to desire; **deja mucho que desear** it leaves a lot to be desired

b) [querer] to want; **¿qué desea?** can I help you?; **estoy deseando que vengas** I'm looking forward to your coming **c) te deseo buena suerte / feliz Navidad** I wish you good luck / a merry Christmas

desecar 1. *vt* [planta, alimento] to dry; [pantano, pozo] to drain **2. desecarse** *vpr* [planta, alimento] to dry up; [pantano, río] to dry out

desechable *adj* disposable, throwaway

desechar *vt* **a)** [tirar] to discard, to throw out o away **b)** [oferta] to turn down, to refuse; [idea, proyecto] to drop, to discard

desecho *nm* **a)** [objeto usado] unwanted object; **material de desecho** [residuos] waste products **b)** [escoria] dregs; **desechos** [basura] *Br* rubbish, *US* garbage, *US* trash; [residuos] waste products

desembarcar [44] **1.** *vt* [mercancías] to unload; [personas] to disembark **2.** *vi* to disembark **3. desembarcarse** *vpr Am* [de autobús, tren] to disembark

desembocadura *nf* mouth

desembocar [44] *vi* **desembocar en** [río] to flow into; [calle, situación] to lead to

desempeñar *vt* **a)** [cargo] to hold, to occupy; [función] to fulfil; [papel] to play **b)** [recuperar] to redeem

desempleo *nm* unemployment; **cobrar el desempleo** to be on the dole

desencadenante 1. *adj* **los factores desencadenantes de la crisis** the factors which triggered the crisis **2.** *nm* trigger

desencadenar 1. *vt* **a)** [perro] to unchain **b)** [pasión, furia] to unleash **2. desencadenarse** *vpr* **a)** [prisionero] to break loose; [viento, pasión] to rage **b)** [conflicto] to start, to break out

desencajar 1. *vt* [pieza] to knock out; [hueso] to dislocate **2. desencajarse**
vpr **a)** [pieza] to come out; [hueso] to become dislocated **b)** [cara] to become distorted

desencaminado, -a *adj* **andar** o **ir desencaminado** [equivocado] to be wrong

desencanto *nm* disenchantment

desenchufar *vt* to unplug

desenfadado, -a *adj* carefree, free and easy

desenfrenado, -a *adj* frantic, uncontrolled; [vicio, pasión] unbridled

desengañar 1. *vt* **desengañar a algn** to open sb's eyes **2. desengañarse** *vpr* **a)** to be disappointed **b)** *Fam* **¡desengáñate!** get real!

desengaño *nm* disappointment; **llevarse** o **sufrir un desengaño con algo** to be disappointed in sth

desenlace *nm* **a)** result, outcome; **un feliz desenlace** a happy ending **b)** CINE & TEATRO ending, dénouement

desenmascarar *vt* to unmask

desenredar *vt* to untangle, to disentangle

desentenderse [3] *vpr* **se desentendió de mi problema** he didn't want to have anything to do with my problem

desenvolver [4] *(pp* desenvuelto*)* **1.** *vt* to unwrap **2. desenvolverse** *vpr* **a)** [persona] to manage, to cope **b)** [hecho] to develop

desenvuelto, -a *adj* relaxed

deseo *nm* wish; [sexual] desire; **formular un deseo** to make a wish

desequilibrado, -a 1. *adj* unbalanced **2.** *nm, f* unbalanced person

desertizarse *vpr* to become desert

desesperación *nf* [desesperanza] despair; [exasperación] desperation

desesperar 1. *vt* to drive to despair; [exasperar] to exasperate **2. desesperarse** *vpr* to despair

desestabilizar *vt* to destabilize

desestatización *nf Am* privatization, sell-off

desestatizar *vt Am* to privatize, to sell off

desfachatez *nf* cheek, nerve

desfallecer [33] *vi* a) [debilitarse] to feel faint; [desmayarse] to faint b) [desanimarse] to lose heart

desfase *nm* a) [desacuerdo] gap b) [desajuste] lag; **desfase horario** jet lag c) *Esp Fam* [barbaridad] madness

desfavorecido, -a *adj* disadvantaged

desfigurado, -a *adj* [persona] disfigured; [verdad, hecho] distorted

desfigurar *vt* [persona] to disfigure; [verdad, hecho] to distort

desfiladero *nm* narrow pass

desfile *nm* MIL parade, march-past; **desfile de modas** fashion show

desforestación *nf* deforestation

desgana *nf* a) [inapetencia] lack of appetite b) [apatía] apathy, indifference; **con desgana** reluctantly, unwillingly

desgastado, -a *adj* worn

desgastar 1. *vt* to wear out 2. **desgastarse** *vpr* [consumirse] to wear out; [persona] to wear oneself out

desgracia *nf* a) misfortune; **por desgracia** unfortunately b) [deshonor] disgrace c) **desgracias personales** loss of life

desgraciadamente *adv* unfortunately

desgraciado, -a 1. *adj* unfortunate; [infeliz] unhappy 2. *nm, f* unfortunate person; **un pobre desgraciado** a poor devil

desgreñado, -a *adj* dishevelled

deshacer [15] (*pp* **deshecho**) 1. *vt* a) [paquete] to undo; [maleta] to unpack b) [plan] to destroy, to ruin c) [acuerdo] to break off d) [disolver] to dissolve; [derretir] to melt 2. **deshacerse** *vpr* a) to come undone *o* untied b) **deshacerse de algn / algo** to get rid of sb / sth c) [afligirse] to go to pieces; **deshacerse en lágrimas** to cry one's eyes out

d) [disolverse] to dissolve; [derretirse] to melt e) [niebla] to fade away, to disappear

deshecho, -a *adj* a) [cama] unmade; [maleta] unpacked; [paquete] unwrapped b) [roto] broken, smashed c) [disuelto] dissolved; [derretido] melted d) [abatido] devastated, shattered e) [cansado] exhausted, tired out

desheredar *vt* to disinherit

deshidratado, -a *adj* dehydrated

deshidratar *vt* to dehydrate

deshielo *nm* thaw

deshonesto, -a *adj* a) dishonest b) [indecente] indecent, improper

deshonor *nm* dishonour

deshonra *nf* dishonour

deshuesar *vt* [carne] to bone; [fruto] *Br* to stone, *US* to pit

desierto, -a 1. *nm* desert 2. *adj* a) [deshabitado] uninhabited b) [vacío] empty, deserted c) [premio] void

designar *vt* a) to designate b) [fecha, lugar] to fix

desigual *adj* a) uneven b) [lucha] unequal c) [carácter] changeable

desigualdad *nf* a) inequality b) [del terreno] unevenness

desilusión *nf* [decepción] disappointment, disillusionment; **llevarse una desilusión con** to be disappointed

desilusionado, -a *adj* disappointed, disillusioned

desilusionar 1. *vt* to disappoint, to disillusion 2. **desilusionarse** *vpr* a) [decepcionarse] to be disappointed b) [desengañarse] to become disillusioned; **¡desilusiónate!** don't get your hopes up!

desinfectante *adj & nm* disinfectant

desinfectar *vt* to disinfect

desinflar 1. *vt* to deflate; [rueda] to let down 2. **desinflarse** *vpr* to go flat

desinhibir 1. *vt* to free from inhibitions 2. **desinhibirse** *vpr* to lose one's inhibitions

desintegración *nf* disintegration

desinterés *nm* **a)** [indiferencia] lack of interest, apathy **b)** [generosidad] unselfishness

desinteresado, -a *adj* selfless, unselfish

desistir *vi* to desist

deslave *nm* landslide *(caused by flooding or rain)*

desliz *nm* mistake, slip; **cometer** o **tener un desliz** to slip up

deslizamiento *nm* sliding

deslizar [40] **1.** *vi* to slide **2. deslizarse** *vpr* **a)** [patinar] to slide **b)** [fluir] to flow

deslocalización *nf* offshoring *(to reduce employment costs)*, relocation *(of jobs to a cheaper country)*

deslocalizar *vt* to offshore *(to reduce employment costs)*, to relocate *(jobs to a cheaper country)*

deslumbrar *vt* to dazzle

desmadrarse *vpr Esp Fam* to go wild

desmanchar *vt Am* to remove the stains from

desmaquillador, -a 1. *nm* make-up remover **2.** *adj* **leche desmaquilladora** cleansing cream

desmaquillarse *vpr* to remove one's make-up

desmayarse *vpr* to faint

desmayo *nm* faint, fainting fit; **tener un desmayo** to faint

desmejorado, -a *adj* deteriorated

desmentir [5] *vt* to deny

desmesurado, -a *adj* excessive

desmontar 1. *vt* **a)** [desarmar] to take to pieces, to dismantle **b)** [allanar] to level **2.** *vi* **desmontar (de)** to dismount, to get off

desmoralizado, -a *adj* demoralized

desmoralizante *adj* demoralizing

desmoralizar [40] *vt* to demoralize

desmotivar 1. *vt* to demotivate **2. desmotivarse** *vpr* to become demotivated

desnatado, -a *adj* [leche] skimmed

desnivel *nm* [en el terreno] drop, difference in height

desnivelado, -a *adj* **a)** [terreno] uneven **b)** [sistema, situación, relaciones] unbalanced

desnivelar 1. *vt* **a)** [terreno] to make uneven **b)** [sistema, situación, relaciones] to unbalance **c)** [balanza] to tip **2. desnivelarse** *vpr* **a)** [mueble] to become wobbly **b)** [terreno] to become uneven

desnudar 1. *vt* to undress **2. desnudarse** *vpr* to get undressed

desnudo, -a 1. *adj* naked, nude **2.** *nm* ARTE nude

desnutrición *nf* malnutrition

desobedecer [33] *vt* to disobey

desobediente 1. *adj* disobedient **2.** *nmf* disobedient person

desocupado, -a 1. *adj* **a)** [ocioso, vacío] unoccupied; [baño] free **b)** [sin empleo] unemployed **2.** *nm, f Am* unemployed person; **los desocupados** the unemployed

desodorante *adj* & *nm* deodorant

desolado, -a *adj* devastated

desorden *nm* untidiness, mess; **¡qué desorden!** what a mess!; **desorden público** civil disorder

desordenar *vt* to make untidy, to mess up

desorganización *nf* disorganization

desorganizado, -a *adj* disorganized

desorientado, -a *adj* disorientated

desorientar 1. *vt* to disorientate **2. desorientarse** *vpr* to lose one's sense of direction, to lose one's bearings; *Fig* to become disorientated

despachar 1. *vt* **a)** [asunto] to get through **b)** [correo] to send, dispatch **c)** [en tienda] to serve **d)** *Fam* [despedir] to send packing, sack **e)** *Am* [facturar] to check in **2. despacharse** *vpr* [hablar francamente] **despacharse (con algn)** to get things off one's chest (with sb)

despacho nm a) [oficina] office; [en casa] study b) [venta] sale c) [comunicación] dispatch

despacio 1. adv a) [lentamente] slowly b) [en voz baja] quietly c) Am [sin ruido] quietly I. 2. interj ¡despacio! quietly!

despampanante adj Fam stunning

desparpajo nm self-assurance; **con desparpajo** in a carefree manner

despecho nm spite; **por despecho** out of spite

despectivo, -a adj derogatory, disparaging

despedida nf a) [adiós] farewell, goodbye; **no me gustan las despedidas** I don't like goodbyes b) [fiesta] leaving party; **despedida de soltera** Br hen party, US bachelorette party; **despedida de soltero** Br stag party, US bachelor party

despedido, -a adj a) [persona] dismissed, fired b) [objeto] **salir despedido** to be ejected

despedir [6] 1. vt a) [empleado] to fire, Br to sack b) [decir adiós] to see off, to say goodbye to c) [olor, humo etc] to give off 2. **despedirse** vpr a) [decir adiós] to say goodbye (**de** to) b) Fig to forget, to give up; **ya puedes despedirte del coche** you can say goodbye to the car

despegar [42] 1. vt to take off, to detach 2. vi AVIACIÓN to take off 3. **despegarse** vpr to come unstuck

despegue nm take-off

despeinado, -a adj unkempt

despeinar 1. vt [pelo] to ruffle; **despeinar a algn** to mess up sb's hair 2. **despeinarse** vpr to get one's hair messed up

despejado, -a adj clear; [cielo] cloudless

despejar 1. vt to clear; [misterio, dudas] to clear up 2. **despejarse** vpr a) [cielo] to clear b) [persona] to clear one's head

despensa nf pantry, larder

despeñadero nm cliff, precipice

desperdiciar [43] vt to waste; [oportunidad] to throw away

desperdicio nm a) [acto] waste b) **desperdicios** [basura] rubbish; [desechos] scraps, leftovers

desperezarse [40] vpr to stretch (oneself)

desperfecto nm a) [defecto] flaw, imperfection b) [daño] damage

despertador nm alarm clock

despertar [1] 1. vt to wake (up), to awaken; Fig [sentimiento etc] to arouse 2. **despertarse** vpr to wake (up)

despido nm dismissal, sacking

despierto, -a adj a) [desvelado] awake b) [vivo] quick, sharp

despilfarrador, -a adj & nm, f spendthrift

despilfarrar vt to squander

despiole nm RP Fam rumpus, shindy

despistado, -a 1. adj a) [olvidadizo] scatterbrained b) [confuso] confused 2. nm, f scatterbrain

despistar 1. vt a) [hacer perder la pista a] to lose, to throw off one's scent b) Fig to mislead 2. **despistarse** vpr a) [perderse] to get lost b) [distraerse] to switch off

despiste nm a) [cualidad] absentmindedness b) [error] slip-up

desplazar [40] 1. vt to displace 2. **desplazarse** vpr to travel

desplegable 1. adj a) [mapa, libro] fold-out b) INFORM [fijo] drop-down; [que desaparece al mover el ratón] pulldown; **menú desplegable** [fijo] dropdown menu; [que desaparece al mover el ratón] pull-down menu 2. nm [folleto] folded leaflet

desplegar [1] 1. vt a) [abrir] to open (out), to spread (out) b) [energías etc] to use, to deploy 2. **desplegarse** vpr a) [abrirse] to open (out), to spread (out) b) MIL to deploy

desplomarse vpr to collapse; [precios] to slump, to fall sharply

despoblarse vpr a) [lugar] to become deserted b) [cabeza] to thin

despojo *nm* **a)** stripping **b)** **despojos** leftovers, scraps

despótico, -a *adj* despotic

despreciable *adj* despicable

despreciar [43] *vt* **a)** [desdeñar] to scorn, to despise **b)** [rechazar] to reject, to spurn

desprecio *nm* **a)** [desdén] scorn, contempt **b)** [desaire] slight, snub

desprender 1. *vt* **a)** [separar] to remove, to detach **b)** [olor, humo etc] to give off **2. desprenderse** *vpr* **a)** [soltarse] to come off o away **b)** **desprenderse de** to rid oneself of, to free oneself from **c) de aquí se desprende que** … it can be deduced from this that…

desprendimiento *nm* **a)** loosening, detachment; **desprendimiento de tierras** landslide **b)** *Fig* [generosidad] generosity, unselfishness

despreocupación *nf* indifference

despreocuparse *vpr* **a)** [tranquilizarse] to stop worrying **b)** [desentenderse] to be unconcerned, to be indifferent (**de** to)

desprevenido, -a *adj* unprepared; **coger** o **pillar a algn desprevenido** to catch sb unawares

desprolijidad *nf RP* messiness, untidiness

desprolijo, -a *adj RP* [casa] messy, untidy; [cuaderno] untidy; [persona] unkempt, dishevelled

desproporcionado, -a *adj* disproportionate

después *adv* **a)** afterwards, later; [entonces] then; [seguidamente] next; **una semana después** a week later; **poco después** soon after **b)** [lugar] next **c) después de** after; **después de la guerra** after the war; **mi calle está después de la tuya** my street is the one after yours; **después de cenar** after eating; **después de todo** after all **d) después de que** after; **después de que viniera** after he came

desquiciar *vt* **a)** [desequilibrar] to upset, to unbalance **b)** [sacar de quicio] to drive mad

desrielar *vi Am* [descarrilar] to derail

destacable *adj* outstanding

destacar [44] **1.** *vt Fig* to emphasize, to stress **2.** *vi* to stand out **3. destacarse** *vpr* to stand out

destajo *nm* piecework; **trabajar a destajo** to do piecework

destapador *nm Am* bottle opener

destapar 1. *vt* to take the lid off; [botella] to open; *Fig* [asunto] to uncover; *RP* [caño] to unblock **2. destaparse** *vpr* to get uncovered

destello *nm* flash, sparkle

destemplado, -a *adj* **a)** [voz, gesto] sharp, snappy; **con cajas destempladas** rudely, brusquely **b)** [tiempo] unpleasant **c)** [enfermo] indisposed, out of sorts **d)** MÚS out of tune, discordant

desteñir [6] **1.** *vt* & *vi* to discolour **2. desteñirse** *vpr* to lose colour, to fade

desterrar [1] *vt* to exile

destierro *nm* exile

destilación *nf* distillation

destilar *vt* to distil

destilería *nf* distillery

destinado, -a *adj* **a)** [predestinado] destined **b)** [carta, paquete] **destinado a algn** adressed to sb; **destinado a Cartagena** bound for Cartagena

destinar *vt* **a)** [dinero etc] to set aside, to assign **b)** [empleado] to appoint

destinatario, -a *nm, f* **a)** [de carta] addressee **b)** [de mercancías] consignee

destino *nm* **a)** [rumbo] destination; **el avión con destino a Bilbao** the plane to Bilbao **b)** [sino] fate, fortune **c)** [de empleo] post

destornillador *nm* screwdriver

destornillar *vt* to unscrew

destrozado, -a *adj* **a)** [objeto] shattered **b)** [plan, proyecto] ruined **c)** [persona, carrera] destroyed

destrozar [40] *vt* **a)** [destruir] to destroy; [rasgar] to tear to shreds o pieces **b)** [persona] to shatter; [vida, reputación] to ruin

destrucción *nf* destruction

destruir [37] *vt* to destroy

desubicado, -a *nm, f Am* **es un desubicado** he has no idea of how to behave

desubicar 1. *vt Am Br* to disorientate, *US* to disorient **2. desubicarse** *vpr Am* to get lost

desuso *nm* disuse; **caer en desuso** to fall into disuse; **en desuso** obsolete, outdated

desvalijar *vt* [robar] to clean out, to rob; [casa, tienda] to burgle

desván *nm* attic, loft

desvanecimiento *nm* [desmayo] fainting fit

desvariar [29] *vi* to talk nonsense

desvelar 1. *vt* to keep awake **2. desvelarse** *vpr* **a)** [despabilarse] to stay awake **b)** [desvivirse] to devote oneself (**por** to) **c)** *CAm, Méx* [quedarse despierto] to stay up o awake

desvencijado, -a *adj* dilapidated

desventaja *nf* **a)** disadvantage; **estar en desventaja** to be at a disadvantage **b)** [inconveniente] drawback

desvergonzado, -a 1. *adj* **a)** [indecente] shameless **b)** [descarado] insolent **2.** *nm, f* **a)** [sinvergüenza] shameless person **b)** [fresco] insolent o cheeky person

desvestir [6] **1.** *vt* to undress **2. desvestirse** *vpr* to undress (oneself)

desviado, -a *adj* diverted

desviar [29] **1.** *vt* [río, carretera] to divert; [golpe, conversación] to deflect; **desviar la mirada** to look away **2. desviarse** *vpr* to go off course; [coche] to turn off; *Fig* **desviarse del tema** to digress

desvío *nm Br* diversion, *US* detour

detallar *vt* to give the details of

detalle *nm* **a)** detail; **entrar en detalles** to go into details **b)** [delicadeza] nice thought, nicety; **¡qué detalle!** how nice!, how sweet! **c)** [toque decorativo] touch, ornament

detallista 1. *adj* perfectionist **2.** *nmf* COM retailer

detectar *vt* to detect

detective *nmf* detective; **detective privado** private detective o eye

detener [24] **1.** *vt* **a)** to stop, to halt **b)** JUR [arrestar] to arrest, to detain **2. detenerse** *vpr* to stop

detenido, -a 1. *adj* **a)** [parado] standing still, stopped **b)** [arrestado] detained **c)** [minucioso] detailed, thorough **2.** *nm, f* detainee, person under arrest

detergente *adj & nm* detergent; *Am* **detergente para la vajilla** *Br* washing-up liquid, *US* dishwashing liquid

deteriorado, -a *adj* dilapidated

deteriorar *vt* to damage

determinación *nf* **a)** determination; **con determinación** determinedly **b)** [decisión] decision

determinado, -a *adj* **a)** [preciso] definite, precise **b)** [resuelto] decisive, resolute **c)** LING definite

determinante *adj* decisive

determinar 1. *vt* **a)** [fecha etc] to fix, to set **b)** [decidir] to decide on **c)** [condicionar] to determine **d)** [ocasionar] to bring about **2. determinarse** *vpr* to make up one's mind to

detestable *adj* detestable, repulsive

detestar *vt* to detest, to hate

detrás *adv* **a)** behind, on o at the back (**de** of) **b)** **detrás de** behind

deuda *nf* debt; **estoy en deuda contigo** [monetaria] I am in debt to you; [moral] I am indebted to you; **deuda del Estado** public debt; **deuda pública** *Br* national debt, *US* public debt

devaluación *nf* devaluation

devaluar [30] *vt* to devalue

devanar 1. *vt* to wind **2. devanarse** *vpr Fam* **devanarse los sesos** to rack one's brains

devoción *nf* **a)** REL devoutness **b)** [al trabajo etc] devotion; *Fam* **Juan no es santo de mi devoción** Juan isn't really my cup of tea

devolución *nf* **a)** giving back, return; COM refund, repayment **b)** JUR devolution

devolver [4] *(pp* **devuelto) 1.** *vt* to give back, to return; [dinero] to refund **2.** *vi* [vomitar] to vomit, to throw *o* bring up **3. devolverse** *vpr Am salvo RP* to come back

devorar *vt* to devour

devoto, -a 1. *adj* pious, devout **2.** *nm, f* **a)** REL pious person **b)** [seguidor] devotee

devuelto, -a *pp de* **devolver**

DGT *nf (abr de* **Dirección General de Tráfico)** *government department responsible for road transport*

di 1. *pt indef de* **dar 2.** *imperat de* **decir**

día *nm* day; **¿qué día es hoy?** what's the date today?; **día a día** day by day; **de día** by day; **durante el día** during the daytime; **de un día para otro** overnight; **un día sí y otro no** every other day; **pan del día** fresh bread; **hoy (en) día** nowadays; **el día de mañana** in the future; *Fig* **estar al día** to be up to date; *Fig* **poner al día** to bring up to date; **día festivo** holiday; **día laborable** working day; **día libre** free day, day off; **es de día** it is daylight; **hace buen/mal día** it's a nice / bad day, the weather is nice / bad today; **¡buenos días!** hello!, good morning!; *RP* **¡buen día!** hello!, good morning!

diabetes *nf inv* diabetes

diabético, -a *adj & nm, f* diabetic

diablo *nm* devil; *Fam* **¡al diablo con …!** to hell with …!; *Fam* **vete al diablo** get lost; *Fam* **¿qué /cómo diablos …?** what / how the hell …?

diablura *nf* mischief

diabólico, -a *adj* **a)** [del diablo] diabolic **b)** [muy malo, difícil] diabolical

diadema *nf* tiara

diagnosticar [44] *vt* to diagnose

diagnóstico *nm* diagnosis

dialecto *nm* dialect

diálogo *nm* dialogue

diamante *nm* diamond

diana *nf* **a)** MIL reveille **b)** [blanco] bull's eye

diapositiva *nf* slide

diariamente *adv* daily, every day

diariero, -a *nm, f Andes, RP* newspaper seller

diario, -a 1. *nm* **a)** PRENSA (daily) newspaper **b)** [memorias] diary; NÁUT **diario de a bordo, diario de navegación** logbook **2.** *adj* daily; **a diario** daily, every day

diarrea *nf* diarrhoea; *Fam* **diarrea verbal** verbal diarrhoea; *Fam* **diarrea del viajero** *Br* traveller's diarrhoea, *US* traveler's diarrhea

dibujar *vt* to draw

dibujo *nm* **a)** drawing; **dibujos animados** cartoons **b)** [arte] drawing; **dibujo artístico** artistic drawing; **dibujo lineal** draughtsmanship

diccionario *nm* dictionary; **buscar** *o* **mirar una palabra en el diccionario** to look up a word in the dictionary

dicha *nf* happiness

dicho, -a 1. *pp de* **decir 2.** *adj* **a)** said; **mejor dicho** or rather; **dicho de otro modo** put another way, in other words; **dicho sea de paso** let it be said in passing; **dicho y hecho** no sooner said than done; **lo dicho** ok, that's settled then **b) dicha persona** [mencionado] the above-mentioned person **3.** *nm* saying

diciembre *nm* December

dictado *nm* dictation; *Fig* **dictados** dictates

dictador, -a *nm, f* dictator

dictadura *nf* dictatorship

dictamen *nm* [juicio] ruling; [informe] report

dictaminar *vt* to declare, to be of the opinion that

dictar *vt* **a)** to dictate **b)** [ley] to enact; [sentencia] to pass

dictatorial *adj* dictatorial

diecinueve *adj & nm inv* nineteen

dieciocho *adj & nm inv* eighteen

dieciséis *adj & nm inv* sixteen

diecisiete *adj & nm inv* seventeen

diente *nm* tooth; TÉC cog; [de ajo] clove; **diente de leche** milk tooth; **dientes postizos** false teeth; *Fig* **hablar entre dientes** to mumble; *Fig* **poner los dientes largos a algn** to make sb green with envy

diera *subj imperf de* **dar**

diéresis *nf inv* diaeresis

diesel *adj & nm* diesel

diestro, -a 1. *adj* **a)** [hábil] skilful, clever **b)** *Esp* **a diestro y siniestro** right, left and centre **2.** *nm* TAUROM bullfighter, matador

dieta *nf* **a)** diet; **estar a dieta** to be on a diet **b)** **dietas** expense o subsistence allowance

dietética *nf* dietetics (*sing*)

dietista *nmf* dietitian

diez *adj & nm inv* ten

diferencia *nf* difference; **a diferencia de** unlike

diferenciar [43] **1.** *vt* to differentiate, to distinguish (**entre** between) **2. diferenciarse** *vpr* to differ (**de** from), to be different (**de** from o (US) than)

diferente 1. *adj* different (**de** from o (US) than) **2.** *adv* differently

diferido, -a *adj* TV **en diferido** recorded

diferir [5] **1.** *vt* [posponer] to postpone, to put off **2.** *vi* [diferenciarse] to differ, to be different; **diferir de algn en algo** to differ from sb in sth

difícil *adj* difficult, hard; **difícil de creer / hacer** difficult to believe / do; **es difícil que venga** it is unlikely that she'll come

dificultad *nf* difficulty; [aprieto] trouble, problem

difundir 1. *vt* to spread **2. difundirse** *vpr* = **difundir**

difunto, -a 1. *adj* late, deceased **2.** *nm, f* deceased

difusión *nf* **a)** [de noticia] spreading; **tener gran difusión** to be widely broadcast **b)** RADIO & TV broadcasting

digerir [5] *vt* to digest; *Fig* to assimilate

digestión *nf* digestion; **corte de digestión** sudden indigestion

digitador, -a *nm, f Am* keyboarder

digital *adj* [gen & INFORM] digital; **huellas digitales** fingerprints

digitalizado, -a *adj* digitized

digitar *vt Am* [teclear] to key, to type

dígito *nm* digit

dignarse *vpr* **dignarse (a)** to deign to, to condescend to

dignidad *nf* dignity

digno, -a *adj* **a)** [merecedor] worthy; **digno de admiración** worthy of admiration; **digno de mención / verse** worth mentioning / seeing **b)** [decoroso] decent, good

digo *indic pres de* **decir**

dilema *nm* dilemma

diligencia *nf* **a)** [esmero, cuidado] diligence **b)** [prontitud] **con diligencia** quickly **c)** [trámite, gestión] errand, job; *Am* **hacer unas diligencias** to run some errands **d)** [vehículo] stagecoach

diligente *adj* diligent

diluviar [43] *v impers* to pour with rain

diluvio *nm* flood; **el Diluvio (Universal)** the Flood

dimensión *nf* **a)** dimension, size; **de gran dimensión** very large **b)** *Fig* [importancia] importance

diminuto, -a *adj* minute, tiny

dimitir *vi* to resign (**de** from); **dimitir de un cargo** to give in o tender one's resignation

Dinamarca *n* Denmark

dinámico, -a *adj* dynamic

dinamita *nf* dynamite

dinamizador, -a *adj* revitalizing

dinastía *nf* dynasty

discrepancia

dinero *nm* money; **dinero contante (y sonante)** cash; **dinero efectivo** *o* **en metálico** cash; **gente de dinero** wealthy people

dinosaurio *nm* dinosaur

diócesis *nf inv* diocese

dios *nm* god; **¡Dios mío!** my God!; **¡por Dios!** for goodness sake!; **a la buena de Dios** any old how; **hacer algo como Dios manda** to do sth properly; *Fam* **ni dios** nobody; *Fam* **todo dios** everybody

dióxido *nm* dioxide; **dióxido de carbono** carbon dioxide

diploma *nm* diploma

diplomacia *nf* diplomacy

diplomado, -a 1. *adj* qualified **2.** *nm, f* holder of a diploma

diplomar 1. *vt* to give a diploma to, to give a certificate to **2. diplomarse** *vpr* to get a diploma, to graduate; **diplomarse en periodismo** to graduate in journalism

diplomático, -a 1. *adj* diplomatic; **cuerpo diplomático** diplomatic corps **2.** *nm, f* diplomat

diplomatura *nf* EDUC ≃ diploma, *qualification obtained after three years of university study*

diptongo *nm* diphthong

diputación *nf Esp* **diputación provincial** *governing body of each province*, ≃ county council

diputado, -a *nm, f* ≃ *Br* Member of Parliament, MP, ≃ *US* representative

dique *nm* dike

dirección *nf* **a)** direction; AUTO **dirección prohibida** [en letrero] no entry; **calle de dirección única** one-way street **b)** [señas] address; INFORM **dirección de correo electrónico** e-mail address **c)** CINE & TEATRO direction **d)** [destino] destination **e)** AUTO & TÉC steering **f)** [dirigentes] management; [cargo] directorship; [de un partido] leadership; [de un colegio] headship

direccional *nm o nf Col, Ecuad, Méx Br* indicator, *US* turn signal

directa *nf* AUTO top gear

directo, -a *adj* direct; TV & RADIO **en directo** live

director, -a *nm, f* [de empresa] director; [de hotel, banco] manager; [de colegio] *Br* headmaster, *f* headmistress, *US* principal; [de periódico] editor; **director de cine** movie *o Br* film director; **director de orquesta** conductor; **director gerente** managing director

directorio *nm* [gen & INFORM] directory; *Am salvo RP* **directorio telefónico** telephone directory

dirigente 1. *adj* leading; **clase dirigente** ruling class **2.** *nmf* leader

dirigir [57] **1.** *vt* to direct; [empresa] to manage; [negocio, colegio] to run; [orquesta] to conduct; [partido] to lead; [periódico] to edit; [coche, barco] to steer; **dirigir la palabra a algn** to speak to sb **2. dirigirse** *vpr* **a)** dirigirse a *o* hacia to go to, to make one's way towards **b)** [escribir] to write; **diríjase al apartado de correos 42** write to PO Box 42 **c)** [hablar] to speak

discar *vt Andes, RP* to dial

discernir [54] *vt* to discern, to distinguish; **discernir algo de algo** to distinguish sth from sth

disciplina *nf* discipline

disciplinado, -a *adj* disciplined

discípulo, -a *nm, f* disciple

disco *nm* **a)** disc; **disco de freno** brake disc **b)** MÚS record; **disco compacto** compact disc **c)** INFORM disk; **disco duro** *o* **fijo / flexible** hard / floppy disk **d)** DEP discus **e)** TEL dial

discolibro *nm* audiobook

discordancia *nf* **a)** [de sonidos, colores] clash **b)** [de opiniones] conflict

discoteca *nf* **a)** [lugar] discotheque **b)** [colección] record collection

discreción *nf* **a)** discretion **b)** **a discreción** at will

discrepancia *nf* [desacuerdo] disagreement; [diferencia] discrepancy

discreto, -a *adj* a) discreet b) [mediocre] average

discriminación *nf* discrimination

discriminador, -a *adj* discriminatory

discriminar *vt* a) to discriminate against b) *Formal* [diferenciar] to discriminate between, to distinguish

disculpa *nf* excuse; **dar disculpas** to make excuses; **pedir disculpas a algn** to apologize to sb

disculpar 1. *vt* to excuse 2. **disculparse** *vpr* to apologize (**por** for)

discurrir *vi* a) [reflexionar] to think b) *Fig* [transcurrir] to pass, to go by c) *Formal* [río] to wander

discurso *nm* speech; **dar** *o* **pronunciar un discurso** to make a speech

discusión *nf* argument

discutible *adj* debatable

discutir 1. *vi* to argue (**de** about) 2. *vt* to discuss, to talk about

disecar [44] *vt* a) [animal] to stuff b) [planta] to dry

diseminar *vt* [semillas] to disperse

diseñador, -a *nm, f* designer; **diseñador gráfico** graphic designer

diseñar *vt* to design

diseño *nm* design; **diseño de interiores** interior design

disfraz *nm* disguise; [para fiesta] fancy dress; **fiesta de disfraces** fancy dress party

disfrazar [40] 1. *vt* to disguise 2. **disfrazarse** *vpr* to disguise oneself; **disfrazarse de pirata** to dress up as a pirate

disfrutar 1. *vi* a) [gozar] to enjoy oneself b) [poseer] **disfrutar (de)** to enjoy 2. *vt* to enjoy

disgustado, -a *adj* upset

disgustar 1. *vt* to upset 2. **disgustarse** *vpr* a) [molestarse] to get upset, to be annoyed b) [dos amigos] to quarrel

disgusto *nm* a) [preocupación] annoyance; **llevarse un disgusto** to get

upset; **dar un disgusto a algn** to upset sb b) [desgracia] trouble; **a disgusto** unwillingly; **sentirse** *o* **estar a disgusto** to feel ill at ease c) [desavenencia] fall-out, disagreement

disidente *adj* & *nmf* dissident

disimular *vt* to conceal, to hide

dislocado, -a *adj* dislocated

dislocarse *vpr* **dislocarse la muñeca** to dislocate one's wrist

disminución *nf* decrease

disminuir [37] 1. *vt* to reduce 2. *vi* to diminish

disolvente *adj* & *nm* solvent

disolver [4] *(pp* **disuelto)** *vt* to dissolve

disparar 1. *vt* [pistola etc] to fire; [flecha, balón] to shoot; **disparar a algn** to shoot at sb 2. **dispararse** *vpr* a) [arma] to go off, to fire b) [precios] to rocket

disparate *nm* a) [dicho] nonsense; **decir disparates** to talk nonsense b) [acto] foolish act

disparo *nm* shot; DEP **disparo a puerta** shot

dispensar *vt* a) [disculpar] to pardon, to forgive b) [eximir] to exempt

dispersar 1. *vt* to disperse; [esparcir] to scatter 2. **dispersarse** *vpr* to disperse

disponer [19] *(pp* **dispuesto)** 1. *vt* a) [arreglar] to arrange, to set out b) [ordenar] to order 2. *vi* **disponer de** to have at one's disposal 3. **disponerse** *vpr* to prepare, to get ready

disponible *adj* available

disposición *nf* a) [uso] disposal; **a su disposición** at your disposal *o* service b) [colocación] arrangement, layout c) **no estar en disposición de** not to be prepared to d) [orden] order, law

dispositivo *nm* device

dispuesto, -a *adj* a) [ordenado] arranged b) [a punto] ready c) [decidido] determined; **no estar dispuesto a** not to be prepared to d) **según lo dispuesto por la ley** in accordance with what the law stipulates

disputa *nf* [discusión] argument; [contienda] contest

disputar 1. *vt* **a)** [premio] to compete for **b)** DEP [partido] to play **2. disputarse** *vpr* [premio] to compete for

disquete *nm* INFORM diskette, floppy disk

disquetera *nf* INFORM disk drive

distancia *nf* distance; **a distancia** from a distance

distanciar [43] **1.** *vt* to separate **2. distanciarse** *vpr* to become separated; [de otra persona] to distance oneself

distante *adj* distant, far-off

distinción *nf* distinction; **a distinción de** unlike; **sin distinción de** irrespective of

distinguido, -a *adj* distinguished

distinguir [59] **1.** *vt* **a)** [diferenciar] to distinguish **b)** [reconocer] to recognize **c)** [honrar] to honour **2.** *vi* [diferenciar] to discriminate **3. distinguirse** *vpr* to distinguish oneself

distintivo, -a 1. *adj* distinctive, distinguishing **2.** *nm* distinctive sign o mark

distinto, -a *adj* different

distracción *nf* **a)** entertainment; [pasatiempo] pastime, hobby **b)** [descuido] distraction, absent-mindedness

distraer [25] **1.** *vt* **a)** [atención] to distract **b)** [divertir] to entertain, to amuse **2. distraerse** *vpr* **a)** [divertirse] to amuse oneself **b)** [abstraerse] to let one's mind wander

distraído, -a *adj* **a)** [divertido] entertaining **b)** [abstraído] absent-minded

distribución *nf* **a)** distribution **b)** [disposición] layout

distribuir [37] *vt* to distribute; [trabajo] to share out

distrito *nm* district; **distrito postal** postal district

disturbio *nm* riot, disturbance

disuelto, -a *pp de* **disolver**

diurno, -a *adj* daytime

diva *nf* MÚS diva, prima donna

diván *nm* divan, couch

divergente *adj* divergent

diversidad *nf* diversity

diversión *nf* fun

diverso, -a *adj* different; **diversos** several, various

divertido, -a *adj* amusing, funny

divertir [5] **1.** *vt* to amuse, to entertain **2. divertirse** *vpr* to enjoy oneself, to have a good time; **¡que te diviertas!** enjoy yourself!, have fun!

dividir 1. *vt* to divide (**en** into); MAT **15 dividido entre 3** 15 divided by 3 **2. dividirse** *vpr* to divide, to split up

divino, -a *adj* divine

divisa *nf* **a)** [emblema] symbol, emblem **b)** COM **divisas** foreign currency

divisar *vt* to make out, to discern

división *nf* division

divorciado, -a 1. *adj* divorced **2.** *nm, f* divorcé, *f* divorcée

divorciar [43] **1.** *vt* to divorce **2. divorciarse** *vpr* to get divorced; **se divorció de él** she divorced him, she got a divorce from him

divorcio *nm* divorce

divulgar [42] *vt* to disclose; RADIO & TV to broadcast

divulgativo, -a *adj* informative

dizque *adv Andes, Carib, Méx Fam* apparently

dnd SMS *written abbr of* **donde**; *written abbr of* **dónde**

DNI *nm (abr de* **Documento Nacional de Identidad***)* Identity Card, ID card

dobladillo *nm* [de traje, vestido] hem; [de pantalón] *Br* turn-up, *US* cuff

doblaje *nm* CINE dubbing

doblar 1. *vt* **a)** to double; **me dobla la edad** he is twice as old as I am **b)** [plegar] to fold o turn up **c)** [torcer] to bend **d)** [la esquina] to go round **e)** [película] to dub **2.** *vi* **a)** [girar] to turn; **doblar a la derecha/izquierda** to turn right/left

b) [campanas] to toll
3. doblarse *vpr* **a)** [plegarse] to fold
b) [torcerse] to bend

doble 1. *adj* double; **arma de doble filo** double-edged weapon **2.** *nm* **a)** double; **gana el doble que tú** she earns twice as much as you do **b)** DEP **dobles** doubles

doce *adj* & *nm inv* twelve

docena *nf* dozen

docente *adj* teaching; **centro docente** educational centre

dócil *adj* docile

doctor, -a *nm, f* doctor

doctorado *nm* UNIV doctorate, PhD

doctorarse *vpr* to get one's doctorate (**en** in)

doctrina *nf* doctrine

documentación *nf* documentation; [DNI, de conducir etc] papers

documental *adj* & *nm* documentary

documento *nm* document; **documento nacional de identidad** identity card

dogma *nm* dogma

dogmático, -a *adj* & *nm, f* dogmatic

dólar *nm* dollar

doler [4] **1.** *vi* to hurt, to ache; **me duele la cabeza** I've got a headache; **me duele la mano** my hand is sore **2. dolerse** *vpr* to be sorry o sad

dolor *nm* **a)** MED pain; **dolor de cabeza** headache; **dolor de muelas** toothache **b)** [pena] grief, sorrow

doloroso, -a *adj* painful

domador, -a *nm, f* [de animales salvajes] tamer; [de caballos] breaker; **domador de leones** lion tamer

domar *vt* to tame; [caballo] to break in

domesticado, -a *adj* **a)** domesticated **b)** [animal] tame

domesticar [44] *vt* **a)** to domesticate **b)** [animal] to tame

doméstico, -a *adj* domestic; **animal doméstico** pet

domiciliar *vt Esp* **a)** [cobro] to be paid direct by bank transfer **b)** [pago] to pay by direct debit

domicilio *nm* home, residence; [señas] address; **sin domicilio fijo** of no fixed abode; **domicilio fiscal** registered office

dominante *adj* **a)** dominant **b)** [déspota] domineering

dominar 1. *vt* **a)** to dominate, to rule **b)** [situación] to control; [idioma] to speak very well; [asunto] to master; [paisaje etc] to overlook **2.** *vi* **a)** to dominate **b)** [resaltar] to stand out **3. dominarse** *vpr* to control oneself

domingo *nm inv* Sunday; **Domingo de Resurrección** o **Pascua** Easter Sunday

dominguero, -a *nm, f Fam* [excursionista] weekend tripper; [conductor] weekend driver

dominical 1. *adj* Sunday **2.** *nm* [suplemento] Sunday supplement

dominio *nm* **a)** [poder] control; [de un idioma] command; **dominio de sí mismo** self-control **b)** [ámbito] scope, sphere; **ser del dominio público** to be public knowledge **c)** [territorio] dominion **d)** INFORM domain

dominó, dómino *nm* dominoes

don¹ *nm* **a)** [habilidad] gift, talent; **tener el don de** to have a knack for; **tener don de gentes** to get on well with people **b)** [regalo] present, gift

don² *nm* **Señor Don José García** Mr José García; **Don Fulano de Tal** Mr So-and-So; **un don nadie** a nobody

donante *nmf* donor; MED **donante de sangre** blood donor

donativo *nm* donation

donde *adv* where; **a** o **en donde** where; **de** o **desde donde** from where;

está donde lo dejaste it is where you left it; *Fam* **está donde su tía** he's at his aunt's

> **donde** combines with the preposition **a** to form **adonde** when following a noun, a pronoun or an adverb expressing location (e.g. **el sitio adonde vamos** the place where we're going; **es allí adonde iban** that's where they were going).

dónde *adv interr* where?; **¿de dónde eres?** where are you from?; **¿por dónde se va a la playa?** which way is it to the beach?

> **dónde** can combine with the preposition **a** to form **adónde** (e.g. **¿adónde vamos?** where are we going?).

donostiarra **1.** *adj* from San Sebastian **2.** *nm, f* native or inhabitant of San Sebastian

dónut® *(pl* **dónuts)** *nm* doughnut

doña *nf* **a)** [tratamiento] ≃ Mrs, ≃ Ms; **doña Ana Bravo** Mrs / Ms Ana Bravo **b)** *Am* [sin nombre] madam; **¿qué va a llevar hoy, doña?** what would madam like today?

dopaje *nm* DEP drug-taking

dopar **1.** *vt* [caballo etc] to dope **2.** **doparse** *vpr* to take drugs

doping *(pl* **dopings)** *nm* DEP drug-taking

dorado, -a **1.** *adj* golden **2.** *nm* TÉC gilding

dormido, -a *adj* **a)** [persona] asleep **b)** [parte del cuerpo] **tengo el brazo dormido** my arm's gone to sleep

dormilón, -ona **1.** *adj Fam* sleepy-headed **2.** *nm, f* sleepyhead

dormilona *nf Am* [de mujer] nightdress; [de hombre] nightshirt

dormir [7] **1.** *vi* to sleep; **tener ganas de dormir** to feel sleepy
2. *vt* **dormir la siesta** to have an afternoon nap
3. **dormirse** *vpr* **a)** [persona] to fall asleep
b) [parte del cuerpo] **se me ha dormido el brazo** my arm has gone to sleep

dormitorio *nm* **a)** [de una casa] bedroom **b)** [de colegio, residencia] dormitory; **ciudad dormitorio** dormitory town

dorsal **1.** *adj* **espina dorsal** spine **2.** *nm* DEP number

dorso *nm* back; **instrucciones al dorso** instructions over; **véase al dorso** see overleaf

dos *adj & nm inv* two; **los dos** both; **nosotros / vosotros dos** both of us / you; *Fam* **cada dos por tres** every other minute; *Fam* **en un dos por tres** in a flash

doscientos, -as *adj & nm* two hundred

dosificación *nf* dosage

dosis *nf inv* dose; **dosis individual** individual dose

dotado, -a *adj* **a)** [persona] gifted **b)** [equipado] equipped; **dotado de** provided with

dotar *vt* **dotar de** to provide with

doy *indic pres de* **dar**

Dr. *(abr de* **doctor)** Dr

Dra. *(abr de* **doctora)** Dr

dragón *nm* dragon

drama *nm* drama

dramático, -a *adj* dramatic

dramaturgo, -a *nm, f* playwright, dramatist

droga *nf* drug; **droga blanda / dura** soft / hard drug

drogadicción *nf* drug addiction

drogadicto, -a *nm, f* drug addict

droguería *nf Esp* shop selling paint, cleaning materials, etc

dto. *(abr de* **descuento)** discount

dual *adj* dual

ducha *nf* shower; **darse / tomar una ducha** to take / have a shower

ducharse *vpr* to shower, to have *o* take a shower

duda *nf* doubt; **sin duda** without a doubt; **no cabe duda** (there is) no doubt; **poner algo en duda** to question sth; **sacar a algn de dudas** to dispel sb's doubts

dudar 1. *vi* **a)** to doubt **b)** [vacilar] to hesitate (**en** to); **dudaba entre ir o quedarme** I hesitated whether to go o to stay **c) dudar de algn** [desconfiar] to suspect sb **2.** *vt* to doubt

duelo[1] *nm* [combate] duel

duelo[2] *nm* [luto] mourning

duende *nm* **a)** [espíritu] goblin, elf **b)** [encanto] magic, charm

dueño *nm* owner; [de casa etc] landlord; *Fig* **ser dueño de sí mismo** to be self-possessed

dulce 1. *adj* **a)** [sabor] sweet **b)** [carácter, voz] gentle **c)** [metal] soft **d) agua dulce** fresh water **2.** *nm* **a)** CULIN [pastel] cake **b)** [caramelo] *Br* sweet, *US* candy

dulzura *nf* **a)** sweetness **b)** *Fig* gentleness, softness

duna *nf* dune

dúo *nm* duet

dúplex *nm* **a)** [piso] duplex, duplex apartment **b)** TEL link-up

duplicar [44] **1.** *vt* to duplicate; [cifras] to double **2. duplicarse** *vpr* to double

durabilidad *nf* ECOLOGÍA durability

duración *nf* duration, length; **disco de larga duración** long-playing record

durante *prep* during; **durante el día** during the day; **durante todo el día** all day long; **viví en La Coruña durante un año** I lived in La Coruña for a year

durar *vi* **a)** to last **b)** [ropa, calzado] to wear well, to last

durazno *nm* [fruto] peach; [árbol] peach tree

Durex® *nm Méx Br* Sellotape®, *US* Scotch® tape

dureza *nf* **a)** hardness; [severidad] harshness, severity **b)** [callosidad] corn

duro, -a 1. *adj* **a)** hard; DEP **juego duro** rough play **b)** [resistente] tough; [severo] hard **c)** [clima] harsh **2.** *nm Esp Antes* [moneda] 5-peseta coin; *Fam* **no tener ni un duro** not to have a penny, to be broke **3.** *adv* hard; **trabajar duro** to work hard

DVD *nm (abr de* **Disco Versátil Digital***)* DVD

E

e *conj* and

> **e** is used instead of **y** in front of words beginning with "i" or "hi" (e.g. **apoyo e interés** support and interest; **corazón e hígado** heart and liver).

ébano *nm* ebony

ebrio, -a *adj* inebriated; **ebrio de dicha** drunk with joy

ebullición *nf* boiling; **punto de ebullición** boiling point

echar 1. *vt* **a)** [lanzar] to throw; **echar una mano** to give a hand; *Fig* **echar una mirada/una ojeada** to have a look/a quick look o glance
b) [carta] to post, *US* to mail; [vino, agua] to pour; **echar sal al estofado** to put salt in the stew; **echar gasolina al coche** to put *Br* petrol o *US* gas in the car
c) [expulsar] to throw out; [despedir] to fire, *Br* to sack
d) [humo, olor etc] to give off
e) *Fam* [película] to show
f) **le echó 37 años** he reckoned she was about 37
g) **echar de menos** o **en falta** to miss
h) **echar abajo** [edificio] to demolish
2. *vi* (+ **a** + *infinitivo*) [empezar] to begin to; **echó a correr** he ran off
3. echarse *vpr* **a)** [tumbarse] to lie down; [lanzarse] to throw oneself
b) **échate a un lado** stand aside; *Fig* **echarse atrás** to get cold feet
c) *Fam* **echarse novio/novia** to get a boyfriend/girlfriend
d) (+ **a** + *infinitivo*) [empezar] to begin to; **echarse a llorar** to burst into tears; **echarse a reír** to burst out laughing; **echarse a perder** [comida] to go bad

eclesiástico, -a 1. *adj* ecclesiastical **2.** *nm* clergyman

eclipse *nm* eclipse

eco *nm* echo; *Fig* **hacerse eco de una noticia** to publish an item of news; **tener eco** to arouse interest

ecología *nf* ecology

ecológico, -a *adj* ecological; [alimentos] organic; [detergente] environmentally-friendly

economía *nf* **a)** economy; **con economía** economically **b)** [ciencia] economics (*sing*)

económico, -a *adj* **a)** economic **b)** [barato] economical, inexpensive **c)** [persona] thrifty

economista *nmf* economist

ecosistema *nm* ecosystem

ecoturismo *nm* ecotourism

ecuación *nf* equation

ecuador *nm* GEOGR equator

Ecuador *n* Ecuador

ecuatoriano, -a *adj & nm, f* Ecuadorian

edad *nf* age; **¿qué edad tienes?** how old are you?; **la tercera edad** senior citizens; **Edad Media** Middle Ages

edición *nf* **a)** [publicación] publication; [de sellos] issue **b)** [conjunto de ejemplares] edition

edificante *adj* edifying

edificar [44] *vt* to build

edificio *nm* building

editar *vt* **a)** [libro, periódico] to publish; [disco] to release **b)** INFORM to edit

editor, -a 1. *adj* publishing **2.** *nm, f* publisher

editorial 1. *adj* publishing **2.** *nf* publisher, publishing house **3.** *nm* PRENSA editorial, leader article

edredón *nm* eiderdown, *Br* duvet

educación *nf* a) education; **educación física** physical education b) [formación] upbringing c) **buena / mala educación** [modales] good / bad manners; **falta de educación** bad manners

educado, -a *adj* polite

educar [44] *vt* [hijos] to raise; [alumnos] to educate; [la voz] to train

educativo, -a *adj* educational; **sistema educativo** education system

EE.UU. *(abr de Estados Unidos)* USA

efectivo, -a 1. *adj* effective; **hacer algo efectivo** to carry sth out; FIN **hacer efectivo un cheque** to cash a cheque 2. *nm* a) FIN **en efectivo** in cash b) MIL **efectivos** forces c) **efectivos** [soldados] troops; [policías] police officers

efecto *nm* a) [resultado] effect; **efectos especiales / sonoros** special / sound effects; **efectos personales** personal belongings o effects; **a efectos de ...** for the purposes of ...; **en efecto** quite!, yes indeed! b) [impresión] impression; **causar o hacer efecto** to make an impression c) DEP spin

efectuar [30] *vt* to carry out; [viaje] to make; COM [pedido] to place

eficacia *nf* [de persona] efficiency; [de remedio etc] effectiveness

eficaz *adj* [persona] efficient; [remedio, medida etc] effective

eficiente *adj* efficient

EGB *nf (abr de Enseñanza General Básica)* EDUC *formerly, stage of Spanish education system for pupils aged 6-14*

Egipto *n* Egypt

egoísmo *nm* egoism, selfishness

egoísta 1. *adj* ego(t)istic, selfish 2. *nmf* ego(t)ist, selfish person

egresado, -a *nm, f Am* [de escuela] high-school graduate; [de universidad] graduate

egresar *vi Am* [de escuela] to leave school after completing one's studies, *US* to graduate; [de universidad] to graduate

egreso *nm Am* [de universidad] graduation

ej. *(abr de ejemplo)* example, ex.

eje *nm* a) TÉC [de rueda] axle; [de máquina] shaft b) MAT axis c) HIST **el Eje** the Axis

ejecución *nf* a) [de orden] carrying out b) [ajusticiamiento] execution c) MÚS performance

ejecutar *vt* a) [orden] to carry out b) [ajusticiar] to execute c) MÚS to perform, to play d) INFORM to run

ejecutivo, -a 1. *adj* executive; POL **el poder ejecutivo** the government 2. *nm* executive

ejemplar 1. *nm* a) [de libro] copy; [de revista, periódico] number, issue b) [espécimen] specimen 2. *adj* exemplary, model

ejemplo *nm* example; **por ejemplo** for example; **dar ejemplo** to set an example

ejercer [49] 1. *vt* a) [profesión etc] to practise b) [influencia] to exert c) **ejercer el derecho de / a ...** to exercise one's right to ... 2. *vi* to practise (**de** as)

ejercicio *nm* a) exercise; [de profesión] practice; **hacer ejercicio** to take o do exercise b) FIN tax year; **ejercicio económico** financial o fiscal year

ejército *nm* army

ejote *nm CAm, Méx* green bean

el, la *(mpl los, fpl las)*

el is used instead of **la** before feminine nouns which are stressed on the first syllable and begin with "a" or "ha" (e.g. **el agua, el hacha**). Note that **el** combines with the prepositions **a** and **de** to produce the contracted forms **al** and **del**.

1. *art det m* a) the
b) [no se traduce] **el Sel García** Mr García; **el hambre / destino** hunger / fate
c) [con partes del cuerpo, prendas de vestir] **me he cortado el dedo** I've cut my finger; **métetelo en el bolsillo** put it in your pocket
d) [con días de la semana] **el lunes** on Monday
2. *pron* a) the one; **el de las once** the eleven o'clock one; **el que tienes en**

la mano the one you've got in your hand; **el que quieras** whichever one you want
b) [no se traduce] **el de tu amigo** your friend's

él *pron pers* **a)** [sujeto-persona] he; [animal, cosa] it **b)** [complemento-persona] him; [animal, cosa] it

Usually omitted in Spanish as a subject except for emphasis or contrast.

elaborar *vt* **a)** [producto] to manufacture, to produce **b)** [teoría] to develop

elasticidad *nf* elasticity; *Fig* flexibility

elástico, -a 1. *adj* elastic **2.** *nm*
a) elastic **b) elásticos** *Br* braces, *US* suspenders

E/LE, ELE *nm (abr de* **español como lengua extranjera)** *Spanish as a Foreign Language*

elección *nf* choice; POL **elecciones** election

electricidad *nf* electricity

electricista *nmf* electrician

eléctrico, -a *adj* electric

electrocutar *vt* to electrocute

electrodoméstico *nm* (domestic) electrical appliance

electrónica *nf* electronics (*sing*)

electrónico, -a *adj* electronic

elefante *nm* elephant

elegancia *nf* elegance

elegante *adj* elegant

elegir [58] *vt* **a)** to choose **b)** POL to elect

elemental *adj* **a)** [fundamental] basic, fundamental **b)** [simple] elementary

elemento *nm* **a)** element **b)** [componente] component, part **c)** *Esp Fam* [persona] *Br* chap, *US* guy; **un elemento de cuidado** a bad lot **d) elementos** elements; [fundamentos] rudiments

elevación *nf* elevation; **elevación de precios** rise in prices; **elevación del terreno** rise in the ground

elevado, -a *adj* **a)** high; [edificio] tall
b) [pensamiento etc] lofty, noble

elevador *nm* **a)** [montacargas] hoist
b) *Méx* [ascensor] *Br* lift, *US* elevator

elevar 1. *vt* to raise **2. elevarse** *vpr*
a) [subir] to rise; [edificio] to stand
b) elevarse a [cantidad] to amount o come to

eliminación *nf* elimination

eliminar *vt* to eliminate

élite *nf* elite, élite

ella *pron pers f* **a)** [sujeto] she; [animal, cosa] it, she **b)** [complemento] her; [animal, cosa] it, her

Usually omitted in Spanish as a subject except for emphasis or contrast.

ello *pron pers neutro* it; **por ello** for that reason

ellos *pron pers mpl* **a)** [sujeto] they
b) [complemento] them

Usually omitted in Spanish as a subject except for emphasis or contrast.

elocuencia *nf* eloquence

elocuente *adj* eloquent; **los hechos son elocuentes** the facts speak for themselves

elogiar [43] *vt* to praise

elogio *nm* praise

elongación *nf* elongation

elote *nm CAm, Méx* [mazorca] corncob, ear of maize o *US* corn; [granos] sweetcorn, *US* corn

eludir *vt* to avoid

e-mail ['imeil] *(pl* **e-mails)** *nm* e-mail

emancipar 1. *vt* to emancipate
2. emanciparse *vpr* to become emancipated

embajada *nf* embassy

embajador, -a *nm, f* ambassador

embalar *vt* to pack

embalsamar *vt* to embalm

embalse *nm* dam, reservoir

embarazada 1. *adj* pregnant; **dejar embarazada** to get pregnant **2.** *nf* pregnant woman, expectant mother

embarazo *nm* **a)** [preñez] pregnancy
b) [obstáculo] obstacle **c)** [turbación] embarrassment

embarcación *nf* **a)** [nave] boat, craft **b)** [embarco] embarkation

embarcadero *nm* quay

embarcar [44] **1.** *vt* to ship **2.** *vi* to embark, to go on board **3. embarcarse** *vpr* **a)** NÁUT **embarcarse (en)** to go on board; AVIACIÓN to board **b) embarcarse en un proyecto** to embark on a project

embargar [42] *vt* **a)** JUR to seize, to impound **b)** *Fig* **le embarga la emoción** he's overwhelmed with joy

embargo *nm* **a)** JUR seizure of property **b)** COM & POL embargo **c) sin embargo** however, nevertheless

embarque *nm* [de persona] boarding; [de mercancías] loading; **tarjeta de embarque** boarding card

embestir [6] *vt* **a)** TAUROM to charge **b)** [atacar] to attack

emblema *nm* emblem

emblemático, -a *adj* emblematic

embolarse *vpr Arg Fam* [aburrirse] to get really fed up

emborrachar 1. *vt* to get drunk **2. emborracharse** *vpr* = **emborrachar**

emboscada *nf* ambush; **tender una emboscada** to lay an ambush

embotellado *nm* bottling

embotellamiento *nm* AUTO traffic jam

embotellar *vt* **a)** to bottle **b)** [tráfico] to block

embrague *nm* clutch

embriagado, -a *adj* drunk

embrión *nm* embryo

embrionario, -a *adj* embryonic

embromado, -a *adj* **a)** *Am Fam* [difícil] tough; **estoy bastante embromado** I'm not feeling too good **b)** [fastidiado] annoyed

embromar *vt Am Fam* [fastidiar] to annoy, to pester

embrujado, -a *adj* **a)** bewitched **b)** [lugar] haunted

embrujar *vt también Fig* to bewitch

embudo *nm* funnel

embustero, -a *nm, f* cheater, liar

embutido *nm* sausage

emergencia *nf* emergency; **salida de emergencia** emergency exit; **en caso de emergencia** in an emergency

emigración *nf* emigration; [de pájaros] migration

emigrante *adj & nmf* emigrant

emigrar *vi* to emigrate; [pájaros] to migrate

eminente *adj* eminent

emisión *nf* **a)** emission **b)** [de bonos, sellos] issue **c)** RADIO & TV broadcasting

emisora *nf* [de radio] radio station

emitir *vt* **a)** to emit; [luz, calor] to give off **b)** [opinión, juicio] to express **c)** RADIO & TV to transmit **d)** [bonos, sellos] to issue

emoción *nf* **a)** emotion **b)** [excitación] excitement; **¡qué emoción!** how exciting!

emocionado, -a *adj* deeply moved o touched

emocionante *adj* **a)** [conmovedor] moving, touching **b)** [excitante] exciting, thrilling

emocionar 1. *vt* **a)** [conmover] to move, to touch **b)** [excitar] to thrill **2. emocionarse** *vpr* **a)** [conmoverse] to be moved **b)** [excitarse] to get excited

empacar [44] **1.** *vt* **a)** [objeto] to wrap **b)** [mercancías] to pack **c)** *Am* to annoy **2. empacarse** *vpr Andes, RP Fam* to dig one's heels in

empacho *nm* [de comida] indigestion, upset stomach; *Fig* surfeit

empalmar 1. *vt* **a)** [tubos, cables] to connect, to join **b)** [planes, ideas] to link **2.** *vi* [medios de transporte] **empalmar (con)** to connect (with) **3. empalmarse** *vpr Esp Vulg* to get a hard-on

empanada *nf* pie

empanadilla *nf* pasty

empañar 1. *vt* [cristales] to steam up **2. empañarse** *vpr* = **empañar**

empapado, -a *adj* soaked

empapar 1. *vt* **a)** [mojar] to soak **b)** [absorber] to soak up **2. empaparse** *vpr* **a)** [persona] to get soaked **b)** *Fam & Fig* **empaparse (de)** to take in

empapelar *vt* to paper, to wallpaper

empaquetar *vt* to pack

emparentado, -a *adj* related

empastar *vt* [diente] to fill

empaste *nm* [de diente] filling

empatado, -a *adj* **estamos** *o* **vamos empatados** it's a draw

empatar 1. *vi* [en competición] to tie; [en partido] to draw **2.** *vt* **a)** DEP **empatar el partido** to equalize **b)** *Andes, Ven* [enlazar, empalmar] to join, to link

empate *nm* DEP draw, tie

empeñar 1. *vt* to pawn **2. empeñarse** *vpr* **a)** [insistir] to insist **(en** on), to be determined **(en** to) **b)** [endeudarse] to get into debt

empeño *nm* **a)** [insistencia] insistence; **poner empeño en algo** to put a lot of effort into sth **b)** [deuda] pledge; **casa de empeños** pawnshop

empeorar 1. *vi* to deteriorate, to worsen **2.** *vt* to make worse **3. empeorarse** *vpr* to deteriorate, to worsen

emperador *nm* emperor

empezar [51] *vt & vi* [a hacer algo] to begin; [algo] to start, to commence

empinado, -a *adj* [cuesta] steep

empinar 1. *vt* **a)** [vasija, jarro etc] to tip *(to drink)*; *Fam* **empinar el codo** to drink, *Br* to prop up the bar **b)** [levantar] to raise **2. empinarse** *vpr* **a)** [perro] to stand on its hind legs **b)** [caballo] to rear **c)** [persona] to stand on tiptoe

empleado, -a *nm, f* employee; [de oficina, banco] clerk; **empleada del hogar** servant, maid

empleador, -a *nm, f* employer

emplear *vt* **a)** [usar] to use; [contratar] to employ **b)** [dinero, tiempo] to spend

emplearse *vpr* to get a job

empleo *nm* **a)** [oficio] job; POL employment **b)** [uso] use; **modo de empleo** instructions for use

emplomar *vt RP* [diente] to fill

empotrado, -a *adj* fitted

emprender *vt* to undertake; *Fam* **emprenderla con algn** to pick on sb

empresa *nf* **a)** COM & INDUST firm, company; **empresa punto com** dot com (company); **empresa de trabajo temporal** temping agency, temporary recruitment agency **b)** POL **la libre empresa** free enterprise **c)** [tarea] undertaking

empresarial 1. *adj* business **2.** *nmpl Esp* **empresariales** Business Studies; **estudia empresariales** she's doing Business Studies

empresario, -a *nm, f* **a)** [hombre, mujer de negocios] businessman, *f* businesswoman **b)** [patrón] employer

empujar *vt* to push, to shove

empujón *nm* push, shove; **dar empujones** to push and shove

empuñar *vt* **a)** [espada, paraguas, raqueta] to grasp **b)** *Fig* [botella, volante, pluma] to grip

ems SMS *written abbr of* **hemos**

emular *vt* **a)** [una persona] **emular a algn** [rivalizar] to vie with sb; [imitar] to emulate sb **b)** INFORM to emulate

en *prep* **a)** [posición] in, on, at; **en Madrid / Bolivia** in Madrid / Bolivia; **en la mesa** on the table; **en el bolso** in the bag; **en casa / el trabajo** at home / work **b)** [movimiento] into; **entró en el cuarto** he went into the room

c) [tiempo] in, on, at; **en 1940** in 1940; **en verano** in summer; *Am* **en la mañana / tarde** in the morning / afternoon; *Am* **en la noche** at night; **cae en martes** it falls on a Tuesday; **en ese momento** at that moment

d) [transporte] by, in; **en coche / tren** by car / train; **en avión** by air

e) [modo] **en español** in Spanish; **en broma** jokingly; **en serio** seriously

f) [reducción, aumento] by; **los precios aumentaron en un diez por ciento** the prices went up by ten percent

g) [tema, materia] **experto en política** expert in politics

h) [división, separación] in; **lo dividió en tres partes** he divided it in three **i)** [con infinitivo] **la conocí en el andar** I recognized her by her walk; **ser sobrio en el vestir** to dress simply

---

enaguas *nfpl* underskirt, petticoat

enamorado, -a 1. *adj* in love **2.** *nm, f* person in love

enamorar 1. *vt* to win the heart of **2. enamorarse** *vpr* to fall in love (**de** with)

enano, -a *adj* & *nm, f* dwarf

encabezar [40] *vt* **a)** [carta, lista] to head; [periódico] to lead **b)** [rebelión, carrera, movimiento] to lead

encadenar *vt* to chain

encajar 1. *vt* **a)** [ajustar] to insert; **encajar la puerta** to push the door to **b)** *Fam* [asimilar] to take **c)** [comentario] to get in; **encajar un golpe a algn** to land sb a blow **2.** *vi* **a)** [ajustarse] to fit **b)** *Fig* **encajar con** to fit (in) with, to square with

encaje *nm* lace

encalar *vt* to whitewash

encamotado, -a *adj Andes, CAm Fam* in love

encamotarse *vpr Andes, CAm Fam* to fall in love

encantado, -a *adj* **a)** [contento] delighted; **encantado de conocerle** pleased to meet you **b)** [embrujado] enchanted

encantador, -a 1. *adj* charming, delightful **2.** *nm, f* magician

encantar *vt* [hechizar] to bewitch, to cast a spell on; *Fig* **me encanta nadar** I love swimming

encanto *nm* **a)** [atractivo] charm; **ser un encanto** to be charming **b)** [hechizo] spell

encapotado, -a *adj* overcast

encapricharse *vpr* **a)** [obstinarse] **encapricharse con algo / hacer algo** to set one's mind on sth / doing sth **b)** *Esp* [sentirse atraído] **encapricharse**

de algn to become infatuated with sb; **encapricharse de algo** to take a real liking to sth

encaramarse *vpr* to climb up

encarar 1. *vt* to face, to confront **2. encararse** *vpr* **encararse con** to face up to

encarcelar *vt* to imprison, to jail

encarecer [33] **1.** *vt* to put up the price of **2. encarecerse** *vpr* to go up (in price)

encargado, -a 1. *nm, f* COM manager, *f* manager, manageress; [responsable] person in charge **2.** *adj* in charge

encargar [42] **1.** *vt* **a)** to put in charge of, to entrust with **b)** COM [mercancías] to order, to place an order for; [encuesta] to commission **2. encargarse** *vpr* **encargarse de** to see to, to deal with

encargo *nm* **a)** [pedido] order; *Esp* **hecho de encargo** tailor-made **b)** [recado] errand **c)** [tarea] job, assignment

encariñarse *vpr* **encariñarse con** to become fond of, to get attached to

encarnado, -a *adj* [rojo] red

encausar *vt* to prosecute

encendedor *nm* lighter

encender [3] **1.** *vt* **a)** [luz, radio, tele] to switch on, to put on; [cigarro, vela, fuego] to light; [cerilla] to strike, to light **b)** *Fig* to inflame, to stir up **2. encenderse** *vpr* **a)** [fuego] to catch; [luz] to go o come on **b)** [cara] to blush, to go red

encendido *nm* ignition

encerado *nm* [pizarra] *Br* blackboard, *US* chalkboard

encerrado, -a *adj* shut away

encerrar [1] **1.** *vt* **a)** to shut in; [con llave] to lock in **b)** *Fig* [contener] to contain, to include **2. encerrarse** *vpr* to shut oneself up o in; [con llave] to lock oneself in

encestar *vi* DEP to score (a basket)

enchilada *nf CAm, Méx* CULIN enchilada *(Mexican tortilla filled with meat, cheese and chilli sauce)*

enchilado, -a 1. *adj Méx* **a)** [alimento] *Br* seasoned with chilli, *US* seasoned with chili **b)** *Fam* [persona] annoyed; **estar enchilado** to be livid **2.** *nm Méx, Cuba* spicy seafood stew

enchilarse *vpr Méx Fam* to get angry

enchinar *vt Méx* to curl

enchufado, -a *adj Fam* **a)** [en un puesto] **su hijo está enchufado en la empresa** he used his connections to get his son a job in the company, he pulled some strings for his son in the company **b)** *RP* [ocupado] **ahora está muy enchufado con la lingüística** he's really into linguistics at the moment

enchufar *vt* **a)** ELEC [aparato] to plug in **b)** [unir] to join, to connect **c)** *Fam* [para un trabajo] to fix up *(with a job)*

enchufe *nm* **a)** ELEC [hembra] socket; [macho] plug **b)** *Fam* [recomendación] connections *(pl)*, string-pulling **c)** *Fam* contact

encía *nf* gum

enciclopedia *nf* encyclopedia

encierro *nm* **a)** [acción] sit-in; **su encierro duró dos días** his sit-in lasted two days **b)** [aislamiento] **lleva semanas sin salir de su encierro** it's been weeks since she's been out **c)** POL [protesta] sit-in **d)** TAUROM *tradition where bulls which are being used in a bullfight are run through the streets towards the ring*; [toril] bullpen

encima *adv* **a)** on top; [arriba] above; [en el aire] overhead; **déjalo encima** put it on top; **ponlo encima** put it on top; **ahí encima** up there; **yo vivo encima** I live upstairs **b)** [además] not only that, on top of that **c)** [sobre sí] **llevar un abrigo encima** to wear a coat; **llevar dinero encima** to have money on you; **¿llevas cambio encima?** do you have any change on you?; *Fig* **quitarse algo de encima** to get rid of sth **d)** **encima de** [sobre] on; [en el aire] above; *Fig* [además] besides; **encima de la mesa** on the table; **encima de tu casa** above your house; **estar encima de algn** to be on sb's back; **encima de ser guapo es gracioso** as well as being good looking, he's funny, he's not only good looking,

he's funny as well **e)** **por encima** over, above, on top; *Fig* quickly; *Fig* **por encima de sus posibilidades** beyond his abilities; **leer un libro por encima** to skip through a book

encimera *nf Esp* [de cocina] worktop

encina *nf* holm oak

encinta *adj* pregnant

encoger [53] **1.** *vi* [contraerse] to contract; [prenda] to shrink
2. *vt* to contract; [prenda] to shrink
3. encogerse *vpr* [contraerse] to contract; [prenda] to shrink; **encogerse de hombros** to shrug (one's shoulders)

encolar *vt* [papel] to paste; [madera] to glue

encolerizar [40] **1.** *vt* to infuriate, to anger **2. encolerizarse** *vpr* to become furious

encomienda *nf* **a)** assignment, mission **b)** [paquete postal] parcel

encontrar [2] **1.** *vt* **a)** [hallar] to find; **no lo encuentro** I can't find it; **lo encuentro muy agradable** I find it very pleasant **b)** [dar con] to meet; [problema] to run into, to come up against **2. encontrarse** *vpr* **a)** [persona] to meet **b)** [sentirse] to feel, to be; **encontrarse a gusto** to feel comfortable **c)** [estar] to be

encriptar *vt* INFORM to encrypt

encrucijada *nf* crossroads

encuadernar *vt* to bind

encuadre *nm* CINE & TV framing

encubierto, -a *adj* [secreto] hidden; [operación] covert

encubrir *vt* to conceal

encuentro *nm* **a)** encounter, meeting **b)** DEP meeting, match; **encuentro amistoso** friendly (match)

encuesta *nf* **a)** [sondeo] (opinion) poll, survey **b)** [investigación] investigation, inquiry

encuestador, -a *nm, f* pollster

endémico, -a *adj* endemic

enderezar [40] **1.** *vt* [poner derecho] to straighten out ; [poner vertical] to set upright **2. enderezarse** *vpr* to straighten up

endeudarse *vpr* to get into debt

endiñar *vt Esp Fam* **endiñar algo a algn** [golpe] to land o deal sb sth ; [tarea] to lumber sb with sth

endivia *nf* endive

endrogarse [42] *vpr Chile, Méx, Perú* [endeudarse] to get into debt

enemigo, -a 1. *adj* enemy ; **soy enemigo de la bebida** I'm against drink **2.** *nm, f* enemy

energía *nf* energy ; **energía hidráulica /nuclear** hydro-electric / nuclear power ; *Fig* **energía vital** vitality

enérgico, -a *adj* energetic ; [decisión] firm ; [tono] emphatic

enero *nm* January

enfadado, -a *adj esp Esp* [enojado] angry ; [molesto] annoyed ; **estamos enfadados** we've fallen out with each other

enfadar *esp Esp* **1.** *vt* to make angry o annoyed **2. enfadarse** *vpr* **a)** to get angry (**con** with) **b)** [dos personas] to fall out

enfado *nm esp Esp* anger ; [desavenencia] fall-out

enfermar 1. *vi* to get sick **2. enfermarse** *vpr Am* = **enfermar**

enfermedad *nf* illness ; [contagiosa] disease

enfermería *nf* infirmary

enfermero, -a *nm, f* [mujer] nurse ; [hombre] (male) nurse

enfermizo, -a *adj* unhealthy, sickly

enfermo, -a 1. *adj* ill ; **caer enfermo** to be taken ill ; *Fam* **esa gente me pone enfermo** those people make me sick **2.** *nm, f* ill person ; [paciente] patient

enfiestarse *vpr Am* to party

enfocar [44] *vt* **a)** [imagen] to focus ; [persona] to focus on **b)** [tema] to approach **c)** [con linterna] to shine a light on

enfoque *nm* **a)** focus ; [acción] focusing **b)** [de un tema] approach

enfrentamiento *nm* clash

enfrentar 1. *vt* **a)** [situación, peligro] to confront **b)** [enemistar] to set at odds **2. enfrentarse** *vpr* **a)** **enfrentarse con** o **a** to face up to, to confront **b)** DEP **enfrentarse (a)** [rival] to meet

enfrente *adv* **a)** opposite, facing ; **la casa de enfrente** the house opposite o across the road **b)** **enfrente de** opposite (to), facing ; **enfrente del colegio** opposite the school

enfriamiento *nm* **a)** [proceso] cooling **b)** MED [catarro] cold, chill

enfriar [29] **1.** *vt* to cool (down), to chill **2.** *vi* to cool down **3. enfriarse** *vpr* **a)** to get o go cold **b)** [resfriarse] to get o catch a cold **c)** *Fig* [pasión] to cool down

enfurecido, -a *adj* **a)** [rostro, voz, gesto] furious **b)** [mar] raging

enfurruñado, -a *adj Fam* grumpy

enganchada *nf Fam* **tener una enganchada con algn** to have a row with sb

enganchar 1. *vt* **a)** to hook ; FERROC to couple **b)** *Fam* [pillar] to nab **2. engancharse** *vpr* to get caught o hooked ; *Fam* **engancharse a** [droga] to get hooked on

enganche *nm* [gancho] hook ; FERROC coupling

engañar 1. *vt* to deceive, to mislead ; [estafar] to cheat, to trick ; [mentir a] to lie to ; [al marido, a la mujer] to be unfaithful to **2. engañarse** *vpr* to deceive oneself

engaño *nm* **a)** deceit ; [estafa] fraud, swindle ; [mentira] lie **b)** [error] mistake, misunderstanding

engañoso, -a *adj* [palabras] deceitful ; [apariencias] deceptive ; [consejo] misleading

engendrar *vt* **a)** BIOL to engender **b)** *Fig* to give rise to, to cause

englobar *vt* to include

engordar 1. *vt* to fatten (up), to make fat **2.** *vi* **a)** to put on weight, to get fat ;

he engordado 3 kilos I've put on 3 kilos **b)** [comida, bebida] to be fattening

engranaje *nm* **a)** TÉC gearing **b)** *Fig* machinery

engrapadora *nf Am* stapler

engrapar *vt Am* to staple

engrasar *vt* **a)** [lubricar] to lubricate, to oil **b)** [manchar] to make greasy, to stain with grease

engreído, -a *adj* vain, conceited

engriparse *vpr CSur* to get a cold

enhorabuena *nf* congratulations; **dar la enhorabuena a algn** to congratulate sb

enigma *nm* enigma

enjabonar *vt* to soap

enjuagar [42] *vt* to rinse

enlace *nm* **a)** [unión] link, connection; **enlace químico** chemical bond **b)** FERROC connection **c)** [casamiento] marriage **d)** [persona] liaison officer; *Esp* **enlace sindical** shop steward **e)** INFORM link; **enlace web** web link

enlatado, -a 1. *adj* [alimento] canned, *Br* tinned **2.** *nmpl* **enlatados** banns; *Am Br* tinned food, *US* canned food

enlazar [40] *vt & vi* to link, to connect (**con** with)

enlistar *vt Am* to list

enloquecer 1. *vt* to drive mad **2.** *vi* to go mad

enloquecido, -a *adj* mad

enlosar *vt* to tile

enmendar [1] **1.** *vt* [corregir] to correct, to put right; JUR to amend **2. enmendarse** *vpr* [persona] to reform, to mend one's ways

enmienda *nf* correction; JUR & POL amendment

enmudecer [33] *vi* [callar] to fall silent; *Fig* to be dumbstruck

enojado, -a *adj* [irritado] angry; [molesto] annoyed

enojar *esp Am* **1.** *vt* to anger, to annoy **2. enojarse** *vpr* to get angry, to lose one's temper

enojo *nm esp Am* anger, annoyance

enorme *adj* enormous

enraizado, -a *adj* deep-rooted

enraizarse *vpr* to put down roots, to settle

enredadera *nf* climbing plant, creeper

enredado, -a *adj* **a)** [lana, hilo, pelo] tangled **b)** [asunto, situación] complicated, messy **c)** [persona implicada] **estar enredado en algo** to be mixed up in sth

enredar 1. *vt* **a)** [lana, hilo, pelo] to entangle, to tangle up
b) *Fig* [asunto, situación] to confuse, to complicate
c) *Fig* [implicar] to involve (**en**)
d) [confundir] to mix up
2. enredarse *vpr* **a)** [lana, hilo, pelo] to get entangled, to get tangled (up) *o* in a tangle
b) *Fig* [asunto, situación] to get complicated *o* confused
c) *Fig* **enredarse con** [involucrarse] to get involved with
d) [confundirse] to get mixed up

enredo *nm* **a)** [maraña] tangle **b)** *Fig* [lío] muddle, mess

enriquecer [33] **1.** *vt* to make rich; *Fig* to enrich **2. enriquecerse** *vpr* to get *o* become rich, to prosper; *Fig* to become enriched

enrojecer [33] **1.** *vt* to redden, to turn red **2.** *vi* [ruborizarse] to blush **3. enrojecerse** *vpr* to blush

enrollar 1. *vt* to roll up; [cable] to coil; [hilo] to wind up **2. enrollarse** *vpr* **a)** *Fam* [hablar] to chatter, to go on and on **b)** *Fam* **enrollarse con algn** [tener relaciones] to have an affair with sb; **¡enróllate!** be cool!

ensaimada *nf* kind of spiral pastry from Majorca

ensalada *nf* salad

ensaladera *nf* salad bowl

ensaladilla *nf Esp* **ensaladilla rusa** Russian salad

ensanchar 1. *vt* to enlarge, to widen; COST to let out **2. ensancharse** *vpr* to get wider

ensartar *vt* **a)** [perlas] to string; [aguja] to thread **b)** [puñal] to plunge **c)** *Am Fam* [engañar] to dupe

ensayar *vt* to test, to try out; TEATRO to rehearse; MÚS to practise

ensayo *nm* **a)** [prueba] test, trial **b)** TEATRO rehearsal; **ensayo general** dress rehearsal **c)** [escrito] essay

enseguida, en seguida *adv* [inmediatamente] immediately, at once, straight away; [poco después] in a minute, soon; **enseguida voy** I'll be right there

ensenada *nf* inlet, cove

enseñanza *nf* **a)** [educación] education **b)** [de idioma etc] teaching **c) enseñanzas** teachings

enseñar *vt* **a)** to teach; **enseñar a algn a hacer algo** to teach sb how to do sth **b)** [mostrar] to show; [señalar] to point out

enseres *nmpl* [bártulos] belongings, goods; [de trabajo] tools

ensopar *vt Andes, RP, Ven Fam* to soak

ensuciar [43] **1.** *vt* **a)** to get dirty **b)** *Fig* [reputación] to harm, to damage **2. ensuciarse** *vpr* to get dirty

ente *nm* **a)** [institución] organization, body; **ente público** public service organization **b)** [ser] being

entenado, -a *nm, f Méx* stepson, *f* stepdaughter

entender [3] **1.** *vt* [comprender] to understand; **a mi entender** to my way of thinking; **dar a algn a entender que ...** to give sb to understand that ... **2.** *vi* **a)** [comprender] to understand **b) entender de** [saber] to know about **3. entenderse** *vpr* **a)** [comprenderse] to be understood, to be meant **b)** *Fam* **entenderse (bien) con** to get on (well) with

entendido, -a 1. *nm, f* expert **2.** *adj* **tengo entendido que ...** I understand that ...

enterar 1. *vt* to inform (**de** about o of) **2. enterarse** *vpr* to find out; **me he enterado de que ...** I understand ...; **ni me enteré** I didn't even realize it

entero, -a 1. *adj* **a)** [completo] entire, whole; **por entero** completely **b)** *Fig* [íntegro] honest, upright **c)** *Fig* [firme] strong **2.** *nm* **a)** MAT whole number **b)** FIN point

enterrar [1] *vt* to bury

entidad *nf* organization; **entidad comercial** company, firm

entierro *nm* **a)** burial **b)** [ceremonia] funeral

entlo. *(abr de entresuelo)* mezzanine

entonces *adv* then; **por aquel entonces** at that time; **el entonces ministro** the then minister

entrada *nf* **a)** entrance **b)** [billete] ticket; [recaudación] takings **c) de entrada** for a start **d)** CULIN entrée **e)** COM entry; **entrada de capital** capital inflow **f)** *Esp* [pago inicial] down payment, deposit **g)** COM **entradas** [ingresos] receipts, takings **h)** [en la frente] receding hairline

entrante 1. *adj* coming; **el mes entrante** next month; **el ministro entrante** the incoming minister **2.** *nm Esp* starter

entrañable *adj* **a)** [lugar] intimate, close **b)** [persona] affectionate, warm-hearted

entrañas *nfpl* bowels

entrar 1. *vi* **a)** to come in, to go in, to enter; *Fig* **no me entran las matemáticas** I can't get the hang of maths **b)** [encajar] to fit **c) el año que entra** next year, the coming year **d)** [venir] to come over; **me entró dolor de cabeza** I got a headache; **me entraron ganas de reír** I felt like laughing **2.** *vt* **a)** to introduce **b)** INFORM to enter

entre *prep* **a)** [dos] between **b)** [más de dos] among(st)

entreabierto, -a *adj* [ojos etc] half-open; [puerta] ajar

entreacto *nm* interval, intermission

entrecejo *nm* space between the eyebrows; **fruncir el entrecejo** to frown, to knit one's brow

entrecot *(pl* entrecots *o* entrecotes*) nm* fillet steak

entrecruzado *nm* crossbreed

entrega *nf* a) [de productos] delivery; [de premios] presentation b) [fascículo] part, instalment c) [devoción] selflessness

entregado, -a *adj* [dedicado] devoted, dedicated

entregar [42] **1.** *vt* to hand over; [deberes etc] to give in, to hand in; COM to deliver **2. entregarse** *vpr* a) [rendirse] to give in, to surrender b) **entregarse a** to devote oneself to; *Despec* to indulge in

entrelazar [40] **1.** *vt* to entwine **2. entrelazarse** *vpr* = **entrelazar**

entremeses *nmpl* CULIN hors d'oeuvres

entrenador, -a *nm, f* trainer, coach

entrenamiento *nm* training

entrenar 1. *vi* to train **2. entrenarse** *vpr* = **entrenar**

entrepierna *nf* crotch, crutch

entresijos *nmpl* a) [de asunto] ins and outs; **conocer todos los entresijos de algo** to know all the ins and outs of sth b) [de negocio] details c) [del poder] secrets

entresuelo *nm* mezzanine

entretanto 1. *adv* meanwhile **2.** *nm* **en el entretanto** in the meantime

entretención *nf Chile* entertainment

entretener [24] **1.** *vt* a) [divertir] to entertain, to amuse b) [retrasar] to delay; [detener] to hold up, to detain **2. entretenerse** *vpr* a) [distraerse] to amuse oneself, to while away the time b) [retrasarse] to be delayed, to be held up

entretenido, -a *adj* enjoyable, entertaining

entretenimiento *nm* entertainment, amusement

entretiempo *nm CSur* half-time ■ **de entretiempo** *loc adj* **ropa de de entretiempo** spring /autumn clothes

entrever [28] *vt* to glimpse, to catch sight of; *Fig* **dejó entrever que ...** she hinted that ...

entreverar *CSur* **1.** *vt* to mix **2. entreverarse** *vpr* to get tangled

entrevero *nm CSur* tangle, mess

entrevista *nf* interview

entrevistador, -a *nm, f* interviewer

entrevistar 1. *vt* to interview **2. entrevistarse** *vpr* **entrevistarse con algn** to have an interview with sb

entristecer [33] **1.** *vt* to sadden, to make sad **2. entristecerse** *vpr* to be sad (**por** about)

entrometerse *vpr* to meddle, to interfere (**en** in)

entroncar *vi* **entroncar con** [familia] to be related to à; [tren etc] to connect with

entusiasmado, -a *adj* excited, enthusiastic

entusiasmar 1. *vt* to fill with enthusiasm **2. entusiasmarse** *vpr* to get excited o enthusiastic (**con** about)

entusiasmo *nm* enthusiasm; **con entusiasmo** enthusiastically

entusiasta 1. *adj* enthusiastic, keen (**de** on) **2.** *nmf* enthusiast

envasar *vt* [embotellar] to bottle; [empaquetar] to pack; [enlatar] to can, to tin

envase *nm* a) [acto] packing; [de botella] bottling; [de lata] canning b) [recipiente] container c) [botella vacía] empty

envejecer [33] **1.** *vi* to grow old **2.** *vt* to age

envenenamiento *nm* poisoning

envenenar *vt* to poison

envergadura *nf* a) [importancia] importance, scope; **de gran envergadura** large-scale b) [de pájaro, avión] span, wingspan; NÁUT breadth (of sail)

enviar [29] *vt* to send

envidia *nf* envy; **tener envidia de algn** to envy sb

envidiar [43] *vt* to envy; **no tener nada que envidiar** to be in no way inferior (**a** to)

envidioso, -a *adj* envious

envío *nm* sending; [remesa] consignment; [paquete] parcel; **gastos de envío** postage and packing; **envío contra reembolso** cash on delivery

enviudar *vi* [hombre] to become a widower, to lose one's wife; [mujer] to become a widow, to lose one's husband

envolver [4] *(pp* **envuelto)** **1.** *vt* **a)** [con papel] to wrap **b)** [cubrir] to envelop **c)** [en complot etc] to involve (**en** in) **2. envolverse** *vpr* **a)** to wrap oneself up (**en** in) **b)** [implicarse] to become involved (**en** in)

envuelto, -a **1.** *pp de* **envolver** **2.** *nm Am* [tortilla] wrap

enyesar *vt* to plaster; MED to put in plaster

epidemia *nf* epidemic

epidermis *nf inv* ANAT epidermis

episodio *nm* episode

época *nf* time; HIST period, epoch; AGRIC season; **en esta época del año** at this time of the year; **hacer época** to be a landmark; **mueble de época** period furniture

equilibrado, -a *adj* **a)** [igualado] balanced **b)** [sensato] sensible

equilibrar *vt* to balance

equilibrio *nm* balance

equilibrista *nmf* tightrope walker

equipaje *nm Br* luggage, *US* baggage; **hacer el equipaje** to pack, to do the packing

equipar *vt* to equip, to furnish (**con** *o* **de** with)

equipo *nm* **a)** [de expertos, jugadores] team **b)** [aparatos] equipment; **equipo de alta fidelidad** hi-fi stereo system **c)** [ropas] outfit

equitación *nf* horse *o US* horseback riding

equivalente *adj* equivalent

equivaler [26] *vi* to be equivalent (**a** to)

equivocación *nf* error, mistake

equivocadamente *adv* by mistake

equivocado, -a *adj* mistaken, wrong

equivocar [44] **1.** *vt* to mix up **2. equivocarse** *vpr* to make a mistake; TEL **se equivocó de número** he dialled the wrong number; **se equivocó de fecha** he got the wrong date

era¹ *nf* [época] era, age

era² *nf* AGRIC threshing floor

era³ *pt indef de* **ser**

eres *indic pres de* **ser**

erguido, -a *adj* upright

erguir [55] **1.** *vt* to raise **2. erguirse** *vpr* to rise up

erizar **1.** *vi Am* [irritar] to make ... stand on end, to really annoy; **ese chirrido me eriza** that screech makes my hair stand on end **2. erizarse** *vpr* to stand on end

erizo *nm* hedgehog; **erizo marino** *o* **de mar** sea urchin

ermita *nf* hermitage

erogar *vt Am* to pay, to settle

erótico, -a *adj* erotic

erotismo *nm* eroticism

errante *adj* wandering

errar [50] **1.** *vt* to miss, to get wrong **2.** *vi* **a)** [vagar] to wander, to roam **b)** [fallar] to err

erróneo, -a *adj* erroneous, wrong

error *nm* error, mistake; INFORM bug; **por error** by mistake, in error; IMPR **error de imprenta** misprint; **caer en un error** to make a mistake

ers, ers2 SMS *(abr de* **eres)** [afirmación] U R; [pregunta] R U

eructar *vi* to belch, to burp

eructo *nm* belch, burp

erudito, -a **1.** *adj* erudite, learned **2.** *nm, f* scholar

erupción *nf* **a)** [de volcán] eruption **b)** [en la piel] rash

es *indic pres de* **ser**

esbelto, -a *adj* slender

esbozo *nm* sketch, outline, rough draft

escabeche *nm* brine

escabechina *nf Fam* [destrozo] destruction

escacharrado, -a, descacharrado, -a *adj Esp Fam* [roto, averiado] bust

escacharrarse, descacharrarse *vpr* a) [mecanismo, aparato, coche] to bust b) *Fig* [plan, proyecto] to fall apart

escala *nf* a) scale; [de colores] range; **escala musical** scale; **en gran escala** on a large scale b) NÁUT [parada] port of call; AVIACIÓN stopover; **hacer escala en** to call in at, to stop over in c) [escalera] ladder, stepladder

escalador, -a *nm, f* climber, mountaineer

escalar *vt* to climb, to scale; *Fam & Fig* **escalar puestos** to climb up the ladder

escalera *nf* a) stair; **escalera de incendios** fire escape; **escalera mecánica** escalator; **escalera de caracol** spiral staircase b) [escala] ladder c) NAIPES run

escalerilla *nf* [de piscina] steps; NÁUT gangway; AVIACIÓN (boarding) ramp

escalofrío *nm* shiver; **me dio un escalofrío** it gave me the shivers

escalón *nm* step; **escalón lateral** [en letrero] ramp

escalope *nm* escalope

escama *nf* ZOOL scale; [de jabón] flake

escampar *vi* to stop raining, to clear up

escandalizar [40] **1.** *vt* to scandalize, to shock **2. escandalizarse** *vpr* to be shocked (**de** at o by)

escándalo *nm* a) [alboroto] racket, din; **armar un escándalo** to kick up a fuss b) [desvergüenza] scandal

escanear *vt* a) INFORM to scan b) MED to have a scan of, to scan

escáner *nm pp de* **scanner**

escaño *nm* [parlamentario] seat

escapar 1. *vi* to escape, to run away **2. escaparse** *vpr* a) to escape, to run away; **se me escapó de las manos** it slipped out of my hands; **se me escapó el tren** I missed the train b) [gas etc] to leak, to escape

escaparate *nm* shop window; **ir de escaparates** to go window shopping

escape *nm* a) [de gas etc] leak, escape b) TÉC exhaust; **tubo de escape** exhaust (pipe) c) [huida] escape; [escapatoria] way out

escarabajo *nm* beetle

escarbar *vt* a) [suelo] to scratch; [fuego] to poke b) *Fig* to inquire into, to investigate

escarcha *nf* hoarfrost, frost

escarmentado, -a *adj* **estar/quedar escarmentado** to learn one's lesson

escarmentar [1] *vi* to learn one's lesson

escarola *nf* curly endive

escasear *vi* to be scarce

escasez *nf* scarcity

escaso, -a *adj* scarce; [dinero] tight; [conocimientos] scant; **escaso de dinero** short of money

escayola *nf* a) plaster of Paris, stucco b) MED plaster

escayolado, -a *adj* in plaster

escayolar *vt* MED to put in plaster

escena *nf* a) scene b) [escenario] stage; **poner en escena** to stage

escenario *nm* a) TEATRO stage b) [entorno] scenario; [de crimen] scene; [de película] setting

escepticismo *nm* scepticism

escéptico, -a *adj & nm, f* sceptic

esclavitud *nf* slavery

esclavo, -a *adj & nm, f* slave

esclusa *nf* lock, sluicegate

escoba *nf* brush, broom

escobilla *nf* brush

escocer [41] **1.** *vi* to sting, to smart **2. escocerse** *vpr* [piel] to chafe

escocés, -esa 1. *adj* Scottish, Scots; **falda escocesa** kilt **2.** *nm, f* Scotsman, *f* Scotswoman

Escocia *n* Scotland

escoger [53] *vt* to choose

escolar 1. *adj* [curso, año] school **2.** *nmf* [niño] schoolboy ; [niña] schoolgirl

escolaridad *nf* schooling

escollo *nm* reef ; *Fig* pitfall

escolta *nf* escort

escombros *nmpl* rubbish, debris

esconder 1. *vt* to hide (**de** from), to conceal (**de** from) **2. esconderse** *vpr* to hide (**de** from)

escondidas *adv* **a escondidas** secretly

escondido, -a *adj* hidden ; [lugar] remote

escondite *nm* **a)** [lugar] hiding place, hide-out **b)** [juego] hide-and-seek

escopeta *nf* shotgun ; **escopeta de aire comprimido** air gun ; **escopeta de cañones recortados** *Br* sawn-off shotgun, *US* sawed-off shotgun

escorpiano, -a *nm, f Am Fam* Scorpio

Escorpio *nmf* Scorpio

escorpión *nm* scorpion

escotado, -a *adj* low-cut

escote *nm* low neckline

escotilla *nf* hatch, hatchway

escribir *(pp escrito)* **1.** *vt* to write ; **escribir a mano** to write in longhand ; **escribir a máquina** to type **2. escribirse** *vpr* **a)** [dos personas] to write to each other, to correspond **b)** **se escribe con h** it is spelt with an h

escrito, -a 1. *adj* written ; **escrito a mano** handwritten, in longhand ; **por escrito** in writing **2.** *nm* writing

escritor, -a *nm, f* writer

escritorio *nm* **a)** [mueble] writing desk, bureau ; [oficina] office **b)** INFORM desktop

escritura *nf* **a)** JUR deed, document ; **escritura de propiedad** title deed **b)** REL **Sagradas Escrituras** Holy Scriptures

escrúpulo *nm* **a)** scruple ; **una persona sin escrúpulos** an unscrupulous person **b)** [esmero] care **c)** **me da escrúpulo** [asco] it makes me feel squeamish

escuadra *nf* **a)** [instrumento] square **b)** MIL squad ; NÁUT squadron ; DEP team ; [de coches] fleet

escucha *nf* [acción] listening, monitoring ; **escucha telefónica** phone tapping ; **permanecer a la escucha** to stay tuned

escuchar 1. *vt* to listen to ; [oír] to hear **2.** *vi* to listen ; [oír] to hear

escudo *nm* **a)** [arma defensiva] shield **b)** [blasón] coat of arms

escuela *nf* school ; **escuela de bellas artes** art school ; **escuela de conducir / de idiomas** driving / language school

escuincle, -a *nm, f Méx Fam* kid

esculcar [44] *vt Méx* to search

esculpir *vt* to sculpt ; [madera] to carve ; [metal] to engrave

escultor, -a *nm, f* sculptor, *f* sculptress ; [de madera] woodcarver ; [de metales] engraver

escultura *nf* sculpture

escupir 1. *vi* to spit **2.** *vt* to spit out

escurrir 1. *vt* [plato, vaso] to drain ; [ropa] to wring out ; **escurrir el bulto** to wriggle out **2. escurrirse** *vpr* **a)** [platos etc] to drip **b)** [escaparse] to run o slip away **c)** [resbalarse] to slip

escusado *nm* toilet

ese, -a *(mpl* **esos,** *fpl* **-esas)** *adj demos* **a)** that **b)** **esos, -as** those

ése, -a *(mpl* **ésos,** *fpl* **ésas)** *pron demos m, f* **a)** that one **b)** **ésos, -as** those (ones) ; *Fam* **¡ni por ésas!** no way! ; *Fam* **¡no me vengas con ésas!** come off it!

Note that **ése** and its various forms can be written without an accent when there is no risk of confusion with the adjective.

esencia *nf* essence

esencial *adj* essential ; **lo esencial** the main thing

esfera *nf* **a)** sphere; *Fig* sphere, field **b)** [de reloj de pulsera] dial; [de reloj de pared] face

esférico, -a 1. *adj* spherical **2.** *nm* [balón] ball

esforzarse [2] *vpr* to make an effort (**por** to)

esfuerzo *nm* effort

esfumarse *vpr Fam* to beat it

esgrima *nf* DEP fencing

esguince *nm* sprain

eslabón *nm* link

eslalon (*pl* **eslalons**) *nm* DEP slalom; **eslalon gigante** giant slalom

eslam, slam *nm* **a)** [poesía] slam **b)** DEP slam; **gran slam** Grand Slam

eslip (*pl* **eslips**) *nm* men's briefs, underpants

Eslovaquia *n* Slovakia

esmalte *nm* enamel; [de uñas] nail polish o varnish

esmeralda *nf* emerald

esmerarse *vpr* to be careful; [esforzarse] to go to great lengths

esmero *nm* great care

esmoquin *nm Br* dinner jacket, *US* tuxedo

esnob (*pl* **esnobs**) **1.** *adj* [persona] snobbish; [restaurante etc] posh **2.** *nmf* snob

eso *pron neutro* that; **¡eso es!** that's it!; **por eso** that's why; *Fam* **a eso de las diez** around ten; *Fam* **eso de las Navidades sale muy caro** this whole Christmas thing costs a fortune

ESO *nf Esp* EDUC (*abr de* **Enseñanza Secundaria Obligatoria**) *the first stage of secondary school education in Spain for students aged 12 to 16*, ≃ *Br* secondary school, ≃ *US* high school

esos, -as *adj* demos pl ver **ese**

espacial *adj* spatial, spacial; **nave espacial** spaceship

espacio *nm* **a)** space; [de tiempo] length; **a doble espacio** double-spaced **b)** RADIO & TV programme

espacioso, -a *adj* spacious, roomy

espada 1. *nf* **a)** sword; **estar entre la espada y la pared** to be between the devil and the deep blue sea; **pez espada** swordfish **b)** NAIPES spade **2.** *nm* TAUROM matador

espaguetis *nmpl* spaghetti

espalda *nf* **a)** ANAT back; **espaldas** back; **a espaldas de algn** behind sb's back; **por la espalda** from behind; **volver la espalda a algn** to turn one's back on sb; *Fam* **espalda mojada** wetback **b)** [en natación] backstroke

espam, spam *nm* INFORM spam

espantapájaros *nm inv* scarecrow

espantar 1. *vt* **a)** [ahuyentar] to scare off **b)** [asustar] to frighten **2.** *vi* [asustar] **la idea espanta** the idea is horrifying **3.** **espantarse** *vpr* to be scared, to be horrified; **espantarse de** o **por** to be scared of o by, to be frightened by

espanto *nm* fright; *Fam* **de espanto** dreadful, shocking

espantoso, -a *adj* dreadful

España *n* Spain

español, -a 1. *adj* Spanish **2.** *nm, f* Spaniard; **los españoles** the Spanish **3.** *nm* [idioma] Spanish

esparadrapo *nm Br* (sticking) plaster, *US* Band-aid®

esparcir [52] **1.** *vt* [papeles, semillas] to scatter; *Fig* [rumor] to spread **2.** **esparcirse** *vpr* **a)** to be scattered **b)** [relajarse] to relax

espárrago *nm* asparagus

espasmo *nm* spasm

espátula *nf* CULIN spatula; ARTE palette knife; TÉC stripping knife; [de albañil] trowel

especia *nf* spice

especial *adj* special; **en especial** especially; **especial para ...** suitable for ...

especialidad *nf* speciality, *US* specialty; EDUC main subject

especialista *nmf* specialist

especializarse [40] *vpr* to specialize (**en** in)

especialmente *adv* [exclusivamente] specially; [muy] especially

especie *nf* a) BIOL species *inv* b) [clase] kind; **una especie de salsa** a kind of sauce c) COM **en especie** in kind

especificar [44] *vt* to specify

específico, -a *adj* specific; **peso específico** specific gravity

espectáculo *nm* a) [escena] spectacle, sight; *Fam* **dar un espectáculo** to make a spectacle of oneself b) TEATRO, CINE & TV show; **montar un espectáculo** to put on a show

espectador, -a *nm, f* DEP spectator; [de accidente] onlooker; TEATRO & CINE member of the audience; **los espectadores** the audience; TV the viewers

especulación *nf* speculation; **especulación del suelo** land speculation

espejismo *nm* mirage

espejo *nm* mirror; AUTO **espejo retrovisor** rear-view mirror

espera *nf* wait; **en espera de ...** waiting for ...; **a la espera de** expecting; **sala de espera** waiting room

esperado, -a *adj* a) [anhelado] eagerly awaited b) [previsto] expected

esperanza *nf* hope; **tener la esperanza puesta en algo** to have one's hopes pinned on sth; **esperanza de vida** life expectancy; **en estado de buena esperanza** expecting, pregnant

esperanzado, -a *adj* hopeful

esperar **1.** *vi* a) [aguardar] to wait b) [tener esperanza de] to hope **2.** *vt* a) [aguardar] to wait for; **espero a mi hermano** I'm waiting for my brother b) [tener esperanza de] to hope for; **espero que sí** I hope so; **espero que vengas** I hope you'll come c) [estar a la espera de] to expect; **te esperábamos ayer** we were expecting you yesterday d) *Fig* [bebé] to expect

esperma *nm* sperm

espeso, -a *adj* [bosque, niebla] dense; [líquido] thick; [masa] stiff

espesor *nm* thickness; **3 m de espesor** 3 m thick

espía *nmf* spy

espiar [29] **1.** *vi* to spy **2.** *vt* to spy on

espiga *nf* a) [de trigo] ear b) TÉC pin

espina *nf* a) BOT thorn b) [de pescado] bone c) ANAT **espina dorsal** spinal column, spine d) *Fig* **ése me da mala espina** there's something fishy about that one

espinaca *nf* spinach

espinilla *nf* a) ANAT shin b) [en la piel] spot

espionaje *nm* spying, espionage; **novela de espionaje** spy story

espiral *adj & nf* spiral

espirar *vi* to breathe out, to exhale

espiritismo *nm* spiritualism

espíritu *nm* a) spirit; **espíritu deportivo** sportsmanship b) REL [alma] soul; **el Espíritu Santo** the Holy Ghost

espiritual *adj* spiritual

espléndido, -a *adj* a) [magnífico] splendid b) [generoso] lavish, generous

esplendor *nm* splendour

espliego *nm* lavender

esponja *nf* sponge

esponjoso, -a *adj* spongy; [bizcocho] light

espontaneidad *nf* spontaneity; **con espontaneidad** naturally

espontáneo, -a **1.** *adj* spontaneous **2.** *nm* TAUROM *spectator who spontaneously joins in the bullfight*

esposas *nfpl* handcuffs

esposo, -a *nm, f* husband, *f* wife

espray *nm* spray

esprint *(pl* **esprints***) nm* sprint

esprínter *nmf* sprinter

espuma *nf* foam; [de olas] surf; [de cerveza] froth, head; [de jabón] lather; **espuma de afeitar** shaving foam

esquela *nf Esp* funeral notice *(in newspaper)*

esqueleto nm **a)** skeleton **b)** CONSTR framework

esquema nm diagram

esquematizar vt **a)** [en forma de gráfico] to draw a diagram of **b)** [resumir] to outline

esquí (pl **esquíes** o **esquís**) nm **a)** [objeto] ski **b)** [deporte] skiing; **esquí acuático** waterskiing

esquiable adj pista esquiable slope suitable for skiing

esquiador, -a nm, f skier

esquiar [29] vi to ski

esquilar vt to shear

esquimal adj & nmf Eskimo

esquina nf corner; DEP **saque de esquina** corner (kick)

esquivar vt [a una persona] to avoid; [un golpe] to dodge

estabilidad nf stability

estable adj stable

establecer [33] **1.** vt to establish; [fundar] to set up, to found; [récord] to set **2. establecerse** vpr to settle

establecimiento nm establishment

establo nm cow shed

estaca nf stake, post; [de tienda de campaña] peg

estación nf **a)** station; **estación de gasolina** o **de servicio** service station, Br petrol station, US gas station; **estación de esquí** ski resort **b)** [del año] season **c)** INFORM workstation

estacionamiento nm AUTO [acción] parking; [lugar] Br car park, US parking lot

estacionar 1. vt AUTO to park **2. estacionarse** vpr = **estacionar**

estada nf stay

estadía nf Am stay; **planeó una estadía de tres días en Lima** he planned a three-day stop in Lima

estadio nm **a)** DEP stadium **b)** [fase] stage

estadística nf statistics (sing); **una estadística** a statistic

estado nm **a)** POL state **b)** [situación] state, condition; **en buen estado** in good condition; **estado de salud** condition, state of health; **estado de excepción** state of emergency; **estar en estado** to be pregnant; **estado civil** marital status **c)** MIL **estado mayor** general staff **d)** [país, división territorial] state; **Estados Unidos de América** United States of America

estadounidense 1. adj American **2.** nmf American

estafa nf swindle

estafador, -a nm, f swindler

estafar vt to swindle

estalactita nf stalactite

estalagmita nf stalagmite

estallar vi **a)** to burst; [bomba] to explode, to go off; [guerra] to break out **b)** Fig [de cólera etc] to explode; **estallar en sollozos** to burst into tears

estallido nm explosion; [de guerra] outbreak

estambre nm BOT stamen

estamento nm HIST estate; Fig [grupo] group

estampado, -a 1. adj [tela] printed **2.** nm **a)** [tela] print **b)** [proceso] printing

estampida nf **a)** [estampido] bang **b)** [carrera rápida] stampede; **de estampida** suddenly

estampilla nf Am (postage) stamp

estancado, -a adj [agua] stagnant; Fig static, at a standstill; **quedarse estancado** to get stuck o bogged down

estancar [44] **1.** vt **a)** [agua] to hold back **b)** Fig [asunto] to block; [negociaciones] to bring to a standstill **2. estancarse** vpr to stagnate; Fig to get bogged down

estancia nf **a)** Esp, Méx [tiempo] stay **b)** [habitación] room **c)** CSur [hacienda] ranch, farm

estanciero, -a nm, f CSur ranch owner, rancher

estanco, -a 1. nm Esp tobacconist's **2.** adj watertight

estándar *adj* & *nm* standard

estanque *nm* pool, pond

estante *nm* shelf; [para libros] bookcase

estantería *nf* shelves, shelving

estaño *nm* tin

estar [13] **1.** *vi* **a)** to be; **está en la playa** he is at the beach; **estar en casa** to be in, to be at home; **estamos en Caracas** we are in Caracas; **¿está tu madre?** is your mother in?; **¿cómo estás?** how are you?; **los precios están bajos** prices are low
b) [+ adj] to be; **está cansado /enfermo** he's tired /ill; **está vacío** it's empty
c) [+ adv] to be; **está bien /mal** it's all right /wrong; **estar mal de dinero** he's short of money; **estará listo enseguida** it'll be ready in a minute
d) [+ ger] to be; **está escribiendo** she is writing; **estaba comiendo** he was eating
e) (+ **a** + *fecha*) to be; **¿a cuántos estamos?** what's the date (today)?; **estamos a 2 de noviembre** it is the 2nd of November
f) [+ precio] to be at; **están a dos euros el kilo** they're two euros a kilo
g) [locuciones] **estar al caer** to be just round the corner; **¿estamos?** OK?
h) (+ **de**) **estar de paseo** to be out for a walk; **estar de vacaciones /viaje** to be (away) on holiday /a trip; **estoy de jefe hoy** I'm the boss today
i) [+ para] **estará para las seis** it will be finished by six; **hoy no estoy para bromas** I'm in no mood for jokes today
j) [+ por] **está por hacer** it has still to be done; **eso está por ver** it remains to be seen; **estoy por esperar** [a favor de] I'm for waiting
k) [+ con] to have; **estar con la gripe** to have the flu, to be down with flu; **estoy con Jaime** [de acuerdo con] I agree with Jaime
l) [+ sin] to have no; **estar sin luz /agua** to have no light /water
m) [+ que] **está que se duerme** he is nearly asleep; *Fam* **está que rabia** he's hopping mad
2. *nm Am* living room

3. estarse *vpr* **¡estate quieto!** stay still!, stop fidgeting!; **¿puedes estarte unos días aquí?** can you stay here a few days?

estárter (*pl* **estárters**), **starter** (*pl* **starters**) *nm* choke

estatal *adj* state; **enseñanza estatal** state education

estático, -a *adj* static

estatua *nf* statue

estatura *nf* **a)** height; **¿cuál es tu estatura?** how tall are you? **b)** [renombre] stature

estatus *nm inv* status; **estatus quo** status quo

estatuto *nm inv* JUR statute; [de ciudad] by-law; [de empresa etc] rules

este¹ 1. *adj* eastern; [dirección] easterly **2.** *nm* east; **al este de** to the east of

este², -a (*mpl* **estos**, *fpl* **esas**) *adj demos* **a)** this **b)** **estos, -as** these

éste, -a (*mpl* **éstos**, *fpl* **éstas**) *pron demos m*, *f* **a)** this one; **aquél ... éste** the former ... the latter **b)** **éstos, -as** these (ones); **aquéllos ... éste** the former ... the latter

> Note that **éste** and its various forms can be written without an accent when there is no risk of confusion with the adjective.

estera *nf* rush mat

estéreo *nm* & *adj* stereo

estéril *adj* **a)** sterile **b)** *Fig* [esfuerzo] futile

esterilizar [40] *vt* to sterilize

esternón *nm* sternum, breastbone

estero *nm* **a)** [pantano] *Am* marsh, swamp **b)** *Ven* [charca] puddle, pool **c)** *Chile* [arroyo] stream

estética *nf* aesthetics (*sing*)

estibador *nm* docker, stevedore

estiércol *nm* manure, dung

estilizado, -a *adj* stylized

estilo *nm* **a)** style; [modo] manner, fashion; **algo por el estilo** something like that; **estilo de vida** way of life

b) [en natación] stroke **c)** LING **estilo directo / indirecto** direct / indirect speech

estilográfica *nf* **(pluma) estilográfica** fountain pen

estima *nf* esteem, respect

estimación *nf* **a)** [estima] esteem, respect **b)** [valoración] evaluation; [cálculo aproximado] estimate

estimado, -a *adj* esteemed, respected; **Estimado Señor** [en carta] Dear Sir

estimulación *nf* stimulation

estimulante 1. *adj* stimulating **2.** *nm* stimulant

estimular *vt* **a)** to stimulate **b)** *Fig* to encourage

estímulo *nm* BIOL & FÍS stimulus; *Fig* encouragement

estirado, -a *adj Fig* stiff

estirar 1. *vt* to stretch; *Fig* [dinero] to spin out; *Fig* **estirar la pata** to kick the bucket **2. estirarse** *vpr* to stretch

estirpe *nf* stock, pedigree

esto *pron neutro* this, this thing, this matter; *Fam* **esto de la fiesta** this business about the party

estofado *nm* stew

estoicismo *nm* stoicism

estoico, -a 1. *adj* stoical **2.** *nm, f* stoic

estómago *nm* stomach; **dolor de estómago** stomach ache

estorbar 1. *vt* **a)** [dificultar] to hinder, to get in the way of **b)** [molestar] to disturb **2.** *vi* to be in the way

estorbo *nm* **a)** [obstáculo] obstruction, obstacle **b)** [molestia] nuisance

estornudar *vi* to sneeze

estornudo *nm* sneeze

estos, -as *adj demos pl ver* **este**

éstos, -as *pron demos m,fpl ver* **éste**

estoy *indic pres de* **estar**

estrafalario, -a *adj Fam* outlandish

estrangulador, -a *nm, f* strangler

estrangular *vt* to strangle; MED to strangulate

estratega *nmf* strategist

estrategia *nf* strategy

estratégico, -a *adj* strategic

estrechar 1. *vt* **a)** to make narrow **b)** [mano] to shake; [lazos de amistad] to tighten; **me estrechó entre sus brazos** he hugged me **2. estrecharse** *vpr* to narrow, to become narrower

estrecho, -a 1. *adj* **a)** narrow; [ropa, zapato] tight; [amistad, relación] close, intimate **b)** *Fig* **estrecho de miras** narrow-minded **2.** *nm* GEOGR strait, straits

estrella 1. *adj inv* **a)** [presentador] star **b)** [producto] flagship **2.** *nf* **a)** ASTRON & ZOOL star; **estrella de mar** starfish; **estrella fugaz** shooting star **b)** *Fig* [celebridad] star; **estrella de cine** movie *o Br* film star **c) tener buena / mala estrella** to be born under a good / bad star

estrellar 1. *vt Fam* to smash **2. estrellarse** *vpr* [morir] to die in a car crash; AUTO & AVIACIÓN **estrellarse contra** [chocar] to crash into

estremecedor, -a *adj* chilling

estremecer [33] **1.** *vt* to shake **2. estremecerse (de)** *vpr* [miedo] to shake *o* to tremble (with)

estrenar *vt* **a)** to use for the first time; [ropa] to wear for the first time **b)** TEATRO & CINE to premiere

estreno *nm* TEATRO first performance; CINE premiere

estreñimiento *nm* constipation

estrepitoso, -a *adj* deafening; *Fig* [fracaso] spectacular

estrés *nm* stress

estría *nf* **a)** [en la piel] stretch mark **b)** ARQUIT flute, fluting

estribillo *nm* [en canción] chorus; [en poema] refrain

estribo *nm* **a)** stirrup; *Fig* **perder los estribos** to lose one's temper, to lose one's head **b)** ARQUIT buttress; [de puente] pier, support

estribor *nm* starboard

estricto, -a *adj* strict

estrofa *nf* verse

estropajo *nm* scourer

estropeado, -a *adj* a) [averiado] broken b) [dañado] damaged c) [echado a perder] ruined, spoiled

estropear 1. *vt* [averiar] to break; [dañar] to damage; [echar a perder] to ruin, to spoil **2. estropearse** *vpr* [máquina] to break down; [comida] to go off, to spoil

estructura *nf* structure; [armazón] frame, framework

estuario *nm* estuary

estuche *nm* case; [para lápices] pencil case

estudiante *nmf* student

estudiar [43] *vt & vi* to study

estudio *nm* a) study; [encuesta] survey; COM **estudio de mercado** market research b) [sala] studio; **estudio cinematográfico / de grabación** film / recording studio c) [apartamento] studio *Br* flat o *US* apartment d) **estudios** studies

estudioso, -a 1. *adj* studious **2.** *nm, f* specialist

estufa *nf* [calentador] heater, *Br* fire; *Méx* [cocina] stove

estupefacto, -a *adj* astounded, flabbergasted

estupendo, -a *adj* super, marvellous; ¡estupendo! great!

estupidez *nf* stupidity

estúpido, -a 1. *adj* stupid **2.** *nm, f* idiot

etapa *nf* stage; **por etapas** in stages

etarra *nmf* member of ETA

etc. *(abr de* etcétera*)* etc

etcétera *adv* etcetera

eternidad *nf* eternity; *Fam* **una eternidad** ages

eterno, -a *adj* eternal

ética *nf* ethic; [ciencia] ethics *(sing)*

ético, -a *adj* ethical

etimología *nf* etymology

etiqueta *nf* a) [de producto] label b) [ceremonia] etiquette; **de etiqueta** formal c) INFORM tag

étnico, -a *adj* ethnic

ETT *nf (abr de* **empresa de trabajo temporall**) temping agency, temporary recruitment agency

eucalipto *nm* eucalyptus

eucaristía *nf* eucharist

eufemismo *nm* euphemism

eufórico, -a *adj* euphoric

euribor *nm* FIN *(abr de* **Euro Inter-Bank Offered Rate**) Euribor

euro *nm* [moneda] euro

Europa *n* Europe

europeo, -a *adj & nm, f* European

Euskadi *n* the Basque Country

euskera *adj & nm* Basque

eutanasia *nf* euthanasia

evacuación *nf* evacuation

evacuar [47] *vt* to evacuate

evadir 1. *vt* [respuesta, peligro, impuestos] to avoid; [responsabilidad] to shirk **2. evadirse** *vpr* to escape

evaluación *nf* evaluation; EDUC assessment; **evaluación continua** continuous assessment

evaluar [30] *vt* to evaluate, to assess

evangelio *nm* gospel

evangelización *nf* evangelization, evangelizing

evaporar 1. *vt* to evaporate **2. evaporarse** *vpr* to evaporate; *Fig* to vanish

evasión *nf* [fuga] escape; *Fig* evasion; **evasión fiscal** o **de impuestos** tax evasion

eventual *adj* a) [posible] possible; [gastos] incidental b) [trabajo, obrero] casual, temporary

eventualidad *nf* contingency

evidencia *nf* obviousness; **poner a algn en evidencia** to show sb up

evidente *adj* obvious

evidentemente *adv* obviously

evitar *vt* to avoid; [prevenir] to prevent; [desastre] to avert

evocar [44] *vt* [traer a la memoria] to evoke; [acordarse de] to recall

evolución *nf* evolution; [desarrollo] development

evolucionar *vi* to develop; BIOL to evolve; **el enfermo evoluciona favorablemente** the patient is improving

exactamente *adv* exactly, precisely

exactitud *nf* accuracy; **con exactitud** precisely

exacto, -a *adj* exact; **¡exacto!** precisely!; **para ser exacto** to be precise

exageración *nf* exaggeration

exagerado, -a *adj* exaggerated; [excesivo] excessive

exagerar 1. *vt* to exaggerate **2.** *vi* to overdo it

exaltar 1. *vt* [ensalzar] to praise, to extol **2. exaltarse** *vpr* [acalorarse] to get overexcited, to get carried away

examen *nm* examination, exam; *Esp* **examen de conducir** driving test; *Am* **examen de manejar** driving test; MED **examen médico** checkup; *Am* **pasar un examen** to pass an exam; *Am* **reprobar un examen** to fail an exam

examinar 1. *vt* to examine **2. examinarse** *vpr Esp* to take o sit an examination

excavación *nf* excavation; [en arqueología] dig

excavadora *nf* digger

excavar *vt* to excavate, to dig

excedencia *nf Esp* leave (of absence)

excedente 1. *adj* a) [producción, dinero etc] excess, surplus b) [empleado, embarazada] on leave c) [funcionario] redundant **2.** *nm* surplus **3.** *nmf* a) [empleado] employee on leave (of absence) b) [funcionario] redundant worker

exceder 1. *vt* to exceed, to surpass **2. excederse** *vpr* to go too far

excelencia *nf* a) excellence; **por excelencia** par excellence b) [título] **Su Excelencia** His / Her Excellency

excelente *adj* excellent

excentricidad *nf* eccentricity

excéntrico, -a *adj* eccentric

excepción *nf* exception; **a excepción de** with the exception of, except for; **de excepción** exceptional; POL **estado de excepción** state of emergency

excepcional *adj* exceptional

excepto *adv* except (for), apart from

excesivo, -a *adj* excessive

exceso *nm* excess; **en exceso** in excess, excessively; **exceso de equipaje** excess baggage; **exceso de velocidad** speeding

excitar 1. *vt* to excite **2. excitarse** *vpr* to get excited

exclamación *nf* exclamation

excluir [37] *vt* to exclude; [rechazar] to reject

exclusiva *nf* PRENSA exclusive; COM sole right

exclusivo, -a *adj* exclusive

excursión *nf* excursion

excusa *nf* [pretexto] excuse; [disculpa] apology

excusar 1. *vt* a) [justificar] to excuse b) [eximir] to exempt (de from) **2. excusarse** *vpr* [disculparse] to apologize

exento, -a *adj* exempt, free (de from)

exhaustivo, -a *adj* exhaustive

exhibición *nf* exhibition

exhibir 1. *vt* a) [mostrar] to exhibit, to display b) [lucir] to show off **2. exhibirse** *vpr* to show off, to make an exhibition of oneself

exigencia *nf* a) demand b) [requisito] requirement

exigente *adj* demanding, exacting

exigir [57] *vt* to demand

exilar 1. *vt* to exile **2. exilarse** *vpr* to go into exile

exiliar [43] = **exilar**

exilio *nm* exile

existencia *nf* a) [vida] existence b) COM **existencias** stock, stocks

existir *vi* to exist, to be (in existence)

éxito *nm* success; **con éxito** successfully; **tener éxito** to be successful

exitoso, -a *adj* successful

exo SMS written abbr of **hecho**

exonerar vt **a)** [de carga, obligación] to exonerate **b)** [de tarea] to relieve **c)** [de impuestos] to exempt

exótico, -a adj exotic

expandible adj **a)** expansible **b)** INFORM expandable

expedición nf expedition

expediente nm **a)** [informe] dossier, record; [ficha] file; EDUC **expediente académico** academic record, US transcript; **abrirle expediente a algn** to place sb under enquiry **b)** JUR proceedings, action

expedir [6] vt **a)** [carta] to send, to dispatch **b)** [pasaporte etc] to issue

expendedor, -a 1. nm, f seller **2.** nm **expendedor automático** vending machine

expendio nm Am Br shop, US store; **expendio de refrescos** soft drinks available

expensas nfpl **a expensas de** at the expense of

experiencia nf **a)** experience; **por experiencia** from experience **b)** [experimento] experiment

experimentado, -a adj experienced

experimental adj experimental

experimentar 1. vi to experiment **2.** vt to undergo; [aumento] to show; [pérdida] to suffer; [sensación] to experience, to feel; MED **experimentar una mejoría** to improve, to make progress

experimento nm experiment

experto, -a nm, f expert

expirar vi to expire

explicación nf explanation

explicar [44] **1.** vt to explain **2.** **explicarse** vpr [persona] to explain (oneself); **no me lo explico** I can't understand it

explícito, -a adj explicit

explorador, -a nm, f **a)** [persona] explorer **b)** MED probe; TÉC scanner

explorar vt to explore; MED [internamente] to explore; [externamente] to examine; TÉC to scan; MIL to reconnoitre

explosión nf explosion, blast; **hacer explosión** to explode; **motor de explosión** internal combustion engine; **explosión demográfica** population explosion

explosivo, -a adj & nm explosive

explotación nf **a)** [abuso] exploitation **b)** [uso] exploitation, working; AGRIC cultivation (of land); [granja] farm

explotar 1. vi [bomba] to explode, to go off **2.** vt **a)** [aprovechar] to exploit; [recursos] to tap; [tierra] to cultivate **b)** [abusar de] to exploit

exponente nmf exponent

exponer [19] (pp expuesto) **1.** vt **a)** [mostrar] to exhibit, to display **b)** [explicar] to expound, to put forward **c)** [arriesgar] to expose **2. exponerse** vpr to expose oneself (**a** to); **te expones a perder el trabajo** you run the risk of losing your job

exportación nf COM & INFORM export

exportar vt COM & INFORM to export

exposición nf **a)** ARTE exhibition; **exposición universal** international exposition o exhibition, US world's fair; **sala de exposiciones** gallery **b)** [de hechos, ideas] exposé **c)** FOTO exposure

expositor, -a 1. adj exponent **2.** nm, f [en feria] exhibitor; [de teoría] exponent

exprés adj express; **(olla) exprés** pressure cooker; **(café) exprés** espresso (coffee)

expresar 1. vt to express; [manifestar] to state **2. expresarse** vpr to express oneself

expresión nf expression; **la mínima expresión** the bare minimum

expresivo, -a adj expressive

expreso, -a 1. adj express; **con el fin expreso de** with the express purpose of **2.** nm FERROC express (train) **3.** adv on purpose, deliberately

exprimidor nm squeezer, juicer

exprimir *vt* [limón] to squeeze; [zumo] to squeeze out; *Fig* [persona] to exploit, to bleed dry

expuesto, -a *adj* **a)** [sin protección] exposed; **estar expuesto a** to be exposed to **b)** [peligroso] risky, dangerous **c)** [exhibido] on display, on show

expulsar *vt* **a)** to expel, to throw out; DEP [jugador] to send off **b)** [gas etc] to belch out

expulsión *nf* expulsion; DEP sending-off

exquisitez *nf* **a)** [cualidad] exquisiteness **b)** [cosa] exquisite thing; [comida] delicacy

exquisito, -a *adj* exquisite; [comida] delicious; [gusto] refined

extasiarse *vpr* **extasiarse (ante / con)** to be enraptured (by / with)

éxtasis *nm inv* ecstasy

extender [3] **1.** *vt* **a)** to extend; [agrandar] to enlarge
b) [mantel, mapa] to spread (out), to open (out); [mano, brazo] to stretch (out)
c) [crema, mantequilla] to spread
d) [cheque] to make out; [documento] to draw up; [certificado] to issue
2. extenderse *vpr* **a)** [en el tiempo] to extend, to last
b) [en el espacio] to spread out, to stretch
c) [rumor, noticia] to spread, to extend
d) *Fig* [hablar demasiado] to go on

extendido, -a *adj* **a)** [estirado] stretched out **b)** [diseminado] widespread

extensión *nf* **a)** [superficie] expanse **b)** [de libro etc] length; [de cuerpo] size; [de terreno] area, expanse; [edificio anexo] extension; **en toda la extensión de la palabra** in every sense of the word; **por extensión** by extension **c)** TELECOM extension **d)** INFORM extension

extenso, -a *adj* [terreno] extensive; [libro, película] long

exterior 1. *adj* **a)** [de fuera] outer; [puerta] outside **b)** [política, deuda] foreign; POL **Ministerio de Asuntos Exteriores** Ministry of Foreign Affairs, ≃ *Br* Foreign Office, ≃ *US* State Department **2.** *nm* **a)** [parte de fuera] exterior, outside **b)** [extranjero] abroad **c)** CINE **exteriores** location

exterminar *vt* to exterminate

externalización *nf* ECON outsourcing

externalizar *vt* ECON to outsource

externar *vt Méx* to display

externo, -a 1. *adj* external; FARM **de uso externo** for external use only **2.** *nm, f* EDUC day pupil

extinguidor *nm Am* fire extinguisher

extinguir [59] **1.** *vt* [fuego] to extinguish, to put out; [raza] to wipe out **2. extinguirse** *vpr* [fuego] to go out; [especie] to become extinct, to die out

extintor *nm Esp* fire extinguisher

extirpar *vt* **a)** MED to remove **b)** *Fig* to eradicate, to stamp out

extra 1. *adj* **a)** [suplementario] extra; **horas extra** overtime; **paga extra** bonus
b) [superior] top-quality
2. *nm* extra
3. *nmf* CINE & TEATRO extra

extracción *nf* **a)** extraction **b)** [en lotería] draw

extracomunitario, -a *adj* non-EU; **países / ciudadanos extracomunitarios** non-EU countries / citizens

extracto *nm* **a)** extract; **extracto de fresa** strawberry extract; **extracto de regaliz** liquorice; FIN **extracto de cuenta** statement of account **b)** [resumen] summary

extractor *nm* extractor

extradición *nf* extradition

extraer [25] *vt* to extract, to take out

extraescolar *adj* EDUC out-of-school

extramarital *adj* extramarital

extramatrimonial *adj* extramarital

extranjero, -a 1. *adj* foreign **2.** *nm, f* foreigner **3.** *nm* abroad; **en el extranjero** abroad

extrañar 1. *vt* **a)** [sorprender] to surprise; **no es de extrañar** it's hardly surprising **b)** [echar de menos] to miss **2. extrañarse** *vpr* **extrañarse de** to be surprised at

extrañeza *nf* **a)** [sorpresa] surprise, astonishment **b)** [singularidad] strangeness

extraño, -a 1. *adj* strange; MED **cuerpo extraño** foreign body **2.** *nm, f* stranger

extraordinario, -a *adj* extraordinary; PRENSA **edición extraordinaria** special edition

extraterrestre *nmf* alien

extravagante *adj* odd, outlandish

extraviar [29] **1.** *vt* to mislay, to lose **2. extraviarse** *vpr* to be missing, to get mislaid

extremar 1. *vt* **extremar la prudencia** to be extremely careful **2. extremarse** *vpr* to take great pains, to do one's utmost

extremaunción *nf* extreme unction

extremidad *nf* **a)** [extremo] end, tip **b)** ANAT [miembro] limb, extremity

extremista *adj* & *nmf* extremist

extremo, -a 1. *nm* [de calle, cable] end; [máximo] extreme; **en extremo** very much; **en último extremo** as a last resort **2.** *nm, f* [en fútbol] winger; **extremo derecha/izquierda** outside right/left **3.** *adj* extreme; **Extremo Oriente** Far East

extrovertido, -a *adj* & *nm, f* extrovert

eys SMS *written abbr of* **ellos**

fabada *nf* stew of beans, pork sausage and bacon

fábrica *nf* factory; **marca de fábrica** trademark; **precio de fábrica** factory o ex-works price

fabricante *nmf* manufacturer

fabricar [44] *vt* **a)** INDUST to manufacture **b)** *Fig* [mentiras etc] to fabricate

fábula *nf* fable

fabuloso, -a *adj* fabulous

faceta *nf* facet

facha 1. *nf* **a)** [aspecto] look **b)** [mamarracho] mess; **vas hecho una facha** you look a mess **2.** *nmf Esp Fam & Despec* [fascista] fascist

fachada *nf* façade

fácil *adj* **a)** easy; **fácil de comprender** easy to understand **b)** [probable] likely, probable; **es fácil que ...** it's (quite) likely that ...

facilidad *nf* **a)** [sencillez] easiness **b)** [soltura] ease **c)** [servicio] facility; **dar facilidades** to make things easy; COM **facilidades de pago** easy terms **d)** **facilidad para los idiomas** gift for languages

facilitar *vt* [proporcionar] to provide, to supply (**a** with)

fácilmente *adv* **a)** [con facilidad] easily **b)** *Fam* [probablemente] at least

factor *nm* **a)** factor **b)** FERROC luggage clerk

factura *nf* **a)** COM invoice **b)** *Arg* [repostería] cakes and pastries

facturación *nf* **a)** COM invoicing **b)** [de equipajes - en aeropuerto] check-in; [en estación] registration

facturar *vt* **a)** COM to invoice **b)** [en aeropuerto] to check in; [en estación] to register

facultad *nf* faculty; **facultades mentales** faculties

faena *nf* **a)** [tarea] task **b)** *Fam* [mala pasada] dirty trick **c)** TAUROM performance

fainá *nf Urug* [plato] baked dough made from chickpea flour, served with pizza

faisán *nm* pheasant

faja *nf* **a)** [corsé] girdle, corset **b)** [banda] sash **c)** [de terreno] strip

fajo *nm* [de ropa etc] bundle; [de billetes] wad

falange *nf* **a)** ANAT & MIL phalanx **b)** POL **la Falange (Española)** the Falange

falda *nf* **a)** [prenda] skirt; **falda pantalón** culottes **b)** [de montaña] slope, hillside **c)** [de mesa] cover **d)** [regazo] lap

falencia *nf* **a)** *Am* COM [bancarrota] bankruptcy **b)** *CSur* [error] fault

falla *nf* **a)** [defecto] defect, fault; **este cajón tiene una falla** there's something wrong with this drawer **b)** *Am* [error] mistake; **un trabajo lleno de fallas** a piece of work full of mistakes **c)** GEOL fault

fallar¹ 1. *vi* JUR to rule **2.** *vt* [premio] to award

fallar² 1. *vi* to fail; **le falló la puntería** he missed his aim; *Fig* **no me falles** don't let me down **2.** *vt* to miss

fallecer [33] *vi Formal* to pass away, to die

fallecido, -a *adj & nm, f Formal* deceased

fallo¹ *nm Esp* **a)** [error] mistake; **fallo humano** human error **b)** [del corazón, de los frenos] failure

fallo² *nm* **a)** JUR judgement, sentence **b)** [en concurso] awarding

falluto, -a *RP Fam* **1.** *adj* phoney, hypocritical **2.** *nm, f* hypocrite

falsedad *nf* **a)** falseness; [doblez] hypocrisy **b)** [mentira] falsehood

falsete *nm* falsetto; **voz de falsete** falsetto voice

falsificar [44] *vt* to falsify; [cuadro, firma, moneda] to forge

falso, -a *adj* **a)** false; **dar un paso en falso** [tropezar] to trip, to stumble; *Fig* to make a blunder; **jurar en falso** to commit perjury **b)** [persona] insincere

falta *nf* **a)** [carencia] lack; **por falta de** for want o lack of; **sin falta** without fail; **falta de educación** bad manners **b)** [escasez] shortage
c) [ausencia] absence; **echar algo /a algn en falta** to miss sth /sb
d) [error] mistake; [defecto] fault, defect; **falta de ortografía** spelling mistake; **sacar faltas a algo /a algn** to find fault with sth /sb
e) *JUR* misdemeanour
f) [en fútbol] foul; [en tenis] fault
g) hacer falta to be necessary; **(nos) hace falta una escalera** we need a ladder; **harán falta dos personas para mover el piano** it'll take two people to move the piano; **no hace falta que ...** there is no need for ...

faltante *nm Am* deficit

faltar *vi* **a)** [no estar] to be missing; **¿quién falta?** who is missing?
b) [escasear] to be lacking o needed; **le falta confianza en sí mismo** he lacks confidence in himself; **¡lo que me faltaba!** that's all I needed!; **¡no faltaría o faltaba más!** [por supuesto] (but) of course!
c) [quedar] to be left; **¿cuántos kilómetros faltan para Managua?** how many kilometres is it to Managua?; **ya falta poco para las vacaciones** it won't be long now till the holidays; **faltó poco para que me cayera** I very nearly fell
d) faltar a su palabra /promesa to break one's word /promise; **faltar al respeto a algn** to treat sb with disrespect

fama *nf* **a)** fame, renown; **de fama mundial** world-famous **b)** [reputación] reputation

familia *nf* family; **estar en familia** to be among friends; **familia numerosa** large family

familiar 1. *adj* **a)** [de la familia] family; **empresa familiar** family business **b)** [conocido] familiar **2.** *nmf* relation, relative

familiarizado, -a *adj* familiarized

familiarizarse [40] *vpr* **familiarizarse con** to familiarize oneself with

famoso, -a 1. *adj* famous **2.** *nm* famous person

fanatismo *nm* fanaticism

fandango *nm* [baile] fandango

fanfarrón, -ona *Fam* **1.** *adj* boastful **2.** *nm, f* show-off

fantasía *nf* fantasy; **joya de fantasía** imitation jewellery

fantasma *nm* **a)** [espectro] ghost **b)** *Esp Fam* [fanfarrón] braggart, show-off

fantástico, -a *adj* fantastic

fardar *vi Esp Fam* [llamar la atención] to stand out; **¡cómo farda esa moto!** wow! That bike certainly stands out!; *Esp Fam* **fardar de** [presumir de] to show off, to boast about

farmacéutico, -a 1. *adj* pharmaceutical **2.** *nm, f* pharmacist, *Br* chemist, *US* druggist

farmacia *nf* **a)** [tienda] pharmacy, *Br* chemist's (shop), *US* drugstore **b)** [ciencia] pharmacology

faro *nm* **a)** [torre] lighthouse **b)** [de coche] headlight, headlamp

farol *nm* **a)** lantern; [en la calle] streetlight, streetlamp **b)** *Fam* [fanfarronada] bragging; **tirarse un farol** to brag **c)** [en naipes] bluff

farola *nf* streetlight, streetlamp

farolillo *nm Fig* **ser el farolillo rojo** to bring up the rear

farsa *nf* farce

farsante *nmf* fake, impostor

fascismo *nm* fascism

fascista adj & nmf fascist

fase nf **a)** [etapa] phase, stage **b)** ELEC & FÍS phase

fashion ['faʃjon] adj hip, fashionable

fastidiar [43] **1.** vt **a)** [molestar] to annoy, to bother; Fam **¡no fastidies!** you're kidding! **b)** Esp Fam [estropear] to damage, to ruin; [planes] to spoil **2. fastidiarse** vpr Esp **a)** [aguantarse] to put up with it, to resign oneself; **que se fastidie** that's his tough luck **b)** Fam [estropearse] to get damaged, to break down **c) me he fastidiado el tobillo** I've hurt my ankle

fastidio nm nuisance

fatal 1. adj **a)** Esp Fam [muy malo] terrible, awful **b)** [mortal] deadly, fatal **c)** [inexorable] fateful, inevitable **2.** adv Esp Fam awfully, terribly; **lo pasó fatal** he had a rotten time

fatalidad nf **a)** [destino] fate **b)** [desgracia] misfortune

fatiga nf **a)** [cansancio] fatigue **b)** **fatigas** [dificultades] troubles, difficulties

fatigar [42] **1.** vt to tire, to weary **2. fatigarse** vpr to tire, to become tired

fauna nf fauna

favor nm favour; **por favor** please; **¿puedes hacerme un favor?** can you do me a favour?; **estar a favor de** to be in favour of; **haga el favor de sentarse** please sit down

favorable adj favourable; **favorable a** in favour of

favorecer [33] vt **a)** to favour **b)** [sentar bien] to flatter

favorecido, -a nm, f **a)** [persona] priviliged person **b)** Am [ganador] lucky winner

favorito, -a adj & nm, f favourite

fax nm **a)** [aparato] fax (machine); **mandar algo por fax** to fax sth **b)** [documento] fax

fayuquero, -a nm, f Méx Fam dealer in contraband

fe nf **a)** faith; **de buena / mala fe** with good / dishonest intentions **b)** [certi-ficado] certificate; **fe de bautismo / matrimonio** baptism / marriage certificate **c)** IMPR **fe de erratas** errata

fealdad nf ugliness

febrero nm February

fecha nf **a)** date; **fecha límite** o **tope** deadline; **fecha de caducidad** sell-by date; **hasta la fecha** so far; **en fecha próxima** at an early date **b) fechas** [época] time; **el año pasado por estas fechas** this time last year

fechar vt to date

fecundo, -a adj fertile

federación nf federation

felicidad nf happiness; **(muchas) felicidades** [en cumpleaños] many happy returns

felicitación 1. nf **a)** [congratulación, deseo] wish fpl **b)** [postal] **tarjeta de felicitación** greetings card **2.** interj Am [enhorabuena] **¡felicitaciones!** congratulations!, well done!; **¡felicitaciones por el nuevo trabajo!** congratulations on the new job!

felicitar vt to congratulate (**por** on); **¡te felicito!** congratulations!

feligrés, -esa nm, f parishioner

feliz adj **a)** [contento] happy; **¡felices Navidades!** Happy o Merry Christmas! **b)** [decisión etc] fortunate

felpudo nm mat, doormat

femenino, -a adj feminine; [equipo, ropa] women's; **el sexo femenino** the female sex, women

feminismo nm feminism

feminista adj & nmf feminist

fémur nm femur

fenomenal 1. adj **a)** phenomenal **b)** Fam [fantástico] great, terrific **2.** adv Fam wonderfully, marvellously; **lo pasamos fenomenal** we had a fantastic time

fenómeno, -a 1. nm **a)** phenomenon **b)** [prodigio] genius **c)** [monstruo] freak **2.** adj Fam fantastic, terrific **3.** interj fantastic!, terrific!

feo, -a 1. adj ugly; [asunto etc] nasty **2.** nm Fam **hacerle un feo a algn** to offend sb

féretro nm coffin

feria nf fair; **feria de muestras/del libro** trade/book fair

feriado, -a Am **1.** adj **día feriado** (public) holiday **2.** nm (public) holiday

fermentación nf fermentation

feroz adj fierce, ferocious; **el lobo feroz** the big bad wolf

ferretería nf Br ironmonger's (shop), US hardware store

ferrocarril nm Br railway, US railroad

ferrocarrilero, -a adj Méx rail

ferroviario, -a adj rail(way), US railroad

ferry nm ferry

fértil adj fertile

fertilidad nf fertility

festival nm festival

festividad nf festivity

festivo, -a 1. adj a) [ambiente etc] festive b) **día festivo** holiday **2.** nm holiday

feta nf RP slice

feto nm foetus

fiaca nf Méx, CSur Fam [pereza] laziness; **¡qué fiaca tener que ponerme a planchar!** what a pain o Br fag having to do the ironing!

fiambre nm a) CULIN Br cold meat, US cold cut b) Fam [cadáver] stiff, corpse

fiambrera nf lunchbox

fiambrería nf RP delicatessen (tienda)

fianza nf [depósito] deposit; JUR bail; **en libertad bajo fianza** on bail

fiar [29] **1.** vt a) [avalar] to guarantee b) [vender sin cobrar] to sell on credit **2. fiarse** vpr **fiarse (de)** to trust

fibra nf fibre; [de madera] grain; **fibra de vidrio** fibreglass

ficción nf fiction

ficha nf a) [tarjeta] filing card; **ficha técnica** specifications, technical data; CINE credits b) [en juegos] counter; [de ajedrez] piece, man; [de dominó] domino

fichar 1. vt a) to put on file b) DEP to sign up **2.** vi a) [en el trabajo - al entrar] to clock in, US to punch in; [al salir] to clock out o off, US to punch out b) DEP to sign

fichero nm card index

ficticio, -a adj fictitious

fidelidad nf [lealtad] loyalty; [de conyuge] faithfulness; **alta fidelidad** high fidelity, hi-fi

fidelizar vt COM to build up loyalty (among customers)

fideo nm noodle

fiebre nf fever; **tener fiebre** to have a temperature

fiel 1. adj a) [leal] faithful, loyal b) [exacto] accurate, exact **2.** nm a) [de balanza] needle, pointer b) REL **los fieles** the congregation

fieltro nm felt

fiera nf a) wild animal; Fam **estaba hecho una fiera** he was hopping mad b) TAUROM bull

fiero, -a adj [salvaje] wild; [feroz] fierce, ferocious

fierro nm Am [hierro] iron

fiesta nf a) [entre amigos] party b) **día de fiesta** holiday c) REL feast; **fiesta de guardar** holiday of obligation d) [festividad] celebration, festivity

fiestero, -a Fam **1.** adj party-loving **2.** nm, f party animal

figura nf figure

figuración nf [invención] **son figuraciones tuyas** it's all just in your head

figurar 1. vi [en lista] to figure **2. figurarse** vpr a) to imagine, to suppose; **ya me lo figuraba** I thought as much b) **¡figúrate!, ¡figúrese!** just imagine!

figurativo, -a adj ARTE figurative

figurín nm fashion sketch; Fig **ir o estar hecho un figurín** to be dressed up to the nines

fijador *nm* a) [gomina] gel b) FOTO fixative

fijar 1. *vt* to fix; **prohibido fijar carteles** [en letrero] post no bills **2. fijarse** *vpr* a) [darse cuenta] to notice b) [poner atención] to pay attention, to watch

fijo, -a *adj* a) fixed; **sin domicilio fijo** of no fixed abode b) [trabajo] steady

fila *nf* a) file; **en fila india** in single file; **poner en fila** to line up b) [de cine, teatro] row c) MIL **filas** ranks; **llamar a algn a filas** to call sb up; **¡rompan filas!** fall out!, dismiss!

filatelia *nf* philately, stamp collecting

filatélico, -a 1. *adj* stamp-collecting, *Formal* philatelic **2.** *nm, f* stamp collector, *Formal* philatelist

filete *nm* [de carne, pescado] fillet

filiación *nf* POL affiliation

filial 1. *adj* a) [de hijos] filial b) COM subsidiary **2.** *nf* COM subsidiary

Filipinas *n pl* **(las) Filipinas** (the) Philippines

filmar *vt* to film, to shoot

filoso, -a *adj Am* sharp

filosofar *vi* to philosophize

filosofía *nf* philosophy; *Fig* **con filosofía** philosophically

filósofo, -a *nm, f* philosopher

filtrar 1. *vt* a) to filter b) [información] to leak **2. filtrarse** *vpr* a) [líquido] to seep b) [información] to leak out

filtro *nm* filter

filudo *adj Andes* sharp

fin *nm* a) [final] end; **dar** o **poner fin a** to put an end to; **llegar** o **tocar a su fin** to come to an end; **en fin** anyway; **¡por** o **al fin!** at last!; **fin de semana** weekend; **al fin y al cabo** when all's said and done b) [objetivo] purpose, aim; **a fin de** in order to, so as to; **a fin de que** in order that, so that; **con el fin de** with the intention of

final 1. *adj* final

2. *nm* end; **al final** in the end; **final de línea** terminal; **final feliz** happy ending; **a finales de octubre** at the end of October
3. *nf* DEP final

finalidad *nf* purpose, aim

finalista 1. *nmf* finalist **2.** *adj* in the final

finalizar [40] *vt & vi* to end, to finish

financiación *nf* financing

financiamiento *nm Am* financing

financiar [43] *vt* to finance

financista *nmf Am* financier

finanzas *nfpl* finances

finca *nf* [inmueble] property; [de campo] country house

finde SMS *(abr de* **fin de semana***)* WKND

fingir [57] **1.** *vt* to feign **2. fingirse** *vpr* to pretend to be

finlandés, -esa 1. *adj* Finnish **2.** *nm, f* [persona] Finn **3.** *nm* [idioma] Finnish

Finlandia *n* Finland

fino, -a 1. *adj* a) [hilo, capa] fine b) [flaco] thin c) [educado] refined, polite d) [oído] sharp, acute; [olfato] keen e) [humor, ironía] subtle **2.** *nm* [vino] *type of dry sherry*

fiordo *nm* GEOGR fiord

firma *nf* a) signature b) [empresa] firm, company

firmar *vt* to sign

firme 1. *adj* a) firm; *Fig* **mantenerse firme** to hold one's ground; **tierra firme** terra firma
b) MIL **¡firmes!** attention!
2. *nm* [de carretera] road surface
3. *adv* hard

firmemente *adv* firmly

firmeza *nf* firmness

fiscal 1. *adj* fiscal **2.** *nmf* JUR ≃ *Br* public prosecutor, ≃ *US* district attorney

fiscalía *nf* JUR [cargo] ≃ *Br* post of public prosecutor, ≃ *US* post of district attorney; [oficina] ≃ Br public prosecutor's office, ≃ US district attorney's office

fiscalidad nf [impuestos] taxation

física nf physics (sing)

físico, -a 1. adj physical **2.** nm, f [profesión] physicist **3.** nm physique

fisioterapeuta nmf physiotherapist

fisonomía nf physiognomy

fisonomista nmf Fam **ser buen/mal fisonomista** to be good/no good at remembering faces

flaco, -a 1. adj **a)** [delgado] skinny **b)** Fig **punto flaco** weak spot **2.** nm, f Am Fam [como apelativo] **¿cómo estás, flaca?** hey, how are you doing?

flamante adj **a)** nuevecito **flamante** [nuevo] brand-new **b)** [vistoso] splendid, brilliant

flamenco, -a 1. adj **a)** MÚS flamenco **b)** [de Flandes] Flemish **2.** nm **a)** MÚS flamenco **b)** ORNIT flamingo **c)** [idioma] Flemish

flan nm crème caramel

flaqueza nf weakness

flash [flaʃ, flas] (pl **flashes**) nm FOTO flash

flato nm Esp **tener flato** to have a stitch

flauta nf flute; **flauta dulce** recorder

flecha nf arrow

fleco nm fringe

flemón nm gumboil, abscess

flequillo nm Br fringe, US bangs

flexibilidad nf flexibility

flexible adj flexible

flexión nf a) LING inflection b) **flexiones de brazo** push-ups, Br press-ups

flojear vi [ventas etc] to fall off, go down; [piernas] to weaken, grow weak; [memoria] to fail; Andes Fam [holgazanear] to laze about o around

flojera nf Fam weakness, faintness

flojo, -a adj **a)** [tornillo, cuerda etc] loose, slack **b)** [perezoso] lazy, idle; [examen, trabajo, resultado] poor

flor nf **a)** flower; **en flor** in blossom; Fig **en la flor de la vida** in the prime of life; Fig **la flor y nata** the cream (of society) **b)** a flor de piel skin-deep

flora nf flora

florecer [33] vi **a)** [plantas] to flower **b)** Fig [negocio] to flourish, to thrive

florero nm vase

florido, -a adj **a)** [con flores] flowery **b)** [estilo] florid

florista nmf florist

floristería nf florist's (shop)

flota nf fleet

flotador nm **a)** [de pesca] float **b)** [para nadar] rubber ring

flotar vi to float

flote nm floating; **a flote** afloat; **sacar a flote un negocio** to put a business on a sound footing

fluido, -a 1. adj fluid; [estilo etc] fluent **2.** nm fluid; **fluido eléctrico** current

fluir [37] vi to flow

flúor nm fluorine

FM nf (abr de **Frecuencia Modulada**) FM

foca nf seal

foco nm **a)** ELEC spotlight, floodlight **b)** [de ideas, revolución etc] centre, focal point **c)** Am [de vehículo] (car) headlight; [farola] streetlight **d)** Andes, Méx [bombilla] light bulb

foie-gras [fwa'ɣras] nm inv (pâté de) foie-gras

folclore nm folklore

folclórico, -a 1. adj traditional, popular **2.** nm, f Esp singer of traditional Spanish songs

fólder nm Andes, CAm, Méx [carpeta] folder

folio nm sheet of paper

folklórico, -a = **folclórico**

follaje nm foliage

follar vi & vt Esp muy Fam to lay, Br to shag

folleto nm leaflet; [turístico] brochure

follón *nm Esp Fam* **a)** [discusión] row **b)** [lío] mess; **me hice un follón con las listas** I got into a real muddle o mess with the lists

fomentar *vt* to promote

fonda *nf* inn

fondo¹ *nm* **a)** [parte más baja] bottom; **a fondo** thoroughly; **tocar fondo** NÁUT to touch bottom; *Fig* to reach rock bottom; *Fig* **en el fondo es bueno** deep down he's kind; **doble fondo** false bottom **b)** [de habitación] back; [de pasillo] end **c)** [segundo término] background; **música de fondo** background music **d)** DEP **corredor de fondo** long-distance runner; **esquí de fondo** cross-country skiing

fondo² *nm* FIN fund; **cheque sin fondos** bad cheque; *Fam* **fondo común** kitty

fono *nm Am Fam* phone

fontanero, -a *nm, f* plumber

footing *nm* jogging; **hacer footing** to go jogging

forastero, -a *nm, f* outsider, stranger

forense 1. *adj* forensic **2.** *nmf* **(médico) forense** forensic surgeon

forestal *adj* forest; **repoblación forestal** reafforestation

forfait [for'fait, for'fe] *(pl* **forfaits***)* *nm* **a)** [para esquiar] ski pass **b)** DEP default

forjar *vt* [metal] to forge; *Fig* to create, to make

forma *nf* **a)** form, shape; **en forma de L** L-shaped **b)** [manera] way; **de esta forma** in this way; **de forma que** so that; **de todas formas** anyway, in any case; **no hubo forma de convencerla** there was no way we could convince her; **forma de pago** method of payment **c)** DEP form; **estar en forma** to be on form; **estar en baja forma** to be off form **d)** **formas** [modales] manners

formación *nf* **a)** formation **b)** [educación] upbringing **c)** [enseñanza] training; **formación profesional** vocational training

formal *adj* **a)** formal **b)** [serio] serious, serious-minded **c)** [fiable] reliable, dependable

formalidad *nf* **a)** formality **b)** [seriedad] seriousness **c)** [fiabilidad] reliability **d)** **formalidades** [trámites] formalities

formar 1. *vt* **a)** to form; **formar parte de algo** to be a part of sth **b)** [educar] to bring up; [enseñar] to educate, to train **2. formarse** *vpr* **a)** to be formed, to form; **se formó un charco** a puddle formed; **formarse una impresión de algo** to get an impression of sth **b)** [educarse] to be educated o trained

formato *nm* [gen & INFORM] format

formidable *adj* **a)** [estupendo] wonderful, terrific **b)** [espantoso] formidable

fórmula *nf* formula; AUTO **fórmula uno** formula one

formular *vt* [quejas, peticiones] to make; [deseo] to express; [pregunta] to ask; [una teoría] to formulate

formulario *nm* form

forofo, -a *nm, f Esp Fam* fan, supporter

forrar 1. *vt* [por dentro] to line; [por fuera] to cover **2. forrarse** *vpr Fam* [de dinero] to make a packet

forro *nm* **a)** [por dentro] lining; [por fuera] cover, case **b)** *RP Fam* [preservativo] rubber

fortaleza *nf* **a)** strength; [de espíritu] fortitude **b)** MIL fortress, stronghold

fortuna *nf* **a)** [destino] fortune, fate **b)** [suerte] luck; **por fortuna** fortunately **c)** [capital] fortune

forzado, -a *adj* forced; **a marchas forzadas** at a brisk pace; **trabajos forzados** hard labour

forzar [2] *vt* **a)** [obligar] to force; **forzar a algn a hacer algo** to force sb to do sth **b)** [puerta, candado] to force, to break open

forzosamente *adv* necessarily

fósforo *nm* [cerilla] match

fósil *adj & nm* fossil

foso *nm* **a)** [hoyo] pit **b)** [de fortificación] moat **c)** [en garage] inspection pit

foto *nf Fam* photo; **sacar / echar una foto** to take a photo

fotocopia *nf* photocopy

fotocopiadora *nf* photocopier

fotocopiar [43] *vt* to photocopy

fotografía *nf* **a)** photograph; **echar** *o* **hacer** *o* **sacar fotografías** to take photographs **b)** [arte] photography

fotografiar [29] *vt* to photograph, to take a photograph of

fotográfico, -a *adj* photographic

fotógrafo, -a *nm, f* photographer

fotomatón *nm* passport photo machine

FP *nf (abr de Formación Profesional)* EDUC vocational training

fra. *(abr de factura)* inv

fracasar *vi* to fail

fracaso *nm* failure

fracción *nf* **a)** fraction **b)** POL faction

fraccionamiento *nm Méx* [urbanización] housing estate

fractura *nf* fracture

fracturar 1. *vt* to fracture **2. fracturarse** *vpr* to fracture

fragancia *nf* fragrance

frágil *adj* **a)** [quebradizo] fragile **b)** [débil] frail

fragmento *nm* fragment; [de novela etc] passage

fraile *nm* friar, monk

frambuesa *nf* raspberry

francamente *adv* frankly

francés, -esa 1. *adj* French; CULIN **tortilla francesa** plain omelette **2.** *nm, f* Frenchman, *f* Frenchwoman **3.** *nm* [idioma] French

Francia *n* France

franco, -a 1. *adj* **a)** [persona] frank **b)** COM **franco a bordo** free on board; **franco fábrica** ex-works; **puerto franco** free port **c)** *CSur, Méx* [día] **me dieron el día franco** they gave me the day off **2.** *nm Antes* [moneda] franc

francotirador, -a *nm, f* sniper

franela *nf* **a)** [tejido] flannel **b)** *Bol, Col, Ven* [camiseta - interior] *Br* vest, *US* undershirt; [exterior] T-shirt **c)** *Bol, Col, Ven* [sudadera] sweatshirt

franja *nf* [de terreno] strip; [de bandera] stripe; COST fringe, border

franqueo *nm* postage

frasco *nm* small bottle, flask

frase *nf* [oración] sentence; [expresión] phrase; **frase hecha** set phrase *o* expression

fraternal *adj* brotherly, fraternal

fraternidad *nf* brotherhood, fraternity

fraude *nm* fraud; **fraude fiscal** tax evasion

fray *nm* REL brother

frazada *nf Am* blanket

frecuencia *nf* frequency; **con frecuencia** frequently, often

frecuente *adj* frequent

fregadero *nm Esp, Méx* (kitchen) sink

fregado¹ *nm* **a)** [lavado] washing **b)** *Fam* [follón] racket

fregado², -a *adj Andes, Méx, Ven Fam* **a)** [persona - ser] annoying; **mi vecino es muy fregado** my neighbour's a real pain **b)** [persona - estar] **perdí las llaves, ¡estoy fregada!** I've lost my keys, I've had it! **c)** [objeto - roto] bust

fregar [1] *vt* **a)** [lavar] to wash; [suelo] to mop **b)** *Andes, Méx, Ven Fam* [molestar] to annoy, irritate **c)** *Andes, Méx, Ven Fam* [estropear] to bust, to break

fregón, -ona *adj Col, Ecuad, Méx* [molesto] annoying

fregona *nf Esp* mop

freír [56] *(pp frito)* **1.** *vt* to fry **2. freírse** *vpr* to fry; *Fig* **freírse de calor** to be roasting

fréjol *nm* = **frijol**

frenar *vt* to brake; *Fig* [inflación etc] to slow down; [impulsos] to restrain

frenazo *nm* sudden braking; **dar un frenazo** to jam on the brakes

frenético, -a *adj* frantic

freno *nm* **a)** brake; **pisar / soltar el freno** to press / release the brake; **freno de disco / tambor** disc / drum brake; **freno de mano** *Br* handbrake, *US* emergency brake **b)** [de caballería] bit **c)** *Fig* curb, check; **poner freno a algo** to curb sth

frente 1. *nm* front; **al frente de** at the head of; **chocar de frente** to crash head on; **hacer frente a algo** to face sth, to stand up to sth **2.** *nf* ANAT forehead; **frente a frente** face to face **3.** *adv* **frente a** in front of, opposite

fresa *nf* **a)** *Esp, CAm, Carib, Méx* [planta, fruto] strawberry **b)** TÉC milling cutter

fresco, -a 1. *adj* **a)** [frío] cool **b)** [comida, fruta] fresh **c)** [reciente] fresh, new **d)** [caradura] cheeky, forward, *US* fresh; **se quedó tan fresco** he didn't bat an eyelid; **¡qué fresco!** what a nerve! **2.** *nm* **a)** [frescor] fresh air, cool air; **al fresco** in a cool place; **hace fresco** it's chilly **b)** ARTE fresco

fresno *nm* ash tree

fresón *nm* (large) strawberry

fresquería *nf Am* soft-drinks *Br* shop o *US* store

friega *nf* **a)** [masaje] rub **b)** *Andes, Méx Fam* **dar una friega a algn** to give sb a beating

friegaplatos *nm inv* dishwasher

frigider *nm Andes* refrigerator, *Br* fridge, *US* icebox

frigorífico, -a 1. *nm Esp Br* refrigerator, *Br* fridge, *US* icebox **2.** *adj* **cámara frigorífica** cold store

frijol, fríjol, fréjol *nm Am salvo RP* bean

friki *nmf Fam* **a)** [persona extravagante] weirdo **b)** [aficionado] fan

frío, -a 1. *adj* **a)** cold **b)** [indiferente] cold, cool, indifferent; **su comentario me dejó frío** her remark left me cold **2.** *nm* cold; *Esp* **coger** o *Am* **tomar frío** to catch cold; **hace frío** it's cold

friolento, -a *adj Am* sensitive to the cold

fritada *nf* fry-up, dish of fried food

fritanga *nf* **a)** *Esp* [comida frita] fry-up **b)** *Am Despec* [comida grasienta] greasy food

frito, -a 1. *adj* **a)** CULIN fried **b)** *Fam* exasperated, fed up; **me tienes frito** I'm sick to death of you **2.** *nm* **fritos** fried food

fritura *nf* fry-up, dish of fried food

frívolo, -a *adj* frivolous

frondoso, -a *adj* leafy, luxuriant

frontera *nf* frontier

fronterizo, -a *adj* frontier, border; **países fronterizos** neighbouring countries

frontón *nm* DEP pelota

frotar 1. *vt* to rub **2. frotarse** *vpr* to rub; **frotarse las manos** to rub one's hands together

fruncir [52] *vt* **a)** COST to gather **b)** [labios] to purse, to pucker; **fruncir el ceño** to frown, to knit one's brow

frustración *nf* frustration

frustrar 1. *vt* to frustrate; [defraudar] to disappoint **2. frustrarse** *vpr* **a)** [esperanza] to fail, to go awry **b)** [persona] to be frustrated o disappointed

fruta *nf* fruit; **fruta del tiempo** fresh fruit

frutal 1. *adj* fruit; **árbol frutal** fruit tree **2.** *nm* fruit tree

frutería *nf* fruit shop

frutero, -a 1. *nm, f* fruit seller, *Br* fruiterer **2.** *nm* fruit dish o bowl

frutilla *nf Bol, CSur, Ecuad* strawberry

fruto *nm* fruit; **frutos secos** nuts; **dar fruto** to bear fruit; *Fig* [dar buen resultado] to be fruitful; **sacar fruto de algo** to profit from sth

fsta SMS *(abr de* **fiesta***)* PRT

FTP *nm* INFORM *(abr de* **File Transfer Protocol***)* FTP *(File Transfer Protocol)*

fuego *nm* **a)** fire; **fuegos artificiales** fireworks **b)** [lumbre] light; **¿me da fuego, por favor?** have you got a light, please? **c)** CULIN **a fuego lento** on a low flame; [al horno] in a slow oven

fuelle *nm* [para soplar] bellows

fuente *nf* a) fountain; *Chile, Col, Méx, Ven* **fuente de soda** [cafetería] *café or counter selling ice cream, soft drinks etc, US* soda fountain (*serving soft drinks and alcohol*) b) [recipiente] dish, serving dish c) [de información] source

fuera¹ *adv* a) outside, out; **quédate fuera** stay outside; **sal fuera** go out; **desde fuera** from (the) outside; **por fuera** on the outside; **la puerta de fuera** the outer door b) **fuera de** out of; **fuera de serie** extraordinary; *Fig* **estar fuera de sí** to be beside oneself c) DEP **el equipo de fuera** the away team; **jugar fuera** to play away; **fuera de juego** offside

fuera² 1. *subj imperf de* **ir** 2. *subj imperf de* **ser**

fuerte 1. *adj* strong; [dolor] severe; [sonido] loud; [comida] heavy; **el plato fuerte** the main course; *Fig* the most important event
2. *nm* a) [fortaleza] fort
b) [punto fuerte] forte, strong point
3. *adv* ¡abrázame fuerte! hold me tight!; **comer fuerte** to eat a lot; ¡habla más fuerte! speak up!; ¡pégale fuerte! hit him hard!

fuerza *nf* a) [fortaleza] strength; *Fig* **a fuerza de** by dint of b) [violencia] force; **a la fuerza** [por obligación] of necessity; [con violencia] by force; **por fuerza** of necessity; **fuerza mayor** force majeure c) FÍS force d) [cuerpo] force; **las fuerzas del orden** the forces of law and order; **fuerza aérea** air force; **fuerzas armadas** armed forces

fuese 1. *subj imperf de* **ir** 2. *subj imperf de* **ser**

fuete *nm Am salvo RP* whip

fuga *nf* a) [huida] escape; **darse a la fuga** to take flight b) [de gas etc] leak

fugarse [42] *vpr* to escape; **fugarse de casa** to run away from home

fugaz *adj* fleeting, brief

fugitivo, -a *nm, f* fugitive

fui 1. *pt indef de* **ir** 2. *pt indef de* **ser**

fulana *nf* whore, tart

fulano, -a *nm, f* so-and-so; [hombre] what's-his-name; [mujer] what's-her-name; **Doña Fulana de tal** Mrs So-and-so

fulminante *adj* [cese] summary; [muerte, enfermedad] sudden; [mirada] withering

fumador, -a *nm, f* smoker; **los no fumadores** nonsmokers

fumar 1. *vt & vi* to smoke; **no fumar** [en letrero] no smoking 2. **fumarse** *vpr* to smoke; **fumarse un cigarro** to smoke a cigarette

función *nf* a) function; **en función de** according to b) [cargo] duties; **entrar en funciones** to take up one's duties; **presidente en funciones** acting president c) CINE & TEATRO performance

funcionar *vi* to work; **no funciona** [en letrero] out of order

funcionario, -a *nm, f* civil servant; **funcionario público** public official

funda *nf* cover; [de gafas etc] case; [de espada] sheath; **funda de almohada** pillowcase

fundación *nf* foundation

fundador, -a *nm, f* founder

fundamental *adj* fundamental

fundamento *nm* basis, grounds; **sin fundamento** unfounded

fundar 1. *vt* a) [empresa] to found b) [teoría] to base, to found 2. **fundarse** *vpr* a) [empresa] to be founded b) [teoría] to be based (**en** on)

fundición *nf* a) [de metales] smelting b) [fábrica] foundry

fundir 1. *vt* a) to melt; [bombilla, plomos] to blow b) [unir] to unite, join 2. **fundirse** *vpr* a) [derretirse] to melt b) [bombilla, plomos] to blow c) [unirse] to merge d) *Am Fam* [arruinarse] to go bust

funeral *nm* funeral

fungir *vi Méx, Perú* to act, to serve (**de** *o* **como** as)

funicular *nm* funicular (railway)

furgón *nm* AUTO van

furgoneta *nf* van

furia *nf* fury; **ponerse hecho una furia** to become furious, to fly into a rage

furioso, -a *adj* furious; **ponerse furioso** to become furious

furor *nm* fury, rage; *Fig* **hacer furor** to be all the rage

fusible *nm* fuse

fusil *nm* gun, rifle

fusilar *vt* to shoot, to execute

fusión *nf* **a)** [de metales] fusion; [del hielo] thawing, melting; **punto de fusión** melting point **b)** COM merger

fustán *nm Am* petticoat

fútbol *nm* soccer, *Br* football

futbolín *nm Esp Br* table football, *US* foosball

futbolista *nmf* soccer *o Br* football player, *Br* footballer

futuro, -a 1. *adj* future **2.** *nm* future; **en un futuro próximo** in the near future; *CSur, Méx* **a futuro** in the future

G

g *(abr de gramo)* g

gabán *nm* overcoat

gabardina *nf* [prenda] raincoat

gabinete *nm* **a)** [despacho] study; **gabinete de abogados** lawyers' office **b)** POL cabinet

gafas *nfpl* **a)** [para ver, proteger, nadar] glasses, spectacles; **gafas bifocales / graduadas o progresivas** bifocal / varifocal glasses, bifocals / varifocals; **gafas de cerca** reading glasses; **gafas oscuras** dark glasses; **gafas de sol** sunglasses; **llevar gafas** to wear glasses **b)** [para submarinismo] goggles; **gafas submarinas** diving goggles

gafe *Esp Fam* **1.** *adj* jinxed; **ser gafe** to be jinxed **2.** *nmf* jinxed person

gafete *nm Méx* badge

gaita *nf* bagpipes

gala *nf* **a)** [vestido] full dress; **de gala** dressed up; [ciudad] decked out **b)** *Esp* [espectáculo] gala; **hacer gala de** to glory in **c)** **galas** finery

galán *nm* **a)** handsome young man; *Hum* ladies' man **b)** TEATRO leading man

galaxia *nf* galaxy

galería *nf* **a)** ARQUIT covered balcony **b)** [museo] art gallery **c)** TEATRO gallery, gods

Gales *n* **(el país de) Gales** Wales

galés, -esa 1. *adj* Welsh **2.** *nm, f* Welshman, *f* Welshwoman; **los galeses** the Welsh **3.** *nm* [idioma] Welsh

Galicia *n* Galicia

gallego, -a 1. *adj* **a)** Galician **b)** *CSur, Cuba Fam* sometimes pejorative term used to refer to a Spanish person **2.** *nm, f* **a)** Galician, native of Galicia **b)** *CSur, Cuba Fam* sometimes pejorative term used to refer to a Spaniard, especially an immigrant **3.** *nm* [idioma] Galician

galleta *nf* **a)** CULIN *Br* biscuit, *US* cookie **b)** *Esp Fam* [cachete] slap

gallina 1. *nf* hen **2.** *nmf Fam* coward, chicken

gallinero *nm* **a)** hen run **b)** TEATRO **el gallinero** the gods

gallineta *nf Am* guinea fowl

gallo *nm* **a)** cock, rooster; *Fam & Fig* **en menos que un canto de gallo** before you could say Jack Robinson **b)** *Fam* MÚS off-key note

galopar *vi* to gallop

galope *nm* gallop; **a galope tendido** flat out

galpón *nm Andes, Carib, RP* shed

gama *nf* range; MÚS scale

gamba *nf* prawn, *US* shrimp

gamberro, -a *Esp* **1.** *nm, f* hooligan, lout, *Br* yob **2.** *adj* loutish

gamonal *nm Andes, CAm, Ven* **a)** [cacique] village, chief **b)** [caudillo] cacique, local political boss

gamuza *nf* **a)** ZOOL chamois **b)** [trapo] chamois *o* shammy leather

gana *nf* **a)** [deseo] wish (**de** for); **de buena gana** willingly; **de mala gana** reluctantly; *Fam* **no me da la gana** I don't feel like it **b)** **tener ganas de (hacer) algo** to feel like (doing) sth; **quedarse con las ganas** not to manage **c)** [apetito] appetite; **comer con ganas** to eat heartily

ganadería *nf* **a)** [crianza] livestock farming **b)** [conjunto de ganado] livestock

ganadero, -a *nm, f* livestock farmer

ganado *nm* **a)** livestock **b)** *Fam & Fig* [gente] crowd

ganador, -a 1. *adj* winning **2.** *nm, f* winner

ganancia *nf* profit

ganar 1. *vt* **a)** [sueldo] to earn **b)** [victoria] to win **c)** [aventajar] to beat **d)** [alcanzar] to reach **e)** [ser superior] **me ganas en astucia** you're more cunning than I am **2.** *vi* to gain; **gana con el trato** he's nice when you get to know him; **gana para vivir** he just earns enough to live on; **hemos ganado con el cambio** the exchange rate has worked out in our *Br* favour o *US* favor; **ganamos en espacio** we've gained more space **3. ganarse** *vpr* **a)** to earn; **ganarse el pan** to earn one's daily bread **b)** [merecer] to deserve; *Esp Fam* **ganarse algo** to win sth; [merecer] to earn sth, to deserve sth; [recibir] to win sth; **ganarse a algn** to win sb over; **ganársela** to get it; **se lo ha ganado** he deserves it; **como no te estés quieto, te la vas a ganar** if you don't stay still, you're going to get it

ganchillo *nm* crochet work

gancho *nm* **a)** hook **b)** *Fam & Fig* [gracia, atractivo] charm **c)** *Andes, CAm, Méx* [horquilla] hairpin **d)** *Andes, CAm, Méx, Ven* [percha] hanger **e)** *Col, Ven* [pinza] *Br* (clothes) peg, *US* clothes pin

gandul, -a *nm, f* loafer

ganga *nf* bargain

ganso, -a 1. *nm, f* **a)** goose; [macho] gander **b)** *Fam* dolt **2.** *adj* *Fam* ginormous; **pasta gansa** bread, dough

gánster *(pl* **gánsters** *o* **gánsteres)** *nm* gangster

garabato *nm* scrawl

garaje *nm* garage

garantía *nf* **a)** guarantee **b)** *JUR* [fianza] bond, security

garbanzo *nm* chickpea

garfio *nm* hook, grappling iron

garganta *nf* **a)** throat **b)** [desfiladero] narrow pass

gargantilla *nf* short necklace

gárgaras *nfpl* gargling (*sing*); *Fam* **¡vete a hacer gárgaras!** get lost!

gárgola *nf* [de catedral] gargoyle

garra *nf* **a)** *ZOOL* claw; [de ave] talon **b)** *Fig* [fuerza] force; **tener garra** to be compelling

garrafa *nf* carafe

garrapata *nf* tick

garúa *nf* *Andes, RP, Ven* drizzle

gas *nm* **a)** gas; *Esp* **gas ciudad** town gas; **gases (nocivos)** fumes; **gas de escape** exhaust fumes **b)** [en bebida] fizz; **agua con gas** fizzy water **c)** *MED* **gases** flatulence

gasa *nf* gauze

gaseosa *nf* **a)** *Esp, Arg* [bebida transparente] pop, *Br* lemonade **b)** *CAm, RP* [refresco con gas] fizzy drink, *US* soda

gaseoso, -a *adj* [estado] gaseous; [bebida] fizzy

gasfitero, -a *nm, f* *Ecuad* plumber

gasóleo, gasoil *nm* diesel oil

gasolina *nf* *Br* petrol, *US* gas, *US* gasoline

gasolinera, *Méx* **gasolinería** *nf* *Br* petrol o *US* gas station

gastar 1. *vt* **a)** [consumir - dinero, tiempo] to spend; [gasolina, electricidad] to consume **b)** *Fig* [malgastar] to waste **c)** *Esp* [ropa] to wear; **¿qué número gastas?** what size do you take? **d) gastar una broma a algn** to play a practical joke on sb **2. gastarse** *vpr* **a)** [zapatos etc] to wear out **b)** [gasolina etc] to run out

gasto *nm* expenditure; **gastos** expenses; **gastos de viaje** travelling expenses

gastritis *nf inv* *MED* gastritis

gastronomía *nf* gastronomy

gastronómico *nf* gastronomy

gatear *vi* **a)** to crawl **b)** [trepar] to climb

gatillo *nm* [de armas] trigger; **apretar el gatillo** to pull the trigger

gato, -a 1. *nm, f* **a)** [animal] cat **b)** *Fam* **dar gato por liebre a algn** to be had, to be conned; **buscar tres pies al gato** to look for complications, to nit-pick; **hay gato encerrado** it smells a bit fishy **2.** *nm* AUTO & TÉC jack

gauchada *nf CSur* favour

gaucho, -a 1. *adj RP Fam* [servicial] helpful, obliging **2.** *nm, f* gaucho

gaveta *nf* drawer

gavilán *nm* ORNIT sparrowhawk

gaviota *nf* seagull

gazpacho *nm* CULIN gazpacho

gel *nm* gel; **gel (de ducha)** shower gel

gelatina *nf* [de carne] gelatine; [de fruta] *Br* jelly, *US* Jell-O®

gemelo, -a *adj* & *nm, f* (identical) twin ■ **gemelos** *nmpl* **a)** [de camisa] cufflinks **b)** [anteojos] binoculars

gemido *nm* groan

geminiano, -a *nm, f Am* Gemini

Géminis *nmf* Gemini

gemir [6] *vi* to groan

generación *nf* generation

generador *nm* ELEC generator

general 1. *adj* general; **por lo o en general** in general, generally **2.** *nm* MIL & REL general

generalizado, -a *adj* widespread, commonly-held

generalizar [40] **1.** *vt* **a)** to generalize **b)** [extender] to spread **2. generalizarse** *vpr* to become widespread o common

generalmente *adv* generally

generar *vt* to generate

género *nm* **a)** [clase] kind, sort **b)** ARTE & LITER genre **c)** [mercancía] article **d)** LING gender **e)** BIOL genus; **el género humano** mankind

generosidad *nf* generosity

generoso, -a *adj* **a)** generous (**con** to) **b)** [vino] full-bodied

genial *adj* great, *Br* brilliant

genio *nm* **a)** [carácter] temperament; [mal carácter] temper; **estar de mal genio** to be in a bad mood **b)** [facultad] genius

genital *adj* genital ■ **genitales** *nmpl* genitals

gente *nf* **a)** people (*sing*) **b)** [familia] folks (*sing*)

gentil *adj* **a)** [amable] kind **b)** [pagano] pagan

gentileza *nf* kindness; *Formal* **por gentileza de** by courtesy of

genuino, -a *adj* [puro] genuine; [verdadero] authentic

geografía *nf* geography

geolocalización *nf* geolocation

geolocalizar *vt* to geolocate

geometría *nf* geometry

geométrico, -a *adj* geometric

geranio *nm* geranium

gerente *nmf* manager

geriátrico *nm* retirement home

germen *nm también Fig* germ

gestante *nf* expectant mother

gestión *nf* **a)** [administración] management **b) gestiones** [negociaciones] negotiations; [trámites] formalities

gestionar *vt* to take steps to acquire o obtain; [negociar] to negotiate

gesto *nm* **a)** [mueca] face **b)** [con las manos] gesture

gestor, -a *nm, f* person who carries out dealings with public bodies on behalf of private customers or companies, combining the roles of solicitor and accountant

gestoría *nf* office of a "gestor"

Gibraltar *n* Gibraltar; **el peñón de Gibraltar** the Rock of Gibraltar

gibraltareño, -a 1. *adj* of /from Gibraltar **2.** *nm, f* Gibraltarian

gigante, -a 1. *nm, f* giant **2.** *adj* giant, enormous

gigantesco, -a *adj* gigantic

gil, -a *nm, f CSur Fam* jerk, *Br* twit

gilipuertas *muy Fam* **1.** *adj inv* idiotic **2.** *nmf inv* jerk

gimnasia *nf* gymnastics

gimnasio *nm* gymnasium

gimnasta *nmf* gymnast

ginebra *nf* [bebida] gin

ginecólogo, -a *nm, f* gynaecologist

gin-tonic, gintonic [jin'tonik] *(pl* **gin-tonics** *o* **gintonics)** *nm* gin and tonic

gira *nf* TEATRO & MÚS tour

girar 1. *vi* **a)** [dar vueltas] to spin **b)** girar a la derecha / izquierda to turn right / left **2.** *vt* **a)** FIN [expedir] to draw **b)** [dinero] to transfer **3. girarse** *vpr* to turn around

girasol *nm* sunflower

giro *nm* **a)** [vuelta] turn **b)** [de acontecimientos] direction **c)** [frase] turn of phrase **d)** FIN draft; **giro telegráfico** money order; **giro postal** postal *o* money order

gis *nm* Méx chalk

gitano, -a *adj & nm, f* gypsy, gipsy

glaciar *nm* glacier

glándula *nf* gland

global *adj* comprehensive; **precio global** all-inclusive price

globo *nm* **a)** balloon **b)** [esfera] globe **c)** [lámpara] globe, glass lampshade

glóbulo *nm* globule

gloria *nf* **a)** [fama] glory **b)** REL heaven; Fam & Fig estar en la gloria to be in seventh heaven **c)** Fam [delicia] delight; es una gloria verte it's a real pleasure to see you; saber a gloria to be delicious

glorieta *nf* **a)** [plazoleta] small square **b)** Esp [rotonda] Br roundabout, US traffic circle **c)** [en un jardín] arbour

glorioso, -a *adj* glorious

glotón, -ona 1. *adj* greedy **2.** *nm, f* glutton

glucosa *nf* QUÍM glucose

gluten *nm* gluten

gobernador, -a 1. *adj* governing **2.** *nm, f* governor; Esp **gobernador civil** ≃ prefect

gobernante *adj* ruling

gobernar [1] **1.** *vt* to govern; [un país] to rule **2.** *vi* NÁUT to steer

gobiernista Andes, Méx **1.** *adj* government **2.** *nmf* government supporter

gobierno *nm* **a)** POL government **b)** [mando] running **c)** NÁUT steering **d)** NÁUT [timón] rudder

goce *nm* enjoyment

godo, -a 1. *adj* Gothic **2.** *nm, f* HIST Goth

gofio *nm* Andes, Carib, RP [harina] roasted maize *o* US corn meal

gol *nm* goal

goleador, -a *nm, f* goal scorer

golf *nm* golf; **palo de golf** golf club

golfo¹, a 1. *nm* [gamberro] lout, Br yob; [pillo] rogue, wide boy **2.** *nf* Fam & Despec tart

golfo² *nm* GEOGR gulf; **el golfo Pérsico** the Persian Gulf

golondrina *nf* swallow

golosina *nf* Br sweet, US candy

goloso, -a *adj* sweet-toothed

golpe *nm* **a)** blow; [llamada] knock; [puñetazo] punch; **de golpe** all of a sudden; **de golpe y porrazo** suddenly, unexpectedly; **golpe de estado** coup d'état; **golpe de suerte** stroke of luck; **golpe de vista** glance; **no dar ni golpe** not to lift a finger **b)** AUTO bump **c)** [desgracia] blow; **un duro golpe** a great blow **d)** [de humor] witticism

golpear 1. *vt* **a)** [objeto] to bang **b)** [persona] to hit **c)** [con el puño] to punch; [cabeza, puerta] to bang **2.** *vi* [dar golpes] to bang **3. golpearse** *vpr* [recibir un golpe] to hit, to bang; **se golpeó en la cabeza** he hit his head

golpiza *nf* Am beating

goma *nf* **a)** rubber; **goma de pegar** glue; **goma de borrar** eraser, Br rubber **b)** [elástica] rubber *o* Br elastic band **c)** Cuba, CSur [neumático] tyre **d)** Fam [preservativo] rubber

gomería *nf* CSur tyre centre

gomero *nm* CSur [planta] rubber plant

gomina *nf* hair cream

góndola *nf* **a)** [embarcación] gondola **b)** Perú [autobús interurbano] (intercity) bus **c)** Bol [autobús urbano] city bus **d)** [en supermercado] gondola

gordo, -a 1. *adj* **a)** [carnoso] fat **b)** [grueso] thick **c)** [importante] big; **me cae gordo** I can't stand him; **de gordo** in a big way **2.** *nm, f* **a)** fat person; *Fam* fatty **b)** *Am Fam* [como apelativo] **¿cómo estás, gordo?** how's it going, big man? **3.** *nm* **el gordo** [de lotería] the jackpot

gordura *nf* fatness

gorila *nm* **a)** [animal] gorilla **b)** *Esp Fig* [en discoteca etc] bouncer

gorjear *vi* [ave] to chirp

gorjeo *nm* chirping

gorra *nf* cap; [con visera] peaked cap; *Esp, Méx Fam* **de gorra** for free

gorrión *nm* sparrow

gorro *nm* **a)** cap **b)** *Fam* **estar hasta el gorro (de)** to be up to here (with)

gorrón, -ona 1. *adj Esp, Méx Fam* **ser gorrón** [aprovechado] to be a scrounger **2.** *nm, f Esp, Méx* scrounger

gorronear *vt Esp, Méx Fam* to scrounge, to sponge; **gorronear cigarros** to scrounge cigarettes

gota *nf* **a)** drop; [de sudor] bead; **gota a gota** drop by drop; **ni gota** not a bit **b)** MED gout

gotera *nf* leak

gótico, -a *adj* Gothic

gozar [40] **1.** *vt* to enjoy **2.** *vi* [disfrutar] **gozar (de)** to enjoy

gozo *nm* pleasure

grabación *nf* recording

grabado *nm* **a)** [arte] engraving **b)** [dibujo] drawing

grabar *vt* **a)** [sonidos, imágenes] to record **b)** INFORM to save **c)** ARTE to engrave

gracia *nf* **a)** [atractivo] grace **b)** [chiste] joke; **hacer** *o* **tener gracia** to be funny **c)** [indulto] pardon **d)** ¡**gracias!** thanks!; **dar las gracias** to thank, to say thank you; **gracias a** thanks to; ¡**muchas gracias!** thank you very much!

gracioso, -a 1. *adj* **a)** [divertido] funny **b)** [garboso] graceful **2.** *nm, f* TEATRO comic character

grada *nf* **a)** [peldaño] step **b)** **gradas** [en estadio] terraces

gradería *nf* **a)** [peldaños] steps (*pl*) **b)** *Esp* [de estadio, teatro] rows (*pl*); [de plaza de toros] stands (*pl*)

graderío *nm* **a)** [peldaños] steps (*pl*) **b)** *Esp* [de estadio, teatro] rows (*pl*); [de plaza de toros] stands (*pl*); DEP terraces (*pl*)

gradiente 1. *nm* gradient **2.** *nf* *CSur, Ecuad* gradient, slope

grado *nm* **a)** [unidad] degree **b)** MIL rank **c)** **de buen grado** willingly, gladly

graduación *nf* **a)** grading **b)** MIL rank

graduado, -a *nm, f* graduate

gradual *adj* gradual

gradualmente *adv* gradually

graduar [30] **1.** *vt* **a)** EDUC to confer a degree on **b)** MIL to confer a rank on, to commission **c)** [regular] to regulate **2. graduarse** *vpr* **a)** EDUC & MIL to graduate **b)** **graduarse la vista** to have one's eyes tested

graffiti *nm* piece of graffiti

grafía *nf* written symbol

gráfico, -a 1. *adj* graphic; **diseño gráfico** graphic design **2.** *nm* graph

gragea *nf* MED pill

grajo, -a 1. *nm, f* ORNIT rook **2.** *nm* *Andes, Carib Fam* [olor] BO, body odour

gramática *nf* grammar

gramatical *adj* grammatical

gramínea *nf* grass

gramo *nm* gram, gramme

gran = **grande**

granada *nf* **a)** [fruto] pomegranate **b)** MIL grenade

Granada *n* **a)** [en España] Granada **b)** [en las Antillas] Grenada

granate 1. *adj inv* [color] maroon **2.** *nm* [color] maroon

grande *adj* **a)** [tamaño] big, large; *Fig* [persona] great; **Gran Bretaña** Great

Britain **b)** [cantidad] large; **vivir a lo grande** to live in style; *Fig* **pasarlo en grande** to have a great time

> **gran** is used instead of **grande** before masculine singular nouns (e.g. **gran hombre** great man).

grandeza *nf* **a)** [importancia] greatness **b)** [grandiosidad] grandeur; **delirios de grandeza** delusions of grandeur

grandioso, -a *adj* grandiose

granel *nm* **a granel** [sin envase] loose; [en gran cantidad] in bulk; [en abundancia] in abundance; **vender/comprar vino a granel** to sell / buy wine from the barrel

granero *nm* AGRIC granary

granito *nm* granite

granizada *nf* hailstorm

granizado *nm* drink of flavoured crushed ice

granizar [40] *v impers* to hail

granja *nf* farm

granjearse *vpr* **a)** [admiración, simpatía] to earn **b)** [desprecio, desconfianza] to engender

granjero, -a *nm, f* farmer

grano *nm* **a)** grain; [de café] bean; **ir al grano** to get to the point **b)** [espinilla] spot

granuja *nm* **a)** [pilluelo] ragamuffin **b)** [estafador] con-man

gránulo *nm* granule

grapa *nf* **a)** staple **b)** CONSTR cramp **c)** *CSur* [bebida] grappa

grapadora *nf* stapler

grapar *vt* to staple

grasa *nf* grease

grasiento, -a *adj* greasy

graso, -a *adj* [pelo] greasy; [materia] fatty

gratificar [44] *vt* **a)** [satisfacer] to gratify **b)** [recompensar] to reward

gratinado *adj* CULIN au gratin

gratinar *vt* CULIN to cook au gratin

gratis *adj inv & adv* free

gratitud *nf* gratitude

grato, -a *adj* pleasant

gratuidad *nf* **garantizar la gratuidad de algo** to guarantee that sth is free

gratuito, -a *adj* **a)** [de balde] free (of charge) **b)** [arbitrario] gratuitous

grave *adj* **a)** [importante] serious **b)** [muy enfermo] seriously ill **c)** [voz, nota] low

gravedad *nf* **a)** [seriedad, importancia] seriousness **b)** FÍS gravity

gravilla *nf* chippings

Grecia *n* Greece

gremio *nm* **a)** HIST guild **b)** [profesión] profession, trade

greña *nf* lock of entangled hair; *Fam* **andar a la greña** to squabble

griego, -a *adj & nm, f* Greek

grieta *nf* crack; [en la piel] chap

grifero, -a *nm, f Perú Br* petrol pump attendant, *US* gas pump attendant

grifo *nm* **a)** *Esp* [llave] *Br* tap, *US* faucet **b)** *Perú* [gasolinera] *Br* petrol station, *US* gas station

grill [gril] *(pl* **grills***) nm* grill

grillo *nm* cricket

gringo, -a *Fam* **1.** *adj* **a)** [estadounidense] gringo, American **b)** *Am* [extranjero] gringo, foreign **2.** *nm, f* **a)** [estadounidense] gringo, American **b)** *Am* [extranjero] gringo, foreigner *(from a non-Spanish speaking country)*

gripa *nf Col, Méx* flu

gripal *adj* flu

gripe *nf* flu; **gripe aviar** *o* **aviaria** bird flu, avian flu

gris *adj & nm* grey

gritar *vt & vi* to shout

grito *nm* shout; **a voz en grito** at the top of one's voice

grosella *nf* [fruto] redcurrant; **grosella negra** blackcurrant; **grosella silvestre** gooseberry

grosería *nf* **a)** [ordinariez] rude word *o* expression **b)** [rusticidad] rudeness

grosero, -a *adj* [tosco] coarse; [maleducado] rude

grosor *nm* thickness

grotesco, -a *adj* grotesque

grúa *nf* a) CONSTR crane b) AUTO *Br* breakdown van o truck, *US* tow truck

grueso, -a 1. *adj* thick; [persona] stout **2.** *nm* [parte principal] bulk

grumo *nm* lump; [de leche] curd

gruñido *nm* grunt

gruñir *vi* to grunt

grupa *nf* hindquarters

grupo *nm* a) group; INFORM **grupo de noticias** newsgroup b) TÉC unit, set

gruta *nf* cave

guaca *nf* a) *Am* [sepultura] pre-Columbian Indian tomb b) *Am* [tesoro] hidden treasure c) *CRica, Cuba* [hucha] moneybox

guacal *nm* a) *CAm, Méx* [calabaza] gourd b) *Carib, Col, Méx* [jaula] cage

guacamayo *nm* macaw

guacamol, guacamole *nm* guacamole, avocado dip

guachada *nf Am Fam* dirty trick

guachafita *nf Col, Ven Fam* racket, uproar

guachimán *nm Am* night watchman

guacho, -a *adj & nm, f Andes, RP* a) *muy Fam* [persona huérfana] orphan b) *Fam* [sinvergüenza] bastard, swine

guaco *nm Am* [cerámica] pottery object found in pre-Columbian Indian tomb

guagua *nf* a) *Andes* [niño] baby b) *Cuba, PRico, RDom* bus

guajiro, -a *nm, f* a) *Cuba Fam* [campesino] peasant b) [de Guajira] person from Guajira *(Colombia, Venezuela)*

guajolote *nm CAm, Méx* a) [pavo] turkey b) [tonto] fool, idiot

guampa *nf Bol, CSur* horn

guampudo, -a *adj Am* cuckolded, deceived

guanábana *nm Am* soursop

guanajo *nm Carib* turkey

guante *nm* glove

guantera *nf* AUTO glove compartment

guapo, -a *adj* a) *esp Esp* [atractivo] good-looking; [hombre] handsome; [mujer] pretty b) *Am* [valiente] gutsy; **ser guapo** to have guts

guaraca *nf Am* sling

guarache *nm Méx* [sandalia] *crude sandal with a sole made from a tyre*

guarangada *nf Bol, CSur* rude remark

guarango, -a *adj Bol, CSur* rude

guarapo *nm Am* a) [zumo] guarapo juice *(extracted from sugarcane)* b) [bebida alcohólica] *alcoholic drink based on fermented sugarcane*

guarapón *nm Andes* large-brimmed hat

guardabarros *nm inv Esp, Bol, RP* [de vehículo] *Br* mudguard, *US* fender

guardacoches *nmf inv* parking attendant

guardaespaldas *nmf inv* bodyguard

guardafango *nm inv Andes, CAm, Carib* [de automóvil, bicicleta] *Br* mudguard, *US* fender

guardameta *nmf* DEP goalkeeper

guardapolvo *nm* overalls

guardar 1. *vt* a) [conservar] to keep b) [un secreto] to keep; **guardar silencio** to remain silent; **guardar cama** to stay in bed c) [poner en un sitio] to put away d) [reservar] to keep e) INFORM to save **2. guardarse** *vpr* **guardarse de hacer algo** [abstenerse] to be careful not to do sth; **guardársela a algn** to have it in for sb

guardarropa *nm* a) [cuarto] cloakroom b) [armario] wardrobe

guardavallas *nmf inv Am* goalkeeper *m*

guardavida *nmf RP* lifeguard

guardería *nf* **guardería infantil** nursery (school)

guardia 1. *nf* a) [vigilancia] watch b) **la Guardia Civil** the civil guard c) [turno de servicio] duty; MIL guard duty; **de**

guardia on duty ; **farmacia de guardia** duty chemist **2.** *nmf* policeman, *f* policewoman

guardián, -ana *nm, f* [de persona] guardian ; [de finca] keeper

guarida *nf* [de animal] lair ; [refugio] hide-out

guarnición *nf* **a)** CULIN garnish **b)** MIL garrison

guarrada *nf Esp Fam* **a)** [cosa sucia, grosería, indecencia] filth **b)** *Despec* [mala jugada] dirty trick

guarro, -a *Esp Fam* **1.** *adj* filthy **2.** *nm, f* pig

guarura *nm Méx Fam* bodyguard

guasa *nf* mockery

guasca *nf Chile, Perú* whip

guaso, -a *adj* **a)** *Chile* [campesino] peasant **b)** *Andes, RP* **ser un guaso** [grosero] to be crude o coarse ; [maleducado] to be rude

guata *nf* **a)** [relleno] padding **b)** *Andes Fam* [barriga] belly

Guatemala *n* **a)** [país] Guatemala **b)** [ciudad] Guatemala City

guatemalteco, -a *adj & nm, f* Guatemalan

guay *Esp Fam* **1.** *adj* cool, mad ; **tope guay** really cool, mad **2.** *adv* **¡lo pasamos guay!** we had a brilliant time! **3.** *interj* [genial] great!, cool!

guayaba *nf* [fruta] guava

guayabera *nf CAm, Carib, Col* guayabera *(lightweight safari-style shirt)*

guayabo, -a 1. *nm, f Am Fam* handsome young man, *f* pretty young girl **2.** *nm* [árbol] guava tree

güero, -a *Méx Fam* **1.** *adj* blond, *f* blonde **2.** *nm, f* [rubio] blond-haired man, *f* blonde-haired woman, blonde

guerra *nf* war; **en guerra** at war; **guerra bacteriológica** germ warfare ; **guerra civil /fría /mundial /nuclear** civil /cold /world /nuclear war ; *Fam* **dar guerra** to be a real nuisance

guerrero, -a 1. *nm, f* warrior **2.** *adj* warlike

guerrilla *nf* **a)** [partida armada] guerrilla force o band **b)** [lucha] guerrilla warfare

guerrillero, -a 1. *adj* guerrilla ; **ataque guerrillero** guerrilla attack **2.** *nm, f* guerrilla

güevón = **huevón**

guía 1. *nmf* [persona] guide **2.** *nf* **a)** [norma] guideline **b)** [libro] guide ; [lista] directory; *Esp, RP* **guía telefónica o de teléfonos** telephone directory

guiar [29] **1.** *vt* **a)** [indicar el camino] to guide **b)** AUTO to drive ; NÁUT to steer ; [caballo, bici] to ride **2. guiarse** *vpr* **guiarse por** to be guided by, to go by

guijarro *nm* pebble

guillotina *nf* guillotine

guinda *nf* [fruto] morello (cherry)

guindilla *nf* chilli

guineo *nm Andes, CAm* banana

guiñar *vt* to wink

guiñol *nm* puppet theatre

guión *nm* **a)** CINE & TV script **b)** LING hyphen, dash **c)** [esquema] sketch

guionista *nmf* scriptwriter

guiri *Fam & Despec* **1.** *adj Esp* foreign **2.** *nmf* foreigner, tourist

guiri *nmf Esp Fam* foreigner

guirigay *nm Esp Fam* **a)** [jaleo] ruckus **b)** [lenguaje] gibberish

guirnalda *nf* garland

guisado *nm* CULIN stew

guisante *nm esp Esp* pea

guisar *vt* to cook

guiso *nm* dish ; [guisado] stew

guita *nf Esp, RP Fam* [dinero] dough

guitarra 1. *nf* guitar **2.** *nmf* guitarist

guitarreada *nf CSur* singalong *(to guitars)*

guitarrista *nmf* guitarist

gurí, -isa *nm, f RP Fam* [niño] kid, child ; [chico] lad, boy ; [chica] lass, girl

gusano *nm* worm; [oruga] caterpillar; *Fam & Despec* [exiliado cubano] *anti-Castro Cuban living in exile*; **gusano de seda** silkworm

gustar 1. *vt* **a)** **me gusta el vino** I like wine; **me gustaban los caramelos** I used to like sweets; **me gusta nadar** I like swimming; **me gustaría ir** I would like to go **b)** *Formal* **¿gustas?** would you like some?; **cuando gustes** whenever you like **2.** *vi* **gustar de** to enjoy

gusto *nm* **a)** [sentido] taste **b)** [en fórmulas de cortesía] **con (mucho) gusto** with (great) pleasure; **tanto gusto** pleased to meet you **c)** **estar a gusto** to feel comfortable o at ease; **por gusto** for the sake of it; **ser de buen / mal gusto** to be in good / bad taste; **tener buen / mal gusto** to have good / bad taste

gustosamente *adv* gladly

H

ha *(abr de* **hectárea)** ha *(hectare)*

haba *nf* broad bean

Takes the masculine articles **el** and **un**.

habano *nm* Havana cigar

haber [14] **1.** *v aux* **a)** (en tiempos compuestos) to have; **lo he visto** I have seen it; **ya lo había hecho** he had already done it
b) **haber de** (+ *infinitivo*) [obligación] to have to; **has de ser bueno** you must be good
2. (*special form of present tense:* **hay)** *v impers* **a)** (*singular used also with plural nouns*) [existir, estar] **hay** there is /are; **había** there was /were; **había un gato en el tejado** there was a cat on the roof; **había muchos libros** there were a lot of books; **hay 500 km entre Madrid y Granada** it's 500 km from Madrid to Granada
b) **haber que** (+ *infinitivo*) it is necessary to; **hay que trabajar** you've got too you must work; **habrá que comprobarlo** we will have to check it
c) [tener lugar] **habrá una fiesta** there will be a party; **hoy hay partido** there's a match today; **los accidentes habidos en esta carretera** the accidents which have happened on this road
d) **había una vez ...** once upon a time ...; **no hay de qué** you're welcome, don't mention it; **¿qué hay?** how are things?
3. **haberse** *vpr* **habérselas con algn** to have it out with sb
4. *nm* **a)** FIN credit; **haberes** assets
b) **en su haber** in his possession

habichuela *nf Esp, Carib, Col* bean

hábil *adj* **a)** [diestro] skilful **b)** [astuto] smart **c)** **días hábiles** working days

habilidad *nf* **a)** [destreza] skill **b)** [astucia] cleverness

habiloso, -a *adj Chile* shrewd, astute

habitación *nf* [cuarto] room; [dormitorio] bedroom; **habitación individual/doble** single /double room

habitacional *adj CSur, Méx* housing; **un complejo habitacional** a housing complex

habitante *nmf* inhabitant

habitar 1. *vt* to live in, to inhabit **2.** *vi* to live

hábito *nm* **a)** [costumbre] habit **b)** REL habit

habitual *adj* usual, habitual; [cliente, lector] regular

hablado, -a *adj* **bien hablado** well-spoken, polite; **mal hablado** foul-mouthed

hablador, -a *adj* [parlanchín] talkative; [chismoso] gossipy

habladuría *nf* [rumor] rumour; [chisme] piece of gossip

hablante *nmf* speaker

hablar 1. *vi* **a)** to speak, to talk; **hablar con algn** to speak to sb
b) **¡ni hablar!** certainly not!; *Fam* **¡quién fue a hablar!** look who's talking!
2. *vt* **a)** [idioma] to speak; **habla alemán** he speaks German
b) [tratar un asunto] to talk over, to discuss
3. **hablarse** *vpr* **a)** to speak *o* talk to one another
b) **se habla español** [en letrero] Spanish spoken

hacendado, -a *nm, f* **a)** [terrateniente] landowner **b)** *CSur* [ganadero] rancher

hacer [15] **1.** *vt* **a)** [crear, producir, fabricar] to make; **hacer una casa** to build a house

b) [obrar, ejecutar] to do ; **eso no se hace** it isn't done ; **hazme un favor** do me a favour ; **¿qué haces?** [en este momento] what are you doing? ; **tengo mucho que hacer** I have a lot to do ; **hacer deporte** to do sports ; **hacer una carrera / medicina** to do a degree / medicine

c) [conseguir - amigos, dinero] to make

d) [obligar] to make ; **hazle callar / trabajar** make him shut up / work

e) [arreglar] to make ; **hacer la cama** to make the bed

f) MAT [sumar] to make ; **y con éste hacen cien** and that makes a hundred

g) [dar aspecto] to make look ; **el negro le hace más delgado** black makes him look slimmer

h) [sustituyendo a otro verbo] to do ; **ya no puedo leer como solía hacerlo** I can't read as well as I used to

i) [representar] to play

j) **¡bien hecho!** well done!

2. *vi* **a)** [actuar] **hacer de** to play ; **hizo de Desdémona** she played Desdemona

b) **hacer por** o **para** (+ *infinitivo*) to try to ; **hice por venir** I tried to come

c) [fingir] to pretend ; **hacer como si** to act as if

d) [convenir] to be suitable ; **a las ocho si te hace** will eight o'clock be all right for you?

3. *v impers* **a)** **hace calor / frío** it's hot / cold

b) [tiempo transcurrido] ago ; **hace mucho (tiempo)** a long time ago ; **hace dos días que no le veo** I haven't seen him for two days ; **hace dos años que vivo en Glasgow** I've been living in Glasgow for two years

4. **hacerse** *vpr* **a)** [volverse] to become, to grow ; **hacerse viejo** to grow old

b) [simular] to pretend ; **hacerse el dormido** to pretend to be sleeping

c) **hacerse con** [apropiarse] to get hold of

d) **hacerse a** [habituarse] to get used to ; **enseguida me hago a todo** I soon get used to anything

hacha *nf* **a)** [herramienta] axe **b)** *Fam* **ser un hacha en algo** to be an ace o a wizard at sth

Takes the masculine articles **el** and **un**.

hachís *nm* hashish

hacia *prep* **a)** [dirección] towards, to ; **hacia abajo** down, downwards ; **hacia adelante** forwards ; **hacia arriba** up, upwards ; **hacia atrás** back, backwards **b)** [tiempo] at about, at around ; **hacia las tres** at about three o'clock

hacienda *nf* **a)** [finca] country estate o property **b)** FIN (**el Ministerio de**) **Hacienda** ≃ *Br* the Treasury, ≃ *US* the Department of the Treasury

hada *nf* fairy ; **cuento de hadas** fairy tale ; **hada madrina** fairy godmother

Takes the masculine articles **el** and **un**.

Haití *n* Haiti

hala *interj Esp* [para dar ánimo, prisa] come on! ; [para expresar incredulidad] no!, you're joking! ; [para expresar admiración, sorpresa] wow!

halago *nm* flattery

halal *adj* halal

halcón *nm* falcon ; **halcón peregrino** peregrine (falcon)

hall [xol] *(pl* **halls***) nm* entrance hall, foyer

hallar 1. *vt* [encontrar] to find ; [averiguar] to find out ; [descubrir] to discover **2. hallarse** *vpr* [estar] to be, to find oneself ; [estar situado] to be situated

halógeno, -a *adj* QUÍM halogenous

halterofilia *nf* weightlifting

hamaca *nf* hammock ; [mecedora] rocking-chair

hambre *nf* [apetito] hunger ; [inanición] starvation ; [catástrofe] famine ; **tener hambre** to be hungry

Takes the masculine articles **el** and **un**.

hambriento, -a *adj* starving

hambruna *nf* famine

hamburguesa *nf* hamburger, *Br* beefburger

hámster ['xamster] *(pl* **hámsters)** *nm* hamster

hangar *nm* hangar

hardware ['xarwer] *nm* INFORM hardware

harina *nf* flour

hartar 1. *vt* **a)** [cansar, fastidiar] to annoy **b)** [atiborrar] to satiate; **el dulce harta enseguida** sweet things soon fill you up **2. hartarse** *vpr* **a)** [saciar el apetito] to eat one's fill **b)** [cansarse] to get fed up (**de** with), to grow tired (**de** of)

harto, -a 1. *adj* **a)** [de comida] full **b)** [cansado] fed up; **¡me tienes harto!** I'm fed up with you!; **estoy harto de trabajar** I'm fed up working **c)** *Am salvo RP* [mucho] lots of; **tiene harto dinero** he's got lots of money **2.** *adv* **a)** *Esp Formal* [muy] very **b)** *Am salvo RP* [muy, mucho] really

hasta 1. *prep* **a)** [lugar] up to, as far as, down to **b)** [tiempo] until, till, up to; **hasta el domingo** until Sunday; **hasta el final** right to the end; **hasta la fecha** up to now; **hasta luego** see you later **c)** [con cantidad] up to, as many as **d)** [incluso] even **e)** *CAm, Col, Ecuad, Méx* [no antes de] **pintaremos la casa hasta fin de mes** we won't paint the house till the end of the month **2.** *conj* **hasta que** until

haya¹ *nf* **a)** BOT [árbol] beech **b)** [madera] beech (wood)

haya² *subj pres de* **haber**

haz¹ *nm* **a)** AGRIC sheaf **b)** [de luz] shaft

haz² *nf* [de hoja] top side

haz³ *imperat de* **hacer**

hazaña *nf* deed, exploit

he¹ *adv* **he ahí/aquí ...** there/here you have ...

he² *indic pres de* **haber**

heavy ['xeβi] **1.** *adj* **a)** [música, grupo] heavy metal **b)** *Fam* [duro] hard **2.** *nm* [música] heavy metal

hebilla *nf* buckle

hebra *nf* thread; [de carne] sinew; [de madera] grain; *Esp* **pegar la hebra** to chat

hebreo, -a 1. *adj* Hebrew **2.** *nm, f* Hebrew

hechizar [40] *vt* **a)** [embrujar] to cast a spell on **b)** *Fig* [fascinar] to bewitch, to charm

hechizo, -a 1. *adj* *Chile, Méx* homemade **2.** *nm* **a)** [sortilegio] spell **b)** *Fig* [encanto] charm

hecho, -a 1. *adj* **a)** made, done; **¡bien hecho!** well done! **b)** [carne] done **c)** [persona] mature **d)** [frase] set; [ropa] ready-made **2.** *nm* **a)** [realidad] fact; **de hecho** in fact; **el hecho es que ...** the fact is that ... **b)** [acto] act, deed **c)** [suceso] event, incident

hectárea *nf* hectare

helada *nf* frost

heladera *nf* *CSur* [nevera] refrigerator, *Br* fridge, *US* icebox

heladería *nf* ice-cream parlour

helado, -a 1. *nm* ice cream **2.** *adj* **a)** [muy frío] frozen, freezing cold; **estoy helado (de frío)** I'm frozen **b)** *Fig* **quedarse helado** [atónito] to be flabbergasted

helar [1] **1.** *vt* [congelar] to freeze **2.** *v impers* to freeze; **anoche heló** there was a frost last night **3. helarse** *vpr* [congelarse] to freeze

hélice *nf* **a)** AVIACIÓN & NÁUT propeller **b)** ANAT, ARQUIT & MAT helix

helicóptero *nm* AVIACIÓN helicopter

hematoma *nm* MED haematoma

hembra *nf* **a)** BOT & ZOOL female **b)** [mujer] woman **c)** TÉC female; [de tornillo] nut; [de enchufe] socket

hemorragia *nf* MED haemorrhage

hendidura *nf* [grieta - pequeña] fissure; [grande] crack

heno *nm* hay

hepatitis *nf inv* hepatitis

herboristería *nf* herbalist's (shop)

heredar *vt* **a)** JUR to inherit **b)** **ha heredado la sonrisa de su madre** she's got her mother's smile

heredero, **-a** *nm, f* heir, *f* heiress; **príncipe heredero** crown prince

hereje *nmf* REL heretic

herejía *nf* REL heresy

herencia *nf* a) JUR inheritance, legacy b) BIOL heredity

herida *nf* [lesión] injury; [corte] wound

herido, **-a** *nm, f* injured person; **no hubo heridos** there were no casualties

herir [5] **1.** *vt* a) [físicamente - lesionar] to injure; [cortar] to wound b) [emocionalmente] to hurt, to wound c) [vista] to offend **2. herirse** *vpr* to injure o hurt oneself

hermana *nf* a) sister b) [monja] sister

hermanastro, **-a** *nm, f* stepbrother, *f* stepsister

hermano *nm* a) brother; **hermano político** brother-in-law; **primo hermano** first cousin b) REL [fraile] brother c) **hermanos** brothers and sisters

hermético, **-a** *adj* a) [cierre] hermetic, airtight b) *Fig* [abstruso] secretive

hermoso, **-a** *adj* beautiful, lovely; [grande] fine

hermosura *nf* beauty

héroe *nm* hero

heroico, **-a** *adj* heroic

heroína *nf* a) [mujer] heroine b) [droga] heroin

heroinómano, **-a** *nm, f* heroin addict

heroísmo *nm* heroism

herradura *nf* horseshoe

herramienta *nf* TÉC tool; **caja de herramientas** toolbox

herrería *nf* forge, smithy

herrero *nm* blacksmith, smith

hervidor *nm* [para líquidos] kettle

hervir [5] **1.** *vt* [hacer bullir] to boil **2.** *vi* a) CULIN to boil; **romper a hervir** to come to the boil b) [abundar] to swarm, to seethe (**de** with)

heteróclito, **-a** *adj* heteroclite

heterosexual *adj* & *nmf* heterosexual

hice *pt indef de* **hacer**

hidalgo *nm* HIST nobleman, gentleman

hidratante *adj* moisturizing; **crema/leche hidratante** moisturizing cream/lotion

hidratar *vt* [piel] to moisturize; QUÍM to hydrate

hidrovía *nf Am* waterway

hiedra *nf* ivy

hielera *nf CSur, Méx Br* cool box, *US* cooler

hielo *nm* ice; *Fig* **romper el hielo** to break the ice

hiena *nf* hyena

hierba *nf* a) grass; **mala hierba** BOT weed; *Fig* [persona] bad lot; *Fam & Hum* **y otras hierbas** among others b) CULIN herb; **hierba luisa** lemon verbena c) *Fam* [marihuana] grass

hierbabuena *nf* mint

hierro *nm* a) [metal] iron; **hierro forjado** wrought iron b) [punta de arma] head, point c) [marca en el ganado] brand

hígado *nm* a) ANAT liver b) *Euf* guts

higiene *nf* hygiene

higiénico, **-a** *adj* hygienic; **papel higiénico** toilet paper

higo *nm* fig; *Fam* **hecho un higo** wizened, crumpled

higuera *nf* BOT fig tree

hija *nf* daughter; **hija política** daughter-in-law

hijastro, **-a** *nm, f* stepson, *f* stepdaughter

hijo *nm* a) son, child; *Despec* **hijo de papá** rich kid; **hijo político** son-in-law; *Vulg* **hijo de puta** o *Méx* **de la chingada** bastard, *US* asshole b) **hijos** children

hilera *nf* line, row

hilo *nm* a) COST thread; [grueso] yarn b) *Fig* [de historia, discurso] thread; [de pensamiento] train; **perder el hilo** to lose the thread; **hilo musical** background music c) TEXT linen

hilvanar *vt* a) COST *Br* to tack, *US* to baste b) *Fig* [ideas etc] to outline

hincapié *nm* hacer hincapié en [insistir] to insist on ; [subrayar] to emphasize, to stress

hincha *Fam* **1.** *nmf* FÚT fan, supporter **2.** *nf* [antipatía] grudge, dislike; *Esp* **me tiene hincha** he's got it in for me

hinchable *adj* inflatable

hinchado, -a *adj* **a)** inflated, blown up **b)** MED [cara etc] swollen, puffed up ; [estómago] bloated **c)** *Fig* [estilo] bombastic, pompous

hinchar 1. *vt* **a)** [inflar] to inflate, to blow up **b)** *Fig* [exagerar] to inflate, to exaggerate **2. hincharse** *vpr* **a)** MED to swell (up) **b)** *Fam* **me hinché de comida** I stuffed myself; **me hinché de llorar** I cried for all I was worth

hinchazón *nf* MED swelling

híper *nm inv Fam* hypermarket

hiperenlace *nm* INFORM hyperlink

hipermercado *nm* hypermarket

hipermetropía *nf* long-sightedness, *Espec* hypermetropia, *US* hypertropia

hipertensión *nf* high blood pressure

hipertexto *nm* INFORM hypertext

hipervínculo *nm* INFORM hyperlink

hípica *nf* horse riding, horesback riding

hipismo *nm* horse riding, horesback riding

hipnotizar [40] *vt* to hypnotize

hipo *nm* hiccups; **me ha dado hipo** it's given me the hiccups

hipoalergénico, -a, hipoalérgico, -a *adj* hypoallergenic

hipocondriaco, -a, hipocondríaco, -a *adj & nm, f* MED hypocondriac

hipocresía *nf* hypocrisy

hipócrita 1. *adj* hypocritical **2.** *nmf* hypocrite

hipódromo *nm* racetrack, racecourse

hipopótamo *nm* hippopotamus

hipoteca *nf* FIN mortgage

hipótesis *nf inv* hypothesis

hipotético, -a *adj* hypothetical

hippy, hippie ['xipi] *(pl* **hippies***) adj & nmf* hippy

hispánico, -a *adj* Hispanic, Spanish

hispano, -a 1. *adj* [español] Spanish ; [español y sudamericano] Hispanic ; [sudamericano] Spanish American **2.** *nm, f* [hispanoamericano] Spanish American ; [estadounidense] Hispanic

Hispanoamérica *nf* Latin America

hispanoamericano, -a *adj & nm, f* Latin American

hispanohablante 1. *adj* Spanish-speaking **2.** *nmf* Spanish speaker

histeria *nf* hysteria; **un ataque de histeria** hysterics

histérico, -a *adj* hysterical; *Fam & Fig* **me pones histérico** you're driving me mad

historia *nf* **a)** history; **esto pasará a la historia** this will go down in history **b)** [narración] story, tale; *Fam* **¡déjate de historias!** don't give me that!

historiar *vt* to recount the story of

histórico, -a *adj* **a)** historical **b)** [auténtico] factual, true; **hechos históricos** true facts **c)** [de gran importancia] historic, memorable

historieta *nf* **a)** [cuento] short story, tale **b)** [tira cómica] comic strip

hizo *pt indef de* **hacer**

hl SMS *(abr de* **hasta luego***)* CUL, CUL8R

hla SMS *written abbr of* **hola**

hobby ['xoβi] *nm* hobby

hocico *nm* **a)** [de animal] snout **b)** [de persona] mug, snout ; *Fam* **meter los hocicos en algo** to stick *o* poke one's nose into sth

hockey ['xokei] *nm* hockey; **hockey sobre hielo** *Br* ice hockey, *US* hockey ; **hockey sobre hierba** *Br* hockey, *US* field hockey

hogar *nm* **a)** [casa] home **b)** [de la chimenea] hearth, fireplace **c)** *Fig* **formar** *o* **crear un hogar** [familia] to start a family

hogareño, -a *adj* [vida] home, family ; [persona] home-loving, stay-at-home

hoguera *nf* bonfire

hoja *nf* **a)** BOT leaf **b)** [pétalo] petal **c)** [de papel] sheet, leaf ; **hoja de cál-**

culo spreadsheet **d)** [de libro] leaf, page **e)** [de metal] sheet **f)** [de cuchillo, espada] blade **g)** [impreso] hand-out, printed sheet **h)** [de puerta o ventana] leaf

hojalata *nf* tin, tin plate

hojaldre *nm* CULIN puff pastry

hola *interj* hello!, hullo!, hi!

holá *interj* Am [al teléfono] hello!

Holanda *n* Holland

holandés, -esa 1. *adj* Dutch **2.** *nm, f* Dutchman, *f* Dutchwoman **3.** *nm* [idioma] Dutch

holgado, -a *adj* **a)** [ropa] loose, baggy **b)** [económicamente] comfortable **c)** [espacio] roomy; **andar holgado de tiempo** to have plenty of time

holgazán, -ana 1. *adj* lazy, idle **2.** *nm, f* lazybones, layabout

hombre 1. *nm* **a)** man; **de hombre a hombre** man-to-man; **¡pobre hombre!** poor *Br* chap o *US* guy!; **ser muy hombre** to be every inch a man; **hombre de estado** statesman; **hombre de negocios** businessman; **hombre orquesta** one-man band; **hombre rana** frogman, diver **b)** [especie] mankind, man **2.** *interj* **a)** **¡hombre, Juan! ¡qué alegría verte!** hey Juan, how nice to see you! **b)** **¡sí hombre!** sure!

hombrera *nf* shoulder pad

hombrillo *nm Ven* [arcén - de carretera] verge; [de autopista] *Br* hard shoulder, *US* shoulder

hombro *nm* shoulder; **a hombros** on one's shoulders; **encogerse de hombros** to shrug one's shoulders; **mirar a algn por encima del hombro** to look down one's nose at sb

homenaje *nm* homage, tribute; **rendir homenaje a algn** to pay homage o tribute to sb

homeopatía *nf* homeopathy

homicida 1. *nmf* murderer, *f* murderess **2.** *adj* homicidal; **el arma homicida** the murder weapon

homicidio *nm* homicide

homosexual *adj* & *nmf* homosexual

hondo, -a *adj* **a)** [profundo] deep; **plato hondo** soup dish **b)** *Fig* [pesar] profound, deep

Honduras *n* Honduras

hondureño, -a *adj* & *nm, f* Honduran

honestidad *nf* **a)** [honradez] honesty, uprightness **b)** [decencia] modesty

honesto, -a *adj* **a)** [honrado] honest, upright **b)** [decente] modest

hongo *nm* **a)** BOT fungus; **hongo venenoso** toadstool **b)** [sombrero] *Br* bowler (hat), *US* derby

honor *nm* **a)** [virtud] honour; **palabra de honor** word of honour **b)** **en honor a la verdad** ... to be fair ...; **es un honor para mí** it's an honour for me **c)** **hacer honor a** to live up to

honorario, -a 1. *adj* honorary **2.** *nmpl* **honorarios** fees, fee

honra *nf* **a)** [dignidad] dignity, self-esteem **b)** [fama] reputation, good name **c)** [honor] honour; **me cabe la honra de** ... I have the honour of ...; **¡a mucha honra!** and proud of it!

honradez *nf* honesty, integrity

honrado, -a *adj* **a)** [de fiar] honest **b)** [decente] upright, respectable

honrar *vt* **a)** [respetar] to honour **b)** [enaltecer] to be a credit to

hora *nf* **a)** hour; *Esp* **hora punta**, *Am* **hora pico** [de mucho tráfico] rush hour; [de agua, electricidad] peak times; **horas extra** overtime (hours); TV **hora de mayor audiencia** prime time; **un programa emitido a la hora de mayor audiencia** a *Br* programme o *US* program broadcast at prime time; **media hora** half an hour; **a altas horas de la madrugada** in the small hours; **dar la hora** to strike the hour; **(trabajo) por horas** (work) paid by the hour **b)** *Fig* time; **¿qué hora es?** what time is it?; **a última hora** at the last moment; *Esp, Andes, Carib, RP* **la hora de la verdad** the moment of truth **c)** [cita] appointment; **pedir hora** [al médico etc] to ask for an appointment

horario, -a 1. *nm Br* timetable, *US* schedule **2.** *adj* time; RADIO **señal horaria** pips

horca *nf* gallows (*sing*)

horchata *nf* CULIN cold drink made from ground tiger nuts, water and sugar

horchatería *nf* café which specializes in serving "horchata", a cold drink made from tiger nuts

horizontal *adj* horizontal

horizonte *nm* horizon

horma *nf* [de zapato] last

hormiga *nf* ant

hormigón *nm* CONSTR concrete; **hormigón armado** reinforced concrete

hormigonera *nf* concrete mixer

hormiguero *nm* **a)** anthill **b)** *Fig* **ser un hormiguero** [lugar] to be swarming (with people)

hormona *nf* hormone

hornear *vt* to bake

hornillo *nm* [de cocinar] stove; [placa] hotplate

horno *nm* [cocina] oven; TÉC furnace; [para cerámica, ladrillos] kiln; CULIN **pescado al horno** baked fish; *Vulg & Fig* **esta habitación es un horno** this room is boiling hot

horóscopo *nm* horoscope

horquilla *nf* **a)** [del pelo] hairpin, *Br* hairgrip **b)** [estadística] chart **c)** **horquilla de precios** price range

hórreo *nm* AGRIC granary

horrible *adj* horrible, dreadful, awful

horror *nm* **a)** horror, terror; **¡qué horror!** how awful!; *Fam* **tengo horror a las motos** I hate motorbikes **b)** *Fam & Fig* **me gusta horrores** [muchísimo] I like it an awful lot

horrorizar [40] *vt* to horrify, to terrify

horroroso, -a *adj* **a)** [que da miedo] horrifying, terrifying **b)** *Fam* [muy feo] hideous, ghastly **c)** *Fam* [malísimo] awful, dreadful

hortaliza *nf* vegetable

hortelano, -a *nm, f Br* market gardener, *US* truck farmer

hortensia *nf* BOT hydrangea

hortera *adj Esp Fam* [decoración, ropa, canción] tacky, *Br* naff; **es muy hortera** he has really tacky o *Br* naff taste

hospedar 1. *vt* to put up, to lodge **2. hospedarse** *vpr* to stay (**en** at)

hospital *nm* hospital

hospitalario, -a *adj* **a)** [acogedor] hospitable **b)** MED hospital; **instalaciones hospitalarias** hospital facilities

hospitalidad *nf* hospitality

hospitalizar [40] *vt* to take o send into hospital, to hospitalize

hostal *nm* guesthouse

hostelería *nf* [negocio] catering business; [estudios] hotel management

hostería *nf* CSur [hotel] country hotel

hostia 1. *nf* **a)** REL host **b)** *Esp Vulg* [golpe] bash **c)** *Esp Vulg* **estar de mala hostia** to be in a foul mood; **ser la hostia** [fantástico] to be *Br* bloody o *US* goddamn amazing; [penoso] to be *Br* bloody o *US* goddamn awful **2.** *interj Vulg* damn!, *Br* bloody hell!

hostigoso, -a *adj Andes, CAm, Méx* annoying

hostil *adj* hostile

hotel *nm* hotel

hotelero, -a 1. *adj* hotel; **el sector hotelero** the hotel sector **2.** *nm, f* hotel-keeper, hotelier

hoy *adv* **a)** [día] today **b)** *Fig* [presente] now; **de hoy en adelante** from now on; **hoy (en) día, hoy por hoy** nowadays

hoyo *nm* **a)** [agujero] hole, pit **b)** [sepultura] grave **c)** [de golf] hole

hoz *nf* AGRIC sickle; **la hoz y el martillo** the hammer and sickle

HTML *nm* INFORM *(abr de* **Hypertext Markup Language***)* HTML *(Hypertext Markup Language)*

HTTP *nm* INFORM *(abr de* **Hypertext Transfer Protocol***)* HTTP *(Hypertext Transfer Protocol)*; **el lenguaje HTTP** HTTP language

huacho = **guacho**

huasipungo *nm Andes small plot of land given by landowner to Indians in exchange for their labour*

huaso, -a *nm, f Chile Fam* farmer, peasant

huasteco, -a *Méx* **1.** *adj & nm, f* Huastec **2.** *nm* [idioma] Huastec

hubiera *subj imperf de* **haber**

hucha *nf Esp* piggy bank

hueco, -a 1. *adj* **a)** [vacío] empty, hollow **b)** [sonido] resonant **2.** *nm* **a)** [cavidad] hollow, hole **b)** [sitio no ocupado] empty space **c)** [rato libre] free time

huelga *nf* strike; **estar en** *o* **de huelga** to be on strike; **huelga de brazos caídos** go-slow; **huelga de celo** *Br* work-to-rule, *US* job action

huella *nf* **a)** [del pie] footprint; [coche] track; **huella dactilar** fingerprint **b)** *Fig* [vestigio] trace, sign; **dejar huella** to leave one's mark

huérfano, -a *nm, f* orphan

huerta *nf* **a)** AGRIC [parcela] *Br* market garden, *US* truck farm **b)** [región] *irrigated area used for cultivation*

huerto *nm* [de verduras] vegetable garden, kitchen garden; [de frutales] orchard

hueso *nm* **a)** ANAT bone; **estar en los huesos** to be all skin and bone **b)** [de fruto] *Br* stone, *US* pit **c)** *Fig* [difícil] hard work; [profesor] hard nut **d)** *Méx* [enchufe] contact; [trabajo fácil] cushy job

huésped, -a *nm, f* [invitado] guest; [en hotel etc] lodger, boarder; **casa de huéspedes** guesthouse

huevada *nf Andes, RP muy Fam* [dicho] crap; **lo que dijiste es una huevada** what you said is a load of crap

huevo *nm* **a)** egg; **huevo duro** hard-boiled egg; **huevo escalfado** poached egg; **huevo frito** fried egg; **huevo pasado por agua**, *Méx* **huevo tibio**, *Andes* **huevo a la copa** soft-boiled egg; **huevos revueltos** scrambled eggs **b)** *Vulg* (usu pl) balls (pl); **hacer algo por huevos** to do sth even if it kills you; **tener huevos** to have guts

huevón, -ona *muy Fam nm, f* **a)** *Cuba, Méx* [vago] **es un huevón** *Br* he's a lazy sod o git, *US* he's so goddamn lazy **b)** *Andes, Arg, Ven* [tonto, torpe] *Br* prat, *Br* pillock, *US* jerk

huida *nf* flight, escape

huipil *nm CAm, Méx* colourful embroidered dress or blouse traditionally worn by Indian women

huir [37] *vi* to run away (**de** from), to flee; **huir de la cárcel** to escape from prison; **huir de algn** to avoid sb

hule *nm* **a)** [tela impermeable] oilcloth, oilskin **b)** [de mesa] tablecloth **c)** *CAm, Méx* [caucho] rubber

humanidad *nf* **a)** [género humano] humanity, mankind **b)** [cualidad] humanity, humaneness **c)** [bondad] compassion, kindness

humanitario, -a *adj* humanitarian

humano, -a 1. *adj* **a)** [relativo al hombre] human **b)** [compasivo] humane **2.** *nm* human (being); **ser humano** human being

humareda *nf* cloud of smoke; **¡qué humareda!** what a lot of smoke!, it's so smoky!

humedad *nf* [atmosférica] humidity; [de lugar] dampness; **a prueba de humedad** damp-proof

humedecer [33] **1.** *vt* to moisten, to dampen **2. humedecerse** *vpr* to become damp o wet o moist

húmedo, -a *adj* [casa, ropa] damp; [clima] humid, damp, moist

humilde *adj* humble, modest; [pobre] poor

humillación *nf* humiliation

humillante *adj* humiliating, humbling

humillar 1. *vt* [rebajar] to humiliate, to humble **2. humillarse** *vpr* **humillarse ante algn** to humble oneself before sb

humita *nf* **a)** *Chile* [pajarita] bow tie **b)** *Andes, Arg* [pasta de maíz] *paste made of mashed (Br) maize o (US) corn kernels mixed with cheese, chilli, onion and other ingredients, wrapped in a (Br) maize o (US) corn husk and steamed*

humo *nm* **a)** smoke ; [gas] fumes ; [vapor] vapour, steam **b)** ¡**qué humos tiene!** she thinks a lot of herself!

humor *nm* **a)** [genio] mood ; **estar de buen / mal humor** to be in a good / bad mood **b)** [carácter] temper ; **es persona de mal humor** he's bad-tempered **c)** [gracia] humour ; **sentido del humor** sense of humour

humorismo *nm* humour

humorista *nmf* humorist ; **humorista gráfico** cartoonist

humorístico, **-a** *adj* humorous, funny

hundido, **-a** *adj* **a)** [ojos] sunken **b)** *Fig* [desmoralizado] demoralized

hundir 1. *vt* **a)** [barco] to sink **b)** [edificio] to bring o knock down **c)** *Fig* [desmoralizar] to demoralize **2. hundirse** *vpr* **a)** [barco] to sink **b)** [edificio] to collapse **c)** *Fig* [empresa] to collapse, to crash

húngaro, **-a 1.** *adj* & *nm, f* Hungarian **2.** *nm* [idioma] Hungarian

Hungría *n* Hungary

huracán *nm* hurricane

hurtadillas *adv* **a hurtadillas** stealthily, on the sly

hurto *nm* petty theft, pilfering

I

ibérico, -a *adj* Iberian

Iberoamérica *n* Latin America

iceberg *(pl* **icebergs)** *nm* iceberg

Icona *nm (abr de* **Instituto Nacional para la Conservación de la Naturaleza)** *Antes Spanish national institute for conservation,* ≃ *Br* NCC

icono *nm* icon; INFORM icon

I+D *nm (abr de* **Investigación y Desarrollo)** R&D

ida *nf* **(billete de) ida y vuelta** *Br* return (ticket), *US* round-trip (ticket); **idas y venidas** comings and goings

idea *nf* **a)** idea; **idea fija** fixed idea **b)** [noción] idea; **hacerse a la idea de** to get used to the idea of; *Fam* **ni idea** no idea, not a clue **c)** [opinión] opinion; **cambiar de idea** to change one's mind **d)** [intención] intention; **a mala idea** on purpose

ideal *adj & nm* ideal

idealismo *nm* idealism

idealista **1.** *adj* idealistic **2.** *nmf* idealist

idéntico, -a *adj* identical

identidad *nf* **a)** identity; **carnet de identidad** identity card **b)** [semejanza] identity, sameness

identificación *nf* identification

identificar [44] **1.** *vt* to identify **2. identificarse** *vpr* to identify oneself; *Fig* **identificarse con** to identify with

ideología *nf* ideology

idilio *nm* **a)** LITER idyll **b)** *Fig* [romance] romance, love affair

idioma *nm* language

idiota **1.** *adj* idiotic, stupid **2.** *nmf* idiot, fool

ídolo *nm* idol

idóneo, -a *adj* suitable, fit

iglesia *nf* **a)** [edificio] church **b) la Iglesia** [institución] the Church

ignorancia *nf* ignorance

ignorante **1.** *adj* **a)** [sin instrucción] ignorant **b)** [no informado] ignorant, unaware (**de** of) **2.** *nmf* ignoramus

ignorar **1.** *vt* **a)** [algo] not to know **b)** [a algn] to ignore **2. ignorarse** *vpr* to be unknown

igual **1.** *adj* **a)** [idéntico] the same, alike; **son todos iguales** they're all the same; **es igual** it doesn't matter; **igual que** the same as
b) [equivalente] equal; **a partes iguales** fifty-fifty
c) DEP [empatados] even; **treinta iguales** thirty all
d) MAT equal; **tres más tres igual a seis** three plus three equals six
e) al igual que just like
f) por igual equally
2. *nm* equal; **sin igual** unique, unrivalled
3. *adv* **a) lo haces igual que yo** you do it the same way I do
b) *Esp* [posiblemente] perhaps; **igual vengo** I'll probably come
c) *Andes, RP* [aún así] all the same; **estaba nublado pero igual fuimos** it was cloudy but we went all the same

igualdad *nf* **a)** equality; **igualdad ante la ley** equality before the law **b)** [identidad] sameness; **en igualdad de condiciones** on equal terms

igualmente *adv* equally; [también] also, likewise; *Fam* **encantado de conocerlo — ¡igualmente!** pleased to meet you — likewise!

ilegal *adj* illegal

ilegítimo, -a *adj* illegitimate

ileso, -a *adj* unhurt, unharmed

ilimitado, -a *adj* unlimited, limitless

ilógico, -a *adj* illogical

iluminación *nf* [alumbrado] illumination, lighting

iluminar *vt* **a)** to illuminate, to light (up) **b)** *Fig* [a persona] to enlighten; [tema] to throw light upon

ilusión *nf* **a)** [esperanza] hope; [esperanza vana] illusion, delusion; **hacerse ilusiones** to build up one's hopes **b)** [sueño] dream **c)** *Esp* [emoción] excitement, thrill; **me hace ilusión verla** I'm looking forward to seeing her; **¡qué ilusión!** how exciting!

ilusionar **1.** *vt* **a)** [esperanzar] to build up sb's hopes **b)** [entusiasmar] to excite, to thrill **2. ilusionarse** *vpr* **a)** [esperanzarse] to build up one's hopes **b)** [entusiasmarse] to be excited o thrilled (**con** about)

ilustración *nf* **a)** [grabado] illustration, picture; [ejemplo] illustration **b)** [erudición] learning, erudition; HIST **la Ilustración** the Enlightenment

ilustrar **1.** *vt* **a)** to illustrate **b)** [aclarar] to explain, to make clear **2. ilustrarse** *vpr* to acquire knowledge (**sobre** of), to learn (**sobre** about)

ilustre *adj* illustrious, distinguished

imagen *nf* **a)** image; **ser la viva imagen de algn** to be the spitting image of sb; **tener buena imagen** to have a good image **b)** REL image, statue **c)** TV picture

imaginación *nf* imagination; **eso son imaginaciones tuyas** you're imagining things

imaginar **1.** *vt* to imagine **2. imaginarse** *vpr* to imagine; **me imagino que sí** I suppose so

imaginario, -a *adj* imaginary

imaginativo, -a *adj* imaginative

imán *nm* magnet

imbécil **1.** *adj* stupid, silly **2.** *nmf* idiot, imbecile

imitación *nf* imitation

imitar *vt* to imitate; [gestos] to mimic; **este collar imita al oro** this necklace is imitation gold

impaciencia *nf* impatience

impaciente *adj* [deseoso] impatient; [intranquilo] anxious

impactante *adj* shocking, powerful

impacto *nm* impact

impar *adj* MAT odd; **número impar** odd number

imparable *adj* DEP unstoppable

imparcial *adj* impartial, unbiased

impasible *adj* impassive

impecable *adj* impeccable

impedimento *nm* impediment; [obstáculo] hindrance, obstacle

impedir [6] *vt* [obstaculizar] to impede, to hinder; [imposibilitar] to prevent, to stop; **impedir el paso** to block the way

impensable *adj* unthinkable

imperativo, -a **1.** *adj* imperative **2.** *nm* LING imperative

imperceptible *adj* imperceptible

imperdible *nm* safety pin

imperdonable *adj* unforgivable, inexcusable

imperfecto, -a *adj* **a)** imperfect, fallible **b)** [defectuoso] defective, faulty **c)** LING imperfect

imperial *adj* imperial

imperio *nm* empire; **el imperio de la ley** the rule of law

impermeable **1.** *adj* impermeable, impervious; [ropa] waterproof **2.** *nm* raincoat, *Br* mac

impersonal *adj* impersonal

impertinencia *nf* impertinence

impertinente **1.** *adj* [insolente] impertinent; [inoportuno] irrelevant **2.** *nmpl* **impertinentes** lorgnette

ímpetu *nm* **a)** [impulso] impetus, momentum **b)** [violencia] violence **c)** [energía] energy

implicancia *nf* CSur implication

implicar [44] **1.** *vt* **a)** [involucrar] to involve, to implicate (**en** in) **b)** [conllevar] to imply **2. implicarse** *vpr* **implicarse en** to get involved in

implícito, -a *adj* implicit, implied

imponer [19] *(pp* **impuesto) 1.** *vt* **a)** to impose
b) [respeto] to inspire
c) FIN to deposit
2. *vi* [impresionar] to be impressive
3. imponerse *vpr* **a)** [infundir respeto] to command respect
b) [prevalecer] to prevail
c) [ser necesario] to be necessary

importación *nf* [mercancía] import; [acción] importing; **artículos de importación** imported goods

importancia *nf* importance, significance; **dar importancia a** to attach importance to; **sin importancia** unimportant

importante *adj* important, significant; **una suma importante** a considerable sum

importar¹ 1. *vi* **a)** [atañer] **eso no te importa a tí** that doesn't concern you, that's none of your business
b) [tener importancia] to be important; **no importa** it doesn't matter; *Fam* **me importa un bledo o un pito** I couldn't care less
c) [molestar] **¿te importaría repetirlo?** would you mind repeating it?; **¿te importa si fumo?** do you mind if I smoke?
2. *vt* [valer] to amount to; **los libros importan 15 euros** the books come to 15 euros

importar² *vt* COM & INFORM to import

importe *nm* COM & FIN amount, total

imposibilidad *nf* impossibility

imposible *adj* impossible; **me es imposible hacerlo** I can't (possibly) do it

impostor, -a *nm, f* [farsante] impostor

impotencia *nf* powerlessness, helplessness; MED impotence

impotente *adj* powerless, helpless; MED impotent

impreciso, -a *adj* imprecise, vague

impredecible *adj* unpredictable

impregnar 1. *vt* to impregnate (**de** with) **2. impregnarse** *vpr* to become impregnated

imprenta *nf* **a)** [taller] printer's, print works **b)** [aparato] printing press **c) libertad de imprenta** freedom of the press

imprescindible *adj* essential, indispensable

impresión *nf* **a)** *Fig* [efecto] impression; **causar impresión** to make an impression **b)** *Fig* [opinión] impression; **cambiar impresiones** to exchange impressions **c)** IMPR [acto] printing; [edición] edition **d)** [huella] impression, imprint

impresionante *adj* impressive, striking; *Fam* **un error impresionante** [tremendo] a terrible mistake

impresionar *vt* **a)** [causar admiración] to impress; [sorprender] to stun, to shock **b)** FOTO to expose

impreso, -a 1. *adj* printed **2.** *nm* **a)** [papel, folleto] printed matter **b)** [formulario] form; **impreso de solicitud** application form **c) impresos** [de correos] printed matter

impresora *nf* INFORM printer; **impresora láser** laser printer; **impresora de chorro de tinta** inkjet printer

imprevisto, -a 1. *adj* unforeseen, unexpected **2.** *nm* [incidente] unforeseen event

imprimir *(pp* **impreso)** *vt* **a)** IMPR & INFORM to print **b)** [marcar] to stamp

improvisación *nf* improvisation; MÚS extemporization

improvisado, -a *adj* [espontáneo] improvised, impromptu, ad lib; [provisional] makeshift; **discurso improvisado** impromptu speech

improvisar *vt* to improvise; MÚS to extemporize

improviso ■ **de improviso** *loc adv* **llegó de improviso** she arrived out of the blue; **todo sucedió de im-**

proviso everything just happened out of the blue o so quickly; *Esp* **nos cogió de improviso** it caught us off guard

imprudente *adj* imprudent, unwise; [indiscreto] indiscreet

impuesto, -a 1. *nm* FIN tax; **impuesto sobre la renta** income tax; **libre de impuestos** tax-free; *Esp* **impuesto sobre el valor añadido,** *Am* **impuesto al valor agregado** value-added tax **2.** *adj* imposed

impulsar *vt* to impel, to drive

impulsivo, -a *adj* impulsive

impulso *nm* impulse, thrust; DEP **tomar impulso** to take a run-up

impuro, -a *adj* impure

inaceptable *adj* unacceptable

inadecuado, -a *adj* unsuitable, inappropriate

inadmisible *adj* inadmissible

inaguantable *adj* unbearable, intolerable

inauguración *nf* inauguration, opening

inaugurar *vt* to inaugurate, to open

incapacidad *nf* a) incapacity, inability; **incapacidad física** physical disability b) [incompetencia] incompetence, inefficiency

incapaz *adj* a) unable (**de** to), incapable (**de** of); **soy incapaz de continuar** I can't go on b) JUR unfit

incendio *nm* fire; **incendio forestal** forest fire

incentivo *nm* incentive

incidente *nm* incident

incinerador *nm* [de basura] incinerator

incinerar *vt* [basura] to incinerate; [cadáveres] to cremate

inciso, -a 1. *adj* **un estilo inciso** an incisive style **2.** *nm* a) [en discurso] interjection b) GRAM interpolation

incitante *adj* provocative

incitar *vt* to incite, to urge

inclinación *nf* a) [de terreno] slope, incline; [del cuerpo] stoop b) [reverencia] bow c) *Fig* [tendencia] tendency, inclination, penchant

inclinado, -a *adj* a) [edificio, torre] leaning b) [tendente] inclined

inclinar 1. *vt* a) to incline, to bend; [cabeza] to nod b) *Fig* [persuadir] to persuade, to induce **2. inclinarse** *vpr* a) to lean, to slope, to incline b) [al saludar] to bow; **inclinarse ante** to bow down to c) *Fig* [optar] **inclinarse a** to be o feel inclined to; **me inclino por éste** I'd rather have this one, I prefer this one

incluido, -a *adj* a) [después del sustantivo] included; [antes del sustantivo] including; **desayuno incluido** breakfast included; **IVA incluido** including VAT; **servicio no incluido** service not included; **todos pagan, incluidos los niños** everyone has to pay, including children b) [adjunto] enclosed

incluir [37] *vt* a) to include b) [contener] to contain, to comprise c) [adjuntar] to enclose

inclusive *adv* a) [incluido] inclusive; **de martes a viernes inclusive** from Tuesday to Friday inclusive; **hasta la lección ocho inclusive** up to and including lesson eight b) [incluso] even

incluso *adv* even; **incluso mi madre** even my mother

incógnita *nf* a) MAT unknown quantity, unknown b) [misterio] mystery

incoherente *adj* incoherent

incoloro, -a *adj* colourless

incómodo, -a *adj* uncomfortable; **sentirse incómodo** to feel uncomfortable o awkward

incomparable *adj* incomparable

incompatibilidad *nf* incompatibility; JUR **incompatibilidad de caracteres** mutual incompatibility

incompetente *adj & nmf* incompetent

incomprensible *adj* incomprehensible

incomunicado, -a *adj* **a)** [aislado] isolated; **el pueblo se quedó incomunicado** the town was cut off **b)** [en la cárcel] in solitary confinement

incondicional 1. *adj* unconditional; [apoyo] wholehearted; [amigo] faithful; [partidario] staunch **2.** *nm* diehard

inconfundible *adj* unmistakable, obvious

inconsciencia *nf* MED unconsciousness; *Fig* [irreflexión] thoughtlessness; [irresponsabilidad] irresponsibility

inconsciente *adj* **a)** (*con estar*) [desmayado] unconscious **b)** (*con ser*) [despreocupado] unaware (**de** of); *Fig* [irreflexivo] thoughtless, irresponsible

incontable *adj* countless, innumerable

inconveniente 1. *adj* **a)** inconvenient **b)** [inapropiado] unsuitable **2.** *nm* **a)** [objección] objection; **poner inconvenientes** to raise objections **b)** [desventaja] disadvantage, drawback; [problema] difficulty; **¿tienes inconveniente en acompañarme?** would you mind coming with me?

incorporación *nf* incorporation

incorporar 1. *vt* **a)** to incorporate (**en** into) **b)** [levantar] to help to sit up **2. incorporarse** *vpr* **a) incorporarse a** [sociedad] to join; [trabajo] to start; MIL **incorporarse a filas** to join up **b)** [en la cama] to sit up

incorrecto, -a *adj* **a)** [equivocado] incorrect, inaccurate **b)** [grosero] impolite, discourteous

incorregible *adj* incorrigible

incrédulo, -a 1. *adj* **a)** incredulous, disbelieving **b)** REL unbelieving **2.** *nm, f* **a)** disbeliever **b)** REL unbeliever

increíble *adj* incredible, unbelievable

incremento *nm* [aumento] increase; [crecimiento] growth; **incremento de la temperatura** rise in temperature

incubadora *nf* incubator

incubar *vt* to incubate

inculpado, -a *nm, f* **el inculpado** the accused

inculto, -a 1. *adj* [ignorante] uneducated, uncouth **2.** *nm, f* ignoramus

incumbencia *nf* responsibility; **no es de mi incumbencia** that's not my (area of) responsibility; **eso no es asunto de tu incumbencia** that does not concern you

incumbir *vi* to be incumbent (**a** upon); **esto no te incumbe** this is none of your business

incurable *adj también Fig* incurable

incurrir *vi* [cometer] to fall (**en** into); **incurrir en delito** to commit a crime; **incurrir en (un) error** to fall into error

incursionar *vi* **a)** [territorio] to make an incursion (**en** into); [en ciudad] to make a raid (**en** into) **b)** [en tema, asunto] to dabble

indecente *adj* **a)** [impúdico] indecent **b)** [impresentable] dreadful

indeciso, -a *adj* **a)** [vacilante] hesitant, irresolute **b)** [resultados etc] inconclusive

indefenso, -a *adj* defenceless, helpless

indefinido, -a *adj* **a)** [indeterminado] indefinite; [impreciso] undefined, vague **b)** LING indefinite

indemnización *nf* **a)** [acto] indemnification **b)** FIN [compensación] indemnity, compensation; **indemnización por despido** redundancy payment

indemnizar [40] *vt* to indemnify, to compensate (**por** for)

independencia *nf* independence

independiente *adj* [libre] independent; [individualista] self-reliant

independizar [40] **1.** *vt* to make independent, to grant independence to **2. independizarse** *vpr* to become independent

indeterminado, -a *adj* **a)** indefinite; [impreciso] vague **b)** [persona] irresolute **c)** LING indefinite

indexar *vt* INFORM to index

India *nf* **(la) India** India

indicación *nf* a) [señal] indication, sign b) [instrucción] instruction, direction; **por indicación de algn** at sb's suggestion

indicador *nm* a) indicator b) TÉC gauge, meter; AUTO **indicador del nivel de aceite** (oil) dipstick; AUTO **indicador de velocidad** speedometer

indicar [44] *vt* [señalar] to indicate, to show, to point out; **¿me podría indicar el camino?** could you show me the way?

indicativo, -a *adj* a) indicative (**de** of) b) LING **(modo) indicativo** indicative (mood)

índice *nm* a) [de libro] index, table of contents b) [relación] rate; **índice de natalidad / mortalidad** birth / death rate; FIN **índice de precios** price index c) ANAT **(dedo) índice** index finger, forefinger

indicio *nm* a) [señal] indication, sign, token (**de** of) b) JUR **indicios** [prueba] evidence

indiferencia *nf* indifference, apathy

indiferente *adj* a) [no importante] unimportant; **me es indiferente** it makes no difference to me b) [apático] indifferent

indígena 1. *adj* indigenous, native (**de** to) 2. *nmf* native (**de** of)

indigestión *nf* indigestion

indigesto, -a *adj* [comida] indigestible, difficult to digest; **me siento indigesto** I've got indigestion

indignación *nf* indignation

indignado, -a *adj* indignant (**por** at o about)

indignante *adj* outrageous, infuriating

indignarse *vpr* to be outraged

indio, -a *adj* & *nm, f* Indian; **en fila india** in single file; *Esp Fam* **hacer el indio** to play the fool

indirecta *nf Fam* [insinuación] hint, insinuation; **tirar** o **lanzar una indirecta** to drop a hint; **coger la indirecta** to get the message

indirecto, -a *adj* indirect; LING **estilo indirecto** indirect o reported speech

indiscreto, -a *adj* indiscreet, tactless

indiscriminado, -a *adj* indiscriminate

indiscutible *adj* indisputable, unquestionable

indispensable *adj* indispensable, essential

indispuesto, -a *adj* indisposed, unwell

individual 1. *adj* individual; **habitación individual** single room 2. *nmpl* DEP **individuales** singles

individualizado, -a *adj* individualized

individuo *nm* a) individual b) [tío] bloke, guy

índole *nf* a) [carácter] character, nature b) [clase, tipo] kind, sort

Indonesia *n* Indonesia

indumentaria *nf* clothing, clothes

industria *nf* industry

industrial 1. *adj* industrial 2. *nmf* industrialist

industrializado, -a *adj* industrialized; **países industrializados** industrialized countries

inédito, -a *adj* a) [libro, texto] unpublished b) [nuevo] completely new; [desconocido] unknown

inepto, -a 1. *adj* inept, incompetent 2. *nm, f* incompetent person

inequívoco, -a *adj* unmistakable, unequivocal

inesperado, -a *adj* [fortuito] unexpected, unforeseen; [imprevisto] sudden

inestable *adj* unstable, unsteady

inevitable *adj* inevitable, unavoidable

inexperto, -a *adj* [inexperto] inexpert; [sin experiencia] inexperienced

infalible *adj* infallible

infancia *nf* childhood, infancy

infanta *nf* infanta, princess

infantería *nf* MIL infantry; **la infantería de marina** the marines

infantil *adj* a) literatura infantil [para niños] children's literature b) [aniñado] childlike; *Despec* childish, infantile

infarto *nm* MED infarction, infarct; **infarto (de miocardio)** heart attack, coronary thrombosis; *Fam* de infarto thrilling, stunning

infección *nf* infection

infeccioso, -a *adj* infectious

infectar 1. *vt* to infect **2. infectarse** *vpr* to become infected (**de** with)

infeliz 1. *adj* unhappy; [desdichado] unfortunate **2.** *nmf Fam* simpleton; **es un pobre infeliz** he is a poor devil

inferior 1. *adj* a) [más bajo] lower b) [calidad] inferior; **de calidad inferior** of inferior quality c) [cantidad] lower, less; **inferior a la media** below average **2.** *nmf* [persona] subordinate, inferior

inferioridad *nf* inferiority; **estar en inferioridad de condiciones** to be at a disadvantage; **complejo de inferioridad** inferiority complex

infición *nf Méx* pollution

infidelidad *nf* infidelity, unfaithfulness

infiel 1. *adj* [desleal] unfaithful **2.** *nmf* REL infidel

infierno *nm* a) REL hell b) *Fig* [tormento] hell; **su vida es un infierno** his life is sheer hell c) [horno] inferno; **en verano esto es un infierno** in summer it's like an inferno here; *Fam* **¡vete al infierno!** go to hell!, get lost!

ínfimo, -a *adj Formal* [mínimo] extremely low; **detalle ínfimo** smallest detail; **ínfima calidad** very poor quality

infinito, -a 1. *adj* infinite, endless **2.** *nm* infinity **3.** *adv Fam* [muchísimo] infinitely, immensely

inflable *adj* inflatable

inflación *nf* ECON inflation

inflar 1. *vt* a) [hinchar] to inflate, to blow up; NÁUT [vela] to swell b) *Fig* [exagerar] to exaggerate **2. inflarse** *vpr* a) to inflate; NÁUT [vela] to swell b) *Fam*

inflarse de to overdo; **se inflaron de macarrones** they stuffed themselves with macaroni

inflexible *adj* inflexible

influencia *nf* influence; **ejercer** *o* **tener influencia sobre algn** to have an influence on *o* upon sb; **tener influencias** to be influential

influenciar [43] *vt* to influence

influir [37] **1.** *vt* to influence **2.** *vi* a) to have influence b) **influir en** *o* **sobre** to influence, to have an influence on

influjo *nm* influence

influyente *adj* influential

información *nf* a) information; **oficina de información** information bureau b) **una información** [noticia] a piece of news, news (*sing*) c) TEL *Br* directory enquiries, *US* information d) [referencias] references

informado, -a *adj* informed

informal *adj* a) [reunión, cena] informal b) [comportamiento] casual c) [persona] unreliable, untrustworthy

informalidad *nf* [incumplimiento] unreliability; [desenfado] informality

informar 1. *vt* to inform (**de** of); [dar informes] to report **2. informarse** *vpr* [procurarse noticias] to find out (**de** about); [enterarse] to inquire (**de** about)

informática *nf* computing, information technology

informático, -a 1. *adj* computer, computing **2.** *nm, f* (computer) technician

informativo, -a 1. *adj* a) RADIO & TV news; **boletín informativo** news (broadcast) b) [explicativo] informative, explanatory **2.** *nm* RADIO & TV news bulletin

informatizar *vt* INFORM to computerize

informe *nm* a) report b) **informes** references; **pedir informes sobre algn** to make inquiries about sb

infracción *nf* [de ley] infringement, breach (**de** of)

infraccionar *Am* **1.** *vt* to violate **2.** *vi* [contra reglamento] to break the rules; [contra la ley] to break the law

infundir *vt* to infuse; *Fig* to instil; **infundir dudas** to give rise to doubt; **infundir respeto** to command respect

infusión *nf* infusion

ingeniería *nf* engineering

ingeniero, -a *nm, f* engineer; **ingeniero agrónomo** agricultural engineer; **ingeniero de telecomunicaciones** telecommunications engineer; **ingeniero técnico** technician

ingenio *nm* **a)** [talento] talent; [inventiva] inventiveness, creativeness; [agudeza] wit **b)** [aparato] device

ingenioso, -a *adj* ingenious, clever; [vivaz] witty

ingenuidad *nf* ingenuousness, naïveté

ingenuo, -a **1.** *adj* ingenuous, naïve **2.** *nm, f* naïve person

Inglaterra *n* England

ingle *nf* ANAT groin

inglés, -esa **1.** *adj* English **2.** *nm, f* Englishman, *f* Englishwoman; **los ingleses** the English **3.** *nm* [idioma] English

ingrato, -a **1.** *adj* **a)** [persona] ungrateful **b)** [noticia] unpleasant **c)** [trabajo] thankless, unrewarding **d)** [tierra] unproductive **2.** *nm, f* ungrateful person

ingrediente *nm* ingredient

ingresar **1.** *vt* **a)** *Esp* [dinero] to deposit, to pay in **b)** MED to admit; **la ingresaron en el hospital** she was admitted to hospital **2.** *vi* **a)** to enter; **ingresar en el ejército** to enlist in the army, to join the army; **ingresar en un club** to join a club **b)** *Esp* **ingresar cadáver** to be dead on arrival

ingreso *nm* **a)** [de dinero] deposit; **hacer un ingreso en una cuenta** to pay money into an account **b)** [entrada] entry (**en** into); [admisión] admission (**en** to) **c)** **ingresos** [sueldo, renta] income; [beneficios] revenue

inhabitable *adj* uninhabitable

inhalar *vt* to inhale

inhibición *nf* inhibition

inhumano, -a *adj* inhumane; [cruel] inhuman

iniciación *nf* **a)** [ceremonia] initiation **b)** [principio] start, beginning

inicial *adj & nf* initial; **punto inicial** starting point

inicializar *vt* INFORM to initialize

iniciar [43] **1.** *vt* **a)** [empezar] to begin, to start; [discusión] to initiate; [una cosa nueva] to pioneer **b)** [introducir] to initiate **2. iniciarse** *vpr* **a)** **iniciarse en algo** [aprender] to start to study sth **b)** [empezar] to begin, to start

iniciativa *nf* initiative; **iniciativa privada** private enterprise; **por iniciativa propia** on one's own initiative

inicio *nm* beginning, start; **a inicios de** at the beginning of

inimaginable *adj* unimaginable

injerto *nm* graft

injusticia *nf* injustice, unfairness

injusto, -a *adj* unjust, unfair

inmaduro, -a *adj* immature

inmediatamente *adv* immediately, at once

inmediato, -a *adj* **a)** [en el tiempo] immediate; **de inmediato** at once **b)** [en el espacio] next (**a** to), adjoining

inmejorable *adj* [trabajo] excellent; [precio] unbeatable

inmenso, -a *adj* immense, vast

inmigración *nf* immigration

inmigrante *adj & nmf* immigrant

inmigrar *vi* to immigrate

inmobiliaria *nf Br* estate agency *o* agent's, *US* real estate company

inmoral *adj* immoral

inmortal *adj & nmf* immortal

inmóvil *adj* motionless, immobile

inmovilizar [40] *vt* **a)** [persona, cosa] to immobilize **b)** FIN [capital] to immobilize, to tie up

inmueble **1.** *adj* **bienes inmuebles** real estate **2.** *nm* building

inmune *adj* immune (**a** to), exempt (**de** from)

inmunidad *nf* immunity (**contra** against); **inmunidad diplomática / parlamentaria** diplomatic / parliamentary immunity

inmunológico, -a *adj* immune

innato, -a *adj* innate, inborn

innecesario, -a *adj* unnecessary

innoble *adj* ignoble

innovación *nf* innovation

inocencia *nf* a) innocence b) [ingenuidad] naïveté

inocentada *nf* Fam ≃ April Fool's joke; **hacer una inocentada a algn** to play an April Fool's joke on sb

inocente 1. *adj* innocent **2.** *nmf* innocent; **día de los Inocentes** Holy Innocents' Day, 28 December, ≃ April Fools' Day

inofensivo, -a *adj* harmless

inoficioso, -a *adj* Am useless

inolvidable *adj* unforgettable

inoperable *adj* RP [aeropuerto] closed

inoportuno, -a *adj* inappropriate; **llegó en un momento muy inoportuno** he turned up at a very awkward moment

inoxidable *adj* **acero inoxidable** stainless steel

inquietar 1. *vt* to worry **2. inquietarse** *vpr* to worry (**por** about)

inquieto, -a *adj* a) [preocupado] worried (**por** about) b) [intranquilo] restless c) [emprendedor] eager

inquietud *nf* a) [preocupación] worry b) [agitación] restlessness c) [anhelo] eagerness

inquilino, -a *nm, f* tenant

inquisición *nf* a) [indagación] inquiry, investigation b) **la Inquisición** [tribunal] the (Spanish) Inquisition

inrayable *adj* scratch-resistant

insaciable *adj* insatiable

insalubre *adj* unhealthy

insatisfacción *nf* a) [disgusto, descontento] dissatisfaction b) [falta, carencia] lack of fulfilment

insatisfecho, -a *adj* dissatisfied

inscribir (pp inscrito) **1.** *vt* a) [registrar] to register; **inscribir a un niño en el registro civil** to register a child's birth b) [matricular] to enrol c) [grabar] to inscribe **2. inscribirse** *vpr* a) [registrarse] to register; [hacerse miembro] to join b) [matricularse] to enrol

inscripción *nf* a) [matriculación] enrolment, registration b) [escrito etc] inscription

inscrito, -a 1. pp de **inscribir 2.** adj inscribed

insecticida *nm* insecticide

insecto *nm* insect

inseguridad *nf* a) [falta de confianza] insecurity b) [duda] uncertainty c) [peligro] lack of safety; **la inseguridad ciudadana** the breakdown of law and order

inseguro, -a *adj* a) [poco confiado] insecure b) [dubitativo] uncertain c) [peligroso] unsafe

insensato, -a 1. *adj* foolish **2.** *nm, f* fool

insensible *adj* a) [indiferente] insensitive (**a** to), unfeeling b) [imperceptible] imperceptible c) MED numb

inseparable *adj* inseparable

insertar *vt* [gen & INFORM] to insert

inservible *adj* useless

insignia *nf* a) [emblema] badge b) [bandera] flag

insignificante *adj* insignificant

insinuar [30] **1.** *vt* to insinuate **2. insinuarse** *vpr* **insinuarse a algn** to make advances to sb

insípido, -a *adj* insipid; Fig dull, flat

insistencia *nf* insistence; **con insistencia** insistently

insistir *vi* to insist (**en** on); **insistió en ese punto** he stressed that point

insolación *nf* MED sunstroke; **coger una insolación** to get sunstroke

insolencia *nf* insolence

insolente *adj* insolent

insólito, -a *adj* [poco usual] unusual; [extraño] strange, odd

insolvente *adj* FIN insolvent

insomnio *nm* insomnia; **noche de insomnio** sleepless night

insoportable *adj* unbearable

inspección *nf* inspection; *Esp* **inspección técnica de vehículos** *compulsory annual test to check vehicle safety,* ≈ MOT (test) *(in UK)*

inspeccionar *vt* to inspect

inspector, -a *nm, f* inspector; **inspector de Hacienda** tax inspector

inspiración *nf* a) inspiration b) [inhalación] inhalation

inspirar 1. *vt* a) to inspire b) [inhalar] to inhale, to breathe in 2. **inspirarse** *vpr* **inspirarse en** to be inspired by

instalación *nf* installation; **instalaciones deportivas** sports facilities

instalar 1. *vt* a) to install b) [puesto, tienda] to set up 2. **instalarse** *vpr* [persona] to settle (down)

instancia *nf* a) [solicitud] request; **a instancia(s) de** at the request of b) [escrito] application form c) JUR **tribunal de primera instancia** court of first instance d) **en primera instancia** first of all; **en última instancia** as a last resort

instantánea *nf* snapshot

instantáneo, -a *adj* instantaneous; **café instantáneo** instant coffee

instante *nm* instant, moment; **a cada instante** constantly; **al instante** immediately, right away; **por instantes** with every second; **¡un instante!** just a moment!

instintivo, -a *adj* instinctive

instinto *nm* instinct; **por instinto** instinctively; **instinto de conservación** survival instinct

institución *nf* institution

institucional *adj* institutional

instituir [37] *vt* to institute

instituto *nm* a) institute b) *Esp* [centro docente] high school

institutriz *nf* governess

instrucción *nf* a) [educación] education b) (*usu pl*) [indicación] instruction; **instrucciones para el o de uso** directions for use c) JUR preliminary investigation; **la instrucción del sumario** proceedings; **juez de instrucción** examining magistrate d) MIL drill

instruir [37] *vt* a) to instruct b) [enseñar] to educate c) MIL to drill d) JUR to investigate

instrumental *adj* instrumental

instrumento *nm* instrument

insuceso *nm Am* unfortunate incident

insuficiente 1. *adj* insufficient 2. *nm* EDUC [nota] fail

insufrible *adj* insufferable

insultante *adj* insulting

insultar *vt* to insult

insulto *nm* insult

insuperable *adj* a) [inmejorable] unsurpassable b) [problema] insurmountable

intacto, -a *adj* intact

integración *nf* [gen & MAT] integration; **integración racial** racial integration

integrar 1. *vt* [formar] to compose, to make up; **el equipo lo integran once jugadores** there are eleven players in the team 2. **integrarse** *vpr* to integrate (**en** with)

íntegro, -a *adj* a) [entero] whole, entire; LITER **edición íntegra** unabridged edition b) [honrado] upright

intelectual *adj* & *nmf* intellectual

inteligencia *nf* [intelecto] intelligence; **cociente de inteligencia** intelligence quotient, IQ

inteligente *adj* [gen & INFORM] intelligent

intemperie *nf* bad weather; **a la intemperie** in the open (air)

intención *nf* intention; **con intención** deliberately, on purpose; **con segunda** *o* **doble intención** with an ulterior motive; **tener la intención de hacer algo** to intend to do sth

intencionado, -a *adj* deliberate

intendencia *nf* a) *RP* [corporación municipal] *Br* town council, *US* city council b) *RP* [edificio] town hall, *US* city hall c) *Chile* [gobernación] regional government

intendente *nm* a) *RP* [alcalde] mayor b) *Chile* [gobernador] provincial governor

intensivo, -a *adj* intensive; *AGRIC* **cultivo intensivo** intensive farming; *EDUC* **curso intensivo** crash course

intenso, -a *adj* intense

intentar *vt* to try, to attempt; *Fam* **¡inténtalo!** give it a go!

intento *nm* attempt; **intento de suicidio** attempted suicide

interactivo, -a *adj* INFORM interactive

intercalar *vt* to insert

intercambiable *adj* interchangeable

intercambiador *nm Esp* **intercambiador (de transportes)** (rail / bus) interchange

intercambiar *vt* to exchange

intercambio *nm* exchange; **intercambio comercial** trade

interceder *vi* to intercede

interceptar *vt* a) [detener] to intercept b) [carretera] to block; [tráfico] to hold up

intercity [inter'θiti] *nm* [tren] intercity (train)

interés *(pl* intereses*) nm* a) interest; **poner interés en** to take an interest in; **tener interés en** o **por** to be interested in b) [provecho personal] self-interest; **hacer algo (sólo) por interés** to do sth (purely) out of self-interest; **intereses creados** vested interests c) *FIN* interest; **con un interés del 11 por ciento** at an interest of 11 percent; **tipos de interés** interest rates

interesado, -a 1. *adj* a) interested (**en** in); **las partes interesadas** the interested parties b) [egoísta] selfish 2. *nm, f* interested person; **los interesados** those interested o concerned

interesante *adj* interesting

interesar 1. *vt* a) [tener interés] to interest; **la poesía no me interesa nada** poetry doesn't interest me at all b) [concernir] to concern 2. *vi* [ser importante] to be of interest, to be important; **interesaría llegar pronto** it is important to get there early 3. **interesarse** *vpr* **interesarse por** o **en** to be interested in; **se interesó por ti** he asked about o after you

interfaz *nm* o *nf* INFORM interface

interferencia *nf* interference; *RADIO & TV* jamming

interino, -a 1. *adj* [persona] acting 2. *nm, f* [suplente] stand-in, deputy; [médico, juez] locum; [profesor] *Br* supply teacher, *US* substitute teacher

interior 1. *adj* a) inner, inside, interior; **habitación interior** inner room; **ropa interior** underwear b) *POL* domestic, internal c) *GEOGR* inland 2. *nm* a) inside, interior; *Fig* **en su interior no estaba de acuerdo** deep down she disagreed b) *GEOGR* interior; *POL* **Ministerio del Interior** ≃ *Br* Home Office, ≃ *US* Department of the Interior

interlocutor, -a *nm, f* speaker; [negociador] negotiator

intermediario *nm* COM middleman

intermedio, -a 1. *adj* intermediate 2. *nm* TV [intervalo] break

interminable *adj* endless

intermitente 1. *adj* intermittent 2. *nm Esp, Col* [en vehículo] *Br* indicator, *US* turn signal

internación *nf* hospitalization

internacional *adj* international

internado, -a 1. *nm, f* inmate 2. *nm* [colegio] boarding school

internar 1. *vt* a) [en colegio] to send to boarding school b) [en hospital] to hospitalize c) [por adicción, problemas psicológicos] to commit 2. **internarse** *vpr* [en lugar] to penetrate, to go deep into

internauta *nmf* Net user

internet *nf* INFORM Internet; **está en internet** it's on the Internet

interno, -a 1. *adj* a) internal; **por vía interna** internally
b) POL domestic
2. *nm, f* [alumno] boarder; MED [enfermo] patient; [preso] inmate
3. *nm RP* [extensión] (telephone) extension; **interno 28, por favor** extension 28, please

interponer [19] (*pp* **interpuesto**) 1. *vt* to insert; JUR **interponer un recurso** to give notice of appeal 2. **interponerse** *vpr* to intervene

interpretación *nf* a) interpretation b) MÚS & TEATRO performance

interpretar *vt* a) to interpret b) TEATRO [papel] to play; [obra] to perform; MÚS [concierto] to play, to perform; [canción] to sing

intérprete 1. *nmf* a) [traductor] interpreter b) TEATRO performer; MÚS [cantante] singer; [músico] performer 2. *nm* INFORM interpreter

interrail *nm* InterRail pass

interrogación *nf* interrogation; LING (signo de) interrogación question *o* interrogation mark

interrogante *nf Fig* question mark

interrogar [42] *vt* to question; [testigo etc] to interrogate

interrogatorio *nm* interrogation

interrumpir *vt* to interrupt; [tráfico] to block

interrupción *nf* interruption; **interrupción del embarazo** termination of pregnancy

interruptor *nm* ELEC switch

interurbano, -a *adj* intercity; TEL **conferencia interurbana** long-distance call

intervalo *nm* interval; **habrá intervalos de lluvia** there will be periods of rain

intervención *nf* a) [participación] intervention, participation (**en** in); [aportación] contribution (**en** to) b) MED intervention

intervenir [27] 1. *vi* [mediar] to intervene (**en** in); [participar] to take part (**en** in); [contribuir] to contribute (**en** to) 2. *vt* a) [confiscar] to confiscate, to seize b) TEL [teléfono] to tap c) MED to operate on

interviú *nf* interview

intestino, -a 1. *adj* [luchas] internal 2. *nm* ANAT intestine

intimidad *nf* [amistad] intimacy; [vida privada] private life; [privacidad] privacy; **en la intimidad** privately, in private

íntimo, -a 1. *adj* a) intimate b) [vida] private; **una boda íntima** a quiet wedding c) [amistad] close 2. *nm, f* close friend, intimate

intocable *adj* [persona, institución] above criticism

intolerable *adj* intolerable

intolerante 1. *adj* intolerant 2. *nmf* intolerant person

intoxicación *nf* poisoning; **intoxicación alimentaria** food poisoning

intoxicar [44] *vt* to poison

intranquilo, -a *adj* [preocupado] worried; [agitado] restless

intransigente *adj* intransigent

intransitable *adj* impassable

intrépido, -a *adj* intrepid

intriga *nf* intrigue; CINE & TEATRO plot

intrigar [42] 1. *vt* [interesar] to intrigue, to interest 2. *vi* [maquinar] to plot

introducción *nf* introduction

introducir [10] *vt* a) to introduce b) [meter] to insert, to put in

introvertido, -a 1. *adj* introverted 2. *nm, f* introvert

intruso, -a 1. *adj* intrusive 2. *nm, f* intruder; JUR trespasser

intuición *nf* intuition

inundación *nf* flood

inundar *vt* to flood; *Fig* [de trabajo etc] to swamp

inusual *adj* unusual

inútil 1. *adj* a) useless; [esfuerzo, intento] vain, pointless b) MIL unfit (for service) 2. *nmf Fam* good-for-nothing

invadir *vt* to invade; *Fig* **los estudiantes invadieron la calle** students poured out onto the street

inválido, -a 1. *adj* **a)** JUR [nulo] invalid **b)** MED [minusválido] disabled, handicapped **2.** *nm, f* MED disabled *o* handicapped person

invalorable *adj CSur* invaluable

invasión *nf* invasion

invasor, -a 1. *adj* invading **2.** *nm, f* invader

invención *nf* [invento] invention; [mentira] fabrication

inventar *vt* to invent; [excusa, mentira] to make up, to concoct

inventariar [43] *vt* to inventory

inventario *nm* inventory

invento *nm* invention

invernadero *nm* greenhouse; **efecto invernadero** greenhouse effect

inversión *nf* **a)** inversion **b)** FIN investment

inversionista *nmf* investor

inverso, -a *adj* opposite; **en sentido inverso** in the opposite direction; **en orden inverso** in reverse order

invertir [5] *vt* **a)** [orden] to invert, to reverse **b)** [dinero] to invest (**en** in); [tiempo] to spend (**en** on)

investigación *nf* **a)** [policial etc] investigation **b)** [científica] research

investigador, -a *nm, f* **a)** [detective] investigator **b)** [científico] researcher, research worker

investigar [42] *vt* to research; [indagar] to investigate

invidente 1. *adj* unsighted **2.** *nmf* unsighted person

invierno *nm* winter

invisible *adj* invisible

invitación *nf* invitation

invitado, -a 1. *adj* invited; **artista invitado** guest artist **2.** *nm, f* guest

invitar *vt* to invite; **hoy invito yo** it's on me today; **me invitó a una copa** he treated me to a drink

involucrado, -a *adj* involved

involucrar 1. *vt* to involve (**en** in) **2. involucrarse** *vpr* **involucrarse en** to get involved in

invulnerable *adj* invulnerable

inyección *nf* injection; **poner una inyección** to give an injection

iPhone® ['aifon, 'ifon] *nm* iPhone®

iPod® ['aipod, 'ipod] *nm* iPod®

ir [16] **1.** *vi* **a)** to go; **¡vamos!** let's go!; **voy a Lima** I'm going to Lima; **¡ya voy!** (I'm) coming!
b) [río, camino] to lead; **esta carretera va a la frontera** this road leads to the border
c) [funcionar] to work (properly); **el ascensor no va** the lift is out of order
d) [desenvolverse] **¿cómo le va el nuevo trabajo?** how is he getting on in his new job?; **¿cómo te va?** how are things?, how are you doing?
e) [sentar bien] to suit; **el verde te va mucho** green really suits you
f) [combinar] to match; **el rojo no va con el verde** red doesn't go with green
g) [vestir] to wear; **ir con falda** to wear a skirt; **ir de blanco/de uniforme** to be dressed in white / in uniform
h) *Fam* [importar, concernir] to concern; **eso va por ti también** and the same goes for you; **ni me va ni me viene** I don't care one way or the other
i) *Fam* [comportarse] to act; **ir de guapo por la vida** to be a flash Harry; *Esp* **¿pero tú de qué vas?** who do you think you are?
j) va para abogado he's studying to be a lawyer
k) (+ **por**) **ir por la derecha** to keep (to the) right; *Esp* [ir a buscar] **ve (a) por agua** go and fetch some water; [haber llegado] **voy por la página 90** I've got as far as page 90
l) [locuciones] **a eso iba** I was coming to that; **¡ahí va!** catch!; **en lo que va de año** so far this year; **ir a parar** to end up; **¡qué va!** of course not!, nothing of the sort!; **va a lo suyo** he looks after his own interests; **¡vamos a ver!** let's see!
2. *v aux* **a)** (+ *gerundio*) **ir andando** to go on foot; **va mejorando** she's improving

b) (+ *pp*) **ya van rotos tres** three (of them) have already been broken **c)** (*a* + *inf*) **iba a decir que** I was going to say that; **va a llover** it's going to rain; **vas a caerte** you'll fall **3. irse** *vpr* **a)** [marcharse] to go away, to leave; **me voy** I'm off; **¡vámonos!** let's go!; **¡vete!** go away!; **vete a casa** go home **b)** [líquido, gas - escaparse] to leak **c)** [direcciones] **¿por dónde se va a …?** which is the way to …?; **por aquí se va al río** this is the way to the river

ira *nf* wrath, rage, anger

Irak *n* Iraq

Irán *n* Iran

Irlanda *n* Ireland; **Irlanda del Norte** Northern Ireland

irlandés, -esa 1. *adj* Irish **2.** *nm, f* Irishman, *f* Irishwoman; **los irlandeses** the Irish **3.** *nm* [idioma] Irish

ironía *nf* irony

irónico, -a *adj* ironic

IRPF *nm* (*abr de* **impuesto sobre la renta de las personas físicas**) ECON income tax

irracional *adj* irrational

irradiar [43] *vt* **a)** [luz, calor] to radiate **b)** *RP* [emitir] to broadcast

irreconciliable *adj* irreconcilable

irrecuperable *adj* irretrievable

irreductible *adj* unyielding

irregular *adj* irregular

irregularidad *nf* irregularity

irremplazable *adj* irreplaceable

irresistible *adj* **a)** [impulso, persona] irresistible **b)** [insoportable] unbearable

irresponsable *adj* irresponsible

irrestricto, -a *adj Am* unconditional, complete

irreversible *adj* irreversible

irrigar [42] *vt* to irrigate, to water

irritable *adj* irritable

irritación *nf* irritation

irritado, -a *adj* irritated

irritante *adj* irritating

irritar 1. *vt* **a)** [enfadar] to irritate, to exasperate **b)** MED to irritate **2. irritarse** *vpr* **a)** [enfadarse] to lose one's temper, to get angry **b)** MED to become irritated

isla *nf* island, isle

islam *nm* REL Islam

islamista *adj & nmf* Islamist

islandés, -esa 1. *adj* Icelandic **2.** *nm, f* [persona] Icelander **3.** *nm* [idioma] Icelandic

Islandia *n* Iceland

islote *nm* small island

Israel *n* Israel

istmo *nm* GEOGR isthmus

itacate *nm Méx* packed lunch

Italia *n* Italy

italiano, -a 1. *adj & nm, f* Italian **2.** *nm* [idioma] Italian

item, ítem *nm* **a)** [cosa & JUR] item **b)** INFORM element

iteración *nf* **a)** [repetición] reiteration **b)** INFORM iteration

itinerancia *nf* TELECOM roaming

itinerario *nm* itinerary, route

ITV *nf Esp* (*abr de* **inspección técnica de vehículos**) compulsory annual test to check vehicle safety, ≃ MOT (test) (*in UK*); **pasar la ITV** ≃ *Br* to pass the MOT

IVA *nm* (*abr de* (**Esp**) **impuesto sobre el valor añadido**, (**Am**) **impuesto al valor agregado**) ECON *Br* VAT, ≃ *US* sales tax

iwal SMS *written abbr of* **igual**

izqda., izqdᵃ (*abr de* **izquierda**) left

izqdo., izqdᵒ (*abr de* **izquierdo**) left

izquierda *nf* **a)** left; **a la izquierda** on the left; **girar a la izquierda** to turn left **b)** [mano] left hand **c)** POL **la izquierda** the left; *Esp* **de izquierdas** left-wing; *Am* **de izquierda** left-wing

izquierdo, -a *adj* **a)** left; **brazo izquierdo** left arm **b)** [zurdo] left-hande

J

jabalí *(pl* **jabalíes)** *nm* wild boar

jabalina *nf* DEP javelin

jabato, -a *nm* **a)** [animal] young wild boar **b)** *Esp Fam* [valiente] daredevil

jabón *nm* soap; **jabón de afeitar / tocador** shaving / toilet soap

jabonera *nf* soap dish

jacal *nm Méx* hut

jacuzzi® [ja'kusi] *nm* Jacuzzi®

jade *nm* jade

jadear *vi* to pant, to gasp

jaguar *nm* jaguar

jaiba *nf Am salvo RP* [cangrejo] crayfish

jalar *vt* **a)** *Esp Fam* [comer] to eat, *Br* to scoff **b)** *Am salvo RP* [tirar de] to pull

jalea *nf* jelly; **jalea real** royal jelly

jaleo *nm* [alboroto] din, racket; [riña] row; [confusión] muddle; **armar jaleo** to make a racket

jalón *nm Am salvo RP* pull

Jamaica *n* Jamaica

jamás *adv* **a)** never; **jamás he estado allí** I have never been there; **nunca jamás** never again **b)** ever; **el mejor libro que jamás se ha escrito** the best book ever written

jamón *nm* ham; **jamón (en) dulce** ham; **jamón serrano** *Spanish cured ham*, Serrano ham, ≃ Parma ham; **jamón (de) York** (boiled) ham

Japón *n* (el) Japón Japan

japonés, -esa 1. *adj* Japanese **2.** *nm, f* [persona] Japanese; **los japoneses** the Japanese **3.** *nm* [idioma] Japanese

jarabe *nm* syrup; **jarabe para la tos** cough mixture

jardín *nm Br* garden, *US* yard; **jardín botánico** botanical garden; **jardín de infancia** nursery school, kindergarten

jardinera *nf* planter

jardinero *nm* gardener

jarra *nf* pitcher; **jarra de cerveza** beer mug; *Fig* **de o en jarras** (with) arms akimbo, hands on hips

jarro *nm* [recipiente] jug; [contenido] jugful; *Fig* **echar un jarro de agua fría a** to pour cold water on

jarrón *nm* vase; [en arqueología] urn

jaula *nf* [para animales] cage

jazmín *nm* BOT jasmine

jazz [jas] *nm inv* jazz

jefatura *nf* **a)** [cargo, dirección] leadership **b)** [sede] central office; **jefatura de policía** police headquarters

jefe *nm* **a)** head, chief, boss; COM manager; **jefe de estación** stationmaster; **jefe de redacción** editor-in-chief; **jefe de ventas** sales manager **b)** POL leader; **Jefe de Estado** Head of State **c)** MIL officer in command; **comandante en jefe** commander-in-chief

jején *nm Am* gnat

jerez *nm* sherry

jerga *nf* [argot-técnica] jargon; [vulgar] slang; **la jerga legal** legal jargon

jeringa, jeringuilla *nf* (hypodermic) syringe

jeroglífico, -a 1. *adj* hieroglyphic **2.** *nm* **a)** LING hieroglyph, hieroglyphic **b)** [juego] rebus

jersey *(pl* **jerseys** *o* **jerséis)** *nm Esp* sweater, *Br* jumper

Jesucristo *nm* Jesus Christ

jesús *interj* [sorpresa] gosh!, good heavens!; *Esp* [tras estornudo] bless you!

jet-set ['ʤetset], **jet** *nf Esp* jet set

jíbaro, -a *nm, f* **a)** [indio] Jivaro **b)** *Ven Fam* [traficante] pusher

jícama *nf* yam bean, jicama

jícara *nf CAm, Méx, Ven* **a)** [calabaza] calabash, gourd **b)** [taza] mug

jinete *nm* rider, horseman

jinetera *nf Cuba Fam* prostitute

jirafa *nf* **a)** giraffe **b)** [de micrófono] boom

jirón *nm* **a)** [trozo desgarrado] shred, strip; [pedazo suelto] bit, scrap; **hecho jirones** in shreds o tatters **b)** *Perú* [calle] street

jitomate *nm Méx* tomato

JJ.OO. *nmpl (abr de* **Juegos Olímpicos)** Olympic Games

joda *nf RP, Ven muy Fam* **a)** [fastidio] pain in the *Br* arse o *US* ass **b)** [broma] piss-take; **¡no te enojes!, lo dije/hice en joda** don't be angry, I was just pissing around **c)** [fiesta] **los espero el sábado en casa, va a haber joda** I'll see you at my place on Saturday, we're having a bash

---

joder *Vulg* **1.** *interj Esp* **¡joder!** shit!, fucking hell!, *Br* bloody hell!

2. *vt* **a)** [fastidiar] to piss off; **¡no me jodas!** you're kidding!

b) [disgustar] to bug, to annoy; **deja ya de joderme** stop being such a pain, stop bugging me

c) *Esp* [copular] to fuck

d) [planes, fiesta] to fuck up

e) [máquina, objeto] to bust, *Br* to bugger up

f) *Esp* [echar a perder] to screw up; **¡la jodiste!** you screwed it up!; **¡como nos pille, la hemos jodido!** if he sees us, we're screwed!

g) [romper] to bugger

3. *vi Esp* **a)** [fastidiar] **¡no jodas!** you've gotta be kidding!, fucking hell!; **eso sí que jode** that's a real pain

b) [copular] to fuck

4. joderse *vpr Esp* **a)** [aguantarse] to put up with it; **¡hay que joderse!** you'll just have to grin and bear it!

b) [echarse a perder] to get screwed up; **¡que se joda!** to hell with him!

c) [romperse] to go bust

---

jogging *nm* **a)** [deporte] jogging; **hacer jogging** to go jogging **b)** *RP* [ropa] tracksuit, jogging suit

Jordania *n* Jordan

jornada *nf* **a)** **jornada (laboral)** [día de trabajo] working day; **jornada intensiva** continuous working day; **jornada partida** working day with a lunch break; **trabajo de media jornada/jornada completa** part-time/full-time work **b)** **jornadas** conference

jornal *nm* [paga] day's wage; **trabajar a jornal** to be paid by the day

jornalero, -a *nm, f* day labourer

jorongo *nm Méx* **a)** [manta] blanket **b)** [poncho] poncho

jota¹ *nf* **a)** *name of the letter j in Spanish* **b)** [cantidad mínima] jot, scrap; **ni jota** not an iota; **no entiendo ni jota** I don't understand a thing

jota² *nf* MÚS *Spanish dance and music*

joven 1. *adj* young; **de aspecto joven** young-looking **2.** *nmf* youth, young man, *f* girl, young woman; **de joven** as a young man/woman; **los jóvenes** young people, youth

joya *nf* **a)** jewel, piece of jewellery; **joyas de imitación** imitation jewellery **b)** *Fig* ser una joya [persona] to be a real treasure o gem

joyería *nf* [tienda] jewellery shop, jeweller's (shop)

joyero, -a 1. *nm, f* jeweller **2.** *nm* jewel case o box

joystick ['ʤoistik] *(pl* **joysticks)** *nm* joystick

JPEG *(abr de* **Joint Photographic Expert Group)** *nm* INFORM JPEG

jubilación *nf* **a)** [acción] retirement; **jubilación anticipada** early retirement **b)** [pensión] pension

jubilado, -a 1. adj retired **2.** nm, f Br pensioner, US retiree; **los jubilados** retired people

jubilar 1. vt [retirar] to retire, to pension off; Fam & Fig to get rid of, to ditch **2. jubilarse** vpr [retirarse] to retire, to go into retirement

judaísmo nm Judaism

judía nf bean; Esp **judía verde** green bean

judío, -a 1. adj Jewish **2.** nm, f Jew

judo nm DEP judo

juego nm a) game; **juego de azar** game of chance; **juego de cartas** card game; Fig **juego de manos** sleight of hand; Fig **juego de palabras** play on words, pun; **juego de rol** fantasy role-playing game; Fig **juego limpio/sucio** fair/foul play
b) DEP game; **Juegos Olímpicos** Olympic Games; **terreno de juego** TENIS court; FÚT field; **fuera de juego** offside
c) [apuestas] gambling; Fig **poner algo en juego** to put sth at stake
d) [conjunto de piezas] set; **juego de café/té** coffee/tea service; Fig **ir a juego con** to match

juerga nf Fam binge, rave-up; **ir de juerga** to go on a binge

jueves nm inv Thursday; **Jueves Santo** Maundy Thursday

juez nmf judge; **juez de instrucción** examining magistrate; **juez de paz** justice of the peace; DEP **juez de salida** starter; **juez de línea** linesman

jugador, -a nm, f player; [apostador] gambler

jugar [32] **1.** vi a) to play; **jugar a(l) fútbol/tenis** to play football/tennis; Fig **jugar sucio** to play dirty
b) **jugar con** [no tomar en serio] to toy with
2. vt a) to play
b) [apostar] to bet, to stake
3. jugarse vpr a) [arriesgar] to risk; Fam **jugarse el pellejo** to risk one's neck
b) [apostar] to bet, to stake

jugo nm juice; Fig **sacar el jugo a** [aprovechar] to make the most of; [explotar] to squeeze dry

jugoso, -a adj a) juicy; **un filete jugoso** a juicy steak b) Fig [sustancioso] substantial, meaty; **un tema jugoso** a meaty topic

juguete nm toy; **pistola de juguete** toy gun; Fig **ser el juguete de algn** to be sb's plaything

juguetería nf toy shop

juguetón, -ona adj playful

juicio nm a) [facultad mental] judgement, discernment; [opinión] opinion, judgement; **a juicio de** in the opinion of; **a mi juicio** in my opinion b) [sensatez] reason, common sense; **en su sano juicio** in one's right mind; **perder el juicio** to go mad o insane c) JUR trial, lawsuit; **llevar a algn a juicio** to take legal action against sb, to sue sb

julepe nm a) [juego de naipes] type of card game b) PRico, RP Fam [susto] scare, fright; **dar un julepe a algn** to give sb a scare

julio nm July

jumper nm CSur, Méx [prenda] pinafore dress

junco nm BOT rush

jungla nf jungle

junio nm June

junta nf a) [reunión] meeting, assembly; POL **junta de gobierno** cabinet meeting b) [dirección] board, committee; **junta directiva** board of directors c) MIL junta; **junta militar** military junta d) [parlamento regional] regional parliament e) TÉC joint

juntar 1. vt a) [unir] to join, to put together; [piezas] to assemble b) [reunir - sellos] to collect; [dinero] to raise **2. juntarse** vpr a) [unirse] to join; [ríos, caminos] to meet; [personas] to gather b) [amancebarse] to live together

junto, -a 1. adj together; **dos mesas juntas** two tables side by side; **todos juntos** all together **2.** adv **junto con** together with; **junto a** next to

jurado *nm* **a)** [tribunal] jury; [en un concurso] panel of judges, jury **b)** [miembro del tribunal] juror, member of the jury

jurar 1. *vi* JUR & REL to swear, to take an oath **2.** *vt* to swear; **jurar el cargo** to take the oath of office; **jurar por Dios** to swear to God **3. jurarse** *vpr* Fam **jurársela(s) a algn** to have it in for sb

jurídico, -a *adj* legal

justicia *nf* justice; **tomarse la justicia por su mano** to take the law into one's own hands

justificación *nf* [gen & INFORM] justification

justificar [44] **1.** *vt* to justify **2. justificarse** *vpr* to clear oneself, to justify oneself

justo, **-a 1.** *adj* **a)** just, fair, right; **un trato justo** a fair deal **b)** [apretado - ropa] tight; **estamos justos de tiempo** we're pressed for time **c)** [exacto] right, accurate; **la palabra justa** the right word

d) [preciso] **llegamos en el momento justo en que salían** we arrived just as they were leaving **e)** **lo justo** just enough **2.** *nm, f* just o righteous person; **los justos** the just, the righteous **3.** *adv* [exactamente] exactly, precisely; **justo al lado** right beside

juvenil 1. *adj* [aspecto] youthful, young; **ropa juvenil** young people's clothes; **delincuencia juvenil** juvenile delinquency **2.** *nmf* **los juveniles** the juveniles

juventud *nf* **a)** [edad] youth **b)** [jóvenes] young people

juzgado *nm* court, tribunal; **juzgado de guardia** *court open during the night or at other times when ordinary courts are shut*

juzgar [42] *vt* to judge; **a juzgar por ...** judging by ...

K

k *nf* **a)** SMS *written abbr of* **que b)** SMS *(abr de* **qué)** wot

karaoke *nm* karaoke

kárate *nm* DEP karate

karateka, karateca *nmf* DEP karateist

kbza SMS *written abbr of* **cabeza**

Kg, kg *(abr de* **kilogramo(s))** kg

kilo, quilo *nm* **a)** [medida] kilo; *Fam* **pesa un kilo** it weighs a ton **b)** *Esp Antes & Fam* [millón] a million (pesetas)

kilogramo, quilogramo *nm* kilogram, kilogramme

kilómetro, quilómetro *nm* kilometre

kimono, quimono *nm* kimono

kíndergarten, *Andes, Méx* **kínder** *nm* kindergarten, nursery school

kitesurf ['kaitsurf] *nm* kitesurf

kiwi *nm* **a)** ORNIT kiwi **b)** [fruto] kiwi (fruit), Chinese gooseberry

kleenex® ['klines, 'klineks] *nm inv* paper hanky, (paper) tissue

kls SMS *written abbr of* **clase**

km a) *(abr de* **kilómetro)** km **b)** SMS *written abbr of* **como**

kntm SMS *written abbr of* **cuéntame**

KO *nm* DEP *(abr de* **knock-out)** [en boxeo] KO; **dejar K.O. a algn** to KO sb

kyat SMS *written abbr of* **cállate**

l *(abr de* **litro(s))** l

la¹ 1. *art det f* the; **la mesa** the table **2.** *pron demos* the one; **la del vestido azul** the one in the blue dress; **la que vino ayer** the one who came yesterday; *ver* **el**

la² *pron pers f* [ella] her; [usted] you; [cosa] it; **la invitaré** I'll invite her along; **no la dejes abierta** don't leave it open; **ya la avisaremos, señora** we'll let you know, madam; *ver* **le**

la³ *nm* MÚS la, A

laberinto *nm* labyrinth

labio *nm* lip

labor *nf* **a)** job, task; **labor de equipo** teamwork; **profesión: sus labores** occupation: housewife **b)** AGRIC farmwork **c)** [de costura] needlework, sewing

laborable *adj* **a)** **día laborable** [no festivo] working day **b)** AGRIC arable

laboral *adj* industrial; **accidente laboral** industrial accident; **conflictividad laboral** industrial unrest; **jornada laboral** working day; **Universidad Laboral** technical training college

laboratorio *nm* laboratory

laborioso, -a *adj* **a)** [persona] hardworking **b)** [tarea] laborious

labrador, -a *nm, f* [granjero] farmer; [trabajador] farm worker

labrar 1. *vt* **a)** AGRIC to till **b)** [madera] to carve; [piedra] to cut; [metal] to work **2. labrarse** *vpr Fig* **labrarse un porvenir** to build a future for oneself

laburar *vi RP Fam* to work; **labura de vendedora** she works in a shop

laburo *nm RP Fam* job

laca *nf* **a)** hair lacquer, hairspray; **laca de uñas** nail polish *o* varnish **b)** ARTE lacquer

lacio, -a *adj* **a)** [pelo] lank, limp **b)** **¡qué lacio!** [soso] what a weed!

lácteo, -a *adj* **productos lácteos** milk *o* dairy products; ASTRON **Vía Láctea** Milky Way

ladera *nf* slope

ladino, -a 1. *adj* [astuto] crafty **2.** *nm, f CAm, Méx, Ven* [no blanco] *non-white Spanish-speaking person*

lado *nm* **a)** side; **a un lado** aside; **al lado** close by, nearby; **al lado de** next to, beside; **dejar de lado, dejar a un lado** [prescindir] to leave out; **ponte de lado** stand sideways **b)** [en direcciones] direction; **por todos lados** on / from all sides **c)** *Fig* **dar de lado a algn** to cold-shoulder sb; **por otro lado** [además] moreover; **por un lado ..., por otro lado ...** on the one hand ..., on the other hand ...

ladrar *vi* to bark

ladrido *nm también Fig* bark

ladrillo *nm* **a)** CONSTR brick **b)** *Fam* [pesado] bore, drag

ladrón, -ona 1. *nm, f* thief, robber; **¡al ladrón!** stop thief! **2.** *nm* ELEC multiple socket

lagartija *nf* small lizard

lagarto 1. *nm* [animal] lizard; *Méx* cayman **2.** *nm Fam* [bíceps] biceps **3.** *interj Esp* touch wood! *(superstitious expression used when you're worried about something you've just said)*

lago *nm* lake

lágrima *nf* **a)** tear; **llorar a lágrima viva** to cry one's eyes out **b)** [en lámpara] teardrop

laguna *nf* **a)** small lake **b)** *Fig* [hueco] gap

laicismo *nf* secularism, *Formal* laicism

lama nm a) [de madera, aluminio] slat b) Am [musgo] moss c) Am [verdín] slime d) Méx [moho] Br mould, US mold

lamber vt Am a) [lamer] to lick b) Fam & Fig [adular] to bootlick

lamentable adj regrettable; [infame] lamentable

lamentablemente adv regrettably

lamentar 1. vt to regret; **lo lamento** I'm sorry 2. **lamentarse** vpr to complain

lamer vt to lick

lámina nf a) sheet, plate; **lámina de acero** steel sheet b) IMPR plate

lámpara nf a) lamp; **lámpara de pie** Br standard lamp, US floor lamp b) ELEC [bombilla] bulb c) RADIO valve

lana nf a) [de oveja] wool; **pura lana virgen** pure new wool b) Andes, Méx Fam [dinero] dough, cash

lanceta nf Andes, Méx [aguijón] sting

lancha nf motorboat, launch; **lancha motora** speedboat; **lancha neumática** rubber dinghy; **lancha salvavidas** lifeboat

langosta nf a) lobster b) [insecto] locust

langostino nm king prawn

lanza nf spear, lance; **punta de lanza** spearhead; Fig **romper una lanza en favor de algn / de algo** to defend sb / sth

lanzar [40] 1. vt a) [arrojar] to throw, to fling b) Fig [grito] to let out c) NÁUT, COM & MIL to launch 2. **lanzarse** vpr a) [arrojarse] to throw o hurl oneself; **lanzarse al suelo** to throw oneself to the ground b) [emprender] **lanzarse a** to embark on; **lanzarse a los negocios** to go into business c) Fam [irse, largarse] to scram

lapa nf a) ZOOL limpet b) **es una verdadera lapa** he sticks to you like glue

lapicera nf CSur ballpoint (pen), Biro®; **lapicera fuente** fountain pen

lapicero nm a) Esp [lápiz] pencil b) CAm, Perú [bolígrafo] ballpoint (pen), Biro®

lápida nf headstone

lápiz nm pencil; **lápiz labial** o **de labios** lipstick; **lápiz de ojos** eyeliner

larga nf a) TAUROM pass with the cape in bullfighting to make the bull run towards it b) **a la larga** in the long run; **está aprendiendo y, a la larga, piensa trabajar** he's studying for now and, in the long run, he plans to work c) **dar largas a algo** to put sth off

largavistas nm inv Bol, CSur binoculars

largo, -a 1. adj a) [espacio] long; [tiempo] long, lengthy; **pasamos un mes largo allí** we spent a good month there; **a lo largo de** [espacio] along; [tiempo] throughout

b) [excesivo] too long; **se hizo largo el día** the day dragged on

c) **largos años** many years

2. nm a) [longitud] length; **¿cuánto tiene de largo?** how long is it?; **siete metros de largo** seven Br metres o US meters long; **pasar de largo** [en el espacio] to walk straight past; **a lo largo de** [en el espacio] along; [en el tiempo] throughout

b) MÚS largo

3. adv **hablar largo y tendido de algo** to discuss sth at great length, to have a long discussion about sth; **esto va para largo** this is going to last a long time

4. interj Fam **¡largo (de aquí)!** scram!, clear off!, get out of here!

largometraje nm feature film, full-length film

laringe nf larynx

las¹ 1. art det fpl the; **las sillas** the chairs; **lávate las manos** wash your hands; **me gustan las flores** (no se traduce) I like flowers 2. pron demos **las que** [personas] the ones who, those who; [objetos] the ones that, those that; **toma las que quieras** take whichever ones you want; ver **la, los**

las² pron pers fpl [ellas] them; [ustedes] you; **las llamaré mañana (a ustedes)**

I'll call you tomorrow; **no las rompas** don't break them; **Pepa es de las mías** Pepa thinks the way I do ; ver **los**

lástima nf pity; **¡qué lástima!** what a pity!, what a shame!; **es una lástima que ...** it's a pity (that) ...; **estar hecho una lástima** to be a sorry sight; **tener lástima a algn** to feel sorry for sb

lastimadura nf Am graze

lata¹ nf a) [envase] can, esp Br tin; **en lata** canned, esp Br tinned b) [hojalata] tin(plate); **hecho de lata** made of tin

lata² nf Esp Fam nuisance, drag; **dar la lata** to be a nuisance o a pest

latido nm [del corazón] beat

látigo nm whip

latín nm Latin

Latinoamérica nf Latin America

latinoamericano, -a adj & nm, f Latin American

latir vi to beat

laucha nf CSur a) [ratón] baby o small mouse b) Fam [persona] **es una laucha** he's a tiny little thing

laurel nm BOT laurel, (sweet) bay; CULIN bay leaf; Fig **dormirse en los laureles** to rest on one's laurels

lava nf lava

lavabo nm a) [pila] Br washbasin, US washbowl b) [retrete] Br lavatory, US washroom

lavadero nm [de coches] car wash

lavado nm wash, washing; Fig **lavado de cerebro** brainwashing; **lavado en seco** dry-cleaning

lavadora nf washing machine

lavanda nf lavender

lavandería nf a) [automática] launderette, US Laundromat® b) [atendida por personal] laundry

lavaplatos nm inv dishwasher

lavar vt to wash; **lavar en seco** to dry-clean

lavarropas nm inv RP washing-maching

lavaseco nm Andes dry cleaner

lavatorio nm a) [en misa] lavabo b) Andes, RP [lavabo] Br washbasin, US washbowl

lavavajillas nm inv [aparato] dishwasher

laxante adj & nm laxative

lazo nm a) [adorno] bow b) [nudo] knot; **lazo corredizo** slipknot c) [para reses] lasso d) Fig (usu pl) [vínculo] tie, bond

le 1. pron pers mf [objeto indirecto - a él] (to) him; [a ella] (to) her; [a cosa] (to) it; [a usted] (to) you; **lávale la cara** wash his face; **le compraré uno** I'll buy one for her; **¿qué le pasa (a usted)?** what's the matter with you? **2.** pron pers m Esp [objeto directo - él] him; [usted] you; **no le oigo** I can't hear him; **no quiero molestarle** I don't wish to disturb you

leal 1. adj loyal, faithful **2.** nmf loyalist

lealtad nf loyalty, faithfulness

lección nf lesson; Fig **dar una lección a algn** to teach sb a lesson; Fig **te servirá de lección** let that be a lesson to you

lechal 1. adj sucking **2.** nm sucking lamb

lechazo nm sucking lamb

leche nf a) milk; ANAT **dientes de leche** milk teeth; **leche descremada o desnatada** skim o skimmed milk b) muy Fam **estar de mala leche** to be in a Br bloody o US goddamn awful mood c) **¡leche!** damn! d) Esp muy Fam [golpe] knock; **dar o pegar una leche a algn** to clobber sb

lechera nf a) [vasija] churn b) muy Fam police car

lechería nf dairy, creamery

lechero, -a 1. adj milk, dairy; **central lechera** dairy co-operative; **vaca lechera** milk cow **2.** nm milkman

lecho nm Literario bed; **lecho del río** river-bed; **lecho mortuorio** death-bed

lechosa nf Carib papaya

lechuga nf lettuce

lechuza nf owl

lector, -a *nm, f* **a)** [persona] reader **b)** *Esp*UNIV lector, (language) assistant **2.** *nm* reader; **lector de CD-ROM** CD-ROM drive; **lector de DVD** DVD player

lectorado *nm Esp*UNIV assistantship

lectura *nf* reading

leer [36] *vt* [un texto & INFORM] to read; **léenos el menú** read out the menu for us; *Fig* **leer entre líneas** to read between the lines

legal *adj* **a)** JUR legal, lawful; **requisitos legales** legal formalities **b)** *Esp Fam* [persona] honest, decent

legalidad *nf* legality, lawfulness

legible *adj* legible

legislación *nf* legislation

legislatura *nf* legislature

legítimo, -a *adj* **a)** JUR legitimate; **en legítima defensa** in self-defence **b)** [auténtico] authentic, real; **oro legítimo** pure gold

legumbre *nf* pulse, pod vegetable; **legumbres secas** dried pulses; **legumbres verdes** green vegetables

lejano, -a *adj* distant, far-off; **parientes lejanos** distant relatives; **el Lejano Oriente** the Far East

lejía *nf* bleach

lejos *adv* far (away); **a lo lejos** in the distance; **de lejos** from a distance; *Fig* **ir demasiado lejos** to go too far; *Fig* **llegar lejos** to go a long way; *Fig* **sin ir más lejos** to take an obvious example

lencería *nf* **a)** [prendas] lingerie **b)** [ropa blanca] linen (goods)

lengua *nf* **a)** tongue; *Fig* **malas lenguas** gossips; *Fam & Fig* **irse de la lengua** to spill the beans; *Fam & Fig* **tirarle a algn de la lengua** to draw sb out **b)** LING language; **lengua materna** native o mother tongue

lenguado *nm* [pez] sole

lenguaje *nm* language; INFORM language; **lenguaje corporal** body language

lengüeta *nf* **a)** [de zapato] tongue **b)** MÚS reed

lente 1. *nf* lens; **lentes de contacto** contact lenses **2.** *nmpl* **lentes** *Am* glasses; **lentes de contacto** contact lenses

lenteja *nf* lentil

lentilla *nf Esp* contact lens; **lentillas blandas /duras** soft / hard lenses; **llevar lentillas** to wear contact lenses

lentitud *nf* slowness; **con lentitud** slowly

lento, -a *adj* slow; **a fuego lento** on a low heat

leña *nf* **a)** firewood; *Fig* **echar leña al fuego** to add fuel to the fire **b)** *Fam* [golpes] knocks

leñador, -a *nm, f* woodcutter

leño *nm* **a)** log **b)** *Fam* [persona] blockhead, halfwit

Leo *nmf* Leo

león *nm* lion

leonino, -a 1. *adj* [rostro, aspecto, cabello] leonine; [piel] lion **2.** *nm, f Am* ASTROL Leo

leopardo *nm* leopard

leotardos *nmpl Esp* thick tights

lépero, -a *adj Fam* **a)** *CAm, Méx* [vulgar] coarse, vulgar **b)** *Cuba* [ladino] smart, crafty

les 1. *pron pers mfpl* [objeto indirecto - a ellos, ellas] (to) them; [a ustedes] you; **dales el dinero** give them the money; **les he comprado un regalo** I've bought you a present **2.** *pron pers mpl Esp* [objeto directo - ellos] them; [ustedes] you; **les esperaré** I shall wait for you; **no quiero molestarles** I don't wish to disturb you

lesbiana *nf* lesbian

leseras *nfpl Chile Fam* [tonterías] nonsense, *Br* rubbish

lesión *nf* **a)** [corporal] injury **b)** JUR [perjuicio] damage

letal *adj* lethal, deadly

letra *nf* **a)** letter; **letra de imprenta** block capitals; **letra mayúscula** capital letter; **letra minúscula** small letter; **letra pequeña** small print **b)** [escritura] (hand)writing **c)** MÚS [texto] lyrics, words **d)** FIN **letra (de cambio)** bill of exchange, draft **e)** UNIV **letras** arts

letrero *nm* [aviso] notice, sign ; [cartel] poster ; **letrero luminoso** neon sign

levantamiento *nm* **a)** raising, lifting ; DEP **levantamiento de pesos** weight-lifting **b)** [insurrección] uprising, insurrection

levantar 1. *vt* **a)** to raise, to lift ; [mano, voz] to raise ; [edificio] to erect ; *Fig* [ánimos] to raise ; **levantar los ojos** to look up
b) [castigo] to suspend
2. levantarse *vpr* **a)** [ponerse de pie] to stand up, to rise
b) [salir de la cama] to get up
c) [concluir] to finish ; **se levanta la sesión** the meeting is closed
d) POL to rise, to revolt ; **levantarse en armas** to rise up in arms
e) [viento] to come up ; [tormenta] to gather

levante *nm* **a) (el) Levante** Levante *(the regions of Valencia and Murcia)*
b) [viento] east wind, Levanter

léxico, -a 1. *nm* LING [diccionario] lexicon ; [vocabulario] vocabulary, word list **2.** *adj* LING lexical

ley *nf (abr de* **leyes***)* **a)** law ; POL bill, act ; **ley del silencio** code of silence ; **aprobar una ley** to pass a bill **b)** **oro de ley** pure gold ; **plata de ley** sterling silver **c) leyes** [derecho] law

leyenda *nf* **a)** [relato] legend **b)** [en un mapa] legend ; [en una moneda] inscription ; [bajo ilustración] caption

liado, -a *adj Fam* **a)** [complicado] complicated, difficult **b)** [ocupado] busy **c)** *Esp* [sentimentalmente] **estar liado (con algn)** to be involved (with sb)

liar [29] **1.** *vt* **a)** [envolver] to wrap up ; [un cigarrillo] to roll **b)** [enredar] to muddle up ; [confundir] to confuse **2. liarse** *vpr* **a)** [embarullarse] to get muddled up **b)** *Esp Fam* [salir con] to get involved ; [besarse] to neck **c)** *Esp* **liarse a bofetadas** to come to blows

libélula *nf* dragonfly

liberal 1. *adj* **a)** liberal ; [carácter] open-minded ; [Partido Liberal] POL **Partido Liberal** Liberal Party ; **profesión liberal** liberal profession **b)** [generoso] generous, liberal **2.** *nmf* liberal

liberar *vt* [país] to liberate ; [prisionero] to free, to release

libertad *nf* freedom, liberty ; **en libertad** free ; JUR **(en) libertad bajo palabra / fianza** (on) parole / bail ; JUR **(en) libertad condicional** (on) parole ; **libertad de comercio** free trade ; **libertad de expresión** freedom of speech

libertador, -a *nm, f* liberator

Libia *n* Libya

libra *nf* [unidad de peso, moneda] pound ; **libra esterlina** pound sterling

Libra *nm* Libra

libramiento *nm* COM payment order

librano, -a *nm, f Am* Libra

librar 1. *vt* **a)** to free ; JUR to free, to release
b) COM [una letra] to draw
c) librar batalla to do o join battle
2. *vi Esp* **libro los martes** [no ir a trabajar] I have Tuesdays off
3. librarse *vpr* to escape ; **librarse de algn** to get rid of sb

libre *adj* free ; **entrada libre** [gratis] admission free ; [sin restricción] open to the public ; **libre cambio** free trade ; **libre de impuestos** tax-free ; *Esp* **estudiar por libre** to study for free, to pay no university fees ; *Esp* **trabajar por libre** to work freelance ; *Esp* **cuando viajo me gusta ir por libre más que ir en grupo** I prefer to travel alone rather than in a group

librería *nf* **a)** [tienda] bookshop, *US* bookstore **b)** *Esp* [mueble] bookcase

librero, -a 1. *nm, f* bookseller **2.** *nm CAm, Col, Méx* [mueble] bookcase

libreta *nf* notebook ; **libreta (de ahorro)** savings book

libretista *nmf Am* [guionista] screenwriter, scriptwriter

libreto *nm Am* [guión] script

libro *nm* book; COM **libro de caja** cashbook; **libro electrónico** e-book, electronic book; FIN **libro mayor** ledger; **libro de texto** textbook

liceal *nmf Urug Br* secondary school *o US* high school pupil

liceano, -a *Chile nm, f* = **liceal**

liceísta *Ven nmf* = **liceal**

licencia *nf* a) [permiso] permission; [documentos] permit, licence; **licencia de armas / caza** gun / hunting licence; *Carib, Chile, Ecuad* **licencia de conducir,** *Méx* **licencia para conducir** *o* **de conductor** *Br* driving licence, *US* driver's license b) [libertad abusiva] licence, licentiousness

licenciado, -a **1.** *adj* UNIV **licenciado en Filología** Language graduate **2.** *nm, f* a) UNIV graduate; **licenciado en Ciencias** Bachelor of Science b) *Am salvo RP* [abogado] lawyer c) *Am* [tratamiento] *form of address used to indicate respect;* **nos atendió el licenciado Sr. López** we were seen by Mr López

licenciar [43] **1.** *vt* a) MIL to discharge b) UNIV to confer a degree on **2. licenciarse** *vpr* UNIV to graduate

licenciatura *nf* UNIV [título] (bachelor's) degree (course); [carrera] degree (course)

liceo *nm* a) [sociedad literaria] literary society b) [escuela] *Br* secondary school, *US* high school

licor *nm* liquor, *US* spirits

licorería *nf* a) [fábrica] distillery b) [tienda] *Br* off-licence, *US* liquor store

licuado *nm Am* [batido] milkshake

licuadora *nf* a) *Esp* [para extraer zumo] juice extractor, juicer b) *Am* [para batir] blender, *Br* liquidizer

licuar *vt* a) [para extraer zumo] to juice b) *Am* [para batir] to blend

líder *nmf* leader

lidia *nf* bullfight, bullfighting

liebre *nf* hare

lienzo *nm* a) TEXT linen b) ARTE canvas

liga *nf* a) DEP & POL league; **hacer buena liga** to get on well together b) [para medias - elástico] garter; [colgante] *Br* suspender, *US* garter

ligar [42] **1.** *vt* a) to join; *Fig* [dos personas] to unite b) *Fam* [coger] to get **2.** *vi Fam* **ligar con algn** [entablar relaciones] *Br* to get off with sb, *US* to make out with sb **3. ligarse** *vpr Esp Fam* **ligarse a algn** *Br* to get off with sb, *US* to make out with sb

ligeramente *adv* a) [levemente] lightly b) [un poco] slightly

ligero, -a **1.** *adj* a) [peso] light, lightweight; **ligero de ropa** lightly clad b) [ágil] light on one's feet; [veloz] swift, quick c) [leve] slight; **brisa / comida ligera** light breeze / meal d) **a la ligera** lightly **2.** *adv* [rápido] fast, swiftly

light [lait] *adj inv* [tabaco] mild; *Fig* [persona] lightweight

ligue *nm Esp Fam* a) [acción] pull; **ir** *o* **salir de ligue** *Br* to go out on the pull, *US* to go out on the pickup; **tener un ligue (con algn)** to have a date (with sb) b) [novio] *Br* bloke, *US* squeeze; [novia] *Br* bird, *US* squeeze

liguero, -a **1.** *adj* DEP league; **partido liguero** league match **2.** *nm Br* suspender belt, *US* garter belt

lija *nf* sandpaper; **papel de lija** sandpaper

lijar *vt* to sand *o* sandpaper (down)

lila¹ **1.** *nm* [color] lilac **2.** *nf* [flor] lilac **3.** *adj inv* lilac

lila² *Fam* **1.** *adj* [tonto] dumb, stupid **2.** *nmf* [tonto] twit

lima¹ *nf* [fruto] lime

lima² *nf* [herramienta] file; **lima de uñas** nail-file

límite *nm* limit; GEOGR & POL boundary, border; **caso límite** borderline case; **fecha límite** deadline; **velocidad límite** maximum speed

limón *nm* lemon

limonada *nf* lemonade (*iced, sweetened lemon juice drink*)

limonero *nm* lemon tree

limosna *nf* alms; **pedir limosna** to beg

limpia *nf Am* **a)** [escarda] clearing **b)** [limpieza] cleaning

limpiabotas *nm inv* shoeshine, *Br* bootblack

limpiacristales *nm inv* window cleaner

limpiador, -a 1. *adj* cleansing **2.** *nm, f* [persona] cleaner **3.** *nm* [producto] cleaner

limpiaparabrisas *nm inv Br* windscreen o *US* windshield wiper

limpiar [43] *vt* **a)** to clean; [con un trapo] to wipe; [zapatos] to polish; *Fig* to cleanse **b)** *Fam* [hurtar] to pinch, to nick

limpieza *nf* [calidad] cleanliness; [acción] cleaning; *Fig* [integridad] integrity; **con limpieza** cleanly

limpio, -a 1. *adj* **a)** [aseado] clean **b)** DEP **juego limpio** fair play **c)** FIN [neto] net; **beneficios en limpio** net profit **d)** pasar algo *Esp* a o *Am* **en limpio** to produce a fair copy of sth **2.** *adv* fairly; **jugar limpio** to play fair

linaje *nm* lineage

lince *nm* lynx; **tiene ojos de lince** he's eagle-eyed

lindo, -a 1. *adj esp Am* [bonito] pretty, lovely; **de lo lindo** a great deal **2.** *adv Am* [bien] very well, beautifully; **dibuja muy lindo** he draws very well o beautifully

línea *nf* **a)** line; **línea aérea** airline; **en líneas generales** roughly speaking; INFORM **fuera de línea** off-line; INFORM **en línea** on-line **b)** **guardar la línea** to watch one's figure

lingote *nm* ingot; [de oro, plata] bar

lingüística *nf* linguistics (*sing*)

lingüístico, -a *adj* linguistic

lino *nm* **a)** BOT flax **b)** TEXT linen

linterna *nf Br* torch, *US* flashlight

linyera *nmf RP* [vagabundo] tramp, *US* bum

lío *nm* **a)** [paquete] bundle **b)** *Fam* [embrollo] mess, muddle; **hacerse un lío** to get mixed up; **meterse en líos** to get into trouble; **armar un lío** to kick up a fuss **c)** *Fam* [relación amorosa] affair

liofilizado, -a *adj* freeze-dried

liofilizar *vt* to freeze-dry

liquidación *nf* **a)** COM [saldo] clearance sale **b)** FIN liquidation

liquidar 1. *vt* COM [deuda, cuenta] to settle; [mercancías] to sell off **2. liquidarse** *vpr Fam* **a)** [gastar] to spend **b)** liquidarse a algn [matar] to bump sb off

líquido, -a 1. *adj* **a)** liquid **b)** FIN net **2.** *nm* **a)** [fluido] liquid **b)** FIN liquid assets; **líquido imponible** taxable income

lira *nf Antes* [moneda] lira

lirio *nm* iris

liso, -a 1. *adj* **a)** [superficie] smooth, even; *Esp* **los cien metros lisos** the one hundred metres sprint **b)** [pelo, falda] straight **c)** [tela] self-coloured **2.** *nm, f Andes, CAm, Ven* cheeky; **es un liso** he's so cheeky

lista *nf* **a)** [relación] list; *Esp* **lista de la compra** shopping list; INFORM **lista de correo** mailing list; **lista de espera** waiting list; [en avión] standby; **pasar lista** to call the register o the roll **b)** [franja] stripe; **a listas** striped

listar *vt* **a)** INFORM to list **b)** *Am* [hacer una lista de] to list

listín *nm Esp* **listín telefónico** telephone directory

listo, -a *adj* **a)** **ser listo** [inteligente] to be clever o smart **b)** **estar listo** [a punto] to be ready

listón *nm* DEP bar; *Fig* **subir el listón** to raise the requirements level

lisura *nf* **a)** *Andes, CAm, Ven* [atrevimiento] cheek **b)** *Andes, CAm, Ven* [dicho grosero] rude remark **c)** *Perú* [donaire] grace

litera *nf* [cama] bunk bed; [en tren] couchette

literal *adj* literal

literario, -a *adj* literary

literatura *nf* literature

litro *nm* litre

llaga *nf* sore; [herida] wound

llama *nf* flame; **en llamas** in flames, ablaze

llamada *nf* call; TEL **llamada interurbana** long-distance call; **señal de llamada** ringing tone

llamado, -a 1. *adj* so-called **2.** *nm Am* **a)** [en general] call; [a la puerta] knock; [con timbre] ring **b)** [telefónico] call; **hacer un llamado** to make a phone call **c)** [apelación] appeal, call

llamar 1. *vt* **a)** to call; **llamar (por teléfono)** to ring up, to call **b)** [atraer] to draw, to attract; **llamar la atención** to attract attention **2.** *vi* [a la puerta] to knock **3. llamarse** *vpr* to be called; **¿cómo te llamas?** what's your name?

llano, -a 1. *adj* **a)** [superficie] flat, level **b)** [claro] clear **c)** [sencillo] simple; **el pueblo llano** the common people **2.** *nm* plain

llanta *nf* **a)** [aro metálico] rim **b)** *Am* [neumático] tyre

llanura *nf* plain

llapa *nf Am* freebie

llave *nf* **a)** [de cerradura] key; **bajo llave** under lock and key; **echar la llave, cerrar con llave** to lock up **b)** [grifo] *Br* tap, *US* faucet; **llave de paso** stopcock; **cerrar la llave de paso** to turn the water / gas off at the mains **c)** [interruptor] **llave de la luz** light switch **d)** [herramienta] spanner; **llave allen** Allen key; **llave inglesa** monkey wrench, *Br* adjustable spanner **e)** [de judo] hold, lock **f)** [signo ortográfico] curly bracket

llegada *nf* arrival; DEP finish

llegar [42] **1.** *vi* **a)** to arrive; **llegar a Madrid** to arrive in Madrid **b)** [ser bastante] to be enough **c)** [alcanzar] **llegar a** to reach; **¿llegas al techo?** can you reach the ceiling? **d)** *Fig* **llegar a las manos** to come to blows; **llegar a presidente** to become president **e)** **llegar a** (+ *infinitivo*) to go so far as to **f)** **llegar a ser** to become **2. llegarse** *vpr* to stop by

llenar 1. *vt* **a)** to fill; [cubrir] to cover **b)** [satisfacer] to satisfy **2.** *vi* [comida] to be filling **3. llenarse** *vpr* to fill (up), to become full

lleno, -a 1. *adj* full (up); *Fig* **de lleno** fully **2.** *nm* TEATRO full house

llevar 1. *vt* **a)** to take; [hacia el oyente] to bring; **¿adónde llevas eso?** where are you taking that?; **te llevaré un regalo** I'll bring you a present **b)** [transportar] to carry; **dejarse llevar** to get carried away; **para llevar** [comida] takeaway **c)** [prenda] to wear; **llevaba falda** she was wearing a skirt **d)** [soportar] to bear; **¿cómo lleva lo de su enfermedad?** how's he coping with his illness? **e)** [tiempo] **llevo dos años aquí** I've been here for two years; **esto lleva mucho tiempo** this takes a long time **f)** [negocio] to be in charge of **2.** *vi* [conducir] **llevar a** to lead to **3.** *v aux* **a)** **llevar** (+ *gerundio*) to have been (+ *present participle*); **llevo dos años estudiando español** I've been studying Spanish for two years **b)** **llevar** (+ *participio pasado*) to have (+ *past participle*); **llevaba escritas seis cartas** I had written six letters **4. llevarse** *vpr* **a)** to take away; [premio] to win; [recibir] to get **b)** [arrastrar] to carry away **c)** [estar de moda] to be fashionable **d)** **llevarse bien con algn** to get on well with sb

llorar *vi* to cry; LITER to weep

llorón, -ona *adj* **un bebé llorón** a baby which cries a lot

llover [4] *v impers* to rain

llovizna *nf* drizzle

lloviznar *v impers* to drizzle

lluvia *nf* rain; **una lluvia de** lots of; **lluvia radiactiva** fallout; **lluvia ácida** acid rain

lluvioso, -a *adj* rainy

lo¹ *art neutro* the; **lo mejor** the best (part); **lo mismo** the same thing; **lo mío** mine; **lo tuyo** yours

lo² (pl **los**) pron pers m & neutro **a)** [cosa] it; **debes hacerlo** you must do it; **no lo creo** I don't think so; **no se lo dije** [no se traduce] I didn't tell her **b)** **lo que ...** what...; **no sé lo que pasa** I don't know what's going on **c)** **lo cual ...** which ... **d)** **lo de ...** the business of ...; **cuéntame lo del juicio** tell me about the trial; ver **le**

lobo nm wolf; **como boca de lobo** pitch-dark; Fam **¡menos lobos!** pull the other one!

local 1. adj local **2.** nm [recinto] premises, site

localidad nf **a)** [pueblo] locality; [en impreso] place of residence **b)** CINE & TEATRO [asiento] seat; [entrada] ticket

localización nf localization

localizar [40] vt **a)** [encontrar] to find **b)** [fuego, dolor] to localize

loción nf lotion

loco, -a 1. adj mad, crazy; **a lo loco** crazily; **loco por** crazy about; **volverse loco** to go mad; Fam **¡ni loco!** I'd sooner die!
2. nm, f madman, f madwoman; **hacerse el loco** to act the fool
3. nm Chile [molusco] false abalone

locomoción nf **a)** [movimiento] transportation; **los gastos de locomoción** transportation costs **b)** Am [transporte] public transport; **los gastos de locomoción** transport costs

locomotora nf locomotive

locura nf [enfermedad] madness, insanity; **con locura** madly; Fam **esto es una locura** this is crazy

locutor, -a nm, f TV & RADIO presenter

locutorio nm telephone booth

lodo nm mud

logaritmo nm logarithm

lógica nf logic; **no tiene lógica** there's no logic to it

lógico, -a adj logical; **era lógico que ocurriera** it was bound to happen

logrado, -a adj [bien hecho] accomplished

lograr vt **a)** to get, to obtain; [premio] to win; [ambición] to achieve **b)** **lograr hacer algo** to manage to do sth

logro nm achievement

lombriz nf worm, earthworm

lomo nm **a)** back; **a lomo(s)** on the back **b)** CULIN loin **c)** [de libro] spine

lona nf canvas

loncha nf slice; **loncha de bacon** rasher of bacon

lonchar vi Méx to have lunch

lonche nm **a)** Perú, Ven [merienda - en escuela] snack eaten during break time; [en casa] (afternoon) tea **b)** Am [comida fría] (packed) lunch **c)** Méx [torta] filled roll

lonchería nf Méx, Ven small fast food restaurant selling snacks, sandwiches etc

Londres n London

longaniza nf spicy (pork) sausage

longitud nf **a)** length; **2 m de longitud** 2 m long; **longitud de onda** wavelength; DEP **salto de longitud** long jump **b)** GEOGR longitude

lonja¹ nf [loncha] slice; **lonja de bacon** rasher of bacon

lonja² nf Esp **lonja de pescado** fish market

loro nm parrot

los¹ 1. art det mpl the; **los libros** the books; **cierra los ojos** close your eyes; **los García** the Garcías; ver **el, las, lo**
2. pron **los que** [personas] the ones who, those who; [cosas] the ones (that); **toma los que quieras** take whichever ones you want; **esos son los míos / tuyos** these are mine / yours; ver **les**

los² pron pers mpl them; **¿los has visto?** have you seen them?

lote nm **a)** set **b)** COM lot **c)** INFORM batch **d)** Esp Fam **darse el lote (con)** to neck (with), Br to snog **e)** Am [solar] plot (of land)

loteamiento nm Bol, Urug parcelling out, division into plots

loteo nm Andes, Méx, RP parcelling out, division into plots

lotería *nf* lottery; **jugar a la lotería** to play the lottery; **me tocó la lotería** I won a prize in the lottery

lotización *nf Ecuad, Perú* parcelling out, division into plots

loza *nf* a) [material] earthenware b) [de cocina] crockery

lubina *nf* sea bass

lubricante *nm* lubricant

lucha *nf* a) fight, struggle; **lucha de clases** class struggle b) DEP wrestling; **lucha libre** freestyle wrestling

luchador, -a *nm, f* a) fighter b) DEP wrestler

luchar *vi* a) to fight, to struggle b) DEP to wrestle

luciérnaga *nf* glow-worm

lucir [35] **1.** *vi* a) [brillar] to shine b) *Am* [parecer] to look; **luces cansada** you seem o look tired c) *Fam* [compensar] **no le luce lo que estudia** his studies don't get him anywhere **2.** *vt* [ropas] to sport; [talento] to display **3. lucirse** *vpr* a) [hacer buen papel] to do very well b) [pavonearse] to show off

lucro *nm* profit, gain; **afán de lucro** greed for money

lúdico, -a *adj* relating to games, recreational

luego 1. *adv* a) [después] then, next, afterwards b) [más tarde] later (on); **¡hasta luego!** so long!; **luego de** after; **luego luego** *Am Fam* [inmediatamente] immediately, straight away; [de vez en cuando] from time to time, now and then c) **desde luego** of course d) *Chile, Ven* [pronto] soon; **acaba luego, te estoy esperando** hurry up and finish, I'm waiting for you; *Méx Fam* **luego luego, luego lueguito** immediately, straight away **2.** *conj* therefore

lugar *nm* a) [place; **en primer lugar** in the first place; **en lugar de** instead of;

sin lugar a dudas without a doubt; **tener lugar** to take place b) **dar lugar a** to cause, to give rise to

lujo *nm* luxury; **productos de lujo** luxury products; **no puedo permitirme ese lujo** I can't afford that

lujoso, -a *adj* luxurious

lujuria *nf* lust

lumbago *nm* lumbago

luminoso, -a *adj* luminous; *Fig* bright

luna *nf* a) moon; *Fig* **estar en la luna** to have one's head in the clouds; **luna creciente / llena** crescent / full moon; *Fig* **luna de miel** honeymoon b) [de escaparate] pane; [espejo] mirror

lunar 1. *adj* lunar **2.** *nm* [redondel] dot; [en la piel] mole, beauty spot; **vestido de lunares** spotted dress

lunes *nm inv* Monday; **vendré el lunes** I'll come on Monday

lupa *nf* magnifying glass

lustrabotas *nm inv Andes, RP* shoeshine, *Br* bootblack

lustrador, -a *nm, f* = **lustrabotas**

luto *nm* mourning

luz *nf* a) light; **apagar la luz** to put out the light; **a la luz de** in the light of; **a todas luces** obviously; *Fig* **dar a luz** to give birth to b) AUTO light; **luces de cruce** *Br* dipped headlights, *US* low beams; **luces de posición** sidelights c) **luces** [inteligencia] intelligence; **corto de luces** dim-witted d) **traje de luces** bullfighter's costume

lycra® *nf* Lycra®

M

m a) *(abr de* **metro(s))** m **b)** *(abr de* **minuto(s))** min

macana *nf a) Andes, Carib, Méx* [garrote] wooden, *Br* truncheon o *US* billy club **b)** *CSur, Perú, Ven Fam* [fastidio] pain, drag **c)** *CAm, Cuba* [azada] hoe

macanear *vt CSur, Ven* [hacer mal] to botch, to do badly

macanudo, -a *adj Fam* great, terrific

macarrones *nmpl* macaroni

macedonia *nf* fruit salad

maceta *nf* [tiesto] plant-pot, flower-pot

machacar [44] **1.** *vt a)* to crush; *DEP* to smash **b)** *Esp Fam* [estudiar] *Br* to swot up on, *US* to bone up on **c)** *Fam* [insistir en] to harp on about, to go on about **2.** *vi a) Fam* [insistir mucho] to harp on, to go on **b)** *Fam* [estudiar con ahínco] *Br* to swot, *US* to grind **c)** [en baloncesto] to smash

machete *nm a)* [arma] machete **b)** *Ven* [amigo] *Br* mate, *US* buddy **c)** *Arg Fam* [chuleta] crib note

machismo *nm* machismo, male chauvinism

machista *adj & nm* male chauvinist

macho 1. *adj a)* [animal, planta] male **b)** *Fam* [viril] manly, virile, macho **2.** *nm a)* [animal, planta] male **b)** *TÉC* [pieza] male piece o part; [de enchufe] (male) plug **c)** *Fam* [hombre viril] macho man, he-man

machote *nm CAm, Méx* [borrador] rough draft

macizo, -a 1. *adj a)* [sólido] solid; **de oro macizo** of solid gold **b)** [robusto] solid, robust; *Fam* [atractivo] well-built **2.** *nm* [masa sólida] mass

macramé *nm* macramé

macro *nf* INFORM macro (instruction)

macuto *nm* [morral] knapsack, haversack

madeja *nf* [de lana etc] hank, skein

madera *nf a)* wood; [de construcción] timber, *US* lumber; **de madera** wood, wooden **b)** *Fig* **tiene madera de líder** he has all the makings of a leader

madrastra *nf* stepmother

madre 1. *nf a)* mother; **es madre de tres hijos** she is a mother of three (children); **madre de familia** mother, housewife; **madre política** mother-in-law; **madre soltera** unmarried mother; *Fig* **la madre patria** one's motherland **b)** [de río] bed **2.** *interj* **¡madre de Dios!, ¡madre mía!** good heavens!

madreselva *nf* honeysuckle

Madrid *n* Madrid

madridista *adj & nm, f* [hincha] Real Madrid supporter; [jugador] Real Madrid player

madriguera *nf* burrow, hole

madrileño, -a 1. *adj* of / from Madrid **2.** *nm, f* person from Madrid

madrina *nf a)* [de bautizo] godmother **b)** [de boda] ≈ bridesmaid **c)** *Fig* [protectora] protectress

madrugada *nf a)* dawn; **de madrugada** in the wee small hours **b)** early morning; **las tres de la madrugada** three o'clock in the morning

madrugador, -a 1. *adj* early-rising **2.** *nm, f* early riser

madrugar [42] *vi* to get up early

madurar 1. *vt Fig* [un plan] to think out **2.** *vi a)* [persona] to mature **b)** [fruta] to ripen

madurez *nf a)* maturity **b)** [de la fruta] ripeness

maduro, -a *adj* a) mature; **de edad madura** middle-aged b) [fruta] ripe

maestría *nf* mastery; **con maestría** masterfully

maestro, -a 1. *nm, f* a) EDUC teacher; **maestro de escuela** schoolteacher b) *Méx* [en universidad] *Br* lecturer, *US* professor c) [especialista] master; **maestro de obras** foreman d) MÚS maestro **2.** *adj* **obra maestra** masterpiece; **llave maestra** master key

mafia *nf* mafia

magdalena *nf* bun, cake

magia *nf* magic; **por arte de magia** as if by magic

mágico, -a *adj* a) magic b) *Fig* [maravilloso] magical, wonderful

magistrado, -a *nm, f* [juez] judge

magistratura *nf* [jueces] magistrature; [tribunal] tribunal

magnate *nm* magnate, tycoon

magnesio *nm* magnesium

magnético, -a *adj* magnetic

magnetófono *nm* tape recorder

magnífico, -a *adj* magnificent, splendid

magnitud *nf* magnitude, dimension; **de primera magnitud** of the first order

magnolia *nf* magnolia

mago, -a *nm, f* wizard, magician; **los tres Reyes Magos** the Three Wise Men, the Three Kings

magrebí *(pl* **magrebíes** *o* **magrebís)** *adj & nm, f* Maghrebi

magro, -a 1. *nm* [de cerdo] lean meat **2.** *adj* [sin grasa] lean

Mahoma *n* Mohammed

mail *nm* INFORM mail

maillot [ma'jot] *(pl* **maillots)** *nm* [malla] leotard; DEP shirt

maíz *nm Br* maize, *US* (Indian) corn

majestuoso, -a *adj* majestic, stately

majo, -a *adj Esp* [bonito] pretty, nice; *Fam* [simpático] nice; **tiene un hijo muy majo** she's got a lovely little boy; *Fam* **ven aquí, majo** come here, dear

---

mal 1. *nm* a) evil, wrong b) [daño] harm; **no le deseo ningún mal** I don't wish him any harm c) [enfermedad] illness, disease; *Fam* **el mal de las vacas locas** mad cow disease **2.** *adj* bad; **un mal año** a bad year *ver* **malo 3.** *adv* badly, wrong; **ir de mal en peor** to go from bad to worse; **lo hizo muy mal** he did it very badly; **menos mal que ...** it's a good job (that) ...; **no está (nada) mal** it is not bad (at all); **te oigo/veo (muy) mal** I can hardly hear/see you; **tomar a mal** [enfadarse] to take badly

malcriar [29] *vt* to spoil

maldad *nf* a) badness, evil b) [acción perversa] evil o wicked thing

maldición 1. *nf* curse **2.** *interj* damnation!

maldito, -a *adj* a) *Fam* [molesto] damned, *Br* bloody b) [endemoniado] damned, cursed; **¡maldita sea!** damn it!

maleable *adj también Fig* malleable

malecón *nm* [muelle] jetty

maleducado, -a 1. *adj* bad-mannered **2.** *nm, f* bad-mannered person

malentendido *nm* misunderstanding

malestar *nm* a) [molestia] discomfort b) *Fig* [inquietud] uneasiness; **tengo malestar** I feel uneasy

maleta 1. *nf* suitcase, case; **hacer la maleta** to pack one's things o case **2.** *nm Fam* [persona] bungler

maletera *Am nf* = **maletero**

maletero, maletera *nm Esp, Cuba* [de automóvil] *Br* boot, *US* trunk

maletín *nm* briefcase

malformación *nf* malformation

malgastar *vt & vi* to waste, to squander

malhablado, -a 1. *adj* foul-mouthed **2.** *nm, f* foul-mouthed person

malhechor, -a *nm, f* wrongdoer, criminal

malhumorado, -a *adj* [de mal carácter] bad-tempered; [enfadado] in a bad mood

malicia *nf* **a)** [mala intención] malice, maliciousness **b)** [astucia] cunning, slyness **c)** [maldad] badness, evil

malintencionado, -a 1. *adj* ill-intentioned **2.** *nm, f* ill-intentioned person

malinterpretar *vt* to misinterpret

malla *nf* **a)** [prenda] leotard **b)** [red] mesh **c)** *Ecuad, Perú, RP* [traje de baño] swimsuit

Mallorca *n* Majorca

malnutrición *nf* malnutrition

malo, -a 1. *adj* **a)** bad; **un año malo** a bad year; **estar a malas** to be on bad terms; **por las malas** by force **b)** [persona - malvado] wicked, bad; [travieso] naughty **c)** [de poca calidad] bad, poor; **una mala canción / comida** a poor song / meal **d)** [perjudicial] harmful; **el tabaco es malo** tobacco is harmful **e) lo malo es que ...** the problem is that ... **f)** [enfermo] ill, sick

> **mal** is used instead of **malo** before masculine singular nouns (e.g. **un mal ejemplo** a bad example). The comparative form of **malo** (= worse) is **peor**, the superlative forms (= the worst) are **el peor** (masculine) and **la peor** (feminine).

2. *nm, f* *Fam* **el malo** the baddy o villain

malograr 1. *vt* *Andes* [estropear] to make a mess of, to ruin **2. malograrse** *vpr* **a)** [fracasar] to fail, fall through **b)** *Andes* [estropearse] [máquina] to break down; [alimento] to go off, to spoil; **se malogró el día** the day turned nasty

malpensado, -a 1. *adj* nasty-minded **2.** *nm, f* nasty-minded person

maltratado, -a *adj* ill-treated, mistreated

maltratar *vt* to ill-treat, to mistreat

malviviente *nmf* *CSur* criminal

mamá *nf Fam Br* mum, *US* mom; *Col, Méx Fam* **mamá grande** grandma

mamacita *nf Am* [mamá] *Br* mum, *US* mom

mamadera *nf RP* [biberón] feeding bottle

mamar *vt* [leche] to suck; **lo mamó desde pequeño** [lo aprendió] he was immersed in it as a child

mameluco *nm* **a)** *Fam* [torpe, necio] idiot **b)** *Méx* [con mangas] *Br* overalls, *US* coveralls; *CSur* [de peto] *Br* dungarees, *US* overalls

mamey *nm* **a)** [árbol] mamey, mammee **b)** [fruto] mamey, mammee (apple)

mamífero, -a *nm, f* mammal

mampara *nf* screen

mamut *(pl* **mamuts***) nm* mammoth

manada *nf* **a)** ZOOL [de vacas, elefantes] herd; [de ovejas] flock; [de lobos, perros] pack; [de leones] pride **b)** *Fam* [multitud] crowd, mob; **en manada(s)** in crowds

manager *(pl* **managers***) nmf* DEP & MÚS manager

manantial *nm* spring

mancha *nf* stain, spot; **mancha solar** sunspot; **mancha de tinta / vino** ink / wine stain

manchar 1. *vt* to stain, to dirty; *Fig* to stain, to blemish **2. mancharse** *vpr* to get dirty

manco, -a 1. *adj* **a)** [de un brazo] one-armed; [sin brazos] armless **b)** [de una mano] one-handed; [sin manos] handless **2.** *nm, f* **a)** [de brazos] one-armed / armless person **b)** [de manos] one-handed / handless person

mancorna *nf CAm, Chile, Col, Méx, Ven* cufflink

mancuerna *nf* **a)** [pesa] dumbbell **b)** *CAm, Chile, Col, Méx, Ven* [gemelo] cufflink

mandado, -a 1. *adj Méx* opportunist **2.** *nm, f Fam* [subordinado] minion **3.** *nm* [recado] errand

mandar 1. *vt* **a)** to order; *Fam* **¿mande?** pardon? **b)** [grupo] to lead, to be in charge o command of; MIL to command **c)** [enviar] to send; **mandar (a) por** to send for; **mandar algo por correo** to post sth, to send sth by post;

mandar recuerdos to send regards **d)** *Am* [encargar] to order, to ask for; **mandó decir que llegaría tarde** he sent a message that he'd be late **2.** *vi Despec* [dar órdenes] to give orders, to be in charge

mandarina *nf* mandarin (orange), tangerine

mandíbula *nf* jaw; *Fam* **reír a mandíbula batiente** to laugh one's head off

Mandinga *nm Am* the devil

mando *nm* **a)** [autoridad] command, control
b) los altos mandos del ejército high-ranking army officers
c) TÉC [control] controls; AUTO **cuadro** *o* **tablero de mandos** dashboard; **mando a distancia** remote control; **palanca de mando** TÉC control lever; [de avión, videojuego] joystick

mandón, -ona 1. *adj Fam* bossy, domineering **2.** *nm, f Fam* bossy *o* domineering person **3.** *nm Chile* [de mina] foreman

manecilla *nf* [de reloj] hand

manejable *adj* manageable; [herramienta] easy-to-use; [coche] manoeuvrable

manejar 1. *vt* **a)** [máquina] to handle, operate; *Fig* [situación] to handle **b)** [negocio] to run, manage **c)** *Fig* [a otra persona] to domineer, boss about **d)** *Am* [conducir] to drive **2.** *vi Am* [conducir] to drive **3. manejarse** *vpr* to manage

manejo *nm* **a)** [uso] handling, use; **de fácil manejo** easy-to-use **b)** *Am* [de vehículo] driving

manera *nf* **a)** way, manner; **a mi / tu manera** (in) my / your way; **de cualquier manera** [mal] carelessly, any old how; [en cualquier caso] in any case; **de esta manera** in this way; **de ninguna manera** in no way, certainly not; **de todas maneras** anyway, at any rate, in any case; **es mi manera de ser** that's the way I am; **no hay manera** it's impossible **b) de manera que** so;

de tal manera que in such a way that **c) maneras** manners; **de buenas maneras** politely

manga *nf* **a)** sleeve; **de manga corta / larga** short- / long-sleeved; **sin mangas** sleeveless; *Fig* **manga por hombro** messy and untidy; *Fig* **sacarse algo de la manga** to pull sth out of one's hat **b)** [de riego] hose **c)** [del mar] arm **d)** DEP leg, round; TENIS set

mango *nm* **a)** [asa] handle **b)** *RP Fam* [dinero] **no tengo un mango** I haven't got a bean, I'm broke

manguera *nf* hose

maní *(pl* **maníes)** *nm* peanut

manía *nf* **a)** dislike, ill will; **me tiene manía** he has it in for me **b)** [costumbre] habit; **tiene la manía de llegar tarde** he's always arriving late **c)** [afición exagerada] craze; **la manía de las motos** the motorbike craze **d)** MED mania

maniático, -a 1. *adj* fussy **2.** *nm, f* fusspot

manicomio *nm Br* mental *o* psychiatric hospital, *US* insane asylum

manicura *nf* manicure

manifestación *nf* **a)** demonstration **b)** [expresión] manifestation, expression

manifestante *nmf* demonstrator

manifestar [1] **1.** *vt* **a)** [declarar] to state, to declare **b)** [mostrar] to show, to display **2. manifestarse** *vpr* **a)** [por la calle] to demonstrate **b)** [declararse] to declare oneself; **se manifestó contrario a ...** he spoke out against ...

manifiesto, -a 1. *adj* clear, obvious; **poner de manifiesto** [revelar] to reveal, to show; [hacer patente] to make clear **2.** *nm* manifesto

manigua *nf Carib, Col* [selva] marshy tropical forest

manigual *nm* = **manigua**

manilla *nf* **a)** [de reloj] hand **b)** *esp Am* [manivela] crank

manillar *nm* handlebar

maniobra *nf* manoeuvre

manipular *vt* to manipulate; [máquina] to handle

maniquí *(pl* **maniquíes)** *nm* [muñeco] dummy

manitas *nmf inv Esp Fam* handyman

manito *nm Méx Fam* pal, *Br* mate, *US* buddy

manivela *nf* TÉC crank

mano **1.** *nf* **a)** hand; **equipaje de mano** hand luggage; **a mano** [sin máquina] by hand; [asequible] at hand; **escrito a mano** hand-written; **de segunda mano** second-hand; **hecho a mano** hand-made; **echar una mano a algn** to give sb a hand; **mano sobre mano, con las manos cruzadas** just sitting there; **¡manos a la obra!** (let's) get down to work!; **manos libres** [dispositivo] hands-free set; **meter mano** [a un problema] to tackle; *Vulg* to touch up; **traerse algo entre manos** to be up to sth
b) [lado] side; **a mano derecha/izquierda** on the right/left(-hand side)
c) mano de pintura coat of paint
d) mano de obra labour (force)
e) *RP* [dirección] direction *(of traffic)*; **calle de una/doble mano** one-/two-way street
2. *nm Am salvo RP Fam* pal, *Br* mate, *US* buddy

manoletina *nf* [zapato] ballet flat

manopla *nf* mitten

manosear *vt* to touch repeatedly, to finger; *Fam* to paw

mansión *nf* mansion

manso, -a *adj* **a)** [persona] gentle, meek **b)** [animal] tame, docile **c)** *Chile Fam* [extraordinario] tremendous; **tiene la mansa casa** he has a gigantic o massive house

manta 1. *nf* **a)** blanket; **manta eléctrica** electric blanket **b)** [zurra] beating, hiding **c)** *Méx* [algodón] *coarse cotton cloth* **d)** *Ven* [vestido] *traditional Indian woman's dress* **2.** *nmf Esp Fam* layabout

manteca *nf* **a)** *Esp* [de animal] fat; **manteca de cacao/cacahuete** cocoa/peanut butter; **manteca de cerdo** lard **b)** *RP, Ven* [mantequilla] butter

mantecado *nm Esp very crumbly shortbread biscuit*

mantel *nm* tablecloth

mantelería *nf* set of table linen

mantener [24] **1.** *vt* **a)** [conservar] to keep; **mantén el fuego encendido** keep the fire burning; **mantener la línea** to keep in trim
b) [entrevista, reunión] to have; **mantener correspondencia con algn** to correspond with sb
c) [ideas, opiniones] to defend, to maintain
d) [familia] to support, to feed
2. mantenerse *vpr* **a)** [sostenerse] to stand
b) mantenerse firme [perseverar] to hold one's ground
c) [sustentarse] to live (**de** on)

mantenimiento *nm* **a)** TÉC maintenance, upkeep; **servicio de mantenimiento** maintenance service
b) [alimento] sustenance, support
c) gimnasia y mantenimiento keep-fit

mantequilla *nf* butter

mantilla *nf* **a)** [de mujer] mantilla **b)** [de bebé] shawl

mantón *nm* shawl

manual 1. *adj* manual; **trabajo manual** manual labour; EDUC **trabajos manuales** handicrafts **2.** *nm* manual, handbook

manubrio *nm Am* [manillar] handlebars

manuscrito *nm* manuscript

mañana 1. *nf* morning; **a las dos de la mañana** at two in the morning; **de mañana** early in the morning; **por la mañana** in the morning **2.** *nm* tomorrow, the future **3.** *adv* tomorrow; **¡hasta mañana!** see you tomorrow!; **mañana por la mañana** tomorrow morning; **pasado mañana** the day after tomorrow

manzana *nf* a) apple b) [de edificios] block

manzanilla *nf* a) BOT camomile b) [infusión] camomile tea c) [vino] manzanilla (sherry)

mañanita *nf* a) [prenda] bed jacket b) *Méx* **mañanitas** *song typically sung for someone on their birthday or saint's day*

manzano *nm* apple tree

mañoco *nm Ven* tapioca

mapa *nm* map; **mapa mudo** blank map; *Fam* **borrar del mapa** to wipe out

maqueta *nf* a) [miniatura] scale model, maquette b) MÚS demo (tape)

maquila *nf CAm, Méx* [de artículos electrónicos] assembly; [de ropa] making-up

maquiladora *nf CAm, Méx US* maquiladora *(bonded assembly plant set up by a foreign firm near the US border)*

maquilar *vt CAm, Méx* [producto, piezas] to assemble

maquillaje *nm* make-up

maquillar **1.** *vt* to make up **2. maquillarse** *vpr* a) [ponerse maquillaje] to put one's make-up on, to make (oneself) up b) [usar maquillaje] to wear make-up

máquina *nf* a) [aparato] machine; **escrito a máquina** typewritten; **hecho a máquina** machine-made; *Fam* **a toda máquina** at full speed; **máquina de afeitar (eléctrica)** (electric) razor o shaver; **máquina de coser** sewing machine; **máquina de escribir** typewriter; **máquina fotográfica** o **de fotos** camera; **máquina** *Esp* **tragaperras** o *Am* **tragamonedas** slot machine, *Br* fruit machine b) *Cuba* [automóvil] car

maquinaria *nf* a) machinery, machines b) [de reloj etc - mecanismo] mechanism, works

maquinilla *nf* **maquinilla de afeitar** safety razor

maquinista *nmf* [de tren] *Br* engine driver, *US* engineer

mar 1. *nm* o *nf* a) sea; **en alta mar** on the high seas; **mar adentro** out to sea; **por mar** by sea; **mar gruesa** heavy sea;

mar picada rough sea b) *Fam* **está la mar de guapa** she's looking really beautiful; **llover a mares** to rain cats and dogs

> Note that the feminine is used in literary language, by people such as fishermen with a close connection with the sea, and in some idiomatic expressions.

2. *nm* sea; **Mar del Norte** North Sea; **Mar Muerto /Negro** Dead /Black Sea

maraca *nf* maraca

maracuyá *nm* [fruto] passion fruit

maratón *nm* marathon

maravilla *nf* marvel, wonder; **de maravilla** wonderfully; **¡qué maravilla de película!** what a wonderful film!; *Fam* **a las mil maravillas** marvellously

maravilloso, -a *adj* wonderful, marvellous

marca *nf* a) mark, sign b) COM brand, make; **marca blanca** own brand; **marca de fábrica** trademark; **marca registrada** registered trademark; **ropa de marca** brand-name clothes c) DEP [récord] record; **batir la marca mundial** to break the world record

marcador *nm* a) marker b) DEP [tablero] scoreboard c) *Am* [rotulador] felt-tip pen; *Méx* [fluorescente] highlighter pen

marcapasos *nm inv* MED pacemaker

marcar [44] **1.** *vt* a) to mark b) TEL to dial c) [indicar] to indicate, to show; **el contador marca 327** the meter reads 1,327 d) DEP [gol, puntos] to score; [a jugador] to mark e) [cabello] to set **2. marcarse** *vpr Esp Fam* **marcarse un detalle** to do something nice o kind

marcha *nf* a) march; **hacer algo sobre la marcha** to do sth as one goes along b) **estar en marcha** [vehículo] to be in motion; [máquina] to be working; [proyecto etc] to be under way; **poner en marcha** to start c) AUTO gear; **marcha atrás** reverse (gear) d) MÚS march e) *Esp Fam* [animación] liveliness, life; **hay mucha marcha** there's a great atmosphere

marchante, -a *nm, f* **a)** [de arte] dealer **b)** *CAm, Méx, Ven Fam* [cliente] customer, patron

marchar 1. *vi* **a)** [ir] to go, to walk; *Fam* ¡marchando! on your way!; ¡una cerveza! — ¡marchando! a beer, please! — coming right up! **b)** [aparato] to be on; **marchar bien** [negocio] to be going well **c)** MIL to march **2. marcharse** *vpr* [irse] to leave, to go away

marchitar 1. *vt* to shrivel, to wither **2. marchitarse** *vpr* = **marchitar**

marchoso, -a *Esp Fam* **1.** *adj* [persona] fun-loving, wild **2.** *nm, f* raver, fun-lover

marciano, -a *adj & nm, f* Martian

marco *nm* **a)** [de cuadro etc] frame **b)** *Fig* [ámbito] framework; **acuerdo marco** framework agreement **c)** FIN [moneda] mark

marea *nf* **a)** tide; **marea alta / baja** high / low tide; **marea negra** oil slick **b)** *Fig* [multitud] crowd, mob

mareado, -a *adj* **a)** sick; [en un avión] airsick; [en un coche] car-sick, travel-sick; [en el mar] seasick **b)** *Euf* [bebido] tipsy **c)** [aturdido] dizzy

mareante *adj* **a)** heady, dizzying **b)** [persona] deadly, tedious

marear 1. *vt* **a)** to make sick; [en el mar] to make seasick; [en un avión] to make airsick; [en un coche] to make car-sick o travel-sick **b)** [aturdir] to make dizzy **c)** *Fam* [fastidiar] to annoy, to pester **2. marearse** *vpr* **a)** to get sick / seasick / airsick / car-sick o travel-sick **b)** [quedar aturdido] to get dizzy **c)** *Euf* [emborracharse] to get tipsy

marejada *nf* heavy sea

maremoto *nm* tidal wave

mareo *nm* **a)** [náusea] sickness; [en el mar] seasickness; [en un avión] airsickness; [en un coche] car-sickness, travel-sickness **b)** [aturdimiento] dizziness, light-headedness

marfil *nm* ivory

margarina *nf* margarine

margarita *nf* daisy

margen 1. *nm* **a)** border, edge; *Fig* **dejar algn / algo al margen** to leave sb / sth out; *Fig* **mantenerse al margen** not to get involved; **al margen de** leaving aside **b)** [del papel] margin **c)** COM **margen de beneficio** profit margin **2.** *nf* [de río] bank

marginación *nf* exclusion

marginado, -a 1. *adj* excluded **2.** *nm, f* dropout

mariachi *nm* **a)** [música] mariachi (music) **b)** [orquesta] mariachi band; [músico] mariachi (musician)

maricón *nm muy Fam Br* poof, *US* fag

marido *nm* husband

marihuana *nf* marijuana

marina *nf* **a)** NÁUT seamanship **b)** MIL navy; **marina de guerra** navy; **marina mercante** merchant navy **c)** GEOGR [zona costera] seacoast

marinero, -a 1. *nm* sailor, seaman **2.** *adj* seafaring

marino, -a 1. *adj* marine; **brisa marina** sea breeze **2.** *nm* sailor

marioneta *nf* marionette, puppet

mariposa *nf* **a)** [insecto] butterfly **b)** [en natación] butterfly

mariquita 1. *nf* [insecto] *Br* ladybird, *US* ladybug **2.** *nm Fam* [marica] fairy

mariscada *nf* seafood meal

marisco *nm* shellfish; **mariscos** seafood

marisma *nf* marsh

marítimo, -a *adj* maritime, sea; **ciudad marítima** coastal town; **paseo marítimo** promenade

marketing ['marketin] *(pl* **marketings)** *nm* marketing

mármol *nm* marble

marqués *nm* marquis

marquesina *nf* canopy; **marquesina (del autobús)** bus shelter

marrano, -a 1. *adj* [sucio] filthy, dirty **2.** *nm, f* **a)** *Fam* [persona] dirty pig, slob **b)** [animal] pig

marrón 1. *adj* [color] brown **2.** *nm*
[color] brown

marroquí *(pl* **marroquíes***) adj & nmf*
Moroccan

Marruecos *n* Morocco

martes *nm inv* Tuesday; **martes y
trece** ≃ Friday the thirteenth

martillero *nm CSur* auctioneer

martillo *nm* hammer

mártir *nmf* martyr

marzo *nm* March

más 1. *adv* **a)** [adicional] more; **no
tengo más** I haven't got any more
b) [comparativo] more; **es más alta /
inteligente que yo** she's taller / more
intelligent than me; **tengo más dinero que tú** I've more money than you;
más gente de la que esperas more
people than you're expecting; **más de**
[con numerales, cantidad] more than,
over **c)** [superlativo] most; **es el más
bonito / caro** it's the prettiest / most
expensive **d)** [interj] so ..., what a ...;
¡qué casa más bonita! what a lovely
house!; **¡está más guapa!** she looks
so beautiful! **e)** [después de pron interr e indef] else; **¿algo más?** anything
else?; **no, nada más** no, nothing else;
¿quién más? who else?; **nadie / alguien más** nobody / somebody else
f) [cada día o vez más** more and more;
estar de más to be unnecessary; **traje
uno de más** I brought a spare one; **es
más** what's more, furthermore; **lo más
posible** as much as possible; **más bien**
rather; **más o menos** more or less; **más
aún** even more **g)** **por más (**+ *adj /adv)*
que (+ *subjuntivo)* however (much), no
matter how (much); **por más fuerte
que sea** however strong he may be;
por más que grites no te oirá nadie
no matter how much you shout nobody
will hear you **2.** *nm inv* **los más** the
majority, most people; **sus más y sus
menos** its pros and cons **3.** *prep* MAT
plus; **dos más dos** two plus o and two

masa *nf* **a)** mass **b)** [de cosas] bulk,
volume; **masa salarial** total wage bill
c) [gente] mass; **en masa** en masse;
medios de comunicación de masas

mass media; *Am* **las masas** [pueblo]
the masses **d)** CULIN dough **e)** *RP* [pas-
telito] cake

masaje *nm* massage; **dar masaje(s)
(a)** to massage

masajista *nmf* masseur, *f* masseuse

mascar [44] *vt & vi* to chew, to mas-
ticate

máscara *nf* mask; **máscara de gas**
gas mask; **traje de máscara** fancy
dress

mascarilla *nf* **a)** mask; **mascarilla
de oxígeno** oxygen mask **b)** MED face
mask **c)** [cosmética] face pack

mascota *nf* mascot

masculino, -a *adj* **a)** ZOOL & BOT
male **b)** [de hombre] male, manly; **una
voz masculina** a manly voice **c)** [para
hombre] men's; **ropa masculina** men's
clothes, menswear **d)** LING masculine

masía *nf traditional Catalan or Ara-
gonese farmhouse*

master *(pl* **masters***) nm* Master's (degree)

masticar [44] *vt* to chew

mástil *nm* **a)** [asta] mast, pole **b)** NÁUT
mast **c)** [de guitarra] neck

matadero *nm* slaughterhouse, ab-
attoir

matador *nm* matador, bullfighter

matambre *nm Andes, RP* **a)** [carne]
flank *o Br* skirt steak **b)** [plato] *flank
steak rolled with boiled egg, olives, red
pepper and cooked, then sliced and served
cold*

matamoscas *nm inv* [pala] fly swat

matanza *nf* slaughter

matar *vt* **a)** to kill; *Fam* **matar el hambre / el tiempo** to kill one's hunger /
the time **b)** [cigarro, bebida] to finish
off **c)** [sello] to frank

matarratas *nm inv* [veneno] rat
poison

matasellos *nm inv* postmark

mate¹ *adj* [sin brillo] matt

mate² *nm* [en ajedrez] mate; **jaque
mate** checkmate

mate³ *nm* [infusión] maté

matemática *nf* mathematics (*sing*)

matemáticas *nfpl* mathematics (*sing*)

matemático, -a 1. *adj* mathematical **2.** *nm,f* mathematician

materia *nf* **a)** matter; **materia prima** raw material **b)** [tema] matter, question; **índice de materias** table of contents **c)** EDUC [asignatura] subject

material 1. *adj* material, physical; **daños materiales** damage to property **2.** *nm* **a)** material; **material escolar/de construcción** teaching / building material o materials **b)** [equipo] equipment; **material de oficina** office equipment

maternidad *nf* maternity, motherhood

materno, -a *adj* maternal; **abuelo materno** maternal grandfather; **lengua materna** native o mother tongue

mates *nfpl* (*abr de* **matemáticas**) *Br* maths, *US* math

matinal *adj* morning; **televisión matinal** breakfast television

matiz *nm* **a)** [de color] shade **b)** [de palabra] shade of meaning, nuance; **un matiz irónico** a touch of irony

matizar [40] *vt* **a)** *Fig* [precisar] to be more precise o explicit about **b)** ARTE to blend, to harmonize **c)** *Fig* [palabras, discurso] to tinge; [voz] to vary, to modulate

matón, -ona *nm, f Fam* thug, bully

matorral *nm* brushwood, thicket

matrero, -a *nm, f Andes, RP* [fugitivo] outlaw

matrícula *nf* **a)** registration; **derechos de matrícula** registration fee; **matrícula de honor** distinction; **plazo de matrícula** registration period **b)** AUTO *Br* number plate, *US* license plate

matricular 1. *vt* to register **2. matricularse** *vpr* = **matricular**

matrimonio *nm* **a)** marriage; **matrimonio civil/religioso** registry office / church wedding; **contraer matrimonio** to marry; **cama de matrimonio** double bed **b)** [pareja casada] married couple; **el matrimonio y los niños** the couple and their children; **el matrimonio Romero** Mr and Mrs Romero, the Romeros

matutino, -a *adj* morning; **prensa matutina** morning papers

maullar *vi* to miaow

maullido *nm* miaowing, miaow

máxima *nf* **a)** METEOR maximum temperature **b)** [aforismo] maxim

maximizar *vt* to maximize

máximo, -a 1. *adj* maximum, highest; **la máxima puntuación** the highest score **2.** *nm* maximum; **al máximo** to the utmost; **como máximo** [como mucho] at the most; [lo más tarde] at the latest

maya 1. *adj* Mayan **2.** *nmf* Maya, Mayan **3.** *nm* [lengua] Maya

mayo *nm* May

mayonesa *nf* mayonnaise

mayor 1. *adj* **a)** [comparativo - tamaño] larger, bigger (**que** than); [edad] older, elder; **mayor que yo** older than me **b)** [superlativo - tamaño] largest, biggest; [edad] oldest, eldest; **la mayor parte** the majority; **la mayor parte de las veces** most often **c)** [adulto] grown-up; **ser mayor de edad** to be of age **d)** [maduro] elderly, mature **e)** [principal] major, main **f)** MÚS major **g)** COM **al por mayor** wholesale **2.** *nm* **a)** MIL major **b) mayores** [adultos] grown-ups, adults

mayoreo *nm Am* wholesale

mayoría *nf* majority; **en su mayoría** in the main; **la mayoría de los niños** most children; **mayoría absoluta** absolute majority; **mayoría relativa** *Br* relative majority, *US* plurality; **mayoría de edad** majority

mayúscula *nf* capital letter

mazapán *nm* marzipan

mazo *nm* mallet

Mb INFORM *(abr de* **Megabit***)* Mb *(megabyte)*

me *pron pers* **a)** [objeto directo] me; **no me mires** don't look at me **b)** [objeto indirecto] me, to me, for me; **¿me das un caramelo?** will you give me a sweet?; **me lo dio** he gave it to me; **me es difícil hacerlo** it is difficult for me to do it **c)** [pron reflexivo] myself; **me he cortado** I've cut myself; **me voy / muero** [no se traduce] I'm off /dying

mear *Fam* **1.** *vi* to (have a) piss **2. mearse** *vpr* to wet oneself; *Fig* **mearse de risa** to piss oneself (laughing)

mecánica *nf* **a)** [ciencia] mechanics *(sing)* **b)** [mecanismo] mechanism, works

mecánico, -a 1. *adj* mechanical **2.** *nm, f* mechanic

mecanismo *nm* mechanism

mecanografía *nf* typewriting, typing

mecanógrafo, -a *nm, f* typist

mecapal *nm CAm, Méx* porter's leather harness

mecedora *nf* rocking-chair

mecer [49] **1.** *vt* to rock **2. mecerse** *vpr* to swing, to rock

mecha *nf* **a)** [de vela] wick **b)** MIL & MIN fuse; *Fam* **aguantar mecha** to grin and bear it **c)** [de pelo] streak; **hacerse mechas** to have one's hair streaked

mechero *nm Esp* (cigarette) lighter

mechón *nm* **a)** [de pelo] lock **b)** [de lana] tuft

medalla 1. *nf* medal **2.** *nmf* DEP [campeón] medallist

medallón *nm* medallion

media *nf* **a)** [prenda interior] **medias** [hasta la cintura] *Br* tights, *US* pantyhose; [hasta medio muslo] stockings **b)** [calcetín - hasta la rodilla] (knee-length) sock; *Am* [de cualquier longitud] sock **c)** [promedio] average; MAT mean; **media aritmética /geométrica** arithmetic /geometric mean **d) a medias** [incompleto] unfinished; [entre dos] half and half; **ir a medias** to go halves

mediado, -a *adj* half-full, half-empty; **a mediados de mes /semana** about the middle of the month /week

medialuna *nf* **a)** [símbolo musulmán] crescent **b)** *Am* [bollo] croissant

mediana *nf* **a)** MAT median **b)** [de autopista] *Br* central reservation, *US* median (strip)

mediano, -a *adj* **a)** middling, average **b)** [tamaño] medium-sized

medianoche *nf* midnight

mediante *prep* by means of, with the help of, using; **Dios mediante** God willing

mediar [43] *vi* **a)** [intervenir] to mediate, to intervene; **mediar en favor de** *o* **por algn** to intercede on behalf of sb **b)** [tiempo] to pass; **mediaron tres semanas** three weeks passed

medicamento *nm* medicine, medicament

medicina *nf* medicine; **estudiante de medicina** medical student

medicinal *adj* medicinal

médico, -a 1. *nm, f* doctor; **médico de cabecera** family doctor, general practitioner **2.** *adj* medical

medida *nf* **a)** measure; **a (la) medida** [ropa] made-to-measure; **a medida que avanzaba** as he advanced; **en gran medida** to a great extent **b)** [dimensión] measurement **c)** [disposición] measure; **adoptar** *o* **tomar medidas** to take steps; **medida represiva** deterrent

medidor *nm Am* [contador] meter

medieval *adj* medieval

medio, -a 1. *adj* **a)** half; **medio kilo** half a kilo; **una hora y media** one and a half hours, an hour and a half **b)** [intermedio] middle; **a media mañana /tarde** in the middle of the morning /afternoon; **clase media** middle class **c)** [normal] average; **salario medio** average wage **2.** *adv* half; **está medio muerta** she is half dead **3.** *nm* **a)** [mitad] half

b) [centro] middle; **en medio (de)** [en el centro] in the middle (of); [entre dos] in between

c) por medio de ... by means of ...

d) medio ambiente environment

e) DEP [jugador] halfback

f) medios means; **medios de transporte** means of transport; **medios de comunicación** o **de información** (mass) media

medioambiental *adj* environmental

mediocre *adj* mediocre

mediocridad *nf* mediocrity

mediodía *nm* **a)** [hora exacta] midday, noon **b)** [período aproximado] early afternoon, lunch-time **c)** [sur] south

medir [6] **1.** *vt* **a)** [distancia, superficie, temperatura] to measure **b)** [moderar] to weigh; **mide tus palabras** weigh your words **2.** *vi* to measure, to be; **¿cuánto mides?** how tall are you?; **mide 2 m** he is 2 m tall; **mide 2 m de alto /ancho /largo** it is 2 m high / wide / long **3. medirse** *vpr* **a)** *Méx Fig* [probarse] to try on **b) medirse al hablar** to watch what one says, to weigh one's words

meditar *vt & vi* to meditate, to ponder; **meditar sobre algo** to ponder over sth

mediterráneo, -a 1. *adj* Mediterranean **2.** *nm* **el Mediterráneo** the Mediterranean

médium *nmf inv* medium

médula *nf* **a)** ANAT marrow, medulla; **médula espinal** spinal chord **b)** [de problema, cosa] heart

medusa *nf* jellyfish

megáfono *nm* megaphone

mejilla *nf* cheek

mejillón *nm* mussel

mejor **1.** *adj* **a)** [comparativo] better **(que** than); **es mejor no decírselo** it's better not to tell her; **es mejor que vayas** you'd better go; **estar mejor** to be better

b) [superlativo] best; **la mejor alumna** the best student; **tu mejor amiga** your best friend; **lo mejor** the best thing

c) [preferible] **(es) mejor que...** it's better that...

2. *adv* **a)** [comparativo] better **(que** than); **cada vez mejor** better and better; **ella conduce mejor** she drives better; **ahora veo mejor (que antes)** I can see better (than before) now; **mejor dicho** or rather, I mean; **¡mucho** o **tanto mejor!** so much the better!

b) [superlativo] best; **es el que mejor canta** he is the one who sings the best; **el que la conoce mejor** the one who knows her best; **¡mejor para ella!** good for her!

3. *nmf* **el mejor de los dos** [comparativo] the better of the two; **el mejor de los tres** [superlativo] the best of the three; **a lo mejor** [quizás] maybe, perhaps; [ojalá] hopefully; **lo mejor es que...** the best thing is to...

mejora *nf* improvement

mejorar 1. *vt* to improve; **mejorar la red vial** to improve the road system; **mejorar una marca** o **un récord** to break a record **2.** *vi* to improve, to get better **3. mejorarse** *vpr* to get better; **¡que te mejores!** get well soon!

mejoría *nf* improvement

melancolía *nf* melancholy

melancólico, -a *adj* melancholic, melancholy

melena *nf* (head of) hair; [de león] mane

mella *nf* **a)** [hendedura] nick, notch; [en plato, taza etc] chip **b)** [en dentadura] gap **c)** *Fig* impression; **hacer mella en algn** to make an impression on sb

mellizo, -a *adj & nm, f* twin

melocotón *nm esp Esp* peach

melocotonero *nm esp Esp* peach tree

melodía *nf* melody, tune

melodrama *nm* melodrama

melodramático, -a *adj* melodramatic

melón *nm* a) [fruto] melon b) *Fam* [tonto] ninny c) *muy Fam* **melones** [tetas] boobs

membresía *nf Am* membership

membrillo *nm* a) BOT quince ; [árbol] quince tree ; [dulce] quince preserve o jelly b) *Fam* [tonto] dimwit

memela *nf Méx* thick corn tortilla, oval in shape

memorable *adj* memorable

memoria *nf* a) [gen & INFORM] memory ; **memoria USB** USB stick ; **aprender/saber algo de memoria** to learn / know sth by heart ; **irse de la memoria** to slip one's mind ; **traer algo a la memoria** to bring sth to mind b) [informe] report, statement ; **memoria anual** annual report c) [recuerdo] memory, recollection d) **memorias** [biografía] memoirs

memorizar [40] *vt* to memorize

menaje *nm* furniture and furnishing ; **menaje de cocina** kitchen equipment o utensils

mención *nf* mention ; **mención honorífica** honourable mention

mencionar *vt* to mention

mendigo, -a *nm, f* beggar

mendrugo *nm* a) [de pan] crust (of bread) b) *Esp Fam* [idiota] fathead, idiot

mene *nm Ven* deposit of oil at surface level

menear 1. *vt* [mover] to move ; [cabeza] to shake ; [cola] to wag **2. menearse** *vpr* [moverse] to move (about) ; [agitarse] to shake

menestra *nf* vegetable stew

menor 1. *adj* a) [comparativo - de tamaño] smaller (**que** than) ; [de edad] younger (**que** than) ; **mal menor** the lesser of two evils ; **ser menor de edad** to be a minor o under age
b) [superlativo - de tamaño] smallest ; [de intensidad] least, slightest ; [de edad] youngest ; **al menor ruido** at the slightest noise ; **el menor de los tres** the youngest of the three ; **es la menor** she's the youngest child
c) MÚS minor

d) COM **al por menor** retail
2. *nmf* minor ; JUR **tribunal de menores** juvenile court

Menorca *n* Minorca

menos 1. *adj* a) [comparativo - con singular] less ; [con plural] fewer ; **menos dinero/leche que** less money / milk than ; **menos libros/pisos que** fewer books / flats than ; **tiene menos años de lo que parece** [con cláusula] he's younger than he looks
b) [superlativo] **el/la/lo menos** the least ; **fui el que perdí menos dinero** I lost the least money ; **lo menos posible** the least possible
2. *adv* a) **menos de** [con singular] less than ; [con plural] fewer than, less than ; **menos de media hora** less than half an hour
b) [superlativo - con singular] least ; [con plural] the fewest ; [con cantidad] the least ; **el menos inteligente de la clase** the least intelligent boy in the class ; **ayer fue cuando vinieron menos personas** yesterday was when the fewest people came
c) [excepto] except
d) [en horas] to ; **son las dos menos diez** it's ten to two
e) MAT minus ; **tres menos dos igual a uno** three minus two equals one
f) [locuciones] **a menos que** (+ *subjuntivo*) unless ; **al menos** o **por lo menos** at least ; **de menos** less ; **hay cinco euros de menos** there's five euros less ; **echar a algn de menos** to miss sb ; **eso es lo de menos** that's the least of it ; **¡menos mal!** just as well! ; **nada menos que** no less o no fewer than ; **todo menos eso** all except that
3. *nm inv* a) [mínimo] **es lo menos que puedo hacer** it's the least I can do
b) MAT minus
4. *prep* a) but, except ; **todo menos eso** anything but that
b) MAT minus ; **tres menos uno** three minus one

menospreciar [43] *vt* to scorn, to disdain

menosprecio *nm* contempt, scorn, disdain

mensaje *nm* message

mensajero, -a *nm, f* messenger, courier

menso, -a *adj Méx Fam* foolish, stupid

menstruación *nf* menstruation

mensual *adj* monthly; **dos visitas mensuales** two visits a month

menta *nf* **a)** BOT mint **b)** [licor] crème de menthe

mental *adj* mental

mente *nf* mind; **se me quedó la mente en blanco** my mind went blank; **mente abierta/tolerante/cerrada** open /broad /closed mind

mentir [5] *vi* to lie, to tell lies

mentira *nf* lie; **aunque parezca mentira** strange as it may seem; **parece mentira** it is unbelievable

mentiroso, -a 1. *adj* lying **2.** *nm, f* liar

mentón *nm* ANAT chin

menú *nm* menu; **menú del día** set menu *(offered by many restaurants for a reasonable fixed price)*

menudeo *nm Andes, Méx* retailing

menudo, -a 1. *adj* minute, tiny; [irónico] tremendous; **la gente menuda** the little ones; **¡menudo lío/susto!** what a mess /fright! **2.** *adv* **a menudo** often

meñique *adj & nm* **(dedo) meñique** little finger, *US, Scot* pinkie

mercadillo *nm* flea market

mercado *nm* market; **mercado de abastos** indoor market *(selling fresh produce daily)*; **Mercado Común** Common Market; **mercado laboral** *Br* labour market, *US* labor market; **mercado negro** black market; **mercado único** single market; **sacar algo al mercado** to put sth on the market

mercancía *nf* merchandise, goods

mercantil *adj* mercantile, commercial

mercería *nf Br* haberdasher's (shop), *US* notions store

mercurio *nm* **a)** QUÍM mercury, quicksilver **b) Mercurio** Mercury

merecer [33] **1.** *vt* **a)** to deserve **b)** [uso impers] **no merece la pena hacerlo** it's not worthwhile doing it **2. merecerse** *vpr* to deserve

merendar [1] **1.** *vt* to have as an afternoon snack, to have for tea **2.** *vi* to have an afternoon snack, to have tea

merendero *nm* [establecimiento] tea room, snack bar; [en el campo] picnic spot

merengue *nm* **a)** CULIN meringue **b)** [música, baile] merengue

meridiano *nm* meridian

meridional 1. *adj* southern **2.** *nmf* southerner

merienda *nf* afternoon snack, tea

mérito *nm* merit, worth; **hacer méritos para algo** to strive to deserve sth

merluza *nf* **a)** [pez] hake **b)** *Fam* [borrachera] **coger una merluza** to get plastered

merluzo, -a *adj & nm, f Esp Fam* [persona] idiot, cretin

mermelada *nf* **a)** jam; **mermelada de fresa** strawberry jam **b)** [de agrios] marmalade; **mermelada de naranja** (orange) marmalade

mero, -a *adj* mere, pure; **por el mero hecho de** through the mere fact of

mes *nm* **a)** month; **el mes pasado/que viene** last /next month **b)** [cobro] monthly salary *o* wages; [pago] monthly payment **c)** *Fam* [menstruación] period

mesa *nf* **a)** table; **poner/recoger la mesa** to set /clear the table; [de despacho etc] desk; **mesa redonda** round table **b)** [junta directiva] board, executive; **el presidente de la mesa** the chairman; **mesa electoral** electoral college

mesada *nf* **a)** *Am* [pago mensual] monthly payment, monthly instalment **b)** *RP* [para adolescentes] pocket money, *US* allowance **c)** *RP* [encimera] worktop

mesero, -a *nm, f Col, Guat, Méx, Salv* waiter, *f* waitress

meseta *nf* plateau, tableland, meseta; **la Meseta** the plateau of Castile

mesilla *nf* **mesilla de noche** bedside table

mesita *nf* side table; **mesita (de noche)** bedside table

mesón *nm* old-style tavern

mesonero, -a *nm, f* a) *Esp* [en mesón] innkeeper b) *Chile, Ven* [camarero] waiter, *f* waitress

mestizo, -a *adj & nm, f* half-breed, half-caste, mestizo

meta *nf* a) [objetivo] goal, aim, objective b) [de carrera] finish, finishing line c) FÚT [portería] goal

metáfora *nf* metaphor

metal *nm* a) metal; **metales preciosos** precious metals b) [timbre de la voz] timbre c) MÚS brass

metálico, -a 1. *adj* metallic 2. *nm* cash; **pagar en metálico** to pay (in) cash

metate *nm Guat, Méx* grinding stone

meteorito *nm* meteorite

meteorología *nf* meteorology

---

meter 1. *vt* a) [poner] to put (**en** in); *Fig* **meter las narices en algo** to poke one's nose into sth

b) [comprometer] to involve (**en** in), to get mixed up (**en** in)

c) *Fam & Fig* [dar] to give; **meter un rollo** to go on and on; **meter prisa a algn** to hurry sb up

d) [hacer] to make; **meter ruido** to make a noise

2. **meterse** *vpr* a) [entrar] to go o come in, to get into

b) [estar] to be; **¿dónde te habías metido?** where have you been (all this time)?

c) [entrometerse] to meddle

d) **meterse con algn** [en broma] to get at sb

---

meterete *nmf RP Fam* busybody, *Br* nosy-parker

metete *nmf Andes, CAm Fam* busybody, *Br* nosy-parker

metiche *nmf Méx, Ven Fam* busybody, *Br* nosy-parker

método *nm* a) method b) EDUC course

metralla *nf* shrapnel

metro *nm* a) [medida] metre b) [tren] *Br* underground, *US* subway

metrópoli *nf* metropolis

mexicanismo *nm* Mexicanism *(Mexican word or expression)*

mexicano, -a *adj & nm, f* Mexican

México *n* Mexico

mezanín, mezanine *nm Am* mezzanine

mezcla *nf* a) [acción] mixing, blending; RADIO & CINE mixing b) [producto] mixture, blend

mezclar 1. *vt* a) [dos o más cosas] to mix, to blend b) [desordenar] to mix up c) [involucrar] to involve, to mix up 2. **mezclarse** *vpr* a) [cosas] to get mixed up; [gente] to mingle b) [relacionarse] to get involved (**con** with)

mezclilla *nf Chile, Méx* denim; **pantalones de mezclilla** jeans

mezquino, -a *adj* a) [persona] mean, stingy b) [sueldo] miserable

mezquita *nf* mosque

mg *(abr de* **miligramo***)* mg

mi[1] *adj* my; **mi casa / trabajo** my house / job; **mis cosas / libros** my things / books

mi[2] *(pl* **mis***) nm* MÚS E; **mi menor** E minor

mí *pron pers* me; **a mí me dio tres** he gave me three; **compra otro para mí** buy one for me too; **por mí mismo** just by myself

miche *nm Ven* [aguardiente] cane spirit flavoured with herbs and spices

mico *nm* a) ZOOL (long-tailed) monkey b) *Fam* [pequeño] **es un mico** he's a midget o *Br* titch

micro 1. *nm Fam* mike, microphone 2. *nm o nf Arg, Bol, Chile* [autobús] bus

microbio *nm* microbe

microbús *nm* a) [autobús] minibus b) *Méx* [taxi] (collective) taxi

microchip *nm* INFORM microchip

microcosmos *nm inv* microcosm

micrófono *nm* microphone

microonda *nf* un (horno) **microondas** a microwave (oven)

microscopio *nm* microscope

miedo *nm* [pavor] fear; [temor] apprehension; **una película de miedo** a horror movie *o Br* film; **tener miedo de algn / algo** to be afraid of sb / sth; *Esp Fam* **lo pasamos de miedo** we had a fantastic time; **un calor de miedo** sizzling heat

miedoso, -a *adj* fearful

miel *nf* honey; **luna de miel** honeymoon

miembro *nm* **a)** [socio] member; **estado miembro** member state **b)** ANAT limb; **miembro viril** penis

mientras 1. *conj* **a)** [al mismo tiempo que] while **b)** [durante el tiempo que] when, while; **mientras viví en Barcelona** when I lived in Barcelona **c) mientras que** [por el contrario] whereas **d)** *Fam* [cuanto más] **mientras más / menos ...** the more / less ... **2.** *adv* **mientras (tanto)** meanwhile, in the meantime

miércoles *nm inv* Wednesday; **Miércoles de Ceniza** Ash Wednesday

mierda *nf Vulg* **a)** shit; **de mierda** [malo] shit; **tienes un buga de mierda** you've got a shit car; **ese libro es una mierda** that book is crap; **¡vete a la mierda!** piss off! **b)** *Fig* [porquería] dirt, filth **c)** *Esp* [borrachera] bender

miga *nf* [de pan etc] crumb; *Fig* **hacer buenas migas con algn** to get on well with sb

migaja *nf* **a)** [de pan] crumb **b)** *Fig* bit, scrap **c) migajas** [de pan] crumbs; *Fig* leftovers

migra *nf Méx Fam & Despec* **la migra** US police border patrol

mil *adj & nm* thousand; **mil euros** a *o* one thousand euros

milagro *nm* miracle

milenario, -a 1. *adj* millenarian, millennial **2.** *nm* millennium

milenio *nm* millennium

milésimo, -a *adj & nm, f* thousandth

mili *nf Esp Antes & Fam* military *o* national service; **hacer la mili** to do one's military service

milico *nm Andes, RP* **a)** *Fam & Despec* [militar] soldier; **los milicos tomaron el poder** the military took power **b)** [policía] pig

miligramo *nm* milligram

mililitro *nm* millilitre

milímetro *nm* millimetre

militante *adj & nmf* militant

militar 1. *adj* military **2.** *nm* military man, soldier **3.** *vi* POL [en un partido] to be a member

milla *nf* mile

millar *nm* thousand

millón *nm* million

millonario, -a *adj & nm, f* millionaire

milonga *nf* popular song or dance from Argentina

milpa *nf CAm, Méx* cornfield

mim SMS *written abbr of* **misión imposible**

mimado, -a *adj* spoilt

mimar *vt* to spoil, to pamper

mímica *nf* mimicry

mimosa *nf* BOT mimosa

mina *nf* **a)** mine; **ingeniero de minas** mining engineer **b)** [explosivo] mine; **campo de minas** minefield **c)** [de lápiz] lead; **lápiz de mina** propelling pencil **d)** *Fig* [ganga] gold mine

minarete *nm* minaret

mineral 1. *adj* mineral **2.** *nm* ore

minero, -a 1. *nm, f* miner **2.** *adj* mining

miniatura *nf* miniature

minibar *nm* minibar

minifalda *nf* miniskirt

mínima *nf* METEOR minimum temperature, low

mínimo, -a 1. *adj* **a)** [muy pequeño] minute, tiny **b)** MAT & TÉC minimum, lowest; **mínimo común múltiplo**

lowest common denominator **2.** *nm* minimum; **como mínimo** at least; **ni lo más mínimo** not in the least

ministerio *nm* **a)** POL *Br* ministry, *US* department **b)** REL ministry

ministro, -a *nm, f* **a)** POL *Br* minister, *US* secretary; **primer ministro** prime minister **b)** REL minister

miniturismo *nm Arg* short trip

minivolumen *nm* AUTO mini-MPV *(mini-multipurpose vehicle)*

minoría *nf* minority; JUR **minoría de edad** minority

minoritario, -a *adj* minority

minucioso, -a *adj* **a)** [persona] meticulous **b)** [informe, trabajo etc] minute, detailed

minúscula *nf* small letter; IMPR lower-case letter

minúsculo, -a *adj* minuscule, minute; **letra minúscula** lower-case *o* small letter

minusválido, -a 1. *adj* handicapped, disabled **2.** *nm, f* handicapped person, disabled person

minuta *nf* **a)** [cuenta] lawyer's bill **b)** [menú] menu **c)** *RP* [comida rápida] *single-course meal which usually consists of meat or fish accompanied by French fries and sometimes vegetables*

minutero *nm* minute hand

minuto *nm* minute

mío, -a 1. *adj poses* of mine; **un amigo mío** a friend of mine; **no es asunto mío** it is none of my business **2.** *pron poses* mine; **ese libro es mío** that book is mine; **lo mío es el tenis** tennis is my strong point; *Fam* **los míos** my people *o* folks

miope *nmf* short-sighted *o US* near-sighted person, *Espec* myopic person

miopía *nf* short-sightedness, *US* near-sightedness, *Espec* myopia

mirada *nf* look; **lanzar** *o* **echar una mirada a** to glance at; **levantar la mirada** to raise one's eyes; **mirada fija** stare

mirador *nm* **a)** [lugar con vista] viewpoint **b)** [balcón] bay window, windowed balcony

mirar 1. *vt* **a)** to look at **b)** [observar] to watch **c) mirar por algn/algo** [cuidar] to look after sb /sth **d)** [procurar] to see; **mira que no le pase nada** see that nothing happens to him **2.** *vi* [dar a] to look, to face; **la casa mira al sur** the house faces south

mirilla *nf* spyhole, peephole

mirlo *nm* blackbird

mirón, -ona *Fam* **1.** *adj* [curioso] nosey; [con lascivia] peeping **2.** *nm, f* [espectador] onlooker; [curioso] busybody, *Br* nosy-parker; [voyeur] peeping Tom

misa *nf* mass

miscelánea *nf* **a)** [mezcla] miscellany **b)** *Méx* [tienda] *small general store*

miserable 1. *adj* **a)** [mezquino - persona] despicable; [sueldo etc] miserable **b)** [pobre] wretched, poor; **una vida miserable** a wretched life **2.** *nmf* **a)** [mezquino] miser **b)** [canalla] wretch

miseria *nf* **a)** [pobreza extrema] extreme poverty **b)** [insignificancia] pittance; **ganar una miseria** to earn next to nothing **c)** [tacañería] miserliness, meanness

misericordia *nf* mercy, compassion

misil *nm* missile; **misil tierra-aire** surface-to-air missile

misión *nf* mission; **misión cumplida** mission accomplished

misionero, -a *nm, f* missionary

mismo, -a 1. *adj* **a)** same **b)** [uso enfático] **yo mismo** I myself; **aquí mismo** right here **2.** *pron* same; **es el mismo de ayer** it's the same one as yesterday; **lo mismo** the same (thing); **dar** *o* **ser lo mismo** to make no difference; **por eso mismo** that is why; **por uno** *o* **sí mismo** by oneself **3.** *adv* **a)** [por ejemplo] for instance; **que venga algn, Juan mismo** ask one of them to come, Juan, for instance **b)** **así mismo** likewise

misterio *nm* mystery

misterioso, **-a** *adj* mysterious

mitad *nf* **a)** half; **a mitad de camino** halfway there; **a mitad de precio** half-price **b)** [centro] middle; **en la mitad del primer acto** halfway through the first act; *Fam* **eso me parte por la mitad** that really screws things up for me

mitin *nm* POL meeting, rally

mito *nm* myth

mitología *nf* mythology

mitote *nm Méx* **a)** *Fam* [alboroto] racket **b)** [fiesta] house party

mixto, **-a** *adj* mixed

mñn SMS *(abr de* **mañana***)* 2MORO

mobiliario *nm* furniture

mocasín *nm* moccasin

mochila *nf* backpack

mochilero, **-a** *nm, f Fam* backpacker

mochuelo *nm* ZOOL little owl

moco *nm* snot; **sonarse los mocos** to blow one's nose

moda *nf* **a)** fashion; **a la moda, de moda** in fashion; **pasado de moda** old-fashioned **b)** [furor pasajero] craze

modalidad *nf* form, category; COM **modalidad de pago** method of payment; DEP **modalidad deportiva** sport

modélico, **-a** *adj* exemplary, model

modelo 1. *adj inv & nm* model **2.** *nmf* (fashion) model; **desfile de modelos** fashion show

módem *(pl* **modems***) nm* INFORM modem; **módem fax** fax modem

moderno, **-a** *adj* modern

modestia *nf* modesty; **modestia aparte** without wishing to be immodest

modesto, **-a** *adj* modest

modificación *nf* alteration

modificar [44] *vt* to modify

modisto, **-a** *nm, f* **a)** [diseñador] fashion designer **b)** [sastre] couturier, *f* couturière

modo *nm* **a)** [manera] way, manner; **modo de empleo** instructions for use **b)** **modos** manners **c)** LING mood

moflete *nm* chubby cheek

mogollón 1. *nm Esp Fam* **a)** [muchos] loads (of people); **llegaron mogollón** loads (of people) arrived; **mogollón de** loads of **b)** [confusión] commotion; [ruido] racket **2.** *adv Esp Fam* really; **me gusta mogollón** I like it loads, I really love it, I think it's fantastic

moho *nm* **a)** BOT mould **b)** [de metales] rust

mojado, **-a 1.** *adj* [empapado] wet; [húmedo] damp **2.** *nm, f Méx Fam* [inmigrante] *immigrant who has crossed illegally into the US*; **irse de mojado** to cross the border illegally

mojar 1. *vt* **a)** to wet; [humedecer] to damp; **mojar pan en la leche** to dip o dunk bread in one's milk **b)** *muy Fam* **mojarla** to have it off **2. mojarse** *vpr* to get wet

mojito *nm* [cóctel] mojito *(cocktail made with rum, lemon juice, sugar, and fresh mint)*

molar *muy Fam* **1.** *vt* **¿te molaría ir a la playa?** do you fancy going to the beach? **¡cómo me mola ese chico!** I really fancy that guy! **2.** *vi Esp* **salir solo no mola** it's not much fun going out on your own; **ese profe mola** that teacher's pretty cool; **¡cómo mola!** that's really cool!, that's mad!; **le mola ese chico** she fancies that guy

molcajete *nm Méx* mortar

molde *nm* mould; **letras de molde** printed letters; **pan de molde** ≃ sliced bread

moldear *vt* to mould

mole 1. *nf* mass, bulk **2.** *nm Méx* **a)** [salsa] *thick, cooked chilli sauce* **b)** [guiso] *dish served in "mole" sauce*

molestar 1. *vt* **a)** [incomodar] to disturb, to bother **b)** *Formal* to bother; **¿le molestaría esperar fuera?** would you mind waiting outside? **c)** [causar malestar a] to hurt **2. molestarse** *vpr* **a)** [tomarse la molestia] to bother **b)** [ofenderse] to take offence, to get upset

molestia *nf* a) bother; **no es ninguna molestia** it is no trouble at all; **perdone las molestias** forgive the inconvenience b) MED [dolor] trouble, slight pain

molesto, -a *adj* a) [irritante] annoying, upsetting b) **estar molesto con algn** [enfadado] to be annoyed o upset with sb

molestoso, -a *adj Am Fam* annoying, upsetting

molino *nm* mill; **molino de agua** watermill; **molino de viento** windmill

molote *nm Méx* [tortilla] *filled Mexican tortilla*

molusco *nm* mollusc

momento *nm* a) [instante] moment; **al momento** at once; **por momentos** by the minute b) [periodo] time; **de momento** for the time being; **en cualquier momento** at any time

momia *nf* mummy

monada *nf Fam* **¡qué monada!** how cute!

monaguillo *nm* REL altar boy

monarca *nmf* monarch

monarquía *nf* monarchy

monasterio *nm* REL monastery

mondar 1. *vt* to peel **2. mondarse** *vpr Esp Fam* **mondarse (de risa)** to laugh one's head off

moneda *nf* a) [pieza] coin; **moneda suelta** small change; **acuñar moneda** to mint money b) FIN currency; **moneda única** single currency

monedero *nm* purse

monitor, -a 1. *nm, f* monitor; [profesor] instructor **2.** *nm* INFORM monitor

monitorear *vt Am* to monitor

monitorizar *vt* to monitor

monja *nf* nun

monje *nm* monk

mono, -a 1. *nm* a) [animal] monkey b) [prenda - con mangas] *Br* overalls, *US* coveralls; [con peto] *Br* dungarees, *Br* boiler suit, *US* overalls; *Ven* [de deporte] tracksuit c) *Esp Fam* [síndrome de abstinencia] cold turkey **2.** *adj Fam* [bonito] pretty, cute

monoambiente *nm Arg* studio

monobloque *nm Arg* tower block

monodosis *nf* single dose

monólogo *nm* monologue

monopatín *nm Esp* skateboard

monopolio *nm* monopoly

monótono, -a *adj* monotonous

monovolumen *nm* people carrier

monstruo *nm* a) monster b) [genio] genius

montacargas *nm inv Br* goods lift, *US* freight elevator

montado *nm Esp* [tapa] *small canapé-style sandwiches served as tapas in the Basque country*

montaje *nm* a) TÉC [instalación] fitting; [ensamblaje] assembling; **cadena de montaje** assembly line b) CINE editing and mounting c) TEATRO staging d) FOTO montage e) *Fam* [farsa] farce

montaña *nf* mountain; **montaña rusa** big dipper

montañismo *nm* mountaineering

montañoso, -a *adj* mountainous

montar 1. *vi* a) [subirse] to get in; [en bici, a caballo] to ride
b) FIN [ascender] **montar a** to amount to, to come to
2. *vt* a) [colocar] to put on
b) [máquina etc] to assemble; [negocio] to set up, to start
c) *Esp* CULIN [nata] to whip
d) CINE & FOTO [película] to edit, to mount; [fotografía] to mount
e) TEATRO [obra] to stage, to mount
f) ZOOL [cubrir] to mount
3. montarse *vpr* a) [subirse] to get on; [en coche] to get in (**en** to)
b) *Fam* [armarse] to break out; *Fam* **montárselo bien** to have things (nicely) worked out o set up

monte *nm* a) [montaña] mountain; [con nombre propio] mount; **de monte** wild b) **el monte** [zona] the hills

montera *nf* bullfighter's hat

montón *nm* heap, pile; **un montón de** a load of; *Fam* **me gusta un montón** I really love it; *Fam* **del montón** run-of-the-mill, nothing special

montura *nf* **a)** [cabalgadura] mount **b)** [de gafas] frame

monumental *adj* **a)** [ciudad, lugar] famous for its monuments **b)** *Fig* [fracaso, éxito] monumental

monumento *nm* monument

moño *nm* **a)** [de pelo] bun **b)** *Am* [lazo] bow **c)** *Méx* [pajarita] bow tie

moqueta *nf Esp* fitted carpet

mora *nf* [zarzamora] blackberry

morado, -a 1. *adj* purple; *Esp Fam* **pasarlas moradas** to have a tough time; *Esp Fam* **ponerse morado** to stuff oneself **2.** *nm* purple

moradura *nf* [en la piel] bruise

moral 1. *adj* moral **2.** *nf* **a)** [ética] morals **b)** [ánimo] morale, spirits; **levantar la moral a algn** to raise sb's spirits

moraleja *nf* moral

moralista 1. *adj* moralistic **2.** *nmf* moralist

moratón *nm* [en la piel] bruise

morcilla *nf Br* black pudding, *US* blood sausage; *Esp Fam* **que te /os den morcilla** you can stuff it, then!

mordaza *nf* gag

mordedura *nf* bite

morder [4] *vt* to bite; **me ha mordido** it has bitten me; *Fig* **morder el anzuelo** to take the bait

mordida *nf CAm, Méx Fam* [soborno] bribe, *Br* backhander

mordisco *nm* bite

moreno, -a 1. *adj* **a)** [pelo] dark-haired; [piel] dark-skinned **b)** [bronceado] tanned; **ponerse moreno** to get a suntan; **pan /azúcar moreno** brown bread /sugar **2.** *nm, f* [persona - de pelo] dark-haired person; [de piel] dark-skinned person

moribundo, -a *adj* & *nm, f* moribund

morir [7] **1.** *vi* to die; **morir de frío / hambre /cáncer** to die of cold / hunger /cancer; **morir de amor** o **pena** to die from a broken heart
2. morirse *vpr* to die; **morirse de hambre** to starve to death; *Fig* to be starving; **morirse de aburrimiento** to be bored to death; **morirse de ganas (de hacer algo)** to be dying (to do sth); **morirse de risa** to die laughing

moro, -a *nm, f* **a)** HIST Moor; *Fam* **no hay moros en la costa** the coast is clear **b)** *Esp* [árabe] Arab *(pejorative term referring to a North African or Arab person)*

morocho, -a 1. *adj* **a)** Andes, RP [moreno] dark-haired **b)** Andes, RP Euf [negro] coloured **c)** Ven [gemelo] twin **2.** *nm, f* **a)** Andes, RP [moreno] dark-haired person **b)** Andes, RP Euf [negro] coloured person **c)** Ven [gemelo] twin

moronga *nf CAm, Méx Br* black pudding, *US* blood sausage

moroso, -a *nm, f* bad debtor

morralla *nf* **a)** [cosas sin valor] rubbish, junk **b)** [chusma] scum

morreo *nm Fam Br* snogging, *US* necking; **darse un morreo** *Br* to have a snog, *US* to neck

morriña *nf Esp* [nostalgia] homesickness *(for one's country)*

morro *nm* **a)** [de animal - hocico] snout **b)** *Esp Fam* [de persona] mouth, (thick) lips; **caerse de morro** to fall flat on one's face; **por los morros** without so much as a by-your-leave; *Fam* **¡vaya morro!** what a cheek! **c)** *Esp* [de coche] nose

morsa *nf* walrus

mortadela *nf* mortadella

mortal 1. *adj* **a)** mortal **b)** [mortífero] fatal; **un accidente mortal** a fatal accident **2.** *nmf* mortal

mortero *nm* CULIN & MIL mortar

mosaico *nm* **a)** [obra, técnica] mosaic **b)** *Am* [baldosa] mosaic tile

mosca *nf* fly; **peso mosca** flyweight; *Esp Fam* **estar mosca** [suspicaz] to be suspicious; [borracho] to be pissed;

Fam **por si las moscas** just in case; *Fam* **¿qué mosca te ha picado?** what's biting you?

moscatel *nm* Muscatel *(dessert wine made from muscat grapes)*; **uvas de moscatel** muscat grapes

mosquearse *vpr Fam* to get annoyed

mosquitera *nf* mosquito net

mosquito *nm* mosquito

mostaza *nf* BOT & CULIN mustard

mostrador *nm* a) [de tienda] counter b) [de bar] bar

mostrar 1. *vt* to show; **muéstramelo** show it to me **2. mostrarse** *vpr* to be; **se mostró muy comprensiva** she was very understanding

mote¹ *nm* nickname

mote² *nm Andes* stewed *Br* maize o *US* corn

motel *nm* motel

motivación *nf* motivation

motivar *vt* a) [causar] to cause, to give rise to b) [inducir] to motivate

motivo *nm* a) [causa] reason; [usu pl] grounds; **con este** o **tal motivo** for this reason; **con motivo de** on the occasion of; **sin motivo** for no reason at all; **bajo ningún motivo** under no circumstances b) ARTE & MÚS motif, leitmotiv

moto *nf* AUTO motorbike, bike; **moto náutica** o **acuática** jet ski

motocicleta *nf* motorbike

motociclismo *nm* motorcycling

motociclista *nmf* motorcyclist

motocross *nm* motocross

motoesquí *nm* [vehículo] snowmobile

motoneta *nf Am* (motor) scooter

motonetista *nmf Am* scooter rider

motor, -a 1. *nm* [grande] engine; [pequeño] motor; **motor de reacción** jet engine; **motor de explosión** internal combustion engine; **motor eléctrico** electric motor; INFORM **motor de búsqueda** search engine **2.** *adj* TÉC motive

motora *nf* motorboat

motorista *nmf Esp* motorcyclist

mousse [mus] *nf (Esp nm)* mousse

mover [4] **1.** *vt* a) to move; **mover algo de su sitio** to move sth out of its place b) [hacer funcionar] to drive; **el motor mueve el coche** the engine drives the car **2. moverse** *vpr* a) to move b) *Fam* [gestionar] to do everything possible c) [darse prisa] to hurry up; **¡muévete!** get a move on!

movida *nf Esp, RP Fam* **hay mucha movida** there's a lot going on

movido, -a *adj* a) FOTO blurred b) [ocupado] busy

móvil 1. *adj* mobile; **teléfono móvil** mobile phone; TV & RADIO **unidad móvil** outside broadcast unit **2.** *nm* a) [de delito] motive b) [teléfono] mobile

movilidad *nf* [en empresa] mobility

movilizar 1. *vt* [poner en movimiento] to mobilize **2. movilizarse** *vpr* [ponerse en movimiento] to mobilize, to get moving

movimiento *nm* a) [gen] movement; FÍS & TÉC motion; **(poner algo) en movimiento** (to set sth) in motion; **movimiento sísmico** earth tremor b) [actividad] activity c) COM & FIN [entradas y salidas] operations d) HIST **el Movimiento** the Falangist Movement

mozárabe 1. *adj* Mozarabic *(Christian in the time of Moorish Spain)* **2.** *nmf* [habitante] Mozarab *(Christian of Moorish Spain)* **3.** *nm* [lengua] Mozarabic

mozo, -a *nm* a) [niño] young boy, young lad; [niña] young girl b) [de estación] porter; [de hotel] bellboy, *US* bellhop c) MIL conscript d) *Andes, RP* [camarero] waiter, *f* waitress e) *Col* [novio] boyfriend; [novia] girlfriend

MP3 *nm* INFORM [formato] MP3; [archivo] MP3 (file)

MP4 *nm* INFORM [formato] MP4; [archivo] MP4 (file)

msj SMS *written abbr of* **mensaje**

mucamo, -a *nm, f Andes, RP* [en hotel] chamberperson, *f* chambermaid

muchacha *nf* girl

muchachada *nf* bunch of kids

muchacho *nm* boy

muchedumbre *nf* [de gente] crowd

mucho, **-a** 1. *adj* a) (*sing*) [usu en frases afirmativas] a lot of, lots of ; [usu en frases negativas] much ; **mucho tiempo** a long time ; **tengo mucho sueño / mucha sed** I am very sleepy / thirsty ; **¿bebes mucho café? — no, no mucho** do you drink a lot of coffee? — no, not much
b) [demasiado] **es mucho coche para mí** this car is a bit too much for me
c) **muchos** [usu en frases afirmativas] a lot of, lots of ; [usu en frases negativas] many ; **tiene muchos años** he is very old
2. *pron* a) a lot, a great deal ; **¿cuánta leche queda? — mucha** how much milk is there left? — a lot
b) **muchos** a lot, lots, many ; **¿cuántos libros tienes? — muchos** how many books have you got? — lots *o* a lot ; **muchos creemos que ...** many of us believe that ...
3. *adv* a) a lot, very much ; **lo siento mucho** I'm very sorry ; **como mucho** at the most ; **mucho antes / después** long before / after ; **¡ni mucho menos!** no way! ; **por mucho (que)** (+ *subjuntivo*) however much
b) [tiempo] **hace mucho que no viene por aquí** he has not been to see us for a long time
c) [a menudo] often ; **vamos mucho al cine** we go to the cinema quite often

mudanza *nf* move ; **estar de mudanza** to be moving ; **camión de mudanza** removal van

mudar 1. *vt* a) [ropa] to change b) [plumas, pelo] to moult ; [piel] to shed, to slough 2. **mudarse** *vpr* **mudarse de casa / ropa** to move house / to change one's clothes

mudéjar *adj* & *nmf* Mudejar

mudo, **-a** 1. *adj* a) [que no habla] dumb ; **cine mudo** silent films b) *Fig* [callado] speechless 2. *nm, f* mute

mueble 1. *nm* piece of furniture ; **muebles** furniture ; **con / sin muebles** furnished / unfurnished ; **mueble bar** cocktail cabinet 2. *adj* movable

mueca *nf* a) [de burla] mocking face ; **hacer muecas** to pull faces b) [de dolor, asco] grimace

muela *nf* a) ANAT molar ; **dolor de muelas** toothache ; **muela del juicio** wisdom tooth b) TÉC [de molino] millstone

muelle¹ *nm* spring

muelle² *nm* NÁUT dock

muerte *nf* death ; **muerte natural** natural death ; **dar muerte a algn** to kill sb ; **odiar a algn a muerte** to loathe sb ; *Esp* **de mala muerte** badly ; *Fam* **un susto de muerte** the fright of one's life

muerto, **-a** 1. *adj* dead ; **muerto de hambre** starving ; **muerto de frío** frozen to death ; **muerto de miedo** scared stiff ; **muerto de risa** laughing one's head off ; **horas muertas** spare time ; AUTO **(en) punto muerto** (in) neutral 2. *nm, f* [difunto] dead person ; **hacerse el muerto** to pretend to be dead ; *Fam* **cargar con el muerto** to do the dirty work ; **hubo dos muertos** two (people) died

muestra *nf* a) [espécimen] sample, specimen b) [modelo a copiar] model c) [prueba, señal] sign ; **dar muestras de** to show signs of ; **muestra de cariño / respeto** token of affection / respect ; **una muestra más de ...** yet another example of ...

mugido *nm* [de vaca] moo ; [de toro] bellow

mugir [57] *vi* [vaca] to moo, to low ; [toro] to bellow

mujer 1. *nf* a) woman ; **dos mujeres** two women ; **mujer de la limpieza** cleaner, cleaning lady ; **mujer de su casa** house-proud woman b) [esposa] wife ; **su futura mujer** his bride-to-be 2. *interj Esp* **pero mujer, no te pongas así** come on, don't be like that

mula *nf Fam* a) [testarudo] **es una mula** he's really pigheaded, he's as stubborn as a mule b) [traficante] mule

mulá *nm* REL mullah

mulato, **-a** *adj* & *nm, f* mulatto

muleta *nf* a) [prótesis] crutch b) TAUROM muleta

mulo, -a *nm, f* [animal] mule

multa *nf* fine ; AUTO ticket

multar *vt* to fine

multicentro *nm* shopping mall, *Br* shopping centre

multinacional *adj & nf* multinational

múltiple *adj* a) multiple ; **accidente múltiple** pile-up b) **múltiples** [muchos] many

multiplicación *nf* MAT multiplication

multiplicar [44] **1.** *vt & vi* to multiply (**por** by) **2. multiplicarse** *vpr* [reproducirse, aumentar] to multiply

múltiplo, -a *adj & nm* multiple

multirriesgo *adj inv* all-risks, fully-comprehensive

multisala(s) *nm inv* [cine] *Br* multiplex cinema, *US* multiplex movie theater

multitud *nf* a) [de personas] crowd b) [de cosas] multitude

mundial 1. *adj* worldwide ; **campeón mundial** world champion ; **de fama mundial** world-famous **2.** *nm* world championship

mundialización *nf* globalization ; **la mundialización de la información / economía** globalization of information / the economy

mundo *nm* world ; **todo el mundo** everyone ; **correr** o **ver mundo** to travel widely ; **nada del otro mundo** nothing special ; **el otro mundo** the hereafter

munición *nf* ammunition

municipal 1. *adj* municipal **2.** *nmf Esp* [guardia] policeman, *f* policewoman

municipio *nm* a) [corporación] local council b) [territorio] town, municipality

m1ml SMS *written abbr of* **mándame un mensaje luego**

muñeca *nf* a) [del cuerpo] wrist b) [juguete, muchacha] doll c) *Andes, RP Fam*

tener muñeca [enchufe] to have friends in high places ; [habilidad] to have the knack d) *Méx* [mazorca] baby sweetcorn

muñeco *nm* [juguete] (little) boy doll ; **muñeco de trapo** rag doll ; **muñeco de nieve** snowman

muñeira *nf* popular Galician dance and music

muñequera *nf* wristband

mural 1. *adj* [pintura] mural ; [mapa] wall **2.** *nm* mural

muralismo *nm* ARTE mural painting

muralla *nf* wall

murciélago *nm* ZOOL bat

muro *nm* wall

musa *nf* muse

músculo *nm* muscle

museo *nm* museum ; **museo de arte** o **pintura** art gallery

musgo *nm* moss

música *nf* music ; **música clásica** classical music ; **música de fondo** background music

musical 1. *adj* musical **2.** *nm* musical

músico, -a 1. *adj* musical **2.** *nm, f* musician

muslo *nm* thigh

musulmán, -ana *adj & nm, f* Muslim, Moslem

mutilado, -a *nm, f* disabled person ; **mutilado de guerra** disabled serviceman

mutua *nf Br* friendly society, *US* mutual benefit society

mutual *nf CSur, Perú Br* friendly society, *US* mutual benefit society

muy *adv* very ; **muy bueno / malo** very good / bad ; **¡muy bien!** very good! ; *Fam* **muy mucho** very much ; **Muy señor mío** Dear Sir ; **muy de los andaluces** typically Andalusian ; **muy de mañana / noche** very early / late

mxa SMS *written abbr of* **mucha**

mxo SMS *written abbr of* **mucho**

N

nº *(abr de* **número***)* no

nabo *nm* **a)** BOT turnip **b)** *muy Fam* [pene] tool, *Br* knob

nacatamal *nm CAm* type of meat-filled corn pasty steamed in banana leaves

nacer [60] *vi* **a)** to be born; **al nacer** at birth; **nací en Montoro** I was born in Montoro; *Fam & Fig* **nacer de pie** to be born under a lucky star **b)** [pájaro] to hatch (out) **c)** [pelo] to begin to grow **d)** [río] to rise

nacho *nm* nacho

nacimiento *nm* **a)** birth; **sordo de nacimiento** deaf from birth; **lugar de nacimiento** birthplace, place of birth **b)** *Fig* [principio] origin, beginning; [de río] source **c)** [belén] Nativity scene, crib

nación *nf* nation; **las Naciones Unidas** the United Nations

nacional 1. *adj* **a)** national **b)** [producto, mercado] domestic; **vuelos nacionales** domestic flights **2.** *nmf* national; HIST **los nacionales** the Francoist forces

nacionalidad *nf* nationality

naco, -a *CAm, Méx Fam & Despec* **1.** *adj* plebby, common **2.** *nm, f* pleb

nada 1. *pron* **a)** [como respuesta] nothing; **¿qué quieres? — nada** what do you want? — nothing
b) [con verbo] not ... anything; [enfático] nothing; **no sé nada** I don't know anything
c) [con otro negativo] anything; **no hace nunca nada** he never does anything; **nadie sabía nada** nobody knew anything

d) [en ciertas construcciones] anything; **más que nada** more than anything; **sin decir nada** without saying anything; **casi nada** hardly anything
e) gracias — de nada thanks — don't mention it; *Fam* **para nada** not at all; **casi nada** almost nothing; **un rasguño de nada** an insignificant little scratch; **nada de eso** nothing of the kind; **nada de nada** nothing at all; **nada más verla** as soon as he saw her **2.** *adv* not at all; **no me gusta nada** I don't like it at all; **no lo encuentro nada interesante** I don't find it remotely interesting
3. *nf* nothingness; **salir de la nada** to come out of nowhere

nadador, -a *nm, f* swimmer

nadar *vi* **a)** DEP to swim; **nadar a braza** to do the breaststroke **b)** [flotar] to float

nadie 1. *pron* **a)** [como respuesta] no one, nobody; **¿quién vino? — nadie** who came? — no one
b) [con verbo] not ... anyone, not ... anybody; [enfático] no one, nobody; **no conozco a nadie** I don't know anyone o anybody; **no vi a nadie** I saw no one
c) [con otro negativo] anyone, anybody; **nunca habla con nadie** he never speaks to anybody
d) [en ciertas construcciones] anybody, anyone; **más que nadie** more than anyone; **sin decírselo a nadie** without telling anyone; **casi nadie** hardly anyone
2. *nm* nobody; **ser un don nadie** to be a nobody

nafta *nf RP* [gasolina] *Br* petrol, *US* gas, *US* gasoline

nagual *nm CAm, Méx* [hechicero] sorcerer

nahua, náhuatl 1. *adj & nmf* Nahuatl **2.** *nm* [idioma] Nahuatl

nailon *nm* nylon

naipe *nm* playing card

nalga *nf* buttock; **nalgas** bottom, buttocks

nana *nf* a) [canción] lullaby b) *Col, Méx* [niñera] nanny c) *Col, Méx* [nodriza] wet nurse

naranja 1. *nf* orange; *Fig* **mi media naranja** my better half **2.** *adj & nm* [color] orange

naranjada *nf* orangeade

naranjo *nm* orange tree

narcotraficante *nmf* drug trafficker

narcotráfico *nm* drug trafficking

nariz *nf* a) nose; *Fam* **me da en la nariz que ...** I've got this feeling that ... b) *Fam* **en mis (propias) narices** right under my very nose; *Fam* **estar hasta las narices de** to be totally fed up with; *Esp Fam* **tenemos que ir por narices** we have to go whether we like it or not

narración *nf* narration

narrador, -a *nm, f* narrator

narrar *vt* to narrate, to tell

narrativa *nf* narrative

nata *nf* a) *Esp* [crema de leche] cream; **nata batida** *o* **montada** whipped cream b) [de leche hervida] skin c) *Fig* cream, best

natación *nf* DEP swimming

natillas *nfpl Esp* custard

nativo, -a *adj & nm, f* native

natural 1. *adj* natural; [fruta, flor] fresh; **de tamaño natural** life-size; **en estado natural** in its natural state; JUR **hijo natural** illegitimate child **2.** *nmf* native

naturaleza *nf* a) nature; **en plena naturaleza** in the wild, in unspoilt countryside; ARTE **naturaleza muerta** still life b) [complexión] physical constitution

naufragar [42] *vi* [barco] to sink, to be wrecked; [persona] to be shipwrecked

naufragio *nm* NÁUT shipwreck

náusea *nf* [usu pl] nausea, sickness; **me da náusea** it makes me sick; **sentir náuseas** to feel sick

náutico, -a *adj* nautical

navaja *nf* a) [cuchillo] penknife, pocketknife; **navaja de afeitar** razor b) [molusco] razor-shell

naval *adj* naval

nave *nf* a) ship; **nave (espacial)** spaceship, spacecraft b) INDUST plant, building c) [de iglesia] nave; **nave lateral** aisle

navegable *adj* navigable

navegador *nm* INFORM browser

navegar [42] *vi* a) to navigate, to sail b) AVIACIÓN to navigate, to fly c) **navegar por Internet** to surf the Net

Navidad(es) *nf (pl)* Christmas; **árbol de Navidad** Christmas tree; **Feliz Navidad, Felices Navidades** Merry Christmas

nazareno, -a 1. *adj & nm, f* Nazarene **2.** *nm* penitent in Holy Week processions; **el Nazareno** Jesus of Nazareth

neblina *nf* mist, thin fog

neblinoso, -a *adj* misty

necedad *nf* a) [estupidez] stupidity, foolishness b) [tontería] stupid thing to say o to do

necesario, -a *adj* necessary; **es necesario hacerlo** it has to be done; **es necesario que vayas** you must go; **no es necesario que vayas** there is no need for you to go; **si fuera necesario** if need be

neceser *nm* [de aseo] toilet bag; [de maquillaje] make-up bag

necesidad *nf* a) necessity, need; **artículos de primera necesidad** essentials; **por necesidad** of necessity; **tener necesidad de** to need b) [pobreza] poverty, hardship c) **hacer sus necesidades** to relieve oneself

necesitar *vt* to need; **se necesita chico** [en anuncios] boy wanted

necio, -a 1. *adj* **a)** [tonto] silly, stupid **b)** *Am* [terco] stubborn, pigheaded **c)** *Méx* [susceptible] touchy **2.** *nm, f* **a)** [tonto] fool, idiot **b)** *Am* [terco] stubborn o pigheaded person **c)** *Méx* [susceptible] touchy person; **es un necio** he's really touchy

nécora *nf* small edible crab

necrológica *nm, f* obituary; **necrológicas** [sección de periódico] obituaries, obituary column

necrológico, -a *adj* **nota necrológica** obituary

negación *nf* **a)** negation **b)** [negativa] denial; [rechazo] refusal **c)** LING negative

negado, -a 1. *adj* **ser negado para algo** to be hopeless o useless at sth **2.** *nm, f* no-hoper

negar [1] **1.** *vt* **a)** to deny; **negó haberlo robado** he denied stealing it **b)** [rechazar] to refuse, to deny; **le negaron la beca** they refused him the grant **2. negarse** *vpr* to refuse (**a** to)

negativa *nf* denial

negativo, -a *adj & nm* negative

negociable *adj* negotiable

negociación *nf* negotiation

negociado *nm* *Andes, RP* [chanchullo] shady deal

negociador, -a *adj* negotiating; **comité negociador** negotiating committee

negociar [43] **1.** *vt* FIN & POL to negotiate **2.** *vi* [comerciar] to do business, to deal

negocio *nm* COM & FIN business; [transacción] deal, transaction; [asunto] affair; **hombre de negocios** businessman; **mujer de negocios** businesswoman

negro, -a 1. *adj* **a)** black; **estar negro** [bronceado] to be suntanned **b)** *Fig* [suerte] awful; [desesperado] desperate; [furioso] furious; **verlo todo negro** to be very pessimistic; **vérselas negras para hacer algo** to have a tough time doing sth

2. *nm, f* [de raza negra] black man, f black woman **3.** *nm* [color] black

nene, -a *nm, f* baby boy, f baby girl

nenúfar *nm* BOT waterlily

nervio *nm* **a)** ANAT & BOT nerve; [de la carne] sinew **b)** *Fig* [fuerza, vigor] nerve, courage **c)** **nervios** nerves; **ataque de nervios** fit of hysterics; **ser un manojo de nervios** to be a bundle of nerves; **tener los nervios de acero** to have nerves of steel

nerviosismo *nm* nerves

nervioso, -a *adj* nervous; **poner nervioso a algn** to get on sb's nerves

neto, -a *adj* **a)** [peso, cantidad] net **b)** [nítido] neat, clear

neumático, -a 1. *adj* pneumatic **2.** *nm* tyre; **neumático de recambio** spare tyre

neurosis *nf inv* neurosis

neutral *adj* neutral

neutro, -a *adj* **a)** [imparcial] neutral **b)** LING neuter

nevada *nf* snowfall

nevar [1] *v impers* to snow

nevera *nf* **a)** [frigorífico] refrigerator, *Br* fridge, *US* icebox **b)** [portátil] cool box

ni *conj* **a)** no … ni, ni … ni neither … nor, not … or; **no tengo tiempo ni dinero** I have got neither time nor money; **ni ha venido ni ha llamado** he hasn't come or phoned; **no vengas ni hoy ni mañana** don't come today or tomorrow **b)** [ni siquiera] not even; **ni por dinero** not even for money; **ni se te ocurra** don't even think about it; **¡ni hablar!** no way!

Nicaragua *n* Nicaragua

nicaragüense *adj & nmf* Nicaraguan

nicho *nm* niche

nido *nm* nest

niebla *nf* fog; **hay mucha niebla** it is very foggy

nieto, -a *nm, f* grandson, f granddaughter; **mis nietos** my grandchildren

nieve *nf* a) METEOR snow; CULIN **a punto de nieve** (beaten) stiff b) *Fam* [cocaína] snow c) *Carib*, *Méx* [dulce] sorbet

ninguno, -a 1. *adj* a) [con verbo] not ... any; **no leí ninguna revista** I didn't read any magazines; **no tiene ninguna gracia** it is not funny at all
b) **en ninguna parte** nowhere; **de ningún modo** no way

ningún is used instead of **ninguno** before masculine singular nouns (e.g. **ningún hombre** no man).

2. *pron* a) [persona] nobody, no one; **ninguno lo vio** no one saw it; **ninguno de los dos** neither of the two; **ninguno de ellos** none of them
b) [cosa] not ... any of them; [enfático] none of them; **me gusta ninguno** I don't like any of them; **no vi ninguno** I saw none of them

niña *nf* a) girl b) ANAT pupil; *Fig* **es la niña de sus ojos** she's the apple of his eye; *ver* **niño**

niñera *nf* nursemaid, nanny

niñez *nf* infancy; [a partir de los cuatro años] childhood

niño, -a *nm, f* a) child; [muchacho] (small) boy; [muchacha] (little) girl; **de niño** as a child; **niño prodigio** child prodigy; *Despec* **niño bien** o **de papá** rich boy, rich kid; *Despec* **niño bonito** o **mimado** mummy's / daddy's boy b) [bebé] baby c) **niños** children; *Fig* **juego de niños** child's play d) METEOR **el Niño** el Niño

níquel *nm* nickel

níspero *nm* [fruto] medlar; [árbol] medlar tree

nítido, -a *adj* [claro] clear; [imagen] sharp

nitrógeno *nm* nitrogen

nivel *nm* a) [altura] level; **a nivel del mar** at sea level b) [categoría] standard; **nivel de vida** standard of living c) [instrumento] level; **nivel de aire** spirit level d) FERROC **paso a nivel** *Br* level crossing, *US* grade crossing

no 1. *adv* a) [como respuesta] no; **¿te gusta? — no** do you like it? — no; **¡pues no!, ¡que no!, ¡eso sí que no!** no way!
b) [en otros contextos] not; **no vi a nadie** I didn't see anyone; **aún no** not yet; **¡cómo no!** of course!; **no sólo... sino que** not only... but...; **no sólo se equivoca, sino que encima es testarudo** not only is he wrong but he's also pig-headed; **¿por qué no?** why not?; **ya no** no longer, not any more
c) **no fumar / aparcar** [en letrero] no smoking / parking
d) **no sea que** (+ subjuntivo) in case
e) **es rubia, ¿no?** she's blonde, isn't she?; **llegaron anoche, ¿no?** they arrived yesterday, didn't they?
f) [como prefijo negativo] non; **la no violencia** non-violence
2. (*pl* **noes**) *nm* no; **un no rotundo** a definite no

noble 1. *adj* noble **2.** *nmf* [hombre] nobleman; [mujer] noblewoman; **los nobles** the nobility

nobleza *nf* nobility

noche *nf* evening; [después de las diez] night, night-time; **de noche**, *Esp* **por la noche**, *Am* **en la noche** at night; **esta noche** tonight; **mañana por la noche** tomorrow night o evening; **buenas noches** [saludo] good evening; [despedida] good night; **son las nueve de la noche** it's nine p.m.

nochebuena *nf* Christmas Eve

nochero *nm* a) *CSur* [vigilante] night watchman b) *Col* [mesilla de noche] bedside table

nochevieja *nf* New Year's Eve

noción *nf* a) notion, idea b) **nociones** smattering, basic knowledge; **nociones de español** a smattering of Spanish

nocivo, -a *adj* noxious, harmful

noctámbulo, -a *nm, f* sleepwalker; *Fam* nightbird

nocturno, -a *adj* a) night; **vida nocturna** night life; **clases nocturnas** evening classes b) BOT & ZOOL nocturnal

nogal *nm* BOT walnut (tree)

nómada 1. *adj* nomadic **2.** *nmf* nomad

nomás *adv* Ame **a)** [sólo] just; **hasta ahí nomás** just to there **b)** [mismo] just; **así nomás** just like that; **ayer nomás** only yesterday

nombrar *vt* **a)** [designar] to name, to appoint; **nombrar a algn director** to appoint sb director **b)** [mencionar] to name, to mention

nombre *nm* **a)** name; **nombre de pila** Christian name; **nombre y apellidos** full name; INFORM **nombre de dominio** domain name; **a nombre de** addressed to; **en nombre de** on behalf of **b)** LING noun; **nombre propio** proper noun

nomeolvides *nm inv* **a)** [flor] forget-me-not **b)** [pulsera] identity bracelet

nómina *nf* **a)** [de sueldo] pay slip **b)** [plantilla] payroll

nórdico, -a 1. *adj* **a)** [del norte] northern **b)** [escandinavo] Nordic **2.** *nm, f* Nordic person

noreste *nm* northeast

noria *nf* **a)** *Esp* [de feria] *Br* big wheel, *US* Ferris wheel **b)** [para agua] water wheel

norma *nf* norm; **norma de seguridad** safety standard

normal *adj* normal, usual; **lo normal** the normal thing, what usually happens

noroeste *nm* northwest

norte *nm* **a)** north; **al norte de** to the north of; **el Norte** [punto cardinal] North; *Am* [Estados Unidos] the US, America **b)** *Fig* aim, goal

Norteamérica *n* North America

norteamericano, -a *adj & nm, f* (North) American

Noruega *n* Norway

noruego, -a 1. *adj & nm, f* Norwegian **2.** *nm* [idioma] Norwegian

nos 1. *pron pers* [directo] us; [indirecto] (to) us; **nos ha visto** he has seen us; **nos trajo un regalo** he brought us a present; **nos lo dio** he gave it to us **2.** *pron* [reflexivo] ourselves; [recípro-

co] each other; **nos hemos divertido mucho** we enjoyed ourselves a lot; **nos queremos mucho** we love each other very much

nosocomio *nm* Am hospital

nosotros, -as *pron pers pl* **a)** [sujeto] we; **nosotros lo vimos** we saw it; **somos nosotros** it is us **b)** [complemento] us; **con nosotros** with us

> Usually omitted in Spanish except for emphasis or contrast.

nostalgia *nf* nostalgia; [morriña] homesickness

nostálgico, -a *adj* nostalgic; [con morriña] homesick

nota *nf* **a)** [anotación] note **b)** [calificación] mark, grade; **sacar** *o* **tener buenas notas** to get good marks **c)** *Fig* [detalle] element, quality; **la nota dominante** the prevailing quality **d)** MÚS note; *Fam* **dar la nota** to make oneself noticed

notable 1. *adj* [apreciable] noticeable; [destacado] outstanding, remarkable **2.** *nm* [nota] very good

notar 1. *vt* [percibir] to notice, to note **2. notarse** *vpr* to be noticeable *o* evident, to show; **no se nota** it doesn't show; **se nota que ...** one can see that ...

notaría *nf* [oficina] notary's office

notario, -a *nm, f* notary (public), solicitor

noticia *nf* news (*sing*); **una noticia** a piece of news; **una buena noticia** good news; **no tengo noticia de esto** I don't know anything about it

noticiario, *Am* **noticiero** *nm* **a)** CINE newsreel **b)** RADIO & TV television news

novatada *nf* **a)** [broma] rough joke, rag **b)** **pagar la novatada** to learn the hard way

novato, -a 1. *adj* [persona] inexperienced; *Fam* green **2.** *nm, f* **a)** [principiante] novice, beginner **b)** UNIV fresher

novecientos, -as *adj & nm* nine hundred

novedad nf **a)** [cosa nueva] novelty; **últimas novedades** latest arrivals **b)** [cambio] change, development **c)** [cualidad] newness

novela nf LITER novel; **novela corta** short story; **novela policíaca** detective story

novelesco, -a adj **a)** [de novela] novelistic, fictional **b)** [extraordinario] bizarre, fantastic

novelista nmf novelist

noveno, -a adj & nm ninth; **la o una novena parte** a ninth

noventa adj & nm inv ninety

novia nf **a)** [amiga] girlfriend **b)** [prometida] fiancée **c)** [en boda] bride

noviar vi CSur, Méx Fam **noviar con algn** to go out with sb, US to date sb; **novian hace tiempo** they've been going out together o US dating for a while

noviazgo nm engagement

noviembre nm November

novillada nf TAUROM bullfight with young bulls

novillero, -a nm, f TAUROM apprentice matador

novillo, -a nm, f **a)** [toro] young bull; [vaca] young cow **b)** Esp Fam **hacer novillos** to play Br truant o US hookey

novio nm **a)** [amigo] boyfriend **b)** [prometido] fiancé **c)** [en boda] bridegroom; **los novios** the bride and groom

nph SMS written abbr of **no puedo hablar**

npn SMS written abbr of **no pasa nada**

nubarrón nm Fam storm cloud

nube nf cloud; Fig **vivir en las nubes** to have one's head in the clouds; Fig **poner a algn por las nubes** to praise sb to the skies

nublado, -a adj cloudy, overcast

nublarse vpr to become cloudy, to cloud over; Fig **se le nubló la vista** his eyes clouded over

nubosidad nf cloudiness, clouds

nuboso, -a adj cloudy

nuca nf nape, back of the neck

nuclear adj nuclear; **central nuclear** nuclear power station

núcleo nm nucleus; [parte central] core; **núcleo urbano** city centre

nudillo nm [usu pl] knuckle

nudismo nm nudism

nudista adj & nmf nudist

nudo nm **a)** knot; **hacer un nudo** to tie a knot; Fig **se me hizo un nudo en la garganta** I got a lump in my throat **b)** [punto principal] crux, core **c)** [de comunicaciones] centre

nuera nf daughter-in-law

nuestro, -a 1. adj poses **a)** our; **nuestra familia** our family **b)** [después del sustantivo] of ours; **un amigo nuestro** a friend of ours **2.** pron poses ours; **este libro es nuestro** this book is ours

Nueva Zelanda n New Zealand

nueve adj & nm inv nine

nuevo, -a 1. adj **a)** new; Fam **¿qué hay de nuevo?** what's new?; **de nuevo** again; **Nueva York** New York; **Nueva Zelanda** New Zealand **b)** [adicional] further **2.** nm, f newcomer; [principiante] beginner

nuez nf **a)** walnut; **nuez moscada** nutmeg **b)** ANAT **nuez (de Adán)** Adam's apple

nulidad nf **a)** [ineptitud] incompetence **b)** JUR nullity

nulo, -a adj **a)** [inepto] useless, totally incapable **b)** [sin valor] null and void, invalid; **voto nulo** invalid vote **c)** **crecimiento nulo** zero growth

núm. (abr de **número**) no

número nm **a)** number; **número de matrícula** Br registration number, US license number; **número de serie** serial number; Fig **sin número** countless **b)** PRENSA number, issue; **número atrasado** back number **c)** [de zapatos] size **d)** [en espectáculo] sketch, act; Fam **montar un número** to make a scene

numeroso, -a adj numerous

numismática nf [estudio] numismatics (sing)

nutritivo

nunca *adv* **a)** [como respuesta] never; **¿cuándo volverás? — nunca** when will you come back? — never **b)** [con verbo] never; [enfático] not ... ever; **no he estado nunca en España** I've never been to Spain; **yo no haría nunca eso** I wouldn't ever do that **c)** [en ciertas construcciones] ever; **casi nunca** hardly ever; **más que nunca** more than ever

nupcial *adj* wedding, nuptial; **marcha nupcial** wedding march

nupcias *nfpl Formal* wedding, nuptials; **casarse en segundas nupcias** to marry again

nutria *nf* otter

nutrición *nf* nutrition

nutricionista *nmf* nutritionist

nutriente *nm* nutrient

nutritivo, -a *adj* nutritious, nourishing; **valor nutritivo** nutritional value

Ñ

ñame *nm CAm, Carib, Col* [planta] yam

ñapa *nf Ven Fam* bonus, extra

ñato, -a *adj Andes, RP* snub-nosed

ñeque *adj CAm, Andes* [fuerte] strong

ñoñería, ñoñez *nf* inanity

ñoño, -a *adj* **a)** [remilgado] squeamish; [quejica] whining **b)** [soso] dull, insipid

ñoqui *nm CULIN* gnocchi

O

o *conj* or; **jueves o viernes** Thursday or Friday; **o ... o** either ... or; **o sea** that is (to say), in other words

> **u** is used instead of **o** in front of words beginning with "o" or "ho" (e.g. **mujer u hombre** woman or man). Note that **ó** (with acute accent) is used between figures.

oasis *nm inv* oasis

obedecer [33] **1.** *vt* to obey **2.** *vi* obedecer a [provenir] to be due to; **¿a qué obedece esa actitud?** what's the reason behind this attitude?

obediencia *nf* obedience

obediente *adj* obedient

obesidad *nf* obesity

obeso, -a *adj* obese

obispo *nm* bishop

objeción *nf* objection; **poner una objeción** to raise an objection, to object

objetar *vt* to object to

objetividad *nf* objectivity

objetivo, -a 1. *nm* **a)** [fin, meta] objective, aim **b)** MIL target **c)** CINE & FOTO lens; **objetivo zoom** zoom lens **2.** *adj* objective

objeto *nm* **a)** object; **objetos perdidos** lost property, *US* lost and found; **mujer objeto** sex object **b)** [fin] aim, purpose; **con objeto de ...** in order to ...; **tiene por objeto ...** it is designed to ... **c)** LING object

obligación *nf* **a)** [deber] obligation; **por obligación** out of a sense of duty; **tengo obligación de ...** I have to ... **b)** FIN bond, security

obligar [42] *vt* to compel, to force

obligatorio, -a *adj* compulsory, obligatory

obra *nf* **a)** [trabajo] (piece of) work; **por obra de** thanks to **b)** ARTE work; **obra maestra** masterpiece **c)** [acto] deed **d)** CONSTR building site **e) obras** [arreglos] repairs; **carretera en obras** [en letrero] roadworks; **cerrado por obras** [en letrero] closed for repairs

obrero, -a 1. *nm, f* worker, labourer **2.** *adj* working; **clase obrera** working class; **movimiento obrero** labour movement

obscuridad = oscuridad

obscuro, -a = oscuro

obsequiar [43] *vt Esp* obsequiar a algn con algo, *Am* obsequiar algo a algn to present sb with sth

obsequio *nm* gift, present

observación *nf* observation

observador, -a 1. *nm, f* observer **2.** *adj* observant

observar *vt* **a)** [mirar] to observe, to watch **b)** [notar] to notice **c)** [cumplir] to observe

observatorio *nm* observatory

obsesión *nf* obsession

obsesionar 1. *vt* to obsess; **estoy obsesionado con eso** I can't get it out of my mind **2. obsesionarse** *vpr* to get obsessed

obstáculo *nm* obstacle

obstante *adv* **no obstante** nevertheless, however

obstinado, -a *adj* obstinate

obstruir [37] **1.** *vt* **a)** [salida, paso] to block, to obstruct **b)** [progreso] to impede, to block **2. obstruirse** *vpr* to get blocked up

obtener [24] **1.** *vt* [alcanzar] to obtain, to get **2. obtenerse** *vpr* **obtenerse de** [provenir] to come from

obvio, -a adj obvious

oca nf goose

ocasión nf a) [momento] occasion; **con ocasión de ...** on the occasion of ...; **en cierta ocasión** once b) [oportunidad] opportunity, chance; **aprovechar una ocasión** to make the most of an opportunity c) COM bargain; **de ocasión** cheap; **precios de ocasión** bargain prices

ocasional adj a) [eventual] occasional; **trabajo ocasional** casual work; **de forma ocasional** occasionally b) [fortuito] accidental, chance

ocaso nm [anochecer] sunset; Fig [declive] fall, decline

occidental adj western, occidental

occidente nm west; **el Occidente** the West

océano nm ocean

ochenta adj & nm inv eighty

ocho adj & nm inv eight

ochocientos, -as adj & nm eight hundred

ocio nm leisure; **en mis ratos de ocio** in my spare o leisure time

ocioso, -a adj a) [inactivo] idle b) [inútil] pointless

ocre nm ochre

octavo, -a adj & nm, f eighth

octeto nm INFORM octet

octubre nm October

oculista nmf ophthalmologist

ocultar 1. vt to conceal, to hide; **ocultar algo a algn** to hide sth from sb **2. ocultarse** vpr to hide

oculto, -a adj concealed, hidden

ocupación nf occupation

ocupado, -a adj [persona] busy; [asiento] taken; [teléfono] Br engaged, US busy; [lavabo] engaged; [puesto de trabajo] filled

ocupar 1. vt a) to occupy b) [espacio, tiempo] to take up; [cargo] to hold, fill c) CAm, Méx [usar, emplear] to use **2. ocuparse** vpr **ocuparse de** [cuidar] to look after; [encargarse] to see to

ocurrir 1. v impers to happen, to occur; **¿qué ocurre?** what's going on?; **¿qué te ocurre?** what's the matter with you? **2. ocurrirse** vpr **no se me ocurre nada** I can't think of anything; **se me ocurre que ...** it occurs to me that ...

odiar [43] vt to detest, to hate; **odio tener que ...** I hate having to ...

odio nm hatred, loathing; **mirada de odio** hateful look

oeste nm west

ofensiva nf offensive

oferta nf offer; FIN & INDUST bid, tender, proposal; COM **de o en oferta** on (special) offer; **oferta y demanda** supply and demand

oficial 1. adj official **2.** nmf a) MIL & NÁUT officer b) [empleado] clerk c) [obrero] skilled worker

oficialismo nm Am a) **el oficialismo** [gobierno] the Government b) **el oficialismo** [partidarios del gobierno] government supporters

oficialista Am **1.** adj pro-government **2.** nm, f government supporter

oficina nf office; **oficina de empleo** Br job centre, US job office; **oficina de turismo** tourist office; **oficina de correos** post office; **horas / horario de oficina** business hours

oficinista nmf office worker, clerk

oficio nm a) [ocupación] job, occupation; [profesión] trade; **ser del oficio** to be in the trade b) [comunicación oficial] official letter o note; **de oficio** ex-officio; **abogado de oficio** state-appointed lawyer c) REL service

ofrecer [33] **1.** vt a) to offer b) [aspecto] to present **2. ofrecerse** vpr a) [prestarse] to offer, to volunteer b) [situación] to present itself c) Formal **¿qué se le ofrece?** what can I do for you?

oftalmología nf ophthalmology

ogro nm también Fig ogre

oído nm a) [órgano] ear b) [sentido] hearing; **aprender de oído** to learn by ear; Fig **hacer oídos sordos** to turn a deaf ear; **ser duro de oído** to be hard of hearing; **ser todo oídos** to be all ears; **tener (buen) oído** to have a good ear

oír [17] *vt* to hear; **¡oye!** hey!; **¡oiga!** excuse me!; *Fam* **como lo oyes** believe it or not

ojal *nm* buttonhole

ojalá 1. *interj* let's hope so!, I hope so! **2.** *conj* (+ *subjuntivo*) **¡ojalá sea cierto!** I hope it's true!

ojeras *nfpl* rings o bags under the eyes

ojo 1. *nm* **a)** [órgano] eye; **ojo de buey** porthole; **ojo morado** black eye; **ojos saltones** bulging eyes; *Fig* **a ojos vista** clearly, openly; *Fig* **calcular a ojo** to guess; **en un abrir y cerrar de ojos** in the blink of an eye; *Fam* **no pegué ojo** I didn't sleep a wink **b)** [de aguja] eye; [de cerradura] keyhole **c)** [de un puente] span **2.** *interj* careful!, look out!

ojota *nf* **a)** *Andes* [zapatilla] sandal **b)** *RP* [chancleta] *Br* flip-flop, *US*, *Austr* thong

okupa *nmf Esp Fam* squatter

ola *nf* wave; **ola de calor** heat wave

ole, olé *interj* bravo!

oleaje *nm* swell

óleo *nm* ARTE oil; **pintura o cuadro al óleo** oil painting

---

oler [65] **1.** *vt* **a)** [percibir olor] to smell **b)** *Fig* [adivinar] to smell, to feel **2.** *vi* **a)** [exhalar] to smell; **oler a** to smell of; **oler bien/mal** to smell good/bad **b)** *Fig* [parecer] to smack (**a** of) **3. olerse** *vpr Fig* [adivinar] to feel, to sense; **me lo olía** I thought as much

---

olfato *nm* sense of smell; *Fig* good nose, instinct

olimpiada *nf* DEP Olympiad, Olympic Games; **las olimpiadas** the Olympic Games

olímpico, -a *adj* Olympic; **Juegos Olímpicos** Olympic Games

oliva *nf* olive; **aceite de oliva** olive oil

olivo *nm* olive (tree)

olla *nf* saucepan, pot; **olla exprés o a presión** pressure cooker

olmeca *adj* & *nmf* Olmec

olmo *nm* smooth-leaved elm

olor *nm* smell; **olor corporal** body odour

olvidar 1. *vt* **a)** to forget; *Fam* **¡olvídame!** leave me alone! **b)** **olvidé el paraguas allí** I left my umbrella there **2. olvidarse** *vpr* to forget; **se me ha olvidado hacerlo** I forgot to do it

olvido *nm* **a)** [desmemoria] oblivion **b)** [lapsus] oversight

ombligo *nm* navel

OMG *nm* (*abr de* **organismo modificado genéticamente**) GMO (*genetically modified organism*)

omitir *vt* to omit, to leave out

ómnibus (*pl* **ómnibus** o **omnibuses**) *nm Cuba, Urug* [urbano] bus; *Andes, Cuba, Urug* [interurbano, internacional] *Br* coach, *US* bus

omnipresente *adj* omnipresent

once *adj* & *nm inv* eleven

ONCE *nf* (*abr de* **Organización Nacional de Ciegos Españoles**) ≈ RNIB

onda *nf* **a)** FÍS wave; *Fam* & *Fig* **estar en la onda** to be with it; **onda expansiva** shock wave; RADIO **onda larga/media/corta** long/medium/short wave **b)** [en el agua] ripple **c)** [de pelo] wave **d)** *Méx, RP* **¿qué onda?** [¿qué tal?] how's it going?, how are things?; **captar o agarrar la onda** [entender] to catch the drift

ondulado, -a *adj* [pelo] wavy; [paisaje] rolling

on-line [onlajn] *adj inv* INFORM online

ONU *nf* (*abr de* **Organización de las Naciones Unidas**) UN(O)

opaco, -a *adj* opaque

opción *nf* **a)** [elección] option, choice; [alternativa] alternative **b)** [posibilidad] opportunity, chance

ópera *nf* MÚS opera

operación *nf* **a)** MED operation; **operación quirúrgica** surgical operation **b)** FIN transaction, deal; **operaciones bursátiles** stock exchange transactions **c)** MAT operation

operador, -a *nm, f* **a)** [técnico] operator **b)** CINE [de cámara] cameraman, *f* camerawoman; [del proyector] projectionist **c)** TEL operator

operadora *nf* [empresa] operator

operar 1. *vt* **a)** MED **operar a algn (de algo)** to operate on sb (for sth) **b)** [cambio etc] to bring about **2.** *vi* FIN to deal, to do business (**con** with) **3. operarse** *vpr* **a)** MED to have an operation (**de** for) **b)** [producirse] to occur, to come about

operario, -a *nm, f* operator; [obrero] worker

opinar *vi* **a)** [pensar] to think **b)** [declarar] to give one's opinion, to be of the opinion

opinión *nf* [juicio] opinion; **cambiar de opinión** to change one's mind

oponer [19] *(pp* **opuesto) 1.** *vt* [resistencia] to offer **2. oponerse** *vpr* [estar en contra] to be opposed; **se opone a aceptarlo** he refuses to accept it

oportunidad *nf* opportunity, chance

oportuno, -a *adj* **a)** [adecuado] timely; **¡qué oportuno!** what good timing! **b)** [conveniente] appropriate; **si te parece oportuno** if you think it appropriate

oposición *nf* **a)** opposition **b)** [examen] competitive examination

oprimido, -a *adj* oppressed

oprimir *vt* **a)** [pulsar] to press **b)** [subyugar] to oppress

optar *vi* **a)** [elegir] to choose (**entre** between); **opté por ir yo mismo** I decided to go myself **b)** [aspirar] to apply (**a** for); **puede optar a medalla** he's in with a chance of winning a medal

optativo, -a *adj* optional, *US* elective

óptica *nf* **a)** [tienda] optician's (shop) **b)** [punto de vista] angle

optimismo *nm* optimism

optimista 1. *adj* optimistic **2.** *nmf* optimist

óptimo, -a *adj* optimum, excellent

opuesto, -a *adj* **a)** [contrario] contrary; **en direcciones opuestas** in opposite directions; **gustos opuestos** conflicting tastes **b)** [de enfrente] opposite; **el extremo opuesto** the other end

oración *nf* **a)** REL prayer **b)** LING clause, sentence

orador, -a *nm, f* speaker, orator

oral *adj* oral; MED **por vía oral** to be taken orally

órale *interj Méx Fam* **a)** [venga] come on! **b)** [de acuerdo] right!, OK!

orangután *nm* orang-outang, orangutan

oratoria *nf* oratory

órbita *nf* **a)** orbit **b)** ANAT eye socket

orca *nf* killer whale

orden 1. *nm* order; **orden público** law and order; **por orden alfabético** in alphabetical order; **de primer orden** first-rate; **orden del día** agenda; **del orden de** approximately **2.** *nf* **a)** [mandato] order; MIL **¡a la orden!** sir! **b)** JUR warrant, order; **orden de registro** search warrant; **orden judicial** court order

ordenado, -a *adj* tidy

ordenador *nm Esp* computer; **ordenador de despacho** *o* **de mesa** desktop computer; **ordenador personal** personal computer; **ordenador portátil** laptop

ordenar 1. *vt* **a)** [organizar] to put in order; [habitación] to tidy up **b)** [mandar] to order **c)** *Am* [pedir] to order **2. ordenarse** *vpr* REL to be ordained (**de** as), to take holy orders

ordeñar *vt* to milk

ordinario, -a *adj* **a)** [corriente] ordinary, common **b)** [grosero] vulgar, common

orégano *nm* oregano

oreja *nf* ear; [de sillón] wing

orgánico, -a *adj* organic

organillo *nm* barrel organ

organismo *nm* **a)** [ser vivo] organism **b)** [institución] organization, body

organización *nf* organization

organizador, -a 1. *adj* organizing **2.** *nm, f* organizer

organizar [40] **1.** *vt* to organize **2. organizarse** *vpr* [persona] to organize oneself

órgano *nm* organ

orgullo *nm* a) [propia estima] pride b) [arrogancia] arrogance

orgulloso, -a *adj* a) **estar orgulloso** [satisfecho] to be proud b) **ser orgulloso** [arrogante] to be arrogant o haughty

oriental 1. *adj* a) [del este] eastern, oriental; [del Lejano Oriente] oriental b) *Am* [uruguayo] Uruguayan **2.** *nmf* a) [del Lejano Oriente] oriental b) *Am* [uruguayo] Uruguayan

orientar 1. *vt* a) [enfocar] to aim (**a** at), to intend (**a** for); **orientado al consumo** intended for consumption b) [indicar camino] to give directions to; *Fig* [aconsejar] to advise c) **una casa orientada al sur** a house facing south d) [esfuerzo] to direct **2. orientarse** *vpr* [encontrar el camino] to get one's bearings, to find one's way about

oriente *nm* East, Orient; **el Extremo o Lejano / Medio / Próximo Oriente** the Far / Middle / Near East

orificio *nm* hole, opening; ANAT & TÉC orifice; **orificio de entrada** inlet; **orificio de salida** outlet

origen *nm* origin; **país de origen** country of origin; **dar origen a** to give rise to

original *adj & nm* original

originariamente *adv* originally

originario, -a *adj* native

orilla *nf* [borde] edge; [del río] bank; [del mar] shore

orillero, -a *adj RP, Ven* common, low-class

orina *nf* urine

orinal *nm* chamberpot; *Fam* potty

orinar 1. *vi* to urinate **2. orinarse** *vpr* to wet oneself

orita *adv Méx Fam* right now

oro *nm* a) gold; **de oro** gold, golden; **oro de ley** fine gold b) NAIPES **oros** [baraja española] *suit in Spanish deck of cards, with the symbol of a gold coin*

orquesta *nf* orchestra; [de verbena] dance band

orquestar *vt* to orchestrate

orquídea *nf* orchid

ortiga *nf* (stinging) nettle

ortodoxo, -a *adj* orthodox

oruga *nf* caterpillar

os *pron pers pl* a) [complemento directo] you; **os veo mañana** I'll see you tomorrow b) [complemento indirecto] you, to you; **os daré el dinero** I'll give you the money; **os escribiré** I'll write to you c) [con verbo reflexivo] yourselves d) [con verbo recíproco] each other; **os queréis mucho** you love each other very much

oscilar *vi* a) FÍS to oscillate b) [variar] to vary, to fluctuate

oscuridad *nf* darkness; *Fig* obscurity

oscuro, -a *adj* a) dark b) [origen, idea] obscure; [asunto] shady; [nublado] overcast

oso *nm* bear; **oso polar** polar bear; **oso hormiguero** anteater; **oso marino** fur seal; *Fam & Fig* **hacer el oso** to play the fool

ostión *nm* a) *Méx* [ostra] Portuguese oyster, Pacific oyster b) *Chile* [vieira] scallop

ostra *nf* oyster; *Fig* **aburrirse como una ostra** to be bored stiff; *Esp Fam* **¡ostras!** *Br* crikey!, *US* gee!

OTAN *nf (abr de* **Organización del Tratado del Atlántico Norte***)* NATO

otoño *nm* autumn, *US* fall

otorrino, -a *nm, f Fam* ear, nose and throat specialist

otorrinolaringólogo, -a *nm, f* ear, nose and throat specialist

otro, -a 1. *adj indef* a) [sin artículo - sing] another; [pl] other; **otro coche**

another car ; **otras personas** other people **b)** [con artículo definido] other ; **el otro coche** the other car **c) otra cosa** something else ; **otra vez** again **2.** *pron indef* **a)** [sin artículo - sing] another (one) ; [pl - personas] others ; [cosas] other ones ; **dame otro** give me another (one) ; **no es mío, es de otro** it's not mine, it's somebody else's **b)** [con artículo definido - sing] **el otro / la otra** the other (one) ; [pl] **los otros / las otras** [personas] the others ; [cosas] the other ones

ovalado, -a *adj* oval

ovario *nm* ovary

oveja *nf* sheep ; [hembra] ewe ; *Fig* **la oveja negra** the black sheep

overol *nm Am* [de peto] *Br* dungarees, *US* overalls ; [completo] overalls, *Br* boiler suit

OVNI *nm (abr de* **objeto volador no identificado***)* UFO

oxidado, -a *adj* **a)** [por óxido] rusty **b)** *Fam & Fig* [anquilosado] rusty

oxidarse *vpr* **a)** [por óxido] to rust **b)** *Fam & Fig* [anquilosarse] to get rusty

óxido *nm* **a)** oxide ; **óxido de carbono** carbon monoxide **b)** [orín] rust

oxígeno *nm* oxygen ; **bomba de oxígeno** oxygen cylinder o tank

oyente *nmf* **a)** RADIO listener **b)** UNIV *Br* occasional student, *US* auditing student

ozono *nm* ozone ; **capa de ozono** ozone layer

P

pa SMS *(abr de* **para)** 4 ; *written abbr of* **padre**

pabellón *nm* **a)** pabellón de deportes sports centre **b)** [en feria] stand **c)** [bloque] wing **d)** [bandera] flag

pacer [60] *vt & vi* to graze, to pasture

pacharán *nm liqueur made from brandy and sloes*

paciencia *nf* patience ; **armarse de paciencia** to grin and bear it

paciente *adj & nmf* patient

pacificación *nf* pacification

pacífico, -a *adj* peaceful

pacifismo *nm* pacifism

pacifista *adj & nmf* pacifist

pack [pak] *(pl* **packs)** *nm* pack ; **un pack de seis** a six-pack

paco, -a *nm, f Andes, Pan Fam* [policía] cop

pacto *nm* pact ; **el Pacto de Varsovia** the Warsaw Pact ; **pacto de caballeros** gentlemen's agreement

padecer [33] *vt & vi* to suffer ; **padece del corazón** he suffers from heart trouble

padrastro *nm* **a)** stepfather **b)** [pellejo] hangnail

padre 1. *nm* **a)** father ; **padre de familia** family man **b)** **padres** [padre y madre] parents ; [antepasados] ancestors **2.** *adj Fam* **a)** *Esp* [tremendo] huge ; **fue el cachondeo padre** it was a great laugh **b)** *Méx* [genial] great, fantastic

padrino *nm* **a)** [de bautizo] godfather ; [de boda] best man ; **padrinos** godparents **b)** [espónsor] sponsor

padrísimo, -a *adj Méx Fam* fantastic, great

padrote *nm* **a)** *Méx Fam* [proxeneta] pimp **b)** *CAm, Ven* [caballo] stallion

paella *nf* paella *(rice dish made with vegetables, meat and/or seafood)*

pág. *(abr de* **página)** p

paga *nf* [salario] wage ; [de niños] pocket money ; **paga extra** bonus

pagadero, -a *adj* payable ; FIN **cheque pagadero al portador** cheque payable to bearer

pagado, -a *adj* paid

pagano, -a *adj & nm, f* pagan, heathen

pagar [42] **1.** *vt* **a)** to pay ; **pagar en metálico** o **al contado** to pay cash ; **pagar por** [producto, mala acción] to pay for ; *Fig* **(ella) lo ha pagado caro** she's paid dearly for it **b)** [recompensar] to repay **2. pagarse** *vpr Am* to pay o.s.

página *nf* page ; **en la página 3** on page 3 ; *Fig* **una página importante de la historia** an important chapter in history ; INFORM **página personal** home page ; INFORM **página de inicio** home page ; INFORM **página web** web page

pago *nm* payment ; **pago adelantado** o **anticipado** advance payment ; **pago contra reembolso** cash on delivery ; **pago inicial** down payment ; **pago por visión** pay-per-view

paila *nf Andes, CAm, Carib* [sartén] frying pan

país *nm* country, land ; **vino del país** local wine ; **los Países Bajos** the Netherlands ; **País Vasco** Basque Country ; **País Valenciano** Valencia

paisaje *nm* landscape, scenery

paisano, -a 1. *adj* of the same country **2.** *nm, f* [compatriota] fellow countryman/countrywoman, compatriot ; **en traje de paisano** in plain clothes

paja *nf* **a)** straw **b)** *Fam & Fig* [bazofia] padding, waffle **c)** *Vulg* **hacerse una** o *Am* **la paja** to jerk off, *Br* to have a wank

pajarita *nf* **a)** *Esp* [corbata] bow tie **b)** [de papel] paper bird

pájaro *nm* **a)** bird; **Madrid a vista de pájaro** a bird's-eye view of Madrid; **pájaro carpintero** woodpecker **b)** *Fam* **tener pájaros** to have daft ideas

paje *nm* page

pala *nf* **a)** shovel; [de jardinero] spade; [de cocina] slice **b)** *DEP* [de ping-pong, frontón] bat, *US* paddle; [de remo] blade

palabra *nf* **a)** word; **de palabra** by word of mouth; **dirigir la palabra a algn** to address sb; **juego de palabras** pun **b)** [promesa] word; **palabra de honor** word of honour **c)** [turno para hablar] right to speak; **tener la palabra** to have the floor

palacio *nm* [grande] palace; [pequeño] mansion; **Palacio de Justicia** Law Courts

paladar *nm* **a)** palate **b)** [sabor] taste

paladear *vt* to savour, to relish

palanca *nf* **a)** lever **b)** [manecilla] handle, stick; *AUTO* **palanca de cambio** *Br* gear lever, gearstick, *US* gearshift, stick shift; **palanca de mando** joystick **c)** [trampolín] diving board

palangana *nf Br* washbasin, *US* washbowl

palco *nm* box

paleta *nf* **a)** [espátula] slice **b)** [de pintor] palette; [de albañil] trowel **c)** *DEP* [de ping-pong] bat **d)** *Andes, CAm, Méx* [piruli] lollipop; *Bol, Col, Perú* [polo] *Br* ice lolly, *US* Popsicle®

paletilla *nf* **a)** shoulder blade **b)** *CULIN* shoulder

pálido, -a *adj* pale

palillo *nm* **a)** [mondadientes] toothpick; **palillos chinos** chopsticks **b)** *MÚS* drumstick

paliza *nf* **a)** [zurra] thrashing, beating; **darle a algn una paliza** to beat sb up **b)** [derrota] beating **c)** *Fam* [pesadez] bore, pain (in the neck)

palma *nf* **a)** *ANAT* palm **b)** *BOT* palm tree **c)** **hacer palmas** to applaud

palmada *nf* **a)** [golpe] slap **b)** **palmadas** applause, clapping

palmera *nf* palm tree

palo *nm* **a)** stick; [vara] rod; [de escoba] broomstick; *Fig* **a palo seco** on its own **b)** [golpe] blow; *Fig* **dar un palo a algn** to let sb down **c)** **de palo** wooden **d)** *DEP* [de portería] woodwork **e)** [de golf] club **f)** *NAIPES* suit

paloma *nf* **a)** [animal] pigeon; *Literario* dove; **paloma mensajera** homing o carrier pigeon **b)** *Méx* [marca] *Br* tick, *US* check **c)** *Méx* [cohete] firecracker

palomar *nm* pigeon house, dovecot

palomitas (de maíz) *nfpl* popcorn

palomo, -a *nm, f* pigeon; *Literario* dove

palpitar *vi* to palpitate, to throb

palta *nf Andes, RP* [fruto] avocado

pamela *nf* broad-brimmed hat

pampa *nf* pampa, pampas

pan *nm* bread; **pan dulce** *Méx* [bollo] bun; *RP* [panetone] panettone; **pan integral** *Br* wholemeal o *US* wholewheat bread; *Arg* **pan lactal** sliced bread; **pan de molde** loaf of bread; **pan rallado** breadcrumbs (*pl*); *Am* **pan tostado** toast; *Fam & Fig* **es pan comido** it's a piece of cake; *Fam & Fig* **más bueno que el pan** as good as gold

panadería *nf* baker's (shop), bakery

panadero, -a *nm, f* baker

panal *nm* honeycomb

Panamá *n* Panama

panameño, -a *adj* & *nm, f* Panamanian

panamericano, -a **1.** *adj* Pan-American **2.** *n* **la Panamericana** the Pan-American Highway

pancarta *nf* placard; [en manifestación] banner

pancho *nm RP* [perrito caliente] hot dog

panda **1.** *adj* **oso panda** panda **2.** *nm* panda **3.** *nf Esp* [de amigos] crowd, gang; [de gamberros, delincuentes] gang

pandereta *nf* tambourine

pandilla *nf Fam* gang

panel *nm* panel

panera nf [para guardar] Br bread bin, US bread box; [para servir] bread basket

pánico nm panic; **sembrar el pánico** to cause panic

panorama nm [vista] panorama, view; Fig panorama

panorámica nf panorama

panorámico, -a adj panoramic

panqueque nm Am pancake

pantaleta nf CAm, Carib, Méx [bragas] panties, Br knickers

pantaletas nfpl = **pantaleta**

pantalla nf a) CINE, TV & INFORM screen; **pantalla de cristal líquido** LCD screen (liquid crystal display screen); **pantalla táctil** touch screen b) [de lámpara] shade c) Fig **servir de pantalla** to act as a decoy

pantalón nm (usu pl) trousers, US pants; **pantalón vaquero** jeans

pantano nm a) GEOGR [natural] marsh, bog b) [artificial] reservoir

pantera nf panther

pantimedias nfpl Méx Br tights, US pantyhose

pantorrilla nf ANAT calf

pantry nm Ven [comedor diario] family dining area off kitchen

pants nmpl Méx [traje] tracksuit, jogging suit; [pantalón] tracksuit bottoms o US pants

panty (pl **pantis** o **pantys**) nm Br tights, US pantyhose

pañal nm Br nappy, US diaper; Fam & Fig **estar en pañales** to be in its infancy

paño nm a) cloth, material; [de lana] woollen cloth; [para polvo] duster, rag; [de cocina] dishcloth; Fig **paños calientes** half-measures b) **paños** [ropa] clothes; **en paños menores** in one's underclothes

pañuelo nm handkerchief; [pañoleta] shawl

papa nf esp Am potato; Am **papas fritas** [de sartén] Br chips, US (French) fries; [de bolsa] Br crisps, US (potato) chips; Fam **no saber ni papa (de algo)** not to have the faintest idea (about sth)

Papa nm **el Papa** the Pope

papá nm Fam dad, daddy, US pop

papachador, -a adj Am cuddly

papachar vt Méx to cuddle, to pamper

papagayo nm a) [animal] parrot b) Carib, Méx [cometa] kite

papalote nm CAm, Méx kite

papear vi & vt Fam to eat

papel nm a) paper; [hoja] piece o sheet of paper; **papeles** [documentos] documents, identification papers; **papel higiénico** toilet paper; Chile **papel confort** toilet paper; INFORM **papel continuo** continuous paper; **papel de aluminio/de estraza** aluminium foil / brown paper; **papel de fumar** cigarette paper; **papel de lija** sandpaper; FIN **papel moneda** paper money, banknotes (pl); **papel pintado** wallpaper; Guat, Ven **papel toilette** o **tualé** toilet paper b) CINE & TEATRO role, part

papeleo nm Fam paperwork

papelera nf a) [en despacho] wastepaper basket o Br bin; [en calle] litter bin b) INFORM [en Windows] recycle bin; [en Macintosh] Br wastebasket, US trash can

papelería nf [tienda] stationer's (shop)

papeleta nf a) [de rifa] ticket; [de votación] ballot paper; [de resultados] report b) Fam [dificultad] tricky problem, difficult job

papeo nm Fam grub

paperas nfpl MED mumps (sing)

papilla nf [de niños] baby food, US formula

papilomavirus nm papillomavirus, Human papillomavirus (HPV)

paquete nm a) [de cigarrillos etc] packet; [postal] parcel, package b) [conjunto] set, package; FIN **paquete de acciones** share package c) INFORM software package; **paquete (de programas o de software)** software package d) Fam [castigo] punishment e) Esp muy Fam [genitales] packet, bulge

Paquistán n Pakistan

paquistaní *(pl* **paquistaníes)** *adj* & *nmf* Pakistani

par 1. *adj* MAT even **2.** *nm* **a)** [pareja] pair; [dos] couple **b)** MAT even number; **pares y nones** odds and evens **c)** [noble] peer **d)** [locuciones] **a la par** [a la vez] at the same time; **de par en par** wide open; *Fig* **sin par** matchless

para *prep* **a)** for; **bueno para la salud** good for your health; **¿para qué?** what for?; **para ser inglés habla muy bien español** for an Englishman he speaks very good Spanish
b) [finalidad] to, in order to; **para terminar antes** to *o* in order to finish earlier; **para que lo disfrutes** for you to enjoy
c) [tiempo] by; **para entonces** by then
d) [a punto de] **está para salir** it's about to leave
e) [locuciones] **decir para sí** to say to oneself; **ir para viejo** to be getting old; **no es para tanto** it's not as bad as all that; **para mí** in my opinion

parabólica *nf* satellite dish

parabólico, -a *adj* parabolic

parabrisas *nm inv Br* windscreen, *US* windshield

paracaídas *nm inv* parachute

paracetamol *nm* paracetamol

parachoques *nm inv* bumper, *US* fender

parada *nf* **a)** stop; **parada de autobús** bus stop; **parada de taxis** taxi stand *o* rank **b)** FÚT save, stop

paradero *nm* **a)** [lugar] whereabouts (*sing*) **b)** *Chile, Col, Méx, Perú* [de autobús] stop

parado, -a 1. *adj* **a)** stopped, stationary; [quieto] still; [fábrica] at a standstill; *Fig* **salir bien/mal parado** to come off well/badly **b)** *Esp* [desempleado] unemployed, out of work **c)** *Fig* [lento] slow **d)** *Am* [en pie] standing **e)** *Chile, PRico* [orgulloso] vain, conceited **2.** *nm, f Esp* unemployed person

paradoja *nf* paradox

paradójico, -a *adj* paradoxical

parador *nm* roadside inn; **parador (nacional)** *state-owned luxury hotel, usually a building of historic or artistic importance*

paragolpes *nmpl inv RP* bumper, *US* fender

paraguas *nm inv* umbrella

Paraguay *n* Paraguay

paraguayo, -a 1. *adj* & *nm, f* Paraguayan **2.** *nm* [fruta] *fruit similar to peach*

paraíso *nm* **a)** paradise; **paraíso terrenal** heaven on earth; FIN **paraíso fiscal** tax haven **b)** TEATRO gods, gallery

paraje *nm* spot, place

paralelo, -a *adj* & *nm* parallel

parálisis *nf inv* paralysis; **parálisis infantil** poliomyelitis

paralítico, -a *adj* & *nm, f* paralytic

paralizar [40] **1.** *vt* to paralyse; [circulación] to stop **2. paralizarse** *vpr Fig* to come to a standstill

parapente *nm* [desde montaña] paragliding, parapenting

parar 1. *vt* **a)** to stop
b) DEP to save
c) *Am* [levantar] to raise
2. *vi* **a)** to stop; **parar de hacer algo** to stop doing sth; **sin parar** nonstop, without stopping; *Fam* **no parar** to be always on the go
b) [alojarse] to stay
c) [acabar] **fue a parar a la cárcel** he ended up in jail
3. pararse *vt* **a)** to stop; **parar a pensar** to stop to think
b) *Am* [ponerse en pie] to stand up

pararrayos *nm inv* lightning rod *o* conductor

parasol *nm* sunshade, parasol

parchís *nm Br* ludo, *US* Parcheesi®

parcial 1. *adj* **a)** [partidario] biased **b)** [no completo] partial; **a tiempo parcial** part-time **2.** *nm* **(examen) parcial** class examination

pardo, -a *adj* [marrón] brown; [gris] dark grey

parecer¹ *nm* a) [opinión] opinion b) [aspecto] appearance

parecer² [33] **1.** *vi* to seem, to look (like); **parece difícil** it seems o looks difficult; **parecía (de) cera** it looked like wax; **parece que no arranca** [uso impers] it looks as if it won't start; **como te parezca** whatever you like; **parece que sí/no** I think/don't think so; **¿qué te parece?** what do you think of it?
2. parecerse *vpr* a) to be alike; **no se parecen** they're not alike
b) **parecerse a** to look like, to resemble; **se parecen a su madre** they look like their mother

parecido, -a 1. *adj* a) alike, similar b) **bien parecido** good-looking **2.** *nm* likeness, resemblance; **tener parecido con algn** to bear a resemblance to sb

pared *nf* wall

pareja *nf* a) pair; **por parejas** in pairs b) [hombre y mujer] couple; [hijo e hija] boy and girl; **hacen buena pareja** they make a nice couple, they're well matched; **pareja de hecho** *common-law heterosexual or homosexual relationship* c) [en naipes] pair; **doble pareja** two pairs d) [de baile, juego] partner

parentesco *nm* relationship, kinship

paréntesis *nm inv* a) parenthesis, bracket; **entre paréntesis** in parentheses o brackets b) [descanso] break, interruption; [digresión] digression

pareo *nm* wraparound skirt

pariente *nmf* relative, relation

parir 1. *vi* to give birth; *Esp Fam* **poner algo/a algn a parir** *Br* to slag sth/sb off, *US* to badmouth sth/sb **2.** *vt* to give birth to

París *n* Paris

parking *(pl* **parkings)** *nm Br* car park, *US* parking lot

parlamentario, -a 1. *adj* parliamentary **2.** *nm, f Br* Member of Parliament, MP, *US* Congressman, *f* Congresswoman

parlamento *nm* parliament

parlanchín, -ina *adj Fam* talkative, chatty

paro *nm* a) [huelga] strike, stoppage b) *Esp* [desempleo] unemployment; **estar en paro** to be unemployed; **cobrar el paro** *Br* to be on the dole

parpadear *vi* [ojos] to blink; *Fig* [luz] to flicker

párpado *nm* eyelid

parque *nm* a) park; **parque de atracciones** funfair; **parque zoológico** zoo; **parque nacional/natural** national park/nature reserve; **parque eólico** wind farm b) [de niños] playpen c) **parque móvil** total number of cars

parqué *nm* parquet (floor)

parqueadero *nm Col, Ecuad, Pan, Ven Br* car park, *US* parking lot

parquear *vt Bol, Carib, Col* to park

parquímetro *nm* AUTO parking meter

parra *nf* grapevine

párrafo *nm* paragraph

parrilla *nf* a) CULIN grill; **pescado a la parrilla** grilled fish b) TÉC grate c) AUTO & DEP starting grid

parrillada *nf* mixed grill

parronal *nm Chile* vineyard

parroquia *nf* parish; [iglesia] parish church

parte 1. *nf* a) [sección] part; [en una repartición] share
b) [lugar] place, spot; **en** o **por todas partes** everywhere; **se fue por otra parte** he went another way
c) JUR party
d) [bando] side; **estoy de tu parte** I'm on your side
e) [locuciones] **por mi parte** as far as I am concerned; **de parte de ...** on behalf of ...; TEL **¿de parte de quién?** who's calling?; **en gran parte** to a large extent; **en parte** partly; **la mayor parte** the majority; **por otra parte** on the other hand, however; **tomar parte en** to take part in
f) **partes** [genitales] privates, private parts
2. *nm* [informe] report

participación *nf* **a)** participation **b)** FIN [acción] share; **participación en los beneficios** profit-sharing **c)** [en lotería] part of a lottery ticket **d)** [notificación] notice, notification

participar 1. *vi* **a)** to take part, to participate (**en** in) **b)** FIN to have a share (**en** in) **c)** *Fig* **participar de** to share **2.** *vt* [notificar] to notify

partícula *nf* particle

particular 1. *adj* **a)** [concreto] particular **b)** [privado] private, personal **c)** [raro] peculiar **2.** *nmf* [individuo] private individual **3.** *nm* [asunto] subject, matter

partida *nf* **a)** [marcha] departure **b)** COM [remesa] batch, consignment **c)** [juego] game **d)** FIN [entrada] item **e)** JUR [certificado] certificate; **partida de nacimiento** birth certificate

partidario, -a 1. *adj* **ser/no ser partidario de algo** to be for/against sth **2.** *nm,f* supporter, follower; **es partidario del aborto** he is in favour of abortion

partidista *adj* biased, partisan

partido, -a 1. *adj* **a)** [roto] broken **b)** [rajado] ripped **2.** *nm* **a)** POL party **b)** DEP game, match *Br*; **partido amistoso** friendly; **partido de vuelta** return match **c)** [provecho] advantage; **sacar partido de** to profit from; **ser un buen partido** to be a good catch **d)** JUR [distrito] district **e)** **tomar partido por** to side with

partir 1. *vt* to break; [dividir] to split, to divide; [cortar] to cut; **partir a algn por la mitad** to mess things up for sb **2.** *vi* **a)** [marcharse] to leave, to set out *o* off **b)** **a partir de** from **3. partirse** *vpr* to split (up), to break (up); *Fam* **partirse de risa** to split one's sides laughing

partitura *nf* MÚS score

parto *nm* childbirth, labour; **estar de parto** to be in labour

parvulario *nm* nursery school, kindergarten

pasa *nf* raisin; **pasa de Corinto** currant

pasable *adj* passable, tolerable

pasaboca *nm Col* snack, appetizer

pasacalle *nm* **a)** [procesión] street procession (*during town festival*) **b)** [banderola] *Col, Urug* banner (*hung across street*)

pasada *nf* **a)** **de pasada** in passing **b)** [jugarreta] dirty trick **c)** *Esp Fam* **es una pasada** [una barbaridad] it's way over the top

pasado, -a 1. *adj* **a)** [último] last; **el año/lunes pasado** last year/Monday **b)** [anticuado] dated, old-fashioned; **pasado (de moda)** out of date *o* fashion **c)** [alimento] bad **d)** CULIN cooked; **lo quiero muy pasado** I want it well done **e)** **pasado mañana** the day after tomorrow **2.** *nm* past

pasaje *nm* **a)** passage **b)** [calle] alley **c)** [pasajeros] passengers **d)** [billete] ticket

pasajero, -a 1. *adj* passing, temporary; **aventura pasajera** fling **2.** *nm,f* passenger

pasamanos *nm inv* [barra] handrail; [de escalera] banister, bannister

pasapalo *nm Ven* snack, appetizer

pasaporte *nm* passport

pasar 1. *vt* **a)** to pass; [mensaje] to give; [página] to turn; **pasar algo a limpio** to make a clean copy of sth **b)** [tiempo] to spend, to pass; **pasar el rato** to kill time **c)** [padecer] to suffer, to endure; **pasar hambre** to go hungry **d)** [río, calle] to cross; [barrera] to pass through *o* over; [límite] to go beyond **e)** [perdonar] to forgive, to tolerate; **pasar algo (por alto)** to overlook sth **f)** [examen] to pass **2.** *vi* **a)** to pass; **¿ha pasado el autobús?** has the bus gone by?; **ha pasado un hombre** a man has gone past; **pasar de largo** to go by (without stopping); **el tren pasa por Burgos** the train goes via Burgos; **pasa por casa mañana** come round to my house tomorrow

b) pasar a [continuar] to go on to; **pasar a ser** to become

c) [entrar] to come in

d) [tiempo] to pass, to go by

e) pasar sin to do without; *Fam* **paso de ti** I couldn't care less about you; *Fam* **yo paso** count me out

3. *v impers* [suceder] to happen; **¿qué pasa aquí?** what's going on here?; **¿qué pasa?** [saludo] how are you?; **¿qué te pasa?** what's the matter?; **pase lo que pase** whatever happens, come what may

4. pasarse *vpr* **a) se me pasó la ocasión** I missed my chance; **se le pasó llamarme** he forgot to phone me

b) [gastar tiempo] to spend o pass time; **pasárselo bien/mal** to have a good / bad time

c) [comida] to go off

d) *Fam* [excederse] to go too far; **no te pases** don't overdo it

e) pásate por mi casa call round at my place

pasarela *nf* [puente] footbridge; [de barco] gangway; [de moda] *Br* catwalk, *US* runway

pasatiempo *nm* pastime, hobby

pascua *nf* **a)** Easter **b) pascuas** [Navidad] Christmas; **¡felices Pascuas!** Merry Christmas!

pascualina *nf RP, Vent* art with spinach and hard-boiled egg

pase *nm* **a)** [permiso] pass, permit **b)** *Esp* [proyección] showing

pasear 1. *vi* to go for a walk, to take a walk **2.** *vt* **a)** [persona] to take for a walk; [perro] to walk **b)** *Fig* [exhibir] to show off **3. pasearse** *vpr* to go for a walk

paseíllo *nm* TAUROM opening parade

paseo *nm* **a)** walk; [en bicicleta, caballo] ride; [en coche] drive; **dar un paseo** to go for a walk / a ride **b)** [avenida] avenue

pasillo *nm* corridor; AVIACIÓN **pasillo aéreo** air corridor

pasión *nf* passion

pasividad *nf* passivity, passiveness

pasivo, -a 1. *adj* passive; [inactivo] inactive **2.** *nm* COM liabilities

paso¹, -a *adj* **ciruela pasa** prune; **uva pasa** raisin

paso² *nm* **a)** step; [modo de andar] gait, walk; [ruido al andar] footstep; *Fig* **a dos pasos** a short distance away; *Fig* **seguir los pasos de algn** to follow in sb's footsteps

b) [camino] passage, way; **abrirse paso** to force one's way through; **prohibido el paso** [en letrero] no entry; **paso de cebra** zebra crossing; **paso a nivel** *Br* level crossing, *US* grade crossing; **paso de peatones** *Br* pedestrian crossing, *US* crosswalk

c) [acción] passage, passing; **a su paso por la ciudad** when he was in town; **el paso del tiempo** the passage of time; **estar de paso** to be just passing through

pasodoble *nm* paso doble

pasta *nf* **a)** paste; **pasta de dientes** o **dentífrica** toothpaste **b)** [de pasteles] dough; [italiana] pasta **c)** [pastelito] shortcake *Br* biscuit o *US* cookie **d)** *Esp Fam* [dinero] dough

pastel *nm* **a)** cake; [de carne, fruta] pie **b)** ARTE pastel **c)** *Fam* **descubrir el pastel** to spill the beans

pastelería *nf* **a)** [tienda] confectioner's (shop) **b)** [dulces] confectionery

pastelero, -a *nm, f* pastry cook, confectioner

pasteurizado, -a, pasterizado, -a *adj* pasteurized

pasteurizar, pasterizar *vt* to pasteurize

pastilla *nf* **a)** tablet, pill; **pastillas para la tos** cough drops **b)** [de jabón] bar **c)** INFORM chip, microchip **d)** *Esp Fam* **a toda pastilla** at top speed, *Br* like the clappers

pasto *nm* **a)** [hierba] grass **b)** [alimento] fodder; **ser pasto de** to fall prey to **c)** *Am* [césped] lawn, grass

pastor, **-a 1.** *nm*, *f* shepherd, *f* shepherdess; **perro pastor** sheepdog **2.** *nm* **a)** REL pastor, minister **b)** [perro] **pastor alemán** Alsatian

pastoreo *nm* shepherding

pata 1. *nf* leg; *Fig* **patas arriba** upside down; **estirar la pata** to kick the bucket; **mala pata** bad luck; **meter la pata** to put one's foot in it; **pata de gallo** crow's foot; **pata negra** *top quality Spanish cured ham* **2.** *nm* *Perú Fam* [amigo] pal, *Br* mate, *US* buddy; [tipo] guy, *Br* bloke

patada *nf* [puntapié] kick, stamp

patata *nf* *Esp* potato; **patatas fritas** [de sartén] *Br* chips, *US* (French) fries; [de bolsa] *Br* crisps, *US* (potato) chips

paté *nm* pâté

patena *nf* paten; *Esp* **limpio o blanco como una patena** as clean as a new pin

patente 1. *nf* **a)** [autorización] licence; [de invención] patent **b)** *CSur* [matrícula] *Br* number plate, *US* license plate **2.** *adj* [evidente] patent, obvious

paterno, **-a** *adj* paternal

patilla *nf* **a)** [de gafas] leg **b)** **patillas** [pelo] sideburns

patín *nm* **a)** skate; [patinete] scooter; **patín de ruedas/de hielo** roller-/ice-skate; **patín en línea** rollerblade **b)** *Esp* [embarcación] pedal boat

patinaje *nm* skating; **patinaje artístico** figure skating; **patinaje sobre hielo/ruedas** ice-/roller-skating

patinar *vi* **a)** to skate; [sobre ruedas] to roller-skate; [sobre hielo] to ice-skate **b)** [deslizarse] to slide; [resbalar] to slip; [vehículo] to skid **c)** *Fam* [equivocarse] to put one's foot in it, to slip up

patinazo *nm* **a)** skid **b)** *Fam* [equivocación] blunder, boob

patinete *nm* scooter

patio *nm* **a)** [de una casa] yard, patio; [de recreo] playground **b)** *Esp* TEATRO & CINE **patio de butacas** stalls

pato *nm* duck; *Fam* **pagar el pato** *Br* to carry the can, *US* to pick up the tab

patoso, **-a** *adj* *Esp* clumsy

patota *nf* *Perú*, *RP* [de gamberros] street gang

patria *nf* fatherland, native country; **madre patria** motherland; **patria chica** one's home town/region

patriota *nmf* patriot

patriótico, **-a** *adj* patriotic

patrocinador, **-a 1.** *adj* sponsoring **2.** *nm*, *f* sponsor

patrón, **-ona 1.** *nm*, *f* **a)** [jefe] boss **b)** *Esp* [de pensión] landlord, *f* landlady **c)** REL patron saint **2.** *nm* **a)** pattern **b)** [medida] standard

patronal 1. *adj* employers'; **cierre patronal** lockout; **clase patronal** managerial class **2.** *nf* [dirección] management

patronazgo *nm* patronage

patrono, **-a** *nm*, *f* **a)** boss; [empresario] employer **b)** REL patron saint

patrulla *nf* **a)** patrol; **estar de patrulla** to be on patrol; **coche patrulla** patrol car **b)** [grupo] group, band; **patrulla de rescate** rescue party; **patrulla ciudadana** vigilante group

patrullero *nm* **a)** [barco] patrol boat **b)** *CSur* [auto] police (patrol) car, *US* cruiser

pausa *nf* pause, break; MÚS rest

pauta *nf* guidelines

pava *nf* **a)** *CAm* [flequillo] *Br* fringe, *US* bangs **b)** *Chile*, *Perú* [broma] coarse o tasteless joke **c)** *Arg* [hervidor] kettle

pavada *nf* *RP* **a)** *Fam* [estupidez] **decir una pavada** to say something stupid; **decir pavadas** to talk nonsense **b)** [cosa sin importancia] silly little thing

pavimento *nm* [de carretera] road (surface), *US* pavement; [de acera] paving; [de habitación] flooring

pavo *nm* **a)** turkey; *Fam* **no ser moco de pavo** to be nothing to scoff at **b)** *Fam* [tonto] twit; *Fam* **estar en la edad del pavo** to be growing up

pay *nm* *Chile*, *Méx*, *Ven* pie

paya *nf* *Am* poem recited to guitar music

payaso *nm* clown; **hacer el payaso** to act the clown

paz *nf* peace; [sosiego] peacefulness; *Fam* **¡déjame en paz!** leave me alone!; **hacer las paces** to make (it) up

pazo *nm* Galician mansion, belonging to noble family

PC *nm* (abr de **personal computer**) PC

pca SMS *written abbr of* **poca**

pco SMS *written abbr of* **poco**

pdt SMS *written abbr of* **piérdete**

peaje *nm* toll; **autopista de peaje** *Br* toll motorway, *US* turnpike

peatón *nm* pedestrian

peatonal *adj* pedestrian; **calle peatonal** pedestrian street

peca *nf* freckle

pecado *nm* REL sin; **pecado capital** o **mortal** deadly sin

pecador, -a *nm, f* sinner

pecar [44] *vi* to sin; *Fig* **pecar por defecto** to fall short of the mark

pecera *nf* fish bowl, fish tank

pecho *nm* **a)** chest; [de mujer] breast, bust; [de animal] breast; **dar el pecho (a un bebé)** to breast-feed (a baby); *Fig* **tomar(se) (algo) a pecho** to take (sth) to heart **b)** *Am* [en natación] breaststroke; **nadar pecho** to do the breaststroke

pechuga *nf* **a)** [de ave] breast **b)** *Fam* [de mujer] boob

pecoso, -a *adj* freckly

peculiar *adj* [raro] peculiar; [característico] characteristic

pedagogía *nf* pedagogy

pedagogo, -a *nm, f* [especialista] educationist; [profesor] teacher, educator

pedal *nm* pedal

pedalear *vi* to pedal

pedante 1. *adj* pedantic **2.** *nmf* pedant

pedazo *nm* piece, bit; **a pedazos** in pieces; **caerse a pedazos** to fall apart o to pieces; **hacer pedazos** to break o tear to pieces, to smash (up); *Fam* **¡qué pedazo de coche!** what a terrific car!

pedestal *nm* pedestal

pediatra *nmf Br* paediatrician, *US* pediatrician

pediátrico, -a *adj Br* paediatric, *US* pediatric

pedicura *nf* pedicure

pedido *nm* **a)** COM order; **hacer un pedido a** to place an order with **b)** [petición] request

pedir [6] *vt* **a)** to ask (for); **pedir algo a algn** to ask sb for sth; **te pido que te quedes** I'm asking you to stay; **pedir prestado** to borrow; *Fig* **pedir cuentas** to ask for an explanation **b)** [mercancía, consumición] to order **c)** [mendigar] to beg

pedo *nm* **a)** [ventosidad] fart; **tirarse un pedo** to fart **b)** *Fam* [borrachera] bender

pedregoso, -a *adj* stony, rocky

pedregullo *nm Am* gravel

pedrisco *nm* hailstorm

pega *nf* **a)** *Fam* [obstáculo] difficulty, hitch; **poner pegas (a)** to find problems (with) **b)** **de pega** [falso] false, fake

pegajoso, -a *adj* [pegadizo] sticky; *Fig* [persona] tiresome, hard to get rid of

pegamento *nm* glue

pegar [42] **1.** *vt* **a)** [adherir] to stick; [con pegamento] to glue; *Fam* **no pegó ojo** he didn't sleep a wink; **pegar fuego a** to set fire to
b) [golpear] to hit
c) INFORM to paste; **cortar y pegar** to cut and paste
d) **pegar un grito** to shout; **pegar un salto** to jump
e) *Fam* [contagiar] to give; **me ha pegado sus manías** I've caught his bad habits
f) [arrimar] **pegar algo a** o **contra algo** to put o place sth against sth
2. *vi* **a)** [adherirse] to stick
b) [armonizar] to match, to go; **el azul no pega con el verde** blue and green don't go together o don't match; *Fig* **ella no pegaría aquí** she wouldn't fit in here
c) [sol] to beat down

3. pegarse *vpr* **a)** [adherirse] to stick; [pelearse] to fight

b) *Fam* [darse] to have, to get; **pegarse un tiro** to shoot oneself

c) [comida] to get burnt; **se me ha pegado el sol** I've got a touch of the sun

d) *Esp Fam* **pegársela a algn** to trick *o* deceive sb

e) [arrimarse] to get close

f) MED [enfermedad] to be catching *o* contagious; *Fig* [melodía] to be catchy

pegatina *nf Esp* sticker

peinado *nm* hairstyle, *Fam* hairdo

peinar 1. *vt* **a)** [pelo] to comb **b)** [registrar] to comb **2. peinarse** *vpr* to comb one's hair

peine *nm* comb

peineta *nf* ornamental comb worn in hair

p.ej. (*abr de* **por ejemplo**) e.g.

Pekín = Beijing

pela *nf Fam & Antes* [dinero] ≃ penny; **no tengo ni una pela** I don't have a penny

peladilla *nf* sugared almond

pelado, -a 1. *adj* **a)** [cabeza] shorn; [piel, fruta] peeled; [terreno] bare **b)** *Fam* **saqué un cinco pelado** [en escuela] I just scraped a pass; **a grito pelado** shouting and bawling **c)** *Fam* [arruinado] broke, *Br* skint **2.** *nm Fam* haircut **3.** *nm*, *f* **a)** *Andes Fam* [niño, adolescente] kid **b)** *CAm, Méx Fam* [persona humilde] common person, *Br* pleb, *Br* oik

pelapatatas *nm inv* potato peeler

pelar 1. *vt* [cortar el pelo a] to cut the hair of; [fruta, patata] to peel; *Fam* **hace un frío que pela** it's brass monkey weather

2. *vi* [despellejar] to peel

3. pelarse *vpr* **a)** [cortarse el pelo] to get one's hair cut

b) *Fam* **corre que se las pela** she runs like the wind

peldaño *nm* step; [de escalera de mano] rung

pelea *nf* fight; [riña] row, quarrel; **buscar pelea** to look for trouble

pelear 1. *vi* to fight; [reñir] to quarrel **2. pelearse** *vpr* **a)** to fight; [reñir] to quarrel **b)** [enemistarse] to fall out

peletería *nf* furrier's; [tienda] fur shop

pelícano *nm* pelican

película *nf* **a)** CINE movie, *Br* film; **película de miedo** *o* **terror** horror movie *o Br* film; **película del Oeste** Western; *Am* **película de suspense** thriller; *Fam* **de película** fabulous **b)** FOTO film

peligro *nm* danger; [riesgo] risk; **con peligro de ...** at the risk of ...; **correr (el) peligro de ...** to run the risk of ...; **poner en peligro** to endanger

peligroso, -a *adj* dangerous, risky

pelirrojo, -a 1. *adj* red-haired; [anaranjado] ginger-haired **2.** *nm*, *f* redhead

pellejo *nm* **a)** [piel] skin **b)** [odre] wineskin **c)** *Fam* **arriesgar** *o* **jugarse el pellejo** to risk one's neck

pellizcar [44] *vt* to pinch, to nip

pellizco *nm* pinch, nip

pelma *nmf Esp* [persona] bore, drag

pelmazo, -a *nm*, *f* = **pelma**

pelo *nm* **a)** hair; **cortarse el pelo** [en la peluquería] to have one's hair cut; *Fig* **tomar el pelo a algn** to pull sb's leg, to take the mickey out of sb; *Fam* **por los pelos** by the skin of one's teeth; *Fam* **me puso el pelo de punta** it gave me the creeps **b)** [de animal] fur, coat, hair **c)** TEXT [de una tela] nap, pile **d)** [cerda] bristle

pelota 1. *nf* **a)** ball; *Fam* **devolver la pelota** to give tit for tat **b)** DEP pelota **c)** *Fam* [cabeza] nut **d)** *Esp* **hacer la pelota a algn** to toady to sb, to butter sb up **e)** *muy Fam* **pelotas** [testículos] balls; **en pelotas** *Br* starkers, *US* butt-naked **2.** *nmf Esp Fam* [persona] crawler

pelotari *nm* pelota player

pelotón *nm* **a)** MIL squad **b)** *Fam* [grupo] small crowd, bunch; [en ciclismo] pack **c)** [amasijo] bundle

pelotudo, -a *adj RP Fam* **a)** [estúpido] damn stupid **b)** [grande] massive

peluca *nf* wig

peludo, -a *adj* hairy, furry

peluquería *nf* hairdresser's (shop)

peluquero, -a *nm, f* hairdresser

pelusa *nf* [de tela] fluff; [de polvo] ball of fluff

pelvis *nf inv* pelvis

pena *nf* **a)** [tristeza] grief, sorrow; *Fig* **me da pena de ella** I feel sorry for her; **¡qué pena!** what a pity! **b)** [dificultad] hardships (*pl*), trouble; **no merece** o **vale la pena (ir)** it's not worthwhile (going); **a duras penas** with great difficulty **c)** [castigo] punishment, penalty; **pena de muerte** death penalty **d)** *CAm, Carib, Col, Méx* [vergüenza] embarrassment; **me da pena** I'm embarrassed about it

penal 1. *adj* criminal **2.** *nm* **a)** [cárcel] prison, *US* penitentiary **b)** *Am* FÚT penalty

penalti *nm* DEP penalty; *Esp Fam* **casarse de penalti** to have a shotgun wedding

pendejo, -a *nm, f* **a)** *Am muy Fam* [tonto] jerk, *Br* tosser **b)** *RP Fam & Despec* [adolescente] spotty teenager

pendiente 1. *adj* **a)** [por resolver] pending; EDUC **asignatura pendiente** failed subject; COM **pendiente de pago** unpaid

b) estar pendiente de [esperar] to be waiting for; [vigilar] to be on the lookout for

c) [colgante] hanging (**de** from) **2.** *nm Esp* earring **3.** *nf* slope; [de tejado] pitch

pendrive, pen drive [pen'draif] *nm* INFORM pen drive, flash drive, USB drive

péndulo *nm* pendulum

pene *nm* penis

penetrar 1. *vt* to penetrate; **penetrar un misterio** to get to the bottom of a mystery **2.** *vi* [entrar] to go o get (**en** in)

penicilina *nf* penicillin

península *nf* peninsula

peninsular *adj* peninsular

penitencia *nf* penance

penitente *nmf* penitent

penoso, -a *adj* **a)** [lamentable] sorry, distressing **b)** [laborioso] laborious, difficult **c)** *CAm, Carib, Col, Méx* [embarazoso] embarrassing **d)** *CAm, Carib, Col, Méx* [persona] shy

pensador, -a *nm, f* thinker

pensamiento *nm* **a)** thought **b)** [máxima] saying, motto **c)** BOT pansy

pensar [1] **1.** *vi* to think (**en** of o about; **sobre** about o over); *Fig* **sin pensar** [con precipitación] without thinking; [involuntariamente] involuntarily

2. *vt* **a)** to think (**de** of); [considerar] to think over o about; **piénsalo bien** think it over; *Fam* **¡ni pensarlo!** not on your life!

b) [proponerse] to intend; **pienso quedarme** I plan to stay

c) [concebir] to make; **pensar un plan** to make a plan; **pensar una solución** to find a solution

pensativo, -a *adj* pensive, thoughtful

pensión *nf* **a)** [residencia] boarding house; [hotel] guesthouse; **media pensión** half board; **pensión completa** full board **b)** [paga] pension, allowance; **pensión vitalicia** life annuity

pensionista *nmf* [jubilado] pensioner

penthouse [pent'xaus] *nm CSur, Ven* penthouse

peña *nf* **a)** rock, crag **b)** [de amigos] club **c)** *Esp Fam* [gente] people

peñasco *nm* rock, crag

peñón *nm* rock; **el peñón (de Gibraltar)** the Rock of Gibraltar

peón *nm* **a)** unskilled labourer; **peón agrícola** farmhand **b)** [en ajedrez] pawn

peonza *nf* (spinning) top

peor 1. *adj* **a)** [comparativo] worse **b)** [superlativo] worst; **en el peor de los casos** if the worst comes to the worst; **lo peor es que** the worst of it is that **2.** *adv* **a)** [comparativo] worse; **¡peor para mí/ti/etc!** too bad! **b)** [superlativo] worst

pepa *nf* a) *Am salvo RP* [pepita] pip; [hueso] stone b) *Méx, RP, Ven muy Fam* [vulva] pussy c) *Ven* [en la piel] blackhead

pepenador, -a *nm, f CAm, Méx* scavenger (*on rubbish tip*)

pepián *nm Andes, CAm, Méx* a) [salsa] *sauce thickened with ground nuts or seeds* b) [guiso] *type of stew in which the sauce is thickened with ground nuts or seeds*

pepino *nm* cucumber; *Fam* **me importa un pepino** I don't give a hoot

pepita *nf* [de fruta] pip, seed; [de metal] nugget

pepito *nm Esp* [de carne] grilled meat sandwich

pequeño, -a 1. *adj* small, little; [bajo] short 2. *nm, f* child; **de pequeño** as a child

pera *nf* a) BOT pear; **pera de agua** juicy pear b) *CSur Fam* [mentón] chin

peral *nm* pear tree

percebe *nm* a) [marisco] goose barnacle b) *Fam* [persona] twit

percha *nf* [colgador] (coat) hanger; [de gallina] perch

perchero *nm* clothes rack

percibir *vt* a) [notar] to perceive, to notice b) [cobrar] to receive

perdedor, -a 1. *adj* losing 2. *nm, f* loser

perder [3] 1. *vt* a) to lose
b) [tren, autobús] to miss; [tiempo] to waste; [oportunidad] to miss
c) [pervertir] to be the ruin o downfall of
2. *vi* to lose; **echar (algo) a perder** to spoil (sth); **echarse a perder** to be spoilt; **salir perdiendo** to come off worst
3. **perderse** *vpr* a) [extraviarse] (persona) to get lost; **se me ha perdido la llave** I've lost my key; **no te lo pierdas** don't miss it
b) [pervertirse] to go to rack and ruin

pérdida *nf* a) loss; *Esp* **no tiene pérdida** you can't miss it b) [de tiempo, esfuerzos] waste c) MIL **pérdidas** losses

perdigón *nm* pellet

perdiz *nf* partridge

perdón *nm* pardon, forgiveness; **¡perdón!** sorry!; **pedir perdón** to apologize

perdonar *vt* a) [remitir] to forgive b) **¡perdone!** sorry!; **perdone que le moleste** sorry for bothering you c) [eximir] to pardon; **perdonarle la vida a algn** to spare sb's life; **perdonar una deuda** to write off a debt

peregrinación *nf* pilgrimage

peregrinaje *nm* pilgrimage

peregrino, -a 1. *nm, f* pilgrim 2. *adj* **ideas peregrinas** crazy ideas

perejil *nm* parsley

pereza *nf* laziness, idleness

perezoso, -a *adj* [vago] lazy, idle

perfección *nf* perfection; **a la perfección** to perfection

perfeccionista *adj & nmf* perfectionist

perfectamente *adv* perfectly; **¡perfectamente!** [de acuerdo] agreed!, all right!

perfecto, -a *adj* perfect

perfil *nm* a) profile; [contorno] outline, contour; **de perfil** in profile b) GEOM cross-section

perforación *nf* perforation; MIN drilling, boring; INFORM [de tarjetas] punching

perforado *nm* = **perforación**

perforar *vt* to perforate; MIN to drill, to bore; INFORM to punch

perfumar 1. *vt* to perfume 2. **perfumarse** *vpr* to put on perfume

perfume *nm* perfume, scent

perfumería *nf* [tienda, arte] perfumery

pergamino *nm* parchment

pérgola *nf* pergola

periferia *nf* periphery; [alrededores] outskirts

periférico, -a 1. *adj* peripheral 2. *nm* a) INFORM peripheral b) *CAm, Méx* [carretera] *Br* ring road, *US* beltway

periódico, -a 1. *nm* newspaper **2.** *adj* periodic(al); QUÍM **tabla periódica** periodic table

periodismo *nm* journalism

periodista *nmf* journalist, reporter

periodo, período *nm* period

periquito *nm* budgerigar, *Fam* budgie

peritaje *nm* [estudios] technical studies

perito, -a *nm, f* technician, expert; **perito industrial/agrónomo** ≃ industrial/agricultural expert

perjudicado, -a *adj* **los más perjudicados** those worst off, the people worst affected

perjudicar [44] *vt* to harm, to injure; [intereses] to prejudice

perjuicio *nm* harm, damage; **en perjuicio de** to the detriment of; **sin perjuicio de** without prejudice to

perla *nf* pearl; *Fig* [persona] gem, jewel; *Fam* **me viene de perlas** it's just the ticket

permanecer [33] *vi* to remain, to stay

permanencia *nf* **a)** [inmutabilidad] permanence **b)** [estancia] stay

permanente 1. *adj* permanent **2.** *nf* [de pelo] permanent wave, perm; **hacerse la permanente** to have one's hair permed

permiso *nm* **a)** [autorización] permission **b)** [licencia] licence, permit; **permiso de conducción** *o* **de conducir** *Br* driving licence, *US* driver's license; **permiso de residencia/trabajo** residence/work permit **c)** MIL leave; **estar de permiso** to be on leave

permitir 1. *vt* to permit, to allow; **¿me permite?** may I? **2. permitirse** *vpr* **a)** to permit *o* allow oneself; **me permito recordarle que** let me remind you that **b) no se permite fumar** [en letrero] no smoking

pernoctar *vi* to stay overnight

pero 1. *conj* but; **pero, ¿qué pasa aquí?** now, what's going on here? **2.** *nm* objection

perpendicular *adj* & *nf* perpendicular

perpetuo, -a *adj* perpetual, everlasting; JUR **cadena perpetua** life imprisonment

perplejo, -a *adj* perplexed, bewildered

perra *nf* **a)** bitch **b)** *Esp Fam* [dinero] penny; **estar sin una perra** to be broke

perro, -a 1. *nm* dog; *Fam* **un día de perros** a lousy day; *Fam* **vida de perros** dog's life; CULIN **perro caliente** hot dog **2.** *adj Fam* [vago] lazy

persa 1. *adj* & *nmf* Persian **2.** *nm* [idioma] Persian, Farsi

persecución *nf* **a)** pursuit **b)** POL [represión] persecution

perseguir [6] *vt* **a)** to pursue, to chase; [correr tras] to run after, to follow **b)** [reprimir] to persecute

persiana *nf* blinds

persona *nf* person; **algunas personas** some people; *Fam* **persona mayor** grown-up

personaje *nm* **a)** CINE, LITER & TEATRO character **b)** [celebridad] celebrity, important person

personal 1. *adj* personal, private **2.** *nm* **a)** [plantilla] staff, personnel **b)** *Esp Fam* [gente] people

personalidad *nf* personality

personalizado, -a *adj* personalized, customized

personalizar *adj* to personalize, to customize

personero, -a *nm, f Am* **a)** [representante] representative **b)** [portavoz] spokesperson

perspectiva *nf* **a)** perspective **b)** [futuro] prospect

persuadir *vt* to persuade; **estar persuadido de que** to be convinced that

persuasión *nf* persuasion

pertenecer [33] *vi* to belong (**a** to)

perteneciente *adj* belonging

pertenencia *nf* **a)** possessions, property **b)** [a un partido etc] affiliation, membership

pértiga *nf* pole; DEP **salto con pértiga** pole vault

Perú *n* Peru

peruano, -a *adj* & *nm, f* Peruvian

pesa *nf* weight; **levantamiento de pesas** weightlifting

pesadez *nf* a) heaviness; [de estómago] fullness b) *Fam* [fastidio] drag, nuisance

pesadilla *nf* nightmare; **de pesadilla** nightmarish

pesado, -a 1. *adj* a) heavy b) [aburrido] tedious, dull; **¡qué pesado!** what a drag! **2.** *nm, f* bore

pesadumbre *nf* grief, affliction

pésame *nm* condolences, sympathy; **dar el pésame** to offer one's condolences; **mi más sentido pésame** my deepest sympathy

pesar 1. *vt* to weigh; *Fig* [entristecer] to grieve
2. *vi* a) to weigh; **¿cuánto pesas?** how much do you weigh?
b) [ser pesado] to be heavy
c) *Fig* [tener importancia] **este factor pesa mucho** this is a very important factor
3. *nm* a) [pena] sorrow, grief
b) [arrepentimiento] regret; **a su pesar** to his regret
c) **a pesar de** in spite of

pesca *nf* fishing; *Fam* **y toda la pesca** and all that

pescadería *nf* fish shop, fishmonger's (shop)

pescadero, -a *nm, f* fishmonger

pescadilla *nf* whiting

pescado *nm* fish

pescador, -a 1. *adj* fishing **2.** *nm, f* fisherman, *f* fisherwoman

pescar [44] **1.** *vi* to fish **2.** *vt* a) to fish
b) *Fam* [coger] to catch

pesebre *nm* manger, stall

pesero *nm Méx* a) [vehículo] collective taxi (*with a fixed rate and travelling a fixed route*) b) [persona] collective taxi driver

peseta *nf* a) *Antes* peseta b) [dinero] money

pesimismo *nm* pessimism

pesimista 1. *adj* pessimistic **2.** *nmf* pessimist

pésimo, -a *adj* very bad, awful, terrible

peso *nm* a) weight; **al peso** by weight; **peso bruto/neto** gross/net weight; *Fig* **me quité un peso de encima** it took a load off my mind; **peso mosca/pesado** [en boxeo] flyweight/heavyweight
b) [importancia] importance; **de peso** [persona] influential; [razón] convincing

pesquero, -a 1. *adj* fishing **2.** *nm* fishing boat

pestaña *nf* a) eyelash, lash b) TÉC flange; [de neumático] rim

peste *nf* a) [hedor] stench, stink b) MED plague; HIST **la peste negra** the Black Death c) **decir** *o* **echar pestes de algn** *Br* to slag sb off, *US* to badmouth sb

pesticida *nm* pesticide

pestillo *nm* bolt, latch

pestiño *nm* CULIN *type of honey fritter*

petaca *nf* a) [para cigarrillos] cigarette case; [para bebidas] flask b) *Méx* [maleta] suitcase c) *Méx Fam* **petacas** [nalgas] buttocks

pétalo *nm* petal

petanca *nf* petanque

petardo *nm* a) firecracker, *Br* banger; MIL petard b) *Fam* [persona aburrida] bore c) *Esp Fam* [porro] joint

petenera *nf Esp Fam* **salir por peteneras** to go off at a tangent

petición *nf* request; JUR petition, plea

petiso, -a *adj Andes, RP Fam* short

peto *nm* **pantalón de peto** dungarees

petróleo *nm* petroleum, oil

petrolero *nm* oil tanker

petrolífero, -a *adj* oil; **pozo petrolífero** oil well

petulancia *nf* arrogance

petulante *adj* arrogant, vain

petunia *nf* petunia

peúco *nm* bootee

pez¹ *nm* fish; **ella está como pez en el agua** she's in her element; **pez gordo** big shot

pez² *nf* pitch, tar

pezón *nm* nipple

pezuña *nf* hoof

pf, pls, xfa SMS *(abr de* **por favor)** PLS, PLZ

pianista *nmf* pianist, piano player

piano *nm* piano

piar [29] *vi* to chirp, to tweet

pibe, -a *nm, f* Fam **a)** Esp [hombre] guy; [mujer] girl **b)** Arg [niño] kid, boy; [niña] kid, girl

pica *nf* **a)** [lanza] pike **b)** picas [palo de baraja] spades

picada *nf* **a)** RP [tapas] appetizers, snacks **b)** RP Br mince, US ground beef **c)** Am [de avión] nosedive; **hacer una picada** to dive

picadillo *nm* **a)** [de carne] minced meat; [de verduras] vegetable salad **b)** Chile [tapas] appetizers, snacks

picado, -a 1. *adj* **a)** [gen] chopped **b)** [triturado - carne] minced, US ground; [verdura] finely chopped; [hielo] crushed **c)** [muela] decayed **d)** Fig [enfadado] annoyed **e)** Am Fam [por alcohol] tipsy **2.** *nm* **a)** Esp [de avión] nosedive; Fig **caer en picado** [ventas, precios] to nose-dive **b)** CULIN **un picado de cebolla y ajo** finely chopped onion and garlic

picador *nm* TAUROM mounted bullfighter, picador

picadora *nf* Esp, RP mincer

picadura *nf* **a)** [mordedura] bite; [de avispa, abeja] sting **b)** [en fruta] spot; MED [de viruela] pockmark; [en diente] decay, caries *(sing)*; [en metalurgia] pitting

picante *adj* **a)** CULIN hot, spicy **b)** Fig [chiste etc] risqué, spicy

picantería *nf* Andes [restaurante] cheap restaurant

picar [44] **1.** *vt* **a)** [de insecto, serpiente] to bite; [de avispas, abejas] to sting; [barba] to prick
b) [comer - aves] to peck (at); [persona] to nibble, to pick at
c) [de pez] to bite
d) [perforar] to prick, to puncture
e) CULIN [carne] Br to mince, US to grind
f) [incitar] to incite, to goad; **picar la curiosidad (de algn)** to arouse (sb's) curiosity
2. *vi* **a)** [escocer] to itch; [herida] to smart; [el sol] to burn
b) CULIN to be hot
c) [pez] to bite
d) Fig [dejarse engañar] to swallow it
3. picarse *vpr* **a)** [hacerse rivales] to be at loggerheads
b) [fruta] to spot, to rot; [ropa] to become moth-eaten; [dientes] to decay
c) [enfadarse] to get cross
d) [drogadicto] to shoot up

pícaro, -a 1. *adj* **a)** [travieso] naughty, mischievous; [astuto] sly, crafty **b)** [procaz] risqué **2.** *nm, f* rascal, rogue

pichincha *nf* RP Fam snip, bargain

pichón *nm* young pigeon; **tiro al o de pichón** pigeon shooting

pickles *nmpl* RP pickles

picnic *(pl* **picnics)** *nm* picnic

pico *nm* **a)** [de ave] beak, bill; Fam [boca] mouth, esp Br gob; **tener un pico de oro** to have the gift of the gab **b)** [punta] corner **c)** GEOGR peak **d)** [herramienta] pick, pickaxe **e)** [cantidad] odd amount; **cincuenta y pico** fifty odd; **las dos y pico** just after two **f)** [drogas] fix

picor *nm* itch, tingling

picoso, -a *adj* Méx spicy, hot

picotear *vt* Fam to nibble

picoteo *nm* [entre las comidas] snacking *(in between meals)*

pie *nm* **a)** foot; **pies** feet; **a pie** on foot; Fig **al pie de la letra** to the letter, word for word; **andar con pies de plomo** to tread carefully; **buscarle (los) tres pies al gato** to make things difficult; Fig **dar pie a** to give cause for; **de pie** standing up; **en pie** standing; **hacer pie** to touch the bottom; **no tener ni**

pies ni cabeza to make no sense at all **b)** [de instrumento] stand; [de copa] stem **c)** [de página] foot; [de ilustración] caption **d)** [medida] foot **e)** TEATRO cue

piedad *nf* **a)** devoutness, piety **b)** [compasión] compassion, pity

piedra *nf* stone; [de mechero] flint; **poner la primera piedra** to lay the foundation stone; *Fam & Fig* **me dejó** *o* **me quedé de piedra** I was flabbergasted

piel *nf* **a)** skin; **piel de gallina** goose pimples **b)** [de fruta, de patata] skin, peel **c)** *Esp, Méx* [cuero] leather **d)** [pelo] fur

piercing ['pirsin] *nm* piercing

pierna *nf* leg

pieza *nf* **a)** piece, part; **pieza de recambio** spare part, *US* extra; *Fig* **me dejó** *o* **me quedé de una pieza** I was speechless *o* dumbfounded *o* flabbergasted **b)** [habitación] room **c)** TEATRO play

pijama *nm* pyjamas

pila *nf* **a)** ELEC battery **b)** [montón] pile, heap; *Fig* **una pila de** [muchos] piles *o* heaps *o* loads of **c)** [lavadero] basin **d)** *Fig* **nombre de pila** Christian name

pilar *nm* **a)** ARQUIT pillar **b)** [fuente] waterhole

píldora *nf* pill; **píldora abortiva** morning-after pill; *Fig* **dorar la píldora a algn** to butter sb up

pileta *nf RP* **a)** [en baño] washbasin; [en cocina] sink **b)** [piscina] swimming pool

pillar 1. *vt* **a)** [robar] to plunder, to loot **b)** [coger] to catch; [alcanzar] to catch up with; **lo pilló un coche** he was run over by a car **c)** *Fam* to be; **me pilla un poco lejos** it's a bit far for *o* from me **2. pillarse** *vpr* to catch; **pillarse un dedo / una mano** to catch one's finger/hand

pilotar *vt* AVIACIÓN to pilot, to fly; AUTO to drive; NÁUT to pilot, to steer

piloto *nm* **a)** AVIACIÓN & NÁUT pilot; AUTO driver; **piso piloto** show flat; **programa piloto** pilot programme **b)** [luz] pilot lamp *o* light

pimentero *nm Br* pepper pot, *US* pepper shaker

pimentón *nm* paprika, red pepper

pimienta *nf* pepper

pimiento *nm* [fruto] pepper; [planta] pimiento; **pimiento morrón** sweet pepper; *Fam* **me importa un pimiento** I don't give a damn, I couldn't care less

pin *(pl* **pins)** *nm* pin, (lapel) badge

pincel *nm* brush, paintbrush

pinchar 1. *vt* **a)** [punzar] to prick; [balón, globo] to burst; [rueda] to puncture **b)** *Fam* [incitar] to prod; [molestar] to get at, to nag **c)** MED to inject, to give an injection to **d)** TEL to bug **2.** *vi* AUTO to get a puncture

pinchazo *nm* **a)** [punzadura] prick; AUTO puncture, blowout **b)** [de dolor] sudden *o* sharp pain

pinche 1. *nmf* kitchen assistant **2.** *adj Méx Fam* [maldito] blasted

pinche *nm* **a)** [de cocina] kitchen boy, *f* maid **b)** *RP Fam* [en oficina] office junior

pincho *nm* **a)** [púa] barb **b)** *Esp* [tapa] **pincho moruno** ≃ shish kebab; **pincho de tortilla** *small portion of omelette*

pinga *nf Andes, Méx, Ven Vulg* prick, cock

ping-pong [pim'pon] *nm* ping-pong, table-tennis

pingüino *nm* penguin

pino *nm* pine; *Esp Fig* **hacer el pino** to do a handstand; *Esp Fam* **en el quinto pino** in the back of beyond

pinol, pinole *nm CAm, Méx* [harina] *Br* maize flour, *US* corn flour

pintada *nf* graffiti

pintado, -a *adj* **recién pintado** [en letrero] wet paint; *Fam & Fig* **nos viene que ni pintado** it is just the ticket; *Fam & Fig* **te está que ni pintado** it suits you to a tee

pintalabios *nm inv* lipstick

pintar 1. *vt* **a)** [dar color] to paint **b)** [dibujar] to draw, to sketch **2.** *vi* [importar] to count; *Fig* **yo aquí no pinto nada** I am out of place here

3. pintarse *vpr* **a)** [maquillarse] to put make-up on
b) *Fam* **pintárselas** to manage

pintor, -a *nm, f* painter

pintoresco, -a *adj* **a)** [lugar] picturesque **b)** [raro] eccentric, bizarre

pintura *nf* **a)** painting; **pintura rupestre** cave painting; *Fam & Fig* **no la puedo ver ni en pintura** I can't stand the sight of her **b)** [materia] paint

piña *nf* **a)** [de pino] pine cone; [ananás] pineapple **b)** *Fig* [grupo] clan, clique **c)** *Fam* [golpe] thump

pinza *nf* [para tender] *Br* clothes peg, *US* clothes pin; [de animal] pincer, claw; **pinzas** [para depilar] tweezers; [para hielo] tongs

piñón *nm* **a)** pine seed *o* nut **b)** TÉC pinion

piojo *nm* louse

piola *adj RP Fam* **a)** [simpático] fun **b)** *Irón* [listo] smart, clever **c)** [lugar] cosy

piolet *nm* ice axe

piolín *nm Andes, RP* cord

pipa *nf* **a)** [de fumar] pipe; **fumar en pipa** to smoke a pipe **b)** [de fruta] pip; [de girasol] sunflower seed

pipí *nm Fam* pee, *Br* wee-wee; **hacer pipí** to pee, *Br* to wee-wee

pipián = **pepián**

pique *nm* **a)** resentment **b)** [rivalidad] needle **c)** **a pique de** on the point of **d)** **irse a pique** NÁUT to sink; [un plan] to fall through; [un negocio] to go bust

piragua *nf* canoe

piragüismo *nm* canoeing

pirámide *nf* pyramid

piraña *nf* piranha

pirata *adj & nmf* pirate

piratear *vt* to pirate; INFORM to hack into

pirateo *nm Fam* piracy; INFORM hacking

Pirineo(s) *nm(pl)* Pyrenees

pirómano, -a *nm, f* MED pyromaniac; JUR arsonist

piropo *nm* **echar un piropo** to pay a compliment

pirrar 1. *vt Fam* **me pirran las albóndigas** I'm mad about meatballs **2. pirrarse** *vpr Fam* **pirrarse por algo** to be mad about sth; **pirrarse por algn** to be crazy about sb

pirueta *nf* pirouette; *Fig* POL **hacer una pirueta** to do a U-turn

pisada *nf* step, footstep; [huella] footprint

pisar *vt* to tread on, to step on

piscina *nf* swimming pool

Piscis *nm* Pisces

pisco *nm* pisco *(Andean grape brandy)*

piso *nm* **a)** *Esp* [vivienda] apartment, *Br* flat; POL **piso franco** safe house **b)** [planta] floor; [de carretera] surface

pisotón *nm* **me dio un pisotón** he stood on my foot

pista *nf* **a)** track; **pista de baile** dance floor; DEP **pista de esquí** ski run *o* slope; DEP **pista de patinaje** ice rink; DEP **pista de tenis** tennis court; **pista de aterrizaje** landing strip; **pista de despegue** runway **b)** [rastro] trail, track **c)** **dame una pista** give me a clue

pistacho *nm* pistachio nut

pistola *nf* **a)** gun, pistol **b)** [para pintar] spray gun

pistolero *nm* gunman, gangster

pitada *nf* **a)** [silbidos de protesta] booing, whistling **b)** *Am Fam* [calada] drag, puff

pitar 1. *vt* **a)** [silbato] to blow **b)** DEP **el árbitro pitó un penalti** the referee awarded a penalty **2.** *vi* **a)** to whistle **b)** AUTO to toot one's horn **c)** DEP to referee **d)** *Esp Fam* **salir pitando** to fly off

pitillera *nf* cigarette case

pitillo *nm* **a)** [cigarrillo] cigarette **b)** *Col* [paja] drinking straw

pito *nm* **a)** whistle; AUTO horn; *Fam* **me importa un pito** I don't give a hoot **b)** *Fam* [cigarrillo] *Br* fag **c)** *Fam* [pene] *Br* willie, *US* peter

pitón *nm* **a)** [serpiente] python **b)** [de toro] horn

píxel ['piksel] *nm* INFORM pixel

pizarra *nf* a) [encerado] *Br* blackboard, *US* chalkboard b) [roca, material] slate

pizarrón *nm Am Br* blackboard, *US* chalkboard

pizza ['pitsa] *nf* pizza

pizzería [pitse'ria] *nf* pizzeria, pizza parlour

placa *nf* a) plate b) [conmemorativa] plaque

placer [33] **1.** *vi* to please; **nos place comunicarle que...** we are pleased to let you know that...; **haz lo que te plazca** do what you like **2.** *nm* pleasure; **ha sido un placer (conocerle)** it's been a pleasure (meeting you); *Formal* **tengo el placer de** it gives me great pleasure to; **un viaje de placer** a holiday trip

plagiar [43] *vt* a) [copiar] to plagiarize b) *CAm, Col, Perú, Méx* [secuestrar] to kidnap

plagiario, -a *nm, f CAm, Col, Perú, Méx* [secuestrador] kidnapper

plan *nm* a) [proyecto] plan b) [programa] scheme, programme; EDUC **plan de estudios** syllabus; **estar a plan** to be on a diet c) *Fam* **en plan de broma** for a laugh; **si te pones en ese plan** if you're going to be like that (about it); **en plan barato** cheaply d) *Fam* [cita] date

plancha *nf* a) iron; [de metal] plate b) CULIN hotplate; **sardinas a la plancha** grilled sardines c) IMPR plate

planchar *vt* to iron

planeta *nm* planet

planilla *nf* a) *Am* [formulario] form b) *Am* [nómina] payroll

plano, -a 1. *nm* a) [de ciudad] map; ARQUIT plan, draft b) CINE shot; **un primer plano** a close-up; *Fig* **estar en primer / segundo plano** to be in the limelight / in the background c) MAT plane **2.** *adj* flat, even

planta *nf* a) plant b) [del pie] sole c) [piso] floor, storey; **planta baja** *Br* ground floor, *US* first floor

plantar 1. *vt* a) [árboles, campo] to plant b) [poner] to put, to place; **plantar cara a algn** to stand up to sb c) *Fam* **plantar a algn en la calle** to throw sb out; *Fam* **dejar plantado a algn** to stand sb up; **le ha plantado su novia** his girlfriend has ditched him **2.** **plantarse** *vpr* a) to stand b) [llegar] to arrive; **en cinco minutos se plantó aquí** he got here in five minutes flat

planteamiento *nm* [enfoque] approach

plantear 1. *vt* a) [problema] to pose, to raise b) [planear] to plan c) [proponer] to put forward d) [exponer] to present **2.** **plantearse** *vpr* a) [considerar] to consider b) [problema] to arise

plantilla *nf* a) [personal] staff, personnel b) [de zapato] insole c) [patrón] model, pattern

plástico, -a 1. *adj* plastic **2.** *nm* a) plastic b) [disco] record

plastificar [44] *vt* to coat o cover with plastic

plastilina® *nf* Plasticine®

plata *nf* a) silver; [objetos de plata] silverware; *Fam* **hablar en plata** to lay (it) on the line; **plata de ley** sterling silver b) *Am Fam* [dinero] money

plataforma *nf* platform

platal *nm Am Fam* **un platal** a fortune

plátano *nm* a) [fruta] banana b) [árbol] plane tree; **falso plátano** sycamore

platea *nf Br* stalls, *US* orchestra

platense 1. *adj* from the River Plate **2.** *nmf* native or inhabitant of the River Plate region

plateresco, -a *adj* plateresque

plática *nf CAm, Méx* [charla] talk, chat

platicar [44] *vi CAm, Méx* to chat, to talk

platillo *nm* a) saucer; **platillo volador**, *Esp* **platillo volante** flying saucer b) MÚS cymbal

plato *nm* a) plate, dish b) [parte de una comida] course; **de primer plato** for starters; **plato fuerte** main course; **plato combinado** one-course meal c) [guiso] dish d) [de balanza] pan, tray e) [de tocadiscos] turntable

platudo, -a *adj Am Fam* loaded, rolling in it

playa *nf* **a)** beach ; [costa] seaside **b)** *Am* **playa de estacionamiento** *Br* car park, *US* parking lot

play-back ['pleißak] *(pl* **play-backs)** *nm* **hacer play-back** to mime (the lyrics)

playera *nf* **a)** [zapatilla] canvas shoe, *Br* sandshoe, *US* sneaker **b)** *Méx* [camiseta] T-shirt

playero, -a *adj* beach

plaza *nf* **a)** square **b)** [mercado] market, marketplace **c)** AUTO seat **d)** [laboral] post, position **e) plaza de toros** bullring

plazo *nm* **a)** [periodo] time, period ; [término] deadline ; **a corto / largo plazo** in the short term / in the long run ; **el plazo termina el viernes** Friday is the deadline **b)** FIN **comprar a plazos** to buy on *Br* hire purchase *o US* an installment plan ; **en seis plazos** in six instalments

plegable *adj* folding, collapsible

pleito *nm* **a)** JUR lawsuit, litigation ; **poner un pleito (a algn)** to sue (sb) **b)** *Am* [discusión] argument

plenitud *nf* plenitude, fullness ; **en la plenitud de la vida** in the prime of life

pleno, -a 1. *adj* full ; **en plena noche** in the middle of the night ; **los empleados en pleno** the entire staff **2.** *nm* plenary meeting

pliegue *nm* **a)** fold **b)** [de vestido] pleat

plomería *nf Méx, RP, Ven* **a)** [negocio] plumber's **b)** [instalación] plumbing

plomero *nm Méx, RP, Ven* plumber

plomo *nm* **a)** [en metalurgia] lead **b)** ELEC [fusible] fuse **c)** [bala] slug, pellet

plotter *(pl* **plotters)** *nm* INFORM plotter

pls = **pf**

pluma *nf* **a)** [de ave] feather **b)** [estilográfica] fountain pen **c)** *Carib, Méx* [bolígrafo] (ballpoint) pen **d)** *Carib, Col, Méx* [grifo] *Br* tap, *US* faucet

plumaje *nm* plumage

plumero *nm* **a)** [para el polvo] feather duster **b)** *Fam* **se te ve el plumero** I can see through you

plumier *(pl* **plumiers)** *nm* pencil box

plumón *nm* [de ave] down

plural *adj & nm* plural

pluralidad *nf* diversity

pluralismo *nm* pluralism

plurilingüismo *nm* multilingualism

plusmarca *nf* record

plusmarquista *nmf* record breaker

p.m. *(abr de* **post meridiem)** p.m.

PM *nf (abr de* **policía militar)** MP

PMF *nfpl* INFORM *(abr de* **preguntas más frecuentes)** FAQ *(Frequently Asked Questions)*

población *nf* **a)** [ciudad] town ; [pueblo] village **b)** [habitantes] population **c)** *Chile* [barrio] **población (callampa)** shanty town

poblado, -a *adj* **a)** populated ; *Fig* **poblado de** full of **b)** [barba] bushy, thick

poblar [2] *vt* **a)** [con gente] to settle, to people ; [con plantas] to plant **b)** [vivir] to inhabit

pobre 1. *adj* poor ; **¡pobre!** poor thing! ; **un hombre pobre** a poor man ; **un pobre hombre** a poor devil **2.** *nmf* poor person ; **los pobres** the poor

pobreza *nf* poverty ; *Fig* [de medios, recursos] lack

pocho, -a *adj* **a)** [fruta] bad, overripe **b)** *Fig* [persona - débil] off-colour ; [triste] depressed, down **c)** *Méx Fam* [americanizado] Americanized

pochoclo *nm Arg* popcorn

pocilga *nf* pigsty

pocillo *nm* **a)** *RP* [pequeño] small cup **b)** *Méx, Ven* [grande] enamel mug

---

poco, -a 1. *nm* **a) un poco** [con adj o adv] a little ; **un poco tarde / frío** a little late / cold
b) un poco [con sustantivo] a little ; **un poco de azúcar** a little sugar
2. *adj* **a)** not much, little ; **poco sitio / tiempo** not much o little space / time ; **poca cosa** not much
b) pocos not many, few ; **pocas personas** not many o few people
c) unos pocos a few

3. *pron* **a)** [escasa cantidad] not much; **queda poco** there isn't much left

b) [breve tiempo] **poco antes /después** shortly *o* a little before /afterwards; **a poco de** shortly *o* a little after; **dentro de poco** soon

c) pocos [cosas] few, not many; **tengo muy pocos** I have very few, I don't have very many

d) pocos [personas] few people, not many people; **vinieron pocos** few people came, not many people came

4. *adv* **a)** [con verbo] not (very) much, little; **ella come poco** she doesn't eat much, she eats little

b) [con adj] not very; **es poco probable** it's not very likely

c) [en frases] **poco a poco** little by little, gradually; **por poco** almost

---

podadera, *Am* **podadora** *nf* garden shears

podar *vt* to prune

poder[1] *nm* power; ECON **poder adquisitivo** purchasing power

---

poder[2] [18] **1.** *vi* **a)** [capacidad] to be able to; **no puede hablar** she can't speak; **no podré llamarte** I won't be able to phone you

b) [permiso] may, might; **¿puedo pasar?** can *o* may I come in?; **aquí no se puede fumar** you can't smoke here

c) [uso impers - posibilidad] may, might; **puede que no lo sepan** they may *o* might not know; **no puede ser** that's impossible; **puede (ser) (que sí)** maybe, perhaps

d) [deber] **podrías haberme advertido** you might have warned me

e) to cope (**con** with); **no puede con tanto trabajo** he can't cope with so much work; **no puedo más** I've had enough, I can't go on

2. *vt* [batir] to be stronger than; **les puede a todos** he can take on anybody

---

poderoso, -a *adj* powerful

podio, pódium *nm* DEP podium

podrido, -a *adj* **a)** [putrefacto] rotten, putrid **b)** [corrupto] rotten; *Fam* **estar podrido de dinero** *o* *Am* **en plata** to be filthy rich **c)** *RP Fam* [harto] fed up, sick

poema *nm* poem

poesía *nf* **a)** [género] poetry **b)** [poema] poem

poeta *nmf* poet

poético, -a *adj* poetic

polar *adj* polar

polea *nf* pulley

polémica *nf* controversy

polémico, -a *adj* controversial

polen *nm* pollen

polera *nf* **a)** *Arg, Chile* [polo] polo shirt **b)** *Urug* [de cuello alto] turtleneck *o* *Br* polo neck sweater

polichinela *nm* **a)** [personaje] Punchinello **b)** [títere] puppet, marionette

policía 1. *nf* police (force) **2.** *nmf* policeman, *f* policewoman

policíaco, -a, policiaco, -a, policial *adj* police; **novela /película policíaca** detective story /movie *o* *Br* film

polideportivo *nm* sports centre

poliéster *nm* polyester

políglota *adj* & *nmf* polyglot

polígono *nm* polygon; **polígono industrial** *Br* industrial estate, *US* industrial area

politécnico, -a *adj* & *nm* polytechnic

política *nf* **a)** politics (*sing*) **b)** [estrategia] policy

político, -a 1. *adj* **a)** political **b)** [pariente] in-law; **hermano político** brother-in-law; **su familia política** her in-laws **2.** *nm, f* politician

póliza *nf* **a)** [sello] stamp **b)** **póliza de seguros** insurance policy

polla *nf* *Vulg* dick

pollera *nf* **a)** *CSur* [occidental] skirt **b)** *Andes* [indígena] *long skirt worn in layers by Indian women*

pollo *nm* **a)** chicken **b)** *Fam* [joven] lad

polluelo *nm* chick

polo *nm* **a)** ELEC & GEOGR pole; **Polo Norte/Sur** North/South Pole **b)** [helado] *Brice* lolly, *US* Popsicle® **c)** [prenda] polo shirt **d)** DEP polo

pololear *vi Chile Fam* to go out (together)

pololo, -a *nm, f Chile Fam* boyfriend, *f* girlfriend

Polonia *n* Poland

polución *nf* pollution

polvera *nf* powder compact

polvo *nm* **a)** dust; **limpiar** *o* **quitar el polvo** to dust; **en polvo** powdered **b)** *Fam* **estar hecho polvo** [cansado] to be *Br* knackered *o US* bushed; [deprimido] to be depressed **c)** *muy Fam* **echar un polvo** to have a screw *o Bra* shag **d)** **polvos** [maquillaje] face powder; **polvos de talco** talcum powder

pólvora *nf* gunpowder

polvoriento, -a *adj* dusty

polvorón *nm* sweet pastry

pomada *nf* ointment

pomelo *nm* [fruto] grapefruit; [árbol] grapefruit tree

pomo *nm* [de puerta] knob

pompa *nf* **a) pompa (de jabón)** (soap) bubble **b)** [suntuosidad] pomp **c)** *Méx Fam* **pompas** behind, bottom

pómulo *nm* cheekbone

ponchar 1. *vt* **a)** *CAm, Carib, Méx* [rueda] to puncture **b)** *Am* [en béisbol] to strike out **2. poncharse** *vpr* **a)** *CAm, Carib, Méx* [rueda] to blow **b)** *Am* [en béisbol] to strike out

poner [19] *(pp* **puesto)** **1.** *vt* **a)** to put; [mesa, huevo] to lay; [gesto] to make; [multa] to impose; [telegrama] to send; [negocio] to set up
b) [tele, radio etc] to turn *o* switch on
c) [+ adj] to make; **poner triste a algn** to make sb sad; **poner colorado a algn** to make sb blush
d) **¿qué llevaba puesto?** what was he wearing?
e) *Esp* [decir] **¿qué pone aquí?** what does it say here?

f) [suponer] to suppose; **pongamos que Ana no viene** supposing Ana doesn't turn up
g) TV & CINE to put on, to show; **¿qué ponen en la tele?** what's on the telly?
h) *Esp* TEL **ponme con Manuel** put me through to Manuel
i) [nombrar] **le pondremos (de nombre) Pilar** we are going to call her Pilar
2. ponerse *vpr* **a)** to put oneself; **ponte en mi lugar** put yourself in my place; **ponte más cerca** come closer
b) [vestirse] to put on; **se puso el jersey** she put her sweater on
c) [+ adj] to become; **ponerse furioso/malo** to become furious/ill
d) [sol] to set
e) TEL **ponerse al teléfono** to answer the phone
f) **ponerse a** to start to; **ponerse a trabajar** to get down to work
g) *Am Fam* [tener la impresión de que] **se me pone que...** it seems to me that..., I get the sense that...

---

pongo *indic pres de* **poner**

poniente *nm* **a)** [occidente] West **b)** [viento] westerly (wind)

ponqué *nm Col, Ven* fruit or custard-filled cake

popa *nf* stern; *Fig* **ir viento en popa** to go full speed ahead

popote *nm Méx* (drinking) straw

popular *adj* **a)** folk; **arte/música popular** folk art/music **b)** [medida] popular **c)** [actor] well-known

popularidad *nf* popularity

popularización *nf* popularization

popularizar [40] **1.** *vpr* to popularize **2. popularizarse** *vpr* to become popular

póquer *nm* poker

---

por *prep* **a)** [agente] by; **pintado por Picasso** painted by Picasso
b) por qué why
c) [causa] because of; **por sus ideas** because of her ideas; **por necesidad/amor** out of need/love; **suspendió por no estudiar** he failed because he didn't study

d) [tiempo] **por la mañana/noche** in the morning/at night; **por ahora** for the time being

e) [en favor de] for; **lo hago por mi hermano** I'm doing it for my brother('s sake)

f) [lugar] **pasamos por Córdoba** we went through Córdoba; **¿por dónde vamos?** which way are we taking o going?; **por la calle** in the street; **mirar por la ventana** to look out the window; **entrar por la ventana** to get in through the window

g) [medio] by; **por avión/correo** by plane/post

h) [a cambio de] for; **cambiar algo por otra cosa** to exchange sth for sth else

i) [distributivo] **por cabeza** a head, per person; **por hora/mes** per hour/month

j) MAT **dos por tres, seis** two times three is six; **un 10 por ciento** 10 percent

k) [+ infinitivo] in order to, so as to; **hablar por hablar** to talk for the sake of it

l) [locuciones] **por así decirlo** so to speak; **por más o muy ... que sea** no matter how ... he/she is; **por mí** as far as I'm concerned

porcelana *nf* porcelain

porcentaje *nm* percentage

porche *nm* porch

porción *nf* portion, part

porno *adj inv Fam* porn

pornografía *nf* pornography

pornográfico, -a *adj* pornographic

poroto *nm Andes, RP* kidney bean

porque *conj* **a)** [causal] because; **¡porque no!** just because! **b)** [final] (+ *subjuntivo*) so that, in order that

porqué *nm* reason

porro *nm* **a)** *Fam* [de droga] joint **b)** *Am* [puerro] leek

porrón *nm* glass wine vessel used for drinking wine from its long spout

portaaviones *nm inv* aircraft carrier

portabultos *nm inv Méx* roof rack

portada *nf* **a)** [de libro etc] cover; [de periódico] front page; [de disco] sleeve **b)** [fachada] front, facade

portador, -a *nm, f* COM bearer; MED carrier

portaequipajes *nm inv* **a)** AUTO [maletero] *Br* boot, *US* trunk; [baca] roof o luggage rack **b)** [carrito] luggage trolley

portafolios *nm inv* briefcase

portal *nm* **a)** [zaguán] porch, entrance hall **b)** [puerta de la calle] main door **c) portal de Belén** Nativity scene **d)** INFORM portal

portamaletas *nm inv Am Br* boot, *US* trunk

portarse *vpr* to behave; **portarse mal** to misbehave

portátil *adj* portable

portavoz *nmf* spokesperson, spokesman, *f* spokeswoman

portazo *nm* **oímos un portazo** we heard a slam o bang; **dar un portazo** to slam the door

porteño, -a 1. *adj* from Buenos Aires **2.** *nm, f* native or inhabitant of Buenos Aires

portería *nf* **a)** [de casa, colegio] *Br* caretaker's office, *US* super(intendent)'s office; [de hotel, ministerio] porter's office **b)** DEP goal, goalmouth

portero, -a 1. *nm, f* **a)** [de casa, colegio] *Br* caretaker, *US* super(intendent); [de hotel, ministerio - en recepción] porter; [a la puerta] doorman **b)** DEP goalkeeper **2.** *nm* **portero automático** entryphone

portezuela *nf* **a)** small door **b)** AUTO fuel filler door

portorriqueño, -a *nm, f pp de* **puertorriqueño**

Portugal *n* Portugal

portugués, -esa 1. *adj & nm, f* Portuguese **2.** *nm* [idioma] Portuguese

porvenir *nm* future; **sin porvenir** with no prospects

posada *nf* inn

posar 1. *vi* [para retrato etc] to pose **2.** *vt* to put o lay down **3. posarse** *vpr* to settle, to alight

posavasos *nm inv* coaster

posdata *nf* postscript

pose *nf* **a)** [postura] pose **b)** [afectación] posing

poseedor, -a *nm, f* possessor

poseer [36] *vt* to possess, to own

posesión *nf* possession; **estar en posesión de** to have; **tomar posesión (de un cargo)** to take up (a post)

posesivo, -a *adj* possessive

posibilidad *nf* possibility; [oportunidad] chance

posible 1. *adj* possible; **de ser posible** if possible; **en (la medida de) lo posible** as far as possible; **haré todo lo posible** I'll do everything I can; **lo antes posible** as soon as possible; **es posible que venga** he might come **2.** *nmpl* **posibles** means

posición *nf* position

positivar *vt* to print

positivizar [40] *vi* to think positive

positivo, -a *adj* positive

posmoderno, -a *adj* postmodern

poso *nm* dregs, sediment

postal 1. *adj* postal **2.** *nf* postcard

poste *nm* pole; DEP [de portería] post

póster *(pl* **pósters** o **posters)** *nm* poster

posterior *adj* **a)** [lugar] posterior, rear **b)** [tiempo] later (**a** than), subsequent (**a** to)

posteriormente *adv* subsequently

postre *nm* dessert, *Br* pudding

postular 1. *vt* **a)** [defender] to call for **b)** *Am* [proponer de candidato] to nominate **2.** *vi* [en colecta] to collect **3. postularse** *vpr Am* **a)** POL [para cargo] to stand, to run **b)** *CSur* [para trabajo] to apply (**para** for)

póstumo, -a *adj* posthumous

postura *nf* **a)** position, posture **b)** *Fig* [actitud] attitude

potable *adj* drinkable; **agua potable /no potable** drinking water / not drinking water

potaje *nm* hotpot, stew

potencia *nf* power; **en potencia** potential

potenciar [43] *vt* to promote, to strengthen

potito *nm* [comida para bebés] baby food

potrero *nm Am* field, pasture

potro *nm* ZOOL colt; [de gimnasia] horse

pozo *nm* well; MIN shaft, pit

pozole *nm CAm, Carib, Méx* [guiso] *stew made with maize kernels, pork or chicken and vegetables*

pq, xq SMS *(abr de* **porque)** COZ; *written abbr of* **por qué**

práctica *nf* **a)** practice; **en la práctica** in practice **b)** [formación] placement; **período de prácticas** practical training period

practicante 1. *adj* REL practising **2.** *nmf* MED medical assistant

practicar [44] **1.** *vt* to practise; [operación] to carry out **2.** *vi* to practise

practicidad *nf CSur* practicality

práctico, -a *adj* practical; [útil] handy, useful

pradera *nf* meadow

prado *nm* meadow, field

precario, -a *adj* precarious

precaución *nf* **a)** [cautela] caution; **con precaución** cautiously **b)** [medida] precaution

precintar *vt* to seal

precinto *nm* seal

precio *nm* price; **precio de costo** cost price; **a cualquier precio** at any price

preciosidad *nf* **a)** [hermosura - cosa] lovely thing; [persona] darling **b)** *Formal* [cualidad] preciousness

precioso, -a *adj* **a)** [hermoso] lovely, beautiful **b)** [valioso] precious, valuable

precipicio *nm* precipice

precipitación *nf* **a)** [prisa] haste **b)** [lluvia] rainfall

precipitado, -a *adj* [apresurado] hasty, hurried; [irreflexivo] rash

precipitar 1. *vt a)* [acelerar] to hurry, to rush **b)** [arrojar] to throw, to hurl down **2. precipitarse** *vpr a)* [persona] to hurl oneself; [acontecimientos] to gather speed **b)** [actuar irreflexivamente] to hurry, to rush

precisamente *adv* [con precisión] precisely; [exactamente] exactly; **precisamente por eso** for that very reason

precisar *vt a)* [determinar] to determine, to give full details of; [especificar] to specify **b)** [necesitar] to require, to need

preciso, -a *adj a)* [necesario] necessary, essential **b)** [exacto] accurate, exact; **en este preciso momento** at this very moment **c)** [claro] concise, clear

precoz *adj a)* [persona] precocious **b)** [fruta] early

predicar [44] *vt* to preach

predilecto, -a *adj* favourite, preferred

predominar *vi* to predominate

preeminente *adj* preeminent

preescolar *adj* preschool; **en preescolar** in the nursery school

preferencia *nf* preference

preferencial *adj* preferential

preferible *adj* preferable; **es preferible que no vengas** you'd better not come

preferido, -a *adj & nm, f Br* favourite, *US* favorite

preferir [5] *vt* to prefer

prefijo *nm a)* TEL *Br* dialling code, *US* area code **b)** LING prefix

pregón *nm a)* [bando] proclamation, announcement **b)** [discurso] speech

pregonar *vt* [anunciar] to announce publicly; *Fig* [divulgar] to reveal, to disclose

pregonero, -a *nm, f* [de pueblo] town crier; *Fig* [bocazas] blabbermouth

pregunta *nf* question; **hacer una pregunta** to ask a question

preguntar 1. *vt* to ask; **preguntar algo a algn** to ask sb sth; **preguntar por algn** to ask after o about sb **2. preguntarse** *vpr* to wonder; **me pregunto si ...** I wonder whether ...

prehistoria *nf* prehistory

prehistórico, -a *adj* prehistoric

prejuicio *nm* prejudice; **tener prejuicios** to be prejudiced, to be biased

prematuro, -a *adj* premature

premeditación *nf* premeditation; **con premeditación** deliberately

premiado, -a *adj* winning

premiar [43] *vt a)* to award a prize to **b)** [recompensar] to reward

premio *nm* prize, award; [recompensa] reward

premisa *nf* premise

prenatal *adj* antenatal, prenatal

prenda *nf a)* [prenda] garment **b)** [garantía] token, pledge

prensa *nf* press; *Fig* **tener buena / mala prensa** to have a good / bad press

preocupación *nf* worry, concern

preocupado, -a *adj* worried, concerned

preocupar 1. *vt* to worry; **me preocupa que llegue tan tarde** I'm worried about him arriving so late **2. preocuparse** *vpr* to worry, to get worried (**por** about); **no te preocupes** don't worry; **preocuparse de algn** to look after sb; **preocuparse de algo** to see to sth

prepa *nf Méx* EDUC ≃ *Br* sixth form, ≃ *US* high school

preparación *nf* preparation; [formación] training

preparar 1. *vt a)* to prepare, to get ready; **preparar un examen** to prepare for an exam **b)** DEP [entrenar] to train, to coach **2. prepararse** *vpr a)* to prepare oneself, to get ready **b)** DEP [entrenarse] to train

preparativo *nm* preparation

preparatorio, -a *adj* preparatory

preponderante *adj* preponderant

preposición *nf* LING preposition

prepotente *adj* domineering; [arrogante] overbearing

preprogramado, -a *adj* preprogrammed

prerrequisito *nm* prerequisite

presa *nf* **a)** prey; *Fig* **ser presa de** to be a victim of; **presa del pánico** panic-stricken **b)** [embalse] dam

prescindencia *nf Am* **con prescindencia de** disregarding, dispensing with

prescindir *vi* **prescindir de** to do without

presencia *nf* presence; **hacer acto de presencia** to put in an appearance; **presencia de ánimo** presence of mind

presenciar [43] *vt* [ver] to witness

presentable *adj* presentable; **no estoy presentable** I'm not dressed for the occasion

presentación *nf* presentation; [aspecto] appearance; [de personas] introduction

presentador, -a *nm, f* RADIO & TV presenter, host, *f* hostess

presentar 1. *vt* **a)** to present; [mostrar] to show, to display; [ofrecer] to offer

b) [una persona a otra] to introduce; **le presento al doctor Ruiz** may I introduce you to Dr Ruiz

2. presentarse *vpr* **a)** [comparecer] to present oneself; [inesperadamente] to turn o come up

b) [ocasión, oportunidad] to present itself, to arise

c) [candidato] to stand; **presentarse a unas elecciones** to stand for election, *US* to run for office; **presentarse a un examen** to sit an examination

d) [darse a conocer] to introduce oneself (**a** to)

presente 1. *adj* present; **la presente (carta)** this letter; **hacer presente** to

declare, to state; **tener presente** [tener en cuenta] to bear in mind; [recordar] to remember **2.** *nm* present

presentimiento *nm* presentiment, premonition; **tengo el presentimiento de que ...** I have the feeling that ...

preservante *nm Am* preservative

preservar *vt* to preserve, to protect (**de** from; **contra** against)

preservativo, -a 1. *adj* protective **2.** *nm* **a)** [condón] condom, *US* prophylactic **b)** *Am* [en alimento] preservative

presidencia *nf* **a)** POL presidency **b)** [de una reunión] chairmanship

presidenciable *nmf esp Am* potential presidential candidate

presidencial *adj* presidential

presidente, -a *nm, f* **a)** POL [de nación] president; **presidente (del gobierno)** prime minister **b)** [de una reunión] chairperson

presidiario, -a *nm, f* prisoner, convict

presidir *vt* **a)** POL to rule, to head **b)** [reunión] to chair, to preside over

presión *nf* pressure; **a o bajo presión** under pressure; **grupo de presión** pressure group, lobby; **presión arterial o sanguínea** blood pressure; **presión atmosférica** atmospheric pressure

preso, -a 1. *adj* imprisoned **2.** *nm, f* prisoner

préstamo *nm* loan

prestar 1. *vt* **a)** to lend, to loan; **¿me prestas tu pluma?** can I borrow your pen? **b)** [atención] to pay; [ayuda] to give; [servicio] to do **2. prestarse** *vpr* **a)** [ofrecerse] to offer oneself (**a** to) **b)** **prestarse a** [dar motivo] to cause; **se presta a (crear) malentendidos** it makes for misunderstandings

prestigio *nm* prestige

presumido, -a 1. *adj* vain, conceited **2.** *nm, f* vain person

presumir 1. *vt* [suponer] to presume, to suppose **2.** *vi* **a)** [ser vanidoso] to show off **b)** **presume de guapo** he thinks he's good-looking

presunción *nf* a) [suposición] presumption, supposition b) [vanidad] vanity, conceit

presunto, -a *adj* supposed; JUR alleged

presuntuoso, -a *adj* a) [vanidoso] vain, conceited b) [pretencioso] pretentious, showy

presupuesto *nm* a) FIN budget; [cálculo] estimate b) [supuesto] supposition, assumption

pretencioso, -a *adj* pretentious

pretender *vt* a) [intentar] to try; ¿qué pretendes insinuar? what are you getting at? b) [afirmar] to claim c) [aspirar a] to try for d) [cortejar] to court, to woo

pretendiente, -a *nm, f* a) [al trono] pretender b) [a un cargo] applicant, candidate c) [amante] suitor

pretensión *nf* a) [aspiración] aim, aspiration b) [presunción] pretentiousness

pretexto *nm* pretext, excuse

prever [28] (*pp* previsto) *vt* a) [prevenir] to foresee, to forecast b) [preparar de antemano] to cater for

previo, -a *adj* previous, prior; **previo pago de su importe** only on payment; **sin previo aviso** without prior notice

previsión *nf* a) [predicción] forecast; **previsión del tiempo** weather forecast b) [precaución] precaution; **en previsión de** as a precaution against c) *Andes, RP* **previsión social** social security

previsor, -a *adj* careful, far-sighted

previsto, -a *adj* foreseen, forecast; **según lo previsto** as expected

prieto, -a *adj* a) [ceñido] tight; **íbamos muy prietos en el coche** we were really squashed together in the car b) *Méx* [oscuro] dark

primaria *nf* [enseñanza] primary education

primario, -a *adj* primary

primavera *nf* spring

primer (*delante de nm*) *adj ver* **primero**

primera *nf* a) [en tren] first class b) AUTO [marcha] first gear c) **a la primera** at the first attempt; *Fam* **de primera** great, first-class

primero, -a 1. *adj* first; **a primera hora de la mañana** first thing in the morning; **primera página** *o* **plana** front page; **de primera necesidad** basic

> **primer** is used instead of **primero** before masculine singular nouns (e.g. **el primer hombre** the first man).

2. *nm, f* first; **a primero(s) de mes** at the beginning of the month
3. *adv* a) first
b) [más bien] rather, sooner

primitiva *nf* [lotería] *Spanish national lottery,* ≃ National lottery (*in UK*)

primitivo, -a *adj* primitive

primo, -a 1. *nm, f* a) cousin; **primo hermano** first cousin b) *Fam* [tonto] fool, drip, dunce **2.** *adj* a) **materia prima** raw material b) [número] prime

primogénito, -a *adj & nm, f* firstborn

princesa *nf* princess

principado *nm* principality

principal *adj* main, principal; **lo principal es que ...** the main thing is that ...; **puerta principal** front door

príncipe *nm* prince

principiante 1. *adj* novice **2.** *nmf* beginner, novice

principio *nm* a) beginning, start; **a principio(s) de** at the beginning of; **al principio, en un principio** at first, in the beginning b) [fundamento] principle; **en principio** in principle c) **principios** rudiments, basics

pringoso, -a *adj* [grasiento] greasy; [sucio] dirty

prioridad *nf* priority

priorizar [40] *vt* to prioritize

prisa *nf* a) [rapidez] hurry; **date prisa** hurry up; **tener prisa** to be in a hurry; **de /a prisa** in a hurry b) **correr prisa** to be urgent; **me corre mucha prisa** I need it right away

prisión *nf* prison, jail

prisionero, -a *nm, f* prisoner

prisma *nm* prism

prismáticos *nmpl* binoculars, field glasses

privacidad *nf* privacy

privado, -a 1. *adj* private **2.** *nm* **a)** [lugar reservado] private room **b)** [retrete] *Br* toilet, *US* bathroom **c)** [del rey] protégé

privar 1. *vt* [despojar] to deprive (**de** of) **2.** *vi* **a)** *Fam* [gustar] to like; [estar de moda] to be fashionable o popular **b)** *Fam* [beber] to booze **3. privarse** *vpr* [abstenerse] to deprive oneself (**de** of), to go without

privilegiado, -a 1. *adj* privileged **2.** *nm, f* privileged person

privilegio *nm* privilege

PRM *nf* (*abr de* **persona con movilidad reducida**) PRM (*person with reduced mobility*)

proa *nf* prow, bows

probabilidad *nf* probability, likelihood; **tiene pocas probabilidades** he stands little chance

probable *adj* probable, likely; **es probable que llueva** it'll probably rain

probador *nm* fitting room

probar [2] **1.** *vt* **a)** [comida, bebida] to try **b)** [comprobar] to test, to check **c)** [intentar] to try **d)** [demostrar] to prove, to show **2.** *vi* to try; **probar a** to attempt o to try to **3. probarse** *vpr* [ropa] to try on

probeta *nf* test tube; **niño probeta** test-tube baby

problema *nm* problem

problemático, -a *adj* problematic

procedencia *nf* origin, source

procedente *adj* **a)** [originario] coming (**de** from) **b)** [adecuado] appropriate; JUR proper

proceder 1. *vi* **a)** **proceder de** [provenir] to come from **b)** [actuar] to act **c)** [ser oportuno] to be advisable o appropriate; JUR **la protesta no procede** objection overruled **d)** **proceder a** [continuar] to go on to **2.** *nm* [comportamiento] behaviour

procedimiento *nm* **a)** [método] procedure **b)** JUR [trámites] proceedings

procesado, -a 1. *nm, f* accused **2.** *nm* INFORM processing

procesador *nm* INFORM processor; **procesador de textos** word processor

procesar *vt* **a)** JUR to prosecute **b)** [elaborar, transformar] to process; INFORM to process

procesión *nf* procession

proceso *nm* **a)** process; INFORM **proceso de datos** data processing **b)** JUR trial

proclamación *nf* proclamation

proclamar *vt* to proclaim

procuraduría *nf Méx* **procuraduría general de justicia** Ministry of Justice

procurar *vt* **a)** [intentar] to try, to attempt; **procura que no te vean** make sure they don't see you **b)** [proporcionar] (to manage) to get

prodigar [42] *Formal* **1.** *vt* [dar generosamente] to lavish **2. prodigarse** *vpr* **prodigarse en** to be lavish in

producción *nf* [acción] production; [producto] product; CINE production; **producción en cadena/serie** assembly-line /mass production

producir [10] **1.** *vt* **a)** to produce; [fruto, cosecha] to yield, to bear; [ganancias] to yield **b)** *Fig* [originar] to cause, to bring about **2. producirse** *vpr* to take place, to happen

productividad *nf* productivity

productivo, -a *adj* productive; [beneficioso] profitable

producto *nm* product; AGRIC [producción] produce

productor, -a 1. *adj* producing **2.** *nm, f* producer

profe *nmf Fam* (*abr de* **profesor**) teacher

profecía *nf* prophecy

profesión *nf* profession; **de profesión** by profession

profesional *adj* & *nmf* professional

profesionista *adj* & *nmf Méx* professional

profesor, -a *nm, f* teacher; UNIV *Br* lecturer, *US* professor

profeta *nm* prophet

profundidad *nf* depth; *Fig* [de ideas etc] profundity, depth; **un metro de profundidad** one metre deep o in depth

profundo, -a *adj* deep; *Fig* [idea, sentimiento] profound

programa *nm* programme; INFORM program; EDUC syllabus

programable *adj* programmable

programación *nf* RADIO & TV programme planning

programador, -a 1. *nm, f* INFORM programmer **2.** *nm* INFORM programmer

programar *vt* to programme; INFORM to program

progresar *vi* to progress, to make progress

progresivo, -a *adj* progressive

progreso *nm* progress; **hace grandes progresos** he's making great progress

prohibición *nf* prohibition, ban

prohibido, -a *adj* forbidden, prohibited; **prohibida la entrada** [en letrero] no admittance; **prohibido aparcar/fumar** [en letrero] no parking/smoking

prohibir *vt* to forbid, to prohibit; **se prohíbe pasar** [en letrero] no admittance o entry

prójimo, -a *nm, f* one's fellow man, one's neighbour

proliferación *nf* proliferation; **proliferación nuclear** proliferation (of nuclear arms)

prolijo, -a *adj* [persona] tedious, prolix; [explicación, descripción etc] longwinded

prólogo *nm* prologue

prolongar [42] **1.** *vt* [alargar] to prolong, to extend **2. prolongarse** *vpr* [continuar] to carry on

promedio *nm* average; **como promedio** on average

promesa *nf* promise; *Fig* **la joven promesa de la música** the promising young musician

prometer 1. *vt* to promise; **te lo prometo** I promise **2.** *vi* to be promising **3. prometerse** *vpr* [pareja] to get engaged

prometido, -a 1. *adj* promised **2.** *nm, f* fiancé, f fiancée

promoción *nf* promotion; EDUC **promoción universitaria** class, year

promocionar *vt* [cosas] to promote; [personas] to give promotion to

promotor, -a 1. *adj* promoting **2.** *nm, f* promoter

pronóstico *nm* [del tiempo] forecast; MED prognosis

pronto, -a 1. *adj* quick, prompt; *Formal* [dispuesto] prepared **2.** *nm* [impulso] sudden impulse **3.** *adv* **a)** [deprisa] quickly, rapidly; **al pronto** at first; **de pronto** suddenly; **por de** o **lo pronto** [para empezar] to start with **b)** [dentro de poco] soon; **¡hasta pronto!** see you soon! **c)** *Esp* [temprano] early; **salimos pronto** we left early

pronunciación *nf* pronunciation

pronunciar [43] **1.** *vt* to pronounce; [discurso] to deliver **2. pronunciarse** *vpr* **a)** [opinar] to declare oneself **b)** [sublevarse] to rise up

propaganda *nf* [política] propaganda; [comercial] advertising, publicity

propasarse *vpr* to go too far, to overstep the mark

propensión *nf* tendency, inclination

propenso, -a *adj* **a)** [inclinado] prone, inclined **b)** MED susceptible

propiciar [43] *vt* [causar] to cause

propicio, -a *adj* propitious, suitable; **ser propicio a** to be inclined to

propiedad *nf* a) [posesión] ownership; [cosa poseída] property b) [cualidad] property, quality; *Fig* **con propiedad** properly, appropriately

propietario, -a *nm, f* owner

propina *nf* tip; **dar propina (a algn)** to tip (sb)

propio, -a *adj* a) [de uno] own; **en su propia casa** in his own house b) [correcto] suitable, appropriate; **juegos propios para su edad** games suitable for their age c) [característico] typical, peculiar d) [mismo - hombre] himself; [mujer] herself; [animal, cosa] itself; **el propio autor** the author himself e) **propios** themselves; **los propios inquilinos** the tenants themselves f) LING proper

proponer [19] *(pp* **propuesto)** **1.** *vt* to propose, to suggest **2. proponerse** *vpr* to intend

proporcionado, -a *adj* [mesurado] proportionate, in proportion

proporcionar *vt* [dar] to give, to supply, to provide

proposición *nf* a) [propuesta] proposal b) [oración] clause

propósito *nm* a) [intención] intention b) **a propósito** [por cierto] by the way; [adrede] on purpose, intentionally; **a propósito de viajes ...** speaking of travelling ...

propuesta *nf* suggestion, proposal

propuesto, -a *pp de* **proponer**

prórroga *nf* a) [prolongación] extension; DEP *Br* extra time, *US* overtime b) [aplazamiento] postponement; MIL deferment

prorrogar [42] *vt* a) [prolongar] to extend b) [aplazar] to postpone; MIL to defer

prosa *nf* prose

proscrito, -a 1. *adj* [persona] exiled, banished; [cosa] banned **2.** *nm, f* exile, outlaw

prospecto *nm* leaflet, prospectus

próspero, -a *adj* prosperous, thriving; **¡próspero año nuevo!** Happy New Year!

prostíbulo *nm* brothel

prostitución *nf* prostitution

prostituto, -a *nm, f* [hombre] male prostitute; [mujer] prostitute

protagonista *nmf* a) main character, leading role; **¿quién es el protagonista?** who plays the lead? b) *Fig* [centro] centre of attraction

protección *nf* protection

proteger [53] *vt* to protect, to defend

protegido, -a 1. *adj* a) protected b) INFORM protected; [transacción, pago] secure; **protegido contra escritura** write-protected **2.** *nm, f* [hombre] protégé; [mujer] protégée

proteína *nf* protein

protesta *nf* protest; JUR objection

protestante *adj & nmf* REL Protestant

protestar *vi* a) to protest; JUR to object b) *Fam* [quejarse] to complain

protocolo *nm* a) [gen & INFORM] protocol b) JUR **protocolo (notarial)** registry

provecho *nm* profit, benefit; **¡buen provecho!** enjoy your meal!; **sacar provecho de algo** to benefit from sth

provechoso, -a *adj* beneficial

provenir [27] *vi* **provenir de** to come from

proverbio *nm* proverb

provincia *nf* province

provisional, *Am* **provisorio, -a** *adj* provisional

provocación *nf* provocation

provocar [44] *vt* a) [causar] to cause; **provocar un incendio** to start a fire b) [instigar] to provoke c) *Carib, Col, Méx Fam* [apetecer] **¿te provoca ir al cine?** would you like to go to the movies?, *Br* do you fancy going to the cinema?

provocativo, -a *adj* provocative

próximo, -a *adj* a) [cercano] near, close b) [siguiente] next

proyección *nf* a) projection b) CINE showing

proyectar *vt* a) [luz] to project b) [planear] to plan c) CINE to show

proyecto *nm* [plan] project, plan; **tener algo en proyecto** to be planning sth; **proyecto de ley** bill

proyector *nm* CINE projector

prudencia *nf* prudence, discretion; [moderación] care

prudente *adj* prudent, sensible; [conductor] careful; **a una hora prudente** at a reasonable time

prueba *nf* a) proof; **en prueba de** as a sign of b) [examen etc] test; **a prueba** on trial; **a prueba de agua/balas** waterproof/bullet-proof; **haz la prueba** try it c) DEP event

psicoanálisis *nm inv* psychoanalysis

psicología *nf* psychology

psicológico, -a *adj* psychological

psicólogo, -a *nm, f* psychologist

psicópata *nmf* psychopath

psicoterapeuta *nmf* psychotherapist

psiquiatra *nmf* psychiatrist

psiquiátrico, -a 1. *adj* psychiatric; **hospital psiquiátrico** psychiatric hospital 2. *nm* psychiatric hospital

psíquico, -a *adj* psychic

pta. *(pl ptas.) (abr de peseta) Antes* peseta(s)

púa *nf* a) [de planta] thorn; [de animal] quill, spine; [de peine] tooth; **alambre de púas** barbed wire b) MÚS plectrum

pub *(pl pubs) nm* pub

pubertad *nf* puberty

pubis *nm inv* pubes

publicación *nf* publication

publicar [44] *vt* a) [libro etc] to publish b) [secreto] to publicize

publicidad *nf* a) COM advertising b) [conocimiento público] publicity

publicitario, -a *adj* advertising

público, -a 1. *adj* public 2. *nm* public; TEATRO audience; DEP spectators

pucha *interj Andes, RP Fam & Euf* a) [lamento, enojo] *Br* sugar!, *US* shoot! b) [sorpresa] wow!

pucho *nm Fam* a) *Andes, RP* [cigarrillo] cigarette, *Br* fag b) *Andes, RP* [colilla] cigarette butt c) *Chile, Ecuad* [hijo menor] youngest child

pudor *nm* modesty

pudrir 1. *vt* to rot, to decay 2. **pudrirse** *vpr* = **pudrir**

pueblo *nm* a) [población - pequeña] village; [grande] town b) [gente] people; **el pueblo español** the Spanish people

puente *nm* a) bridge; AVIACIÓN **puente aéreo** [civil] air shuttle service; MIL airlift; **puente colgante** suspension bridge; **puente levadizo** drawbridge b) [entre dos fiestas] ≃ long weekend

puerco, -a 1. *adj* filthy 2. *nm, f* pig 3. *nm* **puerco espín** porcupine

puerro *nm* leek

puerta *nf* door; [verja, en aeropuerto] gate; DEP goal; **puerta corredera/giratoria** sliding/revolving door; *Fig* **a las puertas, en puertas** imminent; *Fig* **a puerta cerrada** behind closed doors

puerto *nm* a) [de mar] port, harbour; **puerto deportivo** marina b) [de montaña] (mountain) pass c) INFORM port

Puerto Rico *n* Puerto Rico

puertorriqueño, -a, portorriqueño, -a 1. *adj* Puerto Rican 2. *nm, f* Puerto Rico

pues *conj* a) [puesto que] as, since b) [por lo tanto] therefore c) [entonces] so d) [para reforzar] **¡pues claro que sí!** but of course!; **pues como iba diciendo** well, as I was saying; **¡pues mejor!** so much the better!; **¡pues no!** certainly not!

puesta *nf* a) **puesta de sol** sunset b) *Fig* **puesta a punto** tuning, adjusting; *Fig* **puesta al día** updating; TEATRO **puesta en escena** staging; **puesta en marcha** starting-up, start-up; *ver* **puesto**

puestero, -a *nm, f Am* stallholder

puesto, -a 1. *conj* **puesto que** since, as

2. *nm* a) [lugar] place; [asiento] seat b) [empleo] position, post, job; **puesto de trabajo** job, post c) [tienda] stall

d) MIL post

3. *adj* **a)** [colocado] set, put
b) llevar puesto [ropa] to have on; *Fam*
ir muy puesto to be all dressed up
c) *Fam* [borracho] drunk
d) *Fam* **estar puesto en una materia**
to be well up in a subject

pulga *nf* flea; *Fam* **tener malas pulgas**
to be bad-tempered, *Br* to be stroppy

pulgar *nm* thumb

pulidora *nf* polisher

pulir *vt* **a)** [metal, madera] to polish
b) [mejorar] to polish up

pulmón *nm* lung

pulmonía *nf* pneumonia

pulpa *nf* pulp

pulpería *nf* *Am* general store

pulpo *nm* octopus

pulque *nm* *CAm, Méx* pulque *(fermented
agave cactus juice)*

pulquería *nf* *CAm, Méx* "pulque" bar

pulsar *vt* [timbre, botón] to press; [te-
cla] to hit, to strike

pulsera *nf* [aro] bracelet; [de re-
loj] watchstrap; **reloj de pulsera**
wristwatch

pulso *nm* **a)** pulse; *Fig* **tomar el pulso
a la opinión pública** to sound out
opinion **b)** [mano firme] steady hand; **a
pulso** freehand; **ganarse algo a pulso**
to deserve sth **c)** *Fig* trial of strength;
echarse un pulso to arm-wrestle

puma *nm* puma

puna *nf* *Andes* **a)** [llanura] Andean
plateau **b)** [mal de altura] altitude
sickness

punk [pank] *(pl* **punks)** *adj, nm & nmf*
punk

punki ['panki] *adj & nmf* punk

punta *nf* **a)** [extremo] tip; [extremo
afilado] point; [de cabello] end; **sacar
punta a un lápiz** to sharpen a pencil;
tecnología punta state-of-the-art
technology; **me pone los nervios
de punta** he makes me very nervous
b) [periodo] peak; **hora punta** rush

hour **c)** [pequeña cantidad] bit; **una
punta de sal** a pinch of salt **d)** [clavo]
nail

puntada *nf* **a)** [pespunte] stitch **b)** *RP*
[dolor] stabbing pain **c)** *Méx* [broma]
witticism

puntaje *nf* *Am* [calificación] mark, *US*
grade; [en concursos, competiciones]
score

puntapié *nm* kick

puntera *nf* [de zapato] toecap; [de
calcetín] toe

puntería *nf* aim; **tener buena / mala
puntería** to be a good / bad shot

puntero, -a 1. *adj* leading **2.** *nm, f CSur*
DEP winger

puntiagudo, -a *adj* pointed, sharp

puntilla *nf* **a)** [encaje] lace **b) dar la puntilla** TAUROM to finish (the bull) off; *Fig*
[liquidar] to finish off **c) de puntillas**
on tiptoe

punto *nm* **a)** point; **a punto** ready; CULIN
en su punto just right; **a punto de** on
the point of; **hasta cierto punto** to a
certain o some extent; **punto muerto**
AUTO neutral; *Fig* [impase] deadlock;
punto de vista point of view
b) [marca] dot; **línea de puntos** dot-
ted line
c) [lugar] place, point
d) [grado de temperatura] **punto de
ebullición** boiling point
e) punto y aparte *Br* full stop o *US* period,
new paragraph; **punto y coma**
semicolon; **punto y seguido** *Br* full
stop, *US* period *(no new paragraph)*;
dos puntos colon
f) [tiempo] **en punto** sharp, on the dot
g) DEP [tanto] point
h) COST & MED stitch; **hacer punto** to
knit

puntuación *nf* **a)** LING punctuation
b) DEP score **c)** EDUC mark

puntual 1. *adj* **a)** punctual **b)** [exac-
to] accurate, precise **c)** [caso] specific
2. *adv* punctually

puntualidad *nf* punctuality

puntualización *nf* clarification

puntualizar [40] *vt* to specify, to clarify

puntuar [30] **1.** *vt* [al escribir] to punctuate **2.** *vi* **a)** [marcar] to score **b)** [ser puntuable] to count

puñado *nm* handful; *Fam* **a puñados** by the score, galore

puñal *nm* dagger

puñalada *nf* stab; *Fig* **puñalada trapera** stab in the back

puñeta *nf Fam* **hacer la puñeta a algn** to pester sb, to annoy sb; **¡puñetas!** damn!; **¡vete a hacer puñetas!** go to hell!

puñetazo *nm* punch

puñetero, -a *Esp Fam* **1.** *adj* **a)** [persona] damn **b)** [cosa] tricky, awkward **2.** *nm, f* pain

puño *nm* **a)** fist **b)** [de camisa etc] cuff **c)** [de herramienta] handle

punzón *nm* [herramienta] punch

pupa *nf* **a)** [herida] cold sore **b)** *Fam* [daño] pain

pupitre *nm* desk

puré *nm* purée; **puré de patata** mashed potatoes; **puré de verduras** thick vegetable soup

puritano, -a 1. *adj* puritanical **2.** *nm, f* puritan, Puritan

puro, -a 1. *adj* **a)** [sin mezclas] pure; **aire puro** fresh air; **la pura verdad** the plain truth; *POL* **puro y duro** hardline **b)** [mero] sheer, mere; **por pura curiosidad** out of sheer curiosity **c)** [casto] chaste, pure **2.** *nm* [cigarro] cigar

puta *nf Vulg* whore; **de puta madre** great, terrific; **de puta pena** *Br* bloody *o US* goddamn awful; **no tengo ni puta idea** I haven't (got) a *Br* bloody *o US* goddamn clue; **pasarlas putas** to go through hell, to have a rotten time

puteada *nf RP muy Fam* [insulto] swearword

putear *vt muy Fam* **a)** [fastidiar] **putear a algn** to screw *o* bugger sb around **b)** *Am* [insultar] **putear a algn** to call sb for everything, to call sb every name under the sun

puzzle *nm* jigsaw puzzle

PVP *nm (abr de* **precio de venta al público***)* RRP

Pza. *(abr de* **Plaza***)* Sq

q SMS *written abbr of* **que**; *written abbr of* **qué**; **q haces?** *written abbr of* **¿qué haces?**; **q plomo!** *written abbr of* **¡qué plomo!**; **q qrs!** *written abbr of* **¿qué quieres?**; **q risa!** *written abbr of* **¡qué risa!**; **q tal?** *written abbr of* **¿qué tal?**

qand, **qando** SMS *written abbr of* **cuando**; *written abbr of* **cuándo**

qdms SMS *written abbr of* **quedamos**

que¹ *pron relat* **a)** [sujeto - persona] who; [cosa] that, which; **el hombre que vino** the man who came; **la bomba que estalló** the bomb that o which went off **b)** [complemento - persona] that, who, *Formal* whom; [cosa] that, which; **la chica que conocí** the girl (that o who o whom) I met; **el coche que compré** the car (that o which) I bought **c) lo que** what; **lo que más me gusta** what I like best **d)** [+ infinitivo] **hay mucho que hacer** there's a lot to do

que² *conj* **a)** that; **dijo que llamaría** he said (that) he would call; **quiero que vengas** I want you to come **b)** [consecutivo] that; [en comparativas] than; **habla tan bajo que no se le oye** he speaks so quietly (that) he can't be heard; **más alto que yo** taller than me **c)** [causal] **date deprisa que no tenemos mucho tiempo** hurry up, we haven't got much time **d)** [enfático] **¡que no!** no!; **¡que te calles!** I said be quiet! **e)** [deseo, mandato] **¡que te diviertas!** enjoy yourself! **f)** [final] so that; **ven que te dé un beso** come and let me give you a kiss **g)** [disyuntivo] whether; **me da igual que suba o no** it doesn't matter to me whether he comes up or not **h)** [locuciones] **¿a que no ...?** I bet you can't ...!; **que yo sepa** as far as I know; **yo que tú** if I were you

qué **1.** *pron* **a)** [interrogativo] what; **¿qué quieres?** what do you want?; *Fam* **¿y qué?** so what? **b)** [exclamativo + adj] how; **¡qué bonito!** how pretty! **c)** [+ nombre] what a; **¡qué lástima!** what a pity! **d)** *Fam* **¡qué de ...!** what a lot of ...! **2.** *adj interr* which; **¿qué libro quieres?** which book do you want?

Quebec *n* **(el) Quebec** Quebec

quebequense **1.** *adj* Quebec **2.** *nmf* Quebecer, Quebecker

quebrada *nf Am* [arroyo] stream

quebrado *nm* MAT fraction

quebrar [1] **1.** *vt* [romper] to break **2.** *vi* FIN to go bankrupt **3. quebrarse** *vpr* to break; MED to rupture oneself

quedar **1.** *vi* **a)** [restar] to be left, to remain; **quedan dos** there are two left **b)** [en un lugar] to arrange to meet; **quedamos en el bar** I'll meet you in the bar **c) me queda corta** [ropa] it is too short for me; **quedaría muy bien allí** [objeto] it would look very nice there **d)** [acordar] to agree (**en** to); **¿en qué quedamos?** so what's it to be?; **quedamos en traer cada uno una cosa** we agreed we would each bring one thing **e)** [estar situado] to be; **¿dónde queda la estación?** where's the station? **f) quedar bien / mal** to make a good / bad impression **2. quedarse** *vpr* **a)** [permanecer] to stay; **se quedó en casa** she stayed (at) home; **quedarse sin dinero / pan** to run out of money / bread; **quedarse con hambre** to still be hungry

b) quedarse (con) [retener] to keep; **quédese (con) el cambio** keep the change
c) *Esp Fam* **quedarse con algn** to make a fool of sb

quehacer *nm* task, chore

quejarse *vpr* to complain (**de** about)

quejido *nm* groan, cry

quejoso, -a *adj* [persona] complaining; **estar quejoso de** to complain about

quemadura *nf* burn

quemar 1. *vt* to burn; *Fig* [agotar] to burn out
2. *vi* to be burning hot; **este café quema** this coffee's boiling hot
3. quemarse *vpr Fig* to burn out

quepa *ver* **caber**

quepo *indic pres de* **caber**

queque *nm Andes, CAm, Méx* sponge (cake)

querer [20] **1.** *vt* **a)** [amar] to love
b) [desear] to want; **¿cuánto quiere por la casa?** how much does he want for the house?; **sin querer** without meaning to; **queriendo** on purpose; **¡por lo que más quieras!** for heaven's sake!; **¿quiere pasarme el pan?** would you pass me the bread?
c) querer decir to mean
d) no quiso darme permiso he refused me permission
2. quererse *vpr* to love each other
3. *nm* love, affection

querido, -a 1. *adj* dear, beloved; **querido amigo** [en carta] dear friend
2. *nm, f* [amante] lover

quesadilla *nf* **a)** *CAm, Méx* [salada] *filled fried tortilla* **b)** *Ecuad* [dulce] *sweet, cheese-filled pasty*

queso *nm* cheese; **queso rallado** grated cheese; **queso de cerdo** *Br* brawn, *US* headcheese

quiebra *nf* FIN [bancarrota] bankruptcy; [en Bolsa] crash

quien *pron relat* **a)** [con prep] **el hombre con quien vino** the man she came with; *Formal* the man with whom she came **b)** [indefinido] whoever, anyone who; **quien quiera venir que venga** whoever wants to can come; **hay quien dice lo contrario** some people say the opposite; *Fig* **quien más quien menos** everybody

quién *pron interr* **a)** [sujeto] who?; **¿quién es?** who is it? **b)** [complemento] who, *Formal* whom; **¿para quién es?** who is it for?; **¿de quién es esa bici?** whose bike is that?

quienquiera *(pl* **quienesquiera)** *pron* whoever; **quienquiera que venga** whoever comes

quieto, -a *adj* still; [mar] calm; **¡estáte quieto!** keep still!, don't move!

quilla *nf* keel

quillango *nm Arg, Chile* fur blanket

quilo = **kilo**

quilombo *nm RP muy Fam* **a)** [burdel] whorehouse **b)** [lío, desorden] **se armó un gran quilombo** all hell broke loose

quimbambas *nfpl Fam* **¡vete a las quimbambas!** get lost!

química *nf* chemistry

químico, -a 1. *adj* chemical **2.** *nm, f* chemist

quince *adj & nm inv* fifteen

quincena *nf* fortnight, two weeks

quincenalmente *adv* fortnightly

quincho *nm Andes, RP* **a)** [techo] thatched roof **b)** [refugio] thatched shelter

quinielas *nfpl Esp Br* (football) pools, *US* sports lottery

quinientos, -as *adj & nm* five hundred

quinqué *nm* oil lamp

quinteto *nm* quintet

quinto, -a 1. *adj & nm, f* fifth **2.** *nm* MIL conscript, recruit

quiosco *nm* kiosk; **quiosco de periódicos** newspaper stand

quipos, **quipus** *nmpl Andes* quipus, *knotted cords used for record keeping by the Incas*

quirófano *nm* operating *Br* theatre o *US* room

quisquilla *nf* **a)** [crustáceo] shrimp **b)** [pequeñez] triviality

quisquilloso, -a 1. *adj* fussy, finicky **2.** *nm, f* fusspot

quitamanchas *nm inv* stain remover

---

quitar 1. *vt* **a)** to remove ; [ropa] to take off ; [la mesa] to clear ; [mancha] to remove ; [dolor] to relieve ; [hipo] to stop ; [sed] to quench ; [hambre] to take away

b) [apartar] to take away, to take off ; *Fig* **quitar importancia a algo** to play sth down ; *Fig* **quitar las ganas a algn** to put sb off

c) [robar] to steal, to take ; *Fig* [tiempo] to take up ; [sitio] to take

d) [descontar] to take off

e) *Fam* [apagar] to turn off

f) eso no quita para que … that's no reason not to be …

2. quitarse *vpr* **a)** [apartarse] to move away

b) [mancha] to come out ; [dolor] to go away ; **se me han quitado las ganas** I don't feel like it any more

c) [ropa, gafas] to take off

d) quitarse de beber / fumar to give up drinking / smoking

e) quitarse a algn de encima to get rid of sb

---

quizá, **quizás** *adv* perhaps, maybe

R

rábano nm radish; *Fam* **me importa un rábano** I couldn't care less

rabia nf **a)** *Fig* [ira] fury, rage; **¡qué rabia!** how annoying!; **me da rabia** it gets up my nose; **me tiene rabia** he's got it in for me **b)** MED rabies (*sing*)

rabieta nf *Fam*; **coger una rabieta** to throw a tantrum

rabioso, -a adj **a)** MED rabid; **perro rabioso** rabid dog **b)** *Fig* [enfadado] furious **c) de rabiosa actualidad** up-to-the-minute

rabo nm tail; [de fruta etc] stalk

racha nf [de viento] gust, squall; *Fam* [período] spell, patch; **a rachas** in fits and starts

racial adj **discriminación racial** racial discrimination; **disturbios raciales** race riots

racimo nm bunch, cluster

ración nf portion

racismo nm racism

racista adj & nmf racist

radar nm TÉC radar

radiación nf radiation

radiador nm radiator

radial adj **a)** [en forma de estrella] radial **b)** *Am* [de la radio] radio

radiante adj radiant (**de** with)

radiar [43] vt to broadcast, to transmit

radical adj radical

radio 1. nf **a)** nf [medio] radio; *Esp, CSur* [aparato] radio (set) **2.** nm **a)** radius; **radio de acción** field of action, scope **b)** [de rueda] spoke

radioaficionado, -a nm, f radio ham

radiocasete nm radio cassette

radiodespertador nm clock radio

radiodifusión nf broadcasting

radiograbador nm *CSur* radio cassette

radiograbadora nf *CSur* radio cassette

radiografía nf [imagen] X-ray

radiólogo, -a nm, f radiologist

radionovela nf radio soap opera

radiotaxi nm [aparato de radio] *taxi driver's two-way radio*; [taxi] taxi (*fitted with two-way radio*)

radioyente nmf listener

ráfaga nf [de viento] gust, squall; [de disparos] burst

rafting nm DEP rafting

raíl nm rail

raíz nf root; **raíz cuadrada** square root; *Fig* **a raíz de** as a result of; **echar raíces** to take root

raja nf [corte] cut, slit; [hendidura] crack, split

rajar 1. vt [hender] to crack, split; *Fam* [acuchillar] to cut up
2. vi *Esp Fam* to natter on, to witter on
3. rajarse vpr **a)** [partirse] to crack
b) *Esp Fam* [echarse atrás] to back o pull out

rajatabla ▪ a rajatabla loc adv to the letter, strictly

ralentizar [40] **1.** vt to slow down
2. ralentizarse vpr to slow down

rallador nm grater

rallar vt to grate

rally ['rrali] (pl **rallys** o **rallies**) nm rally

rama nf branch; *Fam* **andarse** o **irse por las ramas** to beat about the bush

rambla nf [avenida] boulevard, avenue

ramo nm **a)** [de flores] bunch, bouquet **b)** [sector] branch

rampa *nf* ramp; **rampa de lanzamiento** launch pad

rana *nf* frog; *Fam* **salir rana** to be a disappointment

ranchera *nf* a) *MÚS popular Mexican song* b) [automóvil] *Br* estate (car), *US* station wagon

rancho *nm* a) [granja] ranch b) MIL [comida] mess c) *RP* [en la playa] *thatched beachside building* d) *CSur, Ven* [en ciudad] shack, shanty e) *Méx* [pequeña finca] *small farmhouse and outbuildings*

rancio, -a *adj* a) [comida] stale b) [antiguo] ancient

rango *nm* rank; [jerarquía elevada] high social standing

ranura *nf* slot

rap *nm* [música] rap

rape *nm* a) [pez] angler fish b) *Fam* **cortado al rape** close-cropped

rápel, rapel *nm* abseiling

rápidamente *adv* quickly

rapidez *nf* speed, rapidity

rápido, -a 1. *adj* quick, fast, rapid **2.** *adv* quickly **3.** *nm* a) [tren] fast train b) **rápidos** [de río] rapids

raptar *vt* to kidnap, to abduct

raqueta *nf* a) [de tenis] racquet; [de ping-pong] *Br* bat, *US* paddle b) [de nieve] snowshoe

raro, -a *adj* a) rare; **rara vez** seldom b) [extraño] odd, strange

rasca *nf Fam* [frío] **¡qué rasca que hace aquí!** it's freezing here!

rascacielos *nm inv* skyscraper

rascador *nm* [herramienta] scraper

rascar [44] **1.** *vt* [con uñas] to scratch; [guitarra] to strum **2.** *vi* to chafe

rasgar [42] *vt* to tear, to rip

rasgo *nm* [característica] characteristic, feature; [de rostro] feature; *Fig* **a grandes rasgos** broadly speaking

raso, -a 1. *adj* [llano] flat, level; [vuelo] low; [cielo] clear, cloudless; **soldado raso** private **2.** *nm* satin

rastrillo *nm* a) [rake] b) [mercado] flea market

rastro *nm* a) trace, sign; [en el suelo] track, trail b) **el Rastro** *the Madrid flea market*

rasurador *nm* electric razor

rata 1. *nf* rat **2.** *nm Fam* [tacaño] mean o stingy person

ratero, -a *nm, f* pickpocket

ratificación *nf* ratification

ratificar [44] *vt* to ratify

rato *nm* a) [momento] while, time; **a ratos** at times; **al poco rato** shortly after; **hay para rato** it'll take a while; **pasar un buen / mal rato** to have a good / bad time; **ratos libres** free time b) *Esp Fam* **un rato** [mucho] very, a lot

ratón *nm* [animal] mouse; *Esp* INFORM mouse

raya *nf* a) [línea] line; [del pantalón] crease; *Esp, Andes, RP* [del pelo] *Br* parting, *US* part; **camisa a rayas** striped shirt b) *Fig* **tener a raya** to keep at bay; **pasarse de la raya** to go too far c) [de droga] fix, dose

rayo *nm* a) ray, beam; **rayos X** X-rays b) [relámpago] (flash of) lightning; **¡mal rayo la parta!** to hell with her!

rayuela *nf* hopscotch

raza *nf* a) [humana] race b) [de animal] breed c) *Méx Despec* [populacho] **la raza** the masses d) *Perú* [descaro] cheek, nerve

razón *nf* a) [facultad] reason; **uso de razón** power of reasoning b) [motivo] reason; **razón de más para** all the more reason to c) [justicia] rightness, justice; **dar la razón a algn** to say that sb is right; **tienes razón** you're right d) [proporción] ratio, rate; **a razón de** at the rate of e) **razón aquí** [en letrero] enquire within, apply within

razonable *adj* reasonable

razonamiento *nm* reasoning

razonar 1. *vt* [argumentar] to reason out **2.** *vi* [discurrir] to reason

reacción *nf* reaction; **avión de reacción** jet (plane); **reacción en cadena** chain reaction

reaccionar *vi* to react

reactor nm reactor; [avión] jet (plane)

real¹ adj [efectivo, verdadero] real; **en la vida real** in real life

real² adj [regio] royal

realeza nf royalty

realidad nf reality; **en realidad** in fact, actually; **la realidad es que ...** the fact of the matter is that ...

realismo nm realism

realizable adj feasible

realización nf [ejecución] carrying out; CINE & TV production

realizar [40] **1.** vt a) [hacer] to carry out; [ambición] to achieve, to fulfil b) CINE & TV to produce c) FIN to realize **2. realizarse** vpr [persona] to fulfil oneself; [sueño] to come true

realmente adv really; [en realidad] actually, in fact

reanimación nf revival

rebaja nf [descuento] reduction, discount; **rebajas** sales; **precio de rebaja** sale price

rebajado, -a adj a) [precio] reduced b) [diluido] diluted (**con** with)

rebajar 1. vt a) [precio] to cut, to reduce; [cantidad] to take off b) [color] to tone down, to soften; [intensidad] to diminish c) [trabajador] to excuse, to exempt (**de** from) d) [humillar] to humiliate **2. rebajarse** vpr [humillarse] to humble oneself

rebanada nf slice

rebanar vt to slice, to cut into slices

rebaño nm [de ovejas] flock; [de otros animales] herd

rebasar vt a) [sobrepasar] to rise above b) CAm, Méx [vehículo] to overtake

rebelarse vpr to rebel, to revolt

rebelde 1. nmf rebel **2.** adj rebellious; Fig **una tos rebelde** a persistent cough

rebeldía nf a) rebelliousness b) JUR default

rebelión nf rebellion, revolt

rebenque nm RP [fusta] (riding) crop, whip

rebotar vi to bounce (**en** off), to rebound (**en** off)

rebote nm a) [bote] bounce, bouncing; Fig **de rebote** by chance, indirectly b) DEP rebound; **de rebote** on the rebound

rebozado, -a adj CULIN coated in batter or breadcrumbs; Fig **rebozado de** o **en** [barro] covered in

rebozo nm Am wrap, shawl; **sin rebozo** [con franqueza] frankly

recado nm [mandado] errand; [mensaje] message; **dejar un recado** to leave a message

recaer [39] vi a) MED to relapse b) [culpa, responsabilidad] to fall (**sobre** on)

recalcar [44] vt to stress, to emphasize

recalentar [1] vt [comida] to reheat, to warm up; [calentar demasiado] to overheat

recámara nf a) [de rueda] tube b) [habitación] dressing room c) CAm, Col, Méx [dormitorio] bedroom

recamarera nf CAm, Col, Méx chambermaid

recambio nm a) [repuesto] spare (part); **rueda de recambio** spare wheel b) [de pluma etc] refill

recarga nf recharge; **desconectar tras la recarga** unplug after recharging

recargar [42] **1.** vt a) ELEC to recharge b) [sobrecargar] to overload; [adornar mucho] to overelaborate c) FIN to increase **2. recargarse** vpr Méx [apoyarse] to lean (**contra** against)

recato nm [cautela] caution, prudence; [pudor] modesty

recepción nf reception; [en hotel] reception (desk)

recepcionista nmf receptionist

receptor, -a 1. nm, f [persona] recipient **2.** nm RADIO & TV receiver

recesión nf recession

receta nf recipe; MED prescription

recetar vt MED to prescribe

rechazar [40] vt to reject, to turn down; MIL to repel, to drive back

rechazo *nm* rejection

recibidor *nm* entrance hall

recibimiento *nm* reception, welcome

recibir 1. *vt* to receive ; [en casa] to welcome ; [en la estación etc] to meet **2. recibirse** *vpr Am* [graduarse] to graduate, to qualify (**de** as)

recibo *nm* **a)** [factura] invoice, bill ; [resguardo] receipt ; **recibo de la luz** electricity bill **b)** JUR to appeal acknowledge receipt of

reciclable *adj* recyclable

reciclado, -a 1. *adj* recycled **2.** *nm* [reciclaje] recycling

reciclaje *nm* [de residuos] recycling ; *Fig* [renovación] retraining ; **curso de reciclaje** refresher course

reciclar *vt* [residuos] to recycle ; *Fig* [profesores etc] to retrain

recién *adv* **a)** [recientemente - antes de pp] recently, newly ; **café recién hecho** freshly-made coffee ; **recién casados** newlyweds ; **recién nacido** newborn baby **b)** *Am* [apenas] just now, recently ; **regresó recién ayer** she only o just got back yesterday **c)** *Am* [ahora mismo] (only) just ; **recién me entero** I've (only) just heard **d)** *Am* [sólo] only ; **recién el martes sabremos el resultado** we'll only know the result on Tuesday, we won't know the result until Tuesday

reciente *adj* recent

recientemente *adv* recently, lately

recinto *nm* [cercado] enclosure ; **recinto comercial** shopping precinct

recipiente *nm* receptacle, container

recital *nm* MÚS recital ; LITER reading

recitar *vt* to recite

reclamación *nf* **a)** [demanda] claim, demand **b)** [queja] complaint

reclamar 1. *vt* to claim, to demand **2.** *vi* **a)** to protest (**contra** against) **b)** JUR to appeal

reclamo *nm* **a)** [publicitario] appeal **b)** [en caza] decoy bird, lure ; *Fig* inducement **c)** *Am* [queja] complaint **d)** *Am* [reivindicación] claim

recluir [37] *vt* to shut away, to lock away ; [encarcelar] to imprison, to intern

reclusión *nf* seclusion ; [encarcelamiento] imprisonment, internment

recobrar 1. *vt* to recover, to retrieve ; [conocimiento] to regain ; **recobrar el aliento** to get one's breath back **2. recobrarse** *vpr* to recover, to recuperate

recogedor *nm* dustpan

recoger [53] **1.** *vt* **a)** [del suelo etc] to pick up **b)** [datos etc] to gather, to collect **c)** [ordenar, limpiar] to clean ; **recoger la mesa** to clear the table **d)** [ir a buscar] to pick up, to fetch **e)** [cosecha] to gather, to pick **2. recogerse** *vpr* **a)** [irse a casa] to go home **b)** [pelo] to lift up

recogida *nf* collection ; AGRIC [cosecha] harvest, harvesting

recolección *nf* AGRIC harvest, harvesting ; [recogida] collection, gathering

recomendado, -a *adj Am* [carta, paquete] registered

recomendar [1] *vt* to recommend

recompensa *nf* reward

recompensar *vt* to reward

reconcomerse *vpr* **reconcomerse de** [envidia] to be eaten up with ; [impaciencia] to be itching with

reconocer [34] *vt* **a)** to recognize **b)** [admitir] to recognize, to admit **c)** MED [paciente] to examine

reconocimiento *nm* **a)** recognition **b)** MED examination, checkup

reconquista *nf* reconquest

récord *(pl* **récords***) nm* record

recordar [2] **1.** *vt* **a)** [rememorar] to remember **b)** **recordar algo a algn** to remind sb of sth **2.** *vi* to remember

recorrer *vt* [distancia] to cover, to travel ; [país] to tour, to travel through o round ; [ciudad] to visit, to walk round

recorrida *Am nf* = **recorrido**

recorrido *nm* [distancia] distance travelled ; [trayecto] trip, journey ; [itinerario] itinerary, route

recortar *vt* to cut out

recostar [2] **1.** *vt* to lean **2. recostarse** *vpr* [tumbarse] to lie down

recreo *nm* **a)** [diversión] recreation **b)** [en el colegio] break, recreation

recta *nf* GEOM straight line ; [de carretera] straight stretch ; DEP **la recta final** the home straight

rectangular *adj* rectangular

rectángulo *nm* rectangle

rectitud *nf* straightness ; *Fig* uprightness, rectitude

recto, -a 1. *adj* **a)** [derecho] straight **b)** [honesto] upright, honest **c)** GEOM right **2.** *nm* ANAT rectum **3.** *adv* straight (on)

rector, -a 1. *adj* [principio] guiding, ruling **2.** *nm* REL rector

recuerdo *nm* **a)** [memoria] memory **b)** [regalo etc] souvenir **c) recuerdos** regards

recuperación *nf* recovery ; [examen] resit

recuperar 1. *vt* [salud] to recover ; [conocimiento] to regain ; [tiempo, clases] to make up **2. recuperarse** *vpr* to recover

recurrir *vi* **a)** JUR to appeal **b) recurrir a** [a algn] to turn to ; [a algo] to make use of, to resort to

recurso *nm* **a)** resource ; **recursos naturales** natural resources ; **como último recurso** as a last resort **b)** JUR appeal

red *nf* net ; [sistema] network ; COM [cadena] chain of supermarkets ; *Fig* [trampa] trap ; **la Red** [Internet] the Net ; **red de área extendida** wide area network *(WAN)* ; **red de área local** local area network *(LAN)* ; **Red Digital de Servicios Integrados** integrated services digital network *(ISDN)* ; **red social** social network

redacción *nf* [escrito] composition, essay ; [acción] writing ; PRENSA editing ; [redactores] editorial staff

redactar *vt* to draft ; PRENSA to edit

redactor, -a *nm, f* PRENSA editor

redil *nm* fold, sheepfold

redirigir *vt* to redirect

redistribución *nf* redistribution

redistribuir *vt* to redistribute

redondeado, -a *adj* rounded

redondel *nm Fam* [círculo] circle, ring ; TAUROM ring, arena

redondo, -a *adj* **a)** round ; *Fig* **caer redondo** to collapse **b)** [rotundo] categorical ; [perfecto] perfect

reducción *nf* reduction

reducir [10] **1.** *vt* [disminuir] to reduce **2. reducirse** *vpr* **a)** [disminuirse] to be reduced, to diminish **b)** [limitarse] to confine oneself

reembolsar *vt* to reimburse ; [deuda] to repay ; [importe] to refund

reembolso *nm* reimbursement ; [de deuda] repayment ; [devolución] refund ; **contra reembolso** cash on delivery

reemplazar [40] *vt* to replace (**con** with)

reenviar *vt* to resend

reestreno *nm* **a)** CINE rerun, re-release ; **cine de reestreno** second-run cinema **b)** TEATRO revival

reestructurar *vt* to restructure

refacción *nf* **a)** *Andes, CAm, RP, Ven* [reforma] refurbishment **b)** *Andes, CAm, RP, Ven* [reparación] restoration **c)** *Méx* [recambio] spare part

refaccionar *vt Andes, CAm, Ven* **a)** [reformar] to refurbish **b)** [reparar] to restore

referencia *nf* reference ; **con referencia a** with reference to

referéndum (*pl* **referéndums**) *nm* referendum

referente *adj* **referente a** concerning, regarding

referir [5] **1.** *vt* to tell, to relate **2. referirse** *vpr* [aludir] to refer (**a** to) ; **¿a qué te refieres?** what do you mean?

refinería *nf* refinery

reflectante *adj* reflective

reflector, -a 1. *adj* reflecting **2.** *nm* ELEC spotlight, searchlight

reflejar 1. *vt* to reflect **2. reflejarse** *vpr* to be reflected (**en** in)

reflejo, -a 1. *nm* a) [imagen] reflection b) [destello] gleam, glint c) ANAT reflex d) **reflejos** [en cabello] streaks, highlights **2.** *adj* [movimiento] reflex

reflexión *nf* reflection

reflexionar *vi* to reflect (**sobre** on), to think (**sobre** about)

reforestación *nf* reforestation

reforma *nf* a) reform; **reforma fiscal** tax reform b) [reparación] repair

reformar 1. *vt* to reform; [edificio] to renovate **2. reformarse** *vpr* to reform

reforzar [2] *vt* to reinforce, to strengthen

refrán *nm* proverb, saying

refrescante *adj* refreshing

refresco *nm* soft drink

refrigerado, -a *adj* air-conditioned

refrigerador *nm* refrigerator, *Br* fridge, *US* icebox

refugiado, -a *adj & nm*, *f* refugee

refugiarse [43] *vpr* to shelter, to take refuge

refugio *nm* refuge

regadera *nf* a) [para regar] watering can; *Esp Fam* **estar como una regadera** to be as mad as a hatter b) *Col, Méx, Ven* [ducha] shower

regadío *nm* [tierra] irrigated land

regalar *vt* a) [dar] to give (as a present); [en ofertas etc] to give away b) **regalar el oído a algn** to flatter sb

regaliz *nm* liquorice

regalo *nm* a) gift, present; **de regalo** as a present b) [comodidad] pleasure, comfort

regalón, -ona *adj CSur Fam* [niño] spoilt

regañar 1. *vt* [reprender] to tell off **2.** *vi Esp* [pelearse] to nag

regar [1] *vt* to water

regata *nf* boat race

regatear 1. *vi* a) to haggle, to bargain b) DEP to dribble **2.** *vt* **no regatear esfuerzos** to spare no effort

regazo *nm* lap

regenerar *vt* to regenerate

regente 1. *nmf* POL regent **2.** *nmf* a) [director] manager b) *Méx* [alcalde] mayor, *f* mayoress

régimen *(pl* **regímenes)** *nm* a) POL regime b) MED diet; **estar a régimen** to be on a diet

regio, -a *adj* a) [real] royal, regal b) *Andes, RP* [genial] great, fabulous

región *nf* region

regional *adj* regional

regir [58] **1.** *vt* to govern **2.** *vi* to be in force **3. regirse** *vpr* to be guided, to go (**por** by)

registrado, -a *adj* a) [patentado, inscrito] registered; **marca registrada** registered trademark b) *Am* [certificado] registered

registradora *nf Am* cash register

registrar 1. *vt* a) [examinar] to inspect; [cachear] to frisk b) [inscribir] to register c) [grabar] to record **2. registrarse** *vpr* a) [inscribirse] to register, to enrol b) [detectarse] to be recorded

registro *nm* a) inspection b) [inscripción] registration, recording; [oficina] registry office c) MÚS register d) INFORM [datos] registry; [señal] bookmark

regla *nf* a) [norma] rule; **en regla** in order; **por regla general** as a (general) rule; **regla de oro** golden rule b) [instrumento] ruler c) MAT rule d) MED [periodo] period

reglaje *nm* adjustment

reglamento *nm* regulations, rules

regresar 1. *vi* to return **2.** *vt Am salvo RP* [devolver] to give back **3. regresarse** *vpr Am salvo RP* [yendo] to go back, to return; [viniendo] to come back, to return

regreso *nm* return

regulable *adj* adjustable

regular **1.** *vt* **a)** to regulate, to control **b)** [ajustar] to adjust **2.** *adj* **a)** regular; **por lo regular** as a rule; **vuelo regular** scheduled flight **b)** *Fam* [mediano] average, so-so **3.** *adv* so-so

regularidad *nf* regularity; **con regularidad** regularly

rehabilitar *vt* to rehabilitate; [edificio] to convert

rehén *nm* hostage

rehidratarse *vpr* to rehydrate

rehogar [42] *vt* to brown

reina *nf* queen

reinado *nm* reign

reinar *vi* to reign

reincorporar **1.** *vt* MIL [puesto] to reinstate **2. reincorporarse** *vpr* **reincorporarse al trabajo** to return to work, to go back to work

reino *nm* kingdom; **el Reino Unido** the United Kingdom

reinstalar *vt* [INFORM] to reinstall

reintegro *nm* [en lotería] winning of one's stake

reír [56] **1.** *vi* to laugh **2. reírse** *vpr* **a)** to laugh **b)** [mofarse] to laugh (**de** at), to make fun (**de** of)

reiteradamente *adv* repeatedly

reivindicación *nf* claim, demand

reivindicar [44] *vt* to claim, to demand; **el atentado fue reivindicado por los terroristas** the terrorists claimed responsibility for the attack

reja *nf* **a)** [de ventana] grill, grating; *Fam* **estar entre rejas** to be behind bars **b)** AGRIC ploughshare

rejilla *nf* [de ventana, ventilador, radiador] grill; [de horno] gridiron; [para equipaje] luggage rack

rejuvenecer [33] *vt* to rejuvenate

relación *nf* **a)** relationship; [conexión] connection, link; **con** *o* **en relación a** with regard to; **relaciones públicas** public relations **b)** [lista] list **c)** [relato] account **d)** MAT & TÉC ratio

relacionar **1.** *vt* to relate (**con** to), to connect (**con** with) **2. relacionarse** *vpr* **a)** to be related, to be connected **b)** [alternar] to mix, to get acquainted

relajación *nf* relaxation

relajado, -a *adj* relaxed

relajar **1.** *vt* to relax **2. relajarse** *vpr* to relax; [moral] to deteriorate

relajo *nm* **a)** *Am Fam* [alboroto] **se armó un relajo** there was an almighty row; **esta mesa es un relajo** this table is a complete mess **b)** *Méx, RP* [complicación] nuisance, hassle **c)** *CAm, Carib, Méx* [broma] joke

relámpago *nm* flash of lightning; *Fig* **pasó como un relámpago** he flashed past; *Fig* **visita relámpago** flying visit

relampaguear *v impers* to flash

relatar *vt* to narrate, to relate

relativo, -a *adj* relative (**a** to); **en lo relativo a** with regard to, concerning

relato *nm* [cuento] tale, story

relevo *nm* relief; DEP relay

relieve *nm* ARTE relief; *Fig* **poner de relieve** to emphasize

religión *nf* religion

religioso, -a **1.** *adj* religious **2.** *nm, f* [hombre] monk; [mujer] nun

relinchar *vi* to neigh, to whinny

relincho *nm* neigh, whinny

rellano *nm* landing

rellenar *vt* **a)** [impreso etc] to fill in **b)** [un ave] to stuff; [un pastel] to fill

relleno, -a **1.** *nm* [de aves] stuffing; [de pasteles] filling **2.** *adj* stuffed

relocalizar *vt* to relocate

reloj *nm* clock; [de pulsera] watch; **reloj de arena** hourglass; **reloj de sol** sundial; **reloj despertador** alarm clock

relojería *nf* [tienda] watchmaker's, clockmaker's; **bomba de relojería** time bomb

relojero, -a *nm, f* watchmaker, clockmaker

remar *vi* to row

remediar [43] *vt* **a)** to remedy; [enmendar] to repair, to make good **b)** [evitar] to avoid, to prevent; **no pude remediarlo** I couldn't help it

remedio *nm* [cura] remedy, cure; [solución] solution; **¡qué remedio!** what else can I do?; **no hay más remedio** there's no choice; **sin remedio** without fail; *Fam* **¡no tienes remedio!** you're hopeless!

remendar [1] *vt* [ropa] to patch

remera *nf Am* [prenda] T-shirt

remero, -a *nm, f* rower

remezcla *nf* remix

remezón *nm Am* (earth) tremor

remise *nm RP* taxi *(in private car without meter)*

remisero, -a *nm, f RP* taxi driver *(of private car without meter)*

remite *nm* [en carta] *sender's name and address*

remitente *nmf* sender

remitir **1.** *vt* **a)** [enviar] to send **b)** [referir] to refer **2.** *vi* [fiebre, temporal] to subside **3. remitirse** *vpr* **si nos remitimos a los hechos** if we look at the facts; **remítase a la página 10** see page 10

remo *nm* oar; [deporte] rowing

remoción *nf Andes, RP* [de escombros] removal; [de heridos] transport

remojar *vt* to soak **(en** in)

remojo *nm* **dejar** *o* **poner en remojo** to soak, to leave to soak

remolacha *nf* [planta] *Br* beetroot, *US* beet

remolcador *nm* **a)** NÁUT tug, tugboat **b)** AUTO *Br* breakdown van *o* truck, *US* tow truck

remolcar [44] *vt* to tow

remolque *nm* [acción] towing; [vehículo] trailer; *Fig* **ir a remolque de algn** to trundle along behind sb

remontar **1.** *vt* **a)** [subir] to go up **b)** [superar] to overcome **2. remontarse** *vpr* **a)** [pájaros, aviones] to soar **b)** [datar] to go back, to date back **(a** to)

remordimiento *nm* remorse

remotamente *adv* vaguely, remotely

remoto, -a *adj* remote, faraway; **no tengo la más remota idea** I haven't got the faintest idea

remover [4] *vt* **a)** [trasladar] to move over **b)** [tierra] to turn over; [líquido] to shake up; [comida etc] to stir; [asunto] to stir up

remuneración *nf* remuneration

renacuajo *nm* tadpole; *Fam* [niño pequeño] shrimp

rencor *nm* rancour; [resentimiento] resentment; **guardar rencor a algn** to have a grudge against sb

rendición *nf* surrender

rendimiento *nm* [producción] yield, output; [de máquina, motor] efficiency, performance

rendir [6] **1.** *vt* **a)** [fruto, beneficios] to yield, to produce **b)** [cansar] to exhaust, to wear out **c) rendir culto a** to worship; **rendir homenaje a** to pay homage to **2.** *vi* [dar beneficios] to pay, to be profitable **3. rendirse** *vpr* **a)** to surrender, to give in; **¡me rindo!** I give up! **b)** [cansarse] to wear oneself out

RENFE *nf* *(abr de* **Red Nacional de los Ferrocarriles Españoles***)* Spanish state railway company

rengo, -a *adj Andes, RP* lame

renguear *vi Andes, RP* to limp, to hobble

reno *nm* reindeer

renombrar *vt* INFORM to rename

renovación *nf* [de contrato, pasaporte] renewal; [de una casa] renovation

renovado, -a *adj* [edificio] renovated

renovar [2] *vt* to renew; [edificio] to renovate

renta *nf* **a)** FIN [ingresos] income; [beneficio] interest, return; **renta per cápita** per capita income; **renta fija** fixed-interest security **b)** [alquiler] rent

rentable *adj* profitable

rentar 1. *vt* **a)** [rendir] to produce, yield **b)** *Méx* [alquilar] to rent; [vehículo] to hire **2.** *vi* to be profitable

renunciar [43] *vi* **a) renunciar a** to renounce, to give up; [no aceptar] to decline **b)** [dimitir] to resign

reñir [6] **1.** *vt* [regañar] to scold, to tell off **2.** *vi* [discutir] to quarrel, to argue; [pelear] to fight; **reñir con algn** to fall out with sb

reo *nmf* [acusado] defendant, accused; [culpable] culprit

reparación *nf* repair; [compensación] reparation, amends

reparar 1. *vt* to repair; [ofensa, injuria] to make amends for; [daño] to make good **2.** *vi* **reparar en** [darse cuenta de] to notice; [reflexionar sobre] to think about

repartidor, -a *nm, f* distributor

repartir *vt* **a)** [dividir] to distribute, to share out **b)** [regalo, premio] to give out, to hand out; [correo] to deliver; NAIPES to deal

reparto *nm* **a)** distribution, sharing out **b)** [distribución] handing out; [de mercancías] delivery **c)** CINE & TEATRO cast

repasador *nm RP* [trapo] tea towel

repasar *vt* **a)** to revise, to go over **b)** [ropa] to mend

repaso *nm* revision

repelente 1. *adj* [repugnante] repulsive, repellent; *Fam* **niño repelente** little know-all **2.** *nm* [contra insectos] (insect) repellent

repente *nm Fam* [arrebato] fit, outburst; **de repente** suddenly, all of a sudden

repentino, -a *adj* sudden

repercusión *nf* repercussion

repertorio *nm* repertoire, repertory

repetición *nf* repetition; **repetición de la jugada** action replay

repetidamente *adv* repeatedly

repetidor, -a 1. *adj* repeating **2.** *nm, f Fam* EDUC student who is repeating a year

repetir [6] **1.** *vt* **a)** to repeat **b)** [plato] to have a second helping **2.** *vi* EDUC to repeat a year **3. repetirse** *vpr* **a)** [persona] to repeat oneself **b)** [hecho] to recur **c) el pepino se repite** cucumber repeats (on me / you / him *etc*)

réplica *nf* **a)** answer, reply **b)** [copia] replica

replicar [44] **1.** *vt* to answer back **2.** *vi* **a)** to reply, to retort **b)** [objetar] to argue **c)** JUR to answer

repoblación *nf* repopulation; **repoblación forestal** reafforestation

repoblar [2] *vt* to repopulate; [bosque] to reafforest

reponer [19] **1.** *vt* **a)** to put back, to replace **b)** TEATRO [obra] to put on again; CINE [película] to rerun; TV [programa] to repeat **2. reponerse** *vpr* **reponerse de** to recover from, to get over

reportaje *nm* PRENSA & RADIO report; [noticias] article, news item

reportar 1. *vt* **a)** [beneficios etc] to bring **b)** *Andes, CAm, Méx, Ven* [informar] to report **c)** *CAm, Méx* [denunciar] to report (to the police) **2. reportarse** *vpr CAm, Méx, Ven* [presentarse] to report (**a** to)

reporte *nm Andes, CAm, Méx, Ven* [informe] report; [noticia] news item o report; **recibí reportes de mi hermano** I was sent news by my brother; **el reporte del tiempo** weather report o forecast

reportero, -a *nm, f* reporter

reposera *nf RP Br* sun-lounger, *US* beach recliner

reposo *nm* rest; **en reposo** at rest

repostería *nf* confectionery; [tienda] confectioner's (shop)

representación *nf* **a)** representation **b)** TEATRO performance

representante *nmf* representative

representar *vt* **a)** to represent **b)** [significar] to mean, to represent **c)** TEATRO [obra] to perform

representativo, -a *adj* representative

represión *nf* repression

represor, -a 1. *adj* repressive **2.** *nm, f* [que oprime] oppressor

reprimir *vt* to repress

reprobar [2] *vt* [cosa] to condemn; [a persona] to reproach, reprove; *Am* [estudiante, examen] to fail

reprochar *vt* to reproach; **reprochar algo a algn** to reproach sb for sth

reproche *nm* reproach

reproducción *nf* reproduction; **reproducción asistida** assisted reproduction

reproducir [10] **1.** *vt* to reproduce **2. reproducirse** *vpr* **a)** to reproduce, to breed **b)** [repetirse] to recur, to happen again

reptar *vi* to slither

reptil *nm* reptile

república *nf* republic; **la República Dominicana** the Dominican Republic; **la República Checa** the Czech Republic; **la República Popular (de) China** the People's Republic of China

republicano, -a *adj & nm, f* republican

repuesto, -a 1. *pp de* reponer **2.** *adj* recovered (*from an illness, etc*), better **3.** *nm* [recambio] spare part, spare; AUTO **rueda de repuesto** spare wheel

repugnar *vt* to disgust, to revolt

repuntar *vi Am* [mejorar] to improve

repunte *nm* [aumento] rise, increase; **un repunte en las ventas** an improvement o increase in sales

reputación *nf* reputation

requerir [5] *vt* **a)** to require **b)** [solicitar] to request **c)** JUR [avisar] to summon

requesón *nm* cottage cheese

res *nf* animal

resaca *nf* **a)** hangover **b)** NÁUT undertow, undercurrent

resbalada *nf Am Fam* slip; **dar** *o* **pegar una resbalada** to slip

resbaladizo, -a *adj* slippery

resbalar *vi* to slip; AUTO to skid

resbalarse *vpr* = **resbalar**

rescatar *vt* [persona] to rescue; [objeto] to recover

rescate *nm* **a)** [salvamento] rescue; [recuperación] recovery **b)** [suma] ransom

resentimiento *nm* resentment

reserva 1. *nf* **a)** [de entradas etc] reservation, booking **b)** [provisión] reserve, stock; **un vino de reserva** a vintage wine **c)** MIL reserve, reserves **d)** [duda] reservation **2.** *nmf* DEP reserve, substitute

reservación *nf Méx* reservation

reservado, -a 1. *adj* [persona] reserved, quiet **2.** *nm* private room

reservar 1. *vt* **a)** [billetes etc] to reserve, to book **b)** [dinero, tiempo etc] to keep, to save **2. reservarse** *vpr* **a)** to save oneself (**para** for) **b)** [sentimientos] to keep to oneself **c) reservarse el derecho de** to reserve the right to

resfriado, -a 1. *nm* [catarro] cold; **coger un resfriado** to catch (a) cold **2.** *adj* **estar resfriado** to have a cold

resfriarse *vpr* to catch (a) cold

resfrío *nm Andes, RP* cold

resguardar *vt* [proteger] to protect, to shelter (**de** from)

resguardo *nm* **a)** [recibo] receipt **b)** [protección] protection, shelter

residencia *nf* residence; **residencia de ancianos** old people's home

residuo *nm* **a)** residue **b) residuos** waste

resignarse *vpr* to resign oneself (**a** to)

resistencia *nf* **a)** resistance **b)** [aguante] endurance, stamina **c)** ELEC element

resistente *adj* **a)** resistant (**a** to) **b)** [fuerte] tough, hardy

resistir 1. *vi* **a)** to resist **b)** [aguantar] to hold (out) **2.** *vt* [situación, persona] to put up with; [tentación] to resist **3. resistirse** *vpr* to resist; [oponerse] to offer resistance; [negarse] to refuse

resolver [4] (*pp* resuelto) **1.** *vt* [problema] to solve; [asunto] to settle **2.** *vi* [decidir] to resolve, to decide

3. resolverse *vpr* **a)** [solucionarse] to be solved **b)** [decidirse] to resolve, to make up one's mind (**a** to)

resonancia *nf* **a)** [sonora] resonance **b)** [repercusión] repercussions

resorte *nm* **a)** [muelle] spring **b)** *Fig* means

respaldo *nm* [de silla etc] back ; *Fig* [apoyo] support, backing

respectivo, -a *adj* respective; **en lo respectivo a** with regard to, regarding

respecto *nm* **al respecto, a este respecto** in this respect; **(con) respecto a, respecto de** with regard to; **respecto a mí** as for me, as far as I am concerned

respetable 1. *adj* respectable **2.** *nm Fam* **el respetable** the audience

respetar *vt* to respect ; **hacerse respetar de todos** to command everyone's respect

respeto *nm* **a)** respect ; **por respeto** out of consideration **b)** [recelo] fear

respiración *nf* [acción] breathing, respiration ; [aliento] breath ; **respiración artificial** artificial resuscitation

respirar *vi* to breathe ; **¡por fin respiro!** well, that's a relief!

respiro *nm* **a)** breathing **b)** [descanso] breather, break

resplandor *nm* [brillo] brightness ; [muy intenso] brilliance ; [de fuego] glow, blaze

responder 1. *vt* to answer **2.** *vi* **a)** [una carta] to reply **b)** [reaccionar] to respond **c)** [protestar] to answer back **d)** **responder de algn** to be responsible for sb ; **responder por algn** to vouch for sb

responsabilidad *nf* responsibility

responsable 1. *adj* responsible **2.** *nmf* **el /la responsable** [encargado] the person in charge ; [de robo etc] the perpetrator

respuesta *nf* answer, reply ; [reacción] response

resta *nf* subtraction

restar 1. *vt* **a)** MAT to subtract, to take away **b)** **restar importancia a algo** to play sth down **2.** *vi* [quedar] to be left, to remain

restauración *nf* restoration

restaurador, -a 1. *nm, f* restorer **2.** *adj* restoring

restaurante *nm* restaurant

restaurar *vt* to restore

resto *nm* **a)** rest, remainder ; MAT remainder **b)** **restos** remains ; [de comida] leftovers

restricción *nf* restriction

resucitar *vt & vi* to resuscitate

resuelto, -a *adj* [decidido] resolute, determined

resultado *nm* result ; [consecuencia] outcome; **dar buen resultado** to work, to give results

resultar *vi* **a)** [ser] to turn o work out ; **así resulta más barato** it works out cheaper this way ; **me resultó fácil** it turned out to be easy for me **b)** [ocurrir] **resulta que …** the thing is … ; **y ahora resulta que no puede venir** and now it turns out that she can't come **c)** [tener éxito] to be successful ; **la fiesta no resultó** the party wasn't a success

resumen *nm* summary ; **en resumen** in short, to sum up

resumir 1. *vt* to sum up ; [recapitular] to summarize **2. resumirse** *vpr* **a)** [abreviarse] **se resume en pocas palabras** it can be summed up in a few words **b)** **resumirse en** [saldarse con] to result in

retablo *nm* altarpiece

retal *nm* [pedazo] scrap

retardar *vt* to delay

retardo *nm* delay

rete *adv Am Fam* very

retén *nm* **a)** **retén (de bomberos)** squad (of firefighters) **b)** *Am* [de menores] reformatory, reform school

retención *nf* retention ; FIN withholding ; **retención de tráfico** (traffic) hold-up, traffic jam

retirado, -a 1. *adj* **a)** [alejado] remote **b)** [jubilado] retired **2.** *nm, f* retired person, *US* retiree

retirar 1. *vt* to take away, to remove; [dinero] to withdraw; [ofensa] to take back **2. retirarse** *vpr* **a)** [apartarse] to withdraw, to draw back; [irse] to retire **b)** [jubilarse] to retire **c)** MIL to retreat, to withdraw

reto *nm* challenge

retocar [44] *vt* to touch up

retoque *nm* [de foto] retouching

retorcer [41] **1.** *vt* [cuerda, hilo] to twist; [ropa] to wring (out) **2. retorcerse** *vpr* to twist, to become twisted; **retorcerse de dolor** to writhe in pain

retórica *nf* rhetoric

retornable *adj* returnable; **envase no retornable** non-deposit bottle

retorno *nm* [gen & INFORM] return; **(tecla de) retorno** return key

retransmisión *nf* broadcast, transmission

retransmitir *vt* to broadcast

retrasado, -a 1. *adj* **a)** [tren] late; [reloj] slow; **voy retrasado** I'm behind schedule **b)** [país] backward, underdeveloped **c)** [mental] retarded, backward **2.** *nm, f* retrasado (mental) mentally retarded person

retrasar 1. *vt* **a)** [retardar] to slow down **b)** [atrasar] to delay, to postpone **c)** [reloj] to put back **2. retrasarse** *vpr* to be late; [reloj] to be slow

retraso *nm* delay; **con retraso** late; **una hora de retraso** an hour behind schedule; **retraso mental** mental deficiency

retratar 1. *vt* [pintar] to paint a portrait of; FOTO to take a photograph of; *Fig* [describir] to describe, to depict **2. retratarse** *vpr* FOTO to have one's photograph taken

retrato *nm* [pintura] portrait; FOTO photograph; **retrato robot** Identikit® picture, *Br* Photofit® picture; **ser el vivo retrato de** to be the spitting image of

retrete *nm Br* toilet, *US* bathroom

retribuir [37] *vt* **a)** [pagar] to reward, to pay for **b)** *Am* [por un favor] to return

retroceder *vi* to move back, to back away

retrospectivo, -a *adj* & *nf* retrospective

retrovisor *nm* AUTO rear-view mirror

reúma *nm* rheumatism

reunión *nf* meeting; [reencuentro] reunion

reunir 1. *vt* to gather together; [dinero] to raise; [cualidades] to have, to possess; [requisitos] to fulfil **2. reunirse** *vpr* to meet, to gather; **reunirse con algn** to meet sb

reutilizable *adj* reusable

revancha *nf* revenge; DEP return match

revelado *nm* FOTO developing

revelar *vt* **a)** to reveal, to disclose **b)** FOTO [película] to develop

reventar [1] **1.** *vt* **a)** to burst **b)** [romper] to break, to smash **c)** [fastidiar] to annoy, to bother **2.** *vi* [estallar] to burst; **reventar de ganas de hacer algo** to be dying to do sth **3. reventarse** *vpr* [estallar] to burst, to explode

reventón *nm* [de neumático] blowout, *Br* puncture, *US* flat

reverencia *nf* **a)** [respeto] reverence **b)** [inclinación - de hombre] bow; [de mujer] curtsy

reversa *nf Méx* reverse

reversible *adj* reversible

reverso *nm* reverse, back

revés *nm* **a)** [reverso] reverse; **al o del revés** [al contrario] the other way round; [la parte interior en el exterior] inside out; [boca abajo] upside down; [la parte de detrás delante] back to front; **al revés de lo que dicen** contrary to what they say **b)** [bofetada] slap; TENIS backhand (stroke) **c)** *Fig* [contrariedad] setback, reverse; **los reveses de la vida** life's misfortunes; **reveses de fortuna** setbacks, blows of fate

revestimiento *nm* TÉC covering, coating

revisar *vt* to check; [coche] to service

revisión *nf* checking; [de coche] service, overhaul; **revisión médica** checkup

revisor, -a *nm, f* ticket inspector

revista *nf* a) magazine b) **pasar revista a** to inspect, to review c) TEATRO revue

revistero *nm* [mueble] magazine rack

revolcar [2] **1.** *vt* Fam [oponente] to floor, to crush **2. revolcarse** *vpr* to roll about

revoltijo, revoltillo *nm* jumble

revoltoso, -a *adj* [travieso] mischievous, naughty

revolución *nf* revolution

revolucionario, -a *adj & nm, f* revolutionary

revolver [4] *(pp revuelto)* **1.** *vt* [mezclar] to stir, to mix; [desordenar] to mess up; **me revuelve el estómago** it turns my stomach **2. revolverse** *vpr* a) [agitarse] to roll b) Fig **revolverse contra algn** to turn against sb c) [tiempo atmosférico] to turn stormy; [mar] to become rough

revólver *nm* revolver

revuelta *nf* a) [insurrección] revolt b) [curva] bend, turn

revuelto, -a *adj* a) [desordenado] jumbled, in a mess b) [tiempo] stormy, unsettled; [mar] rough c) [agitado] excited

rey *(pl reyes)* *nm* king; REL **(el día de) Reyes** (the) Epiphany, 6 January

rezar [40] **1.** *vi* a) [orar] to pray b) [decir] to say, to read **2.** *vt* [oración] to say

rezo *nm* prayer

ría *nf* estuary

riachuelo *nm* brook, stream

riada *nf* flood

ribera *nf* [de río] bank; [zona] riverside, waterfront

ribete *nm* edging, border

rico, -a 1. *adj* a) **ser rico** [adinerado] to be rich o wealthy; [abundante] to be rich; [bonito] to be lovely o adorable; [fértil] to be rich o fertile b) **estar rico** [delicioso] to be delicious **2.** *nm, f* rich person

ridículo, -a 1. *adj* ridiculous **2.** *nm* ridicule; **hacer el ridículo, quedar en ridículo** to make a fool of oneself; **poner a algn en ridículo** to make a fool of sb

riego *nm* watering, irrigation; **riego sanguíneo** blood circulation

rienda *nf* rein; Fig **dar rienda suelta a** to give free rein to; Fig **llevar las riendas** to hold the reins, to be in control

riesgo *nm* risk; **correr el riesgo de** to run the risk of; **seguro a todo riesgo** fully comprehensive insurance

riesgoso, -a *adj* Am risky

rifar *vt* to raffle (off)

rigidez *nf* rigidity, stiffness; Fig [severidad] strictness, inflexibility

rígido, -a *adj* rigid, stiff; Fig [severo] strict, inflexible

rigor *nm* rigour; [severidad] severity; **con rigor** rigorously; **de rigor** indispensable

riguroso, -a *adj* rigorous; [severo] severe, strict

rima *nf* rhyme

rímel *nm* mascara

rincón *nm* corner; Fam [lugar remoto] nook

ring [rrin] *(pl rings)* *nm* (boxing) ring

rinoceronte *nm* rhinoceros

riña *nf* [pelea] fight; [discusión] row, quarrel

riñón *nm* kidney; Fam **costar un riñón** to cost an arm and a leg; MED **riñón artificial** kidney machine

riñonera *nf* [pequeño bolso] Br bum bag, US fanny pack

río *nm* river; **río abajo** downstream; **río arriba** upstream

rioja *nm* Rioja (wine)

RIP [rrip] *(abr de requiescat in pace)* RIP

riqueza *nf* a) wealth b) [cualidad] wealthiness

risa *nf* laugh; [carcajadas] laughter; **es (cosa) de risa** it's laughable; **me da risa** it makes me laugh; **tomarse algo a risa** to laugh sth off; *Fig* **morirse** o **mondarse de risa** to die o fall about laughing; *Fam* **mi hermano es una risa** my brother is a laugh; *Fam & Fig* **tener algo muerto de risa** to leave sth lying around

ristra *nf* string

ritmo *nm* a) rhythm b) [paso] rate; **llevar un buen ritmo de trabajo** to work at a good pace

rito *nm* a) rite b) [ritual] ritual

ritual *adj & nm* ritual

rival *adj & nmf* rival

rizado, -a *adj* a) [pelo] curly b) [mar] choppy

rizo *nm* a) [de pelo] curl b) [en el agua] ripple

RNE *nf* (abr de **Radio Nacional de España**) *Spanish state radio station*

robar *vt* a) [objeto] to steal; [banco, persona] to rob; [casa] to burgle; *Fig* **en aquel supermercado te roban** they really rip you off in that supermarket b) NAIPES to draw

roble *nm* oak (tree)

robo *nm* robbery, theft; [en casa] burglary; *Fam* [timo] rip-off

robot *(pl robots) nm* [gen & INFORM] robot; **robot de cocina** food processor

robusto, -a *adj* robust, sturdy

roca *nf* rock

roce *nm* a) [fricción] rubbing; [en la piel] chafing b) [marca - en la pared etc] scuff mark; [en la piel] chafing mark, graze c) [contacto ligero] brush, light touch d) *Fam* [trato entre personas] contact e) *Fam* [discusión] brush

rociar [29] *vt* [salpicar] to spray, to sprinkle

rocío *nm* dew

rock *nm inv* rock; **rock duro** hard rock; **rock and roll** rock and roll

rocoso, -a *adj* rocky, stony

rodaballo *nm* [pez] turbot

rodaje *nm* a) [filmación] filming, shooting b) AUTO running-in

rodar [2] **1.** *vt* [película etc] to film, to shoot **2.** *vi* to roll, to turn

rodear 1. *vt* to surround, to encircle **2. rodearse** *vpr* to surround oneself (**de** with)

rodeo *nm* a) [desvío] detour b) [al hablar] evasiveness; **andarse con rodeos** to beat about the bush; **no andarse con rodeos** to get straight to the point c) [espectáculo] rodeo

rodilla *nf* knee; **de rodillas** [arrodillado] kneeling; **hincarse** o **ponerse de rodillas** to kneel down, to go down on one's knees

rodillo *nm* roller; **rodillo de cocina** rolling pin

roedor *nm* rodent

roer [38] *vt* [hueso] to gnaw; [galleta] to nibble at; *Fig* [conciencia] to gnaw at, to nag at; *Fig* **un hueso duro de roer** a hard nut to crack

rogar [2] *vt* [pedir] to request, to ask; [implorar] to beg; **hacerse de rogar** to play hard to get; **se ruega silencio** [en letrero] silence please; **rogamos disculpen la molestia** please forgive the inconvenience

rojo, -a 1. *adj* a) red; FIN **estar en números rojos** to be in the red b) POL [comunista] red **2.** *nm* [color] red; **al rojo vivo** [caliente] red-hot; *Fig* [tenso] very tense **3.** *nm, f* POL [comunista] red

rollo *nm* a) [de papel etc] roll b) *Fam* [pesadez] drag, bore; **es el mismo rollo de siempre** it's the same old story; **un rollo de libro** a boring book c) *Esp Fam* [amorío] affair

romana *nf* **calamares a la romana** squid in batter

románico, -a *adj & nm* Romanesque

romano, -a 1. *adj* Roman; REL Roman Catholic **2.** *nm, f* Roman

romántico, -a *adj & nm, f* romantic

rombo *nm* rhombus

romería *nf* REL pilgrimage

romero *nm* BOT rosemary

romo, -a *adj* **a)** blunt **b)** [nariz] snub

rompecabezas *nm inv* [juego] (jigsaw) puzzle; *Fig* [problema] riddle, puzzle

rompeolas *nm inv* breakwater, jetty

romper *(pp* roto*)* **1.** *vt* **a)** to break; [papel, tela] to tear; [vajilla, cristal] to smash, to shatter
b) [relaciones] to break off
2. *vi* **a)** [olas, día] to break
b) [acabar] to break (**con** with); **rompió con su novio** she broke it off with her boyfriend
c) romper a llorar to burst out crying
3. romperse *vpr* to break; [papel, tela] to tear; **se rompió por la mitad** it broke *o* split in half; *Fig* **romperse la cabeza** to rack one's brains

rompevientos *nm* RP [jersey] *Br* polo neck, *US* turtleneck; [anorak] windcheater

rompimiento *nm* Am break

ron *nm* rum

roncar [44] *vi* to snore

ronco, -a *adj* hoarse; **quedarse ronco** to lose one's voice

ronda *nf* **a)** round; [patrulla] patrol **b)** [carretera] ring road; [paseo] avenue **c) pagar una ronda** to pay for a round of drinks

rondín *nm* Andes **a)** [vigilante] watchman, guard **b)** [armónica] mouth organ

ronquido *nm* snore

ronronear *vi* to purr

ronroneo *nm* purring

ropa *nf* clothes, clothing; *Fig* **a quema ropa** point-blank; **ropa blanca** (household) linen; **ropa interior** underwear

roquefort [rroke'for] *nm* Roquefort (cheese)

rosa **1.** *adj inv* [color] pink; **novela rosa** romantic novel
2. *nf* BOT rose; [en la piel] birthmark; **rosa de los vientos** compass (rose)
3. *nm* [color] pink

rosado, -a **1.** *adj* [color] pink, rosy; [vino] rosé **2.** *nm* [vino] rosé

rosal *nm* rosebush

rosario *nm* REL rosary; [sarta] string, series (*sing*)

rosco *nm* ring-shaped bread roll; *Esp Fam* **nunca se come un rosco** he never gets off with anyone

roscón *nm* ring-shaped bread roll; **roscón de Reyes** ring-shaped pastry eaten on 6th January

rosetón *nm* rose window

rosquilla *nf* ring-shaped pastry; *Fam & Fig* **venderse como rosquillas** to sell like hot cakes

rosticería *nf* Chile, Méx shop selling roast chicken

rostro *nm* face; *Fam* **tener mucho rostro** to have a lot of nerve; *Fam* **¡vaya rostro!** what a cheek!

rotar *vt & vi* to rotate

rotativo, -a **1.** *adj* rotary, revolving **2.** *nm* newspaper

roto, -a **1.** *adj* broken; [papel] torn; [ropa] in tatters, tattered **2.** *nm* [agujero] hole, tear **3.** *nm*, *f* Chile Fam **a)** [tipo] guy; [mujer] woman **b)** Despec [trabajador] worker

rotonda *nf* **a)** [glorieta] roundabout **b)** [plaza] circus

rotoso, -a *adj* Andes, RP ragged, in tatters

rotulador *nm* felt-tip pen

rótulo *nm* [letrero] sign, notice; [titular] title, heading

rotundo, -a *adj* categorical; **éxito rotundo** resounding success; **un no rotundo** a flat refusal

rozar [40] **1.** *vt* to touch, to rub against, to brush against **2.** *vi* to rub **3. rozarse** *vpr* to rub, to brush (**con** against)

Rte. *(abr de* remite, remitente*)* sender

RTVE *nf (abr de* Radiotelevisión Española*)* Spanish state broadcasting company

ruana *nf* **a)** Andes [cerrado] poncho **b)** RP [abierto] wraparound poncho

rubí *(pl* rubís *o* rubíes*)* *nm* ruby

rubio, -a 1. *adj* [pelo, persona] fair, blond, *f* blonde; **rubio de bote** peroxide blonde; **tabaco rubio** Virginia tobacco **2.** *nm, f* blond, *f* blonde

rubor *nm* blush, flush

ruborizarse [40] *vpr* to blush, to go red

rudimentario, -a *adj* rudimentary

rudo, -a *adj* rough, coarse

rueda *nf* **a)** wheel; AUTO **rueda de recambio** spare wheel; AUTO **rueda delantera/trasera** front/rear wheel; **rueda de prensa** press conference; *Fam* **ir sobre ruedas** to go very smoothly **b)** [rodaja] round slice

ruedo *nm* **a)** TAUROM bullring, arena **b)** [de falda] hem

ruego *nm* request

rugby *nm* rugby

rugido *nm* [de animal] roar; [del viento] howl; [de tripas] rumbling

rugir [57] *vi* to roar; [viento] to howl

rugoso, -a *adj* rough

ruido *nm* noise; [sonido] sound; [jaleo] din, row; *Fig* stir, commotion; **hacer ruido** to make a noise

ruidoso, -a *adj* noisy, loud

ruin *adj* **a)** [vil] vile, despicable **b)** [tacaño] mean, stingy

ruina *nf* ruin; [derrumbamiento] collapse; [de persona] downfall

ruinoso, -a *adj* dilapidated, tumbledown

ruiseñor *nm* nightingale

ruleta *nf* roulette

ruletear *vi CAm, Méx Fam* [en taxi] to drive a taxi

ruletero *nm CAm, Méx Fam* [de taxi] taxi driver

rulo *nm* **a)** [para el pelo] curler, roller **b)** CULIN rolling pin

ruma *nf Andes, Ven* heap, pile

rumba *nf* rhumba, rumba

rumbo *nm* direction, course; **(con) rumbo a** bound for, heading for

rumiante *nm* ruminant

rumiar [43] **1.** *vt* **a)** [mascar] to chew **b)** *Fig* [pensar] to ruminate, to reflect on, to chew over **2.** *vi* to ruminate, to chew the cud

rumor *nm* **a)** rumour **b)** [murmullo] murmur

rumorearse *v impers* to be rumoured

ruptura *nf* breaking; [de relaciones] breaking off

rural *adj* rural, country

Rusia *n* Russia

ruso, -a 1. *adj & nm, f* Russian **2.** *nm* [idioma] Russian

ruta *nf* route, road

rutina *nf* routine; **por rutina** as a matter of course

S

S *(abr de* **Sur)** S

S.A. *(abr de* **Sociedad Anónima)** ≃ *Br* PLC, ≃ *US* Inc

sábado *nm* Saturday

sábana *nf* sheet; *Fam* **se me pegaron las sábanas** I overslept

sabañón *nm* chilblain

saber¹ *nm* knowledge

saber² [21] **1.** *vt* **a)** to know; **hacer saber** to inform; **que yo sepa** as far as I know; **ya lo sé** I know; **¡y yo qué sé!** how should I know!; *Fig* **a saber** namely **b)** [tener habilidad] to be able to; **¿sabes cocinar?** can you cook?; **¿sabes hablar inglés?** can you speak English? **c)** [enterarse] to learn, find out; **lo supe ayer** I found this out yesterday **2.** *vi* **a)** [tener sabor a] to taste (**a** of); **sabe a fresa** it tastes of strawberries; *Fig* **me sabe mal** I feel guilty o bad about that **b)** *Am* [soler] **saber hacer algo** to be in the habit of doing sth **3. saberse** *vpr* to know; **me lo sé de memoria** I know it (off) by heart

sabiduría *nf* wisdom

sabio, -a 1. *adj* [prudente] wise **2.** *nm, f* scholar

sable *nm* sabre

sabor *nm* [gusto] taste, flavour; **con sabor a limón** lemon-flavoured; **sin sabor** tasteless; **me deja mal sabor de boca** it leaves a bad taste in my mouth

saborear *vt* [degustar] to taste; *Fig* [apreciar] to savour

sabotaje *nm* sabotage

sabroso, -a, sabrosón, -ona *adj* **a)** tasty; [delicioso] delicious **b)** [agradable] delightful

sacacorchos *nm inv* corkscrew

sacapuntas *nm inv* pencil sharpener

sacar [44] **1.** *vt* **a)** to take out; [con más fuerza] to pull out; **sacar dinero del banco** to withdraw money from the bank; **sacar la lengua** to stick one's tongue out; *Fig* **sacar faltas a algo** to find fault with sth; **sacar provecho de algo** to benefit from sth; **sacar algo en claro** o **en limpio** to make sense of sth **b)** [obtener] to get; [dinero] to get, to make; [conclusiones] to draw, to reach; [entrada] to get, to buy **c)** [producto, libro, disco] to bring out; [nueva moda] to bring in **d)** [fotografía] to take; [fotocopia] to make **e)** TENIS to serve; FÚT to kick off **2. sacarse** *vpr* [conseguir] avoir; **sacarse el carné (de conducir)** *Br* to get one's driving licence, *US* to get one's driver's license

sacarina *nf* saccharin

sacerdote *nm* priest; **sumo sacerdote** high priest

saciar [43] *vt* to satiate; [sed] to quench; [deseos, hambre] to satisfy; [ambiciones] to fulfil

saco *nm* **a)** sack; **saco de dormir** sleeping bag **b)** MIL **entrar a saco en una ciudad** to pillage a town **c)** *Am* [abrigo de tela] jacket; [de punto] cardigan

sacramento *nm* sacrament

sacrificar [44] **1.** *vt* to sacrifice **2. sacrificarse** *vpr* to make a sacrifice o sacrifices

sacrificio *nm* sacrifice

sacristán *nm* verger, sexton

sacudida *nf* **a)** shake; [espasmo] jolt, jerk; **sacudida eléctrica** electric shock **b)** [de terremoto] tremor

sacudir *vt* **a)** [agitar] to shake ; [alfombra, sábana] to shake out ; [arena, polvo] to shake off **b)** [golpear] to beat **c)** [conmover] to shock, to stun

safari *nm* [cacería] safari ; [parque] safari park

sagitariano, -a *nm, f Am* Sagittarius

Sagitario *nmf* Sagittarius

sagrado, -a *adj* sacred

sal¹ *nf* **a)** salt ; **sal fina** table salt ; **sal gema** salt crystals ; *Esp* **sal gorda** cooking salt **b)** *Fig* [gracia] wit

sal² *imperat de* salir

sala *nf* room ; [en un hospital] ward ; JUR courtroom ; **sala de estar** lounge, living room ; **sala de espera** waiting room ; **sala de exposiciones** exhibition hall ; **sala de fiestas** nightclub, discotheque ; **sala de lectura** reading room

saladito *nm RP* savoury snack o appetizer

salado, -a *adj* **a)** [con sal] salted ; [con exceso de sal] salty ; **agua salada** salt water **b)** *Esp* [gracioso, simpático] amusing ; [encantador] charming **c)** *CAm, Carib, Méx* [desgraciado] unlucky

salamandra *nf* salamander

salar *vt* to salt, to add salt to

salario *nm* salary, wages ; **salario mínimo** minimum wage

salchicha *nf* sausage

salchichón *nm* salami-type sausage

salchichonería *nf Méx* delicatessen

saldo *nm* **a)** saldos sales ; **a precio de saldo** at bargain prices **b)** FIN balance **c)** [de una deuda] liquidation, settlement **d)** [resto de mercancía] remainder, leftover

salero *nm* **a)** [recipiente] saltcellar, *US* saltshaker **b)** *Fig* [gracia] charm

salida *nf* **a)** [partida] departure ; [puerta etc] exit, way out ; **callejón sin salida** dead end ; **salida de emergencia** emergency exit
b) DEP start ; **línea de salida** starting line

c) **te vi a la salida del cine** I saw you leaving the cinema
d) [de astro] rising ; **salida del sol** sunrise
e) [profesional] opening ; COM outlet
f) [recurso] solution, way out ; **no tengo otra salida** I have no other option
g) *Fam* [ocurrencia] witty remark, witticism
h) INFORM output

salina *nf* salt mine

salir [22] **1.** *vi* **a)** [de un sitio] to go out, to leave ; [venir de dentro] to come out ; **salió de la habitación** she left the room ; **salir de la carretera** to turn off the road
b) [tren etc] to depart
c) [novios] to go out (**con** with)
d) [aparecer] to appear ; [revista, disco] to come out ; [ley] to come in ; [trabajo, vacante] to come up
e) [resultar] to turn out, to turn out to be ; **el pequeño les ha salido muy listo** their son has turned out to be very clever ; **¿cómo te salió el examen?** how did your exam go? ; **salir ganando** to come out ahead o into the
f) **salir a** [precio] to come to, to work out at ; **salir barato / caro** to work out cheap / expensive
g) **ha salido al abuelo** she takes after her grandfather
h) [problema] to work out ; **esta cuenta no me sale** I can't work this sum out
i) INFORM [de un programa] to exit, to quit
j) **¡con qué cosas sales!** the things you come out with!
2. **salirse** *vpr* **a)** [líquido, gas] to leak (out) ; *Fig* **salirse de lo normal** to be out of the ordinary ; **se salió de la carretera** he went off the road
b) *Fam* **salirse con la suya** to get one's own way

saliva *nf* saliva

salmón 1. *nm* [pescado] salmon **2.** *adj inv* [color] salmon pink, salmon

salmonete *nm* [pescado] red mullet

salón *nm* **a)** [en una casa] lounge, sitting room **b)** **salón de actos** assembly hall ;

salón de baile dance hall **c) salón del automóvil** motor show; **salón de belleza** beauty salon; **salón de té** tearoom, teashop

salpicadera *nf Méx Br* mudguard, *US* fender

salpicadero *nm Esp* dashboard

salpicar [44] *vt* **a)** [rociar] to splash; **me salpicó el abrigo de barro** he splashed mud on my coat **b)** *Fig* [esparcir] to sprinkle

salpicón *nm* **a)** splash **b)** CULIN cocktail

salpimentar [1] *vt* to season

salsa *nf* sauce; [de carne] gravy; *Fig* **en su (propia) salsa** in one's element

salsera *nf* gravy boat

saltamontes *nm inv* grasshopper

saltar **1.** *vt* [obstáculo, valla] to jump (over)
2. *vi* **a)** to jump; *Fig* **saltar a la vista** to be obvious
b) [cristal etc] to break, to shatter; [plomos] to go, to blow
c) [desprenderse] to come off
d) [encolerizarse] to explode, to blow up
3. saltarse *vpr* **a)** [omitir] to skip, to miss out; **saltarse el semáforo / turno** to jump the lights / the queue
b) [botón] to come off; **se me saltaron las lágrimas** tears came to my eyes

salteado, -a *adj* **a)** [espaciado] spaced out **b)** CULIN sauté, sautéed

saltear *vt* CULIN to sauté

salto *nm* **a)** [acción] jump, leap; *Fig* [paso adelante] leap forward; **a saltos** in leaps and bounds; **dar** *o* **pegar un salto** to jump, to leap; **de un salto** in a flash; *Fig* **a salto de mata** every now and then; **salto de agua** waterfall; **salto de cama** negligée **b)** DEP jump; **salto de altura** high jump; **salto de longitud** long jump; **salto mortal** somersault

salud *nf* health; **beber a la salud de algn** to drink to sb's health; *Fam* **¡salud!** cheers!

saludable *adj* **a)** [sano] healthy, wholesome **b)** *Fig* [beneficioso] good, beneficial

saludar *vt* **a)** [decir hola a] to say hello to, to greet; **saluda de mi parte a** give my regards to; **le saluda atentamente** [en una carta] yours faithfully **b)** MIL to salute

saludo *nm* **a)** greeting; **un saludo de** best wishes from **b)** MIL salute

salu2 SMS *written abbr of* **saludos**

salvación *nf* salvation

Salvador *nm* **a)** REL **el Salvador** the Saviour **b)** GEOGR **El Salvador** El Salvador

salvadoreño, -a *adj & nm, f* Salvadoran

salvaje *adj* **a)** BOT wild, uncultivated; ZOOL wild; [pueblo, tribu] savage, uncivilized **b)** *Fam* [violento] savage, wild

salvamanteles *nm inv* [plano] table mat; [con pies] trivet

salvapantallas *nm inv* INFORM screensaver

salvar **1.** *vt* **a)** to save, to rescue (**de** from)
b) [obstáculo] to clear; [dificultad] to get round, to overcome
c) [exceptuar] to exclude, to except; **salvando ciertos errores** except for a few mistakes
d) INFORM [un fichero] to save
2. salvarse *vpr* **a)** [sobrevivir] to survive, to come out alive; *Fam* [escaparse] to escape (**de** from); **¡sálvese quien pueda!** every man for himself!
b) REL to be saved, to save one's soul

salvavidas *nm inv* life belt

salvo, -a **1.** *adj* unharmed, safe; **a salvo** safe **2.** *adv* [exceptuando] except (for); **salvo que** unless

san *adj* saint

sanador, -a *nm, f* healer

sanatorio *nm* sanatorium

sanción *nf* **a)** sanction **b)** [aprobación] sanction, approval **c)** JUR penalty

sancocho *nm Andes* [comida] *stew of beef, chicken or fish, vegetables and green bananas*

sandalia *nf* sandal

sandía *nf* watermelon

sánduche *nm Am* sandwich

sándwich ['sanwitʃ, 'sanwis] (*pl* **sándwiches**) *nm* sandwich

sangrar 1. *vt* **a)** to bleed **b)** *Fam* [sacar dinero] to bleed dry **2.** *vi* to bleed

sangre *nf* blood; **donar sangre** to give blood; **sangre fría** sangfroid; **a sangre fría** in cold blood

sangría *nf* **a)** MED bleeding, bloodletting; *Fig* drain **b)** [timo] rip-off **c)** [bebida] sangria **d)** IMPR indentation **e)** INFORM indent

sangriento, -a *adj* [guerra etc] bloody

sánguche *nm Am* sandwich

sanidad *nf* health; **Ministerio de Sanidad** Department of Health

sanitario, -a 1. *adj* health **2.** *nm* toilet, *US* bathroom

sanjacobo *nm* CULIN *breaded escalope with cheese filling*

sano, -a *adj* **a)** [bien de salud] healthy; **sano y salvo** safe and sound **b)** [comida] healthy, wholesome **c)** **en su sano juicio** in one's right mind

Santa Claus, *Méx, Ven* **Santa Clos** *n* Santa Claus

santería *nf* **a)** [religión] santería *(form of religion common in the Caribbean in which people allegedly have contact with the spirit world)* **b)** *Am* [tienda] *shop selling religious mementoes such as statues of saints*

santero, -a *nm, f* **a)** [en ermita, santuario] santero, Santeria priest **b)** [curandero] religious healer **c)** [devoto] devotee

santiguarse [45] *vpr* to cross oneself

santo, -a 1. *adj* **a)** holy, sacred **b)** [bueno] saintly; **un santo varón** a saint; **todo el santo día** the whole blessed day **2.** *nm, f* **a)** saint; *Fam* **¡por todos los santos!** for heaven's sake!; *Fig* **se me fue el santo al cielo** I clean forgot **b)** [día onomástico] saint's day; *Fig* **¿a santo de qué?** why on earth?

santuario *nm* sanctuary, shrine

sapo *nm* toad; *Fam* **echar sapos y culebras** to rant and rave

saque *nm* **a)** FÚT **saque inicial** kick-off; **saque de banda** throw-in; **saque de esquina** corner kick **b)** TENIS service

saquear *vt* [ciudad] to sack, to plunder; [casas, tiendas] to loot

sarampión *nm* measles (*sing*)

sarcástico, -a *adj* sarcastic

sardana *nf* sardana (*Catalan dance and music*)

sardina *nf* sardine

sargento *nm* sergeant

sarna *nf* MED scabies (*sing*); ZOOL mange

sarpullido *nm* rash

sarro *nm* [sedimento] deposit; [en dientes] tartar; [en lengua] fur

sartén *nf* frying pan, *US* fry-pan; *Fam & Fig* **tener la sartén por el mango** to call the shots

sastre *nm* tailor

sastrería *nf* [oficio] tailoring; [taller] tailor's (shop); CINE & TEATRO wardrobe (department)

satélite *nm* satellite; *Fig* **país satélite** satellite state; **televisión vía satélite** satellite TV

sátira *nf* satire

satírico, -a *adj* satirical

satisfacción *nf* satisfaction; **satisfacción de un deseo** fulfilment of a desire

satisfacer [15] (*pp* **satisfecho**) *vt* **a)** [deseos, necesidades] to satisfy **b)** [requisitos] to meet, to satisfy **c)** [deuda] to pay

satisfecho, -a *adj* satisfied; **me doy por satisfecho** that's good enough for me; **satisfecho de sí mismo** self-satisfied, smug

sauce *nm* willow; **sauce llorón** weeping willow

sauna *nf* sauna

saxofón *nm* saxophone

sazonar *vt* to season, to flavour

sbs SMS *written abbr of* **¿sabes?**

---

se¹ *pron* **a)** [reflexivo - objeto directo - a él mismo] himself; [animal] itself; [a ella misma] herself; [animal] itself;

[a usted mismo] yourself; [a ellos mismos] themselves; [a ustedes mismos] yourselves

b) [objeto indirecto - a él mismo] (to / for) himself; [animal] (to /for) itself; [a ella misma] (to /for) herself; [animal] (to /for) itself; [a usted mismo] (to / for) yourself; [a ellos mismos] (to /for) themselves; [a ustedes mismos] (to / for) yourselves; **se compró un nuevo coche** he bought himself a new car; **todos los días se lava el pelo** she washes her hair every day

c) [recíproco] one another, each other

d) [voz pasiva] **el vino se guarda en cubas** wine is kept in casks

e) [impersonal] **nunca se sabe** you never know; **se habla inglés** [en letrero] English spoken here; **se dice que …** it is said that …

se² *pron pers* [a él] (to /for) him; [a ella] (to /for) her; [a usted o ustedes] (to / for) you; [a ellos] (to /for) them; **se lo diré en cuanto les vea** I'll tell them as soon as I see them; **¿se lo explico?** shall I explain it to you?; **¿se lo has dado ya?** have you given it to him yet?

sé¹ *indic pres de* **saber**

sé² *imperat de* **ser**

sea *subj pres de* **ser**

secador *nm* dryer; **secador de pelo** hairdryer

secadora *nf* tumble dryer

secamanos *nm inv* hand dryer

secano *nm* dry land

secar [44] **1.** *vt* to dry **2. secarse** *vpr* **a)** to dry; **sécate** dry yourself; **secarse las manos** to dry one's hands **b)** [marchitarse] to dry up, to wither

secarropas *nm inv RP* dryer

sección *nf* section

seco, -a *adj* **a)** dry; **frutos secos** dried fruit; **limpieza en seco** dry-cleaning; *Fig* **a palo seco** on its own; *Fig* **a secas** just, only **b)** [tono] curt, sharp; [golpe, ruido] sharp; *Fig* **frenar en seco** to pull up sharply; *Fig* **parar en seco** to stop dead **c)** [delgado] skinny

secretaría *nf* [oficina] secretary's office; **Secretaría de Estado** [en España] *government department under the control of a (Br) junior minister o (US) under-secretary*; [en Latinoamérica] ministry; [en Estados Unidos] State Department

secretariado *nm* **a)** [oficina] secretariat **b)** EDUC secretarial course

secretario, -a *nm, f* secretary; **secretario de dirección** secretary to the director; **secretario de Estado** [en España] *Br* junior minister, *US* under-secretary; [en Latinoamérica] *Br* minister, *US* secretary; [en Estados Unidos] Secretary of State

secreto, -a 1. *adj* secret; **en secreto** in secret, secretly **2.** *nm* secret; **guardar un secreto** to keep a secret; **con mucho secreto** in great secrecy

secta *nf* sect

sector *nm* **a)** sector **b)** [zona] area; **un sector de la ciudad** an area of the city

secuestrador, -a *nm, f* **a)** [de persona] kidnapper; [de un avión] hijacker **b)** JUR sequestrator

secuestrar *vt* **a)** [persona] to kidnap; [aviones] to hijack **b)** JUR to confiscate

secuestro *nm* **a)** [de persona] kidnapping; [de un avión] hijacking **b)** JUR confiscation

secundario, -a *adj* secondary

sed *nf* thirst; **tener sed** to be thirsty

seda *nf* silk

sedante *adj & nm* sedative

sede *nf* **a)** headquarters, head office; [de gobierno] seat **b)** **la Santa Sede** the Holy See

sedentario, -a *adj* sedentary

sediento, -a *adj* thirsty; *Fig* **sediento de poder** hungry for power

seductor, -a 1. *adj* seductive; [persuasivo] tempting **2.** *nm, f* seducer

segador, -a *nm, f* [agricultor] reaper

segadora *nf* [máquina] reaper, harvester

segar [1] *vt* to reap, to cut

segmento *nm* segment

seguidamente *adv* **a)** [inmediatamente] immediately **b)** [acto continuo] immediately after

seguido, -a 1. *adj* **a)** [continuo] continuous **b)** [consecutivo] consecutive, successive; **tres veces seguidas** on three consecutive occasions; **tres lunes seguidos** three Mondays in a row **2.** *adv* **a)** [en línea recta] straight on; **todo seguido** straight on o ahead **b)** *Am* [a menudo] often

seguir [6] **1.** *vt* **a)** to follow
b) [camino] to continue
c) [perseguir] to chase
2. *vi* **a)** to follow
b) seguir (+ *gerundio*) [continuar] to continue, to go on, to keep on; **siguió hablando** he continued o went on o kept on speaking
c) seguir (+ *adj/pp*) to continue to be, to be still; **sigo resfriado** I've still got the cold; **sigue con vida** he's still alive
3. seguirse *vpr* to follow, to ensue

según 1. *prep* **a)** according to; **según la Biblia** according to the Bible **b)** [en función de] depending on; **varía según el tiempo (que haga)** it varies depending on the weather **2.** *adv* **a)** depending on; **según estén las cosas** depending on how things stand; **¿vendrás mañana? — según** will you come tomorrow? — it depends **b)** [tal como] just as; **estaba según lo dejé** it was just as I had left it **c)** [a medida que] as; **según iba leyendo ...** as I read on ...

segunda *nf* **a)** AUTO second (gear); **meter (la) segunda** to go into second (gear) **b)** AVIACIÓN & FERROC second class; **viajar en segunda** to travel second class

segundero *nm* second hand

segundo¹, -a 1. *adj* second; *Fig* **decir algo con segundas (intenciones)** to say sth with a double meaning **2.** *nm, f* [de una serie] second (one)

segundo² *nm* [tiempo] second; **sesenta segundos** sixty seconds

seguramente *adv* **a)** [seguro] surely **b)** [probablemente] most probably; **seguramente no lloverá** it isn't likely to rain

seguridad *nf* **a)** security; **cerradura de seguridad** security lock **b)** [física] safety; **seguridad en carretera** road safety; **para mayor seguridad** to be on the safe side **c)** [confianza] confidence; **seguridad en sí mismo** self-confidence **d)** [certeza] sureness; **con toda seguridad** most probably; **tener la seguridad de que ...** to be certain that ... **e) Seguridad Social** ≃ Social Security

seguro, -a 1. *adj* **a)** [cierto] sure; **estoy seguro de que ...** I am sure that ...; **dar algo por seguro** to take sth for granted **b)** [libre de peligro] safe; *Fig* **ir sobre seguro** to play safe **c)** [protegido] secure **d)** [fiable] reliable **e) está segura de ella misma** she has self-confidence **f)** [firme] steady, firm **2.** *nm* **a)** SEGUROS insurance; **seguro a todo riesgo** fully comprehensive insurance; **seguro de vida** life insurance **b)** [dispositivo] safety catch o device **c)** *CAm, Méx* [imperdible] safety pin **3.** *adv* for sure, definitely

seis *adj & nm inv* six

seiscientos, -as *adj & nm* six hundred

selección *nf* **a)** selection **b)** DEP team

seleccionador, -a *nm, f* **a)** selector **b)** DEP manager

seleccionar *vt* to select

selectividad *nf* selectivity; *Esp* [prueba de] **selectividad** [examen] entrance examination

selecto, -a *adj* select; **ambiente selecto** exclusive atmosphere

selector, -a 1. *adj* selecting **2.** *nm* selector (button)

self-service *nm* self-service cafeteria

sello *nm* **a)** [de correos] stamp; [para documentos] seal **b)** [precinto] seal

selva *nf* jungle

semáforo *nm* traffic lights

semana *nf* week; **entre semana** during the week; **Semana Santa** Holy Week

semanada *nf Am* (weekly) pocket money,

semanal *adj & nm* weekly

semanalmente *adv* weekly

semanario *nm* weekly magazine

sembrar [1] *vt* **a)** AGRIC to sow **b)** *Fig* **sembrar el pánico** to spread panic

semejante 1. *adj* **a)** [parecido] similar; **nunca he visto nada semejante** I've never seen anything like it **b)** *Despec* [comparativo] such; **semejante desvergüenza** such insolence **2.** *nm* [prójimo] fellow being

semejanza *nf* similarity, likeness

semen *nm* semen

semestre *nm* six-month period, *US* semester

semidesnatado, -a *adj* semi-skimmed

semidesnudo, -a *adj* half-naked

semidirecto, -a 1. *adj* express **2.** *nm* [tren] *through train, a section of which becomes a stopping train*

semifinal *nf* semifinal

semilla *nf* seed

semiprecioso, -a *adj* semi-precious

sémola *nf* semolina

senado *nm* senate

senador, -a *nm, f* senator

sencillo, -a 1. *adj* **a)** [fácil] simple, easy **b)** [natural] natural, unaffected **c)** [billete] *Br* single, *US* one-way **d)** [sin adornos] simple, plain **2.** *nm Andes, CAm, Méx Fam* [cambio] loose change

senda *nf* path

senderismo *nm* hiking

senderista *nmf* hiker

sendero *nm* path

seno *nm* **a)** [pecho] breast **b)** *Fig* bosom, heart; **en el seno de** within **c)** MAT sine

sensación *nf* **a)** sensation, feeling; **tengo la sensación de que …** I have a feeling that … **b)** [impresión] sensation; **causar sensación** to cause a sensation

sensacional *adj* sensational

sensacionalismo *nm* sensationalism

sensacionalista *adj* sensationalist; **prensa sensacionalista** gutter press

sensato, -a *adj* sensible

sensibilidad *nf* **a)** [percepción] feeling; **no tiene sensibilidad en los brazos** she has no feeling in her arms **b)** [emotividad] sensitivity; **tener la sensibilidad a flor de piel** to be easily hurt, to be very sensitive

sensible *adj* **a)** sensitive **b)** [perceptible] perceptible

sensual *adj* sensual

sentado, -a *adj* [establecido] established, settled; **dar algo por sentado** to take sth for granted; **dejar sentado que …** to make it clear that …

sentar [1] **1.** *vt* **a)** to sit **b)** [establecer] to establish; **sentar las bases** to lay the foundations **2.** *vi* **a)** [color, ropa etc] to suit; **el pelo corto te sienta mal** short hair doesn't suit you **b)** **sentar bien/mal a** [comida] to agree/disagree with; **la sopa te sentará bien** the soup will do you good **c)** **le sentó mal la broma** she didn't like the joke **3.** **sentarse** *vpr* to sit, to sit down

sentencia *nf* **a)** sentence; **visto para sentencia** ready for judgement **b)** [aforismo] maxim, saying

sentenciar [43] *vt* JUR to sentence (**a** to)

sentido, -a 1. *nm* **a)** sense; **los cinco sentidos** the five senses; **sentido común** common sense; **sentido del humor** sense of humour **b)** [significado] meaning; **doble sentido** double meaning; **no tiene sentido** it doesn't make sense

c) [dirección] direction; **(de) sentido único** one-way
d) [conciencia] consciousness; **perder el sentido** to faint
2. *adj* deeply felt; *Formal* **mi más sentido pésame** my deepest sympathy

sentimental 1. *adj* sentimental; **vida sentimental** love life **2.** *nmf* sentimental person

sentimiento *nm* **a)** feeling **b)** [pesar] sorrow, grief; *Formal* **le acompaño en el sentimiento** my deepest sympathy

sentir¹ *nm* **a)** [sentimiento] feeling **b)** [opinión] opinion, view

sentir² [5] **1.** *vt* **a)** to feel; **sentir hambre/calor** to feel hungry/hot **b)** [lamentar] to regret, to be sorry about; **lo siento (mucho)** I'm (very) sorry; **siento molestarle** I'm sorry to bother you **2. sentirse** *vpr* to feel; **me siento mal** I feel ill; **sentirse con ánimos de hacer algo** to feel like doing sth

seña *nf* **a)** mark **b)** [gesto] sign; **hacer señas a algn** to signal to sb **c)** [indicio] sign **d) señas** [dirección] address

señal *nf* **a)** [indicio] sign, indication; **en señal de** as a sign of, as a token of **b)** [placa] sign; **señal de tráfico** road sign **c)** [gesto etc] signal, sign **d)** [marca] mark; [vestigio] trace **e)** TEL tone; **señal de llamada** *Br* dialling tone, *US* dial tone **f)** COM deposit

señalado, -a *adj* [importante] important; **un día señalado** a red-letter day

señalar *vt* **a)** [indicar] to mark, to indicate; **señalar con el dedo** to point at **b)** [resaltar] to point out **c)** [precio, fecha] to fix, to arrange

señalero *nm Urug Br* indicator, *US* turn signal

señor *nm* **a)** [hombre] man; [caballero] gentleman **b)** REL **El Señor** the Lord **c)** [con apellido] Mr; [tratamiento de respeto] sir; **el Sr. Gutiérrez** Mr Gutiérrez; **muy señor mío** [en carta] Dear Sir **d)** [con título - no se traduce] **el señor ministro** the Minister

señora *nf* **a)** [mujer] woman, *Formal* lady; **¡señoras y señores!** ladies and gentlemen! **b)** REL **Nuestra Señora** Our Lady **c)** [con apellido] Mrs; [tratamiento de respeto] madam; **la Sra. Salinas** Mrs Salinas; **Muy señora mía** [en carta] Dear Madam **d)** [con título - no se traduce] **la señora ministra** the Minister **e)** [esposa] wife

señorita *nf* **a)** [joven] young woman, *Formal* young lady **b)** [tratamiento de respeto] Miss; **Señorita Padilla** Miss Padilla **c)** EDUC **la señorita** the teacher, Miss

señorito, -a 1. *adj Fam & Despec* [refinado] lordly **2.** *nm* **a)** *Anticuado* [hijo del amo] master **b)** *Fam & Despec* [niñato] rich kid

seo *nf* cathedral

sepa *subj pres de* saber

separación *nf* **a)** separation; JUR **separación conyugal** legal separation **b)** [espacio] space, gap

separado, -a *adj* **a)** separate; **por separado** separately, individually **b)** [divorciado] separated

separar 1. *vt* **a)** to separate **b)** [desunir] to detach, to remove **c)** [dividir] to divide, to separate **d)** [apartar] to move away **2. separarse** *vpr* **a)** to separate, to part company **b)** [matrimonio] to separate **c)** [apartarse] to move away (**de** from)

separatista *adj & nmf* separatist

separo *nm Méx* cell

sepia 1. *nf* [pez] cuttlefish **2.** *adj & nm* [color] sepia

septentrional *adj* northern

septiembre *nm* September; **el 5 de septiembre** the 5th of September; **en septiembre** in September

séptimo, -a *adj & nm, f* seventh; **la o una séptima parte** a seventh

sepulcro *nm* tomb

sequía *nf* drought

ser¹ *nm* being; **ser humano** human being; **ser vivo** living being

ser² [23] *vi* **a)** [+ adj] to be; **es alto y rubio** he is tall and fair; **el edificio es gris** the building is grey

b) [+ profesión] to be a(n); **Rafael es músico** Rafael is a musician

c) ser de [procedencia] to be o come from; **¿de dónde eres?** where are you from?, where do you come from?

d) ser de [+ material] to be made of

e) ser de [+ poseedor] to belong to; **el perro es de Miguel** the dog belongs to Miguel; **¿de quién es este abrigo?** whose coat is this?

f) ser para [finalidad] to be for; **esta agua es para lavar** this water is for washing

g) [+ día, hora] to be; **hoy es 2 de noviembre** today is the 2nd of November; **son las cinco de la tarde** it's five o'clock

h) [+ cantidad] **¿cuántos estaremos en la fiesta?** how many of us will there be at the party?

i) [costar] to be, to cost; **¿cuánto es?** how much is it?

j) [tener lugar] to be; **el estreno será mañana** tomorrow is the opening night

k) [ocurrir] **¿qué es de Gonzalo?** what has become of Gonzalo?

l) [auxiliar en pasiva] to be; **fue asesinado** he was murdered

m) [locuciones] **es más** furthermore; **es que ...** it's just that ...; **como sea** anyhow; **lo que sea** whatever; **o sea** that is (to say); **sea como sea** in any case, be that as it may; **a no ser que** unless; **de no ser por ...** had it not been for ...; **no es para menos** you can't blame them

The auxiliary verb **ser** is used with the past participle of a verb to form the passive (e.g. **la película fue criticada** the film was criticized).

---

serenar 1. *vt* [calmar] to calm **2. serenarse** *vpr* [calmarse] to calm down

serenidad *nf* serenity

sereno¹ *nm* [vigilante] nightwatchman

sereno², **-a** *adj* **a)** calm **b)** *Fam* **estar sereno** [sobrio] to be sober

serie *nf* **a)** series *(sing)* **b)** RADIO & TV series *(sing)* **c) lleva ABS de serie** it has ABS fitted as standard; **fuera de serie** out of the ordinary; **en serie** [industria] mass; INFORM serial; **producir / fabricar en serie** to mass produce; **producción / fabricación en serie** mass production; INFORM **puerto en serie** serial port

seriedad *nf* **a)** seriousness **b)** [formalidad] reliability, dependability; **falta de seriedad** irresponsibility

serio, **-a** *adj* **a)** [severo] serious; **en serio** seriously **b)** [formal] reliable, responsible

sermón *nm* sermon

serpentina *nf* [de papel] streamer

serpiente *nf* snake; **serpiente de cascabel** rattlesnake; **serpiente pitón** python

serrar [1] *vt* to saw

serrín *nm* sawdust

serrucho *nm* handsaw

servicentro *nm* CAm, RP service station

servicio *nm* **a)** service; **servicio a domicilio** delivery service **b)** MIL service; **servicio militar** military service; **estar de servicio** to be on duty **c)** Esp [WC] toilet, US bathroom

servidor, **-a 1.** *nm, f* [yo] este pastel lo ha hecho un servidor the cake was made by yours truly **2.** *nm* INFORM server

servidumbre *nf* **a)** [criados] servants **b)** [dependencia] servitude

servilleta *nf* napkin, Br serviette

servir [6] **1.** *vt* to serve; **¿en qué puedo servirle?** what can I do for you?, may I help you?; **¿te sirvo una copa?** will I pour you a drink?

2. *vi* **a)** to serve

b) [valer] to be useful, to be suitable; **no sirve de nada llorar** it's no use crying; **ya no sirve** it's no use; **¿para qué sirve esto?** what is this (used) for?

c) servir de to serve as, to act as

3. servirse *vpr* **a)** [comida etc] to help oneself

b) *Formal* **sírvase comunicarnos su decisión** please inform us of your decision

sesenta *adj & nm inv* sixty

sesión *nf* a) [reunión] meeting, session; JUR session, sitting b) CINE showing

seso *nm* brain

seta *nf Esp* [comestible] mushroom; **seta venenosa** toadstool

setecientos, -as *adj & nm* seven hundred

setenta *adj & nm inv* seventy

setiembre *nm* September

seto *nm* hedge

seudónimo *nm* pseudonym

severidad *nf* severity

severo, -a *adj* severe

Sevilla *n* Seville

sevillana *nf* Andalusian dance and song

sexismo *nm* sexism

sexista *adj* sexist

sexo *nm* a) sex b) [órgano] genitals

sexto, -a *adj & nm, f* sixth

sexual *adj* sexual; **vida sexual** sex life

sexualidad *nf* sexuality

short *nm Am* shorts

shorts [ʃorts] *nmpl* shorts

show [ʃou, tʃou] (*pl* **shows**) *nm* show

si¹ *conj* a) [condicional] if; **como si** as if; **si no** if not; **si quieres** if you like, if you wish b) [pregunta indirecta] whether, if; **me preguntó si me gustaba** he asked me if I liked it; **no sé si ir o no** [disyuntivo] I don't know whether to go or not c) [sorpresa] **¡si está llorando!** but she's crying!

si² (*pl* **sis**) *nm* MÚS B; [en solfeo] ti

sí¹ *pron pers* a) [singular - él] himself; [ella] herself; [cosa] itself; [plural] themselves; **de por sí, en sí** in itself; **hablaban entre sí** they were talking among themselves o to each other; **por sí mismo** by himself b) [uno mismo] oneself; **decir para sí** to say to oneself

sí² **1.** *adv* a) yes; **dije que sí** I said yes, I accepted, I agreed; **¿por qué lo quieres? — porque sí** why do you want it? — because I do o just because; **¡que sí!** yes, I tell you!; **un día sí y otro no** every other day b) [uso enfático - no se traduce] **sí que me gusta** of course I like it; **¡eso sí que no!** certainly not! **2.** (*pl* **síes**) *nm* yes; **los síes** [en parlamento] the ayes

sida *nm* (*abr de* **síndrome de inmunodeficiencia adquirida**) AIDS

sidecar *nm* sidecar

sidra *nf Br* cider, *US* hard cider

siega **1.** *ver* segar **2.** *nf* a) [acción] reaping, harvesting b) [época] harvest (time)

siembra **1.** *ver* sembrar **2.** *nf* a) [acción] sowing b) [época] sowing time

siempre *adv* a) always; **siempre pasa lo mismo** it's always the same; **como siempre** as usual; **a la hora de siempre** at the usual time; **para siempre** forever; **siempre que** [cada vez que] whenever; [a condición de que] provided, as long as; **siempre y cuando** provided, as long as b) *Am* [todavía] still; **siempre viven allí** they still live there c) *Méx Fam* [enfático] **siempre sí quiero ir** I do still want to go; **siempre no me marcho** I'm still not leaving

sien *nf* temple

sierra *nf* a) saw; **sierra mecánica** power saw b) GEOGR mountain range, sierra

siesta *nf* siesta, nap; **dormir la siesta** to have a siesta o an afternoon nap

siete **1.** *adj & nm inv* seven **2.** *nf RP Fam & Euf* **¡la gran siete!** *Br* sugar!, *US* shoot!

sifón *nm* siphon; **whisky con sifón** whisky and soda

sigla *nf* acronym

siglo *nm* century; **el siglo veintiuno** the twenty-first century; *Fam* **hace siglos que no le veo** I haven't seen him for ages

significado *nm* meaning

significar [44] *vt* to mean

significativo, -a *adj* significant; [expresivo] meaningful

signo *nm* **a)** sign; **signo del zodiaco** zodiac sign **b)** LING mark; **signo de interrogación** question mark

siguiente *adj* following, next; **¡el siguiente!** next, please!; **al día siguiente** the following day

sílaba *nf* syllable

silbar *vi* to whistle; [abuchear] to hiss, to boo

silbato *nm* whistle

silbido *nm* whistle, whistling; [agudo] hiss

silenciador *nm* [de arma] silencer; [de coche, moto] *Br* silencer, *US* muffler

silencio *nm* silence; **imponer silencio a algn** to make sb be quiet

silencioso, -a *adj* [persona] quiet; [motor etc] silent

silicona *nf* silicone

silla *nf* **a)** chair; **silla de ruedas** wheelchair; **silla giratoria** swivel chair **b)** [de montura] saddle

sillín *nm* saddle

sillita *nf* buggy, *US* stroller

sillón *nm* armchair

silueta *nf* silhouette; [de cuerpo] figure

silvestre *adj* wild

símbolo *nm* symbol

simétrico, -a *adj* symmetrical

similar *adj* similar

similitud *nf* similarity

simpatía *nf* liking, affection; **le tengo mucha simpatía** I am very fond of him

simpático, -a *adj* [amable] nice, likeable; **me cae simpático** I like him

simpatizante *nmf* sympathizer

simpatizar [40] *vi* **a)** to sympathize (**con** with) **b)** [llevarse bien] to hit it off (**con** with)

simple 1. *adj* **a)** simple **b)** [fácil] simple, easy **c)** [mero] mere **d)** [persona] simple, simple-minded **2.** *nm* [persona] simpleton

simplicidad *nf* simplicity

simular *vt* to simulate

simultáneo, -a *adj* simultaneous

sin *prep* **a)** without; **sin dinero / ti** without money / you; **estamos sin pan** we're out of bread; **sin hacer nada** without doing anything; **cerveza sin** alcohol-free beer; **sin más ni más** without further ado **b)** [+ infinitivo] **está sin secar** it hasn't been dried

sinagoga *nf* synagogue

sinceridad *nf* sincerity; **con toda sinceridad** in all sincerity

sincero, -a *adj* sincere

sincronizar [40] *vt* to synchronize

sindicar *vt* Andes, RP, Ven to accuse; **sindicar a algn de algo** to accuse sb of sth

sindicato *nm* (*Br* trade o *US* labor) union

sinfonía *nf* symphony

sinfónico, -a *adj* symphonic

singani *nm* Bol grape brandy

single *nm* **a)** [disco] single, 7-inch **b)** CSur [habitación] single room

singular 1. *adj* **a)** singular **b)** [excepcional] exceptional, unique **c)** [raro] peculiar, odd **2.** *nm* LING singular; **en singular** in the singular

siniestro, -a 1. *adj* sinister, ominous **2.** *nm* disaster, catastrophe

sinnúmero *nm* **un sinnúmero de** countless

sino¹ *nm* Formal fate, destiny

sino² *conj* **a)** but; **no fui a Madrid, sino a Barcelona** I didn't go to Madrid but to Barcelona **b)** [excepto] **nadie sino él** no one but him; **no quiero sino que me oigan** I only want them to listen (to me)

sinónimo, -a 1. *adj* synonymous **2.** *nm* synonym

sinsentido *nm* absurdity

síntesis *nf inv* synthesis; **en síntesis** in short; INFORM & LING **síntesis del habla** speech synthesis

sintético, -a *adj* synthetic

sintetizador *nm* synthesizer

síntoma *nm* symptom

sintonía *nf* **a)** ELEC & RADIO tuning **b)** MÚS & RADIO [de programa] theme tune, *Br* signature tune **c)** *Fig* harmony

sintonizar [40] *vt* **a)** RADIO to tune in to **b)** [simpatizar] **sintonizaron muy bien** they clicked straight away

sinvergüenza 1. *adj* [desvergonzado] shameless; [descarado] cheeky **2.** *nmf* [desvergonzado] rogue; [caradura] cheeky devil

siquiera 1. *adv* [por lo menos] at least; **ni siquiera** not even **2.** *conj Formal* [aunque] although, even though

sirena *nf* **a)** siren, mermaid **b)** [señal acústica] siren

sirviente, -a *nm, f* servant

sisa *nf* **a)** [de manga] armhole **b)** [de dinero] pilfering

sistema *nm* [gen & INFORM] system; **por sistema** as a rule; **sistema nervioso** nervous system; **sistema montañoso** mountain chain; INFORM **sistema operativo** operating system

sitiar [43] *vt* to besiege

sitio¹ *nm* **a)** [lugar] place; **en cualquier sitio** anywhere; **en todos los sitios** everywhere; *Fig* **quedarse en el sitio** to die **b)** [espacio] room; **hacer sitio** to make room **c)** *Méx* [parada de taxis] taxi *Br* rank o *US* stand **d)** INFORM site; **sitio web** website

sitio² *nm* siege; **estado de sitio** state of emergency

situación *nf* **a)** situation; **su situación económica es buena** his financial position is good **b)** [ubicación] situation, location

situar [30] **1.** *vt* to locate **2. situarse** *vpr* to be situated o located

skinhead [es'kinxeð] *(pl* **skinheads)** *nmf* skinhead

S.L. *(abr de* **Sociedad Limitada)** ≃ *Br* Ltd, ≃ *US* Inc

slam *nm* = **eslam**

S.M. *(abr de* **Su Majestad)** [rey] His Majesty; [reina] Her Majesty

smartphone® [es'martfon] *nm* smartphone

s /n *(abr de* **sin número)** *abbreviation used in addresses after the street name, where the building has no number*

snowboard [ez'noußorð] *nm* snowboarding

sobaco *nm* armpit

sobar *vt* [tocar] to finger, to paw; *Fam* [persona] to touch up, to fondle

soberbia *nf* pride

soberbio, -a *adj* **a)** proud **b)** [magnífico] splendid, magnificent

soborno *nm* [acción] bribery; [dinero etc] bribe

sobra *nf* **a)** de sobra [no necesario] superfluous; **tener de sobra** to have plenty; **estar de sobra** not to be needed; **saber algo de sobra** to know sth only too well **b)** sobras [restos] leftovers

sobradamente *adv* perfectly

sobrado, -a *adj* [suficiente] **tener tiempo sobrado** to have more than enough time; **tener sobrados motivos para creerlo** to have good enough reason to believe it; **andar** o **estar sobrado (de dinero)** to be very comfortably off

sobrar *vi* **a)** to be more than enough; [sg] to be too much; [pl] to be too many; **sobran tres sillas** there are three chairs too many; **sobran comentarios** I've nothing further to add; *Fam* **tú sobras aquí** you are not wanted here **b)** [quedar] to be left over; **ha sobrado carne** there's still some meat left

sobrasada *nf* sausage spread

sobre¹ *nm* **a)** [para carta] envelope **b)** [de sopa etc] packet

sobre² *prep* **a)** [encima de] on, upon, on top of **b)** [por encima] over, above **c)** [acerca de] about, on **d)** [aproximadamente] about; **vendré sobre las ocho** I'll come at about eight o'clock **e)** sobre todo especially, above all

sobreactuar *vt* & *vi* to overact

sobrecarga *nf* overload

sobrecoste *nm* overspend

sobrecualificado, -a *adj* overqualified

sobredosis *nf inv* overdose

sobrehumano, -a *adj* superhuman

sobremesa¹ *nf* afternoon

sobremesa² *nf* **ordenador de sobremesa** desktop computer

sobrenombre *nm* nickname

sobrepasar 1. *vt* to exceed, to surpass; [rival] to beat **2. sobrepasarse** *vpr* to go too far

sobreponer [19] **1.** *vt* **a)** [poner encima] to put on top **b)** *Fig* [anteponer] **sobreponer algo a algo** to put sth before sth **2. sobreponerse** *vpr* **sobreponerse a algo** to overcome sth

sobresaliente 1. *nm* [nota] ≈ A **2.** *adj* [que destaca] outstanding, excellent

sobresalir [22] *vi* to stick out, to protrude; *Fig* [destacar] to stand out, to excel

sobresaltado, -a *adj* startled

sobresalto *nm* [movimiento] start; [susto] fright

sobretiempo *nm Andes* **a)** [en trabajo] overtime **b)** [en deporte] *Br* extra time, *US* overtime

sobrevivir *vi* to survive

sobrevolar [2] *vt* to fly over

sobrino *nm* nephew

sobrio, -a *adj* sober

sociable *adj* sociable, friendly

social *adj* social

socialista *adj & nmf* socialist

sociedad *nf* **a)** society; **sociedad de consumo** consumer society **b)** [asociación] association, society **c)** COM company; **sociedad anónima** *Br* public (limited) company, *US* incorporated company; **sociedad limitada** private limited company

socio, -a *nm, f* **a)** [miembro] member; **hacerse socio de un club** to become a member of a club, to join a club **b)** COM [asociado] partner

sociología *nf* sociology

sociológico, -a *adj* sociological

sociólogo, -a *nm, f* sociologist

socorrer *vt* to help, to assist

socorrismo *nm* first aid; [en la playa] lifesaving

socorrista *nmf* life-saver, lifeguard

socorro *nm* help, assistance; **¡socorro!** help!; **puesto de socorro** first-aid post

soda *nf* soda water

sofá *nm* sofa, settee; **sofá cama** sofa bed, studio couch

sofisticado, -a *adj* sophisticated

sofocante *adj* suffocating, stifling; **hacía un calor sofocante** it was unbearably hot

sofoco *nm* **a)** *Fig* [vergüenza] embarrassment; [disgusto] **le dio un sofoco** it gave her quite a turn **b)** MED **sofocos** hot flushes

sofrito *nm* fried tomato and onion sauce

software *nm* software

sol¹ *nm* **a)** sun **b)** [luz] sunlight; [luz y calor] sunshine; **hace sol** it's sunny, the sun is shining; **tomar el sol** to sunbathe; **al** *o* **bajo el sol** in the sun; **de sol a sol** from sunrise to sunset **c)** FIN *standard monetary unit of Peru*

sol² *nm* MÚS G; [solfeo] so

solamente *adv* only; **no solamente** not only; **solamente con mirarte lo sé** I know just by looking at you; **solamente que …** except that …

solapa *nf* [de chaqueta] lapel; [de sobre, bolsillo, libro] flap

solar¹ *adj* solar; **luz solar** sunlight

solar² *nm* [terreno] plot; [en obras] building site

solario, solárium *(pl* **solariums***) nm* solarium

soldado *nm* soldier; **soldado raso** private

soldador, -a 1. *nm, f* welder **2.** *nm* soldering iron

soldar [2] *vt* [cable] to solder; [chapa] to weld

soleá *nf* typical folk song and dance from Andalusia with a melancholic tone

soleado, -a *adj* sunny

soledad *nf* [estado] solitude; [sentimiento] loneliness

solemne *adj* **a)** [majestuoso] solemn **b)** *Despec* downright

solemnidad *nf* solemnity

soler [4] *vi* **a)** [en presente] to be in the habit of; **solemos ir en coche** we usually go by car; **sueles equivocarte** you are usually wrong **b)** [en pasado] **solía pasear por aquí** he used to walk round here

solicitar *vt* [información etc] to request, to ask for; [trabajo] to apply for

solicitud *nf* [petición] request; [de trabajo] application

solidaridad *nf* solidarity

sólido, -a *adj* solid, strong

solista *nmf* soloist

solitario, -a 1. *adj* [que está solo] solitary, lone; [que se siente solo] lonely **2.** *nm* **a)** [diamante] solitaire **b)** NAIPES *Br* patience, *US* solitaire

sollozar [40] *vi* to sob

sollozo *nm* sob

solo, -a 1. *adj* **a)** only, single; **ni un solo día** not a single day; **una sola vez** only once, just once **b)** [solitario] lonely **c) hablar solo** to talk to oneself; **se enciende solo** it switches itself on automatically; **a solas** alone, by oneself **2.** *nm* MÚS solo

sólo *adv* only; **tan sólo** only; **no sólo ... sino (también)** not only ... but (also); **con sólo, (tan) sólo con** just by

> Note that the adverb **sólo** can be written without an accent when there is no risk of confusion with the adjective.

solomillo *nm* sirloin

soltar [2] **1.** *vt* **a)** [desasir] to let go of; **¡suéltame!** let me go! **b)** [prisionero] to release **c)** [humo, olor] to give off **d)** [bofetada] to deal; [carcajada] to let out; **me soltó un rollo** he bored me to tears **2. soltarse** *vpr* **a)** [desatarse] to come loose **b)** [perro etc] to get loose, to break loose **c)** [desprenderse] to come off

soltero, -a 1. *adj* single, unmarried **2.** *nm* bachelor, single man, *f* single woman, *f* spinster

solterón, -ona *nm*, *f* old bachelor, *f* old maid

soltura *nf* [agilidad] agility; [seguridad] confidence, assurance; **habla italiano con soltura** he speaks Italian fluently

solución *nf* solution

solucionar *vt* to solve; [arreglar] to settle

solvente *adj* **a)** FIN solvent **b)** [fiable] reliable

sombra *nf* **a)** shade **b)** [silueta proyectada] shadow; **sombra de ojos** eyeshadow; **sin sombra de duda** beyond a shadow of doubt **c) tener buena sombra** [tener suerte] to be lucky

sombrero *nm* hat; **sombrero de copa** top hat; **sombrero hongo** *Br* bowler hat, *US* derby

sombrilla *nf* parasol, sunshade

someter 1. *vt* **a)** to subject; **someter a prueba** to put to the test; **someter algo a votación** to put sth to the vote **b)** [rebeldes] to subdue, to put down **2. someterse** *vpr* **a)** [subordinarse] to submit **b)** [rendirse] to surrender, to yield **c) someterse a un tratamiento** to undergo treatment

somier *nm* spring mattress

somnífero *nm* sleeping pill

son *nm* sound; **al son del tambor** to the sound of the drum; **venir en son de paz** to come in peace

sonajero *nm* baby's rattle

sonar [2] **1.** *vi* **a)** to sound; **sonar a** to sound like; **suena bien** it sounds good **b)** [timbre, teléfono] to ring; **sonaron las cinco** the clock struck five **c) tu nombre / cara me suena** your name / face rings a bell **2. sonarse** *vpr* **sonarse (la nariz)** to blow one's nose

sonido *nm* sound

sonoro, -a *adj* **a)** CINE sound; **banda sonora** soundtrack **b)** [resonante] loud, resounding **c)** LING voiced

sonreír [56] **1.** *vi* to smile; **me sonrió** he smiled at me **2. sonreírse** *vpr* = **sonreír**

sonriente *adj* smiling

sonrisa *nf* smile

sonrojarse *vpr* to blush

sonso, -a *adj Am* foolish, silly

soñado, -a *adj* dream; **mi casa soñada** my dream home

soñar [2] *vt & vi* a) to dream; **soñar con** to dream of o about; *Fig* **¡ni soñarlo!** not on your life! b) [fantasear] to daydream, to dream

sopa *nf* soup; **sopa juliana** spring vegetable soup; *Fig* **quedar hecho una sopa** to get soaked to the skin

sope *nm Méx* fried corn tortilla, with beans and cheese or other toppings

sopera *nf* soup tureen

soplar 1. *vi* [viento] to blow **2.** *vt* a) [polvo etc] to blow away; [para enfriar] to blow on b) [para apagar] to blow out c) [para inflar] to blow up d) [en examen etc] **me sopló las respuestas** he whispered the answers to me

soplete *nm* blowlamp, blowtorch

soplido *nm* blow, puff

soplo *nm* a) [acción] blow, puff; [de viento] gust b) MED murmur

soportable *adj* bearable

soportal *nm* porch; **soportales** arcade

soportar *vt* a) [peso] to support, to bear b) *Fig* [calor, ruido] to bear, to endure; [situación] to put up with, to bear; **no te soporto** I can't stand you

soporte *nm* a) [gen & INFORM] medium; **soporte publicitario** advertising medium b) *Fig* support

soprano *nmf* soprano

sorber *vt* a) [beber] to sip b) [absorber] to soak up, to absorb

sorbete *nm* sorbet, sherbet

sorbetería *nf CAm* [tienda] ice-cream *Br* parlour o *US* parlor

sordo, -a 1. *adj* a) [persona] deaf; **sordo como una tapia** stone-deaf b) [golpe, ruido, dolor] dull **2.** *nm, f* deaf person; **los sordos** the deaf *pl*; *Fam & Fig* **hacerse el sordo** to turn a deaf ear

sordomudo, -a 1. *adj* deaf and dumb, deaf-mute **2.** *nm, f* deaf and dumb person, deaf-mute

soroche *nm* a) *Andes, Arg* [mal de altura] altitude sickness b) *Chile* [rubor] blush, flush

sorprendente *adj* surprising

sorprender *vt* a) [extrañar] to surprise b) [coger desprevenido] to catch unawares, to take by surprise

sorprendido, -a *adj* surprised

sorpresa *nf* surprise; **coger de o por sorpresa** to take by surprise

sorpresivo, -a *adj Am* surprise, unexpected

sortear *vt* a) to draw o cast lots for; [rifar] to raffle (off) b) [evitar] to avoid, to get round

sorteo *nm* draw; [rifa] raffle

sortija *nf* ring

SOS *nm* SOS

sosiego *nm* [calma] calmness; [paz] peace, tranquillity

soso, -a *adj* lacking in salt; *Fig* [persona] insipid, dull

sospechar 1. *vi* [desconfiar] to suspect; **sospechar de algn** to suspect sb **2.** *vt* [pensar] to suspect

sospechoso, -a 1. *adj* suspicious; **sospechoso de** suspected of **2.** *nm, f* suspect

sostén *nm* a) [apoyo] support b) [sustento] sustenance c) [prenda] bra, brassière

sostener [24] **1.** *vt* a) [sujetar] to support, to hold up b) [con la mano] to hold c) *Fig* [teoría etc] to defend, to uphold; **sostener que ...** to maintain that ... d) [conversación] to hold, to sustain e) [familia] to support **2. sostenerse** *vpr* a) [mantenerse] to support oneself b) [permanecer] to stay, to remain

sota *nf* NAIPES jack, knave

sotana *nf* cassock, soutane

sótano *nm* basement, cellar

soy *indic pres de* ser

spam *nm* = espam

SPE *nmpl* (abr de **Servicios Públicos de Empleo**) Spanish national job search *service,* ≃ job centre *(in UK)*; **una oficina de los SPE** ≃ a job centre office *(in UK)*

spro SMS *written abbr of* **espero**

squash [es'kwas] *nm inv* DEP squash

Sr. *(abr de* **Señor***)* Mr

Sra. *(abr de* **Señora***)* Mrs

Sres. *(abr de* **Señores***)* Messrs

Srta. *(abr de* **Señorita***)* Miss

SS.MM. *(abr de* **Sus Majestades***)* their Royal Highnesses

Sta., sta. *(abr de* **Santa***)* St

starter *nm* = **estárter**

Sto., sto. *(abr de* **Santo***)* St

stock [es'tok] *(pl* **stocks***) nm* COM stock

stop [es'top] *(pl* **stops***) nm* **a)** [señal de tráfico] stop sign **b)** [en telegrama] stop

su *(pl* **sus***) adj poses* [de él] his; [de ella] her; [de usted, ustedes] your; [de animales o cosas] its; [impersonal] one's; [de ellos] their; **su coche** his / her / your / their car; **su pata** its leg; **sus libros** his / her / your / their books; **sus patas** its legs

suave *adj* **a)** smooth; [luz, voz etc] soft **b)** METEOR [templado] mild

suavidad *nf* **a)** smoothness; [dulzura] softness **b)** METEOR mildness

suavizante *nm* [para el pelo] (hair) conditioner; [para la ropa] fabric softener

subasta *nf* auction

subcampeón *nm* DEP runner-up

subconsciente *adj & nm* subconscious

subdesarrollado, -a *adj* underdeveloped

subdesarrollo *nm* underdevelopment

subdirector, -a *nm, f* assistant director / manager

subdirectorio *nm* INFORM subdirectory

súbdito, -a *nm, f* subject, citizen; **súbdito francés** French citizen

subida *nf* **a)** [de temperatura] rise; [de precios, salarios] rise, increase **b)** [ascenso] ascent, climb **c)** [pendiente] slope, hill **d)** INFORM [de fichero] upload **e)** *Fam* [drogas] high

---

subir **1.** *vt* **a)** to go up **b)** [llevar arriba] to take up, to bring up **c)** [cabeza, mano] to lift, to raise **d)** [precio, salario] to raise, to put up **e)** [volumen] to turn up; [voz] to raise **f)** INFORM [fichero] to upload **2.** *vi* **a)** [ir arriba] to go up, to come up **b) subir a** [un coche] to get into; [un autobús] to get on; [un barco, avión, tren] to board, to get on **c)** [aumentar] to rise, to go up **3. subirse** *vpr* **a)** to climb up; *Fig* **el vino se le subió a la cabeza** the wine went to his head **b) subirse a** [un coche] to get into; [un autobús, avión, tren] to get on, to board; [caballo, bici] to get on **c)** [cremallera] to do up; [mangas] to roll up

---

súbito, -a *adj* sudden

subjetivo, -a *adj* subjective

subjuntivo, -a *adj & nm* subjunctive

sublevamiento *nm* uprising

sublevar **1.** *vt Fig* [indignar] to infuriate, to enrage **2. sublevarse** *vpr* to rebel, to revolt

sublime *adj* sublime

submarinismo *nm* skin-diving

submarinista *nmf* scuba diver

submarino, -a **1.** *adj* submarine, underwater **2.** *nm* submarine

subrayar *vt* to underline; *Fig* [recalcar] to emphasize, to stress

subsidio *nm* allowance, benefit; **subsidio de desempleo** unemployment benefit

subsistencia *nf* subsistence

subsuelo *nm* subsoil

subte *nm RP* metro, *Br* underground, *US* subway

subterráneo, -a 1. *adj* underground **2.** *nm* [túnel] tunnel, underground passage

subtítulo *nm* subtitle

subtotal *nm* subtotal

suburbio *nm* [barrio pobre] slums; [barrio periférico] suburb

subvención *nf* subsidy

sucedáneo, -a *adj* & *nm* substitute

suceder 1. *vi* a) [ocurrir - uso impers.] to happen, to occur; **¿qué sucede?** what's going on?, what's the matter? b) [seguir] to follow, to succeed **2. sucederse** *vpr* to follow one another, to come one after the other

sucesión *nf* a) [serie] series (*sing*), succession b) [al trono] succession c) [descendencia] issue, heirs

sucesivo, -a *adj* following, successive; **en lo sucesivo** from now on

suceso *nm* [hecho] event, occurrence; [incidente] incident; PRENSA **sección de sucesos** accident and crime reports

sucesor, -a *nm, f* successor

suciedad *nf* a) dirt b) [calidad] dirtiness

sucio, -a 1. *adj* dirty; **en sucio** in rough; *Fig* **juego sucio** foul play; *Fig* **negocio sucio** shady business **2.** *adv* **jugar sucio** to play dirty

suculento, -a *adj* succulent, juicy

sucumbir *vi* to succumb, to yield

sucursal *nf* COM & FIN branch, branch office

sudadera *nf* sweatshirt

Sudáfrica *n* South Africa

Sudamérica, Suramérica *n* South America

sudamericano, -a, suramericano, -a *adj* & *nm, f* South American

sudar *vt* & *vi* to sweat; *Fam* & *Fig* **sudar la gota gorda** to sweat blood

sudeste *nm* southeast

sudoeste *nm* southwest

sudor *nm* sweat; *Fig* **con el sudor de mi frente** by the sweat of my brow

Suecia *n* Sweden

sueco, -a 1. *adj* Swedish **2.** *nm, f* [persona] Swede **3.** *nm* [idioma] Swedish

suegro *nm* father-in-law; **mis suegros** my in-laws

suela *nf* [de zapato] sole

sueldo *nm* salary, wages

suelo *nm* a) [superficie] ground; [de interior] floor; *Fig* **estar por los suelos** [precios] to be rock-bottom b) [territorio] soil, land c) [campo, terreno] land; **suelo cultivable** arable land d) [de carretera] surface

suelto, -a 1. *adj* a) loose; [desatado] undone b) *Fig* **dinero suelto** loose change; **hojas sueltas** loose sheets (of paper); **se venden sueltos** they are sold singly o separately o loose c) [en libertad] free; [huido] at large d) [vestido, camisa] loose, loose-fitting **2.** *nm* [dinero] (loose) change

sueño *nm* a) sleep; [ganas de dormir] sleepiness; **tener sueño** to feel o be sleepy b) [cosa soñada] dream

suero *nm* MED serum; [de la leche] whey

suerte *nf* a) [fortuna] luck; **por suerte** fortunately; **probar suerte** to try one's luck; **tener suerte** to be lucky; **¡que tengas suerte!** good luck! b) **echar algo** *Esp* **a suertes** o *Am* **a la suerte** to draw lots for sth c) [destino] fate, destiny d) *Formal* [género] kind, sort, type

suéter *nm* sweater

suficiente 1. *adj* [bastante] sufficient, enough **2.** *nm* EDUC pass

sufragar [42] **1.** *vt* [gastos] to pay, defray **2.** *vi Am* to vote

sufragio *nm* POL suffrage; [voto] vote

sufrido, -a *adj* [persona] long-suffering

sufrimiento *nm* suffering

sufrir 1. *vi* to suffer; **sufrir del corazón** to have a heart condition **2.** *vt* a) [accidente] to have; [operación] to undergo; [dificultades, cambios] to experience; **sufrir dolores de cabeza** to suffer from headaches b) [aguantar] to bear, to put up with

sugerencia *nf* suggestion

sugerir [5] *vt* to suggest

suiche *nm Col, Ven* switch

suicidio *nm* suicide

suite *nf* suite

Suiza *n* Switzerland

suizo, -a 1. *adj & nm, f* Swiss **2.** *nm Esp* [bollo] *type of sugared bun*

sujetador *nm Esp* bra, brassière

sujetar 1. *vt* **a)** [agarrar] to hold **b)** [fijar] to hold down, to hold in place **c)** *Fig* [someter] to restrain **2. sujetarse** *vpr* [agarrarse] to hold on

sujeto, -a 1. *nm* subject; [individuo] fellow, individual **2.** *adj* [atado] fastened, secure; **sujeto a** [sometido] subject to, liable to

suma *nf* **a)** [cantidad] sum, amount **b)** MAT sum, addition; **suma total** sum total **c) en suma** in short

sumar 1. *vt* MAT to add, to add up **2. sumarse** *vpr* **sumarse a** [huelga] to join; [propuesta] to support

sumario, -a 1. *adj* summary, brief; JUR **juicio sumario** summary proceedings **2.** *nm* JUR summary

sumergible *adj & nm* submersible

sumergir [57] **1.** *vt* to submerge, to submerse; [hundir] to sink, to plunge **2. sumergirse** *vpr* to submerge, to go underwater; [hundirse] to sink

suministrar *vt* to supply, to provide; **suministrar algo a algn** to supply sb with sth

suministro *nm* supply

sumiso, -a *adj* submissive, obedient

súper *Fam* **1.** *adj* super, great **2.** *nm* **a)** [supermercado] supermarket **b)** [gasolina] *Br* four-star (petrol), *US* regular

superación *nf* overcoming; **afán de superación** drive to improve

superar 1. *vt* **a)** [obstáculo etc] to overcome, to surmount; [prueba] to pass **b)** [aventajar] to surpass, to excel **2. superarse** *vpr* to improve o better oneself

superficial *adj* superficial

superficie *nf* surface; [área] area; COM **grandes superficies** hypermarkets

superfluo, -a *adj* superfluous

superior 1. *adj* **a)** [posición] top, upper **b)** [cantidad] greater, higher, larger (**a** than) **c)** [calidad] superior; **calidad superior** top quality **d)** EDUC higher **2.** *nm* [jefe] superior

supermercado *nm* supermarket

superponer [19] *vt* to superimpose

superpuesto, -a 1. *pp de* **superponer 2.** *adj* superimposed

superstición *nf* superstition

supersticioso, -a *adj* superstitious

superviviente 1. *adj* surviving **2.** *nmf* survivor

suplemento *nm* supplement; **sin suplemento** without extra charge

suplente *adj & nmf* [sustituto] substitute, stand-in; DEP substitute

supletorio, -a *adj* supplementary, additional; **cama supletoria** extra bed; **teléfono supletorio** extension

súplica *nf* entreaty, plea

suplir *vt* **a)** [reemplazar] to replace, to substitute **b)** [compensar] to make up for

suponer [19] (*pp* **supuesto**) *vt* **a)** [significar] to mean **b)** [implicar] to entail **c)** [representar] to account for **d)** [pensar] to suppose; **supongo que sí** I suppose so; **supongamos que …** let's assume that … **e)** [adivinar] to guess; **(me) lo suponía** I guessed as much

suposición *nf* supposition

supositorio *nm* suppository

suprimir *vt* **a)** [ley, impuesto] to abolish; [restricción] to lift; [palabra] to delete, to take / leave out; [rebelión] to suppress **b)** [omitir] to omit

supuesto, -a 1. *adj* **a)** [asumido] supposed, assumed; **¡por supuesto!** of course!; **dar algo por supuesto** to take sth for granted **b)** [presunto] alleged **2.** *nm* assumption; **en el supuesto de que** on the assumption that

sur *nm* south

surco *nm* AGRIC furrow; [en un disco] groove

sureño, -a 1. *adj* southern **2.** *nm, f* southerner

surf, surfing *nm* surfing

surfear *vt & vi Fam* INFORM to surf

surfista *nmf* surfer

surgir [57] *vi* [aparecer] to arise, to emerge, to appear; [problema, dificultad] to crop up

surrealista *adj* & *nmf* surrealist

surtido, -a 1. *adj* **a)** [variado] assorted **b) bien surtido** well-stocked **2.** *nm* selection, assortment

surtidor *nm* spout; **surtidor de gasolina** *Br* petrol pump, *US* gas pump

susceptible *adj* susceptible; [quisquilloso] oversensitive, touchy

suscribir *(pp* suscrito*)* **1.** *vt* **a)** to subscribe to, to endorse **b)** *Formal* [firmar] to sign **2. suscribirse** *vpr* to subscribe (**a** to)

suscripción *nf* subscription

suspender 1. *vt* **a)** [ley] to suspend; [reunión] to adjourn **b)** *Esp* [examen] to fail; **me han suspendido** I've failed (the exam) **c)** [colgar] to hang, to suspend **2.** *vi* [alumno] to fail

suspense *nm* suspense; **novela/película de suspense** thriller

suspenso, -a 1. *adj* **a)** [colgado] hanging, suspended **b)** *Esp* [no aprobado] failed **c)** *Fig* [desconcertado] disconcerted **2.** *nm* **a)** *Esp* EDUC [en examen] fail; [en asignatura] ≃ U *(unclassified)*; **sacar un suspenso** to fail; **me he llevado un suspenso en historia** I got a

U in History **b) en suspenso** [asunto, trabajo] pending; **estar en suspenso** to be pending

suspensores *nmpl Am Br* braces, *US* suspenders

suspirar *vi* to sigh

suspiro *nm* sigh

sustancia *nf* substance

sustancial *adj* **a)** substantial **b)** [fundamental] essential, fundamental

sustantivo, -a 1. *adj* substantive **2.** *nm* LING noun

sustituir [37] *vt* to substitute, to replace

susto *nm* fright, scare; **llevarse** *o* **darse un susto** to get a fright

sustracción *nf* **a)** [robo] theft **b)** MAT subtraction

sustraer [25] *vt* **a)** MAT to subtract **b)** [robar] to steal, to remove

susurrar *vt* to whisper

suyo, -a *adj* & *pron poses* [de él] his; [de ella] hers; [de usted, ustedes] yours; [de animal o cosa] its; [de ellos, ellas] theirs; **los zapatos no son suyos** the shoes aren't hers; **varios amigos suyos** several friends of his / hers / yours / theirs; *Fam* **es muy suyo** he's very aloof; *Fam* **hacer de las suyas** to be up to one's tricks; *Fam* **ir (cada uno) a lo suyo** to mind one's own business; *Fam* **salirse con la suya** to get one's (own) way

T

t *(abr de* **tonelada(s)**) t

tabaco *nm* **a)** [planta, hoja] tobacco; **tabaco rubio** Virginia tobacco **b)** [cigarrillos] cigarettes

tábano *nm* horsefly

tabasco® *nm* Tabasco® *(sauce)*

taberna *nf* pub, bar; [antiguamente] tavern

tabique *nm* **a)** [pared] partition (wall) **b)** ANAT **tabique nasal** nasal wall

tabla *nf* **a)** board; DEP **tabla de surf** surfboard; DEP **tabla de windsurf** sailboard **b)** [de vestido] pleat **c)** MAT table **d)** **tablas** [en ajedrez] stalemate, draw; **quedar en tablas** [juego] to end in a draw **e)** TAUROM **tablas** fence **f)** TEATRO **las tablas** the stage; *Fig* **tener (muchas) tablas** to be an old hand

tablao *nm* *Fam* flamenco bar or show

tablero *nm* **a)** [tablón] panel, board; **tablero de mandos** [de coche] dash(board) **b)** [en juegos] board; **tablero de ajedrez** chessboard

tableta *nf* **a)** [de chocolate] bar **b)** [medicamento] tablet, pill **c)** INFORM tablet; **tableta de lectura digital** e-reader; **tableta táctil** (touchscreen) tablet

tablón *nm* plank; [en construcción] beam; **tablón de anuncios** *Br* noticeboard, *US* bulletin board

tabú *(pl* **tabúes**) *adj* & *nm* taboo

taburete *nm* stool

tacaño, -a **1.** *adj* mean, stingy **2.** *nm, f* miser

tachar *vt* **a)** to cross out **b)** *Fig* **tachar de** to accuse of

tachero *nm* *RP Fam* [de taxi] taxi driver

tacho *nm* *Andes, RP* [metálico, de hojalata] tin; [de plástico] container; [papelera] *Br* waste paper bin o basket, *US* waste basket

tácito, -a *adj* tacit

taco *nm* **a)** plug; [de billetes] wad; [de bota de fútbol] stud; [en billar] cue **b)** [cubo - de jamón, queso] cube, piece **c)** CULIN [tortilla de maíz] taco *(rolled-up tortilla pancake)* **d)** *Esp Fam* [palabrota] swearword **e)** *Esp Fam* [lío] mess, muddle; **armarse** o **hacerse un taco** to get all mixed up **f)** *Esp Fam* **tacos** [años] years

tacón *nm* heel; **zapatos de tacón** high-heeled shoes

tacto *nm* **a)** [sentido] touch **b)** *Fig* [delicadeza] tact; **tener tacto** to be tactful

taekwondo *nm* tae kwon do

Taiwán [tai'wan] *n* Taiwan

tajada *nf* **a)** slice; *Fig* **sacar** o **llevarse tajada** to take one's share **b)** *Fam* [borrachera] drunkenness

tajo *nm* **a)** [corte] deep cut **b)** *Esp* [trabajo] workplace, work

tal **1.** *adj* **a)** [semejante] such; [más sustantivo singular contable] such a; **en tales condiciones** in such conditions; **nunca dije tal cosa** I never said such a thing
b) [indeterminado] such and such; **tal día y a tal hora** such and such a day and at such and such a time
c) [persona] **una tal Amelia** someone called Amelia
d) [locuciones] **tal vez** perhaps, maybe; **como si tal cosa** as if nothing had happened
2. *adv* **a)** [así] just; **tal cual** just as it is; **tal (y) como** just as
b) **¿qué tal?** how are things?; **¿qué tal este vino?** how do you find this wine?

3. *conj* as; **con tal (de) que** (+ *subjuntivo*) so long as, provided

4. *pron* [cosa] something; [persona] someone, somebody; **tal para cual** two of a kind; **y tal y cual** and so on

taladradora *nf* drill

taladrar *vt* to drill; [pared] to bore through; [papeles] to punch

taladro *nm* **a)** [herramienta] drill **b)** [agujero] hole

talasoterapia *nf* thalassotherapy

talco *nm* talc; **polvos de talco** talcum powder

talento *nm* talent

Talgo *nm fast passenger train*

talla *nf* **a)** [de prenda] size; **¿qué talla usas?** what size are you? **b)** [estatura] height; *Fig* stature; *Fig* **dar la talla** to make the grade **c)** [escultura] carving, sculpture **d)** [tallado] cutting, carving

tallarines *nmpl* tagliatelle

taller *nm* **a)** [obrador] workshop; AUTO **taller de reparaciones** garage **b)** INDUST factory, mill

tallo *nm* stem, stalk

talón *nm* **a)** [de pie] heel **b)** [cheque] cheque

talonario *nm* [de cheques] cheque book; [de billetes] book of tickets

tamal *nm* [comida] tamale (*steamed maize dumpling with savoury or sweet filling, wrapped in maize husks or a banana leaf*)

tamaño, -a 1. *adj* such a big, so big a **2.** *nm* size; **de gran tamaño** large; **del tamaño de** as large as, as big as

tambero *nm* **a)** *RP* [granjero] dairy farmer **b)** [dueño - de una tienda] storekeeper; [de un tenderete] stall holder

también *adv* [igualmente] too, also, as well; **tú también puedes venir** you can come too; **¿lo harás? yo también** are you going to do it? so am I

tambo *nm* **a)** *Andes* [posada] wayside inn **b)** *Andes* [tienda] shop; [tenderete] stall **c)** *RP* [granja] dairy farm **d)** *Méx* [recipiente] drum

tambor *nm* **a)** [Mús, de lavadora, de freno] drum **b)** ANAT eardrum

tampoco *adv* **a)** [en afirmativas] nor, neither; **Juan no vendrá y María tampoco** Juan won't come and neither will Maria; **no lo sé — yo tampoco** I don't know — neither do I **b)** [en negativas] either, not ... either; **la Bolsa no sube, pero tampoco baja** the stock market isn't going up, but it's not going down either

tampón *nm* tampon

tan *adv* **a)** such; [más sustantivo singular contable] such a; **es tan listo** he's such a clever fellow; **no me gusta tan dulce** I don't like it so sweet; **¡qué gente tan agradable!** such nice people!; **¡qué vestido tan bonito!** what a beautiful dress!
b) [comparativo] **tan ... como** as ... as; **tan alto como tú** as tall as you (are)
c) [consecutivo] so ... (that); **iba tan deprisa que no lo vi** he was going so fast that I couldn't see him
d) tan siquiera at least; **tan sólo** only

tanda *nf* [conjunto] batch, lot; [serie] series (*sing*); **por tandas** in groups

tándem *nm* tandem

tanga *nm* tanga

tango *nm* tango

tanque *nm* tank

tanto, -a 1. *nm* **a)** [punto] point
b) [cantidad imprecisa] so much, a certain amount; **tanto por ciento** percentage
c) un tanto a bit; **la casa es un tanto pequeña** the house is rather *o* somewhat small
d) estar al tanto [informado] to be informed; [pendiente] to be on the lookout
2. *adj* **a)** [+ singular] so much; [+ plural] so many; **no le des tanto dinero** don't give him so much money; **¡ha pasado tanto tiempo!** it's been so long!; **no comas tantas manzanas** don't eat so many apples

b) cincuenta y tantas personas fifty-odd people; **en el año sesenta y tantos** in nineteen sixty-something
c) tanto como as much as; **tantos como** as many as
3. *pron* **a)** [+ singular] so much; **otro tanto** as much again, the same again; **no es o hay para tanto** it's not that bad **b)** [+ plural] so many; **otros tantos** as many again; **uno de tantos** run-of-the-mill; *Fam* **a las tantas** very late, at an unearthly hour
4. *adv* **a)** [cantidad] so much; **tanto más cuanto que** all the more so because **b)** [tiempo] so long
c) [frecuencia] so often
d) tanto ... como both ... and; **tanto tú como yo** both you and I; **tanto si vienes como si no** whether you come or not
e) [locuciones] **por lo tanto** therefore; **¡y tanto!** oh yes!, and how!
5. *conj* **a) en tanto (que)** insofar as **b) tanto (es así) que** so much so that

tapa *nf* **a)** [cubierta] lid; *Andes, RP* [de botella] top; [de libro] cover; [de zapato] heelplate; AUTO [de cilindro] head **b)** *Esp* [de comida] appetizer, snack; **ir de tapas** to go for tapas

tapabarros *nm inv* **a)** [de hombre primitivo] loincloth **b)** [tanga] tanga briefs

tapadera *nf* [tapa] cover, lid; *Fig* cover, front

tapado *nm* *CSur* [abrigo] overcoat

tapar 1. *vt* **a)** to cover; [botella etc] to put the lid / top on; [con ropas o mantas] to wrap up **b)** [ocultar] to hide; [vista] to block **c)** [encubrir] to cover up **2. taparse** *vpr* [cubrirse] to cover oneself; [abrigarse] to wrap up

tapear *vi* to have tapas; **ir a tapear** to go for tapas

tapeo *nm* **ir de tapeo** to go for tapas

tapete *nm* **a)** [de mesa] (table) runner, (table) cover, small table cloth *(used for decoration)*; *Fig* **poner algo sobre el tapete** to table sth **b)** INFORM **tapete de o para ratón** *Br* mouse mat, *US* mouse pad **c)** *Am* [alfombra] mat, rug

tapia *nf* garden wall

tapicería *nf* **a)** tapestry; [de muebles, coche] upholstery **b)** [tienda] upholsterer's shop / workshop

tapiz *nm* tapestry

tapizar [40] *vt* to upholster

tapón *nm* **a)** [de lavabo etc] stopper, plug; [de botella] cap, cork; **tapón de rosca** screw-on cap **b)** [de oídos] earplug **c)** [en baloncesto] block **d)** AUTO traffic jam **e)** *Am* [plomo] fuse

taquería *nf* *Méx* [quiosco] taco stall; [restaurante] taco restaurant

taquigrafía *nf* shorthand

taquilla *nf* **a)** ticket office, booking office; CINE & TEATRO box office; **un éxito de taquilla** a box-office success **b)** [recaudación] takings **c)** [armario] locker

taquillero, -a 1. *adj* popular; **película taquillera** box-office hit **2.** *nm, f* booking o ticket clerk

tara *nf* **a)** [peso] tare **b)** [defecto] defect, fault

tardar 1. *vt* [llevar tiempo] to take; **¿cuánto va a tardar?** how long will it take?; **tardé dos horas en venir** it took me two hours to get here
2. *vi* [demorar] to take long; **si tarda mucho, me voy** if it takes much longer, I'm going; **no tardes** don't be long; **a más tardar** at the latest
3. tardarse *vpr* **¿cuánto se tarda en llegar?** how long does it take to get there?

tarde 1. *nf* **a)** [hasta las cinco] afternoon **b)** [después de las cinco] evening **c) la tarde noche** late evening **2.** *adv* **a)** late; **siento llegar tarde** sorry I'm late **b)** [locuciones] **de tarde en tarde** very rarely, not very often; **(más) tarde o (más) temprano** sooner or later

tarea *nf* job, task; **tareas** [de ama de casa] housework; [de estudiante] homework

tarifa *nf* **a)** [precio] tariff, rate; [en transportes] fare **b)** [lista de precios] price list

tarima *nf* platform, dais

tarjeta *nf* card ; **tarjeta postal** postcard ; **tarjeta de crédito** credit card ; **tarjeta de visita** visiting card, *US* calling card ; INFORM **tarjeta perforada** punch o punched card

tarro *nm* **a)** [vasija] jar, pot **b)** *Esp Fam* [cabeza] nut, *Br* bonce

tarta *nf* tart, pie

tartaleta *nf* tartlet

tartamudo, -a 1. *adj* stuttering, stammering **2.** *nm, f* stutterer, stammerer

tas SMS *(abr de* **estás)** R ; **tas OK?** R U OK?

tasa *nf* **a)** [precio] fee ; **tasas académicas** course fees **b)** [impuesto] tax ; **tasas de aeropuerto** airport tax **c)** [índice] rate ; **tasa de natalidad / mortalidad** birth / death rate **d)** [valoración] valuation, appraisal

tasca *nf* cheap bar

tata 1. *nf Esp* [niñera] nanny **2.** *nm Am Fam* [papá] dad, *US* pop

tatuaje *nm* tattoo

taurino, -a *adj* bullfighting

Tauro *nm* Taurus

tauromaquia *nf* tauromachy, (art of) bullfighting

taxi *nm* taxi

taxímetro *nm* taximeter, clock

taximoto *nm* motorcycle taxi

taxista *nmf* taxi driver

taza *nf* **a)** cup ; **una taza de café** [recipiente] coffee cup ; [contenido] a cup of coffee **b)** [de retrete] bowl

tazón *nm* bowl

tb SMS *written abbr of* **también**

te *pron pers* **a)** [complemento directo] you ; [complemento indirecto] (to / for) you ; **no quiero verte** I don't want to see you ; **te compraré uno** I'll buy one for you, I'll buy you one ; **te lo dije** I told you so **b)** [reflexivo] yourself ; **lávate** wash yourself ; **bébetelo todo** [sin traducción] drink it up ; **no te vayas** don't go

té *nm* tea ; **té con limón** lemon tea

teatral *adj* **a)** **grupo teatral** theatre company ; **obra teatral** play **b)** *Fig* [teatrero] theatrical

teatro *nm* **a)** theatre ; **obra de teatro** play ; **autor de teatro** playwright **b)** LITER drama

tebeo *nm Esp* (children's) comic

techo *nm* [de habitación] ceiling ; [tejado] roof ; AUTO **techo corredizo** sun roof

tecla *nf* [gen & INFORM] key ; *Fig* **dar en la tecla** to get it right

teclado *nm* keyboard ; INFORM **teclado expandido** expanded keyboard

teclear 1. *vt* to key in **2.** *vi* to drum with one's fingers

técnica *nf* **a)** [tecnología] technology **b)** [método] technique **c)** [habilidad] skill

técnico, -a 1. *adj* technical **2.** *nm, f* technician, technical expert

tecnología *nf* technology

tecnológico, -a *adj* technological

tecolote *nm CAm, Méx* [búho] owl

tecomate *nm CAm, Méx* calabash

teja *nf* CONSTR tile ; *Fam & Fig* **a toca teja** on the nail

tejado *nm* roof

tejanos *nmpl* jeans

tejer *vt* [en el telar] to weave ; [hacer punto] to knit ; [telaraña] to spin ; *Fig* [plan] to plot, to scheme

tejido *nm* **a)** fabric ; **tejido de punto** knitted fabric **b)** ANAT tissue

tejo *nm Esp Fam* **tirar los tejos a algn** to make a play for sb

tel. *(abr de* **teléfono)** tel.

tela *nf* **a)** TEXT material, fabric, cloth ; [de la leche] skin ; **tela de araña** cobweb ; **tela metálica** gauze **b)** *Fam* [dinero] dough **c)** ARTE canvas **d)** *Fig* **poner en tela de juicio** to question ; *Fig* **tiene mucha tela** it's not an easy thing

telaraña *nf* cobweb, spider's web

tele *nf Fam* TV, *Br* telly

telearrastre *nm* ski lift

teleasistencia *nf* telecare

telebanca *nf* telebanking, telephone banking, home banking

telecabina *nf* cable car

telecompra *nf* teleshopping

telecomunicaciones *nfpl* telecommunications

telediario *nm* television news

teledirigido, -a *adj* remote-controlled

telefax *nm* telefax, fax

teleférico *nm* cable car / railway

telefonazo *nm* **dar un telefonazo (a algn)** to give (sb) a buzz *o Br* ring

telefonear *vt & vi* to phone, *Br* to ring

telefonía *nf* telephony

telefónico, -a *adj* telephone; **llamada telefónica** telephone call

telefonista *nmf* (telephone) operator

teléfono *nm* telephone, phone; **teléfono inalámbrico** cordless telephone; **teléfono portátil** portable telephone; **teléfono móvil** *o Am* **celular** *Br* mobile phone, *US* cellphone; **descolgar / colgar el teléfono** to pick up / hang up the phone; **está hablando por teléfono** she's on the phone; **te llamó por teléfono** she phoned you

telégrafo *nm* **a)** telegraph **b) telégrafos** post office

telegrama *nm* telegram, cable

telenovela *nf* television serial

teleobjetivo *nm* telephoto lens (*sing*)

telepago *nm* electronic payment; **telepago segurizado** secure electronic payment

telepatía *nf* telepathy

telepeaje *nm* electronic road toll

telescopio *nm* telescope

telesilla *nm* chair lift

telespectador, -a *nm, f* TV viewer

telesquí (*pl* **telesquíes** *o* **telesquís**) *nm* ski lift

teletexto *nm* teletext

teletipo *nm* teleprinter

teletrabajo *nm* teleworking

televidente *nmf* TV viewer

televisar *vt* to televise

televisión *nf* **a)** [sistema] television **b)** *Fam* [aparato] television set; **televisión en color / en blanco y negro** colour / black-and-white television; **televisión digital** digital television; **televisión por cable** cable television; **ver la televisión** to watch television

televisor *nm* television set

télex *nm inv* telex

telón *nm* TEATRO curtain; HIST **telón de acero** Iron Curtain; **telón de fondo** TEATRO backdrop; *Fig* background

tema *nm* **a)** [asunto] topic, subject; [de examen] subject; **temas de actualidad** current affairs **b)** MÚS theme

temática *nf* subject matter

temático, -a *adj* thematic

temblar [1] *vi* [de frío] to shiver; [de miedo] to tremble (**de** with); [voz] to quiver; [pulso] to shake

temblor *nm* tremor, shudder; **temblor de tierra** earth tremor

temer 1. *vt* to fear, to be afraid of; **temo que esté muerto** I fear he's dead; **temo que no podrá recibirte** I'm afraid (that) he won't be able to see you **2.** *vi* to be afraid **3. temerse** *vpr* to fear, to be afraid; **¡me lo temía!** I was afraid this would happen!

temor *nm* **a)** fear **b)** [recelo] worry, apprehension

temperamento *nm* temperament; **tener temperamento** to have a strong character

temperatura *nf* temperature

tempestad *nf* storm; *Fig* turmoil, uproar

templado, -a *adj* **a)** [agua] lukewarm; [clima] mild, temperate **b)** MÚS [afinado] tuned

templo *nm* temple

temporada *nf* **a)** season; **temporada alta** high *o* peak season; **temporada baja** low *o* off season **b)** [período] period, time; **por temporadas** on and off

temporal 1. *adj* temporary, provisional **2.** *nm* storm

temporario, -a *adj Am* temporary

temprano, -a *adj & adv* early

tenaza *nf* [herramienta] pliers, pincers; [para el fuego] tongs ■ **tenazas** *nfpl* = **tenaza**

tendedero *nm* clothes line, drying place

tendencia *nf* tendency

tender [3] **1.** *vt* **a)** [mantel etc] to spread out; [para secar] to hang out
b) *Am* [cama] to make; [mesa] to set, to lay
c) [red] to cast; [puente] to build; [vía, cable] to lay; [trampa] to lay, set
d) [mano] to stretch o hold out
e) [tumbar] to lay
2. *vi* to tend (a to), have a tendency (a to)
3. tenderse *vpr* to lie down, stretch out

tenderete *nm* [puesto] market stall

tendero, -a *nm, f* shopkeeper

tendón *nm* tendon, sinew

tenedor *nm* fork

tener [24] **1.** *vt* **a)** to have, have got; **tenemos un examen** we've got o we have an exam; **va a tener un niño** she's going to have a baby, she's expecting
b) [poseer] to own, possess
c) [sostener] to hold; **tenme el bolso un momento** hold my bag a minute; **ten, es para ti** take this o here you are, it's for you
d) tener calor / frío to be hot / cold; **tener cariño a algn** to be fond of sb; **tener miedo** to be frightened
e) [edad] to be; **tiene dieciocho (años)** he's eighteen (years old)
f) *Am* [llevar] **tengo tres años aquí** I've been here for three years
g) [medida] **la casa tiene cien metros cuadrados** the house is 100 square metres
h) [mantener] to keep; **me tuvo despierto toda la noche** he kept me up all night

i) tener por [considerar] to consider, think; **me tienen por estúpido** they think I'm a fool; **ten por seguro que lloverá** you can be sure it'll rain
j) tener que to have (got) to; **tengo que irme** I must leave; **tienes / tendrías que verlo** you must / should see it
2. tenerse *vpr* **a) tenerse en pie** to stand (up)
b) tenerse por [considerarse] to think o consider oneself; **se tiene por muy inteligente** he thinks he's very intelligent

tenga *subj pres de* **tener**

tengo *indic pres de* **tener**

teniente *nm* **a)** MIL lieutenant **b) teniente (de) alcalde** deputy mayor

tenis *nm* tennis

tenista *nmf* tennis player

tenor¹ *nm* MÚS tenor

tenor² *nm* **a tenor de** according to

tensión *nf* **a)** tension; **en tensión** tense **b)** ELEC tension, voltage **c)** MED **tensión arterial** blood pressure; **tensión nerviosa** nervous strain **d)** TÉC stress

tenso, -a *adj* **a)** [cuerda, cable] tense, taut **b)** [persona] tense; [relaciones] strained

tentación *nf* temptation; **ser una tentación** to be tempting; **tener la tentación de** to be tempted to

tentáculo *nm* tentacle

tentempié *nm Fam* **a)** [comida] snack, bite **b)** [juguete] tumbler

tenue *adj* **a)** [luz, sonido] subdued, faint **b)** [delgado] thin, light

teñir [6] **1.** *vt* **a)** [pelo etc] to dye **b)** *Fig* to tinge with **2. teñirse** *vpr* **teñirse el pelo** to dye one's hair

teología *nf* theology

teoría *nf* theory; **en teoría** theoretically

tepache *nm Méx* non-alcoholic drink made from fermented pineapple juice

terapeuta *nmf* therapist

terapia *nf* therapy

tercera *nf* AUTO third (gear)

tercerización *nf Am* COM outsourcing

tercermundista *adj* third-world

tercero, -a 1. *adj* third

> **tercer** is used instead of **tercero** before masculine singular nouns (e.g. **el tercer piso** the third floor).

2. *nm, f* [de una serie] third; *Esp* **a la tercera va la vencida** third time lucky **3.** *nm* [mediador] mediator; JUR third party

tercio *nm* **a)** [parte] (one) third **b)** [de cerveza] *medium-sized bottle of beer* **c)** TAUROM stage, part *(of a bullfight)*

terciopelo *nm* velvet

terco, -a *adj* stubborn, obstinate

tereré *nm Arg, Par* [mate] cold maté

tergal® *nm type of synthetic fibre containing polyester*

termas *nfpl* [baños] spa, hot baths o springs

terminal 1. *adj* terminal **2.** *nf* **a)** [de aeropuerto] terminal; [de autobús] terminus **b)** ELEC & INFORM terminal

terminar 1. *vt* [acabar] to finish, to complete; [completamente] to finish off

2. *vi* **a)** [acabarse] to finish, to end; **termina en seis** it ends with a six; **no termina de convencerse** he still isn't quite convinced

b) [ir a parar] to end up (**en** in); **terminó por comprarlo** he ended up buying it **c)** **terminar con** [eliminar] to put an end to

3. terminarse *vpr* **a)** to finish, to end, to be over

b) [vino, dinero etc] to run out

término *nm* **a)** [final] end, finish **b)** [palabra] term, word; **en otros términos** in other words; **en términos generales** generally speaking **c)** **término municipal** district **d)** **por término medio** on average **e)** *Fig* **en último término** as a last resort

terminología *nf* terminology

termita *nf* termite

termo *nm* Thermos® (flask), flask

termómetro *nm* thermometer

termostato *nm* thermostat

ternera *nf* calf; [carne] veal

ternero *nm* calf

terno *nm* **a)** [trío] trio **b)** [traje] three-piece suit

ternura *nf* tenderness

terraja *adj RP Fam* [persona] flashy, tacky; [decoración, ropa, canción] tacky, *Br* naff

terrajada *nf RP Fam* **esos zapatos son una terrajada** those shoes are tacky

terral *nm Am* [polvareda] dust cloud

terraplén *nm* embankment

terrateniente *nmf* landowner

terraza *nf* **a)** [balcón] balcony **b)** [de café] terrace, patio **c)** [azotea] terrace roof

terremoto *nm* earthquake

terreno, -a 1. *adj* land **2.** *nm* **a)** [tierra] (piece of) land, ground; GEOL terrain; [campo] field; **ganar / perder terreno** to gain / lose ground; **sobre el terreno** [in situ] at home, in situ; [improvisando] on-the-spot **b)** DEP field, *Br* pitch **c)** *Fig* [ámbito] territory, field, sphere

terrestre *adj* **a)** [de la tierra] terrestrial, earthly **b)** [por tierra] by land; **por vía terrestre** by land

terrible *adj* terrible, awful

territorio *nm* territory

terrón *nm* [de azúcar] lump; [de tierra] clod

terror *nm* terror; CINE horror

terrorismo *nm* terrorism

terrorista *adj & nmf* terrorist

tertulia *nf* get-together; **tertulia literaria** literary gathering

tertuliar *vi Am* to get-together to discuss politics, the arts, etc

tesis *nf inv* thesis; [opinión] view, theory

tesoro *nm* **a)** treasure **b)** [erario] exchequer; **Tesoro Público** Treasury

test [test] *(pl* **tests)** *nm* test

testamento *nm* **a)** JUR will; **hacer** *o* **otorgar testamento** to make *o* draw up one's will **b)** REL Testament

testarudo, -a *adj* stubborn, obstinate

testear *vt CSur* to test

testículo *nm* testicle

testigo 1. *nmf* witness; JUR **testigo de cargo** /**descargo** witness for the prosecution /defence; JUR **testigo ocular** /**presencial** eyewitness; REL **Testigos de Jehová** Jehovah's Witnesses **2.** *nm* DEP baton

testimonio *nm* JUR testimony; [prueba] evidence, proof

teta *nf Fam* **a)** tit, boob; **niño de teta** breast-feeding baby **b)** [de vaca] udder

tetera *nf* teapot

tetero *nm Col, Ven* [biberón] baby's bottle

tetrabrik® (*pl* **tetrabriks**) *nm* tetrabrik®; **un tetrabrik® de leche** a carton of milk

textil *adj* & *nm* textile

texto *nm* text; **libro de texto** textbook

textura *nf* TEXT texture; [en minerales] structure

ti *pron pers* you; **es para ti** it's for you; **hazlo por ti** do it for your own sake; **piensas demasiado en ti mismo** you think too much about yourself

tianguis *nm inv CAm, Méx* open-air market

tibia *nf* shinbone, tibia

tibio, -a *adj* tepid, lukewarm; *Fam* **ponerse tibio de cerveza** to get pissed

tiburón *nm* shark

TIC *nfpl* INFORM (*abr de* **Tecnologías de Información y Comunicación**) ICT (*Information and Communications Technology*)

ticket (*pl* **tickets**) *nm* [billete] ticket; [recibo] receipt

tico, -a *adj* & *nm, f Am Fam* Costa Rican

tiempo *nm* **a)** time; **tiempo libre** free time; **a tiempo** in time; **a su (debido) tiempo** in due course; **a un tiempo, al mismo tiempo** at the same time;

al poco tiempo soon afterwards; **antes de tiempo** (too) early *o* soon; **con el tiempo** in the course of time, with time; **¿cuánto tiempo?** how long?; **¿cuánto tiempo hace?** how long ago?; **demasiado tiempo** too long; **en tiempos de Maricastaña** back in the good old days; **estar a tiempo de** to still have time to; **hacer tiempo** to kill time; **matar el tiempo** to kill time; **¿nos da tiempo de llegar?** have we got (enough) time to get there?

b) [meteorológico] weather; **¿qué tiempo hace?** what's the weather like?; **hace buen** /**mal tiempo** the weather is good /bad

c) [edad] age; **¿cuánto** *o* **qué tiempo tiene tu niño?** how old is your baby / child?

d) MÚS movement

e) DEP half

f) LING tense

tienda *nf* **a)** shop, store; *CAm, Andes, Méx* **tienda de abarrotes** grocery, grocer's; **tienda libre de impuestos** *Br* duty-free shop, *US* duty-free store; **ir de tiendas** to go shopping **b)** **tienda (de campaña)** tent

tierno, -a *adj* **a)** [blando] tender, soft **b)** [reciente] fresh

tierra *nf* **a)** [planeta] earth **b)** AGRIC land, soil **c)** [continente] land; **tocar tierra** to land **d)** [país] country; **tierra de nadie** no-man's-land **e)** [suelo] ground; *Fig* **echar** *o* **tirar por tierra** to spoil **f)** ELEC **(toma de) tierra** *Br* earth, *US* ground

tierral *nm Am* [polvareda] dust cloud

tieso, -a *adj* [rígido] stiff, rigid; [erguido] upright, erect

tiesto *nm* flowerpot

tigre *nm* **a)** tiger **b)** *Am* [jaguar] jaguar

tijeras *nfpl* (pair of) scissors

tila *nf* [flor] lime *o* linden blossom; [infusión] lime *o* linden blossom tea

tilde *nf* written accent

tilma *nf Méx* woollen blanket

tilo *nm* a) BOT [árbol] lime o linden (tree) b) *CSur* [infusión] lime o linden blossom tea

timbal *nm* kettledrum

timbrar 1. *vt* to stamp 2. *vi CAm, Andes, Méx* [llamar] to ring the bell

timbre *nm* a) [de la puerta] bell b) [sello] stamp, seal; FIN fiscal o revenue stamp c) MÚS [sonido] timbre

tímido, -a *adj* shy, timid; *Fig* [mejoría] light; [intento] cautious

timo *nm* swindle, fiddle; **es un timo** it's a rip-off

timón *nm* a) [de barco - palanca] tiller, helm; [rueda] wheel, helm; [pieza articulada] rudder; **estar al timón** to be at the helm b) *Andes, Cuba* [de vehículo] steering wheel

tímpano *nm* ANAT eardrum

tina *nf* a) [tinaja] pitcher b) [gran cuba] vat c) *CAm, Col, Méx* [bañera] bathtub

tino *nm* a) [puntería] (good) aim; **tener buen tino** to be a good shot b) [tacto] (common) sense, good judgement

tinta *nf* a) ink; **tinta china** Indian ink; **tinta simpática** invisible ink b) *Fig* **medias tintas** ambiguities, half-measures

tintero *nm* inkpot, inkwell; *Fig* **se quedó en el tintero** it wasn't said

tinto 1. *adj* [vino] red 2. *nm* a) [vino] red wine b) *Col, Ven* [café] black coffee

tintorería *nf* dry-cleaner's

tío *nm* a) [pariente] uncle; **mis tíos** my uncle and aunt b) *Esp Fam* guy, *Br* bloke

tiovivo *nm* merry-go-round, *US* carousel

tipear *Am* 1. *vt* to type 2. *vi* to type

típico, -a *adj* a) typical; **eso es típico de Antonio** that's just like Antonio b) [baile, traje] traditional

tipo *nm* a) [clase] type, kind b) *Fam* [persona] guy, *Br* bloke; **tipo raro** weirdo c) ANAT [de hombre] build, physique; [de mujer] figure d) FIN rate; **tipo de cambio/interés** rate of exchange/interest e) **el político tipo de la izquierda** the typical left-wing politician

tipografía *nf* typography

tira *nf* a) [banda, cinta] strip b) [de dibujos] comic strip c) *Fam* **la tira de gente** a lot o loads of people d) *Méx Fam* **la tira** [la policía] the law, *US* the heat e) **tira y afloja** tug of war

tirabuzón *nm* ringlet

tirada *nf* a) [lanzamiento] throw b) [impresión] print run

tirador *nm* a) [persona] marksman b) [pomo] knob, handle; [cordón] bell pull c) [tirachinas] *Br* catapult, *US* slingshot

tiraje *nm Am* print run

tiranía *nf* tyranny

tirano, -a *nm, f* tyrant

tirante 1. *adj* [cable etc] tight, taut; [situación, relación] tense 2. *nm* a) [de vestido etc] strap; **tirantes** *Br* braces, *US* suspenders b) TÉC brace, stay

tirar 1. *vt* a) [echar] to throw b) [dejar caer] to drop c) [desechar] to throw away; *Fig* [dinero] to squander d) [derribar] to knock down; **tirar la puerta (abajo)** to smash the door in e) [beso] to blow 2. *vi* **tirar de** [cuerda, puerta] to pull b) [chimenea, estufa] to draw c) [funcionar] to work, to run d) **ir tirando** to get by e) **tirar a** to tend towards; **tira a rojo** it's reddish f) **tira a la izquierda** turn left; **¡venga, tira ya!** come on, get going! g) [disparar] to shoot, to fire 3. **tirarse** *vpr* a) [lanzarse] to throw o hurl oneself; **tirarse de cabeza al agua** to dive into the water b) [tumbarse] to lie down c) *Fam* [tiempo] to spend; **me tiré una hora esperando** I waited (for) a good hour d) *Vulg* **tirarse a algn** to lay sb

tirita *nf Br* (sticking) plaster, *US* Band-aid®

tiritar *vi* to shiver, to shake

tiro *nm* a) [lanzamiento] throw b) [disparo, ruido] shot; FÚT **tiro a gol** shot at goal; **tiro al blanco** target shooting;

tiro al plato clay pigeon shooting; **tiro con arco** archery **c)** [de vestido] shoulder width **d)** [de chimenea] draught; **animal de tiro** draught animal

tirón *nm* pull, tug; [del bolso] snatch; *Fam* **de un tirón** in one go

tisú *nm* tissue, paper hankie

títere *nm* [marioneta] puppet; **no dejar títere con cabeza** to spare no one

titular¹ 1. *nmf* [persona] holder **2.** *nm* PRENSA headline **3.** *adj* appointed, official

titular² 1. *vt* [poner título] to call **2. titularse** *vpr* **a)** [película etc] to be called; **¿cómo se titula?** what is it called? **b)** EDUC to graduate (**en** in)

título *nm* **a)** title **b)** EDUC degree; [diploma] diploma **c)** PRENSA [titular] headline **d) a título de ejemplo** by way of example

tiza *nf* chalk; **una tiza** a piece of chalk

tlapalería *nf Méx* ironmonger's (shop)

toalla *nf* towel; *Am* **toalla higiénica** *Br* sanitary towel, *US* sanitary napkin; **tirar la toalla** to throw in the towel

toallita *nf* (wet-)wipe

tobillo *nm* ankle

tobogán *nm* slide, chute

tocadiscos *nm inv* record player; **tocadiscos digital** *o* **compacto** CD player

tocador *nm* **a)** [mueble] dressing table **b)** [habitación] dressing room; **tocador de señoras** powder room

tocar [44] **1.** *vt* **a)** [objeto, persona] to touch **b)** [instrumento, canción] to play; [timbre, campana] to ring; [bocina] to blow **c)** [tema, asunto] to touch on **d)** [afectar] to concern; **por lo que a mí me toca** as far as I am concerned **2.** *vi* **a)** **¿a quién le toca?** [en juegos] whose turn is it? **b) me tocó el gordo** [en rifa] I won the jackpot **c)** *Fig* **tocar a su fin** to be coming to an end

d) [llamar] **tocar a la puerta** to knock on the door **3. tocarse** *vpr* [una cosa con otra] to touch each other

tocino *nm* lard; **tocino ahumado** smoked bacon; **tocino de cielo** *sweet made with egg yolk*

tocuyo *nm Andes, Arg* coarse cotton cloth

todavía *adv* **a)** [aún] still; [en negativas] yet; **todavía la quiere** he still loves her; **todavía no** not yet; **no mires todavía** don't look yet **b)** [para reforzar] even, still; **todavía más/menos** even more/less

todo, -a 1. *adj* **a)** all; **todo el pan** all the bread; **todo el mundo** (absolutely) everybody; **todo el día** all day, the whole *o* entire day **b)** [cada] every; **todo ciudadano de más de dieciocho años** every citizen over eighteen years of age **c)** [entero] complete, thorough; **es toda una mujer** she is every inch a woman **d) todos** all; [con expresiones de tiempo] every; **todos los niños** all the children; **todos los martes** every Tuesday **2.** *nm* [totalidad] whole **3.** *pron* **a)** [sin excluir nada] all, everything; **ante todo** first of all; **del todo** completely; **después de todo** after all; **eso es todo** that's all, that's it; **estar en todo** to be really with it; **hay de todo** there are all sorts; **lo sé todo** I know all about it; **todo lo contrario** quite the contrary *o* opposite **b)** [cualquiera] anybody; **todo aquél** *o* **el que quiera** anybody who wants (to) **c)** [cada uno] **todos aprobamos** we all passed; **todos fueron** they all went **4.** *adv* completely, totally; **volvió todo sucio** he was all dirty when he got back

todoterreno *adj inv & nm* [vehículo] four-by-four

toga *nf* **a)** gown, robe **b)** HIST toga

toldo *nm* [cubierta] awning

tolerancia *nf* tolerance

tolerante *adj* tolerant

torcer

tolerar *vt* to tolerate; [situación] to stand; [gente] to put up with

tolteca *adj & nmf* Toltec

toma *nf* **a)** [acción] taking; ELEC **toma de corriente** power point, socket **b)** MED dose **c)** MIL capture **d)** CINE take, shot **e) toma de posesión** swearing-in **f)** *Fam & Fig* **toma y daca** give and take

tomacorriente *nm Am* socket

tomado, -a *adj* **a)** [voz] hoarse **b)** *Am Fam* [persona] tight, tanked up **c) tenerla tomada con algn** to have it in for sb

tomar 1. *vt* **a)** [coger] to take; [autobús, tren] to catch; [decisión] to make, take; **toma** here (you are); **tomar el sol** to sunbathe; AVIACIÓN **tomar tierra** to land; *Fam* **tomarla con algn** to have it in for sb

b) [comer, beber] to have

c) tomar algo a mal to take sth badly; **tomar en serio / broma** to take seriously / as a joke

d) [confundir] to take (**por** for)

e) MIL to take

2. *vi Am* [beber alcohol] to drink

3. **tomarse** *vpr* **a)** [comer] to eat; [beber] to drink; **tomarse una cerveza** to have a beer

b) *Fam* **no te lo tomes así** don't take it like that

tomate *nm* tomato; **salsa de tomate** [de lata] tomato sauce; [de botella] ketchup

tómbola *nf* tombola

tomillo *nm* thyme

tomo *nm* volume; *Fam* **de tomo y lomo** utter, out-and-out

tonada *nf* **a)** MÚS tune, song **b)** *Am* [acento] (regional) accent

tonel *nm* barrel, cask

tonelada *nf* ton; **tonelada métrica** tonne

tongo *nm* fix

tónico, -a 1. *nm* MED tonic; [cosmético] skin tonic 2. *adj* **a)** LING tonic, stressed **b)** MÚS & MED tonic ■ **tónica** *nf* **a)** [tendencia] tendency, trend; **tónica general** overall trend **b)** [bebida] tonic (water) **c)** MÚS tonic

tono *nm* tone; **a tono con** in tune o harmony with; **subir de tono** o **el tono** to speak louder; **un tono alto / bajo** a high / low pitch; *Fig* **darse tono** to put on airs; *Fig* **fuera de tono** inappropriate, out of place; **dar el tono** to set the tone

tontería *nf* **a)** stupidity, silliness **b)** [dicho, hecho] silly o stupid thing **c)** [insignificancia] trifle

tonto, -a 1. *adj* silly, dumb 2. *nm, f* fool, idiot; **tonto de remate** o **de capirote** prize idiot

topadora *nf RP* bulldozer

tope 1. *nm* **a)** [límite] limit, end; *Fam* **a tope** [al máximo] flat out; *Fig* **estar hasta los topes** to be full up; **fecha tope** deadline **b)** TÉC stop, check **c)** FERRO buffer 2. *adv Fam* incredibly; **tope difícil** really difficult

tópico, -a 1. *nm* cliché 2. *adj* MED & FARM for external use

top manta ['top 'manta] *nm Fam* illegal selling of goods, especially pirate CDs and DVDs

topo *nm* mole

toque *nm* **a)** ring; **toque de difuntos** death knell; **toque de queda** curfew **b)** [matiz] touch; **dar los últimos toques a algo** to add the final touches to sth **c)** [aviso] **dar un toque a algn** *Fam* [llamar] to call for sb; [por teléfono] to call sb, to give sb a call; [amonestar] to warn sb

tórax *nm* thorax

torbellino *nm* **a)** [de viento] whirlwind **b)** *Fig* [confusión] whirl, turmoil

torcer [41] 1. *vt* **a)** [metal] to bend; [cuerda, hilo] to twist; MED to sprain; *Fig* [esquina] to turn

b) [inclinar] to slant

2. *vi* to turn (left o right)

3. **torcerse** *vpr* **a)** [doblarse] to twist, to bend

b) MED **se me torció el tobillo** I sprained my ankle

c) [plan] to fall through
d) [desviarse] to go off to the side

torcido, -a *adj* twisted ; [ladeado] slanted, lopsided ; [corbata] crooked

tordo, -a 1. *adj* dapple-grey **2.** *nm* ORNIT thrush

torear 1. *vt* to fight ; *Fam* **torear a algn** to tease *o* confuse sb ; *Fam* **torear un asunto** to tackle a matter skilfully **2.** *vi* to fight

torera *nf* [prenda] bolero (jacket)

torero, -a *nm, f* bullfighter

tormenta *nf* storm

tormentoso, -a *adj* stormy

torneo *nm* **a)** DEP tournament, *US* tourney **b)** HIST tourney, joust

tornillo *nm* screw

torniquete *nm* **a)** turnstile **b)** MED tourniquet

toro *nm* bull ; **¿te gustan los toros?** do you like bullfighting?

torpe *adj* **a)** [sin habilidad] clumsy **b)** [tonto] dim, thick **c)** [movimiento] slow, awkward

torpedo *nm* torpedo

torpeza *nf* **a)** [física] clumsiness ; [mental] dimness, stupidity **b)** [lentitud] slowness, heaviness **c)** [error] blunder

torre *nf* **a)** tower **b)** MIL & NÁUT turret **c)** [en ajedrez] rook, castle

torrente *nm* **a)** [de agua] torrent **b)** *Fig* **torrente de voz** strong *o* powerful voice

torrija *nf* French toast

torta *nf* **a)** CULIN [de harina] *flat, round plain cake* ; *CSur, Ven* [dulce] cake ; *Andes, CAm, Carib, RP* [salada] pie ; *Méx* [sandwich] filled roll **b)** *Fam* [golpe] slap, punch

tortazo *nm Fam* **a)** [bofetada] slap, punch **b)** [golpe] whack, thump

tortería *nf Méx* sandwich shop

tortilla *nf* **a)** [de huevo] omelette ; **tortilla española** Spanish *o* potato omelette ; **tortilla francesa** French *o* plain omelette **b)** [de maíz] tortilla *(thin maize pancake)*

tortita *nf* pancake

tórtola *nf* dove

tortuga *nf* [de tierra] tortoise, *US* turtle ; [de mar] turtle

torturar *vt* to torture

tos *nf* cough ; **tos ferina** whooping cough

toser *vi* to cough

tostada *nf* **a)** [de pan] (slice of) toast **b)** *Méx* [de tortilla] tostada *(deep-fried Mexican tortilla with a topping of mince, beans and vegetables)*

tostado, -a *adj* [pan] toasted ; [color] tan ; [tez] tanned

tostador *nm* toaster

tostar [2] *vt* [pan] to toast ; [café] to roast ; [carne, pescado] to brown ; *Fig* [la piel] to tan

total 1. *adj* [completo] total **2.** *nm* **a)** [todo] whole ; **en total** in all **b)** MAT total **3.** *adv* so, in short ; **¿total para qué?** what's the point anyhow? ; *Fam* **total que …** so …; **total, tampoco te hará caso** he won't listen to you anyway

totalidad *nf* whole, totality ; **la totalidad de** all of ; **en su totalidad** as a whole

totuma *nf Am* squash

tóxico, -a 1. *adj* toxic, poisonous **2.** *nm* poison

toxicomanía *nf* drug addiction

toxicómano, -a 1. *adj* MED addicted to drugs **2.** *nm, f* MED drug addict

tp SMS *written abbr of* **tampoco**

tq SMS *written abbr of* **te quiero**

tqi SMS *written abbr of* **tengo que irme**

trabajador, -a 1. *nm, f* worker, labourer **2.** *adj* hard-working

trabajar 1. *vi* to work ; **trabaja mucho** he works hard ; **trabajar de camarera** to work as a waitress **2.** *vt* **a)** to work (on) ; [la tierra] to till **b)** [asignatura etc] to work on **c)** *Fam* [convencer] to (try to) persuade

trabajo *nm* **a)** [ocupación] work ; **trabajo a destajo** piecework ; **trabajo eventual** casual labour ; **trabajos ma-**

nuales arts and crafts **b)** [empleo] employment, job **c)** [tarea] task, job **d)** EDUC [redacción] report, paper **e)** [esfuerzo] effort; **cuesta trabajo creerlo** it's hard to believe

trabalenguas nm inv tongue twister

trabar 1. vt **a)** [sujetar] to tie (up); [unir] to join **b)** [iniciar - lucha, conversación] to start; **trabar amistad con** to strike up a friendship with, to become friends with **c)** [obstaculizar] to hold back **2. trabarse** vpr [enredarse] to become involved, to get mixed up, to get in a muddle; **se le trabó la lengua** he got tongue-tied

traca nf string of firecrackers

tractor nm tractor

tradición nf tradition

tradicional adj traditional

traducción nf translation; **traducción directa / inversa** translation from / into a foreign language

traducir [10] **1.** vt to translate (**a** into) **2. traducirse** vpr Fig to result (**en** in)

traductor, -a nm, f translator

traer [25] **1.** vt **a)** to bring; **trae** give it to me **b)** [llevar puesto] to wear **c)** [llevar consigo] to carry **d)** [problemas] to cause; **traerá como consecuencia ...** it will result in ... **2. traerse** vpr [llevar consigo] to bring along; Fig **¿qué se trae entre manos?** what is he up to?

traficante nmf [de drogas etc] trafficker, pusher

traficar [44] vi [ilegalmente] to traffic (**con** in)

tráfico nm **a)** AUTO traffic; **tráfico rodado** road traffic **b)** COM traffic, trade; **tráfico de drogas** drug traffic

tragar [42] **1.** vt **a)** [ingerir] to swallow **b)** Fam [engullir] to gobble up, to tuck away **c)** Fig [a una persona] to stand, to stomach **d)** Fig [creer] to believe, to swallow **2. tragarse** vpr **a)** [ingerir] to swallow **b)** Fig [creer] to believe, to swallow

tragedia nf tragedy

trágico, -a adj tragic

tragicomedia nf tragicomedy

trago nm **a)** [bebida] swig; **de un trago** in one go **b)** Fig **pasar un mal trago** to have a bad time of it

traición nf treason, betrayal; **a traición** treacherously; **alta traición** high treason

traje[1] nm **a)** [de hombre] suit; **traje de baño** swimming costume, bathing suit o Br costume; **traje de paisano** civilian clothes; **traje de luces** bullfighter's costume **b)** [de mujer] dress; **traje de chaqueta** two-piece suit; **traje de novia** wedding dress

traje[2] pt indef de traer

trama nf **a)** TEXT weft, woof **b)** LITER plot

tramar vt to plot, to cook up; **¿qué tramas?** what are you up to?

tramitar vt **a)** [gestionar] to take the necessary (legal) steps to obtain **b)** Formal [despachar] to convey, to transmit **c)** COM, JUR & FIN to carry out, to process

tramo nm [de carretera] section, stretch; [de escalera] flight

tramontana nf north wind

tramoya nf [maquinaria] stage machinery; [trama] plot, scheme

trampa nf **a)** [de caza] trap, snare **b)** [puerta] trapdoor **c)** [engaño] fiddle; **hacer trampa(s)** to cheat **d)** [truco] trick

trampolín nm **a)** [de piscina] diving board **b)** [de esquí] ski jump

trancar 1. vt [asegurar - con cerrojo] to bolt; [con tranca] to bar **2. trancarse** vpr Am [atascarse] to get stuck; **la llave se trancó en la cerradura** the key got stuck in the lock

trance nm **a)** [coyuntura] (critical) moment; **estar en trance de ...** to be on the point of ... **b)** [éxtasis] trance

tranquilidad nf calmness, tranquillity; **con tranquilidad** calmly; **pídemelo con toda tranquilidad** don't hesitate to ask me

tranquilo, -a adj **a)** [persona, lugar] calm; [agua] still; [conciencia] clear; Fam **tú tranquilo** don't you worry **b)** [despreocupado] placid, easy-going

transar *Fam vi* **a)** *Am* [transigir] to compromise, to give in **b)** *Am* [negociar] to come to an arrangement, to reach a compromise **c)** *RP* [droga] to deal

transbordador *nm* (car) ferry; **transbordador espacial** space shuttle

transbordar 1. *vt* to transfer; NÁUT [mercancías] to tranship **2.** *vi* FERROC to change trains, *US* to transfer

transbordo *nm* **a)** FERROC change, *US* transfer; **hacer transbordo** to change, *US* to transfer **b)** NÁUT transhipment

transcurrir *vi* **a)** [tiempo] to pass, to go by **b)** [acontecer] to take place

transeúnte *nmf* **a)** [peatón] passer-by **b)** [residente temporal] temporary resident

transferencia *nf* transference; FIN transfer; **transferencia bancaria** banker's order

transformación *nf* transformation

transformador *nm* ELEC transformer

transformar 1. *vt* to transform, to change **2. transformarse** *vpr* to change, to turn (**en** into); [algo plegable] to convert

transfusión *nf* transfusion

transición *nf* transition

transigir [57] *vi* to compromise

transistor *nm* transistor

tránsito *nm* **a)** AUTO traffic **b)** [movimiento] movement, passage; **pasajeros en tránsito** passengers in transit

translúcido, -a = **traslúcido**

transmisor, -a 1. *adj* [aparato] transmitting; **estación transmisora** transmitter **2.** *nm* RADIO transmitter

transmitir *vt* **a)** to transmit, to pass on **b)** RADIO & TV to transmit, to broadcast **c)** JUR to transfer, to hand down

transparente 1. *adj* transparent; POL open **2.** *nm* **a)** [visillo] net curtain **b)** [pantalla] shade, blind

transportar *vt* to transport; [pasajeros] to carry; [mercancías] to ship

transporte *nm* **a)** transport, *US* transportation **b)** COM freight; **transporte de mercancías** freight transport; **transporte marítimo** shipment

transportista *nmf* haulage contractor

transversal *adj* transverse, cross

tranvía *nm* *Br* tram, *US* streetcar

trapecio *nm* trapeze

trapecista *nmf* trapeze artist

trapo *nm* **a)** [viejo, roto] rag **b)** [bayeta] cloth; *Fam* **poner a algn como un trapo** to tear sb to pieces; **trapo de cocina** *Br* tea towel, *US* dish towel; **trapo del polvo** dust cloth, *Br* duster

tráquea *nf* trachea, windpipe

tras *prep* **a)** [después de] after; **uno tras otro** one after the other **b)** [detrás] behind; **sentados uno tras otro** sitting one behind the other **c)** **andar / ir tras** to be after; **la policía iba tras ella** the police were after her

trasero, -a 1. *adj* back, rear; **en la parte trasera** at the back **2.** *nm* *Euf* backside

trasladar 1. *vt* [cosa] to move; [persona] to move, to transfer **2. trasladarse** *vpr* to go, to move

traslado *nm* [de casa] move, removal; [de personal] transfer; EDUC **traslado de expediente** transfer of student record

traslúcido, -a *adj* translucent

trasnochar *vi* **a)** [acostarse tarde] to stay up later **b)** [no dormir] to stay up all night, to pull an all-nighter

traspasar *vt* **a)** [atravesar] to go through; [río] to cross **b)** [negocio, local] to transfer; **se traspasa** [en letrero] for sale **c)** *Fig* [exceder] to exceed, to go beyond

traspié *nm* stumble, trip; **dar un traspié** to trip

trasplantar *vt* to transplant

trasplante *nm* transplant; **trasplante de corazón** heart transplant

traste¹ *nm* MÚS fret

traste² *nm* **a)** *Am salvo RP* [utensilio de cocina] cooking utensil ; **fregar los trastes** to wash the dishes **b)** *CSur Fam* [trasero] bottom, *US* tush **c)** *Fig* **dar al traste (con un plan)** to spoil (a plan) ; **irse al traste** to fall through

trasto *nm* [objeto cualquiera] thing ; [cosa inservible] piece of junk

tratado *nm* **a)** [pacto] treaty **b)** [estudio] treatise

tratamiento *nm* **a)** treatment **b)** TÉC processing, treatment **c)** INFORM processing ; **tratamiento de textos** word processing

tratar **1.** *vt* **a)** [atender] to treat ; **tratar bien/mal** to treat well / badly
b) MED to treat
c) [asunto] to discuss
d) INFORM & TÉC to process
e) **me trata de tú** he addresses me as "tú"
2. *vi* **a)** **tratar de** [intentar] to try
b) **tratar de** o **sobre** o **acerca** to be about ; **¿de qué trata?** what is it about?
c) **tratar con** [tener tratos] to deal with ; [negociar] to negotiate with ; [relacionarse] to move among
3. **tratarse** *vpr* **a)** [relacionarse] to be on speaking terms
b) **se trata de** [es cuestión de] it's a question of ; **se trata de un caso excepcional** it's an exceptional case

tratativas *nfpl CSur* negotiation

trato *nm* **a)** [de personas] manner ; [contacto] contact ; **malos tratos** ill-treatment **b)** [acuerdo] agreement ; **¡trato hecho!** it's a deal ! **c)** COM deal

trauma *nm* trauma

traveller ['traβeler] *nm* [cheques] *Br* traveller's cheque, *US* traveler's check

través **1.** *prep* **a)** **a través de** [superficie] across, over ; [agujero etc] through ; **a través del río** across the river ; **a través del agujero** through the hole **b)** *Fig* **a través de** through ; **a través del periódico** through the newspaper **2.** *adv* **de través** [transversalmente] crosswise ; [de lado] sideways

travesaño *nm* FÚT crossbar

travesía *nf* [viaje] crossing

travestí, travesti *(pl* **travestíes** o **travestís)** *nmf* transvestite

travieso, -a *adj* mischievous

trayecto *nm* **a)** [distancia] distance ; [recorrido] route ; [trecho] stretch **b)** [viaje] journey

trayectoria *nf* **a)** [de proyectil, geométrica] trajectory **b)** *Fig* [orientación] line, course

trazado *nm* **a)** [plano] layout, plan **b)** [de carretera, ferrocarril] route

trazar [40] *vt* [línea] to draw ; [plano] to design ; *Fig* [plan] to sketch out

trazo *nm* **a)** [línea] line **b)** [de letra] stroke

trébol *nm* **a)** [trefoil **b)** NAIPES club

trece **1.** *adj inv* thirteen **2.** *nm inv* thirteen ; *Fig* **estar** o **mantenerse** o **seguir en sus trece** to stick to one's guns

tregua *nf* MIL truce ; *Fig* respite

treinta *adj & nm inv* thirty

trekking ['trekin] *nm* trekking

tremendo, -a *adj* **a)** [terrible] terrible, dreadful **b)** [muy grande] enormous ; *Fig* tremendous

tren *nm* **a)** train **b)** AVIACIÓN **tren de aterrizaje** undercarriage ; **tren de lavado** car wash **c)** **tren de vida** lifestyle

trenza *nf* [de pelo] plait, *esp US* braid

trepar *vt & vi* to climb

tres **1.** *adj inv* [cardinal] three ; [ordinal] third ; *Fam* **de tres al cuarto** cheap, of little value ; *Fig* **ni a la de tres** not for the life of me **2.** *nm* three ; **tres en raya** *Br* noughts and crosses, *US* tick-tack-toe

tresillo *nm* **a)** [mueble] (three-piece) suite **b)** MÚS triplet

trial *nm* DEP trial

triangular *adj* triangular

triángulo *nm* triangle ; *Fig* **triángulo amoroso** eternal triangle

tribu *nf* tribe

tribuna *nf* **a)** [plataforma] rostrum, dais ; **tribuna de (la) prensa** press box **b)** DEP stand

tribunal *nm* **a)** JUR court; **tribunal de apelación** court of appeal; **el Tribunal Supremo** ≃ *Br* the High Court, ≃ *US* the Supreme Court **b)** [de examen] board of examiners

triciclo *nm* tricycle

trigo *nm* wheat

trigueño, -a *adj Am* [pelo] light brown, corn-coloured; [persona] light brown-skinned

trilladora *nf* threshing machine; **trilladora segadora** combine harvester

trillar *vt* to thresh

trillizo, -a *nm, f* triplet

trimestral *adj* quarterly, three-monthly

trimestre *nm* quarter; EDUC term

trineo *nm* sledge, sleigh

trío *nm* trio

tripa *nf* **a)** [intestino] gut, intestine; *Esp Fam* tummy; **dolor de tripa** stomach ache **b)** **tripas** innards

triple *adj & nm* triple

trípode *nm* tripod

tripulación *nf* crew

tripulante *nmf* crew member

trisomía *nf* trisomy; **trisomía 21** trisomy 21

triste *adj* **a)** [persona, situación] sad **b)** [lugar] gloomy

tristeza *nf* sadness

triturar *vt* [machacar] to grind (up)

triunfal *adj* triumphant

triunfalista *adj & nmf* triumphalist

triunfar *vi* to triumph

triunfo *nm* **a)** [victoria] triumph, victory; DEP win **b)** [éxito] success

trivial *adj* trivial

triza *nf* bit, fragment; **hacer trizas** to tear to shreds

trocar [64] *vt* **a)** [transformar] **trocar algo (en algo)** to change sth (into sth) **b)** [intercambiar] to swap, to exchange

trocha *nf Am* path

trofeo *nm* trophy

trombón *nm* trombone

trombosis *nf inv* thrombosis

tromba *nf* **a)** MÚS horn **b)** [de elefante] trunk **c)** ANAT tube **d)** *Fam* **estar tromba** to be sloshed o plastered

trompazo *nm Fam* bump; **darse** o **pegarse un trompazo** to have a bump

trompear 1. *vt Am Fam* to thump **2. trompearse** *vpr Am Fam* to have a fight

trompeta *nf* trumpet

trona *nf* [silla] highchair

tronar [2] **1.** *vi* to thunder **2.** *vt Méx Fam* **a)** [destruir, acabar con] to get rid of; **este remedio es para tronar anginas** this remedy will clear up tonsillitis **b)** [suspender] to fail

tronco *nm* **a)** ANAT trunk, torso **b)** BOT [de árbol] trunk; [leño] log; *Fam & Fig* **dormir como un tronco** to sleep like a log

trono *nm* throne

tropa *nf* **a)** squad **b)** **tropas** troops

tropero *nm Am* cattle herder

tropezar [1] *vi* **a)** to trip, to stumble (**con** on) **b)** **tropezar con algo** to come across sth; **tropezar con algn / dificultades** to run into sb / difficulties

tropezón *nm* **a)** [traspié] trip, stumble; **dar un tropezón** to trip **b)** [error] slip-up, faux pas **c)** [de comida] chunk of meat

tropical *adj* tropical

trópico *nm* tropic

tropiezo 1. *nm* **a)** [obstáculo] trip **b)** *Fig* [error] blunder, faux pas **2.** *indic pres de* **tropezar**

trotar *vi* to trot

trote *nm* **a)** trot; **al trote** at a trot **b)** *Fam* **ya no está para esos trotes** he cannot keep up the pace any more

trozar *vt Am* [carne] to cut up; [res, tronco] to butcher, to cut up

trozo *nm* piece

trucado, -a *adj* [cuentas] rigged; [fotos] retouched

trucar [44] *vt* [una fotografía] to touch up; [las cuentas] to rig; [motor, mecanismo] to soup up

trucha *nf* trout

truco *nm* **a)** [ardid] trick; **aquí hay truco** there's something fishy going on here **b) coger el truco (a algo)** to get the knack o hang (of sth)

trueno *nm* thunder; **un trueno** a thunderclap

trueque *nm* swap

trufa *nf* truffle

trusa *nf* **a)** *Carib* [traje de baño] swimsuit **b)** *Perú* [short] briefs **c)** *RP* [faja] girdle

tu *(pl* **tus)** *adj poses* your; **tu libro** your book; **tus libros** your books

tú *pron* you; **de tú a tú** on equal terms

Usually omitted in Spanish except for emphasis or contrast.

tuberculosis *nf inv* tuberculosis

tubería *nf* **a)** [de agua] piping, pipes **b)** [de gas] pipeline

tubo *nm* **a)** tube; **tubo de ensayo** test tube **b)** [tubería] pipe; *AUTO* **tubo de escape** exhaust (pipe)

tuerca *nf* nut

tuerto, -a 1. *adj* one-eyed, blind in one eye **2.** *nm, f* one-eyed person

tul *nm* tulle

tulipán *nm* tulip

tullido, -a *adj* crippled, disabled

tumba *nf* grave, tomb

tumbado, -a *adj* **a)** [recostado] lying down **b)** [derribado] knocked over

tumbar 1. *vt* to knock down o over **2. tumbarse** *vpr* [acostarse] to lie down, to stretch out

tumbona *nf Br* sun-lounger, *US* (beach) recliner

tumor *nm* tumour

tumulto *nm* tumult, commotion

tuna *nf* **a)** [agrupación musical] *group of student minstrels* **b)** *Am* [higo chumbo] prickly pear

túnel *nm* tunnel; **el túnel del Canal de la Mancha** the Channel Tunnel

Túnez *n* **a)** [país] Tunisia **b)** [ciudad] Tunis

túnica *nf* tunic

tupido, -a *adj* thick, dense

turbina *nf* turbine

turbio, -a *adj* [agua] cloudy; [negocio etc] shady, dubious

turbulencia *nf* turbulence

turco, -a 1. *adj* Turkish **2.** *nm, f* [persona] Turk; *Fig* **cabeza de turco** scapegoat **3.** *nm* [idioma] Turkish

turismo *nm* **a)** tourism; **ir de turismo** to go touring; **turismo rural** rural tourism **b)** *AUTO* car

turista *nmf* tourist

turístico, -a *adj* tourist; **de interés turístico** of interest to tourists

túrmix® *nf inv* blender, liquidizer

turno *nm* **a)** [en juegos etc] turn, go **b)** [de trabajo] shift; **estar de turno** to be on duty; **turno de día/noche** day / night shift

Turquía *n* Turkey

turrón *nm* nougat

tute *nm Fam* **darse o pegarse un (buen) tute** to slog one's guts out

tutear 1. *vt* to address as "tú" **2. tutearse** *vpr* to address each other as "tú"

tutor *nm* **a)** *JUR* guardian **b)** *EDUC* tutor

tuyo, -a 1. *adj poses* [con personas] of yours; [con objetos] one of your; **¿es amigo tuyo?** is he a friend of yours?; **unas amigas tuyas** some friends of yours; **un libro tuyo** one of your books **2.** *pron poses* yours; **éste es tuyo** this one is yours; *Fam* **los tuyos** [familiares] your family

TV *nf (abr de* **televisión***)* TV

u *conj* or; *ver* **o**

ubicación *nf Am* location

ubicar [44] **1.** *vt* **a)** [situar - edificio, fábrica] to locate
b) *Am* [colocar] to put
c) *Am* [encontrar] to find, to locate; **no veo su ficha por acá, pero en cuanto la ubique le aviso** I can't see your card here, but as soon as I find it I'll let you know
2. ubicarse *vpr* **a)** [edificio] to be situated o located
b) *Am* [persona] to get one's bearings; **¿ya te ubicas en la ciudad?** are you finding your way around the city all right?

UCI ['uθi] *nf (abr de* **unidad de cuidados intensivos)** ICU, intensive care unit

Ud. *(abr de* **usted)** you

Uds. *(abr de* **ustedes)** you

UE *nf (abr de* **Unión Europea)** EU

újule *interj Am* ¡újule! wow!

úlcera *nf* ulcer

ultimador, -a *nm, f Am* murderer, killer

ultimar *vt* **a)** [terminar] to finalize
b) *Am* [asesinar] to kill

último, -a 1. *adj* **a)** last; **el último día** the last day; **por último** finally **b)** [más reciente] latest; **últimas noticias** latest news **c)** [más alto] top; **el último piso** the top flat **d)** [más bajo] lowest **e)** [más lejano] back, last; **la última fila** the back row **f)** [definitivo] final **2.** *nm, f* **llegar el último** to arrive last; **a últimos de mes** at the end of the month; **en las** últimas on one's last legs; *Fam* **a la última** up to the minute; **el último de la lista** the lowest in the list

ultramarinos *nmpl* groceries; **tienda de ultramarinos** greengrocer's (shop)

ultravioleta *adj inv* ultraviolet

umbral *nm* threshold

un, -a 1. *art indet* **a)** a; [antes de vocal] an; **un coche** a car; **un huevo** an egg; **una flor** a flower **b)** **unos, -as** some; **unas flores** some flowers **2.** *adj* [delante de *nm sing*] one; **un chico y dos chicas** one boy and two girls; *ver* **uno**

unánime *adj* unanimous

UNED *nf (abr de* **Universidad Nacional de Educación a Distancia)** *Spanish open university*

únicamente *adv* only, solely

único, -a *adj* **a)** [solo] only; **es el único que tengo** it's the only one I've got; **hijo único** only child; **lo único que quiero** the only thing I want; **el Mercado Único** the Single Market; **el Acta Única** the Single European Act **b)** [extraordinario] unique

unicornio *nm* unicorn

unidad *nf* **a)** unit **b)** [cohesión] unity

unido, -a *adj* united; **están muy unidos** they are very attached to one another; **una familia muy unida** a very close family

unifamiliar *adj* **vivienda unifamiliar** detached house

unificación *nf* unification

uniforme 1. *nm* [prenda] uniform **2.** *adj* **a)** [igual] uniform **b)** [superficie] even

unión *nf* union; **la Unión Europea** the European Union

unipersonal *adj* individual

unir 1. *vt* [juntar] to unite, to join (together); **esta carretera une las dos comarcas** this road links both districts **2. unirse** *vpr* [juntarse] to unite, to join

unisex *adj inv* unisex

universal *adj* universal; **historia universal** world history

universidad *nf* university; **universidad a distancia** *distance learning university*; ≃ Open University; **universidad laboral** technical college

universitario, -a 1. *adj* university **2.** *nm, f* university student

universo *nm* universe

---

uno, -a 1. *nm inv* one; **el uno** (number) one; **el uno de mayo** the first of May **2.** *nf* **es la una** [hora] it's one o'clock **3.** *adj* **unos** some; **unas cajas** some boxes; **habrá unos veinte** there must be around twenty **4.** *pron* **a)** one; **uno a uno** one to one; **uno (de ellos)** one of them; **uno tras otro** one after the other; **unos cuantos** a few; **de uno en uno** one by one; **uno a otro** each other; **se miraron el uno al otro** they looked at each other **b)** [persona] someone, somebody; **uno que pasaba por allí** some passer-by; **unos ... otros** some people ... others **c)** [impers] you, one; **uno tiene que ...** you have to ...

---

untar *vt* to grease, to smear; [mantequilla] to spread

uña *nf* **a)** nail; **morderse o comerse las uñas** to bite one's fingernails; *Fig* **ser uña y carne** to be hand in glove **b)** ZOOL [garra] claw; [pezuña] hoof

uralita® *nf* material made of asbestos and cement, usually corrugated and used mainly for roofing

uranio *nm* uranium

urbanización *nf* **a)** [barrio] housing development o estate **b)** [proceso] urbanization

urbano, -a *adj* urban, city; **guardia urbano** (traffic) policeman

urgencia *nf* **a)** urgency **b)** [emergencia] emergency

urgente *adj* urgent; **correo urgente** express mail

urinario *nm* urinal, *US* comfort station

URL *nm o nf* INFORM (*abr de* **uniform resource locator**) URL (*uniform resource locator*)

urna *nf* **a)** POL ballot box **b)** [vasija] urn

urraca *nf* magpie

urticaria *nf* MED hives

Uruguay *n* Uruguay

uruguayo, -a *adj & nm, f* Uruguayan

usado, -a *adj* [ropa] second-hand, used

usar 1. *vt* **a)** to use **b)** [prenda] to wear **2. usarse** *vpr* to be used o in fashion

USB [u 'ese be] *nm* INFORM (*abr de* **universal serial bus**) USB (*universal serial bus*); **memoria USB** USB stick; **puerto USB** USB port

usina *nf Andes, RP* plant; **usina eléctrica** power station, power plant; **usina nuclear** nuclear power station, nuclear power plant

uso *nm* **a)** use; FARM **uso externo/tópico** external/local application **b)** [de poder, privilegio] exercise **c)** [de prenda] wearing; **haga uso del casco** wear a helmet **d)** [costumbre] usage, custom; **al uso** conventional

usted (*pl* **ustedes**) *pron pers Formal* you; **¿quién es usted?, ¿quiénes son ustedes?** who are you?

Usually omitted in Spanish except for emphasis or contrast. Although formal in peninsular Spanish, it is not necessarily so in Latin American Spanish.

usual *adj* usual, common

usuario, -a *nm, f* user

utensilio *nm* utensil; [herramienta] tool

útero *nm* uterus, womb

útil 1. *adj* useful; [día] working **2.** *nm* [herramienta] tool, instrument

utilidad *nf* usefulness, utility; [beneficio] profit

utilitario, -a 1. *adj* utilitarian **2.** *nm* **a)** [coche] utility vehicle **b)** INFORM utility (program)

utilizar [40] *vt* to use, to utilize

uva *nf* grape; **uva blanca** green grape

V

vaca *nf* **a)** cow **b)** [carne] beef

vacacional *adj Br* holiday, vacation

vacaciones *nfpl* holiday, *Br* holidays, *US* vacation; **durante las vacaciones** during the holidays; **estar/irse de vacaciones** to be /go on *Br* holiday *o US* vacation

vacacionista *nmf Am Br* holiday-maker, *US* vacationer

vacante **1.** *adj* vacant **2.** *nf* vacancy

vaciar [29] **1.** *vt* **a)** [recipiente] to empty; [contenido] to empty out **b)** [terreno] to hollow out **c)** ARTE to cast, to mould **2. vaciarse** *vpr* to empty

vacilar *vi* **a)** [dudar] to hesitate; **sin vacilar** without hesitation **b)** [voz] to falter **c)** [luz] to flicker **d)** *Fam* [jactarse] to show off

vacilón, -ona *Fam* **1.** *adj* **a)** [fanfarrón] swanky **b)** *Esp, Carib, Méx* [bromista] jokey, teasing **2.** *nm, f* **a)** [fanfarrón] show-off **b)** *Esp, Carib, Méx* [bromista] tease **3.** *nm CAm, Carib, Méx* [fiesta] party

vacío, -a **1.** *adj* **a)** empty; [hueco] hollow **b)** [sin ocupar] vacant, unoccupied **2.** *nm* **a)** emptiness, void **b)** [hueco] gap; [espacio] (empty) space **c)** FÍS vacuum; **envasado al vacío** vacuum-packed

vacuna *nf* vaccine

vacunación *nf* vaccination

vacunar **1.** *vt* to vaccinate (**contra** against); *Fig* to inure **2. vacunarse** *vpr* to get oneself vaccinated

vado *nm* **a)** [de un río] ford **b)** AUTO **vado permanente** [en letrero] keep clear

vagabundo, -a **1.** *adj* [persona] vagrant; **perro vagabundo** stray dog **2.** *nm, f* [sin casa] tramp, vagrant, *US* bum

vagina *nf* vagina

vago, -a **1.** *adj* **a)** [perezoso] lazy **b)** [indefinido] vague **2.** *nm, f* **a)** [holgazán] layabout **b)** JUR vagrant

vagón *nm* [para pasajeros] carriage, coach, *US* car; [para mercancías] truck, wagon, *US* freight car, *US* boxcar

vagoneta *nf* wagon

vaho *nm* [de aliento] breath; [vapor] vapour

vaina **1.** *nf* **a)** [de espada] sheath, scabbard **b)** BOT pod **c)** *Col, Perú, Ven muy Fam* [persona o cosa molesta] pain (in the neck); **ése es un vaina** he's a pain **2.** *nmf* [persona] dimwit

vainilla *nf* vanilla

vajilla *nf* crockery, dishes; **una vajilla** a set of dishes, a dinner service

vale¹ *interj Esp* all right!, OK!

vale² *nm* **a)** [comprobante] voucher **b)** [pagaré] promissory note, IOU (I owe you) **c)** *Méx, Ven Fam* [amigo] pal, *Br* mate, *US* buddy

valenciano, -a **1.** *adj & nm, f* Valencian **2.** *nm* [idioma] Valencian

valentía *nf* courage, bravery

valer [26] **1.** *vt* **a)** [ser válido] to be worth; **no vale nada** it is worthless; **no vale la pena (ir)** it's not worth-while (going) **b)** [costar] to cost; **¿cuánto vale?** how much is it? **c)** [proporcionar] to earn **2.** *vi* **a)** [servir] to be useful, to be of use **b)** [ser válido] to be valid, to count; **no vale hacer trampa** cheating isn't on **c)** **más vale** it is better; **más vale que te vayas ya** you had better leave now **3. valerse** *vpr* **valerse de** to use, to make use of; **valerse por sí mismo** to be able to manage on one's own

valeriana *nf* valerian, allheal

validación *nf* validation

validar *vt* to validate

validez *nf* validity

válido, -a *adj* valid

valiente *adj* a) [valeroso] brave, courageous b) *Irón* ¡**valiente amigo eres tú!** a fine friend you are!

valioso, -a *adj* valuable

valla *nf* a) [cerca] fence; [muro] wall; **valla publicitaria** billboard, *Br* hoarding b) DEP hurdle; **los 100 metros vallas** the 100 metres hurdle race

valle *nm* valley

valor *nm* a) [valía] value, worth; [precio] price; **objetos de valor** valuables; **sin valor** worthless; **valor alimenticio** food value b) [valentía] courage c) FIN **valores** securities, bonds

valoración *nf* valuation

valorar *vt* to value, to calculate the value of

vals *nm* waltz; **bailar el vals** to waltz

válvula *nf* valve; **válvula de seguridad** safety valve

vanguardista 1. *adj* avant-garde **2.** *nmf* avant-gardist

vanidad *nf* vanity

vanidoso, -a *adj* vain, conceited

vano, -a *adj* a) [vanidoso] vain, conceited b) [esfuerzo, esperanza] vain, futile; **en vano** in vain

vapor *nm* a) [de agua hirviendo] steam; CULIN **al vapor** steamed b) [gas] vapour; **vapor de agua** water vapour

vaporizador *nm* vaporizer, spray

vaquero, -a 1. *nm* cowherd, cowboy **2.** *adj* **pantalón vaquero** jeans, pair of jeans **3.** *nmpl* **vaqueros** [prenda] jeans, pair of jeans

vara *nf* pole, rod

variable *adj & nf* variable

variado, -a *adj* varied; **galletas variadas** assorted *Br* biscuits o *US* cookies

variar [29] **1.** *vt* to vary, to change **2.** *vi* to vary, to change; *Irón* **para variar** as usual, just for a change

varicela *nf* chickenpox

variedad *nf* a) variety b) TEATRO **variedades** variety, *Br* music hall

varios, -as *adj* several

varita *nf* [vara] wand; **varita mágica** magic wand

variz *nf* varicose vein

varón *nm* [hombre] man; [chico] boy; **hijo varón** male child; **sexo varón** male sex

varonil *adj* manly, virile

vasallo, -a *nm, f* HIST vassal

vasco, -a *adj* Basque; **el País Vasco** the Basque Country

vasija *nf* pot

vaso *nm* a) [para beber] glass b) ANAT vessel

vasto, -a *adj* vast

Vaticano *nm* **el Vaticano** the Vatican

vaya¹ *interj* a) [sorpresa] ¡**vaya!** wow! b) [contrariedad] ¡**vaya con las huelgas otra vez!** here we go with all the strikes again! c) [énfasis] ¡**vaya moto!** wow! That's some bike!; ¡**vaya tontería!** that's just stupid!; ¡**vaya lío!** what a mess!

vaya² *subj pres de* **ir**

Vd. *(abr de* **usted***)* you

Vds. *(abr de* **ustedes***)* you

ve a) *imperat de* **ir** b) *indic pres de* **ver**

vecindad *nf* a) [área] neighbourhood, vicinity b) [vecinos] community, residents (*pl*) c) *Méx* [vivienda] *communal dwelling where poor families each live in a single room and share a bathroom and kitchen with others*

vecindario *nm* = **vecindad**

vecino, -a 1. *nm, f* a) [persona] neighbour; **el vecino de al lado** the next-door neighbour b) [residente] resident **2.** *adj* neighbouring, nearby

vegetación *nf* a) BOT vegetation b) MED **vegetaciones** adenoids

vegetal *nm* vegetable

vegetariano, -a *adj & nm, f* vegetarian

vehicular *vt* to transport

vehículo nm vehicle

veinte adj & nm inv twenty

vejestorio nm Despec **a)** [persona] old fossil **b)** Am [cosa] relic

vejez nf old age

vejiga nf bladder

vela¹ nf **a)** candle **b)** Fam **quedarse a dos velas** to be in the dark **c) pasar la noche en vela** to have a sleepless night

vela² nf NÁUT sail

velador 1. nm **a)** [mesa] table **b)** Andes, Méx [mesilla de noche] bedside table **c)** Méx, RP [lámpara] bedside lamp **2.** nm, f Méx [sereno] night watchman

velcro® nm Velcro®

velero nm sailing boat o ship

veleta 1. nf weather vane, weathercock **2.** nmf Fam fickle o changeable person

velista nmf [hombre] yachtsman ; [mujer] yachtswoman

veliz nf Méx suitcase

vello nm hair

velo nm veil

velocidad nf **a)** [rapidez] speed ; [de proyectil etc] velocity ; AUTO **velocidad máxima** speed limit ; INFORM **velocidad de transmisión** bit rate ; INFORM **velocidad operativa** operating speed **b)** AUTO [marcha] gear

velódromo nm cycle track, velodrome

velomotor nm moped

velorio nm wake

veloz 1. adj swift, rapid **2.** adv quickly, fast

vena nf vein

venado nm deer, stag ; CULIN venison

vencedor, -a 1. nm, f winner **2.** adj winning

vencejo nm ORNIT swift

vencer [49] **1.** vt **a)** [al enemigo] to defeat ; [al contrincante] to beat **b)** [dificultad] to overcome, to surmount **2.** vi **a)** [pago, deuda] to fall due, to be payable **b)** [plazo] to expire **3. vencerse** vpr [torcerse] to warp

vencido, -a adj **a)** MIL [derrotado] defeated ; DEP beaten ; Fig **darse por vencido** to give up, to accept defeat **b)** [pago, deuda] due, payable **c)** [plazo] expired **d)** Fam **a la tercera va la vencida** third time lucky

vencimiento nm **a)** COM maturity **b)** [de un plazo] expiry

venda nf bandage

vendaje nm dressing

vendar vt to bandage ; Fig **vendar los ojos a algn** to blindfold sb

vendaval nm gale

vendedor, -a nm, f seller ; [de coches, seguros] salesman, f saleswoman

vender 1. vt to sell ; **vender a plazos / al contado** to sell on credit / for cash ; **vender al por mayor / menor** to (sell) wholesale / retail **2. venderse** vpr **a)** to sell ; **este disco se vende bien** this record is selling well ; **se vende** [en letrero] for sale **b)** [claudicar] to sell out

vendimia nf grape harvest

vendimiador, -a nm, f grape picker

vendimiar [43] **1.** vt [uvas] to harvest **2.** vi to pick grapes

veneno nm poison ; [de serpiente] venom

venenoso, -a adj poisonous

venezolano, -a adj & nm, f Venezuelan

Venezuela n Venezuela

venga subj pres de venir

venganza nf vengeance, revenge

vengar [42] **1.** vt to avenge **2. vengarse** vpr to avenge oneself ; **vengarse de algn** to take revenge on sb

vengo indic pres de venir

venida nf coming, arrival

venir [27] **1.** vi **a)** to come ; Fig **venir a menos** to come down in the world ; **el año que viene** next year ; Fig **me viene a la memoria** I remember ; Fam **¡venga ya!** [vamos] come on! ; [expresa incredulidad] come off it! **b) venir grande / pequeño** [ropa] to be too big / small ; **venir mal / bien** to

be inconvenient / convenient; **el metro me viene muy bien** I find the *Br* underground o *US* subway very handy **c)** (*delante de infinitivo*) [aproximarse] **viene a ser lo mismo** it's all the same, it amounts to the same thing
d) [en pasivas] **esto vino provocado por …** this was brought about by …
e) esto viene ocurriendo desde hace mucho tiempo this has been going on for a long time now
2. venirse *vpr* **venirse abajo** to collapse

venta *nf* **a)** sale; **en venta** for sale; **a la venta** on sale; **venta al contado** cash sale; **venta al por mayor / al por menor** wholesale / retail; **venta a plazos** sale by instalments, *Br* hire purchase **b)** [posada] country inn

ventaja *nf* advantage; **llevar ventaja a** to have the advantage over; **le sacó 2 metros de ventaja** he beat him by 2 metres

ventana *nf* **a)** [gen & INFORM] window; INFORM **ventana de información** pop-up **b)** [de la nariz] nostril

ventanilla *nf* **a)** window **b)** [de la nariz] nostril

ventero, -a *nm, f* innkeeper

ventilación *nf* ventilation; **sin ventilación** unventilated

ventilador *nm* ventilator; [de coche] fan

ventisca *nf* blizzard; [de nieve] snowstorm

ventosa *nf* sucker; MED cupping glass

ventoso, -a *adj* windy

ventrílocuo, -a *nm, f* ventriloquist

ver¹ *nm* **de buen ver** good-looking

ver² [28] **1.** *vt* **a)** to see; [televisión] to watch; **a ver** let me see, let's see; **a ver si escribes** I hope you'll write; *Fam* **había un jaleo que no veas** you should have seen the fuss that was made; *Fam* **no poder ver algo / a algn (ni en pintura)** not to be able to stand the sight of sth / sb; **(ya) veremos** we'll see
b) no tener nada que ver con to have nothing to do with

2. verse *vpr* **a)** [imagen etc] to be seen **b)** [encontrarse con algn] to meet, see each other; **véase anexo 1** see appendix 1; **¡nos vemos!** see you later!

veraneante *nmf Br* holidaymaker, *US* (summer) vacationer

veranear *vi* **veranear en** to spend one's summer *Br* holidays o *US* vacation in

veraneo *nm* summer *Br* holidays o *US* vacation

veraniego, -a *adj* summer

verano *nm* summer

veras *nfpl* **de veras** really, seriously

verbena *nf* street party

verbo *nm* verb

verdad *nf* **a)** truth; **es verdad** it is true; **a decir verdad** to tell the truth; **¡de vverdad** really!, truly!; **un amigo de verdad** a real friend **b)** [en frase afirmativa] **está muy bien, ¿(no es) verdad?** it is very good, isn't it?; [en frase negativa] **no te gusta, ¿verdad?** you don't like it, do you?

verdadero, -a *adj* true, real

verde 1. *adj* **a)** green **b)** [fruta] unripe **c)** *Fam* [chiste, película] blue; **viejo verde** dirty old man **d)** *Fam & Fig* **poner verde a algn** to call sb every name under the sun **2.** *nm* **a)** [color] green **b)** POL **los verdes** the Greens

verdulería *nf* greengrocer's (shop)

verdulero, -a *nm, f* greengrocer

verdura *nf* vegetables, greens

vereda *nf* **a)** [camino] path, lane **b)** *CSur, Perú* [acera] *Br* pavement, *US* sidewalk **c)** *Col* [distrito] area, district

veredicto *nm* verdict

vergonzoso, -a *adj* **a)** [penoso] shameful, disgraceful **b)** [tímido] shy, bashful

vergüenza *nf* **a)** shame; **¿no te da vergüenza?** aren't you ashamed?, have you no shame?; **¡es una vergüenza!** it's a disgrace! **b)** [timidez] shyness, bashfulness; **tener vergüenza** to be shy; **me da vergüenza** I'm too embarrassed

verificar [44] **1.** *vt* [comprobar] to check **2. verificarse** *vpr* to take place, to occur

verja *nf* [reja] grating; [cerca] railing, railings; [puerta] iron gate

vermut *(pl* vermuts*)*, **vermú** *(pl* vermús*)* *nm* **a)** [licor] vermouth **b)** [aperitivo] aperitif **c)** *esp Andes, RP* [en cine] early-evening showing; [en teatro] early-evening performance

verosímil *adj* probable, likely; [creíble] credible

verruga *nf* wart

versión *nf* version; **película en versión original** movie *o Br* film in the original language

verso *nm* **a)** [poesía] verse **b)** [línea] line

vertedero *nm* [de basura] *Br* rubbish tip *o* dump, *US* garbage dump

verter [3] **1.** *vt* **a)** to pour (out) **b)** [basura] to dump **2.** *vi* [río] to flow, to run (**a** into)

vertical *adj* vertical

vértice *nm* vertex

vertido *nm* [residuo] waste; **vertidos radiactivos** radioactive waste

vertiente *nf* **a)** [de una montaña, un tejado] slope; *Fig* aspect **b)** *CSur* [manantial] spring

vértigo *nm* vertigo; **me da vértigo** it makes me dizzy

vestíbulo *nm* [de casa] hall; [de edificio público] foyer

vestido, -a 1. *nm* [ropa] clothes; [de mujer] dress **2.** *adj* dressed; **policía vestido de paisano** plain-clothes policeman

vestimenta *nf* clothes, garments

vestir [6] **1.** *vt* **a)** [a algn] to dress **b)** [llevar puesto] to wear **2.** *vi* **a)** to dress; **ropa de (mucho) vestir** formal dress **b)** *Fam* **la seda viste mucho** silk always looks very elegant **3. vestirse** *vpr* **a)** to get dressed, to dress

b) vestirse de to wear, to dress in; [disfrazarse] to disguise oneself as, to dress up as

vestuario *nm* **a)** [conjunto de vestidos] clothes, wardrobe; TEATRO wardrobe, costumes **b)** [camerino] dressing room **c)** DEP changing room, *US* locker room

veterano, -a *adj & nm, f* veteran

veterinario, -a *nm, f* vet, *Br* veterinary surgeon, *US* veterinarian ■ **veterinaria** *nf* veterinary medicine *o* science

vez *nf* **a)** time; **una vez** once; **dos veces** twice; **cinco veces** five times; **a** *o* **algunas veces** sometimes; **cada vez** each *o* every time; **cada vez más** more and more; **de vez en cuando** now and again, every now and then; **¿le has visto alguna vez?** have you ever seen him?; **otra vez** again; **a la vez** at the same time; **tal vez** perhaps, maybe; **de una vez** in one go; **en vez de** instead of **b)** [turno] turn **c)** **hacer las veces de** to do duty as

vía 1. *nf* **a)** FERROC track, line **b)** [camino] road; **vía pública** public thoroughfare; **Vía Láctea** Milky Way **c)** ANAT passage, tract; FARM **(por) vía oral** to be taken orally **d)** *Fig* **por vía oficial** through official channels; **por vía aérea / marítima** by air / sea **e)** **en vías de** in the process of; **países en vías de desarrollo** developing countries **2.** *prep* [a través de] via, through; **vía París** via Paris; **transmisión vía satélite** satellite transmission

viaducto *nm* viaduct

viajar *vi* to travel

viaje *nm* [recorrido] journey, trip; [largo, en barco] voyage; **¡buen viaje!** bon voyage!, have a good trip!; **estar de viaje** to be away (on a trip); **irse** *o* **marcharse de viaje** to go on a journey *o* trip; **viaje de negocios** business trip; **viaje de novios** honeymoon

viajero, -a 1. *nm, f* **a)** traveller **b)** [en transporte público] passenger **2.** *adj* **cheque viajero** traveller's cheque

vianda *nf* **a)** *Méx, RP* [tentempié] packed lunch **b)** *Méx, RP* [fiambrera] lunchbox

víbora *nf* viper

vibrar *vt & vi* to vibrate

vicepresidente, -a *nm, f* a) POL vice-president b) [de compañía, comité] vice-chairman, *f* vice-chairwoman, *US* vice-president

viciar [43] **1.** *vt* a) [corromper] to corrupt b) [estropear] to waste **2. viciarse** *vpr* a) [deformarse] to go out of shape b) [corromperse] to become corrupted

vicio *nm* a) vice b) [mala costumbre] bad habit c) *Fam* [destreza] skill

vicioso, -a **1.** *adj* a) [persona] depraved, perverted b) **círculo vicioso** vicious circle **2.** *nm, f* depraved person; **vicioso del trabajo** workaholic

víctima *nf* victim

victimar *vt Am* to kill, to murder

victimario, -a *nm, f Am* killer, murderer

victoria *nf* victory

vid *nf* vine, grapevine

vida *nf* life; [período] lifetime; **de toda la vida** lifelong; **en mi vida** never in my life; **de por vida** for life; **ganarse la vida** to earn one's living; **¿qué es de tu vida?** how's life?; **estar con / sin vida** to be alive / dead

vidente *nmf* clairvoyant

vídeo, *Am* **video** *nm* video; **grabar en vídeo** to videotape

videocámara *nf* video camera

videocasete *nm* video, videocassette

videoconsola *nf* games console

videojuego *nm* video game

videoteléfono *nm* videophone

vidriera *nf* a) stained-glass window b) *Am* [escaparate] shop window

vidrio *nm* glass

vieira *nf* scallop

viejo, -a **1.** *adj* old; **hacerse viejo** to grow old; **un viejo amigo** an old friend **2.** *nm, f* a) [hombre, padre] old man; [mujer, madre] old woman; **los viejos** old people; *Fam* **mis viejos** my parents b) *Am Fam* [amigo] pal, *Br* mate, *US* buddy; [amiga] girl, *US* girlfriend c) *Chile* **el Viejo Pascuero** Father Christmas

viento *nm* wind; **hace** *o* **sopla mucho viento** it is very windy; *Fam & Fig* **¡vete a tomar viento!** get lost!

vientre *nm* a) belly; **hacer de vientre** to have a bowel movement b) [útero] womb

viernes *nm inv* Friday; **Viernes Santo** Good Friday

Vietnam *n* Vietnam

viga *nf* [de madera] beam; [de hierro] girder

vigencia *nf* validity; **entrar en vigencia** to come into force *o* effect

vigente *adj* in force

vigilante *nm* watchman; [de banco] guard

vigilar **1.** *vt* to watch; [un lugar] to guard; **vigila que no entren** make sure they don't get in **2.** *vi* [gen] to keep watch

vigor *nm* a) vigour; [fuerza] strength b) **en vigor** in force

vigoroso, -a *adj* vigorous

vil *adj Formal* vile, base

villa *nf* a) [población] town b) [casa] villa, country house c) *Arg, Bol* **villa miseria** shanty town

villancico *nm* (Christmas) carol

vinagre *nm* vinegar

vinagreras *nfpl* cruet set

vinagreta *nf* vinaigrette sauce

vincha *nf Andes, RP* headband

vinculación *nf* link, connection

vincular *vt* to link, to bind; [relacionar] to relate, to connect

vino *nm* wine; **tomar un vino** to have a glass of wine; **vino blanco / tinto** white / red wine; **vino dulce / seco** sweet / dry wine; **vino rosado** rosé

viña *nf* vineyard

violación *nf* a) [de una persona] rape b) [de ley, derecho] violation, infringement

violador *nm* rapist

violar *vt* a) [persona] to rape b) [ley, derecho] to violate, to infringe

violencia *nf* a) violence; **la no violencia** non-violence b) [incomodidad] embarrassment

violento, -a *adj* a) violent b) [situación] embarrassing, awkward c) **sentirse violento** [incómodo] to feel embarrassed o awkward

violeta 1. *adj & nm* [color] violet **2.** *nf* [flor] violet

violín *nm* violin; *Fam* fiddle

violinista *nmf* violinist

violoncelo, violonchelo *nm* violoncello, cello

VIP [bip] *nmf* (*abr de* **very important person**) VIP

virgen 1. *adj* a) [persona, selva] virgin b) [aceite, lana] pure; [cinta] blank **2.** *nmf* virgin; *Fam* **ser un viva la virgen** to be a devil-may-care person

virginiano, a *nm, f Am* Virgo

Virgo *nmf* Virgo

virtud *nf* a) virtue; *Fig* **en virtud de** by virtue of b) [propiedad] property, quality

viruela *nf* smallpox; **viruelas** pockmarks

virus *nm inv* [gen & INFORM] virus

viruta *nf* shaving

visa *nf Am* visa

visado *nm* visa

víscera *nf* a) internal organ b) **vísceras** viscera, entrails

viscosa *nf* [tejido] viscose

visera *nf* [de gorra] peak; [de casco] visor

visible *adj* visible; [evidente] evident

visillo *nm* net curtain, lace curtain

visita *nf* a) [acción] visit; **hacer una visita** to pay a visit; **estar de visita** to be visiting b) [invitado] visitor, guest

visitante 1. *nmf* visitor **2.** *adj* [equipo] away

visitar *vt* to visit

vislumbrar *vt* to glimpse

víspera *nf* [día anterior] day before; [de festivo] eve; **en vísperas de** in the period leading up to

vista *nf* a) sight; **a la vista** visible; **a primera** o **simple vista** at first sight, on the face of it; **con vistas a** with a view to; **en vista de** in view of, considering; **en vista de que** in view of the fact that, seeing as; **corto de vista** short-sighted; **conocer a algn de vista** to know sb by sight; *Fig* **tener mucha vista para** to have a good eye for; *Fam* **¡hasta la vista!** goodbye!, see you!
b) [panorama] view; **con vista(s) al mar** overlooking the sea
c) JUR trial, hearing

vistazo *nm* glance; **echar un vistazo a algo** [ojear] to have a (quick) look at sth; [tener cuidado de] to keep an eye on sth

visto, -a 1. *adj* a) **está visto que …** it is obvious that …; **por lo visto** evidently, apparently; **visto que** in view of the fact that, seeing o given that b) **estar bien visto** to be well looked upon, to be considered acceptable; **estar mal visto** to be frowned upon c) **estar muy visto** to be old hat **2.** *nm* **visto bueno** approval, OK

vistoso, -a *adj* eye-catching

visualizador *nm* visual display unit

visualizar *vt* a) to visualize b) [imaginar] to imagine c) INFORM to display

vital *adj* a) vital b) [persona] full of vitality

vitalidad *nf* vitality

vitamina *nf* vitamin

vitícola *adj* grape-producing

vitrina *nf* [aparador] glass o display cabinet; [de exposición] glass case, showcase; *Am* [escaparate] shop window

vitrocerámica *nf* [cocina] glass ceramic hob

viudo, -a *nm, f* [hombre] widower; [mujer] widow

viva *interj* hurrah!

vivaquear *vi* to bivouac

víveres *nmpl* provisions, supplies

vivienda *nf* a) housing b) [casa] house; [piso] flat

vivir **1.** *vi* to live; **vive de sus ahorros** she lives off her savings; **viven de la pesca** they make their living by fishing
2. *vt* to live through
3. *nm* life

vivo, -a **1.** *adj* **a)** alive; **de viva voz** verbally, by word of mouth; **en vivo** [programa] live; *Fam* **es el vivo retrato** *o* **la viva imagen de** she is the spitting image of **b)** **al rojo vivo** red-hot **c)** [vivaz] lively, vivacious **d)** [listo] sharp, clever **e)** [color] vivid, bright **f)** [descripción] lively, graphic **2.** *nm, f* **los vivos** the living

vns? SMS *written abbr of* **¿vienes?**

vocabulario *nm* vocabulary

vocación *nf* vocation, calling; **con vocación europea** with leanings towards Europe

vocal **1.** *nf* LING vowel **2.** *nmf* member

voceador, -a *nm, f* Col, Ecuad, Méx newspaper seller

vocero, -a *nm, f esp Am* spokesperson, spokesman; *f* spokeswoman

vodka *nm* vodka

vol. *(abr de* **volumen***)* vol

volador, -a *adj* flying

volante **1.** *nm* **a)** AUTO steering wheel; **ir al volante** to be driving **b)** COST frill, ruffle **c)** *Esp* [del médico] (referral) note **2.** *adj* flying; **platillo volante** flying saucer

volantín *nm* Carib, Chile kite

volar [2] **1.** *vi* **a)** to fly; *Fig* **lo hizo volando** he did it in a flash
b) *Fam* [desaparecer] to disappear, to vanish
2. *vt* [edificios] to blow up; [caja fuerte] to blow open; MIN to blast
3. **volarse** *vpr* [papel etc] to be blown away

volcán *nm* volcano

volcánico, -a *adj* volcanic

volcar [2] **1.** *vt* **a)** [cubo etc] to knock over; [barco, bote] to capsize
b) [vaciar] to empty out

c) [tiempo] to invest
2. *vi* [coche] to turn over; [barco] to capsize
3. **volcarse** *vpr* **a)** [vaso, jarra] to fall over, to tip over; [coche] to turn over; [barco] to capsize
b) *Fig* **volcarse con** to do one's utmost for

voleibol *nm* volleyball

volquete *nm* dumper truck, US dump truck

voltaje *nm* voltage

voltear **1.** *vt* **a)** *Am* [derribar - objeto] to knock over; [gobierno] to overthrow, to bring down
b) *Am salvo RP* [poner del revés - boca abajo] to turn upside down; [lo de dentro fuera] to turn inside out; [lo de detrás delante] to turn back to front
c) *Am salvo RP* [cabeza, espalda] to turn
2. *vi* Méx [doblar la esquina] to turn
3. **voltearse** *vpr* **a)** *Am salvo RP* [volverse] to turn around
b) *Méx* [vehículo] to overturn

voltereta *nf* somersault

volumen *nm* volume

voluntad *nf* will; **fuerza de voluntad** willpower; **tiene mucha voluntad** he is very strong-willed; **a voluntad** at will

voluntario, -a **1.** *adj* voluntary
2. *nm, f* volunteer; **ofrecerse voluntario** to volunteer

voluntarioso, -a *adj* willing

volver [4] *(pp* **vuelto***)* **1.** *vi* **a)** to return; [venir] to come back; [ir] to go back; **volver en sí** to come round, to recover consciousness
b) **volver a hacer algo** to do sth again
2. *vt* **a)** [convertir] to turn, to make; **me vas a volver loco** you are driving me mad
b) [dar vuelta a] to turn; [boca abajo] to turn upside down; [de fuera adentro] to turn inside out; [de atrás adelante] to turn back to front; [dar la vuelta a] to turn over; **volverle la espalda a algn**

to turn one's back on sb; *Fig* **volver la vista atrás** to look back; **al volver la esquina** on turning the corner
3. volverse *vpr* **a)** to turn
b) [regresar - venir] to come back; [ir] to go back
c) [convertirse] to become; **volverse loco, -a** to go mad

vomitar 1. *vi* to vomit, to be sick; **tengo ganas de vomitar** I feel sick, I want to be sick **2.** *vt* to vomit, to bring up

vos *pron pers* **a)** *Am* [tú] you **b)** SMS *written abbr of* **vosotros**

The **vos** form is used alongside **tú** in many Latin American countries, and in some countries (Argentina, Paraguay and Uruguay) is the preferred form.

V.O.S.E. *nf (abr de* **versión original subtitulada en español**) *original language version subtitled in Spanish*

voseo *nm use of the polite* **vos** *form instead of the familiar* **tú** *form when speaking to sb*

vosotros, -as *pron pers pl Esp* **a)** [sujeto] you **b)** [con prep] you; **entre vosotros** among yourselves; **sin vosotras** without you

Usually omitted in Spanish except for emphasis or contrast. In Latin America, **vosotros** is not used. Instead, **ustedes** is used as the second person plural in all contexts, without necessarily suggesting formality.

votación *nf* **a)** [voto] vote, ballot **b)** [acción] voting

votante *nmf* voter

votar *vi* to vote; **votar a algn** to vote (for) sb

voto *nm* **a)** vote; **tener voto** to have the right to vote; **voto secreto** secret ballot **b)** REL vow

voy *indic pres de* **ir**

voz *nf* **a)** voice; **en voz alta** aloud; **en voz baja** in a low voice; **a media voz** in a low voice, softly; **de viva voz** verbally **b)** [grito] shout; **a voces** shouting; **dar voces** to shout; *Fig* **estar pidiendo**

algo a voces to be crying out for sth; *Fig* **secreto a voces** open secret; **a voz en grito** at the top of one's voice **c)** **no tener ni voz ni voto** to have no say in the matter; *Fig* **llevar la voz cantante** to rule the roost **d)** LING **voz pasiva** passive voice

vuelo *nm* **a)** flight; **vuelo chárter / regular** charter /scheduled flight; **vuelo sin motor** gliding; *Fig* **cazarlas** *o* **cogerlas al vuelo** to be quick on the uptake **b)** COST **una falda de vuelo** a full skirt

vuelta *nf* **a)** [regreso] return; [viaje] return journey; **estar de vuelta** to be back; DEP **partido de vuelta** return match
b) [giro] turn; [en carreras] lap; DEP [ciclista] tour; **dar media vuelta** to turn round; *Fig* **la cabeza me da vueltas** my head is spinning; *Fig* **no le des más vueltas** stop worrying about it; **vuelta de campana** somersault
c) [dinero] change
d) dar una vuelta [a pie] to go for a walk *o* stroll; [en coche] to go for a drive *o* a spin (in the car)

vuelto, -a 1. *pp de* **volver 2.** *adj* **jersey de cuello vuelto** rollneck sweater **3.** *nm Am* [de dinero] change; **dar el vuelto a algn** to give sb their change

vuestro, -a *Esp* **1.** *adj poses* [antes del sustantivo] your; [después del sustantivo] of yours; **vuestro libro** your book; **un amigo vuestro** a friend of yours **2.** *pron poses* yours; **éstos son los vuestros** these are yours; **lo vuestro** what is yours, what belongs to you

vulgar *adj* **a)** vulgar **b)** **el término vulgar** the everyday term

W

walkman® ['walman] *(pl* **walkmans)** *nm* Walkman®

wáter *(pl* **wáteres)** *nm Fam* toilet

waterpolo *nm* water polo

WC *[Esp* uβe'θe, *Am* doβleβe'se] *nm (abr de* **water closet)** WC

web ['weβ] *nf* INFORM **la web** the web; **una (página) web** a web page; **un sitio web** a website

webcam ['weβkam] *(pl* **webcams)** *nf* INFORM webcam

webmáster, **webmaster** [weβ'master] *nmf* INFORM webmaster

whisky ['wiski] *nm* [escocés] whisky; [irlandés, US] whiskey

wi-fi, **wifi** ['wifi] *nm inv (abr de* **Wireless Fidelity)** Wi-Fi

windsurf, **windsurfing** *nm* windsurfing

windsurfista *nmf* windsurfer

wpa SMS *written abbr of* **guapa**

wpo SMS *written abbr of* **guapo**

WWW ['uβe 'doβle 'uβe 'doβle 'uβe 'doβle, 'tres 'uβe(s)'doβles, 'triple 'uβe 'doβle] *nm o nf (abr de* **World Wide Web)** WWW

x SMS *written abbr of* **por**

xa, **xra** SMS *(abr de* **para***)* 4

xdon SMS *(abr de* **perdón***)* sry

xenofobia *nf* xenophobia

xenófobo, -a 1. *adj* xenophobic **2.** *nm, f* xenophobe

xerocopia *nf* photocopy

xfa = **pf**

xilofón, xilófono *nm* xylophone

xq = **pq**

xro SMS *written abbr of* **pero**

Y

y *conj* **a)** and; **una chica alta y morena** a tall, dark-haired girl; **son las tres y cuarto** it's a quarter past three **b)** **¿y qué?** so what?; **¿y si no llega a tiempo?** what if he doesn't arrive in time?; **¿y tú?** what about you?; **¿y eso?** how come?; **y eso que** although, even though; **¡y tanto!** you bet!, and how!; *ver* **e**

ya **1.** *adv* **a)** already; **ya lo sabía** I already knew; **ya en la Edad Media** as far back as the Middle Ages
b) [ahora mismo] now; **es preciso actuar ya** it is vital that we act now; **¡hazlo ya!** do it at once!; **ya mismo** right away
c) [en el futuro] **ya hablaremos luego** we'll talk about it later; **ya nos veremos** see you!
d) ya no no longer; **ya no viene por aquí** he doesn't come round here any more
e) [refuerza el verbo] **ya era hora** about time too; **¡ya está!** that's it!; **ya lo creo** of course, I should think so; **ya lo sé** I know; **ya veremos** we'll see; **¡ya voy!** coming!
2. *conj* **ya que** since

yacer [61] *vi* **a)** [estar tumbado, enterrado] to lie; **aquí yace …** here lies … **b)** [tener relaciones sexuales] to lie together
yacimiento *nm* bed, deposit; **yacimientos petrolíferos** oilfields
yanqui *Despec* **1.** *adj* Yankee **2.** *nmf* Yankee, Yank
yaraví *nm Am* type of melancholy Indian song
yate *nm* yacht
yaya *nf* **a)** *Perú* [insecto] mite **b)** *Cuba, PRico* [árbol] lancewood

yayo, -a *nm, f Fam* granddad, *f* grandma
yegua *nf* mare
yema *nf* **a)** [de huevo] yolk **b)** BOT bud **c) yema del dedo** fingertip **d)** CULIN *sweet made from sugar and egg yolk*
yen *nm* [moneda] yen
yerba *nf* **a)** = **hierba b)** *RP* maté; **yerba mate** (yerba) maté leaves
yerbatero, -a **1.** *nm, f Andes, Carib* [curandero] witch doctor who uses herbs; [vendedor de hierbas] herbalist **2.** *adj RP* maté
yerno *nm* son-in-law
yeso *nm* **a)** GEOL gypsum **b)** CONSTR plaster
ymam, ymm SMS *written abbr of* **llámame**
yo *pron pers* I; **entre tú y yo** between you and me; **¿quién es? — soy yo** who is it? — it's me; **yo no** not me; **yo que tú** if I were you; **yo mismo** I myself

Usually omitted as a personal pronoun in Spanish except for emphasis or contrast.

yodo *nm* iodine
yoga *nm* yoga
yogur (*pl* **yogures**), **yogurt** (*pl* **yogurts**) *nm* yogurt, yoghurt
Yugoslavia *n* Yugoslavia
yunque *nm* anvil
yunta *nf* yoke *o* team of oxen
yuyería *nf RP* herbalist *Br* shop *o* *US* store
yuyo *nm* **a)** *CSur* [mala hierba] weed; [hierba medicinal] medicinal herb **b)** *Andes* [hierba silvestre] wild herb

z

zacate *nm CAm, Méx* fodder

zafiro *nm* sapphire

zaguán *nm* hall, hallway

zambo, -a 1. *adj* [piernas, persona] knock-kneed **2.** *nm, f Am* [hijo de persona negra y otra india] *person who has one Black and one Indian parent*

zambullida *nf* plunge

zambullirse *vpr* to plunge

zanahoria *nf* carrot

zancadilla *nf* ponerle la zancadilla a algn to trip sb up

zanco *nm* stilt

zancudo, -a 1. *adj* **a)** long-legged **b)** ORNIT wading; **ave zancuda** wading bird, wader **2.** *nm Am* mosquito

zanja *nf* ditch, trench

zapallito *nm CSur Br* courgette, *US* zucchini

zapallo *nm* **a)** *Andes, RP* **zapallo (italiano)** *Br* courgette, *US* zucchini **b)** *Andes, RP* [calabaza] pumpkin **c)** *RP Fam* [bobo] mug, *Br* wally

zapateado *nm type of flamenco dance where the dancers stamp their feet rhythmically*

zapatería *nf* shoe shop

zapatero, -a *nm, f* [vendedor] shoe dealer; [fabricante] shoemaker, cobbler

zapatilla *nf* slipper; **zapatillas de deporte** *Br* trainers, *US* sneakers

zapato *nm* shoe; **zapatos de tacón** high-heeled shoes

zapear *vi* to channel-hop

zapping ['θapin] *nm inv Fam* channel-hopping, *US* channel-surfing; **hacer zapping** to channel-hop

zarandear 1. *vt* to shake **2. zarandearse** *vpr* **a)** [dar bandazos] to bounce around **b)** *Am* [contonearse] to strut about

zarpar *vi* to weigh anchor, to set sail

zarpazo *nm* clawing; **dar** *o* **pegar un zarpazo a** to claw

zarza *nf* bramble, blackberry bush

zarzamora *nf* [zarza] blackberry bush; [fruto] blackberry

zarzuela *nf* **a)** *Spanish operetta* **b) la Zarzuela** *royal residence in Madrid* **c)** CULIN *fish stew*

zenit *nm* zenith

zinc *nm* zinc

zíper *nm CAm, Méx Br* zip, *US* zipper

zipizape *nm Fam* squabble, set-to

zócalo *nm* **a)** [de pared] skirting board **b)** [pedestal] plinth

zodiaco, zodíaco *nm* zodiac

zona *nf* zone; [región] region; **zona euro** euro zone; **zona verde** park, green area

zoo *nm* zoo

zoología *nf* zoology

zoológico, -a 1. *adj* zoological; **parque zoológico** zoo **2.** *nm* zoo

zopenco, -a *nm, f Fam* dope, halfwit

zopilote *nm CAm, Méx* black vulture

zoquete 1. *nmf Fam* blockhead **2.** *nm CSur* [calcetín] ankle sock

zorra *nf* **a)** vixen **b)** *Esp Fam* slut

zorro, -a 1. *nm* fox **2.** *adj* **a)** [astuto] cunning, sly **b)** *Esp muy Fam* **no tengo ni zorra (idea)** I haven't got a *Br* bloody *o US* goddamn clue

zueco *nm* clog

zumbado, -a *Fam* **1.** *adj* crazy **2.** *nm, f* nutcase

zumbar 1. *vi* to buzz, to hum; **me zumban los oídos** my ears are buzzing; *Fam* **salir zumbando** to zoom off **2.** *vt Fam* to thrash

zumbido *nm* buzzing, humming

zumo *nm Esp* juice

zurcir [52] *vt* COST to darn; *Fam* **¡que te zurzan!** go to hell!

zurdo, -a 1. *nm, f* [persona] left-handed person **2.** *adj* left-handed

zurrar *vt* [pegar] to beat, to flog

zzz SMS *written abbr of* **dormir**